Encyclopaedia
of Underwater
and Maritime
Archaeology

Encyclopaedia *of* Underwater *and* Maritime Archaeology

EDITED BY JAMES P. DELGADO

BRITISH MUSEUM PRESS

For
Ann, John and Beth

and especially for
Rebecca C. Magallanes

without whom this encyclopaedia
would not have happened

© James P Delgado 1997

Published by British Museum Press
A division of The British Museum Company
46 Bloomsbury Street, London WC1B 3QQ

British Library Cataloguing in Publication Data
A catalogue record for this book is available from
the British Library

ISBN 0 7141 2129 0

Designed and typeset by Harry Green

Printed and bound in Slovenia

Frontispiece: Excavating a ceramic *krater*
from the Kaş wreck at Uluburun, Turkey,
using an airlift. (© INA)

This spread: Reconstruction drawing of the
stern of *Vasa*. (courtesy of the Vasa Museum,
Stockholm, Sweden)

Jacket: (FRONT, FROM TOP CENTRE): ROV *Merlin*
launched from support vessel. (Jack Cosgrove);
Greek red-figure vase showing Odysseus and the
Sirens. (Courtesy of the Trustees of the British
Museum); ships depicted on the Bayeux Tapestry.
(© Michael Holford); *Mary Rose* from the
Anthony Roll, 1546. (By kind permission of
the Master and Fellows of Magdalene College
Cambridge); gold coins and artefacts from
a shipwreck off the coast of Uruguay. (Courtesy of
the Trustees of the British Museum); Sutton Hoo
helmet. (Courtesy of the Trustees of the British
Museum); divers with amphora. (© Mensun
Bound, Oxford University MARE); hard-hat
diver. (Royal Navy Submarine Museum, Gosport).
(SPINE): Reconstructed vessel *Philadelphia II*.
(Courtesy of Lake Champlain Maritime Museum,
Basin Harbor, Vermont).
(BACK, FROM TOP): 'Diving bell'. (Vancouver
Maritime Museum); steamship *Tennessee*.
(Courtesy of San Francisco Maritime National
Historical Park); excavation on the Pandora site.
(© Queensland Museum/Patrick Baker); lifting a
tray of fragile hull remains from the Kaş wreck at
Uluburun. (© Institute of Nautical Archaeology).

Contents

Preface *and* acknowledgements

The last great frontier on earth is the deep ocean. It is also our last archaeological frontier. As new technology unlocks the ocean's depths, long lost (and in some cases long forgotten) shipwrecks, sunken cities, and other submerged antiquities have been discovered. The media attention, be it in print or on the television, is usually intense and at times frenzied, as anyone who remembers the discovery of the wreck of *Titanic* in 1985 can attest. A number of popular books have been written, as well as scholarly articles, but until now there has been no comprehensive encyclopaedia dealing with archaeology underwater, as well as the archaeology of maritime matters from shipwrecks to harbours.

Both underwater and maritime archaeology are relatively new sciences that are rapidly evolving, both in response to new avenues of inquiry among the archaeological profession, and because of new technological advances that allow archaeologists and explorers to work in ocean depths previously thought unreachable. With recent technological advances, there is no place on the ocean floor too deep for human exploration. The result is a scientific explosion of discoveries, including several that were made while this encyclopaedia was in production. This undoubtedly means that by the time this encyclopaedia is published, new sites will have been found that are not included in this work. This rapid pace of new discoveries will always put any reference work on underwater and maritime archaeology a little behind the times, no matter how hard we editors work to bring new finds, new images, and new facts into print.

Of course, not every underwater or maritime archaeological site or shipwreck that has been found in the world is listed in this encyclopaedia. The volume has always been planned and intended for an international audience, but its North American genesis is inevitably reflected to some extent in its attention to North American concerns. We have endeavoured to include every major site around the world, as well as other significant sites that the contributors have brought to our attention. In some cases, while a site may not be the subject of a specific entry, it will be noted and discussed in a larger entry, usually in one of the overview essays (such as the **Arctic**, **Ancient wrecks**, **Mediterranean**, or **United Kingdom** entries). Nonetheless, we have doubtless not included sites or topics that merit inclusion, and request that readers contact us with suggestions for such entries to be included in future editions. We are specifically interested in entries that have hitherto not been published in English, notably of sites in Asia and in those countries formerly behind the Iron Curtain.

Appropriate ways of exploring and interacting with the submerged past is a contentious issue in the underwater and maritime archaeological profession, and a number of sites, particularly shipwrecks, have been subjected to various levels of non-archaeological recovery for monetary gain, particularly in the past four decades. Some of this has been outright treasure-hunting, while in other cases it has been profiting through the sale of artefacts. While these activities have all been conducted under the legal authority of the states or countries involved, they have raised ethical and professional questions that are the subject of intense debate. One response by the profession has been not to allow the presentation of papers at professional conferences or the publication of articles in some professional journals when a site is deemed to have been 'commercially exploited'. Without offering any comment on the merits of these practices, nor condoning the commercial exploitation of archaeological sites, this volume is intended for the general public, and not just the profession. Many 'commercially exploited' sites are well known to the public, and some meaningful, although incomplete, information about the past has been obtained from them. These sites are included to make this encyclopaedia as inclusive a reference work as possible. In those cases where a site has been the subject of commercial exploitation, we append an editor's note.

Because maritime and underwater archaeology is a relatively new science, the terms 'underwater' and 'maritime' archaeology require some explanation. Underwater archaeology is the practice of archaeology, on any type of site, in a submerged environment. Mayan sites, Roman sites, prehistoric sites, and shipwrecks are thus all included in this volume. Maritime archaeology refers to the archaeological study of maritime culture through sites such as shipwrecks, buried ships, and harbours. Not all archaeologists who practise in the field adhere to these definitions of what they do; some refer to their work as 'nautical' or 'shipwreck' archaeology. Others may simply refer to themselves, for example, as prehistoric archaeologists who sometimes work underwater, as well as on land.

In compiling this encyclopaedia, we contacted more than 150 archaeologists around the world who have worked or who are working underwater or on maritime sites. Rather than ask a small, select group to author the various entries, we decided to seek, whenever possible, the contributions of those who actually did the work, and who were therefore the best possible source of information. The result is a large number of entries written by the acknowledged experts in the field, from around the world, who have actually excavated, dived, and recorded the sites included in the encyclopaedia, from the wreck of *Titanic* to the ancient wreck at Uluburun. The same is true for the technology and techniques articles; here we asked the actual inventors, or leading practitioners of the methods and equipment, to write the entries. In those entries where legal or legislative matters are discussed, we again consulted with the experts, many of whom have worked with these laws, either in helping draft them or adjudicating them in court.

We would like to thank our contributors for their efforts to ensure accuracy and comprehensiveness within the space limitations inevitable in a work of this kind. A number of them, particularly members of the advisory board, took time from exceptionally busy schedules and fieldwork to write their entries. Some of the authors who rose to the challenge above and beyond the call of duty by offering advice and preparing several extensive entries (especially after the book was taken on by British Museum Press) were not members of the advisory board, and we specifically wish to acknowledge the contributions of John Broadwater, Christopher Dobbs, Valerie Fenwick, Richard A. Gould, Jeremy Green, D.L. Hamilton, Colin Martin, Larry Murphy, and Roger Smith. The general editor acknowledges the support and assistance of the editorial board, and especially those members who assumed the task of writing entries for whom authors could not be found, or who could not complete their entries. I specifically thank George Bass, Carl Olof Cederlund, Norm Easton, Paul Johnston, Dan Lenihan, and Seán McGrail for exceptional and much appreciated extra assistance.

The interest and support of the Advisory Council on Underwater Archaeology since the beginning of this project is also greatly appreciated, as is the support of Valerie Fenwick and the *International Journal of Nautical Archaeology*. Much of the essential behind-the-scenes work, including maintaining voluminous correspondence, retyping many entries, and a great deal of other editorial work, was done by Rebecca C. Magallanes of the Vancouver Maritime Museum, without whom this encyclopaedia would not have happened. Johanna Nicholson, Roland Limcaco, Rosario Leonor, and Randall Graham also assisted. We also thank the Board of Trustees of the Vancouver Maritime Museum for their support during the four years this project lasted. We are indebted to the numerous scientific illustrators and providers of photographs for their contributions, and for the permission to reproduce them in this work. Last, but not least, we are very grateful for the support of Emma Way, Head of the Press, and the editorial hand and guidance of Carolyn Jones, Senior Editor, at the British Museum Press.

List of contributors

EDITOR

James P. Delgado
Vancouver Maritime Museum
Vancouver, British Columbia, Canada

EDITORIAL ADVISORY BOARD

Dr George F. Bass
Institute of Nautical Archaeology/
Texas A&M University
College Station, Texas, USA

Dr Carl Olof Cederlund
Swedish National Maritime Museum
Stockholm, Sweden

Dr Norman A. Easton
Yukon College
Whitehorse, Yukon Territory, Canada

Dra Pilar Luna Erreguerena
Instituto Nacional de Antropologia
e Historia
Mexico DF

Graeme Henderson
Western Australia Maritime Museum
Fremantle, Western Australia, Australia

Dr Paul F. Johnston
National Museum of American History
Washington, DC, USA

Daniel J. Lenihan
National Park Service, Submerged
Cultural Resources Unit
Santa Fe, New Mexico, USA

Prof. Seán McGrail
Institute of Archaeology,
University of Oxford
Oxford, England

Dr William N. Still, Jr
University of Hawaii
Kailua-Kona, Hawaii, USA

CONTRIBUTORS

Dr D.K. Abbass (D.K.A.)
Rhode Island Marine Archaeology Project
Newport, Rhode Island, USA

J.R. Adams (J.R.A.)
Centre for Maritime Archaeology,
University of Southampton,
Southampton, England

Christos S. Agouridis (C.S.A.)
Hellenic Institute of Marine Archaeology
Athens, Greece

Richard Fontanez Aldea (R.F.A.)
Consejo para la Conservacion y Estudio
de Sitios y Recursos Arqueológicos Subacuáticos
San Juan, Puerto Rico

Christopher Amer (C.A.)
South Carolina Institute of Archaeology
and Anthropology
Columbia, South Carolina, USA

Philip L. Armitage (P.A.)
Sanibel Island, Florida, USA

Tim Armour (T.A.)
Jason Foundation for Education
Waltham, Massachusetts, USA

Beat Arnold (B.A.)
Musee Cantonal d'Archéologie
Neuchâtel, Switzerland

J. Barto Arnold III (J.B.A.)
Texas Historical Commission
Austin, Texas, USA

Adriane Askins (A.A.)
National Park Service, Submerged
Cultural Resources Unit
Santa Fe, New Mexico, USA

Michele Aubry (M.A.)
National Park Service
Washington, DC, USA

Arthur J. Bachrach (A.B.)
Taos, New Mexico, USA

Dr George F. Bass (G.F.B.)
Institute of Nautical Archaeology/
Texas A&M University
College Station, Texas, USA

Thomas F. Beasley (T.F.B.)
Past President, Underwater Archaeological
Society of British Columbia
Vancouver, British Columbia, Canada

Dr Owen Beattie (O.B.)
University of Alberta
Edmonton, Alberta, Canada

Jan Bill (J.B.)
Centre for Maritime Archaeology
Roskilde, Denmark

Dr Mensun Bound (M.B.)
Oxford University MARE
Oxford, England

Leslie S. Bright (L.B.)
North Carolina Dept. of Cultural Resources
Kure Beach, North Carolina, USA

John D. Broadwater (J.D.B.)
National Oceanic and Atmospheric
Administration
Fort Eustis, Virginia, USA

John Brooks (J.B. 2)
National Park Service, Submerged
Cultural Resources Unit
Santa Fe, New Mexico, USA

Vincent J. Bruno (V.J.B.)
Brooklyn, New York, USA

Claire Calcagno (C.C.2)
Oxford, England

Javier Fernando García Cano (J.F.G.C.)
Fundación Albenga
Buenos Aires, Argentina

Toni L. Carrell (T.L.C.)
Ships of Discovery/Corpus Christi Museum
Corpus Christi, Texas, USA

Dr Carl Olof Cederlund (C.O.C.)
Swedish National Maritime Museum/
University of Stockholm
Stockholm, Sweden

Dr Arne Emil Christensen (A.E.C.)
Viking Ship Museum
Oslo, Norway

Philip D. Claris (P.D.C.)
National Trust
Cirencester, England

John F. Coates (J.F.C.)
SABINAL
Bath, England

Wilburn Cockrell (W.C.)
Tallahassee, Florida, USA

Arthur B. Cohn (A.B.C.)
Lake Champlain Maritime Museum
Vergennes, Vermont, USA

Mark Collard (M.C.)
City of Edinburgh Museums
Archaeological Service,
Edinburgh, Scotland

David L. Conlin (D.L.C.)
Brown University
Providence, Rhode Island, USA

Gregory D. Cook (G.D.C.)
Institute of Nautical Archaeology/
Texas A&M University
College Station, Texas, USA

David J. Cooper (D.J.C.)
State Historical Society of Wisconsin
Madison, Wisconsin, USA

Dr Kevin Crisman (K.C.)
Institute of Nautical Archaeology/
Texas A&M University
College Station, Texas, USA

Clive Cussler (C.C.)
National Underwater and Marine Agency
Paradise Valley, Arizona, USA

Jack E. Custer (J.E.C.)
Steamboat Masters & Associates, Inc.
Louisville, Kentucky, USA

Dr Peter Davies (P.D.)
University of Liverpool
Liverpool, England

Janette Deacon (J.D.)
National Monuments Council
Cape Town, South Africa

Martin Dean (M.D.)
Archaeological Diving Unit,
University of St Andrews,
Fife, Scotland

Nicholas Dean (N.D.)
Edgecombe, Maine, USA

James P. Delgado (J.P.D.)
Vancouver Maritime Museum
Vancouver, British Columbia, Canada

Eusebio Z. Dizon (E.D.)
National Museum of the Philippines
Manila, Philippines

Christopher Dobbs (C.D.)
Mary Rose Trust
Portsmouth, England

Dr Sarah Dromgoole (S.D.)
University of Leicester
Leicester, England

Toby Durden (T.D.)
National Monuments Council
Cape Town, South Africa

Dr Norman A. Easton (N.A.E.)
Yukon College
Whitehorse, Yukon Territory, Canada

Lars Einarsson (L.E.)
Kalmar County Museum
Kalmar, Sweden

Dr Ricardo Elia (R.E.)
Boston University
Boston, Massachusetts, USA

Dr Pilar Luna Erreguerena (P.L.E.)
Instituto Nacional de Antropología e Historia
Mexico DF

Angela C. Evans (A.C.E.)
British Museum
London, England

Lawrence H. Feldman (L.H.F.)
Wheaton, Maryland, USA

Enrico Felici (E.F.)
Rome, Italy

Valerie Fenwick (V.F.)
International Journal of Nautical Archaeology
London, England

Michael A. Fitzgerald (M.A.F.)
Institute of Nautical Archaeology/
Texas A&M University
College Station, Texas, USA

John W. Foster (J.W.F.)
State of California Department of Parks
and Recreation
Sacramento, California, USA

Honor Frost (H.F.)
London, England

Dr Ervan Garrison (E.G.)
University of Georgia
Athens, Georgia, USA

William H. Garzke, Jr (W.H.G.)
Gibbs & Cox
Arlington, Virginia, USA

Jerzy H.J. Gawronski (J.H.J.G.)
VOC Ship *Amsterdam*
Amsterdam, Holland

Peter Gesner (P.G.)
Queensland Museum
South Brisbane, Queensland, Australia

Dr Richard A. Gould (R.A.G.)
Brown University
Providence, Rhode Island, USA

Jeremy Green (J.G.)
Western Australia Maritime Museum
Fremantle, Western Australia

Captain Max Guerout (M.G.)
Association CSS *Alabama*
Paris, France

Dr Elpida Hadjidaki (E.H.)
Dept. of Maritime Antiquities
Athens, Greece

Dr Cheryl Haldane (C.H.)
Bilkent University
Ankara, Turkey

Jerome Lynn Hall (J.L.H.)
San Diego, California, USA

Dr Christopher E. Hamilton (C.E.H.)
US Army Infantry Center, Environmental
Management Division
Fort Benning, Georgia, USA

Dr D.L. Hamilton (D.L.H.)
Institute of Nautical Archaeology/
Texas A&M University
College Station, Texas, USA

Dr Iris A. Hardy (I.A.H.)
Geological Survey of Canada
Dartmouth, Nova Scotia, Canada

Dr Edward C. Harris (E.C.H.)
Bermuda Maritime Museum
Mangrove Bay, Bermuda

Lynn Harris (L.H.)
South Carolina Institute for Archaeology
and Anthropology
Charleston, South Carolina, USA

Jay B. Haviser (J.B.H.)
Institute of Archaeology and Anthropology
of the Netherlands Antilles
Willemstad, Curaçao, Netherlands Antilles

Graeme Henderson (G.H.)
Western Australia Maritime Museum
Fremantle, Western Australia, Australia

List of contributors

Alex Hildred (A.H.)
Mary Rose Trust
Portsmouth, England

Martin Hiscutt (M.H.)
Department of Communications and the Arts
Canberra, Australia

Dr Frederick M. Hocker (F.M.H.)
Institute of Nautical Archaeology/
Texas A&M University
College Station, Texas, USA

Dr Olaf Höckmann (O.H.)
Römish-Germanisches Zentralmuseum
Mainz, Germany

Paul E. Hoffman (P.E.H.)
Louisiana State University
Baton Rouge, Louisiana, USA

Robert A. Holcombe Jr. (R.A.H.)
Confederate Naval Museum
Columbus, Georgia, USA

Jonathan Howland (J.H.)
Woods Hole Oceanographic Institution
Woods Hole, Massachusetts, USA

Fraser Hunter (F.H.)
National Museums of Scotland
Edinburgh, Scotland

Jack Hunter (J.H. 2)
District Archaeologist, Stae of California
San Luis Obispo, California, USA

George Indruszewski (G.I.)
National Museum of Denmark
Roskilde, Denmark

Robin R. Inglis (R.R.I.)
Vancouver, British Columbia, Canada

Keith Jarvis (K.J.)
Poole Museum Service Archaeological Unit
Poole, Dorset, England

W.F. Jeffery (W.F.J.)
Australian Institute for
Maritime Archaeology, Inc.
Adelaide, South Australia

Dr Paul F. Johnston (P.F.J.)
National Museum of American History
Washington, DC, USA

Yaacov Kahanov (Y.K.)
Recanati Centre for Maritime Studies
Haifa, Israel

Dr Donald H. Keith (D.H.K.)
Ships of Discovery/Corpus Christi Museum
Corpus Christi, Texas, USA

Trevor J. Kenchington (T.J.K.)
Underwater Archaeology Society of Nova Scotia
Halifax, Nova Scotia, Canada

Martin Klein (M.K.)
Andover, Massachusetts, USA

Lars Åke Kvarning (L.Å.K.)
Vinklevógen, Sweden

C. Patrick Labadie (C.P.L.)
Canal Park Marine Museum
Duluth, Minnesota, USA

Denise Lakey (D.L.)
Ships of Discovery
Dallas, Texas, USA

Susan B.M. Langley (S.B.M.L.)
Maryland Historical Trust Archaeology Office
Crownsville, Maryland, USA

Brenda Lanzendorf (B.L.)
Brown University
Providence, Rhode Island, USA

Richard Lawrence (R.L.)
North Carolina Underwater Archaeology Unit
Kure Beach, North Carolina, USA

Daniel J. Lenihan (D.J.L.)
National Park Service, Submerged Cultural
Resources Unit
Santa Fe, New Mexico, USA

Margaret E. Leshikar-Denton (M.E.L.)
Cayman Islands National Museum
Grand Cayman, Cayman Islands,
British West Indies

Michel L'Hour (M.L.'H.)
Direction des Recherches Archéologiques
Subaquatiques et Sous-Marines
Marseille, France

Marilyn L. Lytle (M.L.L.)
Thatcher Proffitt & Wood
New York, USA

Dr Anna Marguerite McCann (A.M.M.)
Pawlet, Vermont, USA

Mike McCarthy (M.M.)
Western Australia Maritime Museum
Fremantle, Western Australia

Prof. Seán McGrail (S.M.)
Institute of Archaeology, University of Oxford
Oxford, England

Ian MacLeod (I.M.)
Western Australia Maritime Museum
Fremantle, Western Australia, Australia

Dr Teresita Majewski (T.M. 2)
Statistical Research Inc.
Tucson, Arizona, USA

Corey Malcom (C.M. 2)
Mel Fisher Maritime Heritage Society
Key West, Florida, USA

Roxani E. Margariti (R.E.M.)
Institute of Nautical Archaeology/
Texas A&M University
College Station, Texas, USA

Samuel Mark (S.M. 2)
Institute of Nautical Archaeology/
Texas A&M University
College Station, Texas, USA

Dr Colin Martin (C.M.)
Scottish Institute of Maritime Studies
University of St Andrews
Fife, Scotland

Andrew Mason (A.M.)
Golder Associates Ltd
Burnaby, British Columbia, Canada

Gustav Milne (G.M.)
Institute of Archaeology, University College
London
London, England

David Moore (D.M.)
North Carolina Maritime Museum
Beaufort, North Carolina, USA

Jonathan D. Moore (J.D.M.)
Cataraqui Archaeological Research Foundation
Kingston, Ontario, Canada

Ian A. Morrison (I.A.M.)
Edinburgh, Scotland

Dr Torao Mozai (T.M.)
Tokyo University of Mercantile Marine
Ichikawa, Chiba-Pref, Japan

Larry E. Murphy (L.E.M.)
National Park Service, Submerged
Cultural Resources Unit
Santa Fe, New Mexico, USA

Dr William Murray (W.M.)
University of South Florida
Tampa, Florida, USA

Michael Nash (M.N.)
Tasmanian Parks and Wildlife Service
Hobart, Tasmania, Australia

Dr Robert S. Neyland (R.S.N.)
US Naval Historical Center
Washington, DC, USA

Alexander V. Okorokov (A.V.O.)
Russian Ministry of Culture
and Academy of Sciences
Moscow, Russia

Ian Oxley (I.O.)
Archaeological Diving Unit,
University of St Andrews,
Fife, Scotland

Michael Paris (M.P.)
Past President, Underwater Archaeological
Society of British Columbia
Vancouver, British Columbia, Canada

Claire Peachey (C.P.)
Institute of Nautical Archaeology
Bodrum, Turkey

Dr Charles E. Pearson (C.E.P.)
Coastal Environments, Inc.
Baton Rouge, Louisiana, USA

Scott M. Peters (S.M.P.)
Michigan Historical Museum
Lansing, Michigan, USA

Patrice Pomey (P.P.)
Centre Camille Julian, University de Provence
Aix en Provence, France

Kenneth R. Pott (K.R.P.)
Michigan Maritime Museum
South Haven, Michigan, USA

Dr S.R. Rao (S.R.R.)
National Institute of Oceanography
Goa, India

Mark Redknap (M.R.)
National Museum of Wales
Cardiff, Wales, UK

Eduard G. Reinhardt (E.G.R.)
Dalhousie University
Halifax, Nova Scotia, Canada

Dr Warren Riess (W.R.)
Darling Marine Center
Warpole, Maine, USA

Captain J. Ashley Roach (J.A.R.)
US Department of State
Washington, DC, USA

Wilfredo Ronquillo (W.R. 2)
National Museum of the Philippines
Manila, Philippines

Dr Margaret Rule (M.R. 2)
Mary Rose Trust
Portsmouth, England

Nick Rule (N.R.)
Emsworth, Hampshire, England

Matthew Russell (M.R. 3)
National Park Service, Submerged
Cultural Resources Unit
Santa Fe, New Mexico, USA

Bill Sauder (B.S.)
Houston, Texas, USA

Eric Sauder (E.S.)
Houston, Texas, USA

Donald G. Shomette (D.G.S.)
DGS and Cultural Resource Management
Dunkirk, Maryland, USA

Steven Shope (S.S.)
Sandia Research Associates, Inc.
Albuquerque, New Mexico, USA

Dr Patricia Sibella (P.S.)
Institute of Nautical Archaeology/
Texas A&M University
College Station, Texas, USA

KC Smith (K.C.S.)
Museum of Florida History
Tallahassee, Florida, USA

Roger Smith (R.S.)
Florida Department of State
Tallahassee, Florida, USA

Timothy G. Smith (T.G.S.)
National Park Service, Submerged
Cultural Resources Unit
Santa Fe, New Mexico, USA

Donna J. Souza (D.J.S.)
Brown University
Providence, Rhode Island, USA

Michael Stammers (M.S.)
Merseyside Maritime Museum
Liverpool, England

Mark Staniforth (M.S. 2)
The Flinders University of South Australia
Adelaide, South Australia

Dr Richard J. Steffy (R.S.2)
Institute of Nautical Archaeology/
Texas A&M University
College Station, Texas, USA

Willis Stevens (W.S.)
Parks Canada
Ottawa, Ontario, Canada

Dr William N. Still, Jr (W.N.S.)
University of Hawaii
Manoa, Hawaii, USA

Melanie J. Stright (M.J.S.)
US Dept. of the Interior
Hemdon, Virginia, USA

Leif Svalesen (L.S.)
Brattekliev
Arendal, Norway

Dr David Switzer (D.S.)
Plymouth State College
Plymouth, New Hampshire, USA

Bruce Terrell (B.T.)
National Oceanic and Atmospheric
Administration
Silver Spring, Maryland, USA

Dr Richard W. Unger (R.W.U.)
University of British Columbia
Vancouver, British Columbia, Canada

Dr Frederick H. Van Doorninck (F.H.D.)
Institute of Nautical Archaeology/
Texas A&M University
College Station, Texas, USA

Dr Robert Lindley Vann (R.L.V.)
University of Maryland
College Park, Maryland, USA

Karel Vlierman (K.V.)
Institute of Nautical Archaeology/
Texas A&M University,
College Station, Texas, USA

Kenneth J. Vrana (K.J.V.)
Michigan State University
East Lansing, Michigan, USA

Dr Shelley Wachsmann (S.W.)
Institute of Nautical Archaeology/
Texas A&M University
College Station, Texas, USA

Barrie B. Walden (B.B.W.)
Woods Hole Oceanographic Institution
Woods Hole, Massachusetts, USA

Dr M.D. de Weerd (M.D.W.)
Instituut voor Pre- en Protohistorische
Archeologie
Amsterdam, Netherlands

Shirley A. Whitfield (S.A.W.)
Cardiff Law School
Cardiff, Wales

Mark Wilde-Ramsing (M.W.-R.)
North Carolina Dept. of Cultural Resources
Kure Beach, North Carolina, USA

Dr Hector Williams (H.W.)
University of British Columbia
Vancouver, British Columbia, Canada

Robyn P. Woodward (R.P.W.)
Vancouver, British Columbia, Canada

E.V. Wright (E.V.W.)
Gloucestershire, England

Dana Yoerger (D.Y.)
Woods Hole Oceanographic Institution
Woods Hole, Massachusetts, USA

Joseph Zarzynski (J.Z.)
Bateaux Below, Inc.
Wilton, New York, USA

How to use this book

The *Encyclopaedia of Maritime and Underwater Archaeology* is alphabetically arranged, with over 500 topic headings. About a quarter of these are cross-references to articles that deal with the subject concerned. Further cross-references are given in the text of the entries themselves. The entry **Reconstruction**, for example, yields cross-references for Buried ships, Ronson Ship, Quebec Bateaux, Archival research, Experimental archaeology, Red Bay, Yassiada Wrecks, Kyrenia Ship, Khufu Ship, Bremen Cog, Skuldelev Ships, Sea of Galilee Wreck, *Vasa*, IJsselmeerpolders Wrecks, and Quanzhou Ship, all entries that deal in a more detailed fashion with subjects and sites discussed in the Reconstruction entry. Cross-referenced article headings are shown in **bold type** in the text.

A full index will be found at the end of the book.

The encyclopaedia's entries cover sites, be they individual shipwrecks, groups of wrecks, or submerged cities and harbours; as well as research themes and topics of study, legislation, and other legal matters; and finally the technology and techniques employed in the practice of maritime and underwater archaeology. To help readers locate topic headings relevant to a given area, the Subject List by Topic cites headings by general subject, each followed by a major category heading. These major headings are listed alphabetically, as is the order of the topic headings that follow. In addition, each entry supplies cross-references to other articles in the volume that bear on the subject in question. Despite the unavoidable overlap among articles dealing with related subjects, readers should consult all entries thus indicated to be certain of obtaining full information.

Most of the entries are accompanied by suggestions for ADDITIONAL READING. These reference lists are not exhaustive bibliographies, but are pointers to (primarily) recent and easily accessible works to which readers can refer for more information. With the improved access to university resources through interlibrary loans and the Internet, we have included unpublished masters' theses and doctoral dissertations, as they are the greatest source of information on the discipline and many of the sites cited in the entries. Each entry, where possible, also includes an item with a longer bibliography that may serve as an entry point into the popular and technical literature on the subject.

Subject list by topic

Sites

MARITIME/UNDERWATER SITES (NON-SHIPWRECK)
Actian Naval
 Monument
Alexandria
Caesarea Maritima
Cosa, harbour of
Cramond Lioness
Dublin
Dvaraka
Franklin Expedition
 graves
Harbour studies
Hoff's Store
Högholmen Island
Kenchreai
USS *Macon*
Pontia
Port Royal, Jamaica
Quetico-Superior sites
Red Bay
Thera
Zwammerdam

PREHISTORIC ARCHAEOLOGICAL SITES
Chichén Itzá Cenote
Crannogs
Lake Neuchâtel
Lake Phelps Canoes
Lake Zürich
Lithic artefacts
Little Salt Spring
Montague Harbour
Palos Verdes anchor
 stones
Prehistoric
 archaeology
Quaternary coastlines
 and land bridges
Reef netting
Shell midden
Warm Mineral
 Springs

SHIP BURIALS/ BURIED SHIPS/ VESSEL SITES ON LAND
Barland's Farm Boat
Beached shipwreck
 sites
Bjorke Boat

Brigg Logboat
Brigg 'Raft'
Bryggen
Buried ships
County Hall Ship
Dashur Boats
Dover Boat
Gedesby Ship
Gokstad Ship
Graveney Boat
Halsenoy Boat
Hasholme Logboat
Hjortspring Boat
Herculaneum Boat
IJsselmeerpolders
 Wrecks
James River Bateaux
Kalmar Harbour
 Wrecks
Khufu Ship
Lisht timbers
Mainz Boats
Marseille Bourse
 Wreck
New Guy's House
 Boat
Niantic
Nydam Boat
Oseberg Ship
Quebec Bateaux
Ronson Ship
St Mary
Severn Wrecks
Ship burials
Snape Boat
Sparrow Hawk
Sutton Hoo
Tune Ship
Tyjger
Utrecht Boats

SHIPWRECK SITES, ARRANGED BY DATE
Ancient (BC)
Albenga Wreck
Ancient wrecks
Antikythera Wreck
Athlit Ram
Bon-Porté Wreck
Cape Gelidonya
 Wreck
Capo Rasocolmo
 Wreck
Comacchio Wreck
Dattilo Wreck

Dramont Wreck
Ferriby Boats
Giglio Wreck
Grand Congloué
Humber Wrecks
Kyrenia Ship
La Chrétienne
La Madonnina Wreck
Liburnian Sewn Boat
Madrague de Giens
 Wreck
Mahdia Wreck
Marsala Punic
 Warship
Sea of Galilee Wreck
Serçe Limani
Sheytan Deresi Wreck
Straits of Messina
 Wreck
Uluburun

AD 1–750
Blackfriars Wreck I
Butuan Boats
Guernsey Wreck
Isis Wreck
Iskandil Burnu
 Shipwreck
La Chrétienne
Lake Nemi ships
Sea of Galilee Wreck
Skuldelev Ships
Yassiada Wrecks
Zwammerdam

Medieval (AD 750–1500)
Blackfriars wrecks III,
 IV
Bozburun Wreck
Bremen Cog
Bryggen
Butuan boats
Grace Dieu
Kublai Khan Fleet
Magor Pill Boat
Quanzhou Ship
Serçe Limani
Shinan Gun
 Shipwreck
Virolahti Boat
Yassiada wrecks

16th century
Alderney Wreck
Bahía Mujeres Wreck

Cattewater Wreck
Æl Gran Grifon
Emanuel Point Ship
Girona
Highborn Cay Wreck
Kravel Wreck
La Belle
La Gallega
Lake Garda Galley
La Trinidad Valencera
Lomellina
Mary Rose
Molasses Reef Wreck
Padre Island wrecks
San Agustin
Santa Lucia
São Bento
Spanish Armada
Studland Bay Wreck

17th century
Anne
L'Anse aux Bouleaux
 Wreck
Batavia
Blackfriars Wreck II
Dartmouth
Duart Wreck
Kennemerland
Kronan
Mary
Mauritius
Monte Cristi Wreck
Mulan Wreck
Nassau
Nossa Senhora de
 Atalaia do Pinheiro
Nuestra Señora de
 Atocha
Nuestra Señora de la
 Concepción
St John's Bahamas
 Wreck
San Diego
San Juan de Sicilia
Santa Maria de la Rosa
Santíssimo Sacramento
 (1647)
Santíssimo Sacramento
 (1668)
Santo Antonio de Tanna
HMS *Sapphire*
Seahawk
Sea Venture
Trial

Vasa
Vergulde Draeck
Witte Leeuw

18th century
Adelaar
Albion
Älvsnabben Wreck
Amsterdam
Anna Maria
'Battering' Ships of
 Gibraltar
HMS *Betsy*
Boscawen
Bounty
Brown's Ferry Vessel
HMS *Charon*
Colebrooke
Cornwallis Cave
 Wreck
Curaçao
HMS *De Braak*
Defence
Doddington
Dry Tortugas National
 Park
El Nuevo Constante
Evstafii
Flota of 1715
Flota of 1733
Fredensborg
Griffin
Henrietta Marie
Hollandia
Jutholmen Wreck
Land Tortoise
La Pérouse ships
L'Orient
Louisbourg Wrecks
Machault
Malcolm Boat
Marguerite
Meresteyn
Nanking Cargo Wreck
Nieuwe Rhoon
Pandora
Penobscot Expedition
Philadelphia
Prince de Conty
Reader's Point Wreck
Risdam
Ronson Ship
St Nikolai
Sankt Mikael
Sirius

Slot ter Hooge
Stirling Castle
Sussex
Sydney Cove
Ten Sail, Wreck of the
Terence Bay Wreck
Whydah Galley
Wiawaka Bateaux
 Cluster
Yorktown shipwrecks
Zeewijk
Zuytdorp

19th century
Actaeon
HMS *Agamemnon*
CSS *Alabama*
Arabia
Arniston
Beaver
Bertrand
HMS *Birkenhead*
Breadalbane
Brown's Bay Vessel
Brunswick
USS *Cairo*
Cape Fear Civil War
 Shipwreck Group
Central America
Charles Cooper
CSS *Chattahoochee*
Chesapeake Flotilla
Cleopatra's Barge
Clydesdale Plantation
 Vessel
SS *Columbus*
USS *Cumberland*
Day Dawn
Dry Tortugas National
 Park
Dry Tortugas National
 Park Shipwreck
 DRTO-036
Eagle
Earl of Abergavenny
East Key Wreck
Egeria
E. Nordevall
Ericsson
Frolic
CSS *Georgia*
Hamilton and *Scourge*
USS *Hatteras*
Hindostan
H.L. *Hunley*

13

General

Abandoned Shipwreck Act (US)

Law of 1987 that establishes government ownership over the majority of abandoned shipwrecks located in waters of the United States of America and creates a framework within which shipwrecks are managed. Enacted in 1988, it affirms the authority of State governments to claim and manage abandoned shipwrecks on State submerged lands. It makes the laws of salvage and finds not apply to any shipwreck covered under the Act and asserts that shipwrecks are multiple-use resources.

Since the 1950s, citing the Submerged Lands Act of 1953, State governments have claimed title to and control over abandoned shipwrecks on State submerged lands. By the 1980s, over half of the States had enacted laws and established programmes to manage abandoned historic shipwrecks in State waters. However, Federal Admiralty Court also claimed jurisdiction over abandoned shipwrecks. Admiralty courts often treated historic shipwrecks as commodities lost at sea that were in marine peril and in need of salvage to be returned to commerce. Salvage awards often disregarded a shipwreck's historical or archaeological values, thereby causing a loss of important scientific information. Nonetheless, some States prevailed in their claims to title and management authority over abandoned shipwrecks in State waters. The result was confusion and inconsistency from court to court and from State to State over ownership and regulatory control of abandoned shipwrecks.

These problems were resolved by the Abandoned Shipwreck Act. Under the statute, the US Government asserted title to three classes of abandoned shipwrecks located within three nautical miles of the US coastline and in the internal navigable waters of the United States. The Act covers abandoned shipwrecks that are embedded in submerged lands, abandoned shipwrecks that are embedded in coralline formations protected by a State, and abandoned shipwrecks that are on submerged lands and included in or determined eligible for inclusion in the **National Register of Historic Places**. Upon asserting title to these shipwrecks, the US Government transferred its title to the government entity that owns the submerged lands containing the shipwrecks. As a result, State governments have title to shipwrecks

The remains of Chisholm *in the Isle Royale National Park, USA. (National Park Service/Larry Murphy)*

located on State lands, the US Government has title to shipwrecks located on Federal lands, and Indian tribes have title to shipwrecks located on Indian lands. However, the US Government continues to hold title to sunken US warships and other shipwrecks entitled to **Sovereign Immunity**, no matter where the vessels are located. Such vessels are not affected by the statute.

One of the statute's most important provisions specifies that the laws of salvage and finds do not apply to abandoned shipwrecks claimed by the government under the Act (see **Salvage Law**). This provision removes those shipwrecks from the jurisdiction of Federal Admiralty Court. It means that the shipwrecks and their cargo and contents are no longer treated only as commodities lost at sea and in need of salvage. This means that an historically valuable shipwreck can be treated as an archaeological or historical site instead of a commercial property.

Another important provision of the statute addresses rights of public access. Shipwrecks are identified as resources having multiple values and uses that are not to be set aside for any one purpose or interest group. This includes recreational and educational opportunities for sport divers and fishermen, historical values important to archaeologists and historic preservationists, and habitat areas for marine life. In addition, shipwrecks may

generate tourism and other forms of commerce and contain valuable cargoes and objects of interest to commercial salvors and treasure-hunters.

States are directed to provide reasonable access by the public, protect natural resources and habitat areas, guarantee recreational exploration of shipwreck sites, and allow appropriate public and private sector recovery when the shipwreck's historical values and surrounding environment are protected. In addition, States are encouraged to create underwater parks to provide additional protection for shipwrecks. States are authorized to use Federal funds from the Historic Preservation Fund grants programme to study, interpret, protect, and preserve historic shipwrecks.

As required under the statute, the National Park Service, US Department of the Interior, prepared guidelines to assist States and Federal agencies in carrying out their responsibilities under the Act. Issued in 1990, the guidelines provide advice on establishing and funding shipwreck management programmes and technical guidance on surveying, identifying, documenting, and evaluating shipwrecks. In addition, they suggest ways to make sites publicly accessible and to recover shipwrecks using public and private entities. They also include advice on establishing volunteer programmes, interpreting shipwreck sites, and creating and operating underwater parks.

The constitutionality of the Abandoned Shipwreck Act has been challenged and affirmed in Federal Admiralty Court. One case involved a shipwreck believed to be *Seabird*, which sank in Lake Michigan in 1868. This case examined whether Congress exceeded its authority to legislate in admiralty and maritime law when it made the laws of salvage and finds not apply to abandoned shipwrecks covered under the Act. The court ruled that the Constitution was not violated, noting that the law of salvage was unaffected by the Act since it does not apply to abandoned shipwrecks and that, while the law of finds does apply to abandoned shipwrecks, shipwrecks embedded in a State's submerged lands belong to the State under the embeddedness doctrine.

Another case involved a shipwreck from the time of Columbus that lay in the territorial waters of the US Virgin Islands. In this case, the court also upheld the constitutionality of the statute, noting that it does not introduce an element of non-uniformity into admiralty law and does not violate the Due Process Clause of the Fifth Amendment to the Constitution.

The Abandoned Shipwreck Act applies in the fifty States of the United States, the District of Columbia, **Puerto Rico**, Guam, the US Virgin Islands, American Samoa, and the Northern Mariana Islands. A shipwreck is defined to include the vessel or wreck, its cargo, and other contents. The term embedded means firmly affixed in submerged lands or coralline formations such that tools of excavation are required to move bottom sediments to gain access to the shipwreck, its cargo, and any part. M.A.

ADDITIONAL READING

Abandoned Shipwreck Act of 1987. Public Law 100–298, 43 USC. 2101–2106, approved 28 April, 1988.

Aubry, M.C., 1992, 'Federal and State Shipwreck Management in the United States of America', *Bulletin of the Australian Institute for Maritime Archaeology*, 16, 1, 19–22.

Croome, A. , 1992, 'The United States' Abandoned Shipwreck Act Goes into Action: A Report', *International Journal of Nautical Archaeology*, 21, 1, 39–53.

Sunken Treasure, Inc. v. Unidentified, Wrecked, and Abandoned Vessel 857 F. Supp. 1129 (DVI 1994).

US Department of the Interior National Park Service's Abandoned Shipwreck Act Guidelines, Federal Register 55:50116–50145, 4 December, 1990; Federal Register 55:51528–51529, 14 December, 1990; Federal Register 56:7875, 26 February , 1991, Washington, DC.

Zych vs. Unidentified, Wrecked and Abandoned Vessel 19 F.3d 1136 (7th *Cir.* 1994), aff'g 811 F. Supp. 1300 (ND Ill. 1992).

Absolute dating

Various scientific means used to precisely date artefacts or assemblages, often down to a particular calendar year (with an error factor usually cited as well). Many absolute, or chronometric, dating methods use applied chemistry or nuclear physics; others relate observed geological or botanical phenomena to the objects being dated. They are distinctly different from relative chronological dating methods (geochronology, stratigraphy, seriation, cross-dating), which provide comparative dating (earlier/later) between artefacts, assemblages, or sites. There are a number of different techniques or types of absolute dating available to archaeologists, depending on the nature and age of a particular artefact and its site or context.

The simplest and most accurate of the absolute dating techniques is dendrochronology, developed by astronomer A.E. Douglas of the University of Arizona in 1929 to study past climatic variations. It is based upon the observation that trees produce concentric growth rings each year, with dry years producing thin rings and wet years yielding thicker rings. Distinct and unique patterns of thick and thin rings emerge over series of decades; by comparing the patterns from archaeological samples with known tree ring sequences, precise dates can be derived. A dendrochronological date provides only a *terminus post quem*, since the cutting of a tree used in a wooden artefact does not necessarily indicate the year the artefact was made nor if and when a piece of wood may have been reused. In North America the technique is most useful in the American West and Southwest, where the derived sequence of the bristlecone pine goes back thousands of years. European sequences go back at least as far as the Middle Ages, and they are continually being pushed backwards.

Obsidian hydration dating, a geological technique, was first developed by the US Geological Survey in the 1960s. It is based upon the observation that obsidian, a glassy volcanic product, absorbs water in its outer surface when exposed to the elements. The absorption rate depends upon local climatic conditions and temperatures at the sample source, since warmer climates yield a faster hydration rate. By measuring the hydration

thickness layer on a worked surface of an exposed obsidian sample, a *terminus post quem* can be derived for the working of the piece. Problems with interpretation of the dating results may arise when reworked or reburied samples provide conflicting or unclear results. Local and regional hydration rates are still being developed and refined.

Varve dating is also useful in North America and Scandinavia, where glacial studies have produced distinctive chronologies for the past 10,000 years. Developed by Swedish researchers de Geer and Antevs, this technique is based upon the observation that in a year's warmer months, flowing water from melting glaciers deposits measurable sediments that overlap one another, much like stratigraphic lenses in an archaeological balk on a terrestrial site. Known as varves, these sediment deposits have been cross-dated with others back to the last glacial retreat, providing absolute dates for cultural deposits within them. Problems can arise from particularly dry or wet years, when no (or multiple) deposits can result; moreover, only regional chronologies are currently available. In addition, samples must usually be collected by geologists, who may not be readily available.

One of the most widespread types of radioactive dating is radiocarbon age determination, abbreviated as carbon-14 (C^{14}). This outgrowth of post-World War II atomic research, based on measuring the rate of decay of the radioactive isotope of carbon, was developed by Dr Walter Libby in 1948. Normal carbon has twelve protons and neutrons in its nucleus; its radioactive isotope, which is produced in the upper atmosphere at a constant rate, has an additional pair of neutrons. All living things (plant and animal) contain the same ratio of the two carbons, which are absorbed by respiration. When an organism dies, it ceases absorbing carbon, and the radioactive isotope begins to revert to normal carbon at a known rate. After 5,730 (+/-40) years, only half of the C^{14} will be left, and after another equal interval, half of that amount will remain, and so on. Thus, the half-life of C^{14} is 5,730 years. By measuring the amount of radioactivity, the age of an organic artefact can be determined precisely. This is done by purifying and converting an artefact sample to gas (by burning) and then placing it in a thick lead-lined container to prevent contamination by cosmic-ray bombardment. The radioactivity is then measured by extremely sensitive instrumentation, and the count is converted to a chronological scale. Errors can be introduced by a number of circumstances, which are recognized and compensated for by a date range generally expressed as a plus or minus factor, such as 2300 +/-200 years BP (Before Present [1950]). The technique is most accurate for the past 50,000 years, although samples can be radioactively 'enhanced' to increase their datable range.

Potassium-argon dating was developed in 1950 by Professor Koroff at New York University; this procedure is similar to C[14] dating but is based upon potassium, whose half-life conversion to argon takes 1.3 billion years. This technique is useful for dating back from 50,000 BP to millions of years ago and is applied mostly to early man sites. Samples must be inorganic crystalline or glassy materials (rock, pottery) with some potassium content, and must not have been exposed to weathering. This dating method has a number of limitations and is still undergoing refinement.

Less accurate and therefore of less relative use to archaeologists is the thermoluminescence dating method (TO), devised by Professor Jonson at Dartmouth College in 1964. It is mainly used for dating pottery from 300,000 to 10,000 BP, although it also works for many rocks and minerals. It is based upon the principle that when crystalline materials are heated, vibrations in their lattice matrix release electrons, which recombine with lattice atoms, emitting light in the process. The amount of light is related to the amount of radiation (particles or rays) absorbed by the object since last heated; for pottery, this would be either the original firing or subsequent hearth fire, conflagration, etc. The older the sample, the more light or thermoluminescence is produced. This is calibrated against a base sample, obtained by placing a test phosphor at the site for up to a year to absorb ambient radiation and mitigate seasonal vibrations. Accuracy is affected by over a dozen known agents and a number of unknowns, aggravated by the need to make ten to fifteen different measurements, each with its own random error factor. Consequently, TO is seldom used unless other dating techniques are unavailable.

Fission track or alpha recoil dating is best for volcanic products or glass, but can also be used for fossilized bones, minerals, or pottery containing them (or measurable amounts of uranium). Developed in the mid-1960s by Fleischer, its useful date range extends from *c.* 20 BP back several billions of years. It is reliant upon the small marks or tracks left behind in mineral crystals or glasses when uranium or thorium atoms decay into other substances. After undergoing neutron illumination, these tracks are compared with those in specimens of known date, after which the sample is etched, polished, and recounted. The polished surface is then placed against a mica or plastic sheet and undergoes neutron bombardment in a reactor, which allows a uranium count. The tracks in the mica or plastic sheet are then counted; their number is proportional to the uranium count and neutron matrix, thereby allowing derivation of an absolute date. The technique is labour-intensive and expensive; also, there are few laboratories capable of offering this technique, making it impractical when other dating methods are applicable.

These and other newly developing chronometric dating methods, such as coralline growth and lead-210 dating, all have their strong and weak points. It is to be hoped that in the future more variables and error factors can be minimized or eliminated for these techniques, allowing more precise date ranges and reduced chance of error or misinterpretation. In the meantime, samples for dating must be taken with care and in sufficient numbers to mitigate these error-introducing factors, bearing in mind that these methods support rather than replace the older, more reliable methods used by archaeologists to derive dates for their findings. P.F.J.

ADDITIONAL READING

Deetz, J., 1967, *Invitation to Archaeology*, Garden City, New York.

Joukowsky, M., 1980, *A Complete Manual of Field Archaeology*, Englewood Cliffs, New Jersey.

Michael, H.N. and Ralph, E.K., (eds), 1971, *Dating Techniques for the Archaeologist*, Cambridge, Massachusetts.

Michels, J.W., 1973, *Dating Methods in Archaeology*, New York.

Radiocarbon, 1959

Sharer, R.J. and Ashmore, W., 1993, *Archaeology: Discovering Our Past*, Mountain View, California.

Actaeon

Wooden barque built at Miramichi, New Brunswick, Canada in 1838 and condemned in the **Falkland Islands** in 1853 while on a voyage from Liverpool to San Francisco with a cargo of coal. *Actaeon* lies as a hulk with a list to port in Stanley Harbour inshore from the hulk of the American packet ship **Charles Cooper**. The 561 ton vessel is one of the oldest known examples of Canadian wooden shipbuilding, and has some iron hanging knees in her construction. Cut down to her 'tween-decks she served for many years as a jetty. Her condition is deteriorating and her aft end collapsed a number of years ago. Piled on the remains of the hull is a varied collection of marine hardware including capstans and windlass of unknown provenance, as well as some material taken from the hulks of *Fennia* and SS *Great Britain*. As far as can be determined there has been no detailed survey of *Actaeon* beyond a few rough drawings. N.D.

ADDITIONAL READING

Smith, J., 1985, *Condemned at Stanley*, Picton Press, Wiltshire.

Bound, M., 1981, *The Falkland Islands 19 cent. Sailing Ships*, Report to the World Ship Trust.

Actian Naval Monument

A war memorial built by Octavian (the future emperor Augustus) on the site of his camp near Actium to commemorate his victory over Mark Antony and Cleopatra in the Actian War (32–31 BC). Five ancient authors (Dio Cassius 51.1.3; Suetonius *Aug.* 18.2, 96.2; Plutarch *Ant.* 65.3; Philippus in *Anth. Pal.* 6.236; Strabo 7.7.6) describe the site as an open-air shrine with at least two statues and an impressive display of warship rams. Still surviving on the side of Mt Michalitsi near modern-day Proviso (western Greece), the monument preserves unexpected information concerning the final naval battle of the war (2 September 31 BC) and the largest warships in the vanquished fleet.

Sporadic excavations since the monument's discovery in 1913 have uncovered a rectangular podium, supported on three sides by a massive retaining wall, and the foundations of a long covered portico or stoa. The southern retaining wall amazingly preserves 23 elaborately carved sockets which originally held the rams of a grand rostral display along the front of the hillside

The inscription on the Actian Naval Monument. (W.M.Murray)

podium. Considering that 15 m of the wall have not survived intact, the original dedication probably included as many as thirty-five weapons, and represents a 10 per cent offering or tithe from the 350 ships that were captured during the course of the war. The entire display was crowned with a long inscription (which partly survives), carved in 30 cm high letters, recording the name of the dedicant, the date (29 BC), the deities honoured (Neptune and Mars), and the reason for the dedication. Partly Hellenistic in its grandeur, partly Roman in the use of a rostral display, Octavian's memorial served as the victory monument for the city called Nikopolis ('Victory City') that he built at the foot of the hill.

In addition to its obvious importance as a major Augustan monument, the Campsite

at the battle's close. Of the 500 ships that accompanied Antony and Cleopatra to Greece, for example, almost 90 remain unaccounted for (350 were captured while only a few more than 60 escaped back to Egypt). Did these weapons somehow detach from their vessels' burning timbers and sink beyond the range of Octavian's salvors? Whatever the answer, those wishing to understand the battle and its ships must carefully consider the evidence from the Campsite Memorial. Someday, perhaps, a careful investigation of the monument's platform will complete our picture of this important Augustan naval monument.W.M.M.

ADDITIONAL READING

Murray, W.M., 1993, 'Le Trophée naval de la Victoire d'Actium', *Marine Antique, Les Dossiers d'Archéologie*, 128, 66–73.

The Actian Naval Monument. (W.M. Murray)

Memorial also preserves important evidence about the Battle of Actium – the last major sea battle of antiquity – and the warships that took part in it. For example, the wall's carefully carved sockets correspond closely to the sectional shape of the **Athlit Ram** and reveal that the Actian bows were constructed in a manner similar to the Athlit bow. The Actian examples, however, were much more massive, and were designed to deliver and withstand ramming blows of much greater force. The sockets, moreover, are arranged in a progression of generally decreasing sizes from west to east, and represent a range of warship sizes from *dekereis* (i.e. with ten banks of oars) to *hexereis* (six), or perhaps to *pentereis* (five). The numbers behind the dedication also seem to confirm the ferocity of the final battle and support the accounts that describe a great conflagration

Murray, W.M., in press, 'Polyremes from the Battle of Actium: Some Construction Details', in H. Tzalas, (ed.), *Tropis IV: Proceedings of the 4th International Symposium on Ship Construction in Antiquity, 1991.*

Murray, W.M. and Petsas, M., 1988, 'The Spoils of Actium', *Archaeology*, 41, 5, 28–35.

Murray, W.M. and Petsas, M., 1989, 'Octavian's Campsite Memorial for the Actian War', *Transactions of the American Philosophical Society*, 79, 4.

Adelaar

Dutch East Indiaman wrecked off Barra in the Outer Hebrides, Scotland, in 1728. *Adelaar* ('Eagle') was built for the Zeeland chamber of the company in 1722 to the standard specifications of a medium-sized vessel for the Indies route (length 44 m,

beam 11 m, and laden draught 4.7 m). She had a laden displacement of about 700 tons and carried an armament of thirty-six muzzle-loading guns, two of which (those nearest the compass) were bronze, and the rest cast iron. Eight light breechloading swivel guns were mounted on the upper works to counter the threat of small-boat piracy in Asian waters.

Between 1722 and 1727 *Adelaar* made two round trips to Batavia, and in early 1728 preparations were made for a third voyage under a new skipper, Willem de Keyser. She left her home port of Middelburg on 21 March with a general cargo and seventeen chests of specie, mainly in the form of silver ingots and coins, for the purchase of her return lading of spices, tea, and porcelain. Her route took her around the north of the British Isles, and on 4 April, in severe weather, she struck the exposed northwesterly headland of Barra, which she had evidently been trying to weather. There were no survivors.

A remarkable salvage operation to recover the treasure was set in train by Alexander Mackenzie, an official of the Scottish Court of Admiralty in Edinburgh, who used his family connections to engage the services of Captain Jacob Rowe, a diving pioneer with a patented 'engine'. This machine, in effect a closed cylinder with sealed sleeves through which the diver's arms protruded, could be used (albeit with great discomfort) at depths of up to 18 m. *Adelaar* lay in less than half that. Almost all of the specie was recovered and brought to Edinburgh, where subsequent litigation over its division has left a wealth of documentary information about *Adelaar*, the circumstances of her wrecking, and the saga of the salvage operation.

Information derived from this documentation, together with a surviving local tradition about the wreck, led to its discovery in 1972. Two years of investigative work conducted under the direction of Colin Martin of the **Scottish Institute of Maritime Studies** at St Andrews University revealed that a combination of the site's extreme exposure, and the thoroughness of the 18th-century salvage, had scrambled, degraded, and dispersed much of the archaeological evidence. Nevertheless the site was significant in showing that valid conclusions can still be drawn from such an apparently unpromising wreck formation. This was possible because the extensive documentation provided a set of 'answers' about the ship's size, type, origin, and cargo which could be tested against the reality of the remains as they appeared on the seabed. The conclusion to be drawn is that most wrecks, however dispersed and

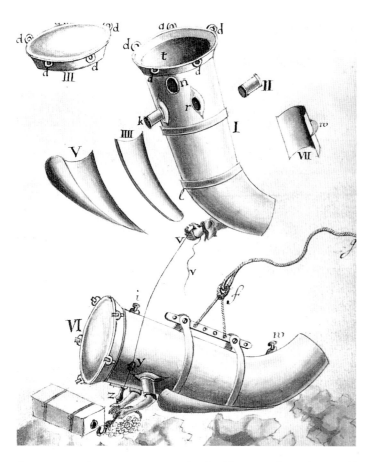

fragmentary they may seem, retain significant levels of archaeological cohesion which only systematic investigation can identify and interpret. C.M.

ADDITIONAL READING

Martin, C.J.M., 1992, 'The Wreck of the Dutch East-Indiaman *Adelaar* off Barra in 1728', in R. Mason and N. MacDougall, (eds), *People and Power in Scotland: Essays in Honour of T.C. Smout*, Edinburgh, 145–69.

Admiral Graf Spee

Wreck of a German pocket battleship scuttled in the estuary of the Rio de la Plata (River Plate), Uruguay, in December 1939. In 1997 **Oxford University MARE** (under the direction of Mensun Bound), at the request of the Uruguayan Government, and in collaboration with the Uruguayan Navy, embarked on a survey of the German panzerschiff *Admiral Graf Spee*. Although bad conditions (extremely strong currents, near-zero visibility, and fishing nets) made a full survey impossible, vital information on the nature, disposition, and deterioration of the wreck was gathered which resulted in the recovery of one of the 150 mm guns for display in Montevideo.

The panzerschiff *Admiral Graf Spee* (named after Count Graf von Spee, the victor of Coronel, who died when his fleet was later destroyed by the British during the Battle of the Falklands on 8 December 1914) was launched at Wilhelmshaven, Germany, on 30 June 1937. The ship was 610 ft (186 m) long, had a maximum beam of 71 ft (21.6 m) and was powered by four two-stroke diesel engines capable of providing 54,000 hp, giving *Graf Spee* a top speed of 28.5 knots. The main armament consisted of six 280 mm guns fitted to triple turrets on rotating mounts. Its medium or side artillery was comprised of eight 105 mm guns in single positions on pivoting mounts. The remaining ordnance consisted of six 105 mm, eight 37 mm, and twelve 20 mm anti-aircraft machine guns. At the stern *Graf Spee* mounted eight torpedo tubes. Below the funnel the ship carried two catapult-launched reconnaissance aircraft. The wartime crew of *Graf Spee* numbered 1,188.

Graf Spee was intended as a surface raider. On 21 August 1939, in anticipation of the war which started eleven days later, she slipped out of Wilhelmshaven and took up a waiting position in a remote area of the Atlantic between Brazil and Africa. The commander was Kapitan Zur See Hans Langsdorff. On 26 September the German Admiralty ordered Langsdorff to begin operations; on 30 September *Graf Spee* stopped and sank the British freighter

Clement. In total, *Graf Spee* sank nine British merchant ships, without sustaining a single loss of life. An indication of the seriousness with which the Allies viewed its activities can be surmised from the fact that nine hunting groups, comprising twenty-three capital ships – aircraft carriers, battleships, and cruisers – that were badly needed for coastal defence and convoy duty, were despatched to find and destroy *Graf Spee*. On 13 December 1939 she was located off the River Plate by a British force consisting of the cruisers *Exeter*, *Ajax*, and *Achilles*. Following a fierce action in which *Exeter* was nearly lost, the badly damaged *Graf Spee* ran for neutral Montevideo. Obliged to leave without proper repairs, Langsdorff scuttled *Graf Spee* a short distance from Montevideo on 17 December. Three days later, Langsdorff committed suicide in Buenos Aires.

The wreck of *Graf Spee* sits deep in the mud, listing heavily to starboard. The conning tower and smokestack have collapsed, and the after hull has separated from the main body of the ship. The aft turret itself, and one of *Graf Spee*'s torpedo mounts, were not located during the survey. M.B.

ADDITIONAL READING

Campbell, A., 1940, *The Battle of the Plate*, Toronto.

Garzke, W.H. *et al.*, 1988, *Battleships: Axis and Neutral Battleships in World War II*, Annapolis, Maryland.

Millington-Drake, E., 1964, *The Drama of Graf Spee and the Battle of the Plate*, London.

Advisory Committee on Historic Wreck Sites (UK)

The body that advises Secretaries of State in the UK on all matters pertaining to the **Protection of Wrecks Act** of 1973. Its headquarters are in the Heritage Branch of the Department of the Environment. It works closely with the **Archaeological Diving Unit**. J.P.D.

Advisory Council on Underwater Archaeology (US)

An international body of archaeologists, government employees (State and Federal), conservators and professional museum staff, incorporated in the United States. The Advisory Council on Underwater Archaeology's (ACUA) purposes are: (1) to preserve and protect underwater archaeological sites; (2) to organize the underwater sessions of the Society for Historical Archaeology's (SHA) Annual Conference on Historical and Underwater Archaeology; (3) to provide opportunities for professional archaeologists to share information, efforts and knowledge; (4) to cooperate with and advise individuals, organizations and government agencies working in related and allied fields;

(5) to encourage publication and dissemination of underwater archaeological research; (6) to encourage the highest ethical and professional standards in underwater archaeology; (7) to publish the *Underwater Proceedings* of the annual SHA conference; (8) to encourage interpretation and educational activities relating to underwater archaeological research for the sport diving community and the general public; and (9) to educate the public and sport diving community on the need to conserve underwater archaeological resources. The twelve members of the ACUA are elected by their peers for four-year terms from the general membership of the SHA, for which they also serve as a standing committee.

The roots of the organization date back to 1959 and retired San Francisco businessman John Huston, who had participated on several underwater archaeological expeditions. Recognizing that the budding discipline lacked effective communications among its international practitioners, Huston organized the Council on Underwater Archaeology (CUA), a non-profit corporation. His advisory committee included Fernand Benoit, Lionel Casson, James Dugan, Edward Link, Spyridon Marinatos, George Mylonas, Pablo Bush Romero, Robert Marx, Mendel Peterson, Froelich Rainey, Rodney Young, and other notable pioneers. Initially, the CUA served as an information clearing house on underwater sites and excavation techniques, but in April 1963 it co-organized its first international conference in St Paul, Minnesota. More than 150 people came to hear twenty-three papers by fourteen speakers at the two-day meeting, and the proceedings were published the following year. Two more conferences were held biannually prior to Huston's death in late 1967, which essentially ended the original council.

Around this time the SHA was created, and many members of the original council and its committee joined. In 1971 a nine-paper session of the SHA conference was devoted to underwater work, and the underwater community decided to hold joint meetings with the SHA for a while owing to mutual interests. Two years later, they formally created the twelve-member ACUA, and in 1978 J. Barto Arnold III edited the next formal *Underwater Proceedings*, which were published by the Texas Antiquities Committee. Various other publishers produced the *Proceedings* until 1985, when the SHA took them on as part of their special publication series on a trial basis. From 1987 to the present, they have been published annually by the SHA, and the ACUA

has gradually increased its presence within the SHA. At the 1995 annual conference in Washington, DC, the underwater archaeological community presented two workshops, seven round table luncheons, thirteen sessions and ninety-one individual papers, one third of which were on international topics. The scope of the underwater sessions is worldwide, and the annual conferences are the largest annual gatherings of underwater archaeologists in the world.

The ACUA also has fostered preservation legislation both in North America as well as overseas, providing advice to institutions and nations attempting to preserve their submerged cultural heritage. In addition, it has developed standards for underwater archaeology courses and conservation methodology, investigated and promoted promising new technologies, and supported the international dissemination of information and knowledge. P.F.J.

ADDITIONAL READING

Fischer, G.R., 1993, 'The Conference on Underwater Archaeology and the Advisory Council on Underwater Archaeology: A Brief History', in S.O. Smith, (ed.), *Underwater Archaeology Proceedings from the Society for Historical Archaeology Conference, Kansas City, Missouri,* Ann Arbor, Michigan.

Marx, R.F., 1978, 'History of the Council of Underwater Archaeology', in J.B. Arnold, (ed.), *Beneath the Waters of Time: The Proceedings of the Ninth Conference on Underwater Archaeology*, Texas Antiquities Committee Publication 6, Austin.

Holmquist, J. and Wheeler, A., (eds), 1964, *Diving into the Past: Theories, Techniques, and Applications of Underwater Archaeology*, St Paul, Minnesota.

HMS *Agamemnon*

British warship once commanded by Nelson, which ran aground and was lost in Maldonado Bay, River Plate, Uruguay, on 16 June 1809. *Agamemnon* was famous throughout the world both for her distinguished list of battle honours and, more particularly, for her links with Britain's great national hero, Vice-Admiral Viscount Horatio Nelson. The victor of the Nile, Copenhagen, and Trafalgar had pronounced her his favourite command. *Agamemnon* was also the ship upon which Nelson had first romanced Lady Hamilton, beginning one of the most famous love affairs since Antony and Cleopatra.

Agamemnon, the first of three Royal Navy vessels to be so named, was of the third-rate 'Ardent' class designed by Thomas Slade; that is to say, a two-decker of sixty-four guns. She had a gun deck length of 160 ft 2 in (48.8 m), a beam of 44 ft 5 in (13.54 m),

and a crew of about five hundred. She was built by Henry Adams at Bucklers Hard, a rural shipbuilding centre on the Beaulieu River in Hampshire, and launched on 10 April 1781. At the time of her commissioning, one of her officers was Thomas Masterman Hardy, who twenty-four years later would be flag-officer of *Victory* under Nelson at Trafalgar.

Before the year was out *Agamemnon* had seen action as part of Rear-Admiral Richard Kempenfeldt's victorious squadron off Ushant. The following year she took part in the Battle of the Saints, Sir George Rodney's famous defeat of the French in the West Indies. After a lay-up at Chatham, *Agamemnon* was recommissioned, under Nelson, upon the entry of Britain into the War of the French Revolution in 1793. During his three-year command she took part in many engagements, including the sieges of Toulon, Bastia, and Calvi (during which Nelson lost the use of his right eye), the capture of *Ça Ira*, the action in Loano Bay, and the blockade of Genoa.

In 1801 *Agamemnon* under Robert Devereux was part of the North Sea fleet which, commanded by Vice-Admiral Lord Nelson (who by that time had been promoted and elevated to the peerage following his great victory at the Nile), fought and won the Battle of Copenhagen. Unfortunately, *Agamemnon* ran aground during the approach and sat out the engagement on a mudbank. She was not in action again until 1805 when, under John Harvey, she took part in Sir Robert Calder's victory against a Franco-Spanish fleet 190 km off Cape Finisterre.

Agamemnon's most famous action was at Trafalgar on 21 October 1805 when, under Sir Edward Berry, she fought as number eight in Nelson's column. The Franco-Spanish fleet consisted of thirty-three ships of the line and the British numbered twenty-seven. It was a decisive victory for the British, who took or destroyed eighteen of the enemy ships.

Following Trafalgar, *Agamemnon* participated in the blockade of Cadiz then went to the West Indies where she took part in further actions. In 1807 she was one of a British fleet of sixty-five ships under Admiral Gambier at the second famous Battle of Copenhagen; this time the Danes surrendered their entire fleet of seventy vessels. Soon after, *Agamemnon* was assigned to the South American station. On 16 July 1809, while part of a small squadron of four ships and two sloops, she ran aground on a mudbank beside Gorriti Island, just inside the mouth of the River Plate. In the course of trying to free herself she was holed on a fluke of her own anchor. When further efforts to save her failed, she was abandoned. At a court martial in Rio de Janeiro two months later, the loss was attributed to the 'incorrectness of the chart' and Captain Rose and his officers were acquitted of blame.

In the early 1990s *Agamemnon* was discovered by Uruguayan divers Hector Bado and Sergio Pronczuk. In 1993 an archaeological evaluation of the site was conducted by Mensun Bound of **Oxford University MARE**, which he followed up with a survey in 1997. The wreck, which is situated in 8–10 m of water, consists mainly of lower hull timbers with a large number of ballast blocks on top. A row of vertical copper bolts marks the keel. Finds include fastenings, sheaves, and other fittings and furnishings, almost all of which are marked with the broad arrow. Of particular importance was a commemorative seal bearing the name of Nelson in reverse. During the 1997 survey the only cannon not to have been salvaged at the time of the vessel's loss was raised for examination then redeposited on the seabed. M.B.

ADDITIONAL READING

Bound, M. and Bardo, H., 1997, 'Nelson's *Agamemnon*, River Plate, Uruguay, 1809', in M. Bound (ed.), *Excavating Ships of War*, Maritime Archaeology Series, vol. 2, Oxford.

Deane, A., 1996, *Nelson's Favourite*, London.

Airlift

An underwater excavation device. Archaeologists have been using airlifts since Jacques-Yves Cousteau's excavation of the **Grand Congloué** wrecks in the 1950s, which were the first ships excavated with **SCUBA** equipment. Airlifts and scuba were soon in use at **Chichén Itzá Cenote**, **Port Royal**, **Caesarea Maritima**, **Mahdia**, in Minnesota rivers on fur-trade sites and in Swiss lakes on inundated terrestrial sites. George Bass refined the basic airlift design in 1961 to include submerged filter baskets to catch artefacts and allow sediment to pass through. Airlifts have since become standard excavation support tools.

The primary archaeological application of large airlifts is removal of sterile overburden and secondarily to lift sediments to the surface; small airlifts are used to remove delicate sediments. Excavation of archaeological sediments is done by hand, trowel, or brush. An airlift, cheap and easily constructed, can move several cubic metres of sterile bottom sediment per hour. The airlift is a deceptively simple instrument consisting in its basic form of a large tube with a (usually) surface-supplied air hose and diver-operated valve attached near the working end. As air is introduced into the airlift, a mixture of air and water is produced that has much less density than the surrounding water. The

decreasing pressures within the tube created as air bubbles rise and expand throughout the airlift's length cause considerable suction at the lower end of the tube.

Suction begins immediately upon opening the air valve. As long as introduction of air continues, and the pipe remains at least partially submerged, the airlift will rapidly suck water and seabed sediments into the intake end and exhaust material from the upper end of the airlift.

Diameter, air pressure and volume, location of air inlet, working depth, size and density of material being lifted, and height of surface discharge determine the amount of material moved by an airlift. These are the chief design and operation parameters. Two basic designs are the simple tube and the air chamber. The air chamber is a larger enclosed tube that forms a chamber into which compressed air is introduced, with air entering the airlift tube through multiple smaller, ideally angled, holes creating an emulsified mixture of small bubbles and water. Airlifts fitted with air chambers have proven to be more efficient than a simple tube. Additional accessories include a handle near the intake to increase handling ease, a reduced intake to prevent obstruction of the airlift tube, and weight to reduce buoyancy. A blocked airlift presents a safety hazard because it becomes buoyant and may rapidly surface; airlifts are often secured to the seabed. Flexible hoses may be added to the discharge end so material can be surface screened.

Surface air pressure and volume must be sufficient for proper operation, and some experimentation may be necessary to obtain maximum efficiency for a specific airlift configuration for particular working conditions. Air sources are usually surface-supplied, industrial-type, low pressure, high-volume compressors. Airlift sizes range from 8 cm to 60 cm or more in diameter. Air volume requirements range from 1.5 to more than 11 cubic metres per minute delivered at sufficient over bottom pressure to allow full volume at the intake. For example, a 10–15 cm diameter airlift should have at least 1.5

cubic metres per minute and can operate well with more than 5 cubic metres per minute.

There are some disadvantages to airlifts for archaeological excavation. Airlifts do not work well in shallow water, and they can be difficult to control. Large airlifts may bounce and will dig deep very quickly in soft sediments; they can also be very powerful, able to lift heavy objects and, if not carefully controlled, can quickly decimate archaeological features. However, small airlifts may allow very controlled excavation. In deep overburden, in-water discharge becomes inefficient because heavier sediments fall back into the excavation. Surface discharge or some means of horizontal displacement

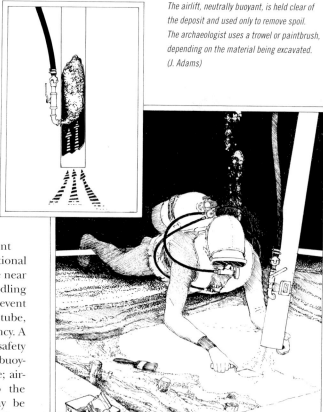

The airlift, neutrally buoyant, is held clear of the deposit and used only to remove spoil. The archaeologist uses a trowel or paintbrush, depending on the material being excavated. (J. Adams)

is required, which increases rigging complexity and further reduces manoeuvrability. Few artefacts pass through the airlift undamaged, and provenance is easily lost – surface screening is no substitute for *in situ* documentation. Consequently, large airlifts are best deployed only for removal of sterile overburden and are appropriate for large operations. For most applications, **Water dredges** are often more useful and allow greater control. L.E.M.

ADDITIONAL READING

Bass, G.F., 1966, *Archaeology Under Water*, New York.

CSS *Alabama*

Confederate warship sunk in 1864 off Cherbourg, France. A 1,023 ton, three-masted, sail and steam barque, 209 ft (64 m) long and 31 ft (9.5 m) at her beam, CSS *Alabama* was built in the John Laird shipyard at Birkenhead near Liverpool. Launched in 1862, she left the Mersey for the Azores where she fitted out as a Confederate warship. She operated for twenty-two months during the American Civil War as a commerce raider in the Atlantic and Indian oceans and in the China seas, capturing, sinking, or ransoming sixty-four United States merchant vessels and destroying USS **Hatteras** off Galveston. She suffered the same

Captain Raphael Semmes standing by Alabama's 110 pounder rifled gun. (US Naval Historical Center)

Left: Recovery of the Blakely gun from Alabama. (© Rod Farb)

Right: Excavations on the site of Alabama. (National Park Service/J. Brooks)

fate on 19 June 1864 off Cherbourg, where she was sunk by USS *Kearsarge*.

Thanks to its sonar, on 30 October 1984 the French Navy mine hunter *Circé* located the *Alabama* wreck 7 nautical miles off Cherbourg, at a depth of 58 m. In 1988, with the authorization of the French Ministry of Culture, the 'Association CSS Alabama' archaeologist Max Guérout, assisted by Gordon Watts of East Carolina University and French divers, undertook the archaeological survey of the wreck site and, in 1994, its exploration and excavation.

The wreck and its artefacts are United States property situated in French territorial waters. The two countries signed an agreement in Paris on 3 October 1989 defining the procedures for the exploration and the protection of the site and creating a Joint Scientific Committee to follow and evaluate its archaeological exploration, to advise the Minister of Culture as to the quality of each year's work and to recommend methods and goals for future work as authorized by Min-

istry of Culture permits. This is the framework in place to date.

The natural environment of the wreck is extremely hostile owing to the depth, the strong current that limits diving time to the period of slack tide (less than an hour per day), and the cold, turbid water. Between 1988 and 1993 the wreck site was mapped and its archaeological potential and stratigraphy studied, as well as its environment, particularly the current and the sediment. The research objectives defined by the Joint Scientific Committee concern living conditions on board, industrial innovations, such as naval artillery and mechanical propulsion, and evidence of the ship's operations.

The remains of the vessel lie on the ocean floor perpendicular to the tidal current, inclined about 20 degrees to starboard. Amidships, the four boilers have protected the hull structure from the effects of the current, but the destruction at the two extremities is much greater; for example, at the stern, the propeller shaft is exposed to

the full force of the current. Many elements of the ship's equipment are visible: two anchors, the capstan, two fire pumps, the galley stove, mooring bitts, portholes, mainmast and foremast bitts, dead-eyes, and the propeller hoisting device. Also visible are parts of the propulsion system, including boilers, funnel, engines, and steam collector, and seven of the eight guns with associated equipment.

Approximately one hundred objects from the officers' mess and pantry areas document life on board. Many are kitchen and table ceramics manufactured in Staffordshire; others are customary or personal items. Some artefacts bear witness to the ship's career, for example, a raw sperm whale tooth, probably from one of the thirteen American whalers sunk by the Confederate warship, a wooden crate for soap from Boston removed perhaps from an *Alabama* prize, and Brazilian coins that evoke the raider's port call at Bahia in 1863.

The most significant results obtained to

date concern artillery in general and the Blakely gun in particular. The study of the Blakely *in situ* culminated during fieldwork in 1994 when the gun and its pivoting platform were retrieved and added to the thirty-odd objects already recovered: gun carriage wheels, cannon balls, lead projectile sabots, bronze sweeps, and pivots used to orient the guns. A shell with its percussion fuse in place was found in the Blakely's barrel and before conservation treatment could begin it had to be defused. That operation was successfully performed in March 1995 by official French bomb disposal experts. Subsequent study of the pivoting platform has also indicated that the loading of the gun was interrupted suddenly, perhaps by the order to abandon ship.

Great care has been made to solve difficult and costly conservation problems, including the availability of qualified laboratories in both France and the United States and of sufficient funds to pay for the conservation treatment of objects retrieved from salt water. Excavation continues on this site which has become an experimental laboratory for the development of marine archaeology techniques applicable to a hostile environment. M.G.

ADDITIONAL READING

Delaney, N.C., 1973, *John McIntosh Kell of the Raider Alabama*, Tuscaloosa.

Guérout, M., 1988, 'The Engagement between the C.S.S. *Alabama* and the U.S.S. *Kearsarge* 19 May 1864: The Archaeological Discovery 1984–1988', *Mariner's Mirror*, 74, 355–62.

Guérout, M., 1995, 'CSS *Alabama*: Evaluation du Site 1988–1992', in M. Bound, (ed.), *The Archaeology of Ships of War*, Oswestry, Shropshire.

Semmes, R., 1869, *Memoirs of Service Afloat During the War Between the States*, Baltimore, reprinted 1987.

Sinclair, A., 1896, *Two Years on the Alabama*, London.

Summersell, C.G., (ed.), 1973, *The Journal of Georges Townley Fullam, Boarding Officer of the Confederate Sea Raider Alabama*, Tuscaloosa.

Albany

see **Arctic** (Archaeology)

Albenga Wreck

The largest known wreck of a Roman cargo ship (40 by 10–12 m), which lies at a depth of about 40 m in the sea off Albenga, Italy. A partial excavation began in 1961 and yielded Campana 'A' and 'C' and 'inside red painted' pottery. The ship carried between 11,000 and 13,000 amphoras, most of which were Dressel 1 type, unstamped,

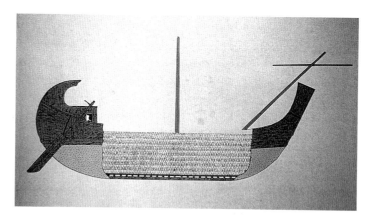

wine-holding amphoras. On board were also Lamboglia 2 type amphoras and one Dressel 27 type. Also found were seven bronze helmets. The hull had double planking and was lead sheathed. Lead pipes from the bilge pump and tiles which perhaps covered some cabins were also found. E.F.

ADDITIONAL READING

Lamboglia, N., 1964, 'Il primo saggio di scavo sulla nave romana di Albenga', in *Rivista di Studi Liguri*, 30, 3 ff.

Lamboglia, N., 1971, 'Il rilievo totale della nave romana di Albenga', in *Atti del III Congresso*, 167 ff.

Lamboglia, N., 'L'ottava e la nona campagna di scavi sottomatini (1970–1971) sulla nave romana di Albenga, in *Rivista Ingaunia e Intemelia*, 26, 71 ff.

Albion

English East Indiaman wrecked on Long Sand in the Thames Estuary, England on 16 January 1765. Having followed the preceding East Indiaman, *Horsendon*, which found herself in shoal water but neglected to make a signal of distress, *Albion*, under Captain John Larkins, proceeded unaware of the danger. Passengers and crew appear to have been taken off after she struck the sandbank, and forty-six of the forty-seven chests of treasure on board for the outward journey to China were saved. Of 844 lead ingots on board, half were saved.

The wreck of *Albion* was discovered in 1985 by salvors who believed it to be that of the homeward-bound *Walpole*, wrecked on Margate Sand in 1803. However, examination of some of the finds soon confirmed that the wreck contained outward-bound merchandise, earlier in date: a musket from the wreck was identified as an EEIC (English East India Company) musket of Lawrence pattern for land service, manufactured between 1760 and 1769, and lead ingots bore the mark UEIC (United East India Company, as the EEIC became) and the numbers 63 or 64 (the year). The appear-

ance of 'Albion knowl' on William Heather's early 19th-century chart of the Thames estuary in a position which corresponded with the wreck site provided further evidence, and archive research confirmed that *Albion* was lost westward of Knock Sand in 1765.

Some sixteen floor timbers were salvaged from the site, each 3–4 m in length, 335 mm wide and 345 mm deep. All fastenings were wooden treenails (diameter 41 mm), irregularly spaced. Wedge-shaped 'filling pieces' on the undersides of the floors took up the void created by the turn of the garboard strakes. At least seventy-one lead ingots were recovered from the site, each weighing between 165 and 175 lb. They varied between 0.94 and 1.05 m in length, and all bore at least one UEIC stamp, the year mark, and single letters L, B, or S, together with merchant's marks. The EEIC financial records list her most valuable commodities on the voyage (destined for India and China) as silver, copper, iron, lead, stuffs, long ells (cloth), and broad cloth. Other finds recovered from the wreck included two tourniquets of Petit type, a penknife, and a brass pistol butt cap (possibly the property of one of the three Madras Army officers due to sail on *Albion*). Rectangular and circular cakes or ingots of transparent green, blue, and purple glass from the wreck have been analysed by energy dispersive X-ray analysis in the scanning electron microscope, and found to be potash-lead-silica glasses coloured by copper, cobalt, and manganese. It is possible that these were being exported for use in Chinese glassworks. M.R.

ADDITIONAL READING

Redknap, M., 1990, 'The *Albion* and *Hindostan*: The Fate of Two Outward-bound East Indiamen', *International Journal of Nautical Archaeology*, 19, 23–30.

Redknap, M. and Freestone, I.C., 1995, 'Eighteenth-Century Glass Ingots from England: Further Light on the Post-Medieval Glass Trade', in D.R. Hook and D.R.M.

Gaimster (eds), *Trade and Discovery: The Scientific Study of Artefacts from Post-Medieval Europe and Beyond*, London, 145–58.

Alderney Wreck

A 16th-century ship, probably an English military transport, wrecked off the island of Alderney in the Channel Islands, English Channel. The Alderney Wreck was a troubled archaeological operation which began in 1991 but which has yet to realize its full potential. For various reasons, work on the site was never established under a proper archaeological authority, and as a result the project became something of a political football. **Oxford University MARE** withdrew from the programme in 1994. Finally in 1996 a specially established maritime trust took over the project from local government and a new director was brought in to stabilize and reorganize operations.

The wreck was found by a crab fisherman around 1980 when a musket came up entangled in the lines of one of his pots. The local dive club examined the site and found several cannon in 26–28.5 m of water on a mixed rock and sand bottom. Strong currents meant that diving on the wreck could only take place between tides, a gap of about forty minutes twice a day. Over 90 per cent of the objects so far recovered from the wreck were raised by this dive club.

Timbers were found scattered around the site but the only significant assemblage was the remains of the rudder which was raised in 1995. Two ports were also found, one of which was certainly a gun port. Other fittings and accoutrements included a sounding lead, a pump handle, two lead scuppers, a dead-eye, and various pieces of cordage. Ship's supplies and equipment included barrel staves, a lead ingot, tools, and two disc weights, both of which were stamped with the Guildhall dagger and the crowned royal cipher of Elizabeth I. The weights gave a *terminus post quem* of 1588 for the wreck.

The ship's heavy ordnance consisted of a minimum of six to eight iron cannon. All (judging from the shot and two of the guns that were examined) were of 3 1/2 inch bore, making them sakers. Shot included star-shot, bar-shot, and ball shot. Pieces from over thirty-five muskets were also recovered and many more examples still survive on the site. The great majority were matchlocks; only one could be securely identified as a wheel lock. One heavy musket has a pintel on the underside of the forestock, indicating that it had been for shipboard use. Accessories included two powder flasks and over twenty small conical powder containers, known as 'apostles', which were hung

from a bandolier across the soldier's chest. Bladed weapons included swords, rapiers, and daggers. Ceramic incendiary grenades were also found. Body armour recovered includes morion and burgonet helmets, 'peascod' breastplates and back plates. A pair of stirrups and a spur may also have had a military role.

Personal possessions such as shoes, spoons, tobacco pipes, a razor, a comb, and manicure items have been found. A pewter bowl was inscribed with the name A DE BOURCE (or A DE POURCE). The pottery was nearly all of North European origin.

The nationality of the vessel is uncertain, but it is most likely that she is the small, unnamed English vessel known to have been 'cast away about Alderney' in 1592 while employed as a despatch carrier and military transport for an English expeditionary force that was active in France at the time. M.B.

ADDITIONAL READING
Bound, M., 1995, 'An Elizabethan Wreck off Alderney', *Minerva*, 6, 2, 11-14.

Aleutians

A windswept chain of islands forming an east–west arc in the Pacific off central Alaska; politically part of the state of Alaska, USA. Although the Aleutians may have underwater cultural resources related to prehistoric times or Russian and American colonial incursions in the area, thus far the World War II sites have drawn the most attention. The Aleutians came under Japanese attack in June 1942 simultaneously with the Battle of Midway. The islands of Attu and Kiska fell to Japanese forces and were recaptured by US and Canadian forces in 1943.

In August 1989 Daniel Lenihan, Larry Murphy, and Mike Eng of the National Park Service Submerged Cultural Resources Unit (SCRU) in association with other NPS, US Fish and Wildlife, US Air Force, and US Navy personnel surveyed Kiska Harbor for ships and planes. The work was accomplished from the USS *Safeguard*, a Navy Rescue and Salvage vessel which was assigned to help in the operation as a part of the NPS/Navy cooperative arrangement known as Project Seamark. The harbour was first scanned with **Side scan sonar** and **Magnetometer**, and divers documented significant finds. All diving operations were conducted by SCRU and Navy divers from the ship and Mobile Diving and Salvage Unit 2 based out of Pearl Harbor.

Sites located included several armed transports (some only partly submerged), two submarine chasers, two landing craft, and a largely intact Vickers Class Japanese subma-

rine, RO 65. On shore, there were very well-preserved remains of one Japanese midget submarine and part of an anchor. The material was used to further support the National Historic Landmark justification for Kiska. Long-term plans for the site include protection in place by the US Fish and Wildlife Service and the possibility of additional research and interpretation efforts by concerned State and Federal agencies. D.J.L.

ADDITIONAL READING
Lenihan, D.J., 1992, 'Aleutian Affair', *Natural History Magazine*, June, 50-61.
Murphy, L.E. and Lenihan, D.J., 1995, 'Underwater Archaeology of the World War II Aleutian Campaign', in F. Chandonnet, (ed.), *Alaska at War 1941–1945*, Anchorage.
Politzer, G., 1990, 'Rising Sun Over Alaska', *American History Illustrated*, 25, 2, 36-9.

Alexandria

Major seaport of ancient and modern Egypt founded by Alexander the Great after his conquest of Egypt in 332 BC. Located at the westernmost mouth of the Nile, and equipped with harbour facilities on the inhospitable North African coast as well as on inland Lake Maerotis, Alexandria became one of the great cities of the ancient Mediterranean and capital of the Ptolemaic Empire until the death of its last ruler, Cleopatra, and its capture by Rome in 30 BC. The city was provided with an Eastern and Western harbour on either side of an artificial mole (the Heptastadion, *c.* 1300 m long) which ran out to an offshore island that was the site of the famous Pharos, one of the Seven Wonders of the ancient world and the first known lighthouse. It was especially necessary as a guide to ships travelling to the new city along the relatively featureless coast. It was begun under Ptolemy I *c.* 297 BC, possibly by one Sostratos, and survived until the Middle Ages when it collapsed in earthquakes; its site was occupied from the late 15th century by a Mamluk fortress that still stands there. Various representations on Roman coins of the 2nd century AD give us a good idea of its appearance – three successive levels about 100 m in height in all.

Although a number of ancient and medieval descriptions survive of the harbour and lighthouse only in the 1990s has underwater archaeology allowed a look at ancient submerged remains both of harbour installations and possible royal palaces that are known to have been by the sea or on a small island offshore. Work by a team of sixteen divers led by Frank Goddio of the European Institute of Marine Archaeology in 1996 appears to have located the ancient island of Antirrhodos, site of the Ptolemaic royal

Highly imaginative
interpretation of the
lighthouse on the island of
Pharos, near the port of
Alexandria, as depicted in a
Renaissance print.
(Bridgeman Art Library)

palace, in about 6 m of water on the eastern side of the East Harbour; large quantities of architectural elements, some inscribed with hieroglyphics and reused from earlier periods, appeared on the seabed. Earlier work by Jean Yves Empereur of the French Institute had located colossal statues underwater. Only limited areas of ancient Alexandria and its monumental cemeteries are visible on land owing to the depth of later habitation deposits – in places 12 m thick – over the ancient city.

The Byzantine port on Lake Maerotis may have been located in Egyptian-American archaeological excavations following leads from a group of Canadian and American psychics who also claimed to have located Ptolemaic monuments and palaces in the area of the ancient harbours. H.W.

ADDITIONAL READING

Clayton, P. and Waywell, G., 1988, *The Seven Wonders of the Ancient World*, London.

Fraser, P.M., 1972, *Ptolemaic Alexandria*, Oxford.

Älvsnabben Wreck

An 18th-century wreck in the **Baltic Sea**. Analysis of historical sources performed in 1994 by Dr C. Ahlström of Helsinki, in order to identify an old wreck at Älvsnabben in the southern part of the Stockholm archipelago, Sweden, showed that the wreck was the galliot *Concordia* of Stralsund, Pomerania. She was of 54 lasts burden and had a crew of eight men. In October 1754 she was commanded by Jochim Lemcke on a voyage from Stralsund to Stockholm with a cargo of grain and also other wares, when she was lost at Älvsnabben Point in a storm. The skipper, crew, and passengers lost their lives.

The Älvsnabben Wreck was discovered in 1968. The uniquely well-preserved ship was investigated by the Swedish National Maritime Museum between 1974 and 1980; the investigation was directed towards developing methods for archaeological recording under water of the hull and its fittings.

Concordia is lying with the stern at 12.5 m and the bow at 17 m depth. Apart from some damage to the stern, the hull of the ship is intact. Most of the rig is gone, and the deckhouse aft of the main hatch has disintegrated. This two-masted galliot was evidently rigged with a gaff sail on the mainmast, and with a small mizzen mast, also with gaff sail at the stern. It was a carvel-built, double-ended ship with a length to stern of 21 m, breadth to the bulwarks of 5.3–5.4 m and a depth of the hold

of approximately 2.6 m. She had a length/beam ratio of 3.8–3.9:1, and a slightly raked stem and a straight sternpost. The construction, shape, and rig corresponds closely to that of the galliot.

A cargo of grain made up of rye but also including barley and oats remains in the hold. It was probably originally loaded in bulk. Objects such as cooking utensils, personal effects of the crew, and ship fittings were found and recorded in the stern and on deck during the archaeological investigation. The origins of the grain cargo were established through analysis of fragments of weeds mixed in it as coming from northwest Germany, Denmark, or possibly western Sweden. An analysis of the coins and utensils found on board suggested that the crew had come from the northwestern region of present Germany, a fact which fits well with the homeport of *Concordia* in Stralsund. C.O.C.

ADDITIONAL READING

Ahlström, C., 1995, *Spår av Hav, Yxa och Penna. Historiska sjöolyckor öster sjön avspeglade i marinarkeologiskt källmaterial*, Bidrag till kännedom av Finlands natur och folk. utgivna av Finska Vetenskaps-Societeten 148, Helsingfors, 123–5.

Cederlund, C.O., 1977, 'Preliminary Report on Recording Methods used for the Investigation of Merchant Shipwrecks at Jutholmen and Älvsnabben in 1973–74', *International Journal of Nautical Archaeology*, 6, 2, 87–99.

Cederlund, C.O., 1981, *Vraket vid Älvsnabben - Fartygets byggnad*, Statens sjöhistoriska museum Rapport 14.

Cederlund, C.O., 1983, *The Old Wrecks of the Baltic Sea, Archaeological Recording of the Wrecks of Carvel-built Ships*, British Archaeological Reports International Series 186.

Kaijser, I., 1981, *Vraket vid Älvsnabben - Dokumentation Last och Utrustning*, Statens sjöhistoriska museum Rapport 13.

Amateur archaeologists

see **Avocationals**

Amsterdam

Ship of the Dutch East India Company (VOC) which ran ashore at Hastings in southern England in January 1749 on its maiden voyage to Batavia in Indonesia. The fully loaded ship sank rapidly into the mud to a depth of approximately 6 m with its contents virtually intact. As a result, *Amsterdam* is the best preserved VOC wreck known to date. The site is located in the surf zone of the beach and is exposed during low spring tides. After its discovery in 1969, the wreck became internationally renowned because of its fine state of preservation. *Ams-*

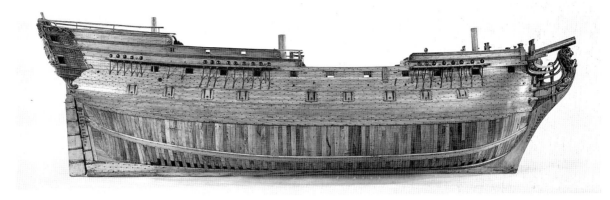

Model of a 150 ft (45.7 m) Dutch East Indiaman like Hollandia and Amsterdam. (Rikjsmuseum, Amsterdam)

The site of Amsterdam with the diving platform, at low tide. (VOC-Ship Amsterdam Foundation)

terdam played an important role in the scientific development of underwater and shipwreck archaeology during the 1970s and 1980s and its research contributed to a variety of aspects, such as legislation, conservation, fieldwork techniques, and the integration of documentary evidence in material culture studies on the VOC.

Archaeological investigations of Amsterdam were triggered by the treasure-hunting activities of a local contractor who removed objects from the wreck with mechanical excavators. Following this event, archaeologist Peter Marsden surveyed the site in 1969–70 during low tides. On the basis of his preliminary data further study was strongly advocated. When the 1973 **Protection of Wrecks Act** became law, Amsterdam was one of the first historic wrecks in the UK to be designated. Due to growing interest in the wreck in Holland the VOC Ship Amsterdam Foundation was

established in 1974. This organization initiated plans for a dry-land excavation and subsequent salvage of the hull. In the early 1980s the research programme shifted towards underwater archaeology. Three large-scale excavation campaigns were organized in 1984, 1985, and 1986 in cooperation with a number of British and Dutch institutions. In view of the difficult working conditions on this shallow site and the complex three-dimensional structure of the wreck, strong emphasis was put on the development and refinement of methods and techniques for survey, excavation, registration, and conservation.

The wreck is about 50 m long, 12 m wide and 6 m high. As the ship heeled to port at an angle of approximately 20 degrees, the hull survived erosion on the port side up to the upper gun deck and on the starboard side to the lower gun deck. Diving activities concentrated on the stern area, where the lower deck at a depth of 2–3 m under the seabed has been uncovered over a length of 15 m. The deposit on this deck was largely undisturbed and consisted of a dense layer of artefacts and organic and ecological components, such as insects, botanical, and faunal remains. Although the excavated area was relatively small, the archaeological data output was dense. Finds were varied, well conserved, and were functionally related to different locations in the stern area, such as the captain's cabin on the upper deck and the constable's room and the sick bay on the lower deck.

The wreck of Amsterdam not only represents an outstanding archaeological site, but its historical significance is also considerable. The ship was newly built in 1748 in the VOC yard in Amsterdam and dated from a period which was essentially the technical and organizational peak of the company in the two centuries of its existence (1602–1795). These years were characterized by reforms which, among other things, also affected the practice of building and

equipping the ocean-going vessels of the VOC. Amsterdam belonged to the charter of VOC ships of 150 ft (45 m) which had just been introduced in 1742. This design was developed by the English shipwright, Charles Bentam, who was then in service of the Admiralty of Amsterdam. The adoption of the new charter theoretically meant that there would be standardization in VOC shipbuilding. An important question of research is to establish if the building process of Amsterdam had been entirely based on these new instructions and to what extent the VOC master shipwright, Willem Theunisse Blok, who had more than forty years' experience, had applied personal and more traditional building methods. The excavation has provided some clues for different constructional solutions in the stern, but further survey of the hull will offer a unique possibility to compare theory and practice of mid-18th-century shipbuilding.

Apart from the ship's construction, the archaeological research covered a large number of other topics such as equipment, armament, cargo and provisions for oversea settlements, personal belongings, nutrition, health, state of technology, environmental, and living conditions on board. A vessel like Amsterdam should be considered a multifunctional tool designed to fulfil several specific tasks within the general policy of the VOC. In other words, a VOC-(Ship)wreck represents a condensed configuration of the technological, socio-economic, and cultural features of the company. Since archaeological data deal with 'real life' and practical aspects of the production and trade of the VOC, they offer unique possibilities for a more detailed understanding of the functioning of the enterprise as a whole. In order to use this theoretical approach, however, more data on the historical context of Amsterdam was needed. Finally, the aim was to develop coherent standards for archaeological analysis and interpretation of VOC ships in general. Extensive archival and his-

A selection of finds from Amsterdam. (VOC-Ship Amsterdam Foundation)

torical studies were therefore started to provide documentary evidence on the organizational and logistical aspects of the building and equipment of the ship. Historical data were also gathered on the supply and manufacture of raw materials and products which were used by the VOC yard in the city of Amsterdam. This provided the first example of the supply network, with indications of professions, addresses, and social status of the persons involved, on which the VOC relied for its intercontinental shipping and trading activities. J.H.J.G.

ADDITIONAL READING

Gawronski, J., (ed.), 1985, *Annual Report of the VOC-ship Amsterdam Foundation 1984*, Amsterdam.

Gawronski, J., (ed.), 1986, *Annual Report of the VOC-ship Amsterdam Foundation 1985*, Amsterdam.

Gawronski, J., (ed.), 1987, *Annual Report of the VOC-ship Amsterdam Foundation 1986*, Amsterdam.

Gawronski, J., 'The Amsterdam Project', *International Journal of Nautical Archaeology*, 19.2, 53-61.

Gawronski, J., 1996, *De equipagie van de Hollandia en de Amsterdam: VOC-bedrijvigheid in 18de-eeuws Amsterdam*, Amsterdam.

Marsden, P., 1985, *The Wreck of the Amsterdam*, New York.

van Rooij, H. and Gawronski, J., 1989, *East Indiaman Amsterdam*, Haarlem.

Anchors

see **Bronze Age stone anchors (Eastern Mediterranean)**

Ancient wrecks

The remains of sunken ships from pre-medieval times. The archaeological and historical value of such wrecks has been amply demonstrated by the relatively new field of nautical archaeology. Most obviously, shipwreck excavations have expanded knowledge of the history of seafaring, providing directions for future research. One goal in any geographic area is the excavation of a wreck of every past century, or even generation, to provide a clear picture of the development of basic shipbuilding techniques in that area. Further excavations of specific types of watercraft through the ages will ultimately write the stories of warships, merchantmen, fishing boats, pleasure craft, ferries, and other craft in each of many areas.

Shipwreck excavations have already shown that ancient Mediterranean ships, from the Late Bronze Age to Greek and Roman times, were usually built shell-first with their planks held together by thousands of mortise-and-tenon joints pegged in place (the slow evolution to the modern, frame-first method of construction has been documented by the excavations of Late Roman to medieval wrecks). The earliest examples of this are from the **Uluburun** and **Cape Gelidonya** wrecks, both in Turkey, from the 14th and 13th centuries BC respectively. Some Mediterranean ships, however, at least as early as the 6th century BC, were held together instead by rope lashings, as revealed by possibly Etruscan wrecks excavated at **Bon-Porté** in France and **Giglio** in **Italy**. A 5th-century BC (?) wreck of uncertain origin off Ma'agan Mikhael in **Israel**, on the other hand, was a hybrid and its planks were fastened by a combination of those two techniques. Future archaeologists may have sufficient data to determine the cultural origin of any hull by the details of its construction.

Ancient wrecks outside the Mediterranean also show early evidence of shell-first construction, but from a different tradition. Three boats taken from the banks of the River Humber at North Ferriby in England (see **Ferriby boats**), dating to about the same time as the Cape Gelidonya Wreck, were laced together with withies; interior cleats may be the forerunners of cleats carved in the planking of medieval Viking ships. Later in England, from the time of the Roman occupation, two methods of construction may be seen in London. A 3rd-century AD hull found near the River Thames during the construction of the County Hall in London was built in the Mediterranean manner with mortise-and-tenon joints (see **County Hall Ship**), whereas a 2nd-century AD wreck found in the Thames near Blackfriars Bridge was built by nailing planks to frames, as in more modern shipbuilding (see **Black-friars wrecks** (Wreck I)). The latter vessel may represent Celtic methods.

The importance of ancient wrecks lies not only in what they tell about the history of ships. Of greater interest to all archaeologists is the fact that they also provide unique information on early technology, art, metrology, medicine, religion, literacy, economics, and other facets of daily life. This is because artefacts of all types are usually found on shipwrecks in better condition, in greater quantity, and in better dated contexts than similar artefacts excavated outside unplundered tombs on land.

Some types of ancient materials, such as raw goods, recyclable scrap, and certain foods, are found almost uniquely in the sea because unless lost on a voyage they would have disappeared soon after arrival in port, either manufactured into finished products or consumed, leaving no trace of their passing. The 14th-century BC wreck at Uluburun, Turkey, for example, yielded a tonne of tin ingots, 200 glass ingots, logs of Egyptian ebony, and a tonne of terebinth resin; although not a single example of any had ever been found on a Bronze Age site on land, many tonnes of such materials must have been traded at the time of their loss. In addition to ostrich eggshells, elephant tusks, cedar logs, and tortoise shells, the same ship carried the largest quantities of pure copper (10 tonnes), hippopotamus teeth, and *Murex opercula* ever found on an archaeological site. Roman wrecks off Greece, Italy, Turkey, and elsewhere have similarly been found with the unfinished stones for buildings and sarcophagi that seldom show up on land.

Although recyclable scrap from antiquity is found in bits and pieces on land, tonnes of it comes from the sea. Another Bronze Age ship, at Cape Gelidonya in Turkey, an Archaic ship from the 6th century BC off Rochelongues in France, and a Roman ship sunk off Bari in Italy all carried cargoes of bronze scraps broken from tools, weapons, and even statues. Because even finished

A diver examines a row of copper ingots from the Kaş wreck at Uluburun. (© INA)

Because travel by watercraft is at least 40,000 years old, as proved by the movement of people across water to Australia, and is at least 11,000 years old in the Mediterranean, there are myriad ancient wrecks to be found. A.J. Parker of Bristol University has catalogued nearly 700 wrecks that have already been discovered from the Roman period alone, and along the relatively short coastline between Bodrum and Antalya, Turkey, the **Institute of Nautical Archaeology** at Texas A&M University has located a hundred ancient and medieval wrecks. The careful excavation of chosen examples will not only add significantly to a history of seafaring but to the history of humankind.
G.F.B.

ADDITIONAL READING

Archaeonautica, 1977–.

Bass, G.F., 1970, *Archaeology Under Water*, Harmondsworth and Baltimore.

Enalia, 1989–.

Institute of Nautical Archaeology Quarterly, 1974–.

International Journal of Nautical Archaeology, 1972–.

Muckelroy, K., (ed.),1980, *Archeology Under Water: An Atlas of the World's Submerged Sites*, New York and London.

Parker, A.J., 1992, *Ancient Shipwrecks of the Mediterranean and the Roman Provinces*, Oxford.

Steffy, J.R., 1994, *Wooden Ship Building and the Interpretation of Shipwrecks*, College Station, Texas.

Throckmorton, P., (ed.), 1987, *The Sea Remembers: Shipwrecks and Archaeology*, New York.

Anna Maria

A large shipwreck situated in the harbour of Dalarö, a small coastal settlement in the Stockholm archipelago. The wreck is known locally as 'Saltskutan', the 'Salt vessel'. The nearly 40 m long hull was first thought to be the wreck of a barge sunk in the 19th century which had been carrying salt. Investigations performed by the Department of Archaeology at Stockholm University during the 1980s revealed that the wreck is that of the fluteship *Anna Maria*, one of the largest merchant ships built in Stockholm around 1700.

Anna Maria had a length of 132 ft (40 m) and a width of 28 ft (8.5 m) and was of 250 tons burden. When she sank on the evening of 9 February 1709 she was not carrying the usual crew of twenty-four men plus the skipper on board. Instead the ship was manned by a handful of men who guarded her at her winter anchorage in Dalarö Harbour, where she had been stopped by the strong winter in November 1708. *Anna Maria* was built in Amsterdam in 1694 at the order of a group of merchantmen and shipowners in Stock-

products were generally broken by accident, melted down as scrap, burned for lime, or otherwise destroyed in the past, ancient shipwrecks are also beginning to yield the best preserved and most complete collections of tools, weapons, ceramics, and weights for every century of antiquity. Further, because objects and collections of objects found on a shipwreck are usually contemporaneous with the time of the ship's sinking, and because wrecks can often be dated precisely by coins, other written evidence, and dendrochronology, the excavation of a ship of every generation of antiquity will provide the most closely dated examples of many types of artefacts, as is already the case with some. One result will be the most complete history of technology: if a future scholar should want to study the development of tools or weapons or lamps or games or glass or jewellery, that scholar will need to turn first to the shelves of publications on the complete excavations of early ships. The ultimate history of each of these categories and others, will eventually be writ-

ten by the excavations of shipwrecks of every century of the past.

A significant example is art. Most Classical Greek bronzes, considered by the Greeks to be their finest works of art, have come from shipwrecks: the Piombino Apollo in the Louvre; the Riace warriors in Calabria; the Youth in the Getty Museum; the Mourning Lady in the Izmir Museum; the Bearded Head from Porticello (see **Straits of Messina Wreck**); the sculptures from the **Mahdia Wreck**, Tunisia; and the **Antikythera** Youth, the Artemision Zeus, and the Marathon Boy, all in the National Museum of Greece, are among the best known, but others, like a female statue netted off Greek Kalymnos, continue to appear.

Further, because preservation of organic materials in water is usually better than that on land, a single wreck, as did that at Uluburun, can yield coriander, safflower, sumac, black cumin, pomegranates, figs, grapes, wheat, and barley, providing firsthand evidence not only of diet in their time, but of the contemporary trade in such commodities.

The bow part of Anna Maria *as it is preserved today.*
(Painting © Jonathan Adams)

holm. After delivery, she sailed from Stockholm with iron, copper, timber, and other kinds of Swedish export wares to London or Amsterdam, carrying salt, wine, and other kinds of merchandise from Lisboa or Setubal in Portugal back to Stockholm. The owners of *Anna Maria* were well-established Stockholm merchantmen. The ship was supposedly named after the wife of the merchant and part owner of *Anna Maria*, Claes Wittmach, who was the biggest shipowner in Stockholm at this time.

Underwater archaeological research on the wreck has been performed by a research group of diving students in Stockholm. One student developed a special documentation method to record the lines of the hull, which lies in 18 m of water. The fore part of the ship is well preserved but the stern part is burnt down. At the bow, the hull still stands 6 to 7 m above the bottom. The midship part of the hold contains piles of pine planks that were part of the ship's last cargo. Other parts of the cargo, in the hold further aft, have been recovered, including barrels filled with steel staves, and rolls of copper plate.

The wreck was identified following a dendrochronological dating of the pine planks in the hold. According to this, the planks had been cut in the counties of Dalarna or Hrjedalen in Sweden between the years 1705 and 1708. With this information, the historian and marine archaeologist Dr

Christian Ahlström was able to identify a court protocol of May 1709 in the city archives of Stockholm charging the members of the small winter guard on *Anna Maria* for not watching the fire in the galley. The ship caught fire and sank. In the same protocol the events in Dalarö Harbour and on board *Anna Maria* during the evening of the fire were thoroughly described.

Extensive underwater documentation led to the construction of a scale model. Serious damage to the wreck of *Anna Maria* because of intensive scuba diving on the site led authorities to prohibit, under the **Swedish Ancient Monuments Act**, any unauthorized diving on it, in order to protect the valuable find.
C.O.C.

ADDITIONAL READING

Ahlström, C., 1988, 'Flöjtskeppet "Anna Maria" från Stockholm', in *St. Eriks Årsbok*, 135–48.

Ahlström, C., 1995, *Spår av Hav, Yxa och Penna: Historiska sjöolyckor i östersjön avspeglade i marinarkeologiskt källmaterial*, Bidrag till knnedom av Finlands natur och folk, Utgivna av Finska Vetenskaps-Societeten 148, Helsingfors, 70–87.

Petersen, B.M., 1987, 'The Dutch Fluitship Anna Maria, Foundered in Dalarö Harbour in 1709', in *International Journal of Nautical Archaeology*, 16, 4, 293–304.

Anne

The bottom of a large wooden ship lying in the mud on the English Channel coastline midway between Hastings and Rye in Sussex, and identified as the warship *Anne*, lost in battle near that location in 1690. The

70 gun ship-of-the-line *Anne* was built at Chatham and launched in 1678. The 150 ft (45.7 m) long, 1,089 ton ship was a medium-sized warship of her time. *Anne* was part of an allied Anglo-Dutch fleet that faced a superior French force in the English Channel at the Battle of Beachy Head on 30 June 1690. Badly crippled by French cannon fire, *Anne* was towed out of danger, then left behind by retreating friendly ships. *Anne* was run ashore in Rye Bay, near the township of Pett Horse Race, and set on fire.

Mid-19th- and early 20th-century accounts noted the presence of visible remains of *Anne* at extreme low tides. In early 1974 the wreck, again visible, was disturbed by a group of relic seekers working with a mechanical excavator and a bulldozer. A survey of the wreck was made under the supervision of Peter Marsden in June 1974. The wreck lies on a firm clay bottom, surrounded by mud, in circumstances similar to the nearby wreck of **Amsterdam** (1749), which lies 10 km to the west of the *Anne* site. The remains on the site are primarily the bottom two metres of the ship's hull, filled with a soft silt. As a result of the mud, and the presence of a sandbar that covered the offshore end of the wreck, most of the observations made in June 1974 were accomplished by manual probing and an analysis of materials dredged from the site by the relic seekers.

Fourteen cast-iron cannon balls, parts of six cast-iron grenades, a musket ball, and a number of barrel staves were recovered from the site and handed to the Portsmouth Museum, on behalf of the Receiver of Wrecks. Other artefacts reportedly removed but not turned in included a spoon, a pewter plate, and clay pipes.

On the basis of Marsden's brief survey, the site was designated as a protected site under the **Protection of Wrecks Act 1973**. The site has potential to reveal information about 17th-century shipbuilding, and the presence of artefacts inside the hull should reflect the armament and life aboard *Anne*. Comparisons could be made with the wreck of **Dartmouth**, lost off Mull, Scotland in 1690.
J.P.D.

ADDITIONAL READING

Marsden, P. and Lyon, D., 1977, 'A Wreck Believed to be the Warship Anne, Lost in 1690', in *International Journal of Nautical Archaeology*, 6, 1, 9–20.

L'Anse aux Bouleaux Wreck

Wreck of a 17th-century New England vessel, part of Sir William Phips's fleet which besieged the city of Québec in 1690. L'Anse aux Bouleaux is a small cove located near Baie-Trinité, Province of Québec, Canada, on the north shore of the Gulf of St Lawrence, 9 km east of Pointe des Monts. The wreck, which lies in less than 4.5 m of water, was discovered in December 1994 by a local sport diver and subsequently identified as one of Phips's vessels.

In the spring of 1689 war broke out in Europe between France and the League of Augsburg, a coalition of countries led by England. After troops from New France had sacked a number of its villages in the winter of 1690, residents of New England, under the leadership of the State of Massachusetts launched two successive sea attacks on the rival colony. Appointed commander of both expeditions, Phips first led his troops against Acadia. He arrived at Port Royal on 22 May 1690 and easily captured the post. On 19 August the same year Phips set sail for Québec with over 2,000 men and a fleet of about thirty ships. Most of the ships taking part in the expedition were small unarmed privately owned vessels.

The fleet reached the city of Québec on 16 October after several delays. After being summoned by Phips to surrender the city, Governor Frontenac responded with the now famous words that he would 'answer through the muzzles of his cannon and muskets'. Phips attacked Québec on 18 October, but was driven back. He had to resign himself to returning to Boston a few days later. Phips's squadron encountered several storms on the return voyage. Although his own vessel reached its destination in December and others in February, a number were wrecked. According to Cotton Mather, four ships never returned to Boston.

Artefacts found at l'Anse aux Bouleaux enabled marine archaeologists from Parks Canada, the Canadian national parks service, to identify the wreck as one of the unsuccessful fleet's vessels. Initialled objects even permitted them to establish that the Dorchester Company, under the orders of Captain John Withington, travelled on board the ship. This squadron's fate had remained a complete mystery in New England. Archival research has left little doubt as to the identity of the ship itself: it is most probably *Elizabeth and Mary*, a 45 ton New England-built barque owned by Caleb Lamb of Massachusetts.

Archaeological work at l'Anse aux Bouleaux started in May 1995 with a three-week pre-disturbance project. Twenty-one **Nautical Archaeology Society**-trained sport divers helped Parks Canada archaeologists map the site and recover exposed artefacts. Systematic excavation of the site started in June

1996. During a two-month project, five Parks Canada marine archaeologists, helped once again by NAS-trained sport divers, uncovered the hull area and part of the surrounding artefact deposits. The treenailed assembled structure comprised oak hull planks, frames, and wale, along with white pine ceiling planks. Remains of the keel, bow, and stern components of the ship have yet to be found. Artefacts recovered illustrate mostly the military nature of the expedition. Muskets, pistols, swords, boarding and belt axes, cartridge pouches and boxes, bandoleers, and powder horn ornaments testify to the New England militiaman's

A diver recovers a musket from the l'Anse aux Bouleaux Wreck. (Parks Canada)

equipment. Since the militiamen had to supply their own muskets, the firearms found show great diversity and many bear personalized decorations, including their owners' initials. The diversified artefact assemblage also includes objects representing life on board (iron cauldrons, lead oil lamp, ceramics, glass bottles), clothing (buckles, leather footwear, textile fragments), personal belongings (seal, clay pipes, comb) and ship-related activities (rope, cable, dead-eye). The important number of fish and mammal bones found during excavation correlates to the known use of *Elizabeth and Mary* as a victualler in addition to carrying troops.

The underwater excavation at l'Anse aux Bouleaux was conducted by Parks Canada's

Marine Archaeology Section, with the collaboration of divers from the Groupe de Préservations des Vestiges Subaquatiques de Manicouagan. The conservation of the artefacts was managed by the Ministère de la Culture et des Communications du Québec through the Centre de Conservation du Québec, with assistance from Historic Resource Conservation, Parks Canada.

The importance of the Anse aux Bouleaux Wreck project is multiple. Apart from being a testimony to one of Canada's most famous episodes, it is one of the oldest wrecks found in Canadian waters. It could also be one of the earliest examples of a New England-built ship. However, the successful collaboration between professionals and sport divers in a large-scale Canadian marine archaeological excavation might turn out to be one of the true highlights of this project. Work is continuing. W.S.

ADDITIONAL READING

Bernier, M., 1995, *Epave De L'Anse aux Bouleaux*, MS on file, Federal Archaeology Office, Ottawa.

Filteau, G., 1990, *Par la Bouche de mes Canons*, Sillery.

Mather, C., 1697, *Pietas in Patriam: The Life of His Excellency Sir William Phips*, ed. Mimi van Doren, 1929, New York.

Myrand, E., 1925, *Sir William Phips devant Québec*, Montréal.

Watkins, W.K., 1898, *Soldiers in the Expedition to Canada in 1690 and Grantees of the Canada Townships*, Boston.

Antikythera Wreck

A Greek shipwreck of the early 1st century BC, best known for its bronze sculptures and a unique clockwork mechanism with technology otherwise unrepresented in the ancient world. Discovered by sponge divers at a depth of 55 m in 1900 and first published in 1901, the Antikythera Wreck was the first ancient shipwreck ever discovered and studied. It was named after the Greek island beside which it was found, midway between Crete and the Greek mainland. A half-century after its discovery, the clockwork mechanism was re-studied and published, prompting scholars in other disciplines to re-examine their areas of expertise in what remained of the wreck in the National Archaeological Museum in Athens.

Only a few pieces of the hull were preserved, but enough to indicate mortise-and-tenon carvel construction, copper-fastened elm strakes with oak tenons, and lead hull sheathing. Commercial amphoras found aboard were variously sourced from the Greek islands of Rhodes and Kos, along with a single Roman example. Hellenistic household pottery probably used by the crew included a bowl, jugs and pitchers of various sizes, mugs and cups, and a lamp; Roman wares included eleven coarse pottery plates. Eleven high-quality glass bowls and cups also were recovered; their quality and condition indicated that they were cargo rather than objects used by the ship's crew. The most spectacular artworks were large, fine bronze statues of the 4th and 3rd centuries BC, including a nude hero or god, a 'philosopher's' head, two male statuettes, and a fragmentary male group with six figures. The thirty-six marble statues, all poorly preserved, included seated and standing male and female figures, as well as four horses. These marbles are considered to be 1st-century Roman copies of earlier Greek masterpieces. A gold earring, a bronze bed, metal ingots, lead weights, and anchors were also raised. The curious clockwork mechanism was briefly inspected, labelled an ancient astrolabe, and largely forgotten.

In the 1950s the mechanism was resurrected and investigated, revealing a remarkably complex instrument. It was a wooden-cased bronze calculator containing thirty-one bronze gears arranged around a differential turntable that marked lunar, solar, and constellation movements on a four-year cycle. It was inscribed on both front and back, and 793 letters have been deciphered from the fragments. A driveshaft out of the bottom was probably driven by a water clock, and the device seems to have been mounted upon a display pedestal or possibly set in the hand of one of the statues, for a truly remarkable effect. Made c. 87 BC by an artisan probably associated with the school of Posidonios of Rhodes, it shows evidence of several repairs. By an enormous factor, it is the most complex technological artefact preserved from the ancient world and is particularly interesting in that it may have served no purpose other than instruction. Its existence in the ancient world implies an astonishingly sophisticated grasp of science and technology that is otherwise undocumented.

Scholars have concluded from various studies of the overall contents of the Antikythera Wreck that it was a Roman ship sailing around 80–70 BC from the Aegean to Rome with a cargo of artworks when it sank. P.F.J.

ADDITIONAL READING
Bass, G.F., 1966, *Archaeology Under Water*, New York.
Bol, P.C., 1972, 'Die Skulpturen des Schiffsfundes von Antikythera', in *Mitteilungen des deutschen archäologischen Instituts Athenische Abteilung*, 2.
Burgess, R.F., 1980, *Man: 12,000 Years under the Sea*, New York.
De Solla Price, D., 1974, 'Gears from the Greeks: The Antikythera Mechanism – A Calendar Computer from *circa* 80 B.C.', *Transactions of the American Philosophical Society*, 64, 7.
Frost, H., 1963, *Under the Mediterranean*, Englewood Cliffs, New Jersey.
Price, D., 1959, 'An Ancient Greek Computer', in *Scientific American*, 200, 6, 60–7.
Throckmorton, P., 1969, *Shipwrecks and Archaeology: The Unharvested Sea.*, Boston, 4, 113–68.
Weinberg, G.D. *et al.*, 1965, 'The Antikythera Shipwreck Reconsidered', *Transactions of the American Philosophical Society*, 55, 3.

USS *Apogon*
see **Crossroads ships**

Arabia

Buried wreck of a US Western Rivers steamboat excavated by amateur archaeologists in a Kansas field along the former alignment of the Missouri River in 1988–9. The steamboat *Arabia* was built at Brownsville, Pennsylvania on the Monongahela River by John Snyder Pringle in 1853. The sidewheel steamer was 171 ft (52.1 m) long, with a breadth of 29 ft (8.8 m), and a 4 ft 9 in (1.45 m) depth of hold. Registered at 222 tons, *Arabia* carried passengers and freight along the Ohio and Mississippi rivers. Steamboats like *Arabia* carried the bulk of commerce and passengers through the American heartland, then a frontier, in the mid-19th century.

In 1855 *Arabia* was sold to a new owner and shifted to service on the Missouri River. On 5 September 1856, after departing St Louis, Missouri, the steamboat struck a submerged snag near the site of modern Kansas City and sank. The passengers were saved, but the majority of the cargo and some passenger baggage was lost. The superstructure and engines were salvaged, but the river's sediments buried the wreck. Over the next century the river's course shifted, and the wreck site was buried beneath a field.

Rumours of treasure aboard the steamboat prompted several later salvage efforts, including two which reached the wreck in 1877 and 1897 by excavating to the buried wreck by means of a caisson. The discovery of the well-preserved wreck of *Bertrand*, also buried in a field along a former riverbed, led to renewed interest in *Arabia*. In 1988 a partnership formed by local residents Robert, David, and Greg Hawley, and Jerry

Mackey, as well as their families, began a **Magnetometer** search for the wreck in 1987. The buried steamboat was found 13.7 m below ground, 0.8 km from the modern river bank.

Between November 1988 and February 1989 the wreck was excavated with heavy equipment and high-pressure water while pumps kept the site clear. The burial in wet mud resulted in an outstanding level of preservation with intact cases, barrels and crates of goods, including tools, firearms, clothing, boots, hats, bottled foods, liquor, ceramics, hardware, textiles, and personal items. The excavation ended in the recovery of nearly 100 tonnes of artefacts, including the boilers, paddlewheels, and the hull and stern of the steamboat.

The recovered artefacts were conserved with the cooperation of the Canadian Conservation Institute (CCI). Rather than sell the collection, the partners opened the Arabia Steamboat Museum in Kansas City in November 1991. Conservation and analysis of the collection continues, including comparative studies with the *Bertrand* collection. This includes work on the clothing by a graduate student from **East Carolina University's Program in Maritime History and Underwater Archaeology**. J.P.D.

ADDITIONAL READING
Hawley, D., 1995, *The Treasures of the Steamboat Arabia*, Kansas City.

Archaeological Diving Unit (UK)

A team of diving archaeologists which provides technical support to the Department of National Heritage for the implementation of the 1973 **Protection of Wrecks Act** in UK territorial seas. The ADU works closely with the **Advisory Committee on Historic Wreck Sites**. This non-statutory committee of experts, chaired by Lady Merrison, advises the appropriate Secretaries of State and officials responsible for administering the 1973 Act in England, Wales, Scotland and Northern Ireland.

The ADU is based at the University of St Andrews in Fife, Scotland. It has been contracted to the various government departments that have had responsibility for the Protection of Wrecks Act 1973 since 1986. The field staff of the ADU are academically qualified archaeologists who specialize in a range of topics relating to archaeology underwater. They also have relevant commercial diving and sea safety qualifications. In addition, most are trained diver medics. In 1997 the ADU consisted of five archaeologists supported by secretarial staff, augmented on occasions by suitable students gaining work experience.

The work of the ADU includes:

- Searching for new historic wreck sites that could benefit from legal protection.
- Assessing sites found by others that may be candidates for designation.
- Monitoring the standards of survey and excavation work carried out under licence on designated wreck sites.
- Offering help and advice to licensees and their diving teams on all aspects of archaeology.
- Assessing the nature of threats, man-made and natural, to designated sites.
- Providing advice on all aspects of underwater archaeology to the home country statutory heritage organizations.
- Providing unbiased information to the Advisory Committee on Historic Wreck Sites.

Each summer the ADU follows a programme agreed by the Advisory Committee. This normally involves a circumnavigation of much of the UK, diving on wrecks designated under the 1973 Act, and any newly discovered wrecks needing assessment. The ADU also links up with the individuals and groups associated with each wreck. Additional information about underwater sites in obtained using sonars and **Magnetometers** linked to the ADU's electronic navigation and survey systems.

ADU diving operations involve the type of equipment developed for commercial diving. The archaeologist in the water is tethered to the surface by an umbilical carrying two-way voice communications, depth monitoring, and the breathing gas (normally oxygen-enriched air). In addition, the archaeologist wears a diving helmet with a video camera mounted on it to provide the surface team with a real-time image of what the diver is seeing. Combined with the clear voice communications this allows immediate discussion about archaeological and related issues without waiting for the diver to surface at the end of the dive. The images and the diver-to-surface communications are recorded in Hi-8 video tape and archived.

Further information about the ADU and designated historic wrecks can be found on the Internet at *http://www.st-and.ac.uk/-www_shir/adu.html*. I.O., M.D.

Archaeological record

The entirety of material produced, altered, and used by humans in the past. The term material record generally includes material in current use; often archaeologists use the terms interchangeably. The archaeological record covers most of the earth's surface with a highly variable density of material residues of human behaviour that include artefacts, ecofacts, features, and structures. Artefacts are any material made or altered by humans. Ecofacts are material not created directly by humans but used or produced culturally, often unintentionally, such as seeds, pollen, natural objects spatially altered, magnetic alterations by heating, geochemical alterations, etc. Some archaeologists do not use the term ecofacts and choose to include all objects made, used, or altered by humans as artefacts. Features normally mean non-portable artefacts and associations, for example, reef scars, sediment stains, etc. Some archaeologists use feature to mean any collection of artefacts associated in a localized area within a site and discussed *in situ*. Structures include physical structures such as intact hulls and those represented by features such as traces of hull fasteners or piling stains in sediment. Hull fragments would be considered features by most archaeologists.

In 1995 the Ethics Committee of the Society for American Archaeology offered a more inclusive definition of archaeological record: '*in situ* archaeological materials and sites, archaeological collections, records, and reports' (Lynott and Wylie, p. 23). The intention was to include material produced by archaeologists as part of the archaeological record. The archaeological record, then, is the contemporary object of study for archaeology, and products of archaeological research become part of the record available for archaeological inquiry. This definition reinforces the necessity of maintaining archaeological collections, and also notes, publications, images, recordings, and digital information, intact and publicly accessible so as to be available for future research.

Future archaeological research will necessarily include restudy of recovered materials for comparative analysis, corroboration, and verification of past research. Regardless of the quality of the original fieldwork and how well the artefact is recorded, unless the artefacts are available for restudy and reinterpretation the original archaeological work can only be considered unscientific because no future independent verification can take place. Disbursed artefacts and other materials cease to be part of the archaeological record available for scientific inquiry. L.E.M.

ADDITIONAL READING
Lynott, M.A. and Wylie, A., (eds), 1995, *Ethics in American Archaeology: Challenges for the 1990s*, Society for American Archaeology Special Report, Washington, DC.

Archaeology

The scientific study of our past human culture through material remains. Archaeology is often considered an academic sub-discipline of anthropology (the study of mankind) or, more broadly, history. One of the social sciences, archaeology is the only destructive scientific discipline. Most scientific endeavour and 'laws' are reliant upon the repeatability of results according to the known laws of physics or chemical reactions, etc. By its nature, however, archaeological excavation to uncover, document, and recover an artefact or assemblage destroys its site context forever, and it can never be put back to preserve the relationships between the artefacts and their ambient environment. Many artefacts that do not survive in the **Archaeological record**, such as delicate organic items, are lost but can be hypothesized or reconstructed into the record by other deductive means.

Writing in the 5th century BC, the ancient Greek historian Herodotus was the world's first archaeologist. His interest in his own and earlier cultures often led him to study and record their material culture, as exemplified by his fascination with Egyptian pyramids and embalming techniques. In the medieval period the discovery of ancient sculptures and structures in Rome excited great interest, and Michelangelo modelled many of his peerless sculptures on Classical paradigms unearthed on the Palatine Hill in Rome. In 1711 a villager in the Bay of Naples uncovered some antiquities while digging a well; similar discoveries thirty-seven years later 14 km away revealed to the general public the ancient cities of Herculaneum and Pompeii, respectively. Widespread fascination with these remarkably preserved sites, inundated by an eruption of volcanic ash and lava from Mt Vesuvius on 24 August AD 79, made them a stop on the grand tour of every European tourist thereafter, although at this time they were little more than romantic and titillating curiosities. It was not until the 1860s under Fiorelli that the random digs around the Bay of Naples became systematic excavations. Also in the mid-18th century, the British architects J. Stuart and N. Revett toured ancient sites in Greece, drafting beautiful line reconstructions of ancient temples and public building in Athens and publishing them in 1762, adding that city to the grand European tour. Similarly, on his 1798 Egyptian campaign, Napoleon took artists and scholars who documented many magnificent Egyptian antiquities; together with the sensational Rosetta Stone discovery they created an Egyptian style revival back in mainland Europe, later fuelled by the sensational plundering of royal tombs by circus strongman Giovanni Belzoni. And in the United

States, Thomas Jefferson pioneered early archaeological interest in 1782 with his systematic 'layer cake' excavation of an Indian mound in Virginia. But all of these discoveries were eclipsed in 1870 by retired German industrialist Heinrich Schliemann, who found the ancient city of Troy on the northwestern shore of Turkey, guided by little more than a copy of Homer's *Iliad* and a vivid and persistent imagination. Subsequent excavations by Schliemann at Mycenae, Tiryns, and other Greek sites helped establish archaeology as a scientific discipline and paved the way for the equally unique discovery of Egyptian king Tutankhamen's tomb in the Valley of the Kings by British archaeologist Howard Carter in 1922.

There are many different sorts of archaeology. For example, prehistoric archaeology in the Old World studies the human record prior to the invention of writing, from the earliest sites involving early humankind several million years ago to around 3,000 BC. In the western hemisphere, the temporal limits for prehistory range from around 14,000 BC, with man's first migration across Bering Strait, to AD 1492, when Columbus made contact. Historical archaeology investigates mankind's history since the development of writing, up to the present. In the western hemisphere this is refined to include the post-contact period from Columbus's first voyage to the modern era. Industrial and commercial archaeology fall under this category, as does the relatively new study known as 'garbology', which studies modern dumps, landfill sites, and their contents. Paleo- or archaeobotany comprises the study of ancient plant remains; forensic archaeology focuses upon 19th- and 20th-century sites with human remains, usually in connection with legal matters. Classical archaeology is the study of ancient civilizations around the Mediterranean, particularly the Greeks and Romans. Nautical or **Maritime archaeology** is concerned with the sunken or shoreside material evidence for waterborne enterprise – trade, travel, exploration, communication, warfare, recreation, subsistence, etc.

In short, nearly every past human endeavour has left behind some physical or material evidence of its existence, and archaeologists attempt to reconstruct that past and its meaning from the extant evidence and reconstruction of the missing elements. New approaches and techniques are constantly under development to document, investigate, and place the past within some form of meaningful context. P.F.J.

ADDITIONAL READING
American Journal of Archaeology.
Archaeology Magazine.
Bass, G.F. (ed.), 1972, *A History of Seafaring Based on Underwater Archaeology*, New York.
Bass, G.F. (ed.), 1988, *Ships and Shipwrecks of the Americas*, London.
Dean, M. *et al.* (eds), 1992, *Archaeology Underwater: The NAS Guide to Principles and Practice*, London.
Deetz, J., 1967, *Invitation to Archaeology*, Garden City, New York.
Gould, R.A. (ed.), 1983, *Shipwreck Anthropology*, Albuquerque.
Green, J., 1990, *Maritime Archaeology: A Technical Handbook*, London.
Hole, F. and Heizer, R.F., 1973, *An Introduction to Prehistory*, 3rd edition, New York.
Historical Archaeology.
International Journal of Nautical Archaeology, 1972-
Joukowsky, M., 1980, *A Complete Manual of Field Archaeology*, Englewood Cliffs, New Jersey.
Muckelroy, K., 1978, *Maritime Archaeology*, Cambridge and London.
Throckmorton, P. (ed.), 1987, *The Sea Remembers: Shipwrecks and Archaeology from Homer's Greece to the Rediscovery of the Titanic*, New York.
Underwater Archaeology Proceedings, 1978 –

Archival research

The use of archives and other resources for historical shipwreck research. Archival research is an essential element in any historical shipwreck project. There are two approaches: research to aid in the location of a wreck, and research to identify a wreck site that has already been found. In the first approach, the investigator has a vessel name and year with which to begin a search of the catalogues, indexes, calendars, and bundles of documents within a particular archive. The second approach is far more demanding. Unless artefacts with very well-defined chronological ranges – particularly coins – are recovered, it is difficult to assign a narrow scope to the wreck and hence limit the span of documents that must be searched. Given the international nature of waterborne transport, it is sometimes impossible to determine the nationality of the wreck. Even if the nationality is established through artefact analysis, the researcher must remember that interest in the lost ship, cargo, personnel, and passengers can span a number of nations. Documents pertaining to the ship and the incident may be found in archives scattered around the globe.

While research approaches are specific to each archive, some fundamentals apply. Knowledge of the nautical history of the period and area is essential. It is also helpful to understand the organization of government and commerce. A number of resources are useful in identifying archives and published primary sources pertaining to nautical matters. Bibliographies are useful in locating document repositories and guides, catalogues, inventories, indexes, calendars, and other tools useful to archival research. Both maritime bibliographies and bibliographies of resource materials for geographic areas and historical periods should be consulted. The bibliographies of well-documented histories are also excellent starting points. Archival handbooks provide brief descriptions of various archives, their holdings, the range of dates of the documents, the archives' locations, contact information, and hours of operation.

More specific than archival handbooks are the guides to individual archives, although not all archives have them. These guides provide further information on the archive's holdings and organization and offer a history of the archive and its documents. Archives are usually organized into sections which represent the institution, governmental body, office, or other entity which submitted the documents to be archived.

The documents in each section of the archive may be inventoried, but not all archives or sections have inventories. Inventories are more detailed than archival guides. Some will describe individual documents; some will describe document bundles or boxes in general terms, such as 'Letters from the governors'. Descriptions usually include dates, although they are sometimes in error. A section inventory will usually be subdivided into smaller groupings. This subdivision means that the inventory is not chronological from beginning to end. The researcher must consult the inventory in several places. The degree of organization and detail varies from archive to archive, from section to section of an archive, and even within sections of an archive.

In some cases selected documents are calendared. Each entry will provide the document date, document type, a brief summary of the contents, the names of key persons, and the archival designation. Sometimes investigators publish inventories of selected documents as the result of their many years of work in an archive. Many archives have indexes. Some are useful; some are not. A few examples of useful archives and research tools are detailed below.

France

The Département des Manuscrits and the Département des Cartes et Plans of the Bibliothèque Nationale in Paris are excellent sources. Documents of French, Spanish, Portuguese, Italian, and Dutch origin can be found there, as well as a number of important 15th- and 16th-century portolans and cosmographies. There are good reference materials to assist investigators in their work. Research should be concentrated in the following sections: Saint-Domingue, Colonies, Admiralty papers from the Ministers de la Marine, and personal papers of former governors of the colonies.

The Département des Cartes et Plans offers an incredible selection of charts and maps. Initially, the repository was composed of maps which had been in the Département des Estampes and included many decorative maps as well as royal map collections, maps deposited by publishers since the middle of the 17th century, and maps confiscated during the French Revolution, including the important collection from the abbey Saint-Victor. In 1924 the Département des Cartes et Plans acquired the entire d'Anville collection from the Affaires Etrangers. In 1942 and 1947 the Service Hydrographique de la Marine gave the Département manuscript maps predating 1800. The Société de Géographie's collection of books, periodicals, maps, manuscript documents, and photographs was transferred to the department in 1942.

The Archives Nationales de France in Paris is an important repository for archival material relating to shipwrecks. Naval papers dating from the 17th to 19th centuries are housed in the Marine section. Some papers from the Affaires Etrangers are kept there as well. The Colonies section was recently transferred to Aix-en-Provence, in southern France. As in the case of the Bibliothéque Nationale, documents are not restricted to French material, but include Spanish, Italian, and Dutch documents as well.

The most important sections for researchers of shipwrecks, particularly for ships lost in the Americas, are Marine and Colonies. In the Marine section, Series B4, B5, B6, B7, and B8, Series C1, C2, C3, C4, C5, C6, and C7, and Series G, should all be consulted. In the section Service Hydrographique, Series 3 JJ (Observations Scientifiques et Géographiques), Series 4 JJ (Journaux de Bord), Series 5 JJ (Voyages et Missions Hydrographiques), and Series 6 JJ (Cartes) should all be consulted.

Other French repositories of interest are Service Historique de la Marine in Vincennes and the Archives Diplomatiques du Ministre des Affaires Etrangers in Paris.

Great Britain

Great Britain's Public Record Office (PRO) is a well-organized repository housed in a new building in Kew, just outside London. Reports from flag officers or captains describing the loss of ships under their command will be found among other official letters to the Admiralty in ADM 1 dating from c. 1698. There is no subject index to records dating before 1793. In order to locate a report, it is necessary to know the name and station of the writer. Beginning in 1793, the Admiralty digest, ADM 12, provides an onomastic and subject index to the class. Similar reports from c. 1850 may be found in ADM 116, to which there is a subject index with the class list. Letters addressed to the Navy Board, or written by that board to the Admiralty, occasionally deal with shipwrecks. Those letters dating to 1832 can be found in ADM 106.

The logs of navy ships from the 1660s are in ADM 51–54, arranged alphabetically by ship name. While these logs may provide the most accurate known location of a loss, the wrecked ship's log was often lost with the ship. It was customary for the Royal Navy to inquire into the loss of a ship by means of a court-martial of the captain and surviving officers. These trials were often omitted in the case of losses to enemy action or when no officers survived. For the years 1680 to 1839, the records of those courts-martial can be found in ADM 1/5253–5494. After 1839 the records are located in ADM 1 'General Series' for each year. The court-martial records are often the most detailed narratives of a loss available, but the court's concern was to establish the circumstances of the loss and the blame, if any. Thus, court-martial papers do not necessarily provide an exact position for the wreck.

Although many classes of records contain incidental references to the loss of merchantmen, almost no systematic attempt was made before the 19th century to collect information about them. The registration system established by the Merchant Shipping Acts of 1786, 1825, and 1854 required the fact of a ship's loss to be officially recorded. The Transcripts of Registration transmitted to the Registrar of Shipping show when the registry was closed on a vessel, that is, when the ship was lost or missing. Transcripts of Registration from 1786 onwards are found in BT 107, BT 108, and BT 110. Indexes are in BT 111. The 19th-century records often include the date and place of the loss.

Lists of shipboard ordnance may be found in WO 55 (Ordnance Office Miscellanea). Maps and charts are preserved among the Admiralty records, and a few of them relate to the loss of warships.

The largest collection of both manuscript and printed charts is held by the Map Library of the British Library in London and by the Hydrographic Department of the Ministry of Defence in Taunton. These charts often help establish the precise location of a wreck but do not usually identify it.

Spain

The Archivo General de Indias (AGI) in Seville is the main repository for documents concerning the Spanish colonies. A researcher wishing to learn a ship's origin, mission, personnel, wrecking, salvage, and precise geographic location will need to consult a number of sections in the AGI since no single section is devoted to seafaring. The most important section for shipwreck research at the AGI is Contratación. The Casa de Contratación governed trade between Spain and the colonies from the 16th to the 18th century. The Casa's responsibilities and authority can be classified into three areas: (1) it organized the fleets that carried on the trade with the colonies and received all goods coming from these colonies, both royal and private; (2) it incorporated the school of navigation and cosmography which trained and certified pilots for the Indies routes and drew together the maps and charts of the New World discoveries; and (3) it held legal jurisdiction over all matters under its authority, both civil and criminal. The majority of the papers from the Casa's original archives are housed in the Contratación section, but some are located in Patronato Real (an artificial section created when archivists segregated papers they deemed to be of greater historical value), Contaduría, the Indiferente subsection of Gobierno, and Juzgado de Arribadas.

Papers in the above sections, particularly Contaduría and Gobierno (divided into the governing Audiencias) papers which do not belong to the Casa de Contratación are also valuable. Also of importance are Consulados. The Consulado de Mercantes was created in 1543 to take charge of civil pleas arising from the Indies trade. These cases had previously been handled by the Casa, but with the growth of traffic the Casa had become clogged with litigation. The creation of the Consulado allowed for simpler, faster, more direct settlement of civil disputes.

Within Contratación, the section on ships' registers is vital. It must be noted that information other than registers is often found here. In the case of *Genovesa*, wrecked on Pedro Bank in 1730, documents concerning the wrecking, salvage, and subsequent incarceration of the second-in-command for attempted fraud during the salvage were included with the registers from Portobelo and Cartagena.

The Libros de Registro, located in Contratación 2898–2902B, are immensely valuable to shipwreck research. These books are the Casa's inventories of the ships' registers that were submitted. Since many of the registers have disappeared, these inventories provide important data on ship traffic. Hugette and Pierre Chaunu based their monumental study of Spanish colonial ship traffic, cargos, and tonnage on these Libros. In addition to their detailed analyses, the Chaunus published tables of raw data drawn primarily from the Libros de Registro and supplemented by other documents. Each item of information in these tables is meticulously cited, making the Chaunu work an excellent resource for locating specific Spanish colonial ship information. Every effort was made to note those ships that were lost, but many shipwrecks in the early years of the study were not noted because that information was not stated in the Libros de Registro.

Other Spanish repositories are the Archivo General de la Marina at the Museo Naval (Madrid) and the Archivo General de Simancas (near Villadolid), particularly the sections Marina and Guerra y Marina.

United States

The wealth of material available precludes any detailed discussion of any single archival source. Before engaging in research in the various archives throughout the country, the investigator must learn what historical data has already been gathered. The offices of many state archaeologists and/or many State Historic Preservation Officers have compiled databases of shipwrecks that have been located in their state's waters. These databases sometimes contain historical material and references concerning these sites as well as the archaeological information which these databases were designed to maintain.

City, county, or state historical societies, local libraries, and local newspaper morgues can provide important data for sites that are not contained in these databases. Unlike research into European seafaring history of many centuries ago, United States maritime history research has benefited from the better organization of the records of naval and commercial shipping of the last two centuries. A large quantity of this material has been published, particularly documents and document guides concerning the Civil War. Compilations of data concerning steamships, such as that by Lytle and Holdcamper, and other

shipping, such as *Lloyd's Register of Shipping*, are particularly useful. D.L.

ADDITIONAL READING

Anderson, R., Jr, 1988, *Guidelines to Recording Historic Ships*, Washington, DC, 2.1.7-13, 2.2.1.-17.

Bass, G. (ed.), 1988, *Ships and Shipwrecks of the Americas: A History Based on Underwater Archaeology*, London, 263-7.

Bryon, R.V. and Bryon, T.N., 1993, *Maritime Information: a Guide to Libraries and Sources of Information in the UK*, London

Chaunu, H. and Chaunu, P., 1955–9, *Seville et l'Atlantique: 1504–1650*, 8 vols, Paris.

Gropp, A., 1965, Bibliografía de fuentes archivísticas relacionadas con iberoamérica (catálogos, guías, indices, inventarios, listas y publicaciones periódicas), in *Anuario de Estudios Americanos*, 22, 919–73.

Lloyd's Register of Shipping, 1764–present, London.

Lytle, W. and Holdcamper, F., 1975, *Merchant Steam Vessels of the United States: 1790–1868*, rev. ed. C. Mitchell, New York.

Munde, K.W. and Beers, H.P., 1962, *Guide to Federal Archives Relating to the Civil War*, Washington, DC.

Official Records of the Union and Confederate Navies in the War of the Rebellion, 1894–1922, 30 vols, Washington, DC.

Peña y Cámara, J. de la, 1958, *Archivo General de Indias de Sevilla: Guía del Visitante*, Madrid.

Phillips, C., 1986, 'Bibliography: Archives and Published Primary Sources', in C.R. Phillips, *Six Galleons for the King of Spain: Imperial Defense in the Early Seventeenth Century*, Baltimore and London, 293–299.

Arctic

The world's smallest ocean, encompassing approximately 13,986,000 sq. km and bordered almost entirely by the land masses of North America, Europe, Asia, and Greenland.

Geography

The Arctic is the world's northernmost body of water, and is centred on the North Pole. At its fringes are the many islands that make up the North American Arctic archipelago in Canada, such as Ellesmere, Melville, Victoria and Baffin islands, Iceland, and numerous islands off Norway and Russia, including Svalbard (Spitsbergen), Novaya Zemlya, and Novosibirskye Ostrova. The Arctic Ocean is also bordered by a number of sea arms – the Barents, Beaufort, Chukchi, East Siberian, Greenland, Kara, and Laptev seas. The principal entrances to the Arctic Ocean are through the Bering Strait from the Pacific, and the Greenland Sea from the Atlantic. Four major rivers drain into the Arctic – the

Mackenzie in Canada, and the Lena, Ob, and Yenisei in Siberia.

About half of the ocean is covered with ice that ranges in depth from 0.6 to 4 m. Much of the rest of the Arctic is covered by ice-floes. The ice moves seasonally, and in some years a passage or inlet that is usually choked with ice may be open water. The ice generally drifts southward and eastward, and some of it is carried out of the Arctic and into the Atlantic; this includes icebergs that calve off the west coast of Greenland. The circular current of the Arctic creates a heavy-pressure ice system in the archipelago and the Northwest Passage, and lighter ice off Siberia. The greatest concentration of ice, and the gathering place for many ice-floes, is the Beaufort Sea, where the greatest average ice thickness in the Arctic region is found. Converging ice creates ridges and hummocks of ice in the Beaufort, and in the Northwest Passage.

The Arctic Ocean has a wide continental shelf that extends about 1,219 km from Siberia. Water depths on the shelf, notably in the archipelago, are shallow, until the shelf terminates in a deep, oval basin that is on average 3,658 m deep. The ocean's greatest depth is 5,441 m, just north of the Chukchi Sea.

The Arctic region is generally defined as the region lying north of the Arctic Circle (latitude 66 degrees, 30 minutes north) but extending further south to the tree line, and the shifting July isotherm of 10 degrees C. It is characterized by long dark winters and short summers, by temperatures that drop to -51 degrees C, and by persistent winds.

Human habitation and exploration

Human habitation of the Arctic region dates back several thousand years, at a time when the climate was warmer, and may have been the result of a spread of peoples northward from Asia. The indigenous peoples of the Arctic lived in relative isolation from the rest of the world until interest in both the Northwest and Northeast passages spurred European exploration of the region. Previous incursions into the Arctic had been made by Vikings several centuries previously, probably beginning in the 9th century with the exploration of Iceland and subsequent settlements there and in Greenland, but it was not until the 16th century that the rest of the world began to probe the fringes of the Arctic. Explorers such as Martin Frobisher (1576–8), John Davis (1585), William Baffin and Robert Bylot (1616), William Barentz, Semen Dezhnev (1648), and Vitus Bering (1728, 1741) probed the Atlantic and Pacific entrances to the Arctic in the 16th, 17th, and early 18th centuries. Other explor-

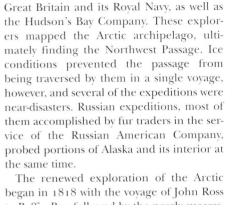

Great Britain and its Royal Navy, as well as the Hudson's Bay Company. These explorers mapped the Arctic archipelago, ultimately finding the Northwest Passage. Ice conditions prevented the passage from being traversed by them in a single voyage, however, and several of the expeditions were near-disasters. Russian expeditions, most of them accomplished by fur traders in the service of the Russian American Company, probed portions of Alaska and its interior at the same time.

The renewed exploration of the Arctic began in 1818 with the voyage of John Ross to Baffin Bay, followed by the nearly successful transit of the Northwest Passage by William Edward Parry in 1819–20. Parry was stopped by thick ice from the Beaufort Sea off Melville Island; he had nearly cleared the

'The Franklin search ship Fox *caught in the ice, 1958'. Painting by Captain Allen Young, RN. (Vancouver Maritime Museum)*

The Arctic coast in winter. (NWT Dept. of Development and Tourism)

ers, such as Henry Hudson (1610), Jens Munk (1619), Thomas James (1631), James Knight (1719–20), and Christopher Middleton (1742), probed the shores of Hudson's Bay in a vain attempt to reach the Arctic and the Northwest Passage, while overland fur traders and explorers Samuel Hearne and Alexander Mackenzie marched across the tundra to reach the shores of the Arctic in 1771–2 and 1789. In 1778 British explorer James Cook revisited and mapped the Bering Strait and sailed as far north as 70 degrees, through the Chukchi Sea, reaching

a solid wall of ice at the edge of the Arctic Ocean during his third and last expedition, again focusing attention on the Northwest Passage. The voyages of George Vancouver (1791–5) conclusively ended speculation on an entrance to the Northwest Passage from the coast south of the Bering Strait. The intervention of the Napoleonic Wars, and the subsequent War of 1812 put off further exploration until 1818.

A renewed interest in the Northwest Passage in the early 19th century led to decades of exploration, largely under the auspices of

archipelago. Other expeditions, by land and led by John Franklin in 1820–21, and again in 1825–7, William Frederick Beechey (1826), George Back and Richard King (1833–4), and Peter Dease and Thomas Simpson (1838–9), successfully mapped much of the Arctic coast at the edge of North America. Subsequent voyages by sea, again by Parry (1821–3) and John Ross (1829–34), probed at various sea approaches in the archipelago. Ross nearly came to grief when his ship, *Victory*, was lost and he was forced to make an arduous overland trek in 1832. He and his men had been given up for lost when they were rescued by a passing whaler in 1834. Ross managed to bring his charts and records out of the Arctic, including observations taken by Ross's nephew, naval officer James Clark Ross, that first pinpointed the magnetic North Pole.

In 1845 the British Admiralty mounted a two-ship expedition, under the command of Sir John Franklin, to attempt another probe of the archipelago and find the Northwest Passage, this time by working south of where Parry had stopped in 1820. Franklin, his 128-man crew, and his two ships, HMS *Erebus* and HMS *Terror*, disappeared into the Arctic in 1845. By 1847, when no word had been heard from the expedition, plans for a search and relief of Franklin were made. Between 1847 and 1879, several expeditions, with dozens of ships and on land, searched for Franklin, in the process completing much of the mapping of the archipelago and finding areas that, when not frozen, would serve as a northwest passage. Several of the rescue ships were caught in desperate circumstances and were nearly lost. During the expedition of Sir Edward Belcher (1853–4), the supply ship **Breadalbane** was crushed by ice and sunk off Beechey Island, and four vessels, including the ship *Resolute*, were abandoned to the ice off Melville Island. The expedition of Elisha Kent Kane (1853–5) also resulted in the loss of a ship, the 144 ton brig *Advance*, which was abandoned to the ice near Ellesmere Island in May 1855.

The first traces of the lost Franklin expedition (see **Franklin Expedition graves**) were located on Beechey Island, where Franklin had wintered in 1845 and 1846, and where the graves of three of his crew, the first to die, were located. From there the trail was cold, but renewed traces of Franklin's expedition were found by Hudson's Bay Company trader and explorer John Rae in 1854. Rae interviewed local Inuit and recovered items abandoned by the crews and taken from the ships after 1846. In 1859 an expedition led by Francis Leopold M'Clintock discovered a cairn of stones with a brief written record noting that *Erebus* and *Terror* had been trapped by ice for two years, that Franklin had died, and that the survivors were attempting to march south, overland, to safety. A trail of abandoned gear, ship's boats, and skeletons led along the shores of King William Island and the Adelaide Peninsula. None of Franklin's men survived, and no major trace of *Erebus* or *Terror* was ever found. With the tragedy of the Franklin expedition, exploration of the archipelago

ceased for decades, although commercial voyages – Arctic whalers – continued well to the end of the century.

Whalers had begun to probe the eastern Arctic in the early 19th century, and by the 1860s a fleet of whalers was operating in the western Arctic in the Chukchi and Beaufort seas. Ice and winter conditions proved just as disastrous to the whalers as it did to explorers. Individual vessels were lost to the ice in the western Arctic in the 1850s and 1860s, and entire fleets of whaling ships were caught, crushed, and sunk, particularly off the west and north coast of Alaska. In 1871 thirty-three ships were crushed by ice off Point Belcher, followed by another ten ships crushed at Point Barrow in 1876. In 1897 ice trapped several ships and crushed and sank two steam whalers.

The British returned to the Arctic in 1875–6 with their final Arctic expedition, led by George Nares. Nares and his crew intended to pass through a region of ice to reach an 'open polar sea' and then sail to the North Pole. Instead they found ice, and sledged to within 644 km of their goal.

In 1879 an American Navy expedition, led by George DeLong, attempted to drift in the ice to the North Pole in the steamer *Jeannette*, but it was caught and crushed in the ice. Only a handful of men survived the over-ice and overland trek to Siberia. Norwegian explorer Fridtjof Nansen, in the motor vessel *Fram*, attempted to drift across the North Pole in the ice between 1893 and 1896, but was thwarted, and subsequent polar expeditions used ships only to reach their starting-off points at the edge of the permanent ice pack. After expeditions led by Adolphus Washington Greeley (1882–4) and Robert Peary (1892–5, 1902, 1906) failed to reach the pole, Peary apparently succeeded in 1909, although his achievement remains controversial.

Exploration of the Arctic archipelago resumed in the 20th century with expeditions led by Norwegian explorer Otto Sverdrup (1902), Norwegian Roald Amundsen (1903–5, 1918–20), Canadian Joseph Bernier (1906–7, 1908–9, 1910–11), American Donald B. MacMillan, and Canadian Vilhjalmur Stefansson (1913–14, 1915, 1916, and 1918–20). Amundsen, in the small sloop *Gjoa*, sailed through the Northwest Passage on his first expedition, becoming the first man to traverse the long-sought and heavily-paid-for sea route. The Northeast Passage, across the top of Russia, was conquered in 1879 by Norwegian Nils A.E. Nordenskjold in the ship *Vega*. Amundsen, in the motor vessel **Maud**, traversed it for the second time in 1918–20. The northern

islands of the archipelago, including Banks, Ellesmere, Axel Heiberg, Amund Ringnes, Ellef Ringnes, Borden, Brock, Bathurst Longheed, and Melville, were completely or partially circumnavigated by ship and sledge, and mapped. Only one expedition, Stefansson's 1913–14 trip, resulted in shipwreck, when his steamer *Karluk* was crushed by ice and sunk near Wrangel Island in August 1913.

By the 1930s settlement in the Arctic was increasing as the Hudson's Bay Company and the Royal Canadian Mounted Police established outposts. In addition, the Canadian Government began to enforce policies to end the nomadic existence of the indigenous Inuit peoples and settle them, at times far from their traditional lands, in an effort to assert sovereignty. Hudson's Bay supply ships and private vessels engaged in trade and supply worked the waters of the archipelago. The RCMP schooner *St Roch*, in a series of voyages between 1929 and 1947, visited many of the islands, and in two voyages (1940–42 and 1944) again conquered the Northwest Passage, the last time by way of the northernmost route that had stymied Parry in 1820. The Hudson's Bay Company lost some of its ships in the north, including the floating supply ship and radio station *Baymaud* (Amundsen's former *Maud*) in 1930, the steamer *Baychimo* in 1931, and the supply ship *Fort James* in 1937.

The last great phase of exploration in the Arctic took place in the last half of the 20th century as air transportation opened the distant reaches to scientists and explorers, and as nuclear submarines capable of deep and protracted dives penetrated beneath the ice cap. USS *Nautilus* was the first, in 1958, followed by USS *Skate*, the first to surface through the ice at the North Pole, in 1959, and USS *Seadragon*, the first to navigate the Northwest Passage submerged, in 1960. Icebreakers with reinforced hulls and powerful engines, including nuclear-powered Soviet icebreakers, opened the Northwest Passage to commercial traffic, which remains a limited and rare activity, and to research. In 1977 the Soviet nuclear icebreaker *Arktika* became the first surface ship to reach the North Pole. **Side scan sonar**, depth sounders, and satellite imaging have largely completed the job of mapping the Arctic Ocean.

Archaeology

The long history of exploration and settlement, the rugged conditions, and the loss of many vessels have combined to create a potentially rich underwater archaeological record in the Arctic. A number of shipwreck sites have probably been discovered as a result of military excursions in Arctic waters, although these records remain classified. Rumours persist that a US nuclear submarine has sonar-imaged the intact wrecks of *Erebus* and *Terror*, although this is officially denied. Meanwhile, given the distance and logistical difficulties, little maritime or underwater archaeological work has been undertaken.

Archaeological remains from various expeditions have been the subject of research by Canadian and American researchers, including surveys, some excavation, and the recovery of artefacts. Numerous relics of the Franklin Expedition, as well as others, were gathered, at first by searchers, later by relic-hunters, throughout the last decades of the 19th century and for much of the 20th century. More serious scientific work, conducted under the supervision of the Prince of Wales Northern Heritage Centre in Canada, has resulted in the documentation and stabilization of a number of sites, and careful archaeological excavation of a few, including the scavenged remains of the steam engine of *Victory*, removed and cached ashore by John Ross prior to abandoning the ship on his expedition of 1831–4, and a site discovered in 1994 with the remains of one of the ship's boats and skeletal remains of some of Franklin's crew. This latter work complements and enhances work done by forensic anthropologist Owen Beattie, who in 1984 opened the graves of Franklin's crew buried on Beechey Island and autopsied the frozen corpses. The exceptional level of preservation included the men's coffins, clothing, and bodies. Beattie found elevated levels of lead in the bodies, and has suggested lead poisoning from canned provisions as one of the causes of the Franklin Expedition's fate.

On Baffin Island a joint Smithsonian Institution/Canadian Museum of Civilization project led by Dr William Fitzhugh of the National Museum of Natural History has excavated the remains of Martin Frobisher's camp and settlement from his expeditions of 1577 and 1578, offering the first archaeological evidence of European explorers in the Arctic. House sites, hearths, tent rings, and mining trenches have been documented, and a number of artefacts including iron ingots and ceramics, have been recovered. As part of the 'Meta Incognita' Project, the Canadian and American teams have pursued a rigorous programme of archival research and have gathered Inuit oral traditions, including some transcribed by later explorers, to obtain the first comprehensive understanding of Frobisher's expedi-

tions, the first to probe for the Northwest Passage, and the first recorded encounter between Europeans and the Inuit.

Another recent maritime discovery is related to a lost expedition of 1719. In June 1719, Hudson's Bay Company fur trader and explorer James Knight sailed from England for Hudson's Bay 'to find the Streights of Anian' (the Northwest Passage). Knight also hoped to find gold mines that local natives had told him about during his previous tenure as the Governor of Hudson's Bay. Knight, with a crew of thirty-seven men, sailed in the ships *Albany*, a 100 ton vessel, and *Discovery*, a 40 ton vessel. Reaching the

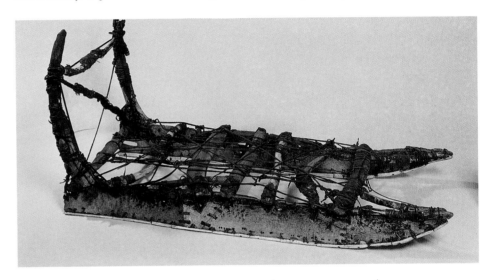

Sled collected by John Ross from the Polar Inuit, and now in the British Museum. (Courtesy of the Trustees of the British Museum)

western shores of Hudson's Bay, he established a settlement on Marble Island, close to Chesterfield Inlet, which was believed to be the opening of the 'streights'. Instead, he and his men, trapped by an early winter and thick ice, vanished without a trace. In 1722 the Hudson's Bay Company's ship *Whalebone*, passing by the island, landed and discovered the ruins of a house built by the explorers, a medicine chest, ice poles and parts of a ship's mast, but no trace of the men. The Inuit people of the region claimed that some of Knight's men had survived to at least 1720.

Archaeological investigation by Owen Beattie between 1989 and 1991 at Marble Island disclosed traces of the settlement where Knight and his men had wintered. This included the foundation of the house that Knight built, and a number of artefacts, but no traces of graves or human remains rumoured to be on the island. Knight, Beattie theorized, took his men and escaped from the island to find an unknown fate in another area. Knight's two ships were not used in the escape, however. The submerged hulks of *Albany* and *Discovery* were

pinpointed by Beattie's expedition, and were subsequently identified by a Parks Canada diving expedition led by Robert Grenier in 1994. The wrecks of *Albany* and *Discovery*, as yet largely unstudied, are the earliest discovered wrecks of Arctic exploration vessels.

Despite several searches, and much speculation, the wrecks of *Erebus* and *Terror* have never been found. However, in 1980 Canadian physician and diver Joe MacInnis led a team to the Arctic to discover the intact wreck of **Breadalbane**, lost during Belcher's expedition in 1853. This is the northernmost shipwreck yet discovered, and, while

not yet archaeologically studied, is an amazing intact time capsule of mid-19th-century Arctic exploration. Significant work focusing on this period has been undertaken by archaeologist James M. Savelle, from the University of Alberta. Savelle has examined the effects of European exploration on the Arctic on the indigenous Inuit population. This includes an analysis of the effects of the introduction of new and exotic materials from the explorers, notably items abandoned or cached by Ross, Franklin, and Franklin search expeditions.

Searches for a number of the whaling ships caught and sunk by ice in the Arctic off Alaska have taken place in the late 1980s and 1990s. Pieces of some ships, crushed and ground by the ice, have been documented on the Alaska coastline, but no sunken ship has yet been located. From the late 1980s to 1997 efforts have focused on the steam whaler *Orca*, sunk off Point Barrow in 1897 and believed to be intact.

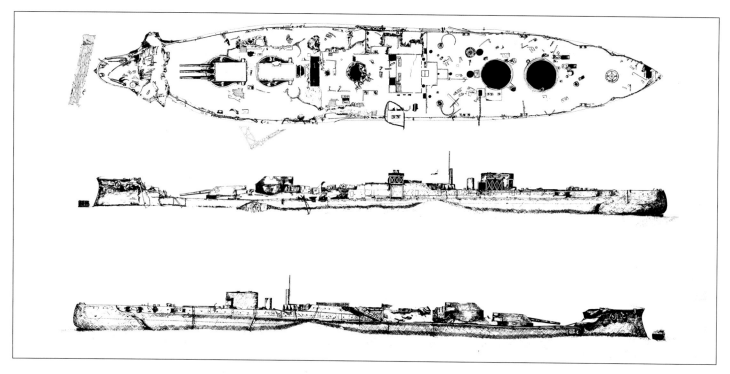

The first detailed archaeological documentation of a shipwreck in the Arctic was undertaken in 1995–6 by a team led by US/Canadian archaeologist James Delgado, which studied the intact, largely submerged hulk of *Baymaud*, ex-**Maud**, near Cambridge Bay on Victoria Island. This work documented the condition of the wreck, assessed site formation processes, and compared *Maud*'s construction to that of *Fram* and *St Roch*, two other Arctic vessels. *Fram* was said to be the 'prototype' of *Maud*, while *Maud* was in many ways found to be a prototype for *St Roch*.

Future discoveries in the Arctic will involve high cost and tremendous logistics. Searchers continue to hunt for *Erebus* and *Terror*, but additional work on *Albany*, *Discovery*, *Breadalbane* and the various land sites associated with various Arctic expeditions, as well as a better understanding of indigenous maritime practices, is needed first. J.P.D.

ADDITIONAL READING

Beattie, O. and Geiger, G., 1987, *Frozen in Time: Unlocking the Secrets of the Franklin Expedition*, New York.

Berton, P., 1988, *The Arctic Grail: The Quest for the Northwest Passage and the North Pole, 1818–1909*, Toronto.

Bockstoce, J.R., 1986, *Whales, Ice and Men: The History of Whaling in the Western Arctic*, Seattle.

Eber, D.H., 1989, *When the Whalers Were Up North: Inuit Memories of the Eastern Arctic*, Montreal and Kingston.

Fitzhugh, W.W. and Olin, J.S. (eds), 1993, *Archeology of the Frobisher Voyages*, Washington, DC.

Geiger, J., and Beattie, O., 1993, *Dead Silence: The Greatest Mystery in Arctic Discovery*, Toronto.

Sutherland, P. (ed.), 1985, *The Franklin Era in Canadian Arctic History, 1845–1859*, Ottawa.

Woodman, D., 1991, *Unravelling the Franklin Mystery: Inuit Testimony, Montreal and Kingston*, Montreal and Kingston.

Argentina

see **South America**

USS *Arizona*

United States battleship (BB39) sunk on 7 December 1941 during the carrier-based air raid by the Japanese Navy on US forces in **Pearl Harbor**. *Arizona* was sunk in the first moments of the attack with a loss of 1,177 sailors and marines. After initial attempts at salvage the decision was made by US authorities to let the ship remain in place as both a war grave and shrine. The superstructure was removed and in 1962 a memorial designed by architect Alfred Preis was built over the vessel. The site is visited by over 5,000 people each day and is meant to be a commemoration of all those who lost their lives in the Pearl Harbor attack.

Arizona's keel was laid in 1914. The ship was launched in 1915 and commissioned on 16 October 1916. It was the second and last of the Pennsylvania class of battleships, and had an overall length of 608 ft (185.3 m), a beam of 97 ft (29.6 m), and displaced 31,400 tons. Its main armament consisted of twelve 14 inch guns mounted three apiece in four turrets, two forward and two aft.

Drawings of USS Arizona *developed from data obtained in the intense underwater mapping sessions of 1983-4.*
From top: planimetric view; port elevation; starboard elevation.
(Submerged Cultural Resources Unit, National Park Service; final rendering by Jerry Livingston)

The operational history of *Arizona* included patrol service during World War I off the US coast, various voyages to convey emissaries on diplomatic missions, and service as flagship of various battleship divisions. At no time in its career did the ship use its immense firepower in battle. The main significance of the ship came at its demise when its remains became a symbolic rallying point for the American people to 'Remember Pearl Harbor'.

When management of the memorial was turned over to the US National Park Service (NPS) in 1980, Superintendent Gary Cummins determined he had insufficient knowledge of the ship remains to intelligently carry out his stewardship responsibilities. He requested the assistance of the NPS underwater archaeology team, the **Submerged Cultural Resources Unit** (SCRU). He met the unit chief Daniel Lenihan in 1982 and plans were laid to survey the vessel in its resting place using a non-intrusive methodology in deference to the ship's role as a war grave.

During field sessions in 1983 and 1984 involving approximately five weeks of work on site, the ship was mapped and video- and photo-documented. Lenihan led a team composed of NPS personnel from his team in Santa Fe, the USS *Arizona* Memorial's park staff, and a contingent of **US Navy** divers to complete the task. Archaeologist Larry Murphy was his chief assistant and primary mapping personnel included scientific illustrator Jerry Livingston and archaeologist Larry Nordby.

No object approaching this size had ever been mapped underwater. The task was further complicated by conditions in the harbour which had an average water visibility of 1.5–1.8 m. Lenihan's team used a form of

Porthole of Arizona *partially filled with air. (National Park Service)*

Baseline trilateration which relied on nylon line and plastic markers to serve as physical controls on the site. Hundreds of dives were made to gradually build planimetric and elevation views of the ship from the initial skeleton of string and plastic.

Success of the technique on this project generated interest in its applications from other archaeologists, the Navy salvage community, and recreational divers. The ship's planimetric view was mapped in more detail in 1986 when Lenihan's team returned to Pearl Harbor to work on the **USS *Utah***. A model of the wreck was being constructed by Robert Sumerall and he requested more deck detail. Larry Nordby was in charge of this aspect of the 1986 project.

During this time a new superintendent, Bill Dickinson, asked Lenihan to initiate a study of the corrosion dynamics on the site (see **Corrosion studies**). Scott Henderson, a civilian scientist working with the Navy, was contracted to take prime responsibility for the data acquisition needed to establish a baseline for deterioration studies. Henderson, working with NPS and Navy divers, established permanent monitoring points on the site after collecting information on variables thought to have most effect on corrosion in the Pearl Harbor environment.

The study determined that the biofouling had created a fairly uniform layer on the ship that served to inhibit further corrosion. The worst areas for damage were those areas

in the splash zone, 1.8 m above and below the water surface. Interior spaces of the ship not subject to flushing were comparatively stable. Henderson and Lenihan both strongly recommended annual monitoring of survey stations on the vessel by park divers. Such a programme has yet to be firmly established. During brief follow-up operations by SCRU on the site in 1988 NPS maritime historian James P. Delgado examined the ship to develop a National Historic Landmark nomination for *Arizona* and *Utah*. The sites were accepted for designation as NHLs in 1989.

This project and all the previous efforts were reported on in a monograph edited by Dan Lenihan and published in 1989. The 1986 work was also the subject of a segment of a major documentary film produced by the BBC, which was first aired in 1988 as part of its Discoveries Underwater series. The film, entitled *Science, Salvage or Scrap?*, was widely distributed throughout the world by cable companies and other outlets during the early 1990s. D.J.L.

ADDITIONAL READING

Delgado, J.P., 1992, 'Recovering the Past of U.S.S. *Arizona*:: Symbolism, Myth and Reality', *Historical Archaeology*, 26, 4, 69–80.

Lenihan, D.J. (ed.), 1989, *Submerged Cultural Resources Study: U.S.S. Arizona Memorial and Pearl Harbor National Historic Landmark*, Santa Fe, New Mexico.

Linenthal, E. Tabor, 1991, *Sacred Ground: Americans and Their Battlefields*, Urbana and Chicago.

Murphy, L., 1987, 'Preservation at Pearl Harbor', *APT Bulletin*, 9, 1, 10-14.

Stillwell, P., 1991, *Battleship Arizona: An Illustrated History*, Annapolis, Maryland.

USS *Arkansas*
see **Crossroads Wrecks**

Armada, Spanish
see **Spanish Armada**

Arniston

A British troopship of twenty-two guns and with many invalid soldiers on board, sunk en route from Ceylon. *Arniston* wrecked near Cape Agulhas, east of Cape Town, in 1815. In 1982 a permit was issued to the Archaeology Department at the University of Cape Town to conduct a survey and excavation of the site. The project team was composed of a graduate student, Jim Jobling, working in conjunction with salvors Brian Clark, Tubby Gericke, and Pete Leube. The results of the project were intended to be written up as an honours thesis.

This project is often referred to as the first attempt at underwater archaeology in South

Africa. A semi-permanent steel grid was erected for excavation and documentation processes. Excavation equipment used on the site included an airlift, diamond gravel pump, and a sandblaster or blower. The wreck was briefly described as composite in construction, but no architectural features were actually documented. A significant number of artefacts were recovered from the site including ceramics, coins, jewellery, ferrous and non-ferrous metals, and other organic materials. All artefacts were numbered and accessioned in a register based on a system developed in Western Australia. L.H., T.D.

ADDITIONAL READING

Cape Town Gazette, 29 July 1815.

Jobling, J., 1982, *The Arniston (1815)*, unpublished report, NMC Library.

Asherah

The first submersible designed specifically for underwater archaeology. Built by the Electric Boat Division of General Dynamics, and named after a Phoenician sea goddess, *Asherah* was launched on 28 May 1964 for the University Museum of the University of Pennsylvania. Her purpose was fourfold: to survey for and inspect ancient shipwrecks, to allow mapping of shipwrecks by stereo photogrammetry, to extend the bottom time of an archaeological director by allowing extended inspection of work in progress by rotating teams of diving excavators, and to aid excavation by manipulating a PVC **Airlift** pipe by means of an external mechanical arm. Although her working depth of 180 m allowed archaeologists to go deeper than was possible with **SCUBA**, the rationale for an archaeological submarine was mostly economic: to allow more work to be done on the seabed during an excavation campaign.

Asherah provided forty-eight hours of life support for a crew of two in a spherical steel pressure hull 1.5 m in diameter. Ballast tanks and batteries were carried aft in a free-flooding conical fairing of fibreglass, partly filled with syntactic foam for buoyancy, which gave a reasonable hydrodynamic shape to the vessel. Its overall length was 5.2 m; its weight was 3,810 kg. Lead-acid batteries powered a pair of propellers, one mounted on either side of the pressure hull, that were manually rotated by hand-cranks inside to move the submarine in any direction at a maximum speed of 2 knots. The main ballast tank, open to the sea at its bottom, provided surface buoyancy. Neutral buoyancy was obtained under water, after the main tank had fully flooded, by means of a spherical variable ballast tank of steel. For economy, *Asherah*

The submersible Asherah *at Yassiada. (© INA)*

was designed to need little surface support and was never lifted from the water during her summers in use; instead, she was towed from place to place by the US Army boat *Virazon* (on loan from the US Office of Naval Research) and simply moored like a dinghy when not in use.

Pilot and observer entered the pressure hull through a top hatch that was protected from the waves by a Plexiglas canopy. Inside, they used a high-pressure oxygen tank to replenish the oxygen they breathed; carbon dioxide was removed from the air by a fan that forced the air through a canister of absorbent that was changed before each dive. Visibility was through six view ports, but after this proved insufficient a closed-circuit television system was added.

First tested in Turkey in 1964, *Asherah* accomplished three of the four functions for which she was designed on a return trip in 1967 when she allowed visual observation of an ancient wreck, discovered with **Side scan sonar**, 85 m deep near Yalikavak, carried the externally mounted stereo cameras that mapped a late 4th- or early 5th-century AD wreck being excavated 40 m deep off **Yassiada**, and then allowed the excavation director to monitor the excavation. The planned external arm was not built before *Asherah* was sold in 1969 because of the cost of the liability insurance that university lawyers determined she must carry. G.F.B.

ADDITIONAL READING

Bass, G.F., 1975, *Archaeology Beneath the Sea*, New York, 147–84.

Bass, G.F. and Rosencrantz, D.M., 1977, 'The

Asherah: A Pioneer in Search of the Past', in Geyer, R.A. (ed.), *Submersibles and Their Use in Oceanography and Ocean Engineering*, Amsterdam, Oxford, and New York.

Assemblage

A set of contemporary artefact types found together in a context that reflects definite archaeological association. A basic assumption regarding artefact assemblage is that it reflects shared activity of a social group or community. In contrast, a group of types of uncertain chronology and association can be considered an 'aggregation'. 'Site assemblage' denotes the complete set of artefacts found at a site. In maritime archaeological practice, a ship can be viewed as a highly structured assemblage in systemic (cultural) context. A shipwreck is the same assemblage after undergoing a series of transformations to become part of the archaeological record.

'Subassemblage' refers to artefacts that share a factor or factors in common with each other, distinguishing them from others of the assemblage. Subassemblages involve artefact classification, and archaeologists differ on how they classify artefacts. Archaeologists working with prehistoric materials may differentiate types based on artefact attributes, for example edge angles of morphologically similar stone tools. A basic question for this type of research is whether assemblage variations result from different functions or different populations. Such questions are rarely asked of maritime assemblages.

For analytical purposes, maritime assemblages have been variously divided. Many archaeologists classify along material lines; other schemes involve functional divisions. Maritime subassemblages may be grouped as specific to a particular activity, for example the gunnery or mess subassemblage of a military wreck; however, some archaeologists use subassemblage to mean artefacts of similar composition, such as glass, wood, or ceramics. Generally, historical archaeologists find functional categories analytically superior. Some maritime archaeologists separate ship-related, cargo-related, and personal effects, or one of many elaborations on this basic scheme.

Use of assemblage as an analytic concept is not widespread in maritime archaeology, particularly in US practice. However, using assemblage analytically can be very productive. For example, examination of co-occurrence of different artefact types and frequencies of particular maritime cultures' wrecks may lead to determination of a specific assemblage characteristic of that culture for a specific period that can serve as interpretative tools for unknown sites. Here, the signature assemblage can be considered a 'cultural assemblage'. This concept is not often used overtly, but it is assumed by many historical archaeologists.

A cultural assemblage is a set of specific artefact types that are found in similar ratios in groups of assemblages occurring during a limited time and geographic area, or in related sites for maritime archaeology. Cultural assemblages are composed from a limited set of artefact types that repeatedly co-occur in varying combinations, although each separate assemblage does not necessarily contain all artefact types. Cultural assemblages may be useful in areas of multiple sites to designate associated artefact types as an aid to establishing archaeological associations or investigating assemblages that are anomalous to expected patterns. The problem is deciding which types co-occur. The concept may be analytically useful in finding which artefacts from a dense artefact distribution from multiple maritime casualties compose separate sites. It may also be possible to develop cultural assemblages for particular shipwreck sites and study their variation over time. For example, in many periods ceramic artefacts significantly outnumber metalwares on Spanish sites, whereas the opposite is true for British sites of similar periods.

Examples from US terrestrial historical archaeology relying heavily on the assemblage concept are the many studies devoted to questions of intrasite patterning. For example, Stanley South in 1977 defined two archaeological patterns based on relative percentage frequencies of artefacts commonly found on British colonial period sites. South's methodology involved examining assemblages in terms of ratios of artefact groups and classes, for example, wine bottles to ceramics to nails, arms to furniture, or single percentages of bones or military objects. His recognition of the Carolina Pattern, which is based on high ratios of 'kitchen group' artefacts compared with 'architecture group' artefacts from sites in settled areas, and the Frontier Pattern, which is based on high 'architecture group' artefacts compared with 'kitchen group' ones from peripheral sites, suggests assemblage regularity that he attributed to differences in these broad settlement patterns. Although South's methodology has been criticized, later studies confirmed his general patterns and substantiated that settlement regularities in form and organization are reflected in assemblage variations. South's patterns were not meant to be explanatory tools, but are descriptive models. They were developed to show the presence of underlying regularities, which have not yet been explained in terms of cultural process or human behaviour.

Demonstration of assemblage patterning is not remarkable – the basic assumption of archaeology is that human behaviour is non-random. Assemblage patterns become interesting and important to archaeology when they provoke archaeologists to explain why they occur. Pattern recognition, based on quantitative analysis of assemblages, assists in moving archaeologists beyond the 'reconstruction of past lifeways' or 'undocumented life aboard ship' approaches towards attempts to explain archaeological variability in terms of human behaviour. Artefact assemblage investigation through pattern analysis may produce a move to more explanatory interpretations of shipwreck materials, and it provides an important impetus to the generation of truly interesting anthropological questions, rather than elaboration of historical documents.

Maritime sites, because of their synchronic nature and narrow range of activities, offer more controlled assemblages than many contemporary land sites. The cultural phenomena producing observed patterns may be more limited, which simplifies pattern recognition and utilization for explanatory purposes. Because of excellent preservation, shipboard assemblages can also be much more representative of the original cultural assemblage than terrestrial sites, which may lead to a refinement of analytical assemblage pattern models used on land.

The most challenging questions involve explanation of the archaeological record and the cumulative processes that produced it. These questions as they pertain to what we find on maritime sites point archaeologists towards explaining assemblage variation, for example, in terms of differences in national origins, ethnicity, role of status and function, or the nature of worldwide distribution systems and their change over time – essentially investigating the cultural system of which the site was once a part. L.E.M.

ADDITIONAL READING

South, S., 1977, *Method and Theory in Historical Archaeology*, New York.

Astrolabe

see **La Pérouse ships**

Athlit Ram

A well-preserved bronze warship ram found near Athlit, just south of Haifa, Israel in 1980. Discovered by Yehoshua Ramon and recovered by Haifa University's Centre for Maritime Studies, the weapon now resides in the foyer of the National Maritime Museum in Haifa.

Originally mounted on the bow of its warship at or near the waterline, the ram was used to shatter an enemy's hull through a carefully controlled collision powered by the oarsmen of its galley. Measuring 2.26 m in length, 0.76 m in maximum width, and 0.96 m in maximum height, the weapon weighed more than 600 kg when pulled from the sea, and preserved in its hollow interior were sixteen timbers from the bow of the vessel that once carried it. This stunning artefact represents the only warship ram ever found by archaeologists in a documented context. Moreover, the Athlit Ram provides our best surviving evidence from the bow of an ancient warship – the most complex part of a vessel type for which little physical evidence of any kind has survived.

When repeated searches failed to produce more pieces from the ram's ship, attention shifted to the weapon itself – its appearance, composition, and design. Initial testing revealed that the ram's casting was made from 465 kg of high-grade bronze (90 per cent copper and 10 per cent tin) with a thickness that generally varied between 7 and 10 mm. X-ray analysis of the metal revealed that the ram was expertly cast in a single pour and that a sand mould was used, a casting technique previously thought to date to no earlier than the 14th century AD.

Four separate symbols carefully cast into the ram's surface as government marks of ownership also appear on Cypriot coins minted between 204 and 164 BC. On this evidence, the ram was probably manufactured at one of Cyprus's naval ports such as Paphos (the largest at the time) and used on a ship in the Cyprian fleet of Ptolemy V Epiphanes or his successor, Ptolemy VI Philometor. The precise circumstances surrounding the ram's loss remain unknown. As for the relative size of the Athlit ship, a comparison of the weapon's cross-section with the sockets on the **Actian Naval Monument** is instructive. Because it is smaller in size than the smallest socket on Octavian's display, the Athlit Ram must belong to a moderately small (by Hellenistic standards) class of ship such as a *tetreres* (i.e. with four banks of oars).

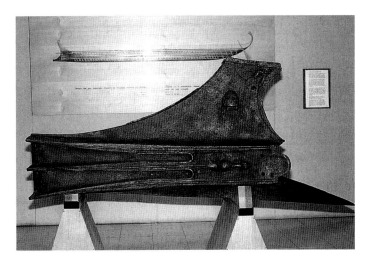

The Athlit Ram on display.
(W.M. Murray)

Careful study of the sixteen timbers inside the ram's casing reveal that the weapon was expertly designed to distribute the considerable forces of the ramming blow to the bottom timbers of its own ship. Moreover, the three-finned design of the ram's head minimized the chance of penetration into the enemy hull and ensured a safer, more effective strike. The ram's timbers also reveal that the Athlit ship's bottom was strong and heavy and that its hull probably weighed at least one tonne per metre of length. Considering the great value of the bronze employed in its manufacture, this heavy construction confirms the Athlit Ram as the primary armament of its vessel and underscores the importance of ramming to warships with bows of the Athlit type. W.M.

ADDITIONAL READING

Casson, L. and Steffy, J.R., 1991, *The Athlit Ram*, College Station, Texas.

Linder, E. and Ramon, Y., 1981, 'A Bronze Ram from the Sea of Athlit, Israel', *Archaeology*, 34, 6, 62–4.

Steffy, J.R., 1983, 'The Athlit Ram: A Preliminary Investigation of its Structure', *Mariner's Mirror*, 69, 229–47.

Atocha

see ***Nuestra Señora de Atocha***

Australia

Continent with several thousand shipwrecks in its waters. Interest in old shipwrecks developed in Australia in the early 1960s as snorkelling technology became accessible to recreational swimmers. In 1963 Graeme Henderson was the first diver (with several companions) to find an early Dutch shipwreck, ***Vergulde Draeck***, of 1656. Later in the same year divers found ***Batavia***, a wreck of 1629. The silver coins on these sites attracted divers from throughout Australia, and some divers used explosives to remove saleable artefacts.

Among the divers who found the early wrecks were several journalists, who used the press to argue against the destruction of these wrecks and to interest the community in their history. The finders of *Vergulde Draeck* saw the need to get museum interest in the early wrecks, and developed a deed whereby they formally transferred their rights under common law to the Western Australian Museum. The museum then pressed for protective legislation, which was passed in 1964.

The museum sought divers' cooperation in their efforts to have the wrecks left undisturbed on the seabed, and they employed watchkeepers to protect the integrity of the sites. However, many divers

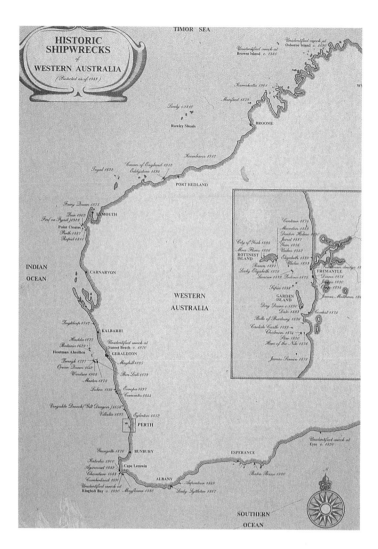

Protected wreck sites, Western Australia. (© Western Australia Maritime Museum)

Part of Batavia's hull, and human remains, on display in the Western Australia Maritime Museum. (© Western Australia Maritime Museum/ Patrick Baker)

observed continued looting, and saw the museum's appropriate role as being more active. So in 1971 the museum commenced a comprehensive fifteen-year programme aimed at archaeological excavation of the sites considered to be most at threat. This programme was linked with the provision of materials conservation and exhibition facilities. The result was the creation of a specialist maritime archaeology museum in 1981. The exhibits proved popular with both the diving community and the general community, and this increased the effectiveness of the legislation. The diving community took the view that the museum was managing the sites effectively, and they in turn took a conservation stance towards the sites underwater.

Meanwhile, events during the 1970s extended the geographical scope of the research/management programmes for historic shipwrecks throughout Australia. A Western Australian treasure-hunter challenged the State legislation in the High Court of Australia, arguing that the Commonwealth

rather than the State had the right to legislate over the seabed. The High Court agreed, but before the finding was given, the Commonwealth prepared its own protective legislation, the 1976 Historic Shipwrecks Act, thus extending protection from one State to the entire Australian coastline.

With the Commonwealth legislation in place other Australian States were encouraged to develop programmes, and all States now have programmes. The programme in Western Australia is museum-based and has a strong emphasis on maritime archaeology. The programmes in Queensland and the Northern Territory are also museum-based. However, in South Australia, Tasmania, Victoria, and New South Wales the programmes are more explicitly based in cultural resource management organizations. The development of programmes in different types of organizations has had the positive effect of adding to the diversity of approach within Australia. Professional staff in all States have been trained at the postgraduate diploma course run by Curtin University and the Western Australian Maritime Museum. This, together with the influence of the professional association, has led to close cooperation between the staff of the various State programmes.

Since the enactment of the **Australian Historic Shipwrecks Act** the Commonwealth Government has gradually increased its level of funding to the States, and through the direction of its programmes it has shifted the emphasis from maritime archaeology towards cultural resource management. In 1996 the Commonwealth Government established the Western Australian Maritime

Under the Act, wrecks and relics may be protected in one of three principal ways. These are: a specific declaration made by the Minister that a certain wreck/relic be protected (Section 5); a wreck/relic reaching seventy-five years of age (Section 4A); and the declaration of a protected zone (Section 7) or an area of exclusion around a wreck. A fourth means of protection is available, although it only operates for a maximum of five years; it is called a Provisional Declaration (Section 6). Such a declaration would be made in a case where further investigation was required to justify the rea-

that point forward, of wrecks and relics seventy-five years old or older, regardless of whether they had been previously declared or not. The seventy-five-year criterion is also referred to as the 'rolling date'.

Australia's Constitution created two levels of government: Commonwealth and State/ Territory. In order to carry out the day-to-day administration of the Act, the Minister has delegated a number of powers to senior government officers at both Commonwealth and State/Territory level. These officers are known as 'delegates' and have primary responsibility for the administration of certain functions of the Act. There is one delegate at Commonwealth level and one in each State and the Northern Territory.

The power currently delegated to the Commonwealth official is the power to appoint inspectors (Section 22). The ambit of inspectors' powers is dealt with in Sections 23, 24, and 25 of the Act; these powers relate to arrest, seizure, and forfeiture of items protected by the Act. Inspectors are usually appointed from the ranks of government parks and wildlife organizations because of their experience in matters of enforcement.

The powers currently delegated to State/Territory officials are the power to require persons to provide reports about the location of historic shipwrecks and relics (Section 10(1)), for instance, penalties apply if false or misleading information is provided; power to give directions in relation to custody etc. of historic wrecks/relics (Section 11(1)), for instance, if items are being incorrectly cared for or are required for display purposes, a direction under Section 11 may be issued; and the power to issue permits for the exploration or recovery of historic shipwrecks and relics (Section 15), for instance, if an institution wants to carry out research work on a wreck in a protected zone or if a commercial charter operator wants to take recreational divers to a wreck for sightseeing purposes into a protected zone.

In addition to the Commonwealth legislation, each State and the Northern Territory has enacted legislation (which is largely complementary) to protect shipwrecks and related relics in their waters, such as inland lakes, rivers, and tributaries.

It is estimated that there are several thousand shipwrecks in Australian waters and Section 12 of the Act provides for the creation and maintenance of a register of wrecks and relics. M.H.

Museum as a national centre of excellence in maritime archaeology. This new status comes with triennial funding which will enlarge the Maritime Museum's programmes at the national level. G.H.

ADDITIONAL READING
Henderson, G., 1986, *Maritime Archaeology in Australia*, Nedlands, Western Australia.

Australian Historic Shipwrecks Act

Legislation to provide for the protection of historic shipwrecks and relics, including old Dutch shipwrecks in Australian waters, and the maintenance of a register of historic shipwrecks and relics. The Australian Commonwealth Historic Shipwrecks Act (the Act) came into effect on 15 December 1976. It consists of three parts and thirty-two sections. The Commonwealth Government Minister for Communications and the Arts has responsibility for the Act. The Act applies within Australia and extends to its external territories, which include Norfolk Island, east of the mainland; and Cocos and Keeling (Christmas) Islands, northwest of the mainland.

sons for a full declaration under Section 5, or to protect the wreck/relic until it reached the age of seventy-five years, if it were already close to reaching that age.

Recommendations for the declaration of shipwrecks as historic (i.e. less than seventy-five years) and the creation of protected zones are normally made to the Minister by delegates, whose powers are described below. However, a recommendation could also be made by any member of the public.

In order to have the force of law, a declaration made by the Minister, under the Act, must be published in the Commonwealth Government's gazette – a publication which is issued on a regular basis and is available to members of the public. However, as mentioned above, when a wreck reaches the age of seventy-five years, it is automatically protected. It is not necessary to publish the fact each time a wreck reaches this age because a notice called a 'Blanket Declaration' was placed in the gazette in February 1993. The effect of this notice was the protection, from

ADDITIONAL READING
Henderson, G., 1986, *Maritime Archaeology in Australia*, Nedlands, Western Australia.

Australian Institute for Maritime Archaeology (AIMA)

Organization formed in 1982 to assist in developing the maritime archaeology profession and furthering the aims of programmes and projects in Australia and in other parts of the world. The first International Conference on Maritime Archaeology in Australia was held in Perth, Western Australia in 1977 and it was at this conference that the idea of AIMA was born. A National Maritime Archaeological Committee was formed from representatives of various Australian States in order to assess the potential and resources in their States. It was hoped that through this committee, active programmes in other States could be initiated and encouraged. This activity was further developed following the establishment of AIMA in 1982, the year of the second conference. Towards the end of the 1980s each State and the Northern Territory had staff employed to implement a programme, and by 1996 about twenty qualified maritime archaeologists were active in the profession in Australia.

The Council of the Australian Institute for Maritime Archaeology comprises many of these archaeologists but it also includes some people that work in other professions and have a special interest in the field. In the 1980s some of these individuals came from 'voluntary' maritime archaeology associations in each of the States. Today there is still a sprinkling of 'volunteers' in the council of AIMA. In addition to the annual general meetings, the AIMA council 'meets' about every two months through telephone conferences.

The objectives of the Institute are: to undertake scientific research in the field of maritime archaeology; to promote the advancement of the field of maritime archaeology; to promote international cooperation in the excavation of maritime archaeological sites and the research and studies related to this field; to cooperate with Australian State Maritime Archaeological Associations and any other body or person having similar aims; to publish periodically a bulletin and a newsletter or such other publications as may be determined from time to time; to inform and make recommendations to government and organizations of matters relating to maritime archaeology; to cooperate with Australian State and Federal organizations working in the field of maritime archaeology; and to subsidize or contribute to any institutions, organizations, and scholarships agreeable to any of the objects specified.

AIMA has been very active in a number of these areas. Former president Jeremy Green has led a number of excavations and training projects in Thailand, while more recently Tom Vosmer has studied existing traditional vessels in Oman. These AIMA projects have involved a number of AIMA members, as have the non-AIMA projects in China, other parts of Southeast Asia, Sri Lanka, New Zealand, and throughout Australia. Australian excavation projects in the 1980s and 1990s have been on the shipwrecks *Sirius*, *Sydney Cove*, and *Pandora*.

The Australian Government has contracted AIMA to compile a National Shipwrecks Database. In cooperation with the State agencies, a database of approximately 7,000 shipwrecks will soon be available to anyone wishing to research Australia's shipwrecks. The Australian Government also asked AIMA recently to prepare guidelines for the management of Australia's shipwrecks.

One of the associated activities that AIMA is keen to play a role in is diving, where it has representation on a national committee preparing a code of practice for occupational (scientific) diving.

Publications have been given a high profile throughout AIMA's existence. A bulletin has been published twice a year since 1982, which comprises good quality and refereed articles on a variety of aspects of maritime archaeological work in Australia and internationally. Ten special publications have also been published. Members are presented with a newsletter four times a year. The Australian Federal Government assists financially with the publications.

An annual AIMA conference has been held since 1982. The conferences, which have attracted many international participants, are well regarded in Australia, drawing financial aid from State and Federal governments, and support from politicians. One of the projects discussed at a few of the AIMA conferences in the mid-1990s has been the concept of a National Research Plan for Australian shipwrecks.

Many of the State maritime archaeological practitioners – who are AIMA members – have come through the Curtin University (Western Australia) course on maritime archaeology. At the present time this postgraduate diploma is the only course specializing in maritime archaeology. Other universities such as Flinders University (South Australia) and James Cook University (Queensland) teach maritime archaeology as a subject in an archaeology degree. One of the things AIMA is looking at in the future is making available a small scholarship for people who want to undertake some relevant study and disseminate the results.

Another important achievement, and an indication of the high regard for maritime archaeology in Australia, can be seen in the fact that the ICOMOS International Committee on the Underwater Cultural Heritage is chaired by Graeme Henderson, an AIMA past president.

AIMA has lobbied governments, individuals, and groups about the proper manner of protecting, managing, and carrying out work on historic shipwrecks, in Australia and internationally. In Australia, the National and State laws covering shipwrecks together with the active programmes – involving the community – have made a big impact on protecting sites, in addition to educating people about how to care for them. But much work still remains to be done, particularly in international waters.

A new and exciting leap into the future for maritime archaeology has come with the advent of the Internet. Through the Western Australian Maritime Museum, AIMA publishes on the World Wide Web its latest bulletin and newsletter, a list of all AIMA publications, and information on the National Shipwrecks Database. An experimental shipwreck database in which it is possible to search for any Australian shipwreck is on trial. W.F.J.

ADDITIONAL READING

Clark, P., 1990, *Shipwreck Sites in the South-East of South Australia 1838–1915*, Australian Institute for Maritime Archaeology Special Publication 5, Fremantle.

Edmonds, L. *et al.*, 1995, *Historic Shipwrecks National Research Plan*, Canberra.

Gesner, P., 1991, *Pandora: An Archaeological Perspective*, Brisbane.

Green, J. (ed.), 1977, *Papers from the First Southern Hemisphere Conference on Maritime Archaeology*, Melbourne.

Green, J. and Harper, R., 1983, *The Excavation of the Pattaya Wreck Site and Survey of Three Other Sites: Thailand 1992*, Australian Institute for Maritime Archaeology Special Publication 1, Fremantle.

Henderson, G. (ed.), 1994, *Guidelines for the Management of Australia's Shipwrecks*, Canberra.

Henderson, G. and Stanbury, M., 1988, *The Sirius: Past and Present*, Australia.

Jeffery, B., 1994, 'National Shipwrecks Project', *Bulletin of the Australian Institute for Maritime Archaeology*, 18, 1, 5–10, Fremantle.

Stanbury, M., 1994, *H.M.S. Sirius, 1790: An Illustrated Catalogue of Artefacts Recovered from the Wreck Site at Norfolk Island*, Australian Institute for Maritime Archaeology Special Publication 7, Fremantle.

Strachan, S., 1986, *The History and Archaeology of*

the *Sydney Cove Shipwreck (1797): A Resource for Future Site Work*, Australian National University Occasional Papers in Prehistory 5, Canberra.

Vosmer, T., Margariti, R., and Tilley, A., 1993, *The Omani Dhow Research Project: Final Report*, Watertown, Massachusetts.

Avocationals

Amateur underwater archaeological groups. Avocationals are a pivotal user group, and can be an effective protector of submerged cultural resources. Avocationals have discovered, mapped, and analysed with professionals, but often work in isolation. Regional avocational groups have evolved from these efforts. The main goal of these groups is resource protection through education and legislation.

In some jurisdictions, these groups have created a 'take only pictures' ethic for submerged cultural sites. However, in other jurisdictions, the removal of artefacts by sport divers continues to damage this non-renewable resource. Sport divers and sponge divers with an interest in history were the first underwater archaeologists. As Bass said in 1966 (p. 18), 'It was the amateur, the diver, and not the professional archaeologist who led the way, found the sites, pioneered their excavation, and showed the promise of the future. We owe these amateur archaeologists a debt of gratitude in spite of errors they may have made.' Since the mid-1960s, amateur shipwreck divers have evolved into avocational underwater archaeologists. College level courses are being taught to sport divers around the world. Avocationals have led non-intrusive shipwreck inventories, mapped sites, and, with professional support, have undertaken limited excavations.

Despite this evolution, some professionals view avocationals as a threat; some even consider them to be licensed looters. Others fear that untrained avocationals will take their jobs and create inaccurate information. Similarly, some dive organizations fear that professional underwater archaeologists want to prevent diving on all shipwrecks. Treasure-hunters seeking unlimited access to 'potential' gold often exploit these fears.

In jurisdictions with effective communication between avocationals and professionals, these fears are diminished and avocationals have become para-professionals who undertake resource inventories. The professional archaeologist provides training, education, and on site expertise. Avocational archaeologists can provide more than volunteer labour, bringing varied skills and professional knowledge to underwater archaeological projects. However, in jurisdictions where

Amateur (avocational) diver surveying the wreck of Barnard Castle. *(UASBC/Mike Paris)*

these fears predominate, avocationals' role is limited to diver support.

Avocational underwater archaeological groups are ideally placed to minimize distrust between professional underwater archaeologists and the many other resource users. Those other users include sport divers, dive charter operators, dive certification agencies, treasure salvors, site developers, subsea companies, maritime museums, government underwater archaeologists, consulting underwater archaeologists, universities, academic underwater archaeologists, and aboriginals (submerged native sites). Avocational groups are often the only link between these users.

Thus, the role of avocational groups is to communicate between users, mediate disputes between users, educate sport divers, lobby for resource protection legislation, broker resource projects, inventory and analyse resources, and provide front-line resource protection. Their success in these roles will depend on the willingness of government archaeologists to work with avocationals. Without that support, avocationals fight an uphill battle for recognition. By working with avocationals, government archaeologists can deliver a preservation message more effectively than by direct contact with sport divers. Divers usually trust other divers in preference to government archaeologists. When disputes arise, avocationals are well placed to mediate a solution for resource protection.

Sport divers are increasingly eager for courses which are beyond the 'shipwreck' courses offered by dive certification agencies but are less rigorous than a university course. The **Nautical Archaeology Society**'s four-part training scheme fills that gap and is being taught around the world. Once

informed, most people respect the conservation principles for a non-renewable resource which are taught in these courses. However, some do not. Treasure salvors view the resource as a private resource. Most discount or ignore the interests of other users, including recreational divers.

Most jurisdictions have maritime salvage laws which are based on a 19th-century risk/reward system. Those laws encourage treasure salvage and were developed before archaeology was a science and long before technology permitted underwater exploration and excavation. Avocationals have played a significant role in some jurisdictions in lobbying for legislative change to treat underwater archaeological sites in the same manner as terrestrial sites.

Non-profit avocational groups have been brokers between industry, academics, and sport divers, to create projects at low or no cost. The potential for this brokerage synergy is limited only by imagination. With training and experience, avocationals have undertaken site surveys and other resource analysis tasks. Surveys are significant resource management tools, especially for government archaeologists. Avocationals should call in professional archaeologists for the difficult tasks.

Most submerged cultural resources are discovered by local divers and not by professional archaeologists. By bridging the gap between local divers and professional archaeologists, more resources become available to the public. Avocationals can also be very effective 'eyes and ears' for local resource protection. Professionals are often viewed as outsiders and they have limited resources for local site protection.

Professionals need avocationals as much as the avocationals need professionals. With time, experience, and training avocationals can become para-professional archaeologists. Some perceived barriers remain but that acceptance is near. T.F.B.

ADDITIONAL READING

Bass, G.F., 1966, *Archaeology Under Water*, London.

Beasley, T.F., 1994, 'Avocationals: Expedition Grunts or Para-archaeologists', in R.P. Woodward and C.D. Moore (eds), *Underwater Archaeology Proceedings from the Society for Historical Archaeology Conference, Vancouver, British Columbia*, Ann Arbor, Michigan.

Cooper, D.J., 1994, '"Come All Ye Gentlemen Volunteers": Perspectives on Avocationals in Underwater Archaeology', in R.P. Woodward and C.D. Moore (eds), *Underwater Archaeology Proceedings from the Society for Historical Archaeology Conference, Vancouver, British Columbia*, Ann Arbor, Michigan.

Bahía Mujeres Wreck

Early 16th-century wreck discovered near Cancun, Mexico by fishermen, subsequently partially recovered by the Mexican **Avocational** group CEDAM, and later documented by **Mexico**'s Instituto Nacional de Antropologia e Historia and the **Institute of Nautical Archaeology** (INA) in 1984. The wreck was discovered in 1958 in a small bay off the Isla de Mujeres, near Cancun on the Yucatan Peninsula, and a wrought-iron cannon was recovered. The find was reported to a nearby CEDAM team, which visited the site and recovered additional ordnance and anchors. CEDAM identified the wreck as *La Nicolesa*, a vessel belonging to conquistador Francisco de Montejo, who spearheaded Spain's efforts to pacify and colonize the Yucatan Peninsula. However, *La Nicolesa* was not lost in Mexico, and the identity of the wreck remains unknown. It is, however, the oldest shipwreck yet discovered in Mexico.

In 1983 a team of INA archaeologists working on the 16th-century Molasses Reef Wreck learned about the Bahía Mujeres Wreck and were able to document some of the artefacts raised by CEDAM, including a *falconete*, a *bombardeta*, a *verso*, two *bombardeta* breech-blocks, and a *verso* breech-block, as well as a grapnel anchor, which confirmed the 16th-century date for the wreck. In 1984 INA and archaeologists from the Instituto Nacional de Antropologia e Historia relocated the wreck site, which was marked by a pile of coral-covered ballast, and marked it for future excavation and research. J.P.D.

ADDITIONAL READING

Smith, R.C. and Keith, D.H., 1986, 'The Archaeology of Ships of Discovery', *Archaeology*, 39, 2, 30–35.

Smith, R.C., 1993, *Vanguard of Empire: Ships of Exploration in the Age of Columbus*, Oxford and New York.

Baltic Sea

A small intracontinental sea, and the largest brackish body of water in the world, measuring 366,000 sq. km.

Geography

The Baltic Sea is fairly shallow with an average depth of about 60 m. The entrance to the Baltic is made up by Öresund (The Sounds), the Stora Bält (Great Belt), and the Lilla Bält (Little Belt), as well as the Belt Sea. The sill between Öresund and the Baltic runs through the belts and the Belt Sea at a depth of 17 m. The Baltic consists of three main sections: the Baltic proper, the Gulf of Bothnia, and the Gulf of Finland.

In the Baltic proper, the Gulf of Riga is distinguished as a separate part. The Gulf of Bothnia is divided into three main areas: the Sea of Åland, the southern part of the Gulf of Bothnia, and the northern part of the Gulf of Bothnia. The area between Åland and Finland is usually called the Ålands Hav or the Skärgårdshavet ('Archipelago Sea'). The Baltic reaches its greatest depth off Landsort just outside the southern part of Stockholm archipelago. At this point it is 459 m deep.

To the east the seabed is made of sedimentary rock that stretches all the way to the Fennoscand shield in the west. To the north and northeast the bottom is made up mostly of primary rock. In the vicinity of Gotland accumulations of gravel and sand have been found. Massive submarine boulder ridges are located in and slightly to the north of the Bay of Gävle. Thinner layers of sand and gravel are found along the shorelines of southern Sweden. Along the coasts, quaternary sediment is common.

In the northern and middle parts of the Baltic the land mass is constantly undergoing gradual uplift, which creates a regression of the waterline. This uplift amounts, at its greatest rate, to about one metre per hundred years. The maximum uplift takes place around Ångermanland county on the Swedish side. Farther north and south these uplifts gradually diminish. In the south it diminishes until Kalmar Sound is reached, south of which the land level is subsiding. These processes are the result of the pressure by glaciers on the land mass during the Ice Age and play an important role in the archaeological and historical interpretation of the shoreline of the Baltic.

Several lake systems and rivers empty into the Baltic imparting particular qualities to the water. The fresh water of these lakes and rivers maintains a low level of salinity, a level which continues to drop to the north and which, in the northernmost part of the Gulf of Bothnia, is almost non-existent.

Visibility in certain parts of the Baltic is relatively low owing to heavy sedimentation. This is particularly true in the northern part of the Gulf of Bothnia, the central part of the Swedish Baltic coastline, and the Gulf of Finland. In coastal waters visibility often varies between 2 and 5 m. The Baltic rarely freezes completely, but heavy floes of ice are formed. These run to great depths under the waterline, particularly in pack ice.

Large sections of the Swedish Baltic coast-line are made up of larger or smaller archipelagos, or groups of islands. At its most northerly section can be found the broad and fairly flat Haparanda archipelago in which the islands are often built up of sand. In the so-called High Coast area in the county of Ångermanland, the archipelago is characterized by high and fairly steep islands. The Uppland and Södermanland archipelagos form Sweden's largest contiguous archipelago region with over 24,000 islands. The Östergötland and northern Småland archipelagos are of a similar nature but less extensive. The southern Småland coastal archipelago is more open and low lying. The coastline of Skåne is characterized by open sandy beaches. This type of coastal geography is also found in the northern part of the Gulf of Bothnia. Rocky and stony shorelines play a significant role in other areas of the Baltic Sea and the Gulf of Bothnia, for example at the island of Gotland.

An archipelago type of landscape is also the dominant feature of the Finnish coastline. Along the southeastern and southern Baltic Sea shores the most common form is sandy bottom and sandy beaches. The most characteristic features are the lagoon or 'haff' formations along the Polish and German coastlines. Even the Danish Baltic coastline is dominated by open and low shores with sandy bottoms.

Archaeological factors

Several natural conditions influence the state and preservation of archaeological remains in the Baltic in certain decisive ways. A few of the factors which are pivotal to the preservation of the submerged cultural resources of the Baltic can be listed: (1) the geographical outline of the coast, e.g. archipelago, open coastline; (2) the position of the remains in relation to the surface of the water, e.g. in deep or shallow water; (3) the topography of the sea bottom, e.g. hard bottom littered with large rocks or a sandy bottom; (4) the geological make-up of the sea bottom, e.g. sedimentation or erosional bottom; (5) the differences in height on the bottom, e.g. caused by movements in the sand on the seabed; (6) the existence of ice down to a great depth; (7) the existence of currents; (8) the existence of heavy wave movements; (9) the existence of special chemical, botanical, or biological conditions influencing the state of archaeological remains under water.

As a rule an open coastline provides less protection for old shipwrecks or other remains than a coastline dotted with islands. Shipwrecks lying off an open coast are often subjected to, and destroyed by, heavy wave formation. The depth of the site is significant as this also affects the remains: remains in shallow waters are more susceptible to various forms of damaging agents.

The character of the bottom is also of significance. Rocky sea bottoms and shorelines with large stones can – due to the wave movement – have a disastrous effect on the remains of ships foundered at such a place, particularly on an open coast. Ships that sink onto sandy sea bottoms, however, may be protected by the very fact that they become buried in the sand. Underwater sedimentation such as in the case of silt also provides a form of protection. Ice, currents, and wave movement all act negatively on sunken ships. The islands in the inner archipelagos can, on the other hand, offer good protection to archaeological remains. The existence of large archipelagos may thus be one of the most decisive factors for the existence of well-preserved remains in the Baltic.

Thus far, few remains are known in the open sea. One reason for this is that fewer remains exist on the bottom there; another is that little work has been done to study archaeological remains there.

Owing to several different conditions marine archaeological remains in the Baltic are uniquely well preserved compared to those in many other types of environments, for example, the big oceans. One reason for this is the absence of the shipworm (*Teredo navalis*) in the brackish waters of the Baltic. Thus wood and other organic materials are devoured and destroyed to a much lesser degree, and can thus be preserved better than they can in environments with a higher degree of salinity. Yet this is not the only reason, and possibly not the most important. The sheltered conditions in the Baltic permit the preservation of structures of organic material under water there. The vast archipelagos, with thousands of skerries and islands, serve as an effective protection against heavy wave action, currents, and other types of impact by the sea which in other seas has a much stronger effect on archaeological remains. Similar sheltering conditions have focused the ongoing process of sedimentation of silt, especially along the shores of middle and north Sweden and Finland. The same effects have formed the thick layers of sand along the shores in the southern part of the Baltic, for example along the coasts of Poland, Germany, Denmark, and southern Sweden.

Chemical, botanical, and biological conditions also act to protect or destroy archaeological remains in the Baltic. One factor of decisive importance in these circumstances

is the presence of galvanic currents existing in the water. These are created between cathodes and anodes, often of metal, especially iron, in old, submerged structures, with the water or organic material, for example wood, as the medium. The galvanic current created is stronger in higher concentrations of salinity, and thus is relatively low in the brackish water of the Baltic (and still lower in fresh water).

Although the shipworm is absent in the Baltic, other organisms interact with or affect archaeological remains under water. These include micro-organisms which devour the cellulose in wood at a rate which is correlated to the degree of oxygen in the surrounding water. The rate of this decay is lower in the Baltic than in other seas with a higher rate of salinity and oxygen.

The concept of maritime archaeology in this context is viewed as the study of material remains of maritime society, located under water, at the shore, or in soil. The description of maritime archaeology of the Baltic Sea must also encompass sites in fresh water on nearby land areas. Prehistoric and also later phases of society at the Baltic have to a high degree been directed towards the sea for living and communications. Coastal and inland habitation sites for fishing and hunting were thus common in the prehistoric periods as well as during the historic period. Due to the fact that the Baltic and surrounding inland areas have had an active role in European trade and seafaring since prehistory, various cultures have developed trading centres (some of them later becoming seafaring towns) on its shores.

The Baltic was one of the most important areas in European trade during the medieval and post-medieval periods. This has left a large number of remains, in the shape of wrecks of merchant ships, remains of harbours, evidence of old sea routes, and so on from these periods. These remains are located either on the bottom in the different areas of the Baltic, or in the coastal sediments, or in inland maritime environments.

The nations bordering the Baltic competed to control and dominate seagoing trade and the harbours developed bustling naval activity, including the establishment of mighty naval bases, the building and use of a great number of naval vessels, as well as the execution of many large naval battles through time.

What we call maritime archaeology seems in most of the countries at the Baltic – in the case of the scientific activities involved in it – to start in the middle of the 19th century, and then develop successively thereafter. This development seems, to a substantial

degree, to express the national characters or historical identities of the respective societies around the Baltic that have engaged in this activity.

The development of maritime archaeology in the Baltic encompasses individual developments within Denmark, Sweden, Finland, the Baltic countries, Poland, and northern Germany. In other words it comprises several separate evolvements based on natural and other conditions in each country, and is also influenced by the cultural patterns within each of these societies. Thus the developments have to a high degree been steered by cultural, social, and economic factors in the different areas of the Baltic up to and during the 20th century.

National developments

Denmark

Danish society has developed a strong sense for its prehistory and its archaeological remains. A high cultural value has in this context been given to the impressive megalithic tombs of Neolithic times. Stone Age sites of habitation also exist. A large part of Danish and south Swedish land has – due to the geological circumstances described earlier – been subjected to a transgression since the latest ice age. This means that a large number of coastal habitation sites of the Ertebölle culture (*c.* 5500–4000 BC) are today submerged under water in Denmark and southern Sweden. Professional research activities have been undertaken, especially by the Department of Prehistoric Archaeology at Aarhus University, to survey and excavate such sites under water. The most extensive excavation of this character is the one of the deposit layers outside an Ertebölle site at Tybrind Bay on the island of Fyn.

Danish maritime archaeology has also, to a high degree, been directed towards the studies of remains of prehistoric Iron Age and medieval vessels, several of which have been investigated and analysed. The boat finds dating from the period before AD 900 are relatively few, but after that date are more numerous. Stone Age boat finds are all of logboats. Some of the oldest known are finds from the Mesolithic Ertebölle period. Examples include a find from Korshavn Bay, dated to *c.* 5200 BC, and two logboats excavated under water at the Tybrind Bay site, and dated to the younger phase of the Ertebölle culture. At such logboat finds, or separately, archaeologists have also found several paddles from the Mesolithic period. About thirty logboats are known which have been dated to the Neolithic period, as well as some from the Bronze Age.

The first find of a plank-built boat in Denmark was the 3rd-century BC **Hjortspring Boat**. This find, a bog offering, spurred a great interest in Danish ship archaeology, partly because of its relevance as evidence of shipbuilding in the Nordic Bronze Age (c. 1800–500 BC), and partly the similarity it has with the rock carving depictions of vessels from the same period.

The Slusegård boat graves from the Roman Iron Age at the island of Bornholm contain remains of lightly built expanded logboats. These have a similar shape to, and are seen as forerunners of, clinker-built vessels. Danish ship archaeologists hold the opinion that clinker-built boats appeared during the early Iron Age, and that the expanded logboat played an important role in that development. The Slusegård boat remains have, therefore, attracted interest as examples of both smaller and bigger coastal vessels of their time. These more coarsely cut logboats, without the sheer of expanded craft, were used especially in inland waters, where they did not need the same seaworthiness required for coastal waters.

The clinker-building technique dominated in shipbuilding in northern Europe for more than a thousand years, until carvel-building emerged in the late medieval period. The first bigger clinker-built vessels known are the bog finds from Nydam on the border between Denmark and Germany, dating to the late Roman Iron Age (see **Nydam Boat**). These are seen as offerings in connection with tribal wars and migrations in the same period. The studies around these finds are carried by a strong ideological interest in the Germanic tribes and their historic roles in early European society. It is no coincidence that these Danish research activities have been and are developed in close contact with the same interest in Germany.

From the latter part of the Iron Age a growing number of ship finds have been made and studied in Denmark. The dominant feature of this ship archaeological material and the work on it is the high level of interest manifested in connection with ships from the Viking period, and the massive investment of resources made to excavate, treat, study, preserve, and exhibit these finds. A series of finds have been made and studied in Danish and adjacent waters. The best known are the five **Skuldelev ships** sunk in Roskilde Fjord as part of a barricade built in the latter part of the 11th century. The ships were raised in 1962 and are now preserved and displayed in a special Viking ship hall in the town of Roskilde.

Other well-known ship finds from late Iron Age in Denmark are the Ladby Ship, a

man of war c. 22 m long, found and excavated as part of a burial from the early 10th century; Foteviken I, a smaller man of war found as part of an underwater barricade from the latter part of the 11th century in southern Sweden (formerly Denmark), and a large 11th-century man of war found in the harbour of the Viking age trading centre at Hedeby.

A special position in Danish ship archaeology directed towards this period is occupied by the excavations of a shipyard from the

The raising of Vasa. *Released from her salvaging pontoons,* Vasa *moves into the Beckholmen dock on her own keel. (Courtesy of the Vasa Museum, Stockholm, Sweden)*

second half of the 11th century at Fribrödre stream on the island of Falster. This site, with rich archaeological material including parts of boats under construction or repair, mirrors strong influences of Slavonic boatbuilding traditions in Danish society between the Iron Age and medieval times.

Another eminent trait in Danish ship archaeology is the interest developed around the archaeological finds of mer-

chant ships from the Viking and medieval periods, and used in the expansive trading systems in northern Europe at this time. Several ship finds have been investigated and analysed; for example, two cargo carriers among the five Skuldelev finds; the remains of a seagoing trading ship from the 11th century, excavated under Danish leadership in the harbour of Haithabu; the Lynäs Ship, another seagoing cargo carrier from about AD 1150; several medieval ship finds, such as the Kyholm Boat and the Ellingå Boat, both

from the 13th century; as well as cog finds from the middle of the medieval period, such as the Kollerup Cog from the late 12th century, and the Vejbystrand Cog, dated to the latter half of the 14th century.

The studies of archaeological ship finds from the earlier part of the Iron Age and the Viking age have been combined with studies of the remains of defence barriers in coastal waters. These were built both in the Late Roman Iron Age and the early Migration period in connection with the tribal wars, and also in the late Iron Age and early medieval period. The latter are supposed to have been built in connection with the creation of a Danish state organization about a thousand years ago.

Research reconstructing and interpreting old sea routes and navigation techniques in early times has followed the studies of boat remains from the Iron Age and the medieval period. These studies are concentrated both on information about how old sailing routes passed through the coastal landscape, and how open sea sailing and navigation was performed. As well as boats and ships, material remains studied in this context include those of sailing marks, beacons, observation posts, navigation instruments, and other ancient monuments or artefacts once part of a sea route system and its use. Integrated as part of this research is information about old natural landmarks and place names along the coasts that indicate the former existence of sailing routes.

Maritime archaeological interest in periods later than the Middle Ages has not developed to the same degree as that directed towards earlier phases. Since the 19th century, in Sweden, some have managed salvage operations from wrecks of naval ships from the post-medieval period. Archaeologists have also studied the remains of Danish naval ships placed as foundations for defence installations in the water outside Copenhagen in the early 19th century. Surveys as well as excavations have been performed on the wrecks of two English ships of the line – *St George* and *Defence* – which were stranded on the west coast of Jutland in 1811. Interest has also developed in the wrecks of merchant ships from the post-medieval period, which are usually located by skin divers.

Sweden

In the southern coastal waters, as in Denmark, remains of Mesolithic settlements exist. Such finds were first subjected to investigation and study around 1870. The dredging of the harbour of the town of Ystad brought artefacts both from this and later periods to the eyes of archaeologists of that time, who treated and published them. Submerged Stone Age settlements in Swedish waters are still a largely unexploited submerged cultural resource.

Interest in submerged cultural resources was increased by the introduction of the heavy diving suit in the middle of the 19th century. Naval officers and divers at this time began to dive and salvage the wrecks of old men of war from the 17th and 18th centuries. Their aim was to raise guns, ship timbers, and other objects from the wrecks. This was done partly to commemorate

these famous ships and partly for commercial reasons. Salvors sold the objects to antique collectors or museums, and the timber, the 'black oak', was sold to furniture manufacturers. A series of these salvage operations were performed from the middle of the 19th century well into the 20th century.

Another early phase in Swedish maritime archaeology has its background in the first big ship excavations in Scandinavia: prehistoric and Iron Age ship remains excavated in the latter part of the 19th century such as the Nydam ships in Denmark and the **Gokstad Ship** in Norway. From the start, Sweden was not as fortunate as its neighbouring nations in the discovery or excavation of early ship finds. However, a few decades into the 20th century, several ship finds were located and excavated. The finds included the remains of a 12th-century merchant ship at Galtabäck, Halland county, excavated at the end of the 1920s; and a few years later, a 10th-century merchant ship at Äskekärr, on the Göta Älv River, Västergötland county, both on the west coast. To the same find group also belongs a 14th-century merchant ship at Falsterbo, Skåne county, on the south coast, and two dozen ship finds from the medieval and early post-medieval periods excavated in the 1930s in the harbour of the town of Kalmar (see **Kalmar Harbour wrecks**).

In Sweden, as well as in Finland, a special branch of archaeology developed to study medieval sea routes. These studies to a great extent are concentrated on a document of the 13th century that describes the sea passage from the coast of Denmark (starting in Blekinge county, which at this time belonged to Denmark) along the Swedish east coast, over the Åland islands to the Finnish south coast, and finally across the Gulf of Finland to Estonia. The studies include not only the run of the sea road itself and sailing along it, but also more than a hundred places along the route that are mentioned in the document, and a diverse spectrum of archaeological remains at the same places.

Between the two world wars a third type of maritime archaeological enterprise was also realized for the first time. This was the survey of a big lake fortress, the Bulverket, in Tingstäde Träsk lake on the island of Gotland. The investigation included an extensive recording of the structure. Since the end of the 1980s, archaeologists have executed a modern underwater archaeological investigation and analysis of the big lake fort, which has been dated to the early 12th century. The aim of the latter project has

been to widen the understanding of the fort and its role in medieval society.

The continued interest in the wrecks of old warships in the same period led at this time to the first modern underwater excavation, from 1933 to 1938, performed with heavy diving equipment on the wreck of the big kravel *Elefanten*, which foundered in Kalmar Sound in 1564.

The 1940s and 1950s were a period of consolidation when archaeologists, on the basis of information retrieved earlier, worked to treat, reconstruct, publish, and exhibit the results gathered and the finds made. Around 1950 two different marine archaeological research programmes were also presented. One was established in Gothenburg in cooperation between avocational maritime archaeologists and the maritime museum there. The programme contained a plan to record archaeological underwater and coastal remains in western Sweden, following a differentiated classification and also containing methodology recommendations. The other programme was aimed at the locating and identification of a selected number of wrecks of old naval ships. This programme was developed by Anders Franzen, who was engaged in the locating of such wrecks on the east coast of Sweden. This programme can be seen as an expression of the Navy's interest in its own old men of war.

The interest in old naval warship wrecks reached its climax in 1961 when **Vasa**, which sank in 1628, was raised from the bottom of Stockholm Harbour. This led to increased interest in such wrecks and in marine archaeology among the public.

The development of **SCUBA** diving at the same time focused interest on a large and hitherto little known group of maritime archaeological remains, namely the big and often well-preserved remains of carvel-built ships from the post-medieval period in Swedish waters. These wrecks, about 90 per cent of which are of merchant ships, are unusually well preserved in certain areas of the Baltic Sea, especially in the Swedish and Finnish archipelagos.

In the 1970s a series of investigations of different types of ship remains were performed to gain experience of the problems of underwater recording and excavation in the waters of the Baltic Sea. Two of these projects were performed on the remains of bigger merchant ship wrecks from the post-medieval period, as these were seen as very typical of the marine archaeological environment of eastern Swedish waters. In 1983 this development work was summarized by Carl Cederlund in a monograph on the theme of archaeological recording and documentation of carvel-built wrecks in the Baltic Sea. A parallel research programme since developed by Christian Ahlström has been directed towards the same type of remains and the methodology of identification of the same type of shipwrecks in archival and other written sources.

At present, Swedish marine archaeology is still strongly dominated by the traditional lines of interest described. One example of this is the excavation since the early 1980s of the big warship *Kronan* which foundered in the open sea at the island of Öland in a battle against the Danish Navy in 1676. The early interest in medieval ships has been followed up by the excavation of ten ship remains from this and later periods at Helgeandsholmen, Stockholm, in 1978–80.

Investigation and research activities in the 1990s have, on the other hand, also embraced wider research, expanding towards the recognition of hitherto unrecognized submerged cultural resources. Especially important in this respect are the remains of structures of many different kinds, for example defence installations, harbours, jetties, caissons, and systems of fishing traps, built under water or on shores later inundated through transgression; and also cultural layers in water at shore habitations.

Finland

The main marine archaeological source materials are boat and ship remains, and old defence and harbour structures connected to the coastal seafaring systems. The first category has been the principal area of study.

Diving and salvage operations were already being performed on old wrecks in the latter part of the 19th century. This activity increased during the first half of the 20th century, and was followed by a growing interest in marine archaeology. From the 1960s marine archaeology was introduced and developed as a scientific activity, coordinated and conducted by the Bureau of Maritime History, now the National Maritime Museum, at the Board of National Antiquities, Helsinki.

At Lapuri, at the eastern end of the Finnish coast, archaeologists in the 1970s and 1980s located, investigated, and raised a clinker-built vessel of between 12 and 13.5 m in length, dated to about AD 980. The vessel is believed to have been built in south-western Scandinavia. A special part of Finnish ship archaeology has been the study of remains of traditional inland vessels, characteristic of the woodlands. As well as logboats there exist the remains of more than twenty boats built with the sewing tech-

nique, most commonly found in eastern and northern Finland. Of the remains the oldest is a small boat from Alatornio, which has been dated to the 10th century AD.

There is considerable interest in the remains of naval vessels sunk in the battles between the Swedish/Finnish and the Russian navies in the war of 1788–90. Several such wrecks are located at Svensksund (Kotka) from the battle there in 1790. One of them, the wreck of the Russian frigate *St Nikolai*, has been subject to extensive salvaging and investigation operations since the 1940s.

Wrecks of merchant or other transport vessels from the post-medieval period came into the focus of interest from the 1950s. Several such remains, in a well-preserved state, have been found in coastal waters. Several have been surveyed and investigated. One important find of this type is the well-preserved three-masted galliot *St Michael*, which foundered in 1747 at Borstö island in the southeastern part of the archipelago. Another is the so-called Mulan Wreck, located near Hangö peninsula on the south coast. This vessel is believed to have been a cargo carrier for the Swedish Navy or Army, lost in the early 17th century on its way from Russia to Stockholm with war booty.

Archaeological investigations and studies have been performed on the remains of harbour installations and defences in the waters around medieval and post-medieval forts and in passages along the coast. Defence installations have been recorded around the medieval fort of Raseborg; similar defences, in the shape of big sunken vessels, date from the 19th century at the Sveaborg fort in the outer part of Helsinki Harbour. Another type is the fort and harbour from the medieval period at **Högholmen Island**, Hitis, where substantial underwater remains of jetties and defences have been investigated. Still another type is the Gäddtarmen lagoon harbour near Hangö, where a large number of rock carvings were made on the surrounding rock surfaces by visiting seafarers during the later medieval and post-medieval periods.

Russia

Studies have centred around the remains of vessels and other finds of a maritime character in connection with the excavations of the medieval trading centre at Novgorod, south of Lake Ladoga. Studies of traditional boatbuilding in the medieval period and later in western Russia, including studies of ship remains, have been carried out in the 1990s.

Since the downfall of the Soviet regime, marine archaeological interest in old ship finds in the Gulf of Finland has developed.

Particular attention has been paid to the remains of several Swedish naval ships sunk in 1790, during the war between Sweden/ Finland and Russia in 1788–90. (See also **Russia and the ex-Soviet Union.**)

Estonia, Latvia, and Lithuania

Estonia and Latvia have several marine archaeological research areas in common. Several wrecks of merchant ships from the medieval and post-medieval periods have been located in the waters of both countries. Of a special character among these are the remains of indigenous clinker-built vessels, some of which have been built using the sewing technique. In the medieval period vessels of this type were used as transports between the trading centre at Novgorod and the Baltic Sea ports; in later periods they were also used as other inland transports on lakes and rivers.

Both Estonia and Latvia are interested in the remains of ships belonging to the Swedish Navy in the 17th and 18th centuries. One expression of this is the recording and salvaging of guns from the remains of Swedish men of war that foundered in battle with the Russian Navy in the Bay of Reval, Estonia, in 1790; another is the survey to locate the remains of several Swedish warships which in 1626 were wrecked at the shores of the Domesnäs peninsula, Latvia, on their way to Sweden.

A special feature of both Estonian and Latvian marine archaeology is the remains of prehistoric and medieval pile-dwellings in inland lakes. The most well-known site in Estonia is the pile-dwelling in Lake Valgjärv, dated to the second half of the first millennium AD, near the Latvian border. Other pile-dwellings have been located and investigated in lakes in Latvia. The well-preserved pile-dwelling site in Lake Araisi, near the town of Cesis, has been subject to an extensive investigation; it is believed to have been used in the 9th and 10th centuries AD.

Marine archaeology in Lithuania has not yet developed to the same extent as in Estonia and Latvia.

Poland

There is growing interest in several marine archaeological subjects in Poland, closely bound up with the nation's history. The earliest type of activity has been the excavation and study, during the late 19th and early 20th century, of the remains of clinker-built Slavonic boats from the Late Iron Age and the early medieval period. Several smaller boats of a similar character from the medieval and post-medieval periods, found in soil near the coast, have also been the subject of investigation from the 1970s (see Smolarek).

After World War II the Polish Maritime Museum in Gdansk developed a differentiated marine archaeology directed towards systematic survey, and a programme of investigations of ship remains in the Polish waters of the Baltic Sea. One reason for this was that much of the nation's maritime heritage had been destroyed during the war. Retrieval and studies of submerged cultural resources could compensate for these losses.

A register of older ship founderings and ship finds in Polish waters has been built up at the museum, with an emphasis on shipwrecks in Gdansk Bay, which has long been a central area of seafaring. A very large number of merchant ships have passed through the port over the centuries. An important example of finds connected to maritime trade in Gdansk Bay is the wreck of the so-called Copper Ship, a late medieval cargo ship, clinker-built in oak, originally about 25 m long. When it was located and raised, its hold still contained a differentiated cargo of export goods from Poland. Among the items were copper ingots, iron bars, tar, and other forest products. Several wrecks of merchant ships from the post-medieval period have also been located and surveyed.

The same waters have also witnessed naval engagements and battles, for example between the Polish and Swedish navies in the 17th century. One ship find illustrating the naval developments in the area is the wreck of the Swedish man of war *Solen* ('Sun') which was sunk by the Polish Navy in a battle in Gdansk Bay in 1627. The wreck became subject to an extensive excavation, performed by the Polish Maritime Museum; finds included twenty ship's guns of Swedish and Polish origin, as well as a large number of artefacts from the ship's equipment and the crew's belongings.

Pile-dwellings similar to those found in lakes in Estonia and Latvia have also been found and surveyed in the Mazurian lake district. The oldest of these pile-dwellings has been dated to the second millennium BC, and the most recent to the medieval period. (See also **Poland**.)

Northern Germany

The coastal areas of northern Germany were inhabited by Vendic tribes into the medieval period. The maritime culture of the area at this period constitute an important realm for north German marine archaeology. The remains of early clinker-built vessels, influenced by Slavonic clinker-building techniques, have been studied, such as the vessels excavated at the Viking age trading centre at Ralswiek on the island of Rugen, dating from the end of the 9th to the 11th century. In the harbour of the Viking age trading centre of Haithabu, Schleswig-Holstein, near the present border between Germany and Denmark, investigations of the remains of Viking ships have been carried out. In 1994 a project was started to survey extensive Viking age defence installations in the bay of Schlei, where Haithabu is situated.

From the 12th century the coastal areas in the southern part of the Baltic Sea became dominated by merchant townships established there. These later amalgamated into the trading organization known as the Hanseatic League. They developed a vital and extensive trade and seafaring network which prospered for several hundred years, persisting long after the Hanseatic League had been dissolved in the 16th century. Characteristic of the historical image of these towns was the symbol of the medieval sea trader, the cog ship, which had been projected ideologically in the medieval period as a symbol of seafaring and merchant capability. Marine archaeologists following this symbolism have been engaged in the raising and excavation of wrecks of cog ships from the 13th and 14th centuries, not only in the home waters of the Hanseatic League but also elsewhere in the Baltic Sea and the North Sea. The most well-known of the cog finds is the **Bremen Cog** from the later 14th century, found and raised in the harbour of Bremen in 1962, and now on exhibition at the German Maritime Museum in Bremerhaven.

Post-medieval marine archaeology in northern Germany has developed rapidly since the reunion of the two German states. An important reason for this is the fact that a large part of the shores of the Baltic Sea coast, as well as the related submerged cultural resources, then became accessible. One example of post-medieval archaeological remains studied underwater at the Baltic Sea coast is the wreck of a naval ship from the early 17th century, located at the Arcona Reef at the northern part of the island of Rugen. C.O.C.

ADDITIONAL READING

Ahlström, C., 1995, *Spår av Hav, Yxa och Penna: Historiska sjöolyckor i östersjön avspeglade i marinarkeologiskt källmaterial*, Helsingfors.

Cederlund, C.O., 1971, 'Archaeology Underwater', *Swedish Archaeological Bibliography 1966–1970*, Stockholm, 155–83.

Cederlund, C.O., 1983, *The Old Wrecks of the Baltic Sea: Archaeological Recording of the Wrecks of Carvel-built Ships*, British Archaeological Reports International Series 186, Oxford.

Cederlund, C.O., 1994, 'The Regal Ships and Divine Kingdom', *Current Swedish Archaeology*, 2, 47–85.

Cederlund, C.O., 1995, 'The Ships of Scandinavia and the Baltic', in *The Heyday of Sail: The Merchant Sailing Ship 1650–1830*, London.

Crumlin-Pedersen, O., 1978, *Sövejen til Roskilde*, Roskilde.

Crumlin-Pedersen, O., (ed.), 1991, *Aspects of Maritime Scandinavia 200–1200 A.D.*, Roskilde.

Flink, G., 1995, *Kung Valdemars Segelled*, Västerås.

Forsell, H., 1983, *Fynd av sydda bätar i Finland: Bätar 1*, Skrifter utgivna av Skärgårdsmuseet, Lovisa.

Grönquist, H., 1988, 'Svensk sjöhistorisk bibliografi 1976–1986', in *Sjöhistorisk Årsbok 1987*, Borås.

Grönquist, H. and Anderson, S., 1994, *Svensk sjöhistorisk bibliografi, 1987–1991*, Borås.

Maritime Museum of Finland, 1973, *Annual Report*, Helsinki.

Nachrichenblatt Arbeitskreis Unterwasserarchäologie, herausgegeben von der Kommission fur Unterwasserarchäologie im Verband der Landesarchäologen in der Bundesrepublik Deutschland, Heft 1/1994.

Newig, J. and Theede, H. (eds), 1985, *Die Ostsee, Natur und Kulturraum*, Husum.

Ohrelius, B. and Kvarning, L.-Å., 1990, *Vasa, Kungens Skepp*, Kristianstad.

Rieck, F. and Crumlin-Pedersen, O., 1988, *Bäde fra Danmarks Oldtid*, Roskilde.

Rönnby, J. and Adams, J., 1994, *Ostersjöns sjunkna skepp*, Stockholm.

Rönnby, J., 1995, *Bålverket: Om samhällsförändring och motständ med utgångspunkt från det tidigmedeltida Bulverket i Tingstäde träsk på Gotland*, Riksantikvarieämbetet Arkeologiska Undersökningar 10, Stockholm.

Selirand, J. and Tönisson, E., 1984, *Through Past Millennia: Archaeological Discoveries in Estonia*, Tallinn.

Smolarek, P., 1979, 'Underwater Archaeological Investigations in the Gdansk Bay', in *Yearbook of the International Association of Transport Museums 6*, Gdansk, 48–66.

Sorokin, P., 1994, 'Some Results of the Study of Medieval Boatbuilding Traditions in Northwest Russia', *International Journal of Nautical Archaeology*, 23, 2, 129–39.

Barland's Farm Boat

A plank boat of the Romano-Celtic tradition dated by dendrochronology to the 3rd century AD. It was found in late 1993 during the early stages of building a supermarket distribution centre at Barland's Farm, near Magor, Gwent, in southeast Wales. The find-spot is not far from the northern foreshore of the Severn estuary; in the Roman period it was in or near a river which flowed south into that estuary. The site was subsequently excavated by the Glamorgan Gwent Archaeological Trust; the boat timbers were then lifted in manageable units and taken to Newport for further research. The timbers are now being conserved and will be reassembled for display in Newport Museum.

Four types of boat timbers survived to be excavated, all of them oak:

1. A plank-keel, consisting of two adjacent, thick planks;

2. A post, probably the stempost (the other post had not survived;

3. Framing timbers, consisting of: (i) three bow frames (the corresponding frames at the stern had not survived); (ii) nine main floor timbers, extending across

Photogrammetric drawing and site plan of the Barland's Farm Boat. (Drawing: Glamorgan-Gwent Archaeological Trust)

the bottom and part-way up each side. Most floors had a side frame overlapping them to port or to starboard (occasionally both), which extended to (near) the top of the sides. One main floor and about a dozen side timbers did not survive to be excavated. Interspersed among the floor timbers were: (iii) five pairs of half frames, each one in a pair extending from the top of one side to the bottom of the other, and overlapping its partner for the breadth of the boat's bottom;

4. Planking, consisting of: (i) two outer bottom planks; (ii) two bow bottom planks (those presumed to be at the stern had not survived); (iii) parts of five port side strakes; (iv) parts of three starboard side strakes.

A mast-step timber was also found, fastened to a floor and to two paired half-frames, about one-third of the waterline length of the boat from the presumed bow.

The post-excavation work was still being carried out in 1997 but it is already clear that this boat has several characteristics in common with other vessels of the Romano-

Celtic tradition, such as **Blackfriars Wreck I** and St Peter Port I:

1. She is built frame-first, her framing, or a significant proportion of it, determining the shape of the boat. This framework was not fully erected before planking was fastened to it; on the contrary, it was built up in stages as necessary to define the hull shape. Some of the frames, for example the bow frames, were probably not added to the structure until planking-up was effectively completed.

2. Her flush-laid planking is fastened to the framework by large iron nails driven through pre-inserted treenails and clenched inboard by turning the emerging point through 180 degrees back into the frame. A caulking of wood particles mixed with resin and some other substance was placed along the edge of each plank before the adjacent plank was fastened in position.

3. Her framework consists of relatively closely spaced groups of framing, each of which consists of two or three relatively massive timbers. The timbers within each group lie alongside and overlap one another, but are not fastened together.

4. She has a plank-keel and raked, L-shaped posts.

5. Her mast-step is well forward of amidships: this suggests that she had a fore-and-aft rig.

The Barland's Farm Boat differs from these two ships in size, but also in having a flat bottom rather than a full-bodied lower hull. Nevertheless, her sides are as gracefully curved as those of the ships. Barland's Farm was probably an estuary boat rather than a fully seagoing vessel.

The Barland's Boat was originally double-ended and measured c. 12 × 3.2 × 1 m overall. This makes her hull volume about one-fifth that of Blackfriars I: she could therefore probably carry about 3 tonnes of cargo. She was sailed up and down the many rivers flowing into the Severn estuary, using tidal flows to advantage. In the right conditions she was probably capable of crossing the estuary under sail.

When excavated she was found to be closely associated with a 3rd-century AD stone and timber structure; her final role may have been as a river landing stage or possibly a reinforcement of the river bank. Research now being undertaken may clarify these and other doubtful points. S.M.

ADDITIONAL READING

McGrail, S., 1995, 'Romano-Celtic Boats and Ships: Characteristic Features', *International Journal of Nautical Archaeology*, 24, 139–45.

Nayling, N., Maynard, D., and McGrail, S., 1994, 'Barland's Farm, Magor, Gwent: A Romano-Celtic Boat', *Antiquity*, 68, 596–603.

Baseline trilateration

A technique for two-dimensional site-mapping that has gained considerable popularity for use on underwater archaeological sites. It is a variation on the basic survey technique of triangulation in which angles and distances are measured from a known point. In baseline trilateration a survey string or line is laid straight along the bottom and marked at measured increments. From this 'base' line, a map is built by measuring distances to any item of archaeological interest from any two known points on the line. Line points are chosen whose distance from each other approximates the distance to the artefact being mapped. Points that, in distance and positioning, will provide the closest match to an equilateral triangle provide the best geometric advantage for accuracy using this technique.

By measuring two ends of a large object back to the baseline in this manner it is possible to determine orientation of the object in relation to the line. It is only necessary to take angles underwater if the baseline happens to make a turn. Otherwise, all three linear dimensions of a triangle are obtained and no angles are required. Thus the technique is commonly referred to as **Trilateration** rather than triangulation.

Major advantages of this technique are that it is simple and works in a wide variety of water conditions including low visibility, surge, and currents. It is also usually easier in an underwater environment to work with measured distances rather than to obtain angles. Materials needed to carry out trilateration-based mapping can be easily obtained at most convenience stores.

The technique was first refined and popu-

Trilaterating and recording SS Winfield Scott.
(National Park Service)

larized by the US National Park Service **Submerged Cultural Resources Unit** (SCRU). It received a high degree of exposure in the early 1980s when it was presented as the technique of choice in the work that SCRU accomplished on the **Isle Royale Shipwrecks** and on the large remaining shipwrecks in **Pearl Harbor**.

As used by SCRU, the baseline employs no. 18 braided nylon line string identical to that used by the American cave diving community. Cave diving reels are used to lay the line. Clips cut from frosted Plexiglas and grooved to accommodate the string are placed at previously determined increments and carefully measured into place. Objects to be mapped are marked with clothes-pegs modified by the addition of small numbered Plexiglas tabs. Although used by SCRU since 1981, trilateration was first discussed in print by Toni Carrell in 1985 in a site report on the shipwreck **Noquebay** in the Submerged Cultural Resources report series.

Future applications of the technique may involve taking the lateral distances with red or green lasers rather than string, but the principle will remain the same. D.J.L.

ADDITIONAL READING

Carrell, T., 1985, *Submerged Cultural Resources Site Report: Noquebay, Apostle Islands National Lakeshore*, Southwest Cultural Resources Center Professional Papers 7, Santa Fe.

Batavia

Australia's second oldest known shipwreck (the oldest is the English East India Com-

pany ship *Trial*, lost off the northwest of Western Australia in 1622). Contrary to popular opinion it was the Dutch who discovered Australia in 1606, not Captain Cook. In 1616 Dirk Hartog left a plate on Dirk Hartog Island, Shark Bay, commemorating his landfall. This is Australia's earliest European artefact and is at present in the Rijksmuseum in Amsterdam. The Vlamingh Plate which replaced it in 1697 may be seen in the Maritime Museum.

Many people wonder why there are 17th-century European shipwrecks on the Western Australian coast. The answer is spice. In the 16th and 17th centuries, Europe had an almost insatiable need for spice. Large quantities were brought to Europe by sea in the 16th century by the Portuguese. By the early 17th century, companies formed by the English and the Dutch were trading in competition with each other and with the Portuguese. The route the Dutch East India

Company (VOC) took to the East Indies across the Indian Ocean was long, unhealthy, and slow. In 1611 the VOC pioneered a new route: ships sailed south from the Cape of Good Hope, then east, and finally turned north to Batavia. This route was much faster and more healthy, but passed close to the mythical and as yet undiscovered Terra Australis Incognita. This land was finally sighted in 1616 and disasters soon followed. Ironically it was an English ship following the Dutch route, that was first to be wrecked in 1622. *Batavia* met the same fate in 1629, followed by **Vergulde Draeck** (1656), **Zuytdorp** (1712), and **Zeewijk** (1727). Surprisingly, out of 8,190 outward and homeward voyages by the VOC, only 305 ended in disaster. Only one English and four VOC ships are known to have been lost on the Western Australian coast, and they have all been found.

On the morning of 4 June 1629, the VOC ship *Batavia* was wrecked on the Houtman Abrolhos, off the coast of Western Australia. The shipwreck was a prelude to an extraordinary tragedy. Commander Francisco Pelsaert, all the senior officers, some crew and passengers, forty-eight in all, deserted 268 people on the wreck and on two waterless islands while they went in search of water. Abandoning the search on the mainland coast, they made their way to Batavia (modern Jakarta) to obtain help; the journey took thirty-three days. On arrival, the high boatswain was executed, on Pelsaert's indictment, for outrageous behaviour before the loss of the ship. Skipper Adrien Jacobsz was arrested for negligence. The Governor General despatched Pelsaert in the yacht *Sardam* to rescue the survivors. With extraordinary bad luck, it took sixty-three days to find the wreck site, almost double the time it took the party to get to Batavia. At the Abrolhos, Pelsaert discovered that mutiny had taken place. A small group of mutineers had mas-

Batavia's 'graveyard'.
(© Western Australia Maritime Museum)

Batavia's iron guns. (© Western Australia Maritime Museum/Patrick Baker)

Raising timbers from Batavia. (© Western Australia Maritime Museum/Patrick Baker)

sacred 125 men, women, and children. Pelsaert arrested the mutineers and executed some of them. When *Sardam* finally returned to Batavia, some of the lesser offenders, who had been flogged, keelhauled, and dropped from the yard arm as punishment on the voyage, were executed. Out of 316 people aboard *Batavia*, only 116 survived. Pelsaert died in the following year. For the VOC it was a political and financial disaster. In the years that followed the events were not forgotten: a book was published entitled *Ongeluckige voyagie van 't schip Batavia* and it was through this and Pelsaert's journal that the wreck was finally rediscovered.

In 1840 John Stokes and John Wickham visited the Abrolhos in HMS *Beagle*, as part of an early survey of the Western Australian coast. They erroneously identified the very southern end of the Abrolhos as the site where *Batavia* was lost. For many years the shipwreck was thought to lie in the Pelsaert Group. In the 1950s Western Australian historian Henrietta Drake-Brockman published a book, *Voyage to Disaster*, which included a translation of Pelsaert's journal. Drake-Brockman suggested that the wreck site was to the north, in the Wallabi Group. Subsequently, journalist Hugh Edwards searched unsuccessfully for the site. In 1963 a crayfisherman, Dave Johnson, took Geraldton divers Max and Graham Cramer and Greg Allen to the wreck. They were the first people to dive on the site. Following the discovery of the wreck site in 1963, an expedition was made to *Batavia*. Many items were recovered and Edwards published an account of this as *Islands of Angry Ghosts*. In 1964 the State Government enacted legisla-

tion (later revised to the Maritime Archaeology Act 1973) to protect this and other historic wrecks. In 1972 the Netherlands Government transferred their rights to the Dutch shipwrecks on the Western Australian coast to the Australian Government. Finally, in 1976 the Commonwealth Government enacted Federal legislation which also helps to protect this site (see **Australian Historic Shipwrecks Act**). Legislation is designed to protect all shipwreck sites for the Australian community. The public is encouraged to explore and enjoy these sites, either in the water or in the museums. All that is asked is that the wreck sites should not be disturbed so that they may be available for future generations.

Between 1972 and 1976 the Department of Maritime Archaeology conducted a series of excavations of *Batavia*. The artefacts from these excavations were treated by the Museum Conservation Laboratory and may now be seen in the Maritime Museum in Fremantle and in the Geraldton Region Museum. During the excavation, part of the hull of the vessel was uncovered. This was carefully recorded and raised. After a number of years of treatment by the Conservation Laboratory, the remains were rebuilt in the Western Australian Maritime Museum and now provide the centrepiece for the Maritime Museum display. The section is the stern quarter of the port side of the ship up to the top of the first gun-deck and includes the transom and sternpost. The vessel was built in an unusual manner with a double layer of planking, and was constructed by building the vessel up from the keel with planks and later adding the ribs. Many unusual and interesting artefacts

were recovered from the site. These include a prefabricated portico, ornate silverware, ceramics, and bricks, all of which were part of the 'paying' ballast of the vessel. The silver coins were the main cargo; this was used by the VOC to pay for their trade in the Indies. The coins from *Batavia* are mainly Rijksdaalders from the Netherlands together with German thalers. The word thaler is the origin of the modern word 'dollar'. Some of the German coins were quite old, the oldest dated from 1542, suggesting that the coins were collected as bullion. It is known that Pelsaert recovered eight of the ten chests that *Batavia* carried; the museum has recovered about 7,700 coins, 80 per cent of which are in poor condition and represent the main contents of the missing two chests.

During the excavation of the site, 137 shaped sandstone blocks were raised from the wreck site. On return to Fremantle and after conservation, work was started to establish the significance of their presence on board the ship. It became obvious that the blocks made up a portal or portico façade. Research in the archives identified it as destined for the waterport of the castle at Batavia. An engraving by Pieter van den Broecke in 1629 at Batavia shows the castle, with scaffolding in place and the waterport unfinished. Van den Broecke even recorded in his journal the arrival of Pelsaert in the *Batavia*'s boat. An illustration from the mid-1630s shows the completed waterport with a new portal, obviously sent out to replace the one lost on *Batavia*.

In the Netherlands, a foundation based in Lelystad is building a full-scale replica of

Hull remains of Batavia. *(© Western Australia Maritime Museum/Patrick Baker)*

Batavia based on historical research and information obtained from the Western Australian excavations. Research between the two organizations is helping to provide a better understanding of both the archaeology, the history, and the craft skills that were involved in the building of 17th-century vessels. It is hoped that after the new *Batavia* is launched it will visit Western Australia. J.G.

ADDITIONAL READING

Baker, P.E. and Green, J.N., 1976, 'Recording Techniques Used During the Excavation of the *Batavia*, January 14, 1997', *International Journal of Nautical Archaeology and Underwater Exploration*, 5, 2, 143–58.

Edwards, H., 1966, *Islands of Angry Ghosts*, New York.

Green, J., 1973, 'The Wreck of the Dutch East Indiaman the *Vergulde Draeck*, 1656', *The International Journal of Nautical Archaeology*, 2, 2, 267–90.

Henderson, G., 1986, *Maritime Archaeology in Australia*, Nedlands, Western Australia.

Bateaux

see **James River Bateaux**; **Quebec Bateaux**; **Wiawaka Bateaux Cluster**

'Battering' Ships of Gibraltar

Siege ships designed to retake the Rock of Gibraltar from the British in the 18th century. Rooke's capture of Gibraltar in 1704 during the War of the Spanish Succession, and the retention of this strategically important site by England under the Treaty of Utrecht, was a continuous source of humilia-

tion to the Spanish. Two attempts to retake Gibraltar followed, but the Rock was found to be almost impregnable. In June 1779, when England was struggling with her American colonies, Spain again declared war. Her purpose was to oust the British and re-establish control over the entrance to the Mediterranean. Spain besieged the Rock by land and sea for three years without success. In frustration the Spanish turned to the esteemed French engineer Chevalier Michaud d'Arcon to design special siege ships to devastate the British defensive positions and then take the Rock by storm.

Under d'Arcon's direction, ten massively timbered, gable-roofed 'battering ships' or 'junk ships' were constructed and during the night of 12/13 September 1782 were sailed into position a short distance from the fortifications. At first the action went very much as the Spanish and French had planned, with the British shot seeming 'incapable of making any visible impression upon the hulls', but at midday they began to use red-hot shot; by the following morning all the siege ships had been destroyed, making it 'one of the completest defensive victories on record'.

In the 1960s the remains of what was believed to be one of the siege ships was found in Gibraltar Harbour. It was examined by divers, but before a scientific evaluation could be made it was buried during land-reclamation activities. In the 1970s Gibraltar diver Stewart Mason found a large deposit of cannon and shot on the seabed just outside the detached mole. In 1992 **Oxford University MARE**, under the direction of Mensun Bound in collaboration with the

Gibraltar Museum, the German Society for Underwater Archaeology, DEGUWA, and Bangor University, began a survey of the site. In difficult conditions some 40 cannon and a mound of shot were mapped. Although this might seem to be too many guns for one of the siege ships, it is known that they carried spares to avoid overheating and it is likely that exhausted guns from the siege were used for ballast. Work on the site continues and in 1997 the archaeologists were still unable to confirm if this was indeed one of d'Arcon's famous battering ships. Models, plans, and prints of the siege ships have been published by Bound and Finlayson (1995). M.B.

ADDITIONAL READING

Bound, M. and Finlayson, C., 1995, 'Surveying and Excavating the Spanish "Battering" Ships from the Great Siege of Gibraltar', in M. Bound (ed.), *The Archaeology of Ships of War*, Maritime Archaeology Series, vol. 1, Oswestry, Shropshire, 64–76.

Drinkwater, J., n.d., *A History of the Late Siege of Gibraltar*, Spilsbury, London.

Baymaud

see *Maud*

Beached shipwreck sites

Shipwrecks and portions of wrecks discovered on beaches and in intertidal zones. Periodically, the remains of vessels are exposed on beaches owing to environmental factors that lead to beach erosion. At times these exposures are seasonal, and the result of geomorphological processes, while at other times they are occasional, as the result of exceptional winter storms. Shipwreck remains have been encountered on beaches throughout the world; a number of these wrecks have been studied by archaeologists since the 1980s. While **Maritime archaeology** began with the study of deep and shallow water sites, it has, within the past few decades, begun to consider other specific zones of site deposition, such as littoral and beach zones; at the same time maritime archaeologists began to integrate their work with geomorphologists. This expansion of field work has challenged the 'common-sense' notion that shallow water and littoral deposition shipwrecks disintegrate and are scattered into jumbles that make provenance data unnecessary because it would be meaningless. The 'scatter pattern' of a disintegrated wooden ship on a beach can be discerned through an interdisciplinary assessment of wave and current patterns, beach erosion and accretion, and other natural processes.

Recording the starboard bow of SS Point Arena, a buoyant structure site. (J.P. Delgado)

The preservation of shipwreck remains on a beach are indicative of natural **Site formation processes**; work on wooden shipwreck remains in dynamic, high surf environments, specifically in California, Massachusetts, North Carolina, and Florida in the United States, when compared with work done in Great Britain, notably on the wreck of **Amsterdam**, has conclusively shown that three basic types of beached shipwreck remains exist. These are: (1) a 'buoyant hull'; (2) a 'buoyant hull fracture'; and (3) a 'buoyant structure'. A buoyant hull is a site where an intact or nearly intact wooden vessel washes ashore, is sanded in, and then buried. This type of site has the highest data return, as these hulls often contain artefacts other than the vessel itself. An excellent example is again *Amsterdam*, on the beach near Hastings, Sussex, which sanded in soon after her loss in 1749 and contains a large number of its original contents. This type of site is not unknown in the United States; perhaps the best known example is the wreck termed **Sparrow Hawk** which is now displayed at Plymouth Plantation, Massachusetts. The wreck was discovered on 6 May 1863 after the sand washed away on the beach and exposed it.

A buoyant hull fracture is where an intact or nearly intact vessel washes ashore, and then breaks up, with its components scattering along the beach, where they sand in and

are buried. At times, some or all of the components may be re-exposed, and during those times may be broken up into smaller components, and redistributed through a dynamic, recurrent site formation process. A number of wreck sites along the Outer Banks of North Carolina, and along Cape Cod provide evidence for this type of activity, and were documented by the National Park Service (NPS) in the mid-1980s. A team led by James Delgado of the NPS documented the wrecks in North Carolina in 1985, after previously documenting the site formation process and distribution of the 1900 wreck of the schooner *Neptune* and the 1913 wreck of the wooden steamer *Pomo* in California, and providing the first empirical proof of buoyant hull fracture site formation processes and redistribution. This work culminated in a 1984 **Magnetometer** survey of two intermingled shipwreck sites where the 1902 buoyant hull fracture wreck of the schooner *Reporter* overlay **King Philip**, a buried buoyant hull wreck of 1878. The site forma-

tion process that resulted in the deposition of both ships at the site, and the relationship of the remains was further tested when exceptional beach erosion after severe winter storms exposed remains from both.

Buoyant structure sites are portions or components of wooden vessels that sink or break up offshore, wash into a beach, and are sanded in and buried. In many cases, discoveries of these sites have been characterized as a recent phenomenon in which the structure has just 'washed ashore'. Analysis of several sites has shown that buoyant structure sites can be buried after the wreck event, reach a state of equilibrium, and reappear on the beach where they washed ashore at the time of the shipwreck.

Beached shipwreck sites can also consist

of more than wooden vessel remains; when a vessel wrecks on a beach, artefacts inside the hull, including cannon, steam engines, specie, ceramics, and other materials will be distributed and buried on a beach. When exposed by beach erosion, usually in exceptional storm circumstances that rival or exceed those at the time of the wreck event, these materials can be found in remarkable states of preservation that belie constant exposure to surf and abrasion. A number of Spanish shipwreck sites, notably from the flota of 1715, recovered from Florida beaches, include beached gold coins which despite their soft metal surfaces have little or no abrasion, indicating they were distributed on the beach in 1715 and remained *in situ* until recovered in the 20th century. One buoyant structure site, the starboard bow of the steamer *Point Arena*, lost in 1913, was re-exposed on the beach south of San Francisco in 1983, with intact carvings (including the vessel's name) and paint.

Recent research on beached shipwreck

Bow of Peter Iredale, beached at Fort Stevens, Oregon, USA. (J.P. Delgado)

remains has included a detailed survey of recurrent exposures of buoyant hull fracture and buoyant structure sites in North Carolina, a survey of three buoyant hull fracture sites in California's Channel Islands, and the documentation of other beached shipwreck remains elsewhere in the United States.

The indications from beached shipwreck remains, other than particular observations from specific sites about the vessels wrecked there and the circumstances of their loss, demonstrates a general patterning of the ability of a wide range of ship construction types, of various ages, that are able to survive in a wide range of environments, most of which can be considered high energy environments formerly deemed to provide little or no scientific return. J.P.D.

ADDITIONAL READING

Bascom, W., 1980, *Waves and Beaches*, Garden City, New York.

Bright, L., 1993, 'Beached Shipwreck Dynamics', in S.O. Smith (ed.), *Underwater Archaeology Proceedings from the Society for Historical Archaeology Conference, Kansas City, Missouri*, Ann Arbor, Michigan.

Delgado, J.P., 1984, 'Erosion Exposed Shipwreck Remains: Winter 1982', in L.E. Murphy (ed.), *Submerged Cultural Resources Survey: Portions of Point Reyes National Seashore and Point Reyes - Farallon Islands National Marine Sanctuary*, Santa Fe.

Delgado, J.P., 1985, 'Skeleton in the Sand: Documentation of the Environmentally Exposed 1856 Ship *King Phillip*', in P.F. Johnston (ed.), *Proceedings of the Sixteenth Annual Conference on Historical Archaeology*, Ann Arbor, Michigan.

Delgado, J.P., 1986, 'Documentation and Identification of the Two-Masted Schooner *Neptune*', *Historical Archaeology*, 20.

Gearhart, R.C., 1988, *Cultural Resources Magnetometer Survey and Testing: Great Highway Ocean Beach Seawall Project, San Francisco, California*, Austin, Texas.

Marsden, P., 1975, *The Wreck of the Amsterdam*, New York.

Morris, D.P. and Lima, J., 1996, *Channel Islands National Park and Channel Islands National Marine Sanctuary: Submerged Cultural Resources Assessment*, National Park Service Submerged Cultural Resources Unit Intermountain Cultural Resource Centers Professional Papers 56, Santa Fe.

Smith, H.A., Arnold, J.B., III, and Oertling, T., 1987, 'Investigations at a Civil War Anti-Torpedo Raft on Mustang Island, Texas', *International Journal of Nautical Archaeology*, 16, 2, 149–57.

Beaver

Canada's earliest located steamship wreck. The paddle steamer *Beaver* was built in London in 1835 for the Hudson's Bay Company for fur trading on the Pacific northwest coast of North America. The 101 ft (31 m) long steamer was two-masted, carried a fore-and-aft rig, and was powered by two 35 hp sidelever engines.

In August 1835 *Beaver* departed Gravesend under sail for the northwest coast of America, arriving at Fort Vancouver on the Columbia River in April 1836. *Beaver* was the first steamship to reach and work along the Pacific coast of North America. The tiny steamer remained in the employ of the Hudson's Bay Company for four decades. Trading voyages for fur and occasional expeditions to survey coastal inlets occupied *Beaver* from 1836 until 1853. After a

Earliest known photograph of *Beaver*, c. *1863*. (Vancouver Maritime Museum)

Wreck of *Beaver*, view of the bow. (Vancouver Maritime Museum)

short career transporting general freight and passengers between the Hudson's Bay Company's British Columbia outposts, *Beaver* was laid up until 1862. The steamer was chartered by the Royal Navy for use as a survey vessel until 1870, when the HBC again retired it. Sold in 1874, *Beaver* worked as a towboat and tramp freighter until wrecked on 26 July 1888 at the entrance to Burrard Inlet at the site of the modern city of Vancouver.

Salvage of the steamer was not economical, and *Beaver* was left to disintegrate on the rocks. Over the next four years, she was subjected to intensive stripping by souvenir hunters as it fell apart. The deteriorated hulk largely disintegrated on 26 June 1892, when a large wake from the passing steamer

Yosemite swept over the wreck. Scuba-divers rediscovered the wreck of *Beaver* in 1960, and from then until 1974 removed artefacts from the site. Beginning in 1991, however, the wreck became the subject of a detailed archaeological survey by the **Underwater Archaeological Society of British Columbia** and the Vancouver Maritime Museum.

Considerable remains, such as the bottom of the hull in the engine room area, the base plates and lower castings for the engines and other machinery, and brass and copper artefacts such as drifts, spikes, copper pipes, and valves remain untouched on the site. Most artefacts and the hull lie exactly where the ship wrecked in 1888 and have not been disturbed by human activity. Oriented in an almost straight line on the wreck site, for example, is a row of nine widely spaced cast-iron hanging knees. Iron hanging knees were an original construction feature of *Beaver*, and these nine specimens are presumed to date to 1835. They originally lined the upper starboard hull, which apparently fell off the steamer and came to rest on the bottom as the ship disintegrated in 1892.

Archaeological survey of the *Beaver* wreck site, and the documentation of materials on the site as well as previously recovered vessel remains have provided a more detailed view of the pioneer steamship on the Pacific coast of North America. Of particular significance and worthy of study and analysis is the social process that transformed *Beaver* from wreck to relic. This process is ably reflected in a rich and diverse material record. Also of note is the dynamic of the **Site formation process**. Despite strong tides, deposition on an exposed steep rocky bottom, and intensive salvage operations between 1888 and 1892, and 1960 and 1973, a substantial, articulated, and well-preserved archaeological record has survived. J.P.D.

ADDITIONAL READING

Delgado, J.P., 1993, *The Beaver: First Steamship on the West Coast*, Victoria.

Pethick, D., 1970, *The Beaver: The Ship that Saved the West*, Vancouver.

Benthic bioturbation

The disturbance and mixing of sediments by the life activities of organisms, both flora and particularly fauna, which live on sea, lake, and riverbeds. Root channels and burrowing behaviour that transport sediments from their original settlement have a significant impact on our ability to interpret the history of underwater archaeological sites. Our current understanding of the effect of benthic bioturbation on submerged archaeological sites is poorly developed. Most of our knowledge is derived from natural history studies in marine biology and geomorphological research of sediment dynamics.

Within marine biology the study of benthic community structures provides data on the bioturbative capacity of specific species (see McCall and Tevez). Examples include the surface disturbances of ground fish, the small excavations of spaces by crustaceans, and the burrowing of molluscs. The range of the latter is extensive between species, from a few centimetres for *macoma* to a metre or more for *saxidomus*. Thus the identification of species present in an underwater site by faunal analysis should turn the archaeologist toward an examination of

their habitat use and an attempt to understand their potential impact on the distribution of archaeological remains.

This impact can be considerable. Sedimentary geomorphology, the study of the creation and transformation through time of sediments, provides some indication of this. These studies are particularly concerned with the effect of bioturbation on the stratigraphic record and with how disturbances might have mixed paleological elements (see Johnson and Watson-Stegner). E.C. Dapples in 1942 undertook one of the first reviews of animal–sediment relations in the benthic zone, with particular emphasis on the profound effect of macro-invertebrates; contributions in McCall and Tevez's book summarize the effects of the marine benthos on the physical and chemical properties of underwater sediments.

The utility of these biological and geomorphological studies to archaeology are effected by the methodologies on which they are based and the timescale with which they are concerned. Biological studies are generally time limited to short periods of observation, with a focus on the life activities of a single or small community of species; often these studies are undertaken within an aquarium setting in a laboratory, which oversimplifies the complex interactions within the natural environment. Earth science studies tend to have an interest in sedimentary effects over geological periods of tens or hundreds of thousands of years.

What underwater archaeology needs is an integrated study of benthic bioturbation built on the principles of taphonomy, similar to that developed and applied over the past thirty years within terrestrial archaeology. Experimental and field studies of the life and death of bioturbative flora and fauna of the benthos will undoubtedly strengthen our ability to extract meaning from the distribution of cultural remains located in underwater sediments. N.A.E.

ADDITIONAL READING

Dapples, E.C., 1942, 'The Effect of Macro-organisms upon Near Shore Marine Sediments', *Journal of Sedimentary Petrology*, 12, 118–26.

Ferrari, B. and Adams, J., 1990, 'Biogenic Modifications of Marine Sediments and Their Influence on Archaeological Material', *International Journal of Nautical Archaeology*, 19, 2, 139–51.

Johnson, D.L. and Watson-Stegner, D., 1990, 'The Soil-evolution Model as a Framework for Evaluating Pedoturbation in Archaeological Site Formation', in N.P. Lasca and J. Donahue (eds), *Archaeological Geology of North America*, Boulder, Colorado.

McCall, P. and Tevez, M.J.S., 1982, *Animal Sediment Relations: The Biogenic Alteration of Sediments*, New York.

Bertrand

Steamboat wrecked on the Missouri River in 1865 and rediscovered by salvors in 1968, buried beneath a former river channel. The well-preserved remains of *Bertrand* and its cargo were subsequently excavated by the salvors working with the US Fish and Wildlife Service and the National Park Service.

The sternwheel river steamboat *Bertrand* was a 251 ton, 161 ft (49 m) long wooden hull vessel built at Wheeling, West Virginia in 1864. Like many river steamers, *Bertrand* was built with a shallow draft to better navigate the shallow western rivers in the heartland of the United States. The hull was built to be flexible, and was braced and in part held together with large hogging trusses. *Bertrand*'s initial career was probably spent carrying passengers and cargo from Wheeling and Pittsburgh down the Ohio to its confluence with the Mississippi, and then up that river to St Louis. The discovery of gold in the Montana Territory, coupled with the impending end of the American Civil War, led *Bertrand*'s owners to advertise her for a trip to Montana in February 1865.

Bertrand departed St Louis on 18 March 1865 with several passengers and cargo valued at $300,000. The steamer struck a submerged snag and sank at DeSoto Bend, 40 km north of Omaha, Nebraska, on 1 April 1865. The superstructure remained above water, and the passengers and crew were rescued. Before *Bertrand* disappeared into the river, portions of the vessel, notably the boilers and the engines, were salvaged.

Led by tales of $35,000 worth of mercury and barrels of whisky, a salvage party attempted to find and salvage *Bertrand* in 1896 but did not find the vessel. The course of the river had shifted, and the former riverbed where *Bertrand* had wrecked was now dry land. Test borings around the area failed to find the now buried steamboat. In 1967 salvors Jesse Pursell and Sam Corbino of Omaha began to search for the wreck, which now lay within the boundaries of the DeSoto Wildlife Refuge, managed by the US Fish and Wildlife Service. The US Government granted permission for the salvage, but stipulated that all work had to be done under the archaeological supervision of the National Park Service's Midwest Archaeological Center in Omaha.

The buried wreck was located after a **Magnetometer** survey of the area disclosed a series

Hull of Bertrand *during excavation, 1969. (National Park Service)*

Modern painting of Bertrand *under way, by Jerry Livingston.*
(National Park Service)

Excavation of Bertrand *recovered many intact crates and barrels*
of well-preserved cargo. (National Park Service)

of promising anomalies. A series of test borings brought up wood and artefacts from a depth of 6 to 8.5 m below the ground surface. Work to excavate the wreck began in March 1968, and in November of the same year the deck of the steamboat was reached. Excavation proceeded with constant pumping to keep groundwater from submerging the wreck. Among the first artefacts recovered were wooden crates stencilled 'Bertrand Stores', which provided conclusive identification of the wreck.

Excavation of the wreck and the removal of the cargo, much of it still packed in its original crates, boxes, and barrels, continued through the summer of 1969. More than two million artefacts were recovered. The site was described as a 'time capsule' with well-preserved foodstuffs, clothing, and items with original paper labels intact and readable after conservation. The collection from *Bertrand* included foodstuffs, patent medicines, and liquor; textiles, clothing, and sewing supplies; household goods; mining supplies and equipment; agricultural supplies; and hardware, tools, and building supplies. Miscellaneous artefacts included personal possessions of passengers, ammunition, cigars, tobacco and clay pipes, and blank ledgers and day books. None of the reputed treasure of mercury, whisky, or gold was found, and the salvors transferred their 60 per cent interest in the cargo to the Federal Government, which had previously monitored the project and now assumed all responsibility for the artefacts and the wreck.

A detailed analysis and **Conservation** of the cargo was undertaken by the National Park Service; in all, more than 300,000 artefacts were treated and preserved in the next few decades. As a collection, the *Bertrand* artefacts offered a unique and unparalleled look at the goods sent to supply a mining community on the American frontier. Detailed studies of the artefacts included a groundbreaking analysis of the bottles from the site. The *Bertrand* bottles remain the major study collection to which most other bottles found in land and underwater mid-19th-century excavations throughout the United States are compared.

Bertrand's excavation and the subsequent treatment of its artefacts was the first major maritime archaeological project of its type in the United States until the excavation of the buried 1856 wreck of the river steamboat **Arabia**. Important lessons about field treatment of artefacts and conservation were learned since the well-preserved materials and their sheer numbers placed incredible demands on the excavators and in the laboratory. The hull, although badly contorted and warped by sinking and subsequent burial, was well preserved. It was carefully documented to provide the first detailed assessment of a mid-19th-century American steamboat's construction and characteristics. This work led to a detailed graphic reconstruction of *Bertrand* and the publication of a set of plans.

Plans to raise, or display *Bertrand*'s hull *in situ* proved too expensive and technically difficult. The hull was covered with a protective covering of plastic and sand. Ground-water was allowed to rise and cover the site, and today *Bertrand* reposes beneath a small man-made lake. The artefacts are housed in a nearby museum, which is administered by the Fish and Wildlife Service as part of the DeSoto Wildlife Refuge. In addition to public interpretation, the *Bertrand* collection is available for scholars to study. J.P.D.

ADDITIONAL READING

Petsche, J.E., 1974, *The Steamboat Bertrand: History, Excavation, and Architecture,* Washington, DC.

HMS *Betsy*

A British naval transport vessel sunk during the Battle of Yorktown (Virginia) in 1781 (see **Yorktown shipwrecks**). This site, 44YO88, was the first shipwreck ever to be excavated underwater from within a **Cofferdam**, a steel enclosure that helped offset the adverse environmental conditions. The excavation took place during 1982–8 under the direction of John D. Broadwater, Senior Underwater Archaeologist, Virginia Department of Historic Resources, as the final phase of the Yorktown Shipwreck Archaeological Project. Research confirmed that the excavated vessel was the brig *Betsy*, built in 1772 in Whitehaven, Cumberland (now Cumbria), England, and employed in the coal trade. Around the mid-18th century, Whitehaven was one of the leading coal and coal-ship producing ports in the UK.

Archaeological data established that *Betsy* was a solidly built, two-masted vessel constructed of oak frames and planking, with a preserved length of 72 ft (21.9 m) and a capacity of 176-32/94 tons burthen. *Betsy*'s reconstructed hull lines demonstrate that the vessel had a broad, flat underbody, full-floored with a round chine, and bluff bows that gave way to a full midships section with a relatively fine run aft. *Betsy*'s hull exhibits an unusual pattern of floors and first futtocks. There is no discernible midships bend, or master couple, and all first futtocks were positioned forward of their respective floors. Only seven sets of floors and futtocks were actually through-fastened to create compound frames, and even those had no fasteners between the floors and first futtocks. The hull also incorporates sets of unique horizontal timbers that take the place of the apron in the bow, and in the stern formed lower transoms.

The hull contained a variety of interesting and diagnostic objects. Seven uniform buttons from the 43rd Regiment of Foot, recovered from the hold, were the key to the vessel's identity. The regiment's order book for the summer of 1781 recorded that men of the 43rd Regiment were transported from Portsmouth to Yorktown on board three vessels, only one of which, *Betsy*, matched the size of the wreck at site 44YO88. A surprising array of furniture and furnishings was recovered from the stern cabin, including wall panelling, a ladder, parts of chairs, tables and bookshelves, and components from a unique china cupboard.

Betsy operated as a collier carrying coal to Dublin. Lloyd's Register of Shipping lists *Betsy* as a brig registered in the port of Whitehaven at 180 tons, having a partially planked lower deck and wooden outer hull sheathing. Lloyd's also records that *Betsy* was owned by her master, John Younghusband, and his crew. In 1780 *Betsy* was leased as a naval transport by the British Navy Board and placed into service as a victualler, even-

tually joining British vessels under the command of Major General Charles Cornwallis at Yorktown, Virginia. When a blockade trapped Cornwallis's forces at Yorktown, *Betsy*, along with other vessels, was purposely scuttled, sunk by a single hole cut into its starboard side just below the lower deck. Fortunately, the hull and contents were covered and protected by the deep silt on the river bottom. J.D.B.

ADDITIONAL READING

Broadwater, J.D., 1988, 'Secrets of a Yorktown Shipwreck', *National Geographic*, June, 173, 6, 804-23.

Broadwater, J.D., 1992, 'Shipwreck in a Swimming Pool: An Assessment of the Methodology and Technology Utilized on the Yorktown Shipwreck Archaeological Project', *Historical Archaeology*, Special Issue 4, 36–46.

Broadwater, J.D., 1995, 'In the Shadow of Wooden Walls: Naval Transports During the American War of Independence', in M. Bound (ed.), *The Archaeology of Ships of War*, Oswestry, Shropshire.

Broadwater, J.D., Adams, R.M., and Renner, M., 1985, 'The Yorktown Shipwreck Archaeological Project: An Interim Report on the Excavation of Shipwreck 44YO88', *International Journal of Nautical Archaeology*, 14, 4, 301–14.

MacGregor, D.R., 1985, *Merchant Sailing Ships, 1775–1815*, London.

Sands, J.O., 1983, *Yorktown's Captive Fleet*, Charlottesville, Virginia.

Bikini Atoll wrecks
see Crossroads wrecks

The wreck of the steamship Birkenhead *off Danger Point, Cape of Good Hope. (© National Maritime Museum Picture Library)*

HMS *Birkenhead*

A British troopship wrecked en route to Algoa Bay and Buffalo River, on South Africa's eastern frontier. An iron-hulled, steam paddle wheel frigate, *Birkenhead* was converted into a troopship in 1848. The vessel was carrying troops, passengers, and munitions to the eastern frontier when it was wrecked at Danger Point off Cape Colony, South Africa in 1852. During the wreck, 445 men were lost. The history of the vessel is associated with the heroic naval tradition of placing 'women and children first' in the lifeboats.

In 1983 a salvage permit for *Birkenhead* was issued to commercial salvors led by Allan Kayle of the Depth Recovery Unit, who were lured by historic reports of 120 boxes of specie. Both the South African and the British governments became involved with ownership claims to the wreck; the British Government considered the site a British war grave. The depth of the wreck, at 30 m, and the extremely adverse diving conditions resulted in decompression problems for the divers and a dubious level of accurate or systematic recording. The hull or machinery of the vessel was not documented because, it was argued, the plans of the vessel were available. An historically significant collection of artefacts was recovered including regimental badges and the personal effects of the soldiers and passengers. Some of these artefacts are housed at the South African Cultural History Museum, while others were auctioned by Sotheby's in 1994. L.H., T.D.

ADDITIONAL READING

Addison, A.C., 1902, *The Story of the Birkenhead*, London.

Bevan, D., 1989, *Drums of the Birkenhead*, London.

Kayle, A., 1990, *Salvage of the Birkenhead*, Johannesburg.

Bismarck. *(US Naval Institute Photo Library/James C. Fahey collection)*

An anti-aircraft gun points at the empty Atlantic Ocean over the hull of the sunken German battleship Bismarck. *(Quest Group Limited)*

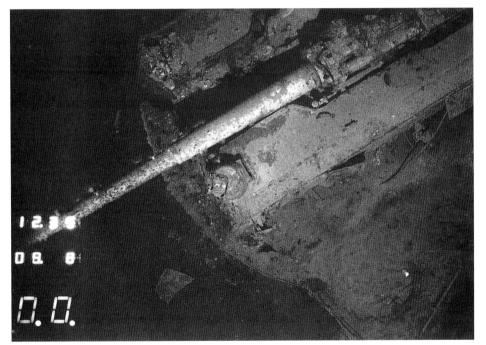

Bismarck

German battleship, sunk in battle in the North Atlantic in 1940 and rediscovered in 1989 at a depth of 4,600 m. *Bismarck* was the largest battleship completed by a European naval power. Its design began during the spring of 1934. Envisioned as a 35,000 ton battleship, *Bismarck* was to be armed with eight 330 mm guns in four twin turrets, twelve 150 mm guns in twin turrets, and sixteen 105 mm guns in twin mounts. The ship required a main belt of 350 mm face-hardened armour and a 100 mm armour deck with slopes of 120 mm. It soon became apparent to German designers that this scale of armour protection and gunpower could not be achieved in a vessel with a standard displacement of 35,000 tons and a speed of 30 knots. When the design was

finally completed, the standard displacement rose to 42,600 tons and the armour was reduced on the sides to 320 mm but the main battery was increased to 380 mm. Although the German Navy had signed a naval agreement with Great Britain in 1935 that she would abide by all navy treaties and restrict her battleship displacement to 35 per cent of the Royal Navy, the true displacement of *Bismarck* and her sister ship *Tirpitz* were kept a secret until Germany capitulated in May 1945.

Bismarck's keel was laid down at the Blohm and Voss Shipyard in Hamburg on 1 July 1936 and the vessel was launched on 14 February 1939 amid great splendour by Frau Dorothea von Loewenfeld, granddaughter of Prince Otto von Bismarck, with Adolf Hitler in attendance. *Bismarck* was

commissioned in August 1940 and spent the next seven months in training. She sortied with the heavy cruiser *Prinz Eugen* in May 1941 to attack British convoys in the North Atlantic. Although the Germans tried to conceal her deployment, British military forces found her in Norway. On 24 May 1941 she was engaged in battle with the battlecruiser *Hood* and the newly completed *Prince of Wales* in the Denmark Strait. During a spectacular battle that lasted sixteen minutes, one of *Bismarck*'s shells penetrated to the aft magazines of *Hood*, leading to a spectacular deflagration that destroyed her. Only three of her crew of 1,418 were saved. *Prince of Wales* was also damaged, but so was *Bismarck*.

The German battleship headed for a French seaport for repairs, but was hit by a torpedo from the aircraft carrier *Victorious* late on 24 May. She managed to evade her British pursuers for the next thirty-two hours. Discovered by a PBY Catalina on 26 May, she was attacked at dusk the same day by British Swordfish torpedo planes from the carrier *Ark Royal*. A torpedo hit jammed her rudders and steering gear. Unmanoeuvrable, she was brought to battle early on the morning of 27 May 1941 by the battleships *King George V* and *Rodney* and the heavy cruisers *Norfolk* and *Dorsetshire*. In an eighty-eight minute battle, these British warships fired 2,876 shells at the *Bismarck*. Several shell hits and five or six torpedo hits finally caused her to sink at 10.40 p.m. Of the crew of 2,206 men, only 115 survived the action.

Bismarck now rests on the seabed of the Atlantic Ocean *c.* 650 km west of Brest, France. In June 1989 Dr Robert Ballard, using new underwater **Submersible** technology, explored the wreck, but has concealed her location. Analysis of the wreck's condition confirmed historic accounts of the battle damage, and also apparently verified

German reports that the crippled ship was scuttled to hasten its sinking. W.H.G.

ADDITIONAL READING

Ballard, R.D., 1990, *The Discovery of the Bismarck*, New York.

Garzke, W.H. and Dulin, R.O., 1990, *Battleships, Axis and Neutral Battleships in World War II*, Naval Institute Press.

Müllenheim-Rechberg, Baron von, 1980, *Battleship Bismarck, A Survivor's Story*, Annapolis, Maryland.

Bjorke Boat

A vessel dating to *c.* AD 100 found on an island near Stockholm. The 7.16 m long craft has been described by J. Richard Steffy as an improvement in the methodology of clinker construction over that of the **Hjortspring Boat**. The boat is constructed of just three planks, with single planks on each side of a expanded dugout fastened together with iron rivers. Cleats, part of the dugout's base, held lashings for the heavy frames. J.P.D.

ADDITIONAL READING

Steffy, J.R., 1994, *Wooden Shipbuilding and the Interpretation of Shipwrecks*, College Station, Texas.

Blackfriars Wrecks

A series of wrecks discovered during the construction of a riverside embankment wall on the shores of the **River Thames** in London, England.

Blackfriars I

The earliest known indigenous seagoing sailing ship yet found in northern Europe. The wreck dates to the 2nd century AD, in the Roman period, and appears to belong to a native Celtic tradition of shipbuilding. It was discovered on 6 September 1962 during construction of a new riverside wall between the Blackfriars Road bridge and railway bridge, and 20 m southward of the then Thames riverside wall. The riverside wall built after 1962 now bisects the wreck site. Brief excavations mandated by extreme low tide conditions, and supervised by Peter Marsden, then of the Guildhall Museum, in October and November 1962 revealed the bottom of the vessel and the sternpost. The exposed portions of the wreck's forward half were excavated, dismantled, and removed from the site to the Guildhall Museum in July 1963 with considerable publicity. The ship was analysed and was the subject of a 1967 report which offered an initial reconstruction. However, re-analysis by Marsden has substantially added to the understanding of the ship and led to a new reconstruction.

The remains of the ship that were excavated were the bottom of the hull and the

collapsed port side, as well as the stone cargo. The starboard side had been present but was removed by construction dredging before the nature of the discovery was apparent. The port side lies outboard of the wreck, while the starboard side had collapsed inboard.

The planking, framing, and posts of this ship were of oak (*Quercus* sp.) which dendrochronological analysis has shown came from southeast England. Instead of a keel the ship had two thick planks placed side by side to form a broad plank-keel *c.* 1.32 m wide, 0.08 m thick, and 11.3 m long. The frames at bow and stern were formed from natural crooks (compass timber), as were the curving side frames, while the floors in the main body of the hull were from substantial straight logs.

Blackfriars I was built 'frame-first': the planking was fastened to a pre-erected framework by large iron nails which were driven through pre-positioned treenails and then clench-fastened by turning the emergent points back into the inner face of the framing. A caulking of pine resin and hazel wood shavings (*Corylus* sp., probably *C. avellana* from southeast England) was placed along the edges of the planks before they were fastened. Marsden suggests that the plank-keel was first fastened to the posts; then three or more floors were fastened to the plank-keel. The planking out to the turn of the bilge was then fastened to this framework. The remaining floor timbers were next added to the structure to complete the lower hull. The lower ends of the side frames were then fastened to the side planking in between the floors, and the upper side planks were fastened to this extension of the framework. Finally the ceiling planking, deck beams, and other structural timbers were installed.

Semi-circular limber holes on the underside of the floors allowed free drainage of the ship's interior. One floor (floor timber

number seven), had a built up mast-step, with a 0.336 by 0.25 m socket, 0.127 m deep and reinforced on either side by iron nails and a 50 mm thick oak plank. A worn bronze votive coin of the Emperor Domitian, minted in Rome in either AD 88 or 89, was found in the mast socket, with the reverse of the coin upright and in a position where it would have touched the foot of the mast. The reverse of the coin shows Fortuna, the goddess of luck, holding a ship's rudder. Coins have not been found in other Romano-Celtic wrecks in central or northern Europe, or in Scandinavian ships of the first millennium AD. However, votive coins have been found in Mediterranean wrecks, the earliest known example being the Chretienne A wreck of the first half of the 1st century BC.

Small mortises cut into the timber on each side of the mast-step appear to have been for upright stanchions to help support the deck around the mast. No decking or deck beams were found in the wreck, although a loose knee was found. Marsden was able to reconstruct, nonetheless, a deck height of approximately 1.7 m, in part using the size of the cargo, evidence from other wrecks, and the average height of a male adult of the period (as determined by an examination of hundreds of skeletons in a Roman period cemetery).

Ceiling planking 25 mm thick was fastened to the inner faces of the floor timbers in the main hold with iron nails, but was so badly damaged by the stone cargo that its width and length could not be determined. The ship had wrecked while carrying a cargo of building stone. The cargo remained in the wreck – in all 20 cu. m of stone weighing about 26 tonnes, identified as Kentish ragstone (a blue-grey sandy limestone from the Hythe Beds of Kent) which suggested a final voyage from the Maidstone area, along the River Medway past Rochester into the Thames, and thence up the Thames to London, where the ship was lost before unloading. There was also an unfinished millstone lying on the floor timbers near the bow. While the exact origin of the millstone could not be determined, Marsden believed it to be from Belgium. This and evidence of marine borers suggested a prior voyage across the Channel. Extensive evidence of borers (*Teredo* and *Limnoria*) also suggested a prolonged career in the ocean or in a tidal estuary as opposed to freshwater river trade.

Marsden commented that while the wreck was from the Roman period it was of a very different construction from Roman ships of the Mediterranean tradition. The fastening of the ship was different from the **County Hall Ship**, another Roman period wreck found in London, which was built plank-first with the planking fastened together with mortise-and-tenon joints. Blackfriar I's construction seemed to Marsden to be more Celtic than Roman. One possible reconstruction of the bow, for example, has the stempost as the base of a protruding forefoot, which was probably a pre-Roman feature of Celtic ships in Britain and which was definitely illustrated on native craft in northern Europe at roughly the same time. A Celtic identification would fit with an analysis of the ship's timbers, which showed that it had been built in or near southeast England. Marsden's reconstruction of Blackfriars I shows a single mast, carrying either a square sail or a spritsail. The placement of the mast forward of midships suggests that a fore-and-aft rig such as a sprit or a lugsail was more likely than a square sail. It is also possible that the large hold amidships necessitated a mast stepped slightly forward so that the yard could be used as a crane.

The *c.* 18.5 by 6.12 m Blackfriars I was closely dated. The votive coin of Domitian (AD 88–9) and a pottery sherd (*c.* AD 150) dated the wreck to a period of great expansion and construction in Roman London during the late 1st and early 2nd centuries, which would explain the ragstone cargo. No evidence of living accommodation was found in the bow area, suggesting that the unexcavated stern was the location of the crew's quarters, as was the case with other excavated Roman period wrecks. Four non-construction related artefacts were found in addition to the millstone: two pottery sherds (the fragments of a ceramic bowl), a wooden mallet, and a piece of leather pierced to create a fish decoration.

Marsden deduced from the position of the wreck, far from the Roman period river bank and heeled to port with the stone cargo shifted, that the ship had probably sunk after a collision with another vessel. The wreck lay across the flow of the river and probably drifted before sinking. Portions of the wreck would have been accessible at low tide, and salvage probably accounts for the lack of anchors, mast, and the rudders or steering oars. The ship's sides collected gravel and driftwood before the sides collapsed, and gradually the wreck was buried, only to be exposed again as the former riverbed was slowly reclaimed by an expanding London.

Blackfriars II

Remains of a 17th-century river barge lost with a cargo of brick, rediscovered two metres below the River Thames east of Blackfriars Bridge, London in June 1969, during excavation for a **Cofferdam**. Before construction work was stopped, the west and north ends of the vessel were torn away. Excavation of the wreck by R. Inman and Peter Marsden of the Guildhall Museum revealed a cargo of new red bricks, clay pipes, and pottery that dated the wreck to *c.* 1660–80, leading Marsden to conclude that the wreck was carrying building material to London during the extensive rebuilding of the City after the Great Fire of 1666.

The wreck was approximately 14 m long, and the surviving end was sharp. The sides had not survived, and Marsden suggests a beam of 3–4 m. The surviving bottom, from chine to chine, was 2 m wide. A clinker-built, flat-bottomed craft, the vessel was iron fastened with rivets. The narrow (4–7 cm) floors were overlaid with transverse planks to protect the hull from the brick cargo. The wreck was similar to 15th-century wrecks found near by (see Blackfriars III and IV) and, through its retention of medieval shipbuilding techniques, demonstrated to Marsden that 'our knowledge of the history of shipbuilding is not sufficient for us to be able to date small boats simply by their construction', which has become a maxim of archaeologists engaged in **Small craft studies**.

Blackfriars III and IV

Two wrecks, dating to *c.* 1500 when they both sank in the River Thames, possibly as a result of a collision between them, and rediscovered in 1970. Both wrecks lie off the riverfront in the City of London, close to the site of Blackfriars I and II. Blackfriars III is the most complete medieval sailing vessel yet found in Britain. A sailing barge built around 1400, Blackfriars III was approximately 14.64 m long, 4.3 m wide and 0.88 m high amidships. The vessel was sharp at both ends, clinker built, and was made of oak. Archaeologist Peter Marsden believes it closely fits a common type of river vessel known as a 'shout', and that it dates to between 1380 and 1415. Rigged with a single mast amidships and probably fitted with a steering oar, the vessel was empty when it was lost. Hydrostatic analysis of the hull, however, indicates that it could carry a 7.5 tonne cargo.

The vessel was partially destroyed by the contractor's grab prior to discovery, and the cofferdam did not expose the entire hull. Nonetheless, a major area of the hull was available for excavation and study. The vessel was documented *in situ* and then cut up and removed in portions for future study ashore. The removed timbers were stored at the National Maritime Museum, Greenwich.

The wreck contained no cargo, but was filled with layers of clean sand and gravel with rubbish (mostly ceramics and animal bones). In addition, 1,109 lead net weights were recovered, although a similar number could not be recovered. They were all evidence of a large net, probably a seine net, that snagged on the wreck about the time of its loss, as it silted in and was buried rapidly after sinking. Archaeologists excavating in and around the hull also found two pewter badges, the bronze arm of a pair of shears,

Blackfriars III.
(Museum of London)

two larger lead weights, and an iron grapnel. These, as well as the fragments of pottery and building materials (a roofing slate fragment, peg, and a roof edging tile) provided the suggested date for the filling of the sunken hull, and hence its sinking.

The hull of Blackfriars III evidences many repairs – both replacements and patches to the planking. It was built with iron rivets, wooden treenails, and the planks were caulked with animal hair. If it is a 'shout', as the evidence suggests, then it offers the first substantial material evidence of the most common Thames river transport vessel of the 14th and 15th centuries.

Lying near by, and discovered within a few days of Blackfriars III, Blackfriars IV was a clinker-built vessel, probably of the 15th century, which was lost with a cargo of Kentish ragstone. Its position, just a few metres away, and on a north–south axis, suggested to Marsden that Wreck IV had collided with, swamped, and sunk Wreck III. The remains of Wreck IV were exposed inside a cofferdam being excavated for construction on 1 December 1970, cutting through the hull and exposing a cross-section. As the sides of the excavation were collapsing, no additional excavation was done. The cross-section was cleaned and better exposed for photography, and a measured drawing was made before construction continued.

Blackfriars IV lay at the same level of the riverbed as Wreck III. It was of very light construction; the garboard strake was 23 cm wide while the other planks ranged from 24 to 30 cm wide. The keel was 41.5 by 10 cm thick. The vessel's size was estimated to be only 3.2 to 3.5 m wide. It was possibly a local river craft, perhaps even a lighter used to unload larger vessels as its size and light construction would not have been sufficient to transport the ragstone for a long distance. J.P.D.

ADDITIONAL READING

Marsden, P., 1966, *A Ship of the Roman Period From Blackfriars in the City of London*, London.

Marsden, P., 1972, 'A Seventeenth-Century Wreck in London', *Mariner's Mirror*, 58, 2, 129–34

Marsden, P., 1994, *Ships of the Port of London: First to Eleventh Centuries A.D.*, London.

Marsden, P., 1996, *Ships of the Port of London: Twelfth and Seventeenth Centuries A.D.*, London.

Boat archaeology

A subset of maritime archaeology in which research is focused on structural and performance aspects of early water transport. The subject matter includes not only *boats*, but also: *floats*, which are personal aids to flotation; *rafts*, which are not watertight but 'flow

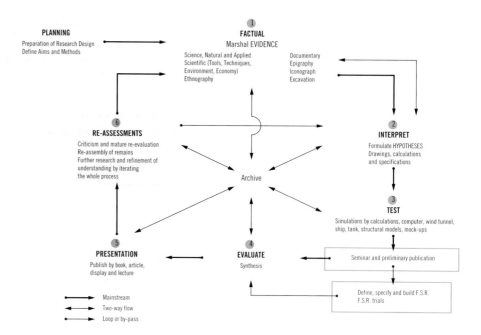

Flow diagram showing the phases of research when building a reconstruction of an ancient boat.
(Institute of Archaeology, Oxford)

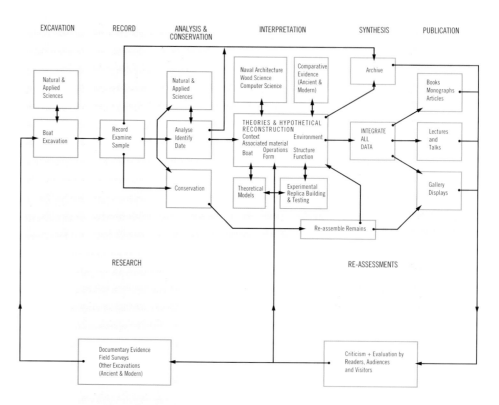

Flow diagram illustrating research methods in boat archaeology.
(Institute of Archaeology, Oxford)

through' and derive their buoyancy from that of individual components; and *ships*, larger versions of the boat, usually decked and capable of sustained voyages at sea, and which, like boats, derive their buoyancy from the displacement of water by their hollow watertight hulls.

Boat archaeologists are not particularly concerned with the historical, environmental, social, and economic contexts of water transport, and they tend to leave to others the study of land-based aspects of this subject – landing places, harbours, warehouses, cargo-handling facilities, and the other fixed structures which are essential to the successful operation of water transport, be it riverine or seagoing. Boat archaeologists thus concentrate on the technical aspects of water transport, the building and use of floats and float rafts, logboats and log rafts, bundle boats and bundle rafts, and boats of pottery, bark, hide, and planks.

Research

Research topics in boat archaeology include: methods of building water transport, from the selection of raw materials and the choice of tools, to in-service repairs and maintenance; the processes by which hulls were 'designed' before technical design, scale models and scale drawings became commonplace; the hypothetical reconstruction of the distorted, fragmented, and fragmentary remains of excavated water transport, and estimates of the performance of the original vessel; the manufacture and use of nautical equipment such as sails, rigging, anchors, and guns; methods of propulsion and steering; cargo stowage and uses of ballast; and seafaring, including pilotage and navigational techniques. Generally speaking, such studies follow the excavation of water transport remains from land, inter-tidal, or underwater sites, and are undertaken in library, laboratory, workshop, and afloat.

Using data from excavation records and post-excavation research, and the techniques of naval architecture and other sciences, the boat archaeologist first seeks to reconstruct, as a small-scale drawing or model, the original full form and structure of the raft, boat, or ship under investigation, its means of propulsion, and its steering arrangements – in so far as sound deductions and hypotheses are possible, without over-dependence on indirect evidence. Where there are insufficient data to produce a single definitive reconstruction, two or three may be needed, each one compatible with the excavated evidence. The computer plays an increasing role in the formation of these hypotheses.

Assessments of performance are made using scale drawings or models of the reconstruction hypothesis or hypotheses. Desk-based assessment methods include the use of computers to compile hydrostatic curves and to undertake related calculations. They may also be used to investigate such aspects of performance as seakeeping abilities in different sea states. Small-scale models are sometimes used in ship tanks and in wind tunnels to investigate other aspects. For simple craft, such methods produce reasonably accurate assessments of stability, cargo capacity, and potential speeds at different waterlines. But for more complex craft, and particularly those propelled by sail, these methods can prove inadequate, and it may be necessary to build a full-scale reconstruction ('replica') if the full potential of the evidence is to be realized. This building and testing of a reconstruction, sometimes known as experimental boat archaeology, is both difficult and expensive as a vessel has to be built which is as authentic as the specific aims of the project require, and lengthy and rigorous trials have to be undertaken. It may, however, be the only way to ensure that the results of 20th-century investigations can validly be applied to the ancient prototype and thus increase our knowledge of early boatbuilding and seafaring.

The end product of this research is publication in books, monographs, and articles, through lectures, talks, and museum displays. In this way information about these aspects of the maritime past is disseminated at all levels and to many sectors. The resulting feedback should ensure that the boat archaeologist reassesses his or her aims, assumptions, methods, and results. This reappraisal, and the boat archaeologist's own mature reflections, can result in a re-evaluation of the original project, or it may lead to a new research design for another, but related, project.

Projects

Recent examples of boat archaeology projects may be found in the publications of J. Richard Steffy, formerly Professor of Nautical Archaeology at Texas Agricultural and Mechanical University, who has worked for over twenty-five years with ancient boat and ship structures ranging from Mediterranean Classical wrecks to post-colonial wrecks in American waters. Steffy's work extends from the on-site recording of excavated vessels to the use of drawings, graphics, and three-dimensional models to establish the original form and structure of such vessels as the **Kyrenia Ship** of the 4th century BC, the **Herculaneum Boat** and the **Sea of Galilee Wreck** of the 1st century BC/AD, and the 11th-century **Serçe Limani** vessel – all from the eastern Mediterranean. Of these, only the Kyrenia project, to date, has reached the stage of building and testing a reconstruction, and this has yet to be published in detail.

Ole Crumlin-Pedersen and colleagues in Roskilde, Denmark, have been involved in boat archaeology since the 1960s, in the wake of their excavation of five Viking age wrecks in Roskilde Fjord (see **Skuldelev Ships**). Their work on some of these ships and others from the medieval period has progressed beyond the small-scale model and theoretical assessment stage to the building and trials of full-scale reconstructions. The final report on the Skuldelev ships will significantly increase the medieval data available to boat archaeologists and will describe the research methods used by the Roskilde team who are internationally recognized as leading specialists in this field.

A third example of a project in boat archaeology is that undertaken by the British-based Trireme Trust. In 1984, after more than five years of research, this *ad hoc* and part-time research team, led by ancient historian John Morrison and naval architect John Coates, designed a reconstruction of an Athenian trireme, an oared warship of the 5th century BC. A full-size ship was built by the Hellenic Navy in 1985–7, and since that date the vessel has undergone several seasons of trials, under sail as well as oars. An unusual feature of this project is that the reconstruction was primarily based on written and iconographic evidence, rather than on excavated remains. This project has been criticized by those who consider that such experiments can only be valid when based on a specific find rather than a general class of ship. There would seem to be no intrinsic reason why this should be so: both methods – one using specific, mainly excavated evidence, the other using general, mainly non-excavated evidence – are valid as research techniques, providing that they are applied with scientific rigour.

Boat archaeologists and other nautical specialists discuss their research projects and topics of a more general nature at the triennial meetings of an informal group known as the International Seminars on Boat and Ship Archaeology (ISBSA). The first meeting of this academic forum was at Greenwich, London, England in 1976, since when there have been meetings at Bremerhaven, Germany; Stockholm, Sweden; Oporto, Portugal; Amsterdam, Netherlands; Roskilde, Denmark; and Tatihou, France. The publications of the ISBSA conference proceedings are among the works cited in the bibliography below.

There are other groups, with their own

means of publication, which also hold conferences to discuss aspects of boat archaeology: the Southern Hemisphere Conferences on Maritime Archaeology, organized by the Australian Institute for Maritime Archaeology, deals with the Indian Ocean and Oceania; the International Symposia on Ship Construction in Antiquity, organized by the Hellenic Institute for the Preservation of Nautical Tradition, concentrates on the Classical world; the United States' Society for Historical and Underwater Archaeology has broader interests; and there are regionally focused conferences in Scandinavia and elsewhere. Articles on topics in Boat Archaeology may also be found in the *International Journal of Nautical Archaeology*, published in Britain by the **Nautical Archaeology Society**, and occasionally in the journal of the British-based Society for Nautical Research, *The Mariner's Mirror*, and similar organs worldwide.

Achievements

Boat archaeology has made uneven progress in research as regards periods, regions, and the types of water transport covered. If we take the period before the 16th century AD, there are no excavated remains other than those of log boats, plank boats, vestigial hide boats, and an insignificant number of log rafts, anywhere in the world. For the other types of craft, we have to turn to documentary and representational evidence, much of it from the 16th century and later, and to recent ethnographic studies. In the temporal dimension, the earliest known boat, a log boat from Pesse, in the Netherlands, is dated to *c.* 9000 BC; the earliest planked vessel, the **Khufu Ship** from the pyramids at Giza, Egypt, is as late as 2600 BC while it is not until the mid-2nd millennium BC that there is direct evidence for seagoing ships. In total this is very little, especially when it is realized that the first sea voyages, those from Southeast Asia to Australia, were undertaken as early as 40,000 years ago.

The evidence for early vessels, such as it is, is mainly from Europe and ancient Egypt. In China there are log boats dated from the 5th millennium BC, three small plank boats from the 2nd century BC–3rd century AD, and a handful of ship remains from the 11th to 14th centuries. In Southeast Asia there are three or four log boats and plank boats from the early centuries AD, and a few 12th- to 16th-century ships. In Russia there are a few log boats dated to the medieval period. Some of the log boats excavated in the Americas have been dated to the pre-Columbian era, while there is fragmentary evidence for early hide boats from the circumpolar region. Elsewhere, there are virtually no excavated remains of water

transport. Standards of excavation, recording, and publication vary widely.

Techniques for classifying ancient plank boats and ships into meaningful groups are in the early stages of development. However, using just one attribute – whether and how the planking is fastened together – seven main groups or traditions of boat and ship-building can be identified in Europe from medieval times and earlier.

1. Vessels from the Mediterranean, dated from the mid-2nd millennium BC to the 7th century AD, have flush-laid planking fastened by tenons locked within mortises by treenails.

2. A number of wrecks from the central Mediterranean dated from *c.* 600 BC to the 11th century AD have stitched plank fastenings.

3. Some Mediterranean wrecks from the 7th century have upper side planking which is not fastened together but to the framing. The 11th-century wreck from **Serçe Limani** has none of its hull planking fastened together, only to the framing – this ship was built skeleton-first.

4. Several boat finds from northwest Europe, dated from the mid-2nd millennium BC to *c.* 300 BC, have stitch-fastened planking.

5. There are twenty or so finds from northwest Europe, of the 1st to 4th centuries AD, which have their planking not fastened together but fastened to the framing by nails clenched by turning the point 180 degrees back into the inboard face of the frame. The building sequence of the riverine boats of this Romano-Celtic tradition is unclear, but the three seagoing vessels were built skeleton-first.

6. There are many finds in northern and western Europe of vessels of the Viking/Norse tradition (4th to 15th century) with their overlapping planking fastened by iron nails clenched inboard by deforming the tip over a rove. A variant technique in the southern Baltic was to use wedged treenails instead of iron nails.

7. The cog of 12th- to 14th-century northern and northwestern Europe had overlapping side planking fastened together by iron nails, similar to but smaller than those used in the Romano-Celtic tradition to fasten planking to framing.

Outside Europe, there are as yet no regions with a sufficient number of well-recorded planked vessels to justify detailed classification. However, it seems possible to suggest tentatively that Chinese and Southeast Asian ships of the 13th to 16th centuries may be differentiated by reference to their plank fastenings: Southeast Asian ships

used wooden treenails, while Chinese ships used obliquely driven iron nails. The five plank boats known so far from early Egypt appear to fall into two groups: the mid-3rd millennium BC Khufu vessel has unlocked tenons in mortises and transverse stitched fastenings across the planking; while the **Dashur boats** of *c.* 1800 BC have unlocked tenons and double-dovetail wooden clamps set into the plank faces, across the seam.

Boat archaeology has made great strides in the past twenty-five years, but our knowledge of early forms of water transport in large areas of the maritime world is still negligible: the pre-Columbian Americas; Africa outside Egypt; Arabia; India and Oceania. The discovery and scientific excavation of early water transport in those regions is essential if an unbiased worldwide view of water transport is to be obtained.

It is being increasingly realized that boat archaeology on its own cannot be considered a viable academic specialization. The study of rafts, boats, and ships is sterile unless associated with the study of shore-based facilities and the environmental, economic, social, and historical contexts. Boat archaeologists are now in an excellent position to give a factual basis to maritime archaeology and to enrich their own studies by contact with other aspects of the discipline – many have already taken the plunge. S.M.

ADDITIONAL READING

Cederlund, C.O. (ed.), 1985, *Post Medieval Boat and Ship Archaeology*, British Archaeological Reports S 256, Oxford.

Coates, J. *et al.*, in press 'Experimental Boat and Ship Archaeology: Principles and Methods', *International Journal of Nautical Archaeology*.

Crumlin-Pedersen, O., and Vinner, M., eds, 1986, *Sailing into the Past*, Roskilde.

Filgueiras, O.L. (ed.), 1988, *Local Boats.*, 2 vols, British Archaeological Reports S 438, Oxford.

Greenhill, B., 1995, *New Archaeology of the Boat*, London.

McGrail, S. (ed.), 1977, *Sources and Techniques in Boat Archaeology*, British Archaeological Reports S 29, Oxford.

McGrail, S. (ed.), 1979, *Archaeology of Medieval Ships and Harbours*, British Archaeological Reports S 66, Oxford.

McGrail, S., 1987, *Ancient Boats in N.W. Europe*, London.

McGrail, S., 1987, *Ancient Boats of the World*, Oxford.

Morrison, J.S. and Coates, J. 1986, *Athenian Trireme*, Cambridge.

Olsen, O., Madsen, J.S., and Rieck, F. (eds), 1995, *Shipshape*, Roskilde.

Reinders, R. and Paul, K. (eds), 1991, *Carvel Construction Techniques*, Oxbow Monograph 12, Oxford.

Shaw, T. (ed.), 1993, *Trireme Project*, Oxbow Monograph 31, Oxford.

Steffy, J.R., 1994, *Wooden Shipbuilding and the Interpretation of Shipwrecks*, College Station, Texas.

Westerdahl, C., 1994, *Crossroads in Ancient Shipbuilding*, Oxbow Monograph 40, Oxford.

Bolivia

see *South America*

Bon-Porté Wreck

A wreck from the 6th century BC found near Saint-Tropez, **France**. In spite of its modest dimensions and its subsequent plundering, the Bon-Porté Wreck is important because of its antiquity and the interest of its cargo and hull. Discovered in 1971, the wreck lies at a depth of 48 m in Bon-Porté bay, not far from Saint-Tropez. After a preliminary investigation in 1973, Jean-Pierre Joncheray undertook the full excavation of the site in 1974.

At the time of its discovery, the wreck finds included over 30 wine amphoras of which 4–5 were Greek – some from Corinth (Type A), others from Clazomenae (or Chios) – about 10 are now identified as being Archaic amphoras (Type 1) from Massalia (Marseille), and about 20 were Etruscan (Type 3A). Moreover, an *oenochoe* (wine jug) now considered as a Massalian product and a lead ingot were also found on the wreck. The artefacts allow us to date the shipwreck to between 530 and 525 BC, making this wreck one of the oldest known in the western Mediterranean. At first thought to be a Greek or Etruscan boat, the Bon-Porté Wreck, according to the new identification of some artefacts as coming from Massalia, is today regarded as evidence of the emergence during that period of Massalian trade when merchants redistributed Greek and Etruscan wine while exporting the wine of their own city.

Only some remains of the ship, of slight tonnage and not exceeding 10 m in length, have been preserved: a keel fragment, some frames, of large section but widely spaced, into which a part of the mast-step timber was still fitted, and some strakes of the planking. The planks are assembled by means of horizontal treenails and tetrahedral hollows filled with pegs which have since been identified as holes for the passage of lashings of vegetable fibre locked in place by pegs. So, the Bon-Porté ship is a sewn boat which testifies to the archaic tradition of assembly by lashings found in ancient texts. Since that discovery, this assembly system has been found on other ancient wrecks from the archaic period at

Divers constructing a grid before lowering it over the submerged remains of Boscawen *to provide excavation control. (Courtesy of Lake Champlain Maritime Museum, Basin Harbor, Vermont)*

Giglio in Etruria, Gela in Sicily, and in Marseille itself on a little boat very similar to the Bon-Porté one and particularly well preserved, with the sewing still in place between the planks and on the frames. P.P.

ADDITIONAL READING

Joncheray, J.-P., 1976, 'L'épave grecque, ou étrusque, de Bon-Porté', *Cahiers d'Archéologie Subaquatique*, 5, 5–36.

Pomey, P., 1981, 'L'épave de Bon-Porté et les bateaux cousus de Méditerranée', *Mariner's Mirror*, 67, 3, 225–43.

Pomey, P. and Long, L., 1992, 'Les premiers échanges maritimes du Midi de la Gaule du VIe au IIIe s. av. J.-C. à travers les épaves', *Etudes Massaliètes*, 3, 189–98.

Borstö Wreck

see *Sankt Mikael*

Boscawen

A sixteen-gun sloop built at Fort Ticonderoga in 1759 for service in the British naval flotilla on **Lake Champlain** during the 'French and Indian War'. To date it is the earliest inland lake warship archaeologically excavated in North America. *Boscawen* was constructed during British General Jeffery Amherst's invasion of the French-controlled Champlain Valley in 1759. Amherst's objectives were to seize fortifications at Ticonderoga and Crown Point at the southern end of the lake, then to advance north over Lake Champlain and into French Canada. The first British goal was accomplished with little difficulty in July, but the advance down the lake had to await the assembly of a naval flotilla at Ticonderoga. Captain Joshua Loring of the Royal Navy directed the con-struction of two small warships: a twenty-gun brig, *Duke of Cumberland*, and *Boscawen* (named after Admiral Edward Boscawen). Loring's warships were not completed until early October, at which time they sailed in search of the French flotilla of three sloops and a schooner. The French sloops were cornered by Loring in the northern lake and scuttled by their crews. The delay in gaining naval control forced Amherst to postpone his invasion until the following year. In 1760 British advances on Montreal from three directions, including Lake Champlain, led to the surrender of New France.

Boscawen was abandoned after the war at Ticonderoga, and allowed to sink beneath the lake. A survey of the waters off the old 'King's Shipyard' in 1983, sponsored by the Champlain Maritime Society, the Fort Ticonderoga Museum, and the Vermont Division for Historic Preservation turned up the buried hull of the sloop. The Fort Ticonderoga Museum sponsored a two-year excavation of the wreck in 1984–5, during which time the interior of the sloop was entirely exposed, a variety of artefacts were recovered and conserved, and the hull was documented.

The hold of *Boscawen* contained rigging elements such as blocks, dead-eyes, and rope; tools; munitions and small arms parts; and many personal possessions lost or abandoned by the crew, including buttons, buckles, cufflinks, shoes, pipes, eating utensils,

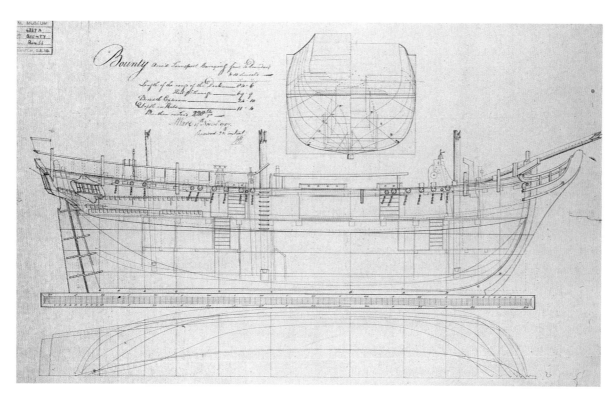

Outboard plan of Bounty, drawn in November 1787. (© National Maritime Museum Picture Library)

and fragments of ceramics, as well as evidence of their diet in the form of bones, nuts, and seeds. One whole and many broken alcohol bottles testify to drinking among the crew, a problem noted by Amherst and his officers.

Boscawen originally measured about 75 ft (23 m) in length and 25 ft (7.6 m) in beam. About 40 per cent of the original hull remained, namely the keel, endposts, keelson, and the frames and planking out to the turn of the bilge. The hull was fashioned from white oak, and fastened with a combination of iron bolts and spikes and wooden treenails. While Boscawen was strongly constructed, the level of workmanship was crude, as might be expected in a vessel built in about three weeks in a wilderness shipyard. K.C.

ADDITIONAL READING

Crisman, K. and Cohn, A., 1994, 'Lake Champlain Nautical Archaeology Since 1980', Journal of Vermont Archaeology, 1, 153–66.

Krueger, J. et al., 1985, 'The Fort Ticonderoga King's Shipyard Excavation', Ticonderoga Bulletin, 14, 6, 335–436.

Bounty

Wreck of a British armed transport, the subject of one of the most famous mutinies in the history of the Royal Navy, subsequently scuttled by the mutineers off Pitcairn Island in the Pacific. His Majesty's Armed Transport Bounty was built as Bethia in Hull, England in 1784 for trade between London and the Carolinas in North America. A 230 ton ship, Bethia was 69 ft 11 in (21.36 m) long at the keel, with a 24 ft 4 in (7.4 m) beam, and an 11 ft 4 in (3.4 m) depth of hold. Bethia was purchased by the Admiralty in May 1787 and fitted out to carry breadfruit from the East Indies to the West Indies, where it would provide a cheap source of food for plantation slaves. Commissioned as the armed transport Bounty, the ship was placed under the command of Lt William Bligh, who was assigned a 45 man crew. After refitting and provisioning, Bounty finally sailed for the Pacific on 23 December 1787.

Bounty arrived at the Pacific island of Tahiti in October 1788 to load breadfruit. The ship remained at Tahiti for five months, sailing on 4 April 1789. The ship sailed westward and stopped at several islands while discontent among the crew, many of whom had not wished to leave Tahiti, reached breaking point. On the morning of 28 April most of the crew joined in a mutiny led by officer Fletcher Christian. Bligh and eighteen of the crew who did not join the mutiny were placed in a 23 ft (7 m) long launch and set adrift. In an amazing feat of seamanship, Blight navigated his launch 5,820 km to Timor without the loss of a single man, and ensured that a vengeful Admiralty would pursue Fletcher Christian and his fellow mutineers. Bounty, meanwhile, with the mutineers aboard, landed some of the crew at Tahiti. Christian and the remaining crew, supplemented by a group of Tahitian men and women, sailed to the uncharted Pitcairn Island, 2,100 km southeast of Tahiti, where Bounty was stripped and burned in Bounty Bay on 23 January 1790.

The Bounty mutineers who remained at Tahiti were apprehended by HMS Pandora in 1791. On her trip home, however, Pandora wrecked on Australia's Great Barrier Reef. The survivors, including some of the Bounty mutineers, ultimately reached home. After a trial, six of the ten men returned to England were convicted of mutiny, and three were hanged. The others were pardoned. Their fate was better than that of those who had sailed off with Christian. Tension between the mutineers and the Tahitians led to an outbreak of violence on Pitcairn. When it ended, only one mutineer, John Adams, was left alive. He and the Tahitians, including the Tahitian children of his fellow mutineers, were left in isolation until 1808, when the ship Topaz of Boston arrived at Pitcairn and resolved the mystery of the final fate of Bounty and the mutineers who sailed off in her. In 1838 Pitcairn became a British colony; it remains an isolated outpost to this day, with many of its residents descendants of the original mutineers.

In 1841 HMS Curaçao anchored in Bounty Bay and Captain Jenkin Jones fished up some of the charred timbers of Bounty. In 1933 Bounty's rudder was recovered from the wreck by Pitcairn islander Parkin Christian and was ultimately placed in the museum at Suva, Fiji. The main body of the wreck was discovered by National Geographic Society writer-photographer Luis Marden in January 1957. Diving with two Pitcairn islanders, Marden discovered iron ballast (kentledge) and yellow metal fasteners and fittings from the wreck. Some of these were cut free of the coral bottom and recovered.

Bounty's anchor was discovered in February 1957 by diver Wilford Fawcett, a crew member aboard the yacht *Yankee*, which anchored outside Bounty Bay. The anchor, found in 15 m of water, was raised by *Yankee*'s crew and is displayed ashore at Pitcairn. J.P.D.

ADDITIONAL READING

McKay, J., 1989, *Anatomy of the Ship: The Armed Transport Bounty*, London.

Marden, L., 1957, 'I Found the Bones of the *Bounty*', *National Geographic Magazine*, 112, 6, 725–90.

Bousolle
see **La Pérouse ships**

Hull remains and in situ *amphoras* exposed during the 1996 excavation season on the Bozburun Byzantine shipwreck. (© INA/Donald A. Frey)

Exploring the wreck of Breadalbane in the Arctic Ocean. Diver Doug Osborne in the revolutionary 'Wasp' suit. (National Geographic Society/Emory Kristof)

Bozburun Wreck

A merchantman with a primary cargo of wine amphoras wrecked on the southwest coast of Asia Minor in the late 9th or early 10th century AD. Preliminary indications are of a vessel approximately 20 m long with a cargo of between 1,000 and 1,500 relatively small amphoras similar to those from contemporary Crimean vessels. The vessel was wrecked at the mouth of the large natural harbour of Selimiye and may have been engaged in supplying one of several naval stations along the Byzantine coast. The site was identified in 1973 by the **Institute of Nautical Archaeology**; excavation began in 1995. F.M.H.

Brazil
see **South America**

Breadalbane

Wreck of an Arctic exploration vessel sunk by ice in 1853 and rediscovered in 1980. It is the northernmost shipwreck yet discovered. The search for the Northwest Passage across the top of North America occupied the attention of the world's great maritime powers for centuries (see **Arctic**). Great Britain assumed the leading role in searching for the passage in the early 19th century, and by 1845 subsequent British expeditions had probed the far reaches of the Arctic and had come close to achieving their goal. In 1845 a Royal Navy expedition led by Sir John Franklin sailed from England in what

was intended to be the final leg of mapping an Arctic route from the Atlantic to the Pacific. Franklin, his two ships, and 128 man crew disappeared. In response, more than forty vessels and a number of expeditions searched for more than twenty years, at first for Franklin himself and then finally for evidence of his fate.

The rugged Arctic also claimed some of the searchers and their ships. Among them was *Breadalbane*, a former merchantman assigned to the expedition led by Sir Edward Belcher. Built at Glasgow in 1844, *Breadalbane* was a 125 ft (38 m) long, 428 ton barque with a beam of 24 ft (7.3 m) and a depth of hold of 18 ft (5.4 m). In March 1853 *Breadalbane* was hired by the British Admiralty to carry provisions – clothing, food, spirits, timber, canvas, and equipment, as well as coal – to the Arctic rendezvous of Beechey Island. Sailing from Sheerness on 19 May 1853 in company with HMS *Phoenix*, a steam screw sloop, *Breadalbane* was caught in ice upon her arrival. On 21 August 1853 the barque was holed by the ice and sank in only fifteen minutes. The crew managed to reach safety as *Breadalbane* went down.

Between 1978 and 1980 Toronto physician and diver Dr Joe MacInnis began searching for *Breadalbane*. Using a Klein **Side scan sonar** operated by Garry Kozak, and working from the Canadian icebreaker *John A. MacDonald*, MacInnis's team located the intact wreck of *Breadalbane* in August 1980. She was found lying upright in 97.5 m of water. In September 1981 MacInnis returned with a new expedition, sponsored by the **National Geographic Society**, to film the wreck using a remotely operated vehicle. A subsequent expedition in April 1983 sent divers down in one-atmosphere 'Wasp' suits. Four dives, for a total of six hours, resulted in more filming and the recovery of the ship's wheel, as well as other artefacts, despite the objections of the Canadian Government archaeological official assigned to monitor the project.

The wheel, kept in a refrigerated freshwater bath, is held by Parks Canada in Ottawa. No additional work, including archaeological survey, has been done on the wreck. The discovery of *Breadalbane* sparked tremendous international interest, and demonstrated that remarkable levels of preservation are possible in the Arctic. This has spurred renewed interest in searching for the wrecks of Franklin's and other lost ships in the Arctic. J.P.D.

ADDITIONAL READING

Booda, L.L., 1981, 'Exploration Without Desecration Planned for H.M.S. *Breadalbane*', *Sea Technology*, December, 29–31.

MacInnis, J., 1985, *The Search for the Breadalbane*, London.

Bremen Cog

The best example yet found and studied of the dominant northern European bulk cargo carrier and most powerful warship of the North and Baltic Seas in the high Middle Ages. The ship was built about 1380, the date established using the tree ring pattern in the timbers. The wreck was found in Bremen Harbour in 1962. It had come to rest after breaking away from moorings during construction and so was unfinished. When uncovered the vessel was immediately identified as a cog. This type of vessel predated the Middle Ages but it was transformed by the 13th century into a vessel capable of moving bulky cargo over the open ocean relatively efficiently. The type appeared on the seals of a number of north German towns which belonged to the Hanseatic League and so the cog was permanently associated with that powerful association of towns.

Using varied methods of excavation, including dredging the riverbed and using a diving bell to reach the timbers of the ship, the remains were recovered by 1965 and placed in solution to prepare for the job of reconstruction. This work has gone on at

The Bremen Cog, reassembled and displayed in the Deutsches Schiffahrtsmuseum, Bremerhaven. (Deutsches Schiffahrtsmuseum/ E. Laska)

the Deutsches Schiffahrtsmuseum in Bremerhaven where the vessel is housed. An unprecedented opportunity, the investigation and preservation of the Bremen Cog has led to an extensive programme for the study of cogs and similar vessels from throughout the Middle Ages. In addition to the research programmes of that museum, two replicas of the cog have now been built for experiments on the handling of such a vessel. The Bremen Cog, if nothing else, has played an important role in the development of nautical archaeology and in promoting the study of maritime history over the last thirty years.

Cogs typically had a flat bottom with the planking fastened to the floor timbers, a sharp turn at the bilges and overlapping edge-fastened planking on the sides. The stempost and sternpost were set at sharp angles to the keel to which each was scarfed. The cog carried a single mast to which was fixed a single square sail. A rudder was fixed to the sternpost. The Bremen Cog, an example from the type's heyday, displayed all these features; indeed, it was in such good condition that it offered much more detailed evidence about the construction and design of cogs.

The Bremen Cog was about 23 m long, about 7.6 m wide and somewhat over 3 m deep in the hold. It was not among the largest of vessels of its type, the estimated tonnage being about 130. It took more than seven years to put all the pieces of wood back together. It proved possible to identify the precise process of construction beginning with the laying of the keel, the erecting of the posts, and the placing of the hull planking. Reconstruction showed that the keel was not one single piece of wood but was in three parts, consistent with some early medieval illustrations of cogs. The

largest of the three parts, the middle piece of the keel, was 8.3 m long and 4.73 m wide. The other two pieces of the keel were 3.73 and 4.78 m long. The slightly angled portions toward bow and stern were presumably to make it easier for the vessel to get off sandbars as well as to make possible the use of lighter timbers in keel construction.

Shipbuilders used treenails throughout the ship to attach planks, the holes drilled for them after the planks were set in place. The builders also relied on nails which were bent over small triangular pieces of iron and then bent again at the tip to make hooks. The rudder was not salvaged but its shape could be inferred from the shape and size of the sternpost. The hull planks typically weighed over 90 kg. A total of eight longitudinal deck beams added stiffness to the hull and formed part of the base for the deck. Deck planks were at right angles to the sides and were not watertight so that water on the deck spilled into the bilges. The decking was probably nailed down. With so much water below decks all cargo had to be shipped in watertight containers which meant barrels.

There was a main castle at the stern which was 7.37 m long and narrowed from 6.88 m to 6.44 m aft. The castle was trapeziform and extended out on both the port and starboard sides as well as over the stern. Even a ship's toilet was preserved, designed to hang over the starboard side. The vessel had both a capstan and a windlass. The latter, 3.53 m long and operated with handspikes, was of a sophisticated construction, balanced and fitted so that sailors could lubricate it easily. The capstan, which probably came from the same workshop, was 2.1 m long with its reconstructed head, and weighed about 686 kg. The two were operated in much the same way. Presumably sailors used one to raise the anchor and the yard but whether the other was there to supplement those tasks or to control the mast is not certain. The function of some of the excavated pieces has proved elusive, as with a violin-shaped thick piece of oak which was attached to the inner stempost and extended above it.

The continuing process of investigation and reconstruction has revealed a great deal about each aspect of the ship type. The examination of the Bremen Cog has confirmed many conclusions based on other sources but also advanced far beyond what could be learned from images and written records. It has also made possible a better understanding of the sailing quali-ties of the cog. Conservation of the vessel continues. It sits in a preserving bath in a tank surrounded by windows so visitors to the museum at Bremerhaven can see this wreck which has inspired so much work. R.W.U.

ADDITIONAL READING

Ellmers, D., 1994, 'The Cog as Cargo Carrier', in R.W. Unger (ed.), *Cogs, Caravels and Galleons*, London.

Heinsius, P., 1956, *Das Schiff der Hansischen Fruühzeit*, Weimar.

Hoffmann, P., 1986, 'The Bremen Cog Sails a New Course', *International Journal of Nautical Archaeology*, 15, 215–19.

Kiedel, K.-P. and Schanall, U. (eds), 1985, *The Hanse Cog of 1380*, Bremerhaven.

Lahn, W., 1992, *Die Kogge von Bremen: Band I, Bauteile und Bauablauf*, Hamburg. (With an abbreviated English version translated by Judith Rosenthal.)

Pohl-Weber, R. *et al.*, (eds), 1969, *Die Bremer Hanse-Kogge Fund Konservierung Forschung*, Bremen.

Brigg Logboat

A large Bronze Age boat dated by radio-carbon to *c.* 1000 BC. This near-complete, but damaged and fragile, logboat was found in 1886 during excavations for a gas works near the River Ancholme (a trib-utary of the River Humber: see **Humber wrecks**), at Brigg in northern Lincolnshire, England. After being excavated, it was first displayed in Brigg, then moved to Hull where she was destroyed by fire during an air raid in 1942. This notable find attracted both popular and scholarly attention: within twenty years of excavation there were at least thirty publications about the logboat, including an account of a court case in the Chancery Division, London, 'Elwes v. The Brigg Gas Company', to deter-mine ownership.

The Brigg logboat was hewn from a single large oak tree with a bole at least 15 m long

and a girth of *c.* 6 m (1.9 m diameter) at its lower end. There was heart rot at this end of the tree, which, as it was broadest, was to become the stern of the boat. A two-piece transom board had therefore to be fash-ioned, caulked with moss and wedged within a groove worked around the inside of the stern to make that end of the boat water-tight. The upper, narrower end of the log, which was rot-free, became the bow, and knot holes left on either side of this bow after the removal of two large branches were filled with protruding wooden plugs to become the 'eyes' of the boat.

Three shallow ridges were left in the solid wood across the boat's bottom, all in the for-ward 40 per cent of the boat, and spaced 1.4 m and 1.85 m apart. Such integral ridges,

The Brigg logboat after excavation in 1886. (National Maritime Museum, Greenwich)

some 50 to 100 mm in height, are commonly found in logboats, recent as well as ancient: some are at regular intervals, some are not. There seems to be no one explanation for this feature: the Brigg ridges may have marked sta-tions for paddlers, two at each ridge, port and starboard, with cargo further aft.

At the stern there was a raised platform or deck for two steersmen who probably used large paddles port and starboard. There was a smaller platform at the bow for a lookout. A 3.66 m split, low down on the starboard side, had been repaired using several oak patches caulked with moss. One of these patches was held in place by a cleat and transverse timber arrangement similar to

that used to link together the planking of the prehistoric **Ferriby Boats** and the Brigg sewn plank boat (the so-called **Brigg 'Raft'**). Some of these patches had been sewn to the boat with a fine rope of natural fibre.

Originally this boat measured *c.* 14.78 × 1.37 × 1 m, the broadest and deepest dimensions being at the stern; thus it retained the tapered shape of its parent It could carry a maximum of two steersmen and twenty-six paddlers at a draft of 35 cm and a freeboard of 65 cm. With a five-man crew the boat could carry *c.* 5.5 tonnes of cargo at a draft of 60 cm and a freeboard of 40 cm.

The Brigg Logboat was steered and pro-pelled by paddles or poles. It was used in the tidal creeks and rivers of the Humber estu-ary to ferry people and goods. It is also pos-sible that it had a prestigious ceremonial role, and it may have been used on occa-sions as a war boat. S.M.

ADDITIONAL READING

McGrail, S., 1978, *Logboats of England and Wales*, BAR British Series 51, Oxford.

McGrail, S., 1996, 'Bronze Age in N. W. Europe', in A.-E. Christensen (ed.), *The Earliest Ships*, Conway's History of the Ship, vol. 1, London, 24–38.

Brigg 'Raft'

A Bronze Age sewn plank boat, generally similar in construction to the **Ferriby Boats**, and dated by radiocarbon to *c.* 800 BC. It was found in 1888 by workmen digging for brick clay in a field at Brigg, Lincolnshire, England, close to the River Ancholme and some 500 m northwest of the find-spot of the prehistoric **Brigg Logboat**. The remains were left exposed from February to June 1888; then a large proportion was lifted and the remainder back-filled and left in the ground in a degraded state. Of the portion lifted, only one small fragment in Lincoln Museum has so far been traced. The site was relocated by the National Maritime Museum, Greenwich in 1974, when about three-fifths of the original bottom planking and part of a lowest side strake were excavated, lifted, and taken to Greenwich for further research, conservation, and display.

This was a flat-bottomed boat, of near-rectangular form, for which there are many ethnographic parallels on the rivers and lakes of the world. The bottom of the boat consisted of five planks of equal thickness fashioned from slow-growing, straight-grained forest oaks: two planks were from the same tree, two others were from a second tree, while the fifth plank was from a third. These oaks were more than 12.2 m in height up to the crown, with girths of 2.7 to 3.03 m near their lower ends, tapering to c. 2.07 m at the top.

The five planks were butted edge to edge, and fastened together by a continuous zig-zag stitching with a two-stranded rope of split willow, over a moss caulking capped by a longitudinal lath of hazel along each seam. The edges of each plank, where the sewing holes were bored, were much thinner than elsewhere: thus the sewing was kept well above the outer surface of the boat so that it would not be worn away by the river bed when the boat was berthed.

The bottom planks were also linked by ten transverse oak timbers wedged within cleats carved in the solid wood on each plank; there are parallels here with the Ferriby boats. These transverse timbers not only minimize the stresses imposed on the stitching when under way and when berthing, but could also be used to realign the planking

after periodic dismantling for maintenance as is done today by sewn plank boats crews in Arabia, India, and elsewhere.

The lowest side strakes, also of oak, were fastened to the outer bottom planks so that they overlapped. There was formerly at least one more strake of side planking. Since the bottom planking is now incomplete at both ends, the bow and stern of the boat are more conjectural, but they may have had transoms fitted.

The minimum reconstruction of this boat resembles a 'lidless box', generally tapering towards one end which was probably the bow. Its overall dimensions were 12.20 × 2.27 m with a height of sides either 34 or 55 cm. Propelled and steered by paddles or by poles in the shallows, it was used as a ferry on the middle reaches of the River Ancholme which, in the Bronze Age, was a tidal creek of the Humber estuary (see **Humber wrecks**). Brigg was a natural point to cross this creek since it was not only where the highlands to east and west were closest together, but it was also near the head of the tide. Depending on draft and freeboard requirements, this boat could have carried between 1.54 tonnes (say four men and twenty-six sheep) and 7.16 tonnes (say six men and seventeen cattle). When no longer needed as a boat she was moored on the eastern approaches to the creek and used as a landing stage by which people and animals could cross the marsh margins of the creek to embark in boats in the deep water channel. S.M.

ADDITIONAL READING

McGrail, S., 1981, *The Brigg 'Raft' and her Prehistoric Environment*, BAR British Series 89, Oxford.

McGrail, S., 1994, 'The Brigg "Raft": A Flat-bottomed Boat', *International Journal of Nautical Archaeology*, 23, 283–8.

McGrail, S., 1996, 'Bronze Age in N.W. Europe', in A.-E. Christensen (ed.), *The Earliest Ships*, Conway's History of the Ship, vol. 1, London, 24–38.

Roberts, O., 1992, 'The Brigg "Raft" Reassessed as a Round Bilge Bronze Age Boat', *International Journal of Nautical Archaeology*, 21, 245–58.

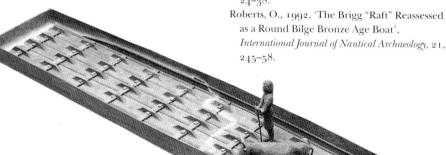

Reconstruction model of the Brigg sewn plank boat, called the Brigg 'Raft'. (National Maritime Museum, London)

Bronze Age stone anchors (Eastern Mediterranean)

Anchors are instruments for immobilizing floating objects from fishing-tackle to oil-rigs. Lives and fortunes depend on their 'hold', especially when they keep vessels at a safe distance from hazards; hence the universal symbolism attributed to them. In the Christian religion, for example, they remain the emblem of hope. Symbolism does, however, vary with period and place, while its importance fluctuates with the degree of risk involved. The sea remains perilous despite successive design improvements (to the shape of sails, propulsion by engines, etc.) which reduce its dangers to some measure. Archaeologically, the utilitarian and the symbolic aspects of anchors are so closely interrelated that it is impossible to follow one line of research without taking the other into account. Bronze Age wrecks are rare, but lost anchors are not and each one of them, by marking the passage of a ship, gives a potential clue to its ownership and size. It follows that the relative importance of ancient merchant fleets and sea-lanes can be deduced, providing the provenance and date of anchors is established.

Sites: Numbers of ancient anchors mark certain offshore shallows where the square sails of Mediterranean antiquity forced craft to ride out adverse winds by dropping their inefficient pierced stones wherever their cables could reach. These improvised moorings could be dangerous, so cables often had to be cut – hence the groups of anchors lost in such places, as well as those found off flat, sandy, windswept shorelines. The typological identification of various 'families' of stone anchors is mainly based on specimens excavated on land in sacred contexts of known date. Unfortunately, before the 1950s (when discoveries by **SCUBA**-divers began to confirm their use) pierced stones were not always identified and recorded on land, despite J. Zvoronos's references to stone anchors published in 1914. Nevertheless, the temples and tombs of three great east Mediterranean ports, Byblos (Lebanon), Ugarit (Syria), and Kition (Cyprus), have produced typological material of key importance.

Various meanings are implied by the positioning of anchors in sacred contexts. At Ugarit, where the acropolis (which is 2 km inland) was crowned by twin tower-like temples, respectively dedicated to a weather god and an earth god, no anchors were found in the latter. To judge from a recently discovered Ugaritic tablet recording the burning of sacrifices on its roof, the weather god's temple may also have served as a beacon tower (a precursor of the lighthouse). The same may apply to the Tower Temple at Byblos, where unfinished anchors form the first step of a flight leading to its unique entrance. Besides being associated with sea-marks, the placing of votive anchors reflects the general preoccupations of seafarers: taking on water (anchors in wells), and a safe passage in this life and the next (anchors in temples and in tombs). Further shades of meaning are, for instance, suggested at Kition by anchors standing upright as baetyls, over pits wherein unwanted religious objects had been burned. They are

the Iron Age. Consequently, size gives the first indication of the date of an anchor lost undersea. There is also an obvious correlation between anchor and ship size (although given the number of unknown variables in the structure of Bronze Age ships, this correlation cannot as yet be reduced to a precise mathematical formula). Furthermore, the inefficiency of stone anchors meant that large complements had to be carried, and that individual anchors were dispensable. The 19th-century BC wreck at Newe Yam off Israel had a complement of seventeen anchors, and the

from Newe Yam: Corrections and Additions', *International Journal of Nautical Archaeology*, 16, 2, 167–8.

Green, J.N., 1973, *An Underwater Survey off Cape Andreas 1969–1970*, Colston Papers 23, London, 141–80.

Pulak, C., 1988, 'Excavations in Turkey: 1988 Campaign', *INA Newsletter*, University of Texas A&M, 15, 4, 12–17.

Pulak, C., 1989, 'Uluburun 1989 Excavation Campaign', *INA Newsletter*, University of Texas A&M, 16, 4, 9.

Zvoronos, J., 1914, 'Stylides, ancreshierae, aphlaste, stoloi, ackrostolia, embola, proembola et totems marins', *Journal international d'archéologie numismatique*, Athens, 105–10.

Brown's Bay Vessel

An early 19th-century converted British gunboat, wrecked or abandoned at Brown's Bay, a small inlet on the north shore of the St Lawrence River, 50 km from the eastern end of Lake Ontario, Canada. The site was first investigated in 1966, during a survey of shipwrecks in the Lake Ontario/St Lawrence region, when archaeologists from the National Historic Sites Service of the Canadian Department of Indian Affairs and Northern Development (now the Canadian Parks Service) were informed of the presence of the wreck by local divers. The wreck was excavated, raised, conserved, and put on display in nearby St Lawrence Islands National Park. An in-depth study of the vessel was made by Christopher Amer in 1985 to record hull construction and to re-evaluate the previous identification of the remains.

The hull form can be favourably compared to representations and descriptions of British Admiralty flat-bottomed boats of the period. The first recorded building and use of these craft was during the Seven Years War when the British sent an expeditionary force against France in 1758 and invaded Havana in 1762. They were also used in the conquest of French Canada in 1758–60. The boats were propelled by sails and sweeps. In 1813 many of these craft were fitted with bow guns and operated as a gunboat fleet, patrolling Lake Ontario and the St Lawrence River.

Military artefacts from the site confirm its military origin and suggest an early 19th-century date for the vessel. However, the presence of features on the hull which were uncharacteristic of British gunboats of that period – a centreboard, a wide blade rudder, a heavy keelson – and an apparent lack of evidence for a gun, suggest that the vessel had once undergone an extensive refit. In

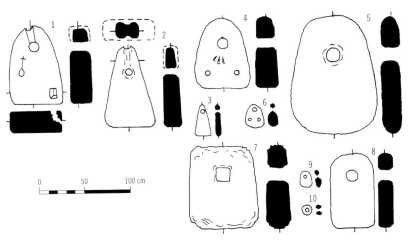

Bronze Age stone anchors. **1** *Byblos, Egyptian type, limestone, 188.8 kg.* **2, 3** *Byblian form: limestone, 150 kg and 6 kg, from the 16th and 19th century BC phases of the 'Obelisk Temple'.* **4–6** *Cypriot forms (Kition Temples), respectively yellowish sandstone, coarse pebbly sandstone and coraline limestone, weighing 100 , 1035 and 6 kg respectively;* **7–10** *Ugaritic forms from the Baal Temple area and from 'Tomb 36' (no. 8). All fine local limestone (except no. 9, basalt); 400kg, c.120 kg and (the fishermen's weights) only a kilo or so. All from late Bronze Age levels. (Honor Frost)*

also found in the thresholds and foundation courses of sacred buildings: singly, in groups, or placed as cornerstones. In reused tombs, anchors sometimes mingle with the fill thrown back into the entrance corridors, but in Tomb 36 at Ugarit an identical pair stands upright, flanking the entrance itself. Pairs may represent oared ships, since oars could carry a vessel to safety when the wind turned against it, while the seating of oarsmen did not leave space to stow the large complements of anchors essential to 'round' cargo-ships; in his sixth *Olympic Ode* Pindar likens an athlete to a fast (i.e. 'long' and oared) vessel needing few anchors 'on a stormy night'. Finally, fishing tackle for immobilizing set-long lines, nets, baskets, etc. is also found in sacred contexts where it represents the fertility of the sea. It often takes the form of miniature anchors weighing about a kilogram.

Size and weight are of prime importance in recording Bronze Age anchors which, for boats and ships, range from some 20 kg to half a ton or more. In many parts of the world, including the Mediterranean, stone anchors light enough to be handled by a single man are still used on small boats by inshore fishermen, whereas the larger sizes became obsolete on cargo-carriers during

14th-century BC wreck at **Uluburun** off Turkey had twenty-four. An anchor's shape and the kind of stone from which it is made indicate its place of origin. All such factors need to be taken into account in recording anchors, and in analysing existing records. H.F.

ADDITIONAL READING

Frost, H., 1969, 'The Stone Anchors of Byblos', *Mélanges de l'Université Saint-Joseph*, 65, 26, 425–42.

Frost, H., 1985, 'The Kition Anchors', *Kition V*, Part I, App. 1, Cyprus.

Frost, H., 1991, 'Anchors Sacred and Profane', *Ras Shamra-Ougarit 6, Arts et Industries de la Pierre*, E.R.C., Paris.

Galili, E., 1985, 'A Group of Stone Anchors from Newe Yam', *International Journal of Nautical Archaeology*, 14, 2, 143–53.

Galili, E., 1987, 'A Group of Stone Anchors

addition, the hull had been strengthened with the installation of a second set of futtocks, and a second layer of hull planking. Modifications made during the conversion are characterized by the use of iron nails and threaded bolts, and suggest a change of assignment to that of a commercial cargo carrier. A late date for some of the non-military artefacts found in the hull suggests a long period of use for the vessel.

The reconstructed hull is 54 ft 2 in (16.5 m) long, has a beam of 16 ft 6 in (5 m) and a depth of hold of 4 ft 1 in (1.3 m). It is a broad, shallow-draft craft with a slight sheer over its length, a transom stern, and a wide buff bow. The vessel would have drawn less than one metre of water when carrying a 21 ton load. Originally built of clinker, or lap-strake construction, the frames were fastened with copper nails, while the planks were attached to each other with copper rivets. The hull form was well suited to navigation in shallow waters. The modification, done after 1820, retained those features of the original hull form which made the craft a good military craft – light and flexible, yet strong and durable – while strengthening the hull and making the vessel more economical to operate. The nearly flat bottom of the boat necessitated the addition of a centreboard and a wide-blade rudder to reduce leeway when sailing close to the wind.

The Brown's Bay Vessel is the only known Royal Navy flat-bottomed boat that dates to the period of the War of 1812. While some of the gunboat fleet in Canada were evidently sold and operated commercially after their military role had ceased, this vessel holds the only evidence for the continued use of such a boat. C.A.

ADDITIONAL READING

Amer, C.F., 1986, 'The Construction of the Brown's Bay Vessel', MA thesis, Texas A&M University, College Station, Texas. (Published 1987 as Canada Parks Microfiche Report Series 266, Ottawa.)

Beattie, J.A., 1967, *Gunboats on the St. Lawrence River 1763–1839*, Canada Parks Manuscript Report Series 15, Ottawa.

Chapelle, H.I., 1949, *The History of the American Sailing Navy*, New York.

Cuthbertson, G.A., 1931, *The Great Lakes*, New York.

Pearsall, A.W.H. (ed.), 1984, 'Naval Aspects of the Landings on the French Coast, 1758', in N.A.M. Rodger (ed.), *The Naval Miscellany, V*, London, 207–43.

Preston, R.A., 1952, 'The Fate of Kingston's Warships', in *Ontario Historical Society*, 44, 3, 85–100.

Syrett, D. (ed.), 1970, *The Siege and Capture of Havana*, London.

Zacharchuck, W., 1968, 'The Raising of the Mallorytown Wreck', in S. South (ed.), *The Conference on Historic Site Archaeology Papers 1967*, 2, 1, Raleigh, North Carolina, 85–94.

Zacharchuck, W., 1969, *One of a Thousand Wrecks*, MS on file at Canadian Parks Service, Ottawa.

Zacharchuck, W., 1981, *Architectural Report on the Brown's Bay Gunboat*, MS on file at Canadian Parks Service, Ottawa.

Brown's Ferry Vessel

A schooner-rigged, flat-bottomed inland transport vessel of the first half of the 18th century, discovered in the Black River near Georgetown, South Carolina in 1971 and

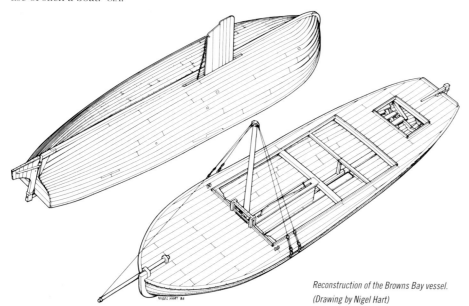

Reconstruction of the Browns Bay vessel.
(Drawing by Nigel Hart)

excavated and raised in 1976 by the South Carolina Institute of Archaeology and Anthropology (SCIAA). A second excavation season in 1984 recovered several loose pieces of the vessel and documented other remains in the area. Following conservation in SCIAA's facility in Columbia, South Carolina in 1992 the vessel was transferred to the Rice Museum in Georgetown for display.

The vessel was discovered embedded in the bank of the river near the site of a 19th- and 20th-century ferry landing, and forms the lowest stratum of a complex deposition of abandoned vessels and rubbish. A cargo of nearly 12,000 building bricks, probably destined for Georgetown or Charlestown, overloaded the open hold and probably rendered the hull prone to swamping. Other artefacts found in the vessel include lead and wax seals, bottles, four millstones, and three iron cooking pots. Among the personal items recovered from the site were several smoking pipes, a straight razor, and an inkwell. Ceramic vessels include a slipware cup and a delph bowl. A Davis quadrant, found in the vicinity, may be associated with the vessel. If so, its presence suggests that the craft may sometimes have operated out of sight of land.

At a reconstructed length of 15.65 m, with a breadth of 4.36 m and depth amidships of only 1.28 m, the Brown's Ferry Vessel is not particularly large, nor is it exceptionally burdensome for its dimensions, the maximum displacement being only 29 tonnes. Although flat-bottomed, the flat is narrow and tapers toward the ends. The midships section is relatively full, with only slight deadrise outboard of the bottom and soft bilges, but both the entrance and run are long and easy. The bilge curvature is carried fairly far forward and aft, but rises well above the bottom, producing exaggerated hollows low in the ends. Stem and sternpost rakes are both relatively short, and the stern terminates in a small high transom. The hold was probably open, with a small deck and windlass forward and possibly a small deck or steering platform aft.

The most distinctive element of the hull structure is the flat bottom, a platform made of three straight thick cypress planks. There is no rabbet, just a shallow bevel on the upper surface; the lower part of the outer edge is also bevelled. The curved and rabbeted live oak stem sits directly on top of the bottom in a shallow recess. The joint is reinforced by a live oak apron nailed to the stem and with a broad foot treenailed to the bottom. The forward edge of the stem is extended by a narrow grip or false stem nailed in place. All three stem components are fastened together by at least two iron forelock bolts. Little survives of the stern, only the eroded end of the bottom and the broad foot of an inner sternpost similar to the apron, but the construction is similar to the bow.

The vessel is framed in a mixed technique, twenty approximately symmetrical floor timbers are treenailed to the upper surface of the bottom; nineteen of these are joggled to fit the irregularities of the bottom planks, and the midships frame is set on a flat carefully dubbed across the bottom. Two more floor timbers are treenailed to the top of the apron foot. Each floor timber is matched with a pair of futtocks set against or close to its after face; all the planks except the garboards are backed out to fit the frames. In fifteen of the frames, the futtocks are free elements, but in five frames, evenly spaced over the length of the hull and including the midships frame, the futtocks are nailed and treenailed to the floor timber. The five made frames have identical bilge and side curvature, narrowing and rising toward the ends, and were the first frames erected after the bottom was assembled. As is frequently the case with such crude forms of whole moulding, this produces the exaggerated hollows seen in the entrance and run. At two frames, there are second futtocks in line with the floor timbers, a possible indication of beam locations. In addition to the primary frames, there is a series of free futtocks set in every third room; these are dubbed flat to fit the planks and are probably a later addition.

A broad cypress keelson with deeply chamfered edges is treenailed through eighteen of the floor timbers and into the bottom, with its forward end resting on the apron. Two mast-steps, simple rectangular mortises, are cut into the upper surface, one at the forward end and one just abaft amidships; the spacing and size conform with the schooner rig often used on vessels of this size and type.

Eight strakes of yellow pine planking are nailed and treenailed to the frames below a thick narrow wale, nailed and bolted through the frames to a now missing stringer. The forward ends of several strakes were kerfed on the inboard face with an adze to make them more flexible so that they could be bent into the rabbet. The garboard was probably attached to the first five frames and its surface used to determine the deadrise of the remaining frames. The wale was nailed and bolted through the frames to a now missing stringer and surmounted by a thick toerail edge-nailed to the wale. Two vertical holes in the wale probably carried thole pins for a single pair of sweeps.

In the mid-18th century small flat-bottomed inland schooners with open holds were often referred to as periaugers or pettiaugers, but the term usually indicates a vessel of dugout or log-based construction. Such vessels were often locally built and crewed by slaves. The Brown's Ferry Vessel, although built by a craftsman at least vaguely familiar with traditional whole moulding and planked construction, may retain some elements of a log-based tradition in the heavy bottom hewn from three planks. The bottom construction may also reflect the builder's familiarity with traditional methods of flat-bottomed construction practised in northwestern Europe since the Iron Age. F.M.H, C.A.

ADDITIONAL READING

Albright, A.B. and Steffy, J.R., 1979, 'The Brown's Ferry Vessel: Preliminary Report', *International Journal of Nautical Archaeology and Underwater Exploration*, 8, 2, 121–42.

Amer, C.F. and Hocker, F.M., 1995, 'A Comparative Analysis of Three Sailing Merchant Vessels from the Carolina Coast', in W.C. Fleetwood (ed.), *Tidecraft: The Boats of South Carolina, Georgia and Northern Florida, 1550–1950*, Georgia.

Hocker, F.M., 1985, 'The Place of the Brown's Ferry Vessel in the Evolution of the Flat Bottomed Boat', MS on file at Nautical Archaeology Program, Texas A&M University.

Hocker, F.M., 1992, 'The Brown's Ferry Vessel: An Interim Hull Report', in D.H. Keith and T.L. Carrell (eds), *Underwater Archaeology Proceedings from the Society for Historical Archaeology Conference, Kingston, Jamaica*, Ann Arbor, Michigan.

Leader, J.M., 1992, 'The Brown's Ferry Vessel Project: Assessing the Conservation of a Mid-1700s Merchantman from South Carolina', in D.H. Keith and T.L. Carrell (eds), *Underwater Archaeology Proceedings from the Society for Historical Archaeology Conference, Kingston, Jamaica*, Ann Arbor, Michigan.

Nylund, R.C., 1989, 'The Historical Background of the Brown's Ferry Vessel', MA thesis, University of South Carolina, Columbia.

Steffy, J.R., 1978, *Preliminary Report: Hull Construction Features of the Brown's Ferry Vessel*, Notebook 5, 1, 13–33, South Carolina Institute of Archaeology and Anthropology, University of South Carolina, Columbia.

Steffy, J.R., 1978, 'Construction Details of the Brown's Ferry Ship', in J.B. Arnold III (ed.), *Proceedings of the Ninth Conference on Underwater Archaeology*, Texas Antiquities Committee, Austin.

Brunswick

A homeward-bound East Indiaman that sank while at anchor in Simon's Bay, near Cape Town, South Africa. The vessel had been captured as a prize by French Admiral Linois in the Indian Ocean and brought to the Cape. *Brunswick* carried a cargo of sandalwood and iron knees. Sandalwood logs scattered around the wreckage aided in site verification. The site consists of well-preserved sections of hull wreckage. Few artefacts remain on the site owing to past vandalism. In 1993 participants in the first public maritime archaeology programme offered by the South African National Monuments Council (NMC) selected the site for a prototype avocational archaeology project with no commercial intent.

Joint collaboration with the staff of the NMC, SA Maritime Museum, and the SA Institute of Maritime Technology has resulted in a state-of-art survey of the hull Pre-disturbance site plans were digitized and included in a GIS Arcview database (see **Geographic Information Systems**). The intention is eventually to create a GIS database of other wreckage in the Simon's Bay area with photographs and other site data. L.H., T.D.

ADDITIONAL READING

Boshoff, J., Durden, T., and Kruyshaar, C., 1994, *Proposal for Protection of Underwater Archaeology Sites in Simon's Bay*, Cape Town.

Hardy, C., 1813, *A Register of Ships in the Service of the English East India Company*, Cape Town.

Bryggen

Historic waterfront district of Bergen, Norway, which was the site of extensive excavation following a major fire in 1955. In the Middle Ages Bryggen, also known as the German Wharf, had been part of the commercial district of one of the busiest ports in Scandinavia, one of the four *kontore* (overseas depots and distribution centres) of the Hanseatic League. Excavation between 1955 and 1968 (with smaller campaigns in the 1970s) revealed that the long, multi-storey tenements with narrow street fronts and passages between that had been destroyed in the fire were built on top of many layers of the remains of similar buildings interspersed with ash layers from previous fires. Many of these ash layers could be correlated with historic accounts of fires to allow reasonably accurate dating of the cultural material.

Among the fragments of medieval architecture dating back to the 12th century were numerous pieces of ships and boats, reused as building material: beams and frames turned into foundation timbers, and planking used for walls. In some cases, several pieces of planks were still fastened together and used as panels to stabilize foundations. The finds also included a large variety of rigging elements, from masts to parrels and cleats. Virtually all of the hull fragments came from clinker-built vessels squarely in the Nordic tradition of boatbuilding. Despite the prominence of Bergen as a Hanseatic port, only one fragment of thick planking with the characteristic marks of iron caulking clamps, or *sintels*, testifies to the presence of cogs, the vessel normally assumed to be the dominant long-distance carrier of the 13th and 14th centuries.

The vessels represented by these remains span a wide range of sizes, from small rowed craft to large sailing cargo-carriers. No individual vessel is sufficiently preserved to allow detailed reconstruction, but several substantial timbers deposited in the rebuilding after the 1248 fire appear to be from a single vessel, which provides a unique view of a type of ship not widely attested in the cog-dominated historical sources. This vessel, often referred to as the 'Big Ship', was of a size comparable to the largest cargo-carriers of its day, with a length of over 30 m, a beam of perhaps 9 or 10 m, and a cargo space of at least 165 cu. m (twice that of the **Bremen Cog**). Its construction appears to be a development of the clinker tradition seen in vessels of the Viking age, but accommodating the greatly increased requirements for size of the High Middle Ages. The frames are spaced much more closely than in early ships, just under 0.5 m apart. The *bite* (lower beam) of the Viking ships is set much lower, so low that it rests on top of a very short, sharp floor timber and extends past it to carry the planking directly on its joggled underside. Heavy knees on top of the *bite* continue the framing up the sides. The mast-step is a very long timber, nearly a full keelson, similar to the mast-step of the Skuldelev 2 vessel (see **Skuldelev Ships**), but reinforced by a pair of unusual beams laid directly over it. These two beams have greatly expanded central sections, and each has a vertical notch in one side. The notches meet when the beams are assembled against each other and form an upward extension of the mortise in the mast-step. The ship probably had an open hold with small decks fore and aft, and was equipped with a large windlass.
F.M.H.

Additional Reading

Christensen, A.E., 1985, 'Boat Finds from Bryggen', in A.E. Herteig (ed.), *The Bryggen Papers*, Main Series I, Bergen and Oslo.

Herteig, A.E., 1985, 'The Archaeological Excavations at Bryggen, "The German Wharf", in Bergen, 1955–68', in A.E. Herteig

(ed.), *The Bryggen Papers*, Main Series I, Bergen and Oslo.

Buried ships

The remains of ships found buried beneath 'dry' land. Ships and ship remains may be buried as a deliberate act, such as Ship burials (see **Gokstad Ship**, **Oseberg Ship**, **Tune Ship**, and **Sutton Hoo**), or when geomorphological change or human activity transforms submerged areas into dry land, such as the steamer *Bertrand* (1865), buried in a former river course in Nebraska, USA, the steamer *Arabia* (1856), also buried in a former riverbed in Missouri, USA, and the wrecks of the famous **IJsselmeerpolders wrecks** in Holland. Buried ship archaeology has mainly focused

Aerial view of the buried ship Niantic *during excavation in downtown San Francisco. (National Park Service)*

on ship burials and on ships buried in landfill along the former waterfronts of major port cities.

Chance encounters with buried ships during construction activity has occurred with great frequency in London, New York, and San Francisco. Archaeological work on buried ships in urban settings has likewise taken place in all three locales. Construction work along the Thames riverfront in London has uncovered substantial remains of waterfront structures, including revetments, wharves, docks, and buildings, as well as buried ships from the Roman period to the 18th century (see **River Thames**). Numerous other examples have been found since the discovery in 1910 of the **County Hall Ship**, a vessel of the late 3rd–early 4th century AD. In 1958 the well-preserved remains of a

2nd-century AD boat were discovered during foundation work for New Guy's House near the south end of London Bridge (see **New Guy's House Boat**); the remains were excavated, documented, and analysed by Peter Marsden. Discoveries have included portions of dismantled ships reused as dockside structures and subsequently buried as the London riverfront has advanced. In the last decades of the 20th century this work has been conducted by the Museum of London's Archaeological Service and has included the 1974 excavation of broken boat timbers from the 10th century found on top of a Saxon foreshore embankment at New Fresh Wharf, as well as planking from Billingsgate, Fennings Wharf, Southwark, in the early and mid-1980s. Work on the London foreshore and former waterfront continues, and new discoveries are coming to light. Excavations in Dublin, Ireland have unearthed portions of ships and timbers from the medieval period. These finds, like those in London, show the high potential for well-preserved materials from waterfronts, especially from periods where intact wooden structures add a great amount of detailed information to the submerged record.

In San Francisco as many as fifty or more ships were buried as the former waterfront was filled in during the boom years of the California Gold Rush (1849–56). Since 1872 more than dozen buried vessels have been encountered during downtown construction, notably the ships *Niantic* and *William Gray*. Most have been found since the 1970s, as deep excavation for the construction of highrise blocks has reached the former beach level, 7.3–9.1 m below the present-day street level. In 1994 a nearly intact vessel, believed to be the ship *Roma*, was discovered during subsurface tunnelling along the waterfront for a streetcar tunnel. The vessel was bored through and removed in pieces.

Construction work in New York has also recovered vessel remains, including an early vessel believed to be the Dutch ship *Tyjger*, in 1916. Substantial remains of another buried ship in New York were found in 1982, when construction on Water Street, several blocks from the waterfront, discovered the well-preserved remains of an early 18th-century vessel buried nearly 6 m below the street level. Known variously as the Water Street Ship or the **Ronson Ship**, the nearly complete hull had been abandoned on the site sometime prior to 1750, sunk in place and filled with rubble to support a wharf, and then buried in succeeding years as landfill reclaimed the waterfront.

There have also been construction-related discoveries of buried bateaux (see **James River bateaux**; **Quebec bateaux**). J.P.D.

Burra Charter

The standard for heritage conservation practice in Australia. Australia has a different heritage landscape to that of Europe; heritage managers deal with sites which may have had a history of human occupation for over 40,000 years but buildings for only 200 years. Australia **ICOMOS** started to review the applicability of the Venice Charter in 1977. In 1979, at a meeting in the South Australian town of Burra, the Australian ICOMOS Charter for the conservation of places of cultural significance was adopted, with the short title of the Burra Charter. A series of guidelines has been developed to explain aspects of the charter. G.H.

ADDITIONAL READING
Marquis-Kyle, P. and Walker, M., 1992, *The Illustrated Burra Charter*, Sydney.

Bursledon Wreck
see **Grace Dieu**

Butuan boats

Large plank-built wooden boats discovered in Ambangan, Butuan City, Agusan del Norte, southern Philippines, in the late 1970s. A total of eight boats are known to exist. Three have been excavated by the National Museum of the Philippines. Two of the boats are on exhibit and a third is undergoing conservation treatment. Butuan Boat One, excavated in 1977, has a radiocarbon date of AD 320; Butuan Boat Two, excavated in 1978, dates to 1250; and Butuan Boat Five, excavated in 1986, dates to 990. The locations of the wooden boats appear to be a former shoreline, a former estuary, and former tributaries of the Masao River. As the Philippines is a series of archipelagos, boats played a vital role in transportation, in commerce, and in helping to expand social contacts among population centres during the protohistoric period (AD 1000 to 1600).

The three boats average 15 m in length and 3 m across the beam. The remains indicate a manufacturing technique where the hull was built first like a shell and, plank by plank, was carved to fit together. Since the shell-first technique of boat-making provided no solid ribs to fasten the planks to, the planks could not have been steamed, bent, or held in place by nails, but instead had to be carved to shape in advance. The edges of the planks of the excavated boats were connected with dowels. The planks of Butuan Boat Two are made of two sections of hardwood joined by Z-shaped scarfs. The boats are characterized by a lashed-lug construction which is typical of Southeast Asian boat-making technology.

A distinctive feature of the wooden planks is a succession of flat rectangular protrusions or lugs which are carved out of the planks on the side which is on the inside of the boats. Placed exactly opposite one another on each plank, these lugs are 78 cm apart and have holes along their edges through which cords or lashings can be passed. The recovery of remains of the cordage, which are fibres of the palm *Arenga pinnata*, confirmed the function of the lugs.

In 1993 a careful examination and detailed analysis of Butuan Boat Two resulted in a more accurate reconstruction of the boat revealing some interesting details. The planks are made of a hardwood locally called 'Dongon' (*Heretiera litorales*). A series of scarf joints was observed at one end of the boat, two of which connected to a stem or sternpost. The stem or sternpost is of the 'winged' type, common in Southeast Asia and the Pacific and also frequently seen in Viking boats. A careful study and analysis of an excavation photograph of Butuan Boat Two showing one end of the boat indicated the relationship between the planks and the scarf joints. It was noted that all the scarf joints are of the hooked variety. This type is commonly used when the prime consideration is longitudinal strength since it locks the ends of planks together. An abrupt change in the shape at one end of the boat was made possible by the large number of scarf joints noted. This sudden change in shape could not have been possible by following the normal lines of the planks. The presence of the scarfs where the planks were fitted was the solution to address the problem of the need for more radically curved strakes. The practice of stacking a number of scarfs one on top of another, possibly in an attempt to increase the strength of the boat, is still common today in Southeast Asia and the Pacific.

Butuan Boat Five, the most complete of the three boats excavated, appears to have had eight strakes. Here, the uppermost strake had a different lug style which is triangular in cross-section. This could be the sheer strake where the frames terminated and a thwart was likely to have been fitted. This lug style was not found in the other boats because their upper strakes were missing. Butuan Boat Two might have had a total of eight strakes.

From the hypothetical form of Butuan Boat Two and the available surface area of the boat an estimate of the displacement of the hull was undertaken. A computation of the weight of the lashing material was also considered. With the density of the timber known, the estimated weight of the shell, the frames, and the assumed thwarts was calculated. The reconstructed empty hull is calculated to have weighed about 1,800 kg.

Whether the wooden boats originally had outriggers and where these would have been positioned in the boats cannot yet be ascertained. What is known, through computer simulations, is that the presence of outriggers could result in a dramatic increase in stability without greatly increasing the weight. Ronquillo believes that the Butuan boats did have outriggers.

The Butuan archaeological sites are waterlogged, and indicate both habitation and burial areas. The archaeological assemblage includes low-fired ceramics, high-fired tradeware ceramics from China dating from the Five Dynasties (907–60) to the Ming dynasty (1366–1644) as well as from Thailand and Vietnam; hundreds of palm-sized and thick earthenware crucibles; wooden tools, some in the shape of a pincer, a pick, and a knife; metal artefacts made of iron, bronze, lead, and gold in the form of an adze, a basin, bells, a blade, a cymbal, ear pendants, and iron slags; and a variety of animal and fish bone remains from ancient middens which include wild pigs, chicken, and small game. All indicate the existence of large population centres and coastal communities engaging in an active maritime trade network in Southeast Asia in the protohistoric period. W.R.2

ADDITIONAL READING
Cembrano, M.R., n.d., *Excavation in the Balangay Area, Butuan, Northeastern Mindanao*, Manila.
Clark, P. *et al.*, 1993, 'The Butuan Two Boat Known as a Balangay in the National Museum', *International Journal of Nautical Archaeology*, 22, 2, 143–8.
Horridge, G.A., 1982, *Lashed-lug Boats of the Eastern Archipelagoes*, National Maritime Museum Monographs 5, Greenwich, London.
Peralta, J.T., 1980, 'Ancient Mariners of the Philippines', *Archaeology*, 33, 5, 41–8.
Ronquillo, W.P., 1987, 'The Butuan Archaeological Finds: Profound Implications for Philippine and Southeast Asian Prehistory', *Man and Culture in Oceania*, 3, 71–8.
Scott, W.H., 1981, *Boat-building and Seamanship in Classic Philippine Society*, National Museum Archaeological Paper 9, Manila.

Caesarea Maritima

Harbour built by Herod the Great in the 1st century BC at Caesarea Maritima, Israel, and one of the most dramatic experiments in construction in the ancient world. It is the earliest example of a harbour of substantial size to be built with Roman concrete; the builders employed hydraulic cement (*pozzolana*) for concrete that was poured in place and underwater. The site has been recorded, excavated, and studied by a number of research teams over the past twenty years, and their results, combined with the literary testimonial of an eye-witness account, gives an excellent, yet incomplete, view of this vast project. A useful summary of various early teams and their work including Edwin Link, the Israel Undersea Exploration Society, the Center for Maritime Studies Survey for the Israel Electric Company, the CMS workshops, and the Joint Expedition Underwater Survey has been provided by Hohlfelder in J.P. Oleson's *The Harbours of Caesarea Maritima*, vol. 1, part 1, pp. 65–98. The results of the Caesarea Ancient Harbour Excavation Project (CAHEP) have appeared in two volumes of final reports edited by Oleson, as well as Robert L. Vann's *Caesarea Papers*, and the more popular *King Herod's Dream* by Holum *et al.*. General results of the Combined Caesarea Expeditions (CCE) are provided by Raban and the extraordinary work on the concrete formwork by Brandon.

The harbour and its host city were both parts of a vast building programme by the king of Judaea to improve his country's position in the lucrative arena of international trade for tariffs collected in a harbour of this size. In doing so, Herod was ultimately in competition with **Alexandria**, the greatest harbour in the ancient Mediterranean. Rome was also part of this scenario. After originally supporting Mark Antony and Cleopatra against the young Octavian – soon to be renamed Augustus and raised to position of Rome's first emperor – Herod skilfully realigned his political allegiance to serve as a client king for the empire. He built a great new city named for the emperor (Caesarea) and called its harbour Sebastos (Greek equivalent for 'emperor'). In return it appears that Rome provided architects and engineers to assist in building this strategically important harbour. The facility was of revolutionary design with enormous con-

crete breakwaters set directly into the open sea along a coast that had few suitable natural anchorages. The Romans had already developed and built in concrete (*opus caementicum*) for two centuries but never on such dramatic scale. Although its commercial promise was perhaps never achieved, and despite the fact that there were debilitating structural failures, the harbour of Caesarea Maritima has provided an excellent opportunity for underwater archaeologists from around the world. Here is a major harbour of the Roman period, important for its design, part of the record of written history, and perhaps most important, it remains submerged and available for investigation.

Herod built his harbour on the site of a delapidated but not yet abandoned settlement called Straton's Tower. Although the exact nature and extent of this first town remains in question, it appears to have been built around what later became the inner harbour and on the higher elevations of the site immediately to the north. An observation tower probably gave its name to the site. Raban has suggested that the principal anchorage was at the mouth of a stream and in the lee of a rocky outcropping to the south. Discovery of a suspected warehouse, including among other items a cache of more than two dozen terracotta jars for pickled fish, suggested the presence of a secondary anchorage further north in Area J (CAHEP).

According to historical accounts Herod and his builders completed the harbour at Caesarea in approximately ten years. How did they accomplish this feat and upon what models were their design and logistical organization based? We cannot be as certain of the predecessors of this harbour as we can be of its descendants. Caesarea appears to have been the first harbour in a series of later Roman examples that utilized the benefits of hydraulic cement. In the case of Sebastos, this material was used to pour huge concrete blocks that created artificial building platforms in open water. These, in turn, served as island bases for construction teams to simultaneously work on the breakwaters from both ends.

The harbour plan is easily recognized from the air and corresponds in its basic outline with the description of Josephus, the Jewish historian who visited the city 70 years later during the First Jewish Revolt. Two breakwaters defined its protected basin; that forming the southern and western sides measured 500 m and that on the north 250 m. The entrance lay to the northwest. Along these breakwaters were walls and towers, the tallest and grandest of which was called the

'Drusion' in honour of Augustus' deceased son-in-law. This feature, probably associated with the collapse of a major building near the harbour mouth at the tip of the west breakwater, has been identified by Vann as the site of Caesarea's lighthouse. Three towers stood outside the harbour entrance, two on the port side of an approaching ship and one to the starboard. Josephus states that on these platforms stood six columns carrying sculpted figures: these were probably statues of the imperial Roman family. Warehouses stood along the breakwaters.

The extensive archaeological record at Caesarea reinforces this literary description. Trenches (Areas A–C) by CMS and CAHEP defined the inner eastern edge of the western breakwater, revealing a long-established Levantine tradition of header construction used previously in Phoenician breakwaters. Later work by CAHEP (Areas D and G) explored the harbour entrance and Area H set the inner, southern side of the northern breakwater. The submerged twin towers standing west of the harbour entrance and the single tower to the east, Areas K and G respectively, proved to be enormous monoliths of concrete, some of the largest found in the harbour. The western towers stood 6.1 m and 3.3 m above the seabed and measured 5–7.5 m on a side. Horizontal cavities 20 by 30 cm were left from timber beams providing stability during construction.

The most significant discoveries during the excavations underwater at Caesarea have been in Areas G and K where the largest concrete blocks were located. In 1983 explorations in the former revealed a single block 11.5 m wide (east-west), 15 m long (noth-south) and preserved to a height of 2 m (4–5 m below sea-level). A visible vertical wall of concrete emerging from the sand led to the excavation and recovery of portions of timber framing of the forms into which concrete had been poured to form the northwest corner of the northern breakwater. A double wall stood on sleeper beams 29 sq. cm. Interior and exterior planking attached to vertical posts left a series of cavities around the perimeter of the block that were filled with the same concrete mixture as the block itself. The interior of the huge block had no floor but was stabilized by a series of horizontal and vertical supports which can still be recognized by their hollow horizontal cavities (18 sq. cm placed 1.6 m apart or approximately five Roman feet). Uprights, spaced 1.3 m apart, reinforced the horizontal beams until the concrete mixture set. The formwork was primarily of pine and fir while the mortise-and-tenon joints were fastened with oak and poplar. Subsequent analysis by Oleson and Brandon indicated that the timber as well as the cement for the concrete mixture came from the western Mediterranean.

Beginning in 1990, excavations in Area K-2 uncovered the remains of additional timber formwork belonging to the foundations of the large structure identified as the 'Drusion' or lighthouse of Caesarea. These remarkably preserved forms were carefully built in mortise-and-tenon technique and were probably the work of shipwrights well trained in that technique. The remains of several more wooden structures appeared during excavations in the early 1990s but this time with timber flooring. Chris Brandon has studied these forms and postulates that they were constructed south of the harbour so that they might be launched on the beach, and partially filled with concrete in order that they might lie lower in the water and be more stable during their brief trip north to the construction site. The offshore current which moves from south to north along this portion of the Mediterranean would have assisted this journey. Brandon believes that the builders first constructed artificial islands at the end of the western breakwater (Area K-2), at the bend between the southern and western portions of the larger breakwater, and at the western terminus of the northern breakwater (Area G). This practice is well known in later Roman construction, as at Ostia, where a large obelisk freighter was filled with concrete and sunk to create the basis of Claudius' lighthouse. Another such artificial island is recorded in one of the letters of Pliny the Younger, in his description of seeing a similar process being carried out at Centum Cellae.

More recent excavations by the CCE have included excavations in the silted inner harbour (CAHEP Area I). R.L.V.

ADDITIONAL READING

Holum, K.G. *et. al.*, 1988, *King Herod's Dream: Caesarea on the Sea*, London.

Oleson, J.P. (ed.), 1994, *The Harbours of Caesarea Maritima: Results of the Caesarea Ancient Harbour Excavation Project 1980–85, Vol. II: The Finds and the Ship*, BAR International Series 594, Oxford.

Raban, A., 1989, *The Harbours of Caesarea Maritima: Results of the Caesarea Ancient Harbour Excavation Project 1980–85, Vol. I, The Site and the Excavations*, BAR International Series 491, Oxford.

Raban, A. and Holum, K.G. (eds), *Caesarea Maritima: A Retrospective after Two Millenia*, Leiden and New York.

Vann, R.L., 1992, *Caesarea Papers: Straton's Tower, Herod's Harbour, and Roman and Byzantine Caesarea*, Journal of Roman Archaeology Supplementary Series no. 5.

USS *Cairo*

American Civil War ironclad gunboat salvaged in 1964 and reconstructed as an outdoor exhibition with an attached museum in Vicksburg, Mississippi. During the American Civil War, the Union's naval strategy against the Confederacy was primarily devoted to a blockade of Southern ports and harbours, and control of the Mississippi River, effectively dividing and isolating the rebellious Southern states. Specialized warships, drawing on the experience of western river steamboats, were built on the Mississippi and its tributaries. Known as the City class gunboats, most were built in late 1861 and early 1862. The City class gunboats merged both steam power and iron armour, inside a shallow draft, casemated, wooden hull. Steam inclined, reciprocating steam engines drove a recessed paddle wheel protected from gunfire by the casemates. Railroad iron laid over the casemates also protected the crew and the ship's armament.

USS *Cairo*, named for Cairo, Illinois, was built at Mound City, Illinois by James B. Eads in 1862. Displacing 888 tons, the 175 ft (53 m) long vessel was extremely broad, with a 51 ft (15.5 m) beam, and a shallow 6 ft (1.8 m) draft. She was lost on 12 December 1862 during naval operations in support of General U.S. Grant's siege of Vicksburg. *Cairo* and a flotilla of other ironclads advanced up the Yazoo River to assault Vicksburg's northern defences. 'Torpedoes' (mines) were electronically detonated under *Cairo*, tearing two holes in the hull. Settling rapidly, the ironclad was beached to allow the crew to escape. *Cairo* sank in twelve

The remains of USS Cairo *displayed in Vicksburg, Mississippi, USA, bow view. (J.P. Delgado)*

minutes. Despite interest in recovering the ironclad in 1864 and 1882, it was never salvaged.

The wreck of *Cairo* was rediscovered in 1956 by Edwin C. Bearss, research historian at Vicksburg National Military Park, and a companion, local historian Warren Grabau. Plotting the ironclad's location with naval records and old maps, they located the wreck with a handheld compass and an iron bar used to probe beneath the water and mud. In 1959–60, a series of dives by local divers surveyed the exterior of the wreck, and in September 1960 a salvage crane was used to pull the armoured pilothouse off the wreck and raise it to the surface. An 8 in naval gun was also pulled free of the casemate at the same time.

The intact hull of *Cairo*, filled with sand and silt, was a perfectly preserved, encapsulated archaeological site filled with the ship's ordnance, equipment, tackle, and the personal items of the crew who had so hastily abandoned the ship in December 1862. A local group, Operation Cairo, raised funds to recover the ship, with assistance from the State of Mississippi and local governments. Funds for raising the ironclad from the Yazoo were secured, but no money was raised to house or preserve the wreck, or its contents. The project failed to conduct the recovery with any archaeological controls, and materials were recovered in a primitive fashion without recording or mapping.

In 1963 an effort to raise the wreck intact

resulted in the removal of decking and hardware, which was discarded. Despite a well-publicized and highly successful contemporary effort by archaeologists to raise the intact warship **Vasa** in Sweden, *Cairo* was left in the hands of marine salvors who underestimated the ship's weight. In October 1964 crane barges, using lifting wires, tried to raise the hulk from the river. Filled with mud, the water-saturated hulk was cut and partially crushed by the cables, and only the bow was raised relatively intact. The midships portion of *Cairo* was crushed and demolished, and the stern collapsed and fell back into the river. A large amount of material that fell into the river, such as armour, the wheelhouse, entire sections of the casemates, and smaller artefacts, were never recovered. *Cairo*'s recovery was an archaeological disaster. The surviving pieces of the ship were barged to Pascagoula, Mississippi for cleaning, partial reassembly, and, hopefully, reconstruction. The smaller artefacts were cleaned, sorted, and catalogued by volunteers. These artefacts, as well as the ironclad's guns, were conserved and curated by the National Park Service at Vicksburg National Military Park.

Cairo's hull, machinery, and armour slowly rotted at Pascagoula. In 1977, after title to the wreck was passed from the State of Mississippi to the National Park Service, the surviving remains were barged back up the river to Vicksburg. Between 1977 and 1984 the wreck was stabilized, and its remaining fabric (about 15 per cent of the original vessel) was reinstalled on a laminated wooden framework that provides an exoskeleton support system while approximating the original appearance of *Cairo* in a 'ghosted' format. The wreck is displayed outside, beneath a cover structure. A nearby museum houses the *Cairo* artefacts and interprets the story of the ship, her loss, and the recovery and detailed reconstruction. Archaeologists and ship preservationists now view *Cairo* as an object lesson in how not to recover a shipwreck. J.P.D.

ADDITIONAL READING

Bearss, E.C., 1980, *Hardluck Ironclad: The Sinking and Salvage of the Cairo*, rev. edn. Baton Rouge, London.

McGrath, T.H., Jr, 1981, 'The Eventual Preservation and Stabilization of the USS *Cairo*', *International Journal of Nautical Archaeology and Underwater Exploration*, 10, 2, 79–94.

Caldicot Boat fragment
see **Severn wrecks**

Cape Fear Civil War Shipwreck District
The largest collection of American Civil War shipwrecks anywhere in the world. Cape Fear is one of three prominent capes that define the coast of North Carolina in the United States. Cape Fear, the southernmost, extends nearly 80 km seawards and is formed by shoals, inlets, and barrier islands that create a navigational hazard for vessels entering the Cape Fear River, which leads to the major port of Wilmington. The Cape Fear Civil War Shipwreck District represents the full range of rapidly evolving merchant vessels used to elude the Union naval blockade, as well as a complement of naval warships involved either in restricting or assisting merchant traffic.

The civil war came at a time in history when great technological changes were taking place in maritime construction. The two major innovations were the use of the steam engine both as a primary means of propulsion and as a supplement to sail and the use of iron in hull construction. Great Britain was the major area involved in developing these new techniques, though the United States and the other European powers were to a lesser extent also experimenting with and changing their ship designs. For many years, British ship makers had experienced increasing difficulty in procuring an adequate supply of high-quality timber with which to build ships, particularly oak. By the second decade of the 19th century iron manufacturing had developed to the point that it became economically and technologically feasible, in Great Britain, to use iron in the construction of ships. Along with this trend was the continued development of the steam engine and its use connected to a paddle wheel or screw to power ships.

The lack of marine facilities in the South forced the Confederacy to rely on seized vessels, or those that could be purchased abroad, in order to carry on vital foreign trade. The fleet of available vessels was quickly exhausted, with most being pressed into naval service. Great Britain with its active shipbuilding industry and established transatlantic trade relations became the logical supplier of merchant vessels for Southern trade.

The most vital element in blockade-running was acquiring a vessel capable of successfully eluding the Union blockade of Southern ports, which began in 1861. Sailing vessels carried the bulk of commerce early in the war. In 1861 there were 253 different sailing vessels known to have run the blockade off North and South Carolina. This number dropped to 145 in 1862, fifty-three in 1863, and fourteen in 1864. This reduction resulted from the realization that large sailing vessels were too slow to avoid the blockaders while the quicker schooners simply could not carry enough cargo. As Union strategists understood that steam vessels clearly would form the best blockade, the South arrived at a similar counter solution: steamships were needed to successfully run that blockade. Consequently, the number of blockade-running steamers arriving at Carolina ports increased from twenty-one in 1861, to forty-nine in 1862, seventy-three in 1863, and ninety-eight in 1864.

Shipping was of paramount importance during the civil war since the vast majority of both raw materials and manufactured goods, necessary to sustain the Confederate war effort, were transported across the Atlantic. The examination of such cargoes can add knowledge to the general understanding of Confederate trade and its economic system during the civil war. Bogus manifests and port records often obscured the actual supplies a blockade-runner was carrying. Content studies of surviving cargoes can point out the types of materials being exchanged with foreign markets. The proportions of imported items, particularly war supplies, civilian staples, and luxuries, reflect the needs and demands of the Confederacy and its attempt to regulate maritime trade.

During the Civil War, Wilmington, North Carolina, situated on the Cape Fear River several miles from the ocean, was one of the most valuable ports in the Confederacy. Blockade-running activities began early in 1861 and continued until January 1865, when Fort Fisher, a large earthwork fortification that guarded the entrance to the river, fell into Union control. The Cape Fear port provided blockade-runners with a geographically excellent entrance to the Confederacy, and the Union blockading squadron with a unique problem. Two inlets provided access to the Cape Fear River, separated by Smith Island and Frying Pan Shoals, which extend eastward into the Atlantic. This created the necessity for two blockading fleets isolated by almost 100 km of hazardous navigation. For the blockade-runners, this phenomenon provided the possibility of selecting the most opportune route of entrance and exit. The unique configuration, in conjunction with a complex series of fortifications that the Confederates constructed at the inlets and along the river, combined to frustrate Union attempts to close the port until the last months of the war.

During the Civil War at least thirty-one steam and twenty-two sail blockade-runners, as well as a wide assortment of Federal and

Confederate military vessels were lost in the Cape Fear River area. With the exception of USS *Peterhoff*, which was lost in a collision, all wrecks were stranded along the beach or on inlet shoals and sank in water less than 10 m deep. Upon wrecking, a vessel became the focus of furious attempts to save it and its cargo. The Federals had the decided advantage in efforts to recover the total vessel since they could approach from the sea with tugboats. The Confederates concentrated on a wreck's cargo, which was not only more important to their specific need, but could be unloaded with ease onto the beaches, which they controlled. Rough weather and artillery fire from the enemy hampered salvage attempts by either side. In only a few cases was a whole vessel refloated, or the cargo of a wrecked vessel completely salvaged. In most cases the Confederates recovered a small portion of the cargo before Union boarding parties destroyed both the vessel and cargo by setting them on fire. Steam machinery was often rendered useless at the time of wrecking by the removal or destruction of key parts by the vessel's crew.

Despite the destructive activities, Civil War wrecks were never as intensely salvaged as they might have been during peacetime. Time and conditions of the war did not permit major recovery of a wreck's machinery, cargo, or hull structure. After the war, when commercial salvors resumed normal activities, few of the Civil War wrecks were of interest. However, wreckers charged with removing or levelling sunken vessels that posed a threat to navigation did affect several Civil War wrecks.

On the whole, vessels lost during the Civil War have rested on the ocean or river bottom undisturbed by man's activities. However, the continuous pounding of the waves, shifting sands, and marine fouling organisms have degraded their structural integrity over the years. The degree and nature of deterioration has been directly affected by the type of wreck.

Steamers, with their heavy metal engines, support stanchions, and reinforced hulls, have held up the best. Those with iron hulls have fared far better than their wooden counterparts and often remain intact to the upper deck level in the stern and bow areas. In the fore and aft cargo compartments, the hull has generally broken near the turn of the bilge and fallen out, exposing the inner portions of the vessel, or fallen in on itself, offering some protection of artefact remains.

Wooden sailing vessels have most often broken apart, usually in large sections, which are widely scattered. Only heavy materials associated with the wreck, such as anchors, ballast, certain cargoes, and armament generally, remain on a wooden wreck site. Hull preservation *in situ* is often limited to the keel/keelson, floor frames, and bottom planking, which are weighted and covered by ballast.

Wrecks submerged in sea water are subject to deterioration by natural processes of decay, oxidation, and electrolysis, which occur rapidly at first and gradually diminish as a heavy layer of encrustation forms. Through time a delicate equilibrium is achieved which aids in a vessel's protection. Currently the Civil War wrecks lying in the lower Cape Fear area are in a relatively stable condition.

The locations of several wrecks have survived through oral tradition. Strong identifications have even been applied to a few blockade-runners, since a portion of each is still visible at low tide. However, most Civil War wrecks were forgotten soon after the war and their locations and identities were lost to the sea for nearly a century.

The invention of self-contained underwater breathing apparatus (**SCUBA**) and its popularization during the 1950s began a period of rediscovery of many wrecks in the Cape Fear area. Historians, most notably the late Charles Foard, curator of the Blockade Runner Museum in Carolina Beach, worked with pilots, who spotted menhaden for the fishing fleets, to search out, explore, and identify the forgotten hulks. When the water was very clear they were able to see wrecks lying below, mark them with buoys, and then return in boats to scuba dive. This was an exciting time of rediscovery for these early explorers. Local sport divers of the late 1950s and 1960s avidly examined and collected from at least ten Civil War wrecks. Although findings were often not recorded, helpful information has been gained from interviewing the divers. Some individuals set up backyard facilities to clean and stabilize small artefacts.

In 1962 local divers informed a team of **US Navy** frogmen, on vacation in the area, of the whereabouts of the blockade-runner *Modern Greece*. They reported that the wreck held a wealth of intact artefacts which had been exposed by a fierce storm earlier the same year. The US Navy and the North Carolina Division of Archives and History subsequently conducted a full-scale salvage operation at the wreck site and recovered over 10,000 artefacts – the largest single cache of Civil War period materials yet analysed.

During the early 1970s a group of very energetic sport divers began to collect accurate archaeological data on the blockade-runner *Ella* shipwreck site, and also began to address the problems inherent in working in the difficult nearshore environment. From 1974 to 1977 the State underwater archaeology programme spent a large part of their energies on the Cape Fear Civil War shipwrecks. They conducted bathometric and **Magnetometer** surveys along the nearshore waters from New Topsail Inlet to New Inlet. Subsequent site assessments and coal sampling were conducted on six wrecks.

Beginning in 1978 several survey and assessment projects conducted in the State as a result of the environmental review process took place in the Cape Fear area because of the possibility of encountering Civil War vessels. Because it was necessary to determine the significance of these shipwrecks, existing site data was compiled to gain an understanding of the overall Civil War shipwreck resource. This intensive focus by State underwater archaeologists resulted in the creation of the Cape Fear Civil War Shipwreck District, which was listed on **the National Register of Historic Places** in 1985.

The distribution of Civil War wrecks scattered along the coast as far south as Little River, at the North Carolina/South Carolina line, and to New Topsail Inlet, North Carolina, follows the historic boundaries originally established by Union naval leaders for the Wilmington flotilla. Shipwrecks are densest in the vicinity of the Cape Fear River inlets where the most intensive naval activities took place, and thin out from there in both directions. All wrecks lie close to shore and within the present State three mile (5 km) limit.

Currently there are twenty-one Civil War vessels listed on the National Register of Historic Places as part of Cape Fear Civil War Shipwreck District. As future survey and assessment activities are expanded, that number may nearly double. Fifteen wrecks are blockade-running steamers and represent each key step in the evolution of the classic Civil War blockade-runner. Furthermore, those fifteen wrecks represent nearly 20 per cent of all steam blockade-runners lost during the Civil War. The wreck of a British barque attempting to run the blockade is also a part of this group. Nowhere in the world is there a comparable concentration of vessel remains from this period.

Four Union and one Confederate military vessels are also included in the district. Although not nearly as significant in terms of the percentage of overall Civil War naval losses, this group represents a good cross-section of ships used in conjunction with blockade-running activities. Two bar tenders, an ex-blockade-runner, and an ironclad are part of the military wreck assemblage.

Cape Gelidonya Wreck

Late Bronze Age shipwreck site near Finike on the south coast of Turkey, excavated in 1960 and dated to approximately 1200 BC by comparative artefact studies and radio-

VESSELS LISTED IN THE CAPE FEAR CIVIL WAR SHIPWRECK DISTRICT

BLOCKADE-RUNNERS	DATE LOST	VESSEL TYPE	DATE BUILT
Modern Greece	27 Jun 1862	Iron screw steamer	1859
Sophia	5 Nov 1862	Wood bark sail	unknown
Hebe	18 Aug 1863	Iron twin screw steamer	1863
Elizabeth	3 Sep 1863	Wood sidewheel steamer	1852
Arabian	15 Sep 1863	Wood sidewheel steamer	1851
Phantom	23 Sep 1863	Steel screw steamer	1863
Duoro	11 Oct 1863	Iron screw steamer	1863
Venus	21 Oct 1863	Iron sidewheel steamer	unknown
Beauregard	11 Dec 1863	Iron sidewheel steamer	1858
Bendigo	4 Jan 1864	Iron sidewheel steamer	1863 (?)
Ranger	11 Jan 1864	Iron sidewheel steamer	1863
Wild Dayrell	1 Feb 1864	Iron sidewheel steamer	1863
Lynx	26 Feb 1864	Steel sidewheel steamer	1864
Condor	1 Oct 1864	Iron sidewheel steamer	1864
Ella	3 Dec 1864	Iron sidewheel steamer	1864
Stormy Petrel	15 Dec 1864	Iron sidewheel steamer	1864
USS *Iron Age*	11 Jan 1864	Wood screw steamer – bar tender	1862
USS *Peterhoff*	6 Mar 1864	Iron screw steamer – ex-blockade-runner	Pre-war
CSS *Raleigh*	7 May 1864	Wood screw steamer – ironclad	1863/64
USS *Aster*	8 Oct 1864	Wood screw steamer – bar tender	unknown
USS *Louisiana*	24 Dec 1864	Iron screw steamer – powder ship	1860

The Cape Fear Civil War Shipwreck District preserves a physical record of an important part of United States history. The shipwrecks within it provide the means to understand more fully the Civil War period through the development and utilization of their historical, archaeological, educational, and recreational potential. M.W.R.

ADDITIONAL READING

Bright, L.S., 1977, *The Blockade Runner Modern Greece and Her Cargo*, Raleigh, North Carolina.

Naval History Division, 1964–5, *Civil War Naval Chronology, Parts IV and V: 1864 and 1865*, Washington, DC.

Selfridge, T.O., Jr, 1956, 'The Navies at Fort Fisher', in *Battles and Leaders of the Civil War, Vol. IV*, New York.

Soley, J.R., 1898, *The Navy in the Civil War: The Blockade and the Cruisers*, New York.

Wilkinson, J., 1877, *The Narrative of a Blockade Runner*, New York.

Wise, S.R., 1988, *Lifeline of the Confederacy: Blockade Running During the American Civil War*, Columbia, South Carolina.

carbon analysis. At the time the world's oldest known shipwreck and the only one to be excavated in its entirety on the seabed, the site yielded more than a tonne of metal cargo along with metalworking tools and personal possessions, which suggest it was the ship of an itinerant smith of Syrian or Cypriot origin. The site provided valuable information about the nature and materials of international trade in the Late Bronze Age Mediterranean region.

In 1959 Turkish sponge divers led journalist and amateur archaeologist Peter Throckmorton to the site of a shipwreck at Cape Gelidonya, approximately 32 km west of Finike, near Antalya. The sponge divers had planned to dynamite the site and sell the concreted pieces of bronze visible on the seabed for scrap. Instead, at the invitation of the Turkish Government, George F. Bass, a graduate student of classical archaeology at the University of Pennsylvania, and Throckmorton led a three-month excavation of the site in 1960. It was the first underwater exca-

vation in the Mediterranean region in which the directing archaeologist dived and excavated. Despite the difficulties presented by working under water, the team adhered to standards of land excavation, adapting methods as necessary for the underwater environment.

The site lay just offshore between 26 and 30 m deep on an irregular rocky bottom. The team camped near by at the base of a sheer cliff on a narrow strip of beach that offered two freshwater springs for drinking and for artefact desalination, and a cave that was used as a darkroom. Diving operations were conducted from two sponge boats moored directly over the site and equipped with a winch and air compressors.

As a mapping aid, a photographic montage was composed by means of a diver swimming over the site at a fixed height along evenly spaced lines of string. All objects were labelled with plastic identification tags, and their positions measured to within a few centimetres by triangulation from datum points (iron spikes driven into the seabed). Detailed pencil drawings were made on sheets of frosted plastic attached to clipboards. An average of fifty photographs was taken and processed each day to record artefact positions and excavation methods, and to allow for discussion of the following day's work, as team members could not confer on the seabed.

Sandy areas were excavated by hand-fanning the sand towards one of two hand-held **Airlifts**, or long suction pipes 5 cm and 10 cm in diameter, which carried the explored sand away from the site. Small artefacts were brought to the surface in plastic bags, larger ones in wicker or steel baskets raised either with the boat's winch or with air-filled balloons. Most of the objects were firmly attached to one another and to the seabed by a thick overgrowth of rock-hard marine concretion. Rather than chisel free each object under water, which would have required many additional months of work, large lumps of concreted artefacts, some weighing several hundred kilos, were freed with hammer and chisel and a hydraulic jack. These were raised and reassembled on the beach-camp as they had lain on the seabed, in an effort to preserve the original lading pattern of the ship. The concretion was then cleaned away, and the artefacts were drawn in their original positions.

Bass and a team from the **Institute of Nautical Archaeology** (INA), which he founded in 1973, returned to Cape Gelidonya in 1987 and unexpectedly found several more artefacts. Realizing that the site had not been excavated as completely as had been thought in

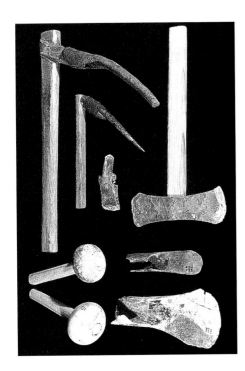

Stone hammers and bronze tools found at Cape Gelidonya. (© INA)

1960, the team returned in 1988 and 1989 to conduct a systematic survey and found many artefacts outside the area originally explored.

The primary cargo of the ship consisted of copper and bronze ingots and ingot fragments of the so-called 'ox-hide' (four-handled), 'bun' (plano-convex discoid), and 'slab' (flat oval) shapes. Many were still stacked on the seabed as they had been in the hold of the ship, with traces of matting and brushwood dunnage, used as protective cushioning, preserved beneath. The thirty-four copper oxhide ingots (averaging 60 cm long, 45 cm wide, 4 cm thick, and 21 kg in weight) are of a type found at many Bronze Age sites in the Mediterranean region and depicted in Egyptian tomb paintings of the 15th to 12th centuries BC, almost always as tribute brought to the pharaoh by men of Retenu (Syria). Several bear stamped or incised marks that are still undeciphered. Lead-isotope analyses indicate they are made of copper ore from Cyprus. Remains of tin ingots were found in the form of a white toothpaste-like corrosion product.

Also on board were hundreds of whole and fragmentary bronze tools, weapons, and other objects, some with well-preserved traces of the wicker baskets that carried them: picks, hoes, double axes, adzes, chisels, awls, knives, hooks, a needle, a shovel, a mattock, a sickle, a spatula, spearheads, fragments of one or two tripods and an offering stand, unworked castings, casting waste, and unidentifiable scrap. Nearly all the tools are

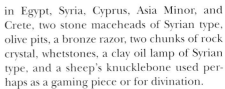

Cemal Pulak carries a large stirrup jar found intact at Cape Gelidonya. (© INA)

Cypriot or Syrian types, and taken together closely resemble metal hoards found on Cyprus that are dated with some controversy to either the 13th or the 12th century BC. Except for a few complete and unique pieces, the Cape Gelidonya metals are presumed to have been scrap to be sold, remelted, and made into new objects. Hammerstones, a whetstone, stone polishers, two stone 'anvils', and a bronze swage block for hammering out pins and similar items were undoubtedly tools used on board to make new objects.

Careful mapping of each artefact on the site revealed that all the personal items came from an area at one end of the ship (the east end of the site), probably the cabin or living quarters of the captain and crew. These items include a Syrian cylinder seal for marking official documents, five scarabs made on the Syro-Palestinian coast in imitation of Egyptian ones, several sets of haematite pan-balance weights containing the standards that would have allowed trade

in Egypt, Syria, Cyprus, Asia Minor, and Crete, two stone maceheads of Syrian type, olive pits, a bronze razor, two chunks of rock crystal, whetstones, a clay oil lamp of Syrian type, and a sheep's knucklebone used perhaps as a gaming piece or for divination.

Artefacts found elsewhere on the wreck include a bronze sword, a bronze pan-balance weight in the shape of a bull's head, several hundred glass beads, ballast stones, a large ceramic *pithos*, and a fragment of lead-tin alloy. Ceramics, mainly fragmentary, include water jars, cooking pots, bowls, two large Mycenaean stirrup jars dated to the late 13th century BC, and Cypriot wares.

The rocky bottom did not allow more than a few fragments of the wooden hull to survive attack by shipworm. Tenons with wooden treenails driven through them suggest mortise-and-tenon joinery typical of 'shell-first' hull construction, in which a shell of planks is partly or completely erected before any framing elements are added.

Bass interprets the shipwreck as that of a 9 m vessel which had been sailing along the south Anatolian coast with a merchant-smith on board, stopping to barter scrap metal, other cargo items, and newly fashioned tools. The artefacts interpreted as personal possessions rather than cargo suggest that this merchant was Syrian. The ship may have sailed from a Syro-Palestinian port, stopped in Cyprus to pick up a metal cargo, then continued westward. The primarily Cypriot cargo requires that a Cypriot origin for the ship not be ruled out, however.

Bass's research led him to propose that maritime activity in the Bronze Age Mediterranean was not controlled by Mycenaean

Syrian cylinder seal found at Cape Gelidonya, and its impression in clay. (© INA)

Greeks, as held by many scholars, but that Near Eastern (particularly Syrian, or 'proto-Phoenician') seafarers played a significant if not dominant role, trading along routes similar to those used by Phoenician merchants two to four centuries later. He also suggested that Homer's mention of 'Phoenician' sailors in the Bronze Age, at the time of the Trojan War, was not an anachronism of the period in which he wrote, the 8th century BC. Mycenaean dominance had been assumed by many because large numbers of Mycenaean trade items are found in eastern Mediterranean lands, but few eastern items in Greek lands. Bass and others suggested a return trade from east to west in raw materials and perishables, such as metals, ivory, spices, and textiles, which

would leave little trace on land sites. Excavation between 1984 and 1994 of another Late Bronze Age shipwreck at **Uluburun**, 48 km to the west of Cape Gelidonya, also appears to support this theory.

The Cape Gelidonya ship is dated to 1200 ± 50 BC by comparative analysis of the bronze tools, scarabs, and pottery, and by carbon-14 analysis of brushwood dunnage. The well-dated Mycenaean jars found in 1988 favour a date for the shipwreck (and therefore for the Cypriot metal hoards) before rather than after 1200 BC.

The artefacts raised from Cape Gelidonya in 1960 were deposited in the 15th-century Crusader castle of the Knights of St John, in the small harbour town of Bodrum, forming the first collection of what is now the Bodrum Museum of Underwater Archaeology. C.P.

ADDITIONAL READING

Bass, G.F., 1967, 'Cape Gelidonya: A Bronze Age Shipwreck', *Transactions of the American Philosophical Society*, 57, 8.

Bass, G.F., 1975, *Archaeology Beneath the Sea*, New York.

Bass, G.F., 1988, 'Return to Cape Gelidonya', *Institute of Nautical Archaeology Newsletter*, 15, 2, 3–5.

Bass, G.F., 1989, 'Cape Gelidonya – Once More', *Institute of Nautical Archaeology Newsletter*, 16, 4, 12–13.

Bass, G.F., 1991, 'Evidence of Trade from Bronze Age Shipwrecks', in N.H. Gale (ed.), *Bronze Age Trade in the Mediterranean: Studies in Mediterranean Archaeology*, Jonsered, 90, 69–82.

Pulak, C., 1988, 'Excavations in Turkey: 1988 Campaign', *Institute of Nautical Archaeology Newsletter*, 15, 4, 13–17.

Throckmorton, P., 1987, 'Sailors in the Time of Troy', in Throckmorton, P. (ed.), *The Sea Remembers: Shipwrecks and Archaeology*, New York.

Capo Rasocolmo Wreck

Roman wreck, dating between 43 and 36 BC, discovered in 1991 near the reef of Capo Rasocolmo on the northeast coast of Sicily. In 1991 the Milan-based Cooperativa Aquarius, under the direction of Alice Freschi, conducted a survey of the area for the Soprintendenza ai Beni Culturali of Messina. A number of ancient wrecks have been discovered in the area, including the **Straits of Messina** (or Porticello) **Wreck**, and unfortunately many have been looted.

Cooperativa Aquarius divers surveying the eastern side of Capo Rasocolmo discovered the wreck in 8 m of water on a sand and rock bottom in an area c. 21 by 12 m. The site was marked by a number of small mill-

stones, melted lead sheathing, and a bronze swan-shaped artefact identified as a boat cleat. Metal detector survey of the surrounding area defined a site for excavation, which was conducted with an **Airlift**.

A number of artefacts were recovered whose positions and type indicated that the remains were those of a warship's port side. A number of iron nails, pieces of copper sheathing, nine of the swan-shaped cleats, several other bronze objects, an iron anchor, half of a removable anchor stock, and concretions were recovered. Particularly diagnostic were fifteen broken lavic millstones lying on an axis. This, and the fact that a functional pair could not be assembled, indicated that the millstones had been used as ballast, as had been the case with the **Kyrenia Ship** and other wrecks.

The presence of 131 *glans* (sling shots) and the absence of cargo suggest that the wreck is that of a warship. A number of bronze coins were excavated along with a small copper plaque. The coins, *asses* or *semisses*, have a double-headed Janus on the obverse and the word MAGNVS and the prow of a ship with the words PIVS IMP. The Janus represents Pompeius Magnus (Pompey the Great); the coins may be coins struck by Sextus Pompeius, son of Magnus, just prior to his defeat at the Battle of Naulochus in 36 BC. Sextus Pompeius used Sicily as his base of operations against Rome between 43 and 36 BC, when he was defeated by Agrippa, one of the lieutenants used by Octavian (the future Augustus) to consolidate his control of the emerging Roman Empire. The copper plaque is inscribed C . . .P. MAGNVS, another association with Pompey.

The Cooperativa Aquarius, noting the location of the wreck near the site modern scholars identify as Naulochus, the association with Pompeius Magnus or Sextus Pompeius, and the approximate date of the wreck, have tentatively ascribed it as either a Battle of Naulochus battle loss in 36 BC or an earlier foundering of one of Sextus' fleet between 43 and 36 BC. J.P.D.

ADDITIONAL READING

Freschi, A., 1995, 'An Ancient Warship in the Waters off Capo Rasocolmo, Sicily', in M. Bound (ed.), *The Archaeology of Ships of War*, Oswestry, Shropshire.

Capricieux

see **Louisbourg wrecks**

Caribbean

Region encompassing the Caribbean Sea, rich in maritime history from prehistoric times onwards. The Caribbean was a major crossroads of shifting colonial power and

Aerial view of the treacherous reefs where the wreck of the Ten Sail occurred. (Dennis Denton)

waterborne commerce among European nations, particularly Spain, England, France, and the Netherlands from the 16th to the 19th centuries. It is, therefore, the location of thousands of significant maritime archaeological sites, including prehistoric and historical coastal settlements, fortifications, lighthouses, shipbuilding sites, ports, and harbours as well as shipwrecks and related contemporary salvage sites.

Most islands in the West Indies were occupied prehistorically by aceramic and/or ceramic-age cultures, though their origins and routes of migration are matters of debate. There is no doubt, however, that settlement was accomplished by people who used watercraft. Upon his arrival in the New World in 1492, Columbus was greeted by indigenous people paddling dugout canoes. While few examples of surviving craft have been discovered by archaeologists, it is apparent that prehistoric Caribbean seafarers were adapted to coastal settlement and procured marine resources. **Mexico**, Central American, **South American**, and island countries bordering the Caribbean Sea, as well as overseas academic institutions from the **United States**, Canada, **United Kingdom**, **France**, the Netherlands, and Spain, have focused attention on the study of prehistoric sites in the region. In 1995, for example, a ceremonial Lucayan canoe was found in the 'Stargate' blue hole (a submerged cenote) of Andros Island. The

vessel was investigated by the University of South Carolina Institute of Archaeology and Anthropology at the invitation of the Bahama Islands Government.

The first recorded European explorations of the Caribbean were accomplished by Christopher Columbus during four Spanish voyages undertaken between 1492 and 1504. The *nao Santa Maria* wrecked during the first voyage, while the caravels *Mariagalante*, **La Gallega**, *San Juan*, and *Cardera* were lost during the second, all off the north coast of Hispaniola. The third voyage claimed no shipwrecks, but the fourth brought the loss of the caravels *Gallega* at Rio Belén and *Vizcaína* at Portobelo, Panama. The caravels *Capitana* and *Santiago de Palos* were run aground in St Ann's Bay, Jamaica. Since the early 1980s the **Institute of Nautical Archaeology** (INA) has mounted archaeological surveys and test-excavations to locate remains of Columbus's ships in Hispaniola, Jamaica, and Panama, while Ships of Exploration and Discovery Research (SEDR) has launched expeditions in search of *Gallega* in Panama. In the late 1990s a cooperative Indiana University/Panamerican Consultants project continues the quest for Columbus's ships off Hispaniola.

Remains of other early 16th-century ships of exploration and discovery have been found in the Caribbean region. Although positive identifications are lacking, three

wreck sites were investigated in the 1980s by the INA: the **Molasses Reef Wreck** in the Turks and Caicos Islands; the **Highborn Cay Wreck** in the Bahamas; and in cooperation with the Instituto Nacional de Antropología e Historia (INAH), the **Bahía Mujeres Wreck** off the northeast coast of Mexico's Yucatán Peninsula. The Molasses Reef Wreck was fully excavated in the 1980s, all artefacts were conserved, and SEDR, working in cooperation with the Turks and Caicos National Museum, prepared an exhibition which today forms the central exhibition of the National Museum. Further investigations were undertaken on the Bahía Mujeres Wreck in a joint INAH/SEDR project in the 1990s. The site of another 16th-century vessel, the **St John's Bahamas Wreck**, was discovered on the Little Bahama Bank in 1991.

European navigators in the 16th century knew that it was advantageous to follow prevailing winds and ocean currents when sailing to and from the New World, so they set about learning them. Entering the Caribbean through the Lesser Antilles, ships could exit through the Windward, Mona, and Anegada passages. It was even more expedient to maintain a westward course to the Leeward Passage, by which ships would exit through the Yucatán Channel, enter the Gulf Stream, and follow the currents through the Straits of Florida out into the Atlantic for the return passage to Europe. Soon, distant colonies and seaborne trade

Archaeologist examining anchor, probably from the Wreck of the Ten Sail. (Mike Guderian)

networks were established in the West Indies.

Spain claimed a monopoly on all the New World territories encountered during Spanish voyages until the latter half of the 17th century. The country capitalized on procuring precious metals, though these were quickly depleted in the West Indies. While Spanish interests shifted to exploit the gold and silver resources of Mexico, Bolivia, and Peru, Spain's main administrative centre remained in Hispaniola. By 1535, however, Mexico City displaced Santo Domingo, and in 1544 a second centre was created in Lima, Peru. Cuba, adjacent to the Leeward Passage and Straits of Florida, remained strategically valuable to Spain. Although single armed merchantmen made the passage, by 1537 Spain organized a regularly scheduled convoy system, whereby merchant ships loaded with cargoes of gold, silver, and pearls would sail together under the protection of armed vessels to ensure a safe passage back to Spain. But Caribbean shoals and hurricanes claimed numerous Spanish treasure ships over the course of three centuries. In recent decades, archaeologists have investigated Spanish merchantmen, including ships of the 1554 flota excavated by the Texas Antiquities Committee off Padre Island, Texas (see **Padre Island Wrecks**), and the Cayo Nuevo Wreck documented by a joint INA/INAH project in the Gulf of Mexico, but the majority of sites that have been located have been salvaged by treasure-hunters, whose methods and ethics regarding historical resources are not consistent with those of scientific archaeology. Among shipwreck sites worked by salvors are well-known names such as *San Pedro* and *San Antonio* off Bermuda, *Nuestra Señora de Atocha* in the Florida Keys, *Nuestra Señora de la Concepción* on the Silver Bank of Hispaniola, and *Nuestra Señora de Guadalupe* and *Conde de Tolosa* off the northeast coast of Hispaniola. Although vessels of the **Flota of 1715** located off the east coast of Florida were compromised by treasure-hunters, archaeologists investigated the *Urca de Lima*. In 1987 the site became Florida's first Underwater Archaeological Preserve. Likewise, remains of the **Flota of 1733** that wrecked in the Florida Keys were first impacted by salvors. In recent times, however, State of Florida archaeologists have begun scientific studies of a number of these ships. In 1996 East Carolina University began a general survey of the waters of Anguilla which will include assessment of two 1772 inbound Spanish merchantmen.

In the 16th and 17th centuries England, France, and the Netherlands challenged Spain's monopoly to weaken her trade with the Spanish colonies and to establish their own presence in the New World. Both official and entrepreneurial ventures were undertaken. By the early 1600s the English and French began to settle the eastern Caribbean; the Dutch established an extensive commercial network. Meanwhile, the Spanish colonies frequently engaged in the illicit import of European products and African slaves from passing foreign merchant ships. In the Dominican Republic, the Pan-American Institute of Maritime Archaeology is in the late 1990s investigating a 17th-century interloper into the Spanish colonies, though it is hypothesized that the ship was en route from Europe to North America via the Caribbean when it wrecked. The **Monte Cristi Wreck** appears to be an English-built merchantman carrying a Dutch cargo, primarily clay tobacco pipes of Amsterdam manufacture, which wrecked between 1652 and 1656 off the north coast of Hispaniola.

During the mid-17th century England and France moved to establish permanent settlements in the western Caribbean. In 1655 the English seized Jamaica from Spain, although Spain did not recognize the English claim until 1670, by the Treaty of Madrid. In 1655 the French took Tortuga and later occupied the western third of Hispaniola. Known to the French as St Dominique, Spain finally recognized France's right to the colony in 1697, by the Treaty of Ryswick. The century was an era of pirates and privateers. In 1979 the INA investigated the Turtle Wreck, an English turtle-fishing vessel thought to have been burned in 1670 by a Spanish privateer, Manuel Rivero Pardal, in the Cayman Islands. In 1692 an earthquake devastated the thriving English colonial city of **Port Royal, Jamaica**. As a result large portions of the town, as well as contemporary ships, were buried in the sediments of Kingston harbour. Several groups have conducted archaeological investigations at the site, but the most recent and comprehensive work was undertaken by Texas A&M University in cooperation with the Jamaican Government. The Trinidad and Tobago National Museum has been successful in having their government enact legislation to protect newly discovered French Louis XIV-period ship-wrecks buried in the harbour sediments of Trinidad.

In the 18th century, Britain and France were the dominant European powers in the Caribbean. Both capitalized on the lucrative sugar-producing industry which served international markets. Both countries protected their colonies and their merchant

Two divers excavating with water dredges within the brick walls of a structure at Port Royal, Jamaica. (Donny Hamilton)

trade with naval strength. Through a series of wars, these two nations found themselves on opposing sides: the War of Spanish Succession (1702–13), the Seven Years War (1756–63), the American War of Independence (1775–83), the French Revolutionary Wars (1792–1802), and the Napoleonic Wars (1803–15). Spain and the Netherlands were inconsistently allied with the two major powers. Numerous European merchantmen and warships wrecked during this period in the Caribbean. At least six 18th-century wrecks have been discovered in the 1990s in St Ann's Bay, Jamaica, by the INA working in cooperation with the Jamaican government; one British sloop, the **Reader's Point Wreck**, was investigated in detail. Between 1990 and 1993 research was accomplished on the wreck of the **Ten Sail**, under the auspices of the Cayman Islands National Museum and with additional support from Texas A&M University. This disaster, which occurred in 1794, involved HMS *Convert* and nine produce-laden merchantmen of a Europe-bound convoy. The study resulted in a special 200th anniversary exhibition, in 1994, at the Cayman Islands National Museum. Between 1994 and 1995 investigations were undertaken in St Maarten, Netherlands Antilles, on HMS *Proselyte*, a captured Dutch frigate previously named *Jason* which wrecked in 1801; this was a cooperative project between the St Maarten National Heritage Foundation, the St Maarten Department of Planning and Environment, and Maritime Archaeology and Research. The Dutch frigate *Alphen* which exploded and sank in 1778 in St Annabay, Curacao is in the late 1990s under investigation by the Institute of Archaeology and Anthropology of the Netherlands Antilles.

The 19th century marked the end of the Age of Sail and the flourishing of the Age of Steam. The Underwater Archaeological Council in **Puerto Rico** has investigated two Spanish steamships of this era, the *Alicante* which was lost in 1881, and the *Antonio López* which wrecked in 1898 during the Spanish-American War.

Even 20th-century sites in the Caribbean attract the attention of archaeologists. *Geneva Kathleen*, a three-masted schooner which wrecked with a load of lumber in the Cayman Islands in 1930, is being non-intrusively documented by Ball State University.

Unless treasure salvors are allowed to severely compromise sites, much work remains to be undertaken in Caribbean maritime and underwater archaeology.
M.E.L.

ADDITIONAL READING

Bass, G.F. (ed.), 1988, *Ships and Shipwrecks of the Americas*, London.

Keith, D.H., 1987, *The Molasses Reef Wreck*, Ph.D. thesis, Texas A&M University, University Microfilms, Ann Arbor, Michigan.

Leshikar, M.E., 1993, *The 1794 'Wreck of the Ten Sail', Cayman Islands, British West Indies: A Historical Study and Archaeological Survey*, Ph.D. thesis, Texas A&M University, University Microfilms, Ann Arbor, Michigan.

Smith, R.C., 1993, *Vanguard of Empire*, New Yale.

Throckmorton, P. (ed.), 1987, *The Sea Remembers*, London.

USS *Carlisle*
see **Crossroads wrecks**

Casting

The process of casting the natural moulds left by corroded metal artefacts. The importance of this process in nautical archaeology cannot be over-emphasized: in some cases, only through casting can the object be saved or its form determined. Metal objects, even within an encrustation, can continue to corrode until little or no metal remains. In such cases, the original surfaces with identification marks, stamps, letters, or numbers are lost. Fortunately, the encasing encrustation begins to form immediately at the onset of the corrosion process, forming a mould and preserving details of the original form as well as marks or stamps. Occasionally, the encrustation is more informative than the deteriorated or badly oxidized object. It is this critical part of conservation that is often overlooked, and the older the site the more critical it becomes. For instance, the majority of the small iron artefacts from **Port Royal, Jamaica** which date from 1692, and the 1554 **Padre Island Wrecks** have completely corroded, leaving only a void within the encapsulating encrustation. These artefacts can be recovered by breaking into a strategic area of the encrustation, cleaning out the void, filling the void with epoxy, and then using a pneumatic air scribe to remove the marine encrustation surrounding the epoxy cast. It is through casting the natural moulds inside encrustations that the complete array of

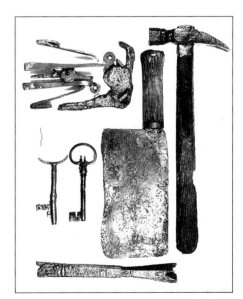

Array of iron objects recovered by casting natural moulds left in the encrustation formed around iron artefacts. They include a hammer head and a cleaver blade cast on original wood handles, a side lock mechanism for a door, two keys, and a socketed chisel. (© INA/Donny Hamilton)

small iron tools present at both sites could be recovered. Hundreds of epoxy casts of iron objects from Port Royal have been made and include items such as keys, hammers, cleavers, and a number of door locks. In many instances the epoxy cast of an object such as a hammer is made around the surviving wood handle.

The first published account of casting used in marine **Conservation** as a means of retrieving completely oxidized artefacts is that reported by Katzev and van Doorninck in 1966. Utilizing a lapidary saw, they sectioned small encrustations containing natural moulds left by oxidized Byzantine iron tools. Some specimens required only one cut, other more complicated objects required several cuts. The corrosion residue was removed from the natural moulds and a cardboard or plastic gasket made to fit between the sawn halves to compensate for the material removed by the saw blade. The mould was then filled with a flexible compound and the halves fitted together. After the compound cured, the rubber cast was removed and the excess rubber along the seams of the mould was cut off with scissors or knives, resulting in a flexible replica of the disintegrated artefact. This technique is seldom used any more because of the difficulties in cutting even simple encrusted objects, the need to place a gasket between the cut halves to replace the thickness cut away by the saw blade, the difficulties in aligning the two halves, the short life of the cast objects, and the need to make another mould and cast it in epoxy for a permanent cast. When X-ray facilities are available, some of the problems of casting natural moulds can be overcome because the conservator is able to determine the condition and shape of the object before casting starts.

Natural moulds of disintegrated metal objects are often encountered in very large encrustations, where they cannot be detected on radiographs even if they could be X-rayed. To avoid destroying possible valuable information, close observation is required when the encrustations are being taken apart with the air chisels to detect the moulds before they are destroyed. Once exposed, it is usually possible to clean the mould out and fill it with epoxy. Complex artefacts and multiple artefacts encrusted together present some very difficult problems.

The recommended procedure is to break open the encrustation and fill the void with epoxy. If possible, in the case of long, spike-shaped encrustations, the piece is merely snapped in half. The exposed void is then cleaned out with jets of water and wire

probes. After cleaning the natural mould left by the disintegrated object, it is filled with an epoxy and the two halves placed back together. By breaking the object, a rough irregular surface is produced which allows the conservator to align the pieces exactly with little or no resulting flash line. After curing, the object is then removed with a pneumatic chisel and a permanent cast is produced. Black epoxy can be used, or black paint or graphite can be applied to white epoxy casts to create a more realistic-looking cast.

Casting is not just required for corroded iron artefacts. Various casting techniques are often used in recovering stamps from corroded silver specimens. The surfaces of silver discs and bars found on mid-16th- and 17th-century Spanish shipwrecks often are stamped with a variety of marks or stamps indicating ownership, mines, and tax marks. Frequently the stamps are obliterated in the corrosion process. The encrustation that forms on the surface of silver in marine environments often forms a perfect mould of the original surface of the silver, preserving reverse impressions of the stamp. When processing silver objects, the adhering encrustation should be removed as intact as possible in order to preserve any marks. If any marks are detected, they can be cleaned with fine brushes to remove any adhering corrosion products. A flexible casting compound peel can then be applied to the impression of the mark. Once the peel cures, it can be removed, revealing the original marks that may now be missing from the silver. Many otherwise lost stamps have been recovered by this procedure, which should be routinely incorporated into the conservation of all encrusted silver objects.

A very strong case can be made for the value and significance of casting in the conservation of marine shipwreck material. If casting is not routinely resorted to, then considerable data will be lost. This fact emphasizes the reasons why marine shipwreck material should be processed by personnel familiar with the material culture and the alternative techniques of salvaging and preserving the maximum amount of data. Casts of objects and marks provide the archaeologist with data obtainable from no other source. There is no limit to what can be recovered by casting if one proceeds cautiously and deliberately. D.L.H.

ADDITIONAL READING

Hamilton, D.L., 1976, *Conservation of Metal Objects from Underwater Sites: A Study in Methods*, Texas Memorial Museum Miscellaneous Papers 4; Texas Antiquities Committee Publication 1, Austin, Texas.

Katzev, M.L. and van Doorninck, F., 1966, 'Replicas of Iron Tools from a Byzantine Shipwreck', *Studies in Conservation*, 11, 3, 133–42.

Muncher, D.A., 1988, 'Composite Casting of Partially Degraded Iron Artefacts', *Studies in Conservation*, 33, 94–6.

Cattewater Wreck

Early 16th-century armed merchantman wrecked at Plymouth, Devon, England. The wreck is of primary importance in our understanding of the development of 16th-

Model at a scale of 1:10 of the Cattewater Wreck. The black area was not excavated. (Model by M. Redknap)

century European ship design. Contemporary shipwrights' plans do not exist for this period, at a time when the three-masted skeleton-built (frame-oriented) ship had developed as a standard seagoing vessel in northern Europe. Devon ships probably shared this tradition, but there is little first-hand information about their construction, rig, or equipment. Ships of this type, of carvel or flush-laid hull form, which may have developed from Portuguese caravels (first recorded trading to England in 1448) are generally thought to have been established on the north and south coasts of the county by the 1480s.

The Cattewater Wreck was discovered in 1973 during dredging operations in the last reach of the River Plym as it flows into Plymouth Sound. The Cattewater, sheltered from all but prevailing southwest to westerly winds, was the principal anchorage for the town of Plymouth during the early post-medieval period. Following emergency designation under the 1973 **Protection of Wrecks Act**, detailed survey and selective excavation took place between 1976 and 1979. The surviving section of hull, which ran from one end to the midships area (total length 12 m), was recorded. All the main timbers were of oak (keel, garboard strakes, floor timbers, and futtocks); ceiling planking of mixed species (pine, oak); and treenails of oak or elm. A total of fourteen equal-armed floor timbers (the lowest elements of the frames, directly over the keel), with fish tails in way of garboard strakes and offset rectangular limber holes, were found *in situ*, each measuring about 20 cm in cross-section. The sawn outer planking (6–7 cm thick) had been fastened carvel-fashion by a combination of treenails and iron nails. Ceiling planking varied in thickness, and included one possible inspection hatch for the bilges. The keelson was notched on its lower surface to fit over the floor timbers, and swelled at its centre for a main mast-step, where it measured 54 cm in width by 40 cm in height; adjacent to the mast-step was a tapered elliptical pump pipe hole. Filling pieces (short planks) had been fitted horizontally between the first futtocks (frame timbers) at the floor timber heads to prevent material falling through to the bilges.

The radiocarbon date for the hull is 340 ± 80 BP (Har-3310) or AD 1420–1600, with a midpoint at 1510. Structural indications of date are the skeleton-build of the hull, with no sign of refit from clinker, the form of the keelson (parallels with Rye vessel A, and **Mary Rose**, sunk in 1545), and the date of the associated ceramics and leather from the wreck (c. 1495–1530). Three composite wrought-iron swivel guns from the site are of a type popular during the 16th century. The gun tubes (bore about 5.5 cm) were secured to carefully trenched beds of oak by three iron retaining straps contoured around the assembly and nailed. Parallels for the guns include two fragments from Castle Rising, Norfolk, those from the Kattegat (Denmark), and one found in 1986 off the east Kent coast (now in the collection of the Royal Armouries). The vessel would appear on this evidence to have sunk in the early 16th century.

Recent debate since the publication of the site has concentrated on the identification of what were termed 'lapped dovetails' fastening the floor timbers to the first futtocks. Similar dovetail mortises have since been recognized on other 16th-century wrecks: on Spanish and Basque ships such as *San Juan* (1560/65; see **Red Bay**), and wrecks at Villefranche (thought to be the Genoese *Lomellina*, 1516), Studland Bay (c. 1520; see **Studland Bay Wreck**) and Calvi, Corsica (late 16th century), all thought to be of Mediterranean build, as well as the wreck at Highborn Cay, Bahamas (c. 1520–70), Western Ledges Reef, Bermuda (late 16th century) and the **Molasses Reef Wreck**, Turks and Caicos Islands (c. 1500–25). It has therefore been suggested that the wreck may belong to the Iberian (Iberico-Atlantic) group of ships on the basis of construction. However, the number of wrecks from this period which have been investigated is small, and native manufacture in the British Isles cannot be ruled out. The character of the artefact assemblage suggests that the ship was English-operated (rather than Iberian), the distinctive shape of the floor timbers differs from some of the wrecks cited above, and the dovetail mortise probably represents one of those minor developments within 16th-century shipbuilding traditions to improve construction method, strength, and carrying capacity. The source of ballast stone, which may have run right through the ship, indicates activities along the coast of south/southwest England. The dominant lithology of the ballast was local limestone, together with granite and slate. Chalk and flint from Dorset or Kent/the Cinque Ports, and lower carboniferous limestone from Bristol/South Wales area were also represented. The ballast gravel contained only nine species of freshwater mollusc, and a complete absence of marine organisms, indicating that this came from a fairly lime-rich river at the limit of saline influence, or upstream from it; the present distribution of several of the species suggests somewhere east of the Lyme Regis longitude, possibly the Hampshire or Sussex areas.

Most of the artefactual evidence came from deposits in the southernmost section of the hull associated with the ballast. Elements of ship's equipment include a parrel truck (for the running rigging of the vessel); a marlinspike or fid of hardwood; rope of varying diameters; and small ragged fragments of vegetable fibre, possibly flax, thought to be deteriorated sail cloth. Galley utensils were represented by floor and peg tiles from the hearth, fuel in the form of charred wood, and cooking utensils by two, or possibly three, earthenware tripod cooking pots, a redware jar base, a North Devon ware cooking pot, a wooden bucket lid, and wooden bungs of various sizes. Eating and drinking equipment (excluding knives) included a wooden bowl, a fragment of Siegburg jug or beaker, and a Raeren drinking mug. Such stoneware is commonly found on English coastal sites, and the Raeren form is particularly common during the second quarter of the 16th century. Victuals were represented by animal bone (mainly cow, with some sheep/goat and pig, one dog, and cod), and victual storage was represented by barrel parts and olive jar sherds. (See also **Faunal studies**.)

The excavation and extant remains were too limited to permit a convincing reconstruction of her lines, but the earliest known English method for calculating tonnage (Bakers Old Rule) and maximum and minimum estimates for beam and depth provide approximate, though unreliable, figures of between 186 and 282 tons burden. The wreck provides useful *comparanda* to her close-contemporary, the warship *Mary Rose*. M.R.

ADDITIONAL READING

Duffy, M., *et al.* (eds), 1992, *The New Maritime History of Devon, Vol. I: From Early Times to the Late Eighteenth Century*, Exeter.

Mortlock, B. and Redknap, M., 1979, 'The Cattewater Wreck, Plymouth, Devon: Preliminary Results of Recent Work', *International Journal of Nautical Archaeology*, 7, 195–204.

Redknap, M., 1984, *The Cattewater Wreck: The Investigation of an Armed Vessel of the Early Sixteenth Century*, British Archaeological Reports 131, National Maritime Museum Archaeological Series 8, Greenwich.

Redknap, M., 1985, 'The Cattewater Wreck: A Contribution to 16th Century Maritime Archaeology', in C.O. Cederlund (ed.), *Postmedieval Boat and Ship Archaeology*, British Archaeological Reports International Series 256, 39–59.

Steffy, J.R., 1994, *Wooden Ship Building and the Interpretation of Shipwrecks*, College Station, Texas.

Cayman Islands

British Dependent Territory in the Caribbean, whose government invited assistance from professional underwater archaeologists in 1978. The **Institute of Nautical Archaeology** conducted an underwater survey of Little Cayman, Cayman Brac, and Grand Cayman between 1979 and 1980; seventy-seven archaeological sites were located. Documentary files on these sites form the core of a National Shipwreck Inventory which is archived and being enlarged by the Cayman Islands National Museum. In the mid-1980s

Exhibition at the Cayman Islands National Museum of the 200th anniversary of the Wreck of the Ten Sail. (M. Leshikar-Denton)

Indiana University undertook additional surveys.

Between 1990 and 1993 archaeology, archival research and folklore studies were undertaken on the Wreck of the **Ten Sail** by M.E. Leshikar, a Texas A&M University Ph.D. candidate working under the auspices of the Cayman Islands National Museum. In 1993 the museum made a commitment to the Islands' archaeological resources by employing a full-time professional archaeologist. In 1992, 1993, and 1995 surveys for prehistoric sites on all three islands were undertaken by the Institute of Archaeology, University College London, and by the Florida Museum of Natural History in cooperation with the museum, with negative results. In 1994 the museum staged an exhibition to commemorate the 200th anniversary of the Wreck of the Ten Sail, and worked with other organizations to bring the historical event to the public in a Philatelic Bureau stamp issue, a Currency Board commemorative coin, a National Archive Publication, a Visual Arts Society art competition, public lectures, and radio and television appearances. In 1996 the museum participated with water sports operators in an initial educational programme for Caymanian students on a shipwreck site. Future plans include involving overseas academic institutions and the sport-diving community in the preservation and interpretation of shipwrecks.

In the 1990s the Ministry of Culture formed a Marine Archaeology Committee to advise them regarding replacement of the outdated Abandoned Wreck Law of 1966. The Committee has prevented permits from being issued to salvagers under the present law. M.E.L.

ADDITIONAL READING

Drewett, P.L., 1992, *The Cayman Islands: Their Potential in Prehistoric Research*, University College London Institute of Archaeology Report, London.

Leshikar, M.E., 1993, *The 1794 'Wreck of the Ten Sail', Cayman Islands, British West Indies: A Historical Study and Archaeological Survey*, Ph.D. thesis, Texas A&M University, College Station, Texas.

Leshikar-Denton, M.E. (ed.), 1994, *Our Islands' Past, Vol. II: The 'Wreck of the Ten Sail'*, Georgetown, Grand Cayman .

Smith, R.C., 1981, *The Maritime Heritage of the Cayman Islands: Contributions in Nautical Archaeology*, MA thesis, Texas A&M University, College Station, Texas.

Stokes, A.V. and Keegan, W.F., 1993, *A Settlement Survey for Prehistoric Archaeological Sites on Grand Cayman*, Florida Museum of Natural History Dept. of Anthropology Miscellaneous Project Report 52, Gainesville, Florida.

Célèbre

see **Louisbourg wrecks**

Central America

Steamship wreck off the South Carolina coast, USA, lost in 1857 and rediscovered in 1987 by a treasure-hunting consortium, the Columbus-America Discovery Group. The group's search was spurred by *Central America*'s cargo of gold specie and bullion, valued at $2,189,000 in 1857 dollars. The discovery of the wreck led to protracted litigation between various claimants.

The sidewheel steamship *Central America* was built in New York in 1852 as the steamer *George Law* for the United States Mail Steamship Company. The 2,141 ton, 278 ft (84.7 m) long steamer carried passengers and mail between New York and Aspinwall, Panama. One of many steamships working on the Panama Route, which connected the east and west coasts of the United States, *George Law* saw service only on the Atlantic side of the route. At Aspinwall, the steamer would meet trains arriving from Panama City on the Pacific. *George Law* and other Atlantic mail steamers loaded passengers, mail, and gold transhipped across the Isthmus of Panama for the voyage back to New York.

George Law was renamed *Central America* in July 1857. On 12 September 1857, en route from Aspinwall to New York, the steamer encountered a severe storm at sea and sank after being battered by the waves. Lost with *Central America* were 423 lives and $2,189,000 in California gold. The steamer foundered in deep water, and other than floating wreckage, no trace of it was ever found.

The accounts of 'treasure' aboard *Central America* led to several modern attempts to find the wreck, and at least two treasure-hunters claimed to have found it. A Columbus, Ohio consortium, the Columbus-America Discovery Group (CADG), led by engineer Thomas Thompson, discovered the wreck of *Central America* in 2,500 m of water, 320 km off the South Carolina coast, in 1987. The wreck site is reportedly marked by the sidewheels and engine machinery, some hull timbers, and a number of artefacts, some of which are scattered on the seabed near the wreck. These include intact leather trunks and other baggage.

Utilizing a remotely operated vehicle, *NEMO*, the Columbus-America Discovery Group recovered a large amount of gold bullion and coins, as well as the ship's bell and a number of other artefacts. By the end of the summer of 1989, over one tonne of gold was brought into the jurisdiction of the Federal District Court in Norfolk, Virginia. CADG sought to be declared the owner of the treasure or, as an alternative, to be given a salvage award of $1 billion. As required by admiralty law, CADG gave notice to the underwriters who were known to have insured the gold. Insurers immediately filed their claim to the treasure.

Central America litigation is one of the first disputes pitting the rights of owners of long-lost property against the claims of salvors. CADG alleged that the insurers had abandoned their interest in the gold. Did the maxim 'finders keepers' apply, or would the courts rely on the traditions of maritime law which encourage rescue of property lost at sea while protecting the rights of owners? According to the maritime law of salvage, when property is taken involuntarily from an owner's control, the law is hesitant to say the property is abandoned. Abandonment must be proven by clear and convincing evidence, such as an express declaration abandoning title. Neither failure to exercise control over property nor lapse of time alone can support a finding of abandonment when an owner appears in a salvage award proceeding and establishes his ownership. The law of finds awarding title to the salvor may only be applied where the former owner specifically abandoned his property or where no one comes forward to claim property recovered from an ancient shipwreck.

At trial in 1990, the insurance companies faced the difficult task of proving that they had become the subrogated owners of the commercial shipment upon payment of claims more than a century before. They could locate neither the original bills of lading nor the insurance policies, and the trial court held that the underwriters had abandoned their claim to the gold. According to the lower court, insurers had intentionally destroyed documents, and title to the treasure was awarded to CADG under

The sinking of the steamship Central America *in 1857.*
From Frank Leslie's Illustrated Newspaper, *3 October 1857.*
(San Francisco Maritime National Historical Park)

the law of finds. That decision was overturned by the United States Court of Appeals for the Fourth Circuit in 1992, as there was no evidence of intentional destruction of documents. In reversing the trial court decision, the Fourth Circuit noted that almost all of the evidence introduced showed an intention on the part of the underwriters to retain ownership of the treasure.

The litigation was returned to the lower court for a salvage award proceeding as well as a determination of the interests of each of the underwriters. The law of salvage was to be applied by the trial court in setting the amount of the award for CADG with respect to the insured commercial shipment. The Court of Appeals anticipated that CADG would eventually be awarded the largest share of the treasure. The law of finds was to be applied to passenger gold (for which no owner had made a claim), to the artefacts, and to the wreck itself. Title to those objects was to be awarded to the salvors.

The importance of *Central America* litigation lies in the guidelines established to evaluate the actions of salvors in connection with historic wrecks. Traditionally, admiralty courts use six criteria, established in 1869, in setting the amount of the salvage award. The key factors to be considered in determining an award were: (1) the labour expended by the salvors in rendering the salvage service; (2) the promptitude, skill, and energy displayed in rendering the service and saving the property; (3) the value of the property employed by the salvors in

rendering the services and the danger to which such property was exposed; (4) the risk incurred by the salvors in securing the property from the impending peril; (5) the value of the property saved; and (6) the degree of danger from which the property was rescued. The Court of Appeals added a new consideration for historic shipwreck cases: the degree to which the salvors have protected the historical and archaeological provenance of the wreck and its artefacts.

After weighing the various criteria imposed by the Court of Appeals, the lower court awarded 90 per cent of the treasure to CADG. The Court of Appeals later upheld this generous award: the long days CADG spent at sea locating and recovering the treasure, in comparison to the normal salvage operation requiring just a few days or hours, was an important factor. The court concluded that no one could demonstrate more diligence, skill, and energy than CADG had in assembling experts and designing equipment for the project, and noted that when such meritorious service is combined with high worth of the recovered property, salvors should receive a high award. The sale of the treasure is expected to yield one of the highest values in history, although it is possible that the value will not approach the $1 billion originally speculated.

CADG's testimony about care they had taken in preserving *Central America*, benefiting several disciplines and sciences, also weighed heavily in the lower court's generous award. The particular care exercised by CADG in recovering and handling jewellery, china, cloth, newspapers, and even cigars from the wreck had been demonstrated at trial. The publication of a book, production

of a television account about the wreck, and the development of educational materials for school history classes led the lower court to conclude that CADG's efforts to preserve the wreck site and the artefacts were unequalled.

CADG was awarded sole control over the marketing of the treasure. The matter has been returned to the lower court for supervision of the marketing and a precise determination of the rights of each underwriter in the 10 per cent reserved for owners.

Until the *Central America* case, most of the treasure salvage disputes in the United States have been between salvors and State governments. The States claimed ownership of sunken wrecks embedded in State soil based on the law of finds, while salvors sought ownership of the ancient wrecks based on their services. A growing public concern over the ability to protect the historic and archaeological aspects of shipwrecks led to Congressional action. The rights of salvors and governmental entities were clarified with the enactment of the **Abandoned Shipwreck Act** of 1987, under which United States has title to all abandoned shipwrecks in territorial waters embedded in submerged lands or listed in the **National Register of Historic Places**. Except for shipwrecks located on Federal lands, title to such shipwrecks is transferred to the States under the Act. If the shipwreck is abandoned, it is State law, rather than the laws of salvage or finds, that controls salvage activities associated with the wreck. In cases such as *Central America*, which are excluded from application of the Act, Federal admiralty courts continue to apply the venerable traditions of maritime law while recognizing the public interest in the preservation of historic shipwrecks.

The two Court of Appeals' decisions in *Central America* litigation established important precedents for resolving disputes over the salvage of historic wrecks: (1) owners do not lose their rights merely because of passage of time, particularly when the wreck has been inaccessible; (2) preservation of historic shipwrecks and related artefacts will increase a salvage award; and (3) traditions of admiralty law can adapt to advances in technology and to an evolving public interest.

Because of extensive litigation over ownership of the recovered gold, CADG has not disclosed exactly how much of the 'Treasure' they have recovered. No overall site photographs, a site map, or any other archaeological information has been released. Some artefacts, including well-preserved clothing and newspapers from an intact leather trunk, were conserved and placed on display in Ohio.

Archaeological study and documentation of *Central America* would be particularly significant because no detailed record of a Panama Route steamship of the period exists. More importantly, the apparent high degree of preservation of passenger baggage, which is very similar to that observed at the *Titanic* wreck site, would offer a detailed opportunity to assess the material culture of the period, and its use and transportation on a vessel travelling from the 'frontier' of Gold Rush California, and could be compared with collections of the same period from the wrecks of *Bertrand* and *Arabia*. M.L.L., J.P.D.

ADDITIONAL READING

Columbus-America Discovery Group vs. Atlantic Mutual Ins. Co., 974F.2d 450, 455, 1992 A.M.C. 2705 (4th Cir. 1992), *cert. denied*, 113 S. Ct. 1625 (1993).

Columbus-America Discovery Group vs. Atlantic Mutual Ins. Co., 56F.3d 556, 565, 1995 A.M.C. 1985 (4th Cir. 1995), *cert. denied*, 116 S. Ct. 352 (1995).

Delgado, J.P., 1990, *To California by Sea: A Maritime History of the Gold Rush*, Columbia.

Herdendorf, C. and Conrad, J., 1992–3, 'The Steamship *Central America* and her Era', *Sea History*, 26.

Kemble, J., 1943, *The Panama Route: 1848–1869*, Berkeley and Los Angeles.

Klare, N.E., 1992, *The Final Voyage of the Central America, 1857*, Spokane, Washington.

Centre for Maritime Archaeology, Roskilde

Research centre established in affiliation with the Danish National Museum in September 1993 on the basis of a five-year grant from the Danish National Research Foundation. The purpose of the centre is to make research on an international level into questions related to man's use of the sea throughout history. The centre was established in continuation of the research efforts at the Viking Ship Museum and the National Museum's Institute of Maritime Archaeology in Roskilde, and the three institutions are closely cooperating. The director of the centre is Ole Crumlin-Pedersen. The research at the centre falls into three areas: ship archaeology, archaeological and historical studies into the effect of the sea on Danish history, and development of methods within maritime archaeology, including conservation. The centre publishes, together with the Institute and the Viking Ship Museum, the semi-annual *Maritime Archaeological Newsletter from Roskilde*, with information on current research, seminars, and publications. J.B.

ADDITIONAL READING

Crumlin-Pedersen, O., 1993–, *Maritime Archaeological Newsletter from Roskilde*.

Crumlin-Pedersen, O., 1993, Danish Marine

Archaeology Research Centre Wetland Research Project 14, *Newswarp*, 12-14.

Centre for Maritime Archaeology, Southampton

see **Southampton Centre for Maritime Archaeology**

Ceramic studies

Methods used to analyse a specific material class from underwater contexts, primarily in order to establish site chronology, but also to link the functions of the artefacts with use contexts such as trade and foodways, and their distributions with post-event formation processes. Ceramics usually preserve well under water because of their fired clay composition and the fact that they are often glazed, which provides a protective coating. General categories found include earthenware, stoneware, and porcelain, a distinction made based on firing temperature and type of clay body. Ceramic bodies fired at lower temperatures, such as earthenwares, are less likely to survive intact than are porcelains.

Ceramics are generally found on all wreck sites, but also occur in other underwater contexts, such as the submerged town of **Port Royal, Jamaica**; ancient anchorages and ports throughout the world; at the bottom of rivers near South Carolina rice plantations (after being thrown in as offerings by African and African American slaves); and in Central American and Mesoamerican cenotes and lakes where they were thrown by the ancient Maya (also as offerings). Controversy surrounds the issue of how ceramic artefacts should be recovered from underwater sites and whether collections taken from non-scientifically investigated wrecks should be studied at all.

Artefacts found on accurately dated shipwrecks provide unique uncontaminated contexts rarely found on terrestrial sites. The quantity of ceramics found on wrecks often far exceeds that found on terrestrial sites, thus allowing the researcher to generalize about recurring characteristics.

However, the sheer volume of ceramic material associated with wrecks often leads to the recovery only of 'diagnostic' sherds (e.g. glazed and decorated sherds, or partially intact or rim portions) that provide clues to dating. When many examples of apparently similar vessels occur, past practice has often led to the recovery of 'representative' examples rather than the full assemblage. Researchers are cautioned against this because of the loss of information that can occur, and are urged to use scientific methods to collect as much of the assemblage as possible from each wreck investigated.

Provenance data (where the item was found within the site and its relationship to other items found, both ceramic and non-ceramic) also must be collected for the ceramics recovered. This information can allow the researcher to answer such questions as: 'How was the ship loaded?', 'Were some of the ceramics used as part of shipboard life?', and 'How did the wrecking process actually occur?' To maximize the potential of a collection for study, it should be curated together in a location accessible to researchers. Conservation of ceramic items found in underwater contexts is usually less problematic and labour-intensive than for other material classes, because of the nature of the material itself.

Underwater wreck sites are unique laboratories for studying material culture from a particular point in time. Ceramic items can

An excavated ceramic bowl and jar at Port Royal, Jamaica, alongside a pewter plate and half-coconut. (Donny Hamilton)

be decorated or undecorated, but the study of decorated ceramics has taken precedence because decorative motifs can change rapidly, giving the archaeologist a useful tool for dating. In addition, many complete vessels occur in underwater contexts, providing reliable baseline data for classification and typology building. Basic descriptive data should be collected for all ceramics recovered, including quantitative and qualitative observations about each vessel and its contents. Common quantitative measurements record a vessel's dimensions, including volume, weight, and thickness. Qualitative observations subsume descriptions of surface treatments, especially decoration. The most effective way to analyse sherds is to regroup and refit them into whole vessels, and this technique should be used whenever possible. Careful drawings (including profiles and cross sections) of as many representative examples as feasible should be made, with photographs and descriptions as additional guides, to allow other researchers to make use of the material for comparative purposes.

Scientific techniques such as thermoluminescence dating can be used to determine the 'age' of a particular ceramic specimen, but the more usual approach is to appeal to specialists familiar with particular kinds of ceramics to place finds within a temporal framework. When there are written records, both historical and archaeological information should be used to document the age of the recovered artefacts. When written documentation is incomplete or appears to contradict the archaeological evidence, the latter may be particularly important. A good example of this situation relates to ceramics recovered from Southeast Asian wrecks that are helping researchers to grasp the complexity of the trade in Asian porcelains prior to European involvement in the region. Documented collections from wrecks of known age are helping to illuminate the skills of Thai, Vietnamese, and Korean potters and to place their products in perspective *vis-à-vis* the products of the Chinese, which have to date received the bulk of scholarly attention (see **Koh Talu Wreck**).

Ceramic collections from underwater sites are also used together with those from terrestrial sites to construct more accurate typologies. John Goggin's classic 1960 study of the Spanish olive jar employed ceramics from land sites throughout southeast USA as well as materials from the salvaged Spanish **Flota of 1733**. Study of the ceramic materials being shipped up the Missouri River on the sunken steamboats *Arabia* (1856) and *Bertrand* (1865) not only help to flesh out our picture of goods being shipped to western markets in the mid-19th century but tie into what is found in terrestrial sites from the same period in the trans-Mississippi West. Work on ceramic finds from wrecks in the waters surrounding the British Isles and the former English colonies has increased our understanding of everyday and exotic ceramics from late medieval times into the post-medieval, increasingly industrial era. Finally, dated wrecks can provide the temporal context for many little-studied types of ceramics, such as undecorated plainwares, which are often very difficult to date.

One of the difficulties faced by archaeologists is the lack of comparative ceramic materials in museums for 'common' wares, i.e. those used on an everyday basis and most often recovered archaeologically in the form of sherds from terrestrial sites. Shipwrecks, however, often contain a full range of ceramics, recovered as intact pieces or as reconstructable vessels. Functional classes include ceramics as vessels used for cooking and eating (both for use on-ship and as part of private and commercial cargoes), for storage and shipment of foodstuffs and other goods (amphoras, olive jars), as religious offerings, as mementos (e.g. aboriginal pottery from the Americas found on Spanish ships returning to Europe), and in the form of other goods made from clay such as building materials (e.g. roof tiles), smoking pipes, incendiary weapons (firepots), and oil lamps. To link ceramics with their functional contexts it is important to record the locations of ceramics found on a wreck and to recover the most complete assemblage possible. Historical documentation in the form of ships' manifests is also useful, as are contemporary renditions of the ceramics in use (as in period paintings or other artistic media). The researcher must resist the temptation to interpret an object in terms of 'modern' ceramic functional categories.

Amphoras have been called the 'jerrycans of antiquity', and served as storage and shipping containers for centuries. Research on residues left inside them indicate that they contained a wide range of products, from wine, olive oil, almonds, fish and fish products, to tesserae, the small stones used for making mosaics. Classic contextual studies of amphoras from the 1st-century BC **Madrague de Giens Wreck** and the 7th-century AD Byzantine wreck near Yassiada (see **Yassiada wrecks**) are particularly instructive. At each wreck, researchers found that small differences existed among the thousands of vessels recovered, allowing them to be grouped stylistically and temporarily – a conclusion made possible by the fact that all of the amphoras from each wreck were studied within their context as an **Assemblage**. These findings have been linked to different manufacturing and marketing locations. Many of the amphoras even had graffiti. Several vessels also bore inscriptions indicating their contents and even their makers. From these data, researchers have begun to reconstruct the history of trade and commerce on the ancient Mediterranean with a high degree of certainty.

The locations of ceramics (and other artefacts) found on wreck sites, when carefully recorded, can help to reconstruct the 'wrecking process' of the vessel as well as provide an understanding of the ways in which onboard space was utilized. This study emphasis, as well as those briefly outlined above, illustrate how the analysis of ceramics from submerged sites can contribute to a more thorough understanding of the historical and cultural processes operating at a particular time. Because ceramics are generally so plentiful – on both underwater and terrestrial sites – their study in both of these often interrelated contexts can lead to a more holistic understanding of the past. T.M.2

ADDITIONAL READING

Andrews, A.P. and Corletta, R., 1995, 'A Brief History of Underwater Archaeology in the Maya Area', *Ancient Mesoamerica*, 6, 101–17.

Bass, G.F., 1990, 'After the Diving is Over', in T. Carrell (ed.), *Underwater Archaeology Proceedings from the Society for Historical Archaeology Conference, Tucson, Arizona*, Ann Arbor, Michigan.

Deagan, K., 1987, *Ceramics, Glassware, and Beads: Artefacts of the Spanish Colonies of Florida and the Caribbean, 1500–1800*, vol. I, Washington, D.C.

Ferguson, L., 1992, *Uncommon Ground: Archaeology and Early African America, 1650–1800*, Washington, DC.

Goggin, J., 1960, 'The Spanish Olive Jar: An Introductory Study', in *Papers in Caribbean Anthropology*, Yale University Publications in Anthropology 62, New Haven.

Green, J. and Harper, R., 1987, *The Maritime Archaeology of Shipwrecks and Ceramics in Southeast Asia*, AIMA Special Publication 4.

Marken, M.W., 1994, *Pottery from Spanish Shipwrecks 1500–1800*, Gainesville, Florida.

Miller, G.L., 1987, 'The Second Destruction of the *Geldermalsen*', *The American Neptune*, 47, 275–81; reprinted 1992 in *Historical Archaeology*, 26, 4, 124–31.

Pearson, C., 1987, *Conservation of Marine Archaeological Objects*, London.

Throckmorton, P. (ed.), *The Sea Remembers: Shipwrecks and Archaeology*, New York.

Charles Cooper

Last surviving example of a 19th-century transatlantic packet ship and the most intact survivor of all the square-rigged merchant vessels built in the United States. *Cooper* now lies as a hulk in the harbour of Port Stanley in the Falkland Islands in seriously deteriorating condition (see also **Falklands wrecks and hulks**).

A packet was a vessel that sailed on a regular schedule carrying passengers and freight. Built in Black Rock, Connecticut in 1856, *Cooper* was originally intended for the New York to Le Havre run, and a major cargo out of New York after the inauguration of packet service in 1818 was American cotton destined for British and French mills. In 1866, bound from New York to San Francisco, *Cooper* put into Stanley for repairs, which tended to be expensive in that remote port, and as sometimes happened in that situation she was sold as a floating warehouse. About 1870 she was grounded next to the

Stern of Charles Cooper.
(Nicholas Dean)

Remains of Charles H.
Spencer at Lee's Ferry.
(Daniel Lenihan)

Charles H. Spencer

Steamboat wreck in the Arizona desert, United States. Both the man and the paddle wheel steamboat that bears his name were controversial figures on the Colorado River at the turn of the 20th century, the man because of his questionable business ventures and the boat for causing the collapse of a poorly conceived mining operation. Born in Walsenberg, Colorado, Spencer spent his early years learning how to mine gold. Despite the failure of other large, well-funded mining operations on the upper Colorado, Charlie Spencer had a penchant for attracting investors who could bankroll his activities. When one project failed or was inconclusive, his 'western' manners, the magnitude of his projects, and their poten-

Canadian barque **Actaeon**; protected by a metal roof, she saw further service for nearly a century.

In 1968 a New York newspaper purchased *Cooper* for New York's South Street Seaport Museum with the hope that all or part of the hull might eventually be salvaged for exhibit. Between 1976 and 1981 three museum expeditions recorded and attempted to stabilize *Cooper*. In 1978 the 30 ft (9.1 m) long stern carving was removed to the Falkland Islands Museum in Stanley, though a few carvings remain at the bow. In 1991 South Street Seaport Museum transferred ownership to the Falkland Islands Government. As the hull's condition continued to deteriorate, with the danger that falling debris might pose a threat to harbour traffic, in the mid-1990s the Falklands authorities literally wrapped the hull in surplus fish net. Given available resources, whether portions of the hull eventually can be retrieved for shoreside exhibit remains problematic.

Cooper's significance lies in three areas: first, as a relic of the oceanic commerce with Europe which put America's balance of payments account firmly in the black; second, as an example of a passenger vessel (Liverpool's Merseyside Maritime Museum used the 'tween-decks as its model for the exhibit on emigration); and third, as an important glimpse of naval architecture. Unlike the sleek clippers, the packets, with their relatively bluff bows and somewhat boxy hulls, were designed and built to cross the Atlantic reliably and safely rather than with great speed. Fortunately, as stabilization efforts took place it was possible to study and record the hull in some detail as it was still remarkably intact, even to the 19th-century interior paint. It was massively built with deck beams supported by large timber

knees. A large wooden windlass still rests in the forepeak.

Cooper also exemplifies a dilemma in maritime preservation, which is that without a great deal of careful and extremely expensive care, large wooden hulls eventually deteriorate at an accelerating rate, leaving the question of what eventually can and should be salvaged once documentation has been carried out. N.D.

ADDITIONAL READING

Albion, R.G., 1938, *Square Riggers on Schedule*, Princeton.

Brouwer, N., 1981, 'The 1856 Packet Ship *Charles Cooper*', *Seaport*, Fall, 18–21.

Brouwer, N., 1993, *International Register of Historic Ships*, 2nd edition, New York.

Cutler, C., 1961, *Queens of the Western Ocean*, Annapolis.

Hill, A.T., 1977, *Voyages*, New York.

Throckmorton P., 1976, The American Heritage in the Falklands, *Sea History*, 4, 36–40.

tial return enabled him to attract new investors. In 1910, following the failure of his operations in Colorado, Spencer moved men and machinery to Lee's Ferry, Arizona.

Even before locating the necessary deposits of coal to support a mining operation, a large steam boiler and pumps were set up along the Colorado River, with the flumes assembled and the amalgamator prepared. While everything worked fine at first, it soon became apparent that the gold was passing out with the tailings instead of being absorbed by the mercury. In addition, there was an insufficient supply of fuel for the boilers.

In late 1910 a sizeable vein of coal was located in a tributary canyon 47 km upstream from the mine. Company backers were convinced that the only economical way to move coal from the tributary to the mine was by boat. In 1911 a paddle wheel steamboat was ordered from the San Francisco firm of Shultze, Robertson, Shultze. Remarkably for the time, the paddle wheeler was designed to be framed up, temporarily pinned together, dismantled, transported by train and then wagon to the mouth of the tributary canyon, and there reassembled under the direction of a company shipwright.

Launched sometime in late February 1912, the flat-bottomed hull of *Charles H. Spencer* was designed with considerable flare in order to allow the current to run under the boat. Its construction and machinery were well within the mainstream of paddle wheel vessel design, yet it has been referred to as a technological failure, underpowered and unable to carry enough coal to support the mine. Unfortunately, by the time the boat was completed, the mining operation was on the verge of collapsing. The fouling of the mercury plates on the amalgamator was becoming an insurmountable problem and the value of the mercury required exceeded the value of the gold recovered. Finally, in the spring or summer of 1912, the entire mining operation was shut down, and by 1913 even Spencer had moved on to other business ventures.

Blamed for the failure of the mine, the boat became a scapegoat and was abandoned. A 1987 study of the boat and the mining operation disproved allegations of its technological shortcomings (see Carrell, Bradford and Rusho). The history of the steamboat, how it was later used to help decide a Supreme Court water rights case, and Charlie Spencer's exploits, is a story that mirrors western river exploration and development. T.L.C.

ADDITIONAL READING

Carrell, T.L., Bradford, J.E., and Rusho, W.L., 1987, *Submerged Cultural Resources Site Report: Charles H. Spencer's Mining Operation and Paddle Wheel Steamboat*, Southwest Cultural Resources Center Professional Papers 13, Santa Fe, New Mexico.

Colton, H.S., 1957, 'The Colorado River Steamboat *Charles H. Spencer*', *Steamboat Bill*, 61, 6–7.

Crampton, G.C., 1959, *Outline History of the Glen Canyon Region*, University of Utah Anthropological Papers 42, Salt Lake City.

Crampton, G.C., 1986, *Ghosts of Glen Canyon: History Beneath Lake Powell*, St George.

Rusho, W.L., 1962, 'Charles Spencer and his Wonderful Steamboat', *Arizona Highways*, 37, 8, 34–9.

Rusho, W.L. and Crampton, G.C., 1981, *Desert River Crossing: Historic Lee's Ferry on the Colorado River*, Salt Lake City.

HMS *Charon*

A British warship that was burned and sunk during the Battle of Yorktown (Virginia) on 10 October 1781 (see **Yorktown shipwrecks**).

Charon was a fifth-rate warship, mounting forty-four guns. Built in 1778 in Harwich, *Charon* was 140 ft 3 in (42.7 m) in length on the main gundeck, 116 ft 1 in (35.36 m) on the keel, with a beam of 38 ft (11.6 m), a draught of 16 ft 4 in (5 m), and displacing 891 tons. Sometimes mistakenly referred to as a frigate, she belonged to a new class of twenty-five two-deck warships, with a battery consisting of 18 and 12 pounders, and a crew of 300. *Charon*, Captain Thomas Symonds commanding, was assigned to protect a convoy of transport vessels supporting the Southern British Army, under the command of Major General Charles, Earl Cornwallis.

During the summer of 1781 Cornwallis moved his army to Yorktown, Virginia, where he established a fortified post. The deep water of the York River provided an ample anchorage for the fleet of five warships and some fifty transports. On 10 October 1781, a combined French and American army commenced a siege on Cornwallis's position. On that first night HMS *Charon*, the largest of Cornwallis's warships, was set afire by red-hot shot from a French battery. The ship drifted across the river, eventually grounding and sinking near Gloucester Point.

During the Yorktown Shipwreck Archaeological Project, *Charon*'s remains were rediscovered in 1978 and positively identified in 1980. Although only an estimated 5 per cent of the hull survived, positive identification was accomplished by comparing the preserved hull remains with the ship's as-built plans, obtained from the National Maritime Museum, Greenwich. Because so little of the hull survived, and because previous unscientific salvage had damaged the site and its contents, no further excavation was conducted. J.D.B.

ADDITIONAL READING

Sands, J.O., 1983, *Yorktown's Captive Fleet*, Charlottesville, Virginia.

Sands, J.O., 1988, 'Gunboats and Warships of the American Revolution', in G.F. Bass (ed.), *Ships and Shipwrecks of the Americas: A History Based on Underwater Archaeology*, London.

Steffy, J.R. *et al.*, 1981, 'The Charon Report: Underwater Archaeology', in *The Challenge Before Us: Proceedings of the Twelfth Conference on Underwater Archaeology*, San Marino, California.

CSS *Chattahoochee*

Confederate ironclad scuttled in 1865 off Columbus, Georgia and partially raised in 1865. *Chattahoochee* was a twin propeller, sail- and steam-powered Confederate gunboat of conventional wooden construction designed by naval constructor John L. Porter. Built on the banks of the Chattahoochee River at Saffold, Georgia, pursuant to a contract dated 19 October 1861 between the Confederate States Navy Department and David S. Johnston, the vessel measured 130 ft (39.6 m) between perpendiculars, 30 ft (9.1 m) in moulded beam, and 10 ft (3 m) in depth of hold. It stepped three schooner-rigged masts and mounted six cannon: four 32 pounder smoothbores in broadside, a 9 inch Dahlgren smoothbore aft, and a rifled and banded 32 pounder forward.

Entering service on 1 January 1863, under the command of Lt Catesby ap R. Jones, *Chattahoochee* patrolled the Apalachicola-Chattahoochee-Flint river system against potential Federal attack from the Gulf of Mexico. Five months later the gunboat suffered a disastrous boiler explosion near Blountshown, Florida, which caused it to sink in shallow water with the loss of nineteen crew members. The following August *Chattahoochee* was raised and taken to the navy yard at Columbus, Georgia for repairs. Refitted except for the installation of new boilers, the hard-luck warship saw limited service during the spring of 1864 before returning to Columbus for the completion of its overhaul. Still unfinished, *Chattahoochee* was sunk by its crew 20 km below Columbus after Federal forces captured the city on 16 April 1865.

Damaged amidships by fire, but with steam engines mostly intact, *Chattahoochee*'s wreck remained largely undisturbed for nearly one hundred years. The centennial observance of the American Civil War in the early 1960s inspired Columbus citizens to seek and raise the remains of *Chattahoochee* and the Confederate ironclad *Jackson*, which had also been sunk in the Chattahoochee River in 1865. After the successful retrieval of *Jackson*'s hull in 1963, local salvors working with Georgia Historical Commission officials and the US Army Corps of Engineers' snagboat *Montgomery* began the recovery of *Chattahoochee* in November 1964. Working in accordance to a plan developed by the three parties, a series of cables were run under the gunboat's keel, while sediment and debris were dredged from within the hull in order to lighten it. Time constraints placed on the use of *Montgomery* resulted in a premature recovery effort four weeks after the project began. As a result, only a 9 m stern section of the 130 ft (40 m) gunboat was raised. This hull remnant, containing *Chattahoochee*'s two unique Confederate-made steam engines, was later transferred to the Confederate Naval Museum in Columbus for permanent display alongside the previously recovered *Jackson*.

In 1984, at the invitation of the Confederate Naval Museum, East Carolina University's field school (see **East Carolina University Program in Maritime History and Nautical Archaeology**) spent four weeks investigating the submerged portion of *Chattahoochee*'s hull. Through artefact recovery and extensive mapping of the hull remains, a greater understanding was gained of *Chattahoochee* and the Confederate Navy's early war efforts to construct conventional wooden gunboats. R.A.H.

ADDITIONAL READING

Still, W.N., Jr, 1987, *Confederate Shipbuilding*, 2nd edition, Columbia.

Turner, M., 1988, *Navy Gray: A Story of the Confederate Navy on the Chattahoochee and Apalachicola Rivers*, Tuscaloosa, Alabama.

Watts, G.P., Jr *et al.*, 1988, *CSS Chattahoochee: An Investigation of the Remains of a Confederate Gunboat*, Greenville, Carolina.

Chesapeake Flotilla

Group of wrecks of American gunboats scuttled in the Patuxent River, Maryland, USA, in 1814, and rediscovered in 1980. With the onset of the War of 1812, the Chesapeake Bay of Maryland and Virginia, known as the Tidewater, emerged as a principal seat of American privateering. The British response was to institute a stringent blockade of the bay by the Royal Navy in February 1813. Thereafter, British forces under the command of Admiral Sir George Cockburn commenced a campaign of seaborne depredations that devastated shipping, towns, and plantations throughout the region. Lacking sufficient land and naval forces to contend with the invaders, the Tidewater defenders were virtually powerless to combat the attacks.

On 4 July 1814 Captain Joshua Barney, a Revolutionary War hero and acclaimed privateersman from Baltimore, submitted a plan entitled 'Defense of the Chesapeake' to Secretary of the Navy William Jones. Barney's design called for the construction of a fleet of shallow-draft armed barges that could be both rowed and sailed, and used to interdict the enemy in the shoally waters of the bay during their landing attempts. The plan was accepted. Barney was appointed Commodore, and instructed to build, man, and field the fleet. The barges were to be constructed at shipyards at the ports of Baltimore and St Michaels, Maryland. The force would officially be referred to as the Chesapeake Flotilla, and was authorized by the Navy Department to serve only in the Chesapeake Tidewater.

By the spring of 1814 the fleet, though

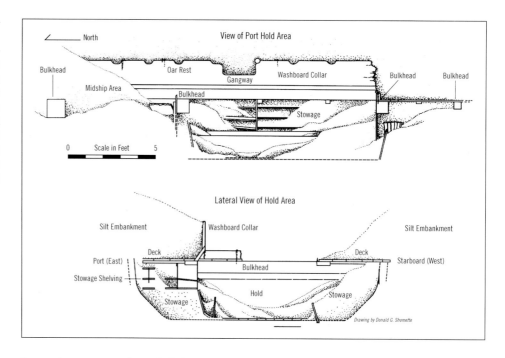

Plan view of the forward port hold area of USS Scorpion, *and lateral view of the same area looking towards the stern. Note the remnant of the port washboard collar and stowage compartments. The starboard compartment is believed to have been employed as a sail and rope locker. (Drawing by Donald G. Shomette)*

incomplete, was put through field trials and readied for its first mission, a raid against the main enemy base in the bay at Tangier Island, and then a link-up with a gunboat fleet defending Norfolk, Virginia. In May Barney sallied from Baltimore with his flagship, the sloop *Scorpion*, the row galley *Vigilant*, gunboats 137 and 138, seven 75 ft (22.9 m) barges, six 50 ft (15.2 m) barges, and a lookout boat, armed with carronades, long guns, and gunnades, and accompanied by a fleet of merchantmen under convoy.

On 31 May 1814 the flotilla encountered a strong British naval force off Cedar Point, Maryland and, after a spirited engagement, withdrew into the nearby Patuxent River. After the appearance of overwhelmingly superior British naval reinforcements, the flotilla retired into St Leonard's Creek, a shallow tributary of the river into which the great ships of the invaders could not penetrate. Between 8 and 10 June, utilizing his own large force of barges and schooners, the British commander, Captain Robert Barrie, attempted and failed six times to destroy the flotilla. Then, in a calculated effort to draw Barney into the open river, where the heavy British broadsides could be brought to bear, he initiated a deliberate campaign of destruction along the Patuxent drainage, destroying towns and plantations alike.

On 26 June 1814, reinforced by units of the US Marines, Army, and local militia, Barney launched a surprise pre-dawn land and sea assault on the blockading squadron. Two British frigates, HMS *Loire* and *Narcissus*, were driven off in sinking condi-

tion. Leaving gunboats 137 and 138 and a number of merchantmen behind to be scuttled in the creek, but accompanied by as many as a dozen merchantmen and the transport schooner *Islet*, Barney escaped upriver. The British blockade of the Patuxent, however, was maintained.

On 17 August 1814 a British armada of forty-six warships and transports, carrying over 4,000 troops under General Robert Ross, entered Maryland waters. The British objective was the capture of Washington, DC, and their main avenue of invasion was to be the Patuxent River. A landing at the town of Benedict, the destruction of the flotilla, and an overland march against the 'backdoor' of the capital was planned. On 20 August, even as the British landed unopposed, Secretary Jones instructed Barney, then anchored well above Benedict at the riverport of Nottingham, to retire to the head of navigation at Queen Anne's Town and destroy the flotilla if it were imperilled. The fleet, however, could proceed no higher than Scotchman's Hole, near the town of Upper Marlboro. Two days later, as advancing British gunboats rounded a bend in the river at Pig Point, sixteen vessels of the flotilla were scuttled to prevent capture. A single barge was captured. Several merchantmen were quickly burned by the British, and the remainder taken off as prizes. On 24 August, following the American defeat at the Battle of Bladensburg, Washington fell to the invaders.

Soon after the British departure from the Patuxent, salvor John Weems was contracted by the government to recover the flotilla but raised only several vessels. In October Barney's flotillamen returned to the fleet and recovered most of the guns, carriages, anchors, cables, and shot. All of the salvaged goods were removed to Mount Pleasant Landing and then shipped to Baltimore and sold at auction. For nearly a century afterwards the unsalvaged remains of the flotilla could be seen from time to time. As late as 1907 the Army Corps of Engineers reported the hulks were still visible at low water.

In 1978, when the Patuxent River Submerged Cultural Resources Survey was initiated by Nautical Archaeological Associates, of Upper Marlboro, and the Calvert Marine Museum, of Solomons, Maryland, with funding by the Heritage, Conservation, and

Destruction of the Chesapeake Flotilla, detail from an untitled engraving. (Courtesy of the Library of Congress, Washington, DC)

Recreation Service of the Department of the Interior, archaeological research on the flotilla began. The following year a **Magnetometer** survey of the Patuxent was carried out. The remains of several vessels believed to be the gunboats sunk in St Leonard's Creek were located and examined. The sites could not be positively identified owing to extensive damage inflicted by the Maryland Derelict Removal Program. Upriver, where the main fleet had been lost, however, nearly 3 km of significant targets were recorded. One of the sites investigated was found to be the remains of a vessel. The site was dubbed the Turtle Shell Wreck after the only artefact recovered during the testing.

In 1980 an extensive test excavation was conducted at the Turtle Shell Wreck site. The lie and condition of the site was determined by the construction of a small test **Cofferdam**, within which a preliminary excavation was undertaken. The overall parame-

ters of the wreck were determined through probing with a high-pressure waterjet tube. The wreck measured nearly 15 m in length and 4.9 m abeam. A larger cofferdam, 8.5 m long and 4.6 m wide, was then erected over a segment of the site, and excavation proceeded within.

As excavation proceeded into the forward hold of the vessel, buried beneath 1.5 m of sediments, the wreck was found to be intact and in an anaerobic condition. Moreover, the soils of the site possessed a distinct stratigraphy which revealed the settling sequences of the wreck. Fire-charred wood and the disposition of splayed cant frames indicated that an explosion had destroyed approximately 1.8 m of the bow. Fortunately, owing to bulkheads immediately aft the bow, the explosion had been blocked from damaging the hold itself. Intact stowage compartments, with adjustable shelving, were discovered on the port side, along with domestic materials stowed within. A washboard collar, with oar rests and a gangway, was located still in position. A section of a contoured oarsman's bench and a companion ladder were found in the hold. Decorative red trim suggested that the vessel had not been constructed in haste, as were the barges of the fleet. High resolution lowlight **Underwater video**, the first ever deployed in a Tidewater marine archaeology project, revealed that the starboard and port decks and ceiling were intact but showed signs of erosion and shrinkage from alternating exposures to water and air.

Only limited artefact recovery was conducted owing to funding constraints for conservation. Artefacts were classified in six categories: medical, military, carpentry, domestic, maritime-related, and architectural. A set of surgical tools belonging to fleet surgeon Thomas Hamilton and manufactured by the London firms of Hague and Nowill, and John Evans and Company, were recovered, along with pill tiles, a pestle, spatulas, pharmaceutical bowls, plates, and containers, some with salves and unguents still contained within. Military items included gun flints, a swivel gun grip, gunner's picks, and an intact munitions box. Carpentry tools, probably belonging to fleet carpenter Charles Fleming, included a draw knife, a punch, plane blades, and kegs of dried paint. Domestic items included mess gear, a ration cup bearing the initials of cook Caesar Wentworth, coins, a sandstone galley stove, coal, clothing and shoe fragments, a chamber pot, water jugs, padlocks, and an inkwell. Maritime artefacts included a sounding lead, lantern, pulley block, and dunnage. Architectural features recovered

included an oarsmen's bench, companion ladder, leather pump gasket, and fragments of trim and shelving. A total of 151 artefacts in all were recovered. The remainder were left *in situ* and reburied with the site. Conservation was carried out at a laboratory erected for the purpose in the museum's Lore Oyster House at Solomons.

Following the test excavation, the site was reburied to restore it to the anaerobic environment in which it had been found. From the archaeological evidence and historic record, architectural and dimensional characteristics, site location, and artefacts, the vessel has been tentatively identified as USS *Scorpion*. D.G.S.

ADDITIONAL READING

Shomette, D.G., 1981, *Flotilla: Battle for the Patuxent*, Solomons, Maryland.

Shomette, D.G., 1981, 'The Much Vaunted Flotilla: An Underwater Survey of 1-TSW, an Early 19th-Century Federal Warship in Patuxent River', *Maryland Archaeology*, 17, 2, 1–18.

Shomette, D.G., 1995, *Tidewater Time Capsule: History Beneath the Patuxent*, Centreville, Maryland.

Shomette, D.G. and Hopkins, F.W., Jr, 1981, *War on the Patuxent, 1814: A Catalog of Artifacts*, Solomons, Maryland.

Shomette, D.G. and Hopkins, F.W., Jr, 1983, 'The Search for the Chesapeake Flotilla, *The American Neptune*, 43, 1, 5–19.

Chichén Itzá Cenote

A special well among the numerous natural water-filled limestone sinkholes, called *dzonot* in Maya or *cenotes* in Spanish, existing on the Yucatán Peninsula, Mexico, containing thousands of Mayan goods and artefacts. The *cenotes* played a vital role as a source of fresh water and it was around them that the Mayas built their cities.

The most important ancient well in Mexico is the Sacred Cenote, or Cenote of Sacrifice, which is located near the main plaza of Chichén Itzá, one of the largest Maya ceremonial sites in pre-Columbian times. Chichén Itzá is located approximately 120 km east of Mérida, in the northeast portion of the Yucatán Peninsula, a low flat limestone shelf. It is different from the Xtoloc Cenote located in the same city, and other wells or *cenotes* in the surrounding area which provided water for daily needs: the Sacred Cenote had a totally religious character since it was devoted to rites, offerings and human sacrifices made by the different groups that inhabited the area from as early as the 5th century AD and as late as the 13th century.

One of the most important Maya groups

established there were the Itzaes, who arrived in the area in AD 968. Chichén Itzá takes its name from the Sacred Cenote, as well as from the Itzaes. It means: in the mouth of the well of the water sorcerers (*chi* = mouth, *chen* = well, *its* = sorcerer, and *há* or *a* = water). The first chronicler who described the city of Chichén Itzá and the ceremonies that took place in the Sacred Cenote was the Spanish bishop Diego de Landa, in his book *Relación de las cosas de Yucatán*, written around 1566. According to this text, the well was linked to the principal structure of the ancient city by a *sacbe*, a wide and beautiful man-made road 170 m long. De Landa describes the *cenote* itself, the structure on the south side where the deities were honoured, the human sacrificial rites to Chac, the god of water, which took place especially during the dry season, and the kind of offerings thrown.

In 1841 John L. Stephens published the book *Incidents of Travel in Central America, Chiapas and Yucatan*, with splendid illustrations by Frederick Catherwood; it incorporated a detailed description of the two *cenotes* located at Chichén Itzá, supposing that they were underground rivers. Special reference was made to the sacred well.

The sinkhole is elliptical in shape, 56 by 68 m; from the mouth of the cenote to the surface of the water is a 22 m drop. The water is 14 m deep, and the bottom of the cenote is lined with silt and mud 3 m deep. Its walls are almost vertical and the water has a greenish dark colour due to the seaweed and micro-organisms it contains as well as the shadow of the vegetation that surrounds it.

According to the chronicles, the offerings contained artefacts made of gold, silver, and precious stones, especially jade, as well as other materials. This made the Sacred Cenote a very attractive place to look for **Treasure**. Many of the objects appear to have been intentionally damaged before they were thrown, some by the effects of fire and cold water, others broken or cut, or both, and some others even melted. It seems that this was due to different purposes in Maya rituals. The first attempt to recover these treasures was made in 1882 by Desiré Charnay, a French antiquarian. However, due to the characteristics of the *cenote* as well as the fact that the bottom is full of mud, fallen trees, and loose stones, the dredge equipment he used was not adequate and his work was fruitless.

Edward Herbert Thompson, who came to Mexico in 1885, was fascinated by the Maya civilization. He wrote an article entitled, 'Archaeological Research in Yucatán' for the *Proceedings of the American Antiquarian Society* in Massachusetts. Nine years later, as the first consul of the United States in Yucatán, he bought the Hacienda of Chichén Itzá for the small amount of 300 pesos; his property included most of the ruins and the Sacred Cenote. Between 1904 and 1907, using a dredge, he recovered a large amount of important archaeological artefacts. During the 1909 season he hired a Greek sponge diver to search the bottom, joining him in the operation. However, due to the lack of visibility they went back to dredging. The number of objects (complete and broken) recovered by Thompson varies from hundreds to thousands according to different authors. Most of them were taken to the Peabody Museum, at Harvard University, and to the Field Museum of Natural History of Chicago. Some of these pieces have subsequently been presented to Mexico by the Peabody Museum in exchange for study collections of ancient Mexican and Spanish colonial ceramics.

In 1926 Theodore A. Willard published a book, *The City of the Sacred Well*, describing the work done and the objects recovered by Thompson, who said that the huge amount of artefacts he had obtained was not even a tenth of the treasures that remained at the bottom of the *cenote*. This information inspired the Mexican Government to sue Thompson for ownership of the antiquities. He insisted that he was the owner of the land, but according to Mexican legal dispositions as old as the Leyes de Indias from colonial times, and the Law of Archaeological Monuments, issued on 11 May 1897, even if he was the owner of the land the ruins belonged to the nation. This legal quarrel lasted forty years but, due to administrative problems, Mexico lost the case even though it was believed that Thompson had violated the law because the government never granted him a permit to dig.

In 1954 divers from the Club de los Hombres Rana de México tried to use aqualungs for the first time in the *cenote*; but the lack of visibility forced them to abandon the enterprise. The first successful project, which involved archaeologist Dr Román Piña Chán, took place in 1960–61. The National Institute of Anthropology and History (INAH), together with the Club de Exploraciones y Deportes Acuáticos de México (CEDAM), the **National Geographic Society**, and Norman Scott, a private professional diver, worked during four months on the site using an **Airlift** to recover hundreds of artefacts. The project was cancelled by INAH when they realized that proper stratigraphical data was not being obtained and that

The Sacred Cenote, which is located near the main plaza of Chichén Itzá. (Warwick Bray)

many of the objects were breaking when they passed through the airlift.

According to William Folan's thesis, *The Sacred Cenote of Chichén Itzá, Yucatán, Mexico*, presented in 1965 but never published, the ideal way to keep stratigraphic control was drying the *cenote* and digging it as land archaeology. This method was employed in the last attempt to dig the Sacred Cenote, in 1967–8, when INAH, CEDAM, and Expeditions Unlimited, Inc. joined efforts again and worked together during two and a half months. The water level was lowered 4 m and terrestrial archaeological techniques were used in a kind of peninsula made by Thompson in the west side of the well. The water was treated with chemical products to purify it and to increase the visibility. The *cenote* was divided into quadrants and scuba-divers explored the site using an airlift.

Archaeological studies conclude that there were two main phases in the use of *cenote* as an offering place, AD 800–1150 and 1250–1539. The Early Phase was over in the 12th century, when Chichén Itzá was apparently abandoned by most of its population. The Late Phase probably began when Mayapán was founded in the southwest of the peninsula, and started to diminish in 1450 with the fall of this important capital city.

The Sacred Cenote has yielded a large number of precious goods: pieces made of gold, copper, jade, pottery, obsidian, stone, wood, bone, shell, textile, rubber, and *copal* (incense). Most of these were unfortunately recovered without stratigraphic or contextual control. However, it is evident that they belong to different cultures and times. Many of them were manufactured in different parts of Mesoamerica and Central America. They are a vital proof of almost eight centuries of history of the Maya civilization. As Alfred M. Tozzer observed, 'There is perhaps no other single collection in New World archaeology that has afforded so comprehensive a view of the aesthetic life of an ancient people'. P.L.E.

ADDITIONAL READING

Bush Romero, P., 1972, 'The Sacred Well of Chichén-Itzá and Other Freshwater Sites in Mexico', in *Underwater Archaeology, a Nascent Discipline*, Lausanne.

Coggins, C.C. and Shane, O.C., III (eds), 1984, *Cenote of Sacrifice, Maya Treasures from the Sacred Well at Chichén Itzá*, Austin, Texas.

Guzmán Peredo, M., 1991, *Subaquatic Archaeology in Mexico*, Mexico.

Olivé Negrete, J.C., 1991, 'Para la historia de la arqueología mexicana', *Arqueología*, 5 (2nd series), 119-27.

Piña Chán, R., 1970, *Informe preliminar de la reciente exploración del Cenote Sagrado de Chichén Itzá*, Mexico City.

Piña Chán, R., 1990, *Chichén Itzá. La ciudad de los brujos del agua*, Mexico City.

Proskouriakoff, T., 1974, *Jades from the Cenote of Sacrifice, Chichén Itzá, Yucatan*, Memoirs of the Peabody Museum of Archaeology and Ethnology, Hardvard University vol 10/1, Cambridge, Massachusetts.

Tozzer, A.M., 1957, *Chichen Itza and its Cenote of Sacrifice*, Memoirs of the Peabody Museum, Harvard University 11–12, Cambridge, Massachusetts.

Chile
see South America

Cleopatra's Barge

The first deepwater yacht built in the United States. *Cleopatra's Barge* began life in Salem, Massachusetts. In 1815 the local shipping firm of George Crowninshield & Sons was dissolved upon the death of its founder, who was among the wealthiest individuals in the United States. In the spring of 1816 his eldest son and namesake George, Jr commissioned a new vessel. Built for his private leisure on the lines of *America IV* – another Crowninshield ship and the most successful privateer of the War of 1812 – the new hermaphrodite brig measured 100 ft (30.5 m)

Hull sheathing from Cleopatra's Barge, *being pieced together at the Smithsonian Institution.*

Cleopatra's Barge *painted in full sail in 1818 by artist George Roper.*

on deck, 23 ft (7 m) in beam, 11ft 6 in (3.5 m) in depth of hold, and 192 41/95 tons. Named *Cleopatra's Barge*, the first ocean-going yacht built in the nation cost $50,000 to construct and as much again to fit out and furnish. No expense was spared at a time when a conventional deep water merchant vessel cost one-tenth as much; Crowninshield commissioned special china and silver for his fancy new toy and as many as 2,600 people per day visited the unique ship during the winter of its construction and fitting-out.

Crowninshield embarked upon a 'voyage of pleasure' in March 1817; this turned into a six-month Mediterranean cruise, during which he underwent a series of adventures (and misadventures) in sixteen ports, hosting up to 8,000 curious visitors per day. He returned in August 1817 and died that November while planning his next cruise. After an unsuccessful attempt by a brother to steal the *Barge*, it was auctioned in July 1818 for $15,400. It subsequently made a coffee voyage to Rio and then worked briefly as a packet between Boston and Charleston, South Carolina.

In 1820 the Boston merchant firm of Bryant & Sturgis sent the *Barge* to Hawaii under Captain John Suter. Active China traders, Bryant & Sturgis planned to sell the famous yacht to Hawaiian king Kamehameha II (Liholiho) in exchange for Hawaiian sandalwood, a commodity highly prized by Chinese artisans for incense and the decorative arts. Within a day of its arrival on 6 November 1820 at Lahaina Roads, the king inspected the famous ship; nine days later it was his for $80,000 in sandalwood. He renamed it *Ha'aheo o Hawaii* ('Pride of Hawaii') and used it as his royal yacht for the next three years; it also saw limited use as an inter-island merchant vessel.

In late 1823 Liholiho went to England to meet King George IV. He embarked upon a British whaler with his wife and $25,000, most of which was stolen at Rio. While awaiting a royal audience, he and his wife died of the measles. Meanwhile his royal court had taken *Ha'aheo* for a cruise around the island of Kauai. On 5 April 1824 the brig grounded on a reef in Hanalei Bay, on the north end of the island.

Despite a valiant rescue attempt by local Hawaiians, *Ha'aheo* could not be salvaged and was declared a total loss. The effort was witnessed by Boston missionary Hiram Bingham, who described it in his memoirs. A section of the hull washed ashore during a storm on 30 December 1844 and was declared 'in quite a sound state'; the last historical reference to the *Barge* dates from the mid-1850s, when Hawaiian A.S. Nuuanu obtained a permit to salvage its remains. He ceased operations after recovering two cannon and a wooden and metal object – possibly a capstan.

In 1995 the Smithsonian Institution's National Museum of American History conducted a survey for the wreck of the famous yacht. It was located against a reef at the littoral by the mouth of the Waioli River in Hanalei Bay, precisely where Reverend Bingham said it lay in 1824. Ambient environmental conditions has caused the loss of a hull structure; however, other artefacts are preserved, including copper hull sheathing, hull and sheathing fasteners, ceramics, glass, lead patching, personal items, a leather holster, tableware, animal bones, local wood fragments, and even a sample of smithsonite, the mineral named after James

Smithson, found of the Smithsonian Institution. A second and final season of excavation in 1996 discovered substantial remains of the hull and the artefacts. P.F.J.

ADDITIONAL READING

Alexander, W.D., 1906, 'The Story of Cleopatra's Barge', *Papers of the Hawaiian Historical Society*, 13, 27–9.

Bingham, H., 1847, *A Residence of Twenty-one Years in the Sandwich Islands*, 4th edition, 1981, Rutland, Vermont.

Crowninshield, F.B., 1913, *The Story of George Crowninshield's Yacht Cleopatra's Barge on a Voyage of Pleasure to the Western Islands and the Mediterranean 1816–1817*, Boston.

Dodge, E.S., 1954, 'Cleopatra's Barge: America's First Deepwater Yacht', *Motor Boating*, December, 18–106.

Ferguson, D.L., 1976, *Cleopatra's Barge: The Crowninshield Story*, Boston.

Johnston, P.F., 1996, 'The Wreck of America's First Yacht: Cleopatra's Barge (Ha'aheo o Hawaii): 1995 Survey', in T.L. Carrell (ed.), *Underwater Proceedings from the Society for Historical Archaeology Conference, Tucson, Arizona*, Ann Arbor, Michigan.

Lydgate, J.M., 1919, *The Story of Cleopatra's Barge*, Kauai Historical Society Paper 36, Lihue, Hawaii, partially reprinted in Kauai Historical Society, *The Kauai Papers*, 1991, Lihue, 20–22.

Whitehead, W.M., 1953, 'George Crowninshield's Yacht Cleopatra's Barge', *The American Neptune*, 13, 235–51.

Whitehead, W.M., 1959, *George Crowninshield's Yacht Cleopatra's Barge*, Salem, Massachussetts.

Clydesdale Plantation Vessel

A small sloop of the late 18th/early 19th century excavated in the Back River, near Savannah, Georgia, USA in 1992. The remains consist of the keel, keelson, lower stern assembly, and most of the starboard side. The bow and port side were removed when the vessel was buried. The hull was found in association with the remains of a wooden pier and a concentration of domestic refuse dating from the mid- to late 18th century, but the burial postdates the abandonment of the pier.

The vessel, although only 13.34 m long, 4.65 m in beam and no more than 2 m deep amidships, was heavily built to a seagoing standard. The hull form, with moderate, straight deadrise, a short, sharp entrance, long, straight run, long stem rake, and considerable drag, is generally similar to that seen in pilot schooners of the early Federal period. The hull is clearly built for speed and sail-carrying ability rather than capacity, and displaces just over 30 tonnes at a draft of 1.35 m amidships; it

Hull remains of the Clydesdale Plantation Vessel: view from the bow. (INA/F.M. Hocker)

Reconstructed lines of the Clydesdale Plantation Vessel. (Drawing by F.M. Hocker)

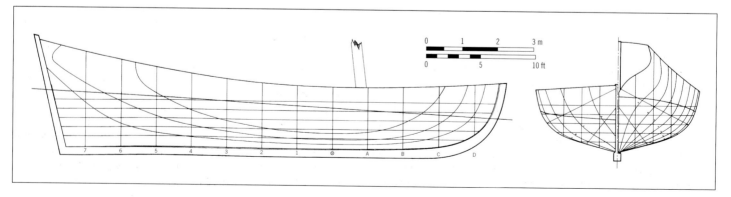

would have been rated between 20 and 25 tons burden.

The vessel is heavily built of Southern timber. The simple but robust backbone consists of a yellow pine keel with a pine deadwood, live oak knee, and sternpost bolted to its upper surface aft. The stem is missing but the foot of the live oak apron is still bolted to the top of the keel. A pine keelson, bolted through every third or fourth frame, the apron, and stern knee to the keel completes this massive assembly. The keelson supported a thwartship mast-step timber relatively far forward. The framing, also of live oak, consisted of floor timbers, notched over and bolted to the keel, alternating with free half-frames spaced evenly between. Futtocks in line with the floor timbers, and top timbers fitted between the futtocks and half-frames, support the topsides. Planking of long, wide, yellow pine boards is nailed and treenailed to the frames. Similar planks make up a tightly fitted ceiling covering the central portion of the hull. Although the deck had been removed when the vessel was buried, loding knee fragments indicated a strongly built structure. Cuttings in the ceiling suggest a trunk cabin aft and perhaps a small fo'c's'le.

Vessels of this size and rig are recorded in customs records of the 18th century clearing for ports in Bermuda and the West Indies, although few such vessels were Southern built; and the tightly fitted, caulked ceiling suggests that this vessel probably carried rice, the principal cash crop of the region, although it seems unlikely that the vessel was originally built for this purpose. It is more likely to have been built either as a pilot boat serving one of the Carolina or Georgia ports or a general-purpose carrier for use along the coast. After its useful career was over, it was deliberately buried as levee cribbing on one of the numerous rice plantations of the lower Savannah River. F.M.H.

Coastal migration theory

The proposition that the initial human occupation of the Americas occurred by maritime adapted populations travelling along now submerged Pleistocene shorelines. The timing and course of first arrival of human populations to a new area are basic questions asked in the study of prehistory. Archaeology has always concerned itself with origins and beginnings, and in every region in the world archaeologists work to discover the evidence that will answer the questions: When did people first arrive at this place? How did they get here?

What were their lives like and how did they adapt to their new environment? Underwater archaeology has important contributions to make to the resolution of these questions in coastal regions.

The spread of the species *Homo* to occupy nearly every area of the earth occurred during the latter portion of the two million year long geological period known as the Quaternary, which itself contains two epochs, the Pleistocene and the Holocene. The Pleistocene, which lasted for most of the Quaternary, was an age of fluctuating, widespread glaciation, while the Holocene represents the current post-glacial period of the last ten thousand years. During the Quaternary, geophysical and climatological factors have caused wide fluctuations in sea-levels throughout the world (see **Sea-level changes**). Foremost among these are tectonic (the movement of continental crusts) and eustatic (the volume of water in global oceans) variables. More regionally specific factors may have important effects on sea-level as well, such as local and regional climatic changes, and their effect on erosion processes and sediment supplies. Generally speaking, all coastlines are dynamic, in a state of constant flux, as the sum of these and other factors combine, compound, cancel, and ultimately control the development of coastlines in terms of both relative sea-level and its geophysical morphology.

Sea-level dynamics during the Quaternary have important archaeological implications to our study of human migrations. Changes in the coastal land mass would have had a direct bearing on the patterns of movement and settlement of human populations. Marine regressions have everywhere resulted in coastal archaeological sites being found on present-day hillsides, sometimes high above current coastlines, while marine transgressions have inundated critical occupational phases of human history. Within the Pacific Basin, Quaternary glacial marine regressions of 100 m or more are generally believed to have played a key role in the settlement of Australasia, Japan, and the Americas, as exposed land masses provided dry land, or at least foreshortened maritime, approaches to these previously inaccessible land masses.

In the case of Australia, Melanesia, and Japan, it is clear that some form of water craft, and hence maritime adaptation, was necessary for the first migrations to these lands, since at no time during the Quaternary were sea-levels so low that human populations could simply walk across dry land to occupy them. The questions that are unresolved concern the timing and routing of

these migrations. In the case of the Americas, however, there is a cleavage among archaeologists since there are two possible vectors of migration, one along an interior continental route, the other along the northeast Pacific coast.

Prehistorians agree that there has never been any evidence uncovered to date to suggest that the species *Homo* arrived in the Americas prior to its full evolution into *Homo sapiens* about thirty thousand years ago; no Neanderthal or *Homo erectus* skeletons or artefacts generally associated with these earlier *Homo* forms have been found in the New World. After this agreement, however, archaeologists concerned with the first people of the Americas divide into two broad camps: those who favour an interior routing along the 'ice-free corridor'; and those who argue for a 'coastal migration' route.

The interior route is assumed to have led from Beringia, the broad plain of the Bering Sea, exposed between Siberia and western Alaska by lowered glacial sea-levels. After a period of occupation in eastern Beringia, the migrant population spread into central North America and beyond by moving through a terrestrial corridor along the eastern edge of the continental divide, created by the decay of the Cordilleran and Laurentide ice sheets at the end of the Pleistocene. There are several weaknesses to this theory, however, not the least of which is that no sites of the appropriate age (c. 10,000 to 14,000 years old) have ever been located within the presumed boundaries of the ice-free corridor. It is also incongruent with the analysis by historical linguistics of the distribution of Amerindian languages, which suggests the oldest resident languages of the Americas are found along the Pacific coast, not inland. Despite these weaknesses, this theory has dominated North American archaeology.

Similarly, the alternative coastal migration theory is supported by only the most circumstantial evidence. This includes the linguistic data and the fact that the earliest sites on the northwest coast of America represent fully adapted maritime societies, although none of these sites predates the earliest interior ones. Proponents of the coastal migration theory do not find this surprising since they argue that the evidence for earlier sites will be found on the now submerged Pleistocene paleo-shoreline. To hold this position, however, immediately raises three important problems which many believe to be insurmountable.

First, is it even possible to locate archaeological evidence in the submarine environment? Second, even if a submerged archaeological site were found, would it have integrity or would the deposit be so heavily degraded by environmental processes subsequent to its original deposition as to be impossible to evaluate? Third, if a site with archaeological integrity were found would it be possible to carry out controlled excavation of it in the underwater environment in which it is located?

All of these concerns have merit and they must be resolved in order to actually test the coastal migration theory. Thus the operationalization of the coastal migration theory necessarily requires the application of an interdisciplinary research programme. This would include: additional research to determine more exactly the rate and direction of changing Quaternary sea-levels; the continued development and testing of prediction models for archaeological sites along paleoshorelines; higher resolutions in **Remote sensing** technology to recognize archaeological site signatures; the examination of coring data (core samples of bottom sediments; see **Submarine coring**) from industry-driven surveys; refinement of our understanding of underwater **Site formation processes**, through detailed field study; the continued exploration of underwater methods of archaeological survey, testing, and excavation; and, ultimately, the direct excavation of a located site in order to recover archaeological remains within acceptable standards of the discipline.

The advances within underwater archaeology over the past three decades suggest that many of these apparent obstacles may be overcome through continued focused research. N.A.E.

ADDITIONAL READING

Allen, J., Golson, J., and Jones, R. (eds), 1977, *Sunda and Sahul: Prehistoric Studies in South-Asia, Melanesia, and Australia*, London.

Easton, N.A., 1992, 'Mal de Mer over Terra Incognita; or, "What Ails the Coastal Migration Theory?"', in M. Moss and J. Erlandson (eds), 'Maritime Cultures of Southern Alaska: Papers in Honour of Richard H. Jordan', *Arctic Anthropology*, 29, 2, 28–41.

Gruhn, R., 1988, 'Linguistic Evidence in Support of the Coastal Route of Earliest Entry into the New World, *Man*, New series, 23, 1, 77–100.

Masters, P.M. and Flemming, N.C., 1983, *Quaternary Coastlines and Marine Archaeology*, New York.

Stright, M.J., 1986, 'Human Occupation of the Outer Continental Shelf During the Late Pleistocene/Early Holocene: Methods for Site Location', *Geoarchaeology*, 1, 4, 347–64.

Cofferdam

A watertight enclosure, usually temporary, constructed within a body of water such as a river or lake, to allow the interior space to be pumped dry so that construction or other work can take place. Cofferdams have been used effectively for the excavation of shipwrecks, including the Viking **Skuldelev Ships** (Roskilde Fjord, Denmark, 1962), Asker Wreck (near Oslo, Norway, 1964), and Hedeby Wreck (near Schleswig, Germany, *c.* 1977–9); the Roman **Blackfriars Wreck I** (London, 1962); the British transport **Betsy** (Yorktown, Virginia, 1982–8); and the French barque **La Belle** (Galveston Bay, Texas, 1966-7).

The steel cofferdam at Yorktown was the first within which the water was retained during the excavation of a shipwreck. Dry, or dewatered, cofferdams are practical for water depths of up to several metres, but in the 6 to 7 m depth of water over *Betsy* at Yorktown a 'stilling basin' was a more cost-effective alternative. This demonstrated that retaining and filtering the water greatly improved diving conditions while, at the same time, helping preserve the ship's hull and contents during excavation. J.D.B.

ADDITIONAL READING

Bass, G.F., ed., 1972, *A History of Seafaring Based on Underwater Archaeology*, New York.

Broadwater, J.D., 1992, 'Shipwreck in a Swimming Pool: An Assessment of the Methodology and Technology Utilized on the Yorktown Shipwreck Archaeological Project', *Historical Archaeology*, Special Issue 4, 36–46.

Muckelroy, K. (ed.), 1980, *Archaeology Underwater: An Atlas of the World's Submerged Sites*, New York.

Colebrooke

An English Indiaman wrecked in False Bay near Cape Town in 1778. The site is one of the few known 18th-century shipwreck sites in South Africa with extant structural remains and well-preserved organic materials such as leather and cordage. In 1984 a salvage group, under the leadership of Charlie Shapiro, was granted a permit to work on the site in collaboration with the South African Maritime Museum.

Although the divers claim to have used a system of triangulation, few fixed archaeological controls could be maintained. This was due to countless problems with a heavy overburden of sand, several metres deep, which necessitated the use of controversial **Propwash deflection**. To date, the architecture of the vessel has not yet been properly documented. Artefacts including bottles of snuff, leather-bound packages of scissors, filled bottles of Madeira wine, bale seals, glassware, and musket components are in the

collection housed at the South African Maritime Museum. L.H., T.D.

ADDITIONAL READING

Hardy, C., 1800, *A Register of Ships in the Service of the East India Company*, Cape Town.

Colombia

see **South America**

SS *Columbus*

One of seven submerged anomalies targeted for investigation by the US Army Corps of Engineers in a channel widening project, and found to be the remains of a steamboat including the only known example of a Baltimore-built crosshead engine. Not only the engine but the entire side-wheeler *Columbus* was built in 'Charm City' in 1828. At 138 ft (42 m) it was one of the larger vessels on Chesapeake Bay. Although designed as a freighter, it was considered a pretty ship and boasted a ladies' lounge panelled in mahogany and curly maple as well as eight staterooms. It was altered several times, including being lengthened to 174 ft (53 m) in 1836, which increased its tonnage commensurately. The vessel also changed hands on a number of occasions, ending up eventually with the Powhattan Steamboat Company and serving on the Baltimore to Richmond route until its fiery demise.

Columbus left Baltimore late in the afternoon of 27 November 1850 bound for Richmond via Norfolk. The steamer carried only sixteen passengers and crew and six horses. At the entrance to the Potomac River the engine room caught fire. Only seven people reached the lifeboat, which followed the burning ship in search of survivors until the superstructure collapsed. The lifeboat then made for the Smith Point light ship from which the survivors watched the burning wreck. At one point it drifted sufficiently near for its heat to be felt. It subsided at dawn into about 18 m of water, 15 km from shore in Maryland waters.

With more than 600 steamers plying the waters of the bay and with fire a chief source of loss for these ships, the significance of *Columbus* lies not in its death. The hull of the ship was unusual as it represented a transitional form; an evolution from what was essentially a sailing hull with an engine added, to a vessel designed specifically for steam propulsion. There was insufficient remaining of the burned hull to consider recovery. The engine, though, was a different matter. *Columbus* was equipped with a crosshead engine, the creation of Charles Reeder, one of the first designers of marine steam engines in Maryland. Both *Columbus* and the crosshead engine are known only from written descriptions; formal plans do not exist for either entity.

The remains, first recorded by the National Oceanic and Atmospheric Administration's (NOAA) Automated Wreck and Obstruction Information System (AWOIS) in 1987, were investigated when the area was surveyed in 1991, preparatory to an Army Corps of Engineers' dredging project to deepen and widen the existing approach channel to Baltimore Harbour (see Morrison *et al.*). Examination of anomalies that might be affected by the project revealed one with an unusual engine within hull remains that might represent one of several steamers known to be submerged in the area. Identification of the engine type correlated with dimensional measurements permitted professional photographer Michael Pohuski to positively identify the remains as those of *Columbus*.

In compliance with Federal and State regulations, the site was mapped and wood samples collected in 1992. Although it lies in only 18 m of water, conditions including strong currents and an almost complete lack of visibility complicated operations on the site. The fragile state of the engine and its precariously balanced position made its lift particularly hazardous. Ultimately the engine was raised in its constituent pieces.

The project was undertaken jointly by the Army Corps of Engineers, using military divers, and the archaeological consulting firm of R. Christopher Goodwin and Associates, Inc. which employed both underwater archaeologists and professional divers trained in underwater archaeology. Raising the engine was accomplished over a year due to restricted availability of equipment and personnel, and inclement weather.

Although heavily graphitized on the exterior, the internal portions of the engine contained much sound metal. The components were sent for conservation treatment in a Louisiana laboratory (scheduled for completion in 1997). The engine will be returned to Maryland, where the elements will be reassembled for display, possibly at the Baltimore Museum of Industry which would place them within blocks of the Federal Hill steamworks where they were built on Baltimore's Inner Harbour. S.B.M.L.

ADDITIONAL READING

Irion, J.B. and Beard, D.V., 1995, *Data Recovery on the Wreck of the Steamship Columbus, 18ST625, St Mary's County, Maryland*, Frederick, Maryland.

Morrison, P.H. *et al.*, 1992, *Phase II Archaeological Investigations of Three Shipwreck Sites in the Baltimore Harbor and Channels: Federal Navigation 50 Ft. Project, Chesapeake Bay, Maryland and Virginia*, Frederick, Maryland.

Comacchio Wreck

An important Roman wreck of the late 1st century BC discovered in 1980 under 3.5 m of silt in the Po delta near the town of Comacchio (Ferrara), just north of Ravenna, Italy. It was excavated, lifted to a local museum, and published by a team led by Dr Fede Berti. The wreck contained a cargo of freshly cut boxwood logs and 3 tonnes of lead ingots stamped with the name of Agrippa, the emperor Augustus's son-in-law. The ingots as well as dendrochronological study of ship's timbers (boxwood and elm) and logs from the cargo along with lamps and pottery confirmed a date *c.* 12 BC or a little earlier. The site is noteworthy for its excellent prompt publication and its affording the possibility of a 513-year master chronology through the boxwood timber of the cargo, the best available dendrochronological sequence for this poorly represented period.

The ship was 21 m long, 5.62 m wide, and about 130 tonnes burden; it is the only known example of an ancient wreck transporting timber. The technique of the ship was interesting too, as the hull timbers are sewn together (see also **Bon-Porté Wreck**). Also preserved were pieces of rigging and cordage, fishing implements and wooden tools and utensils, leather garments and shoes, storage amphoras and pottery for daily use, a variety of terracotta oil lamps (including a common late Hellenistic eastern Aegean type, the so-called 'Ephesos lamp', rarely found in the West), and a number of small lead temple models. H.W.

ADDITIONAL READING

Berti, F. (ed.), 1990, *Fortuna Maris: La Nave Romana di Comacchio*, Bologna.

Kunniholm, P., *et al.*, 1994, 'Comacchio (Ferrara): A 513–Year Buxus Dendrochronology for the Roman Ship', *Bolletino di Archeologia*, 291–9.

Computer modelling

The generation of a representation of a set of conditions and variables that have enough in common with observed conditions to be useful as a simplified example, demonstration, or for prediction. Computer models have not often been used by maritime archaeologists, although modelling has become increasingly common in terrestrial archaeology for two decades.

Modelling can be static or dynamic. Static modelling is generating a hypothetical synthesis of complex observations and processes that has predictive or heuristic utility; a simplified generalization of a complex situation that accurately presents empirical data. A simple example of a static model is a flow chart. Dynamic computer models, or simulation studies, usually have two main attributes: the ability to manipulate variables and the ability to move the model through time to observe how alterations of the variables affect the outcome. Dynamic model utility is in using existing knowledge to forecast trends, or retrodict to develop explanatory hypotheses. A computer's data synthesis capabilities can help solve very difficult and complex problems, which of course require complex data sets for the model. Most models use both theoretical and empirical data, and increase in validity through refinement by incorporation of tested data.

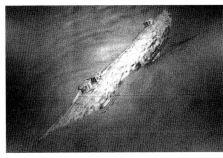

Computer model of H.L. Hunley. (SCIAA)

Flow charts and simulation models have become common to archaeology since systems theory influenced archaeology in the 1970s, and they continue to reflect the influence of computers on the discipline. Flow charts as models represent relationships between variables and, like models overall, reduce a complicated amount of interactive data into a more comprehensible form. For example, models can represent anything from shipbuilding material procurement, to interactive trade networks over wide areas or dynamically through time, or perhaps the flow of energy during a voyage or complicated **Site formation processes**.

Analysis of natural site formation processes is one area that has a high potential for productive computer modelling. Running computer simulations of wind, current, and wave variables can be very useful for site interpretation. Once a tested model that validly accounts for initial and post-wreck site distribution is developed, it can be used to find areas of high probability for additional materials and to generate some idea of the site's vulnerability to future large weather events. Simulations also enhance interpretation by aiding the separation of cultural and natural processes in explaining how the site came to be the way it appears today.

Recent advances in computer assisted

design (CAD) programs have immediate application to hull studies. There have been several experimental archaeological hull reconstructions conducted to determine sailing qualities, building sequence, or structural strength. Detailed documentation of hull remains and presentation of the data in a three-dimensional CAD program can go a long way to answering questions that previously required scale reconstructions, particularly when combined with one of the sophisticated nautical architecture analysis computer programs available. Nautical architecture software is particularly useful for quantifying hull sailing qualities under different variables, whether reproducing historical conditions or determining seasonally variable sailing times (the technical distance) between ports.

Three-dimensional modelling coupled with animation can be particularly powerful for processual or interpretive applications. In the 1990s, the National Park Service **Submerged Cultural Resources Unit** developed an analytical and three-dimensional model for public interpretation of the HMS *Fowey* site in Biscayne National Park, Florida. Spatial or geographic models are becoming more common in terrestrial archaeology and have been used especially for predicting site locations and accounting for settlement patterns through their relation to environmental variables. Development of **Geographic Information Systems (GIS)** software programmes have made sophisticated spatial modelling possible through its ability to capture, interrelate, manipulate, and ultimately create data for analysis and display. The added dimension of time depth provided by archaeological data can be portrayed by combining sites of similar periods on a single GIS theme. Observing multiple timeperiod overlays produces a chronological simulation that relates data temporally as well as spatially. GIS modelling can also be useful in testing different sea-level models and affects of inundation of local topography. Assuming application of terrestrial site location models can productively be expanded underwater for similar geomorphological feature, GIS modelling can effectively indicate areas of high submerged site potential.

The temporal dimension of GIS allows modelling of such processes as population migration and growth, the development of trade networks, and the maritime trade route alterations that result. Another spatial-temporal correction used in maritime archaeology is the correction of chart distances for predicted sailing times and assessing risk variables of different routes under varying weather and hull conditions,

which can be useful for historical site prediction and explanation. Computer models can easily simulate historically documented or predicted seasonal trade networks to account for a particular wreck distribution located at a specific location. The model would incorporate information about raw materials, finished goods, markets, populations, navigation hazards, and wind and oceanographic currents to simulate the trade that the wreck collection reflects. These variables could be altered to observe the results of the introduction of new trade materials, market vagaries, and the impact of new port and market introductions on trade variation and port longevity, as an aid to maritime site interpretation at the regional level.

One of the earliest examples of computer modelling to answer a maritime process question was the simulation of Polynesian settlement, a problem that had been debated for decades. More than 100,000 hypothetical drift voyages from nearly seventy different starting islands were generated and analysed by Levison, Ward, and Webb. Variables such as the distance land would be visible, seasonal current and wind, boat speed, voyager survival length probabilities, and storm risk were included in this computer model. The simulation model indicated that drift voyages from New Zealand and the American continent were unlikely; only elementary navigation would be required for major Polynesian settlement voyages; and drift could have been responsible for the settlement of Tonga and Samoa once Western Polynesia was settled.

Computer modelling will probably become as common in underwater archaeology as it has in terrestrial archaeology as researchers become more familiar with computer capability and modelling methodology. There are many questions that can benefit from modelling techniques, and it will prove to be one of the most useful tools in maritime archaeology for developing explanation and generating hypotheses. L.E.M.

ADDITIONAL READING

Levison, M., Ward, R.G., and Webb, J., 1972, 'The Settlement of Polynesia: A Report on a Computer Simulation', in Clarke (ed.), 'Archaeology and Physical Anthropology', *Oceania*, 7, 234–45.

Clarke, D.L., 1978, *Analytical Archaeology*, New York.

Concepción
see *Nuestra Señora de la Concepción*

Concordia
see **Älvsnabben Wreck**

Concretions
see **Casting**; **Conservation**

Conservation
The scientific process of preserving and restoring archaeological materials; in the case of underwater and maritime sites conservation usually involves waterlogged materials from submerged environments. **Underwater archaeology** is the only branch of archaeology that is totally dependent on the conservation laboratory for its ultimate success. Because of the corrosion and deterioration processes that the material from underwater sites undergoes before recovery,

Conserving a pintle from Sirius. *(© Western Australia Maritime Museum/Patrick Baker)*

extensive conservation is required before it can be identified and analysed. Over the decade to 1997 there has been a dramatic increase in all aspects of underwater archaeology and with this increased activity comes the responsibility to conserve the material properly. Often the conservator is the first and, in the case of some very fragile items, may be the only person to see the tenuous remains of some artefacts. Conservation, like archaeology, is not just a set of techniques, procedures, and treatments; it is a state of mind that holds a deep concern for the integrity of the artefacts and what they represent as remnants of history. The conservator's responsibilities are those of archaeologist, mender, caretaker, and recorder of the artefacts that come into his or her care. Archaeological conservation, therefore, should always include documentation, analysis, cleaning, and stabilization of an object.

The objectives of cleaning and stabilization are to protect artefactual, faunal, and other archaeological materials and to prevent their reacting adversely with the environment after recovery. In the conservation of archaeological material, be it siliceous, organic, or metallic, there are different deterioration and corrosion processes to consider (see **Corrosion studies**). In the majority of the cases, it is iron and wood that present the most overwhelming problems for the conservator. This is especially true when dealing with marine shipwreck sites.

The conservation of metal artefacts from marine sites, and to a lesser degree from freshwater sites, is only remotely related to the conservation problems presented by metal artefacts from most land sites. When artefacts are recovered from the sea, especially warm areas such as the Caribbean and the Mediterranean, they are commonly encrusted with thick layers of calcium carbonate, magnesium hydroxide, metal corrosion products, sand, clay, and various forms of marine life such as shells, coral, barnacles, and plant life. The term 'encrustation' or 'conglomerate' refers to the encrusted whole that may contain one or more artefacts. These conglomerates may range from the size of a single coin to masses weighing several thousand kilograms containing hundreds of individual objects made of many different materials. In the process of dealing with encrusted metal artefacts, which are in most cases iron, one will encounter artefacts of other metals along with ceramics, glass, and various organic materials such as wood, leather, and bone. Thus the conservation of encrustations with their concealed contents is analogous to an excavation square within a site.

Any laboratory that processes these encrustations has the responsibility to preserve and stabilize the artefacts as well as conservation technology permits and to recover as much archaeological data as possible. In many instances information exists in the form of associations recoverable only by *in situ* observations made by the conservator. Extensive records have to be maintained which include notes on the encrustation, the objects it contains, the preservation techniques used, measured drawings, and colour, black and white, and X-ray photographs. The laboratory must have sufficient space and equipment to take a conglomerate, and both extract and conserve the encased specimens. It may even be necessary to prepare the conserved artefacts for display. The laboratory has to have forklifts, chain hoists, large vats, specialized DC power supplies, hundreds of kilograms of chemicals, and thousands of litres of deionized water, among other resources, to perform the job.

Casts have to be made of disintegrated objects and of significant impressions left in the encrustations (see **Casting**). The conservatory must be able to detect such things as potsherds, cloth fragments, spikes, straps, and animal bones that are randomly distributed in the encrustation. Even less obvious remains like the impressions of seeds and even insects, for example the impressions and egg cases of cockroaches found in several encrustations from the 1554 Spanish Plate Fleet, and the remains of a 17th-century cricket found in a bottle from Port Royal, Jamaica, must be detected and recorded. The conservator is in a unique position to supply the archaeologist with valuable evidence and to provide the laboratory with basic conservation data for research.

It is necessary for the conservator to be aware of the corrosion processes that the different metals go through and to know what corrosion products have to be eliminated for the safety of the artefact and which corrosion products can remain, or be removed for aesthetic reasons only. Chloride corrosion compounds, for instance, are detrimental to the long-term survival of all artefacts of iron, copper, and alloys containing copper. The corrosion processes of these metals are accelerated unless precautions are taken as soon as they have been recovered from a marine environment. However, the chloride corrosion products of lead and silver and their alloys are stable. They may be unsightly or even disfiguring, but they do not take part in chemical reactions that attack the remaining metal. Lead and silver artefacts need to be cleaned only for aesthetic reasons and to reveal surface details under the corrosion layers. Electrolytic reduction is commonly used to clean most metals; however, a number of chemical treatments are also effective.

Encrusted metal artefacts from a marine environment may not be conserved for months or even years after recovery, so they must be properly stored in inhibited aqueous solutions until treatment can begin. It is important that any adhering encrustation or corrosion layers be left intact until the objects are treated because they form a protective coating which retards corrosion. If iron artefacts are left encrusted, they can usually be stored in plain tap water for long periods of time. If the encrustation is removed, then an alkaline solution is required to prevent the iron from corroding. Once properly stored, conservation can proceed in an orderly fashion with no need to rush the process.

The mechanical cleaning process is one of the most important parts of conserving encrusted iron artefacts. For it is during this phase that most of the observations on overall associations are made. Where possible, X-rays are used to determine the content of each encrustation, the condition of the objects, the presence of moulds, and as guides in extracting the artefacts from the encrustation. A variety of tools from hammers and chisels to pneumatic air scribes are used to remove and mechanically clean the artefacts.

Electrolytic reduction is one of the most utilized techniques for the conservation of metal artefacts from marine sites and, to a large degree, metal objects from any environment. Because of its effectiveness in removing chloride ions, it is often the treatment of choice for iron artefacts as well as other metals. It can also be used to reduce the corrosion products on non-ferrous metal artefacts back to a metallic state. Chemical reduction treatments such as alkaline sulphite treatment for iron, and the dithionite treatment for cupreous and silver artefacts, can be used in lieu of electrolytic reduction to reduce the corrosion products and eliminate aggressive ions. Depending on the degree of chloride contamination, electrolytic reduction may not be required and satisfactory results can be obtained with alkaline rinses. For cupreous and iron artefacts with reasonably low chloride contamination, it is possible to rinse the chlorides out in successive changes of alkaline baths until the chlorides are removed. The object is then thoroughly rinsed in several baths of deionized water.

After metal artefacts have been treated, it is imperative that their surfaces be covered with a protective coating to insulate the metal from the effects of moisture, chemically active vapours, and gases. For iron artefacts several coats of tannic acid are put on before applying a final sealant. The tannic acid reacts with the surface of the iron and forms a black-coloured ferric tannate which is aesthetically pleasing and more corrosion resistant than metallic iron. A protective sealant, such as microcrystalline wax, polyurethane coatings, or zinc phosphate based anti-corrosion primers is then applied to prevent further corrosion. In general, the sealant selected should be impervious to water vapour and gases, be natural-looking so that it does not detract from the appearance of the artefact, be reversible, and transparent or translucent so any corrosion of the metal surface can be quickly detected. Immersion in molten microcrystalline wax is one of the best sealants for a variety of metals, especially wrought and cast iron. With the exception of microcrystalline wax, all present a problem if there is ever need to retreat the artefacts. Clear acrylic sprays are generally applicable for the final coating on non-ferrous artefacts; however, microcrystalline wax can be used.

ganic artefacts of wood, extiles are found on most organic material normally decays under combined biological and chemical attack when buried in the ground and submerged in water. It can, however, survive for prolonged periods when in either a very dry or a waterlogged environment. When wood is deposited in an underwater site, the water-soluble substances such as starch and sugar disappear first, along with mineral salts, colouring agents, tanning matters, and other bonding materials. In time, through hydrolysis, cellulose in the cell walls disintegrates, leaving a lignin network to support the wood. The loss of cellulose tissue does not cause much alteration in the gross volume of wood, but the porosity is increased and the wood absorbs water like a sponge. As long as waterlogged wood objects are kept wet they will retain their shape. If the wood is exposed to the air, the excess water evaporates and the surface tension of the evaporating water will cause the weakened cell walls to collapse, causing considerable shrinkage and distortion.

Waterlogged wood is commonly conserved by a process that involves removing the excess water by replacing it with cellular bulking materials such as different molecular weights of polyethylene glycol, sucrose, or acetone/rosin. Another alternative is to remove the excess water by freeze drying or solvent dehydration in order to keep the wood dimensionally stable. While these treatments are effective, each has its own drawbacks. Research is continuing on a number of substances that may provide less expensive and more reliable methods of treatment.

Generally speaking, the conservation of ceramics and siliceous material recovered from archaeological sites is very straightforward and only minimal treatment is required. One of the main things that needs to be determined first when one conserves ceramics is whether they are earthenware, stoneware, or porcelain. The latter two are fired at higher temperatures and are relatively impervious and therefore do not absorb soluble salts. Earthenware, which constitutes the bulk of the ceramics from any period, is fired at much lower temperatures and will adsorb soluble substances that may be in the archaeological environment; thus earthenware pieces require soaking in a series of water baths to remove the soluble salts. If the soluble salts are not removed from any porous material, they will go through cycles of liquefying and recrystallizing as the relative humidity rises and falls. Over time this action will exfoliate the surface of the material and even break up the piece through internal stresses and fractures. Chemical cleaning and/or mechanical cleaning is required to remove the insoluble salts. Pottery recovered from freshwater sites seldom have sufficient soluble salts (chlorides, phosphates, nitrates) in the body of the sherd to present a problem and no treatment other than rinsing off dirt and possibly consolidation of the earthenware is required. In marine sites, and even many wetland sites, black sulphide staining of ceramic glazes and even glass is very common. This type of staining is easily removed by immersing in a diluted solution of hydrogen peroxide for a short period of time until the stains disappear.

Only a few of the basic conservation considerations have been addressed here. The preservation of antiquities should produce objects that are chemically stable with an aesthetically acceptable appearance. All treatments should be reversible in the event that the object should require additional preservation. Just because an object has been successfully conserved, does not mean it will not deteriorate in the future. Only if stored or displayed under optimum conditions can stability be assured. Metal artefacts, as well as those made of organic or siliceous material, can become chemically unstable from a myriad causes and require periodic inspection and evaluation, as well as possible re-treatment. At our present stage of knowledge, perhaps it is most realistic to say that the objective of archaeological conservation is to delay reprocessing as long as possible by proper storage and to make any necessary re-treatment simple and brief. It is obvious that the conservation laboratory can play a major role in archaeology, when the objective is to produce the maximum amount of archaeological data from the excavation of underwater sites.
D.L.H.

ADDITIONAL READING

Grattan, D.W., ed., 1982, *Proceedings of the ICOM Waterlogged Wood Working Group Conference*, Ottawa.

Hamilton, D.L., 1975, *Conservation of Metal Objects from Underwater Sites: A Study in Methods*, Texas Antiquities Committee Publication 1, Austin.

Pearson, C. (ed.), 1987, *Conservation of Marine Archaeological Objects*, London.

Plenderleith, H.J. and Werner, A.E.A., 1977, *The Conservation of Antiquities and Works of Art*, London.

Singley, K., 1988, *The Conservation of Archaeological Artifacts from Freshwater Environments*, South Haven, Michigan.

Contextual relationships

The relationship between the site and its context. Evaluation of archaeological findings requires an organized effort to identify and control for context. While archaeologists generally agree about the need to recognize contextual factors that affect their conclusions, they do not always concur about what constitutes relevant context. For maritime archaeologists, special factors arise in fresh- and salt-water environments that distinguish underwater archaeology from the land-based variety. But the basic reasoning involved applies equally to the conduct of land and underwater research.

Post-depositional context

Physical associations of cultural remains in the archaeological record are affected by factors that intervene from the moment of deposition to the recording of those associations by archaeologists. Michael Schiffer has identified transformational factors of this kind that affect land sites, and in a general way his approach parallels that of Keith Muckelroy in relation to **Maritime archaeology**. Schiffer distinguishes between the cultural context of the past cultural system as a living, adapting entity, and the **Archaeological record**, where the discards and remains of that cultural system become progressively altered due to transformational factors after deposition. For marine archaeology, these factors include natural processes of erosion, chemical destruction and alteration, corrosion, biological effects of marine growth, turbation due to tectonic activities, wave action, ice damage, and a wide range of seabed-altering actions that can change the material associations archaeologists use to build their ideas about the human past. These factors also include intervention due to human activity following deposition – for example, salvage, dredging, looting, destruction due to warfare, effects of construction, and others that operate to alter the archaeological record.

Muckelroy's parallel distinction between scrambling devices and extracting filters in relation to post-depositional processes has been widely adopted in maritime archaeology. Filters are processes that affect the archaeological context by removing or obliterating materials from the physical associations at a site. These processes include decomposition and destruction by marine organisms (such as the action of gribbles, also known as shipworms, in removing exposed timbers), flotation (when wooden items float away from a shipwreck site after wrecking), and salvage activities resulting in the removal of materials from the site. Scramblers are processes that operate to cause mixture of materials in such a way as to alter the physical associations at the site. Strong surge and wave action, for example, may jumble the parts of a shipwreck and alter their position on the seabed in ways that had nothing to do with the ship's original character or with its wrecking.

One of the most important scramblers described by Muckelroy is mixing of deposits of different shipwrecks by current, wave action, and other factors, especially in high-risk locations where multiple shipwrecks tend to occur. Maritime archaeologists are fond of referring to shipwrecks as 'time capsules' representing units of contemporaneity. That is, materials found associated at wreck sites are often assumed to have been deposited simultaneously and exclusively in the context of a single moment in time (the wreck event). Such units of contemporaneity are relatively rare in land archaeology and are sometimes referred to as the 'Pompeii premise' because of their Pompeii-like way of presenting material associations in relation to a single moment in time. Undisturbed tombs and grave associations are probably the most common occurrence on land of this kind of association. More often, land archaeologists must deal with sites that have accumulated through successive occupations, with factors of disturbance and alteration from one occupational level to the next.

A careful review of potential scrambling factors at maritime sites reveals that the archaeological 'time capsule' is often an illusion. Many, if not most, shipwrecks are found in so-called **Ship traps** such as the North Carolina capes (including Cape Hatteras), Bermuda, the Dry Tortugas (Florida), **Yassiada** (Turkey), and **Isle Royale** (Lake Superior, Michigan), to name a few. These are places where the geography, weather, and sea conditions conspire to put ships at risk. The result is a large number of wrecks and strandings within limited areas, with the possibility of mixed deposits produced by overlapping debris fields.

The Nine Cannon site in the **Dry Tortugas National Park**, studied by Larry Murphy, provides an extreme case of disassociated materials from multiple shipwrecks from different periods spread across more than 319 m of Loggerhead Reef. This reef was indicated by archival research as the most dangerous ship trap within the National Park. Also on Loggerhead Reef, there are wrecks that, while relatively coherent and well preserved, present some anomalous associations. The wooden sailing cargo ship recorded as DRTO-036, which burned and sank sometime around 1850 while trans-

porting construction materials to Fort Jefferson, has a chainplate and dead-eye resting nearby that is too large to have been used on this ship and probably derives from another, larger and later-period sailing ship. Strong waves sweep across Loggerhead Reef during storms and hurricanes, and even in good weather there are current and surge. Archaeological surveys there are revealing the extent to which such 'scramblers' have disassociated and recombined materials from wrecks in different parts of the reef. No final or convincing assessment of the archaeological associations at this location will be possible until the filtering and scrambling factors in the post-depositional context of Loggerhead Reef are identified and controlled.

Cultural context

There is little agreement among anthropologists about the culture concept, but there is widespread recognition of the need to recognize and control for factors arising from human behaviour beyond the post-depositional factors of natural and cultural origin, and it should be possible to identify archaeological associations that relate to the human society that produced them. Instead of worrying about anthropologically correct definitions of 'culture', maritime archaeologists are encouraged to apply pragmatic, minimalist reasoning to this question. This means regarding the physical associations at shipwreck sites that cannot be accounted for by post-depositional factors as products of cultural factors pertaining to the ship's construction and contents on the one hand and the cultural system that produced both the ship and the wreck on the other.

There are differing points of view about what constitutes cultural context in archaeology. At the risk of oversimplification, two principal views need to be considered:

1 *The primacy of post-depositional context.* Simply put, this means that post-depositional factors of whatever kind relevant to a particular underwater site or survey area must be evaluated before attempting cultural explanations of any kind. Cultural context pertains to the living human society that produced the shipwreck in the first place, but our understanding about this must be as free as possible of distortions arising from the obscuring or filtering effects of post-depositional factors.

2 *Materialist vs. mentalist cultural contexts.* The relevance of competing materialist and mentalist culture concepts to the findings of land archaeology is currently being debated. This debate is unlikely to be resolved soon. So maritime archaeologists need to decide

for themselves which kind of cultural context offers the best explanation for the physical associations encountered at their particular sites.

Archaeology, by virtue of its reliance on material remains to understand the human past, is predisposed to rely upon materialist theories of culture, especially theories of Marxist origin. Such theories tend to regard material relations of production and distribution as primary determinants of the social order, with technology playing a key role. Marxist-materialist explanations (without political rhetoric) historically have been important in archaeological theory. This trend began with V. Gordon Childe in the 1940s as he developed his concept of the 'Neolithic Revolution' to explain the growth of urban civilizations following the rise of agriculture. His theory attempted to explain their evolution of food surpluses, sedentarism, full-time craft specialists, and class-structured societies. Following Childe, this trend continued during the 1950s and 1960s with the study of prehistoric economies and the rise, in the 1960s and 1970s, of the 'new archaeology', with its emphasis on ancient cultures as adaptive systems known through the scientific analysis of their material remains in relation to paleoecology, paleodiet, and other ecosystemic indicators. Without attributing such materialist approaches to any particular school of thought or to individual scholars, one can argue that the mainstream of modern archaeological science is founded upon materialist assumptions, although no longer necessarily Marxist in origin or character.

Ship traps of the sort referred to earlier are good places to test theories of cultural behaviour based upon materialist expectations. Why would shipowners and captains risk their vessels in such places? And what accounts for the historical persistence of such high-risk behaviour in such localities? Murphy has proposed the concept of 'one more voyage' as a hypothesis that shipowners will always push their vessels one more voyage beyond their safe operating limits or intended use-life. Research at such conspicuous ship traps as Bermuda and the Dry Tortugas has enabled archaeologists to refine and to start testing this concept in relation to the cultural context of the shipwreck sites there. In true Marxist fashion, this concept stresses economic and technological relations as primary indicators of socio-cultural behaviour. It specifically relates to the Western mercantile-capitalist historical tradition and is not presented as a universal, cross-cultural principle of human behaviour. And, finally, it includes an awareness of geographical, meteorological, and other situational variables as essential components of these material relations.

For sailing ships, the dangers were measurably different (and usually greater) in these localities than for steamships. But during the late 19th century sail was engaged in prolonged competition with steam for the transport of bulk cargoes such as lumber, coal, cotton, and grain. It was still possible for shipowners to make profitable voyages under sail provided economies were achieved in the form of reduced crew sizes, efficiently constructed ships combined with low capital investment, and routes that would reduce passage times. Both in Bermuda and in the Dry Tortugas, archaeologists have encountered wrecks best understood within a cultural context involving a willingness to accept risks for the sake of profits. Evidence for such economies appears in the form of large-displacement (over 2,000 tons) sailing ships constructed of wrought iron according to standardized designs pioneered by Scottish shipyards from the 1870s onwards.

The wreck of *North Carolina* on Chubb Reef off Bermuda's west end while transporting a cargo of cotton in 1888, and *Killian* (later renamed *Avanti*), wrecked on Loggerhead Reef in the Dry Tortugas in 1907 while carrying lumber, are good examples of this class of ship. Examination of both wrecks revealed features that are best explained in relation to the cultural context of the capitalist economies of late 19th-century Europe and America. Each ship was big but lacked internal bulkheads (a feature already in use in civil and military ships of the period). Structural support for the hull was provided by rail-like longitudinal stringers and stiffeners attached to the vertical frames. By avoiding the use of bulkheads, the builders made almost the entire hull into cargo-carrying space, with no obstructions to the efficient loading and unloading of bulk materials. Neither ship had steam propulsion, which was costly and required valuable space for machinery and coal that shipowners preferred to use for cargo. But each ship had steam-powered deck engines to operate winches for raising and lowering sails and other heavy tasks. This was necessary because the masts and yards were made of iron, with iron (and later, steel) cables that were too heavy for a small number of sailors to raise and lower by hand. Historical accounts describe the working and living conditions on these ships as difficult, with relatively small crews pushed hard in a manner comparable to industrial mill and factory workers of the same period in Europe and America.

Extant examples of ships of this kind are found as wrecks or hulks as far afield as French Polynesia (*County of Roxborough*) and Chile (*County of Peebles*) and as preserved ships in such places as Hawaii (*Falls of Clyde*), New York City (*Wavertree*), and San Francisco (*Balclutha*). The location of wrecks recorded so far of this class of ship is indicative of the risk-taking associated with this kind of voyaging. For example, the Dry Tortugas lie between Florida and Cuba in the Straits of Florida, the shortest passage for ships travelling between Gulf ports and the open Atlantic. The reefs and shoals of the Dry Tortugas, some of which change their shape and shift their position due to storms and current, were a major hazard to navigation. Archival sources studied by a National Park Service team produced at least 241 cases of sinkings or strandings within the 250 sq. km Dry Tortugas National Park. Of these, 215 were well documented, with Loggerhead Reef heading the casualty list. Surveys conducted by the National Park Service there since 1990 have located and documented additional wrecks, many of which were not listed in the archival sources. These wrecks include at least one large late 19th-century sailing cargo ship of composite wood and iron construction that is being compared to *Killian* and its contemporaries and analysed in relation to the cultural context of the late 19th-century maritime-mercantile economies that produced them.

Materialist perspectives on cultural context are presently being challenged by mentalist views that regard culturally constructed attitudes, with their attendant symbolic and ideational constructs, as relevant to archaeological interpretation. Sometimes referred to as 'post-processual' archaeology, this movement has been influential in historical archaeology on land, where documentary sources are available. The most favoured approach at this time is one that advocates reading the archaeological record as a form of text, with controls applied to that text through the deconstruction of dominant cultural influences and assumptions. Historically particular and culturally constructed issues such as gender, race, colonialism and neo-colonialism, status, and political power are seen as the relevant context against which to interpret the text provided through archaeology. By peeling back layers of received wisdom and preconceptions about the past – including those acquired and perpetuated by archaeologists – archaeology can achieve a relatively unbiased view of the human past.

This approach attempts to identify culturally constructed attitudes and values in the minds of people living in the past. In some ways, this seems like the materialist approach just described for late 19th-century commercial shipwrecks, and it, too, has strongly Marxist roots. But the conduct of this approach so far has generally failed to control for post-depositional effects upon the archaeological record. Post-processual archaeologists prefer instead to read the archaeological record directly as the historical product of human cultural constructions at particular times and places. The result in historical archaeology has been the rise of a subjective, non-scientific (sometimes anti-scientific) mode of archaeological interpretation.

It remains to be seen whether or to what extent maritime archaeologists will embrace the post-processual approach. The unwillingness so far of post-processual archaeologists to recognize or control for post-depositional context makes the adoption of their ideas uncertain. A pragmatic, minimalist approach to matters of archaeological context, with primary consideration to the effects of post-depositional factors as measured and evaluated by good archaeological science, remains the most promising and convincing alternative for maritime studies. R.A.G.

ADDITIONAL READING

Muckelroy, K., 1978, *Maritime Archaeology*, Cambridge.

Murphy, L.E. (ed.), 1993, *Dry Tortugas National Park: Submerged Cultural Resources Assessment*, National Park Service, Santa Fe.

Schiffer, M.B., 1972, 'Archaeological Context and Systemic Context', *American Antiquity*, 37, 156–65.

Schiffer, M.B., 1976, *Behavioral Archaeology*, New York.

Cordelière and *Regent*
see **Oxford University MARE**

Cornwallis Cave Wreck

A British shipwreck of the American Revolutionary War period in the York River off Yorktown, Virginia, USA (see also **Yorktown Shipwrecks**). Towards the end of the American War for Independence, British commander-in-chief General Clinton withdrew most of his forces from Charlestown, South Carolina to New York in anticipation of the imminent arrival of the colonists' French allies. He left his second-in-command, Lord Earl Cornwallis, in charge of the Southern campaign. By the summer of 1781, Cornwallis had moved his remaining forces north to Virginia, where he was ordered to winter and establish an ice-free port. He chose Yorktown, Virginia, on the York River due to the town's commanding view of the bluffs, a natural deep water harbour, and the possibility of fortifying the opposite shore at Gloucester Point. In addition to his ground troops, Cornwallis commanded a fleet of around fifty naval and merchant vessels, along with an equal number of prize craft, privately owned, and small craft.

American general George Washington coordinated and concentrated his ground troops and two French naval fleets in the region, greatly outnumbering the British forces. To prevent an amphibious invasion and to force enemy shipping into the river middle within range of his cannon, Cornwallis fortified both sides of the river and scuttled at least fourteen ships along the Yorktown shoreline. Although indecisive, the ensuing siege of Yorktown, starting on 9 October 1781, forced Cornwallis to attempt a crossing of the York River six days later for a retreat to New York. Foiled by a thunderstorm, his disorganized troops scattered, and he was forced to request a truce on the 17th. The Battle of Yorktown became the last battle of the American Revolution, with the final British surrender two days later on 19 October.

General Washington turned over all shipping in Yorktown harbour to his French allies, who mounted a salvage effort the following winter. An unknown quantity of ships was raised, and subsequent salvage efforts in 1852 and 1934 recovered more material from the scuttled vessels. In the early 1970s, a wreck was discovered by sport divers and named the Cornwallis Cave Wreck after the nearest landmark on shore. In 1976 archaeologists with the American **Institute of Nautical Archaeology** directed by George Bass surveyed it for date, origins, condition, and size, also searching the immediate vicinity for other sites revealed by an earlier electronic survey. Due to extremely low visibility, several innovative excavation tools were developed, including a portable floating **Cofferdam** and a clear, freshwater 'pillow' for photography.

Test trenches revealed that around 10 per cent of a large ship-rigged British merchant or transport vessel (possibly HMS *Fowey*) was preserved, originally measuring *c*. 118 ft (36 m) in length and 550 tons burthen. Heavy cant frames were present at bow and stern. Outer hull planking was 3 in (75 mm) thick, while the square-butted ceiling varied in thickness between 3 in and 5 in (90 and 130 mm). Remains of three bulkheads were located in the bow area, and the stern was decked above the ceiling.

Although the ship was certainly stripped before scuttling and partially salvaged thereafter, there was a wide variety among the 433 artefacts recovered and catalogued. Organics included wood, bone, leather, cork, pine pitch, coal, rope, fruit pits, nuts, and nutshells; among the highlights were wooden ship's tackle, rigging, shot garlands, leather buttons, shoe fragments, and a well-preserved powder flask. Inorganics of ceramics, glass, metal, and stone included uniform buttons, gun flints, iron grape or canister shot and lead musket balls. All artefacts were transferred to the Yorktown Victory Center for conservation, curation, and display. P.F.J.

ADDITIONAL READING

Bass, G.F.,(ed.) *et al*., 1976, *The Cornwallis Cave Shipwreck 1976*, unpublished MS, Texas A&M University, College Station, Texas.

Johnston, P.F., Sands, J.O., and Steffy, J.R., 1978, 'The Cornwallis Cave Shipwreck, Yorktown', *International Journal of Nautical Archaeology*, 7, 3, 205–22.

Sands, J.O., 1983, *Yorktown's Captive Fleet*, Charlottesville, Virginia.

Corrosion studies

The investigation of long-term interactions of materials in a marine environment, which has applications to the management and conservation of all shipwreck sites. Without access to pre-disturbance chemical, biological, and electrochemical surveys it is all too easy to lose valuable information regarding

Iron ballast on the site of Sirius. *(© Western Australia Maritime Museum/Patrick Baker)*

the nature of the site and the way in which the forces of deterioration have worked to bring about the current nature of the archaeological deposit. *In situ* corrosion studies provide the practitioner with a new and sensitive management tool.

All metals used in the construction of ships were mined as minerals. These raw materials are compounds of the metal which are found as oxides, sulphides, chlorides, and carbonates. The conversion of minerals into metals is made possible by a series of chemical reduction reactions. Following from their use in building a ship or being made part of a cargo, their placement on a shipwreck site begins to reverse this energy intensive process. The electrons 'forced' back into iron during the high temperatures of the blast furnace will flow back into oxygen to bring about a return to a form that approximates their original nature as a mineral. The addition of alloying elements such as carbon will greatly change the inherent reactivity of the parent metal and lead to the selective corrosion of the phases of the alloy that have the lowest carbon content. This corrosion reaction ultimately manifests itself in the common problem of graphitization of cast iron, where the outermost parts of the surface have lost all or most of their iron content.

The addition of other metals will alter the energy level of the parent metal which alters the corrosion resistance of the alloy. Properties such as mechanical hardness and melting point also alter dramatically with alloying. Depending on the rate at which the metal or alloy cools, the microstructure will be changed and this has a subsequent effect on the rate of corrosion. Mechanical working such as hammering, drawing, and rolling also change the microstructure. If the stresses imparted to the metal are not relieved after fabrication, stress corrosion will manifest itself as a series of finely etched lines on copper fastening bolts or as cracks around the heads of drifts and clinch rings.

Different phases in an alloy have non-identical chemical and physical properties and corrode at different rates; examples of this phenomena are readily seen in dezincification of Muntz sheathing and similar fastenings. The contact between dissimilar alloys and metals will normally result in differential corrosion, as observed in the first attempts to copper sheath wooden ships fastened with iron bolts. The more reactive metal or alloy is selectively corroded while the less reactive phase or component acts as the cathodic half of the corrosion cell where oxygen reduction is normally the dominant process. On shipwreck sites it is possible to observe a form of galvanic corrosion in which the metals do not have to be in direct physical contact. This 'proximity corrosion' explains why so many iron artefacts are adversely affected by the presence of significant amounts of copper alloy fastenings and fittings. Since all metallic shipbuilding materials will ultimately decay, it is the rate of decay that is of vital significance to the maritime archaeologist. From a combination of *in situ* corrosion potential measurements and the depth of graphitization of cast iron, it is possible to obtain quantitative data on the rate of iron corrosion.

The corrosion potential is the voltage of the corrosion cell which normally consists of metal oxidation (corrosion) and oxygen reduction. In anaerobic environments the corrosion potential consists of the oxidation of metal and the reduction of water as the cathodic process. The voltage for concreted metals such as iron is controlled by the rate of reduction of dissolved oxygen at the concretion/sea water interface. Experimental details of how to obtain these measurements have been reported. After decades of immersion metals are corroding at a quasi-equilibrium rate. Thus determination of corrosion potentials prior to any site disturbance provides a unique insight into the nature of the processes controlling the decay of the wreck. Repeated measurements on the boiler of SS **Xantho** (1872) have shown that the method of measurement does not significantly impact on the overall corrosion process. Concreted iron gradually develops an acidic and chloride-rich microenvironment. If this reactive mixture is exposed to direct contact with oxygen then the overall corrosion rate will be dramatically

increased. The acidity results from hydrolysis of metal ions, and the increased concentration of chloride ions is due to inward diffusion from the surrounding sea water to achieve electrical neutrality of the corrosion products.

The wreck of **HMS Sirius** (1790) on Norfolk Island showed a most unusual phenomenon: sea urchins had burrowed through the encapsulating concretion around a carronade and a series of cast-iron ballast pigs. The biologically attacked artefacts are corroding at a 70 per cent faster rate than objects which are in the same microenvironment but without the influence of the sea urchins. Clearly the impact of the marine organisms is a major factor to consider in the management of this site.

The *in situ* measurement of corrosion potential values and typical depths of graphitization enable the archaeologist to make a comparison of the present rate of corrosion and the extent of decay if the current rate were to have been in place for the past centuries. Data collected from *Swan* (1653) (see **Duart Wreck**) has demonstrated that site disturbance had increased the long-term corrosion rates by factors which varied from 76 to 1,100 per cent. Site stabilization techniques of sand bagging the areas of major archaeological deposits has resulted in a reduction of 25 per cent in the corrosion rate of two of the cannon that had previously recorded the greatest rate of deterioration. In other areas of the site where no intervention had occurred the overall corrosion rates of the cannon remained either unchanged or were slightly elevated.

The *in situ* conservation of iron artefacts on historic shipwreck sites began with the stabilization of the Penn's horizontal trunk engine on the SS *Xantho* (1872) site off Port Gregory in Western Australia. Data obtained at the time the engine was excavated indicated that the pre-treatment had assisted in the stabilization of the 5.5 tonne cast-iron engine. Further work was performed on the best bower anchor of HMS *Sirius*, which after one year of cathodic treatment from a sacrificial anode was recovered in an excellent state of preservation. Data obtained from the anchor and from a three-year *in situ* treatment of the second carronade have confirmed that this method of stabilization is the most acceptable form of archaeological intervention on a site. The use of cheap aluminium alloy engine blocks was successful in removing 80 per cent of all the chloride sales before the carronade was recovered. Accidental damage to the protective layer of concretion around the carronade occurred

during its excavation in the surf zone, but there was no localized corrosion because of the cathodic protection and the effects of several years of pre-treatment. Future work may involve the routine pre-treatment of artefacts on the seabed prior to their being excavated in subsequent seasons. Not only would this minimize the treatment time above the ground but the procedures would also halt corrosion during the remaining time on the seabed.

Work on the wreck of the iron ship *Santiago* (1860) in Port River, Adelaide has shown that it is possible to bring about a significant reduction of the rate of deterioration of a vessel that is half in and half out of the water. The structural elements that remained above water or in the intertidal zone were protected with commercially available protective coatings, while the iron below the waterline was protected by ten sacrificial anodes.

A series of inspections of iron shipwrecks in Port Phillip Bay, Victoria (Australia) provided the opportunity to assess the impact of water movement and the loss of the encrusting mixture of corrosion products and marine growth on iron hull plating. The wreck of *City of Launceston* (1865) lies in 22 m of water in the middle of the bay and is subject to a steady current associated with normal tidal movements. The lack of the thick protective marine concretion that characterizes the warm sub-tropical iron shipwrecks of Western Australia resulted in a higher long-term corrosion rate than would be expected on the basis of the water depth. Another iron shipwreck, *Eliza Ramsden*, lies in a similar depth but much closer the entrance of the bay. The higher corrosion rate on *Eliza Ramsden* is primarily due to its location at the entrance to the bay where it is subjected to massive water movement.

The wrecks of the paddle steamers and barges that plied the River Murray in South Australia during the 19th century provide a rich source of sites for assessing the effects of fresh water on metal corrosion. Since the turbid waters of the river preclude visual inspection methods, a study of the metal corrosion potentials provides a set of 'remote sensing' eyes since the traditional imaging methods of assessment cannot be used in the river. Owing to the difficulties of working in total darkness, no depths of graphitization were obtained on cast-iron fittings and so it was not possible to generate a corrosion equation for these sites. However, a comparison of the average corrosion potential values of the iron frames and engine components from different sites along a 520 km stretch of the river shows a very strong correlation with the average water depth. Since all the metal was covered with a thin and dense layer of accretion, the physical separation of anode and cathode of the corrosion cell is similar to that of sea water. The combination of pH and corrosion potential data for the ten sites indicate that the pH is controlled by the equilibrium between magnetite, Fe_3O_4 and Fe^{2+} ions. Within each region of the river the average corrosion potential data was the same when the wrecks were in a similar physical environment. The higher corrosion potentials are associated with greater water movement across the site. Reduction of dissolved oxygen exerts a major influence on the corrosion rates. Through repeated measurements of the corrosion potentials on the sites it is possible to monitor the effects of increased water movement, associated with flooding and irrigation activities, on the fate of the wrecks in this special environment.

A series of measurements on seven shipwrecks in the Fathom Five National Park, Lake Huron has shown that this approach works as a sensitive indicator of the microenvironment for the iron fastenings in this alkaline freshwater lake. Because of the alkalinity of the fresh water, iron fastenings holding together the wooden vessels are covered in a dense and thin layer of calcium carbonate.

The measurements of *in situ* corrosion parameters on a wide variety of shipwreck sites ranging from turbulent open ocean waters to sheltered freshwater rivers and lakes has provided a unique insight into the mechanism of deterioration. The insights obtained on the long-term interactions of materials in a marine environment has applications to the management of all shipwreck sites. I.M.

ADDITIONAL READING

Kentish, P., 1995, 'Stabilization of *Santiago*', *Report to the Australian Heritage Commission for the Dept. of Environment and Natural Resources*, University of South Australia Report MET 1291, Part 1, Adelaide, 1–56.

MacLeod, I.D., 1987, 'Conservation of Corroded Iron Artefacts – New Methods for On-site Preservation and Cryogenic Deconcreting', *International Journal of Nautical Archaeology*, 16, 1, 49–56.

MacLeod, I.D., 1989, 'The Application of Corrosion Science to the Management of Maritime Archaeological Sites, *Bulletin of the Australian Institute of Maritime Archaeology*, 13, 2, 7–16.

MacLeod, I.D., 1992, 'Conservation Management of Iron Steamships: The SS *Xantho* (1872)', *Multi-disciplinary Engineering Transactions*, GE 16, 1, 45–51.

MacLeod, I.D., 1994, 'Conservation of Corroded Metals: A Study of Ships' Fastenings from the Wreck of HMS *Sirius*', in D.A. Scott, J. Podany and B.B. Considine (eds), *Ancient and Historic metals: Conservation and Scientific Research*, Los Angeles.

MacLeod, I.D., 1995, '*In-situ* Corrosion Studies on the Duart Point Wreck, 1994', *International Journal of Nautical Archaeology*, 24, 1, 53-9.

MacLeod, I.D., 1996, '*In-situ* Conservation of Cannon and Anchors on Shipwreck Sites', in R. Ashok and P. Smith (eds) *Archaeological Conservation and its Consequences*, Copenhagen.

MacLeod, I.D. and North, N.A., 1980, '350 years of Marine Corrosion in Western Australia', *Corrosion Australasia*, 5, 3, 11-15.

MacLeod, I.D., North, N.A., and Beegle, C.J., 1986, 'The Excavation, Analysis and Conservation of Shipwreck Sites, in *Preventative Measures During Excavation and Site Protection*, Rome.

North, N.A., 1982, 'Corrosion Products on Marine Iron', *Studies in Conservation*, 27, 75–83.

North, N.A. and MacLeod, I.D., 1987, 'Corrosion of Metals', in C. Pearson (ed.), *Conservation of Marine Archaeological Objects*, London, 68-98.

Cosa, Harbour of

A Roman commercial port and fishery serving the Latin colony of Cosa founded in 273 BC on the Tyrrhenian coast of Italy about 138 km northwest of Rome. This earliest of known Roman harbours is protected on the northwest by a limestone headland rising to a height of about 114 m above sea-level. A man-made ancient breakwater of limestone rocks, now submerged, was thrown out directly eastward from the cliffs for a distance of about 110 m. Unconnected rock piles gave further protection to the south and east to enclose a protected basin of some 25,000 sq. m. The remains of four ancient concrete piers extend in a southerly direction out from the beach. An additional pier, probably supporting a lighthouse, rests upon the eastern tip of the submerged breakwater.

To the north of the port lies the once-attached fishing lagoon that occupies a former barrier-lagoon complex. Today over two-thirds of the ancient lagoon has been silted over. Originally, the lagoon stretched to the east as far as the Tafone River 20 km away. At its western Cosan end, the fishing lagoon communicated with the sea through a series of channels cut into the harbour cliffs, known as the Tagliata and the Spacco della Regina. Several freshwater springs gush from fractures in the cliffs as well as along the western embankment of the lagoon. The existence of fresh water in abundance was of prime importance for the original location of the port and fishery and for its success as an industrial centre, since both the hill town of Cosa above and the ancient port of Hercules (modern Port' Ercole) opposite on the Argentario peninsula had to rely on rainwater alone.

The earliest description of the ancient remains is that of G. Santi in 1798, followed by G. Dennis in the 1840s. The first detailed study of the port was made by R. Del Rosso in 1905 who first noted that the channels and cavern in the cliffs might be associated with an ancient fishing industry. Later scholars such as R. Cardarelli and F.E. Brown interpreted the fishing lagoon as an inner harbour. E. Rodenwaldt and H. Lehmann doubted the presence of either an inner or outer harbour and suggested that the cliff channels were used in antiquity for drainage as part of a large-scale land reclamation project. They located the ancient port in the Orbetello lagoon or on the Tombolo di Feniglia. The first excavation of the port and western lagoon area took place between 1965 and 1978 by A.M. McCann with a team of archaeologists, scientists, and engineers. Excavations were carried out both underwater and on land in the silted lagoon with mechanical help.

Four major chronological periods of the port's Roman use were established. The limestone breakwater probably dates from the first period in the 3rd century BC. In the first half of the 2nd century BC, the lagoon temple, identified by McCann with Neptune/Poseidon, was built on the present site of Le Rocce hotel. From this second period comes 9 per cent of the total amphora finds – the Greco-Italic amphoras (Will Type 1d) associated by E.L. Will with the famous long-lived Sestius family. In the recent deep water exploration off the northwestern tip of Sicily near the **Isis Wreck**, several Type 1d Sestius amphoras were found. One is stamped with SES and a trident shown right side up. This unique stamp is the earliest Sestius stamp thus far discovered.

The period of greatest commercial activity for the port occurred from the last quarter of the 2nd century to the 1st century BC. In this third period, the port was transformed into an elaborate harbour/fishery complex for the export of wine, garum, and other fish products by the Sestius family. From this time date the concrete piers of the harbour and lighthouse, as well as Beach Wall M, the fishing lagoon structures that include extensive fish tanks more than 100 m in length and covering about 1 ha, and a Spring House linked to piers for an aquaduct leading eastward. All were made of the same Volsinian tufa-and-pozzolana concrete, providing the earliest date for this important hydraulic building material invented by the Romans. Strabo (5.2.8) in the late 1st century BC mentions a watch for tuna on the Cosa promontory. Within the Spring House the excavations released a gushing spring with water flowing into a collecting basin at about 1,800 litres per

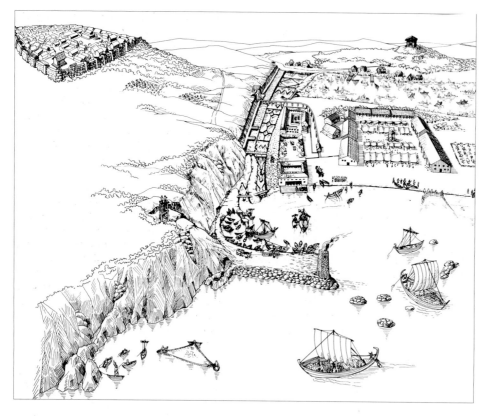

Reconstruction of the early Roman harbour at Cosa.
(Drawing by A. M. McCann)

minute. A water-lifting device was discovered buried in Room 2 of the Spring House. Remains of seven wooden, pitchlined, pine buckets were uncovered. They originally formed a chain of twenty-four and each held 7 litres of water to lift 156 litres in all. Linked together by rope loops, the chain had an estimated length of 27 m and lifted water about 13 m up the sloping hillside to a cistern. While these remains date from the fourth and last period of the port's use in Imperial times when the site was occupied by an elaborate maritime villa, the archaeological evidence indicates that the Spring House was originally designed in the 1st century BC for such a water-lifting mechanism. The Cosa machinery gives the earliest archaeological evidence for the presence of a geared water-lifting device in the ancient world (see Oleson).

From these peak years belong the well-

known Will Type 4 amphoras also identified with the Sestii. Type 4 comprises 70 per cent of the total amphora material. Mineralogical analysis of the Sestius amphoras shows that the clay and sand come from the Cosa area. Although the remains of an amphora factory and saltery for fish have not as yet been found, they probably stood on the sand behind the harbour. So extensive were the finds of the Sestius amphoras that it seems highly likely that this famous plebeian family

that had a villa at Cosa (Cicero *Att.* 15.27.1) and produced amphoras for several centuries had their major factory at the port near the ships that were to transport them around the Mediterranean world. Will has identified their trade marks from over thirty sites in the western Mediterranean as well as in the Agora at Athens. It is highly likely that the famous **Grand Congloué** upper shipwreck containing about 1,200 amphoras of Will Type 4a and most marked with the stamp of Sestius was loaded at the port of Cosa. Only a factory the size of the one at the port could have produced such a shipment and 86 per cent of all the stamps from the port site are those of the Sestii.

Besides amphoras, pottery material in greatest quantity is the thin-walled ware

dating mainly from about 75 BC into Augustan times. These vessels were found largely in the Spring House area, giving new evidence for their use as drinking cups.

This active commercial period for the port and fishery complex of Cosa appears to have come to a sudden end in the closing years of the 1st century BC. Analysis of the sediments of the lagoon indicates the presence of a layer of grey sea sand within the polygonal channel leading into the lagoon and inside the fish tanks. A single storm on the high seas could have produced such a disaster. From the viewpoint of history, the need for a port in Etruria had passed. The centres of trade were now to the south of Rome, namely Puteoli followed by Ostia, to receive grain from Alexandria.

In the fourth and last period of the harbour's ancient use from about the mid-1st to the 3rd century AD, a large Imperial villa occupied the sand dunes. The port was now for import only. Beach walls made of layered courses of brick and limestone date the villa from the Claudian period or later. It remains unexcavated and lies on the site of a 16th-century watch tower owned in the early 20th century by the Italian composer Giacomo Puccini, known as Torre Puccini. In the lagoon, the Spring House is rebuilt to lift water 13 m up the hillside to a cistern, probably serving a bath. The date of the destruction of the water-lifting machinery by fire in about AD 150 is confirmed by pottery finds. Another spring source, however, remained in use about 50 m north, enclosed in a small structure (YZ). Finds indicate its use from about the last quarter of the 1st century AD until about the mid-3rd century AD. By the early 5th century AD when Rutilius Namatianus (1.293) sailed by on his way home to Gaul, Cosa with its port lay in ruins.

The importance of the port and fishery of Cosa lies in its early date. Founded with the colony in 273 BC, the port provides new evidence that economic rivalry with Carthage for western Mediterranean trade may have also played a role in the establishment of colonies along with defensive needs on the Tyrrhenian coast. Moreover, as this is the earliest Roman harbour and commercial fishery thus far known, the origins of Roman international trade are pushed back at least two centuries. The concrete piers of the port provide the earliest dated examples of hydraulic concrete made with tufa-and-*pozzolana* concrete. In its harbour design, Cosa combines the use of nature with man-made protection, forming a link between the Greek maritime and the Roman Imperial worlds. The unique water-lifting machinery is the earliest archaeological evidence for such a gear-driven bucket chain still in use in the Near East today and known as a 'saqiya'. The amphora finds reveal startling new evidence for the importance of the Sestii for the advancement of Roman state-of-the-art technology as well as for the early development of Italy's export trade in both wine and garum. A.M.M.

ADDITIONAL READING

Del Rosso, R., 1905, *Pesche e peschiere antiche e moderne nell'Etruria marittima*, Florence.

Oleson, J.P., 1984, *Greek and Roman Mechanical Water-Lifting Devices: The History of a Technology*, Toronto.

McCann, A.M. *et al.*, 1987, *The Roman Port and Fishery of Cosa: A Center of Ancient Trade*, Princeton.

McCann, A.M., 1988, 'The Roman Port of Cosa', *Scientific American*, 256, 3, 102–9.

Council of American Maritime Museums

Organization of American and Canadian maritime museums, established in 1974 to promote cooperation between institutions working towards the preservation and interpretation of America's maritime heritage. The Council of American Maritime Museums (CAMM) also promotes legislation that supports maritime preservation and ethical standards for the field, including archaeological standards. To accomplish its mission, it serves as a formal network for more than seventy member institutions and sponsors an annual meeting. Full members of CAMM must be maritime museums or museums with significant maritime collections, located within the United States or Canada, be open to the general public on a regular basis, for a minimum of 120 days per year, and be institutions that abide by the policies of the American Association of Museums, UNESCO, and CAMM.

Many, if not most, members of CAMM hold maritime archaeological materials in their collections. These include major collections at the Mariner's Museum, in Newport News, Virginia, which holds all artefacts archaeologically recovered from the wreck of USS *Monitor*; San Francisco Maritime National Historical Park, whose holdings include artefacts from a number of California shipwrecks and the collection excavated in 1978 from the storeship *Niantic* in San Francisco; the Smithsonian Institution, whose extensive collections include the engine of *Indiana* and the intact hull of the Continental gondola *Philadelphia*. Some CAMM institutions support active maritime and underwater archaeological programmes and research. The Vancouver Maritime Museum hosts the avocational

Underwater Archaeological Society of British Columbia, the Bermuda Maritime Museum conducts regular research on a number of Bermuda shipwrecks, including excavation, and an active maritime archaeological programme on the Great Lakes is conducted by the Michigan Maritime Museum. The Columbia River Maritime Museum, on the Pacific Coast, initiated an ongoing research programme with the 1830 wreck *Isabella*. Many other CAMM institutions also hold collections and participate in maritime archaeological research.

In 1986, in response to controversies over the display of materials from shipwrecks that had been systematically recovered by salvors and treasure hunters, sold privately, and then offered, often without context, to member institutions, CAMM established an archaeology committee to advise CAMM on professional policies, ethics, and standards. In April 1987 CAMM passed an archaeological bylaw prepared by the committee. The bylaw states that 'CAMM member institutions shall adhere to archaeological standards consistent with those of the American Association of Museums/International Congress of Museums (AAM/ICOM), and shall not knowingly acquire or exhibit artefacts which have been stolen, illegally exported from their country of origin, illegally salvaged or removed from commercially exploited archaeological or historical sites.' The by law excluded artefacts already acquired and in the collection of member museums.

The purpose of the bylaw was to explicitly exclude major maritime museums from the purchase, acquisition, or display of commercially salvaged shipwreck artefacts. Considerable discussion has since ensued over the definition of 'commercial exploitation' and whether amendments are needed to more specifically address the issues of proper archaeological methodology, conservation, and what would constitute trafficking in antiquities. J.P.D.

ADDITIONAL READING

Johnston, P.F., 1989, 'Beneath the Devil and the Dark Blue Sea: Archaeology and the Council of American Maritime Museums', in J.B. Arnold III (ed.), *Underwater Archaeology Proceedings from the Society for Historical Archaeology Conference, Baltimore, Maryland*, Ann Arbor, Michigan.

County Hall Ship

The central part of a ship dating to the late 3rd to early 4th century AD, discovered during construction of the County Hall, on the south bank of the Thames, London, in 1910. It was the first Roman Age wreck in

the world to be documented and studied in detail.

The wreck was discovered 6.55 m beneath the street level, and 91.44 m east of the Embankment river retaining wall, between the Westminster and Hungerford bridges, in February 1910, but was not removed from the ground until August 1911. The drying timbers, shrinking and brittle, were transported to the London Museum at Kensington Palace. The hull, in a poor condition, was partially 'restored' with plaster. After World War II, the remains, in even greater disrepair, were again 'restored' with an additional three quarters of a ton of plaster. In 1978 the London Museum decided to dismantle the remains. Peter Marsden was assigned the task, and found that little other than the frames and other major timbers had survived. With a better understanding of Roman vessel construction then available from subsequent discoveries, including underwater work, Marsden was able to generate new plans, make a scale model, and clarify details of the County Hall Ship's construction.

Marsden found that the remains were of the midships portion of the hull, extending towards what may have been the bow. Both ends of the wreck were destroyed, however, and it is not clear which end is which to this day. The hull remains were approximately 13 m in length and 5.5 m wide, representing the bottom and one collapsed side of the hull. The side of the hull extended past the deck level, but not the gunwale. The vessel was built entirely of oak and was treenail fastened. Iron nails had been used in antiquity to strengthen or replace treenails. Marsden found evidence that the outboard face of the hull planks had been treated with pine resin that had only been slightly heated.

The keel was cut from a single log, and was 10.3 m long. A slight rise at one end corresponded with a closer coincidence of mortise-and-tenon joints than elsewhere, and may suggest a slight 'rocker' or curve, as was found with the keel of the **Kyrenia Ship**. Evidence of a now missing false keel was also found. The planks, all cut from oak logs, were probably sawn, although the condition of the timbers has not preserved tool marks. The hull was built in the Classical Mediterranean tradition, with the planks fastened edge to edge with mortise-and-tenon joints. The planks were apparently so tight that caulking was not necessary. The strakes averaged 26.7 to 38.1 cm in width, and although now in fragments, suggest that several were substantial. One garboard strake was 10.5 m long, 0.38 m wide, and 0.076 m thick.

The frames were generally 11.4 cm broad,

The bottom of the County Hall Ship; the white dotted lines are an early attempt to indicate what the missing parts might have looked like. (Museum of London)

16.5 cm deep, and cut from grown crooks of trees. Very few scarf joints were found; some were later repairs. Limber holes, shaped like a V, were found on the underside of the frames close to the keel. Frames and strakes were fastened together with treenails 3.2 cm in diameter, with two treenails through each strake. One strake was actually a heavy fore and aft strengthening wale, 15.2 cm square. A stringer, inside the hull and fastened with iron nails atop the frames to one side of the keel, was one of an apparent pair. It was 14 cm wide by 8.9 cm thick.

Marsden, using average ratios for length to beam, reconstructed the ship as a Mediterranean style of vessel 19.1 m long, with a 1:6.3 ratio. It may be similar in this ratio to the Yassiada and Kinneret (**Sea of Galilee**) wrecks. Some cross timbers found in the wreck were determined to be deck beams, fastened into slots in a wale and supported by stanchions in the hull. Marsden further postulated that, based on the height of the deck, the vessel was a sailed, not rowed craft. The County Hall Ship was built plank first with oak which dendrological examination showed had grown in southeast England. The ship was probably built in southern England by a shipwright familiar with Mediterranean construction methods. Dendrochronological evidence and other factors suggest a probable construction date of AD 300. First interpreted as a 'warship', the poor condition of the wreck and the lack of substantial remains even when excavated in 1910 leads Marsden to caution that

only a minimal reconstruction of the vessel's type is possible, and to restrict conjecture. Four bronze coins found in the wreck provide a *terminus post quem* of AD 293, and a fragment of Roman grey coarse ware flanged bowl suggests that it was abandoned, not wrecked, soon after AD 300. J.P.D.

ADDITIONAL READING

Marsden, P., 1974, 'The County Hall Ship', *International Journal of Nautical Archaeology and Underwater Exploration*, 3, 1, 55–65.

Marsden, P., 1994, *Ships of the Port of London: First to Eleventh Centuries AD*, London.

Cramond Lioness

A magnificent Roman sculpture of a lioness, found in early 1997 in the River Almond, west of Edinburgh, Scotland. It lay in the intertidal zone at Cramond, and had only been exposed by erosion for a short time when it was noticed by the local ferryman. Excavations were carried out by the City of Edinburgh Museums' Archaeological Service and the National Museums of Scotland, and it was lifted by crane from the riverbed. Its condition is remarkably good: the carving is fresh and unworn, and it cannot have been exposed to the Scottish climate for long before its burial.

The 1.5 m long sculpture depicts a lioness devouring a bearded man, with his head in her jaws and his naked torso under her paws. The base, which had broken off, shows two snakes crawling from under the lioness's stomach. This is standard Roman funerary symbolism, representing the destructive power of death on the one hand and the survival of the spirit (represented by the snakes) on the other. However, it is very uncommon to see a lioness, rather than a

The Cramond Lioness, viewed from the side; the base has been detached. (Trustees of the National Museums of Scotland)

lion, and human rather than animal prey. Also, snakes are not found on other British examples. Although it is a Roman theme, the carving is not Classical in style, and it was most probably carved by an auxiliary from one of the Celtic provinces.

The find has many interesting implications. Funerary sculpture of this quality is otherwise unknown in Scotland, and it must have come from the tomb of a high-ranking Roman, perhaps the commander of the nearby fort (occupied mid-2nd to early 3rd century AD). The commissioning of such a work of art certainly points to a patron of wealth, and a belief that the Roman presence in Scotland was going to last.

This raises the question of how the lioness ended up in the river. It was found in the Roman channel, and may have fallen off a boat during unloading. However, it is just as likely that it was deliberately deposited in the water when the fort was abandoned, perhaps because it was seen by the Romans as too important and powerful a symbol to be left behind. Alternatively, it may have been consigned to the river by the native tribes.

A chance discovery, the Cramond Lioness has both excited the public imagination and forced archaeologists to rethink their view of the period. It also guides us to further work: not just the intriguing possibility of a companion lion still lurking under the silts of the Almond, but a pointer to the whereabouts of the Roman harbour which must lie in the area. F.H., M.C.

Crannogs

Lake-dwellings. Crannogs are distinct from the accidentally submerged lakeside settlements characteristic of the Alpine lakes (see **Lake Neuchâtel**; **Lake Zürich**). Their basic characteristic is that they are built-up islets (not necessarily wholly artificial) which have

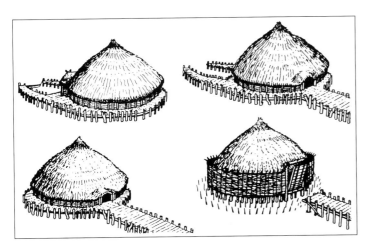

Despite good preservation of crannog sites underwater, loss of organic material above the lake surface means that several alternative reconstructions may be considered for each site, as shown here for Milton Loch I. (Ian Morrison)

been deliberately set in lakes, marshes, and less commonly in estuarine or sheltered marine locations. There are substantial numbers in Ireland and Scotland, perhaps of the order of a thousand in each country. One has been excavated at Llangorse Lake in Wales. England's Lake District deserves investigation.

The Gaelic term (crannog in Ireland, crannag in Scotland) was current through medieval times, but continuity of usage was lost, and the precise original meaning is not now entirely clear. Since its subsequent adoption by archaeologists, 'crannog' has become a portfolio term, embracing sites of a wide range of dates, sizes, locations, and possible functions.

Views vary on whether some Neolithic or Mesolithic sites should be classed as crannogs. Certainly by the Bronze Age, well-developed built-up islet sites are apparent, especially in the Early Christian period. Interesting full-size attempts to recreate crannogs from these characteristic periods may be viewed in Scotland (Late Bronze Age: Loch Tay; Dr N. Dixon) and Ireland (Early Christian: Craggaunowen, Co. Clare; Professor E. Rynne). Crannogs did not become obsolete until the 17th century. It would thus be misleading to think in terms of a 'crannog culture' *per se*. They were elements in the landscapes of several millennia, and of varying regional cultures. The structures and artefacts associated with them accordingly tend to reflect whatever was contemporarily characteristic. Their high standard of preservation of organic materials thus offers valuable cultural as well as environmental information to supplement that available from land sites, for both prehistoric and historic periods.

In size, they range from some large enough for prestigious establishments (royal crannogs, the establishments of local kings, are documented in Ireland) down to

mere fishing or fowling stances. Their locations also suggest differing priorities. Some were sited close inshore, with a gangway. Others were set as far offshore as the underwater terrain allowed, seemingly with security overriding convenience of access. Some were equipped as self-sufficient homesteads, but others appear to have had specialized functions, complementing other sites on shore. Documentary evidence suggests these were not necessarily near by. When documents are absent, one approach to interpretation is to attempt to identify consistently repeated patterns in the relationships of sites to their landscapes. There is a good prospect of valid distribution maps, since because of their lake-bed setting, crannog remains tend not to be obliterated by later activities. Thus it seems clear that while some large lakes have many crannogs, nucleated 'lake villages' are not characteristic. Instead they tend to be set apart, many juxtaposed to land of good arable potential.

It has become apparent that a wide range of functions needs to be considered. A primary role was to provide security for people and goods, but not only for innocents (some were bases for cattle raiders).

Local kings utilized 'royal crannogs', although these were not necessarily their full-time residences. Some crannogs acted as treaty Islands, neutral ground for diplomatic exchanges; others were aggressive emplacements of strongpoints in the territory of rivals. Several had routeway functions, from hospices offering secure stopovers to control stations where short-cuts were taken by drovers swimming cattle across lochs. All sizes of crannog, from major homesteads down to small ancillary establishments, could have agricultural functions. Byre deposits on some with gangways show that beasts were kept on them, presumably to protect them from wolves as much as from

two-footed predators. Several crannogs were used as manufactories for homestead blacksmithery and weaving, etc.; Moynagh Lough (Ireland) even has a 'high-security industrial estate'. Finally, there was a recreational function. Besides their direct use by wildfowlers and fishers, some crannogs were 'hunting lodges' for deer hunting; so-called Tigh nam Fleadh ('House of Feasting') islets saw notable drinking bouts.

In both Scotland and Ireland, research momentum has been gathering, and it is perhaps time to ask whether the continuing use of 'crannog' as a portfolio term is unproductive, since it tends to gloss over so many intriguing complexities. I.A.M.

ADDITIONAL READING

Campbell, E. and Lane, A., 1989, 'Llangorse: A 10th Century Royal Crannog in Wales', *Antiquity*, 63, 675–81.

Morrison, I., 1985, *Landscape with Lake Dwellings: The Crannogs of Scotland*, Edinburgh.

Crossroads Wrecks

Vessels sunk in 1946 in Kwajalein and Bikini atolls as part of the US atomic bomb test Operation Crossroads. Following the end of World War II, the first large-scale atomic weapons effects tests were conducted by the United States at Bikini Atoll. The Able and Baker detonations, which took place on 1 July and 25 July 1946, were the first two atomic bombs tests of a three-part weapon test named Operation Crossroads. The third scheduled test, code-named Charlie, was cancelled.

Representing the 'crossroads' from conventional to nuclear war, Operation Crossroads was a momentous event. In all, 42,000 men, a fleet of 242 ships, 156 airplanes, thousands of tons of military equipment, ordnance, and material, and relocation of the inhabitants of Bikini were involved. Conceived as a means for testing the potency of atomic explosives against naval vessels, Operation Crossroads bombs were dropped on surviving enemy merchant and warships, and United States Navy combatant ships struck off the active list. Prior to the tests, the vessels were examined for structural integrity, installed with test equipment, and stripped of armament and items of either historical interest or of critical nature, before being loaded with munitions, fuel, and water that replicated their battle or operating displacement.

The initial impact of the bombs produced mixed reactions. Military and public interest had been focused on the blasts' effects: while many vessels sunk on impact, the bombs had less than a cataclysmic result. Initially, observers and press representatives were unimpressed. It was not until the potency of the aftermath, radiation, was studied, that the true destructive powers of the bombs were fully realized.

In 1989 and 1990, the National Park Service's **Submerged Cultural Resources Unit** (NPS-SCRU), led by Daniel J. Lenihan, documented nine of the twenty-one vessels sunk in Kwajalein and Bikini atolls during the 1946 Operation Crossroads atomic bomb tests. Invited by the Bikini Council and the United States Department of Energy, the team's efforts focused on the historical, archaeological, and recreational potential of these historic sites. Logistical support was provided by the United States Navy under the auspices of the National Park Service's Project Seamark.

Investigation of Operation Crossroads sites, limited by both field session lengths and diving constraints, forced NPS-SCRU to customize documentation techniques. The size and depths of the sites (most dives were decompression dives between 30 and 55 m) made many traditional documentation methods prohibitive. NPS illustrators systematically sketched the sites, using the original ship plans as templates. At the end of each dive they observed video footage of the sites to augment their drawings. Site descriptions were logged on video. As an experimental video camera hookup, a full face mask (AGA) installed with a microphone was connected to the video camera in order to narrate field notes congruently with video footage.

Nine of the twenty-one wrecks accessible to divers was examined. Two others were observed by ROV and later assessed by NPS-SCRU. The aircraft carrier *Saratoga* (CV-3) was the major focus of the documentation project. Other sites investigated included the battleships *Nagato* and *Arkansas* (BB-33), submarines *Pilotfish* (SS-386) and *Apogon* (SS-308), YO-160, LCT-1175, LCM-4, and the attack transports *Gilliam* (APA-57) and *Carlisle* (APA-69). These vessels were investigated at Bikini, while the cruiser **Prinz Eugen** was examined at Kwajalein.

In addition to developing site descriptions, **site formation processes** were evaluated. The effects of the blasts on the different categories of vessels were compared. Site descriptions focused on ship class, proximity and orientation to the blast, pre-blast vessel condition, and alterations.

Sites examined

USS *Gilliam*, the accidental surface zero target, was the only Able test vessel dived by the SCRU team. The hulk of *Gilliam* sits upright on the bottom at 55 m. It suffered severe hull damage, its successive decks com-

pressed into the hold and hull sides above the waterline bent inwards up to 3 m. The documentation dive made by NPS-SCRU revealed most of the damage was in the bow area. Of the Operations Crossroads sites examined, *Gilliam* suffered the most damage.

USS *Carlisle*, also sunk during the Able test, was dived by the Navy ROV in 1989. *Carlisle*, 123 m from surface zero, with its port side facing the blast, had been loaded to 95 per cent of its fuel and oil capacity. The blast moved the vessel approximately 45 m, knocked down the stacks and mainmast, pushed the superstructure to the starboard, and damaged the foremast. Although *Carlisle*, an identical sister ship to *Gilliam*, was further from surface zero, it too suffered considerable damage. Its decks were also compressed down and its shell plating buckled, dented, and dished.

USS *Arkansas*, dived by the Navy ROV and NPS dive team during 1989 and 1990, was exposed to both atomic detonations. During Able, its superstructure was severely damaged, but hull and turrets remained intact. The second blast capsized the vessel, sinking it to the bottom. The vessel now lies inverted in about 55 m of water. The 1946 report suggests that the vessel was smashed nearly straight down into the lagoon floor. The vessel's inverted position, the flattened condition of its hull bottom, and the position of the superstructure located directly beneath the hull verify this supposition.

USS *Saratoga*, the most accessible site to divers and therefore of primary interest for evaluation, became the principal focus of the documentation project. Prior to the test, its armament was stripped and fixtures removed, and blast gauge towers and other

instruments designed to measure the effects of the blast, as well as aircraft, vehicles, and radars, were mounted on its decks. The blast from Baker blew the vessel 730 m from its position and inundated it with a 29 m tall blast wave, sinking it to the bottom.

Investigation of the site revealed a virtually intact vessel sitting upright in 55 m. Sections of *Saratoga* rise to within 12 m of the surface, with its mast and island visible from the surface. The worst damage, aft on the starboard side of the hull, is where the blast ripped loose shell plating and exposed frames. The flight deck also suffered extensive damage. The blast wave and the thousands of tons of water that rained down from the blast column smashed the wood decking and ruptured the steel deck. The vessel's superstructure remains recognizable, although the ship's funnel was toppled and crushed onto the flight deck. *Saratoga*'s island and mast remain standing, though various components were shattered or blown off. All five of the aircraft secured to the deck for the test were swept from the ship by either the blast or the waves. The four aircraft stowed in the hangar remained at their stations. Five 20 mm anti-aircraft guns were observed on the site, two on the lagoon floor near the sheared-off stern sponson gun platform. Test equipment installed prior to the blast still remains. NPS divers penetrated several of *Saratoga*'s interior compartments, including the flag plot bridge, navigation bridge, pilothouse, and the aerological office.

USS *Pilotfish* was on the surface during Able. It was about 400 m from surface zero and suffered some scorching and charring of superstructure paint during the detona-

tion. Its operational capacity was determined to be unimpaired and it was subsequently submerged for the Baker test. *Pilotfish* was the closest submarine to the Baker blast. Investigation during post-blast evaluations in 1946 suggested that its compartments flooded, sending it to the bottom at a depth of 53 m. In 1989, NPS divers found the vessel upright, tilting about fifteen degrees to starboard. The hull is intact, but the aft section is dished up to 15 cm between frames. The superstructure remains intact, but dented.

USS *Apogon*, like the other submarines used during Able, was on the surface during detonation. It received moderate scorching and charring on its port side exterior, and pressure distorted three internal bulkheads. For the Baker blast, it was submerged 777 m from the bomb at 30 m. After the detonation, the Navy attempted to raise the vessel, but salvage efforts were abandoned before it was raised. Investigation of the site was made only by ROV. The *Apogon* is in better condition than *Pilotfish*. There is no dishing between frames and damage seems confined to the ship's superstructure. A major section of the forward superstructure near the forward torpedo loading hatch is missing. This area appears to have been cut away. Perhaps

this section was removed during the 1946 salvage attempt.

YO-160, heavily damaged during Able, swamped and sank during the Baker blast. The vessel is sitting upright, on an even keel, in 43 m of water. The deck is littered with broken equipment, pipes, and steel plates. Only observations of the midships deck area were made by NPS-SCRU.

Nagato, the one-time flagship of the Imperial Japanese Navy, was subjected to both blasts. It received no modification prior to the detonations, though it is likely that it was fitted with blast gauge towers. NPS-SCRU found the *Nagato* inverted in 52 m of water. The vessel appears to have capsized stern first, the transom striking the sea bottom, causing the hull to fold across the aft deck. Aft of the rudders and screws is a major break in the stern hull. Torn plates reveal twisted and splayed frames in the interior, a result of the deadly force that struck the vessel.

Located between the high and low tide mark in Bikini Lagoon, LCT-1175 was scuttled after the Baker test. It had been listed as a derelict vessel prior to the test and its 20 mm gun armament removed. It was moored close to the beach during the test and sank from heavy wave action caused by the detonation.

The German cruiser *Prinz Eugen* survived both Bikini test blasts. Lost during a storm, which drove it ashore and capsized it at Kwajalein Atoll, the vessel was dived by NPS-SCRU twice. The team did not observe any damage that could be clearly attributable to the blasts.

The vessels examined during the NPS Operation Crossroads documentation project represent all but four of the major vessels sunk during the blasts. The sites documented in Bikini and Kwajalein portray much more than the surviving remnants of atomic test subjects. Many had long and significant military careers or successful lives as merchant vessels, some starting as early as World War I. Collectively, they illustrate over thirty years of naval design and development, as well as a range of ship types, hull forms, and construction methods.

The documentation project included a management plan for the sites. NPS-SCRU devised guidelines for their use as a dive park, outlining provisions for their protection, preservation, and interpretation. A.A.

ADDITIONAL READING

Delgado, J.P., 1990, 'Documenting the Sunken Remains of USS *Saratoga*', *United States Naval Institute Proceedings*, 116, 10, 45-50.

Delgado, J.P., 1993, 'Operation Crossroads', *American History Illustrated*, 28, 3, 50-59.

Delgado, J.P., 1996, *Ghost Fleet: The Sunken Ships of Bikini Atoll*, Honolulu.

Delgado, J.P., Lenihan, D.J., and Murphy, L.E., 1991, *The Archaeology of the Atomic Bomb: A Submerged Cultural Resources Assessment of the Sunken Fleet of Operation Crossroads at Bikini and Kwajalein Lagoons*, Santa Fe.

Eliot, J.E., 1992, 'Bikini's Nuclear Graveyard', *National Geographic*, 181, 6, 70-83.

Lenihan, D.J., 1993, 'Bikini Beneath the Waves', *American History Illustrated*, 28, 3, 60-67.

Weisgall, J.M., 1994, *Operation Crossroads: The Atomic Tests at Bikini Atoll*, Annapolis.

Cultural Heritage Act (Sweden)
see **Swedish Ancient Monuments Act**

Cultural resources management (CRM)
An activity that involves the identification, evaluation, and treatment of the full range of cultural properties under one's jurisdiction. Inherent in the use of the term is the assumption that certain products of human endeavour may deserve protection because they are unique or typical to a particular culture or important to humankind in general. Cultural resources may include buildings, bridges, art, archaeological artefacts, or even extant lifeways that are in threat of extinction.

As it refers to underwater archaeology, cultural resources are the remains of human activity in submerged environments. This may include the residues of early man in sinkholes and springs (e.g. the **Chichén Itzá Cenote** in Mexico or **Warm Mineral Springs** in Florida); the hulks of ships in marine, lacustrine, or riverine environments; and the variety of inundated archaeological sites found in the conservation pools of many dams.

Managing submerged cultural resources may include inventory of sites, protection in place, interpretation to the public in the form of educational programmes, excavation and display to the public in museums, or the decision to take no action if they are discovered. Some of the more dramatic options for management may include total recovery and display of an entire vessel or aggressive attempts at inhibiting the process of deterioration on an underwater site. The latter may include the placing of sacrificial anodes on a metal vessel to slow the corrosion process.

The simple act of avoidance of a significant cultural resource in a public works project is a viable management strategy. All land management or resources management agencies engage in CRM decision-making even if only in the sense of *de facto* neglect. Although generally CRM does not involve the commercial exploitation of sites for their intrinsic value, where submerged sites are concerned a double standard exists. Some resource management agencies have incorporated commercial salvage as one of their options for treatment for underwater sites.

In the United States Federal legislation has mandated that antiquities receive special attention by agencies of jurisdiction. In the case of shipwrecks the primary responsibility for management of the sites has been put on the States through the passage of the **Abandoned Shipwreck Act** of 1987. In other nations the responsibility for underwater sites is highly centralized and not separated from the treatment of sites on land.

An area of question for any nation in managing its cultural resources is that of jurisdiction. How far from its shores does it claim jurisdiction or title to historic shipwrecks? This varies, but is normally 3–12 statute miles (5–19 km) or occasionally marine leagues. In some cases the nations refer to the physical bounds of their outer contintental shelf; in others, to a generic 200 mile (322 km) area of influence.

A special case in jurisdiction develops when a sovereign vessel of a particular nation is involved, that is usually a naval vessel owned by the state at the time of sinking. In the United States it applies also to vessels owned by the Confederacy in the American Civil War. The US Navy retains title to those vessels and has pursued that claim even in foreign waters such as the case of the CSS **Alabama** in the English Channel off France.

For those actively engaged in the management of submerged cultural resources a phased programme of site inventory, protection, and interpretation (in the sense of interpretation for public educational purposes) is adopted. The inventory phase of CRM activities is often partially an exercise in archival work and partially a listing of known sites in the field. The latter can be accompanied by comprehensive underwater remote sensing of large areas of a nation's territorial waters. Whatever the discovery process, be it in the library or through accounts of divers or state-sponsored fieldwork, there follows a process of evaluation of significance.

The latter usually results in a list of sites that are deemed important to the nation's heritage and which will be accorded a greater degree of protection than those deemed less significant. In the United States the most important are listed on a **National Register of Historic Places**. Criteria for such listing can include age, integrity, and archaeological or marine architectural data likely to be lost in the destruction of the site in question. Australia, the UK and Canada have preserve systems that offer special protection, and some nations have blanket protec-

tion of all sites older than a certain date in the nation's waters.

In some cases the agencies charged with submerged cultural resources management responsibilities actually carry out research activities; in others it is contracted out or done in conjunction with marine salvage activities. In the latter case the results have proved particularly problematic. When a survey is conducted within the parameters of a profit motive it often compromises the state's ability to maintain control and true management authority over archaeological resources.

In the last decades of the 20th century there have been increasing attempts to set international standards for submerged cultural resources management of offshore sites through the efforts of UNESCO, **ICOMOS**, and the International Law Association. These efforts are complicated by larger geopolitical issues relating to the Law of the Sea and ambivalence in the relations of various states to the United Nations. D.J.L.

USS *Cumberland*

US Navy shipwreck of 1864, sunk as a result of damage sustained from the Confederate ironclad CSS *Virginia* during the Battle of Hampton Roads, rediscovered in 1980, and subsequently subjected to dredging and looting. USS *Cumberland* was a 1,726 ton frigate built at the Boston Navy Yard and launched in May 1842. After a long career, including service in the Navy's Home, Mediterranean, and African squadrons, *Cumberland* was assigned to the Union Navy's large fleet of wooden vessels blockading the James River in the early months of 1862 during the American Civil War.

On 8 March 1862 the Confederate ironclad *Virginia*, built on the razed hull of the scuttled Union warship *Merrimac*, attacked the blockading fleet. USS *Congress* was the first Union vessel attacked, and was seriously damaged. *Congress*'s guns failed to penetrate *Virginia*'s armour. Approaching *Cumberland*, *Virginia*'s captain called for her surrender. Lt. George Morris, *Cumberland*'s executive officer, was in command and answered, 'Never! I'll sink alongside!' *Virginia* then rammed *Cumberland*, backing off as the wooden warship began to sink. *Cumberland* fired a broadside into *Virginia*, damaging the ironclad and killing or wounding nineteen of her crew. *Cumberland* quickly sank with a loss of 120 lives, the world's first casualty of an ironclad warship. *Virginia*'s onslaught against the remaining Union fleet was halted by the timely arrival of the Union's new ironclad, USS **Monitor**.

The wreck of *Cumberland* was partially salvaged by the US Navy after sinking, but in time the wreck was forgotten, although *Cumberland* was declared a war grave. In early 1981 Underwater Archaeological Joint Ventures, under contract to the non-profit **National Underwater and Marine Agency** (NUMA), located the wreck in approximately 20 m of water. Limited visibility hampered site observations, but intact decking, a bilge pump pipe, and an anchor were observed by divers. A number of small artefacts were recovered, including the unmarked ship's

The sinking of USS Cumberland *by the ironclad* CSS Virginia *off Newport, 8 March 1862. (Courtesy of the Beverly Robinson Collection, Naval Academy Museum, Annapolis, MD. US Naval Historical Center)*

bell, ordnance stores, including a wooden sabot, calipers, and two fuses, and ceramics. A copper alloy pan, dated 1856, provided a *terminus post quem*. This, and the location of the wreck, led NUMA to identify the site as the wreck of *Cumberland*. The wreck was ultimately nominated to and listed in the **National Register of Historic Places**.

Despite its listing in the National Register, the wreck was subjected to extensive dredging and looting by local watermen and clammers following its discovery. The nearby wreck of the Confederate raider CSS *Florida*, also located by NUMA in 1981, was also dredged and looted. A number of artefacts were recovered and sold through antique dealers to private collectors and museums. Following a tip from the Confederate Naval Historic Society, the FBI launched an investigation in December 1989 that culminated in a series of raids in March 1990. Many artefacts were recovered, and prosecution of the looters commenced. Four persons ultimately pleaded guilty in United States District Court in 1993. Both wrecks, as warships, are owned by the US Government. In the aftermath of the case, the recovered artefacts were turned over to the Navy's Norfolk Navy Museum for conservation and curation. J.P.D.

ADDITIONAL READING
Cussler, C. and Dirgo, C., 1996, *The Sea Hunters: True Adventures with Famous Shipwrecks*, New York.

Curaçao

The largest of the five islands comprising the Netherlands Antilles, situated *c.* 40 km off the northwest coast of Venezuela. Since 1987 the Archaeological-Anthropological Institute of the Netherlands Antilles (AAINA) has conducted two major underwater archaeological projects at Curaçao. The largest underwater project is at the site of the Dutch frigate *Alphen* in Santa Anna Bay. This ship exploded in the harbour on 15 September 1778, and sank on the spot. A 130 m baseline was established in the 20 m deep water, with survey and test excavations coordinated from it. Of interest was the far greater proportion of artefacts of English manufacture, compared to those of Dutch manufacture, in the collections. The *Alphen* shipwreck site has been included as the only underwater archaeological site on the official Curaçao monuments list.

The second underwater research project conducted by AAINA on Curaçao was a survey and limited surface collection along the main commercial wharf area called Handelskade, at the entrance to Santa Anna Bay, in 1993. This project consisted of establishing a 210 m baseline parallel to the wharf, from which collections were mapped. This area was apparently a trash dumping location for the colony, from the mid-17th until the early 19th century. As with the shipwreck *Alphen*, artefacts of English manufacture outnumber those of Dutch manufacture by a considerable margin, indicative of the extensive trading for which Curaçao is known. J.B.H.

ADDITIONAL READING
Nagelkerken, W., 1989, 'Survey of the Dutch Frigate *Alphen*, which Exploded and Sank in 1778 in the Harbour of Curaçao, in E. Ayubi and J. Haviser (eds), *Proceedings of the Thirteenth International Congress for Caribbean Archaeology*, AAINA Reports 9, Curaçao.
Nagelkerken, W., 1993, 'Onderwater-archeologisch onderzoek van de historische vuilstortplaats langs de Handelskade in de St Annabaai, Curaçao', *Reports of the Archaeological-Anthropological Institute of the Netherlands Antilles*, Curaçao.

Curaçao

Dutch warship wrecked off the Isle of Unst, Shetland, in 1729, and rediscovered in 1972. The warship *Curaçao*, a 145 ft (44 m) long vessel carrying forty-four guns, was built at the naval dockyard at Amsterdam in 1704. *Curaçao* was lost while convoying a fleet of Dutch East India (VOC) ships through the North Sea. The ship ran aground off the Shetland coast on 31 May 1729 in calm seas, but in extremely foggy weather. *Curaçao* was a complete loss, although 195 men out of a 200 man crew survived.

The wreck was rediscovered by a team led by Robert Stenuit in June 1972, lying in 22 to 28 m of water in three underwater canyons at the base of a large rock known as Ship Stack. The wreck was initially identified by an exposed anchor and the broken remains of up to thirty or more cannon. After mapping the site, Stenuit's team recovered some 200 artefacts from the ship's ordnance stores: buckles, silver spoons, ceramics, brass coin weights, and coils of well-preserved rope. Some portions of the wooden hull were observed, but not studied.

The Netherlands transferred title to the wreck to Stenuit, who sold the artefacts from the site at auction after conservation and inventory. A small portion of the collection was donated to the Shetlands County Museum. J.P.D.

ADDITIONAL READING
Stenuit, R., 1977, 'The Wreck of the *Curaçao*, A Dutch Warship Lost off Shetland in 1729 While Convoying a Fleet of Returning East Indiamen: An Interim Report', *The International Journal of Nautical Archaeology*, 6, 2, 101–25.

Dartmouth

A fifth-rate British warship wrecked in the Sound of Mull, off the west coast of Scotland, in 1690. *Dartmouth* was built at Portsmouth in 1655 by Sir John Tippetts as one of a new class of light and manoeuvrable vessels derived from Dutch and Danish prototypes. Rated at 240 tons, the ship had a keel length of 80 ft (24.4 m), a beam of 25 ft (7.6 m), and carried up to thirty-two cast-iron guns, of which the largest were nine-pounders. Her crew numbered about 120. After a long career which included service in the Mediterranean, Caribbean, and home waters she was involved in a number of events which followed the so-called 'Glorious Revolution' of 1688 which brought William of Orange and his wife Mary to the British throne. *Dartmouth* participated in the Battle of Bantry Bay (May 1689) and the relief of Derry (July 1689). A year later, she was engaged in pursuing adherents of the former James II on the west coast of Scotland, among whom were the Macleans of Duart. While preparing to attack their Mull stronghold on 9 October 1690 *Dartmouth* was struck by a violent storm and wrecked. Her remains were discovered in 1973 by a group of divers from Bristol, and over the following three seasons excavations were conducted under the direction of Colin Martin of the **Scottish Institute of Maritime Studies** at St Andrews University. All the recoveries, including a substantial section of ship structure, are preserved in the Royal Museum of Scotland, Edinburgh.

The wreck lies in shallow water (between 2–8 m) just off the small islet of Rudha an Ridre. She appears to have struck stern-first and to have rolled onto her starboard side before breaking in two. The after part of the lower starboard side, including a 6 m length of keel, survived as an articulated structure encapsulated within an inshore gully. This has yielded evidence of composite skeleton and shell construction (a Dutch characteristic) as well as unconventional repair techniques apparently intended to reinforce an ageing and partly rotten hull. The forward part of the wreck lacks articulated structure but shows a linear cohesion of deposited guns and lead scupper-liners. Work by Keith Muckelroy on spacial distributions of various categories of finds within the wreck formation context shows a strong relationship

A small warship, probably Dartmouth, drawn by Van de Velde the Younger c. 1676. (© National Maritime Museum Picture Library)

between archaeological deposition and their probable original locations within the ship.

Recovered items include the ship's bell (dated 1678, when she underwent a major refit), navigational and surgical instruments, tools, nautical and domestic equipment, and items of weaponry. Organic material, including environmental evidence, has survived in some abundance. The site is protected under the UK's historic shipwreck legislation. C.M.

ADDITIONAL READING

Adams, J.R., 1974, 'The *Dartmouth*, a British Frigate Wrecked off Mull, 1690', *International Journal of Nautical Archaeology*, 3, 2, 269–74.

Holman, R.G., 1975, 'The *Dartmouth*, a British frigate Wrecked off Mull, 1690. 2. Culinary and Related Items', *International Journal of Nautical Archaeology*, 4, 2, 253–65.

McBride, P., 1976, 'The *Dartmouth*, a British Frigate Wrecked off Mull, 1690. 3. The Guns', *International Journal of Nautical Archaeology*, 5, 3, 189–200.

Martin, C., 1978, 'The *Dartmouth*, a British Frigate Wrecked off Mull, 1690. 5. The Ship', *International Journal of Nautical Archaeology*, 7, 1, 29–58.

Martin, P.F. de C., 1977, 'The *Dartmouth*, a British Frigate Wrecked off Mull, 1690. 4. The Clay Pipes', *International Journal of Nautical Archaeology*, 6, 3, 219–23.

Muckelroy, K., 1978, *Maritime Archaeology*, Cambridge.

Dashur Boats

Ceremonial watercraft buried outside the Middle Kingdom pyramid of Senwosret III (called Sesostris by the Greeks; 1878–1859 BC) at Dashur, Egypt, about 33 km south of Cairo. Four of the six hulls originally reported by the archaeologist Jean-Jacques de Morgan after his 1894 excavations provide evidence for Egyptian boatbuilding technology of about 4,000 years ago. The frameless Dashur boats are of mixed construction, with both sewing and mortise-and-tenon fastenings used along plank edges. Beams that support a deck provided the necessary transverse stiffening.

The boats are assumed to belong to Senwosret III because of their location south of his pyramid, but no inscriptions or artefacts prove the relationship. Senwosret III is viewed as a powerful monarch who expanded Egypt's territory both to the south in Nubia (modern Sudan) and north to Syria and Anatolia. It is possible that he was emulating the great kings of the Old Kingdom by having cedar hulls, possibly used in funeral ceremonies, buried in his pyramid precinct. Cedar did not grow in Egypt, and was imported, probably from the Levantine coast, as early as 3200 BC.

Two Dashur boats are exhibited at the Egyptian Museum in Cairo, Egypt (EM 4925 and EM 4926); two others are in the United States, displayed at the Field Museum of Natural History (FMNH) in Chicago, Illinois and at the Carnegie Museum of Natural History (CMNH) in Pittsburgh, Pennsylvania. Although de Morgan described six hulls buried in the sand outside the southern enclosure wall of Senwosret III's pyramid, later maps drawn by him indicate only five hulls. Only three hulls are described as being excavated: the two in Cairo and the FMNH boat, which was purchased as a gift to the Field Museum by Mrs John McCormick. The CMNH hull was purchased by Andrew Carnegie in 1901, and it is certain to have come from Dashur because of its similarities in shape, construction, and date to the other boats. In addition, all of the boats show the same kinds of repair and reconstruction: new tenons in almost all of the mortises, the addition of dovetail tenons and mortises, similar modern tool marks, and iron bands screwed to the outside of the hulls. EM 4925 also had planks replaced following excavation.

Each of the boats is between 9.25 and 9.92 m long today; the ends of all the hulls are slightly eroded. Width varies between 2.15 and 2.43 m, and depth between 0.72 and 0.79 m. Length to beam ratios describe the shape of the hull; the Dashur boats range from 3.8 to 4.6:1, the same range seen in many contemporary models of funerary boats. Thus, the Dashur boats show a design intermediate between the elongated Khufu I (see **Khufu Ships**) at 7:1 and the very common 3.1 proportion for ancient merchant ships such as the 4th-century BC **Kyrenia Ship**. Body sections are round and the sheer is gently curving with slightly raised ends, the stern higher than the bow. Like Khufu I, the hulls are somewhat fuller aft of amidships. Mortises at both ends of the central strakes suggest that they once had decorative finials, perhaps shaped like Khufu I's and the many funerary boat models from Middle Kingdom times.

Wood from the CMNH and FMNH planks identified as cedar is still fragrant. Although no analyses of wood from the Cairo hulls have been completed, physical characteristics such as colour, grain, and odour strongly resemble those of the hulls in the USA. Tamarisk tenons have been identified in the CMNH hulls; tamarisk is native to Egypt. Dendronchronological analysis of some CMNH timbers shows that the wood came from at least eighteen different cedar trees.

The construction sequence for the hulls is typical for shell-built craft. After selecting timber balks of appropriate size and curvature, the shipwrights probably trimmed the logs with axes. Next, plank shapes were roughly marked and sawn out; planks range from 8 to 13 cm thick. All planks in these hulls, and in ancient Mediterranean-area hulls in general, are carved, not bent, to shape. The central strake was laid down first. The Dashur boats have no keels, but the central strake protrudes about 1 cm. Both ends would be supported by shoring, something we see illustrated in pharaonic-era shipbuilding scenes.

Next, the shipwrights marked and cut edge mortises. Most hull mortises measure 7.5 cm wide, 1.8–2.0 cm thick, and 12 cm deep (range of 10–13 cm). These measurements coincide with standard Egyptian measurements of one palm (7.5 cm) and one digit or finger (1.8–2.0 cm). Traces of the black charcoal-based ink or paint used for this job and of the tools they used remain to provide evidence for the stages of construction. After shaping the planks in the next strake and checking the fit, mortises were marked and cut along the inboard edge. As seen in Khufu I, the mortise-and-tenon fastenings line up in transverse rows that would have functioned as internal frames.

The shipwrights designed the hulls to be symmetrical in the distribution and shape of planks and strakes. In addition, lashing channels for ligatures (stitch-like connections between plank edges) also have a symmetrical distribution. Only a few traces of the original ligatures remain on each hull as almost all of these fastenings were crudely

which in illustrations appear only on royal watercraft, topped green-, yellow-, red-, and blue-striped stanchions that supported steering oars beautifully painted with lotus flowers and wedjat eyes.

The proportions, shape, and decoration of the Dashur boats, as well as the high level of craftsmanship in their construction, suggest that they were funerary boats. The hulls demonstrate principles learned in thousands of years of hull construction. It required at least six, and probably ten, tons of imported cedar to build these hulls and bury them outside the pyramid of Senwosret III in the continuation of a practice first seen in the ritualized world of the mortuary cult by the burial of ten or more planked hulls at Abydos (c. 3000–2670 BC). C.H.

the wreck it tends to be remembered in Europe as the wreck that sank within the crater of a live submerged volcano.

The seabed within and surrounding the site is characterized by open vents (fumeroles) that gush forth hot water (hot enough to boil an egg) and gas. The latter, as it bubbles up, dissolves in the water to form dilute sulphuric and sulphurous acid that burned the divers as they were excavating. Also, the hot water, as it rises through the rock of the seabed, leaches out iron salts which are carried in solution to the surface; when the iron-heavy hot water comes into contact with the cold water of the seabed, the reaction is such that the iron salts precipitate out of solution and fall back onto the seabed where, over time, they consolidate to form a thick hard blanket of iron products. Much of the pottery from the wreck had to be cut free from this layer using hammers and chisels. To avoid damage, the more delicate pieces had to be raised in slabs of the brittle ferrous material; some of these can still be seen in that state in the permanent exhibition of the wreck at the museum on Lipari, the main island in the archipelago.

Unfortunately, it was several years before archaeologists learned of the wreck's discovery, in which time the site was much plundered. It is impossible to determine with any accuracy how much of the cargo was taken during this period, but judging from the broken fragments that were left by the looters and the private collections that were amassed, estimates of two to three thousand pieces do not seem unreasonable. Rumours of the discovery first came to the ears of Mensun Bound, the Director of Archaeology of **Oxford University MARE** (Maritime Archaeological Research), in 1985; he immediately went to Panarea where he saw and heard enough to convince him of the wreck's existence. He returned to the island in 1996 with a full team to begin the first of three seasons of survey and excavation.

The team was headquartered on Panarea and operated from the deep-ocean salvage tug *Ghibli* which was loaned to the project by the Palermo-based maritime engineering company Medit. Although some amphora and galleyware pieces were recovered, 98 per cent of the excavated material was fineware made from a cohesive red clay and painted with a high quality, lustrous black glaze. The forms, which could be dated to the early years of the 4th century BC, consisted mainly of *skyphoi* (two-handled tumblers) of Attic and Corinthian type, *pateras* (one-handled cups), seven types of bowl,

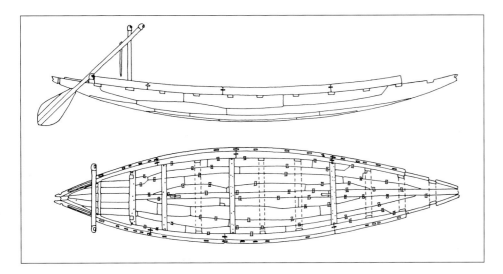

Dashur Boat of Senwosret III. (Drawing by Bjorn Landstrom)

recut during the reconstruction of the hull and filled with modern dovetail tenons. Their original purpose may have been to hold down battens over the plank seams; they are neither numerous nor deep enough to hold hull planks together during construction or use.

The three strakes are topped by a carefully finished bulwark above deck level; notches cut in the sheer strake about every 70–85 cm held beam ends. Beams, each supported by three small stanchions, were lashed in place before being pegged to the sheer strake. The inner surfaces and all areas above the waterline are well finished. Numerous tool marks remain on the outer surfaces and the lower edges of planks, however. Decking, steering gear, superstructure, and decoration completed the boats. Each hull's bulwark has traces of red, black, and blue lines over a white background; at least one of the Cairo hulls was painted green. Blue hawk's heads,

ADDITIONAL READING
Haldane, C.W. and Patch, D.C., 1990, *The Pharaoh's Boat at the Carnegie*, Pittsburgh.
Jones, D., 1995, *Egyptian Bookshelf: Boats*, London.
Landstrom, B., 1970, *Ships of the Pharaohs: 4000 Years of Egyptian Shipbuilding*, Garden City, New York.

Dating
see **Absolute dating**

Dattilo Wreck
A 4th-century BC wreck discovered in the early 1980s near the rock whose name it bears, in front of the island of Panarea, one of the Lipari, or Aeolian, Group in the Tyrrhenian Sea on the northern approaches to the Straits of Messina. The wreck is important as it is one of the very few from the Classical period and one of the even fewer (and certainly the earliest) that went down with a cargo of black glazed finewares. Despite the archaeological importance of

stemmed plates, six types of *oinochoai* (jugs), two types of *lekythoi* (oil jugs), *askoi* (cruets), table amphoras, *pelike* and lamps of so-called padlock type. The forms were mainly duplicate imitations of current Greek tableware fashions. Scientific analyses of the clay were unable to determine their place of manufacture, but they were almost certainly of Sicilian origin. However, the Aeolian Islands themselves cannot be excluded as a possibility.

Because of the acidic environment nothing of an organic nature survived except for several small pieces of wood that had been encapsulated by clay. A quantity of ballast stones was found, but a lead anchor stock, which has frequently been described as having come from the wreck, was found several hundred metres away, too far for this link to be certain. M.B.

ADDITIONAL READING

Bound, M., 1989, 'The Dattilo Wreck (Panarea, Aeolian Islands): First Season Report', *International Journal of Nautical Archaeology*, 18, 203–19.

Bound, M., 1989, 'A Wreck at Dattilo, Panarea (Aeolian Islands): A Preliminary Note', *International Journal of Nautical Archaeology*, 18, 27–32.

Bound, M., 1992, *Archeologia sottomarina alle Isole Eolie*, Pungitopo.

Day Dawn

Mid-19th-century American ship wrecked near Fremantle, Australia. The 398 ton whaling ship *Thomas Nye*, built at Fairhaven, Massachusetts in 1851, made three successful whaling voyages before being sold out of the fishery to South Australian interests in 1864; it was renamed and rerigged as the barque *Day Dawn*. The vessel was used in the Australian timber trade before being wrecked in August 1886 at Busselton, south of Fremantle in Western Australia. Refloated, and apparently unsuitable for use at sea, it seems to have been stripped for conversion to a storage bulk. It was taken to Careening Bay, just south of Fremantle, but was again unsuitable for its intended purpose. The vessel then appears to have been abandoned and burnt to the waterline to recover metallic fastenings and fittings some time around 1890. From then on it became lost to living memory.

Threatened by dredging for a new naval facility in 1976, the then unidentified wreck was moved laterally and vertically to finish below the desired harbour datum. The newly formed Maritime Archaeological Association of Western Australia then conducted a sixteen–month excavation under the guidance of Department of Maritime Archaeology staff. This was designed to assess, record and identify the site. A piece of timber found in the bilge with the marking 'Day Dawn' proved an important clue in the latter process. Discounted as having come from the gold mine of that name, near Meekatharra in Western Australia, it eventually led to the identification of the site as the former whaler. This analysis was supported by timber analysis and archaeological evidence.

Following these investigations, the wreck was declared an historic site, allowed to refill with sediment and was monitored at regular intervals as part of the Western Australia Maritime Museum's site management programme. When it became apparent that vessels using the harbour facility in which the site lay were contributing to the degradation of the site, further attempts at stabilizing it were made. In 1982, for example, an attempt to help stabilize and cover the wreck in sediment was made by using spoil from a hopper barge. This proved unsuccessful. In 1988, the wreck came under more direct threat and a number of submissions mooted the possibilities of sliding the wreck into deeper water again, burying it in landfill, or dismantling the site and then re-burying it.

Owing to alarm at the possibility that the wreck might be cut up, thereby diminishing its archaeological significance, it was moved out of the harbour and deposited on the seabed (see Kimpton and Henderson). Joining the remains of a number of American whalers wrecked on the Western Australian coast in the 1840s, the remains of *Day Dawn* provide a useful archaeological resource pertinent to that industry and to wooden shipbuilding generally. Students have used the site as a field-school and further work will be conducted in monitoring and stabilizing the site. M.M.

ADDITIONAL READING

Henderson, G.J., 1978, *Unfinished Voyages*, Nedlands, Western Australia.

Kimpton, G. and Henderson, G., 1991, 'The Last Voyage of the *Day Dawn* Wreck', *Bulletin of the Australian Institute of Maritime Archaeology*, 15, 2, 25–9.

McCarthy, M., 1979, 'The Excavation and Identification of the ex-American Whaler, *Day Dawn*', *International Journal of Nautical Archaeology*, 8, 2, 143–54.

McCarthy, M., 1980, *The Excavation of the Barque Day Dawn*, Perth.

McCarthy, M., 1986, 'The Protection of

Left: Day Dawn's capstan. (© Western Australia Maritime Museum/ Patrick Baker)

Right: Heavy media coverage of the disastrous attempted salvage of De Braak helped lead to the passage of the Abandoned Shipwreck Act of 1987. (Courtesy of Delaware State Museums)

Australia's Underwater Sites', *Papers from the Conference on Preventative Measures During Excavation and Site Protection*, ICCROM Ghent, 1985, 133–45.

McCarthy, M., 1990, *Charles Edward Broadhurst, 1826–1905: A Remarkable 19th Century Failure*, unpublished M. Phil. thesis, Murdoch University, Western Australia.

Sledge, S.D., 1979, 'On Shifting a Wooden Wreck: Supplementary Notes to the *Day Dawn* and *Dato*', *International Journal of Nautical Archaeology*, 8, 3, 245.

Wolfe, A. and Waterman, P., 1990, *Movement of the Historic Shipwreck Day Dawn from the Small Boats Harbour, Careening Bay, Garden Island, Western Australia*, HMAS *Stirling* EMP Discussion Paper 1/90, Department of Defence, Canberra.

HMS *De Braak*

A British sloop wrecked off Cape Henlopen, Delaware in 1798. On the afternoon of 28 May 1798 HMS *De Braak*, a sixteen–gun brig-sloop, Captain James Drew commanding, entered the Delaware River, accompanied by *Don Francisco Xavier*, a Spanish prize laden with £160,000 worth of copper, and prepared to come to anchor off Cape Henlopen. Sud-

denly the vessel was capsized by a gust of wind and sank, taking with it Drew, thirty-four crewmen, and twelve prisoners. Several survivors made their way to Philadelphia on foot and aboard *Don Francisco Xavier* to inform Phineas Bond, the British consul, of the loss. On 21 July HMS *Assistance* arrived off the Delaware to determine the feasibility of salvage and returned to Halifax, Nova Scotia with news that *De Braak* might be saved. In mid-August HMS *Hind*, accompanied by the

salvage brig *Vixen*, was dispatched from Halifax to raise the wreck. Despite several days of concerted effort, the endeavour failed. Soon, rumours began to circulate along the Delaware coast that the brig had foundered with a treasure of Spanish gold and silver. As time passed, this unfounded legend of the treasure grew, and the search for *De Braak* became a cottage industry at the nearby port of Lewes, Delaware.

In 1805 the location of the wreck site was recorded by Gilbert McCracken, a Delaware pilot, and entered into his family Bible. The record became the primary source guide thereafter for many efforts to relocate the ship. Following the Civil War, the first salvage permit to recover the supposed treasure was sought from the US government by Charles Sanborn. In 1867 Sanborn, 'a noted submarine diver', purportedly conducted research at Halifax and, it was later reported, discovered that the ship carried 'an immense amount of treasure, consisting of gold and silver bars and precious stones'. Sanborn died before launching his salvage effort, but word of the treasure he had supposedly documented added to the growing folklore of *De Braak*.

In 1880 the first of many unsuccessful efforts to locate the alleged treasure was launched by McCracken's grandson Samuel, with backing from the International Submarine Company (ISC) of Connecticut. ISC secured a salvage permit from the US government and commenced a futile search for the wreck. In 1886 Dr Seth Pancoast, of Philadelphia, secured control of ISC and began his own ill-fated three-year treasure quest. In 1888, as Pancoast was conducting

his final expedition to find the ship, the *De Braak* treasure legend was given historical respectability by being included in John Thomas Scharf's *History of Delaware*. Spurred by such scholarly acknowledgement of the fictitious treasure, the Merritt Wrecking Company of New York was contracted in 1889 by an ISC spin-off, the Ocean Wrecking Company, to find the wreck, but searched in vain.

The 20th century saw innumerable efforts to locate *De Braak*. Among the notable expeditions fielded were those led by Ralph Chapman (1932, 1933), the Braak Corporation (1933), Charles N. Colstad (1935, 1937), Archie and Weldon Brittingham, Charles Johnston, and Rod King (1952), William H. Boyce and Robert Howarth (1955), William Strube (1962, 1963), D&D Salvage (1965–70), Tracy Bowden Associates (1970), and Seaborne Ventures, Inc. (1980).

The first scholarly work on the history of *De Braak* and debunking of the treasure legend was produced by Howard Chapelle of the Smithsonian Institution and M.E.S. Laws in 1967. In 1970 Mendel Peterson, Director of Underwater Exploration at the Smithsonian Institution, presented an address at the Lewes Historical Society declaring for the first time that *De Braak* and many other shipwrecks in Delaware waters were of historical and archaeological significance. Treasure hunters paid little heed and proceeded to destroy at least a dozen 18th- and 19th-century shipwrecks in pursuit of the non-existent treasure.

In April 1984 the firm of Sub-Sal, Inc., led by Harvey Harrington, under permit from the State of Delaware, discovered the wreck of *De Braak* by utilizing **Side scan sonar**. The vessel was identified from artefacts, including a carronade, an anchor, silver coins, and other items illegally retrieved from the site. On 26 July a suit was filed by Sub-Sal against the wreck in Wilmington US District Court. The wreck was formally arrested under admiralty law (see **Salvage law**) and placed in custody of Sub-Sal. Despite legal challenges by competitors, Sub-Sal's jurisdiction over the site was upheld, and salvage commenced. As salvage proceeded, violations of State and federal laws by Sub-Sal began. Human remains were illegally disposed of, artefacts requiring expensive conservation were cast overboard, and recovered artefacts of monetary value were illegally employed as collateral for bank loans. Some artefacts, employed as a props to raise investment funds, were of questionable authenticity.

In 1985 L. John Davidson, of New Hampshire, secured control of Sub-Sal and introduced industrial salvage techniques to its operations. On 11 August 1986, believing treasure lay beneath the ship's hull, Sub-Sal raised the ship, severely damaging the intact remains of the hull, and losing uncounted artefacts which spilled into the sea in the process. Finding little treasure, the company then carried out massive clambucket dredging of the entire wreck area, further impacting the archaeological integrity of the site. Spoils were processed on an industrial gravel separator.

Although 26,000 artefacts were recovered, fewer than 650 were coins. The monetary value of the collection, which cost nearly $3,000,000 to recover, was appraised by Christie's of New York at $298,265. The hull was placed in a concrete, water-filled coffer at Lewes where it remained until it was moved on 28 March 1990 to a specially constructed wet-storage building at Henlopen State Park. On 4 February 1992, after much litigation, title to the wreck's remains was awarded by the Wilmington US District Court to the State of Delaware, in whose lands the ship had been embedded.

The *De Braak* salvage was one of the worst maritime archaeological disasters in American history. The disaster was vigorously and successfully employed as a worst-case scenario by historic preservationists to generate Congressional support for passage of the **Abandoned Shipwreck Act** of 1987. On 28 April 1988 the Act was signed into law by President Ronald Reagan. D.G.S.

ADDITIONAL READING

Beard, D., 1989, *HMS De Braak: A Treasure Debunked, a Treasure Revealed*, MA thesis, East Carolina University, Greenville, North Carolina.

Brodeur, P., 1988, 'The Treasure of the *De Braak*', *New Yorker*, 16 April, 33–60.

Shomette, D., 1993, *The Hunt for HMS De Braak: Legend and Legacy*, Durham, North Carolina.

Shomette, D.G. and Hopkins, F.W., Jr, 1991, 'The *De Braak* Legacy: An Analysis of Eighteenth Century Rigging', *American Neptune*, 51, 3, 156–63.

Deep water sites

Submerged archaeological sites, usually shipwrecks, found at depths greater than three hundred metres. In the early Victorian age, British geologist Sir Charles Lyell prophesied that 'it is probable that a greater number of monuments of the skill and industry of man will in the course of ages be collected together in the bed of the oceans, than will exist at any one time on the surface of the continents'. Thousands of years of maritime activity, and the loss of several hundred thousand vessels, perhaps more, have resulted in a tremendous submerged archaeological repository. Technological innovation, principally in the last two centuries, has allowed human exploration below the water and the recovery of a small portion of this archaeological record.

History of discoveries

The invention of **SCUBA** led to increased forays into the ocean after World War II, while new wartime technologies for locating enemy submarines – sonar and **Magnetometers** – were employed to find sunken ships. The result was an explosion of interest and activity, focused in part on the investigation of the submerged past, but in large measure dedicated to the plundering of the underwater cultural heritage – the stripping of most wrecks in shallow waters by souvenir hunters, treasure hunters and professional salvors. In some countries, it is difficult to find a stretch of coast where every wreck exposed on the seabed has not been visited and stripped to depths of up to 60 m or more.

This situation led to the development of **Underwater archaeology** and the careful scientific study of inundated prehistoric sites, submerged cities, and shipwrecks. It also led to various efforts to protect and preserve the submerged past, including regulation and legislation. Throughout the 1970s and early 1980s, as the archaeological community sought increased measures to protect submerged sites, particularly shipwrecks, many took comfort in the fact that inaccessible sites remained in the world, deep down in the ocean, beyond the reach of technology and greed.

The incredible record of the past, and the presence of near-legendary vessels miles down, was the subject of much discussion and interest. In 1976, oceanographer Willard Bascom published *Deep Water, Ancient Ships* and prophesied that a completely intact ancient ship would someday be found in the Mediterranean. Bascom's book fired the imagination of many explorers, treasure seekers, and archaeologists. The thought of perfectly preserved, untouched shipwrecks and lost cargoes was almost too incredible, and so all the more hoped for. And yet there were tantalizing traces and hints of what might be left in the deep ocean's dark depths. Bascom's book cited examples of well-preserved materials from great depths, encountered haphazardly during excursions to the ocean floor to recover missing naval weapons, lost submarines, and crashed aircraft.

The technology for searching the ocean floor and visiting it was available in the 1960s as the first generation of self-propelled **Submersibles** was introduced. In June 1963, a US Navy crew using the bathyscaphe *Triese II* searched for and recovered portions of the nuclear submarine *Thresher*, which had sunk 2.5 km down in the Atlantic after experiencing mechanical problems. In 1965–6, US Navy crews, working with the remotely operated vehicle CURV and the submersible *Alvin* recovered a hydrogen bomb dropped into the sea after a mid-air collision between a bomber and its tanker off Palomares, Spain. Finding ancient wrecks or legendary lost vessels was merely a matter of time.

In 1976, author Clive Cussler published the novel *Raise the Titanic!* and described the discovery and salvage of the sunken liner **Titanic**. Texas oil millionaire Jack Grimm financed a series of unsuccessful searches for the wreck of *Titanic* in the early 1980s. In 1985, a joint French-American expedition led by Woods Hole Oceanographic Institute scientist Dr Robert D. Ballard and

Recent advances in diving technology are expanding the limits for deep dives while unmanned technology allows a human 'telepresence' at extreme depths. (Courtesy of Lake Champlain Maritime Museum, Basin Harbor, Vermont)

Institut Français de Recherche pour l'Exploitation des Mers scientist Jean-Louis Michel discovered the wreck of *Titanic* 4 km down, off the Grand Banks of Newfoundland. Grimm, after his expeditions, had declared the wreck 'beyond reach'. That pronouncement only heightened the drama of discovery. The sense of excitement, and of a new era for deep sea research that followed in the wake of *Titanic*, was like that of early space triumphs. Broken, torn and rusted, the hulk of the once magnificent ocean liner dominated the world's attention. It also opened a Pandora's box of potential benefits and curses for the world's archaeological community.

Considerable debate ensued on what to do with *Titanic* now that the wreck had been found, and, presumably, could be returned to again and again. Some were in favour of leaving it as it lay, untouched, as a memorial to the ship's dead. Others called for salvage for public display. In 1986, the United States Congress passed legislation prohibiting the sale of artefacts from the *Titanic* in the United States and called for international discussion to preserve the wreck as a memorial while developing plans for 'appropriate' recovery and salvage. Congress notwithstanding, that did not stop a 1987 expedition by Titanic Ventures, Inc., a Connecticut-based firm that used French equipment and experts to recover some 1,800 artefacts from the wreck and took them to France for preservation and display. Subsequent expeditions by RMS Titanic, Inc., a New York-based company, also recovered artefacts from the wreck in 1993 and 1994, this time acting under authority of United States District Court decision awarding them salvage rights to the wreck after extensive litigation. In 1994, RMS Titanic, Inc. opened a controversial museum display of *Titanic* artefacts at Britain's National Maritime Museum, and followed it with a controversial but failed attempt to raise a 20 tonne piece of the hull in 1996.

While *Titanic* has been at the centre of a decade-long debate over the future of that wreck, as well as deep water sites in general, other discoveries of wrecks in deep waters also encouraged debate. Robert Ballard subsequently searched for, discovered, and documented the deeply submerged wreck of the German battleship **Bismarck** in the North Atlantic and then a number of US and Japanese vessels sunk in Iron Bottom Sound in the South Pacific (see **Guadalcanal Wrecks**).

In 1987, at the same time as the first salvage of *Titanic* artefacts commenced, the Columbus-America Discovery Group, a private consortium from Ohio, discovered the 1857 wreck of the sidewheel steamer **Central America** in 2.5 km of water off the US east coast near the State of North Carolina, but in international waters. They captured headlines with their high-tech recovery of gold bullion from the lost steamer's $2,100,000 cargo. In 1989, another private company, a Tampa, Florida-based firm named **Seahawk**, discovered and later recovered artefacts from a Spanish galleon believed to be *Buen Jesus y Nuestra Señora del Rosario*, lost in 1622 in 450 m of water. A US/Saudi Arabian team of salvors discovered the American liberty ship *John Barry*, torpedoed off East Africa in 1944, and recovered a significant portion of its $26 million US cargo of silver coin. In 1995, another American firm based in Virginia, the Au Company, located the wreck of the Japanese submarine I-52, sunk by US aircraft off Africa in June 1944 and believed to be carrying a cargo of precious metals, including gold, to Japan's Nazi allies. I-52, lying in 5,500 m of water, is the deepest shipwreck yet discovered.

To date, only one archaeological project with a deep water shipwreck has been undertaken. Dr Anna Marguerite McCann, working with Dr Robert D. Ballard, discovered and documented a 4th-century AD wreck known as the **Isis Wreck** in 900 m of water off Skerki Bank in the Mediterranean.

The future

In the past decade of deep water shipwreck research, commercial interests have prevailed. Within the space of several years, technological innovation has provided most of the tools for conquering the obstacles to exploring and working in the deep ocean. Things thought lost forever in a seemingly fathomless ocean, be they majestic ocean liners or the scattered wreckage of a crashed airliner, are discovered and returned to again and again, with accuracy.

Technology has at last provided the tools to unlock archaeology's final frontier. Humanity's probes, exploration, habitation and work on the ocean floor is now the stuff of science fact, not science fiction. But this bold leap into the future has also provided access to the world's last great archaeological resource – uncounted shipwrecks and lost cargoes, dating from storm-tossed wrecks from the beginnings of civilization to warships sunk by nuclear detonation or supertankers snapped in two by rogue waves. These shipwrecks, and the incredibly rich and diverse record of the past that they contain, are the world's last great archaeological frontier. Thus far, the brief history of human intervention into this final frontier has been one of exploitation. What will the future bring?

Commercial interests, archaeological research, and even recreational diving to depths unheard of today are in the future, just as they are present today. There will always be exploitation of the traces of the past, and centuries of plundering, trafficking in antiquities and private collecting indicate just how futile efforts to eradicate them have been. The debate over these non-sustainable resources has reached new levels of urgency, with technological advantages unheard of in years past. All the more frustrating is the lack of any comprehensive legal regime in international waters that, like national statutes, could regulate work on sites and protect those of significance.

While various nations have taken steps to protect, preserve and manage historic shipwrecks within their territorial waters, the same has not been the case for shipwrecks in international waters. The **UN Law of the Sea Convention** of 1982 specifically excluded efforts to regulate or protect historic wrecks. Initiatives to resolve this situation have included the creation of an international committee of archaeologists and government officials chaired by Graeme Henderson, Director of the Western Australia Maritime Museum, under the auspices of the International Commission on Monuments and Sites (**ICOMOS**), and the drafting of a charter on the protection of underwater cultural heritage by the International Law Association (**ILA**). But to date the discussions have focused within the legal and archaeological community, not the world at large.

In 1995 and 1996, Britain's National Maritime Museum, after criticism from some museum and archaeological colleagues for mounting a display of recovered *Titanic* artefacts, convened two special conferences at Greenwich 'on the protection of historic wrecks in international waters'. The issues of protecting and preserving shipwrecks of historical and archaeological importance have increasingly dominated the discussions of the maritime museum community as well as the world at large. Debates over the passage of an archaeological bylaw by both the **Council of American Maritime Museums** (CAMM) and the International Congress of Maritime Museums, as well more contentious discussions over the **Museum display** of artefacts recovered from the wreck of *Titanic*, have begun to highlight the issue for the maritime museum community and the media.

The Greenwich conferences debated the various legal regimes available for protecting shipwrecks in international waters, and made a number of constructive suggestions for future action. Efforts to amend the Law of the Sea could take place by the end of the decade. The special conference was only a beginning, but it was significant in that for the first time a group of people, representing a variety of interests, some commercial, others archaeological, legal, or governmental, had met, talked and listened to one another. The meetings ended with a pledge to continue the discussion and seek positive solutions, including possible future action by the United Nations. Progress was also made on an international agreement to protect the wreck of *Titanic*.

There are many values, be they memorial, commercial, recreational, or archaeological, or even a combination of values, that are associated with the wrecks that lie on the ocean's bed. Successful strategies for the future will ensure that no one value prevails, that interests are balanced, and that everyone with an interest sits at the table, from whatever sector or nation, as was the case with the National Maritime Museum's conferences. For the archaeological community, that means a realization that we cannot preserve everything, and that mechanisms must be put into place to ensure that commercial interests never override or destroy significant archaeological resources in the name of profit. At the same time, the archaeological community should capitalize on the tremendous research opportunities presented by deep water sites, and undertake projects that develop specific techniques for deep water archaeological survey and excavation of significant sites. Public appreciation and understanding of the cultural values and significance of deep water sites can also be enhanced through publication, media promotion, and educational programmes such as the **Jason Project**. J.P.D.

ADDITIONAL READING

Ballard, R.D., 1987, *The Discovery of the Titanic*, New York.

Bascom, W.D., 1996, *Deep Water, Ancient Ships*, Garden City, New York.

Beasant, J., 1995, *Stalin's Silver*, London.

Delgado, J.P., 1996, 'Lure of the Deep', *Archaeology*, 49, 3 (May/June), 40–46.

Hoffman, W. and Grimm, J., 1982, *Beyond Reach: The Search for the Titanic*, New York.

Lewis, F., 1967, *One of our H-Bombs is Missing*, New York.

McCann, A.M. and Freed, J., 1994, *Deep Water Archaeology: A Late-Roman Ship Sailing from Carthage*, Journal of Roman Archaeology, Supplementary Series no. 13, Ann Arbor, Michigan.

Schultz, F., 1996, 'It's a Carnival: An Interview with Robert Ballard', *Naval History*, 10, 5 (September/October), 20–23.

Defence

A Revolutionary War privateer wreck. A brig mounting sixteen six-pounder cannon, built at Beverly Massachusetts in 1778 or 1779, *Defence* was scuttled by an explosion in Stockton Harbor, Penobscot Bay (Maine) in August 1779 (see **Penobscot Expedition**). From 1975 to 1980 excavation of the hull was carried out by the **Institute of Nautical Archaeology** (INA). The wreck site of *Defence* was discovered in 1972 by the faculty and students of the Maine Maritime Academy. The configuration of the hull was revealed by frame ends protruding a few cm above the seabed. Also protruding were the mast stumps, a wooden bilge pump pipe, and the top of the brick-built cookstove located immediately aft of the foremost stump.

In 1975 the Maine State Museum created a task force to undertake the excavation of the hull of *Defence*. Task force members included the museum, the Maine Maritime Academy and the Institute for Nautical Archaeology. The museum provided conservation and curation facilities, the Maritime Academy provided logistical support, and INA carried out the excavation during summer field-schools. Initially there were thoughts of raising and conserving the hull, as had been done with the Swedish warship **Vasa**. The expense of such an operation prompted an alternative strategy, preservation of the hull by documentation.

The documentation of the hull began in 1975 with the completion of a plan of the hull outline. As the excavation continued the plan recorded more internal structural details. The excavation procedures initiated during the 1975 field season became standard practice during ensuing field seasons, for example use of an **Airlift** emptying into a sieve box, establishing a grid frame for excavation control, and completion of measured drawings. During the 1976 field season the number and variety of artefacts became evident. An athwartship trench in the bow yielded hundreds of finds that were associated with the bosun, carpenter, gunner, the galley, and personal use. These included fids, sailmaker's palms, tool handles, cannon wadding, a rammer, grapeshot stools, mess kid parts, barrel staves, pewter spoons, buttons, buckles, and tobacco pipe fragments. The stratification of the trench contents provided insight as to the course of events in the hull following the sinking. Buoyant objects trapped in 'use areas' became waterlogged and sank. With the deterioration of deck planks silt invaded the hull, burying the contents and creating an anaerobic environment.

Clearance of the bow area provided the opportunity to document the structural characteristics of the bow in plan, perspective, and cross-sectional views. The latter provided evidence that *Defence* had considerable deadrise and a sharp bow. The structural characteristics resemble those recorded in Chesapeake- or Virginia-built vessels. A New England designer of vessels with such features at the time was John Peck. To date, evidence linking Peck to *Defence* has not come to light. Construction details noted in the bow included oak frames and ceiling, a breast hook formed from a natural oak tree crotch, a white pine mast stepped into the keelson, and a cookstove located immediately aft of the foremast stump. The stove, standing over 1.5 m tall and nearly as wide was built of brick and faced with white pine boards. The aft facing fire box was flanked by 'buttresses', and in the top was a 50+ gallon copper cauldron.

When the excavation was carried out around the stove, numerous galley-related finds were recovered. In addition to an intact mess kit, there were pewter spoons bearing graffiti, ceramic mugs and storage jars, a pewter plate, and a wooden trencher with sixteen carved wooden 'tags' 5 to 8 cm in length with initials or graffiti. At first the tags were thought to be gaming pieces or some sort of tally device. They were actually used to identify pieces of beef being boiled down in the stove cauldron: the tag identified a mess section, most likely a gun crew since sixteen tags were recovered. Some of the initials were duplicated on spoons and mess kits. Varieties of bottles were also recovered from the galley area, including tall green wine bottles, clear case bottles, and a number of bottles that probably contained medicine. Two phials were found with their original contents of sulphur and pine turpenoid.

As the excavation moved into the midsection, a variety of ordnance-related finds were recovered, such as tompions, truck carriage wheels, and a quoin. Exhibiting no wear marks, they were probably spares. The most ubiquitous ordnance-related artefacts were wooden grapeshot stools. The stools provided internal and base support for a stand of grapeshot. Several intact stands of grape were recovered along with cannon balls and a shot garland. No cannon was found within the hull. No attempt was made to dig for them outside of the hull for fear of harming the integrity of the structure and hampering documentation efforts.

During the final field seasons, excavation efforts concentrated on the stern area. Two goals were established: documenting of the shot locker/bilge well assemblage and locating the place where the scuttling explosion occurred. The shot locker/bilge well, built around the mainmast, was recovered along with a wooden bilge pump pipe. The locker/well assemblage was built of wide pine boards. The pump pipe was oak. Inside the locker was a concretion of a number of six-pound shot and, in the matrix, grapeshot stools. The concretion, solidly attached to the remains of the mainmast, was left in place. That the explosion took place in the stern was evident from a number of observations. The stern-most structure, stern post and transom features were missing. Beneath the ballast 3 m aft of the mainmast, the keelson was severely cracked, presumably from the downward force of an explosion that also damaged some frames.

The 1980 field season brought an end to the work at the *Defence* site. Since then the artefacts have been conserved and are in the collection of the Maine State Museum, Augusta. Also in the collection are examples of the hull documentation effort. D.S.

ADDITIONAL READING

Mayhew, D.R., 1974, 'The Defence: Search and Recovery', *International Journal of Nautical Archaeology*, 3, 312–13.

Smith, S.O., 1986, *The Defence: Life at Sea as Reflected in an Archaeological Assemblage from an Eighteenth Century Privateer*, unpublished PhD dissertation, University of Pennsylvania.

Switzer, D.C., 1978, 'Provision Stowage and Galley Facilities Onboard the Revolutionary War Privateer *Defence*', in W.A. Cockrell, ed., *Beneath the Waters of Time: The Proceedings of the Tenth Conference on Underwater Archaeology*, Fathom Eight, San Marino, California.

Switzer, D.C., 1981, 'Interpretation of the Stern Area of the Privateer *Defence*', in G.P. Watts, Jr. (ed.), *Underwater Archaeology, the Challenge Before Us: Proceedings of the Twelfth Conference on Underwater Archaeology*, Fathom Eight, San Marino, California.

Switzer, D.C., 1981, 'Nautical Archaeology in Penobscot Bay', in C.L. Symonds (ed.), *New Aspects of Naval History*, Annapolis, Maryland.

Switzer, D.C., 1987, 'Privateers not Pirates', in P. Throckmorton (ed.), *History from the Sea*, New York.

Wyman, D., 1981, 'Developing the Plans for the Revolutionary War Privateer Defence', in W.A. Cockrell (ed.), *Beneath the Waters of Time: The Proceedings of the Tenth Conference on Underwater Archaeology*, Fathom Eight, San Marino, California.

Dendrochronology

see **Absolute dating**

Denmark

see **Baltic Sea**

The Direct Survey Method (DSM) in use by the Foundations Fotevikens Maritima Centrum, on the wreck of a medieval cog near Hollviken, Sweden. (Fotevikens Maritima Centrum)

Direct Survey Method (DSM)

A technique for mapping the x, y, z coordinates of points on a site. It has the ability to mix almost any type of measurement underwater, as long as the resulting geometry defines a point. Distance measurements using a tape measure are the most common, but depths, slopes, bearings, and various types of offsets have been used. The underwater surveyor thus has considerable freedom to use any combination of measurements that suits the underwater geometry, the aim in such cases being to 'keep it simple, stupid (KISS)'. The technique also has the ability to use measurements that are not restricted to the horizontal plane (cf. **Trilateration**). DSM is fully three-dimensional; the name 'direct' refers to the use of distance measurements that record the shortest (i.e. line of sight) distance between two points. It is not necessary to know the coordinates of any of the points in advance.

Great emphasis is placed on the use of redundant 'check' measurements in order to quantify error and isolate and reject rogue measurements. Rule (1995) described how in a database of 3,731 tape measurements from 11 sites, 4 per cent were determined to be 'blunders' (defined as non-systematic errors). If only the minimal number of measurements is taken, DSM will find a plan that fits the measurements, but the archaeologist will have no objective way of knowing if the plan is any good. If a few check measurements are taken DSM will provide a measure of confidence, thereby allowing the project to redeploy resources once the target confidence has been exceeded. If sufficient redundant measurements are taken, it becomes possible to isolate and reject most of the blunders.

DSM originated on the **Mary Rose** project in 1980 when the depth of excavation trenches exceeded the visibility and thus trilateration became very difficult. It has subsequently been extended and used on over thirty sites around the world.

Simplicity underwater is exchanged for complexity on land, and a computer program is used to process the measurements. The mathematical problem can be expressed in terms of the residual error for each measurement, this being defined as the difference between the measurement as observed by the diver, and as measured from the site plan (a sketch is used as an approximate site plan at the start of the process). The aim is to adjust the values for the coordinates of the unknown points to minimize these residual errors; this is a multidimensional minimization problem.

A large number of families of heuristic algorithms can be used to perform the 'best fit' minimization, including least squares (also known as 'variation of coordinates') and multidimensional scaling. In each case the algorithm takes a starting guess, performs a transformation, and (usually) obtains a better guess. This is repeated over and over again as the 'guess' becomes refined into a 'plan'. During this phase data visualization tools draw attention to possible blunders; these can be discarded or preferably re-checked underwater. When the plan fits the measurements with acceptably low residual errors, the process is complete. N.R.

ADDITIONAL READING:

Adams, J. and Rule, N. 1991 'A Comparison of the Application of a Three Dimensional Survey System on Three Underwater Archæological Sites', *Scheepsarcheologie: prioriteiten en lopend onderzoek; inleidingen gehouden tijdens de glavimans symposia in 1986 en 1988*, Flevobericht 322, Holland.

Bomford, G., 1971, *Geodesy*, Clarendon Press, Oxford.

Cross, P.A., 1981, 'The Computation of Position at Sea', *Hydrographic Journal*, 20, 7–16.

Rule, M., 1982, *The Mary Rose*, London, 218–20

Rule, N., 1989, 'The Direct Survey Method (DSM) of underwater survey, and its application underwater', *The International Journal of Nautical Archaeology*, 18, 2, 157–162.

Rule, N., 1995, 'Some Techniques for Cost-effective Three-dimensional Mapping of Underwater Sites', J. Wilcock and K. Lockyear (eds), *Computer Applications and Quantitative Methods in Archaeology 1993*. BAR International Series 598, Oxford.

Spencer, R., 1986, 'Similarity Mapping', *Byte*, August.

Doddington

A British East Indiaman wrecked on Bird Island in Algoa Bay, South Africa in 1755. In 1977 a salvage group led by Allen and Van Niekerk worked in collaboration with the Port Elizabeth Museum and recovered items for display. Little archaeological documentation was conducted due to the salvors' arguments that accuracy was impossible with the local surf and swell conditions.

Public education courses in underwater archaeology methods began to be offered in South Africa in 1994. As a result, a new detailed survey using triangulation, baselines, and shoreline datums was undertaken with fifty cannon and eight anchors. A system of using aerial photographs and buoyed reference points in conjunction with GPS (see **Global Positioning System**) was explored. The data generated by the project has revealed new evidence allowing the team to interpret site formation processes. Close cooperation with Port Elizabeth Museum was maintained throughout this project. L.H., T.D.

ADDITIONAL READING

Hardy, C., 1800, *A Register of Ships in the Service of the East India Company*, Cape Town.

Plaited, B., 1758, *A Journal from Calcutta and a Journal of Proceedings of the Doddington East Indiaman*, London.

Dover Boat

A substantial portion of a Middle Bronze Age stitched plank boat, found in 1992 in Dover, Kent, during roadworks over which the Canterbury Archaeological Trust was maintaining a watching brief. The mid-section was exposed in deep excavations necessary for the construction of an underpass on the seaward flank of the ancient town. A rescue operation was mounted to record and recover it within the six days made available. In view of its importance the Department of Transport and English Heritage agreed to the construction of an adjacent **Cofferdam** so that a further portion, possibly including one of its ends, might be recovered. As a result a total length of 9.5 m of a vessel, perhaps originally about 13 m long and 2.3 m in beam, was revealed. Careful excavation, environmental sampling, and recovery of the second portion was achieved in eight days.

The boat was deeply buried in silt 6 m below ground level and the stratigraphy sup-

Excavation of the Dover Boat. (© English Heritage)

ported a Bronze Age date which provisional radiocarbon dates suggested to be in the 14th century BC. It was clear that the vessel lay to one side of the ancient harbour and had been partly dismantled in antiquity. The recovered portion consisted of four parallel elements each converted from the trunk of an oak. Their southern extremities were complete, but their northern portions lay beyond the first cofferdam which had cut diagonally across them. There was no central plank, but an upstanding 'cleat-rail' carved out of each plank flanked the central seam. This was packed with moss and covered by a lath held in place by wedges passing through mortices in the cleat-rail. No wood or metal pins were used anywhere in the construction. The side planks, or iles,

were carved to form a curved junction with the sides of the craft. They were secured by separate stitches made of thin twisted branches of yew which held in place wads of moss and a covering lath. At intervals on the bottom planks there were pairs of large cleats carved out of the solid wood. These housed wedges up to 60 cm long which also passed through mortices in the cleat-rails. Single smaller cleats were carved at intervals on the side planks. These were empty when found.

The surface of the oak was exceptionally fresh and was covered with hundreds of tool-marks, although the weight of the overlying deposits had caused variable compression and distortion of the timber. The boat showed clear signs of having been partially dismantled. Severed stitches and empty stitch-holes were found along the surviving upper edges of the side planks showing where upper planks had been removed. Unfortunately dismantling had extended to the removal of the element which had evidently closed the southern end of the hull. Here there survived portions of wedges which had fastened the missing element to the ends of the bottom planks. These had been deliberately severed, leaving behind a large pad of moss resting on wide bevels which terminated in finely worked feather edges. Both the design and execution of the pointed ends of the planks was remarkable. The cleat-rails continued to a point 60 cm from their ends and then diverged at an angle of 22 degrees, while the central lath tucked into a rebate carved in a short transverse lath. Each end of this little lath was rebated and in turn was locked in position by other laths housed in slim mortises in the cleat-rails. The craftsmanship may be said to resemble cabinet-making; its function was clearly to provide even pressure over the seam between the bottom planks and the (missing) end element.

The boat had evidently settled and changed shape after it was abandoned. Thus its precise form and that of the missing parts is not immediately apparent. Hypotheses will have to await evidence obtained from the detailed study and recording programme. Its find-spot beside the tiny River Dour, which flows through a gap flanked by many kilometres of chalk cliffs, shows that it must have been seagoing. The size and quality of its components and the effort expended to make good its seams indicate a vessel of the highest status. It seems most probable that it was engaged in cross-Channel trade and contacts. These have hitherto been hinted at by numerous imported artefacts, such as the large group of continental bronzes from Langdon Bay just outside Dover Harbour. v.f.

ADDITIONAL READING

Needham, S. and Dean, M., 1987, 'La cargaison de Langdon Bay à Douvres (Grand Bretagne), *Actes du Colloque de Bronze de Lille*, 119–24.

Parfitt, K., 1993, 'The Discovery of the Dover Bronze Age Boat, *Current Archaeology*, 133, 4–8.

Parfitt, K. and Fenwick, V., 1993, 'The Rescue of Dover's Bronze Age Boat, in J. Coles, V. Fenwick, and G. Hutchinson (eds), *A Spirit of Enquiry*, Wetland Archaeology Research Project, Exeter.

Dramont Wreck

Mid-1st-century BC wreck off Cap Dramont, France. If we consider the numerous ancient shipwrecks found in its area, Cap Dramont, near Saint-Raphaël, must have been particularly dreaded by ancient mariners. The first wreck, called Dramont A, was discovered as early as 1956 by Claude Santamaria in between 35 and 40 m of water. The wreck was then the object of numerous study campaigns. The first, from 1957 to 1960, was led by Santamaria; it was assisted in 1959 by a team led by A. Sivirine. After a long period of abandonment, a second project was undertaken by Santamaria who undertook its systematical excavation between 1971 and 1979.

The site consisted of a large amphora tumulus, 22 by 9 m, which corresponded to the wreck of a merchant ship carrying an important cargo of wine amphoras from south Italy, stacked in three layers and still in place. The amphoras, of the Dressel IB type, included potter's marks of which about ten different stamps have been recovered. The study of their distribution has shown that the amphoras had been loaded by groups of same stamps. At each extremity of the cargo, two series of board artefacts have allowed the identification of a little store-room at the bow and a cabin equipped with a fireplace at the stern. Lastly, on each side of the prow, two sets of two lead stocks indicated that the ship had sunk with the anchors still in place. The characteristics of the artefacts allow us to date the shipwreck to around the middle of the 1st century BC.

The hull remains, preserved for 23.5 m in length and only 4 to 5 m in width, correspond to the port side of the ship, keel included. These dimensions allow us to reconstruct the original size with a length of at least 25 m and a minimum width of 7 m. Besides the keel, a part of the stem post and of the stern post were found in place. The latter was doubled by an important false post working as a centre board. The hull has double planking assembled by tenons pegged on mortises, and a frame consisting of alternated floor-timbers and half-frames, except for the centre part where a succession of eight floor-timbers strengthened the structure under the mast step timber. In spite of some differences and smaller sizes, the structure of the Dramont Wreck reveals numerous analogies with the **Madrague de Giens Wreck**. Study of the construction method demonstrates that the ship had been built according to the shell-first method. P.P.

ADDITIONAL READING

Liou, B. and Pomey, P., 1985, 'Recherches sous-marines', *Gallia*, 43, 2, 568–72.

Santamaria, C.I., 1975, 'L'épave A du Cap Dramont (Saint-Raphaël), Fouilles 1971–1974, *Revue Archéologique Narbonnaise*, 8, 185–98.

Dry Tortugas National Park

An area with numerous wrecks in Florida. The Dry Tortugas are currently composed of

Aerial view of Fort Jefferson, Dry Tortugas National Park. (National Park Service/John Brooks)

seven sand islands surrounded by shallow patchy coral reefs about 100 km west of Key West Florida and 170 km north of Havana, Cuba. The shallow Tortugas reef/island complex is approximately 25 km long by 12 km wide, lying northeast–southwest between 240° 33′–240° 44′ N and 820° 46′–820° 58′ W. The complex consists of three major bank reef systems, which are separated by 10–20 m deep channels, surrounding a 12–30 m deep lagoon that furnishes excellent deepwater anchorage. Water depths are 2–3 m over the shoals; the complex is surrounded by 11–30 m depths.

When discovered and named 'Las Tortugas' by Ponce de Leon in 1513 for the many sea turtles observed, there were eleven islands, of which the smallest have been lost to hurricane erosion. 'Dry' was later added to alert mariners there was no water there. The Tortugas' aridity results from a combination of poor water retention and a high evaporation rate from the nearly constant easterly trade winds. The sand islands are shaped by currents, and their positions and names have varied over time. A 260 sq. km area containing the entire complex was made a national monument in 1936, and it became Dry Tortugas National Park in 1994.

The Dry Tortugas lie on the western edge of the 120 km wide Florida Straits, through which passes the north-flowing Gulf Stream and the major shipping lanes connecting the 3,000 km Gulf coastline with the northeast United States and Europe. The straits have served as a corridor of commerce since the days of Spanish conquest, and as their western terminus, the Dry Tortugas have claimed many a vessel that ventured too close (the park is what archaeologists sometimes call a **Ship trap**, an area that collects numerous wrecks because it presents particular risk to major shipping lanes). In the 19th century, construction of Fort Jefferson – the largest of the US masonry harbour forts built prior to the Civil War – demon-

strated the strategic importance of these islands. Fort Jefferson established America's presence in the Caribbean and denied access to the Tortugas' safe anchorage for any enemy fleet attempting to blockade US ports.

Commercial development and military activity have left numerous wrecks here, as have the competition among maritime nations in the New World, fort construction and support, salvage, fishing, and other activities. Consequently, the park contains a remarkable collection of maritime sites that have occurred over a long period, collectively representing an important international maritime heritage about which little was known. Park managers understood the necessity for an archaeological survey of submerged areas by the early 1970s, and archaeologists began investigations of the area.

In 1971 the National Park Service conducted the first cultural resource management magnetometer survey in North America at the Dry Tortugas. In subsequent years, both the National Park Service and the State of Florida conducted short-term surveys there. In 1993, the NPS **Submerged Cultural Resources Unit** (SCRU) began conducting a model systematic area-wide survey directed by Larry Murphy. The ongoing survey goals are to inventory both cultural and natural submerged resources and evaluate cultural sites. This survey is the first submerged resources survey designed from the outset completely for **Geographic Information System (GIS)** applications. GIS data sets are cumulative, integrated, comparative, and readily accessible, and this technology provides the necessary infrastructure for data collection, storage, manipulation, and presentation required for long-term park management and research applications.

A comprehensive assessment was conducted by Murphy in 1993, and a computer database incorporating more than 250 Tortugas maritime casualties was generated for survey planning purposes. The wreck database allows rapid manipulation of fields and combinations to facilitate analysis of variables and relationships among attributes to discern maritime activity patterns for survey design, particularly regarding methodology, intensity, and sampling methods. Patterns were sought in such things as frequency of location, cargo, hull size, rig type, date, time, and season of loss. One research question is whether historic patterns support wrecks primarily resulting from contingency factors such as weather and currents or from cultural factors, or perhaps as simply a function of ocean travel. If the latter is the case, then the correlation between losses and amount of shipping should be generally constant over time, with variations gradual and generally attributed to war or technology. There was no wreck patterning based on cumulative five- or ten-year intervals for the 19th and 20th centuries. In fact, some periods, such as the Civil War, predicted to have numerous wrecks, had fewer than average. There was only weak correlation between wrecks and poor weather; consequently, cultural factors must be considered in explanation of Tortugas wreck patterns. The database was also useful for determining general cargo assemblages, as well as the general extent and nature of salvage operations and amount of anchoring, repair, and jettisoning activity.

The survey design established basic methodology and research domains. The survey was multi-disciplinary and conducted from a regional approach; site evaluation and significance incorporated the widest possible context; shipwrecks were not treated as discrete, disparate sites but as the result of large-scale cultural patterning. Generation of relevant historical themes aided site interpretation and significance evaluation. Areas shallower than 10 m were comprehensively surveyed with a suite of differentially corrected GPS-positioned remote sensing instruments including the fathometer, **Magnetometer**, and RoxAnn bottom classification device; the applicability of other instruments was tested during the survey. Deeper areas were statistically sampled with randomly and judgementally selected units for a 30 per cent coverage.

Implicit in the regional approach are two basic assumptions: the material record is composed of both wreck sites and activity areas, and the concentration of sites in the survey area is not an accidental, haphazard conglomeration of unfortunate vessels, but rather a more-or-less representative sample of all the maritime activity in the region, which is structured by a complex interaction of natural and cultural factors. Research questions were developed that focused on site-formation processes as well as relationships between patterning and variability of the archaeological record and the past behaviour of all the maritime cultures represented. Principal research topics emphasized cultural processes such as intersocietal contact, acculturation, competition, and conflict among social groups over time. The approach relies on both documentary and material records as it is both archaeological-anthropological and historical.

The long time-depth of the Tortugas material record, as in many similar 'ship trap' areas, allows investigation and interpretation of change in the material record while controlling for environmental and geographical variables. Ships, whether commercial or military, are parts of cultural systems, and it is those larger cultural systems that is the object of investigation through their representation in the material and documentary record. The material record is patterned because it results from patterned behaviour. In short, for the Dry Tortugas project, site interpretation was ultimately directed towards understanding sociocultural patterns responsible for the wrecks by developing and using broad principles of economic and maritime behaviour as well as more traditional approaches. The basic idea is that shipwrecks in this centuries-old crossroads can provide important clues to the

Working on the site of DRTO GUW 0241D. (NPS/John Brooks)

evolution and structure of the global economic system we live in.

The real utility of a comprehensive survey lies in the ability to access and manipulate the data through GIS software, which requires specific post-processing, collation, and archiving procedures. Multiple data sets, portrayed as spatially related themes, can be overlaid and their databases queried with Boolean interrogatives, allowing rapid analytical manipulation and comparison of amounts of data that would otherwise be impossible. One immediate benefit of GIS to the survey project was the ability to generate locations for onsite investigation concurrent with the survey. A point was selected based on magnetic or environmental attributes or material relationships and the computer-generated coordinates were loaded into a portable GPS receiver. One simply followed the range and bearing to the desired point to begin in-water investigation of selected loci. There were no buoys used during the project. The data collected for a locus varied from 'nothing found' to a large volume of information, including site maps, photographs, video, convergent photogrammetric documentation, samples, and feature and artefact narrative descriptions.

In addition to hydrographic survey data, SCRU included aerial photography and historical maps and charts in GIS coverages. One application of this longitudinal temporal database is determination of changes in channels, shoals, and islands through time. Aerial photographs were scanned, georeferenced, and rectified. These photos and maps could then be compared (overlaid) to existing spatial data and examined for clues leading to the location of old island and reef positions, other parts of a wreck site or 'ship tracks', which are scars left on the bottom by a grounding vessel. Location of these tracks has produced sites consisting of nothing more than piles of ballast off-loaded during a grounding, a clear archaeological signature for this activity. Many of these sites have little or no magnetic content, and consequently would likely be overlooked by researchers relying solely on magnetic data.

Digitized historic maps, some from the 1700s, were compared to existing islands. Because the Dry Tortugas are sand islands, they have moved, reshaped, disappeared, and reappeared over time. The islands were referred to by different names at various times. It is important to be able to overlay historic maps upon the existing area to correlate historical documentation and current topography. Static cartographic sources become dynamic analytical tools through comparative GIS manipulation.

The survey used two levels of investigation: examination of specific sites and wide areas. Several sites have been investigated in the traditional manner and reported. Three sites have been the subject of master's degree research – the **East Key Wreck** by Souza, the *Maria Louisa* by Lanzendorf, and **Dry Tortugas National Park Shipwreck DRTO-036**, the 'Cement Barrel Wreck', by Conlin; a dissertation is being completed on B016-32; and other sites have been reported by Richard Gould and Larry Murphy.

In ship traps where numerous casualty sites and activity areas exist, discrete site analysis has to be modified. Many sites, as represented in the Dry Tortugas, are just large areas where there are greater or lesser concentrations of artefacts that must be analytically distinguished. Numerous multiple sites, sometimes from the same period, can be intermingled and altered by activities such as salvage, fishing, anchoring, and refuse deposition in addition to natural processes. There are areas of the Dry Tortugas where magnetic anomalies exceed 200 per square kilometre, with numerous small objects scattered throughout. In these areas, site boundaries become meaningless, and often material relationships must be established one by one. In one area, for example, there are at least four shipwrecks from the 1870s or so – some showing distinctive evidence of salvage – overlaying an area where cannon were dropped perhaps half a century or more earlier, all of which is close to where another vessel ran aground and off-loaded two piles of ballast stones to lighten its hull for release. We are treating spots like this as maritime casualty and activity areas. Thus, through an anthropologically oriented wide-area survey we are learning to seek different evidence about the past than if we had dealt with each wreck separately.

Survey and site evaluation results are still being analysed. However, some preliminary observations can be offered. Wide-area survey and interpretation from a regional approach is potentially much more productive than a single-site approach. Localized shipwreck concentrations are complex, and they require examination of a wide range of data to isolate causal factors forming wreck concentrations. GIS is a remarkably effective tool for regional-scale analysis and is basic to this approach because it makes analysis of complex relationships and archaeological associations over wide areas possible. L.E.M.

ADDITIONAL READING

Conlin, D.L., 1994, 'The Loggerhead Reef Ship Trap: Maritime Site Formation Processes on DRTO-036 and Beyond', Master's research paper, Brown University, Providence.

Gould, R., 1995, 'The Bird Key Wreck, Dry Tortugas National Park, Florida', *Bulletin of the Australian Institute for Maritime Archaeology*, 19, 2, 7–16.

Lanzendorf, B., 1996, 'The Grounding and Abandonment of the *Maria Louisa*: A Behaviourist Approach', Master's research paper, Brown University, Providence.

Murphy, L.E., ed., 1993, *Dry Tortugas National Park: Submerged Cultural Resources Assessment*, National Park Service, Santa Fe.

Souza, D.J., 1991, 'An Archaeological Survey of a 19th Century Shipwreck, Dry Tortugas National Park', Master's research paper, Brown University, Providence.

Dry Tortugas National Park Shipwreck DRTO-036

Nineteenth-century wreck in Florida. Shipwreck DRTO-036 (DRy TOrtuga site 036) was discovered during a systematic survey of Dry Tortugas National Park, Florida, by the National Park Service's **Submerged Cultural Resources Unit** (SCRU) in June 1993, under the direction of Larry Murphy (see **Dry Tortugas National Park**). It was investigated and documented over the course of two seasons (1993–4) as part of an ongoing collaborative research project between the SCRU and Dr Richard Gould and graduate students of Brown University. It has been documented as a MA paper by Conlin.

DRTO-036 represents the wreck of a medium-sized ship of *c*. 150 ft (45 m) in length that sank in shallow water on the southern margins of a shallow reef. A combination of *ante* and *post quem* dates derived from multiple lines of evidence including pottery, Muntz metal, and natural cement set a time for the sinking of DRTO-036 in a period ranging from the late 1840s to the late 1860s. The date and location of the wreck, the cargo of at least 340 barrels of natural cement, greywacke (a hard, metamorphic stone used for flooring at Fort Jefferson and in Loggerhead Lighthouse), and nails point towards an association with either Fort Jefferson or Loggerhead Lighthouse. Furthermore, the makeup of the cargo offers circumstantial evidence for a northern port of origin on the final voyage. Wood samples taken from the 25 m of surviving timbers revealed keelson and outer hull timbers of pine, with birch framing, indicating a North American cultural affiliation for the ship. To date, no name has been conclusively attached to DRTO-036.

Overall, the ship falls well in line with what is known about mid- to late-19th-century North American shipbuilding techniques and shipping technology. A number of things, however, are interesting about the site. Widespread fire onboard is indicated by charred timbers, heat-cracked ballast stones, and a melted glass bottle. Whether the fire was a proximate cause or result of the wreck, or was used later to expedite salvage and/or removal of a hazard to navigation is still under investigation.

However, an examination of shipping records for the region of the Dry Tortugas revealed four ships as having burned in the area. The US Bureau of Customs Annual Listings of Losses has fire as one of the six categories for wreck causes for 1867–1967, indicating vessel loss by fire may be rather common. In addition to the fire, a series of repairs, including replacement and scarfing of a floor timber, and the introduction of siliceous mastic through drilled holes in the ship's timbers, as well as a mended dead-eye on a nearby chainplate, point to a long working life and a quiltwork of stopgap repairs. Taken together these may be material indicators of Murphy's 'one more voyage' hypothesis, where maritime capitalism pushes ships (and their crew) past the point of safety while attempting to maximize profit by minimizing expenditures for things such as comprehensive repairs and new ships.

A final interesting aspect of the site is that

the natural cement barrel casts scattered over several thousand metres of reef can be uniquely sourced to the cargo of DRTO-036. In a relatively small area characterized by multiple shipwreck, stranding, and salvage episodes, the single provenance of the barrels offers some indication of the nature and degree of pre- and post-depositional factors operating on the cultural materials of the Dry Tortugas. Using securely attributable materials (in this case 400 pound barrels of cement) to characterize taphonomic processes in the area, archaeologists from the Submerged Cultural Resources Unit and Brown University have been able to make sense of other, less securely attributable, artefactual distributions. D.L.C.

ADDITIONAL READING

Conlin, D.L., 1994, 'The Loggerhead Reef Ship Trap: Maritime Site Formation Processes on DRTO-036 and Beyond', Master's research paper, Brown University, Providence.

Gould, R., 1995, 'The Bird Key Wreck, Dry Tortugas National Park, Florida', *Bulletin of the Australian Institute for Maritime Archaeology*, 19, 2, 7–16.

Murphy, L.E., 1993, *Dry Tortugas National Park: Submerged Cultural Resources Assessment*, Santa Fe.

Duart Wreck

A small vessel, probably the pinnace *Swan*, wrecked close to Duart Castle, Mull, off the west coast of Scotland. In September 1653 Oliver Cromwell sent a task force to the area to root out the royalist Macleans of Duart. The expedition consisted of six ships under the command of Colonel Ralph Cobbett. When they arrived off Mull they found the castle abandoned, but a sudden storm dispersed the anchored fleet and wrecked three of them – *Martha and Margaret* of Ipswich, *Speedwell* of Lyn, and *Swan*. The latter was a small warship originally belonging to Charles I's navy which, in 1645, had been captured by the parliamentarians. The incident resulted in substantial loss of life, and a witness records how it occurred 'in the sight of our Men att land, who saw their friends drowning, and heard them crying for helpe, but could not save them'.

The wreck was located in 1979 and, apart from some initial recoveries, remained untouched until 1991, when serious environmental destabilization began to threaten its integrity. After investigation by the state-funded **Archaeological Diving Unit** the most vulnerable material was recovered, and the site was designated as a protected historic wreck. Under licence from Historic Scotland, the national regulatory authority,

a long-term programme of survey, assessment, and protection has been initiated by the **Scottish Institute of Maritime Studies** at St Andrews University, under the direction of Colin Martin. At the time of writing, two seasons of work have been conducted (in 1993

Fragile organic material exposed by shifting sediments off Duart Point. The objects include a carved wooden cherub, a stave-built keg, and a human arm bone. (Colin Martin)

and 1994), and sandbags have been used to secure those areas most prone to erosion.

Substantial elements of articulated hull structure have been identified beneath two distinct mounds of stone ballast, and at the eastern end of the site a complex of high-quality wooden panelling suggests that this area contains part of the stern cabin, collapsed in on itself. Among the finds recovered in this area are several well-preserved wooden carvings associated with the ship's exterior embellishment. Other recoveries include pottery, pewter, part of a pistol lock, and a range of wooden artefacts. Radiographs of concretions have revealed an ornate sword hilt and the apparently intact movement of a pocket watch. The finds are being conserved by the Royal Museum of Scotland, Edinburgh, where the entire collection will eventually be housed.

Extensive environmental studies are being conducted in an attempt to understand and perhaps mitigate the processes responsible for the site's destabilization. It is likely that the most threatened parts of it will be excavated under controlled conditions to ensure their preservation. C.M.

ADDITIONAL READING

Martin, C.J.M., 1994, 'The Cromwellian Shipwreck off Duart Point, Mull: An Interim Report, *International Journal of Nautical Archaeology*, 24, 1, 15–32.

Martin, C.J.M., 1995, 'Assessment, Stabilisation, and Management of an Environmentally Threatened Seventeenth Century Shipwreck off Duart Point, Mull', A.Q. Berry (ed.),

Managing Ancient Monuments: An Integrated Approach, Mold.

Dublin

Capital city of Ireland, where excavations have revealed medieval boat and ship timbers (see **Buried ships**). Nearly four hundred timbers from dismantled boats and ships were found during a series of excavations in medieval Dublin undertaken by the National Museum of Ireland between 1962 and 1981. These timbers, and others, had been used to build 10th- to 13th-century defences, waterfronts, houses, drains, and causeways, or they had been discarded as fill along the former waterfront. Although some of the planking was still articulated, no complete, or even near-complete, vessel was excavated, and many of the timbers were isolated finds.

With two exceptions, all the nautical timbers proved to be from the Viking/Norse tradition. There were keels, stems, planking, floors, knees, side timbers, bulkheads, and breast hooks; there were also spar crutches (*c.* 1 m across), oars, paddles, a rudder tiller with part of the stock, parrels for holding a yard to a mast, and a fragment of rope. Other finds which shed light on medieval shipbuilding and seafaring included model boats, wood engravings of sailing ships, an ampulla in the form of a ship, and a number of woodworking tools.

Planking from a 12th/13th-century merchant ship exposed during excavations at the Wood Quay site in Dublin. (National Maritime Museum, Greenwich)

Estimates of the size, shape, and structure of the parent vessels of the Dublin timbers were obtained by comparison with similar elements from nearly complete Viking/Norse boats and ships excavated elsewhere. For example, it was possible to show that four groups of late 12th/early 13th-century planking came from one large ship, 'Dublin 69', which was similar to the mid-12th-century ship from Lynaes, Denmark, and could have carried about 60 tonnes of cargo.

In the 10th, 11th, and 12th centuries, oared boats up to 12 m in length, and small sailing ships up to 20 m, used the port of Hiberno-Norse Dublin. Whereas, from *c.* 1170 onwards, in Anglo-Norman Dublin, there were large sailing ships 25–30 m in length, as well as smaller craft.

The 10th- and 11th-century River Liffey embankments were to constrain the river and to act as town defences, rather than to be used as waterfronts for shipping. During this period boats and ships probably anchored in the *dubh linn* ('blackpool'), a natural harbour in the River Poddle to the east of the Viking town, or they were beached on an adjoining strand below the east end of the ridge on which Dublin Castle now stands. Further earth banks and wooden revetments were built by the Anglo-Normans in the early 13th century, but it was not until the building of a back-braced revetment in the late 13th century and a stone quay in the early 14th that Dublin had a waterfront alongside which large ships could berth. Smaller vessels, however, probably continued to use the River Liffey strand or the pool in the River Poddle. S.M.

ADDITIONAL READING

McGrail, S., 1993, *Medieval Boat and Ship Timbers from Dublin*, Dublin.

Mitchell, G.F., 1987, *Archaeology and Environment in Early Dublin*, Dublin.

Wallace, P.F., 1992, *Viking Age Buildings of Dublin*, Parts 1 and 2, Dublin.

Dvaraka

Late Harappan city submerged in the Arabian Sea. According to ancient Indian traditions, the city of Dvaraka was founded by the epic hero Shri Krishna to shelter his followers (the Yadavas) from the army of their enemy Jarasandha. The *Mahabharata* epic tells how Krishna reclaimed 12 *yojanas* (245 sq. km) of land from the sea to build a port city, which stood for one hundred years before being submerged once again.

In 1979–80 Indian archaeologists undertook a search for the site of Dvaraka in the Arabian Sea. They began with onshore excavations in the enclosure of the 15th-century Dwakaradhish temple in the Jamnagar Dis-

Plotting a bastion of the submerged city identified by Dr Rao as Dvaraka. (S.R.Rao)

The inscription on a votive jar from Dvaraka. (S.R. Rao)

trict of Gujarat, near a modern town also known as Dvaraka. The excavations revealed a 9th-century temple of Vishnu and two earlier temples, one dating to the 2nd century BC and the other to the 3rd–4th centuries AD; the latter had been inundated by the sea. Further digging brought to light the eroded remains of a settlement which the excavators assigned to the 15th century BC. This discovery inspired them to look for further remains underwater, beyond the modern shoreline.

A government-funded marine archaeology centre, headed by Dr S.R. Rao, was established in 1981 in the National Institute of Oceanography (NIO), Goa. Its purpose was to explore the site which the archaeologists identified with ancient Dvaraka. Underwater excavations began in 1983, and the remains of a city were located. In 1989 and 1992 geophysical and **Magnetometer** surveys were used to establish the outer limits of the site. The nearby island of Beyt Dwarka was also explored.

Careful excavations in 10–11 m of water exposed structural remains of a submerged city about 1 km to seaward of the (onshore) remains of the Temple of Samudranaryana at modern Dvaraka. Massive fortified walls, pierced by gateways flanked by bastions, were traced in six sectors, two on the right and four on the left bank of the ancient Gomati Channel. Blocks of finely dressed stone, weighing between 1 and 3 tonnes, were used in the construction of the walls and bastions, which stand on a foundation of dry boulders. This technique is still adopted in reclamation areas to provide firm foundations for buildings on waterlogged ground.

The location of three holed anchors, of triangular and prismatic shape, lying along the ancient harbour wall suggested that large ships could have anchored there. The modification of the natural rock into a wharf suggested to Dr Rao that the city had been a busy port. Larger sea-going vessels could have been berthed at the site about

1 km seaward of the Samudranarayana temple, while smaller vessels sailed further up the Gomati River (a pattern known from the early Islamic period).

In and around the island of Beyt Dwarka, the remains of fortified stone walls were found. This, along with the other excavations, led Dr Rao to conclude that a settlement extending over some 4 km had existed there about 3,500 years ago, now mostly submerged in the sea, and that a second town, on the mainland, was also inundated.

Various artefacts were found during the excavations. A late Indus-type seal of conch shell, inscribed with a three-headed animal figure representing a bull, a unicorn, and a goat, can be assigned to the 15th or 16th century BC. A votive jar found in the intertidal zone is inscribed. The brass, bronze, and iron artefacts found, and the construction of the wharf and walls on reclaimed land, argue for a high level of artistic and engineering skills on the part of the city dwellers. S.R.R.

ADDITIONAL READING

Rao, S.R., 1996, *Lost City of Dvaraka Aditya Prakasham*, Delhi.

Eagle

A US Navy twenty–gun brig built in 1814 at Vergennes, Vermont for service on **Lake Champlain** during the Anglo-American 'War of 1812'. Construction of *Eagle* was authorized in early July 1814 in response to a threatened British invasion of the Champlain Valley by land and water. The contract was let to New York shipwrights Adam and Noah Brown, who hired two hundred shipwrights and completed the 117 ft (35.7 m) vessel in only nineteen days. Following the launch on 11 August *Eagle* was outfitted with twelve 32–pounder carronades and eight 18–pounder long guns, and manned by approximately 150 sailors and US Army soldiers (including convicts from an army chain gang and band musicians).

Eagle joined Commodore Thomas Macdonough's naval squadron on Lake Champlain in late August, and just two weeks later, on 11 September 1814, Macdonough's force met an invading British squadron at the Battle of Plattsburgh Bay. The last-minute addition of *Eagle* gave the two squadrons parity: the US Navy had a 26–gun corvette, the 20–gun *Eagle*, a 17–gun schooner, an armed sloop, and ten gunboats, while the Royal Navy had a 36–gun frigate, a 16–gun brig, two armed sloops, and thirteen gunboats. The British attack upon the anchored line of American ships resulted in a bloody two-and-a-half-hour battle which terminated with the British surrender of all vessels except the gunboats. The US Navy's victory turned back the invasion of northern New York, and hastened the British decision to sign the Treaty of Ghent that ended the war.

After the battle the American and captured British vessels were laid up near Whitehall, New York where they swiftly deteriorated; the half-sunk hulls were sold to salvagers in 1825. Over the next 150 years several of the warships were broken up for fittings or destroyed as navigational hazards. A survey of the Whitehall area in 1982 by the Champlain Maritime Society yielded four 1812–era wrecks: *Eagle*, the US schooner *Ticonderoga*, a US Navy gunboat, and the captured R.N. brig *Linnet*. *Eagle* was particularly well preserved, with the port side of the vessel preserved up to the gunports. The wreck was archaeologically recorded in 1983 and 1984, and the hull was reconstructed on paper.

Like other warships built on the North

Divers working in the early 1980s in lower Lake Champlain locating and documenting the US brig Eagle. *(Courtesy of Lake Champlain Maritime Museum, Basin Harbor, Vermont)*

American lakes during the War of 1812, *Eagle* had a very shallow draft that combined slack bilges amidships with a sharp entrance and fine run. Of particular interest were the short cuts taken by Adam Brown to complete the hull in nineteen days. The brig was entirely iron-fastened, and contained an strange selection of wood types, including weaker white pine and spruce for some frame floors and futtocks. The method of deck construction was particularly unusual for a wooden warship, for no knee timbers were used for reinforcement; instead, the clamp and waterway timbers were greatly enlarged to secure the deck beams. Omitting knees and using inferior woods permitted great savings in time, and speed of assembly was clearly of greater concern to Adam Brown than *Eagle's* long-term durability. K.C.

ADDITIONAL READING

Cassavoy, K. and Crisman, K., 1988, 'The War of 1812: Battle for the Great Lakes', in G. Bass (ed.), *Ships and Shipwrecks of the Americas*, London and New York.

Crisman, K., 1987, *The Eagle: An American Brig on Lake Champlain During the War of 1812*, Annapolis, Maryland and Shelburne, Vermont.

Crisman, K., 1991, 'Nautical Archaeology of the War of 1812: The Lake Brigs *Jefferson* and *Eagle*', *Seaways*, 2, 4, 5–9.

Earl of Abergavenny

An English East India Company (EIC) vessel, wrecked in 1805, periodically salvaged, broken down and stripped from 1805 to the 1960s, and excavated and surveyed by members of the Chelmsford Sub Aqua Club between 1979 and 1989. *Earl of Abergavenny* was built at the Pitcher Yard at Northfleet, Kent in 1796 for the East India Company.

The ship was 176 ft 11 in (53.92 m) long, with a 43 ft 8 in (13.31 m) breadth and was 1,400 tons burthen.

Earl of Abergavenny sailed from the Company's docks in early November 1804 for a voyage to Bengal and thence China under the command of Captain John Wordsworth, brother of poet William Wordsworth. The ship carried a cargo estimated at 200,000 pounds (90 tonnes), nine passengers, and twenty-six EIC cadets. Wordsworth's orders called for the ship to meet a convoy of EIC ships at the Downs by 21 December. While anchored in the Downs, *Earl of Abergavenny* was struck in the bow by another East Indiaman and put into Portsmouth for repairs. After repairs, the ship embarked 109 EIC troops and 45 King's troops and sailed for the next rendezvous with the convoy at Portland Roads.

Arriving off Portland Roads in rough weather on 5 February 1805, *Earl of Abergavenny* met the pilot and made for the Roads. The ship lost the wind, and a strong tide, coupled with poor navigation by the pilot, drove the ship onto a shoal where she pounded for five hours until she beat over it. When the ship was filling with water, and the pumps failing, Captain Wordsworth made for the shore and fired distress signals. Just 2.5 km out, *Earl of Abergavenny* sank on an even keel in 18 m of water. Of the 405 persons aboard, 261 were lost, including Wordsworth. Nearby sloops rescued some of the passengers from the water, while others were pulled from the masts, which rose above the water.

Salvage of the wreck's cargo commenced in September 1805 and ended in 1807. The wreck may have been flattened as a hazard to navigation after then. Periodic visits by divers beginning in the late 1950s to the

1960s resulted in the removal of most visible features and the undocumented recovery of a number of artefacts.

In 1979, members of the Chelmsford Sub Aqua Club commenced a programme to excavate and study the wreck of *Earl of Abergavenny*. Over a ten-year period they spent approximately 2,500 hours underwater, recovering over 1,000 artefacts and exposing and documenting the bottom of the ship. Much of the bottom of the ship survives in a 43 by 8 m long area that comprises most of the original keel length, a 7 m section of the port side, and a 1 m section of the starboard side of the hull. This is because the ship came to rest on a hard chalk seabed covered with a heavy silt, and rests angled to port in approximately one metre of the compacted silt.

In addition to the structural remains of the copper-sheathed bottom, artefacts recovered include pulleys, sections of rope, ornate carvings with red paint, and personal items, including belt buckles, and other fittings from the military forces aboard when *Earl of Abergavenny* sank. J.P.D.

ADDITIONAL READING

Cumming, E.M. and Carter, D.J., 1990, 'The *Earl of Abergavenny* (1805), an Outward Bound English East Indiaman', *International Journal of Nautical Archaeology and Underwater Exploration*, 19, 1, 31–3.

East Carolina University Program in Maritime History and Nautical Archaeology

An interdisciplinary graduate programme that began in 1981, offering a master of arts degree. The Program in Maritime History and Nautical Archaeology (previously named the Program in Maritime History and Underwater Research) is located at East Carolina University, Greenville, North Carolina. It is one of only two graduate level nautical archaeology university programmes in North America. Requirements originally included completion of a curriculum, a thesis/site report, and other university requirements for graduate students. In 1984, the academic requirements were revised and expanded to a two-year, forty-five semester hour degree programme including a thesis. The curriculum was revised to contain an appropriate concentration of history, including courses in maritime history, both classroom and advanced on-site experiences in underwater archaeology, and a variety of cognates associated with underwater archaeological research. Since then, the curriculum has continued to be revised with additional courses in maritime history, archaeology, artefact conservation and museum studies.

Fieldwork includes a summer field-school open to students enrolled in the programme and other qualified students from institutions of higher learning. On-site academic work also includes a 'field semester', and individual student-directed field projects. Programme staff and students have been involved in projects from France to Hawaii, from Florida and the Gulf Coast to the Great Lakes, from Mobile Bay to Bermuda. They have included projects associated with the American Revolutionary War, especially sites near Yorktown, Virginia, as well as projects associated with the American Civil War – the USS *Monitor*, USS *Southfield*, USS *Maple Leaf*, CSS *Gaines*, CSS *Alabama*, CSS *Raleigh*, as well as blockade runners in Bermudian waters and along the southeastern coast of the United States. World War II underwater remains have also been studied, particularly the battleship *Arizona* at **Pearl Harbor** and a PBY Catalina flying boat destroyed at Kaneaohe Bay, Hawaii on 7 December 1941. Underwater projects have also included colonial American vessels, prehistoric dugout canoes, a Hawaiian inter-island steamer, California Gold Rush steamers, the remains of submerged buildings and entire villages, the 'lost colony' on Roanoke Island, North Carolina, and surveys of geographical areas – bays, lakes, harbours, and sections of rivers.

The academic programme staff grew from one archaeologist and one historian in 1981 to four historians and four archaeologists. Faculty in the departments of Anthropology, Planning, Geology, and the Institute for Coastal and Marine Resources also offer courses and work with students in the program. In 1989, the programme moved into its own building, the Admiral Ernest M. Eller House, which is located on the main campus. It houses offices, a computer laboratory, library, and seminar room. In 1990, a conservation facility with wet and dry laboratories, artefact storage, photographic darkroom, and classroom was established in two buildings on a satellite campus.

About fifteen students are admitted to the Programme each year, complementing those in the second-year class. Well over one hundred students have enrolled in the programme to date and about sixty have received the MA. Most of the graduates hold positions with museums, State and national governmental agencies, private cultural resource firms, or are enrolled in PhD programmes. W.N.S.

East Key Wreck

Wreck in **Dry Tortugas National Park**, Florida. The site known as the East Key wreck, located near East Key, remains anonymous like many shipwrecks in the Dry Tortugas and, to date, no records documenting its loss or history have been located. The site is significant because of its relationship to the construction history of Fort Jefferson, built in the Dry Tortugas from 1847 as part of the third-system coastal fortification in the United States.

During its construction, all materials, supplies, and labour force were transported to the Dry Tortugas via ship, many of which ended in shipwreck. Construction ceased in 1874 on the uncompleted fort because it was known to have been obsolete for several years. Archaeological investigation of the East Key site, conducted in 1990 as part of the Dry Tortugas National Park Survey, focused on the unsalvaged construction materials observed at the site and on the impact that the loss of such materials had on the construction history of Fort Jefferson. The most prominent feature of the East Key wreck is the 'cement barrels', which are actually cement casts that were formed when the dry cement packed inside wooden barrels became saturated with seawater. The barrels in which the cement was packed have decomposed due to exposure to seawater and wood-boring organisms, leaving only the cement cast. In addition to the cement casts, more than one hundred slabs of graywacke (a metamorphic limestone) flagging stones are present at the site. The cement, once saturated with seawater, was no longer usable. The flagging stones were, and still are, suitable for construction purposes, yet they were not salvaged and brought to the fort. Comparative analysis of the flagging stones found at Fort Jefferson and those observed at the wreck site demonstrated that the materials lost at East Key were originally intended to be used for the completion of the floor in the large parade-ground magazine at Fort Jefferson.

The East Key ship was a late 19th-century wooden-hulled vessel, possibly a schooner, of approximately 350 tons. Salvage or replacement of the flagging stones for the unfinished, yet obsolete, fort and parade-ground magazine was too costly, and the wreck and the construction materials were abandoned. Archaeological investigation of the East Key wreck site demonstrated that the loss of construction materials on it and on other ships that were wrecked en route to Fort Jefferson significantly contributed to the almost continuous delays in the construction schedule and the high cost of building and maintaining the fort.

These observations have broader significance when considered in a behavioural context and are used to identify and test certain cultural uniformities. For instance, in the evolution of the modern arms race there are numerous examples of the revival of archaic technologies and their continued use well beyond their usefulness. The use and development of these technologies include the concept of 'deterrence', that is, the development of a technology or defence system in order to deter an enemy, either real or imagined, from attacking. The development of these systems is often accompanied by continued investment in them even when it has become obvious that they are obsolete. Fort Jefferson is a prime example of this. D.J.S.

ADDITIONAL READING

Gould, R., 1995, 'The Bird Key Wreck, Dry Tortugas National Park, Florida', *Bulletin of the Australian Institute for Maritime Archaeology*, 19, 2, 7–16.

Murphy, L.E. (ed.), 1993, *Dry Tortugas National Park: Submerged Cultural Resources Assessment*, Santa Fe.

Souza, D.J., 1991, 'An Archaeological Survey of a 19th Century Shipwreck, Dry Tortugas, Florida', Master's research paper, Brown University, Providence.

Souza, D.J., 1993, 'East Key Construction Wreck (FOJE011) Investigations', in L.E. Murphy (ed.), *Dry Tortugas National Park: Submerged Cultural Resources Assessment*, Santa Fe.

Education, precollegiate
see **Precollegiate education**

Egeria

The most intact Canadian-built 19th-century deep water merchant vessel, now a hulk in Port Stanley, Falkland Islands. Launched in 1859 from the New Brunswick shipyard of Thomas Edward Millidge, *Egeria* was built largely of Canadian tamarack (eastern larch) with outer hull planking of pitch pine imported from the southern United States. Diagonal iron hull strapping gave added strength. Iron vertical hanging knees supported deck beams spaced at approximately 4 ft (1.2 m) intervals. These were buttressed by horizontal wooden lodging knees. The sternpost measures 15 in (38.1 cm) square. *Egeria* was a three-masted square-rigged sailing ship of 1,066 tons, with dimensions of 176 ft 6 in × 36 ft 4 in (53.8 × 11.06 m). It had main, 'tween, and poop decks. Headroom in the 'tweendeck was a comfortable 7 ft 11 in (2.4 m).

New Brunswick's shipbuilding heyday was from 1820 to 1890, with its peak in the decade that produced *Egeria*. During that ten-year period New Brunswick yards launched more than eleven hundred ves-

Egeria in Port Stanley Harbour, Falkland Islands. (Nicholas Dean)

sels, a total of nearly 600,000 tons. Millidge operated his yard from 1853 to 1872, building at least twenty-seven vessels besides *Egeria* on speculation. Unfortunately, with the end of the Crimean War in 1856 there was an oversupply of shipping. With twelve of his vessels on the British market, Millidge instructed his agent to sell them for what he could get for them, and he succeeded in selling *Egeria* and its cargo for a profit in October 1859.

Egeria's career of 13 years was about average for a wooden freighter of that period, particularly for a 'softwood' vessel. Shipowners reckoned on roughly a decade of useful service, though that might be lengthened with repair. *Egeria*'s cargoes were not glamorous: general merchandise from England to India or Australia. Cargoes from India home were predominantly agricultural. The ship also ran in the trade of bringing nitrate-rich guano (dried seabird droppings) from the west coast of South America to Europe.

In 1872, bound from England to Peru with a cargo of cement, *Egeria* put into Port Stanley, leaking badly, and a survey revealed that it was not worth repairing. The Falkland Islands Company purchased it cheaply for use as a storage hulk and eventually erected a metal roof over it. The forward section was later cut down for jetty construction but a large portion of the stern has survived, though the outer hull planking, particularly in the intertidal zone, has suffered damage both from vessels moored alongside and from marine organisms. The interior of the stern section is in remarkably

good condition with portions of 19th-century paint still intact. It is possible to discern where cabin partitions, now removed, were once in place. Like other wooden vessels in Stanley Harbour, *Egeria* will ultimately collapse unless stabilization is undertaken. Unremarkable in its career, the ship is the best evidence available today for 19th-century Canadian shipbuilding materials and practices. N.D.

ADDITIONAL READING

Brouwer, N., 1993, *International Register of Historic Ships*, 2nd edn, New York.

Lawson, E., 1986, '*Egeria*: The Nineteenth Century Canadian Sailing Ship at Port Stanley', *Falkland Islands Journal*, 15–19.

El Gran Grifon

Flagship of the **Spanish Armada**'s supply squadron, wrecked on Fair Isle between the Orkney and Shetland Islands to the north of Scotland. She was a Baltic hulk from Rostock, embargoed by the Spanish authorities along with twenty-two vessels of similar type to take part in the projected invasion of England. Such ships had been engaged in ferrying naval stores – canvas, cordage, timber, and artillery – from the Baltic to Lisbon, and were incorporated into the Spanish fleet because of their capacity to carry large cargoes. Unfortunately, this was counterbalanced by poor sailing performance, and throughout the campaign the Armada's overall progress was held in check by the slowness of the hulks. *El Gran Grifon* was rated at 650 tons and carried an armament of thirty-eight guns. Eight of these were newly cast bronze pieces (four *medias culebrinas* and four *medias sacres*) from the

Lisbon foundry, while the remainder comprised her original armament of wrought- and cast-iron guns, all relatively light. The senior officer on board was Juan Gomez de Medina, who also commanded the squadron as a whole, and she carried a complement of forty-three seamen and 243 soldiers.

As the squadron flagship she was regarded, in spite of her clumsy design, as a front-line vessel, and took an active part in the fighting. In the course of one encounter, probably with Sir Francis Drake's *Revenge*, she was severely damaged, and this may have been what caused her to lag behind the fleet during the Armada's homeward passage around the British Isles. The ship arrived at Fair Isle in a sinking condition and drove ashore in the narrow creek of Stroms Hellier near the southeast corner of the island on 27 September 1588. Although most of her crew scrambled to safety the ship quickly went to wreck.

A diving archaeologist from St Andrews University recording El Gran Grifon's *remains off Fair Isle, Scotland. (Colin Martin)*

The site was discovered in 1970, and further investigated in 1977 by the **Scottish Institute of Maritime Studies** at St Andrews University under the direction of Colin Martin. No structural remains had survived in this very high energy location, but heavy material – comprising mainly guns and shot – had worked its way through up to two metres of shingle to stabilize in the gully bottoms. A wide sampling of ordnance was obtained, including one each of the *medias culebrinas* and *medias sacres* which had been issued to the ship at Lisbon. These guns showed evidence of hasty production, and the *media culebrina* had a dangerously off-centre bore. The large collection of roundshot gave the lie to Spanish claims of running out of ammunition during their battles with the English, and prompted more detailed study – in the archives and on the wrecks – into the reasons behind Spain's poor artillery performance in 1588. The recoveries are

preserved in the Shetland Museum, Lerwick. C.M.

ADDITIONAL READING

Martin, C.J.M., 1972, '*El Gran Grifon*: An Armada wreck off Fair Isle', *International Journal of Nautical Archaeology*, 1,59–71.

Martin, C.J.M., 1975, *Full Fathom Five: The Wrecks of the Spanish Armada*, London and New York.

Elizabeth and Mary
see L'Anse aux Bouleaux Wreck

El Nuevo Constante

An 18th-century Spanish merchantman wreck off Central Louisiana in the United States. During the first week of September 1766, a fleet of seven ships was struck by a severe hurricane in the Gulf of Mexico. The vessels were sailing out of Veracruz, on their way to Spain via Havana, loaded with New World cargoes of dyes, medicines, ceramics, copper, and large amounts of gold and silver. Two of the ships were driven north by the hurricane and went aground. One of these ships was the merchantman *El Nuevo Constante*, which went ashore on the central Louisiana coast on 5 September. The other ship, *Corazon de Jesus y Santa Barbara*, was blown ashore west of *El Nuevo Constante*, apparently on the Texas coast. The other ships of the fleet were scattered, but all eventually made safe harbour at Havana, Campeche, or Veracruz.

Within a few days, the captain of *El Nuevo Constante*, Julian Antonio de Urcullu, dispatched the ship's boat to the east to settlements on the Mississippi River. When informed of the disaster, Antonio de Ulloa, the Governor of Spain's new colony of Louisiana, sent ships to rescue the stranded passengers and crew and to recover *Constante*'s cargo. The Spanish salvage efforts were hampered by severe weather and abandoned before *Constante*'s cargo could be entirely removed. Eventually, the ship was forgotten, but the memory of its loss was preserved by the name that soon attached to a nearby stream, Bayou del Constante. In 1979, the wreck was rediscovered by a shrimper sailing out of Port Bolivar, Texas. This discovery set in motion archaeological excavation and historical study of the wreck by the State of Louisiana.

El Nuevo Constante's final voyage began in March 1764 with its purchase at Cadiz, Spain, by Doña Mariana de San Gines and her daughter, Doña Maria de San Gines. These women purchased the ship from the firm of Bewicke-Timmerman, a London-based company engaged in trade between England and Spain. Prior to its purchase by Doña Mariana, *Constante* had been known as

Duke of York. Almost certainly British-built, *Duke of York* was a three-masted ship measuring 121 ft (36.9 m) long, 30 ft (9.1 m) wide, and with a draft of 14 ft (4.3 m). Its cargo capacity was about 475 tons.

El Nuevo Constante was intended to sail with the annual convoy, or New Spain flota, which was to depart for America in February 1765. Delays in obtaining adequate cargo prevented *Constante* from joining the flota when it left Spain, but finally, in December 1765, *El Nuevo Constante* departed from Cadiz loaded with cargo and carrying sixty-three crewmen and three passengers. The ship's principal cargo consisted of 1,334 boxes of mercury, each weighing 150 lb (68 kg). The mercury, all of which belonged to the Spanish Crown, was a necessity in New Spain because it was the critical element used in the process to extract silver from ores.

El Nuevo Constante arrived at the port of Veracruz on the eastern coast of Mexico (then New Spain) on the afternoon of 27 February 1766. The New Spain flota was still in Veracruz, but with intentions of sailing on 15 April for the return voyage to Spain. The 15 April deadline was missed and it was not until 21 August 1766 that the fleet sailed from Veracruz.

The fleet consisted of seven ships: two royal warships and five merchantmen carrying a cargo composed of all varieties of New World riches. This included over 13 million pesos in silver and 600,000 pesos in gold coins, plus copper, cacao beans (for making chocolate), vanilla pods, dyestuffs such as indigo, cochineal, and annato, sugar, leather hides, tobacco, medicines, and pottery. *El Nuevo Constante* carried only a small amount of coin and much of its cargo consisted of dyestuffs, including over 10,000 lb (4.5 tonnes) of cochineal and 40,000 lb (18 tonnes) of dyewood, as well as annato and indigo. Other cargo consisted of 143 copper ingots weighing 12,471 lb (5.6 tonnes), vanilla pods, a medicinal plant known as purga de Jalapa, cacao beans, balsam, copal, turtle shell, and ceramics made in Guadalajara.

Modern excavations on the wreck of *El Nuevo Constante* extended over several months during 1979, 1980, and 1981. Examination of the wreck site involved **Side scan sonar** and **Magnetometer** surveys, collection of geological cores, excavation, and recording of the exposed ship's structure. The excavation revealed that the entire bottom three to four feet of the hull of the ship is extant. The intact hull structure is 127 ft 6 in (39 m) long and *c*. 26 ft (8 m) wide at its maximum width. The hull is constructed of paired, live oak frames covered with 4 in (10 cm) thick white oak hull planking. Portions of the exterior of the hull are sheathed with 1 in (2.5 cm) thick spruce planking, and a number of sheets of lead, apparently used to patch the hull, were recovered. The keelson is intact along much of the length of the hull and a considerable area of interior planking or ceiling is extant. Remnants of the steps for the mainmast and foremast are extant and the bases of two elm pump tubes were found amidship and adjacent to the keel.

Large numbers of artefacts were removed from inside and around the remains of the hull. These included a variety of items associated with the operation of the ship such as two 10 ft (3 m) long wrought-iron anchors, two iron rudder gudgeons, three iron 9-pounder cannons, iron cannon balls, iron and lead grapeshot, and large numbers of hand-wrought nails, spikes, drift bolts, eye bolts, chain-plates, and other ship fittings.

Of particular importance in the artefact collection are the remains of cargo items carried by *El Nuevo Constante*. These include thousands of fragments of Guadalajara Ware, a pottery made in New Spain, primarily for export to Europe. Guadalajara Ware occurs in a variety of moulded forms, including vases, globular bowls, and miniature shoes, musical instruments, and animals. A variety of other ceramics were also recovered, including Rey Ware, El Morro Ware, and a number of olive jar fragments. These may not be cargo items, but ceramics used in the everyday operation of the ship. Examples of the dyes indigo and annato were also recovered, as were examples of logwood, another of the dyestuffs aboard the ship. The logwood, or dyewood, occurs as short logs, about one metre long. Many fragments of well-preserved leather were also recovered. Several of these represent portions of large containers made from complete cow hides. Known as *zurrones*, these bags were used to carry items such as cacao and vanilla beans.

Over a hundred disk-shaped copper ingots were brought up from the wreck. Weighing from 35 to 130 lb (16 to 60 kg) each, these ingots would have been used in the production of items such as bells, cannon, and cauldrons. The historical documents indicate that no gold or silver was left aboard *El Nuevo Constante* after its sinking, but over 50 lb (23 kg) of gold and almost 100 lb (45 kg) of silver were found on the wreck. The gold and silver occurs primarily as small disks, or planchas, and all is presumed to represent contraband being smuggled to Europe. P.E.H., C.E.P.

ADDITIONAL READING
Pearson, C.E. (ed.), 1981, *Investigations of an Eighteenth Century Spanish Shipwreck off the Louisiana Coast*, Anthropological Study no. 4, Louisiana Archaeological Survey and Antiquities Commission, Baton Rouge.
Pearson, C.E. and Hoffman, P.E., 1995, *The Last Voyage of El Nuevo Constante: The Wreck and Recovery of an Eighteenth Century Spanish Ship off the Louisiana Coast*, Baton Rouge.

Emanuel Point Ship

Well-preserved remains of a mid-16th-century galleon found by archaeologists in Pensacola Bay, Florida. The remains are thought to be from the fleet of Tristán de Luna y Arellano, which was lost in a hurricane during one of the first European attempts to colonize what is now the United States. A forgotten chapter in the history of early Spanish America, the Luna expedition consisted of eleven ships carrying a thousand settlers, five hundred soldiers and Aztec mercenaries and their belongings, which embarked in 1559 from Veracruz for Pensacola. Luna had been directed by the Viceroy of New Spain to establish a major colony along the northern rim of the Gulf of Mexico, a Spanish frontier previously discovered by Ponce de León, and explored by Pánfilo de Narváez, Hernando de Soto, and others. A month after their arrival in Pensacola Bay, a hurricane sank most of the anchored ships, some of which had not yet been unloaded. The resulting loss of stores and supplies doomed the fledgling settlement; despite repeated resupply attempts from Mexico and Cuba, the colonists became increasingly disorganized as their leader fell ill. Luna was replaced in 1561 by Angel de Villafañe, who brought the remnants of the failed settlement back to Mexico. Four years later, St Augustine was established on the Atlantic coast of Florida by Pedro de Menéndez de Avilés, and Pensacola's strategic bay was forgotten for over 130 years, until a small *presidio* was built in 1698 to secure West Florida for the Spanish crown.

In 1992, while conducting an inventory of shipwrecks in Pensacola Bay, archaeologists from the Florida Bureau of Archaeological Research discovered a small mound of oyster-encrusted ballast stones protruding from a shallow sand bar near Emanuel Point in the central portion of the bay. The site was detected with a **Magnetometer**, which registered a magnetic anomaly produced by a large wrought-iron anchor at the edge of the ballast stones. Preliminary test excavations at the centre of the mound revealed well-preserved and articulated ship architecture characteristic of 16th-century Iberian con-

Neck and shoulder of olive jar, from the Emanuel Point Ship. (R. Smith)

struction, ceramic shards of early middle-style Spanish olive jars, lead-glaze *melado* wares, and tin-enamelled *majolicas*. Structural damage to the port side of the hull amidships suggested that the ship had pounded violently against the sand bar. Continued excavation of the site revealed that the lower hull of what was once a substantial ship lay entombed beneath a thick stratum of compacted shell that had accumulated around the vessel for centuries after it came to rest on the sand bar. Together with the ballast stones, the hard shell layer had effectively capped the wreck deposit and preserved its contents over time.

Although the absence of cargo above the ballast suggested that the ship had been salvaged after the wrecking event, a broad range of cultural materials was encountered in the ship's bilge and at the periphery of the hull. Galley utensils, such as a large tin-lined copper pitcher and the ship's copper cooking cauldron, were found in the forward area. Amidships, remnants of leather shoes, rope, wooden tools, and an unusual miniature galleon silhouette, carved from fir, were recovered. Botanical deposits included nuts, seeds, stems, pits, husks, and leaves, which represent a variety of European and American plants, from olive to coconut, and from almond to papaya. Faunal examples of ship's provisions included pig, chicken, cow, and fish. The remains of stowaways – cockroaches, a species of beetle associated with stored leather products, and rats – were encountered in the bilge. Study of a large collection of the latter's bones revealed that a cannibalistic colony of black rats, plagued by rickets, had existed in the hold of the ship. (See **Faunal studies**.)

At the ship's stern, the framed and planked tail section was found intact, although the rudder, which lay nearby, had been wrenched away. Partially sheathed with lead, this area of the ship contained additional cultural clues to the site's interpretation. Fragments of red-burnished ceramics, moulded with facial features and decorated with graphite-based pigment, were identified as a post-classic Aztec type from the central valley of Mexico. Over 3,000 g of liquid mercury, brought first in the 1550s to New Spain for the amalgamation of silver, were found between the ship's floors. Stone, lead, and iron shot recovered from this area suggested that the ship had been armed with stone-throwing ordnance in the stern, and smaller verso-type anti-personnel guns along the rails. Buried next to the rudder was found an intact, but fragile, breastplate, of a style worn by 16th-century soldiers. Finally, a small coin turned up among the stern deposits. Identified as a *blanca*, minted of an alloy called *vellón* in Spain during the reign of Enrique IV (1454–74), the coin may have been a keepsake or pocket-piece belonging to a passenger or crew member. More likely, the coin was present among ballast stones that were loaded aboard the ship at a European port, where dumps of recycled stones were available to vessels in need of additional ballast.

Preliminary investigations of the Emanuel Point Ship, which is the earliest wreck yet found in Florida's waters, indicate that it was a large armed vessel which probably came from Mexico to Pensacola and was wrecked in the bay during a violent storm, sometime during the mid-16th century. While the site's association with the 1559 fleet of Tristán de Luna is not yet secure, continued excavation and analysis of its contents, along with additional archival research, can perhaps provide a positive identification of the ship and its role in the early European settlement of the United States. R.S.

ADDITIONAL READING

Bratten, J.R., 1995, 'Olive Pits, Rat Bones, and Leather Shoe Soles: A Preliminary Report on the Organic Remains from the Emanuel Point Shipwreck, Pensacola, Florida', in P.F. Johnston (ed.), *Underwater Archaeology Proceedings: Society for Historical Archaeology Conference, Washington, DC*, Ann Arbor, Michigan.

Scott, D., 1995, 'Unique Artifacts from the Emanuel Point Shipwreck', P.F. Johnston (ed.), *Underwater Archaeology Proceedings: Society for Historical Archaeology Conference, Washington, DC*, Ann Arbor, Michigan.

Smith, R.C., 1994, 'The Emanuel Point Ship: An Examination of Florida's Earliest Shipwreck, in R.P. Woodward (ed.), *Underwater Archaeology Proceedings: Society for Historical Archaeology Conference, Vancouver, British Columbia*, Ann Arbor, Michigan.

Smith, R.C., 1995, 'The Emanuel Point Ship: A Florida Experiment in Research, Development, and Management', P.F. Johnston (ed.), *Underwater Archaeology Proceedings: Society for Historical Archaeology Conference, Washington, DC*, Ann Arbor, Michigan.

Spirek, J., 1995, 'Pinned to the Bottom: Emanuel Point Hull Remains', in P.F. Johnston (ed.), *Underwater Archaeology Proceedings: Society for Historical Archaeology Conference, Washington, DC*, Ann Arbor, Michigan.

Endymion
see **Oxford University MARE**

E. Nordevall

Swedish paddle steamer wrecked in 1856. *E. Nordevall* was one of five paddle steamers built in the 1830s in Sweden for the then newly opened Göta Canal running across the country from the Baltic to the west coast. The vessels were designed by Swedish naval officer and ship designer Johan Gustaf von Sydow. *E. Nordevall* was built in 1832 and was named after engineer and canal builder Eric Nordevall (1753–1835), who played an important role in the realization of the Göta Canal.

The vessel had an overall length at load waterline of 25.75 m, a beam of 3.87 m, a depth of hold of 2.65 m and a load draught of 2.06 m. The hull was carvel-built of oak and pine. The two side-lever engines of 17 hp each were designed by Scottish engineer Daniel Frazer, for a long time the technical leader at the Motala Workshop (Motala Verkstad), where *E. Nordevall*'s engines were manufactured.

E. Nordevall was lost in Lake Vätter in June 1856 after nearly twenty years of service, after grounding near the small island of Jungfrun outside the town of Vadstena, which it had just left. The paddle steamer sank at 45 m of water. The wreck was located in 1980 by a small group of divers. During the latter half of the 1980s, the Swedish National Maritime Museum, in cooperation with other organizations, carried out underwater documentation of the vessel, resulting in a horizontal projection plan, a side view, as well as photo and video recording of the vessel and its state today. In 1995, work began on building a full-scale replica of the vessel. This replica, to be named *E. Nordevall II*, does not aim at being an identical copy of *E. Nordevall*, but a close reconstruction. The replica will be based on and built from the original ship design plans of a vessel similar to *E. Nordevall*, built at Motala Verkstad in 1841, and from the original and very precise plans of the engines of *E. Nordevall*. The replica will be built at Forsvik Shipyard, at the Göta Canal and near Lake Vätter.

E. Nordevall is uniquely well preserved. It is characterized by a low hull with a small sheer. It has one mast, rigged with a gaff sail. Both the mast and the high funnel are still preserved and standing. The wheelhouses are built of steel plates on a wooden framework. The stern part of the hull, aft of the engine room and the funnel, houses the

Fragment of post-Classic Aztec ceramic from the Emanuel Point Ship. (R. Smith)

An ancient Greek sailing ship depicted as part of a scene of Odysseus and the Sirens on a Greek red-figure vase. (Courtesy Trustees of the British Museum)

passenger cabins and aft of these the ladies' saloon. The deck of this part of the hull is raised about one metre above the main deck. Afore of the engine room in the ship's interior is the men's saloon, which is also the ship's mess. Afore of that is the galley and the crew's compartments.

E. Nordevall represents one of the first types of paddle steamers in general use in Europe. Its design has its origin in the paddle steamers built for river and coastal traffic in Scotland in the 1820s. The side-lever engines in *E. Nordevall* represent in their turn the first type of generally manufactured marine steam engines in Europe. The well-preserved intact side-lever engines in the engine room of *E. Nordevall* are the only mid-19th-century marine steam engines of this type preserved in the world. C.O.C.

ADDITIONAL READING

Cederlund, C.O., 1987, 'Eric Nordevall: An Early Swedish Paddle Steamer', *International Journal of Nautical Archaeology and Underwater Exploration*, 16, 190-33

Cederlund, C.O. (ed.), 1989, *Rapport över den marinarkeologiska undersökningen av hjulångfartyget E. Nordevall 1985–1988*, Stockholm.

Epigraphy

The study of inscriptions or depictions, here specifically those of watercraft. Ancient watercraft first became known to scholars from the inscriptions and depictions of these vessels that survived to the present day. In many instances epigraphic evidence is still the primary source of information for some ancient ships. Inscriptions in ancient languages can be found on clay tablets, monuments and grave stones, as graffiti on walls, and on similar surfaces. Vessel representations can be painted, etched, incised, or carved on a variety of materials. These are distributed virtually world-wide, present wherever a seafaring culture developed and became documented in that culture's artistic traditions. Commonly these representations are found on rock faces or stones, as reliefs on temple or burial vaults and as decorations on ceramic or metal vessels, coins, and seals.

Textual references to ships can be tantalizing but enigmatic, for they are generally lacking in details about construction, rig, capacity, and overall appearance. For example, when Urnanshe (Mesopotamian) cuneiform texts mention vessel types as 'Dilmun boat', 'Magan boat', and 'Meluhha boat' it is unclear if these classifications are based upon construction, rig, nationality, or even by the last port of call or the next destination. In the examples of Egyptian tomb and temple reliefs, and in Greek vase paintings, the depictions of water craft are extremely realistic. In other cases, such as Cycladic seals, the representations are crude and abstract.

Epigraphic and archaeological information can be complementary to one another, however, each assisting in interpreting the other. When interpreted together the depictions, the inscriptions, and the archaeological sites provide a more complete reconstruction of the vessel, its cargo, and crew. One example of such complementary usage is the thoughtful interpretations underwater archaeologists were able to make using the remains of the Bronze Age **Uluburun** shipwreck, the representation of the Syrian ship found on the 14th-century Tomb of Kenamon at Thebes, and references to ships and seafaring found in the *Odyssey*.

The original motivations for rendering inscriptions of ships may have been varied, perhaps resulting from votive offerings, decorations, the recording of historic or funerary events, economic transactions, or as personal motifs. Whatever purpose they were originally intended to serve, the depictions are merely the artist's conception of a boat; therefore, the archaeologist should be conservative in interpreting these. In most cases, the ancient artist's purpose was not to educate future generations of man, but simply to give an impression of a boat recognizable to his peers. Certain features may have been excluded, abstracted, or emphasized. This is particularly true when the artist is attempting to fit the boat onto a limited or curved space such as a seal or coin. The more primitive depictions can be misinterpreted and are often the subject of scholarly dispute. One well-known example of such controversy is the Early Bronze Age depictions of boats found on the Cycladic 'frying-pan' vases from Skyros. Deciding which end is the bow and which the stern has been the subject of dispute from the time of their discovery in 1899 until the present.

Despite these problems epigraphic information can often be used successfully to distinguish general developments in ships and their usage. Depictions can mark stages of development such as when masts, sails, figureheads, rudders, or castles appeared on vessels. Some of the more notable examples where epigraphic information has aided in the study of ancient ships of the Bronze Age are those inscriptions found on Egyptian and Assyrian reliefs; representations of Cycladic vessels on vases, models, and rock carvings; Minoan, Mesopotamian, and Bahrainian portrayals on seals; Harappan vessels on amulets, pottery sherds, and seals; and rock carvings of early Scandinavian watercraft. For the Classical age the epigraphic evidence of ships can be found on

Greek, Etruscan, and Roman vase paintings, frescoes, and mosaics, as well as reliefs on monuments, temples, and sarcophagi. In the medieval period town seals, coins, carvings on stone, and religious iconography provide useful sources. R.S.N.

ADDITIONAL READING

Bass, G., 1972, *A History of Seafaring*, New York.

Casson, L., 1971, *Ships and Seamanship in the Ancient World*, Princeton.

Degraeve, M., 1981, *The Ships of the Ancient Near East (c. 2000–5000 B.C.)*, Leuven.

Johnston, P.F., 1980, *The Sea-craft of Prehistory*, Cambridge, MA.

Neyland, R.S., 1992, 'The Seagoing Vessels on Dilmun Seals', D.H. Keith and T.L. Carrell, (eds), *Underwater Archaeology Proceedings from the Society for Historical Archaeology Conference, Kingston, Jamaica*, Ann Arbor, Michigan.

Winkler, H.A., 1939, *Rock-drawings of Southern Egypt*, London.

HMS *Erebus*

see **Arctic**

Eric Nordevall

see *E. Nordevall*

Ericsson

The 'caloric ship' designed by Captain John Ericsson (1803–89) and wrecked in 1892. Ericsson also designed USS *Monitor* and adapted the screw propeller to ship propulsion. *Ericsson* was revolutionary and regarded by Ericsson as his best work but it was not a commercial success.

Launched on 15 September 1852, *Ericsson* was 253 ft 6 in (77.1 m) long, 39 ft 3 in (9.9 m) broad and 26 ft 6 in (7.9 m) deep; it was powered by hot air instead of steam. The four working cylinders, vertical and in-line, were 14 ft (4.25 m) in diameter and had a 6 ft (1.8 m) stroke. These were connected to four supply (or compressor) cylinders which were 11.5 ft (3.3 m) in diameter. This massive caloric engine had a working displacement 2.5 times that of the largest steam engines and was joined with a crankshaft on which revolved 32 ft (10 m) paddle wheels at about nine revolutions per minute. The engine's unique feature was its regenerator. The spent charge, on being exhausted from the cylinder, left its caloric as it passed through to the atmosphere. This hot air was then picked up by the incoming air charge as it passed from the receiver to the working cylinder. Ericsson's theory was that the caloric could be used over and over again, essentially reusing heat wasted in steam engine exhaust.

After extensive tests, *Ericsson* made her first trial run on 11 January 1853. Many of the over sixty scientist and journalist guests took advantage of the low speed to ride up and down on the open tops of the giant pistons. The newspapers trumpeted that the age of steam was closed and 'the age of caloric opens'.

The 'caloric age' lived only a few months and only in the press. Although simpler than side-lever or vertical beam steam engines

Left: The bell from the wreck of Ericsson. *(Underwater Archaeology Society of British Columbia/Mike Paris)*

Right: A diver illuminates the interpretative plaque placed on the wreck of Ericsson *by the UASBC. (Underwater Archaeological Society of British Columbia/Mike Paris)*

and weighing far less, the caloric engines did not develop the necessary power to move *Ericsson* quickly enough. The huge cylinders could not be machined leak proof and the required pressure could not be raised.

Changes were therefore made in the engines. The cylinders were reduced to two double-acting cylinders only 6 ft (1.8 m) in diameter with a 6 ft stroke. Blowers were added to increase the draft under the boilers. On 27 April 1854, on her second trial run after this refit, *Ericsson* heeled over in a squall, took on water in her lower port holes and sank near New York City. Raised two weeks later, the ship's caloric engines were scrapped and replaced by an inclined steam engine. After a reputed $350,000 investment, the caloric engine was a dramatic commercial failure.

After conversion to a steamer, *Ericsson* served on several trans-Atlantic runs, made three New York to Nicaragua trips, and was chartered to the War Department as a troop transport in the Civil War. In 1868, *Ericsson* was converted to a three-masted sailing ship. The deck was altered and a half poop added. Without her heavy machinery, she sailed faster than ever. After several trans-Atlantic crossings, she moved to the Pacific service. In the 1880s, she operated mainly out of San Francisco. On her last voyage, *Ericsson* sailed in ballast from San Francisco for Nanaimo, British Columbia to load coal. Off Cape Flattery she encountered a strong gale and lost her sails. Drifting helplessly north, *Ericsson* ran aground on 19 November 1892 on Leach Island at the entrance to Barkley Sound, British Columbia. Although no life was lost, the ship was a write-off.

Some salvage was undertaken in 1893 but the shipwreck site was unknown to modern divers until it was discovered by members of the **Underwater Archaeological Society of British Columbia** on 25 February 1985. Identification of the site was easy, as two bells with the name *Ericsson* were lying on the bottom. The large number of artefacts and the ship's importance in the history of marine engines led the province to promptly declare it a protected heritage site. Operating under provincial permit, the site was surveyed and artefacts at risk were mapped and then removed for conservation, storage, and display at the Vancouver Maritime Museum. T.F.B.

ADDITIONAL READING

Angas, Commander W.M., 1938, 'Ericsson's Dream', *Motor Boating*, July, 32–7.

Church, W.C., 1907, *The Life of John Ericsson*, New York.

Ferguson, E.S., 1960, 'John Ericsson and the Age of Caloric', *Bulletin 228: Contributions from the Museum of History and Technology*, Paper 20, Washington, DC.

Griffiths, D., 1989, *The Caloric Ship Ericsson: A Historical Overview*, Vancouver, British Columbia.

Ethics

see **Professional ethics**

Evstafii

Wreck of an Imperial Russian naval transport, lost off the Shetlands in 1780 and rediscovered, salvaged, and archaeologically documented in 1972. *Evstafii* was built at Archangel at the Malcov yards and was launched on 1 October 1773. The 130 ft (39.6 m) long vessel was armed with 38 guns. Under the command of a Captain-Lieutenant Markov, *Evstafii* was en route from Archangel to Kronstadt with 180 officers and crew and nine passengers when she was wrecked in the Shetlands on 17 September 1780. The vessel, apparently blown off course by a gale, grounded on the rock Griff Skerry and was lost. Only five members of the crew survived. Local residents salvaged floating debris from *Evstafii* in 1780, and oral tradition two centuries later remembered the circumstances and the name of the wreck.

The wreck was discovered by a team led by Robert Stenuit in the summer of 1972 while searching for other shipwrecks. Two anchors and a broken cannon found in 20–25 m of water led divers to the wreck. After preparing a three-dimensional map of the site, Stenuit's team excavated the wreck, which largely consisted of iron objects and concretion embedded in the rocks, with chisels, hammers, and explosive charges.

A large number of artefacts were recovered, but none of the ship's hull, sheathing or rigging were found. Most of the recovered artefacts were metal, including fragments of eighteen cannon, solid, bar- and grapeshot, metal parts from muskets and pistols, lead shot, brass hardware, iron tools, sword hilts, shoe and belt buckles, 220 Russian and Dutch gold, silver and copper coins, fragments of ceramic containers and pipes,

lumps of tar, fragments of sailcloth and rope preserved in concretion, and a pewter plate. Other significant discoveries included two different sets of nested weights, made of incised and decorated brass, a corroded silver medal struck to commemorate the Russian naval victory against the Turks at the Battle of Tchesme in June 1770, and seven small brass icons, and fragments of icons, that were carried aboard the ship.

The recovered artefacts were conserved, and then sold at auction in 1973 after Stenuit documented and studied them, and identified the wreck. A small sample of artefacts was purchased and donated to the Zetland County Museum in the Shetlands, but the majority of the collection was dispersed and is no longer available for study or reanalysis. J.P.D.

ADDITIONAL READING

Stenuit, R., 1976, 'The Wreck of the Pink *Evstafii*: A Transport of the Imperial Russian Navy, Lost off Shetland in 1780', *International Journal of Nautical Archaeology and Underwater Exploration*, 5, 3, 221–43.

Excavation

The process of uncovering a site by removing spoil or intrusive material, observing and identifying the archaeological material, and then recording and recovering it. Each excavator will have a different approach to a site, and no two sites are ever alike. It is therefore impossible to give more than the broad outlines of methods and techniques of excavation. Because an archaeological site contains unique records of the past, and the process of excavation will dismantle this record, it is important to understand that excavation can only be justified in certain circumstances. The excavator must have a clear understanding of the reasons for undertaking the excavation and of the techniques and methods that will be used. Adequate storage, conservation, and work facilities, together with trained archaeological staff to handle the material, are absolutely essential before excavation can be considered.

Archaeologists undertaking an excavation must not only be experienced in excavation work but must also be used to directing staff. It is, for example, possible to be a good archaeologist and not be able to direct staff; this can result in poor archaeology. However, the converse is also true; one cannot be a good director of people and, with no archaeological skills, direct an archaeological excavation.

The most difficult aspect of excavation is identifying what is archaeological material and interpreting its significance. This is

again where experience is essential. While high standards of excavation are now expected on all maritime archaeological projects, one should always remember that excavation alone is not archaeology, it is merely part of a process whereby information is obtained which allows archaeological interpretation. Excavation is therefore carried out in a systematic manner across the site, in both the horizontal and vertical directions. All the artefacts and their associations are recorded with their three-dimensional coordinate location. Subsequently, the archaeologist has the responsibility, which is no less demanding, of interpreting this information and then publishing it.

It is therefore important to emphasize that minimum archaeological standards include publication, and an excavation that is not published – so that the information is lost – is as bad as, if not worse than, excavating with inadequate techniques. There are two simple approaches to excavation: one is to excavate over large areas of the site, layer by layer; the other is to work the site in small sections, layer by layer, repeating section by section across the site. The former approach is taken where the site lies in relatively calm conditions, there is a large staff available, and there are no time constraints. The latter method tends to be utilized where conditions are rough, or there is a limited number of staff, or where budget constraints restrict the length of excavation. In the latter case, excavation can be rapidly terminated without danger to the site.

In planning excavation work it is important to refer to the pre-disturbance survey. The information from this survey will play an important part in the planning of the excavation. The survey will provide information on the area of the site, the depth of the overburden, the extent of the archaeological material, and its nature. It may be necessary to consider some form of exploratory excavation to complement the pre-disturbance survey. For example, it may be necessary to determine the exact periphery of the site, prior to the main part of the excavation. This process may simply be to excavate the overburden at the periphery until the archaeological layer is exposed. Alternatively, it may be necessary to excavate a test pit in order to determine the depth of the archaeological material. A great deal of caution is necessary when carrying out this form of exploratory work; however, provided the work is done carefully, it provides essential information in planning the excavation strategy. For example, until the extent of the site is fully understood, it is not possible to plan the necessary storage and conservation facilities. There is a

Excavating a square metre of the St Johns Bahamas site. (MFMHS/Dylan Kibler)

great deal of difference between excavating a site which has an average archaeological depth of 0.5 m and that of a site which has an archaeological depth of 4 m.

In planning the excavation, there are a number of advantages and disadvantages to using grid frames. On extensive sites with a large staff, grid frames are often used to help define excavation areas and to orientate staff who may be unfamiliar with the site. Novice archaeological divers inevitably require some form of coordination and, at times, the grid frame is the best solution. Otherwise, when left to their own devices, it is not uncommon to find inexperienced staff excavating totally unsystematically in some far off area. With the grid frame one is confined. (Additionally, grid frames can be used to support the excavators while they are working over a site that has a large quantity of extremely fragile material exposed.) Proper buoyancy control and coordination of the excavation by using more experienced staff may be a better approach in this situation. On many sites it is a requirement that fins are removed since they tend to stir up the sediment, thus reducing the visibility.

Grid frames are rarely used for reference purposes in survey work, because it requires that they are firmly attached to the seabed, and inevitably the grid frames will move if they are bumped by divers or equipment. Ideally, grid frames should be dispensed with altogether simply because they get in the way of the excavation, particularly when one needs to get excavation equipment into a grid frame and then work around the framework. If the excavation is deep, the grid frames will cause the edges of the excavation to slope down towards the centre of the grid, because it is often impossible to get excavation equipment into the edges of the frame. As a result there will be slumping at the sides of the grid. If it is necessary to use a grid, it should be made as large as possible, ideally at least 4 sq. m.

One alternative to the grid frame is the trench system. Instead of square frames, a series of parallel lines or bars can be laid across the site. The lines marking the edges of the trench can be scaled so that the relative position in the trench may be determined. It is also possible to back-fill from one grid square to the previously excavated square, or from one trench to the previously excavated trench. This simplifies excavation techniques considerably, particularly where spoil is too large to be removed with suction devices. The heavy material or even light spoil can be removed quite simply to the adjacent square. Naturally, such a system can never show the whole site completely excavated. This can be a disadvantage where there is a structure which would be best displayed completely excavated. This may be partially resolved by making a **Photomosaic** of the site, section by section.

An excavation without frames has a number of problems, partly because it is difficult to control the excavation. As mentioned above, there is a danger that excavation will progress in random directions unless there is some form of control. However, if a start is made at one end of the site, and excavation proceeds forward across the site, with experienced staff it is possible to excavate quickly and efficiently. A bar or tape can be used to help keep the excavation moving evenly across the site. The great advantage of this technique is that complex structures can be excavated in one piece. When excavating in localized areas, a grid frame or defined trench is essential to confine the extent of the excavation. Excavation proceeds downwards, layer by layer. The process is repeated grid by grid. However, it is often difficult to correlate grid square layers, as structures sometimes extend through several squares creating serious problems. On a site with little vertical component, the trench system works well.

One ingenious method of excavating a hole in order to make a test pit in loose sand or mud is to use an open-ended 200 litre fuel drum as a caisson. By operating an **Airlift** inside the drum, the interior base can be excavated away, and as this happens, the caisson drops lower and lower. The caisson keeps the sand from falling into the hole, and, as a result, it is quite easy to excavate down to about a metre or so. Using this system, it is also possible to make careful records of the different layers excavated and record their depth by measuring how far the drum has penetrated into the seabed.

It is not usually possible to excavate vertical cross-sections underwater, except when working in thick mud; therefore, under water, stratigraphy can be difficult to record. In sand, silt, or gravel areas it is impossible to excavate in vertical sections; thus excavation strategy will need to be carefully thought out if stratigraphy is to be recorded. The merits of working over a large area and excavating systematically downwards have to be considered in relation to the difficulty of doing this evenly over the whole area. The problem with working in small grid squares (*c.* 2 sq. m), as discussed above, is that inevitably one will end up with a conical hole or pit, simply because the sand or silt will not hold any appreciable wall. Working along a front enables systematic recording and some degree of stratigraphy can be observed, although inevitably the working face will have slippage. The methods used will depend on the circumstances and the correct choice will only come with experience.

In many cases on wreck sites there is no stratigraphy to speak of; one simply finds that there is a sterile overburden, followed by an archaeological layer, followed by a sterile layer. This is not always the case, and excavators must be careful not to miss the subtle changes. Additionally, when changes are observed these are often difficult to record because of problems in establishing vertical datum points. This can be an extremely difficult problem and bubble tubes or depth measuring devices will have to be used to make these measurements.

It is worth noting that under water, archaeological chronology can have a significance different to that of an archaeological site on land. In the excavation of a shipwreck, stratigraphy usually relates to a single event in time. Consequently, the stratigraphy may have little or no temporal significance, but it may have a particular spatial significance. Thus a shipwreck lying upright on the seabed will disintegrate in time. Anything lying on top of another thing is there because of a spatial relationship rather than a temporal one. If the ship settled upright on the bottom, material would generally collapse downward and outwards. If a ship sank heeled over on its port side, the guns (for example) on the starboard side would lie on top of the port guns after the wreck collapsed. This would tell the excavator where they had come from on the ship after the interpretation of the events subsequent to wreck from the excavation. The unusual circumstance of a wreck, with the immediacy of the event, makes the spatial aspect of the site of much greater significance than the temporal. This does not mean that one should ignore stratigraphy; the point is simply that the vertical component may be of no more significance than the horizontal. Stratigraphy has played an essential part in the excavation of a number of shipwreck sites, for example, in the **IJsselmeerpolders Wrecks**. Likewise, inundated land sites have an essential stratigraphical component.

Many other new and interesting underwater excavation techniques have been pioneered in the last few years, some of which have been standard on land excavations for many years; as the practice of maritime archaeology improves, so the technology moves with the times. On the *Amsterdam* project, the excavation work has developed into a multi-faceted scientific study which has taken into account a wide variety of excavation strategies. Likewise, the examination of the mud in a late Saxon logboat found at Clapton shows the extent of the information that can be recovered using suitable excavation strategies.

In any archaeological situation, data has to be recorded. Under water, this is not particularly complicated to do, but it needs planning and organization from the start. A simple clipboard or writing slate is ideal for recording. In the simplest form – plastic drawing film – sheets are taped or clipped onto the recording board and a pencil can be attached to this by a string. Although easy to use, it is often no more than just a piece of plastic on to which bits of drawing film have been taped; as a result the system is inconve-

nient and it is time-consuming to replace the writing sheets. It is strongly recommended that proper writing slates be constructed, made of rugged plastic sheet on to which a plastic frame can be clamped. Sheets of pre-cut drawing film can then be clamped between the board and the frame and removed when necessary. The sheets can be pre-punched with ring binder holes and can then be immediately filed for safekeeping. A pencil, compass, ruler, and depth gauge can be attached to the slate and the back of the slate can be used for temporary notes; with a carrying handle the whole makes an extremely useful item of equipment. It is worth making a holder to put the pencil in when it is not in use. Half pencils are more economical, as whole ones usually break or get lost. Ensure you have a suitable diving knife for sharpening. One excellent alternative to a writing pencil is the Poppet Pencil. It consists of a series of short pencil leads mounted in small plastic holders, one on top of each other, in a tube. When the lead is worn away, the lead and holder is removed, inserted in the end of the pencil, and the next new lead is pushed into place.

A simple, large, net catch bag is essential for carrying tools and equipment and for returning robust artefacts to the surface. Ensure that there are no holes in the netting and that the mouth of the bag can be clipped shut. When recovering fragile material such as rope and leather, it is best to utilize a rigid plastic box, an old ice-cream container, or a glass storage jar, which can be filled with sand. A spatula or kitchen fish slice can be used to support the material as it is transferred to the sand box. Slightly more robust material can be placed in a polythene bag filled with water and tied off with a knot. The bag does not collapse when removed from the water. Large objects are best carried in a basket; commercial fish storage baskets or any self-draining basket of reasonable rigidity are useful.

Usually each operator works in one particular area during one session, so it is best that one person's finds are kept together, and not mixed with those of other operators working in the same or different areas. By keeping the material together, the excavator can usually provide notes from the record slate or, subsequently, provide verbal information on the objects during debriefing or registration. Thus, each excavator must have collection equipment available on the site for immediate use. As the excavator works in his or her area, important artefacts can be plotted on a plan of the excavation area or grid. Where there is integrity in the distribution of the material, it may be necessary to

take record photographs and detailed plans. In some cases, the objects can be tagged *in situ*, recorded, and then raised. J.G.

ADDITIONAL READING

Bass, G., 1966, *Archaeology under Water*, New York.

Dean, M. *et al.*, 1992, *Archaeology Underwater: The NAS Guide to Principles and Practice*, London.

Experimental archaeology

A method of deriving information about technology and energy consumption in the past by the study of reconstructed processes, based on primarily, but not exclusively, archaeological source material. Experimental archaeology is working with basically two methods: experimentation and observation. Both have inherited their ideal methodological demands of repeatability and control over all relevant variables from natural science, but due to the human element in archaeological problems those can seldom be fully honoured. The main constraint on the scientific rigidity of experimental archaeology is that it is dealing with situations that are no longer existing, and which can only be hypothetically reconstructed. The value of any data derived from experimental archaeology is therefore dependent on the value of the hypothetical reconstruction on which it is based. This reconstruction includes not only the artefact(s) involved, but also human skills and capabilities, as well as possible environmental factors influencing the process.

The two methods of experimental archaeology are used in different ways. Experimentation is usually used in combination with deductive reasoning – a hypothesis is established and tested through carefully designed experiments. If falsified, the hypothesis is modified or given up. Otherwise, it has been strengthened, but not proven. While experimentation is very useful to test the reconstruction of processes that produce artefacts, structures, waste, or other archaeologically recognizable objects, it is extremely difficult to apply in processes that leave virtually no traces, like the sailing of a ship. Furthermore it demands total control over all variables to say that a hypothesis has been falsified by an experiment. This is very difficult to obtain in most experimental ship and boat archaeology because the reconstruction, building, and navigation of ancient vessels form an extremely complicated process, and vast amounts of human experience are now lost. At best, such experimentation in this field leads to establishing hypothetical possibilities of acting in the past. Thor Heyerdahl's drift-vessel voyages across the Atlantic and the Pacific in vessels of papyrus and balsa are good examples. They showed that it was possible to make those voyages and thus improved the validity of his hypotheses – but any failure of the vessels to make the voyages could be countered by claiming a modern lack in expertise in building the crafts. Studies of building and carpentry techniques through the construction of scale models or mockups are much

ble standards, unless it can be convincingly argued that short cuts will not change the properties of the vessel or the trials.

However, no replica of an archaeological find can be identical to its model. Crucial to the value of the observational projects is therefore the possibility of assessing the accuracy of the reconstructions involved. While this is indeed very difficult when it

likely to differ from that of a past society, any addition so justified has the potential of manipulating the project towards supporting rather than challenging modern views. Apart from producing empirical data, archaeological experiments also produce experience, often leading to the discovery of new information in the original artefacts, or to the reinterpretation of known features. For example, the experience of cleaving oak into radially split planks drew attention to the extraordinary quality of the oak wood in Viking ships and thus initiated research into the field of changes in wood quality in shipbuilding over time. Likewise the experience of producing the thousands of nails for clinker-built vessels generated research into detailed study of their morphology, regional and chronological distribution patterns, and interpretation. Though not readily verified empirically, the process of reconstructing, building, and sailing experimental replicas of well-preserved archaeological ships and boats has proved to be a very important tool in the investigation of those finds.

Reproduction bateau launched on Lake Champlain, USA, being technically evaluated as a water craft. (Courtesy of Lake Champlain Maritime Museum, Basin Harbor, Vermont)

simpler and more efficient ways of using experimentation as they focus on singular problems.

Observation, in experimental ship and boat archaeology, is the recording of the consequences of a given hypothesis in the shape of trials with a reconstructed vessel. Observations might result in minor alterations of the vessel, the rigging, or the handling of one or both, but the purpose is not to challenge a hypothesis on a specific point – the reconstruction is accepted as basically valid and beyond the need of testing before the trials even start, because it has been thoroughly evaluated on the basis of the archaeological evidence. Projects aimed at observations might have limited goals and thus involve only certain variables of, for example, hull shape, rigging, or steering. But they might also try to simulate the entire process of an ancient ship at sea, thus replicating very complex processes, involving every thinkable, relevant variable. Such projects can only be carried out on the basis of minute examination of well-preserved, archaeological finds, and all stages from reconstruction, selection of material, building of an experimental vessel, and training of a crew has to be done to the highest possi-

comes to the skills of the seamen navigating the vessel, the accuracy of a replica can be established by investigating the natural variance of the original. Unintended variations in the symmetry of the original hull, along with such in the dimensioning of planks, fasteners etc., reflect the accuracy to which the vessel was originally built, and thus also determine the necessary accuracy of a replica.

Few archaeological finds allow a total replication of a ship or boat, and usually some portions, often including the means of propulsion and steering, have to be reconstructed from insufficient material in order to make the experimental vessel operational. In such reconstructions, information from other finds, and from historical, iconographical, and ethnographical sources, may be employed on the basis of a critical, scholarly discussion. The demand of functionality, that is, that the vessel should actually be seaworthy and manoeuverable, plays an important part in this discussion. However, as modern opinions about functionality are

Thoroughly published experimental projects with reconstructed boats and ships are few, but many shorter reports have been printed. Experimentations have mainly been concerned with establishing the hypothetical possibility of vessels made from various materials and techniques travelling along certain routes. Such projects have been published by Thor Heyerdahl (the balsa vessel *Kon-Tiki*, the papyrus vessels *Ra I* and *Ra II*, the reed vessel *Tigris*) and Timothy Severin (the leather curragh *Brendan*). The well-published trireme project *Olympias* set out to explore the practical arrangement of oars and the speed potential of this supreme type of rowing ship, and thus both embarked on experimentation and observation. The value of the observations from sea trials with *Olympias* has been discussed intensely, as the choice of hull design is lacking precise archaeological support and is leaning strongly on considerations of functionality.

The projects designed to provide observations of the navigational properties of archaeologically known ships are more numerous. One of the oldest vessels recreated as a sailing replica is the 4th-century BC **Kyrenia Ship** from Greece. The vessel was only preserved to approximately 60 per cent, but due to symmetry about 75 per cent of the vessel could be reconstructed with little uncertainty, including all the underwater hull and even significant parts of the rigging. Sea trials with *Kyrenia II* have shown it to be capable of an average speed of 2.85 knots over an almost 500 nautical mile (925 km) two-way voyage between Greece and Crete, and of surviving gales in those waters.

A number of projects have been carried out in Norway, Germany, and Denmark, by or in cooperation with the Viking Ship Museum and the Danish National Museum's Institute of Maritime Archaeology in Roskilde. Those experiments include the building and trials of replicas of *Skuldelev* 1, 3, and 5 from the 11th century (see **Skuldelev ships**), the late 13th-century **Gedesby Ship**, a replica built in Kiel of the **Bremen Cog** from 1380, as well as the Viking ships from Gokstad and Oseberg (see **Oseberg Ship**). A replica of Skuldelev 1, built in Norway for a modern explorer, Ragnar Thorseth, circumnavigated the globe in 1984–6. During sea-trials and during the voyage, average speeds were calculated and it was established that, given fair conditions, a *dægra sigling* (a 24–hour journey of 144 nautical miles, 267 km) could be counted upon. The results thus support the reflection of fairly regular and predictable ocean seafaring given by such distance measurements as the *dægra sigling*. The many trials with different square-rigged vessels have also shown that, given that the reconstruction of the sails are accepted, those vessels were usually able to advance with a speed of 1.5–2.0 knots upwind, although tacking angles would be only 64–5 degrees. Comparisons between vessels of the same size, like Skuldelev 3 and the Gedesby Ship, confirm the general picture of a sacrifice of speed for cargo capacity and safety from the late Viking Age to the High Middle Ages. Trials with the replica of Skuldelev 5 have shown the capacity of this vessel to provide communication and deployment of forces within any part of the local, 40 km long fjord within a twelve-hour period, no matter the weather conditions. They have thus given us an indication of the military efficiency of the 10th- to 13th-century defence system thought to be an important part of the development of royal power in Denmark.

In Sweden, archaeologists have been involved in the reconstruction and trials of a 14th-century small longship found at Helgeandsholmen, Stockholm, as well as in the building of a 12 m long boat based on the remains found in the Valsgärde 14 boat grave from the 9th century. Both of these projects have been published in Swedish, though not in any great detail. A widely published, and discussed, Swedish project is the reconstruction of the Bulverket Boat (11th century) and its subsequent use for an expedition to Istanbul, exploring the possibility of travelling along the East European riverways in a Scandinavian vessel and at the same time investigating the peculiar type of sail depicted on the Gotlandic picture stones. The project was hampered by the very few remains left of the Bulverket Boat, but also by the fact that the waterways through Europe – and indeed the landscape which surrounds them – have changed to an extent that prohibits any final conclusion from being drawn.

In Great Britain, replicas of the **Gokstad Ship**, the Årby Boat, as well as of a Saxon dugout canoe have been made, contributing to the methodological discussion, as well as to the archaeological record in terms of new observations. Two other British projects conducted by Edwin Gifford, replicated the Graveney and the **Sutton Hoo** I finds in half scale. Though useful, the consequences of the reduction in scale should be seriously considered before drawing conclusions from the experiences of trials with such vessels. The proportions between man and vessel change when scaling down, and so do the structural properties of the vessel as it becomes considerably stiffer.

Experimental archaeology has an important role to play in the study of ships and seafaring in the past, because only this method can provide us with data on speed, manning ratios, seaworthiness, technological and environmental demands, and much more. Some of the experiments will move from the sea surface into the simulation basins and the virtual reality of the computers, but it will still be the task of the archaeologist to transform the archaeological find into a hypothesis, on the basis of which the trials can be performed. J.F.C., J.B.

ADDITIONAL READING

Coates, J. *et al.*, 1995 'Experimental Boat and Ship Archaeology: Principles and Methods', *International Journal of Nautical Archaeology*, 24, 293-301.

Crumlin-Pedersen, O., 1987, 'Aspects of Viking Age Shipbuilding', *Journal of Danish Archaeology*, 5, 209–28.

Crumlin-Pedersen, O., 1995, 'Experimental Archaeology and Ships Bridging the Arts and the Sciences', *International Journal of Nautical Archaeology*, 24, 303-6.

Crumlin-Pedersen, O. and Vinner, M., 1993, *Roar og Helge af Roskilde: Om at bygge og sejle med vikingeskibe*, Copenhagen.

Crumlin-Pedersen, O., and Vinner, M. (eds), 1986, *Sailing into the Past*, Roskilde.

Heyerdahl, T., 1950, *The Kon-Tiki Expedition: By Raft Across the South Seas*, London

Shaw, T. (ed.), 1993, *The Trireme Project*, Oxbow Monograph 31, Oxford.

Vinner, M., 1995, 'A Viking Ship off Cape Farewell', in O. Olsen, J. Skamby Madsen, and R. Flemming (eds), *Shipshape: Essays for Ole Crumlin-Pedersen*, Roskilde.

Falklands wrecks and hulks

A large and diverse collection of predominantly 19th-century wood and iron vessels, with a few 20th-century examples, in varying states of repair and of varying historical significance. Some vessels are unique examples of their type. The largest collection of hulks, some fifteen in number, lie along the 3 mile (4.8 km) length of Port Stanley, capital of the Falklands, on East Falkland Island. Other hulks and wrecks lie at some distance from Port Stanley. Some wrecks, or portions of them, still lie on shore near where they struck; others are accessible only by divers. Collectively the Falkland Islands hulks and wrecks represent an unparalleled resource for the study of maritime history and a management problem of immense magnitude.

The Falklands lie approximately 480 km off the east coast of South America between latitudes 51 degrees and 53 degrees south. There are two major islands, East and West Falkland, and many smaller ones with a land area approximately equal to that of Northern Ireland. The distance from New Island, at the northwest corner of the archipelago, to Port Stanley at the southeast is approximately equal to that from London to Cardiff. The Falklands grew to maritime prominence with the development of the 19th-century sailing route between the Atlantic and Pacific Oceans by way of Cape Horn. Vessels damaged off Cape Horn had but one port of refuge: Port Stanley, where repair was possible, though expensive. Some vessels, condemned and sold as beyond economical repair, became storage hulks in the harbour. Other vessels were wrecked in the attempt to reach Port Stanley. The preferred route to Port Stanley from Cape Horn was to make landfall at Beauchêne Island at the southwest corner of the archipelago, but after a storm there is a strong onshore current off East Falkland, a fact which was not widely known until the late 19th century. In the vicinity of Bull Point on East Falkland there are at least ten known wrecks, the most visible of which is the stern section of *Craigie Lea*, which went ashore in 1879. The yacht *City of Dunedin* also came to grief here in 1893 but was floated off (see Southby Tailyour).

There is a persistent myth that the Falklands' rich maritime trove was 'unknown' until discovered by British and American museums in the 1960s. However, occasional magazine articles as early as the 1930s, such as that by Lellman, dealt with some aspects of the Falklands maritime history. By the late 1950s British interest in the Falklands hulks centred on Isambard Kingdom Brunel's pioneering 1843 SS *Great Britain*, which served as a storage hulk in Port Stanley from 1886 to 1933 before being beached in nearby Sparrow Cove. In the 1960s Karl Kortum, founder of the San Francisco Maritime Museum, made preliminary plans to bring *Great Britain* to San Francisco, but ultimately deferred to British interests. In 1970 *Great Britain* returned to her birthplace of Bristol aboard a barge for restoration in the drydock in which she was built.

Subsequently American museums purchased two other Falklands hulks, the 1841 British barque **Vicar of Bray**, which had entered San Francisco during the Gold Rush of 1849 and now lies as part of a jetty at Goose Green, west of Port Stanley, and the 1856 American packet ship **Charles Cooper** in Port Stanley Harbour, the only remaining example of the type. Though both vessels were extensively surveyed and some repairs made to *Cooper*, neither vessel left the Falklands and ownership of *Cooper* was eventually transferred to the Falkland Islands government. *Cooper*'s condition has been deteriorating severely in recent years to the extent that the hulk is now wrapped in fish net to prevent timbers from falling into the harbour and posing a hazard to navigation. In 1978 American archaeologist Peter Throckmorton recovered a 12 m section from the wreck of the 1890 American downeaster **St Mary** for the Maine State Museum, and between 1983 and 1987 the Snow Squall Project recovered approximately 10 m of the bow of the 1851 Maine-built clipper ship **Snow Squall** for American museums. The one notable failure was the attempted recovery of the 1902 French barque *Fenna ex-Champigny*, the only one of the Port Stanley hulks that was still afloat. In 1967 she left for San Francisco under tow but was scrapped in Uruguay when money ran out.

Two other hulks in Port Stanley have been extensively surveyed with no plans for eventual recovery. These are the 1859 Canadian ship **Egeria** and the 1849 Liverpool-built ship **Jhelum**, hulked in Port Stanley in 1870. In the latter case the Merseyside Maritime Museum has mounted several expeditions to Port Stanley to stabilize the hulk as far as possible (see Stammers and Kearon). In addition, at the east end of Port Stanley harbour the 1879 British iron barque *Lady Elizabeth* lies beached, still with one yard crossed on the mainmast. She struck a rock when headed

for Port Stanley in 1913 and served as a storage hulk until being beached in 1936. In 1983 a team from the Snow Squall Project surveyed her in case it should eventually prove feasible to move her to a more central location in Port Stanley for exhibit, but this has not yet taken place.

Other hulks in Port Stanley include the rapidly deteriorating British *William Shand*

Charles Cooper in Port Stanley Harbour. (Nicholas Dean)

(1839) and Welsh *Fleetwing* (1874). The Canadian *Margaret* (1836) lies filled with rubble under a jetty while the Welsh *Capricorn* (1839) is all but invisible. More modern examples include the British steam fishing boats *Golden Chance* (1914) and *Afterglow* (1918) and the steam tug *Samson* (1888). The after end of *Snow Squall* lies under the Falkland Islands Company jetty, buried under a number of metres of rock fill. Outside Port Stanley, *Vicar of Bray* lies several hours drive away at Goose Green. South of Goose Green, on the east side of Choiseuil Sound, lies the 1865 Liverpool-built iron Barque *Garland*, accessible only by water. She came in in distress early in this century when her cargo of acid broke loose and threatened to eat out her bottom.

It is impossible to list here every Falklands hulk and wreck, if indeed an accurate inventory were available. They range from those mentioned to the Canadian 1943 minesweeper, ex-sealer *Protector*, abandoned at New Island in the 1950s. Nearby is the half-submerged hulk of the steel ship *Glengowan*, towed there after her cargo of coal caught fire in 1895. As has been mentioned, in the vicinity of Bull Point on North Arm there

are at least ten wrecks and the shoreline is littered with maritime debris. At Fox Bay is the submerged hulk of the American iron ship *Clarence S. Bement*, whose cargo of coal caught fire in 1903. All of this presents a management problem of somewhat staggering dimensions, and does not include underwater wreck sites, of which approximately sixty are known, with an estimate of two or three times that number yet to be located and investigated (see Bound 1982).

Over the years there have been attempts by several organizations, most notably the British-based World Ship Trust and the Falkland Islands Foundation, to develop a maritime management plan for the Falklands. The most significant hulks have been inventoried in the *International Register of Historic Ships*. Meanwhile the condition of the Falklands hulks continues to worsen. The wooden hulls in Port Stanley harbour show marked degradation in the intertidal zone, exacerbated by greatly increased harbour traffic following the 1982 Anglo-Argentine conflict. In addition, some hulks, such as *Cooper*, are showing the adverse effects of structural changes, such as the cutting of waterways, resulting from their earlier use as warehouses. Efforts at reinforcing deck beams from below have been only partially successful in slowing down collapse. Portions of some hulks such as *Jhelum* and *Egeria* and the entire length of *Cooper* lie under metal roofs in varying degrees of repair. With the exception of a small shed at the stern, *Vicar* lies completely exposed to the elements and her deterioration was quite noticeable between the 1982 survey and a later examination in 1986. In this respect the fairly dry Falklands climate, with an average rainfall of about 63.5 cm at Port Stanley, and brisk, drying winds, retards but does not eliminate the growth of wood-eating fungi. Finally there is the reported introduction of marine worms, brought in the ballast water of visiting fishing boats. The seriousness of this problem is presently unknown.

The Falklands hulks, in service for many years for storage of wool and coal, are a familiar part of those islands' landscape and cultural heritage, but until recent years the Falklands' economy, though serviced by the quarterly freighter from Britain, was agricultural, not maritime. Sheep farming was the economic mainstay; the Falkanders were not themselves mariners. The extent to which this historical fact may colour preservation

Above: The 'tween deck of Charles Cooper. (Nicholas Dean)

Left: Vicar of Bray. (Nicholas Dean)

priorities in this community of just over 2,000 inhabitants cannot be predicted.

Writing some fourteen years ago archaeologist Mensun Bound, a native of the Falklands, predicted that with the limited resources available in the South Atlantic 'most of the ships will have to go abroad if they are to be saved'. However, given the straitened circumstances of most, if not all, museums and the great expense of the 1987 recovery and conservation of *Snow Squall*, a large-scale further recovery seems problematical. Whether some portions of the Falklands hulks and wrecks may become museum exhibits in the Falklands is also unknown. N.D.

ADDITIONAL READING

Bound, M., 1982, 'Falklands' Other Fleet', *Archaeology*, 4, 2, 11–18.

Bound, M., 1982, 'Should We Restore the Falklands Ships?', *Archaeology*, 4, 3, 24–31.

Brouwer, N., 1993, *International Register of Historic Ships*, 2nd edn, New York.

Goold-Adams, R., 1976, *The Return of the Great Britain*, London.

Lellman, K., 1933, 'The Hulks in Stanley Harbour', *Sea Breezes*, 16,159, 270–71.

Southby-Tailyour, E., 1985, *Falkland Islands Shores*, London.

Stammers, M. and Kearon, J., 1993, *The Jhelum: A Victorian Merchant Ship*, Stroud, Gloucestershire.

Faunal studies

The analysis of archaeological animal remains. Faunal studies may contribute to our understanding of the environment of a site and the diet of its occupants. Differential distribution of dietary elements may reflect social relations among residents and seasonal use of the site. As organic remains, faunal elements often make excellent radio-carbon samples for determining the age of a site. Faunal studies range from the primary identification of types and numbers of species to answering questions such as whether the death of the fauna was natural or cultural. Sampling methods and statistical extrapolation are of particular concern to establishing the representativeness of faunal data.

The primary identification of faunal remains is accomplished by comparative osteology, comparing bones of archaeological specimens with elements of known species of documented age and sex. Because of homologies (similar physical attributes shared between species) it is common to be restricted in our identification to the genus level. Many fish bones, for example, are indistinguishable. Advances in micro-identification using the electron scanning microscope and residual amino acids have allowed for increasingly specific species identification. Species identification of fish scales for salmonids have been recently introduced, for example.

Once each faunal element is identified, the minimum number of individuals (MNI) can be calculated, based on the number of unique elements of a species present. In a sample containing thirty-six ungulate humeri, if twenty-three are right forelegs then the MNI = 23. While MNI estimates are confounded by differential preservation, butchering, and selection patterns, as well as random bias within the sample, it does provide a relative indication of numbers of a specific species or genus within a site.

The minimum numbers of species (MNS)

is the basis for an appreciation of the diversity present within and between components or areas of the site. It is often presented in simple present/absent tabulation. Such distinctions may allow for separating dietary preferences through time (as between hunters and fishers), cultural activities, or differences through space (as between cooking and eating), or natural from cultural deposition. Distinguishing between the latter is the special concern of taphonomy, the study of the natural history of death and decay processes.

Animal remains may be present on a site because of past human activity but an animal may also be present because it simply shared the same environment at the time of its death prior or subsequent to human presence. Faunal studies determine the cause for presence by considering the natural taphonomy of the species as the null hypothesis; the remains are present due to natural, non-cultural circumstances. Contrary evidence, such as burning, breakage, cutmarks, or unusually high proportions of species within the site, suggest its falsification and strengthens our argument for human use.

Cultural use, with its concentrating effect, may in turn confound the use of faunal elements for the environmental reconstruction of a site. The presence of land mammals does not accord with the historic natural environment of the seabed on a shipwreck site, but may if it was once exposed during lower sea-levels. For these reasons, our most reliable environmental data comes from micro-analyses, such as **Foraminifera**, diatoms, or pollens, which are less likely to have been culturally deposited.

Sampling methods are of great concern to faunal studies. It is rare that entire sites, even shipwrecks, are excavated, rarer still that all the material excavated is subjected to analysis. Thus the majority of faunal studies report on only a sample of the entire site's contents. Determination of the representativeness of this sample then becomes critical to establish the reliability and validity of faunal data.

The seemingly ubiquitous human pattern to dispose of trash in the waters fronting shoreline communities along lakes, streams, and seas creates midden deposits of extraordinary analytical richness. Divers at **Red Bay**, Labrador, for example, recovered considerable faunal material relating to the economy and subsistence of the itinerant 16th-century Basque whalers who harboured there. Specific examples of the application of faunal studies to underwater archaeology are discussed in the next section.

The inundated sites of Atlit Yam (see **Israel**) and **Montague Harbour** provide contrasting extremes of the role of faunal studies in underwater archaeology. At Atlit Yam, *in situ* deposition has been little effected and faunal remains can be directly tied to village life on the Israeli coast in the 6th century BC. At Montague Harbour, cultural and natural deposits have been mixed by a more dynamic coastal geomorphology and benthic bioturbation. In the latter case, however, faunal studies have nevertheless contributed to distinguishing distinct stratigraphic and environmental episodes within the site through time. N.A.E.

Vertebrates

Animal bones feature as the most conspicuous of the biological remains recovered from excavations of historic shipwrecks, and their systematic scientific analysis is providing insight into maritime diet and foodways – revealing information in more detail than has been possible to obtain from documentary evidence alone about sources, variety, and the quality of meat provisions carried and consumed on board sailing vessels ranging in period from antiquity to early modern times. Besides food-related faunal remains, shipwrecks also yield osteological evidence of the presence on board of live animals (who perished when the vessel was lost). Studies of these remains further illuminate the kinds of animals, wild (exotic) as well as domestic, that became closely associated with maritime lifeways.

Studies of discrete assemblages of cattle bones, the remains of salted beef packed into barrels and casks unopened and stored in the holds of ships at the time of their loss, have advanced our knowledge of the development of meat-processing technologies from medieval to more recent times in response to the requirements of feeding mariners undertaking extended voyages in the open sea, away from shore-based supplies. Through identification of the various skeletal elements represented, and examination of the manner of their subdivision by means of axe, cleaver, or saw, primary butchering patterns may be reconstructed which indicate exactly how carcasses had been cut into requisite portions for preservation by salting. Such assemblages have come from several shipwrecks: Scheurrak So1 (Dutch Wadden Sea), a late 16th-century merchant vessel; the American privateer *Defence* (1779, Penobscott Bay, Maine); and the brig *William Salthouse* (1841, Port Phillip, Melbourne). Common to all these assemblages is the preponderance of thoracic vertebrae divided along the sagittal plane, with associated (articulated) ribs,

square-cut either across the mid-section or more distally. This butchering pattern is essentially indistinguishable from that recorded in cattle bones from terrestrial archaeological contexts. However, in the disjointing and subdivision of the cattle legs in preparation for salting, the butchering pattern for maritime meat-processing was very different from that practised by retail butchers supplying households, as evidenced from the presence of distinctive square-cut (sawn) fore and hind limb bone elements in the casks of 'prime mess beef' transported from Canada to Australia in the brig *William Salthouse*.

Despite disparaging remarks made by 18th- and early 19th-century sailors regarding the 'infamous quality' of salted pork supplied to their ships, those provisions carried on board at least one English East Indiaman, *Earl of Abergavenny* (1805, Weymouth Bay, Dorset, England), were apparently of the highest grade. The analysis of the pig bones recovered from this shipwreck revealed proportionally higher representation of the better quality (meatier) cuts, including roast, ham, and hindleg. A similar pattern was documented in the pig bones excavated from the shipwreck of the steamboat *Bertrand* (1865, Missouri River), in the remains of barrelled mess pork; while the assemblage from the **Hoff's Store** site (1851, San Francisco), consisting of the lowest grade of barrelled prime pork, was made up of less desirable cuts (jowls and feet) not present in the *Earl of Abergavenny* assemblage. Pigs' heads were clearly regarded by early modern sailors as unappetising, virtually inedible offal, but to their Roman counterparts these seem to have been readily accepted as part of the rations consumed on board their ships, as evidenced by the discovery of a butchered pig skull in the shipwreck of a Roman merchant vessel of *c.* 50 BC excavated off Marseille.

Fish bones found in shipwrecks, recognized as discrete assemblages (contents of barrels or casks), provide further information about preserved foodstuffs carried as part of ships' provisions. Osteological remains of cod (*Gadus morhua*), representative of stockfish (dried or salted cod), were discovered in two 16th-century shipwrecks: the Dutch wreck Scheurrak So1, and the Tudor man-of-war *Mary Rose* (1545, the Solent, southern England). In both shipwrecks, preparation of the cod for salting had involved removal of the head and a large part of the backbone. The presence in the Scheurrak So1 samples of bones of torsk (*Brosme brosme*) and ling/blue ling (*Molva molva/Molva dypterygia*), suggests the fish

Collapsed salt pork barrels
at the Hoff's Store site.
(J.P. Delgado)

had been caught in the northern part of the North Sea.

Recovery of bones of herring (*Clupea harengus*), the contents of a collapsed wooden barrel excavated in the shipwreck of the Dutch East Indiaman **Amsterdam** (1749, Hastings, southern England), provides further evidence of the sorts of fish important in the Dutch maritime diet. Each herring was represented by an almost complete skeleton, but lacking the three bone elements situated behind the gills; this reflects the established Dutch method of preparing this fish for salting, which involved removal of the gill region as well as the stomach. An earlier Dutch East Indiaman, *'t Vliegend Hart* (1735, Flushing, the Netherlands), yielded bones of anchovy (*Engraulis encrasicolus*); but here, their elaborate and highly unusual manner of packaging – in a stoneware jar, contained in a leaden sealed container placed in an oakwood keg – indicated these fish were never intended for consumption during the voyage. Instead, they probably formed part of the cargo destined for sale at Batavia. An even earlier example of preserved fish in transit as cargo was discovered in a 4th-century AD Roman wreck excavated at Randello, Sicily, in which large quantities of sardine (*Sardina pilchardus*) bones were packed in amphoras, and interpreted as remains of whole fish, preserved either as plain salted fish or, perhaps, a form of garum (fish sauce).

Besides preserved fish remains, shipwrecks also yield evidence of fresh caught fish that supplemented the maritime diet. An example is the diverse collection of fish species in the faunal sample from the 11th-century Byzantine merchantman excavated in **Serçe Limani** bay, on the southwest coast of Turkey, which included bones of tunny (*Thunnus spp.*), bass (*Dicentrarchus labrax*),

tub gurnard (*Trigla lucerna*), and drum (*Sciaena spp.*). These species are all recognized as commonly found throughout the Mediterranean Sea, and their exploitation by the merchant sailors on board the Serçe Limani vessel would have been an efficient way to reduce expenditures on provisions.

Other fish species identified among faunal remains from shipwrecks, and known to be abundant locally, may not necessarily have formed part of the diet on board, but rather represent intrusive material of the recent past, either from seabed detritus washed into the wreck site, or the remains of fish that had inhabited and died inside the sunken hull. Those fish whose flesh is known to be inedible to humans would clearly indicate intrusive material, as in the case of green moray eel (*Gymnothorax funebris*) remains from the **Reader's Point Wreck**, Queen Anne's Bay, Jamaica (identified as a late 18th-century 'British' sloop). Moray eel was certainly not eaten by those on board: as ingestion of this animal by humans often causes a debilitating, sometimes fatal, form of poisoning called ciguatera.

Identification of bones of domestic rabbit (*Oryctolagus cuniculus*) from shipwrecks has added to our knowledge of the variety of sources of meat in maritime foodways. Such bones have come from the shipwreck of a mid-15th-century merchantman located off the north coast of Brittany, as well as from two more recent shipwrecks: the English East Indiaman *Earl of Abergavenny* and the late 18th-century 'British' sloop at Reader's Point, Jamaica. As indicated in contemporary documentary sources, rabbits were sometimes carried live on English ships, serving as a ready-to-hand source of fresh meat for the captain's table during extended voyages in the open sea. This practice seems anomalous given the supersti-

tious aversion late 18th-/early 19th-century sailors had for these animals, believing that they brought bad luck to ships foolish enough to carry them. In the early 17th century, cats on ships were also viewed with superstitious mistrust by English sailors, but clearly their value in helping control rat infestation outweighed such prejudice, as evidenced by the presence of cat bones among the faunal remains from the shipwreck **Sea Venture** (1609, Bermuda), and wreck of the English 32–gun frigate HMS **Sapphire** sunk in action against the French at Bay Bulls, Newfoundland, in 1696. An ulna of a young cat was also recovered from the Spanish Armada shipwreck **La Trinidad Valencera** (1588, Donegal coast, Ireland).

Dogs were also frequently taken on board ships, and their skeletal remains from shipwrecks form an interesting subject of study. Recovery of intact skulls has allowed determination of breed-type based on comparative craniometric analysis with modern dogs. The specimen from the Dutch East Indiaman *Amsterdam* had morphological features such as domed forehead, absence of sagittal crest, together with small snout–width index, which indicated a spaniel-type dog (interpreted as a lap dog belonging to one of the female passengers known to have been on board). A very different canid skull found in the hull remains of *Mary Rose*, (possibly a pet of one of the ship's officers) was identified as a whippet-like dog.

As is well known from documentary sources, European mariners operating in the Caribbean and the coastal waters off central and southern America in the 17th and 18th centuries often augmented their regular provisions by catching marine turtles. Studies of faunal remains from shipwrecks of this same period and location have thrown further light on this subject, revealing opportunistic exploitation by European mariners of other reptile species as food sources. This included the South American yellow-footed land tortoise (*Geochelone denticulata*), whose skeletal remains were found in the shipwreck 'New Old Spaniard' (*c.* 1620–40, Bermuda). Plotting the natural range of this tortoise against locations of 17th-century European settlements in South America revealed concordance with those areas settled by the Dutch in what is now Surinam. This fact is of especial significance in view of the current interpretation that this as yet unnamed (unidentified) ship was Dutch and not Spanish as previously proposed. Gopher tortoise (*Gopherus polyphemus*) apparently also featured in the maritime foodways of the New World, as evidenced by the discovery in the Reader's Point shipwreck, Jamaica, of a humerus of this species. Knowledge of the natural distribution of the Gopher tortoise (nowhere found in Jamaica) assisted in charting possible ports-of-call visited by this as yet unidentified vessel, indicating the vessel had at one time reprovisioned along the southeastern seaboard of North America, where during the 16th–18th centuries this animal was a common component in Hispanic colonial subsistence.

Post-excavation research of the **Monte Cristi Wreck**, on the north coast of the Dominican Republic, presented the challenge of using faunal remains in the determination of the crew's nationality. Dendrochronological wood analysis suggested English construction, whereas the artefactual evidence indicated a cargo of Dutch origin, with the shipwreck dated c. 1651–65. The faunal evidence was reviewed in an attempt to resolve the vessel's national identity. Preliminary research of historically and archaeologically known dietary preferences of 17th-century European maritime and terrestrial foodways suggested the following associations for recognition from faunal assemblages: a preponderance of pig bones, with those of both cattle and sheep/goat in equal or near-equal proportional representation, may reflect Dutch consumers, whereas larger quantities of both cattle and sheep bones with proportionally fewer pig bones may indicate English ones. Application of these dietary-bone profiles tentatively identified the Monte Cristi crew as English. However, the proportionally high quantity of pig seemed somewhat atypical of what would perhaps be expected with an entirely English crew. This observation suggested another scenario: the bone evidence may represent cultural preferences of both English and Dutch crews in succession, as not all the faunal remains may be from the vessel's last voyage, but could also include residual food debris from earlier ones that had been discarded into the bilges and elsewhere in the hull. Faunal evidence was also employed in helping confirm the ethnic identity of the merchant sailors and passengers on board the 11th-century merchantman wrecked in Serçe Limani bay, on the Turkish coast. From our knowledge of the dietary traditions and religious regulations of medieval Mediterranean/Near Eastern foodways, all the occupants were identified as Christians (Byzantines) rather than Muslims, mainly on the basis of the presence of pig remains.

Commonplace among the non-food related faunal remains from shipwrecks are bones of commensal rats, whose presence is not unexpected given the numerous con-temporary eyewitness accounts indicating that these unwelcome vermin invariably accompanied sailors on their maritime enterprises. Studies of their skeletal remains, however, are revealing new clues concerning the historical pattern in the changing identity of the 'ship rat' that commonly infested European sailing vessels. Up to the first quarter of the 18th century, it was exclusively the black rat (*Rattus rattus*), but thereafter was largely replaced by its Asian cousin, the brown (or Norway) rat, (*Rattus norvegicus*). This situation reversed with the advent of steamships, when *Rattus rattus* again became the predominant rat species in European and North American shipping. Thus the presence in an undated/unidentified English shipwreck of skeletal remains of *Rattus norvegicus* provides a useful *terminus post quem* of c. 1720–40. Application of this methodology helped confirm the provisional late 18th-century date established for the shipwreck of an English collier-type vessel located off Chubb Head Cut, Bermuda – recently tentatively identified as the merchantman *Industry*, commissioned as a Royal Naval transport in 1765, and lost off Bermuda in 1774.

Investigation of another English collier-type vessel, **Betsy** (York River, Virginia), revealed infestation by both black and brown rats in virtually equal numbers. Like *Industry*, this brig had served as a Royal Naval transport/victualler during the American War of Independence, and was scuttled at the siege of Yorktown in 1781. In this shipwreck, stratigraphic evidence provided unique insight into the food-consuming behaviour and activities of the rats on board. Distribution plots of the locations of rat bones in the wreck revealed a high concentration of rats in the stern bilge area, where also the presence of accumulated food scraps (fragments of cattle, pig, sheep, and chicken bones), together with a skeleton of a kitten – all of this bone material exhibiting distinctive gnawing marks made by rat incisor teeth – indicated the contents of a so-called rat 'larder' similar to those documented for Norway rats living on British farmlands. The stern bilge area would have afforded the rats a reasonably safe harbourage and secluded eating place. Despite proximity to food sources and lack of predators (other than the ship's cat or sailors) life aboard ship for the indigenous rat population was not entirely wholesome: the dark dank recesses of the ship's hull was hardly a propitious environment. For rats that had spent their entire lives since birth under such conditions, away from sunlight, eating foodstuffs deficient in essential growth-pro-moting minerals and vitamins, the toll was severe, as evidenced from the rat bones recovered from the shipwreck of a 16th-century Spanish galleon at Emanuel Point, Pensacola Bay, Florida (see **Emanuel Point Ship**). Several limb bones of young rats from this shipwreck exhibited pathological changes indicative of rickets, while in the jawbones of older individuals there was evidence of very poor dental health (ante-mortem shedding of the molar teeth).

Other non-food/livestock-related shipwreck faunal remains include artefacts fashioned from animal products, which are routinely examined to ascertain the source material used. The cutlery handles recovered from the shipwreck of the English East Indiaman *Earl of Abergavenny*, for example, were identified as horn and bone of cattle, as well as elephant ivory. Such studies sometimes reveal unexpected sources: a 'needle-like implement' from a 4th-century BC Punic wreck on the northern shore of Isola Lunga, Sicily, was made from the radius of white stork (*Ciconia ciconia*). Maritime trade from early times also involved transportation of animal tissues used as raw materials. An early example of such trade is provided by the discovery in a Late Bronze Age shipwreck, at **Uluburun** near Kaş in southern Turkey, of twelve complete hippopotamus incisor teeth, an important source of ivory in the eastern Mediterranean in antiquity.

Invertebrates

Very little research has so far been carried out into invertebrate remains from shipwrecks; but preliminary results from two such published works (both making special reference to insects) serve to illustrate their potential contribution to maritime history.

Analysis of environment samples collected in the wreck of the Dutch East Indiaman *Amsterdam* (1749, Hastings, southern English coast), yielded evidence for the presence on board of grain weevil (*Sitophilus granarius*) and broad-bean weevil (*Bruchus rufimanus*), two common food pests, probably accidentally introduced with the provisions. In this same wreck, a Rhenish stoneware storage jar filled with tamarind fruits (part of the ship's medical supplies) was also discovered to contain large numbers of the tamarind beetle (*Sitophilus linearis*). Such a heavy infestation indicated the fruit had been packed raw (unwashed and unprocessed). For use as a laxative, the ship's surgeon would have prepared a decoction from fermented tamarind fruit purée. Also associated with the ship's medical supplies were the remains of Spanish fly (*Lytta vesicatoria*). Intentionally taken on board, these beetles (in dried and powdered form) served as the source of 'cantharidine' used in the treatment of migraine, rheumatism, and cases of sciatica and pleurisy.

Excavations of the shipwreck of a mid-16th century Spanish galleon at Emanuel Point, Pensacola Bay, Florida, also yielded insect remains (including wings, thoracic segments, and egg cases). The most abundant of these (from the frames and keelson buttresses) were identified as belonging to the American cockroach (*Periplaneta americana*), whose presence reflects unsanitary conditions on board. Found also in this wreck were elytra (wing covers) of the hide beetle (*Dermestes maculatus*), a destructive pest of stored animal tissues used as raw materials, and probably introduced onto the Emanuel Point vessel with a cargo of leather hides. P.A.

ADDITIONAL READING

Armitage, P.L., 1986, 'Mammalian, Bird and Fish Bones: Second Interim Report', J.H.G. Gawronski (ed.), *Annual Report of the VOC-ship 'Amsterdam' Foundation 1985*, Amsterdam, 60–67.

Armitage, P.L., 1989, 'Ship Rats, Salted Meat and Tortoises: Selected Aspects of Maritime Life in the "Great Age of Sail" (1500–1800s)', *Bermuda Journal of Archaeology and Maritime History*, 1, 143–59.

Armitage, P.L., 1991, 'Social Status and Mutton Consumption on Board English East Indiamen: Faunal Evidence from the Shipwreck *Earl of Abergavenny* (1805)', in P.J. Crabtree and K. Ryan (eds), *Animal Use and Culture Change*, MASCA Research Papers in Science and Archaeology, Supplement 8, 53–60.

Bratten, J.R., 1995, 'Olive Pits, Rat Bones, and Leather Shoe Soles: A Preliminary Report on the Organic Remains from the Emanuel Point Shipwreck, Pensacola, Florida', in P.F. Johnston (ed.), *Underwater Archaeology: Proceedings from the Society for Historical Archaeology Conference, Washington, DC*, 49–53.

Brinkhuizen, D.C., 1992, 'Anchovies for Batavia', *Archaeofauna*, 1, 121–6.

Brinkhuizen, D.C., 1994, 'Some Notes on Fish Remains from the Late 16th Century Merchant Vessel Scheurrak So1', *Fish Exploitation in the Past, Annales du Musée Royal de l'Afrique Centrale, Sciences Zoologiques*, 274:197–205.

English, A.J., 1990, 'Salted Meats from the Wreck of the *William Salthouse*: Archaeological Analysis of Nineteenth Century Butchering Patterns', *Australian Journal of Historical Archaeology*, 8, 63–9.

Grayson, D.K., 1984, *Quantitative Zooarchaeology: Topics in the Analysis of Archaeological Faunas*, Orlando, Florida.

Hakbijl, T., 1985, 'Remains of Insects 1984', in J.H. Gawronski (ed.), *Annual Report of the VOC-ship 'Amsterdam' Foundation*, Amsterdam, 72–3.

Hamilton-Dyer, S., 1995, 'Fish in Tudor Naval Diet, with Reference to the *Mary Rose*', *Archaeofauna*, 4, 27–32.

L'Hour, M. and Migaud, P., 1990, 'Reflet d'un aspect de la vie de bord: étude préliminaire des restes osseux de l'épave de L'Aber Wrac'h (Finistère, XVe s.)', *Anthropozoologica*, 12, 3–12.

Smith, R.C. *et al.*, 1995, *The Emanuel Point Ship: Archaeological Investigations, 1992–1995, Preliminary Report*, Bureau of Archaeological Research, Division of Historic Resources, Florida Department of State, Tallahasssee.

Tchernia, A., Girard, M., and Poplin, F., 1986, 'Pollens et ossements animaux de l'épave Romaine 3 de Planier (Provence)', *L'exploitation de la mer, VIèmes Rencontres Internationales d'Archéologie et d'Histoire, Antibes, October 1985*, 231–55.

van Rooij, H.H. and Gawronski, J., 1989, *East Indiaman Amsterdam*, Haarlem.

Ferriby Boats

Middle Bronze Age boats discovered at North Ferriby, East Yorkshire. At the time of the discovery of the first Ferriby boat (F1) in 1937 it was realized that the find was a substantial part of a plank-built boat of an unknown kind, probably of prehistoric age. Subsequent finds (F2, 1940, and F3, 1963) and the application of radiocarbon dating techniques have established that the three, all incomplete parts of separate examples, are probably contemporary at c. 1300 BC. They are, therefore, among the earliest plank-built boats from northwest Europe, being of the Middle Bronze Age and roughly of the same period as underwater finds from the Aegean; but later by more than a millennium than the earliest example from ancient Egypt, the royal craft of Khufu (Cheops) of c. 2600 BC (see **Khufu Ship**). Preserved in an intertidal deposit of silty clay on the north shore of the Humber estuary and kept permanently waterlogged therein, all the details of construction survived intact and were successfully recorded, although for lack of adequate methods of conservation of waterlogged timber at the time of excavation, the actual remains of F1 and F2 have become badly degraded. (F3, impregnated with polyethylene glycol, is somewhat better.) The timbers are at present stored at the Hull and East Riding Museum.

F1 was discovered when the ends of three planks, recognized as oak (*Quercus*), were observed protruding from clay near low water by E.V. Wright in September 1937. Subsequent investigations by him and his brother, C.W. Wright, before World War II revealed both ends of the remains and a little of what turned out to be a part of the lowest side-strake on one side, with a total length of 13.32 m and breadth of 1.67 m. Some parts were removed for safety, but others were carried away by the current during the war years. All but a very small area of F1 was measured and recorded while the plan of the lost part could be confidently inferred from the adjoining timbers. On a visit of inspection by E.V. Wright in November 1940, F2 was located in the same manner as F1 and some 60 m upstream. It proved to be an incomplete keel-strake of a similar boat 11.40 m long, and of this 1 m was washed away between 1942 and 1946, having been recorded earlier. In 1946 the surviving parts of F1 and F2 were excavated and lifted for removal to the National Maritime Museum, Greenwich, the archaeological team under Wright's direction having been drawn from that museum, the British Museum, and Hull Museums together with other supporters. Conservation during the following years was largely unsuccessful, although some of the timber survives in a condition fit for radiocarbon and dendrochronological study. The third of the major boat finds, F3, was made by Wright in 1963 and excavated, lifted, and conserved by Hull Museums. It was found by observation between the first two, but closer to F1, and turned out to be part of the bottom-structure and lowest side-strake of the same type of boat; altogether 8.97 m survived.

Subsequent studies have filled out the environmental history of the deposit, confirming that it covers much of the Bronze Age; explored details of materials and construction; and culminated in the design of a hypothetical reconstruction of a complete boat which remains a preferred option among several possible alternatives. At the time of writing, absolute dating by dendrochronology is still a possibility, the tree-rings of a plank of F3 having been matched with a floating chronology of bog-oaks of similar radiocarbon age from a nearby wetland site. Either may be fitted into a complete chronology at some future date.

Assuming that all three were of similar design, a Ferriby boat would have consisted of a bottom-structure made up of four planks of oak up to 60 cm wide and 18 cm thick, the thickest being joined end to end amidships by a simple box-scarf to form a keel-strake. The outer ends were shaped out of the solid with a pronounced upward curve, the two halves having been derived from a single trunk split down the middle. On either side of this keel-strake were fas-

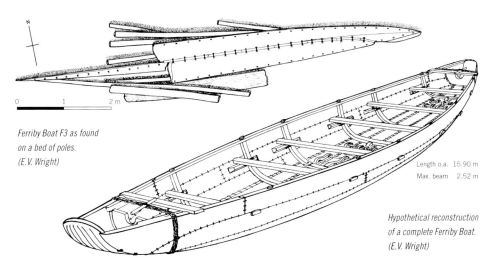

Ferriby Boat F3 as found
on a bed of poles.
(E.V. Wright)

Length o.a. 15.90 m
Max. beam   2.52 m

*Hypothetical reconstruction
of a complete Ferriby Boat.
(E.V. Wright)*

tened somewhat thinner outer bottom-strakes, curved in plan on their outboard edges and terminating 2.65 m short of the protruding keel-strake. The bottom-structure was braced from side to side by transverse timbers passing through openings in cleats left standing integrally on the face of the planks ('cleat-systems'). The planks were fastened to each other by separate stitches of twisted withy of yew at intervals of 20–30 cm. The holes for the stitches in the bottom were of 25 mm square section but turned through a 90 degree path so that the stitches were buried in the seams for protection against damage on grounding. At the ends outboard of the outer bottom-planks, stitches passed through larger oval holes, but were countersunk in grooves on the outside, again for protection. Seams were waterproofed with moss which was kept in place by lengthwise laths of oak under the stitches.

The ends of the lowest side-strakes, present in F1 and F3, were shaped in three dimensions to fit into the space between the outer bottom-strakes and the protruding keel-strake. In the end of the keel-strake which survived only in F1 there were spaces for two more side-strakes per side. Absolute proof of the existence of the second side-strakes was provided by the presence of stitches along the first strake, but the existence of third strakes is confidently inferred from the number and spacing of stitch-holes. There was a single large and elegantly shaped cleat on the under (outer) face of the surviving end of the keel-strake with an oval-sectioned, transverse opening, and outboard of this again the end was carved with convergent grooves.

The seams were fashioned in a variety of ways according to the position in the boat, the prime purposes being to lock the planks securely to their neighbours, to protect the stitching, and to retain the caulking in place between the planks. There was evidence of major ancient repairs in F1 to cracks in the planks and in this case it apparently proved impossible to bend the paths of the stitch-holes within the thickness of the timber. Stitches were therefore cut straight through the edges in spite of the fact that they would have been vulnerable to abrasion on grounding.

There were a number of protuberances left standing proud of the inner surface of the planks of F1 and F2, though the surviving part of F3 had none. Possible purposes for these have been inferred in considering the hypothetical reconstruction of a complete boat.

In recent years (1984 and 1989) two small pieces of timber have been found nearby and these have been interpreted as fragments of boat-planking (F4) and a detached cleat (F5). They have been dated by radiocarbon determination to *c.* 400 BC.

All three major finds showed signs of dismantling before final abandonment. In F1 and F2 stitches or transverse timbers displayed deliberate cut-marks. In the case of F3 the remains had been placed on a rough platform of poles (chiefly of alder), no doubt to prevent them from sinking into the mud.

There is no absolute proof among the finds that there were any timbers other than one more side-strake, fastening for which occurred along the upper edges of the planks recorded in F1 and F3. However, the surviving intact ends of these were fastened to the keel-strake by three (F1) or four (F3) stitches and there were seven unused stitch-holes remaining on that side of the keel-strake in F1. These would have accommodated two more side-strakes without making undue demands in the shaping of the plank-ends. A total of three strakes per side would have provided satisfactory free-board amidships. Alternatives have been suggested of only two such strakes or even two with the addition of screens of hide on top as a protection against spray which could have been a problem with the reduced free-board.

A structure consisting of the shell alone with only the bracing provided by the cleat-systems is thought to have been too easily distorted without some internal ribbing. In both F1 and F2 there are several slots between upstanding projections and other chocks which could have been suitable means of locating transverse ribs to the floor of the boat. Hypothetical reconstruction proceeds on the inference that there were six such stations for grown crooks, each consisting of two timbers scarfed together and secured by treenails. In addition, the structure may have been further strengthened by up to nine thwarts notched to fit over the tops of the second strakes and passing to the outside of the hull through half-round cutouts in the sheer-strakes. Such a cutout was observed in F4 and adopted, even though it is admittedly a thousand years later than Fs 1–3. Another feature recorded in F4 has been borrowed to complete the conjectural system of bracing, in the shape of an internal rail or flange formed along the upper edge of the sheer-strake and pierced by oval holes. These are interpreted as means of securing the rib-ends, as in the 2nd-century AD Romano-Celtic barge, **Zwammerdam** 2 from Holland.

Finally it is suggested that the large cleat on the underside of the keel-strake in F1 was for the purpose of securing and protecting a girth-lashing to bind the plank-ends together. Lodged against a transverse ridge on the inner face in the same plane as the cleat below, a timber of the same sort as the transoms in contemporary logboats has been added to give the lashing a form against which to grip the plank-ends, tautened by a tourniquet. The most convincing suggestion for the purpose of the grooves beyond the cleat is that they were designed to break up the surface in order to facilitate unsticking from mud if the boat were run into a bank.

It is probable that these boats were propelled by paddles, parts of three having been found in the same deposit. Oars for rowing, although known from the Mediterranean earlier than the date of the Ferriby boats, are not identified from northern Europe before *c.* 500 BC. There would be room for eighteen paddlers sitting on the conveniently placed thwarts inferred above. It has been estimated that a complete boat as proposed would have had an unladen weight of 4 tonnes and, allowing adequate free-board amidships, could carry crew, passengers, and cargo of nearly 7 tonnes. With such a load eighteen paddlers could drive it at up to 6 knots for a burst of say thirty minutes, a speed sufficient at high tide to complete the crossing of the estuary which is about 2 km wide at North Ferriby. A smaller crew or an easier rating would give a reasonable cruising speed of about 5 knots.

The possibility of mast and sail has been considered. There are some enigmatic rock-engravings in Norway of Bronze Age date conceivably depicting boats with sails; but otherwise masts and sails are not known from northwestern Europe before the 2nd-century BC Broighter Model (a small gold model of an ancient vessel from Broighter, Co. Derry, Ireland). In F1 there is a feature amidships on the keel-strake which might be a step for a simple mast. If so and with a following wind a rudimentary sail would have given welcome relief to paddlers.

Until recently the only remotely similar plank-built boat recorded from Europe was the so-called **Brigg 'Raft'**, actually the bottom of a flat-bottomed river-boat with low sides (see also **Humber Wrecks**). This was found in 1888, was re-buried in the same year after some months' exposure, and was re-excavated in 1974. The planks were sewn together continuously with twisted willow-branch and secured transversely by timbers passed through integral cleats as in F1 and F2. It has been radiocarbon dated to c. 800 BC. In 1990 part of a substantial boat-plank was excavated at Caldecott Castle, Gwent which has features suggesting that it was from the hull of a boat fastened and braced in ways similar to the Ferriby trio. It has been radiocarbon dated to c. 1600 BC. (See **Severn Wrecks**.) In 1992 a more spectacular find was made during roadworks at Dover, Kent in the form of the lower part of a boat of proportions similar to those from North Ferriby and of approximately contemporary date (see **Dover Boat**).

Some of the details of construction match those from Ferriby, while others are markedly different. Over half of the hull was exposed and lifted from 6 m deep shafts and the remainder left undisturbed. Full publication is awaited.

As far as is known there are no other parallels from Europe, although sewing and stitching of planks in boats was commonplace in prehistory in the classical era, and survived into historical times in northern Scandinavia and Siberia. It is still widely practised around the coasts of the Indian Ocean. The only parallels that can be traced to date for the cleat-systems are in the c. 300

BC **Hasholme Logboat** and a boat from Anapchi Pond, South Korea dated to c. AD 800.
E.V.W.

ADDITIONAL READING

McGrail, S., 1987, *Ancient Boats in N.W. Europe*, London.

Wright, E.V., 1990, *The Ferriby Boats*, London.

Wright, E.V., 1991, 'The North Ferriby Boats: A Final Report', in C. Westerdahl (ed.), *Crossroads in Ancient Shipbuilding: Proceedings of the Sixth International Symposium on Boat and Ship Archaeology*, Roskilde.

Filtering processes

Concepts developed in 1977 by Keith Muckelroy in his seminal work *Maritime Archaeology* to characterize aspects of shipwreck evolution from the organized assemblage of a ship and its contents. Filtering processes combine two concepts developed by Muckelroy to account for the disparity between the ship as a cultural object and its seabed distribution as an archaeological site: extractive filters – processes that remove material during wrecking, and scrambling devices – processes that create varying degrees of disorder as the ship becomes an archaeological site. Muckelroy defined the wrecking process as closed, with the ship as input and the site and filtering processes as output. He developed a basic thesis that filters are constrained and describable through archaeological evidence, which can in turn ultimately inform about the ship itself.

Muckelroy approached shipwreck site formation scientifically by examining twenty shallow-water shipwrecks in varying environments to measure the degree of correlation between quality of archaeological remains and environmental variables. The results of his inquiry had important implications for shallow-water shipwreck archaeology and were instrumental in overturning the prevailing assumption at the time that shallow-water shipwrecks were essentially destroyed and consequently of little interest to archaeologists. He found that seabed variables such as bottom slope, topography, and bottom sediment were more important than depth in their effect on the quality of archaeological preservation. Muckelroy also made the important observation that after initial deposition, filtering processes often had little continuing effect, and shallow shipwrecks could be well preserved with much to offer archaeologists.

Extracting filters include three primary processes that remove material from a shipwreck site: wrecking, salvage operations, and disintegration of perishables. Archaeologists must control for these processes and explain the presence and absence of material in all

cases. During wrecking, some materials simply float away, although some materials that would have floated can be found. Salvage operations can remove much from the ship. Contemporary salvage potential must be assessed by archaeologists to account for its impact to the wreck site. Perishables disintegrate and corrode at varying rates, which must also be determined by the archaeologist through chemical and biochemical analysis; however, general principles may have to be followed in the absence of specific studies regarding disintegration rates.

Scrambling devices rearrange patterns found aboard the ship and introduce disorder in the archaeological record during wrecking and from seabed movement. Scrambling begins during the wrecking process and continues until the material stabilizes as part of the seabed. Further scrambling may occur afterwards from additional seabed movement. Muckelroy proposed a depositional model in which the vessel settles relatively intact to the bottom. Scouring ensues and the vessel heels over into the scour pit with material below the seabed preserved. However, most vessels, he surmised, do not reach the seabed intact and may be disbursed over long distances by tide and current.

Once shipwreck materials are stabilized, they can be affected by seabed movement, which makes geomorphological analysis important in wreck site interpretation. A wreck site may have a very complex stratigraphy that reflects not only chronology, such as in some anchorages, but differential seabed movement. For example, the upper sediment layer may be mobile and in a semi-suspension state that allows artefact sorting by density, or it may allow all artefacts to drop through this mobile layer to more stable strata, such as noted on the Spanish Armada site **La Trinidad Valencera**. Other sites, such as *Dartmouth*, may be very mobile with undisturbed sediment found only beneath the hull. On other sites, Muckelroy observed that the entire wreck deposit had been post-depositionally resorted through seabed movement with artefacts found only at the bottom of bedrock fissures.

Muckelroy suggested wave and current data be recorded in addition to detailed site stratigraphy. Experimenting with introduced objects after excavation may also inform on seabed distribution. He also suggested that flora and fauna tolerant to a narrow range of conditions be recorded as indicators of environmental context. Faunal impact, like sherd concentrations by octopi as observed by George F. Bass in Turkey, should also be noted as they can affect artefact distributions. While archaeologists often turn to natural scientists for analysis of seabed processes, Muckelroy pointed out that archaeologists are in a position to contribute to knowledge about seabed movement and stability very useful to sedimentologists. A striking example is the **Mary Rose** excavation that produced geological and biological data on the past 400 years of that portion of the Solent.

It would be difficult to overstate Muckelroy's methodological contribution and its impact on maritime archaeology. Many concepts currently used for the investigation of **Site formation processes** and site interpretation were first systematically discussed by Muckelroy in *Maritime Archaeology*. L.E.M.

ADDITIONAL READING

Muckelroy, K., 1977, *Maritime Archaeology*, Cambridge.

Finland
see **Baltic Sea**

Fission track dating
see **Absolute dating**

Flota of 1715

Combined fleet of Spanish treasure ships that was lost on the east coast of Florida during a hurricane in 1715. It has attracted generations of treasure hunters who continue to search for coins and jewellery from the disaster. The 1950s beachcomber Kip Wagner is credited with starting a modern-day gold rush after following a trail of oxide-blackened coins from the beach into the shallow waters near Sebastian Inlet, where he found the strewn remains of a shipwreck. Consulting the Spanish Archive of the Indies, Wagner learned to his surprise that a whole convoy of treasure ships had wrecked in the area.

Details of the disaster indicated that it was one of the worst losses of shipping in the history of Spain's maritime empire. A combined fleet of eleven ships of the Tierra Firme squadron and the New Spain flota had embarked from their rendezvous at Havana early on the morning of 24 July 1715 to begin the long voyage back to Spain. The vessels had been in the Indies almost two years and their departure had been retarded well into the hurricane season by delays in lading and paperwork. Total registered cargoes of the convoy in gold and silver amounted to almost seven million pieces-of-eight, in addition to what probably was a vast fortune in contraband bullion being smuggled back to Spain. Sailing with the Spanish ships was a lone French merchantman named *Grifon*, which had been detained at Havana so as not to fall prey to corsairs who might learn of the impending fleet departure.

Both captain generals, Juan Estéban de Ubilla of the New Spain galleons and Antonio de Echeverz y Zubiza of the Tierra Firme fleet, realized the dangers of sailing so late in the summer, but neither man expected the mistake to prove so disas-

Diver on the 'Wedge Wreck', probably a storeship of Miguel de Lima. (Roger Smith)

trous. As the treasure ships made their way north through the Florida Strait borne along by the Gulf Stream, it gradually became apparent to all aboard the vessels that a tremendous storm was bearing down on them from the east. Ubilla ordered all of his consorts to face into the wind and tack at an angle which hopefully would keep them clear of Florida's reefline. But in the early hours of 31 July the hurricane struck with full force, driving the helpless ships one after another over the shallow shoals and onto the sand with grinding impact. Crushed under tonnes of water, the splintered galleons were ripped open in the darkness, drowning people and cargoes in the wild surf. All eleven ships were destroyed; of the 2,500 persons on board, nearly half lost their lives. Only *Grifon*, sailing in the teeth of the wind, somehow managed to stay clear of the reefs. Ironically, her captain had disobeyed fleet orders by heading a half-point further to the northeast, and she escaped destruction.

Wagner and his colleagues organized the

Real Eight Corporation; the shipwreck he initially encountered was dubbed the 'Cabin Wreck'. Initially dug with a dragline from a temporary pier constructed out into the water, timbers and ship's debris were scooped up and dumped on the beach to be combed with a metal detector. A salvage permit was eventually obtained from the State of Florida, which began in 1967 to administer a contract programme to oversee shipwreck recovery and subsequent division of artefacts between the State and salvors. The 'Cabin Wreck' consisted of two main areas of wreckage, and became one of the most productive of the wrecks to be worked by Real Eight, due to large amounts of silver coinage recovered from the site.

Further south, recoveries of gold bullion and specie from the 'Gold Wreck' suggested that, despite lengthy and determined Spanish salvage efforts after the disaster, little of the ship's cargo had been recovered, perhaps because it had been spread over an area of four submerged acres. Discovery of elephant bones and ivory tusk fragments prompted salvors to speculate that the vessel had been involved in the African slave trade. However, subsequent archaeological analysis of the site, which also contained a partial human cranium and stone projectile point, led to the unearthing of an intact stratum of Pleistocene sediments beneath the shipwreck, which produced fragments of prehistoric horses, camels, and mammoths.

Extensively salvaged by the Spaniards,

another site was dubbed the 'Wedge Wreck', due to the discovery of a number of crudely cast silver wedges that originally fit together to form a pie-shaped assemblage which could perhaps have been concealed at the bottom of a barrel. The shallow wreck had originally been found in 1928, and its cannons and anchors salvaged with the help of local officials. Among the most intact of the 1715 fleet sites, a large portion of the ship's lower hull remained stable under a smattering of ballast stones.

Coins found on the beach led to another site, where intermittent deposits of wreckage and cannons had been deposited along the seabed with increasing frequency towards shore. Although no distinct concentrations of ballast were found on the site, which was named 'Corrigan's Wreck', a pattern of deposition typical of the 1715 fleet disaster was encountered. The disabled vessels appear to have been pushed shoreward from a southeasterly direction, striking the shallow reefs and spilling the contents of their lower hulls, while their superstructures and upper decks piled up on the beach, and resulting debris swept northward with the prevailing current along the shore. Another site, called 'Sandy Point Wreck', was found on a hard limestone bottom with clusters of cannons, familiar silver and gold coinage and Mexican pottery, and a brass ship's bell. A sixth site, called 'Rio Mar Wreck', featured nineteen iron cannon and two large anchors, clustered on a reef near a shallow point of land.

Word of Real Eight Corporation's finds prompted other treasure hunters to demand similar salvage permits from the State of Florida. Mel Fisher's Treasure Salvors, Inc. developed magnetic detection tools and **Propwash deflection** to mine the seabed, ushering in a small cottage industry of part-time treasure hunters who continue to comb the 1715 disaster area. Despite almost seventy years of informal and formal salvage activities on Florida's east coast, only six shipwreck sites can be clearly associated with the 1715 fleet. Their individual identities, however, have never been positively determined, due to inadequate archival documentation and artefact cataloguing procedures. Although the State has attempted to regulate and supervise recovery activities, the stupendous amounts of precious metals extracted from the shallow sands blurred the archaeological significance of the wreck sites from the start. Unique discoveries were occasionally retained for the public, but many were dispersed into private collections under the terms of the permits. The largest collection of 1715 materials, once displayed in Real

Eight's museum at Cape Canaveral, suffered a massive burglary and the remaining items were sold. A fraction of the original finds is now housed and displayed in the State's museums at Tallahassee and Sebastian. In 1989 the 'Wedge Wreck', thought to have been a large storeship (*urca*) belonging to Miguel de Lima, was designated as Florida's first Underwater Archaeological Preserve, in an attempt to safeguard its remains for future generations of visitors. R.S.

ADDITIONAL READING

Burgess, R.F. and Clausen, C.J., 1976, *Gold, Galleons, and Archaeology*, New York.

Clausen, C.J., 1965, *A 1715 Spanish Treasure Ship*, Contributions of the Florida State Museum, Social Sciences, no. 12, Gainesville, Florida.

Smith, R.C., 1988, 'The Iberian-American Maritime Empires', in G.F. Bass (ed.), *Ships and Shipwrecks in the Americas: A History Based on Underwater Archaeology*, London.

Smith, R.C., 1991, 'Florida's Underwater Archaeological Preserves', in J.D. Broadwater (ed.), *Underwater Archaeology Proceeding from the Society for Historical Archaeology, Richmond*, Ann Arbor, Michigan.

Wagner, K., 1972, *Pieces of Eight: Recovering the Riches of a Lost Spanish Treasure Fleet*, New York.

Flota of 1733

New Spain treasure fleet that grounded in the Florida Keys during a hurricane in 1733. Commanded by Captain-General Rodrigo de Torres, a convoy of eighteen merchant ships and four armed galleons departed Havana for Spain on Friday 13 July 1733. Next day, as the fleet neared the Florida Keys, the wind shifted abruptly and increased in velocity. Sensing an approaching storm, Torres ordered his captains to turn back to Havana, but it was too late. By nightfall, most of the ships had been sunk or swamped along 130 km of reefs bordering the island chain; only one vessel made it safely back to Havana.

Survivors gathered in small groups throughout the Keys, and were soon rescued by salvage boats carrying food, supplies, soldiers, and divers. Wrecked ships that could not be refloated and towed back to Havana were burned to the waterline to allow divers to descend into cargo holds, and to conceal the sites from freebooters. Salvage work continued for years; when a final calculation of recovered cargoes was made, more gold and silver had been recovered than had been listed on the manifests – a result of inevitable contraband.

Most of the 1733 fleet shipwrecks were relocated by modern fishermen and treasure hunters. They quickly became the

objects of weekend explorers, with little regard for their historical or archaeological integrity. Due to the successful salvage activities of the Spaniards after the disaster, very little treasure has been discovered at the wreck sites. Nonetheless, they have suffered from repeated and illegitimate disturbances during attempts to find non-existent treasure. As a result, most have been thoroughly rummaged and are barren of artefacts.

Torres's *capitana* (flagship), *El Rubi Segundo*, was relocated in the 1930s by a fisherman, who showed the site to Arthur McKee, a local hard-hat diver. For over a decade, McKee and his friends worked on the massive mound of ballast and timbers, recovering over twenty cannons, more than a thousand silver coins, statues and religious medals, small arms and edged weapons, jewellery, navigational instruments, ship's gear, and galley wares. Realizing the historical importance of these items, McKee built a museum in 1949; he also shared the wreck site with thousands of tourists from a glass-bottomed boat, allowing many to dive with his helmet.

From Spain McKee had obtained archival documents of the 1733 disaster, which included a copy of a map depicting locations of the salvaged wrecks. The map led treasure hunters to the shallow reef where *Nuestra Señora de Balvaneda* (alias *El Infante*), had been stranded. The galleon's remains have been worked continuously since 1955; reports of finds include examples of the first silver pesos to be minted in the New World by a screw press, Chinese porcelain, jewellery, ivory fans, and a silver helmet. The site of a Genoese-built freighter, *Nuestra Señora del Carmen, San Antonio de Padua y las Animas,* was the next discovery. The Spanish salvage map had depicted the ship's name as *Chaves*, after her owner, Antonio de Chaves. Although she had carried no registered treasure, and had been extensively salvaged by the Spaniards, her shallow inshore remains were accessible to modern divers, who promptly picked them apart. Nearby, an English-built ship in the convoy had also been stranded with decks awash. Also named after her owner and captain, Luis de Herrera, the merchantman had carried thousands of pesos in silver specie and bullion. *Herrera* became known to modern salvors as the 'Figurine Wreck', due to the recovery of hundreds of small Mexican ceramic statuettes in the form of fish, animal, and human shapes.

Another wreck, thought to be the *almiranta* (vice-flagship) of the fleet *El Gallo Indiana* ('Cock of the Indies'), was accidentally discovered and partially salvaged in the early 1960s by a group of divers. However, it may instead have been an English-built merchantman, *San Francisco de Asis*, according to the Spanish salvage map. Archaeological evidence is insufficient to determine the ship's identity, since diagnostic cargoes have been removed, features of the site altered, and no systematic excavation records kept. Similarly, another 1733 shipwreck is shown on the chart as *El Sueco de*

of Chinese porcelain when she wrecked. Her rediscovery in the 1960s was rewarded by thousands of silver coins in small denominations, dated 1731 to 1733. The hoard of coins may have been lost during Spanish recovery operations, since some of the specie was cemented together in the form of cloth sacks.

By the mid-1960s, most of the 1733 ship-

wrecks had been discovered and worked by various treasure hunters. One important galleon, *San José de las Animas*, had not been located, despite persistent searching by airplane and boat. Eventually in 1968, the wreck was discovered buried under almost a metre of sand and grass. The well-preserved ship's hull contained numerous pieces of ordnance and arms, thousands of coins, assorted fine jewellery and silverware, and an enormous collection of pottery. Despite years of salvage, initial archaeological consultation by the Smithsonian Institution and the National Park Service, and supervision by Florida officials, little scholarly data was generated from this well-preserved galleon site. Another 1733 shipwreck, *Nuestra Señora de las Angustias y San Rafael*, long eluded modern salvors, who wrongly assumed that she had been towed back to Havana. However, archival research and a **Magnetometer** search helped treasure hunters to locate the wreck site in 1972. Situated in the murky water of a channel between two islands, the shipwreck was mapped and salvaged under State supervision. Documented finds included a rare gold four-escudo 'Royal' coin, minted as a proof for the king of Spain.

In 1989, the site of *San Pedro* became Florida's second Underwater Archaeological Preserve with the assistance of local citizens and waterfront organizations. In 1994, after additional archival research and archaeological documentation of the 'Lerri' wreck revealed the ship's identity as *San Felipe*, an English-built merchantman, the site was placed on the **National Register of Historic Places**. R.S.

Above: The site of El Infante *from the Flota of 1733. (Roger Smith)*

Right: Site of the 'Lerri' wreck, San Felipe. *(Roger Smith).*

Arizón; however, the name 'Arizón' can be matched in documents with that of the owner and captain of *Nuestra Señora del Rosario, San Antonio y San Vicente Ferrer,* shown as having wrecked at another location. Another map site was called 'Tres Puentes', which probably referred to the three decks of *Nuestra Señora de Belem y San Juan Bautista*, which stranded inshore of the reefs and was later found through aerial reconnaissance by treasure hunters. A large ballast further inshore was denoted as the site of a vessel nicknamed 'Lerri' or 'Herri' on the map; other documents mention the names 'Tyrri', 'Terri', or 'Lyrri'. Its coral-covered ballast mound was subjected to modern salvage operations in which an anchor and several cannons were removed as trophies, but no treasure was found. A Dutch-built ship, *San Pedro*, was carrying 16,000 pesos of silver and numerous crates

ADDITIONAL READING

Peterson, M., 1975, *The Funnel of Gold*, Boston.

Skrowronek, R.K., 1984, *Trade Patterns of Eighteenth Century New Spain: The 1733 Fleet and St. Augustine*, Historical Archaeology, South Carolina Institute of Archaeology and Anthropology, University of South Carolina, Columbia.

Smith, R.C., 1988, 'The Iberian-American Maritime Empires', in G.F. Bass (ed.), *Ships and Shipwrecks in the Americas: A History Based on Underwater Archaeology*, London.

Smith, R.C., 1991, 'Florida's Underwater Archaeological Preserves', in Broadwater, J.D., (ed.), *Underwater Archaeology Proceeding from the Society for Historical Archaeology, Richmond*, Ann Arbor, Michigan.

Foraminifera

Testate rhizopods belonging to the sub-kingdom Protozoa that inhabit marine and marginal marine environments from coastal marshes to the deep sea. They are microscopic (63 microns to several millimetres), single-celled animals that are very useful for paleoenvironmental reconstruction both in the earth sciences and in underwater archaeology.

Being unicellular, foraminifera perform all life-functions, such as feeding, reproduction, respiration, and test (shell) construction within the confines of a single cell. Net-like extensions of cell protoplasm are used to move, anchor, and retrieve food. Foraminifera may be omnivores, carnivores, herbivores, or detrivores, eating other microorganisms such as diatoms, bacteria, and other protozoans. There are two main groups of foraminifera as differentiated by their life mode: planktic foraminifera that float in the upper water column of the deep sea and benthic foraminifera that live on or within the substrate of the sea-floor.

Foraminiferal classification is largely based upon shell characteristics, with wall composition and microstructure defining the taxa at the suborder and superfamily level. Shell composition includes three main wall types: organic (membranous or tectinous), agglutinated, and calcareous. Agglutinated shells are composed of foreign sediment particles glued together with an organic cement, and calcareous shells are formed from secreted calcium carbonate. Calcareous shells can be further subdivided into hyaline, porcellaneous, and microgranular types as determined by their calcite crystal arrangement.

Benthic foraminifera are a useful tool for paleoenvironmental analysis in coastal areas for a number of reasons: (1) they have a mineralized shell that is well preserved in the sedimentary record; (2) they are abundant in most marine and marginal marine environments with a living population density that can often exceed a million individuals per square metre; (3) due to their small size and their high population density only a small sediment sample is needed to obtain statistically significant results; (4) they are single-celled so they respond very rapidly to environmental changes; (5) as many species have very narrow environmental constraints, their remains provide information on the depositional environment that cannot be derived from sedimentological characters alone; (6) the elemental and isotopic composition of calcareous shells records the environmental water chemistry; and (7) there exists a large body of ecological information on specific foraminiferal species.

Understanding the paleoenvironment is very important for marine archaeological studies. Any coastal site is subject to a wide variety of physical and environmental processes including anthropogenic activity, sea-level changes, tectonism, and shifts in climatic and oceanographic patterns which may affect site formation. Understanding past environmental conditions and their temporal influence provides important information for archaeological interpretations. A good proxy for these environmental changes is provided by both the spatial and temporal distribution of foraminiferal shells in the sedimentary record. An increasing number of researchers recognize the potential uses of foraminifera as a paleoenvironmental proxy in marine archaeology. Several exemplary cases are briefly outlined below.

Foraminifera have been demonstrated to be a very useful tool in the archaeological analysis of ancient harbours. Foraminifera analysis distinguished environments within the ancient harbour at **Caesarea Maritima**, Israel (built by Herod the Great in 21 BC), adding information on the form and function of the harbour and how and when it was destroyed. Foraminiferal analysis of a stratigraphic section from the inner harbour delineated salinity changes over the life of the harbour. Contrary to initial speculation, the analysis revealed that the inner harbour was a brackish water environment which differed from the hypersaline eastern Mediterranean Sea. This brackish water environment was probably created by the city's runoff of freshwater and ground-water flow. Further, since such an environment could only have existed in a confined locality, researchers were able to infer that in antiquity the inner harbour was restricted by a wall that is no longer present. In addition, the inflow of fresh water into the inner harbour may have been an important component of a sluicing system which prevented siltation of the harbour. The foraminiferal evidence also indicated a shift towards normal marine conditions sometime after the 5th century AD, suggesting the structural deterioration of the inner harbour breakwaters.

Similarly, foraminiferal analysis of a sediment core taken from the entrance in the outer portion of the ancient harbour added to the archaeological interpretation. This analysis revealed that the outer harbour environment was typical of a Mediterranean marine or hypersaline lagoon, indicating that the harbour was an effective barrier to the waves and provided a safe haven for shipping. However, this quiet water lagoonal environment was punctuated by large-scale storms that caused the incursion and deposition of sand. The foraminiferal analysis in conjunction with carbon-14 dating determined that the harbour was no longer func- tioning as a quiet water entity after the third century AD and that a purported renovation in AD 500 did not return the harbour to a quiet water state.

Archaeologists have also used foraminiferal analysis to indicate paleopollution and climatic changes in medieval London. This analysis revealed that pollution in the River Fleet, a tributary of the Thames Estuary in London, reached catastrophic levels in 1343. It also indicated periods of short-term drought. The recognition of pollution and climatic perturbations in the sediment record allowed correlations to be made with events in primary medieval documents.

Sea-level changes may have a great impact on coastal archaeological sites. The west coast of Canada has undergone dramatic isostatic, eustatic, and tectonic sea-level changes which have important implications for Amerindian site distribution and early human migration. Through the foraminiferal analysis of an underwater excavation profile from **Montague Harbour** (Gulf Islands, British Columbia, Canada) salinity changes were recognized in the late Holocene that were related to basin physiography and sea-level changes. This enabled researchers to predict paleo-shorelines where older Amerindian habitation sites might be found. Similarly, another study from the more northern Queen Charlotte Islands used micropaleontological analysis to discern salinity changes. These were correlated with fluctuations in sea-level which then enabled archaeologists to predict the location of past Amerindian habitation sites (c. 10,400 carbon-14 years ago) that are presently submerged in one hundred metres of water. E.G.R.

ADDITIONAL READING

Boyd, P.D.A., 1981, 'The Micropaleontology and Paleoecology of Medieval Estuarine Sediments from the Fleet and Thames in London', in J.W. Neale and M.D. Brasier (eds), *Microfossils from Recent and Fossil Shelf Seas*, British Micropalaeontological Society Series, Chichester.

Culver, S.J., 1993, 'Foraminifera', in J.H. Lipps (ed.), *Fossil Prokaryotes and Protists*, Boston, MA.

Josenhans, H.W. *et al.*, 1995, 'Post Glacial Sea Levels on the Western Canadian Continental Shelf: Evidence for Rapid Change, Extensive Subaerial Exposure, and Early Human Habitation', *Marine Geology*, 125, 73–94.

Murray, J.W., 1991, *Ecology and Palaeoecology of Benthic Foraminifera*, London.

Reinhardt, E.G., Easton, N.A., and Patterson, R.T., in press, 'Late Holocene Sea Level Change and Amerindian Habitation at Montague Harbour, British Columbia', *Géographie Physique et Quaternaire*.

Reinhardt, E.G., Patterson, R.T., and Schröder-Adams, C., 1994, 'Geoarchaeology of the Ancient Harbour Site of Caesarea Maritima Israel: Evidence from Sedimentology and Paleoecology of Benthic Foraminifera', *Journal of Foraminiferal Research*, 24, 37–49.

France

The history of underwater archaeology is closely tied up with the success of underwater exploration in general and, in this respect, one of the key moments was the invention of the aqualung in 1943 by Frenchmen Emile Gagnan and Jacques Yves Cousteau. By allowing almost universal access to the underwater world, SCUBA brought about the first underwater excavation in France in the 1950s. The target of the excavations was a cargo of amphoras buried 42 m deep off the island of **Grand Congloué** in Marseille harbour. Fernand Benoît, a university professor who did not himself dive, directed operations from the surface while professional divers worked under the direction of Commander Cousteau. This arrangement had its limitations, however. During the five-year excavations (1952–7) none of the divers noticed that the remains consisted of not one, but two superimposed Roman wrecks, lost within a century of one another (Grand Congloué 1 in the early 2nd century BC, Grand Congloué 2 in the early 1st century BC). Some experts in France, the USA and England began to realise that the development of underwater archaeology required that archaeologists themselves should be trained in diving techniques. This is how the first professional organizations were born in Europe in the 1960s. French underwater archaeology was one of the first to organize itself officially as the Direction des Recherches Archéologiques Sous-Marines (DRASM), set up by a government order of 30 September 1966 and based in Marseille. Since then, under the aegis of the French Ministry of Culture, and as the owner of the 140-tonne research ship *Archéonaute*, DRASM has been in charge of the administrative and scientific management of the French underwater heritage, comprising the French territorial waters from Europe to the Pacific, except the French territories of Polynesia and the Antarctic. At the beginning of 1996, DRASM also acquired scientific control of the cultural heritage of France's inland waters (lakes and rivers), and was renamed Département des Recherches Archéologiques Subaquatiques et Sous-Marines (DRASSM).

Since the 1960s, two main factors – one legal, the other maritime – have contributed to the development of underwater archaeology in France. The first relates to the long-established French legislation on maritime wrecks. In effect, since the 17th century, the French legal system has protected the interests of the wreck owner in the first instance, then, if the owner were not identified, its own. This dynamic legislation has been added to over the years, the most recent acts dating from 1989, 1991 and 1996. All these laws have served to confirm the validity of the fundamental principles established in the 17th century, namely that if the rightful owner of a wreck located in French territorial waters cannot be found, then the wreck belongs to the French state. (The law defines a wreck broadly, as an object or structure of human origin found underwater or on the water's surface.) This legislation has forced the state to ensure the protection and display of wrecks and has *de facto* forbidden their commercial exploitation without permission.

The second favourable factor of the situation in France is the country's exceptional maritime geography. France has in effect two different coasts, the Mediterranean and the Atlantic, where, from early times, totally different maritime societies evolved. So, for instance, while the Greeks and Romans sailed the Mediterranean in ancient times, the Celts visited the harbours of the Atlantic coast. Later, in the 8th-10th centuries, while Muslim flotillas disrupted French Mediterranean harbours, the Vikings were attacking the Atlantic coasts. Finally, in the 17th century, Marseille traders set up a wide shipping network with towns in Turkey, Syria and Egypt and simultaneously traders in Nantes and Saint-Malo, and the administrators of the East India Company at Lorient, built their fortunes on commerce with the Antilles or the Far East. It is a consequence of this activity over thousands of years that the French maritime heritage is so rich and diverse today. Furthermore, the abundant collection of archaeological shipwrecks which traditionally have been in the care of underwater archaeologists is expanded by a number of submerged sites which were originally located on land. The most famous and recent example is the Grotte Cosquer, discovered in 1991 in Marseille harbour. This cave was inhabited twice during the Paleolithic period (around 28,000 years B.P. then again around 18,500 B.P.); its entrance is now 37 m underwater due to transgression.

Nevertheless, the main underwater archaeological sites in France are shipwrecks. Since the 1960s more than 700 wrecks from all periods, from the 6th century BC to the end of the 19th century AD, have been recorded in DRASSM's inventory, and this number continues to grow at the rate of 20 to 25 per year. More than half of the inventoried wrecks have been surveyed or methodically excavated. Every year some 45 to 55 surveys or excavations are authorized by the French Minister of Culture. Annually, a large number of articles and publications are dedicated to these projects. Furthermore, since 1992 DRASSM has published an extensive annual 100-page scientific report which gives a succinct account of important results from each year's underwater excavations in France.

Naturally a great number of underwater excavations have been carried out over the last thirty years, so it is difficult to select particular examples to illustrate the progress of the discipline in France. In fact, from the Etruscan **Bon-Porté Wreck** to the English earthenware of the *Colombian* (1865), including along the way the Greek bronzes of the La Fourmigue C wreck (1st century BC), the Arab wreck of Bataiguier (mid-10th century), and the Chinese porcelain from the French EastIndiaman *Prince de Conty* (1746), there are a multitude of scientific projects dedicated to the history of trade or ship construction which could be quoted. To give a comprehensive account, one would have to include the results of numerous advisory or training missions undertaken by French underwater archaeologists in Asia, the Middle East, Africa and Europe as part of international cultural exchanges.

Nevertheless, some excavations more than others – without necessarily being the most important scientifically – have truly symbolized a new evolution of the discipline. Created by Classical archaeologists, French underwater archaeology naturally showed a bias at the outset towards Antique wrecks of the Mediterranean. Right up to the 1980s this preference led to a relative neglect of more recent wrecks and of archaeological sites on the Atlantic coast. For the first fifteen years of research, it is probably the excavation of the **Madrague de Giens** wreck (1st century BC), situated east of Toulon, which is the most representative. Directed by researchers from the National Centre of Scientific Research (CNRS), and the University of Aix-en-Provence, this excavation acted as a training-ground for several young researchers and as a springboard for the first methodological principles of the discipline. At the beginning of the 1980s, the ruling passion of French researchers for ancient wrecks in the Mediterranean had abated a little and the west coast of France, which had been neglected until then, began to be investigated. The excavation in 1983 of the ancient wreck of Ploumanac'h on the northern Brittany coast (4th century AD), has played an important role in the broadening of French underwater studies by associating Antiquity and the Atlantic for the first time. During the same period, numerous research projects were undertaken on more recent wrecks. The excavation of the wreck Plage d'Arles 1 (1714), *Lomellina* (1516), the study in the Gulf of Guinea of the Dutch East Indiaman *Mauritius* (1609) carried out by DRASSM's archaeologists, at the request of the Gabon government, and finally, the excavation of the wreck Aber

sites already studied during the first decades of the discipline's development. This is true of a study undertaken from 1991 by CNRS experts. The purpose of this study is to draw up dendrochronological referentials, and to classify the types of wood used in ship construction during antiquity by the carpenters of Mediterranean Gaul. This enquiry has required the methodical taking of samples from and around twenty ancient wrecks excavated since 1966 and dating between the 2nd century AD and the 4th century AD.

Given that there was a better balance between the research of ancient wrecks and

from human looting – are generally better preserved and consequently of greater scientific interest to underwater archaeologists. However, the development of offshore engineering, of which the Marseille company Comex was a world leader, has led since the 1970s to more and more frequent surveys of very deep underwater sites. Nearly 70 wrecks out of the 700 recorded today on French coasts are indeed situated beyond the usual limit imposed in France for aqualung diving, that is, 60 m. It is therefore understandable that French archaeologists should soon have become interested in these very deep sites. Consequently, many

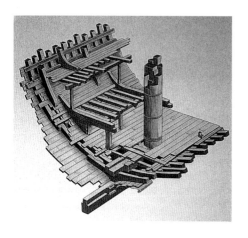

Far left: Reconstruction of the main mast-step of Lomellina. *(© GRAN/N.Blotti)*

Left: Alabama, *a Confederate warship lost off Cherbourg in 1864. Engraving published in* Harper's Weekly, 1862. *(US Naval Historical Center)*

Below: On the site of Alabama. *(NPS/J.Brooks)*

Wrac'h 1 (first half of the 15th century) are highlights in this period. French underwater archaeology began to take its place in research areas which previously had been ignored by its experts. At the end of this period of evolution, at the beginning of the 1990s, the scientific community's acknowledgement of the importance of these operations finally brought about a harmonious equilibrium in French research on both ancient and more modern wrecks. This is evident from the fact that the main projects of the two big professional excavation sites in France in the years 1990 to 1995 were, first, the ancient wrecks of the Pointe Lequin east of Toulon, in particular the Greek wreck Lequin 1A (6th century BC), and, second, the wrecks of five French vessels lost in 1692 at Saint-Vaast-La-Hougue, in Normandy.

Running parallel to the increasingly important role played by detailed analyses resulting from the study of wrecks and their cargo, methods of cutting up wood, spectrometric analyses of clay or isotopic analysis of lead, in addition, new research problems were encountered during the 1990s. Triggered by the scientific achievements of underwater archaeology, the focus of these new problems is sometimes

that of more recent ones in the 1980s, one might say that it is probably the conquest of the very deep ocean which will be the predominant achievement of the 1990s. Deep water wrecks are often lost in more favourable conditions than those near to the shore, which are subsequently destroyed. These sites – protected against marine hazards like sea swell and temporarily saved

experimental excavations have been undertaken on these wrecks since the early 1990s. Usually carried out with the logistical help of Comex or the Institut Francais de Recherche pour l'Exploitation de la Mer (IFREMER), these excavation sites have facilitated the development of excavation strategies and suitable methods. Often judged stimulating for the experience they offer, the operations carried out since 1990 on the wrecks Sud-Caveaux 1 (64 m – late 1st century BC), *Dorothea* (72 m – 1693), *La Lune* (88m – 1664), *Basses de Can 1* (100 to 150m – late 2nd century BC), *Bénat 4* (328 m – late 2nd century BC) or *Arles 4* (660 m – 1st century AD), have also highlighted the sociological, technological and, most of all, financial pressures which hinder the development of deep-water excavations. Nevertheless, much progress has been made and these developments should not be stopped. As well as wrecks in shallow water, deep water sites are presently threatened as more technological facilities for looting become available and trawling activities cause damage. Deep water archaeology will, therefore, probably become one of the major challenges of the early decades of the next millennium.

Running parallel to these developments towards very deep explorations, everything points to the development of ancient coastal sites as important areas of investigation in the next few years. Worthy of particular note are the studies undertaken on the Neolithic coastal installations of the small lake of Thau, or the research on submerged ancient harbour structures, such as those of Olbia, Arles or Fos (the ancient *Fossae Marianae*).

Thirty years after its first halting start, French underwater archaeology is now a well-structured and dynamic discipline which continues to provide new sources of research for today and the future. M.L'H.

Franklin Expedition graves

Graves from the disastrous third Franklin expedition to the **Arctic** of 1845–8. During this ambitious endeavour to complete the charting of a Northwest Passage – one of the most engrossing stories of European Arctic exploration – all 129 men on the expedition lost their lives. Beginning in 1848, and continuing to this day almost to the point of obsession, searchers, explorers, and adventurers have travelled to the Arctic in quest of the lost expedition. During these searches, graves and **Human remains** from the expedition have been found at a number of sites in central and southern Arctic regions. However, the wrecks of the expedition's two ships (HMS *Erebus* and HMS *Terror*) have never been found, though many theories as to their whereabouts have been voiced, and even investigated, over the decades.

The first evidence of the expedition was detected in 1850 by sailors sent out by the British Admiralty as part of a massive search and rescue effort. On 27 August of that year, the Franklin Expedition's 1845–6 winter camp was found on tiny Beechey Island, located off the southwest tip of Devon Island. Found along with many articles of equipment, materials, and structures left behind by Franklin and his men were the graves of three sailors: twenty-year-old Petty Officer and Leading Stoker John Torrington (HMS *Terror*, died 1 January 1846), twenty-five-year-old Able-Bodied Seaman John Hartnell (HMS *Erebus*, died 4 January 1846), and Royal Marine Private William Braine (HMS *Erebus*, died 3 April 1846). The graves are located side by side and on rising ground, 8 m above sea-level, and 75 m upslope from the shoreline overlooking a protected bay. Each grave was originally identified by a wooden headboard (today replaced by replica wooden markers), and the surfaces marked by various outlines and pavings of stones of various sizes.

At this latitude in the Arctic, the top of the permafrost layer can be found within 10 to 15 cm of the surface. The sailors' bodies (which are buried at varying depths from 85 cm to 2 m) have thus remained continually frozen since the day each was buried. However, there have been three occasions when the bodies have been examined. On 7 September 1852, a private search expedition funded by Franklin's widow, Lady Jane Franklin, and led by Commander Edward A. Inglefield, temporarily exposed the frozen body of John Hartnell. The purpose of the exhumation was to establish the medical condition of the sailor. The partially exposed clothed body was described as being perfectly preserved, showing no signs of scurvy, but reflecting the ravages of a wasting disease, probably tuberculosis. In August of 1984 and June of 1986, the preserved bodies of all three sailors were exposed, thawed, and examined by a scientific research team from the University of Alberta. The full autopsies of the sailors identified the presence of tuberculosis in all three. It was also discovered that one of the sailors, John Hartnell, had been autopsied immediately after his death in 1846 by the doctors on the expedition.

All three sailors were found to contain high levels of lead in all body tissues, revealing the occurrence of lead poisoning. The amounts detected indicate that the lead contributed to their deaths. The presence of lead in the soft tissues points to short-term exposures within the time frame of the expedition. Tests have shown that the large store of tinned foods carried by the expedition was almost certainly the source of the lead, with the food being contaminated through prolonged contact with the solder used to seal each tin. Current knowledge of the serious physical and mental effects of lead on humans, when applied to these discoveries, provides a clearer understanding of the possible causes of the disaster. If most, or perhaps even all of the men were exposed to high levels of lead, the results may have significantly compromised the health and safety of the crews.

Other sites yielding human remains from the expedition were located during search expeditions following Dr John Rae's discovery in 1854 of the actual 'fate' of Franklin and his men. Rae, when encountering Inuit on Boothia Peninsula near King William Island, learned that the expedition had met its end on and around that island, probably from starvation. In support of these second-hand observations, Rae was able to purchase many articles from the expedition collected by the Inuit, including a number of personal items linked to some of the officers, even Franklin. He also heard stories of the dying crews resorting to cannibalism, news that was not well received by the British upon his return.

The first to search the King William Island region thoroughly was the Lady Franklin sponsored ship-based expedition of Captain Leopold M'Clintock. In 1859 their sledge surveys of the island located at least two sites where bodies were found. On the south coast, a single skeleton was discovered sprawled on the surface. Near the body were a number of objects probably carried by the sailor, including a notebook attributable to Petty Officer Harry Peglar of HMS *Terror*. On the west coast of the island M'Clintock's group found a lifeboat containing the skeletons of two men. The most significant discovery of this expedition (or perhaps any other) was that of a note left behind by the Franklin Expedition, and stored in a stone cairn on the northwest coast of the island. Its apparent simplicity belies its true complexity, and debate continues today about its contents. It describes the last days of the disaster in the barest language possible. From it we learn that the ships, stuck in the ice off the northwest coast of King William Island since September 1846, were deserted in April 1848, and that of the original crews of 129 men, 105 had survived to begin an overland march to the southeast, towards the mouth of the Back River. Franklin was not one of the survivors, having died in June of the previous year. When the note was written, they must have known there was no hope for survival. The images that are conjured up by this note have provided the driving force for many of the searches that followed.

American explorer Charles Francis Hall found the skeleton of one sailor on the

Erebus and Terror Wintering in the Ice, *an imaginary scene painted by Capt. Allen Young, RN, around 1858 while searching for Franklin's lost expedition. (Vancouver Maritime Museum)*

south coast of the island in 1869. Collecting the remains, he took them back to the United States, though they eventually made their way to England. The presence of a gold filling in a tooth resulted in the sailor being identified as Lieutenant Henry Le Vesconte of HMS *Erebus*.

In 1879, another American expedition, led by Frederick Schwatka, found skeletal evidence for at least four individuals on the west coast of the island, and associated with the remains of a lifeboat. On the northwest coast of the island they found a damaged formal grave structure and a scattered skeleton, which they collected. A medal inscribed with the name of Lieutenant John Irving of HMS *Terror* was found in the vicinity of the grave, and is only circumstantial evidence at best that the skeleton is his. Schwatka had the skeleton collected, and it, too, was eventually returned to England. Schwatka's group also found the remains of one sailor at Starvation Cove, a site on the mainland adjacent to the southeast coast of King William Island.

Since these 19th-century search expeditions, other smaller scale searches, or discoveries made by people living in the King William Island region, have located skeletal remains. Some of these may be from Franklin Expedition crewmen, though many are probably Inuit. All appear to be surface scattered remains. Systematic and planned searches resumed in the early 1980s.

Human skeletal remains from the Franklin Expedition were found on King William Island in 1981 and 1982 during an archaeological survey conducted by a research team

from the University of Alberta. In 1981 the fragmentary remains of a single individual were found scattered around a small tent circle on the southeast corner of the island. One of the bones had clear indications of cut marks made by a metal knife, providing physical evidence to support Rae's reporting of cannibalism on the expedition. In 1982 the fragmentary remains of six to fourteen individuals were located on the west coast and in association with remnants of one of the Franklin expedition lifeboats employed by the men after their desertion of the ships in April 1848. Chemical analysis of all of the bones recovered in both years indicated that the sailors had been exposed to dangerously high levels of lead, and were probably lead poisoned.

In 1982, McGill University archaeologist James Savelle located the skeletal remains of two individuals on a small island off the southeast coast of King William Island. In 1992 amateur historian Barry Ranford from Orangeville, Ontario conducted a survey of the west coast of King William Island and located a site from the expedition containing human remains. Subsequent excavation of the site in 1993 revealed the fragmentary remains of at least eleven sailors also possibly associated with a lifeboat. Analysis of the remains by a research group from McMaster University revealed bone lead levels consistent with lead poisoning. Many of the bones had been cut by a metal knife, evidence now solidly supporting the occurrence of cannibalism during the last weeks and days of the expedition.

Except for the three graves of the sailors from Beechey Island, and the grave of a sailor circumstantially identified as Lieutenant Irving on the northwest coast of King William Island, there is little evidence for

the formal interment of other Franklin crewmen. Most, if not all, of the discoveries of skeletons made by searchers since M'Clintock have been surface scattered remains of sailors who died as they walked along the coast, or who died as a group associated with one or more of the expedition's lifeboats.

Though all of the factors that eventually converged to cause the Franklin Expedition mass disaster may never be completely revealed, the discovery, recovery, and examination of human remains from these explorers has provided some unique insights into life and death during their search for a Northwest Passage. Physical evidence for the occurrence of cannibalism reveals the final desperation of the doomed crews, and the presence of lead levels in the sailors' bodies, even early in the expedition, illuminates the presence of serious health problems that eventually may have become insurmountable.

Various groups are continuing their plans for future searches of King William Island. Motivations for these projects are as varied as they are complex. Indeed, for some, the expedition has never died. O.B.

ADDITIONAL READING

Beattie, O. and Geiger, J., 1993, *Frozen in Time*, London.

Cyriax, R.J., 1939, *Sir John Franklin's Last Arctic Expedition*, London.

Kowal, W.A. *et al.*, 1991, 'Source Identification of Lead Found in Tissues of Sailors from the Franklin Arctic Expedition of 1845', *Journal of Archaeological Science*, 18, 193–203.

Ranford, B., 1994, 'Bones of Contention', *Equinox* , 74 (Spring), 69–87.

Sutherland, P. (ed.), 1985, *The Franklin Era*, Mercury Series, Ottawa.

Woodman, D., 1991, *Unraveling the Franklin Mystery: The Inuit Testimony*, Montreal and Kingston.

Fredensborg

The Danish-Norwegian frigate and slave ship *Fredensborg* was wrecked on 1 December 1768, at Tromøy, an island off Arendal in southern Norway. The long journey in the 'Triangular' trade route (Europe, Africa and the West Indies), was nearly complete. The crew of twenty-nine men, three passengers and two slaves escaped with their lives. Captain Johan Frantzen Ferentz, and the supercargo, Christian Hoffmann, saved the ship's logbook and other journals. These, together with other documents which are in the national archives in Denmark and Norway, make it possible to follow the course of the frigate from day to day, both during the journey and after the wreck.

Fredensborg, 100 ft (30.5 m) and 278 tons, was built in 1752–53 by the Danish West India

Guinea Company in Copenhagen. On its first journey in the 'Triangular' trade, and during five subsequent journeys to the West-Indies, it sailed under the name of *Cron Prindz Christ-ian*. In 1765, when the Guinea Company replaced the West India-Guinea Company, its name was changed to *Fredensborg*.

The ship weighed anchor in Copenhagen on 24 June, 1767 with forty men on board, and anchored off their main fort, Christians-borg, on the Gold Coast 103 days later. Because of an inadequate supply of slaves *Fre-densborg* remained there for 205 days. This had a very adverse effect on the health of the crew; eleven men died, including the Cap-tain, Espen Kiønig. Loaded with a total of 265 slaves – 165 males, 78 females, 9 girls, and 20 boys – they set course for St. Croix. The ship was also carrying 927,75 kg of ivory,

The three divers who found the wreck of the Fredensborg, bringing an elephant tusk to the surface. (Allan Iversen)

and 1250 g of gold. After a seventy-eight day crossing, the surviving slaves were sold. Twenty-nine had died during the journey.

With a new cargo of sugar, dyewood, mahogany, tobacco, cinnamon, and cotton, *Fredensborg* set off, for Copenhagen. There were three slaves on board, one of whom died before the ship was wrecked.

The wreck of *Fredensborg* was found on 15 September 1974 by three Norwegian divers, Odd. K. Osmundsen, Tore Svalesen, and Leif Svalesen. The site of the search was based on the historical documents found during archival research. Marine expedi-tions were carried out, the first one in 1975 and the second in 1977, conducted by the Norwegian National Maritime Museum and the Aust-Agder-Museum.

Because of the frigate's participation in the 'Triangular' trade, certain objects are of spe-cial interest: those from Africa are elephant and hippopotamus tusks, a single animal joint identified as the leg bone of a water chevrotain, and an African millstone off

Accraian sandstone. Of products which were taken on as cargo in the West Indies there were found a large quantity of dyewood and a little mahogany. Other articles found were many so-called 'slave-pipes', clay pipes of a simple quality which were given to the slaves.

Most of the iron was gone, but there remained several clear imprints of the slaves' leg irons. Among the other articles found were: leather bindings for a bible and a prayer book, weights, empty medicine bot-tles, faunal remains from the ship's provi-sions (cattle, sheep, pig bones), ink pots and remains of Chinese porcelain. Among the items for personal use were shoes, a ker-chief, a whistle, a spur and a spinning top. A small personal chest made of wood con-tained, among other things, two seals and three small sticks of sealing wax. One seal bore the initials TBM with a maquis crown over them. Engraved in the other seal was a dove with an olive branch in its beak; and alongside the dove were the words PEACE AND LOVE.

Fredensborg had nearly completed the 'Tri-angular' route when it sank. The materials recovered from the wreck, in combination with the extensive written material which was saved, give a detailed and vivid picture of the slave trade on all three legs of the journey. L.S.

ADDITIONAL READING

Svalesen, L., 1996, *Slaveskipet Fredensborg Og Den Dansk-Norske Slavehandel På 1700-Tallet*, Oslo.

Frolic

A clipper brig wrecked in 1850 while en route to San Francisco, USA. Built in 1844 in Baltimore for the opium trade, *Frolic* spent several years in the illicit and danger-ous trade. In 1850, the brig was loaded with a speculative cargo of Chinese merchandise and sailed for San Francisco, only to wreck

en route approximately 190 km north of San Francisco on the California coast near Point Cabrillo.

The wreck of *Frolic* lies in approximately 4.5 to 7.5 m of water within 45 m of the shore. The wreck site is principally marked by a mound of kentledge (pig iron) ballast. Three admiralty-style iron anchors lie at the northeast end of the ballast pile at the base of a large rock. A small cast-iron cannon lies near the kentledge; it is badly worn by surf abrasion and the cascabel is missing. A large number of ceramic fragments lie scattered among the kentledge and in the rocks in a spreading pattern moving south from the main concentration of wreckage.

The wreck of *Frolic* was discovered by local sport divers in the early 1960s, who made periodic forays and recovered hundreds of artefacts from the site. Dr Thomas Layton of the Department of Anthropology, San Jose State University, discovered ceramic frag-ments and bottle glass shaped into projectile points during his excavation of Three Chop Village, a Mitom Pomo site, in 1984. The salvage and reutilization of shipwreck mater-ial by native cultures is not uncommon; *Frolic* is one of two California sites (the other is the Manila galleon **San Agustin**, wrecked in 1595), where the phenomenon has been documented.

Tracing the artefacts to *Frolic*, Layton grad-ually gathered the hundreds of artefacts taken from the wreck by divers and began a decade-long research project to analyse the collection and research *Frolic*'s history. The result is the most comprehensive assessment of the construction and career of an opium clipper yet done. Material culture from the wreck gathered from sport divers by Dr Layton includes the full range of the cargo intended for the San Francisco Gold Rush market, including jewellery, a prefabricated house, firearms, porcelain and stoneware, ale bottles, furniture, and the remains of chests of tea, as well as fittings and fasten-ings from the ship and personal effects of the crew.

The wreck site was listed on the **National Reg-ister of Historic Places**, and considerable com-munity interest and involvement sparked by Layton's work resulted in an award-winning unique cooperative project that included museum exhibitions, publications, a dra-matic presentation of *Voices of the Frolic*, and the brewing of a popular 'Frolic Shipwreck Ale'. J.P.D.

ADDITIONAL READING

Delgado, J.P., 1990, *To California By Sea: A Maritime History of the Gold Rush*, Columbia.

Layton, T.N., 1997, *Drug Runner: The Story of the Brig Frolic*, Palo Alto, California.

Gedesby Ship

Wreck of a small clinker-built cargo vessel from the last quarter of the 13th century, excavated by the Danish National Museum in 1990. The ship was found in a former fjord on southern Falster, near the village of Gedesby, which is known from written sources as a port of departure for travellers to northern Germany during the Middle Ages. It had wrecked near the entrance of the fjord and was rapidly covered by thick layers of sand. The ship's length is 12.57 m, with a beam of 5.15 m, and a depth of hold of 1.42 m. About 90 per cent of the original hull elements are preserved, along with parts of the shrouds and five shroud pins from the single mast rigging. The hull was built predominantly of radially split planks, although a few were sawn. It was iron riveted. It has fifteen strakes, but only thirteen are taken all the way to the sternpost, and only fourteen to the stem.

The keel is T-shaped, with vertical, diagonal scarfs to the large, knee-shaped lower parts of the stem and the stern. On the upper part of the stern, the planking covers the stern timber completely. Traces of two gudgeons for a stern rudder were found. The frames consist of asymmetrical floor timbers, joggled over the planking, and lashed with horizontal, diagonal scarfs to the futtocks. The ship had only three crossbeams, none of them preserved. They had protruded through the planking, and were secured with heavy vertical knees. Three stringers, fastened with treenails to futtocks and top timbers, provided some longitudinal strength to the very beamy and round-bottomed hull. Along the keelson were found mats of wattle, embedded in dung from cattle transported in the vessel only a few days before it sank in late summer/early autumn. Other finds included domestic waste (small pieces of leather, small ceramic and brick sherds, bones with cut marks, nut shells) and some pieces of chalk-stone from quarries further north in the Sound.

Middelaldercentret in Nykbing Falster and the **Centre for Maritime Archaeology** at the Danish National Museum have cooperated in the reconstruction, building, and trials of a replica of the Gedesby Ship, named *Agnethe* and launched in 1995. A report on this project is under preparation, while the final publication of the find will appear as a volume in the series Ships and Boats of the North, published by the Centre for Maritime Archaeology. J.B.

ADDITIONAL READING

Bill, J., 1991, *Gedesbyskibet: Middelalderlig skude- og færgefart fra Falster*, Copenhagen.

Bill, J. and Vinner, M., 1995 'The Gedesby Ship Under Sail', *Maritime Archaeology Newsletter from Roskilde, Denmark*, 5, 1–8.

Robinson, D. and Aaby, B., 1994, 'Botanical Analyses from the Gedesby Ship: A Medieval Shipwreck from Falster', *Proceedings of the 9th Meeting of the International Workgroup for Palaeoethnobotany*, Denmark.

Gela Wreck

see **Italy**

Geldermalsen

see **Nanking Cargo Wreck**

Geodesy

The branch of applied mathematics that uses observations and measurements to survey exact positions of points, large areas of the earth, and variations in the earth's gravity, size, and shape. Geodesy has become increasingly important because of rapidly expanding **Geographical Information Systems** (GIS) applications. GIS is a computer system allowing query, display, and manipulation of spatially oriented data sets. Currently, there are several sources for spatial data, such as charts, maps, and remote sensing data. A GIS requires all data to be entered in mapping projection coordinates for computer manipulation. Few programs can use geodetic coordinates. Various data sets may have been collected in different projections; combining these introduces gross systematic error into the GIS. Serious site positioning errors result from using instruments that generate positions in a different projection to that of the original coordinates.

Mapping projections place geographic coordinates on spatial data so that they are in a grid or x,y coordinate system. Each projection, such as Universal Transverse Mercator (UTM), uses one of many geodetic datums. A geodetic datum such as the North American Datum of 1983 (NAD-83) is based on a mathematical model of the earth, an ellipsoid, which is produced though precise measurements of the earth's circumference. Geodetic datum coordinates are curved surface coordinates expressed in latitude and longitude; mapping projection coordinates are based on a flat surface and are expressed as x,y or northing, easting. A mapping projection places the ellipsoidal model's curved surface onto a flat surface to generate x,y coordinates for computer mapping. An example is cutting a basketball so that it lies flat on a table.

Many ellipsoidal models of the earth have been produced, mainly the result of refinements in distance measurement technology. An ellipsoid model requires earth axes measurement, the major at the equator and the minor at the poles. Initial attempts by the Greeks and Egyptians used sun angles; others used star angles and other means. More accurate ellipsoid models stem from recent advances in modern technology, especially satellites.

Two important ellipsoids are Clark's spheroid of 1866 and the Geodetic Reference System of 1980 (GARS-1980). Most US maps since the 1920s use the North American Datum of 1927 (NAD-27), which was based on Clark's spheroid. Cartographers optimized the datum model to make production of continental US coordinate systems easy.

Two important changes have occurred since the 1920s: military interest (a principal technological force) has become global and satellites have made it easy and necessary to measure accurately the earth's axes. In the 1980s two new geodetic datums were devised using the most accurate measurements from the GARS-1980 ellipsoidal model: North American Datum of 1983 (NAD-83) and the World Geodetic System of 1984 (WGS-84), which are equivalent for practical purposes. These datums are becoming the world standard because the **Global Positioning System** (GPS) provides geodetic coordinates in WGS-84.

Cartographic adoption of these new, more accurate geodetic datums required coordinate systems or mapping projections such as Universal Transverse Mercator or state plane to be adjusted to fit the new model. Consequently, one must know the mapping projection and which datum produced a set of coordinates before they can be used successfully. Mixing projections and geodetic datums has caused serious site location error and confusion. There can easily be hundreds of metres difference between the same projection coordinates based on two different datums, and even greater differences between coordinates of differing projections. Software programmes are available that simplify conversions between various datums and projections. T.G.S.

Geographic Information Systems (GIS)

A revolutionary combination of computer hardware and software that allows input, editing, storage, retrieval, viewing, manipulation, comparison, interpretation, analysis, and display of spatially referenced data. Tabular relational databases, geographically referenced maps, and graphics comprise basic GIS data sets to which other digital data such as scanned and rectified historic maps, images, and video may be added. In the past, GIS operation required dedicated workstations; current hardware requirements can be met by most top-level, multitasking personal computers with large data storage capabilities. GIS software is increasingly user friendly and menu driven, making it directly accessible to most researchers.

GIS data sets can be presented as tabular database files or sets of layers or themes that can be generated, analysed, combined, superimposed, and displayed through direct user access in unlimited variations. Data themes are presentations of non-spatial data referenced to a common location expressed as geographic coordinates. One way of looking at themes is to consider them x,y horizontal locations that share a category of variable z values, which represent discrete, quantifiable attributes. Analytical techniques include statistical and spatial analysis, measurement, and comparisons that can be used to create additional themes reflecting analytical results.

GIS can be contrasted with computer assisted design (CAD) systems that are generally limited to graphic output such as drawings, pictures, and maps and contain no relational database capability nor generation of new data sets based upon analytic functions. CAD systems generally contain no interrogative capability and are unable to manipulate non-spatial database attributes.

Archaeology, whose primary interest is the interpretation of material culture through analysis of spatial, temporal, and formal relations, is particularly suited to utilize GIS technology. Much of what archaeologists record is spatially distributed, and much archaeological inference is based on maps of artefacts, architecture, sites, landforms, bathymetry, and other spatial variables. GIS provides a means for systematically accessing large varied geographic data sets from such sources as aerial imagery, geophysical instrument data, historical maps, site files, and other digitized data.

Spatial data can be described as attributes (water depths, magnetic intensities, bottom sediment, etc.) represented as a line, point, or area. There are two ways GIS presents these data – in raster or vector format. Raster GIS divides an area into grid cells and assigns each cell with appropriate data, for instance seabed classification type, which is an example of categorical data. Frequency data, such as number of artefacts, can also be attributed to raster cells. Technically, data

are stored as arc-nodes so that adjoining polygons can share a common boundary.

There are advantages and limitations to both raster and vector methods. Raster's gridded format limits data resolution to cell size and consequently produces inexact borders. However, raster data are particularly well suited for mathematical manipulation and predominate analytical and modelling applications. Most remote sensing data, like satellite imagery, is provided as raster data. Vector GIS with exact borders and points is used to produce high quality maps. Vector data allow precise control of spatial entities, where raster precision is limited to cell size. Multiple data sets are more easily displayed in vector format as multiple polygons, while raster GIS typically displays one data set at a time. Vector data are easily converted to raster format for analytical functions. A GIS ideally should be able to utilize both raster and vector data and convert between formats.

Two problems make the creation of GIS data sets expensive and time consuming: accuracy determination and data conversion of various data sets to an appropriate format. Mixing different levels of accuracy among data sets degrades overall GIS accuracy and gives a false sense of comparability that can lead to serious analytical problems in data interpretation. Data set conversions must consider fundamental geodetic concepts such as geoid, ellipsoid, coordinate system, and projection. **Geodesy** factors vary over time and space, and each variation is critical to conversion accuracy. Few archaeologists record a chart's datum and ellipsoid when generating coordinates. In addition, much maritime archaeology is conducted with arbitrary local grids making conversion inaccurate or impossible. Increasing reliance on **Global Positioning System** (GPS) geodetic coordinates will eventually alleviate conversion problems in generating future data sets.

Programmatic maintenance of GIS databases, which includes revision and incorporation of new data sets, is critical to long-term utility. Users must be able to assume their GIS database is current and correct to avoid combining data of different ages and accuracies. GIS maintenance and utility rely on accurate metadata, which is a description about the data incorporated into the system. Metadata includes such information about data sets as accuracy level, generation date, input date, source, analytical functions, and last update.

Terrestrial archaeologists have been using GIS since the late 1980s when a number of pioneering projects were initiated. Although computers have been used for data collection and storage, there are few examples of

integrated GIS applications in maritime archaeology. An early pre-GIS data collection effort in maritime archaeology using CAD technology and database management software was conducted on HMS *Pandora* site by the Queensland Museum of Northern Australia beginning in 1983. Project data were compiled, analysed, and displayed by computer. AutoCad software was used to collate field data, **Photomosaics**, **Sub-bottom profiler** results, artefact data, and vessel plans, produce computer measurements, and model the site in 3 D.

The US National Park Service **Submerged Cultural Resource Unit**'s survey of **Dry Tortugas National Park** begun in 1992 is the first maritime archaeological investigation to be designed totally as a GIS-based project. This survey and inventory project was designed to produce cumulative multi-disciplinary data necessary for research and long-term management requirements. Databases currently combined in the project GIS include: rectified historic charts and maps, past survey datums, coastlines, terrestrial features, aerial and satellite imagery, metereological and oceanographic data, survey vessel track plots, bathymetry, seabed classification, magnetometry, dive loci, site maps, convergent photogrammetric images, artefact drawings, photographs, video, and text. The databases constitute themes accessible in ESRI's vector-based ArcView. Some themes, particularly those involving rectification and mosaicing, are produced with ERDAS software and ArcCAD.

Some strengths of a GIS-based archaeological field investigation that have been demonstrated by the Dry Tortugas National Park Survey Project are: site stratification and sampling are simplified; surveyed areas containing no cultural material though permanently recorded can be eliminated from further consideration; incoming data provide immediate feedback for field investigations including refinement of target selection criteria based on success rates; daily field decisions can be made on cumulative data; holes in data collection become obvious during field operations; environmental and historical data are easily integrated into field decisions; rapid computer analysis facilitates measurement of variables, allowing examination of relationships that would otherwise be impossible; and archaeological associations in multi-site locales are easier to establish. Project data will be available to natural and cultural resource managers, park interpreters, and researchers through the GIS and, ultimately, portions will be available to park visitors through on-site, touch-screen computers.

GIS offers a remarkable tool for maritime and underwater archaeology, and it will ultimately affect the practice of the discipline. Along with this new tool, however, come some potential problems that should be considered in its application. There are in fact four components of the GIS system: hardware, data, software, and, as some have termed it, 'greyware' – the brains of the people involved with the system. Like any technology, it should be approached thoughtfully and critically; it is not neutral but occurs in a social context and its use has social implications. The assumptions and geographic models of GIS must be understood by researchers, and it must be directly accessible and not dependent upon a technician for data manipulation.

A liability of GIS is that one can easily be very impressed with the technology and its visually stunning products and ignore its limitations. The scientific process of archaeology can be subsumed to GIS parameters, for example, data availability driving analysis rather than data collection driven by research questions derived from theory. Debates about differing archaeological interpretations could be influenced by GIS' visual elegance rather than substance. Inaccurate data sets seamlessly combine with ones produced through faulty analytic procedures to generate graphics that are indistinguishable from those of superior positional and analytic accuracy. Digital data and GIS software rely upon Boolean mathematics, which influences the nature of questions, data, and inferences, which tends to emphasize empirical fit rather than archaeological testing. Some archaeological inferences may not be reducible to the assumptions, spatial algorithms, and models inherent in current GIS software. For example, concepts such as 'near' and 'many' are not easily handled; site characteristics are much more easily examined than relations between sites. Like any tool, its appropriateness to addressing archaeological problems must be determined by a well-informed archaeologist. L.E.M.

ADDITIONAL READING

Allen, K.M.S., Green, S.W., and Zubrow, E.B.W., 1990, *Interpreting Space: GIS and Archaeology*, London.

Antenucci, J., 1991, *Geographic Information Systems: A Guide to the Technology*, New York.

Matuire, D., Goodchild, M., and Rhind, D., 1991, *Geographic Information Systems: Principles and Applications*, New York.

Tomlin, C.D., 1990, *Geographic Information Systems and Cartographic Modelling*, Englewood Cliffs, New Jersey.

Geophysical instruments
see **Remote sensing**

CSS *Georgia*

A Confederate ironclad built in 1862 and deployed as part of the Savannah Squadron of the Confederate States Navy until December 1864. Intentionally sunk, the vessel has remained relatively intact except where damaged by harbour development activities. An archaeological and electronic instrumental survey of the wreck site was begun in 1979 and continued at yearly intervals until

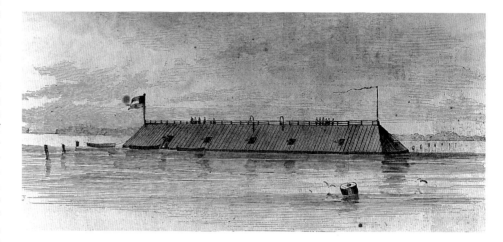

The ironclad Georgia *off Savannah, Georgia. Engraving published in* Harper's Weekly, *1863. (US Naval Historical Center)*

1984. The survey resulted in: (1) the positive identification of the site as that of CSS *Georgia*; (2) a distributional map of exposed features of the site, most notably the armoured casemate; and (3) data to augment the paucity of historical information on the vessel's specific dimensions. Other elements of the study were the analysis and conservation of recovered structural materials and artefacts.

CSS *Georgia* was essentially a floating battery – a barge-type structure roofed over with wood at an inclined angle and then covered with railroad iron cladding. Such ironclads were, according to various historical accounts, also described as 'floating forts'. One observer of the CSS *Georgia* called it 'an ironplated monster à la Merrimac'. The construction of CSS *Georgia* sprang out of the enthusiasm generated by the clash of the CSS *Virginia* and USS **Monitor** at Hampton Roads, March 1862. No definite date is documented for the beginning of her construction but special orders given by Major General Henry Jackson suggest a probable date somewhere between 20 February and 3 March 1862.

From examining various documentary

sources for architectural data, it is obvious that confusion exists concerning the vessel's dimensions. Variously the vessel is reported to have been between 150 to 250 ft (46 to 76 m) long. Very little has been found relevant to its other structural details. Depictions of the vessel survive which illustrate it above the waterline only. No plans were ever drawn, and CSS *Georgia*'s shape and dimensions below the waterline may only be guessed for the present, as the historical records are anything but conclusive. As to its power plant, the supposition that its engines came from the burnt-out wooden steamer *William Jenkins* (1,011 tons) is a tenable one.

Archaeologically it has been possible to characterize the zero visibility wreck site in some detail. The small suite of artefacts, including 6.4 in (163 mm) Brooke and 9 in (229 mm) Dahlgren ordnance recovered during the archaeological survey, clearly indicates that the vessel is CSS *Georgia*.

Magnetometric, bathymetric, sonar, and artefactal data all converge to give a reliable estimate as to the extent of the wreckage. The vessel's orientation still remains a mystery as no key indicators such as funnel, pilot house, rudder, or propeller have been identified. The location of the recovered portside 32 lb rifled gun does support an orientation with bow upstream. This interpretation relies heavily on the original deployment of this gun in the vessel's battery and may not reflect the late 1864 placement of the reduced number (five versus the original ten) of guns known for that time. An attempt to model the wreck site instrumentally has met with mixed success. Computer graphics and image enhancement have filled in large gaps in our understanding of the site, but equally large gaps in archaeological detail remain.

Large timbers (30–60 cm in diameter) protrude from the sand and extend well below the present bottom. No evidence of the vessel's machinery, boilers, or engines has been found; they are believed to be still buried within the remains of the hull. Thanks to archaeology, conflicting reports on her length and breadth can more confidently be evaluated: these varied between 150 and 260 ft (45 and 80 m) for her length, and 50 and 60 ft (15 and 18 m) for her breadth. The observed shape and size of the casemate sections agree well with the two published drawings of the vessel and with most contemporaneous reports that attribute a length of 150 ft (45 m) to the vessel. A width of 50 ft (15 m) giving a length to breadth ratio of 3:1 seems reasonable.

CSS *Georgia* floated for twenty months on the Savannah River, moored near Elba Island where, if the situation required, its broadside could be brought to bear on either channel of the river. On 20 December 1864, the city of Savannah was evacuated and CSS *Georgia* was scuttled, making its resting spot for the next century and more on the bed of the Savannah River. The vessel was considered a 'failure' by some and termed a 'mud tub' and a 'marine abortion' by others. Imperfect and often disappointing vessels as they were, the simple presence of such ironclads prevented many a Union thrust at Southern ports. Today protected as a listed historic site on the **National Register of Historic Places**, it is hoped that CSS *Georgia* will be the subject of more extensive and systematic archaeological studies so that our knowledge of this unique type of vessel can be increased. E.G.

ADDITIONAL READING

Johnson, R.U. and Buel, C.C. (eds), 1962, *Battles and Leaders of the Civil War*, New York.

Kollack, S.M., (ed.), 1950, 'Kollack Letters', *Georgia Historical Quarterly*, 34 (Sept), 36–62, 241–3.

Lytle, W.M. and Holdcamper, F.R., 1975, *Merchant Steam Vessels of the United States, 1790–1868*, Staten Island, New York.

Nordoff, C., 1863, 'Two Weeks at Port Royal', *Harper's New Weekly Magazine*, 27, 115–16.

Scharf, J.T., 1887, *History of the Confederate States Navy*, vols 1 and 2, New York.

Stephens, H., 1985, 'CSS *Georgia*: Memory and Calling', *American Neptune*, 45, 191–8.

Still, W.N., Jr, 1961, 'Confederate Naval Strategy: The Ironclad', *Journal of Southern History*, 27, 330–43.

Still, W.N., Jr, 1971, *Iron Afloat: The Story of the Confederate Armorclads*, Nashville.

Gibraltar

see 'Battering' Ships of Gibraltar

Giglio Wreck

A pre-Classical wreck off the island of Giglio in the Tuscan Archipelago, found in 1961 by Mr Reg Vallintine. The remains of the vessel were situated in 45 to 55 m of water at the base of an offshore reef known as Secca i Pignocchi in Campese Bay on the northwest side of the island. Vallintine alerted the authorities but was unable to prevent the plunder of the site that followed. The following year Vallintine covered over what was still visible of the wreck and left the island. In 1981 Mensun Bound, then a graduate

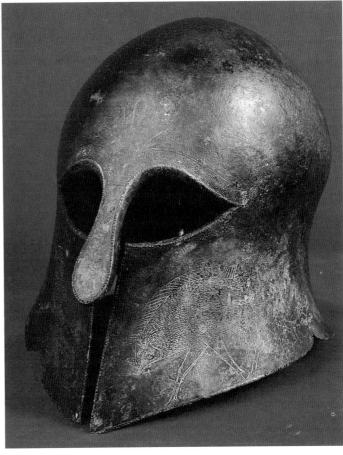

The bronze helmet from the Giglio Wreck, after conservation. (Oxford University MARE)

student at the University of Oxford, by chance spotted in somebody's house one of the items (an Etruscan amphora handle) that had been looted from the wreck in 1961. Recognizing its importance, Bound made enquiries and was put in contact with Vallintine who confirmed the details of his discovery and gave him photographs of some of the material that had been raised. From the photographs it was evident that the vessel had been carrying a mixed cargo of luxury and utilitarian goods and could be dated to soon after 600 BC, making this the earliest known wreck from the Greek post-Dark Ages.

Bound spent a year tracing people who

had been on the island to establish whether they had artefacts or further useful information. In particular he was anxious to locate a bronze helmet that had been sketched by Vallintine in his dive log before it had been taken from the island. The helmet was eventually traced to Germany. The original marine deposits had been removed to reveal beautifully etched charging boars on the cheeks and snakes across the brows. Other early pottery finds from the wreck were traced to Monaco (a Corinthian *kothon*), the United States (an Etruscan amphora), and England (a Lakonian *aryballos*, two bucchero *kantharoi* and a Samian amphora). With this assembled proof of the vessel's importance, licenses were granted by the Italian authorities to conduct an archaeological search and survey.

In 1982 Bound lead an expedition to Giglio with Vallintine as chief diver. The wreck was eventually found in the interface zone at the foot of the reef. Excavation proper began in 1983 and continued until 1986. All work was in collaboration with the Superintendency of Archaeology for Tuscany.

The finewares consisted mainly of

Corinthian, Lakonian, Ionian, and Etruscan fabrics. Of particular interest were the Corinthian *oinochoae* (jugs) which were decorated with animal friezes, and a range of small round pots known as *aryballoi* that were painted with combating warriors, flo-

fittings, and copper and lead ingots. A series of arrowheads raises interesting questions regarding the defensive capability of the vessel. A series of iron bars and copper nuggets, together with nodules of unworked amber, may have functioned as currency.

Left: Diver with painted Etruscan pot from the Giglio Wreck. (Oxford University MARE)

Right: Recovering a copper ingot from the Giglio Wreck. (Oxford University MARE)

rals, animals, and mythological motifs. The Lakonian ware consisted of beakers, wine mixing craters and *aryballoi* that were mostly painted with banded or geometric patterning. The Etruscan pottery consisted of buchero *kantharoi* (chalices) and an *aryballos* with boars painted in a manner imitative of current Corinthian styles. The amphoras were of Etruscan, Samian, East Greek, and Punic-Phoenician origin. The Etruscan amphoras were of both flat and round bottomed type and contained olives and pitch. They were sealed with pinewood discs and there was evidence that some of them had been recycled. The Samian amphoras almost certainly contained olive oil, while the East Greek forms most likely contained wine. Several lamps were also found, two of which were charred at their beaks thus indicating a shipboard role.

Metal finds included fishing weights, ship's

Organic remains included gaming bones, a wooden writing plaque, an elaborately carved wooden lid, fragments of inlaid furniture, and a number of musical pipes (*auloi*). A unique insight into the technical capability of the times came from a pair of boxwood calipers that were of similar design to the modern instrument, with one fixed and one sliding jaw. Traces of incised lettering proved to be of Greek origin.

A well-defined line of artefacts marked the trajectory of the sinking ship. The trail began beneath the edge of the reef where the vessel had struck and ended up at 50 m where the remains of the vessel's keel and some associated planking were found. The keel was of oak; the planks were of pine. The vessel was found to be assembled with monocot cord which threaded through diagonal holes across the seam. The inboard side of the holes featured a triangular notch.

Once the seams had been stitched the holes were jammed and sealed with wooden inserts. This technique, which is reflected in the later **Bon Porté** and Gela ships, has been called the GBG technique. Questions regarding the source of the technique have not yet been solved; compelling arguments can be made for both a north central and western Mediterranean origin.

In broad terms the Giglio Ship is important for the information it provides on early deep water ship construction and for the insight it gives on the Hellenization of Etruria. The material from the wreck went on display at the National Archaeological Museum of Florence in 1994. The excavation of the Giglio Ship led directly to the formation of **Oxford University MARE**, which, since Giglio, has gone on to survey and excavate wrecks all over the world from South America to Southeast Asia. M.B.

ADDITIONAL READING
Bound, M., 1985, 'Il relitto arcarco di Giglio Campes: L'indagine, *Archaeologia Viva* 4, 12, 52-65.
Bound, M., 1986, 'Il relitto arcaico di Giglio Campese: il recipero', *Archaeologia Viva*, 5, 1, 48–63.
Bound, M., 1991, *The Giglio Wreck: A Wreck of the Archaic Period (c.600 BC) off the Tuscan Island of Giglio*, suppl. 1 to *Enalia*, Athens.
Bound, M. and Vallintine, R., 1983, 'A Wreck of Possible Etruscan Origin off Giglio Island', *International Journal of Nautical Archaeology*, 12, 2, 113–22.

USS *Gilliam*

see **Crossroads wrecks**

Girona

Spanish Armada galleass lost on Lacada Point, near the Giant's Causeway in County Antrim, Northern Ireland, on 26 October 1588. The four galleasses that sailed with the Armada came from Naples, and were hybrid warships which combined the weight and armament of a galleon with the oar-given mobility of a galley. But the design was beset with problems, particularly with respect to their awkwardly hung rudders, and only one survived the campaign unscathed. Before they left Lisbon their Mediterranean-style lateen rig was replaced by a square rig more appropriate to Atlantic sailing, and superficially at least they were formidable vessels, each displacing some 600 tonnes and mounting an armament of fifty guns, some of them extremely large.

On the voyage back to Spain, *Girona* was forced by damage and stress of weather to put into Killibegs, on the west coast of Ireland, to make repairs. While there she was joined by the surviving crews of two other Armada ships wrecked in the vicinity. Their leader was Don Alonso de Leiva, a personal favourite of Philip II. Leiva had gathered around him the flower of Spanish aristocracy in his 820 ton ship *Rata Encoronada*, and had been in the thick of the fighting throughout the campaign. *Rata* was wrecked in Blacksod Bay, County Mayo. Leiva brought his men ashore and marched to where another Armada ship, the hulk *Duquesa Santa Ana*, was sheltering at anchor. Eventually, *Duquesa* set sail, only to be stranded in Loughros Mor Bay, Donegal. In coming to shore, Don Alonso was injured, and had to be carried in a litter, but he nevertheless led the combined ships' crews to Killibegs where he took charge of the repaired *Girona*.

Eventually all three crews – amounting to some 1,300 men in all – crammed themselves into the patched-up galleass and headed for neutral Scotland. But off Antrim the jury rudder broke, and the ship was driven onto the jutting fang of Lacada Point. There was only a handful of survivors.

Girona's remains were discovered by Robert Stenuit in 1967, and over the following two years he excavated the complex gully system around Lacada Point. In this extremely high energy zone, no structural remains had survived, but the heavier material – mostly objects of gold and silver – had worked its way through the mobile sediments to stabilize in the deepest fissures. The recoveries included more than a thou-

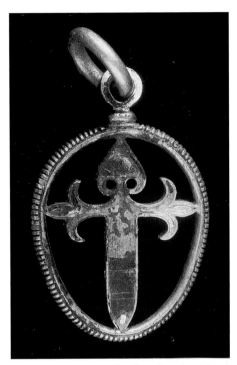

Cross of the Order of Santiago, from Girona. *It may have belonged to Don Alonso de Leiva, Commander Designate of the Spanish Armada. (Ulster Museum, Belfast)*

sand coins, and a remarkable collection of Renaissance jewellery and knightly orders. One of these – the insignia of a knight of Santiago – almost certainly belonged to Don Alonso de Leiva himself, while another – the cross of a knight of Malta – may have been the property of the ship's captain, Fabricio Spinola. The remaining finds, which are much broken and abraded, include three pieces of bronze artillery. The material is preserved in the Ulster Museum, Belfast, and the site is now a protected historic wreck. C.M.

ADDITIONAL READING
Stenuit, R., 1972, *Treasures of the Armada*, Newton Abbot, Devon.

GIS

see **Geographic Information Systems**

Global Positioning System (GPS)

Twenty-four US Department of Defense satellites orbiting the earth at a height of about 20,000 km every twelve hours that transmit signals used for ranging to develop an accurate position on the earth's surface. Satellite position and time information transmitted by these space vehicles are used by GPS receivers to trilaterate an unambiguous location on the earth. Receivers measure the time interval between the transmission of a signal and its reception on earth from at least three, preferably four or more, satellites to generate an accurate position.

GPS, originally developed for military purposes, provides continuous, real-time, three-dimensional (position and elevation) coverage anywhere on earth. The current system produces reliable, repeatable information that is unaffected by rough seas and bad weather, and is highly resistant to multipath errors and interference. (A similar system, known as GLONASS, was developed by the Russians.) Commercial GPS receivers became available to civilian users in 1984; the first hand-held receivers appeared in 1989.

The satellites broadcast on two carrier frequencies in the 'L-band' of the electromagnetic spectrum. One is the 'L1' or 1575.42 MHz and the other is 'L2' or 1227.6 MHz. On these carrier frequencies are broadcast codes, much like a radio or television station broadcasts information on their channels (frequencies). Satellites broadcast two codes, a military-only encrypted code known as Precise Positioning Service (PPS) and a civil-access or Standard Positioning Service (SPS) code.

All commercial and consumer GPS receivers are SPS receivers. There are two basic types of SPS receivers, those that use code to produce positions (code-phase), and those that use carrier measurements (carrier-phase). PPS, Precision-code or 'P-code' receivers use the P-code broadcast on the L1 and L2 carrier frequencies for positioning. These receivers are only available to the military and some US government agencies. Some autonomous PPS receivers produce 4 m accuracy.

Positional accuracies for the code-phase, resource grade, or C/A-code (coarse acquisition) receivers range from 100 m to less than 2 m. Carrier-phase receivers (commonly called geodetic receivers) provide post-processed positions within millimetres. Positional accuracy for both types of receivers strongly depends on a process called 'differential correction' (DGPS), which requires multiple receivers or receiver/transmitter configurations. The US Department of

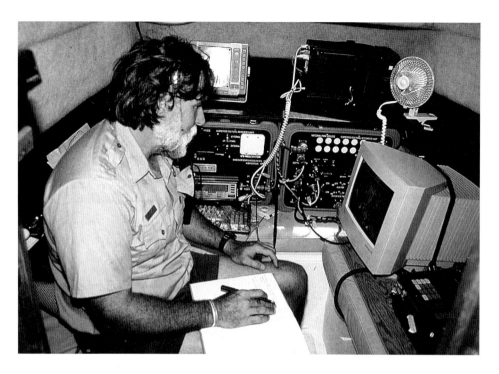

Surveying using Global Positioning System. (NPS/Tim Smith)

Defense maintains control over autonomous receiver accuracies through selective availability (SA), an information degradation procedure that produces intentional errors. With SA implemented, civilian receivers will receive information adequate for positioning within 100 m at a confidence level of 95 per cent. To achieve greater accuracies, one must have a procedure for limiting SA and other errors in GPS positional data, which makes differential corrections necessary.

Differential corrections are achieved by using two GPS receivers, one collecting data on a stable, geodetic point (base station), and one collecting mobile positioning data. Most SA and atmospheric errors are removed by mathematically comparing the two receiver files in a computer post-processing program. Differential corrections can also be transmitted by a radio modem to a receiver so that real-time corrections can be calculated for mobile operations such as surveying, although accuracy is less than post-processed DGPS. Differential corrections are available from many sources, for example from a portable base station, from commercial suppliers through a subscription service, or from the US Coast Guard radio beacon service, all of which supply real-time corrections. Accuracy depends upon equipment and the nature of corrections. DGPS typically provides 1–10 m accuracy. Currently, the most accurate positioning is supplied by Real-Time Kinematic (RTK) receivers, which are capable of centimetre accuracy for moving positions.

GPS has already proved itself as a revolutionary technology and is being used in many underwater and maritime archaeology applications. Receiver costs have dropped precipitously, making GPS the system of choice for navigation and surveying operations in maritime and underwater archaeology. GPS positions have made incorporation of **Geographic Information Systems** technology feasible at virtually any level of modern field-work. L.E.M., T.G.S.

Gokstad Ship

Early 10th-century AD inhumation ship burial found at Gokstad farm, Vestfold, southern Norway. Fragments of a male skeleton were found in the ship with three small boats, a sled, a copper cauldron with iron chain, the wooden parts of a tent, several beds, wooden buckets, a gaming board for two different games, one of them nine men's morris, a horse harness, and other artefacts. Horses, dogs, and a peacock were sacrificed for the burial. A tent-shaped wooden burial chamber was constructed on board. The burial was plundered in antiquity, but it seems certain that the dead man was laid in the burial chamber, which also contained a number of the smaller artefacts. Most male burials from the Norwegian Viking Age contain arms. They are lacking at Gokstad, and this may indicate that the grave-robbers were at work fairly soon after the burial, when the arms were still serviceable and of interest to the robbers.

The mound was excavated in 1880. The excavation was started by the landowner, but the professional archaeologist Nicolay Nicolaysen led the work for most of the time. Local tradition had long believed that the 'King's Mound', as it was called, contained fabulous treasures. The mound is situated on low-lying land near the Viking Age shore-line, and the ship must have been transported a short distance overland from the beach to the burial site.

After the excavation, the ship and other grave goods were taken by sea to Oslo and placed in a temporary building. In 1930 the find was moved to the Viking Ship Museum, and the ship was restored. Analysis of the skeleton shows that the man was about sixty years old at the time of death, and that he was nearly disabled by arthritis. The very rich grave shows that the dead man must have belonged to the highest level of Viking Age society. It has been suggested that he may be Olav Geirstada-Alv, who is mentioned as a member of the Ynglinge dynasty by Snorri Sturlusson in *Heimskringla*, the saga of the Norwegian Kings. According to Snorri, he was king of southern Vestfold, and the uncle of Harald Fairhair, who united Norway. Modern historians tend to reject Snorri as a reliable historical source for this early period, and the combination of archaeology and early written sources is problematic. Even if the 'Gokstad chieftain' remains anonymous, he must have definitely belonged to the ruling class.

Recent dating by dendrochronology places the felling of the timber for the ship at *c.* AD 895 and timber for the burial chamber *c.* AD 900–905. The dates are accepted as the building date for the ship and the date of burial respectively, as Viking wood-workers used unseasoned wood according to all available evidence.

Until the Skuldelev find from Denmark, excavated in 1962, gave examples of other ship types from the late Viking Age (see **Skuldelev ships**), the Gokstad Ship has been widely published as a 'type specimen' Viking ship. The ship is probably of a type called 'karve' or 'karfi' in the Old Norse sources. Such ships were the personal travelling vessels of kings and nobility, adaptable to war, travel, or trade with luxury goods as the situation demanded. The Gokstad Ship is an important source for the study of shipbuilding history and the evolution of ships in the clinker area of northern Europe. Thanks to a number of well-preserved boat and ship finds, we can follow this evolution from the 3rd-century BC **Hjortspring Boat** from Denmark, via the Iron Age rowing ships from Nydam (see **Nydam Boat**) in Denmark, **Sutton Hoo** in

England, and Kvalsund in Norway, to the Viking Age and well into the Middle Ages. In small boats, the tradition is still alive. The three small boats found with the ship had been broken to pieces as part of the burial ritual. Two of them have been reconstructed. The smaller, four-oared boat, 6.5 m long, is remarkably like boats still built in western Norway; information from traditional boatbuilders is an important source for the study of ancient ships in Norway.

The backbone of the Gokstad Ship is a sturdy keel, made from a large oak log. Short intermediate pieces are riveted to the end of the keel as a transition to the naturally curved stems. The keel has a slight curve, so the deepest point is amidships, below the mast-step. In a long-keeled ship like Gokstad, the curve in the keel makes the ship easier to turn when tacking against the wind. The keel is T-shaped in cross section, the stems rabbeted for the plank ends. Sixteen strakes on each side are fastened together with iron nails riveted over square iron roves. The bottom strakes are about 2.5 cm thick. The tenth strake is thicker and wedge-shaped, and forms the transition from bottom to topsides. Above it follow three more 2.5 cm thick strakes, then a nearly 4 cm thick strake with the oar-holes, and two light topstrakes, only *c.* 1.6 cm thick. An important structural detail is the use of cleats on the planking, left in place on the second to eighth strakes at 1 m intervals as the shipwrights cut the planks to shape from oversize stock. The planking material was split radially from large oak logs. The first strake is riveted to the second strake and the keel, but not connected to the ribs. The ribs rest on the top surface of the keel, but they are not fastened to it. The ribs below the waterline were lashed to the planking through holes in the cleats. A narrow lath worked on the underside of the ribs has holes corresponding to those in the cleats. The rib lashings of the Gokstad Ship are of birch or spruce roots. The result is a light and flexible hull. The skipper of a replica ship which sailed across the North Atlantic in 1893 reported that the top strakes twisted up to 15 cm as the ship moved with the waves.

Gokstad is so far the youngest ship found with lashed ribs. The early 11th-century Skuldelev vessels have ribs that are cut to fit the planking closely and the fastenings are treenails. In the Gokstad Ship the ends of the ribs rest on a low triangular cleat on the ninth strake and are let into the underside of the crossbeams wich rest against the ninth and tenth strakes. The beams are rabbeted for loose deckboards. The six strakes above the beams are supported by naturally grown knees standing on the beams and short top ribs. Above the ninth strake, the fastenings between ribs and planking are treenails and rivets instead of the lashings used below the waterline. The thicker fourteenth strake is pierced for sixteen oar ports on each side. Small lids on the inside close the oar ports against spray when the ship is under sail. A sturdy inwale along the upper edge of the sixteenth strake strengthens the hull. The ship has seventeen ribs with crossbeams. Triangular bulkhead-like ribs fore and aft give added strength to the stem areas; these ribs are not lashed, but nailed to the planking. The aft rib also supports the side rudder. Outside the mast-step area, the crossbeams are supported in the middle by a stanchion resting on the rib. When compared to the older **Oseberg Ship**, Gokstad has a higher freeboard and a more seaworthy hull shape. The dimensions are *c.* 24 m total length, 5.2 m maximum beam amidships, 2.2 m height from underside keel to top of sheerstrake amidships. The original stem tops were destroyed by rot, but there is no evidence for dragon heads or other stem decorations. The restored ship has been given neutral, pointed stem tops.

The mast was supported by a 4 m long keelson, mortised to fit over four ribs and supported sideways by knees standing on the ribs. A mast partner resting on five of the crossbeams gave added support at deck level. The mast can be raised and lowered as the mast partner has a long slit opening aft. When the mast is upright, the slit can be closed by a heavy block of oak. A short fragment of the mast was in place when the ship was found. It has been suggested that the support is sufficiently strong for sailing without standing rigging to support the mast. This is not probable, however, as all contemporary illustrations of ships show ropes supporting the mast, and experience with sailing replicas clearly indicates that standing rigging is necessary. It is uncertain how the standing rigging was fastened: rigging details found in the ship are three pairs of cleats aft, presumably for securing running rigging used to handle the sail. Just forward of the mast, there is a block of wood at deck level on each side of the ship. The blocks are securely fastened to two knees, and have two sockets cut into the upper surface. The sockets probably held the butt end of a spar used to spread the foot of the sail when tacking against the wind. The old Norse *beitiass* may be the name of such a spar. One replica built in 1892 and two from recent years have been rigged with single square sails of *c.* 100 to 120 sq. m With a sail of this size, the replicas have proved to be fast, to tack well, and to be seaworthy enough to sail the North Atlantic in summer. During the excavation large fragments of decayed woollen cloth with red stripes sewn on was found. It is uncertain whether this is sail-cloth or was intended for the tent. Medieval written sources indicate that most sails were made of wool, and replica experiments have shown that wool from primitive sheep can be used to produce sailcloth of good quality.

When found, the ship had thirty-two shields placed along each side. The shields were fragmentary, but the excavator reported that they were painted, black and yellow shields alternating. Traces of yellow and black colour were also found on the carved heads which decorate the boards forming the gables of the tents. The carved animal head on the tiller was also decorated with black,

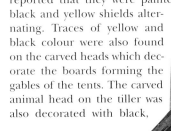

*The Gokstad ship.
(Courtesy Universitets Oldskamling, Oslo)*

yellow, and red. The top strake of the ship has a decoration of fine lines, cut with a knife point to form equal-sided triangles all along the strake. The thin lines would be nearly invisible on their own. The triangular fields may have been painted, probably in the same colours as the shields, yellow and black. A fragmentary boat find from western Norway had remains of similar decorations, and ships with decorated upper strakes are known from medieval ship pictures. A.E.C.

ADDITIONAL READING

Dammann, W., 1989, *Das Gokstadschiff und seine boote*, Heidesheim.

Nicolaysen, N., 1882, *The Viking-ship Discovered at Gokstad in Norway*, Oslo.

Wexelsen, E. (ed.), 1979–80, *Centenary of a Norwegian Viking Find: The Gokstad Excavations*, Sandefjord.

Goldcliff boat fragment
see Severn Wrecks

Grace Dieu

Warship built by Henry V of England, subsequently beached and burned on the banks of the River Hamble, Hampshire after a twenty-one–year career, and periodically excavated and studied since 1874 by antiquarians, historians, and archaeologists. *Grace Dieu*, a two-masted carrack, was laid down in 1416 and launched in 1418 at Southampton. The vessel was the largest northern European warship built up to that time. Reconstruction of the hull on paper suggests an original length of 125 ft (38.1 m) at the keel, 180 ft (54.9 m) overall, and a 50 ft (15.24 m) beam. *Grace Dieu* was rated at 1,400 tons, and a 1430 description by Luca di Maso degli Albizzi, a Florentine naval officer, noted that the ship towered about 16 m above the water.

Grace Dieu was fitted with a towering forecastle, which allowed fighting men, particularly bowmen, to fight another ship after grappling from the advantage of height. *Grace Dieu* was built in response to French naval raids on the English coast. Henry V mounted an effective naval response with a large fleet of small vessels supported by a handful of great ships, and by 1417, while *Grace Dieu* was still under construction, had won naval supremacy in the English Channel.

Grace Dieu made one short voyage in 1420, sailing from Southhampton only 20 miles before a mutiny forced the ship's captain, the Earl of Devon, to put into St Helen's on the Isle of Wight. The crew refused to sail, and *Grace Dieu* was towed to the River Hamble and laid up in reserve. The mainmast was pulled in 1431. In 1433 the ship was moved further upstream to a fenced mud-berth above Burlesdon. In January 1439 a lightning strike set the hulk on fire and burned it out.

The remains of the vessel were gradually buried in mud, although a portion of the wreck was visible during low spring tides. The wreck was first mentioned in mid-19th-century accounts, and an 1859 directory noted the 'timbers of an ancient vessel . . . supposed to have been burnt by the Saxons'. In 1874 and in 1899 the Bursledon Wreck, as the site was known, was excavated by antiquarians and timbers were removed by blasting, some of them for souvenirs.

Dr R.C. Anderson and Mr F.C. Prideaux Naish, undertook a survey of the wreck in March and October 1933; their work led to the identification of the wreck as *Grace Dieu*.

In 1970 the University of Southampton bought the wreck from the Ministry of Defence for £5; and in 1973 the site was designated as 'historic' under the Protection of Wrecks Act (1973). From 1980 to 1985 the site was investigated, underwater and at low water, by the Archeological Research Centre of the National Maritime Museum, Greenwich. The extent of the wreck was established and the outline structure recorded: environmental changes due to deposition of silts and to erosion were monitored; and the state of the timbers exposed at low water was noted and degradation assessed.

Only the bottom of the hull now survives, a metre or so above the keel; in plan the remains reasure *c*. 40 × 12 m. *Grace Dieu* was built in the Nordic ('Viking') tradition, but on a grand scale, with triple-thickness planking caulked with moss and tar, fastened through the overlaps by anils more than 0.22 m in length. The closely-spaced framing timbers were fastened to the planking by treenails *c*. 38 mm in diameter. *Grace Dieu* was one of the last large ships to be built in this way. J.P.D., S.M.

ADDITIONAL READING

Clarke, R. et al., 1993, 'Recent Work on the River Hamble Wreck near Bursledon, Hampshire', *International Journal of Nautical Archaeology*, 22, 21–44.

Friel, I., 1993, 'Henry V's Grace Dieu and the Wreck in the River Hamble near Bursledon, Hampshire', *International Journal of Nautical Archaeology*, 22, 3–19.

McGrail, S., 1993, 'The Future of the Designated Wreck Site in the River Hamble', *International Journal of Nautical Archaeology*, 22, 45–51.

Prynne, M.W., 1968, 'Henry V's Grace Dieu', *The Mariner's Mirror*, 54, 2 (May), 115–28.

Graf Spee
see Admiral Graf Spee

Grand Congloué

Multiple shipwreck site named after a rocky island situated between Marseille and Cassis in southern **France**. The site was discovered by divers during the construction of a sewer outlet, and first reported in 1948 by Christianini. It was excavated by J.-Y. Cousteau and F. Benoît from 1952 to 1957, and then by Y. Girault in 1961. The site lies at the foot of a cliff at the northeastern point of the island, covers an area 28 by 8 m, and ranges from 32 to 45 m in depth. It was a pioneering project in which numerous techniques were established for underwater excavation, such as the employment of divers using scuba gear, the use of **Airlifts** to remove sand and sediment, and balloons to lift heavy artefacts to the surface. This equipment is now considered standard on many underwater excavations.

Benoît was never certain, despite hundreds of dives, whether he was dealing with one ancient shipwreck or with at least two wrecks, one nearly on top of the other. Even before his report was published in 1961, controversy was raised concerning the presence of materials from different time periods. The French Mediterranean coast alone provided several examples of areas with many wrecks in close proximity to each other. For example, eleven wrecks are known from the area around the reef of **La Chrétienne** and at Cap **Dramont** near Saint Raphaël, and seven wrecks are recorded around the island of Planier, off Marseille. Even nearly juxtaposed wrecks are not unique phenomena: Pointe Lequin, near the island of Porquerolles, and L'Anse des Laurons include superimposed shipwrecks.

L. Long's study of Benoît's excavation notes established conclusively that the site of Grand Congloué comprised two shipwrecks, one carrying amphoras predominantly of Greco-Italic type, and the second carrying Roman amphoras. These materials, chronologically distinct, were clearly separated by a stratified layer of wooden hull remains interpreted by Cousteau and Benoît as the ship's deck. However, descriptions and sketches of these remains in the excavation reports show that they in fact represent the hull of a second ship, and that they were mistaken by its excavators for deck planking of the earlier ship. This was despite its sheathing underneath with lead, a practice reserved only for the exterior surface of hulls. Even the disposition of the cargoes indicated that two vessels were involved: the earlier Greco-Italic materials were situated to the northeast and aligned with the hull remains of the lower wreck, while the later Roman materials were generally scattered more to the southwest.

The earlier wreck contained about thirty Rhodian amphoras in two sizes, seven amphoras from the Cyclades, over four hundred Greco-Italic amphoras in two sizes, some of which bore the stamp TI.Q.IVENTI., approximately seven thousand pieces of black glazed table ware of the Campana A class in about thirty shapes including three oil lamps, containers for fragrant oils, and fragments of Ampurian Gray pottery. These materials date the wreck to the last decade of the 3rd century BC. The cargo suggests that the ship started its voyage from Greece, Rhodes, or Delos, and stopped at several ports in Italy before continuing on towards Marseille.

The later wreck is dated to the very end of the 2nd or beginning of the 1st century BC. It contained at least 1,500 long Roman amphoras stacked in three layers. They are similar to examples from the Grand Ribaud A wreck. Most were stamped on their rim with SES, the presumed abbreviated form of the name SESTIUS followed by an anchor, trident, and in one case by a vegetal motif. It has been suggested that the name Sestius be identified with the family that, according to literary sources, owned vast landholdings near Cosa in Etruria, where many amphoras with the Sestius stamp have been found. Other amphoras were stamped DAV.ATEC on their shoulder, while about twenty bore no stamps at all. Several stoppers found inside unspecified amphoras were stamped C.TITI.C.F. All of the amphoras were believed to have been carrying wine, as they were lined with resin. Campanian B and C fine wares were also recovered along with two Punic amphoras and ceramic fragments with moulded Hellenistic decoration, known as Megarian bowls. Similar Punic amphoras were found in association with Roman jars from one of the Dramont shipwrecks, and at Fos-sur-mer.

Some of the artefacts recovered cannot be attributed to either wreck. Among them are roof tiles, a *mortarium* (a basin in which mortar is made), a copper helmet, copper and iron tools, two lead anchor stocks, lead fishnet sinkers, other assorted lead objects, and lead and olive wood rings that may be part of the ship's rigging.

Although both hulls were extensively preserved, only five frames and portions of the keel and planking, presumably all from the later wreck, were raised for study. They reveal that the planks were edge-fastened with mortise-and-tenon joinery, which was used in constructing the shell-first hulls typical of the period. This ship was double-

planked in a fashion similar to that of the **Madrague de Giens Wreck**.

A third wreck was discovered at a depth of 58 to 65 m between the islands of Grand and Petit Congloué. Designated Grand Congloué B or II, the wreck has never been intensively investigated or published, but is known to include ovoid and *garum* (fish sauce) amphoras, probably from southern Spain. These seem to date the wreck to the middle of the 1st century BC.

The importance of the Grand Congloué wrecks lies not so much in their cargoes, but that the project was a pioneering effort in the then unknown field of underwater excavation, despite the initial misidentification of the two wrecks as a single, large wreck. It was demonstrated that shipwreck excavation was feasible and that abundant new information on technology, commerce, and economics in antiquity was accessible. P.S.

ADDITIONAL READING

Benoît, F., 1954, 'Amphores et céramique de l'épave de Marseille', *Gallia*,12, 35–54.

Benoît, F., 1957, 'Typologie et épigraphie amphorique: les marques de Sestius', *Revue d'Études Ligures*, 23, 3–41.

Benoît, F., 1961, *L'épave du Grand Congloué à Marseille*, Gallia supplement 14, Paris.

Carrazé, F., 1971, 'La polémique du Grand Congloué', *Océans* 12 (June–August), 36.

Fibreglass model of the Graveney Boat on display in the National Maritime Museum, London. (© National Maritime Museum Picture Library)

Grace, V.R., 1985, 'The Middle Stoa Dated by Amphora Stamps', *Hesperia*, 54, Appendix 3, 40–41.

Lamboglia, N. and Benoît, F., 1953, 'Fouilles sous-marines en Ligurie et en Provence', *Institut International d'Études Ligures*, 18, 3–4 (July–Dec), 109–27, 237–307.

Long, L., 1987, 'Les épaves du Grand Congloué: étude du journal de fouille de Fernand Benoît', *Archaeonautica*, 7, 9–36.

Thévenot, E., 1953, 'Les importations vinaires

en pays bourguignon avant le développement de la viticulture', *RAECE*, 4, 234–9.

Will, E.L., 1979, 'The Sestius Amphoras: A Reappraisal', *Journal of Field Archaeology*, 6, 339–50.

Gran Grifon
see *El Gran Grifon*

Graveney Boat

Late Saxon clinker-built vessel found on a north Kent marsh in 1970 and recognized as belonging to a distinct non-Scandinavian tradition. The construction and seagoing capability show that it should be termed a 'ship'. The discovery was made during drainage works and led to a combined British Museum and National Maritime Museum (NMM) rescue. The special unit set up in the NMM was charged to record in detail the remains and its context, using them as a test-bed to develop ship archaeological techniques in the UK; it evolved into the Archaeological Research Centre. The methods and data obtained are fully described in the 1978 publication.

Roughly two thirds of the after part of the oak hull survived with portions of eight cleft strakes and nine substantial ribs. Formed from curved branches, the heavy ribs twist out of square, are joggled over the planking and arranged with scarfs alternately to port

and starboard, showing where the top timbers would have fitted. Notches indicated the position of stringers. The plank keel was broadest amidships, tapering to a horizontal box sternpost scarf. The very raking sternpost had clenching grooves inboard to facilitate fastening the ends of the strakes. Completely corroded iron rivets had roughly square-sectioned shanks which had been driven through wooden plugs. The roves were rough quadrilaterals cut from sheet metal. The willow treenails fastening the frames had knobbed heads outboard and oak wedges inboard.

The vessel is reconstructed as 14 m long with eleven strakes and eleven ribs, each completed with short top timbers. A mast-step for a squaresail is presumed to have been fitted in the rabbets in three midships ribs, while either a quarter rudder or stern sweep may have provided steerage. Calculated to have a draft of 45 to 65 cm, the vessel has a high beam/draft ratio and would have operated with a metacentric height of more than 1 m, making her very stable. The design is sophisticated in facilitating good speed at varying loads; its speed is estimated at 3.5 knots when rowed by six men, with a maximum sailing speed of 7 knots. Trials of a half-size reconstruction have confirmed the sailing capability of the hull form. The conserved hull is not currently on display.

The basic reconstruction shows a fairly efficient carrier of heavy concentrated cargoes, such as stone or salt. The discovery in the bilge of fragments of unfinished quern made from a lava which occurs in the Middle Rhine points to the area in which it may have traded, as do remains of hops, which provide the first evidence for the early use of this flavouring in British brewing. Another indicator of cross-Channel contact, this time with the upper Seine, was a Hamwih Class II cooking-pot made in northern France.

The mean radiocarbon calendar date bracket for the construction and abandonment of the ship was AD 944 ± 30. In 1978 efforts to date its construction precisely by dendrochronology produced a date of AD 927 ± 2, revised in 1983 to AD 895 ± 2. However, attempts in 1994 to computer-match the Graveney curves to British and continental chronologies were unsuccessful. V.F.

ADDITIONAL READING

Fenwick, V., (ed.), 1978, *The Graveney Boat*, BAR British Series 53, Oxford.

Gifford, E. and Gifford, J., 1995, 'The Sailing Characteristics of Saxon Ships', *International Journal of Nautical Archaeology*, 24, 121–31.

Great Lakes

A body of freshwater lakes lying on the border of the US and Canada which harbours a unique and well-preserved collection of underwater archaeological resources. The lakes' cold fresh water and great depths (over 400 m in Lake Superior) act as a natural deep-freeze for many shipwrecks and other underwater archaeological remains. The lakes can perfectly preserve not only wooden and metal ship hulls, but their

Left: The boiler of Cumberland, which sank on the Rock of Ages Reef in Lake Superior in 1877. (NPS/John Brooks)

Opposite: ROV-controlled video survey of the remains of Kamloops, lost in 1927 in Lake Superior. (Emory Kristof)

contents as well, including cargo, personal effects of passengers and crew (such as tools, equipment, clothing, and food), and even extremely fragile materials such as paper and **Human remains**. (See also **Isle Royale Shipwrecks**.)

In addition to superb preservation, the Great Lakes present other important opportunities for nautical archaeologists. The Great Lakes are an unusual geographical and ecological entity, and the vessels built to navigate and trade on the lakes were cultural adaptations to the Great Lakes environment. The maritime traditions of various ethnic groups, including Native Americans, northern Europeans, and European-Americans, blended and evolved on the Great Lakes, producing new vessel designs and technology. The exploitation of the lakes' natural resources – iron and copper ore, lead, timber, fish, coal, salt, stone, and agricultural products – led to the development of new technology in resource extraction, processing, and transportation. Great Lakes nautical archaeology offers a microcosm study in the evolution and adaptation of maritime traditions, technology, economics, and culture.

Native American watercraft of the Great Lakes region consisted primarily of the wooden dugout canoe and the birchbark canoe. While numerous examples of the former have been found, few appear to have been studied in an archaeological context. Still fewer archaeological remains of birchbark canoes have been encountered, and much is still to be learned about Native American watercraft of the Great Lakes region. This is also true of Euro-American watercraft used on the Great Lakes, including fur trade canoes, bateaux, skiffs, yawls, and other small craft. The study of small watercraft, both Native American and Euro-

American, is an important area for future Great Lakes nautical archaeological research (see Carrell 1989 and Tolson).

Much of the nautical archaeological research conducted on the Great Lakes has focused on the sailing and steam vessels of the 19th and early 20th centuries. These vessels, generally of American and Canadian manufacture, derived their designs chiefly from the shipbuilding traditions of the North American East Coast and northern Europe. Most Great Lakes shipbuilders were of New England, Scandinavian, English, Scottish, French, or German heritage.

Sailing vessels

The schooner was the principal sailing rig used on the Great Lakes, and was first introduced on Lake Ontario by the French around 1728. Although many other types of rigs, including sloops, brigs, barks, and full-rigged ships, were experimented with by the French, British, Canadians, and Americans, by the mid-19th century, the schooner, usually equipped with a centreboard, had emerged as the most popular and economical sailing rig for general purpose Great Lakes navigation. Schooners of two, three, and in one case five masts, sailed the Great Lakes in huge numbers well into the 20th century, carrying the bulk cargoes and commodities of the rapidly developing region. The typical 19th-century Great Lakes schooner had a full hull with almost flat floors. Some had sharp 'clipper'-type bows with narrow entries and long after runs, but full bows and flat-sided hulls (to maximize cargo-carrying capacity) were most common. Great Lakes schooners were economical, operating with small crews, and flexible enough to transport a wide variety of cargoes such as lumber, grain, coal, salt, ore, stone, and manufactured goods.

Archaeological study of the Great Lakes schooner has revealed a generally well-built, robust, versatile class of commercial sailing craft, equal to and occasionally superior to ocean-going schooners in design and construction. The availability of superb stands of white oak and white pine provided ample building material for the growing Great Lakes fleet, and the rapid development of the Great Lakes iron industry supplied builders with high-quality iron and steel for fastenings, fittings, and equipment.

Great Lakes schooners were generally constructed of white oak, and by the mid-19th century, the use of double-timbered frames and all-iron fastenings became standard. Decks, cabins, and spars were of white pine, which was plentiful in the region. Schooners were generally gaff-rigged, and usually carried a topsail. Beginning in the 1860s, a triangular sail called a raffee was often carried on the forecourse or topsail yard, with its triangular peak brought up to the foremasthead. After about 1870, many schooners were cut down into schooner-barges, functioning as towed bulk cargo carriers, although maintaining enough of a reduced gaff-rig to sail alone if separated from their tow in foul weather. Many three-masted schooners were also cut down into jackass, or 'Grand Haven' rigs. This involved the removal of the mainmast, reducing the sail area, but allowing greater space for deck cargoes in a period when commercial sailing ships were in increased competition from steam vessels and railroads.

Schooners saw service not only as commercial cargo vessels, but as military transports, and in a few cases as armed warships. The discovery of the armed schooners *Hamilton* and *Scourge* in Lake Ontario provide extremely intact archaeological examples of warships of the War of 1812 period, complete down to carronades still mounted on their carriages and boarding cutlasses waiting in racks along the rail.

Archaeological studies of Great Lakes schooners, while numerous, have only scratched the surface of what remains to be learned about these important Great Lakes craft. Excepting the military craft of the War of 1812 period, the earliest known Great Lakes schooner studied by archaeologists is the Millecoquins Shipwreck, a small ship of the 1830s period buried in sand at Millecoquins Creek in the Michigan's Upper Peninsula. The ship, whose identity is unknown at present, represents an important transition link between the ocean-going vessels of the American colonial period and the archetypical Great Lakes centreboard schooner. Archaeological excavations revealed a 19 m long hull with a pronounced deadrise, single-timbered floors, a mix of wooden treenail and wrought-iron fastenings, and a small forecastle cabin and relatively large aftercabin housing a well-preserved collection of artefactual material, including personal effects and ship's equipment. Interestingly, the little ship lacked a centreboard. The ship's hold contained the remains of a barrelled cargo including salted fish, and a small store of perishables including tea and tobacco. The Millecoquins Wreck appears to have been a small general-purpose schooner supplying seasonal American fishing camps on Lake Michigan in the 1830s, probably operating out of Detroit or Cleveland. Apart from a few historical references and sketches, no detailed plans for a Great Lakes schooner exist for this period, nor is the use of these vessels in early exploration, trade, and settlement well documented, making the Milleco-

quins Shipwreck a unique and important archaeological find.

The next generation of Great Lakes schooner is represented by *Alvin Clark*, built near Detroit in 1846 and lost near Chamber's Island, Green Bay, in 1864. Salvaged almost entirely intact in 1969 by amateur salvors, the ship provided a wealth of new information on the architecture and material culture of pre-Civil War Great Lakes schooners. *Clark* was two-masted, and carried a centreboard (offset to the port side of the keelson), as well as an unusual rig. Gaff-rigged on both her fore and mainmast, she carried not only a forecourse, but foretopsail, and foretopgallant. While she was often referred to as a topsail schooner, her rig is technically that of a hermaphrodite or schooner-brig. Another well-preserved example of a schooner of this period is the Port Stanley Shipwreck, a two-masted schooner found on the Ontario side of Lake Erie.

Several important variants of the lake schooner emerged over the thirty years following the construction of *Alvin Clark*. One type was the 'canaller', a narrow, flat-sided schooner built to navigate through the Welland Canal locks separating Lake Ontario from the upper lakes. A well-preserved archaeological example of a canaller is *Bermuda*, built in 1860 and sunk in Murray Bay, Lake Superior, near Munising, Michigan in 1870. The use of wooden hogging arches overlaying the vessel's ceiling is a particularly interesting feature of this vessel.

Another important Great Lakes schooner type was the scow-schooner. Cheap to build and occasionally awkward to sail, the scow-schooner combined an extremely boxy scow hull (usually possessing an angular chine, cross-planked bottom, and often a flat stern and bow) with a two-masted gaff schooner rig. Scow-schooners served in local coasting trades, often carrying rough cargoes such as shingles and stone, where economy of construction and operation were more important than speed and manoeuvrability. The scow-schooner *Rockaway*, built in 1866 and lost on Lake Michigan in 1891 near South Haven, Michigan, has been the subject of an extensive archaeological study, revealing much new information on the construction and use of Great Lakes scow-schooners, and refuting certain historical notions regarding the vessels' alleged design inferiorities.

The zenith of Great Lakes schooner construction followed the dredging of the St Clair Flats in 1871 between Lake St Clair and Lake Huron. This allowed the construction of much larger, deeper draft vessels, including large schooners of over 200 ft

(60 m) in length. Heavily canvassed, and capable of carrying substantial cargoes, these large schooners included *S.P. Ely*, *Wells Burt*, and **Lucerne**. The largest of all the Great Lakes schooners was the five-masted *David Dows*, built in 1881, and 278 ft (84.7 m) in length.

By the 1870s, competition from steamships and railroads was already diminishing the profitability of the lake schooners, and increasing numbers of the vessels (including the massive *David Dows*) were being converted to schooner-barges. Towed behind powerful steamers or large tugs, sometimes in strings of up to six 'consorts', the schooner-barges included former schooners with cut-down gaff-rigs, as well as new vessels specifically built as schooner-barges. Particularly common in the lumber trade, schooner-barges participated in virtually all aspects of the Great Lakes bulk cargo trade.

Archaeological examples of schooner-barges include **Noquebay** and *Pretoria*. The latter vessel represents the pinnacle of Great Lakes schooner-barge construction. At 340 ft (103.6 m) in length, *Pretoria* and her sisters *Chieftain* and *Montezuma* were the longest wooden vessels to sail the lakes, and were among the longest ships built in the world. The ships' exceptional size was permitted by the use of extensive iron reinforcement in the wooden hull, including hogging arches, strapping, keelson plates, and a network of iron cross-bracing fastened over the frames. While the use of schooner-barges prolonged the use of sailing vessels on the Great Lakes, by the 1920s they were unable to compete with either the railroads or the new class of large steel bulk carrier steamers, and the Great Depression saw the last of the schooners and schooner-barges towed to various Great Lakes boneyards and abandoned.

Steam vessels

Commercial steamboats on the Great Lakes evolved from prototypical models not unlike those in other regions of the United States and Canada eventually to satisfy a variety of specialized needs such as towing, package freight (general cargo), bulk freight, and passenger service (see **Steamboat archaeology in North America**). The earliest steamers were paddlewheelers patterned after the pioneer craft of the Hudson and lower St Lawrence rivers, with shallow flat-bottomed hulls, simple radial wheels somewhat forward of amidships, and small passenger cabins in the stern. They were invariably powered by crosshead or vertical beam engines of enormous size and weight which towered above the low superstructure.

Steam vessels were introduced to the Great Lakes in 1816 with construction of the 150 ft (45.7 m) paddlewheeler *Frontenac* on Lake Ontario and *Walk in the Water* on Lake Erie two years later. The remains of *Lady Sherbrooke*, built at Montreal in 1817, have yielded very valuable data about these pioneer craft. By 1840 there were reportedly a hundred steamboats running on the Lakes.

Immigration into the Midwest during the 1830s and 1840s generated dramatic growth in the dimensions and numbers of Lakes steamers. The 780 ton *Great Western*, built in 1838, was the first with an upper deck cabin. *Empire* of 1844 was the first steamer in the country of more than 1,000 tons burden. A whole fleet of lavish 'Palace Steamers' appeared between 1844 and 1856 to ferry settlers from the Erie Canal to the blossoming cities around the shores of Lakes Erie and Michigan. Several of the steamers of this era have been documented, including *Superior* of 1845, *Niagara* of the same date, *Lady Elgin* of 1851, and *Arctic*, also built in 1851. All of these vessels showed extraordinary measures taken by their builders to reinforce long lightly constructed hulls. Besides hogging trusses and great wooden arches, some also used diagonal ceiling planking and great parallel keelsons of heavy oak. The remains of the smaller *Maple Leaf*, built at Kingston, Ontario in 1851, are presently being studied at Jacksonville, Florida, where she was sunk during the Civil War. The intact *Atlantic* (1849), lying 60 m below Lake Erie's waters, offers a rare opportunity to study the construction and outfitting of these fascinating vessels.

It is interesting that while sidewheel steamers survived on the Great Lakes until well into the 20th century, few of their type constructed after 1860 have been documented. A notable exception is the 200 ft (61 m) *Cumberland*, built at Port Robinson, Ontario in 1871. Screw steamers found a niche in Great Lakes commerce as soon as they were perfected in 1840. Eighty-one of their type were in use only ten years later, and they superseded sidewheelers not long after that. 'Propellers' were inexpensive to construct and to operate, and they carried large cargoes for their size because of their compact machinery. They were also better suited for weather conditions on the Lakes, with their submerged screws and high sides. Several of the propellers of the 1840s have been located and studied, most notably the 1846 *Goliath* and **Indiana**, built in 1848 (see Johnston and Robinson). The Smithsonian Institution's methodical study of *Indiana* has provided a wealth of new information about the hulls and machinery of these vessels, much of it in the form of exquisite drawings. They show a vessel type of very efficient design only a handful of years after its introduction in the most experimental form. The seminal *Independence*, constructed at Chicago in 1843 when that place was little more than a wilderness settlement, might have proved an invaluable resource too, except that it was cut up for souvenirs when its remains were found in shallow water near Sault Ste Marie, Michigan in the early 1970s. Only a small portion of its hull was documented.

During the 1850s, screw steamers increased in dimensions and numbers. Dozens were built each year between 1851 and 1856, ranging from 350 to 900 tons, and another surge in propeller construction between 1861 and 1864 produced still larger examples. In the later 1840s and the early 1850s, propellers also diversified to serve different uses. The typical propeller carried freight below and between decks and passengers above. 'Package freighters' evolved around 1845 without passenger accommodation; they were operated chiefly by the railroads bordering the Lakes, who used them to transport all manner of packaged cargo and livestock. Package freighters reached their zenith between 1870 and 1910, when they were the fastest carriers on the Lakes. A good example was the 252 ft (75.8 m) *Conestoga*, built for the prestigious Erie and Western Transportation Line; her remains showed a complex system of internal reinforcing used to stiffen her long wooden hull, characterized by very heavy external arches at her sides and a whole series of longitudinal keelsons in her bottom. The same measures were later used in bulk freighter construction.

Screw tugs were also developed before 1850. Propeller-driven 'steam barges' appeared in 1866 to carry bulky lumber products from the forest regions of Lakes Huron and Michigan to markets in major metropolitan centres such as Buffalo and Chicago. Their usual capacity was from 250 to about 800 tonnes. Steam barges also initiated the 'consort system' which revolutionized the transportation of cheap bulk cargoes; the steamers regularly towed two, three, or more schooner-barges or 'consorts' behind, vastly increasing their trip capacities. The system was used until the 1940s.

Single-decked steam barges intended for the lumber trade evolved within a few years into double-decked 'bulk freighters' designed for bulk grain, coal, and iron ore cargoes. These much larger vessels carried 1,200 to 2,000 tonnes of cargo and towed one or two barges with as much or more of the same products. The earliest steam barge observed in the archaeological record is *Michael Groh* of 1867, one of the first fifteen or twenty of its type. Unfortunately, little remains of the vessel excepting the framing in its bottom, but there is enough structure to demonstrate an obvious relationship between the early steam barges and their schooner predecessors; cross-sectional details of the hulls are virtually identical. Other very early steam barges are known to have sufficient structural integrity to merit eventual study.

There are several fine examples of steam barges dating from 1880 and afterwards. *Thomas R. Scott*, built in 1887, was located intact during 1994 in Fathom Five National Park, Lake Huron; it has yet to be documented. The 152 ft (46.3 m) *Francis Hinton*, constructed in 1889 and now resting in Lake Michigan near Two Rivers, Wisconsin, was recorded between 1992 and 1994; most of her hull and machinery were found and documented. The larger *Herman H. Hettler* (1889) has been studied but not yet thoroughly documented. Some shipwrecks have also been located representing passenger propellers which were later converted to steam barges; these include the propellers *New York* (1856), *Union* (1861), *Passaic* (1862), and *Joseph L. Hurd* (1869), all interesting studies in technological adaptation.

Excellent specimens of bulk freighters and their steam barge forebears have been identified and documented by archaeologists in the waters of the Great Lakes, including examples from virtually every stage of their evolution. The wrecks of the first two bulk freighters ever built lie about 80 km apart in lower Lake Michigan, and both have been investigated in recent years. *R.J. Hackett* was built as the prototypical bulk freighter at Cleveland in 1869, and *William T. Graves* was converted from a barkentine the same year at Buffalo; both communicate much about the technological era in which they were developed and the extraordinary means their builders employed to achieve this efficient new design. The most striking feature of both hulls is the incorporation of numerous heavy parallel keelsons in their bottoms to achieve longitudinal strength, necessitated by the relatively shallow hulls and the unusually great length-to-beam ratio in this vessel type. In spite of the abusive trade in which they served, most of the early bulk freighters survived for thirty or forty years before they were abandoned or dismantled; hull failures were virtually unknown among these vessels.

Sufficient numbers of early Great Lakes

bulk freighters have been targeted for study to enable interesting comparisons. Among the vessels documented have been *Mary Jarecki* (1874), *Smith Moore* (1880), *Henry Chisholm* (1880; see **Isle Royale Shipwrecks**), *Sitka* (1887), *Gale Staples* (1888), *Fedora* (1889), *Louisiana* (1889), *Hesper* (1890), and *Frank O'Connor* (1891). Great Lakes bulk freighters are well represented in historic plans and primary literature (good shipbuilding plans exist for many of these craft constructed after about 1885), but archaeological investigations have added materially to our knowledge of their construction, usage, and manning – information which is not well documented in the literature of the period.

Iron was introduced into Great Lakes shipbuilding in the 1860s, although the technology had been employed in the United Kingdom more than thirty years earlier. Many successful iron steamers were built at Buffalo, New York during the 1870s for the passenger and package freight trades, but it was only in 1882 that the first iron bulk freighter, *Onoko*, was constructed at Cleveland. The wreck of this important steamer has been studied, but because it lies in 60 m of water it has not yet been thoroughly documented. Since no builders' plans have been found for the ship, even a superficial survey of its remains will provide valuable technological data.

Iron was quickly replaced by steel as the preferred medium for ship construction. After several iron bulk freighters were constructed, the steel *Spokane* was built in 1886, and iron went out of fashion. Iron and steel made much larger hulls possible than were allowed by wood, and so vessel dimensions grew rapidly during the 1880s and 1890s, from 285 to 350 ft (87 to 107 m) and, at the turn of the century, 500 ft (152 m); a 500-footer could carry four times the 2,500 ton load of iron ore, coal, or grain of a 250 ft (76.2 m) bulk freighter.

Several fine examples of bulk freight vessels exist from this interesting time when technology developed so rapidly. Field investigations coupled with architectural drawings show that some vessels were not built according to their design, and virtually all went through some degree of adaptation during regular maintenance, repairs, or during modernization. The steel freighter *Sevona* was constructed in 1889 but underwent significant changes before her loss in a November gale in 1905. Lengthening of existing ships became practical with the adoption of steel hulls, and *Sevona* was a good example. She was originally 300 ft (91.4 m) in length, but was lengthened by 72 ft (21.9 m) in 1905, just months before

her loss. It was speculated that the ship broke up because of weaknesses generated by her 'surgery'. Archaeological investigation showed that the hull did not in fact separate where the work had been done earlier that year. Documentation of *Glenlyon* (1893) at Isle Royale resulted in the same conclusion regarding that craft, which had similarly been lengthened and modernized during a thirty-year working career.

Steel bulk freight vessels dating from the present century make up the largest group of intact shipwrecks in the Great Lakes because of the durability of their construction. These wrecks include virtually every class of Great Lakes bulk carriers, including the unique 250 ft (76.2 m) craft built for the Third Welland Canal (around Niagara Falls and linking Lakes Erie and Ontario), and modern 730-footers built for the present St Lawrence Seaway system. *Kamloops*, lost at Isle Royale in Lake Superior in 1927, exemplifies the former, and the well-known *Edmund Fitzgerald* the latter. *Kamloops*'s remains were studied using ROV-controlled video equipment. Although numerous 20th-century wrecks have been located and explored by sports divers, Isle Royale's pristine waters are home to the most carefully documented 20th-century wrecks in the Great Lakes, including the bulk freighters *Chester A. Congdon* (1907) and *Emperor* (1910).

Today's Great Lakes fleet is composed principally of steel bulk carriers ranging from 730 to 1,000 ft (222.5 to 304.8 m) in length, hauling the same commodities as did the wooden schooners and steamers a hundred years ago. The only exception is general cargo or 'package freight', which is now carried by truck or rail. Several commercial vessels have suffered accidental loss in the Great Lakes in recent years, and so the material record continues to grow. These recent wreck sites have not yet been given any priority, but they will undoubtedly become the focus of archaeological investigations in years to come. D.J.C., C.P.L.

ADDITIONAL READING

Amos, A., 1987, *The Port Stanley Shipwreck: An Inquiry*, Malton, Ontario.

Avery Color Studios, 1974, *The Mystery Ship from 19 Fathoms*, AuTrain, Michigan.

Barkhausen, H.N., 1991, *The Riddle of the Naubinway Sands*, Bowling Green, Ohio.

Belisle, J. and Lepine, A., 1988–90, *Le projet Molson I*, Quebec.

Cantelas, F.J., 1993, 'A Portrait of an Early Nineteenth-century Great Lakes Sailing Vessel', in S.O. Smith (ed.), *Underwater Archaeology: Proceedings from the Society for Historical Archaeology Conference*, Ann Arbor, Michigan.

Carrell, T., 1985, *Submerged Cultural Resources Site Report: Noquebay*, Southwest Cultural Resources Centre Professional Papers no. 7, Washington, DC.

Carrell, T., 1989, 'In All Things Remembered: An Oral History Approach to Understanding Small Craft Remains', in J. Barto Arnold III (ed.), *Underwater Archaeology: Proceedings from the Society for Historical Archaeology Conference*, Ann Arbor, Michigan.

Cassavoy, K.A. and Crisman, K.J., 1988, 'The War of 1812: Battle for the Great Lakes', in G.F. Bass (ed.), *Ships and Shipwrecks of the Americas: A History Based on Underwater Archaeology*, New York.

Cooper, D.J., 1989, *Survey of Submerged Cultural Resources in Northern Door County: 1988 Field Season Report*, Office of the State Archaeologist, Technical Publication no. 1, Madison.

Cooper, D.J. (ed.), 1991, *By Fire, Storm, and Ice: Underwater Archaeological Investigations in the Apostle Islands*, Office of the State Archaeologist, Technical Publication no. 3, Madison.

Cooper, D.J. and Jensen, J.O., 1995, *Davidson's Goliaths: Underwater Archaeological Investigations of the Steamer Frank O'Connor and the Schooner-barge Pretoria*, Office of the State Archaeologist, Technical Publication no. 4, Madison.

Fountain, D.R., 1995, 'Preliminary Site Survey: *Arctic* Shipwreck', unpublished manuscript, Marquette, Michigan.

Gegesky, P.S., 1985, 'The Propeller *Goliath*: A Pioneer of the Lakes', *Telescope*, May–June, 66–74.

James, S.R., 1993, 'National Register Assessment of Four Great Lakes Shipwrecks: The *Essex*, *Hesper*, *Amboy*, and *George Spencer*, Lake Superior, Minnesota', in S.F. Anfinson (ed.), *Archaeological and Historical Studies of Minnesota's Lake Superior Shipwrecks*, Minnesota State Historic Preservation Office, St Paul.

Jensen, J.O. *et al.*, 1995, 'Archaeological Assessment of Historic Great Lakes Shipwrecks: Surveys of the Steamers *Niagara* and *Francis Hinton*, unpublished report to the University of Wisconsin Sea Grant Institute (MS. on file, State Underwater Archaeology Program, Division of Historic Preservation, State Historical Society of Wisconsin, Madison).

Johnston, P.F. and Robinson, D.S., 1993, 'The Wreck of the 1848 Propeller *Indiana*: Interim Report', *International Journal of Nautical Archaeology*, 22, 3, 219–35.

Labadie, C.P., 1989, *Investigation of the Schooner S.P. Ely Shipwreck Remains at Two Harbors, Minnesota*, US Army Corps of Engineers, Detroit District.

Labadie, C.P., 1989, 'Submerged Cultural Resources Survey: Pictured Rocks National Lakeshore', Southwest Cultural Resources Centre Professional Papers no. 22, National Park Service Submerged Cultural Resources Unit, Washington, DC.

Lenihan, D.J. (ed.), 1987, *Submerged Cultural Resources Study: Isle Royale National Park*, Southwest Cultural Resources Centre Professional Papers no. 6, National Park Service Submerged Cultural Resources Unit, Washington, DC.

McCutcheon, C.T., Jr, 1983, '*Alvin Clark*: An Unfinished Voyage', *Wooden Boat*, (May–June), 52–9.

Merryman, K., 1989, 'Site Survey, Steamer *Hesper* Shipwreck at Silver Bay, Minnesota', unpublished report, Fridley, Minnesota.

Pott, K.R., 1993, 'The Wreck of the *Rockaway*: The Archaeology of a Great Lakes Scow Schooner', in S.O. Smith (ed.), *Underwater Archaeology: Proceedings from the Society for Historical Archaeology Conference*, Ann Arbor, Michigan.

SOS Conestoga, 1984, *A Report of the Marine Archaeological Survey Conducted by an Ottawa Conservation Group during the Summer of 1983*, Save Ontario Shipwrecks, Ottawa, Ontario.

Tidewater Atlantic Research, Inc., 1991, 'An Underwater Archaeological Assessment of the Steam Tug *A.C. Adams* and Bulk Freighter *Onoko* and Surveys for the Bulk Freighter *Benjamin Noble* and Schooner *Charlie* in Lake Superior near Duluth, Minnesota', St Paul, Minnesota.

Tolson, H., 1991, 'Vernacular Watercraft of Isle Royale National Park', in J.D. Broadwater (ed.), *Underwater Archaeology: Proceedings from the Society for Historical Archaeology Conference*, Ann Arbor, Michigan.

Underwater Archaeological Society of Chicago, 1991, *The Wells Burt Project: A Report of the Survey of a Submerged Nineteenth Century Schooner*, Chicago.

Underwater Archaeological Society of Chicago, 1993, *The Lady Elgin: A Report on the 1992 Reconnaissance Survey*, Chicago.

Greece

Country in the Mediterranean Sea which, with its long coastline, numerous scattered islands, and favourable climate, formed a natural region for early and intensive seafaring. Prehistoric cultures of the area show strong and lasting interactions with the maritime environment, and the Aegean islands formed a natural causeway between the civilizations of the Near East and southeast Europe. Widespread tectonic activity and marine transgression since the beginning of the Holocene have left the waters around Greece full of submerged coastal sites, and the rugged geomorphology of the country-side made the sea a natural avenue of communication and trade. The numerous navigational hazards have resulted in thousands of shipwrecks in the approximately 11,000 years of seafaring attested by archaeology.

The need for exotic raw materials and marine resources turned early inhabitants of Greece towards the sea. The first evidence for seafaring comes from the Mesolithic strata of Franchthi Cave (*c.* 9000 BC) which contained obsidian tools originating from the island of Melos. Furthermore, fishbones from tuna and other large species found at Franchti and at the Mesolithic site of Cyclops' Cave on the island of Gioura in the northern Aegean clearly show that people were involved in open sea fishing during that period as well.

Following the agrarian societies of the Neolithic, the introduction of metalworking in the Bronze Age was concurrent with the emergence of the more commercially oriented island civilizations of Crete, the Cyclades, and the northeast Aegean. These cultures show a shift to coastal settlements and increasing interactions with the civilizations of Anatolia and the eastern Mediterranean. The first representations of sea-going ships in the Aegean are incised on the so-called 'frying pans' found in the Cycladic islands and dating to *c.* 2500 BC. The earliest evidence of ships with sails comes from inscribed seals from the island of Crete dating to *c.* 2000 BC; these probably represent the ships involved in the trade attested to archaeologically between the Minoan civilization of the island and the cultures of Egypt and the eastern Mediterranean. During the middle of the 2nd millennium BC, Minoan influence was replaced by that of the Mycenaean civilization of the Greek mainland. For almost five centuries the Mycenaeans ranged throughout the eastern Mediterranean from Cyprus to Sardinia and beyond. Echoes of these voyages are found both in the heroic epics of Homer and the tale of the Argonauts.

The historic period of Greece begins at *c.* 1100 BC. Early writings and archaeological finds show Greek civilization and colonies spreading throughout the Mediterranean via *penteconters* (oared galleys with fifty rowers) and merchantmen. Classical Greece of the 5th century BC was dominated militarily by the triremes of city states such as Athens. These ships reflected the high cultural and technological levels of Classical Greek society. The centuries which followed produced a series of cultures in Greece: Roman, Byzantine, Venetian, Ottoman, and others. Each competed against the others for control of the islands and anchorages which formed the focal points of maritime communication in the eastern Mediterranean. These conflicts and interactions produced shipwrecks and settlements which have left a rich tapestry of archaeological materials on both land and sea.

Underwater archaeological research

With such a rich maritime tradition and historical background, it is perhaps not surprising that the possibilities of underwater archaeology were appreciated quite early by Greek archaeologists. In 1884 the Keeper of Antiquities, Christos Tsountas, with the help of sponge divers, carried out the first system-

The 5th century BC shipwreck of Alonnesos. Photogrammetric survey, 1995. (Christos Agouridis)

atic underwater survey of the strait between the island of Salamis and Attica. Working under the authority of the Athens Archaeological Society, he attempted to locate the remains of the famous naval battle of 480 BC in which the Greeks, led by Athens, defeated the Persian fleet. Although technical difficulties hindered the success of the investigations, the General Secretary of the Athens Archaeological Society, S Koumanoudis, closed his account of the project with the prediction that there would be more favourable times in the future for such difficult campaigns.

It is, however, thanks to Greek fishermen and sponge divers that numerous masterpieces of the ancient world were brought to light. In 1889 the Poseidon of Kreusis was caught in fisherman's nets in the Gulf of Corinth; in 1925 the Boy of Marathon was found near the east coast of Attica; in 1928 the famous Poseidon (or Zeus) and the Jockey were raised somewhere off Cape Artemision, north of the island of Euboea; and around 1900 Bronze Age copper ingots, similar to those found on the **Cape**

Gelidonya Wreck and at **Uluburun**, were found off the coast of Kymi. In 1994, a fisherman from the island of Kalymnos pulled a bronze statue of a woman from his nets, suggesting that the sea around Greece has not yet offered up all its surprises.

One of the most famous early excavations occurred in 1900 when sponge divers from the island of Symi discovered the **Antikythera Wreck**, dating to about 80 BC, off a nearby island. Immediately afterwards, the first rescue campaign was begun under the authority of the Greek State. The sponge divers worked for several months and brought to the surface remarkable bronze and marble statues, and the famous 'astrolabe'. The expedition, however, left one diver dead and two paralysed – a tragic demonstration of the early hazards of diving.

At the beginning of the 20th century, attempts were made to study coastal changes and submerged harbours by scholars such as P. Negris (1903), A. Georgiades (1907), and J. Paris (1915–1916). Since then, ancient **Harbour studies** have been a small but consistently examined aspect of Greek archaeology.

The revolutionary invention of the aqualung in 1943 by Cousteau and Gagnan (see **Self-Contained Underwater Breathing Apparatus**), offered archaeologists the opportunity to investigate sunken ships and the submerged sites of antiquity for themselves. After World War II several expeditions were undertaken by Greek or foreign scientists. One of the most important of these was at the ancient

site of Pheia in the Peloponnese, by the first Greek archaeologist-diver Nikos Yialouris. Other projects followed in the 1960s at sites such as the two ancient harbours of Corinth, **Kenchreai** and Lechaeum; the Early Bronze Age settlement of Pavlopetri in the south Peloponnese; and the ancient harbour of Halieis/Porto Heli in the northeastern Peloponnese. The 1960s were also marked by the investigations of the late Peter Throckmorton at such sites as Methoni, Porto Logo, Sapienza, etc. with the participation of some young archaeologists.

The 1970s were years of intensive activity as the potential of underwater archaeology began to be appreciated more widely in Greece and around the world. It was, however, only after the extensive looting of a number of wrecks that underwater archaeology was taken seriously. Nikos Yalouris, General Director of Antiquities, personally encouraged young archaeologists of the Ministry of Culture to learn how to dive and work underwater. This decade also saw the foundation of the **Hellenic Institute of Marine Archaeology** in 1973, and the establishment of the Department of Underwater Antiquities by the Ministry of Culture in 1976.

In 1970 ceramics looted from a Byzantine shipwreck near the island of Pelagos appeared in foreign museums. This prompted the first systematic rescue excavation of a shipwreck in Greece, under the supervision of the diving archaeologist Charalabos Kritzas and with the technical assistance of Peter Throckmorton. The project lasted three months and its aim was to map, excavate, and raise all exposed finds, mainly fine decorated plates and commercial amphoras. In this decade several other small projects were completed at various sites around Greece. Between 1975 and 1976 Jacques Cousteau and his team investigated Cape Artemision, Navarino Bay, the **Antikythera Wreck**, and other sites. The projects provided opportunities for young Greek archaeologists to gain experience in diving and underwater work.

Since the 1980s, the Department of Underwater Antiquities has engaged in many surveys and excavations. Ancient harbours such as those of Samos, Naxos, Thasos, Toroni, and Phalasarna have been investigated, some as cooperative projects with foreign archaeological institutions. Highlights of this period include the excavations by Delaporta and Spondylis of the Early Bronze Age settlement of Platygiali in western Greece, the wreck of Louis XIV's flagship *La Térèse* (Lianos 1989), and the post-Byzantine wreck off the island of Zakynthos (see Delaporta and Bound 1997).

Early Bronze Age pottery raised from the cargo site of Dokos in 1992; excavation by the Hellenic Institute of Marine Archaeology. (Christos Agouridis)

Of all the shipwrecks excavated in Greek waters by the Department of Antiquities to date, perhaps the most important is the 5th century BC wreck found near the island of Alonnesos in the northern Aegean and excavated under the direction of Dr Elpida Hatzidaki from 1992 to 1993. Although the excavation has not yet finished, the capacity of the ship at over 100 tonnes and its cargo of three to four thousand amphoras, promises to shed new light on Classical shipbuilding and the economic history of the 5th century BC. Another Classical shipwreck, also of the 5th century BC, has been under excavation by the department in nearby waters since 1994.

Since 1989 the Hellenic Institute of Marine Archaeology has undertaken projects at Dokos (the earliest known wreck) in 1988–92, Point Iria (1991–4) and Kythira (1993–7).

Law and management
In 1824, soon after Greek independence from Turkish rule, the first archaeological law was passed which defined all antiquities as 'the national possession of all Greeks' and established the Archaeological Service for the investigation and protection of the Greek national heritage. Subsequently, various legislative regulations were enacted and finally codified in 1932 into the law which remains in force today. In its opening article, mention is made for the first time of underwater antiquities. Although pioneering for its time, it now seems insufficient to manage the underwater heritage of Greece in light of emerging socio-economic developments.

The law of 1932, coupled with the inabil-ity of the State to monitor over 15,000 km of coastline, has resulted in the general prohibition of the use of the aqualung. To date, only certain coastal areas have been opened for diving, after survey by the Department of Underwater Antiquities. Over one thousand sites had been reported to the Department by 1997, but very few have been thoroughly surveyed, excavated, or published. Furthermore, there currently exist no scientific criteria for the assignment of research priorities and efforts, and a long-range plan for Greece's underwater heritage yet to be formulated.

Part of the reason for this is the fact that the Department of Underwater Antiquities must provide clearance before any type of construction work (such as harbours, fish-farms, coastal industrial installations, etc.) may begin. These responsibilities leave little time for purely scientific research, although its personnel and infrastructure have considerable potential scientific contributions to make.

Other activities of the department include the ambitious restoration of Niokastro, an Ottoman castle in Pylos, to serve as a national museum and centre of maritime archaeological research. The project began in 1982 and work was still in progress in 1997. Proposals for underwater parks have also been submitted but are still in the planning stage.

Education and institutions
Maritime archaeology is not offered as a subject in Greek universities, although graduate seminars have occasionally been organised by the University of Athens and the Hellenic Institute of Marine Archaeology. In 1996 the first undergraduate course containing a measure of maritime archaeology was offered by Professor Yannos Lolos at the University of Ioannina. Currently most archaeologists wishing to pursue maritime archaeology in Greece form their own programme of study or attend universities outside the country.

There are several institutions involved in the field of underwater archaeology. The Hellenic Institute for the Preservation of Nautical Tradition, established in 1981 and based in Athens, organized two experimental boat archaeology projects. The *Kyrenia II* is a full-scale replica of the **Kyrenia Ship**, excavated in Cyprus during the 1960s by Michael Katzev. It was built between 1982 and 1985 using authentic methods and materials. It undertook one experimental voyage from Attica to Cyprus (September 1986) and returned (April 1987) across the eastern Mediterranean and south Aegean. The project was supported by the Greek Navy and the Ministry of Culture. The *papyrella*, built in 1988, was a double-prow reed-boat, propelled by paddles. The Institute undertook trials between Attica and the island of Melos, showing that the straits between the Cycladic islands could have been crossed 10 000 years ago with such wash-through craft, to procure valuable obsidian.

Since 1985 the Institute has organized the biennial International Symposium on Ship Construction in Antiquity, held in Greece. It publishes the proceedings in the volume *TROPIS*.

The Aegean Maritime Museum was established by private initiative and is based on the island of Mykonos. Its main aim is the preservation and promotion of the Greek nautical tradition in the Aegean and beyond. Its displays covers many periods of Greek nautical history, with diaries, boat models, engravings, anchors, and a small archaeological collection. Its major contribution to the preservation of the Aegean's traditional shipbuilding is the maintenance of two traditional vessels: *Evagelistria*, built in 1940, and *Thalis Milisios*, built in 1905. It has also a publications department.

The Piraeus Hellenic Maritime Museum was established under the authority of the Greek Navy at the harbour of Zea, the ancient harbour of the Athenian triremes. Remains of shipsheds have been excavated nearby. The Museum's exhibits cover mainly subjects of Greek nautical history of the last two centuries. It has a notable collection of stone anchors raised from the seabed of the harbour of Zea, and a library. There are several other local nautical museums around the country with small archaeological collections focusing on regional nautical history, such as the museums of Galaxidi, Oinouses, and Hania. C.S.A.

ADDITIONAL READING

See also the Additional Reading sections of the individual site entries in the Encyclopaedia.

Casson, L., 1971, Ships and Seamanship in the Ancient World, Princeton, New Jersey.

Delaporta, K. and Bound, M., 1997, 'A wreck beside the signal reef outside the main port of Zakynthos (Zante), Greece; Preliminary report of 1991-3', in Tzalas, H. (ed.), TROPIS V, in press.

Delaporta, K. and Spondylis, E., 1990, 'Platiyiali-Astakos: A Submerged EH Site in Akarnania', Enalia Annual 1989, vol. 1, 44–6.

Harding, A., Cadogan, G., and Howell, R., 1969, 'Pavlopetri: An Underwater Bronze Age Town in Lakonia', Annual of the British School at Athens, 64, 113–142.

Hatzidaki, E., 1996, 'Excavation of a Classical Shipwreck at Alonnesos', Enalia Annual, 4, 37–45.

Jameson, M. 1969: 'Excavations at Porto Cheli and Vicinity I', Hesperia 38, 311–42.

Koumanoudis, S., 1885, 'Praktika tis en Athinais Archaiologikis Etairias tou etous 1884', Praktika tis en Athinais Archaiologikis Etairias, 7–17.

Kritzas, H., 1971, 'To Byzantino navagio Pelagonnisou-Alonnisou', Athens Annual of Archaeology, 4, 176–182.

Kritzas, H., 1978, 'I upovrihia archaiologia stin Ellada', in H.-W. Rackl, (ed.), Tauchfahrt in die Vergangenheit Archaeologie unter Wasser ein Tatsachenbericht, Vienna and Heidelberg. Greek trans., Gutenberg and Athens, 1978.

Scranton, R. and Ramage, E., 1967, 'Investigations at Corinthian Kenchreai', Hesperia 36, 124–186.

Shaw, J., 1967, 'Shallow-water Excavations at Kenchreai', American Journal of Archaeology 71, 223–31.

Shaw, J., 1969, 'A Foundation in the Inner Harbour at Lechaeum', American Journal of Archaeology, 73, 370–72.

Spathari, E., 1995, Sailing Through Time. The Ship in Greek Art, Athens.

Throckmorton, P., 1987, The Sea Remembers: Shipwrecks and Archaeology, New York.

Throckmorton, P., 1971, 'Exploration of a Byzantine Wreck at Pelagos Island Near Alonnesos', Athens Annals of Arachaeology, IV, 183–5.

Tzalas, H., Proceedings of the International Symposium on Ship Construction in Antiquity (TROPIS), Hellenic Institute for the Preservation of Nautical Tradition, Athens.

Yialouris, N., 1957, 'Dokimastikai erevnai eis ton kolpon tis Pheias Elias', Archaiologiki Efimeris, 31–43.

Griffin

English East India Company shipwreck in the Philippines. *Griffin* was built for the English East India Company at Blackwall, London in 1748 and was *c.* 130 ft (39.6 m) long. Registered at 499 tons, the ship was actually rated at 600 tons. *Griffin* made four trading voyages to China for the East India Company. Departing China on 1 January 1761, *Griffin* struck a reef in the Sulu Sea just three weeks after sailing. The crew was able to lighten the ship and work her off the reef, but the damage was too great and *Griffin* sank on 21 January off the island of Mindanao. Lost with the ship was a cargo of tea, fabrics, and 194 chests of ceramics.

The wreck was discovered in 1985 by Franck Goddio, under contract to the National Museum of the Philippines. It was found in 12 m of water, and was buried in as much as 6 m of sand. Several months of excavation uncovered the substantially intact remains of 29 m of the hull, comprising about 60 per cent of the ship's bottom. The stern section of the ship was not located, but scattered ballast and porcelain on the bottom indicate that the stern may have torn free aft of the mizzen mast after the ship came off the reef where she struck. A **Photomosaic** was made of the hull, which was then reburied.

A large quantity of porcelain, some of it stacked in the remains of the original packing chests and crates, was recovered. In all several thousand pieces, representing 250 types of ceramics, were excavated. Various concretions, lead sheets, cannon balls, metal bars, four brass kettles, musket balls, shoe buckles, and clay pipes were also recovered.

After conservation, a number of the artefacts were displayed at the National Museum in Manila. The disposition of the remaining artefacts is unknown, but since the project was privately financed, and the terms of the recovery provided for a 'split' of the materials, they may have been sold. A popular book has been written about the wreck and excavation, but to date no detailed scholarly monograph on the wreck or the recovered cargo has been published. J.P.D.

ADDITIONAL READING

Daggett, C., Jay, E., and Osada, F., 1990, 'The Griffin, an English East Indiaman Lost in the Philippines in 1761', The International Journal of Nautical Archaeology and Underwater Exploration, 19, 1, 35–41.

Daggett, C. and Shaffer, C., 1990, Diving for the Griffin, London.

Guadalcanal Wrecks

Group of US, Australian, New Zealand, and Japanese warship wrecks lying in close proximity to each other and the South Pacific island of Guadalcanal, in the Solomon Islands. Most of the wrecks were sunk between the months of August to November 1942 during the first major clash between Allied and Japanese forces of World War II.

Following Japan's early victories in the Pacific War, including Pearl Harbor, the fall of the Philippines, and the fall of Hong Kong and Singapore, the Japanese military machine seemed unstoppable. In June 1942, Japanese troops began the construction of an airfield on Guadalcanal, in the recently occupied British Solomon Islands Protectorate in what would be Japan's farthest southeastward expansion in the Pacific. The Japanese thrust was met by the United States, Australia, and New Zealand in a bloody six-month campaign. A number of naval engagements, skirmishes, and battles sank nearly fifty ships off Guadalcanal and nearby islands. The two most famous engagements took place on 8–9 August 1942, the Battle of Savo Island, and 12–16 November 1942, the Battle of Guadalcanal. The waters surrounding the islands were named 'Iron Bottom Sound' because of the many ships sent to the bottom during these battles.

In the autumn of 1991, a team led by Robert D. Ballard surveyed the waters of Iron Bottom Sound, relocating ten wrecks. In the summer of 1992, Ballard and his team returned with **US Navy** assets to survey for additional wrecks and photographically document the ships. In all, Ballard's team surveyed a 800 sq. km area. The **Submersible** *Sea Cliff* and the remotely operated vehicle *Scorpio* made a number of dives. Ballard's team included American, Australian, and Japanese veterans, and historians, including warship specialist Charles Haberlein of the US Naval Historical Centre in Washington, DC, who made the identifications of the sunken ships.

Ballard relocated and photographed thirteen wrecks during his expeditions. These included the Australian heavy cruiser HMAS *Canberra*, and the US cruiser *Quincy*, both sunk in the Battle of Savo Island, as well as the Japanese battleship *Kirishima*, the US cruiser *Atlanta*, the Japanese destroyers *Ayanami* and *Yudachi*, and the US destroyers *Laffey*, *Cushing*, *Barton*, *Monssen*, and a wreck that was either the destroyer *Little* or *Gregory*, but unidentified, all sunk during the Battle of Guadalcanal. Ballard also discovered the wreck of the US cruiser *Northampton*, sunk during the Battle of Tassafaronga on 30 November 1942, and the US destroyer *DeHaven*, sunk by Japanese bombers on

1 February 1943 as the campaign for Guadalcanal ground to a halt.

Ballard's work pinpointed the final location of the wrecks he documented, in some cases within close proximity to where historical accounts placed the ships, but at other times at greater distances, as would be expected when ships sink in fierce battle, at times in the dark, and with great confusion. The wreck of USS *Quincy*, for example, was approximately 1.5 km from her final reported position, while USS *DeHaven* was found 5 km from the destroyer's reported sinking site; the final location of HIJMS *Ayanami* had never been pinpointed. Ballard's team also obtained a more detailed understanding of battle damage to a number of the ships, including heavy shell damage, torpedo damage, and evidence of major detonations and fire, including magazine explosions. The wreck of USS *Quincy* had its bow blown off, and its stern area had partially collapsed, USS *Monssen*, hit by at least thirty-three shells, lost its superstructure, USS *Barton* was blown in half by a torpedo hit (only the bow was discovered by Ballard, on its side), *Laffey*'s stern was torn off by a torpedo, *Yudachi*, shelled and sunk by a magazine explosion, lost its bow when it hit the bottom, and the battleship *Kirishima* is broken up and lies upside down, the bow torn free from a catastrophic magazine explosion.

The majority of the wrecks documented by Ballard were deep, in waters ranging from 300 to 1,110 m. Ballard also located wrecks in shallower waters, but with the exception of a brief photographic survey of the cruiser *Atlanta*, which lies in 130 m of water, did not survey them. In November 1995, a joint US and Australian technical dive team led by Terrence Tysall and Kevin Denlay returned to Guadalcanal to dive and photo-document some of the shallow water wrecks. Their work focused on USS *Atlanta* and the US destroyer *Aaron Ward*, sunk on 7 April 1943 in 74 m of water and discovered by diver Brian Bailey in September 1994.

Other wrecks lying in shallow water and documented by the Tysall/Denlay expedition included the US oiler *Kanawa*, the bow of the US battleship *Minneapolis*, blown off by a torpedo (the battleship survived), the US attack transports *Calhoun* and *John Penn*, the Japanese transports *Asumassan Maru*, *Sasako Maru*, and *Ruaniu*, the Japanese submarine I-123, the New Zealand corvette *Moa*, the US tug *Seminole*, landing barges, and submerged aircraft, including a B-17 'Flying Fortress', and Japanese and American fighters and Kawanishi flying boats. The majority of these wrecks lie in depths ranging from 30 to 80 m.

The significance of the wrecks, apart from their historical association with the battles of Guadalcanal, comes from their unaltered integrity as a submerged battlefield. Ballard noted this at the conclusion of his 1992 expedition, and Denlay, in a 1996 report, commented on the untouched scene in one anti-aircraft gun tub aboard USS *Kanawa* where 'spent shell casings from her last-ditch effort at surviving a final attack lie scattered about, and among them lies the helmet of the gunner'. Ballard commented on the underwater scene off Guadalcanal as 'the literal evidence of war – shell holes in blasted metal, guns and torpedo tubes still trained as if to fire or pointing crazily askew, the wrecked bridge where a captain or an admiral breathed his last'.

The wrecks of Iron Bottom Sound and in the shallow waters off Guadalcanal comprise the largest fleet of sunken warships associated with World War II that have yet been documented, other than the work of the US National Park Service's **Submerged Cultural Resources Unit**'s work at **Pearl Harbor**, Guam, Palau, the Aleutians, and Bikini (see **Crossroads Wrecks**), and the initiative of a few diver/historians at Kwajalein and **Truk Lagoon**. The sunken fleet of Iron Bottom Sound and the warships in shallow waters off Guadalcanal remain with the US, Australian, Japanese, and New Zealand governments. The wrecks are also protected by local Solomon Islands laws. J.P.D.

ADDITIONAL READING

Ballard, R.D. and Archbold, R., 1993, *The Lost Ships of Guadalcanal*, New York.

Denlay, K., 1996, 'Solomon Islands/Guadalcanal', *Immersed: The International Technical Diving Magazine*, 2 (Summer), 44–51.

Guernsey Wreck

A late 3rd-century AD merchant ship from Guernsey, Channel Islands. The wreck lay in a busy shipping channel, 4.8 m below chart datum, in the entrance to St Peter Port, Guernsey; it was discovered in 1982 by Richard Keen, a professional diver and amateur archaeologist, who recognized late medieval and post-medieval pottery scattered around the wreck.

The ship was sunk when she burned to the waterline about AD 280–87. There is no evidence of a mast stump and comparatively little collapsed and partially burnt structure. As the ship was lying in shallow water (probably less than 6 m deep in the 3rd century) it would have been possible, using grapnels, to recover any remnants of the mast or rudder which survived the fire. At some time in the recent past, probably during the German occupation of the Channel Islands during World War II, an attempt was made to remove upstanding timbers, including the sternpost. These were probably fouling the moorings, but their importance was unrecognized and records of the attempted demolition have not been found.

One third of a single-masted sailing vessel was recovered in 1984–5. It had an original length of 25 m, a beam of 6 m and a depth of at least 3 m below the gunwales. Recovery of individual detached timbers allowed the entire length of the hull aft of the stem to be recorded. The finds are displayed in the Museum at Castle Cornet, St Peter Port, and the timbers are being conserved prior to reconstruction for display.

The ship was strongly built in the Celtic shipbuilding tradition, with a central keel-plank and flush-laid planking fastened to the frames by large iron nails clenched in a herringbone pattern on the inner face of the frames. This is quite unlike contemporary Mediterranean or Scandinavian shipbuilding techniques, and there are close similarities with the late 2nd-century AD **Blackfriars Wrecks** and the Roman boat found at Bruges in Belgium.

The flat bottom of the hull was formed by a tripartite keel-plank 14.05 m long, 0.12 m

Plan of the hull of the Guernsey Wreck showing recovered structure and interpretation of missing frames. (M. Rule)

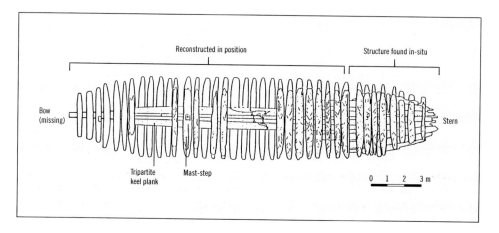

thick, and a maximum of 1.21 m wide. The garboard strakes, about 9 cm thick, were fitted flush with the inboard face of the keel-plank, leaving the thickened keel-plank projecting below the bottom of the ship. Iron nails were driven through pre-drilled holes in the keel-plank and the heads were sunk into carefully cut rebates in the outer face to protect the nail heads when the boat was drawn up on the beach.

The single mast was stepped in a large floor-timber situated approximately one third

second timber was secured. A twisted wad of moss (*Polytrichum* sp.) was placed beneath each nail head to ensure a watertight seal before the nail was driven through the pre-drilled hole in each timber.

The outer planks and the keel-plank were all tangentially sawn from a balk of timber before being trimmed to shape with an adze. The ship had at least forty floor-timbers, of which twenty-three survived reasonably intact. These had been dressed to shape from a log with an adze, taking advantage of

The pottery found in the ship illustrates the trading area of the time: Algeria (amphora), Spain (amphora), western France (flanged bowls in *céramique à l'éponge*), Dorset (black burnished ware), and eastern England (Nene Valley ware). These ceramics represent the crew's domestic possessions: three amphoras, three bowls, three drinking vessels (one being of maple wood), three cooking pots, three flagons, and two *mortaria*. They are all types which were in use from the late 3rd to the early

Clenched nails securing the outer planks to the floor-timber on the Guernsey Wreck; note the rebates for the nail heads beneath the keel-plank and limber holes. (M. Rule)

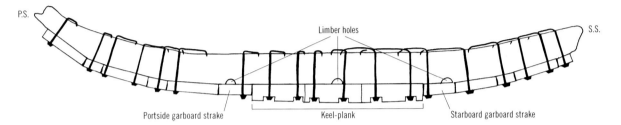

of the overall length from the bow. This timber was thicker and wider than other floor-timbers with a well-defined medial ridge extending laterally on either side of the area around the rectangular socket which served as the mast-step. The mast was missing and there was no evidence for a rudder or steering oar; it is possible that all removable elements were salvaged soon after the ship was lost. An eroded yoke-shaped mast partner and fragmentary charred planks suggest that there was a deck above the hold.

The internal face of the central member of the keel-plank assemblage has an incised line scored along its entire length. Twenty-four incised cuts – prefabrication marks – were made at a mean interval of 56 cm across this line to mark the position of each floor-timber. The position of the mast-step was marked by a modified incised mark: a prominent 'I'. The 56 cm interval does not equate with a standard Roman unit, being approximately 23 Roman inches, or one *uncia* short of two *pes monetalis* (59.2 cm). It would seem that the shipwright either had a measuring stick cut roughly to 'two feet' or he marked out the keel by walking heel to toe along its length. The accuracy of plus or minus 2 per cent is probably all that was required to carry an architectural concept into practical construction.

The seams in the outer skin of the ship were caulked with a mat of oak shavings. The shavings had not been forced into the seam with a caulking tool, but were laid on one timber before the adjoining timber was placed in position. This suggests that a water-soluble glue (fish glue?) was used to secure the material in place while the

the grain of the wood and utilizing, whenever possible, a natural curve in a tree trunk or a branch. The outer faces of the floor-timbers were trimmed with an adze to provide a series of flat facets in order to accommodate the outer planking.

Floor-timbers which overlay the keel-plank had three limber holes cut in their under face to allow free flow of bilge water. Further aft the floor-timbers overriding the stern-post had two limber holes. These holes showed chisel or gouge marks and they had been kept clear of debris until the ship sank.

There was no ballast within the hull, and in spite of the absence of ceiling planking or partitions which might have been required if the ship routinely sailed with ballast in the hold, there was comparatively little wear on the floor-timbers. No alien stones, which might be ballast, were found around the wreck. The conclusion is that the ship was seaworthy when properly laden without ballast.

A layer of solidified 'pitch' or heat-modified pine resin sealed most of the deposits at the stern. The stratified material beneath this layer included coins, ceramics, tile, wooden objects, and cereal grains (mainly *Triticum* sp.). The coins were all found close together in the stern and they may have been stored within a bag in a cabin. A group of six coins of 2nd-century AD date were worn, with little surviving detail. A second group of seventy-four *antoniani* of late 3rd-century AD date contained sixty-six contemporary imitations of regular issues struck between *c.* AD 263 and 284. The total assemblage of coins suggests that they were the personal property of a crew member, lost when the ship sank, around AD 280.

4th century AD and they probably represent items collected during cabotage along the Atlantic coasts of Spain and France and across to southern England.

A large quantity of pitch was recovered, representing the remains of eight blocks which were stored as cargo in the rear hold of the ship. Several near-complete rectangular blocks, weighing between 30 and 50 kilos, survived. These retained the impression of the bottomless wooden casting moulds which had been set onto a sand base. From an examination of the sand entrapped in the lower 2–3 cm of the blocks it appears that they were probably cast in an area of extensive flat ancient coastal sand dunes on the western coast of France.

Vertical supports for a bulkhead, fitted into a floor-timber at the stern, together with a collapsed clay oven and roofing tiles (*tegula* and *imbrex*) suggest a deck house or cabin at the stern of the ship. All the domestic equipment came from this area and the pitch was stored in the hold below. M.R. 2

ADDITIONAL READING

Marsden, P., 1976, 'A Boat of the Roman Period Found at Bruges, Belgium in 1899, and Related Types', *International Journal of Archaeology*, 5, 23–55.

Marsden, P., 1990, 'A Re-assessment of Blackfriars I', in S. McGrail (ed.), *Maritime Celts, Frisians and Saxons*, CBA 71, London.

Rule, M., 1990, 'The Romano-Celtic Ship Excavated at St Peter Port, Guernsey', in S. McGrail (ed.), *Maritime Celts, Frisians and Saxons*, CBA 71, London.

Rule, M. and Monaghan, J., 1993, *A Gallo-Roman Trading Vessel from Guernsey*, Guernsey Museum Monograph no. 5, St Peter Port.

Habbakuk

Unsuccessful attempt in World War II, as part of Operation GE-1, to construct an unsinkable aircraft refuelling platform of ice. Top secret plans progressed to the point of building a 1:10 scale model at Patricia Lake in Jasper National Park, Alberta, Canada from the winter of 1942 to the spring of 1943. By May, logistical problems as well as other developments rendered the project obsolete and the remains, although studied informally through the summer, were allowed to subside into the lake. The site has been the object of archaeological study and monitoring since 1984.

By 1942, U-boat 'wolf packs' were decimating Allied shipping. The German submarines would lie in wait for convoys travelling beyond the escort capabilities of aircraft from either side of the Atlantic, an area that became known as 'U-boat Alley'. An increasingly desperate Britain began to entertain diverse countermeasures including a number of rather unconventional suggestions. *Habbakuk* was the brainchild of eccentric genius Geoffrey Nathaniel Pyke, who was attached to Lord Louis Mountbatten's Combined Operations Headquarters. Pyke was aware of unsuccessful attempts to destroy icebergs undertaken after the sinking of *Titanic* three decades earlier. He proposed the construction of a floating refuelling depot for aircraft escorting convoys by breaking off a 'lozenge' of ice from an Arctic ice field and towing it to the mid-Atlantic. There was also discussion about using the ice platforms as landing craft. Ice was to be the new strategic material to win the war. The nickname *Habbakuk* was derived (though misspelled) from the Old Testament prophet Habakkuk, who cried, 'regard and wonder marvellously: for I will work a work in your days which ye will not believe, though it be told you' (Habakkuk 1:5).

Mountbatten convinced Prime Minister Winston Churchill of the concept's validity and permission to proceed was granted. The scheme was over-simple and flawed. British Admiralty pointed out that aircraft required a 50 ft (15.2 m) freeboard to launch from aircraft carriers and since an iceberg maintains 90 per cent of its bulk underwater, the floes would require almost 500 ft (152 m) of ice below the surface. The enormity of the structures would pose insurmountable problems in just manoeuvring the ice into place

in the ocean let alone utilizing them as landing craft.

Churchill's solution was then to hollow out the bergs and use steel reinforcement to create conventional-looking craft of ice. However, the intrinsic strength of the ice would be lost and some means of maintaining refrigeration as well as a protective outer skin would be necessary. Experiments were undertaken at universities and colleges across Canada and in the United States seeking a resolution to this problem even as the model was begun. A solution was found by Dr Herman Mark at Brooklyn Polytechnical Institution when he discovered that the inclusion of 4 to 10 per cent wood pulp provided sufficient macro-reinforcement to permit the ice to be sawed, hammered, and even turned on a lathe, all the while resisting melting, torpedoes, and even incendiary bombs. He named the substance pykrete in honour of Pyke.

The Canadian National Research Council (NRC), under Dr C.J. MacKenzie, was charged with the construction of the model. Patricia Lake was selected as its location because it had cold winters, was sited at a railhead for supplies within an area already sequestered by the military for training ski paratroopers, and had a ready source of labour in the form of a conscientious objectors' camp of Mennonites and Doukhobors. The model was actually less than 1:10 scale at 60 ft (18.2 m) long by 30 ft (9.1 m) wide and 19.5 ft (6 m) deep and consisted of a wooden shiplap outer shell and a much smaller double-walled refrigeration room suspended in the centre. Galvanized 6 in (15 cm) refrigeration tubing jacketed the inside of the shell, entering and exiting the double-walling of the inner chamber where three generators circulated cold air through the rib-like piping. Original plans called for the circulation of brine water, but the pipes arrived too damaged to be leakproof. The interior of the wooden shell was welded with ice shavings and water. The refrigeration chamber was built into the shell and connected to the pipes when the ice blocks reached a sufficient height inside to support it. Sisal blankets and wood shavings covered the surface and the entire structure was roofed. Despite local mythology which claims it was 'disguised' as a boat house, participants still living claim the roof was just to keep out the weather and protect the machinery. It was described by a Calgary journalist as 'the mother of all ice cubes'.

The full-size vessels were designed to be 2,000 ft (610 m) long with a 300 ft (91.4 m) beam and 200 ft (61 m) depth and with

engines attached to the sides capable of maintaining 7 knots in order to ensure control of *Habbakuk*'s movement. Initial plans called for the construction of a fleet of such craft at Cornerbrook, Newfoundland by 1944. It soon became apparent that even with 2,000 people working in shifts around the clock, it might not be possible to create even a single vessel and that construction would make serious demands on scarce resources such as wood pulp and galvanized piping.

MacKenzie faced the daunting task of reporting to Churchill that the idea was impractical. The Prime Minister did not accept the news graciously. However, the development of the VEL Liberator aircraft, the establishment of air bases in Iceland, and the invention of centimetric radar virtually closed U-boat Alley and turned the tide against the German wolf packs.

The machinery was removed from the model and the roof materials were salvaged for re-use. The remaining wood was inaccessible since it was sealed into the ice block. Scientists monitored the longevity of the model which did not subside into the lake until late summer. It remains relatively upright, although sitting diagonally on a side-slope, at depths of 20 to 30 m at an altitude of 1,170 m above sea-level. The Alberta Underwater Archaeological Society has installed a commemorative plaque, in cooperation with the Canadian Parks Service, near the southwest corner of the model.
S.B.M.L.

ADDITIONAL READING

Langley, S.B.M., 1986, 'Project Habbakuk: World War II Prototype Vessel', *Scientia Canadensis*, 31, 10, 2, 119–31.

Langley, S.B.M., 1994, *Inundation Taphonomy of Selected Submerged Heritage Resources in Alberta*, unpublished doctoral dissertation, University of Calgary, Alberta.

Halsenoy Boat

Remains of a small sewn boat discovered in a bog at Halsenoy, near Bergen, Norway. Fragments of planking, a rib, and a rowlock were recovered. Dated to *c*. AD 350, the remains are the earliest indisputable evidence of the clinker-built tradition. Christensen has discerned that the Halsenoy Boat was an improvement over the **Hjortspring Boat**, in that the rib was a heavy curved piece of wood, and not a light hazel branch, as was used on the former craft. J.P.D.

ADDITIONAL READING

Christensen, A.E., 1972, 'Scandinavian Ships from Earliest Times to the Vikings', in G.F. Bass (ed.), *A History of Seafaring Based on Underwater Archaeology*, New York.

Hamilton and *Scourge*

Two American merchant schooners sunk at the bottom of Lake Ontario during the War of 1812. Purchased by the **US Navy** in 1812, they were converted into warships by adding heavy guns that made the ships top-heavy. They both sank in a sudden squall on 8 August 1813, 10 km off Port Dalhousie, Ontario. They are the best preserved of all historic shipwrecks, lying at a depth of 91 m. No other complete ships from this early period of North America's naval history remain in their original configuration. Fifty-three men were lost but eight survived. One was Ned Myers, who told his story in 1843 to his friend James Fenimore Cooper. Fenimore Cooper preserves a rare contemporary account of the shipwreck in his naval classic, *Ned Myers; or, A life Before the Mast*.

The two ships were found by Dr Daniel A. Nelson of St Catharines, Ontario, in 1973 using a **Magnetometer**, under the auspices of the Royal Ontario Museum. The find was confirmed in 1975 by **Side scan sonar** images. In 1980 films were taken from a manned submersible and in the same year title to the vessels was transferred to the city of Hamilton, Ontario by the United States Navy. In 1982, the Hamilton-Scourge Foundation (aided by the Ontario Heritage Foundation, Ministry of Citizenship and Culture, Province of Ontario) and the **National Geographic Society** sponsored a full-scale photographic survey of the two wrecks, interpreted by project archaeologists Kenneth A. Cassavoy and Kevin J. Crisman.

In 1990, Dr Robert D. Ballard of the Woods Hole Oceanographic Institution and the Jason Foundation for Education took the remotely operated vehicle **Jason** to the site to make a further photographic and sonar survey of the ships as part of his 1990 Jason Project for the education of children in the sciences and technology. Margaret Rule of the **Mary Rose** Trust was the archaeologist. Utilizing three independent sonar systems, Jason produced three-dimensional information about the ships and an electronic still camera (ESC) transmitted digital images to a top-side computer. These were scaled to fit into a composite, black-and-white mosaic of the hull and figurehead of *Hamilton*, accomplished on shipboard during the two-week project. This was the first use of the ESC camera that promises such revolutionary work for the marine archaeologist in the future.

Hamilton, originally named *Diana*, was an approximately 75 tonne vessel built in Oswego, New York in 1809. She is 22 m in length with a 6 m breadth. Nine or ten 18 lb carronades were added when she was refit-

Hamilton: 18 pounder carronade. (Emory Kristof)

ted for war. Later two guns were removed and replaced by a 12 lb long gun, mounted amidships. If becalmed, the ships were propelled by long oars (sweeps), some of which lie around the ships, along with spars, blocks, dead-eyes, powder ladles, grape-shot pedestals, cannisters, cannon balls, and the sailors' bones. Both ships rest upright on the bottom, listing about 16 to 18 degrees to port. Three of their four masts still stand and reach upward some 15 m. *Hamilton* carried two wooden stock type anchors at her bow. A number of cutlasses are preserved. At the stern lies a ship's boat, still fastened on its davits when the ship sank. *Hamilton*'s figurehead of the goddess Diana is well preserved with her quiver slung over her left shoulder. She wears a high-waisted, Empire style dress. An unusual decorative garland rings the base of the bust.

Scourge, lying 400 m away, was originally named *Lord Nelson*. Built in 1810–11 at Niagara in Upper Canada, it has a length of 17.4 m with a 5.4 m breadth and a tonnage estimated at 45 or 50 tons. She carried ten four and six pounder long guns and two iron sliding-stock anchors. Two crossed pairs of cutlasses are fastened above the gun ports in the bulwarks, and boarding axes are stowed inside the starboard stern quarters. The figurehead was originally identified as Admiral Horatio Nelson, but since it has both arms and the admiral had lost his right arm earlier in battle, this suggestion is now doubted. The full figure walking is a common type on ships' figureheads of the 19th century.

Hamilton and *Scourge* were ordinary topsail merchant schooners with shallow draft. They were designed for hard everyday lake transport, not for war. Their importance for archaeology lies in their excellent state of

preservation. They are precious documents about shipbuilding techniques and a sailor's life before the mast from a time in early American naval history when little is known or recorded. The fine video coverage thus far of the wrecks provides the student and tourist with a virtual underwater museum, the first of its kind. A.M.M.

ADDITIONAL READING

Cain, E., 1983, *Ghost Ships* Hamilton *and* Scourge*: Historical Treasures from the War of 1812*, New York and Toronto.

Cain, E., 1987, 'Naval Wrecks from the Great Lakes', in P. Throckmorton (ed.), *The Sea Remembers: Shipwrecks and Archaeology*, New York.

Cassavoy, K.A. and Crisman, K.J., 1988, 'The War of 1812: Battle for the Great Lakes', in G.F. Bass, (ed.), *Ships and Shipwrecks of the Americas*, London.

Cooper, J. Fenimore, 1843, repr. 1989, *Ned Myers; or A Life Before the Mast*, Annapolis.

McCann, A.M., 1991, 'High-tech Link Up for Kids', *Archaeology*, Jan–Feb, 44–5.

Nelson, D., 1983, 'Hamilton and Scourge: Ghost Ships of the War of 1812', *National Geographic*, 163, 3, 289–313.

Harbour studies

The investigation of ancient harbours based upon archaeological and literary evidence. Throughout history, sea transport provided imperial powers with the key to commercial and military dominance. Harbours and docking facilities in conjunction with good land communications allowed the Phoenicians, Greeks, and Romans to dominate the seas, from the prehistoric period until the 7th century AD. Artificial harbours, moles, quays, canals, and sluice gates were invented thousands of years before our time. The importance of harbour studies lies in the information it provides about which parts of the coast were used as trade routes, and at what periods; what kind of trade existed; what imports and exports were made; what was the size, construction, and cargo of ancient ships; what anchors they carried; how advanced and skilful was the society in building construction; what protected the port from the winds; what arrangements were made to prevent silting; and finally in providing insight into the organization of ancient societies. In the last fifty years, information on ancient harbours from literary sources has been supplemented by aerial photography, and excavations both on land and underwater.

The earliest remains of man-made sea installations yet discovered are in India, Mesopotamia, Egypt, the Levantine coast, and Crete. They consisted of basins dug first out of riversides, and later sea coasts, with embankments or quays on which to unload ships too large for beaching. The first examples are from the late 3rd millennium BC, one near the Indus Delta and another at Mesopotamia, from within the city walls of Ur. During the 2nd millennium BC, Egyptian installations appeared along the River Nile, particularly at Thebes, and on the North African coast. Along the exposed Levantine and southern Cretan coasts, reefs and offshore islands provided natural shelter and were adapted as harbours, either by cutting into the rock, or by creating stone breakwaters to reinforce natural protection, as at the eastern Phoenician harbours of Tyre and Sidon. Harbours were kept free of silt by designing their outer parts in such a way as to deflect silt-bearing currents.

The 1st millennium BC saw great advances in harbour construction. One important type is called *cothon*, a land-locked artificial basin, provided with a channel for access to the sea, and surrounded with stone quays against which ships moored for loading and unloading. Such engineering is traditionally ascribed to the western Phoenicians, as at Motya in Sicily, or the famous double harbour at Carthage. In the Greek world, a harbour type frequently referred to by ancient authors was the 'closed harbour', which consisted of a basin, natural or artificial, surrounded by city walls, fortified with towers, and whose entrance could be closed off with a chain. Typical closed harbours were those of Athens at Piraeus, Halieis in the Peloponnesian Argolid, and at the islands of Aigina, Samos, and Thasos. The closed harbours were heavily fortified because they were military installations, while separate commercial harbours were often located outside the city walls, as at Thasos and Cnidos.

Greek harbours typically lay in natural deep bays along steep rocky coastlines, where the principal human intervention was to construct breakwaters to deflect the force of the waves. Ancient moles were built by throwing rubble into the sea, and allowing it to settle. Large rectangular blocks were placed on top, often fastened together by metal clamps, as at **Kenchreai**, the eastern port of Corinth, and Eleusis. Offshore reefs were sometimes joined to the mainland by strong walls or causeways, as at Syracuse, Klazomenai on the Asia Minor coast, and Cyrenaica in Libya. Before they built a harbour, Greek engineers watched for the prevailing winds and currents to determine the amount of sedimentation. Not only were moles designed to prevent silt from entering, as at Halicarnassus on the Asia Minor coast, but a variety of devices were developed to allow silt-free water to sweep into the harbour through channels, and scour it clean, as at Mytilene on the island of Lesbos. The skill of the ancient engineers is attested by the fact that modern 'improvements' sometimes cause a previously clear harbour to silt up in a few years.

A combination of a *cothon* and a closed port is found at Phalasarna, west Crete, a largely intact harbour which was active from the 4th to 1st centuries BC, and which owes its survival to tsunami waves that covered it during massive earthquakes of the 1st and 4th centuries AD. The harbour, now being excavated, is entirely artificial with a long entrance channel cut into the bedrock. This ability to cut stone beneath sea-level originated with the Phoenicians, who passed the tradition on to the Greeks and Romans. Elegant isodomic towers surround the port, connected to one another by long stone walls and quays and with adjacent freshwater basins. A strong acropolis stood on the hilly peninsula above the harbour, protecting it from three sides and making siege difficult.

Each harbour had its own ship sheds for the protection of the fleet. These were long and narrow buildings with a pitched roof, and a gentle slope towards the sea, with a rock-cut slip, as at Piraeus, Carthage, Apollonia in North Africa, and Oeniade in Akarnania. Their length varied from 21 to 47 m, according to the length of the ships to be stored in them.

From the 4th century BC onwards, the conquests of Alexander the Great and the rise of Rome created larger states than those which had previously existed; their economic and military power required the expansion of existing harbours. Commerce was now carried out by larger and more numerous ships. The small quays of the past were replaced by large platforms, at times up to 1 km long and 20 m wide, furnished with flights of steps and special mooring devices, as on the island of Delos, which was the main slave market of Hellenistic Greece. The great harbour at Alexandria, begun under Alexander's orders, featured a causeway 1 km long and 200 m wide, large warehouses and public granaries, and a lighthouse visible 50 km out to sea – one of the wonders of the ancient world.

The absence of natural deep water basins along the Italian coast forced the Roman engineers to construct artificial harbours in lagoons, and in the 3rd century BC they invented hydraulic cement, which made a formidable building material out of limestone and volcanic ash (*pozzolana*). Not only could this cement be formed into any desired shape, it set and became harder underwater than rock, bringing a radical change to civil engineering. Moles, piers, bridges, and archwork could now be built from this concrete. Monumental breakwaters were built at Ostia, Puteoli, and Misenum.

A Roman harbour which has been studied with particular care is at **Cosa**. It demonstrates many characteristic features of Roman harbour architecture: large sturdy breakwaters made of rubble and rough-cut blocks, concrete piers, rock-cut channels, and a lighthouse.

The great Claudian harbour at Ostia dates to the 1st century AD, and was the largest in antiquity, having been dug out from a bare shore with the sinking of large ships used as the base for an artificial mole. The same technique for mole construction was also used at Kenchreai. A further development occurred in the 1st century AD at **Caesarea Maritima**, on the Levantine coast, where a huge harbour was built in the midst of the sea off a sandy coastline without particular benefit of any natural features. This ambitious construction withstood the elements only for around two hundred years. The best preserved of the Late Roman harbours is the 3rd-century AD construction at Leptis Magna on the North African coast. In order to prevent this large and beautiful harbour from silting a river was diverted from its natural course, and the harbour only fell from use when negligence allowed the river to return.

The Roman tradition of harbour building continued in the eastern part of the Roman world, and survived for many centuries. E.H.

ADDITIONAL READING

Blackman, D.J., 1982, 'Ancient Harbours in the Mediterranean, *International Journal of Nautical Archaeology and Underwater Research*, 11, 79–104, 185–211.

Hadjidaki, E., 1988, 'Preliminary Report of Excavations at the Harbor of Phalasarna in

West Crete', *American Journal of Archaeology*, 92, 463–79.

Lehmann-Hartleben, K., 1926, *Die antiken Hafenlagen des Mittelmers*, Klio supplement 14, Leipzig, repr. 1963, Aalen.

McCann, A.M., 1987, *The Roman Port and Fishery of Cosa*, Princeton.

Raban, A., 1989, *The Harbours of Caesarea Maritima: Results of the Caesarea Ancient Harbour Excavation Project 1980–1985*, BAR International Series 491, Oxford.

Scranton, R.L., Shaw, J.W., and Ibrahim, L., 1978, *Kenchreai: Eastern Port of Corinth*, vol. 1, Leiden.

Hasholme Logboat

Iron Age logboat dated by dendrochronology to the period 322 to 277 BC. This boat was found in 1984 when a machine was laying field drains at Hasholme, near Holme-on-Spalding Moor, East Yorkshire, England. Today the site is farmland below sea-level, protected from the Humber estuary by a sea wall; in the prehistoric period it lay in a tidal stretch of a river which flowed southward into that estuary (see **Humber Wrecks**).

Although broken into several pieces, much of this boat survived. It was excavated by a team from the University of Durham, the National Maritime Museum and the East Riding Archaeological Society, and then moved to Greenwich where the timbers were cleaned, the main hull rotated to the vertical through 40 degrees, and recorded after detached and fragmented pieces had been reassembled. The boat is now being conserved in Hull Museum and will then be displayed.

The main hull of this boat was fashioned from an oak bole *c.* 14 m in length, with a lower girth of 5.4 m (diameter 1.72 m) and an upper girth of 4.15 m (diameter 1.32 m). This oak tree was *c.* 800 years old when felled and had heart rot throughout its length. Although this rot meant that hollowing-out was easier, it also meant that openings at both ends of the log had to be closed to make the boat watertight. The lower, broader end became the stern and this was closed by wedging a transom board inside a groove, generally similar to the **Brigg Logboat** in this respect. This transom was further held within its groove by two timbers fastened transversely across the boat: one timber of rounded section bore down on a U-shaped projection from the after face of the tran-som; and a second plank-like timber across the top of the transom not only forced it down into the groove, but also clamped the boat's sides firmly to the transom.

The forward end of the log was closed by two bow timbers which displayed woodworking techniques of a standard hitherto unsuspected in Iron Age Britain. The lower timber was positioned on longitudinal ledges cut along the lower edges of the forward parts of the main hull, and locked there by two rounded transverse timbers driven horizontally through the boat's sides and through holes in a cleat projecting from the lower bow timbers' upper face. This cleat is similar to cleats on the Ferriby and Brigg plank boats (see **Ferriby boats** and **Brigg 'Raft'**) and on a repair to the **Brigg Logboat**. The upper bow timber was worked to a complex shape so that it enveloped the leading edge of the lower bow, the forward ends of the washstrakes, and the upper forward parts of the main hull. The upper and lower timbers were then locked together by three large treenails driven vertically through holes in both timbers.

To give more freeboard to the boat forward, narrow washstrakes were fastened to the upper edges of the main hull for some 4 m from the bow, by treenails driven from outboard and locked inboard by wooden keys like cotters. Two repairs were fastened to the boat by similar means. A steering platform was positioned on, but not fastened to, ledges near the upper edges of the sides, just forward of the transom stern.

A series of large holes, 50 to 60 mm in diameter, through the sides of the boat just below the sheerlines, are thought to be where temporary transverse lashings were fastened to hold the sides together during hollowing. They may also have been used as fastening points for hides to keep perishable cargo dry. Comparable holes in the Brigg Logboat probably had similar functions.

Like any other known boats of prehistoric Britain, the Hasholme Logboat was propelled and steered by paddles, or by poles in the shallows. Originally the boat measured 12.78 × 1.40 × 1.25 m, the broadest and deepest dimensions being at the stern: thus it retained the tapered shape of her parent tree. It was used as a ferry and a cargo-carrier in Humber tidal creeks and tributary rivers, and in the main estuary in fair weather. Like the Brigg Logboat it may also have had a ceremonial or war role. The boat could carry a maximum of two steersmen and eighteen paddlers at a draft of 46 cm and a freeboard of 79 cm. With a five-man crew it could carry *c.* 5.5 tonnes of cargo at a draft of 75 cm and a freeboard of 50 cm.

On what proved to be its final voyage, the Hasholme Logboat appears to have been heading towards a landing place associated with an Iron Age settlement known from excavation to have been inland to the north. The boat foundered in about one metre of water and came to rest on the seabed with a 40 degree list to starboard. Her bow timbers appear to have been broken off during attempts to dismantle the boat or to haul her from the seabed. Much of her cargo appears to have been salvaged, but animal bones, with evidence of butchered joints of meat, and two lengths of partly worked timbers were found onboard when she was excavated. S.M.

ADDITIONAL READING

McGrail, S., 1988, 'Assessing the Performance of an Ancient Boat: The Hasholme Logboat', *Oxford Journal of Archaeology*, 7, 35–46.

Millett, M. and McGrail, S., 1987, 'The Archaeology of the Hasholme Logboat', *Archaeological Journal*, 144, 69–155.

USS *Hatteras*

US warship wreck, sunk in combat in 1863. Subsequently discovered, it was the subject of protracted litigation which ultimately upheld continued US ownership of wrecked and sunken warships in national waters. Built as the steamer *St Mary's*, USS *Hatteras* was a 1,126 ton, 210 ft (64 m) long side-wheel steamship. The ship was purchased new from the Wilmington, Delaware firm of Harland and Hollingsworth by the United States Navy in September 1861. The steamer, renamed USS *Hatteras*, was fitted with four 32 pounder guns and a single 20 pounder gun and commissioned in October. USS *Hatteras* was assigned to the South Atlantic Squadron of the Navy, blockading southern ports during the US Civil War.

Reconstruction model of the Hasholme Logboat. (Institute of Archaeology, Oxford)

CSS Alabama *sinks* USS Hatteras *off Galveston, Texas on 11 January 1863. (US Naval Historical Center)*

USS *Hatteras* was reassigned to the Gulf Squadron in January 1862, and in the course of a year's duty captured seven Southern ships attempting to run the blockade. In early 1863, *Hatteras* was detached from blockading duty and ordered to join the squadron then forming under Rear Admiral David G. Farragut to capture the southern port of Galveston, Texas.

On 11 January 1863, *Hatteras* spotted a sail on the horizon and gave chase. The enemy ship, when hailed, was identified by its officers as a British warship, but when *Hatteras* approached closer the enemy ship was declared to be the Confederate raider CSS **Alabama**. In a twenty-minute battle, the two ships exchanged heavy fire at distances ranging from 23 to 180 m. Badly holed and sinking, *Hatteras* surrendered. As the last boats pulled away from the ship, *Hatteras* sank.

The wreck of USS *Hatteras* was discovered in the early 1970s by a salvage group, USS Hatteras, Inc., in some 9 m of water. The wreck, largely intact, lies on a sandy bottom, and was exposed after storms scoured the wreck site, which lies some 32 km off Galveston. The United States disputed USS Hatteras, Inc.'s claim to the wreck after the salvors filed an admiralty suit. The case, which was won by the government, determined that title to *Hatteras* remained with

the **US Navy**; it is the most frequently cited legal precedent in the US Government's defence of its historic shipwrecks. The wreck of USS *Hatteras* is listed in the **National Register of Historic Places** and is considered significant not only as the only identified wreck site of a victim of CSS *Alabama*, the most successful commerce raider and Confederate warship of the Civil War, but also as a never salvaged, substantially intact warship of the Civil War era.

Eight artefacts removed from the wreck, including the builder's nameplate, were held by the court, but were released in 1996 by the court to the Navy, which has loaned them to the Corpus Christi Museum in Texas for public display. There are no plans for further study of the wreck of *Hatteras* at the time of writing. J.P.D.

Hellenic Institute of Marine Archaeology

A private, non-profit organization, founded in 1973, whose aim is to organize and promote maritime archaeological research in **Greece** and to assist the Greek Ministry of Culture with the difficult task of preserving, studying and promoting Greece's maritime heritage. From 1973 until 1976 (when the Department of Underwater Antiquities in the Greek Ministry of Culture was founded) HIMA acted as official consultant to the Ministry.

HIMA undertakes scientific research, under the supervision or in cooperation with the Greek Ministry of Culture. It has

over 400 members, with diverse academic credentials, all of whom work on a voluntary basis. HIMA's scientific and technical expertise provide a solid foundation for the promotion of underwater archaeology in Greece and beyond. Furthermore, its non-government status and the support of private sponsors give HIMA a flexibility not shared by more bureaucratic organizations.

Between 1973 and 1989 HIMA completed numerous small projects such as a survey of the ancient city of Pheia, the rescue excavation of an early Roman amphora wreck near the village of Limeni in the Peloponnese, and an investigation of the shipwreck of *Mentor*, Lord Elgin's ship (lost while transporting the Parthenon marbles and other Greek antiquities out of the country). Since 1989 HIMA has conducted three full-scale excavations.

From 1989 to 1992, under the direction of Dr George Papathanassopoulos, HIMA organized and led a systematic investigation of a site at the island of Dokos, where the late Peter Throckmorton had located an impressive concentration of Early Helladic II pottery sherds. On the evidence so far, this underwater find dates to *c.* 2200 BC and might well be the cargo of an Early Helladic II ship – in which case it would be the oldest known shipwreck yet discovered. The Dokos finds have an important bearing on the chronology of the Early Helladic II period and on the study of sea routes and trade patterns in the Early Bronze Age Aegean.

A wreck at Point Iria, in the Gulf of Argolid – Peloponnese, was excavated from 1990 to 1994 under the direction of Haralambos Pennas. The pottery assemblage from the wreck dates to 1200 BC and comes from three different areas: Crete, Cyprus, and mainland Greece. It confirms the apparently frequent and direct links between the Argolid and Cyprus at the time, and probably represents an 'everyday' trading expedition within the Mycenaean world.

Dr Dimitris Kourkoumelis has directed excavations of a shipwreck from the islet of Antidragonera, near the island of Kythira, since 1994. This can be dated to the second half of the 4th century BC. Finds to date include nine large pyramidal stone anchors, sherds from coarse ware pottery (lamps, salt-cellars, plates), amphoras and at least two storage jars, along with a considerable number of lead objects, probably part of the ship's rigging.

HIMA publishes the scientific journal *Enalia* (in Greek) and *Enalia Annual* (in English), which mainly document the Institute's various projects.

To date, HIMA has trained more than fifty

young archaeologists in the methods of maritime archaeological research through the Institute's excavation campaigns and training programmes.

HIMA maintains close cooperative links with institutions and scholars throughout Europe and worldwide. Current projects supported by the European Union include the conservation, publication and display of the Iria shipwreck; the Navis I computerized shipwreck image database; and a computerized image database of ship graffiti from Greek monuments.

Further information can be obtained from: Hellenic Institute of Marine Archaeology, 4 Al Soutsou Street, 106 71 Athens, Greece. C.S.A.

Henrietta Marie

Wreck of a small English slaveship on New Ground Reef about 56 km off Key West, Florida, located by commercial salvors in 1972. Over a period of a few weeks in 1972 and 1973, while the commercial salvors extensively worked the site, a small collection of diagnostic artefacts were recovered under the auspices of the State of Florida's salvage programme. In 1983, archaeological control was initiated and the site identified when the ship's bell was located with the embossed inscription 'THE HENRIETTA MARIE 1699', allowing researchers to focus on one particular vessel and period for the vessel's historical background.

Artefacts recovered between 1972 and 1991 provide a rare glimpse into the material culture of both a typically small West Indian merchant vessel and a vehicle associated with the notorious transatlantic African slave trade. Perhaps the most diagnostic items recovered from the site are the dozens of wrought-iron manacles or shackles last used in 1700 to restrain as many as four hundred slaves within the confines of the ship's hold. Other artefacts include copper cauldrons for preparing the meals of both crew and cargo, various types of weapons, thousands of glass trade beads, numerous tools, scale and scale weights, elephant tusks, logwood, 'voyage iron' or iron barstock, and perhaps the largest assemblage of William III pewterware recovered from one site.

In addition, an intact section of the slaver's lower stern is providing insight into the construction practices of shipwrights during the late 17th century and valuable clues into the architecture of a little-recorded class of ship – the smaller transatlantic merchant vessel. The configuration of the stern suggests a situation long suspected by some historians and archaeologists, that

slave merchants frequently utilized faster than normal sailing vessels to facilitate higher profits due to the inherent problem of delivering a live human cargo across the Atlantic.

Records indicate that the ship was a square-sterned, foreign-built vessel of 120 tons burden and registered in London. Archaeological evidence, along with the fact that the English captured almost thirteen hundred prizes during the recently

concluded conflict with France (King William's War, 1689–97), suggests a French origin. The earliest known date of operation as an English slaver is 1697, which is provided by one of six wills located of persons associated with *Henrietta Marie* (PRO PROB II/447). The ship appears to have made two voyages. Sailing as a separate trader and therefore an interloper in 1697, the slaver departed England and made her way to the West African coast. She arrived in Barbados in July the following year, taking on 114 hogsheads of sugar after offloading her cargo of 250 slaves. In 1698 the monopoly on the slave trade held by the Royal African Company was thrown open to all who agreed to pay a 10 per cent duty to the company on those goods utilized for trade in Africa. Hereafter *Henrietta Marie*, while still a separate trader, sailed legally as a 'ten-percenter'. She appears to

have wrecked a few weeks after departing Jamaica in July 1700.

In 1991, the National Association of Black SCUBA Divers in association with the Mel Fisher Maritime Heritage Society placed a bronze memorial plaque down on the site to commemorate the millions of lives lost during the African diaspora. In December 1995, an international travelling exhibition containing many *Henrietta Marie* artefacts began touring the United States. D.D.M.

Henrietta Marie. *Top left: ship's bell. Below left: a set of iron shackles. Above: pewter jug. (© MFMHS Key West FL/Dylan Kibler)*

ADDITIONAL READING

Boudriot, J., 1984, *Traite et navire négrier*, Collection Archeologie Navale Française, Paris.

Davies, K.G., 1970, *The Royal African Company*, Studies in American Negro Life, New York.

Dow, G.F., 1968, *Slave Ships and Slaving*, Cambridge, Maryland.

Minchinton, W.E., 1989, 'Characteristics of British Slaving Vessels, 1698–1775', *Journal of Interdisciplinary History*, 20, 1.

Moore, D.D., 1989, *Anatomy of a 17th Century Slave Ship: Historical and Archaeological Investigations of 'The Henrietta Marie 1699'*, unpublished Master's thesis, East Carolina University, Greenville, North Carolina.

Singleton, T.A. and Bograd, M.D., 1995, 'The Archaeology of the African Diaspora in the Americas', *Guides to the Archaeological Literature of the Immigrant Experience in America* no. 2, Ann Arbor.

Sullivan, G., 1994, *Slave Ship: The Story of the Henrietta Marie*, New York.

Tattersfield, N., 1991, *The Forgotten Trade, Comprising the Log of the Daniel and Henry of 1700 and Accounts of the Slave Trade from the Minor Ports of England, 1698–1725*, London.

EDITOR'S NOTE: This site is included because it is well known and widely reported in the popular media and press. However, sites such as this have primarily been the focus of commercially oriented activity that has often resulted in the sale of recovered artefacts to private owners, the transfer of artefacts to private investors, or the splitting of artefacts between a Government and a private salvor. Despite the presence of an archaeologist on the site, or the recovery of any archaeological data, the long-term potential of a site to yield meaningful information is compromised when the collection of artefacts – the primary data of any archaeological site – has been dispersed. Furthermore, the sale of artefacts from shipwreck sites endorses the concept that the archaeological past and antiquities are commodities for sale on the open market, which has proven detrimental to the protection and study of the past. The inclusion of this site in this encyclopaedia does not sanction or condone this type of activity.

Herculaneum Boat

A Roman boat discovered buried on the former waterfront of Herculaneum, Italy. Herculaneum was buried by pyroclastic mud flows during the eruption of Mount Vesuvius in AD 79, unlike nearby Pompeii, also destroyed in the same eruption and buried in volcanic ash. A tsunami created by the eruption tossed the boat up onto the beach at Herculaneum; when excavated it was upside down. The boat's remains were completely carbonized by the eruption, and to date it has not been possible to examine the interior. However, the exterior of the approximately 9 m long hull was documented by J. Richard Steffy, who found it similar in some ways to the **Sea of Galilee Wreck**, but lighter, more graceful, and better built.

Steffy documented construction characteristics wherever possible and generated a cross-sectional drawing. Only the aft two thirds of the hull were preserved. The keel, moulded 7.2 cm and sided 6 cm, was rectangular with chamfered upper corners to seat the garboards. The 2 cm thick planking was mortised, with pegged joints. No scarfs were found in the surviving planks. A complex, two-part wale surrounded the hull. Steffy discerned from patterns of treenails and bronze nails that the 5 cm square frames were paired, half frames alternating with

Some of the iron artefacts salvaged from the Highborn Cay Wreck in the late 1960s. (© Ships of Discovery/ Courtesy Bob Wilke)

Excavating the main mast step of the Highborn Cay Wreck. (© Ships of Discovery/K.C. Smith)

floor timbers. Thole-pins for six oars were found in a recessed area in the centre of the hull. J.P.D.

ADDITIONAL READING

Steffy, J.R., 1994, *Wooden Shipbuilding and the Interpretation of Shipwrecks*, College Station, Texas.

Highborn Cay Wreck

Site of a very old wooden sailing ship in the cut north of Highborn Cay, northern Exuma Islands, Bahamas. The site, located in 1965 by three American sport divers, is about 150 m from Highborn Cay in water only 6 m deep, but strong currents sweeping through the cut made it difficult to work on the coral-encrusted remains. During the next two years they salvaged the site of all exposed artefacts. Unfortunately, no comprehensive site report was ever issued, and the artefacts were eventually dispersed.

In 1985, limited excavations designed to reveal the remains of the ship's hull were conducted by an archaeological team from Texas A&M University. It appears that the Highborn Cay Wreck, as it came to be known, was probably a Spanish ship that sank in the first half of the 16th century, making it one of the earliest shipwrecks ever found in the Americas. Clues to the ship's identity were provided by the wrought-iron breechloading artillery and ceramic vessels it carried. When discovered, the site consisted of a mound of ballast stones 16 m long and 4 m wide surmounted by two *bombardeta*s and at least fourteen *verso*s, as well as a wrought-iron anchor. Three other anchors found nearby led the discoverers to conclude that the ship sank while at anchor. Largely as a result of the crude manner in which the site was salvaged in the 1960s, its precise date, nationality, and mission remain mysterious. D.H.K.

ADDITIONAL READING

Keith, D.H., 1988, 'Shipwrecks of the

Explorers', in G.F. Bass (ed.), *Ships and Shipwrecks in the Americas*, London.

Lakey, D.C., Keith, D.H., and Smith, R.C., 1985, 'The Highborn Cay Wreck: Further Exploration of a 16th-century Bahaman Shipwreck', *International Journal of Nautical Archaeology*, 14, 1, 63–72.

Oertling, T.J., 1989, 'The Highborn Cay Wreck: The 1986 Field Season', *International Journal of Nautical Archaeology*, 18, 244–53.

Peterson, M., 1974, 'Exploration of a 16th-century Bahaman Shipwreck', *Nautical Geographic Society Research Reports: 1967 Projects*, 231–42.

Hindostan

English East Indiaman wrecked in the Thames Estuary, England, in 1803. *Hindostan* was built in 1796, and registered in Hardy's list at 1,463 tons. She had a keel length of 144 ft (43.9 m), breadth of 43 ft 6 in (13.25 m), a crew of 132 men, and thirty guns. Her fourth voyage was to have been to China, and to have included the delivery of a division of artillery for the garrison at Ceylon. Under the command of Edward Balston, she anchored in the Queen's Channel off Wedge Sand (Thames Estuary), in the face of an increasing easterly wind. On 11 January 1803 her anchor cable parted, and she drifted onto Wedge Sand, striking her at 4.40 a.m. on 12 January. She was eventually abandoned with the loss of fourteen lives. Much of her outward-bound cargo, valued at £70,000, was eventually salvaged after the sinking. It included 45,000 oz silver bullion, copper, lead, tin, iron, and personal property.

The site was salvaged again in 1985 by bucket grab. Some details of the lower hull structure, which was lifted off the seabed, were observed, such as a composite keel to which large floor timbers had been fastened by long copper spikes. Many of her constructional details have also been recognized on the wreck of the East Indiaman *Earl of Abergavenny*, built in the same year.

The site was surveyed by **Side scan sonar** by Marine Archaeological Surveys in 1986. The seabed was characterized by sand waves about 0.5 m high, and a debris field spread over a considerable area. Marine Archaeological Surveys were allowed to record the large collection of artefacts recovered from the site, which included parts of a mercury barometer and medical stores, small copper bar ingots (analysed and shown to have a high bismuth content indicative of a Cornish source), large battery plates of similar composition (also found in *Earl of Abergavenny*), V, X, and XX cash pieces marked 1803 but probably struck in 1802, mercury

and lead cloth seals bearing the UEIC (United East India Company) mark, as well as barrels of leather shoes and boots of a type worn by officers in infantry regiments of the period. M.R.

ADDITIONAL READING

Craddock, P.T. and Hook, D.R., in press, 'The British Museum Collection of Metal Ingots from Dated Wrecks', in M. Redknap (ed.), *Artefacts from Wrecks: Dated Assemblages from the Late Middle Ages to the Industrial Revolution*, Oxford.

Redknap, M., 1990, 'The Albion and Hindostan: The Fate of Two Outward-bound East Indiamen', *International Journal of Nautical Archaeology*, 19, 23–30.

Historic Shipwrecks Act (Australia)
see **Australian Historic Shipwrecks Act**

Hjortspring Boat

A 4th-century BC boat, believed to be a twenty-man war canoe, found in a bog at Hjortspring on the island of Als, southern Denmark. A sacrificial offering, the boat had been placed in a bog with war equipment (spears, swords, etc.) like the later **Nydam Boat**. The style of the weapons allowed archaeologists to date the wreck to *c*. 350 BC. The boat was excavated in 1921; it was recovered in fragments, but archaeologists were able to work up a reconstruction. During the 1980s the timbers were re-conserved, and the reassembled boat is now on display at the Danish National Museum, Copenhagen.

The Hjortspring Boat was a wooden clinker-built vessel with sewn planks and a double up-curved prow and stern. It was reconstructed as a 16 m long vessel, with a broad bottom plank, slightly curved from stem to stern. Fore and aft specially hollowed 'end-pieces' were placed on the bottom plank and lashed in place. Two lime-wood side planks and two garboard strakes made up the boat, which possesses a total of only seven planks. Iron fastenings were not used in the boat. The ribs were formed with thin hazel branches bent in a curve, gunwale to gunwale, and lashed to cleats projecting from the planks. Seats for rowers and the struts supporting them also formed part of the rib structure. J.P.D.

ADDITIONAL READING

Christensen, A.E., 1972, 'Scandinavian Ships from Earliest Times to the Vikings', in G.F. Bass (ed.), *A History of Seafaring Based on Underwater Archaeology*, New York.

Rosenberg, G., 1937, *Hjortspringfundet*, Copenhagen.

Steffy, J.R., 1994, *Wooden Shipbuilding and the Interpretation of Shipwrecks*, College Station, Texas.

H.L. Hunley

The first submarine to successfully sink a warship during time of war. On the night of 17 February 1864 the submarine *H.L. Hunley* attacked and sank the Union blockading warship USS *Housatonic* as she lay at anchor off Charleston Harbour, South Carolina. The feat was not to be repeated for nearly fifty years, when during World War I the German U-boat wolf packs attempted to break the Allied supply convoys.

Hunley was the last of three experimental submarines built between 1861 and 1863 by James McClintock and Baxter Watson. Their first submarine, *Pioneer*, was constructed in New Orleans, but evidently was scuttled in Lake Ponchartrain to avoid capture when the city fell to the Northern forces. The operation moved to Mobile, Alabama, where, with the assistance and financial backing of Horace Hunley, as well as Lieutenant George Dixon and William Alexander, two engineers from the 21st Alabama Infantry, they developed and built *American Diver* and *H.L. Hunley*.

The submarine *H.L. Hunley* was built at the Park and Lyons machine shop in the spring of 1863. Fashioned from an iron steam boiler, with tapered cast ends, the vessel was a true **Submersible**. It featured movable dive planes for diving and surfacing, internal ballast tanks, operated by manual force pumps, to trim the vessel, and a mercury depth gauge to maintain depth. When running, submerged twin snorkels could be raised to the surface to admit air. Designed for a crew of nine, the vessel was powered by an eight-position hand crank connected to a propeller, and under ideal conditions it could make 3 to 4 knots. Steering was facilitated by a compass when submerged, and with glass view ports set into the coamings of the two hatches set along the upper surface of the hull when operating on the surface.

The vessel operated successfully during trials in Mobile Bay. However, Charleston was to become its theatre of operation. On 7 August 1863, Confederate General P.G.T. Beauregard ordered *Hunley* to be transported to Charleston to operate offensively against Admiral Dahlgren's blockading fleet. Its original armament consisted of a floating copper 'torpedo' (mine), which was to be towed and detonated against the side of an enemy ship as the submarine dived beneath its hull. However, this method proved to be untenable in the treacherous currents around Charleston Harbour, and with weighted nets protecting the Union monitors from such an attack. Furthermore, the vessel's first targets lay in too shallow water

CSS H.L. Hunley *at Charleston, 6 December 1863. (US Naval Historical Center)*

Magnetometer readings from the survey of H.L. Hunley. (NPS)

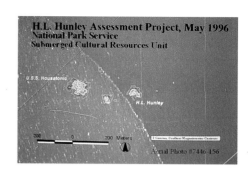

for the submarine to pass beneath them. The towed torpedo was abandoned in favour of a spar fitted with a Singer torpedo containing a 90 lb black powder charge and fitted with a barbed spike. The new plan called for *Hunley* to ram its target, thus firmly affixing the torpedo to the enemy hull below the waterline, pull astern, and detonate the charge by means of a line attached to the trigger mechanism.

Hunley was based at Battery Marshall on Sullivan's Island and for several months conducted trials in Charleston Harbour. While on trials the submarine twice sank, taking thirteen men to their death. After the second sinking, which occurred on 15 October 1863 and claimed the life of the vessel's main financial backer and namesake Horace Hunley, General Beauregard ordered that the submersible be operated solely as a surface craft. Further trials were conducted offshore under the command of Lieutenants Dixon and Alexander. Finally, after successfully detonating a charge against the hull of USS *Housatonic*, the submarine *H.L. Hunley* sank for the last time on the evening of 17 February 1864, off Charleston.

Over the years, numerous attempts were made to locate the ill-fated submarine. A survey of the wreck of *Housatonic* nine months after the attack failed to uncover any evidence of the submarine's presence, as did another survey in 1873, conducted prior to demolishing the remains of *Housatonic* to remove it as an obstruction to navigation. The vessel was located in May 1995 by divers from Clive Cussler's **National Underwater and Marine Agency** (NUMA) working under authority of the State. In the spring of 1996, the National Park Service's **Submerged Cultural Resources Unit** (NPS-SCRU) led by Daniel J. Lenihan (principal investigator), with field operations supervised by Larry E. Murphy, and the South Carolina Institute of Archaeology and Anthropology (SCIAA) led by Christopher Amer, conducted an archaeological assessment of the site on behalf of the US Naval Historical Center and South

Carolina Hunley Commission which oversee the disposition and scientific research of the vessel. The purpose was to assess the vessel's condition for potential archaeological recovery and permanent display.

Hunley is completely buried in the harbour sediments, lying 45 degrees on its starboard side, bow facing the shore, dive planes elevated. The evidence suggests that, after the initial sinking, the hull became buried within ten to fifteen years in a single event. The hull still contains metal with active corrosion taking place throughout the vessel. There is little apparent damage to the hull in the areas investigated (less than one-quarter of the vessel). Nonetheless, the forward face of the forward hatch combing is fractured, possibly where a porthole once existed.

Architecturally, *Hunley* differs in a number of ways from early descriptions of the vessel by Lieutenant Alexander (1902) and Simon Lake (1899) and bears more similarity to a Conrad Wise Chapman painting of the vessel done shortly after it was built. The hull investigated has a hydrodynamic shape with smooth lines converging at bow and stern. The hull is 39 ft 5 in (12 m) long and *c*. 3 ft 10 in (1.2 m) in diameter. A 4 3/4 in (12 cm) external keel runs along the bottom of the hull. Both hatches are present, each located *c*. 2.7 m from either end of the hull. Each hatch coaming contains a small view port on its port side, while the forward hatch coaming apparently contained one facing forward. The dimensions and configuration of the hatches approximate those noted by Alexander. A cutwater, formed from a single plate of iron, angles forward from the forward hatch toward the bow. The air box/snorkel is located directly aft of the forward hatch, although only stubs of the snorkel tubes remain. Between the air box and the aft hatch, evenly spaced along the hull, and to either side of the centreline, are five pairs of flat-glass deadlights, noted on the 1899 Simon Lake drawing, presumably to facilitate illumination of the interior of the vessel. The port dive plane, located

below the air box, is 6 ft 10 in (2.1 m) long (longer than the 5 ft (1.5 m) noted by Alexander), 8 1/2 in (20 cm) wide, and turned on a 3 in (7.6 cm) pivot pin. No evidence for a spar was found during the assessment.

The submarine, particularly, *H.L. Hunley*, was perhaps the most dramatic naval weapon introduced during the American Civil War, a war in which, for the first time, the achievements of the industrial and scientific revolution were used on a large scale. While the submarine *H.L. Hunley* was not much of a factor in the course of the naval aspects of the war, it did foreshadow the important role that submarines were to play in subsequent wars and the balance of world power. C.A.

ADDITIONAL READING

Coker, P.C. III, 1987, *Charleston's Maritime Heritage, 1670–1865*, Charleston, South Carolina.

Kloeppel, J.E., 1987, *Danger Beneath the Waves: A History of the Confederate Submarine H.L. Hunley*, College Park, Georgia.

Perry, M.F., 1965, *Infernal Machines: The Story of Confederate Submarine and Mine Warfare*, Baton Rouge, Louisiana.

Ragan, M.K., 1995, *The Hunley: Submarine, Sacrifice, and Success in the Civil War*, Charleston, South Carolina.

Rich, M.A. (ed.), 1968, *The Confederate States Ship H.L. Hunley*, Journal of the Confederate Historical Society of England, Rickmansworth, Herts.

Scharf, J.T., 1887, *History of the Confederate States Navy from its Organization to the Surrender of its Last Vessel*, New York and San Francisco.

South Carolina Institute of Archaeology and Anthropology Hunley Project Working Group, n.d., 'H.L. Hunley Archaeology Management Plan', MS. on file, Columbia.

Still, W.N., 1969, *Confederate Shipbuilding*, Athens, Georgia.

Still, W.N., 1971, *Iron Afloat: The Story of the Confederate Armorclads*, Nashville, Tennessee.

Wise, S.R., 1988, *Lifeline of the Confederacy: Blockade Running During the Civil War*, Columbia, South Carolina.

Hoff's Store

A ship chandler's shop operated during the California Gold Rush that burned down and collapsed into shallow water in 1851, was subsequently buried by landfill, and excavated in 1986. During the California Gold Rush of 1848–56, large numbers of ships cleared ports around the world for San Francisco, California's principal port. By the end of 1849, more than five hundred vessels had arrived and lay at anchor off the young city. San Francisco's population of a few hundred blossomed into the tens of thousands, and the city rapidly expanded up its steep sand hills and across the shallows of Yerba Buena Cove. The result, by 1850, was a city described by one contemporary as 'a Venice built of pine, rather than marble'. The town's waterfront streets were planked wharves, with buildings perched above the bay on pilings. Some of the buildings were ships hauled in close to shore and converted to other uses.

San Francisco burned down seven times during the Gold Rush, only to rebuild as a larger, more permanent city each time. The worst fire was that of 3–4 May 1851, which consumed more than 2,000 buildings and devastated the waterfront. Among the losses were the ship-buildings **Niantic** and *Apollo*, and a number of prominent mercantile and business establishments. The ship chandlery owned and operated by William C. Hoff and Henry Owner, and located at the southwest corner of Sacramento and Battery Streets, together with the harbourmaster's office on the second floor, was one of the destroyed buildings. It was almost completely consumed by flames before the second floor, loaded with heavy merchandise, collapsed into the bay. Immediately after the fire, sand was dumped over the site, filling in the shallows and encapsulating the remains of the store. Subsequent filling and construction buried the Hoff's Store site 6 m below the modern street level.

Prior to construction of a highrise tower on the site, a series of test borings were done under the supervision of contract archaeologist Allen Pastron to determine whether archaeological remains were present on the site. When the borings disclosed well-preserved Gold Rush artefacts, a comprehensive excavation was planned after pre-construction excavation for the foundation of the new building. A 1.5 m thick layer of charred cultural material was excavated from ten 5 m square units in 1986, under Pastron's supervision, resulting in the recovery of more than 29,000 artefacts.

The burial of the store's remains and its contents in water and mud, which was then sealed beneath 4 m of sand, created an anaerobic environment and near perfect preservation of otherwise perishable objects. Paper, textiles, vegetable fibre, foodstuffs, and wood were all recovered, albeit saturated, in excellent condition.

Architectural remains included the charred stubs of the pilings that supported the store, and intact sections of the wood floor that had collapsed into the bay before burning. One section of floor included a trap door that originally led to the shallows below, perhaps for water access to the ships in the harbour.

A large number of the artefacts reflected the maritime supply activities of the store, including dried and preserved foodstuffs capable of withstanding the long-term storage requisite for prolonged ocean voyages, white lead paint, copper tacks, brushes and brooms for shipboard maintenance, the burned remains of a ship's medicine chest, navigational instruments, and tinware and ceramics for shipboard use. The foodstuffs included barrels of intact hardtack and ship's bread, salt pork, crocks of butter, coffee, bags of rice, jars of preserves and condiments, and a case of whisky. These foodstuffs, other than the hardtack and salt pork, were still edible (see also **Faunal studies** (Vertebrates)).

Other artefacts on the site may have come from nearby stores that collapsed into the bay during the fire and mingled with Hoff's merchandise, or represented a more diverse range of goods for sale to miners. These included shovels and pickaxes, coffee grinders, stacks of tin sheets, rolls of decorated floor cloth, arms and ammunition, including a case of Mexican War (1846–8) surplus carbine rifles, a box of paper cartridges with powder and shot intact, cartridge boxes, swords, the burned remains of an army uniform, chests of Chinese tea, and a considerable amount of Chinese export porcelain.

Following the excavation, construction proceeded at the site. The collection was analysed by scholars under Pastron's direction, and then donated to the Anthropology Museum at the University of California, Berkeley. The Hoff's Store site, like the remains of buried ships from the Gold Rush, including *Niantic*, represents a rich and diverse archaeological record of the rapid maritime beginnings of San Francisco, displaying the wide range of goods and materials afforded on the western frontier because of the availability, if not necessity, of ships for regular supply, and the incredible purchasing power of California gold. J.P.D.

San Francisco's 'Long Wharf' in 1850–51. The two-storey ship chandlery of W.C. Hoff can be seen to the left. (San Francisco National Historical Park)

ADDITIONAL READING

Delgado, J.P., 1991, *To California By Sea: A Maritime History of the California Gold Rush*, Columbia.

Pastron, A.G. and Hattori, E.M. (eds), 1990, *The Hoff Store Site and Gold Rush Merchandise from San Francisco, California*, Society for Historical Archaeology, Special Publication Series no. 7, Ann Arbor, Michigan.

Högholmen Island

A fort and associated harbour located on the southwestern part of the Finnish coast, west of Hanko, on the islet of Högholmen. The site, which is situated near the island of Hitis, along the old sea route that followed the coast, has been archaeologically dated to the medieval period. The remains on land were first investigated by archaeologists in the 1870s and 1880s. A hundred years later, archaeological investigations again commenced, including recording and sampling of the underwater remains of the harbour. The site on land includes the remains of a large defensive stone building on the top of the island of Högholmen, and a not yet dated earthen wall on the eastern side of the island. The artefacts excavated at the site, including coins, glassware, and pottery, have been dated to the end of the 14th and the beginning of the 15th century. Although these finds evidently are from the main occupation phase, there were also signs of activity at the site from the Iron Age.

The material remains under water are situated on the north and west sides of the island. The ones to the north, where a harbour was located, are the remains of timber caissons filled with stones. Those to the west are of a 70 m long stone jetty running parallel to the shore. The harbour basin outside the jetty was about 5 m deep in the 13th century. The jetty has been dated by carbon-14 analysis to the early 14th century.

The original function of the Högholmen site is not yet fully interpreted. One hypothesis is that this fortified harbour was a location where, in the medieval period, wares were unloaded from seagoing ships into smaller vessels. According to oral tradition, the Högholmen harbour was a trading centre. The site was mentioned in written sources in 1347, when the Swedish king Magnus Eriksson visited the island.

Other remains in this area of the coast which might be contemporary with the Högholmen harbour are the medieval cemetery at Kyrkö Island and the ruins of a chapel at nearby Kyrksundet. C.O.C.

ADDITIONAL READING

Edgren, T., 1977, 'Medeltidsarkeologi i skärgårdshavet, *Historisk Tidskrift för Finland*, 4, 404–26.

Edgren, T., 1979, 'Högholmen i Hitis, en hamnplats från medeltiden: en preliminår rapport', *Nordisk Maritimhistorisk Exkursion III Hamnar och Ankarplatser i Sydväst, Helsingfors*, 85–106.

Ericsson, C., 1973, 'A Medieval Harbour Located in the Parish of Hitis: June 1973', *Bureau of Maritime History Report*, 2–3.

Ericsson, C., 1974, 'The Medieval Harbour of the Parish of Hitis: Work Resumed', *Bureau of Maritime History Report*, 7–9.

Holland I

The first submarine of the British Royal Navy, sunk in 1913, rediscovered and raised in 1982, and now being conserved in a conservation tank at Gosport, England. Designed by Irish-American John Philip Holland, *Holland I* represented more than two decades of refinement by the inventor, who began his work to develop a combat **Submersible** in 1878. In 1895, Holland won a contract with the US Government to build a submarine for the US Navy. The design was completed in September 1896, and in May

The launch of HMS Holland I. *(Royal Navy Submarine Museum, Gosport)*

1897 the John P. Holland Torpedo Boat Company launched its first boat at Lewis Nixon's Crescent Shipyard at Elizabethport, New Jersey. Sea trials and protracted negotiations with the government ended in the summer of 1900, when the **US Navy** purchased the submarine and ordered six more.

The British Royal Navy followed suit, and ordered five of the Holland 'boats' in 1900. The submarines were built under licence by Vickers at Barrow-in-Furness. The first to be delivered, HM Submarine No. 1, also known as *Holland I*, was launched on 2 October 1901. The 64 ft (19.6 m) long, 122 ton submarine was powered by electric batteries and fired a Whitehead torpedo.

The adoption of the submarine as a naval weapon was assured by the initial success of the Holland boats, later refinements, and other governments' purchase of the submarines. Obsolete after twelve years of service, *Holland I* was lost while under tow in October 1913, underway to the scrapyard. In April 1981, a Royal Navy minesweeper working off Eddystone Lighthouse rediscovered the wreck in deep water. Navy divers raised the wreck in the summer of 1982 under the supervision of Commander Richard Compton Hall, a submarine expert. After seventy years, the submarine was in an excellent state of preservation.

Holland I was towed to the Royal Navy dockyard at Devonport, cleaned with high pressure hoses and treated with the metal preservative Fertan. It was then cut into three pieces and transported overland to the Navy's submarine museum at Gosport, near Portsmouth, and placed on public display as the earliest surviving Holland submarine in the world. J.P.D.

ADDITIONAL READING

Snow, R.F., 1984, 'The Holland Surfaces', *American Heritage*, 3, 5.

Hollandia

Ship of the Dutch East India Company (VOC) which wrecked with no survivors west of the Scilly Isles off southwest England on 13 July 1743. Historically, *Hollandia* is closely related to *Amsterdam*, which was lost on the English south coast in 1749. Both VOC ships were newly built at the company's shipyard in Amsterdam, belonged to the same rate of 150 ft (42.5 m) and were sunk on their maiden voyage to Batavia in Indonesia. From an archaeological point of view, however, these shipwrecks are rather diverse. In the case of *Amsterdam* the hull is substantially intact, while *Hollandia* belongs to the category of sites where the ship's structure has disintegrated completely.

In 1968, shipwreck explorer Rex Cowan took the initiative to locate the wreck through documentary research and **Magnetometer** surveys. After its discovery in 1971, excavation extended continuously throughout the 1970s, into the 1980s, and was restarted on an irregular basis in the early 1990s. The vessel remains were widely scattered over an area of approximately 180 by 100 m. The find distribution pattern comprised three main regions which allowed the reconstruction of the wrecking process. The southern half of the site contained a trail of finds, such as lead ingots, barrels of nails, iron bars, and two bronze mortars, which originated from the lower part of the hull. This material had fallen to the seabed while *Hollandia* was adrift with a damaged bottom after striking a rock. The ship itself finally came to rest on the rocky seabed north of this area.

As the ship fell apart, artefacts settled in gullies and around heavy remains, such as five anchors and twenty-eight iron guns. Concentrations of debris were found in two areas of 40 by 30 m each. From the presence of four bronze breechloading guns and a large quantity of silver coins on one of these locations, it can be deduced that the stern was facing south. The environmental conditions, however, resulted in a random find distribution which did not allow for a refined spatial reconstruction of the ship's layout. Interpretation of such a complex site was further hampered by the methodological approach of the fieldwork. The excavation during the 1970s reflected the early stage of VOC-wreck explorations in northwest Europe, when underwater archaeological standards were being newly developed.

The collection of finds was heterogeneous and extensive. Some 3,500 items have been recovered, silver coins and lead ingots excluded. Most artefacts were of a durable nature, such as various metals (including parts of the ship's fire engine), ceramics,

International Journal of Nautical Archaeology, 4, 2, 267–300.

Gawronski, J., 1992, 'Functional Classifications of Artefacts of VOC-ships: The Archaeological and Historical Practice', in D. Keith and T.L. Carrell (eds), *Underwater Archaeological Proceedings from the Society for Historical Archaeology Conference 1992*, Ann Arbor.

Gawronski, J., Kist, B., and Stokvis-Boetzelaer, O. (eds), 1992, *Hollandia Compendium: A Contribution to the History, Archaeology, Classification and Lexicography of a 150 ft. Dutch East Indiaman (1740–1750)*, Amsterdam.

Horse Ferry Wreck

A horse-propelled sidewheel ferryboat built for service on **Lake Champlain** in the second quarter of the 19th century and sunk off the city of Burlington, Vermont. The wreck of the horse ferry (also referred to as the horseboat or teamboat) was discovered upright in 15 m of water during a **Side scan sonar** survey in 1983 and was recorded as a

sion for watercraft extends far back in time. Roman engineers in the 4th century AD proposed building a warship propelled by teams of oxen walking around capstans and turning three pairs of side-wheels (there is no evidence that the idea advanced beyond the drawing board, however). The earliest working horseboat that we know of was an 8 hp River Thames boat built in London around 1680 by Prince Rupert. In North America, steamboat inventor John Fitch built a functional horse-propelled boat on the Delaware River in the 18th century, and other designs were built and tested in the earliest years of the 19th century.

Robert Fulton's success with the steamer *North River* in 1807 contributed to the introduction of horseboats seven years later. New York City ferry owners, impressed by the speed and dependability of paddle wheel propulsion, hoped to build steamboats for their crossings, but were prevented by the state monopoly on steam propulsion granted

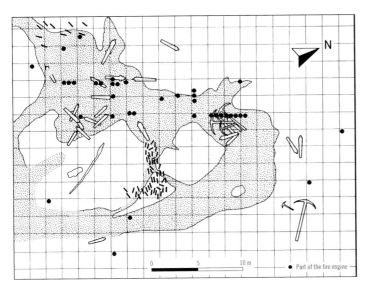

Distribution of the remains of Hollandia's fire engine on the main site. (Rijksmuseum, Amsterdam)

Parts of the ship's fire engine recovered on the main site of Hollandia. (Rijksmuseum, Amsterdam)

and glass, but they were heavily damaged and fragmented. Delicate organic material hardly survived. Analysis of the wreck was enhanced after the acquisition of 80 per cent of these finds in 1980 by the Rijksmuseum in Amsterdam. Research focused on the problem of functional classification of this type of fragmented archaeological remains. This resulted in the *Hollandia Compendium* publication, consisting of a systematic catalogue combined with exhaustive historical documentation on the construction and equipment of VOC ships from the middle of the 18th century. J.H.J.G.

ADDITIONAL READING

Cowan, R., Cowan, Z., and Marsden, P., 1975, 'The Dutch East Indiaman Hollandia Wrecked on Isles of Scilly in 1743',

Photomosaic by Scott Hill and Milton Shares in 1984. The wreck was opened as a Vermont Division for Historic Preservation underwater preserve in 1989, and was the subject of an archaeological study sponsored by the Lake Champlain Maritime Museum, the **Institute of Nautical Archaeology**, and the **National Geographic Society** between 1989 and 1992.

Historical research on the horseboat in Burlington Bay revealed that this vessel was not unique, but was instead one of hundreds of horse-powered ferries built in North America during the 19th and early 20th centuries. The research also showed that horse-propelled craft developed side by side with steamboats, in many cases by inventors working with both forms of propulsion. The concept of animal propul-

to Fulton and his partner Robert Livingston. They turned to horse power instead, and in the summer of 1814 three ferries of this type were launched around Manhattan. The boats proved efficient for short-distance passages, and were cheaper to build and operate than steam-propelled boats. The success of the New York horse ferries led to the construction of many others on the rivers, lakes, and bays of North America.

Horse power mechanisms for ferryboats underwent three stages of evolution between 1814 and 1840. The earliest ferries were powered by a horse whim, a capstan-like device that required the horses to walk in a circle to turn the paddle wheel. Because the whim required a large horse walkway, most boats powered by this mechanism were twin-hulled catamarans with a single paddle wheel – propelled by six to eight horses – mounted in the centre. There were drawbacks to this form of horseboat, however: catamarans were relatively expensive to build, the walkway occupied much deck space, and walking in a circle all day was hard on the horses.

The deficiencies of the whim-catamaran ferries were corrected in 1819 when Barnabus Langdon, an inventor from Troy, New York, created the horizontal treadwheel ferry, a single-hulled craft with a large horizontal wheel, similar to a record turntable, mounted beneath the deck. Openings cut through the deck allowed horses to walk in place on the wheel and, through a system of gears and power shafts, turn a pair of sidewheels. The below-deck configuration of the mechanism permitted maximum use of a ferry's deck space for cargo and passengers. Langdon established a business in Troy to build and install his machinery, and for the next quarter of a century inexpensive horizontal treadwheel horseboats, powered by two, four, or six horses, were a common sight at ferry crossings in the United States and Canada.

The third form of propulsion mechanism for horseboats was the treadmill, a device developed in the late 1820s, perfected in the 1830s, and mass-produced from the 1840s until the early 20th century. Treadmills were compact power sources that proved even cheaper to purchase and maintain than horizontal treadwheels, and because they were mounted on a ferry's deck, they could be installed on simple, shallow-hulled craft. The typical treadmill boat had a pair of one-horse treadmills mounted on either side of the hull, with each mill powering one side-wheel. Other variants included a side-wheel boat with a single two-horse treadmill mounted in the centre, and a sternwheel ferry powered by pair of two-horse mills. Treadmill ferries gradually replaced treadwheel boats in the middle of the 19th century, and remained in use until the 1920s.

When discovered in 1983 the horseboat wreck in Burlington Bay was nearly complete, lacking only the foredeck, paddle boxes, and horse sheds. The ferry was equipped with a two-horse horizontal treadwheel, and measured 62 ft 5 in (19 m) in length, with the hull 15 ft 3 in (4.6 m) in breadth and the deck a maximum of 23 ft 8 in (7.2 m) in breadth. Unusual construction features included frames shaped from straight pieces of white and red oak by sawing across their width, steaming the wood, and then bending them to the proper shape. The 21 ft 11 in (6.7 m) diameter

Human remains: a skeleton found on board Vasa, under a gun carriage on the port side of the lower gun deck. The man's shoes, parts of his dress, hair, and nails have been preserved by the mud which filled the ship. (Courtesy of the Maritime Museum and the Warship Vasa)

treadwheel extended beyond the sides of the hull amidships, and the deck at this location had to be supported from above by a simple bridge structure.

Excavations in the bow and stern of the wreck yielded used gear wheels, broken horseshoes and leather harness fragments, a shattered teapot, a heavily used caulking iron, and (in the bow) the vessel's rudder. The artefacts and the worn state of the hull together suggested that the horseboat had seen many years of service – at least ten years and perhaps as many as twenty – and was intentionally scuttled in the lake when it was no longer of use. The name and precise dates of the ferry have not been determined (horseboat ferries did not operate out of Burlington), but archival and archaeological evidence hint that it was built around 1830 and retired in the 1840s. K.C.

ADDITIONAL READING

Crisman, K., 1993, 'A Horse-powered Sidewheel Ferry Sunk in Burlington Bay, Lake Champlain', in S. Smith (ed.), *Proceedings of the 1993 Conference on Underwater Archaeology, Kansas City*, Ann Arbor, Michigan.

Crisman, K., 1991, 'Horsepower on the Water: The Burlington Bay Horse Ferry Project', *Institute of Nautical Archaeology Newsletter*, 18, 4, 12–15.

Crisman, K. and Cohn, A., in press, 'When Horses Walked on Water', *The History and Archaeology of North America's Horse-powered Boats*, Washington, DC.

Human remains

One of the most difficult issues in underwater archaeology is that of human remains. Not only does their presence remind us of our own mortality, but there is no agreed upon method to address sensitive issues in which scientific, cultural, and religious values must be considered and reconciled. The range of shipwrecks that may contain human remains spans centuries, encompasses diverse cultural and ethnic groups, is

scattered around the globe in a variety of environments, and results from many circumstances.

The earliest human remains discovered to date come from a Roman cargo ship sunk off Spargi in the 1st century BC. Protected by the deep cold water and the helm of the amphora-carrier, a skull was excavated from the site in 1961. Ten centuries later, two Arab ships that sank off Cannes preserved the remains of three more individuals. Excavated in the 1970s, the hull of the 7.5 to 9.1 m long Camp-Long shipwreck contained a male skeleton with his sword and cutlass-sheath. The second shipwreck, off Sainte-Marguerite Island, contained two more incomplete male skeletons. These examples suggest that human remains on even the most ancient shipwrecks should not be discounted.

Warships may be the single greatest source of wrecks that contain human remains. In 1545, while in the midst of battle, Henry VIII's **Mary Rose** plunged to the bottom of Portsmouth Harbour drowning nearly seven hundred seamen and soldiers. The remains of archers, pikemen, and gunners, crushed beneath cannons or trapped below decks, were exhumed during excavations in the 1970s. Eighty-five years after the Portsmouth disaster, the heavily armed warship **Vasa**, considered the epitome of 17th-century Swedish design, proved so unstable it capsized and sank. The cold water and mud not only preserved the ship, but the remains of its crewmen and their wives.

The North American War of 1812 saw the loss of schooners **Hamilton** and **Scourge** on Lake Ontario. On the night of 8 August 1813, during a break in the battle between an American and a Canadian-British squadron, a sudden fierce squall roared across the lake capsizing both schooners. Fifty-three men drowned in the combined disaster. The discovery of the ships and later photographic documentation in 1982 revealed human remains scattered across the lake bottom.

Perhaps the largest single group of shipwrecks that clearly contain human remains are from World War II. More than eleven hundred men remain entombed in the battleships USS *Arizona* and USS *Utah*. The battles at **Truk Lagoon**, Guadalcanal (see **Guadalcanal Wrecks**), Leyte Gulf, Palau, Midway, and submarine attacks in the North Atlantic and Pacific resulted in heavy losses. The sailors, whether in the military or in non-military convoys, hailed from America, Canada, the British Isles, Germany, Japan, the Baltic and Pacific rim. Scuba divers and remotely operated vehicles exploring these shipwrecks have regularly encountered human remains. Submarines, like that of the German U-352 sunk off the North Carolina coast in 1942, efficiently trapped their crews who were to be found 40 years later near their battle stations.

Horrific accidents at sea resulting from squalls, hurricanes, icebergs, and collision have claimed many thousands of ships. During the era of New World exploration, hurricanes destroyed whole fleets of treasure-laden ships. One such fleet left Havana in 1733, among them the galleon *St Jose*. Although salvaged in antiquity, its location was forgotten until 1968 when excavations on the site uncovered a human skull in the floor timbers.

The North American **Great Lakes** have claimed their share of accidents, including *Kamloops*, sunk in 1927, and *Emperor*, wrecked in 1947. Both ships, like *Edmund Fitzgerald*, sank during blizzards on the lakes. Twelve crew members from *Kamloops* are reported to be trapped in the stern while an unknown number remain on *Emperor*. The one crewman recovered from *Emperor* in 1976 was reported to be clothed and in remarkably good condition after twenty-nine years of immersion. The fate of the crew on *Edmund Fitzgerald* remains unknown.

There are also many disasters where the presence of human remains is suspected. In 1912, more than fifteen hundred lives were lost in the **Titanic** disaster. To date, there has been only very limited examination of the ship's interior due to its extreme depth and a worldwide call to treat the site as a memorial. The British-owned passenger ship **Lusitania** was struck by a torpedo in May 1915; nearly twelve hundred passengers drowned.

Although the wreck was surveyed, no effort has been made to examine carefully the dangerous interior spaces.

Two famous American Civil War warships, the Union ironclad USS **Monitor** and the Confederate submarine **H.L.Hunley**, may also contain human remains. In 1862, a few months after *Monitor*'s well-known battle with CSS *Virginia*, the former took on water and slipped beneath the sea off North Carolina carrying with it sixteen members of the crew. On the night of 17 February 1864, the Confederate submarine *H.L. Hunley*, equipped with a spar-mounted torpedo, attacked and sank USS *Housatonic*. While the attack was a success, *Hunley* and its small crew never returned. In 1973, USS *Monitor* was found in 70 m of water. It has been only sporadically investigated in the intervening years, and no human remains have yet been discovered. Whether human remains will be found in the ill-fated CSS *Hunley*, discovered in May 1995, is unknown.

There are numerous recent accidents where human remains are known to exist, including the famous submarines *Thresher* (1963) and *Scorpion* (1968). In these and other cases, the decision was made to leave the individuals entombed. While it is easier to remain dispassionate about human remains from our remote past, their discovery on ships lost in this century is another matter. The issues raised by human remains on sites at or near the fifty-year cutoff for archaeological designation are numerous. As our ability to discover and excavate deep water shipwrecks increases, so does the likelihood of finding human remains. These discoveries will challenge our ability to balance research and reverence for the deceased. T.L.C.

ADDITIONAL READING

Ballard, R.D. and Michel, J.-L., 1985, 'How We Found the Titanic', *National Geographic*, 168, 6.

Cain, E., 1983, *Ghost Ships: Hamilton and Scourge: Historical Treasures from the War of 1812*, Watford, Herts.

Franzen, A., 1960, *The Warship Vasa*, Stockholm.

Lamboglia, N., 1961, 'La seconda campagna di scavo sulla nave romana de Spargi (1959)', in *Atti del III Congresso International di Archeologia Sottomarina di Barcellona*, Bordighera, 205–14.

Lenihan, D.J. (ed.),1987, *Submerged Cultural Resources Study: Isle Royale National Park*, Southwest Cultural Resources Centre Professional Papers no. 8, Santa Fe.

Lovin, B., 1977, 'Argosy Discovers a German U-boat off North Carolina', *Argosy*, 385, 4, 32–7.

McKee, A., 1982, *How We Found the Mary Rose*, New York.

Miller, E.M., 1978, *USS Monitor: The Ship that Launched the Modern Navy*, Annapolis.

Morrison, S.E., 1984, *History of United States Naval Operations in World War II*, vols 3–8, 14, Boston.

Perry, M.F., 1965, *Infernal Machines: The Story of Confederate Submarines and Mine Warfare*, Baton Rouge.

Peterson, M.L., 1972, 'Traders and Privateers Across the Atlantic: 1492–1733', in G.F. Bass (ed.), *History of Seafaring Based on Underwater Archaeology*, New York.

Prange, G.W., 1981, *At Dawn We Slept: The Untold Story of Pearl Harbor*, New York.

Humber Wrecks

The remains of early logboats and plank boats on the Humber estuary foreshore in eastern England, and in the former courses

Ferriby Boat 1 emerging from the northern foreshore of the Humber estuary at low water. (National Maritime Museum, London)

Plan drawing of Ferriby Boat 1. (E.V. Wright)

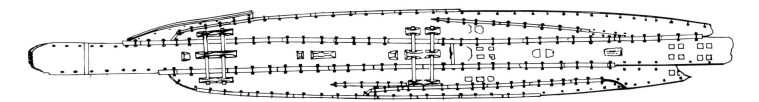

of rivers which used to flow into the Humber. These have been revealed both by chance finds and by planned excavations; none has yet been found underwater. Related plank boats have been excavated from the Severn estuary and at Dover.

The **Ferriby boats** (mid-2nd millennium BC) were used as ferries within the Humber estuary and its many tributaries, from informal landing places on foreshore and riverbank. Fragments of wickerwork hurdles, roughly contemporary with the boats, have been excavated, pinned to the foreshore close to where the boats were found. These were probably either part of a boat hardstanding or a causeway giving access to the landing place.

In the late 19th century, three structures from the early-1st millennium BC were excavated near a Humber tributary at Brigg, Lincolnshire: a causeway, a logboat, and a plank boat. The plank boat, the so-called **Brigg 'Raft'**, was a sewn oak plank boat from *c.* 800 BC, used as a paddled or poled ferry across the upper reaches of a tidal creek of the Humber. When no longer needed as a ferry, she became a landing stage between riverbank and boats. The Brigg causeway probably had a similar use, a century or so earlier. The **Brigg Logboat**, made from one large oak log more than 15 m long and 6 m in girth, no longer survives, but comparison with an excavated logboat of *c.* 300 BC from Hasholme, near another former tributary of the Humber, assists interpretation of the Brigg excavation record. The Brigg boat could carry twenty-eight paddlers at a draft of 35 cm, or five men and 5.49 tonnes of cargo at a draft of 60 cm. Unlike Brigg, the parent **Hasholme Logboat** was open forward as well as aft, probably due to heart rot. The bow was made watertight by two shaped timbers held in position by vertical treenails and by transverse timbers wedged within cleats similar to those used at Ferriby and Brigg. This boat could have carried twenty paddlers at 46 cm draft, or five men and 5.5 tonnes cargo at 75 cm draft.

In addition to Brigg and Hasholme, twenty other logboats have been found in or near rivers flowing into the Humber, ranging in size from 3 to 10 m, and in date from 1400 BC to AD 1100. Logboats were clearly in use for a long time in Britain and their value to economic and social life can hardly be over-emphasized. S.M.

ADDITIONAL READING

McGrail, S., 1978, *Logboats of England and Wales*, British Archaeological Reports 51, Oxford.

McGrail, S., 1981, *Brigg 'Raft' and its Prehistoric Environment*, British Archaeological Reports 89, Oxford.

McGrail, S., 1985, 'Brigg "Raft": A Flat-bottomed Boat', *International Journal of Nautical Archaeology*, 23, 283–8.

McGrail, S., 1987, *Ancient Boats in NW Europe*, London.

McGrail, S., 1988, 'Assessing the Performance of an Ancient Boat', *Oxford Journal of Archaeology*, 7, 35–46.

Millett, M. and McGrail, S., 1987, 'Archaeology of the Hasholme Logboat', *Archaeological Journal*, 44, 96–155.

Wright, E.V., 1990, *Ferriby Boats*, London.

Humboldt

A transatlantic steamer built for the Havre Line in 1851 by Westervelt and Mackay of New York. In common with other early oceanic passenger steamers, it was a wood-hulled paddler and, for its day, was very large - around 2,200 tons. Following fifteen successful voyages, carrying mail, passengers, and high-value cargo, in December 1853 *Humboldt* ran aground while entering Halifax, Nova Scotia, to take on extra coal.

In the 1960s, two large but badly eroded sections of hull were found by sport divers, lying exposed on the seabed about 1 nautical mile (1.9 km) north of the site where the ship ran aground. They had probably been moved there by a hurricane a number of years after the ship broke up. An ongoing survey of this wreckage began in 1989 with the primary aim of documenting some structural details employed by mid-19th-century shipwrights. Very large hulls must be designed to withstand exceptional stresses, while those of steamers (with the weight of their engines concentrated amidships) had to bear loads not faced by sailing ship hulls. *Humboldt*, as one of the last very large ships built before the general adoption of iron, provides an example of the ways in which this challenge was met.

By 1997, work on the site had documented the use of diagonal iron trusses and braces between the frames and the ceiling, of copper planking bolts used in place of treenails, and of edge-bolting of the ceiling planks. The most unusual feature recorded, however, is the large after deadwood. That seems to have been placed on top of the keelson, which apparently extended aft to the sternpost. This arrangement is analogous to one seen on the much smaller, Liverpool-built *Jhelum* of 1849. This combination of features seen on *Humboldt* would not have been employed in any ship of the 1840s, nor would it be expected in one built after 1860. Thus, the survey of her remains illumines one point along the continuous evolution of wooden ship structure, specifically a final attempt to build the biggest ships of wood.

Humboldt was built in the same yard and at the same time as **Winfield Scott**, which is currently being studied where she sank off California. Future work on the two sites may thus illustrate the degree of variability in structural features among such 'sisters', providing an important reference measure for typologies of hull structure. Finally, the survey of *Humboldt* has shown that much can be learned from the close examination of surviving wreckage, even when the site is relatively modern, the hull broken, and its remnants badly eroded. T.J.K.

ADDITIONAL READING

Kenchington, T.J. and Whitelock, C., 1996, 'The United States Mail Steamer *Humboldt*: 1851-53: Initial Report', *International Journal of Nautical Archaeology*, 25, 207-23

Hunley

see *H.L. Hunley*

USS *Huron*

United States gunboat lost during a storm off Nags Head, North Carolina in 1877 with large loss of life. USS *Huron* was built in 1875 at the Delaware River Shipbuilding Company in Chester, Pennsylvania, just down river from Philadelphia. Classified as a 'sloop-of-war', *Huron* was an *Alert*-class, third-rate gunboat, and had a length of 175 ft (53.4 m), a beam of 32 ft (9.75 m), and drew 13 ft (4 m) of water amidships. The ship had a displacement tonnage of 541 tons, 1,020 tons fully loaded, and carried a crew of sixteen officers and 118 enlisted men. Built a decade after the American Civil War, USS *Huron* was constructed during a period of transition between the old and new navy. *Huron* and her two sister-ships were the last American naval vessels to be built of iron rather than steel and to be equipped with sails to supplement the ship's steam engine.

On 24 November 1877, while en route to a surveying expedition in the Caribbean, *Huron* ran aground during a heavy gale on the Outer Banks of North Carolina. Tragically, the nearby Nags Head Lifesaving Station was closed, and the local residents who gathered on the beach were helpless to aid the ship's crew. Only thirty-four sailors made it safely to shore; the rest of *Huron*'s crew perished during the night. The magnitude of the disaster shocked the nation, and eventually prompted Congress to appropriate additional funding for the Lifesaving Service. By 1883, fifteen new stations had been built along the North Carolina coast.

The remains of *Huron* lie approximately 230 m offshore of the Bladen Street beach access in Nags Head, North Carolina. The

USS Huron, *showing her schooner rig. (Courtesy of Mariners Museum, Newport News, Virginia. US Naval Historical Center)*

vessel is totally submerged in 5.5 m of water. Shifting sands alternately expose or cover portions of the wreck, but in recent years the entire hull has been examined and documented from the well-preserved bow that juts nearly 4.5 m above the bottom, to the sternpost and rudder that were badly damaged during salvage efforts in 1877.

For years the wreck of *Huron* has been a popular dive site, and during the summers of 1987 and 1988 archaeologists conducted the first investigation of the vessel and prepared a detailed site map. As a result of those investigations, USS *Huron* was placed in the **National Register of Historic Places**. In 1991 the Secretary of the North Carolina Department of Cultural Resources designated the site as North Carolina's first 'Historic Shipwreck Preserve'. The site is administered cooperatively by the **US Navy**, the town of Nags Head, and the North Carolina Department of Cultural Resources.

In order to relate the story of *Huron* and make the wreck site more accessible, the Department of Cultural Resources and the town of Nags Head built an onshore exhibit gazebo and placed an underwater commemorative marker on the wreck site. During the summer months the town maintains buoys to mark the bow and stern of the wreck. Divers and snorkellers who visit the site can see a wide variety of sea life as they swim over the remains of the historic warship. R.L.

ADDITIONAL READING

Farb, R.M., 1985, *Shipwrecks: Diving the Graveyard of the Atlantic*, Hillsborough, N. Carolina.

Stick, D., 1952, *Graveyard of the Atlantic: Shipwrecks of the North Carolina Coast*, Chapel Hill, N. Carolina.

Hydration dating
see **Absolute dating**

Hydraulic probing

The use of high pressure water and pipe to determine the location and some characteristics of buried cultural material, such as shipwrecks, on a beach or in the surf. During **Magnetometer** surveys of beaches, inlets, shoals, and other shallow areas, anomalies indicating the presence of buried cultural material are occasionally discovered in areas where a considerable sand overburden makes test excavation difficult and expensive. Shipwreck sites, particularly in surf zones on a beach, can be buried beneath three or more metres of sand, small gravel, and shell. Excavation in soft sand of varying densities can be difficult, and **Cofferdams** used on land or in deeper water can be dangerous in surf.

An easy, inexpensive alternative used to test anomalies is the use of a high pressure water jet inside a small diameter (*c.* 10 cm) plastic pipe to penetrate through the sand and probe for the depth, size, and occasionally the shape of buried cultural material. The relative position and outline of buried shipwrecks have been discerned in this fashion, particularly when the probes are arranged on a grid and systematically used. Occasionally smaller cultural material washes to the surface, such as wood, indicating the nature of the contact. J.P.D.

ICMM
see **International Congress of Maritime Museums**

ICOMOS

The International Council on Monuments and Sites, the peak international non-governmental organization dealing with monuments and sites. It is closely linked with UNESCO and has members in over sixty countries and headquarters in Paris. Members in each country are formed into national committees and have the right to participate in the ICOMOS triennial general assemblies. ICOMOS also has a number of specialized international committees.

ICOMOS grew out of a meeting in Venice in 1964 of the International Congress of Architects and Technicians of Historic Monuments, which established the International Charter for the Conservation and Restoration of Monuments and Sites (the Venice Charter), a document laying down on an international basis the principles guiding the preservation and restoration of ancient buildings. The intention was that each country should be responsible for applying the plan within the framework of its own culture and traditions. ICOMOS was subsequently formed in 1965 as the international organization concerned with furthering the conservation, protection, rehabilitation and enhancement of monuments, groups of buildings, and sites. Other objectives were to provide a mechanism for linking those concerned with the conservation of monuments and sites, to disseminate information about their conservation, to cooperate at national and international levels in the development of documentation centres, to encourage the adoption and implementation of international recommendations, to cooperate in training programmes, and to cooperate with UNESCO.

ICOMOS played an important role with UNESCO in the preparation of the World Heritage Convention of 1972, in the organization of exchange and training programmes, and in the preparation of recommendations. In more recent times ICOMOS has turned its attention to the underwater cultural heritage. A 1987 International Symposium held in Washington requested ICOMOS to: (1) petition UNESCO to establish international instruments (a Recommendation and a Convention) to advise member states on the establishment of national legislation protecting shipwrecks in national waters and an agreement to protect them in international waters; and (2) to initiate the development and documentation of appropriate techniques to be used in the protection, investigation, and recovery of material and data from shipwrecks and other underwater sites.

In 1990 ICOMOS adopted a Charter for the Protection and Management of the Archaeological Heritage, which advocates the creation of archaeological reserves by governments. In 1991 it created the **International Committee on the Underwater Cultural Heritage**. G.H.

IFREMER

Institut Français de Recherche pour l'Exploitation de la Mer, one of the world's leading marine research organizations. Founded by government decree on 5 June 1984, IFREMER serves as a finalized-research body and a public establishment, providing scientific and technical support for the Government of Finance and for public and private sector groups involved in marine research and business throughout the world. IFREMER's approximately one billion French franc budget is obtained primarily through government subsidy but is supplemented by incomes generated through its commercial work. As of 1995, IFREMER employed about 1,250 engineers, scientists, technicians, and administrative staff at its headquarters, centres, attached stations, and delegations in France and around the world (Tahiti, the Antilles, Guyana, La Réunion, and New Caledonia). IFREMER maintains a fleet of long-distance general oceanography ships, a deep sea trawler, high seas and coastal fishing ships, a coastal oceanography ship, a long-distance support ship for underwater vehicles, and a number of manned and unmanned **Submersibles**, including towed sonar and cameras.

As a finalized-research body, IFREMER conducts its own basic and applied research and technical activities in the marine environment. It provides advice and assistance, produces and disseminates scientific knowledge, trains engineers and technicians, and is responsible for the construction, maintenance, and deployment of France's oceanographic research fleet. IFREMER has a policy of scientific cooperation and partnership with the domestic and international scientific community, and most of its activities are centred on studying and documenting natural resources in the coastal zones, nearshore areas, and the deep ocean.

IFREMER's work also includes shipwreck research and recovery. In 1985 IFREMER collaborated with the Woods Hole Oceanographic Institute (WHOI) in the United States during the successful search for the wreck of RMS *Titanic*. IFREMER scientist Jean-Louis Michel and WHOI scientist Robert Ballard led the research team. IFREMER returned to the *Titanic* wreck site in 1987, 1992, 1993, and 1996 with New York-based RMS Titanic, Inc. IFREMER's submersible *Nautile* and the remotely operated vehicle *Robin* extensively photographed and filmed *Titanic*'s hull remains and debris field and recovered more than 4,000 artefacts. IFREMER's shipwreck work has also included the non-intrusive documentation of a Roman wreck off the French Mediterranean coast with archaeologists from DRASM (1988) and recovery operations from the 1944 wreck of the liberty ship *John Barry*. Using the GRAB, a heavy intervention system comprising a large set of jaws equipped with thrusters, camera and sounder, IFREMER retrieved some of *Barry*'s cargo: $20 million in Saudi silver dollars from 2,576 m of water. J.P.D.

ADDITIONAL READING

Beasant, J., 1995, *Stalin's Silver*, London.

IFREMER, 1995, *Annual Report*, Issy-les-Moulineaux.

Charpentier, V. (ed.), 1994, *L'archéologie sous les eaux*, Paris.

Montluçon, J. and Lacoudre, N., 1989, *Les objets du Titanic*, Paris.

Institut Français de Recherche pour l'Exploitation de la Mer
see **IFREMER**

IJsselmeerpolders wrecks

Extensive collection of medieval and post-medieval watercraft, found in lands that were formerly the seabed of the Zuider Zee. From 1930 to 1968, a national land reclamation project partitioned the Zuider Zee with a series of dikes and dams. This division created four polders (reclaimed land masses) and several large inland lakes. The polders are now thoroughly inhabited and used extensively for agricultural cultivation. As the waters of the Zuider Zee receded and agricultural development was begun, scores of shipwrecks were discovered. While many of these were deeply embedded in protective wet and anaerobic sediments, others were exposed above the former sea bottom or only covered with a shallow layer of mud. Clearly these wrecks were going to be lost very quickly to the elements. The government of the Netherlands acted to rescue these highly significant archaeological sites and the information contained within them, through the agency overseeing the construc-

tion and development of the polders, the IJsselmeerpolders Development Authority, an agency within the Ministry of Transport and Public Works. This agency created a programme to rescue as much information as possible, through excavation and documentation of the most threatened of the newly found shipwrecks. Scientific research and rescue work has gone on continuously, from the 1940s to the present: over the last fifty years 435 wrecks have been located.

The present **Netherlands Institute of Ship and Underwater Archaeology** (NISA), which was formerly the Centre for Ship Archaeology, located at Ketelhaven in the Province of Flevoland, has its origins in the modest archaeological programme created by the Ijsselmeerpolders Development Authority. NISA now has jurisdiction over all shipwrecks located on terrestrial sites within the Netherlands, as well as those within territorial waters. These shipwrecks represent an unprecedented collection of ships and boats. Nowhere in Europe has there been found such an extensive collection of types of medieval and post-medieval watercraft. R.S.N.

INA
see **Institute of Nautical Archaeology**

India

Country strategically positioned in the Indian Ocean, with a coastline of 6,500 km, which has been a focal point in east–west trade from the dawn of civilization. The peoples of the ancient Indus civilization were apparently a seafaring nation and pioneers in building docks. The Indian archaeologist Dr S.R. Rao believes that their tidal dock, built *c*. 2300 BC at Lothal on the West Indian coast, was designed on scientific principles, taking into account tides, waves, and currents. The basin of the dock, which is 216 m long, 37.8 m wide, and 4.3 m deep, was lined with kiln-fired brick walls. Ships entered the basin at high tide; the lock gate device retained enough water for the vessels to manoeuvre. Cargo was stored, examined, and sealed in the warehouse by the authorities as well as the consigner. Terracotta seals found in the warehouse of Lothal bear mirror impressions of the seal on one side and of packing material on the other. Three types of boats in use can be made out from the terracotta models excavated off Lothal.

After the decline of the Indus civilization (*c*. 1900 BC) there was a lull in overseas trade. S.R. Rao's excavations at the submerged port city of **Dvaraka** indicate it had regained momentum by 1600 BC. The thermoluminescence date of the pottery from the fortified town of Beyt Dvaraka is 1528 BC; inscriptions, pottery, and a seal found at the same site area are also datable to the 16th century BC.

There is little documented evidence for subsequent maritime activities, but important ports such as Sopora near Bombay (Suparaka of Buddhist *Jataka* texts) were known for their brisk trade with Mediterranean and Southeast Asian ports in the 5th century BC, if not earlier. References to Indian shipbuilding are made by Arrian and Curtius. According to Arrian (325 BC) Alexander's fleet of 800 vessels was built of Indian wood by Indian craftsmen. The most reliable mariner's guide book is the *Periplus of the Eritrean Sea* (*c.* AD 50), in which the major ports of India in the 1st century AD are described. Later Indian dynasties maintained sizeable navies to defend the coast and protect the sea trade. The Chalukya ruler Pulikeshi fought a naval battle to take Gharapuri (Elephanta near Bombay) while the Silhara king took Kavadidvipa (Kairali in Lakshadveep).

By the 10th century, Arabs had a monopoly of shipping in the Indian Ocean. By the 16th century, the Maratha navy was a great challenge to them. The Portuguese, under Vasco de Gama, landed at Calicut on 27 May 1498. From the 16th century onwards the struggle among the French, Dutch, British, and Portuguese for control of Indian Ocean trade resulted in naval warfare and the loss of many vessels from Indian, European, and Arab countries. Even so, India-built teak-hulled vessels, which were durable and easily manoeuvrable, were in great demand in Europe. Marco Polo observed that ships built in India were so large that a crew of 300 was needed to man them. Large vessels could carry 6,000 matbags of pepper and nutmeg from Quilon. The English ships of 1600 were of 300 to 350 tons, while the Indian-built ships were of 1,400 to 1,500 tons. A Surat-built ship of 1,500 tons stopped by H. Middleton in 1612 on its voyage to the Red Sea was 153 ft (46.6 m) long with a 42 ft (12.8 m) beam and a 31 ft (9.4 m) depth. The Marathas had several types of merchant vessels and men of war, such as Pal, Galbat and Gurab. The fear of competition from the Indian shipping industry forced the British to issue orders prohibiting the construction of large vessels in India (*Calcutta Gazette*, 27 January 1789). This was a great blow to the industry.

Marine Archaeology Centre (MAC)
Marine archaeological research in India began under Dr S.R. Rao in 1981 after he found onshore evidence of the destruction of the township of Dvaraka of 1500-1400 BC,

during the excavation of a 13th–15th-century AD temple.

The main objective of the Marine Archaeology Centre is to explore and preserve submerged ports and sunken ships with a view to reconstructing the maritime history of India, and to bring to light the rich underwater cultural heritage of the subcontinent and of other countries with which India had commercial and cultural relations. Scientific data on sea-level fluctuations and the rate of sedimentation in river mouths could also be generated for future planning of ports.

The conventional method of survey has been supplemented by optical, mechanical, and electronic surveys for target search. Expert archaeologists, technicians, and photographers are trained in diving, excavation, documentation, and retrieval of submerged objects. Manual survey is supplemented by geophysical and magnetic surveys by deploying **Side scan sonar**, Echosounder, **Sub-bottom profiler**, and **Magnetometer**. For preliminary surveys of a vast area of submerged cities an underwater scooter (Aquazepp) has been pressed into service. The position-fixing of structures and artefacts was done initially with the help of sextant and Miniranger III, but subsequently **Global Positioning System** (GPS) based on satellite data was preferred. Conservation of artefacts of wood and metal is done in the NIO laboratory. Integration of aerial maps of shore and shallow water is done by the Survey of India. As a result of this interdisciplinary study and research by MAC, two ancient ports were discovered and excavated on the west coast and one port and a shipwreck on the east coast between 1983 and 1995.

Offshore exploration of Dvaraka on the mainland and off Beyt Dvaraka island was undertaken with a view to shedding light on the so-called 'Dark Ages of India' (1600-500 BC) and to investigate the possible historical basis of the *Mahabharata*. Underwater excavation was also undertaken at Prabhas (Somnath), a port contemporary with Dvaraka (1500 BC). A rock-cut channel, spheroid mooring stones, and a triangular anchor were found at a depth of 7 m at Somnath. The sea-level fluctuations on the Bahrain coast, submerging Kassite period sites, seem to correspond to fluctuations on the Dvaraka coast in 1500-1300 BC (see Rao 1988).

The early historical port town of Poompuhar, also called Kaveripattanam, situated at the mouth of the River Kaveri on the Tamilnadu coast, was explored by MAC in collaboration with the Department of Archaeology, Tamilnadu. Vestiges of the submerged brick and stone structures were

found at a depth of 5-20 m. The carbon-14 date of the brick wharf excavated in one of the ancient channels of the River Kaveri is 3rd century BC. Coins of Chola rulers as well as Roman and megalithic pottery have been found in the excavation. A semicircular stone structure which is 20 m in its longer axis lies buried in 23 m of water. The ancient Poompuhar town extended over 6 km from Kadakkod up to China Vanageri. As a result of excavations at Poompuhar on the east coast which dated the site to 3rd–6th century AD, the historicity of both the submerged towns has been established.

The data needed for locating shipwrecks in Indian waters have been collected by the researchers of MAC in Indian archives. The Geophysical and Manual Underwater survey was undertaken by NIO in collaboration with MAC off the Tamilnadu coast and a large cargo vessel of the 18th century which was wrecked about 4 km seaward of Poompuhar was discovered in 19 m of water. Lead weights punched with the legend W. BLACKETT 1791-1792 have been recovered. This wooden ship is sheathed with copper sheets. Further excavation of the shipwreck was undertaken in 1996.

The Lakshadveep group of islands, with Kavaratti as the main island, lies 404 km west of Cochin and was an important intermediary station for ships sailing to Europe via the Cape of Good Hope. A large number of ships sank in Lakshadveep waters between the 16th and the 19th centuries. The British ship *Byramgore*, for example, which was carrying valuable cargo, sank on 17 November 1827. Attempts were made to rescue the crew and the vessel, but by the time the rescue ship could reach the station, *Byramgore* had broken up. The Indian Naval Hydrographic Survey ship INS *Sandhayak* carried out a preliminary survey of the wreck of *Byramgore*. MAC also participated in the survey in February 1992. Further survey is needed to pinpoint the wreck, however, which might have slid to a depth of some 200 m.

The research vessel *Gaveshini* of NIO was engaged to carry out a preliminary survey of shipwrecks in Suheli and Minicoy islands in 1994. One of the shipwrecks is partly visible on the reef above the waterline in Suheli. A number of tyres and parts of a military tank can be seen lying on the reef, but divers could not reach it owing to rough seas. Two shipwrecks (LSW2 and LSW3) were discovered by MAC in the waters of Minicoy Island. The wreck LSW2 lies 200 m seaward in waters 4 m to 10 m deep. The divers could identify and document the frame and the beam of the ship. Several parts were identified, among them the steam pipe and flywheel, which are not damaged. The shaft attached to the flywheel is 27 m long. As the length from the engine to the front of the vessel is 75 m, the ship must have been 100 m long, if not more. Although the anchor could not be located, as it may be lying buried at great depth, the anchor chain is in good condition. The brass fixtures of the ship include the portholes. Shipwreck LSW3, which is 100 m long, was discovered 200 m north of the wreck LSW2. Its hull plate and engine part are well preserved but the flywheel could not be traced. Two huge steam boilers are partly visible above the waterline; the engine shaft is broken. LSW2 and LSW3 will be excavated carefully with an eye for technical details.

Near by, a wreck recorded as LSW4, but identified as the German ship *Russell*, is being salvaged by a private company, which is losing much of the archaeological evidence. Another wreck in Kalpani Island has also been robbed of its parts by clandestine divers.

The Society for Marine Archaeology, registered as an autonomous body in 1988, is actively engaged in holding bi-annual conferences on the marine archaeology of Indian Ocean countries and in publishing the proceedings. These conferences and publications have created an awareness of the rich underwater cultural heritage of India, which must be fully surveyed and appropriately excavated. So far, proceedings of four conferences are published. *The Journal of Marine Archaeology* is also published by the society every year. The membership of the society is open to all interested in underwater archaeology, maritime trade, and related subjects. S.R.R.

ADDITIONAL READING

Rao, S.R., 1987, *Program and Prospects of Marine Archaeology in India*, NIO, Goa.

Rao, S.R., 1988, *Marine Archaeology in India*, NIO, Goa.

Rao, S.R. (ed.),1991, *Recent Advances in Marine Archaeology*, NIO, Goa.

Indiana

An early **Great Lakes** propeller steamboat built in 1848 and sunk in 1858. *Indiana* was built in 1848 at Vermilion, Ohio by Joseph M. Keating. Her principal owners were Ahira Cobb and Alva Bradley, after whom inventor Thomas Alva Edison was named. First enrolled at Sandusky, Ohio, *Indiana* measured 146 ft 6 in (44.65 m) and 349–34/95 tons (old measurement). She undertook 378 documented voyages in her career, mostly around the lower Great Lakes. Built during the region's period of widespread settlement and development, *Indiana* transported gen-

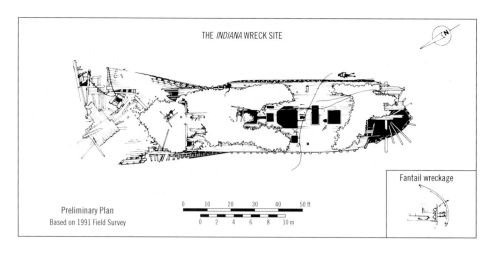

THE *INDIANA* WRECK SITE

Fantail wreckage

Preliminary Plan
Based on 1991 Field Survey

Preliminary site plan of Indiana *shipwreck, 1992. (Smithsonian Institution, Washington, DC)*

Indiana *propeller on display at the Smithsonian Institution's National Museum of American History, Washington, DC. (Smithsonian Institution)*

eral and miscellaneous cargoes (manufactured goods, raw materials, and bulk cargoes of grains, ore, etc.) throughout her working life, much like a modern tramp freighter. In 1851 she suffered the first of eight accidents, carrying away a schooner's bowsprit during a collision. In 1852 she was sold to a company in Buffalo which retained the same basic routes and clients. One 1852 cargo which later proved significant was a merchandise consignment for a regional railroad: ironically, only a few years later most Great Lakes steamboats would be owned or put out of business by the railroads.

In 1853 *Indiana* was sold again (twice) and ran a highly competitive route between Buffalo and Ohio ports; along with common cargoes, she also transported quantities of books, tobacco, whisky, and coffins. In 1854 Francis Perew of Buffalo purchased half-ownership; sixteen days later he ran her against the west pier in Cleveland when 'her machinery became deranged'. Repairs cost $1,500 and may have included a restructuring of the vessel's architecture; she suffered another grounding at Sault Ste Marie later that year while transporting Lake Superior iron ore.

In 1855 Perew bought out his partner. He chartered *Indiana* in Lake Erie all season; highlights of the season included two cargoes of 700 and 800 live hogs for his own account. In 1856 she ran freight between Cleveland and Buffalo. Westward cargoes were light or non-existent; eastbound cargoes remained a miscellany, with flour topping the list in quantity. Four different railroads were clients, as were two steamboat companies allied with railroads. At the end of the season, Perew turned over command to his first mate, who ran *Indiana* ashore on his first voyage.

The following year, *Indiana* was chartered to a railroad, running merchandise between Buffalo and Dunkirk, New York. In October she encountered the same pier met in 1854, causing a $500 loss. The same schedule was planned for 1858, but Perew took a short charter in May transporting ore. On 6 June 1858 *Indiana* cleared Marquette, Michigan with 285 tonnes of iron; early that evening her stuffing box was reported broken, splitting the sternpost. All twenty-one crew and passengers abandoned ship and reached the shore safely, but *Indiana* sank rapidly in Lake Superior off Whitefish Point, Michigan. The ship was insured for $9,000.

In 1975, sport diver John Steele discovered *Indiana*'s wreck, upright and almost perfectly preserved, at a depth of 36 m. On account of her pioneering machinery (predating other regional marine steam technology by forty years), she was declared eligible for the **National Register of Historic Places** in 1978; subsequently the Smithsonian Institution recovered her engine, boiler, propeller and associated machinery, safe, whistle, hand tools, anchor, pump, bell, and ore cargo samples. In 1991–3 additional diving documented her structure and wrecking process. Except for the safe in Lansing, Michigan, all artefacts are at the Smithsonian's National Museum of American History, where portions are on exhibition in the Hall of American Maritime Enterprise.

No palace steamer transporting famous people around the Great Lakes, *Indiana* was a common carrier, far more representative of her time and place. She was part of the transition from sail to steam and ultimately the railroad in the Great Lakes and elsewhere; it is precisely these commonplace aspects of her career which make her significant to modern understanding of the region's settlement and development. P.F.J.

ADDITIONAL READING

Johnston, P.F., 1995, 'Downbound: The 1848 Great Lakes Propeller *Indiana*', *American Neptune*, 55, 4, 61-6.

Johnston, P.F. and Robinson, D.S., 1993, 'The Wreck of the 1848 Propeller *Indiana*: Interim Report, *International Journal of Nautical Archaeology*, 22, 3, 219-35.

Wright, R.J., 1979, 'The Indiana Salvage: Part I', *Detroit Marine Historian*, 33, 4 (Dec), 1-4.

Wright, R.J., 1980, 'The Indiana Salvage: Part II', *Detroit Marine Historian*, 33, 5 (Jan), 2-4.

Institute of Nautical Archaeology

A non-profit-making scientific/educational organization with the purpose of gathering knowledge of the past from the physical remains of maritime activities, and disseminating this knowledge through scholarly and popular publications, films, seminars, and lectures. The Institute of Nautical Archaeology (INA) was founded by George F. Bass and incorporated as the American Institute of Nautical Archaeology in 1972 (the name was shortened in 1978) in Philadelphia, Pennsylvania. It was originally headquartered on Cyprus, but relocated in 1976 to Texas A&M University (TAMU), where INA staff are on the faculty of the Nautical Archaeology Program of the Department of Anthropology and TAMU graduate students form the core staff of most INA projects (see **Texas A&M University Nautical Archaeology Program**). Permanent research centres, including conservation laboratories, are maintained in Bodrum, Turkey and Cairo, Egypt. The institute publishes its own journal, the *Quarterly*.

Following an initial survey for shipwrecks in 1973, INA has excavated six sites in Turkish waters: a Middle Bronze Age cargo near Sheytan Deresi (excavated in 1975; see **Sheytan Deresi Wreck**); a Late Bronze Age ship at

Indiana *bow area with winch in centre, stem on far right; the bow is broken up.*
(P.F. Johnston)

Uluburun (1984–94); a Hellenistic amphora carrier (1979–81) and a medieval merchantman (1978–80) at **Serçe Limani**; a medieval amphora carrier near Bozburun (begun in 1995; see **Bozburun Wreck**); and a 16th-century Ottoman wreck at Yassiada (1967, 1969, and 1982–3; see **Yassiada Wrecks**). Since 1982, regular surveys have located over a hundred ancient and medieval sites on the Aegean and western Mediterranean Turkish coast.

Elsewhere in the Mediterranean region, INA has excavated sites in **Italy**, **Israel**, and Egypt. In 1977, INA archaeologists directed saturation divers in the partial excavation of a Hellenistic wreck at Secca di Capistello, near Lipari. In Israel, work has concentrated since 1994 on Tantura Lagoon, near Haifa. INA-Egypt, established in Cairo in 1993, carried out a survey of the Red Sea coast in 1994 and began excavation of a 17th-century merchant vessel near Sadana Island in 1995.

Since 1976 and the excavation of the **Cornwallis Cave Wreck** near Yorktown, INA has also concentrated on New World archaeology. INA excavations in the western hemisphere have included the privateer *Defence* (1975–80) in Maine (in conjunction with the Maine State Museum), HMS *Charon* (1980) near Yorktown, a ship of the exploration period at **Molasses Reef** in the Turks and Caicos Islands (1982), the **Clydesdale Plantation Vessel** (1992, with the South Carolina Institute of Archaeology and Anthropology), and a number of sites in **Lake Champlain** (with the Lake Champlain Maritime Museum), from a horse-powered ferry to naval vessels of the War of 1812. Between 1981 and 1990, INA excavated several hectares of **Port Royal, Jamaica**, a large commercial port destroyed in an earthquake in 1692. Several seasons have also been spent surveying in Jamaican and Caymanian waters.

Outside the primary research areas of the

Mediterranean and New World, INA projects have included the excavation (1976–80) of a Portuguese frigate *Santo Antonio de Tanna*, lost in 1697, at Mombasa, Kenya and two small excavations of late medieval/Renaissance vessels in the Netherlands, in cooperation with the Centrum voor Scheepsarcheologie in Ketelhaven. Recent surveys and pre-survey reconnaissance have taken place in Albania, the Azores, Bahrain, Bulgaria, the Canary Islands, Eritrea, Poland, and Rumania. F.M.H.

International Committee on the Underwater Cultural Heritage

Organization formed in 1991 by **ICOMOS** to promote international cooperation in the identification, protection, and conservation of underwater cultural heritage sites, and to advise ICOMOS on the development and implementation of programmes in this field. The Committee, based at the Western Australian Maritime Museum and chaired since 1991 by Graeme Henderson, has members from nineteen countries: Argentina, Australia, Canada, Cayman Islands, Denmark, Egypt, **France**, Honduras, India, **Israel**, Kenya, Malaysia, **Mexico**, the Netherlands, the Philippines, **Russia**, Sri Lanka, the **United Kingdom**, and the **United States of America**. Its programme includes assisting the International Law Association's International Committee on Cultural Heritage Law in the development of an International Convention on the Underwater Cultural Heritage, intended for adoption by UNESCO.

The process of UNESCO adoption of a Convention takes some years. In the meantime the ICOMOS Committee, acutely aware that there was no internationally accepted guideline for appropriate behaviour on shipwreck sites, developed the Charter as a stand-alone document titled The ICOMOS Charter on the Protection and Management of the Underwater Cultural Heritage, which was adopted by ICOMOS in

1996. World Heritage Listing, which designates natural and cultural sites of exceptional significance, has long been thought to be a powerful protective and promotional tool that is out of the reach of the managers of underwater cultural heritage. There is not a single underwater shipwreck site that is covered by World Heritage Listing. Part of the reason is that shipwrecks have been considered as 'moveable' heritage. But the World Heritage people have been reexamining their guidelines and giving strong encouragement to the ICOMOS Committee, which in turn is developing several preliminary submissions as test cases. World Heritage Listing has the potential to bring the attention of the international community to responsible management of the underwater cultural heritage. G.H.

International Congress of Maritime Museums

The main international body representing maritime museums. A prime objective of the ICMM is, in the words of its constitution, to promote liaison between museums concerned with maritime history, including the identification, recovery, study, collection, preservation, interpretation, and exhibition of objects and material, and the identification, study, excavation, preservation and display of places, connected with the history and development of all navigation in or upon water. Other objectives are to improve professional standards and encourage research, to publish and sell relevant information, to generally encourage understanding and enjoyment of maritime history and maritime museums, to further the aims of the International Council of Museums (ICOM), and to cooperate with bodies having similar aims.

The ICMM was established to address a perceived need for an international gathering of maritime museum directors. At the First International Congress of Maritime Museums, held at Greenwich, England, in September 1972, delegates from Europe and the United States decided that the Congress should be permanently established. The constitution, set up in 1975, required that the major business of the Congress be conducted at triennial general assemblies, to be held in differing host countries. Since that time the triennial assemblies, held in Europe and the United States, have been supplemented by annual meetings.

In 1990 the Congress was represented in thirty-five countries, and although it is primarily a US and UK organization there are now some initiatives to widen the membership. The triennial general assembly continues to be the *raison d'être* for the Congress,

and the associated conference consists of a mix of show-and-tells, and exploration of current museum issues.

Of particular interest is the Committee for Underwater Archaeology. This Committee, chaired by Graeme Henderson (Director of the Western Australian Maritime Museum) was established in 1987 to address the concern, expressed at the Congress, that different museum policies towards the acquisition of objects from underwater archaeological sites were causing conflicts and confusion among museum curators around the world. The Committee was asked to perform a survey on existing museum acquisition policies as they affected underwater sites, and to set recommendations for ICMM's position with regard to such acquisitions. A questionnaire was sent to all ICMM members with collections and 80 per cent responded. The survey results form an important original data bank and were taken into account in the setting of recommendations for ICMM's policy. The recommendations, adopted as an ICMM Standard at the 1993 Congress, read as follows:

1 That in regard to collecting policy, ICMM member museums should follow the provisions of the *ICOM Code of Professional Ethics*, the ICOMOS Charter, and the *UNESCO Convention*.

2 That ICMM member museums should follow sections 3.1 and 3.2 of the ICOM *Code of Professional Ethics* and that in particular, 'each museum authority should adopt and publish a written statement of its collecting policy ... [and] ... museum[s] should not acquire by purchase [or donation] objects ... where ... their recovery involved the recent unscientific or international destruction or damage of ... archaeological sites'. Museums with collections from underwater sites should each adopt and publish either a written statement of their general collecting policy or a written policy relating specifically to collections from underwater archaeological sites.

3 That ICMM member museums should follow Council of American Maritime Museums (CAMM) policy and 'not knowingly acquire or exhibit artefacts which have been stolen, illegally exported from their country of origin, illegally salvaged or removed from commercially exploited archaeological or historic sites' in recent times [i.e. since the 1990 full Congress of ICMM].

4 That ICMM members should report to the responsible authorities any illegal activities at underwater sites or auction or sale of artefacts from illegally excavated underwater sites in their countries.

5 That ICMM members should recognize that artefacts from underwater sites are integral parts of archaeological assemblages, which should remain intact for research and display.

6 That ICMM members should explore ways for more member institutions to involve students from academic institutions in the study of their underwater archaeological collections.

In these resolutions a commercially exploited heritage site is one which the primary motive for investigation is private financial gain.

These resolutions are the result of a six–year study undertaken by a committee of museum professionals and archaeologists. Maritime museums represent the largest repository of material from underwater cultural sites and the ICMM has thereby taken steps to ensure that appropriate measures are in place to guarantee the integrity of this resource.

Since the Standard was adopted the ICMM has played an important role in major current debates relating to acquisitions from our underwater cultural heritage, such as the exhibition of material salvaged from *Titanic*. G.H.

ADDITIONAL READING

Johnston, W., 1979, 'The International Congress of Maritime Museums: Its First Decade', in *International Congress of Maritime Museums, Third Conference Proceedings, 1978*, Mystic, Connecticut.

International Council on Monuments and Sites
see ICOMOS

International Journal of Nautical Archaeology

The leading academic publication in the subject of nautical archaeology. It was first published in 1972 for the UK Council for Nautical Archaeology by Academic Press of London and New York; its founding editor was Joan du Plat Taylor, a land archaeologist who foresaw the need to give the emerging discipline of nautical archaeology the academic respectability of a specialist periodical. The *Journal* became a quarterly after its third volume; since 1987 it has been published for the Nautical Archaeology Society.

Leading international scholars serve as advisory editors and submitted manuscripts are refereed. The language is English and the contents include main articles, shorter contributions, technical communications, news and museum reports, and book reviews. There is an index to each volume. A cumulative index has yet to be published, although all articles and reviews in volumes 1 to 22 are indexed in the *Bibliography of*

Underwater Archaeology and Related Subjects and volumes from 1996 onwards are available through IDEAL (International Desk-top Electronic Access Library) for authorized users to view, print, and download complete articles in Adobe's Acrobat format. For users of the Internet it will be possible to search freely the contents list of volume 25 onwards, using standard browsers, such as Netscape Navigator.

In common with the longer-established *Mariner's Mirror* – the quarterly publication of the Society for Nautical Research – the *Journal* spans a wide temporal and geographic range, but differs by placing particular emphasis on excavation reports and new developments in recording, reconstruction, and conservation techniques. Initial reports of investigations of ships, as both underwater and as land sites, are well represented, as are re-evaluations of old discoveries and surveys of ethnographic survivals.

clear reflection of the concerns and direction of the emerging discipline, and the development of other subject areas, such as theory, ethics, law, and the management of the underwater heritage. The *Journal* is an indispensable storehouse of information for the student and scholar. V.F.

ADDITIONAL READING

Illesley, J., 1995, *Bibliography of Underwater Archaeology and Related Subjects*, Oswestry, Shropshire.

Inundation Study
see **National Reservoir Inundation Study (US)**

Isabella

British merchantman wreck of 1830 on the west coast of the US, rediscovered and documented in 1986–7, 1994, and 1996. *Isabella* was built at Shoreham, Sussex, on the channel coast of England, in 1825. In all respects *Isabella* was an ordinary vessel, one of hun-

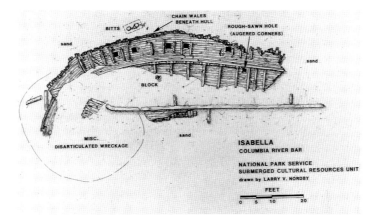

Wreck of Isabella as surveyed in 1987. (National Park Service)

The first volume gave a clear indication of the *Journal's* area of interest. A scene-setting essay reviewed the ancient literature on naval architecture, the potential of underwater archaeology, and its development after 1535 when Demarchi used diving apparatus to measure one of the huge Roman ships sunk in **Lake Nemi**, Italy. Other articles in the same volume spanned in time the 13th century BC to the 18th century AD, and related to Israel, Canada, Kenya, England, Scotland, Sicily, the Crimea, and the Bahamas. The technical articles included: the 'comb' devised to measure sections across the **Kyrenia Ship** under water; a sheet steel cylinder used for controlled test excavation of sandy strata in an ancient harbour; the use of sub-bottom profiling and **Magnetometer** surveys to locate shipwrecks sealed under sediments; aids to packing and transporting ancient ship's timbers; and precision underwater photographic mapping techniques.

Subsequent volumes of *IJNA* provide a

dreds of British brigs built in the early 19th century as carriers of bulk cargoes such as coal and grain. *Isabella* was small, with an estimated length of 25.5 m. After serving four years in trade between London and Mediterranean ports, *Isabella* was sold to the Hudson's Bay Company in 1829. The brig was purchased to carry supplies to the company's new Pacific Coast fur trading outpost at Fort Vancouver, on the Columbia River.

Sailing from London in November 1829, *Isabella* carried a varied cargo that reflected the needs of Fort Vancouver's growing agricultural and industrial community for tools, medicines, stationery supplies, preserved foods, lead and pig iron, and paint, as well as the commodities of the fur trade – guns, ammunition, blankets, beads, copper cooking pots, candles, mirrors, tinware, buttons, combs, tobacco, and tea. Arriving at the bar of the Columbia River on 2 May 1830, *Isabella* was stranded and wrecked on a sand bar when the captain mistook his

bearings. The Hudson's Bay Company was able to salvage two-thirds of the cargo before the brig broke up and sank.

The remains of *Isabella* were discovered in September 1986 by a local fisherman who snagged his nets on the wreck. In 1987 a cooperative effort to study the wreck was led by the National Park Service's **Submerged Cultural Resources Unit** with assistance from the Columbia River Maritime Museum and the US Coast Guard, as well as several local sport divers. Other surveys were conducted in 1994 and 1996 by the Museum, the latter with the assistance of the **Underwater Archaeological Society of British Columbia**.

Isabella's hull was nearly perfectly preserved by the fresh water of the river and constant burial by shifting sand. The hull split open at the bilges. The starboard side is exposed on the bottom and is intact from the bilge to the waterway, or the original deck level. The hull is also lined by a series of six cargo or ballast ports below the sheerstrake. These ports, closed and caulked during voyages, were opened to salvage the cargo when the brig wrecked. Another indication of the salvage was found on the underside of the starboard hull. Below the cargo ports, on the starboard side, a small square hole was cut into the hull. The brig's log entry for 9 May, six days after the wreck, noted that the carpenter 'cut a hole in the side to let the water out, so that we could better get at the cargo'. The hole was one of the conclusive pieces of evidence in identifying the wreck as *Isabella*.

The well-preserved wreck of *Isabella* is the oldest known fur trade vessel yet found on the Pacific coast of North America. It is listed in the **National Register of Historical Places**. The study of *Isabella* also yielded important information about the little documented and yet once common British merchant brigs of the early 19th century. J.P.D.

ADDITIONAL READING

Delgado, J.P., 1995, 'The Brig *Isabella*: A Hudson's Bay Company Shipwreck of 1830', *American Neptune*, 55, 4, 309–22.

Isis Wreck

A Late Roman wreck located about 120 km due west of the northwestern tip of Sicily and about 80 km north of Skerki Bank. It was the first ancient ship to be found and surveyed with the new ROV (remotely operated vehicle) technology. Found at a depth of about 800 m, the Isis Wreck is also the deepest ancient wreck thus far known; it begins a new era of deep water archaeology. It was discovered in 1988 by Robert D. Ballard of the Woods Hole Oceanographic Institution. Explored by A.M. McCann in 1989

Details of central area of the Isis Wreck site, taken in 1988. (Quest Group Ltd)

with the ROV named *Jason*, the Isis was part of the first JASON Project, conceived and directed by Ballard. These projects are aimed specifically for the education of children in the sciences and technology in America and Canada. The 1989 project included the first live interactive television broadcast directly from the sea floor and was also filmed by National Geographic. The shipwreck was nicknamed 'Isis' for the benefit of the television programmes.

The Isis site was mapped and photographed along with the Skerki Bank trade route site about 1.5 km to the northwest where some seventy amphoras dating from the 4th century BC to the 12th century AD were documented. Selected objects were lifted with Jason's robotic manipulator. No digging below the surface occurred and Jason was not as yet equipped with sonar devices. The visible remains of the Late Roman ship are scattered over an area of about 10 sq. m. The main concentration of material fell in an area 5 by 6 m and lay in a line running northeast–southwest. Forty-eight objects were documented, with ten complete amphoras and five complete commonware vessels lifted. Also recovered were a Roman lamp, the upper stone of a cylindrical basalt millstone, sections of iron anchors, and wooden planking. A copper coin of Constantius II, dated AD 355–61, was recovered embedded in a pot of pine tar used on deck in the daily maintenance of the ship. This resinous material is the first example analysed of such an essential naval store. The ship was not sheathed in lead, but lead patching was observed. The finds date the ship probably in the last quarter of the 4th century AD.

The vessel was built of white oak and Mediterranean cedar in the ancient shell-first method with widely spaced mortise-and-tenon joining. The original size of the ship is estimated by the stack of four or more iron anchors. One rectangular shank with a removable iron stock has an estimated length of 1.7 m. It is slightly smaller than the anchors from the Roman Dramont D wreck that had an estimated length of 18–20 m (see **Dramont Wreck**), but larger than those carried by the Dramont F ship with an estimated length of only 10–12 m. The Isis thus may have had a length of between 12 and 15 m with a carrying capacity of under 30 tonnes. She was probably one of the small sturdy traders typical of the Late Roman world, designed to brave the open seas between Carthage and Rome.

Of the ten amphoras recovered, five are large Tunisian cylindrical jars, two are from western Asia, and two probably from Calabria. They appear to have carried oil, fish sauce, and wine. The commonware pottery is largely Tunisian, with a lamp from Carthage and an amphoretta from Mauretania. The cooking pot filled with tar is from Pantelleria. The assemblage of pottery yields two new amphora types and provides new evidence for the Late Roman date and Tunisian origin of Keay Type 35. Some whole pieces of commonware are also unique in their style: a small flat-bottomed table amphora from Tunisia with a tall grooved neck, and a rare miniature version of a large-sized amphora from Mauretania. The basalt millstone from Libya with its concave hopper and protruding handles is also not a form previously known.

These finds and her location suggest that the home port of the Isis was Carthage and that she was en route to Rome. Perhaps in the more distant past she had also sailed in the eastern Mediterranean and called at ports in Italy. The Isis thus provides evidence for a new trade route over the open seas and for worldwide Mediterranean trade in late antiquity. The wreck is also important as one of the few documented shipwrecks from the Late Roman world. The discovery of the Isis in the deep sea with the new ROV technology opens the way for the development of non-destructive archaeology. Not every shipwreck need be excavated and judgements for lifting can be made carefully in collaboration with colleagues. The archaeologist can record with the camera and search wide areas of the sea floor in safety. The challenge is for man and machine and archaeologist and engineer to work together to discover new knowledge about our deep ocean. A.M.M.

ADDITIONAL READING

Ballard, R.D., Archbold, R., and McCann, A.M., 1990, *The Lost Wreck of the ISIS*, Toronto.

McCann, A.M., 1990, 'Diving Into Our Past, World Ocean Floors: Atlantic Ocean', *National Geographic Magazine*, January.

McCann, A.M. and Freed, J., 1994, *Deep Water Archaeology: A Late-Roman Ship from Carthage and an Ancient Trade Route Near Skerki Bank off Northwest Sicily*, Journal of Roman Archaeology, Supplementary Series no. 13, Ann Arbor, Michigan.

Iskandil Burnu Shipwreck

Wreck 50 m off Iskandil Burnu, Turkey, approximately twenty minutes by sail from the ancient harbour at Knidos. The vessel was probably a coastal freighter practising cabotage in the later part of the 6th century AD; she possibly originated in southern Palestine with her final destination a port in the Black Sea.

The wreck was discovered by Tufan Turanli and Ali Uygun at a depth of about 20 m during a survey conducted by the **Institute of Nautical Archaeology** in 1981. It was never excavated, but over a three-year period thirteen diving hours were spent producing two **Photomosaics** of the site and recovering a representative sample of artefacts. Based on this information, it was estimated that the main cargo had a weight of 30 tonnes, at least 10 tonnes less than a ship of this size was capable of carrying. The ship, therefore, may have carried an additional cargo of perishable material.

The egg-shaped amphoras are a type of *havit*, a standard Palestinian sandy, baggy storage jar. Their closest parallels are from the mid-6th to the early 7th century in southern Palestine. The two sizes found on the wreck may correspond to the standard capacities of one and two *se'ah*, as mentioned in the Talmud. The cigar-shaped amphoras come from the Gaza region of southern Palestine and are dated to the 5th and 6th centuries. Two other amphora types were recovered; one is hourglass-shaped, from the 6th and

Archaeologists survey the seabed at Iskandil Burnu, using underwater scooters. (© INA)

7th centuries, and probably from Cyprus or Asia Minor. The second type is carrot-shaped and believed to be an Egyptian wine amphora dating from the 4th to 7th centuries.

Smaller pieces of pottery consisting of jugs, cooking pots, and a covered casserole were found in two groups, one near the stern and the other amidships, but as none of these containers exhibit signs of wear, they probably represent cargoes of individual merchants stored separately from the main cargo. The jugs appear to have originated in southern Palestine or Cyprus and are of a type that is dated to the 5th and 6th centuries. The cooking wares have their closest parallels in 6th- and 7th-century pottery from southern Palestine. Five of the cooking pots may be of the type of vessel known as *kedera*, the most frequently mentioned cooking pot in Talmudic literature.

Also recovered from the wreck is *'ilpas satum*, a two-handled casserole with lid that was fired in one piece. When the clay was leather hard the lid was cut from the body and immediately rejoined before firing to ensure that lid and pan shrunk evenly, resulting in a tight fit and to guarantee that the pot was unused when purchased; the lid was then broken free. These containers were used to improve the flavour of foods precooked in a *kedera*, and to prepare meats.

The closest parallels to this container are found in Palestine and Cyprus, dating from the 5th to 6th centuries. S.M.2

ADDITIONAL READING

Lloyd, M., 1984, *A Byzantine Shipwreck at Iskandil Burnu, Turkey: Preliminary Report*, MA thesis, Texas A&M University, College Station, Texas.

Isle Royale Shipwrecks

A group of shipwrecks at Isle Royale National Park in Lake Superior, North America, documented and assessed by the National Park Service's **Submerged Cultural Resources Unit** (NPS-SCRU). The principal investigator for all phases of the project was Daniel J. Lenihan. The shipwrecks represent a cross-section of **Great Lakes** maritime steam technology from the 1870s to the mid-1900s, and include passenger/package freighters, bulk freighters, a side-wheeler, and wooden- and steel-hulled vessels. Because of the unique research potential, the wrecks were investigated as a population from a regional perspective, not as individual sites. The study was conducted within the context of regional history, vessel evolution, and socioeconomic dynamics, and sought to identify patterns in the maritime behaviour of the region that have relevance to the shipwrecks at Isle Royale. This research approach has not been widely used in underwater archaeology; its first use was in a survey of the Tennessee–Tombigbee waterway by Murphy and Saltus, and the Isle Royale study quickly became the model of the regional approach in the discipline. In addition to a regional approach, the NPS-SCRU employed a totally non-destructive field methodology, which is in line with NPS preservation philosophy.

The study includes eleven separate maritime casualty events, which resulted in ten shipwrecks; the eleventh was a stranding event, which nonetheless left material remains on the bottom. The most noticeable aspect of the study population is that no sailing vessels are represented. Although sailing vessels were common and numerous before the period studied, and even throughout that period, none has been located in Isle Royale's waters.

The earliest vessel studied at Isle Royale National Park is *Cumberland*, a wooden-hulled side-wheel steamer built in 1871. The vessel was involved in the passenger/package trade when it grounded and sank on Rock of Ages reef in 1877. The site contains several large discrete sections of the ship, spread along an underwater ravine ranging in depth from 6 to 24 m. Hull components present at the site include a large section of hull bottom, several sections of

side, and a portion of the stern. The most conspicuous pieces missing are the bow (which was later located approximately 12 km away), and the remaining sections of the vessel's bottom and sides. Also present are several elements of the vessel's propulsion system, including *Cumberland*'s firebox boiler, a condenser, an engine cylinder, several sections of the paddle wheels, and the top portions of the A-frames, which supported the overhead shaft of the walking beam engine. One of the most interesting aspects of the site is *Cumberland*'s hull support structure, which was a 'ceiling arch', or arch-system integrated into curving ceiling planks, beginning at the stern deadwood, curving upwards inside the hull to the main deck clamps, and back down to a point 6 m aft of the stempost. This hull support system is a previously undocumented aspect of Great Lakes steamer construction.

Interestingly enough, the next vessel in the Isle Royale collection built after *Cumberland*, the wooden-hulled, screw-driven bulk freighter *Henry Chisholm*, was wrecked in the exact same spot as *Cumberland* twenty-one years later. When *Chisholm* was launched in August 1880, it was the largest bulk freighter on the lakes. It ran aground on Rock of Ages reef in 1898, and quickly became a total loss. *Chisholm*'s wreckage lies in the same ravine as *Cumberland*, with additional material located some way down the reef in 45 m of water. The material remains of the two vessels are intermingled; one of the archaeologist's first jobs was to determine which hull components were from which vessel. That job proved relatively easy, given the different construction techniques and methods of propulsion of *Cumberland* and *Chisholm*. Much more of *Chisholm* is present at the site than *Cumberland*. Large sections of the vessel's bottom, sides, and stern are present. Also present is the compound engine, propeller shaft, and screw; the Scotch boilers were salvaged shortly after the wreck. *Chisholm*'s hull support structure was a common method of diagonal iron braces fastened to the outside faces of the frames, under the outer hull planking. The relatively intact sections of *Chisholm* made it a straightforward task to determine the natural site formation processes of the wreck. The *Cumberland/Chisholm* site is a remarkable glance at two separate stages of wooden-hull development on the Great Lakes.

One of the first steel-hulled vessels in the Great Lakes was *Algoma*, built in Great Britain in 1883. After only two years in the passenger/package trade, the vessel wrecked on the northeast side of Isle Royale during a gale in 1885. Today the highly scattered site lies between 2 and 45 m deep. *Algoma*'s hull is not so much torn apart as it is disassembled, with the loose hull components lying in random groupings. Salvage after the wreck event was extensive, and therefore no machinery, anchors, chains, propellers, or much of the cargo of steel rails are left on site. Although further documentation needs to be completed on the *Algoma* site, one obvious mystery is the lack of any bow structure or materials remaining.

A further stage in the development of the

gunwale girder that ran along the length of the cabin deck level. Although all the propulsion machinery (engine, boilers, shaft, and screw) were salvaged after the wreck, the engine mount, main bearing, and thrust bearing mount are still visible on the site. Another interesting feature of the site is a portion of the vessel's cargo, including a scatter of bottles and four intact crates of bolts or rivets.

After *Algoma*, the next steel-hulled vessel in the Isle Royale population is *Glenlyon*. This vessel was launched as a package

up. Most of this is due to natural processes, in particular ice scouring.

The passenger/package freight vessel *America*, launched in 1898, is more closely tied to the history of Isle Royale than any other vessel in its waters. For almost twenty-five years, *America* acted as a communication and transportation link for the smaller ports around the island. It was lost after tearing a hole in its bottom on a reef in 1928. Today the vessel is the most heavily dived site in the park, and displays an apparent lack of portable artefacts. In addition, it was sub-

Right: Isle Royale National Park: the bow of Chester A. Congdon. *(Artist's perspective by J.L. Livingston, NPS)*

Left: Isle Royale National Park: Chester A.Congdon. *(NPS/John Brooks)*

Below: Isle Royale National Park: Stanley. *(NPS/John Brooks)*

Great Lakes wooden-hulled steamer is the screw-driven *Monarch*. Like *Cumberland* and *Algoma*, *Monarch* was a passenger/package freight vessel. It was built in 1890, and wrecked off the northeast point of Isle Royale in 1906. *Monarch* broke into large hull components, similar to *Cumberland* and *Chisholm*. Present on the site are most of the hull bottom and sides, including the stern. Much of the bow, except for the port bow assembly, is missing from the site. *Monarch* was a strongly built vessel, with three principal iron hull support structures: the main arch, the sheer strap (running the length of the ship below the main deck level), and a

freighter in 1893. It served under various owners until lost on Isle Royale in 1924. *Glenlyon* was the subject of very little contemporary salvage; only the grain cargo was removed. This makes the site, with its intact propulsion machinery, an excellent opportunity for a detailed study of early 20th-century Great Lakes steam technology. In addition to its engine, screw, and boilers, the majority of the hull components, though badly broken up, are present, as well as auxiliary machinery such as deck winches, windlass, and capstan. Other than *Algoma*, *Glenlyon* is the only other metal-hulled wreck at Isle Royale that has completely broken

jected to a modern salvage attempt in 1965, which did much damage. The vessel's hull is intact, though most of the superstructure and upper cabins have been removed by ice damage and the salvage attempt. *America* rests on a steep slope, with its bow just below the water's surface and its stern resting at a depth of 23 m. The most remarkable aspect of the site is the vessel's totally intact and fully plumbed machinery space, which offers a well-preserved, three-dimensional display of turn-of-the-century engineering details.

Located only a kilometre from the *Cumberland/Chisholm* site on Rock of Ages reef, the steel-hulled passenger steamer *George M. Cox* lies in two main wreckage fields. The vessel's bow section is scattered on a flat shoal, while the nearly intact aft portion is on a sloping ridge 45 m southeast. Although like most Isle Royale sites the wreck of *Cox* is stripped of portable artefacts, documentation of the vessel revealed some interesting features. *George M. Cox* was very lightly built for a vessel of its size, which is evidenced by the massive structural damage incurred during the wrecking process. In addition, an aspect of the site unique to the Isle Royale shipwreck population are the remains of the wooden superstructure present on site. This vessel is an excellent example of a turn-of-the-century steamer built for speed.

The bulk freighter *Chester A. Congdon* is the largest vessel in the Isle Royale population. The 532 ft (162 m) vessel was launched in 1907 and wrecked at Isle Royale in 1918. The site consists of two discrete sections of hull. The intact bow and scattered forward section of the vessel lie on the south side of Congdon Shoal, while the stern section lies to the north. The stern portion of the vessel, resting in 55 m of water, contains an impressive collection of artefacts in the undisturbed engine and cabin areas. *Congdon* is an imposing site, and offers an interesting dive to both visitors and students of Great Lakes vessel technology.

Canoe Rocks, on the northeast end of Isle Royale, contains two maritime casualty sites: the wreck of *Emperor* and the stranding site of *Dunelm*. Although the steel package freighter *Dunelm* was refloated after it stranded in 1910, it left material remains of the event behind. Two anchors and chain cable that were probably dropped from the vessel to lighten it, and the remains of a lifeboat, mark the event. The bulk freighter *Emperor*, launched in 1910, was the largest vessel built in Canada at the time of its completion. Of the vessels in the Isle Royale population, *Emperor* had the longest operational history; it wrecked in 1947. The vessel lies largely intact, from a depth of 9 m at the bow to 45 m at the stern. It is still loaded with its cargo of 10,000 tonnes of ore from the Steep Rock Mine. The most important research potential offered by the site is the intact engine room with nearly four decades of alterations and revision by the many crews that ran the vessel. It could give insight into many anthropological questions regarding the relationship between people and their work environment in a maritime setting.

The final Isle Royale wreck site has the most mystery surrounding its loss. The steel package freighter *Kamloops*, built in 1924, disappeared during a severe gale in 1927.

The vessel's whereabouts and the circumstances of its loss remained a mystery until 1977, when sport divers discovered the vessel's remains near Isle Royale, lying in 55 to 80 m of water. *Kamloops*'s cargo, mixed 'package freight', represents a cross section of 1920s Great Lakes material culture. The remarkable preservation on the site and the relatively low visitation from sport divers have created an archaeological site of unparalleled importance in terms of material culture and subsistence studies. M.R.3

ADDITIONAL READING

Lenihan, D.J. (ed.),1987, *Submerged Cultural Resources Study: Isle Royale National Park*, Submerged Cultural Resources Unit, Santa Fe, New Mexico.

Murphy, L. and Saltus, A.R., 1981, *Phase II Identification and Evaluation of Submerged Cultural Resources in the Tombigbee River Multi-resource District, Alabama and Mississippi: Report of Investigations no. 17*, Office of Archaeological Research, University of Alabama.

Israel

Country at the eastern end of the Mediterranean Sea. The study of marine archaeology in Israel began in 1960 when Elisha Linder brought together a group of ex-Navy divers and established the Undersea Exploration Society of Israel. The society conducted surveys and excavations of dozens of sites along the Mediterranean coast of Israel, the Sea of Galilee, the Dead Sea and the Red Sea. Its activity led to the establishment in 1972 of the Recanati Centre for Maritime Studies (CMS), a research centre, at the University of Haifa. In 1973 an academic programme for graduate students was opened in the Department of Maritime Civilizations. Both the centre and the department are leaders in maritime and underwater archaeological research in Israel, offering an interdisciplinary curriculum in humanistic oceanography. The Marine Branch of the Israel Antiquities Authority (IAA) maintains an ongoing programme of underwater rescue surveys and excavations along Israel's coasts, and is responsible for enforcing the relevant antiquities laws.

This article describes the principal Mediterranean underwater sites (from north to south), the Kinneret Boat, and some relevant organizations.

Shavei Zion, 5 km north of Acco, was excavated underwater from 1972 to 1974 by E. Linder. A large number of hollow terracotta female figurines were found, many of them with the sign of the Punic goddess Tanit appearing on their pedestal. Neutron activation analysis tests of the clay indicated

The bow of the Ma'agan Mikhael ship, south of Haifa, Israel. (Itamar Grinberg)

that their origin was along the southern Phoenician coast.

Acco is mentioned in early literary sources, from the beginning of the Egyptian Middle Kingdom. In antiquity the mouth of the Na'aman River served for anchorage. During the Persian period a harbour was built at the northern side of the natural Bay of Acco where it has remained to this day. Evidence of ancient breakwaters and other harbour installations from the 6th century BC onwards are found, including Phoenician, Hellenistic, and Roman construction, Ibn Tulun's rampart, and Crusader buildings. Remains of shipwrecks and their cargoes have also been located dating from the 5th century BC to the Roman period and up to the time of Napoleon's siege of the city.

The peninsula of Athlit is situated 15 km south of Haifa. In the southern bay there are remains of a crusader jetty. Excavations in the north bay by E. Linder and A. Raban revealed 6th–5th-century BC Phoenician harbour installations including an inner quay and breakwater that probably served as an emporium. Several remnants of shipwrecks and cargoes dating to the same period were identified in the north bay.

A unique example of a naval ram belonging to a warship dating to the 2nd century BC was discovered and excavated in 1980 in the northern bay of Athlit. The ram was the principal weapon of naval warfare. The **Athlit Ram**, the 'three-pronged' type, is a 465 kg bronze casting, 2.26 m long, and is decorated on its sides by three symbols: an eagle, a thunderbolt, and a wreathed helmet of the Dioscuri. A fourth symbol, the *kerukeion (caduceus)*, appears on its nosing surface. A small section of the bow structure of the ship was retrieved, including wooden elements of the ramming complex. The ram is the first of its kind ever to be recovered from the sea.

Also in the northern bay of Athlit, a submerged Pre-Pottery Neolithic settlement has been excavated by E. Galili of the IAA since 1984. Found at a depth of 8–12 m, this settlement is dated to the end of the 7th millennium BC. Excavations have revealed foundations of stone dwellings, human burials, ritual installations, artificially dug water wells, animal and fish bones, and flint and stone tools.

Recent excavations by the CMS on the peninsula of Tel Nami, 20 km south of Haifa, have exposed a coastal settlement and a variety of artefacts, some of gold, silver, and ivory, and numerous bronze objects. The site was inhabited during the Middle and Late Bronze Ages (*c.* 2000–1750 and 1300–1200 BC). Artefacts including imported ceramic and cultic tradition from the Aegean, Anatolia, coastal Syria, and Cyprus are evident. Rock engravings of boats on the nearby Carmel ridge, together with ingots and other finds revealed in a related underwater survey, led the project director, M. Artzy, to conclude that Tel Nami was a maritime trading centre.

Tel Dor is located on the coast 30 km south of Haifa. It is first mentioned in the 13th century BC and known in Wen-Amon's sailing account from *c.* 1100 BC. Land excavations carried out by E. Stern of the Hebrew University of Jerusalem indicate that the site was inhabited at the beginning of the Middle Bronze Age IIA. Two shallow lagoons, one to the north and one to the south, have revealed evidence of more than three thousand years of maritime activities. Two partially protected bays are found to the north of Tel Dor. Maritime activities from the Persian period are evident from the existence of maritime industrial installations, channels cut in the rocks, and three slipways.

Situated to the south of Tel Dor, the shallow Tantura Lagoon is protected by a line of rocks about 150 m from the shore. Remnants of about twenty shipwrecks and cargoes, dating from the 13th century BC to the 19th century AD, have been found here. The Dor Maritime Archaeology Project (DMAP), directed by K. Raveh and S. Kingsley, conducts a study of the maritime history of Dor, through a year-round underwater archaeological survey. The project results, as well as many of the artefacts, are on display in the local museum. Beginning in 1994, excavations directed by S. Wachsmann of the **Institute of Nautical Archaeology**, together with a team from the CMS, revealed hull remains of seven shipwrecks. Two were systematically excavated: Tantura A is a local coaster, 12 m long, constructed frame-based, and dated to the 6th century AD. Tantura B is a long flat-bottomed ship, constructed skeleton-based, and dated to the first half of the 9th century AD. Artefacts found at both sites include a few amphora, organic materials including ropes, and in Tantura B parts of the rigging. The wrecks remain underwater.

The Ma'agan Mikhael Ship was discovered in 1985 about 70 m off the coast of a kibbutz called Ma'agan Mikhael, 35 km south of Haifa. It lay at a depth of 1.5 m and under an additional 1.5 m of sand. The ship was excavated in 1988 and 1989 by a team from the CMS headed by E. Linder and J. Rosloff. Among the finds were 13 tonnes of stones and rocks which were not locally quarried, seventy ceramic vessels, mainly from Cyprus, carpenter's tools, ropes, food remnants, and a one-armed wooden anchor. The ship was unusually well preserved, constructed shell-first with closely set mortise-and-tenon joints; the bow and the stern were partially sewn. The ship is dated to *c.* 400 BC. The archaeological remains measured over 11.15 m and the boat is estimated to have been 13 m long. The hull timbers and all archaeological artefacts were retrieved from the sea and conserved at the CMS. The hull elements will be reassembled and the ship will be exhibited in a special museum at the University of Haifa.

Evidence for artificial harbours at **Caesarea Maritima** dates back as far as the 2nd century BC. The largest and most impressive is that built by Herod and completed in 10 BC. The shape and construction techniques are described in detail by Josephus Flavius (*Antiq.* 15.331–9, *Jewish War* 1.408–15). Twenty-five years of research by A. Raban and colleagues have confirmed Flavius' descriptions and have brought to light sophisticated technology and advanced engineering skills. The excavations have also provided a greater understanding of the writings of Vitruvius (*De Architectura* 5.12). Breakwaters were built in the open sea using a combination of ashlar headers and wooden forms, which were filled and sunk using a mixture of earth, limestone, and volcanic ash. During construction the builders utilized wave-borne sand to fill in spaces between building forms. Special sluice gates made use of wave action to rinse out the completed harbour and prevent siltation by migrating sand. The inner face of the breakwater served as a working wharf and for storage. The harbour area extended over 10 hectares. The research has proved that the harbour was built on tectonically unstable ground; subsidence, which began about one hundred years after completion, has reached 6–7 m by the late 1990s. These undersea excavations are among the most ambitious in the world both in scope and duration.

A Roman shipwreck was discovered in 1976 less than 1 km north of the harbour of Caesarea, 60 m from the shore at a depth of 2.5 m, under a thick layer of sand. Systematic excavation by M. Fitzgerald under the direction of A. Raban began in 1983. The ship was a big merchantman, 40–45 m in length, of shell-first construction with 8 cm thick strakes and 25–28 cm moulded, closely set frames. It is dated to 18–15 BC. Among its cargo were large storage jars known as *dolia*. The shipwreck remains underwater, re-covered by sand.

The coastal survey of the Marine Branch of the IAA has revealed many assemblages of shipwreck cargoes along the Carmel coast from Haifa to Athlit, as well as uncovering several shipwrecks in the Ashkelon Marina development area on the south Mediterranean coast of Israel.

The Kinneret Boat (see **Sea of Galilee Wreck**) was discovered in 1986 on the western shore of the Sea of Galilee ('Kinneret' in Hebrew) and was excavated by S. Wachsmann and K. Raveh on behalf of the IAA. It was retrieved intact from the site and conserved over a period of eight years in Beit Alon at Kibbutz Ginosar, where it is now exhibited. The extant hull remains were 8.2 m long and 2.3 m wide. Its original dimensions are estimated to have been 8.8 m long and 2.5 m wide. It was constructed shell-first and is dated between the 1st century BC and the end of the 1st century AD.

The National Maritime Museum in Haifa was founded in 1953. Its exhibition sections include ship models, Jewish shipping past and present, navigation instruments, marine mythology, a numismatic collection, cartography, and marine archaeology. The latter includes the Athlit Ram, Egyptian funerary boats, an amphora collection, and miscellaneous artefacts retrieved from the sea.

The Man and Sea Society is a non-profit and non-governmental society directed by S. Arenson. The society is engaged in increasing public awareness of the underwater archaeological heritage, protecting sites and artefacts, and developing educational programmes. Y.K.

ADDITIONAL READING

Artzy, M., 1995, 'Nami: A Second Millennium International Maritime Trading Center in the

Mediterranean', in S. Gitin (ed.), *Recent Excavations in Israel: A View to the West*, Iowa.

Casson, L. and Steffy, J.R., 1994, *The Athlit Ram*, Texas.

Fitzgerald, M., 1995, *The Roman Shipwreck at Caesarea*, Ph.D. dissertation, Texas A&M University.

Galili, E. *et al.*, 1993, 'Atlit Yam', *Journal of Field Archaeology*, 20, 2, 133–57.

Galili, E. *et al.*, 1993, 'Underwater Survey and Rescue Excavations Along the Israeli Coast', *International Journal of Nautical Archaeology*, 22, 1, 61–77.

Kingsley, S. and Raveh, K., 1996, *The Ancient Harbour and Anchorage at Dor, Israel*, BAR 626, Oxford.

Linder, E., 1973, 'A Cargo of Phoenicio-Punic Figurines', *Archaeology*, 26, 182–7.

Linder, E., 1992, 'Excavating an Ancient Merchantman', *Biblical Archaeology Review* 18, 6, 24–35.

Raban, A., 1993, 'Acco (Maritime)', in E. Stern (ed.), *The New Encyclopedia of Archaeological Excavations in the Holy Land*, Jerusalem, 29–31.

Raban, A., 1995, 'Dor-Yam', in E. Stern *et al.*, *Excavations at Dor: Final Report*, *1 A*, Jerusalem, 285–354.

Raban, A. and Holum, K. (eds), 1996, *Caesarea Maritima*, Leiden.

Raban, A. and Linder, E., 1993, 'Atlit', in E. Stern (ed.), *The New Encyclopedia of Archaeological Excavations in the Holy Land*, Jerusalem, 117–20.

Stern, E. (ed.), *The New Encyclopedia of Archaeological Excavations in the Holy Land*, Jerusalem.

Wachsmann, S., 1990, *The Excavation of an Ancient Boat in the Sea of Galilee (Lake Kinneret)*, Atiqot (English Series) 19, Jerusalem.

Italy

Country lying at the heart of the **Mediterranean Sea**. Italy is a quintessentially maritime country: its 7,500 km coastline is studded with islands, and its territory boasts the two largest islands in the Mediterranean, Sicily and Sardinia. Italy spawned an ancient empire which claimed the entire sea as its own for several centuries. It fostered maritime ambitions at great port centres such as Venice and Genoa, from which a new world was rediscovered at the height of the Renaissance. Of the almost 1,200 shipwrecks catalogued by A.J. Parker in 1992, over one-third have been recovered from Italian shores, testifying to the markedly maritime focus of the country.

Maritime salvage operations in Italy go back at least to Imperial times when *urinatores*, or specialized divers, were officially employed at Rome's port of Portus; interest in recovering lucrative wreck cargoes inspired efforts and inventions by Leonardo da Vinci and Leonbattista Alberti. Not until early in the 20th century, however, were the first ancient vessels actually raised, when Benito Mussolini's imperial pretensions prompted him to order a spectacular project to recover Caligula's famous pleasure barges from Lake Nemi, southeast of Rome (see **Lake Nemi ships**). Between 1928 and 1932 the lake was entirely drained, revealing two barges with elaborate deck structures and luxurious fittings. For the first time Roman ships, albeit extraordinary ones, could be examined; they were raised, studied, and displayed in a lakeside museum. Regrettably, the museum suffered a devastating arson attack in 1944 which destroyed all but a few metal fittings. Plans to reconstruct a replica of at least one barge are in progress at the time of writing.

The modern history of Italian underwater archaeology may be said to begin with the recovery of the largest known Roman cargo ship at Albenga off the Ligurian coast, carrying over 11,000 wine amphoras arranged in several layers, dating to the late Republican period (see **Albenga Wreck**). Following ill-conceived salvage efforts in 1950, the formal excavation of the site was directed by the archaeologist Nino Lamboglia from 1957 to the early 1970s. This project was fundamental to the establishment of an Italian research strategy carried out by Lamboglia and his successor Francisca Pallarés at the Istituto Internazionale di Studi Liguri, Centro Sperimentale di Archeologia Subacquea at Bordighera (Liguria). The institute, which remained the primary maritime archaeology research centre in the country until the late 1980s, regularly published in its journal Rivista di Studi Liguri a report on current underwater archaeology in Italy. Lamboglia supervised numerous wreck excavations throughout Italy, including the first site where survey grids were used under water (the late 2nd-century BC Spargi Wreck in northeast Sardinia: 1958–9), as well as coastal investigations such as that at the Roman port of Baia, recently reinvestigated by P.A. Gianfrotta.

Sporadic finds by fishermen and sport divers over the decades have included hundreds of isolated amphoras and anchor stocks, as well as spectacular recoveries such as the two Classical bronze statues found off the Calabrian coast near Riace (Reggio Calabria), which were probably part of a cargo of works of art being transported in Roman times. The Late Bronze Age Levantine statuette recovered in dragnets off the southern Sicilian coast near Sciacca (Agrigento), reflects long-distance overseas exchanges in the last centuries of the 2nd millennium BC. Methodical survey and excavation projects have been conducted by local dive clubs and by individuals, including Piero Alfredo Gianfrotta, Gianfranco Purpura, Edoardo Riccardi, Claudio Mocchegiani Carpano, Alessandro Fioravanti, and Luigi Fozzati, to name but a few. Italian waters have also attracted a variety of international organizations including the American **Institute of Nautical Archaeology**, the American Academy of Rome, the British **Oxford University MARE**, the German Instituto Archeologico Germanico of Rome and the Israeli Recanati Centre for Maritime Studies at the University of Haifa (see **Israel**), as well as independent researchers including Gerhard Kapitän, Honor Frost, Peter Throckmorton, and A.J. Parker.

The wealth of shipwrecks along the Italian coasts provides precious information within a range of disciplines, from cargoes illustrating trade patterns, political connections, and even cultural tastes, to developments in ship technology. Several sites are worthy of special mention.

The only known ancient warships were recovered in a lagoon off southwest Sicily by Honor Frost (1971–4; see **Marsala Punic Warship**). Preserved by a covering of ballast stones and lagoonal mud, these two Punic vessels are likely to have sunk during the First Punic War (264–241 BC). The sleek proportions of the first vessel reflect its function as a speedboat, while the second vessel was built more robustly and featured a light ram which has been the subject of various interpretations. Shipwrights' marks in Phoenician lettering indicate building phases and suggest a degree of prefabrication in construction. Regrettably, recent legislation (1995) has condemned the one raised vessel to destruction by not permitting the completion of its conservation, despite long campaigning by local and international experts over the years.

The badly looted Classical (late 5th/early 4th century BC) Porticello Wreck off the Calabrian coast (see **Straits of Messina Wreck**) was excavated by D. Owen and C.J. Eiseman in the 1970s. Its cargo (much of which was eventually recovered from the thieves) included amphoras from the Bosphorus region, southern Italy, and perhaps the Punic region of southwest Sicily, as well as lead ingots from Attica, several globular inkwells, and at least three life-size statues stylistically dated to the third quarter of the 5th century BC. The few remains of the hull, estimated to have measured *c.* 17 m in length, showed this was a typical mortise-and-tenon joined hull, with early use of copper nails to attach the frames. This excavation illustrates the potential value even of a looted wreck, when exiguous material is properly examined and interpreted.

Dozens of shipwrecks spanning centuries provide insight into the evolution of the widespread mortise-and-tenon shipbuilding tradition. A particular feature of the central Mediterranean region, however, is the apparent concentration of a 'sewn' or 'lashed' hull joinery system ranging from Archaic to medieval times. The early 6th-century BC **Giglio Wreck** represents the earliest known example of a lashed hull. Discovered (and subsequently looted) in the early 1960s, and only excavated in the early 1980s by Mensun Bound (Oxford University MARE), it is also considered the earliest known Etruscan ship. Its varied cargo reflects international connections between contemporary markets from several Greek centres as well as from Etruria and Carthage; site conditions contributed to the remarkable preservation of organic objects including musical instruments and calipers, as well as a Corinthian bronze helmet (currently in a private German collection).

The Archaic (early 5th century BC) Greek Gela Wreck from southern Sicily, discovered in 1988 and excavated by Alice Freschi (Cooperativa Aquarius), has the unusual feature of combining lashed with mortise-and-tenon construction. The vessel carried a cargo of Ionian, Corinthian, Attic, and Punic amphoras, as well as fine ware and well-preserved organic objects including baskets and a fragment of a wooden statue; the well-preserved 17.4 m hull has been raised and is undergoing conservation treatment at the time of writing.

The late 1st-century BC **Comacchio Wreck** (or Valle Ponti Ship), a well-preserved beached wreck, represents the lashed hull tradition of the upper Adriatic region which continued into the medieval period. Discovered and excavated by F. Berti in 1980, the vessel carried both local and Aegean amphoras, over 100 lead ingots probably from Spain, consignments of bronze vessels and coarse ware, and a variety of other metal objects. Once again site conditions allowed excellent preservation of organic materials, much of the ship's equipment and items belonging to the crew. The raised hull is to be displayed following final conservation at Comacchio.

Other sites of unusual interest to socio-economic studies include the late 2nd-century BC Torre Sgarrata (Apulia) Wreck, which carried a cargo of sarcophagi; the mid-1st-century AD Diano Marina (Liguria) Vessel known as the Dolia Wreck for its large storage containers (*dolia*) fixed in the hold;

the 2nd-century AD Grado (Veneto) Ship, which carried glass for recycling; the 3rd-century AD Marzamemi (Sicily) Vessel, which was delivering marble building material from Attica; the early 3rd-century AD Ognina (Sicily) Vessel, a luxury yacht with mosaics and columns; and a couple of 12th-century Norman ships at Marsala (Sicily). Of relevance to nautical archaeology is the recovery of various vessel types illustrating a range of technological features and developments: at Fiumicino near Rome boats recovered in the silted harbour include a fishing boat with an internal compartment to keep the catch fresh; the 7th-century AD Pantano Longarini (Sicily) wreck illustrates an early example of a transom stern. Not to be ignored are the numerous investigations of finds from rivers and lakes. Excavations by M.L. Fugazzola Delpino at Lago di Bracciano (northwest of Rome) have revealed a submerged Neolithic village and remarkably well-preserved logboat, perhaps the oldest known oak logboat in Europe.

The **Isis wreck** site, which lies at 818 m on Skerki Bank in the channel between Tunisia and Sicily, was discovered by A.M. McCann and R. Ballard in 1988 with the use of an ROV **Submersible**. The cargo was made up of a variety of Late Roman amphora types; provisional dates based on a coin and diagnostic lamp point to the late 4th century AD. The site is significant as perhaps the deepest known ancient shipwreck and the first archaeologically relevant use of an ROV, pointing to future possibilities of extending the range of underwater archaeology with remotely controlled vehicles.

Coastal studies on geomorphological changes, ports, and harbours along the Italian littoral have been conducted by a number of researchers since Giulio Schmeidt published documentary research based on aerial photographs and surface surveys in the mid-1960s. Projects investigating harbours include collaborations between Italian and Israeli researchers (from the Recanati Centre of Maritime Studies, Haifa) searching for traces of Phoenician ports in Sardinia, and the American Academy project at the 3rd-century BC Roman colony established at Cosa (see **Cosa, Harbour of**) Complex harbourworks included canals to reduce the effect of silting between the lagoonal harbour and the sea, and breakwaters, in which Roman engineering ingenuity is displayed in an early use of hydraulic cement. A recent (1993-6) research project headed by Francisca Pallarés has established a databank of information on coastal installations from prehistoric times to the Middle Ages around the Italian

coastline, as a working tool for the archaeological superintendencies (*soprintendenze*) whose territories include submerged archaeological sites.

Relative sea-levels in the region are estimated to have stabilized *c.* 2,000 years ago, with variations of less than 50 cm since then, according to measurements taken of ancient coastal structures such as fish-tanks. Local variations occur, especially around the volcanic area of Naples, as illustrated in excavations of the submerged Imperial port areas of Baia and Pozzuoli, where continuous changes in sea level due to the local volcanic phenomenon of bradyseism submerged significant buildings and port structures. Italy's volcanic conditions have served nautical archaeology in one instance, by preserving a rare example of a small coastal vessel at Herculaneum which was buried under mud in the famous volcanic eruption of Vesuvius in AD 79 (see **Herculaneum Boat**).

The discipline of maritime archaeology in Italy, which has had a chequered history, has since the 1980s witnessed a number of initiatives aimed at establishing its legal, academic, and formal recognition. The underwater archaeology consultancy service of the Ministry of Culture (STAS), established in 1986, is intended to provide technical assistance to the regional archaeological superintendencies working on maritime research projects. However, the lack of clear objectives, coordinating plans, and infrastructures such as a permanent work vessel and even insurance have seriously hampered its efforts. Thus rescue excavations are often contracted to private groups, of which the Cooperativa Aquarius under the direction of the archaeologist Alice Freschi is one of the most successful. Under the current law (n. 1089, of 1939) underwater finds must be reported immediately to the relevant organization, port authority, or police department, and the finder may claim up to 25 per cent of the object's total value; individuals granted permission to excavate a site must follow scientific archaeological methodologies under the threat of penalties or fines.

Efforts to facilitate proper and thorough protection of Italy's submerged heritage, including proposals to ensure the presence of formally qualified maritime archaeologists in the country's thirty-odd regional archaeological superintendencies, have been spearheaded by the professional Associazione Italiana di Archeologi Subacquei (AIASub) founded in 1993. The AIASub has initiated an international conference series (Anzio, 1996), and also supports a four-monthly journal, *L'Archeologo Subacqueo*. The

Istituto Italiano di Archeologia e Etnologia Navale (ISTIAEN), also established in 1993–4, aims to provide a reference centre for maritime researchers, as well as offering courses in the history of navigation and naval architecture. The Italian archaeology journal *Archeologia Viva*, which publishes a summer issue dedicated to underwater archaeology, has offered summer courses in maritime archaeology for several years on the Sicilian island of Ustica. At the university level, however, while the universities of Viterbo, Venice, and Agrigento offer maritime archaeology courses and the University of Viterbo has begun a scholarly journal of underwater archaeology (*Archeologia subacquea. Studi, ricerche e documenti*), academic qualifications in the discipline are not yet available. The yearly conference on Mediterranean maritime archaeology held since the mid-1980s at Giardini Naxos in northeast Sicily is an important forum at which to review recent research in Italy, at the crossroads of the Mediterranean. C.C.2

ADDITIONAL READING

Berti, F. (ed.), 1990, *Fortuna Maris. La nave romana di Comacchio*, Ferrara.

Bound, M., 1991, 'The Giglio Wreck', *Enalia*, suppl. 1, Athens.

Celuzza, M.G. and Rendini, P. (eds), 1993, *Relitti di storia: Archeologia subacquea in Maremma*, exhibition catalogue, Siena.

Eiseman, C.J. and Ridgway, B.S., 1987, *The Porticello Shipwreck. A Mediteerranean Merchant Vessel of 415-385 BC*, College Station, Texas.

Fugazzola Delpino, M.A., 1995, *Un tuffo nel passato. 8,000 mila anni fa nel lago di Bracciano*, Soprintendeza Speciale al Museo nazionale Preistorico Etnografico 'L. Pigorini', Rome.

Gargiullo, S. and Okely, E. 1993, *Atlante archeologico dei mari d'Italia* (3 vols), Formello.

Gianfrotta, P.A. and Pomey, P., 1981, *Archeologia subacquea: Storia, tecniche, scoperte e relitti*, Milan.

McCann, A.M. (ed.), 1987, *The Roman port and Fishery off Cosa*, Princeton, New Jersey.

McCann, A.M. and Freed, J., 1994, 'Deep Water Archaeology. A Late Roman Ship from Carthage and an Ancient Route near Skerki Bank off Northwestern Sicily', *Journal of Roman Archaeology*, suppl. 13, Ann Arbor

Navigia fundo emergunt: Mostra di archeologia sottomarina in Liguria, Genova.

Parker, A.J., 1992, *Ancient Shipwrecks of the Mediterranean and Roman Provinces, 1500 BC - AD 1500*, Tempus Reparatum/BAR International Series 580, Oxford.

Schmiedt, G., 1964, 'Contribution of photo interpretation to the reconstruction of the geographic-topographic situation of the ports of Italy', *X Congress of International Society of Photogrammetry*, Lisbon.

J

James Matthews

Mid-19th-century wreck off Fremantle, Western Australia. Slave ships of the illegal period were normally destroyed upon capture by the authorities, so although such vessels had a reputation for speed, there are few shipwrecks representing that period of the trade available for study. *James Matthews* is one such shipwreck. The snow brig *Don*

Francisco was a Portuguese slaver, owned by the notorious Francisco Felis da Sousa, slave dealer of the West African fort of Whydah. In 1837 *Don Francisco* was captured off the Caribbean island of Dominica, with a cargo of 433 slaves from Africa. The normal procedure was for such vessels to be taken back to Freetown, Sierra Leone for adjudication, condemnation, and destruction, but *Don Francisco* was adjudicated in the West Indies and, after condemnation, was re-registered as *James Matthews*.

James Matthews left London for Fremantle, Western Australia in March 1841, with a cargo of 7,000 roofing slates, farm implements, general cargo, three passengers, and a crew of fifteen. After arriving safely at Fremantle the vessel was blown ashore in a gale and wrecked. Henry de Burgh, who left a diary describing the wreck, watched aghast as the crew, attempting to lighten the ship, consigned to the deep his chest containing 200 sovereigns.

The wreck was located in 1973 by skin-divers who were granted a reward of $600 under the conditions of the Museum Act. During the 1970s four seasons of excavation

were carried out on the site by archaeologists from the Western Australian Museum under the direction of Graeme Henderson. This work resulted in a fine collection of farming equipment belonging to the pioneer settlers. The hull was in good condition and the survey provided sufficiently comprehensive data for the lines of the vessel to be reconstructed. This has given unique information about one of the vessels representative of the infamous illegal period of the slave trade, so often referred to in the literature but never comprehensively described. G.H.

ADDITIONAL READING

Henderson, G., 1976, '*James Matthews* Excavation, Summer 1974, Interim Report',

Excavating a besom (broom) from James Matthews. *(© Western Australia Maritime Museum/ Patrick Baker)*

Artefacts from James Matthews. *(© Western Australia Maritime Museum/Patrick Baker)*

International Journal of Nautical Archaeology, 5, 3, 245–51.

Henderson, G., 1980,*Unfinished Voyages: Western Australian Shipwrecks 1622–1850*, Nedlands.

James River Bateaux

Keel-less, double-ended, open watercraft used to navigate rapid upland rivers of Virginia between the late-18th and mid-19th centuries. The craft was developed in response to the need to transport tobacco from the agricultural regions of the piedmont James River Valley to the market at Richmond. It became the main vessel of commerce on pre-canal and small upland waters from the Potomac to the Savannah rivers prior to 1860. Bateaux were operated primarily by slaves and free black boatmen.

The James River bateau reflected a national trend prior to steam and canal navigation of using open double-ended boats to carry commerce and travellers on upland rivers. Among many contemporary bateaux-types were Ohio River keelboats, Mohawk River bateaux, and Delaware River Durham boats. Most of these craft were characterized by long narrow dimensions (up to 18 m long), shallow draft, low sheer, and open hulls. They were propelled upstream by poling, towing, and general manhandling, and rode the current downstream steered by long oar-like sweeps. The double-ended hull permitted steering from either end which was useful on narrow waters and for getting unstuck from shoals and rocks.

The introduction of the James River bateaux was credited to Albemarle County planter Anthony Rucker (1740–1821) in about 1771, an event witnessed and documented by neighbouring planter Thomas Jefferson. The hull dimensions and form echo the earlier use of dugout canoes to transport tobacco in the region. Tobacco canoes disappeared due to over-logging and a devastating flood in 1771 and the bateaux were apparently developed in response to the thriving upland commerce. Hull construction features reflect French bateau and dory influences introduced in the Old Northwest by 17th-century French fur trappers. It is unknown whether or how Rucker might have had knowledge of these earlier craft.

Archaeological assessment indicates that bateau frames were precut and numbered for their relative position. They were fastened to the king plank in an inverted position, flipped upright, and the remaining three courses of planks then attached. The ends, attached in a final stage, were composed of a stem and short keelson assembly and short planks which butted at the end frames forming a roughly triangular shape that required no steaming of planks. The crudeness and simplicity of construction permitted construction by plantation carpenters, usually slaves. Bateaux were cheap to build and had short but useful lifespans.

James River bateaux carried approximately 12 tonnes of cargo. Although initially developed for the tobacco trade they were used for most commercial transport on the upland rivers of the Southeast. Bateaux commerce on the James River impelled the rise of Richmond as a significant Southern entrepot and manufacturing centre in the early 19th century. The success of bateaux

navigation hastened the development of the James River Canal and Kanawha Canal system which linked coastal Atlantic trade with the Ohio River system. The canal system was superseded only by the introduction of railroad commerce. Bateaux commerce continued into the early 20th century on lesser rivers.

Numerous remains of James River bateaux were uncovered in emergency archaeological excavations at the site of the James River Canal basin in Richmond between 1983 and 1985. Although lack of State funding precluded conservation of remains, volunteer archaeological support resulted in the documentation of several vessels. Plans from the excavations have resulted in the construction of over thirty replicas which are used in an annual race and cultural heritage celebration along the James River. B.T.

ADDITIONAL READING

Terrell, B., 1992, *The James River Bateaux: Tobacco Transport in Upland Virginia, 1745–1840*, East Carolina University Research Report no. 7, Greenville, North Carolina.

Jason

A remotely operated undersea vehicle used for scientific mapping and sampling tasks to depths of 6,000 m. *Jason* was designed and built at the Woods Hole Oceanographic Institution and is currently operated under the auspices of the US National Deep Submergence Facility. *Jason* is 2.2 m in length and weighs 1,200 kg in air.

Jason has been used for a variety of survey and sampling tasks for a variety of scientific disciplines, including marine geology, biology, chemistry, and archaeology. Archaeo-

logical expeditions have included the survey and recovery of artefacts from the Isis site in the Mediterranean at a depth of 700 m (see **Isis Wreck**), and a photographic and sonar survey of **Hamilton and Scourge** in Lake Ontario. Other expeditions have included surveys of active hydrothermal sites in the Pacific, a deep water dump site and a mid-ocean ridge survey in the Atlantic, and the survey of the wreck of **Lusitania** off the coast of Ireland.

In deep water, *Jason* operates from its companion vehicle *Medea*. *Medea* is connected to the surface by a steel-armoured fibre-optic cable 17 mm in diameter up to 6,000 m long, and to *Jason* by a much shorter neutrally buoyant cable approximately 50 m long. *Medea* stabilizes the system by providing weight to the end of the long steel-armoured cable, isolates *Jason* from the motions and weight of the long cable, and also provides auxiliary cameras, lighting, and navigation references. *Jason*, which is neutrally buoyant, is propelled by seven thrusters and can manoeuvre finely in any direction.

For mapping purposes, *Jason* represents the fine scale component of a multiple vehicle system operated by the National Facility. *Jason*'s fibre-optic telemetry system accommodates a variety of sensors, such as colour video cameras, 35 mm film cameras, a high-dynamic range electronic still camera, and several high resolution imaging sonars. Navigation systems include a long-range system providing resolution of several metres over ranges up to 5 km, and a more precise system (Exact), which provides resolution of several centimetres over a range of 100 m. Data from the sensors are routinely

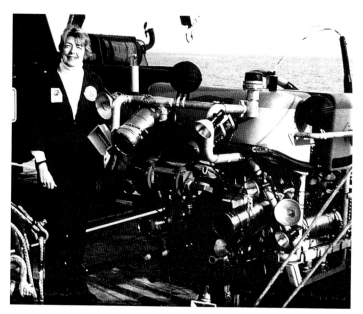

Anna Marguerite McCann with ROV Jason *in 1990. (Quest Group Ltd)*

assembled into a variety of maps and mosaics.

Jason is equipped with a manipulator arm that can recover artefacts and samples. At the Isis site, *Jason* and its manipulator were used to recover over forty artefacts. Jason's manipulator can be fitted with a variety of grippers to accommodate many sizes and shapes of objects, and the grasping forces can be carefully controlled to avoid damage. In the Isis work, the artefacts were transferred to an 'elevator' on the sea-floor, which then returned to the surface when commanded to release ballast weights. D.Y.Z.

ADDITIONAL READING

Ballard, R.D., 1993, 'The Medea/Jason Remotely Operated Vehicle System', *Deep-sea Research I*, 40, 8, 1673–87.

Bowen, A., *et al.*, 1993, *The Woods Hole Oceanographic Institution's Remotely Operated and Towed Vehicle Facilities for Deep Ocean Research*, WHOI Technical Report, Woods Hole, Massachusetts.

McCann, A.M. and Freed, J., 1994, *Deep Water Archaeology: A Late-Roman Ship for Carthage and an Ancient Trade Route Near Skerki Bank off Northwest Sicily*, Journal of Roman Archaeology, Supplementary Series no. 13, Ann Arbor, Michigan.

JASON Project

Educational expeditions administered by the JASON Foundation for Education, whose mission is to excite and engage students in science and technology and to motivate and train their teachers through the use of advanced telecommunications. The Foundation enjoys the support and expertise of a unique alliance of public, private, and non-profit organizations who are committed to the improvement of science and technical education for all students. JASON Project expeditions feature live broadcasts from distinctive sites on our planet through advanced technologies in robotics, fibre optics, television production, computer science, mechanical and electrical engineering, and satellite communications.

The JASON Project is sponsored by science museums, private businesses, educational organizations and government. The strength of the JASON Project comes in no small part from the diversity of its national sponsors which have included EDS, the **National Geographic Society**, Bechtel, Sprint, Sun Microsystems, the **US Navy**, the National Science Foundation, Cray Research, Woods Hole Oceanographic Institution, and the US Department of Education. The Foundation works with the National Science Teachers Association in the development of its curriculum to help in the preparation of participating teachers in each year's Project.

The Project involves teachers and students in a comprehensive programme of teacher workshops; up-to-the-minute curriculum developed around specific expedition topics each year, interactivity through the Internet using JASON's several online systems; viewing of specially produced taped programmes available through educational television; and active participation in live 'you are there' broadcasts from real science expeditions, which have included the archaeological examination of the wrecks of *Hamilton* and *Scourge*.

One recent expedition, JASON Project Voyage VI, Island Earth, took place in March 1995, transporting more than 350,000 teachers and students electronically to the Big Island of Hawaii. There they studied the roles of volcanism in the formation and constant change of the Earth, compared that to volcanism at other points in our solar system, and examined the unique biological adaptations that take place in an isolated island environment.

Other expeditions have examined the rich biology, geology, and anthropology present in the rainforest and coral reefs of Belize; the unique life forms called 'tube worms' on the bottom of the Sea of Cortez, as well as the more typically spectacular migrating grey whales on the Pacific side of Baja California; the unique natural laboratory of the Galapagos Islands; and explorations of sunken ships in the **Great Lakes** and the **Mediterranean Sea**.

JASON Project Voyage VII took place off Key Largo, Florida, in April 1996, and featured a study of the watershed from the Florida Everglades, through Florida Bay to the reefs and into the deeper water of the relic reefs. Students studied the geology of the region, the biological adaptations of the various creatures who live there, and the technological adaptations man has made to study and live in the ocean. T.A.

Jefferson

A **US Navy** twenty-gun brig built at Sackets Harbor, New York for service on Lake Ontario during the Anglo-American 'War of 1812'. *Jefferson* was one of four warships – two large frigates and two brig-rigged sloops of war – added to the American naval squadron of Commodore Isaac Chauncey during a shipbuilding contest in 1814 with the rival Royal Navy squadron on the lake. The builder of *Jefferson* was New York shipwright Henry Eckford, who acquired a reputation during the war for assembling strong fast-sailing ships in a short period of time; *Jefferson*, for example, was started in late January, finished in March, and launched in early April. The brig was outfitted with twenty very heavy guns (sixteen 42-pounder carronades and four 24-pounder long guns) and manned by 160 sailors transferred from the blockaded US Navy sloop-of-war *Erie* at Baltimore.

Chauncey's squadron did not sail until late July 1814, at which time *Jefferson* participated in the destruction of the Royal Navy brig *Magnet* and, together with its sister-brig *Jones*, maintained a blockade of British vessels in the Niagara River. While off this location in September a nor'easter storm knocked *Jefferson* on its side twice and forced the crew to jettison half the guns to keep the brig from capsizing. When news of the war's end reached Sackets Harbor in February 1815, Chauncey's naval squadron was laid up in the harbour and left to rot. Most of the sunken warships were sold to salvagers in 1825, but *Jefferson* was never removed from the harbour.

Jefferson's half-buried hull was relocated in 1984 by the Lake Champlain Maritime Museum, and partially excavated in 1985, 1987, and 1988 with assistance from the New York Bureau of Historic Sites and the **National Geographic Society**. The port side of the hull was preserved to the cap rail for most of its length, although the bow was extensively damaged by the construction of a marina in the 1960s. Test excavations yielded ship's equipment (gratings, deadeyes, glass skylights, and a wooden snowshovel), grape and cannister shot, and crew possessions (pearlware ceramics, mustard bottles, buttons, and a spoon with the owner's name scratched in the bowl).

The excellent state of hull preservation permitted reconstruction of the *Jefferson* on paper and revealed many of Eckford's design and construction practices. The vessel measured 122 ft 11 in (37.5 m) between perpendiculars and had a maximum beam of 32 ft 6 in (9.9 m). The shallow-draft hull was designed for fast sailing, with a sharp entrance, a long, tapering run, and extreme deadrise (giving *Jefferson* a V-shaped hull in section). This form, combined with an extremely heavy battery of cannon, made for a very unstable vessel and explains *Jefferson*'s difficulties in the storm of September 1814. The brig was entirely iron-fastened, and its scantlings were fashioned from white oak and other strong long-lasting hardwoods. Eckford did employ one shortcut to speed the assembly of the hull: there were no knees used in the construction of the hull, and the deck was secured to the hull by enlarged clamp and waterway timbers. Additional interior reinforcement was provided by diagonally oriented rider timbers bolted to the interior of the ceiling and frames. K.C.

ADDITIONAL READING

Cassavoy, K. and Crisman, K., 1988, 'The War of 1812: Battle for the Great Lakes', in G. F. Bass (ed.), *Ships and Shipwrecks of the Americas*, London and New York.

Crisman, K., 1989, *Jefferson: The History and Archaeology of an American Brig from the War of 1812*, doctoral dissertation, University of Pennsylvania.

Crisman, K., 1991, 'Nautical Archaeology of the War of 1812: The Lake Brigs *Jefferson* and *Eagle*', *Seaways*, 2, 4, 5–9.

Crisman, K., 1992, 'Two Deck Lights from the US Navy Brig *Jefferson*', in 'Ships in Scale', *Seaways*, 3, 6, 48–50.

Crisman, K., in press, 'Captain Ridgely's Command: The Archaeology of the War of 1812 Brig *Jefferson*', in V. Brehm (ed.), *A Fully Accredited Ocean*, Ann Arbor, Michigan.

Jhelum

A rare survival of a typical mid-19th-century British merchant ship, which also provides an insight into shipbuilding and shipowning in mid-19th-century Liverpool. *Jhelum* was a three-masted square-rigged wooden sailing ship measuring 118.5 ft (36.1 m) long by 24.6 ft (7.49 m) beam with a registered tonnage of 466 tons, built at Liverpool in 1849 by Joseph Steel and Son for their own use. The ship was stoutly built: keel of rock elm, keelson of 'African oak' with double frames of oak, and hull planking of pine, fastened with treenails, copper bolts, and iron spikes. The internal structural members – longitudinals, inner planking, and deck beams – were mainly of African mahogany, and these were reinforced with iron stanchions and knees including Fell's patent knees for fixing the deck beams to the frames. She had a raised poop and her hold (without tween-decks) was continuous apart from a small partitioned space in the bow for the crew.

Her Indian name seems to have given rise to the myth that she was an East Indiaman. Apart from her maiden voyage to Bombay, *Jhelum* traded mainly between the United Kingdom and the west coast of South America, with various manufactures outwards and copper ore, wool, nitrates, or guano homewards. Steels sold her in 1863. On 18 August 1870, *Jhelum* put into Stanley in the Falkland Islands, leaking badly. She was condemned in March 1871 and sold to the Packe Brothers of Stanley who converted her into a store hulk and workshop by roofing over her main deck from amidships to the stern. By the 1980s *Jhelum* was abandoned and between 1987 and 1990, Mersey-

side Maritime Museum, Liverpool worked with the Falkland Islands Museum to document and conserve the hulk. A full dimensional and visual record of her lines, construction, and fittings, plus documentation, was published in 1992–3. Measuring presented problems because the forward unroofed part of the hull listed at a different angle to the stern section. Traces of the fixtures and equipment of the ship survived which made it possible to develop an almost complete picture of her when in use. These included the crew and officers' accommodation, the anchoring arrangement, mast positions, chain-plates and standard rigging, and pin rails for running rigging, sections of which survived. The two wrought-iron water tanks in the hold amidships were unusual. Contemporary sources and their location proved that they were original to the vessel. The hold also contained large quantities of sand, mud, and stone mixed in with late 19th-century ceramics, glass, and domestic metal objects. Local oral sources suggested that this was domestic refuse rather than a survival from the ship's stores.

The conservation programme included the rebuilding of the stern section's roof, the strengthening and protection of the few remaining forward deck beams, and sheathing the starboard bow to prevent wave damage. The hulk is protected by a local maritime heritage law and is the responsibility of the Falkland Islands Trust and Museum. M.S.

ADDITIONAL READING

Bound, M., 1993, 'Iron Beam-end Fastenings: Fell's Patent no. 8186: A Puzzle Resolved, *Mariner's Mirror*, 79, 338–42.

The starboard bow of Jhelum, 1987. Many of the original bow features are still intact, including the forward rails, starboard cathead and the chain-plates for the four-mast rigging. (Trustees of the National Museums and Galleries on Merseyside (Merseyside Maritime Museum))

Stammers, M.K., 1989, 'The *Jhelum* and the Liverpool Shipbuilders', in V. Burton (ed.), *Liverpool Shipping: Trade and Industry*, Liverpool.

Stammers, M.K. and Baker, J., 1994, 'Fell's Patent Knees: Some Evidence of their Use', *Mariner's Mirror*, 80, 474–6.

Stammers, M.K. and Kearon, J., 1992–3, *The Jhelum: A Victorian Merchant Ship*, Stroud, UK and Wolfeboro Falls, USA.

Jutholmen Wreck

The remains of a cargo-carrying ship which foundered around 1700, situated at Jutholmen Island, in Dalarö Harbour, Sweden. The wreck was located in 1965 at a depth of between 11 and 14 m. Since the Middle Ages, Dalarö has been a port for merchant and naval vessels. A customs office established in 1636 became the most important office for shipping to and from Sweden during the era of mercantilistic policy in the 17th and 18th centuries. All merchant ships carrying foreign goods on their way to or from the capital or the northern part of Sweden were obliged to declare their cargoes there.

The wreck was surveyed and excavated by the Swedish National Maritime Museum between 1970 and 1974. The site has been subjected to selective investigation after that time. The investigation was, together with that of the galliot *Concordia* (see **Älvsnabben**

Wreck), part of a programme for the development of underwater archaeological recording and excavation methods fitted to the waters of the Swedish east coast and the Baltic Sea. The Jutholmen project comprised the surveying of the hull of the wreck, the excavation of the major part of its interior, and the raising and recording of thousands of artefacts.

Both numismatic analysis of coins found in the wreck as well as later dendrochronological dating of the parts of a tar barrel in it, which in all probability was newly manufactured when the ship sank, give evidence that the ship was lost around the year 1700. The ship and its interior showed signs of fire damage, indicating the possibility of fire as the cause of the ship's sinking. Analysis of the structure of the wreck shows that it was a carvel-built, cargo-carrying ship with a round stern and a flush deck. It originally had three masts, the two forward masts square rigged. The hull has a length of 24 m and a moulded breath of 5.35 m. It has a length–breath ratio of 4.5:1. The depth of hold is an estimated 2 to 2.5 m, and the ship has a shallow draught. The capacity of the cargo hold is estimated to be between 190 and 240 cu. m. The ship had a sterncastle with a backboard across the stern. The sides of the hull slope inwards at deck level as do the sides of the aftercastle.

The technique by which the ship was built – as is evident by, for example, the midship frame and details in its structure – is in the Dutch fashion. On a number of essential structural points the Jutholmen Wreck represents a typical cargo-carrying ship from the 17th century, possibly a small flute or a catship. The vessel belongs to the same building traditions as the naval ship **Vasa**, built under the leadership of a Dutch master shipwright in Stockholm in the 1620s, and lost in 1628, and also the flute ship **Anna Maria**, built in Amsterdam in 1694 and lost in Dalarö Harbour in 1709. Dutch merchant vessels, or vessels built by Dutch shipwrights, were the most common trading ships active in the Baltic at the time of the Jutholmen Wreck. The ship seems to have been relatively old when it sank, possibly several decades old.

At the time of the sinking, Sweden was on the verge of a full-blown Nordic War which was to spell the demise of the country as a major political power in Europe. When it sank, the ship had been carrying a cargo of wrought-iron bars, tar in barrels, and a larger amount of firewood. It seems that the ship – according to the coins found on board – had been travelling between Swedish ports and the harbours at the south-

ern part of the Baltic Sea. Some finds indicated that it had military officers aboard.

The artefacts retrieved from the wreck, besides the structural parts of the hull and its rigging, comprised a number of objects from the ship's equipment and crew members' belongings. Among these were remains of household goods, such as plates, glasses, and bowls of different materials, and also artefacts such as hand weapons, clothes, shoes, and coins. Also found were the remains of navigational instruments – part of a sundial and parts of time glasses – as well as remains of ship's armament ranging from a store of cannon balls to guns of smaller size.

The original identity of the Jutholmen Wreck is still not established, although much effort has been expended on this task for more than twenty years. One hypothesis is that the ship was not a merchant ship, but a smaller cargo carrier used in the Navy or the Army at the time. It could have belonged to any of these organizations, or have been hired by the Navy during the pre-Nordic War build-up. Such an explanation indicates why written information has not been found about the foundering of the ship. It might also mean that no or very few notes were made about the accident when it happened, as the ship was merely a small military transport vessel. C.O.C.

ADDITIONAL READING

Cederlund, C.O., 1977, 'Preliminary Report on Recording Methods Used for the Investigation of Merchant Shipwrecks at Jutholmen and Älvsnabben in 1973–74', *International Journal of Nautical Archaeology*, 6, 2, 87–99.

Cederlund, C.O., 1982, *Vraket vid Jutholmen: Fartygets byggnad*, Rapport: Statens Sjöhistoriska Museum no. 16, Stockholm.

Cederlund, C.O., 1983, *The Old Wrecks of the Baltic Sea: Archaeological Recording of the Wrecks of Carvel-built Ships*, British Archaeological Reports International Series 186, Oxford.

Kaijser, I., 1983, *Vraket vid Jutholmen: Last och utrustning*, Rapport 1: Statens Sjöhistoriska Museum no. 17, Stockholm.

Kalmar Harbour Wrecks

Remains of twenty-five ships and boats (Finds I–XXV) recovered from the old harbour of Kalmar, situated on Kalmar Sound in southeast Sweden. The wrecks were recovered between 1933 and 1934 together with pilework for wharves, ballast-beds, anchors, pottery, glass, leather, and objects of tin and bronze after draining Slottsfjärden (Castle Bay) immediately north of medieval Kalmar Castle. Excavations were directed by Harald Åkerlund. The dating of the vessels was based upon typology. The remains of the Kalmar Harbour wrecks are stored in the cellars of Kalmar Castle.

Find I (mid-13th century or slightly later). A small clinker-built ship constructed mainly of oak, with top planking, beams, and other details of pine. All of the timbers are axed. The vessel is c. 11 m long, 4.55 m broad, and 2 m deep from the upper edge of the keel. The sternpost is quite straight with a moderate rake and rudder. Amidships the hull is almost flat-bottomed, but with quite a clean-shaped entrance and run. The ship carried a lowerable mast, standing in a step in the keelson, and steadied by two longitudinal timbers. A powerful windlass was found in the afterbody. The keel was constructed in three sections: the middle part is 5.4 m long and T-shaped; the after-part is made of a knee timber, whose upright part forms the base of the sternpost. This is five-sided in section, where the planks meet in a point astern of the stern. At the stempost, they fit into notches in the stem. The top planking is jointed with small treenails while the rest of the planks are fastened with iron rivets. There are projecting beam ends.

Find II (13th century?). A large clinker-built ship with all preserved parts of oak. Its length is estimated at 19–20 m and the width at 5.8–6 m. The hull is fairly flat-bottomed, with a broader forebody than afterbody. The mast is placed a short distance afore of midships. The hull planks are 25–30 mm thick with the inside planking made with quite close, broad planks of oak. Furthest forward the keel has a knee, in which it is tabled with the sternpost. The extant part of the sternpost is completely straight. The frame timbers are laid quite close together. There are indications of projecting beams through the planking.

Find III (medieval). A small clinker-built rowing boat, almost completely preserved.

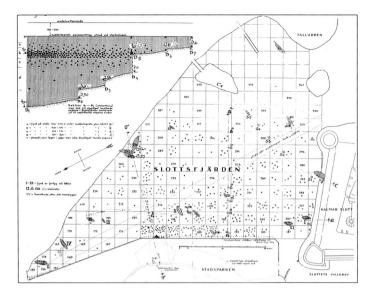

Site plans of the excavated
part of the old harbour in
Kalmar. The boat- and shipfinds are marked with Roman
numerals. (Kalmar County
Museum's Archive)

The hull is all oak, except the upper planking and false-keel. It is 4.4 m long and 1.53 m wide midships. The keel is made of a broad hollowed plank of oak, equipped on the underside with a nogged false-keel. There are two pairs of holes, the sternmost pair being movable. The gunwale saddle is angle-shaped in section at the stempost. The vessel is presumably a ship's boat or a fishing boat.

Find IV (late 15th century?). A clinker-built ship, *c.* 15.6 m long, 4 m broad, and 1.8 m deep from the upper edge of the keel, with quite a raking stem and sternpost. The port side is preserved amidships right up to the gunwale. The keel is high, with broad wing-lists, and is united with the straight sternpost in a knee that is not preserved. The lower part of the stempost has survived. The vessel has alternate floor timbers, coarse and of pine, with the intervening ones less stout and of oak. The garboards are not attached to the floor timbers. There is a keelson with a step for a mast. The vessel was originally fitted with a thin ceiling. There were six cross-beams projecting through the planking, but only one survives.

Find V (*c.* 1500). Ship with part of the port side preserved up to the gunwale. The starboard side and after-part of the top of the port side were destroyed by fire. The ship was *c.* 16.2 m long, 5.6 m wide, and 2.4 m deep; presumably it was round-sterned with a broad after-part. The ship was decked solely at the bow and stern. Timbers as well as the planks are pine. The outer part of the keel, stempost, and beams, etc. are oak. The keel and stempost are built up of two superimposed timbers. The timbers are axed from crooked trunks and coarse branches of pine. The planks are 25–35 mm thick. The keelson is supported at the mast-step by timbers in two pairs. There is a thin inside plank, cross-

Kalmar Harbour Find XII in
situ, with Kalmar Castle in
the background. (Kalmar
County Museum's Archive)

beams, and longitudinal beams with one cross-beam originally projecting through the planking. Pump arrangements were recovered.

Find VI (early 16th century?). A small clinker-built ship, entirely made of oak. Only partly preserved, it is *c.* 11 m long and 4 m wide. The keel is 9.2 m long. The floor-timbers are coarse, with 20–30 cm planks. The keelson is 6.7 m long with a mast-step placed 1 m forward of midships. The stem-post is extant, but the sternpost is missing.

Find VII (16th century?). A small, clinker-built rowing boat without mast and keelson. It is *c.* 6 m long and 2 m wide with frames of juniper, oak, and pine, and the keel, stem and sternpost, and planking of oak. The ceiling planking is 15 mm thick pine.

Find VIII (*c.* 1600). A small clinker-built sailing boat. The preserved structure is entirely of oak. Originally the vessel had a total of only four frames. A small, 5 by 3 cm circular mast-step is placed in the frame immediately forward of midships. The planks are 20 cm broad and 15–18 mm thick. The vessel appears to have been used as a fire-ship.

Find IX (*c.* 1600). A small clinker-built ship, entirely of oak, with only a few parts preserved. The original length from stem to

stern was *c.* 15 m. The keel is 10 m long in three sections. The planks are 3 cm thick and 25–35 cm broad.

Find X (*c.* 1600). A carvel-built ship of oak, destroyed by fire, originally 18–20 m long.

Find XI (17th century). Parts of what appears to be a clinker-built ship-boat made entirely of oak. Its original length was *c.* 10 m. The keel is 6 m long and the planks are 25 mm thick and 20–25 cm broad.

Find XII (presumably the Swedish *boeier Kråkan* ('The Crow'), built in 1636). The only carvel-built ship among the Kalmar Harbour wrecks. It is 18.5 m long and 3–4 m wide. The hull contained piles of cannon-balls, a fragment of a cannon, and in the forebody a heap of tiles from the fireplace. It has double planking with inner planks of oak *c.* 40 cm thick and outer planking of pine *c.* 35 mm thick. The ship probably carried two masts.

Find XIII (17th century). A small clinker-built ship, presumably a *lodja*, a one-masted vessel of eastern Baltic origin which could be rowed as well as sailed. It was originally *c.* 15 m long. The structure is oak, except for a ceiling of pine. The planks are 25 mm thick and *c.* 25 cm broad.

Find XIV (late 17th century). A strong clinker-built ship, entirely of pine, with closely laid timbers. It is *c.* 22 m long and 7 m broad. Only the bottom of the hull is extant but the keelson is missing. The stout method of construction indicates a transport vessel, possibly a *struss*, a one-masted vessel of eastern Baltic origin which could be rowed as well as sailed.

Find XV (early 17th century). A fairly large clinker-built ship, entirely of oak. Very little of the vessel is preserved. Originally at least 25 m long, it has stout floor timbers 30 cm broad and 12–15 cm thick.

Find XVI (undated, probably not older than the 16th century). A small clinker-built vessel of oak. The keel is 8.9 m long. The original length of the vessel is estimated at *c.* 13–14 m.

Find XVII (undated, probably not older than the 16th century). A small, clinker-built vessel of oak, with a 6 m long keel. The original length of the vessel was *c.* 10 m.

Find XVIII (17th century). A large clinker-built boat. The keel, planking, a few frames, stern and the stempost are oak. The frames, keelson, and ceiling are pine. The keel is *c.* 6 m long. The original length of the vessel was *c.* 9.5 m. The planks are 25–35 cm broad and 1.5–2.5 cm thick.

Find XIX (16th or 17th century). Parts of a large clinker-built boat of oak. The keel is 8 m long, in three sections. The original length of the vessel was *c.* 11–12 m.

Find XX (undated, possibly 16th or 17th century). Parts of a small clinker-built ship; the keelson is missing.

Find XXI (undated). An oak ship's keel of oak, 12 m long and made in one piece.

Find XXII (Viking age, AD 800–1050?). Parts of a small boat of oak, including part of a deeply hollowed keel, 1 m long, and two fragments of planks, *c.* 10 mm thick, partly fastened with iron rivets and partly joined with small treenails.

Find XXIII (undated). A small ship's keelson of oak, 4.7 m long.

Find XXIV and XXIV (undated). Oak vessel stems with stage-like notches in the aft-side. L.E.

ADDITIONAL READING

Åkerlund, H., 1951, *Fartygsfynden i den forna hamnen i Kalmar*, Uppsala.

Crumlin-Pedersen, O. (ed.),1991, *Aspects of Maritime Scandinavia*, Roskilde.

Ellmers, D.,1972, *Frühmittelalterliche Handelsschiffart in Mittel- und Nordeuropa*, Neumünster.

Unger, R., 1980, *The Ship in the Medieval Economy 600–1600*, London.

Varenius, B.,1989, *Båtarna från Helgeandsholmen*, Riksantikvarieämbetet och Statens historiska museer Rapport UV, 1989, 3, Stockholm.

Varenius, B., 1992, *Det nordiska skeppet: Teknologi och samhällsstrategi i vikingutid och medeltid*, Stockholm Studies in Archaeology 10, Stockholm.

Kenchreai

Eastern port of the ancient Greek city of Corinth located at the head of the Saronic Gulf. The site was excavated by teams from the University of Chicago and Indiana University under the direction of R.L. Scranton from 1962 to 1968. The project recovered submerged and semi-submerged structures and features as well as others on land. Most important was a complex with an entrance area, an apsidal open court and adjacent temple foundations (interpreted by the excavator as the Temple of Isis mentioned by the 2nd-century AD writers Pausanias and Apuleius) and associated walls at the landward end of the south mole. Over a hundred panels in glass *opus sectile* (i.e. made up of specially shaped pieces) with a variety of scenes of Nile swamps, a city by the sea, fish, and various boats were recovered from the court. Another submerged room contained a mass of preserved wooden remains including a large pulley block, doors, and furniture parts. Much of the area was later covered by an early Christian church and cemetery in the 5th century.

Along the mole other buildings uncovered included warehouses and a *piscina* (fish tank), while just off the quayside a large dump of 1st-century AD pottery, lamps, and other finds was partially excavated. Excavations off the end of the north mole uncovered a large rectangular platform, possibly part of the base for a colossal bronze statue of Poseidon that both coin evidence and Pausanias suggest stood at the harbour entrance; at the water's edge and partly eroded by the sea there is a large Roman brick building with a peristyle and mosaic floors interpreted by the excavator as the Sanctuary of Aphrodite mentioned by Pausanias, but more likely a public or commercial building of some sort.

The glass panels provided extensive evidence for a new art form in glass mosaic and are also a particular important source of iconography of ship representations in the 4th century AD, with a variety of merchant and fishing vessels depicted off a city that may be Alexandria in Egypt; one boat seems to be operating a seine net while another is attached to a large cetaceous creature, thus possibly constituting the earliest known representation of whaling. H.W.

ADDITIONAL READING

Scranton, R.L., 1976-81, *Kenchreai: Eastern Port of Corinth*, 5 vols, Leiden.

Scranton, R. and Ramage, E., 1967, 'Investigations at Corinthian Kenchreia', *Hesperia*, 36, 124-86.

Shaw, J., 1967, 'Shallow-water Excavations at Kenchreai', *American Journal of Archaeology*, 71, 223-31.

Kennemerland

A Dutch East Indiaman wrecked off Shetland, north of Scotland, in December 1664 while travelling outward bound from Texel to Batavia. The richly laden merchantman was on a second trip to the East Indies, taking the northern route around Scotland to avoid hostile ships in the English Channel. Relocated by divers in 1971, the scattered remains of the wreck were the subject of seven seasons of excavation and two further surveys in the subsequent twenty-five years.

Originally laden with treasure, almost all of it recovered by contemporary salvors, the *Kennemerland* site has benefited from being investigated by only archaeologically motivated teams. The importance of the site is partly due to its position in the early development of practice and theory in maritime archaeology in the UK. The wreck is one of forty-three that have been designated by the 1973 **Protection of Wrecks Act (UK)** but prior to that it had some limited protection from a lease of the seabed taken out by the local council around all the major wreck sites in the Shetlands.

The search for *Kennemerland* was aided by local folklore, as a well-known rhyme from the islands mentions the wreck with the verse: 'The Carmelan frac Amsterdam, cam on a *Maunsmas* day, on Stoura Stack she broke her back and in the voe she ca[me].' *Maunsmas* was the feast day of St Magnus, celebrated on 13 December; Stoura Stack was the name of a substantial rock on the edge of the harbour mouth; while 'voe' is the local dialect term for a bay. The positions of the finds surveyed during the excavations support the legend, as the ballast of lead ingots and substantial quantities of yellow Dutch bricks, as well as four of the anchors, were found at the base of this rock with further finds including cannon distributed up the voe. The investigation of this wreck site was one of the first to show that even a scattered wreck site can yield a great deal of archaeological evidence, including stratigraphic relationships. One aim of the excavations was to provide data concerning

Kennemerland wreck site. (Christopher Dobbs)

the distribution of objects on a scattered site so as to create interpretative models of the development of wreck sites. This contributed to the ideas and theoretical framework for the discipline postulated by Keith Muckelroy.

Artefacts found on the site include goods intended for private trade as well as personal possessions and cargo. Many were similar to artefacts found on other East Indiamen such as navigational dividers, a pocket sundial, combs, a shot mould, tobacco boxes, and copious fragments of green bottle glass. One German stoneware flagon was found still full of mercury. The most surprising items located were the heads of five golf clubs, three of which were for left-handed players, while organic material included plum stones, peach stones, and peppercorns. The artefacts from *Kennemerland* are housed at the County Museum in Lerwick, Shetland. c.d.

Additional Reading

Dobbs, C.T.C. and Price, R.A., 1979, 'The *Kennemerland* Site, an Interim Report: The Sixth and Seventh Seasons 1984 and 1987, and the Identification of Five Golf Clubs', *International Journal of Nautical Archaeology*, 20, 111–22.

Forster, W.A. and Higgs, K.B.,1973, 'The *Kennemerland* 1971: An Interim Report', *International Journal of Nautical Archaeology*, 2, 291–300.

Muckelroy, K., 1975, 'A Systematic Approach to the Investigation of Scattered Wreck Sites', *International Journal of Nautical Archaeology*, 4, 173–90.

Muckelroy, K., 1977, 'Historic Wreck Sites in Britain and their Environments', *International Journal of Nautical Archaeology*, 6, 47–57.

Muckelroy, K., 1978, *Maritime Archaeology*, Cambridge.

Price, R. and Muckelroy, K., 1974, 'The Second Season of Work on the *Kennemerland* Site, 1973: An Interim Report', *International Journal of Nautical Archaeology*, 3, 257–68.

Price, R. and Muckelroy, K., 1977, 'The *Kennemerland* Site, the Third and Fourth Seasons 1974 and 1976: An Interim Report', *International Journal of Nautical Archaeology*, 6, 187–218.

Price, R. and Muckelroy, K., 1979, 'The *Kennemerland* Site, the Fifth Season 1978: An Interim Report', *International Journal of Nautical Archaeology*, 8, 311–20.

Price, R., Muckelroy, K., and Willies, L., 1980, 'The *Kennemerland* Site: A Report on the Lead Ingots', *International Journal of Nautical Archaeology*, 9, 7–25.

Khufu Ships

Two planked ships dismantled and buried outside the southern enclosure wall of the

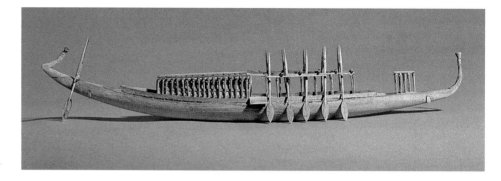

Model of Khufu Ship I in the British Museum. (Courtesy of the Trustees of the British Museum)

Great Pyramid of Khufu (called Cheops by the ancient Greeks), Giza, Egypt, about 2600 BC. In 1954 archaeologists for the Egyptian Antiquities Organization (EAO) discovered two rectangular sealed pits beneath a boundary wall beside Khufu's pyramid. Through an opening made in one of the stones sealing the 32.5 m long eastern pit, archaeologist Kamal el Mallakh saw a steering oar, planks, columns, beams, and the remains of matting and ropes, all extremely well preserved. Thus began the recovery and reconstruction of the largest and most ancient ship yet excavated, the 43 m long Khufu I hull. A non-destructive evaluation of the second pit's contents was made by the EAO and the National Geographic Society, resulting in photographic and visual documentation of the disassembled and unexcavated Khufu II hull which resembles Khufu I in most observable aspects.

The discovery of Khufu I revolutionized knowledge of ancient Egyptian shipbuilding. Despite hundreds of representations and models of boats and ships, written descriptions of watercraft and their dimensions, and at least five **Dashur boats**, the true elegance and magnificence of Egyptian hull construction was unknown. Just as building enormous stone pyramids demonstrated Egypt's wealth and power, so Khufu I transformed a simple means of transportation into a massive ship of state.

Shell-built with timbers 7 to 23 m long, Khufu I represents a tremendous investment of labour and capital. Mortise-and-tenon joints and lashing across the inside of the hull held the 12–15 cm thick planks together, floor timbers loaned strength to the hull's sides, and beams supported a collapsible, prefabricated deckhouse and canopy. Hag Ahmed Mustafa, an EAO conservator, reconstructed Khufu I over a twenty-year period; documentation of this process by the EAO and Paul Lipke provides insight into the original construction of the hull as well.

Six hundred and fifty-one major pieces

and an additional 467 tenons in the hull and 200 tenons in the cabin were removed from the pit. The major pieces included 30 planks, 16 floor timbers, 62 deck beams, 36 stanchions, a carling and 2 stringers, 22 sections of decking, 23 pre-assembled panels of the deckhouse, 12 oars, 58 columns decorated with papyrus or palmette ends, 5 doors, and 3 battens. Rope, lashing knots, matting and other cordage were also retrieved. The reassembled hull measures approximately 42.3 × 5.7 × 1.8 m.

The shipwrights who built Khufu I relied on a regular symmetrical design known 500 years before they began selecting and trimming the logs they would saw and adze to shape. The ancient Egyptians built watercraft and finished plank edges like no others in the world; looking at the planking shapes of Khufu I is like looking at a jigsaw puzzle. Plank edges feature joggles, projections, and notches that fit into notches and projections on adjacent planks; these locked plank edges together and limited longitudinal movement along the seams. Within strakes, curved 'S' scarfs about a metre long connect plank ends.

Egyptian shipwrights also fastened their planks uniquely. Hulls sewn or lashed along plank seams are known from boatbuilding traditions around the world, but as far as we know only Egyptian ships relied on transverse lashing. The practice of lashing hull components together across the vessel rather than along its seams probably resulted from techniques used to build papyrus rafts and boats. Threading ropes through V-shaped channels across the inside of the hull had several advantages. In addition to adding stability to the hull shape in a design that placed little reliance on internal framing, transverse lashing required only 20 per cent of the rope that would be needed to sew planks together along plank seams. This is a significant saving, as the necessary 5,000 m of rope would have cost about the same as a herd of 200 fine cattle 1,400 years later, when industrial production was far advanced over its level in the Old Kingdom.

Fastenings include mortise-and-tenon joints, coaks (half the size of mortise-and-tenon joints, cut perpendicular to the grain in the plank edges), ligatures (stitch-like lashings at points of stress), and the transverse lashing mentioned above. Throughout the hull, mortise-and-tenon joints are spaced 1–1.2 m apart in a regular pattern that creates bands of fastenings across the hull. Coaks are little documented, but seem to be located about every two metres, and may have served to align planks during construction. Superstructure panels include pegged mortise-and-tenon joints, but there are no pegged joints in the hull. Ancient Egyptian shipwrights avoided fastenings that passed through planks below the waterline.

The key to the hull's design is the flat-bottomed central strake, made of eight planks whose edges were fastened with mortise-and-tenon joints, and at the strakes' ends by ligatures. Shoring controlled the degree of bottom curvature (rocker) as the first side strakes were marked, rabbeted, and fit to the central section. As shipwrights added the remaining side planks and sheer strakes, whose upper edges were already notched for beam ends, a few carefully placed beams at midships maintained the hull shape. At this stage, the thin strips of wood (battens) that covered the plank seams were shaped, labelled, and lashed over seams in the midships area. A few floor timbers, spaced 2–3 m apart, were inserted and lashed to the hull before more deck beams were added further aft and forward in the hull.

In the second phase of construction, longitudinal stiffening in the form of carlings and stringers was added, and the remainder of the transverse components were fitted. Stanchions raised the carling to deck level, where lashing secured it to both stanchions and beams. Then the rest of the beams were laid across the hull and their positions marked and cut in the carling before beam ends were notched into the sheer strake. Shipwrights then roughed out and fitted two stringers over the beams, and finally the transverse lashing, including battens, was completed. Huge 'backing timbers' intended to support the decorative ends of the hulls were fastened to the hull's ends with ligatures before the finely shaped and carved finials were added. With the addition of decking panels, deckhouse, and canopies, the hull was finished.

It should be noted that not a single tool mark was found by the hull's reconstructor and conservator, Hag Ahmed Mustafa. The only marks on the hull are the painted symbols that were intended to allow the parts of the hull to be quickly located and matched to surrounding components. With the exception of a few copper staples, no metal was used to fasten any part of Khufu I.

Khufu's upright high ends were carved to resemble those of papyrus boats, so its shape is described as papyriform, a type of vessel that reflects the origin of Egyptian watercraft. When we see papyriform boats illustrated in tombs and elsewhere, or as models, it is almost always in association with ritualistic behaviour. Papyriform boats are used for pilgrimages to sacred sites and by the gods, particularly the sun god Re for his travels across the sky in separate boats for the day and night. The discovery of Khufu I and II sparked a continuing debate about the purpose of these hulls.

Some Egyptologists believe that Khufu I and Khufu II are the solar boats for Khufu to use in his aspect as the sun god Re for daily voyages across the sky; others suggest that these were vessels used, or intended to be used, in holy pilgrimages during Khufu's lifetime or after his death. Arguments about the purpose of the Khufu hulls and three other empty full-sized boat graves within the pyramid complex also feature opinions about whether or not the Khufu I hull was used. Some battens that covered plank seams have rope impressions on them. Some ship scholars have used these as proof that the boat was used at least once. More important than such arguments that are unlikely ever to be proved or disproved is the fact that every aspect of the Khufu I hull was planned, beautifully built, finely finished and fully functional as an authentic example of the ancient Egyptian shipwright's craft. C.H.

ADDITIONAL READING

el Baz, F., 1988, 'Finding a Pharaoh's Funeral Bark', *National Geographic*, 173, 513–33.

Jenkins, N., 1980, *Boat Beneath the Pyramid*, New York.

Lipke, P., 1984, *The Royal Ship of Cheops*, British Archaeological Reports International Series 225, Oxford.

Lipke, P., 1985, 'Retrospective on the Royal Ship of Cheops', in S. McGrail and E. Kently, eds, *Sewn Plank Boats*, British Archaeological Reports, Oxford.

Miller, P., 1988, 'Riddle of the Pyramid Boats', *National Geographic*, 173, 534–50.

Nour, M.Z. *et al.*, 1960, *The Cheops Boats*, Cairo.

King Philip

Wreck lying in the intertidal zone on Ocean Beach in San Francisco, constituting the most complete remains of an American 'medium' clipper of the mid-19th century. Launched in 1856 at Alna, Maine, *King Philip* was a full-rigged ship 186 ft (56.7 m) long and built along lines referred to at the time of her construction as those of a 'medium clipper'. Wrecked at the entrance to San Francisco Bay on 25 January 1878, *King Philip* was buried in beach sands and periodically exposed by winter storms until the early 20th century. The wreck was re-exposed for the first time between 1981 and 1984, when work coordinated by James Delgado documented the ship. Research conducted on *King Philip* was the first major American maritime archaeological project on beached shipwreck remains. The wreck site and remains of *King Philip* are listed in the **National Register of Historic Places**.

A significant portion of the vessel survived the wreck, subsequent salvage, and seasonal

Aerial view of King Philip *wreck site, 1984. (J.P. Delgado)*

exposure by winter beach erosion. When exposed, the ship lies parallel to the surf, and is heeled 8 degrees to port. The port side is breached 6.4 m aft of the stem; the gap in the hull runs to within 6 m of the sternpost. The hull has survived below the level of the lower deck; knees for this deck are present at the stern on the port side. The bow of *King Philip* is reinforced by three massive breasthooks set 2 ft (60 cm) apart at 45 degree angles, one atop the other. The upper breasthook has what seems to be the letter 'W' carved in it, perhaps for 'Weymouth', the shipbuilder who constructed *King Philip*.

Hydraulic probing of the interior of the wreck in 1983 along a baseline established along the centre of the hull from bow to stern and amidships contacted wood, loose gravel, and rock at various levels ranging from 0.3 to 3 m, indicating loose structure rests inside the hull atop the ballast; contacts were made with what appears to be ballast at three stations at a depth of 2.4 m below the beach level. Hydraulic probing and the documentation of exposed structure allowed for an accurate assessment of surviving areas of the hull; an estimated 45 per cent of *King Philip*'s hull has survived as articulated, intact structure.

King Philip's substantial remains comprise the only known surviving architectural link between the sleek and very sharp-lined American-built clipper ships of the 1840s and 1850s and the beamier larger 'downeasters', the typical American deep water ships of the 1860s to 1890s. J.P.D.

ADDITIONAL READING

Delgado, J.P., 1985, 'Skeleton in the Sand: Documentation of the Environmentally Exposed 1856 Ship King Philip', in P.F. Johnston (ed.), *Proceedings of the Sixteenth Annual Conference on Historical Archaeology*, Ann Arbor.

Delgado, J.P. and Haller, S.A., 1989, *Shipwrecks at the Golden Gate*, San Francisco.

Kinneret Boat
see **Sea of Galilee Wreck**

Koh Talu Wreck
Mid-20th-century carvel-built merchant vessel with a cargo of Thai ceramics wrecked in the Gulf of Thailand. The site, located in 1987 and further documented through field seasons in 1988, 1989, and 1991, is located in 18 m of water 10 km off Ban Pah Klong, Klaeng in the Gulf of Thailand near the small island (*Koh*) of Talu, Rayong Province. Tentatively identified as *Tai Luhn,* it was the subject of several international training sessions in underwater archaeology sponsored by the South East Asian Ministers of Education Organization (SEAMEO), an arm of UNESCO, in cooperation with international partners including Canada, Australia, and France. Participants included representatives from Indonesia, Malaysia, Philippines, and Thailand.

When first located the vessel was approximately 60 per cent intact. However, due to the flat and exposed nature of the bottom topography, the area is subject to heavy trawling activities. These damaged the superstructure and removed and smashed artefacts. In addition, use of explosives by fishermen, although illegal, still occurs in the area and resulted in damage to the stern section of the vessel.

A baseline was established south of the wreck and 72 sq. m were gridded. Initial recording permitted the removal of overlying sand and displaced broken sherds and ceramic vessels. Judicious use of a water dredge exposed the *in situ* cargo and the outline of the hull, as well as the keel and mast-step. The grid was corrected to align with the keel and a 5 m transverse excavation was undertaken across the vessel at the step. The ship was 11–12 m long and 4–4.5 m at the beam with both ends tapered. Construction was carvel style, edge joined, and single planked. The planks are hardwood and between 33 and 34 mm thick, attached to nineteen frames per side. The mast-step, which is 40 sq. cm, is situated forward and probably supported a hard sail. The relatively shallow draft indicates that the ship was suitable for navigating muddy flats and rivers as well as for the coastal trade but was not adequate for any serious ocean travel. This type of boat has been in regular use for centuries along the coastal province of Chanthaburi, Rayong, Samuthsakhorn, and Samuthsongkhram.

Through research and informant interviews, archaeologist Sayan Prishanchit was able to determine that a 14 m boat of this type, known as a Chalom style vessel, had sunk in the area fifty years earlier. *Tai Luhn* had been en route to Bangkok laden with cargo of Thai ceramics. The cause of sinking is unknown. Some researchers argue that it sprang a leak and sank gradually because its final disposition is upright and relatively undisturbed. However, there are many examples of vessels sinking in storms and ending up in comparable positions, such as the remains of **Hamilton** and **Scourge**.

A representative sample of ceramic wares numbered sixty-six pieces. Two intact large storage jars with different decorative motifs and one cracked storage jar with its contents in place were recovered. Many were imprinted with the factory's name, Mung Huad, in both Thai and Chinese. This company began production at Ban Tao Moh ('Village of the Pottery Kiln'), Chanthaburi Province 175–200 years ago during the Early Bangkok Period. It was started by Chinese immigrants and has remained in production since. Informants noted that in the past the kilns were fired twice per month (now four times monthly), producing sufficient wares to load two 14–16 m boats. Smaller ceramics were usually packed inside large storage jars that were laid on their sides to reduce breakage. This was exactly how the cargo was distributed in the hull of the wreck. The owner, with a crew of five or six, sailed through the Ta Sala Canal to the Kham Noo River and then to the Gulf at Bangkachai Bay, Chanthaburi. From this point they followed the coast with the entire round-trip journey taking ten days. The canal is presently closed to prevent the incursion of salt water into freshwater rivers and the factory now transports its wares by land.

Four basic types of ceramics were recovered. The large storage jars, when not used as shipping containers, serve to store both liquids, especially water, and dry goods such as rice. These measure 58–64 cm in diameter and stand 61–5 cm high. The three jars raised from the site were selected because they each exhibited a different motif on the shoulder. One has a dragon in an oblong octagonal frame with 'Mung Huad' in Thai. The second has a flying horse in a circle with the Thai characters *Tra Mah Bin* ('flying horse'), and the third has a doe with her head turned looking over her back, within a circle. The latter has no writing in association. Narrow mouthed storage jars sort approximately into small and medium sizes, ranging from 27.5 to 33.5 cm tall and 19 to 29 cm in diameter. The narrow mouths and the historically documented use of this type of vessel indicates their probable use for the production of shrimp paste and fish sauce, both of which require fermentation and which are absolute staples in any Asian kitchen. The jars exhibit a stamped, possibly rolled-on decoration of sets of short vertical lines over the shoulders and upper third to half of the vessels. In an oval frame near the rim are both the Chinese and Thai characters for 'Mung Huad'. Basin-like bowls, unglazed on the rims and bases, vary in size from 14 to 17 cm in diameter, although they all stand about 11 cm high. These are in general use for the preparation and serving of foodstuffs.

The items found in the greatest quantity are ceramic ant-proof table leg supports, an ingenious solution to a common tropical problem. These resemble small steep-sided bowls with a cylinder built into the centre. The table leg is inserted into the cylinder and stays dry, while the outer compartment is filled with water. The 'moat' formed around each leg prevents ants from reaching the table surface. Some people also top the water with a film of oil to prevent mosquitoes from laying eggs on the standing water (flying insects remain a problem).

All of the ceramics are high fired stoneware with a buff coloured body. The glaze is translucent and ranges from yellowish brown to pale green. It is unevenly applied but none of the pieces showed any bubbling, crazing, or cracking. They are basically durable, utilitarian wares made for household use. Thai archaeologists attribute the survival of the assemblage to just this reason; the ceramics were not perceived as having any market value or interest to collectors. The wares certainly resemble closely many of those currently available at local markets. However, fishermen did break off the bottoms of some pots to create favourable fish habitats and so did impact the site without actually collecting the objects.

The only non-ceramic artefacts found on the site were three stingray spines found together near the stern. Whether these were curiosities, meal remnants, or trade items has not yet been determined.

Although less than a century old, the wreck offers insights into aspects of Thai culture which are rapidly disappearing. The site provides information about the last use of sail for Thai coastal trade and about the trade patterns *per se*. Improvements in road networks have opened huge new markets and the increased demand for rural commodities and produce have made speed of delivery a priority. The five-day sailing trip from Chanthaburi to Bangkok can be driven in less than eight hours. The entire interplay of hinterland–coastal socio-economics is shifting with the availability of access to urban markets and their products. The latter have cut the demand for certain ceramic wares. To reduce use of scarce and increasingly costly wood, houses are constructed of poured concrete, which has permitted the inclusion of water cisterns and eliminated the need for large water storage jars. Availability of cheap, colourful, and unbreakable plastics has reduced the demand for other ceramic utilitarian wares, and the rapid industrialization of the region has made factory-produced foodstuffs such as pastes and sauces conveniently and inexpensively available in bottles at stores.

Therefore, in spite of its relatively recent age, the Koh Talu site provides a valuable opportunity to document a rapidly vanishing way of life and the cultural milieu within which it functioned. In addition, it provides an excellent venue for instruction and the practical application of underwater archaeological techniques. S.B.M.L.

ADDITIONAL READING

Prishanchit, S.,1991, *Report on the Intermediate Training Course in Underwater Archaeology, 141b, and the Survey and Excavation of the Koh Talu Wrecksite, Rayong*, Bangkok.

Kravel Wreck

Wreck of an early 16th-century ship discovered in 1990 lying between 30 and 56 m of water in the Nämdöfjärd, near Stockholm, Sweden. It was initially identified as *Lybska Svan* ('Swan of Lubeck'), the flagship of Gustav Eriksson Vasa (1523–63). Preliminary inspection of the wreck indicated that although the ship was certainly from that period, it was too small to be *Swan*. However, it was carvel-built, and carried one of the largest collections of breechloading wrought-iron ordnance so far discovered. The remains were therefore of considerable importance to research into the development of shipping, and of post-medieval European society as a whole.

In 1994 an Anglo-Swedish archaeological team began a survey-orientated non-intrusive research programme. The aim was to salvage, reconstruct, and interpret the ship through the use of computer technology, rather than through the physical recovery of structure. Computer software was used to process primary survey data, in the form of measurements and video, and subsequently for modelling and analysis. In order to increase safety and survey efficiency, **SCUBA**-divers and surface-supplied helmet divers worked together from a wet-bell, breathing enriched air, and heliox when below 36 m.

The archaeological evidence suggests this ship may be the *kravel* ('carvel') mentioned in historical sources. It was despatched by Gustav Vasa to recover guns and other equipment from the abandoned *Swan*. The *kravel* wrecked on its return to Stockholm in 36 m of water, 'between Djiurshamn and Dalarö', a location that describes the Nämdöfjärd. J.R.A.

ADDITIONAL READING

Adams, J., Norman, P., and Rönnby, J., 1991, *Rapport från marinarkeologisk vrakbesiktning, Franska Stenarna, Nämdöfjärden*, Marinarkeologisk tidskrift 2, Stockholm.

Adams, J. and Rönnby, J., in press, *Furstens Fartyg: Marinarkeologiska undersökninga av en tydig 1500–tals 'kravel'*, Stockholm.

Friel, I., 1994, 'The Carrack: The Advent of the Full Rigged Ship', in R. Unger (ed.),*Cogs, Caravels and Galleons*, London.

Kronan

Royal Swedish three-decked warship, which capsized, exploded, and sank on 1 June 1676 before the beginning of an action between the Swedish and the allied Danish–Dutch fleet 6.5 km off the east coast of the Baltic island of Öland. The ship was designed by the English shipwright Francis Sheldon. Her keel was laid on 27 October 1665 at Skeppsholmen, the royal shipyard in Stockholm. Although she was launched on 31 July 1668, *Kronan's* completion was delayed until 1672 due to shortages of funds. The ship's dimen-

Wooden sculpture from Kronan's exterior in the shape of a Roman warrior with royal attributes. (Kalmar County Museum/Rolf Lind)

sions were 178 ft 6 in (54.4 m) on the waterline, 197 ft (60 m) overall with a 43 ft 1 in (13.1 m) beam with a relative beam/length ratio of 1:4.1; her displacement is calculated as 2,140 tonnes. The crew consisted of 500 seamen and 300 soldiers, but at the time of sinking *Kronan* carried an additional number of infantry. *Kronan* was armed with 124 to 128 bronze guns on three flush decks, the quarter-deck, fo'c'sle, and the poop. The weight of the ordnance is estimated at 228 tonnes. The wreck was discovered at a depth of 26 m on 8 August 1980 by Anders Franzén and three associates. Since 1981 the wreck has been the subject of underwater archaeological investigations carried out under the supervision of the Kalmar County Museum.

The wreck, resting on a flat sand bottom with underlying, solid, geologically deposited anaerobic glacial clay, is oriented roughly north–south, with the stern to the north. The wreck site measures 50 by 40 m but parts are spread out over a vast surrounding area. The surviving hull-structure, measuring 40 by 20 m, represents two-thirds of the port side from the stern forward. It appears to be one continuous part, lying flat on the bottom with the outside pressed into the clay. The shock wave from the explosion tore away most of the starboard side, leaving just futtocks and some five to ten strakes. Possibly part of the starboard side from the bilge up to the lower gun deck may have been relatively undamaged by the explosion, and formed part of the initial wreck. Evidence of this is a 25 by 10 m section of

Objects recovered from Kronan: a medicine spoon of solid gold, a circular snuff box, square glass bottles with pewter lids, dice and game-pieces. (Kalmar County Museum/Rolf Lind)

the hull located southwest of the central wreck site. Forward of the mainmast-step, in conjunction with the main hatch, the hull is broken athwartships. The structure forward of the fracture is missing. Most likely, the ship came to rest in her present position on the bottom very quickly, as indicated by *in situ* finds, of both external and internal fittings. The present condition of the wreck is mainly due to the explosion which preceded the sinking, natural erosion, the effects of which were exacerbated by the explosion, and damage caused by human interference such as salvage operations in the 1680s, when sixty of the ship's bronze guns were recovered by means of a diving bell, and later by fishing and minesweeping. A field of debris, concentrated on a 200 m southbound strip extending from the wreck site, indicates a dramatic and fast sinking caused by the hull's severe damage.

Fieldwork on the site is divided into three consecutive phases: (1) complete excavation of the hull structure, in order to secure the entire context; (2) documentation of the uncovered structure; and (3) recovery of the remaining port side, in order to secure and reconstruct *in situ* finds of external decorations beneath the ship's side.

The objects from the wreck are divided into four categories: ship-equipment, objects of warlike nature (weapons and weapon-related objects), common utensils, and private belongings. To date 10,000 numbers have been assigned to more than 23,000 objects recovered from the site, among them forty-four bronze guns, wooden sculpture, musical instruments, the largest quantity of minted gold ever found in Sweden, clothing, navigational instruments, and chests with diverse contents. The wreck offers a rich context of artefacts in good condition with great variation, both in terms of material and function. The presence of considerable quantities of **Human remains** offers an important opportunity to osteological research, given the exact date

of death and the varying age and social and geographical origin.

Conditions for underwater archaeological work on the site are favourable. There is little biological activity, as in the **Baltic Sea** in general, owing to the lack of salinity, thus resulting in the absence of wood boring organisms. The offshore location means no contact with land vegetation and exploited, polluted areas. Currents on the site are normally weak. The temperature seldom exceeds 5 degrees C. These factors, in connection with the flat, bright, and light-reflecting sand-bottom, offer great scope for underwater documentation in general, and the use of video technique and still-photography in particular. The actual excavation of the site is conducted with an **Airlift**.

At the time of discovery in 1980, considerable quantities of objects were lying exposed. A primary recording of the site was carried out and exposed objects were recovered, including one bronze cannon and the ship's bell, found at the edge of the site. The following year sixteen bronze guns were recovered and regular excavations started. Two test trenches were opened, in order to determine the volume and extension of objects and structures. In 1983 test trenches were succeeded by systematic excavation extending from clearly identified sections of ship structure. Previous test excavations showed that the continuous find-layers were concentrated round the hull structure. Deck-levels of the horizontal port side of the upper part of the hull are clearly visible, separated by the deck-clamps. Each deck-level, starting with the upper deck, is excavated systematically from stern forward. Discoveries of internal fittings *in situ* on the upper deck in 1984 were followed by the finding of large quantities of well-preserved exterior sculptures underneath the ship's side. The recovered sculptures have an important bearing on the future of the project, as the presence of exterior decoration *in situ* is a great incentive to recover the ship's structure. L.E.

ADDITIONAL READING

Einarsson, L., 1982–, *Kronanprojektet: Rapport om de marinarkeologiska undersökningar av vraket efter regalskeppet*, Kalmar.

Einarsson, L., 1990, 'Kronan. Underwater Archaeological Investigations of a 17th-century Man-of-war: The Nature, Aims and Development of a Maritime Cultural Project', *International Journal of Nautical Archaeology*, 19, 4.

Franzén, A., 1981, *HMS Kronan: The Search for a Great 17th-century Swedish Warship*, Stockholm Papers in History and Philosophy of Technology, Royal Institute of Technology Library, Stockholm.

Franzén, A., 1989, 'Kronan: Remnants of a Warship's Past', *National Geographic*, 438–66.

Golabiewski-Lannby, M. (ed.),1988, *The Gold Treasure from the Royal Ship Kronan*, The Royal Coin Cabinet Catalogue 24, Kalmar.

Kublai Khan Fleet

Mongol fleet wrecked on the southern shores of Takashima Island, Japan in 1281. Kublai Khan (1215–94), the grandson of Genghis Khan, became emperor of the Mongol empire in 1250, renaming his country Yuan. The first Mongol invasion of Japan took place in 1274. After a sweeping victory the Mongol troops returned to their ships in Hakata Bay, Kyushu. On 20 October a violent wind swept the bay, raging throughout the night, and completely devastated the fleet.

Kublai Khan finally conquered Nan-Sung (southern China) and unified China. Thereafter, encouraged by his success, in 1281 he again invaded Japan. His force consisted of two armies, Tung-lu and Chian-nan. The Tung-lu army, despatched from the Korean peninsula, consisted of 40,000 soldiers and 900 ships; the Chiang-nan army, despatched from Nan-Sung, comprised more than 100,000 soldiers and 3,500 warships.

The scale of the army was vast. The first fleet included 1,170 wooden war junks, each 240 ft (73 m) in length and 400 tonnes burden, with a complement of sixty crew and soldiers. These vessels carried a thousand horse, and each towed a landing craft with twenty soldiers called a *battoru* ('brave'). There were also numerous boats for transporting food and water. The second fleet was built around 300 big two-masted Korean warships. Each carried about 100 men. The rest of this fleet consisted of 600 medium sized and small military craft: 900 vessels in all with 40,000 men.

The Japanese army attacked the Mongol warships in small but skilfully manoeuvred ships, burning their ships at night. The Mongol army, although skilled in cavalry, was at a complete loss at sea, and was successfully prevented from penetrating inland.

Between 27 and 30 July 1281 most of the Mongol ships entered Imari Bay and anchored. During peacetime the bay was smooth as glass; in this quiet bay the Mongol army was finally able to rest, a great relief after many days of pitching and rolling in the rough sea of Genkai. Just before the Mongols were able to make their all-out attack against Japan, a violent typhoon hit Imari Bay on the evening of 30 July, an event very similar in character to the first invasion. According to the *History of Yuan*, the wind was so strong that many ships were damaged. The commander boarded an undamaged ship and fled to his homeland, abandoning his 100,000 Mongol soldiers on Takashima Island. Most of the ships were wrecked on the shores of southern Takashima by southeasterly and southwesterly winds.

Torao Mozai and his group began underwater activities to discover the sunken fleet in 1981, when underwater archaeology in Japan was still at a preliminary stage. Mozai devised a special electronic technique to detect archaeological finds, a technique not used in any other country. Usually sonar is used, which detects remains between the sea surface and the sea bottom through the use

The ancient hull of the Kyrenia Ship restored in the Crusader Castle of Kyrenia. (Michael L. Katzev)

Test sailing the full-scale replica Kyrenia II. (Susan and Michael Katzev)

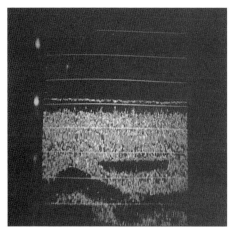
An example of the image from the colour probe invented by Torao Mozai to detect finds from the Kublai Khan Fleet. The centre horizontal line is the seabed at a depth of 25 m. Above that line is sea water, and below is the silt stratum under the seabed. Each space between the white horizontal lines is 2.5 m. A sunken ship-like image is visible about 7 m below the seabed. (Torao Mozai)

of ultrasonic waves; the new sonar detected remains not only underwater but also under the sea bottom, similar to an X-ray photograph. The intention was to ascertain the quality of the remains before extracting them. Fortunately all the experiments were successful and the research group worked very effectively. It continued its work for four years with the support of the Ministry of Education in Japan.

Many remains from the Mongol fleet were excavated: spearheads (from 5 to 30 cm long), many ingots of iron, anchor stones, stone mortars (used for pounding rice or corn), stone hand mills (perhaps for gunpowder preparation), stone balls (used for ballista, almost the same size as a shot put), and many pots (the Mongols must have stored tea, grain, and other commodities). With the cooperation of local people many valuable Mongol artefacts were found, such as a bronze seal (given by Kublai Khan), war

helmets, and a Korean bronze Buddha. Most are now exhibited in the newly established Mongol Museum in Takashima, which had been built at the suggestion of Torao, who gave the first donation of 128.1 thousand yen. The construction fund was finally enlarged to several hundred million yen through the efforts of the inhabitants of Takashima Island. T.M.1

Additional Reading

Mozai, T., 1981, 'Japanese Divers Discover Wreckage of Mongol Fleet', *Smithsonian*, 12, 9.

Mozai, T., 1982, 'The Lost Fleet of Kublai Khan', *National Geographic*, 162, 5.

Kyrenia Ship

A late 4th-century BC Greek merchant vessel lost off Kyrenia, Cyprus, excavated in the 1960s, and now on exhibit in the Kyrenia Crusader Castle. The Kyrenia Ship was found by a Greek Cypriot diver, who showed the site to University of Pennsylvania archaeologist Michael L. Katzev in 1967. The site comprised an untouched mound of ancient Greek amphoras 1 km offshore in 30 m deep water; its manifest state of preservation indicated it to be an ideal candidate for excavation. Katzev excavated the site in 1968 and 1969, first recording and raising the contents. Below lay more than 75 per cent of the original hull, which also was recorded, recovered, conserved in polyethylene glycol (PEG), reconstructed under the supervision of J. Richard Steffy of the **Institute of Nautical Archaeology**, and exhibited in a gallery at the Kyrenia Crusader Castle.

The principal cargo of the Kyrenia Ship was 404 wine amphoras in ten distinct styles: 343 were from the island of Rhodes. Some 10,000 almonds were also recovered, both inside amphoras as well as loose against the ceiling, where they probably had been transported in sacks. Twenty-nine unmatched top and bottom millstones from Kos were found spread out on the ceiling in the cargo area below the amphoras, where they served not only as a cargo but also as ballast.

Small finds and personal pottery were found at both bow and stern, indicating two discrete living areas aboard the little merchantman. The personal pottery (oil jugs, spoons, cups, plates) – found in multiples of four – was from Rhodes, indicating both the crew size and probable ship origin. Cooking utensils, including a large copper cauldron, were found at the stern; however, no hearth or evidence for cooking aboard was discovered, indicating that cooking was done ashore. Lead weights for two fishing nets were also found, indicating a dietary staple as well as a possible leisure activity. A 'sail locker' in the stern area contained lead brail rings for the square sail that propelled the ship, spare rigging parts, bundled iron ingots, small quantities of food (almonds, olives, nuts, lentils, garlic, herbs, grapes, and figs), and a large dished marble pedestal for performing sacrifices. Only a few small bronze coins were found – hardly a long voyage's worth – but the latest dated to 306 BC, providing a *terminus post quem* for the ship's final passage. No personal belongings beyond a fragmentary sandal were found in the wreck.

Measuring 14 m in length by 4.2 m in beam and an estimated 25 tonnes burden, the Kyrenia Ship was built almost entirely of Aleppo pine; Turkey oak was used for the tenons, their pegs, and the false keel. Carbon-14 dates indicate that she was constructed around 389 BC. The ship was built in the traditional ancient Mediterranean shell-first method, with edge-joined outer hull planks (strakes) joined together with mortises and tenons. Two heavier strakes, or wales, were applied above the turn of the bilge. Frames were added after the outer hull was begun; they were fastened to the strakes by treenails with pure copper spikes driven through them and then clenched over the frame. The hull was not caulked, but it was coated with pitch prior to launching. There is considerable evidence for repairs over the course of the craft's long career; these include replacement of rotten strakes and part of the false keel; internal lead patching over leaky hull seams; a block repairing a crack in the keel, and the application of copper-fastened lead sheathing over the entire hull shortly before the ship sank.

The archaeological evidence suggests that the ship and its crew of four were from the island of Rhodes, and that on her final voyage the 80-year-old ship set sail from Samos around 306 BC, travelling to Kos for the millstones. Most of the stones were probably off-loaded at Rhodes, with the mismatched remainder serving as ballast. At Rhodes, a large cargo of wine was loaded aboard, followed by the final leg of the voyage to Cyprus. Only a kilometre from landfall at Kyrenia disaster struck, ostensibly in the form of a pirate attack which removed the crew, their belongings, and valuables and left behind eight iron spearpoints, several of which were found embedded in the outer lead hull sheathing. The crew may have been sold into slavery or ransomed, and the ship was probably scuttled to destroy the evidence.

Between 1982 and 1985 a replica of the Kyrenia Ship was constructed at Perama, near Athens, Greece. Built jointly by the **Institute of Nautical Archaeology** and the Hellenic Institute for the Preservation of Nautical Tradition as an example of experimental archaeology, *Kyrenia II* was launched on 22 June 1985. Her first voyage was in a 4th of July Tall Ships parade in New York; her second was from Greece to Cyprus in September 1986. The following April she cleared Cyprus to recreate her namesake's final voyage, reaching a maximum speed of 12 knots and averaging slightly over 2 knots. Since then *Kyrenia II* has been on display in Greece and Cyprus. P.F.J.

ADDITIONAL READING

Katzev, M.L., 1970, 'Resurrecting the Oldest Known Greek Ship', *National Geographic*, 137, 6, 841–57.

Katzev, M.L., 1974, 'Last Harbor for the Oldest Known Greek Ship', *National Geographic*, 146, 5, 618–25.

Steffy, J.R., 1985, 'The Role of Three-Dimensional Research in the Kyrenia Ship Reconstruction', *Tropis I*, 249–62.

Steffy, J.R., 1985, 'The *Kyrenia* Ship: An Interim Report on its Hull Construction', *American Journal of Archaeology*, 89, 1, 75–101.

Steffy, J.R., 1994, *Wooden Ship Building and the Interpretation of Shipwrecks*, College Station, Texas.

Swiny, H.W. and Katzev, M.L., 1973, 'The Kyrenia Shipwreck: A Fourth-Century BC Greek Merchant Ship', in D.J. Blackman (ed.), *Marine Archaeology*, London, 339–59.

La Belle

A 45 ton *barque longue* of six guns wrecked in a storm in Matagorda Bay in 1686. J. Barto Arnold of the **Texas Historical Commission** (THC) conducted a **Magnetometer** survey and test excavation project of underwater cultural resources in Matagorda Bay in June and July 1995. The project was a continuation of earlier work in the same area by the agency. The wreck of *La Belle* was the most important archaeological site located (site 41MG86). She was one of the ships belonging to the French explorer Rene Robert Sieur de la Salle and part of his abortive attempt to found a colony on the Gulf of Mexico.

THC archaeologists conducted test excavations and recovered artefacts including an ornately decorated bronze 4 pounder cannon, pottery vessels, pewter plates, and trade goods. The trade goods consisted of hawk bells, rings, and straight pins of bronze and glass beads. Hull remains survive below sand and mud, as do barrels still in place in the hold. The THC conducted excavations at the site beginning in the late spring of 1996, using a **Cofferdam** and excavating the site 'dry', as was done with the **Skuldelev Ships** at Roskilde Fjord. The excavations revealed a wide range of artefacts and human remains. J.B.A.

ADDITIONAL READING

Arnold, J.B., III, 1982, *A Matagorda Bay Magnetometer Survey and Site Test Excavation Project*, Texas Antiquities Committee Publication 9, Austin.

Arnold, J.B., III, 1993, 'Matagorda Bay Surveys: Applications of Inexpensive Satellite Navigation', *International Journal of Nautical Archaeology*, 22, 1, 79–87.

Weddle, R.S., 1991, *The French Thorn: Rival Explorers in the Spanish Sea, 1682–1762*, College Station, Texas.

La Chrétienne

A reef situated approximately 800 m offshore from Saint-Raphaël on the Mediterranean coast of **France**. It is exposed frequently to strong east and west winds; at least eight ships are known to have been wrecked here in antiquity.

La Chrétienne A was the first ancient shipwreck found in France. Discovered in 1947, it was partially excavated in 1953, 1954, and 1962. It is located 30 m east of a beacon on the reef, and rests in two pieces in a gully at a depth of 20 m. Substantial

hull remains indicate that the ship was 8 m wide, and an estimated 24 to 32 m long. The oak framing is unusual, with the typical arrangement of alternating floors and half frames found only at the stern. Floor timbers are used exclusively thereafter. It is difficult to determine whether the ship had one or two masts, but the extant mast-step contained a Punic coin dated to 217 BC.

Over 2,000 amphoras were recovered dating to the first third of the 1st century BC. Many were stamped M[ARCUS] [and] C[AIUS] LASS[IUS] and L.TITI.C.F. The family of the Lassii are known from the regions of Pompeii and Sorrento (Campania). Other amphoras were stamped in retrograde on their belly or at the base of their handles SS, ME (?), and BZ, in an alphabet used in the Nocera region of Campania. The amphoras were lined with resin like those from **Grand Congloué**, presumably to carry wine. Other wine amphoras originated from the Adriatic coast of Italy.

La Chrétienne B is located northwest of the beacon at 15 m. This site consists of a heap of broken amphoras dating from the middle of the 1st to the 2nd century AD.

La Chrétienne C is located 300 m west of the beacon at a depth of 35 m. It was discovered in 1953 and excavated by J.P. Joncheray twenty years later. The hull is poorly preserved, but the ship appears to have been new when it sank. It was flat bottomed, 11 m long, 3 to 4 m wide, and constructed in the common mortise-and-tenon method, although the framing is widely spaced. The twenty-three existing frames, and possibly the hull planking, were assembled without metal fasteners. Remains of a mast were found 4 m from the bow; it probably held a single square sail.

Approximately 500 Greco-Italic amphoras constituted the cargo. All the *in situ* examples had their cork stoppers sealed with *pozzolana*, a cement made with volcanic ash that can harden under water. This cement was stamped six times with a square seal, each bearing one or two letters which, when reconstructed, provide the name C. TEREN[TIUS] M[.]. A silver coin from the northern end of the site dates the wreck to 211–170 BC.

La Chrétienne D is at the northeast side of the reef beacon at a depth of 25 m. It was discovered in 1962 and has been entirely looted. The cargo was composed of four types of amphoras, three of which came from the Roman province of Lusitania (Portugal) and carried *garum*, or fish sauce. The other carried olive oil and came from the province of Baetica (southern Spain). These date from the 3rd to the 5th century AD and are similar to transport amphoras from two other wrecks at Les Catalanes and Pampelonne in southern France.

La Chrétienne E was discovered 200 m west of the beacon at a depth of 20 m. The excavation conducted in 1992 revealed material dated to the 16th century AD. The poorly-preserved hull remains were lead-sheathed. There are no published accounts on La Chrétienne F and G.

La Chrétienne H was discovered by fishermen 1 km west of the reef beacon at a depth of 58 m. It was excavated by C. Santamaria from 1975 to 1980 and yielded approximately 300 wine amphoras that originated in Tarraconensis (northern Spain). They are similar to examples from the Sud-Lavezzi 3 and Perduto 1 wrecks. Olive oil and *garum* amphoras from southern Spain, a Punic *garum* amphora, a Rhodian wine amphora, two unknown amphora types, coarsewares, finewares, and glass vessels were also found and help date the wreck to the first quarter of the 1st century AD. The hull could not be examined due to the depth, muddy bottom, and a layer of ballast stones, but it appears to be well preserved and is estimated at 15 m in length and 5 m in width. The ballast originated in the Ampurias region.

La Chrétienne I is northeast of the reef beacon at a depth of 53 m. Discovered in 1974, it now is mostly looted. The site consisted of a resin mound, with *garum* and wine amphoras from Baetica dating from the 1st century BC to the 1st century AD.

La Chrétienne J is located 200 m north of La Chrétienne I at about 55 m. It was discovered in 1984 by J.P. Joncheray and consists of a concreted mound of wine amphoras from the southwest coast of Italy, and tools. It dates from the mid-2nd to the early 1st century BC.

The sites of La Chrétienne K, L (unexcavated) and M (three superimposed wrecks) were all discovered during the 1990s.

These wrecks help to document the history of the wine trade between Italy, Gaul, and Spain from the 2nd century BC to the 4th century AD. However, none should be considered unique. At least eleven other wrecks are known to have carried wine amphoras similar to that of La Chrétienne H, thereby giving some indication of the intensity of the commercial flow and competition between Italian and Spanish wines as early as the 1st century AD. Italian imports appear to cease during the 2nd century AD, being replaced by olive oil and *garum* amphoras from Spain. This suggests an economic change based on local wine production, and allows us to reconsider the chronology for the establishment of vineyards in Gaul and Spain. P.S.

ADDITIONAL READING

Benoit, F., 1956, 'Épaves de la côte de Provence: Typologie des amphoras', *Gallia*, 14, 23–34.

Corsi-Sciallano, M. and Liou, B. 1985, 'Les épaves de Tarraconaise à chargement d'amphores Dressel 2–4', *Archaeonautica*, 5, 78–94.

Dumas, F., 1964, *Épaves antiques: Introduction à l'archéologie sous-marine méditerranéne*, Paris.

Joncheray, J.P., 1972, 'Découverte d'une ancre en bois à jas de plomb sur une épave gréco-italique', *Cahiers d'Archéologie Subaquatique*, 1, 121–3.

Joncheray, J.P., 1975, ''L'épave C de la Chrétienne', *Premier supplément aux Cahiers d'Archéologie Subaquatique*.

Lamboglia, N. and Benoît, F., 1953, *Fouilles sous-marines en Ligurie et en Provence*, Institut International d'Études Ligures 18, 3, 4, 135–6.

Lopez, A. Joncheray, J.-P. and Brandon, C., 1994, 'L'épave post-médiévale Chrétienne K', *Cahiers d'Archeologie Subaquatique* 12, 113-30.

Parker, A.J., 1992, *Ancient Shipwrecks of the Mediterranean and the Roman Provinces*, British Archaeological Reports International Series 580, 140–44.

Santamaria, C., 1984, 'L'épave H de la Chrétienne à Saint-Raphaël (Var)', *Archaeonautica*, 4, 9–52.

Sciallano, M. and Sibella, P., 1991, *Amphoras: comment les identifier?*, Aix-en-Provence.

La Gallega

One of the four ships commanded by Columbus during his fourth and last voyage to the New World. In 1503, following an abortive attempt to found a colony on the Atlantic coast of what is now Panama, the caravel *Gallega* was abandoned in the mouth of a river Columbus named Río Belén. She had been provisioned to keep Santa Maria de Belén, a garrison of sailors-turned-

Right: Morisco green (left) and melado ware (right) from the excavation of El Pozo Viejo on the shore of Río Belén. (Courtesy Ships of Discovery)

Left: The mouth of Río Belén, site of the La Gallega wreck, looking south. (© Ships of Discovery)

colonists, alive for one year, and to serve as their means of escape should things go wrong. Indians attacked and drove the Spaniards out of their garrison and onto the beach even before the other three caravels had disappeared over the horizon. Columbus managed to save most of his men, but the garrison and *Gallega* had to be abandoned. Seven years later, in 1510, a group of conquistadors on their way to Costa Rica saw the remains of *Gallega* in Río Belén.

In 1987 maritime archaeologists began searching the mouth of Río Belén in the hope that if the ship could be found it would be well preserved in the muddy riverbed. At the time of writing, despite intensive surveys incorporating gradiometers, sub-bottom-penetrating sonar and mechanical probing, the caravel has not been discovered, although 16th-century ceramics and a bronze stirrup have been found in the vicinity. *La Gallega* is in reality only the ship's nickname, possibly indicating it was built in the Spanish province of Galicia; its official name is unknown. D.H.K.

ADDITIONAL READING

Columbus, C., 1503, 'Relación del cuarto viaje', in C. Varela (ed.), *Cristóbal Colón: Textos y documentos completos*, 2nd edn, 1984, Madrid, 316–30.

Keith, D.H., Carrell, T.L., and Lakey, D.C., 1990, 'The Search for Columbus' Caravel *Gallega* and the Site of Santa María de Belén', *Journal of Field Archaeology*, 17, 4, 123–40.

Keith, D.H. and Carrell, T.L., 1991, 'The Hunt for the *Gallega*', *Archaeology*, 44, 1, 55–9.

Méndez, D., 1536, 'Testamento de Diego Méndez', in J. Gil and C. Varela (eds), *Cartas de particulares a Colón y relaciones coetáneas*, 1984, Madrid, 333–45.

de Porras, D., 1502–4, 'Informe oficial del cuarto viaje del Almirante a las Indias', in J. Gil and C. Varela (eds), *Cartas de particulares a Colón y relaciones coetáneas*, 1984, Madrid, 300–317.

Right: Excavation at El Pozo Viejo. (© Ships of Discovery)

Below: The 'probe barge' operation. (© Ships of Discovery)

Lake Bienne

see Lake Neûchatel; Lake Zürich

Lake Champlain

Lake on the borders of Vermont and New York States, which may contain the most important collection of wooden shipwrecks in North America. Evidence of human habitation in the Champlain Valley spans over 10,000 years, the vast majority of the time-line being occupied by Native American cultures. These original navigators of the region relied on dugout and birch-bark canoes for their water travel and several examples of dugout canoes have been located and studied in the 1980s–1990s. The Shelburne Pond Dugout was radio-carbon dated to 525 years old; after it had made an unscheduled and destabilizing appearance in 1984, it was studied and then reburied in the preserving mud of the pond.

In July 1609 Samuel de Champlain, explorer of New France, entered the lake from the north with sixty Algonquin warriors in twenty-four canoes. In a battle with his travelling companions' traditional enemy, the Iroquois, Champlain introduced Native American people to the technology and deadly nature of gunpowder. This contact triggered a struggle between France and England to possess and control Lake Champlain. It also helps explain why the lake contains such an extraordinary collection of sunken historic watercraft.

Lake Champlain was a natural transportation corridor. Its 185 km of north–south navigable waterway was in close connection with other navigable waterways both to the north and the south. The colonial struggle occupied the century and a half following Champlain's battle, engulfing Native American peoples in the conflict. Military fortifications were built on the lake shore, most notably the French Fort St Frederic (1734) and British Crown Point (1759) and Carillon (Ticonderoga, 1755). Bateaux, flat-bottomed utilitarian craft, were added to the traditional canoe to move the ever-increasing number of troops engaged in these wilderness outposts. A schooner, Le Vigelente (1742), the lake's first substantial vessel, was built to move troops and supplies from French Canada to St Frederic.

In the final act of the colonial wars (1755–60), the lake witnessed the movement of vast armies consisting of thousands of troops supported by hundreds of bateaux and whale boats. In 1758 the French built sloops of war to prevent a British invasion of Canada, and in the campaign of 1759 the British countered by building the sloop

Boscawen, the brig Duke of Cumberland, and the radeau Ligonier. Successful in ending French domination of the region, this naval activity has left a legacy of submerged archaeological sites. In 1983 three vessels from this era were discovered and a two-year study of Boscawen was undertaken, directed by Arthur Cohn.

Human activity and archaeological potential are directly related and the lake's military episodes during the Revolutionary War and the War of 1812 have added to the collection. From 1775 to 1777 the lake's strategic value caused it to be a major focus in the Revolutionary struggle. American forces seized the lake in 1775 and used it as a highway to invade British Canada. The invasion failed and the campaign of 1776 saw a naval shipbuilding contest on Lake Champlain between American and British shipwrights. Commodore Benedict Arnold was placed in

Diver recovering artefacts from the stern cabin of a vessel from Lake Champlain. (Courtesy of Lake Champlain Maritime Museum, Basin Harbor, Vermont)

command of the American effort which culminated in the crucial Battle of Valcour Island. This hard-fought contest saw the American flagship, schooner Royal Savage, and the gundelo Philadelphia sunk, while during a daring retreat and successive engagements the Americans lost several other vessels. During the winter of 1777 American forces working on the ice enhanced the communication between Ticonderoga and Mt Independence by building a bridge across the lake. The British Army spring offensive quickly cut through the 'Great Bridge' while the Americans abandoned the lake and prepared to deliver a fatal blow to John Burgoyne's army at Saratoga.

During the conflict dozens of naval craft were fielded by both sides; the recovery of some of them has provided great insight into the technology of the time. Philadelphia was raised by Lorenzo Hagglund in 1935, and in 1961 given to the Smithsonian Institution. Sadly, over the past century, a number of other vessels from this fleet have been raised and destroyed by natural deterioration and souvenir hunters. This has led current activities to focus on documenting newly discovered sites underwater. Arnold's second flagship, the row-galley Congress (1776), as well as all the remaining 'caissons', the twenty-two log-cabin style structures that supported the 'Great Bridge', have been located. An extraordinary and threatened collection of Revolutionary War artefacts, thrown into the lake after Burgoyne's defeat by retreating British forces, has been recovered, conserved, and placed on exhibit at a new interpretive centre at Mt Independence.

History repeated itself during the War of 1812 when the conflict turned once again on the Lake Champlain invasion route. After two seasons of preparation and probing by the rival forces, the campaign of 1814 brought a major British advance through Lake Champlain to the heart of America. A British land force advanced south from Canada to Plattsburgh, New York and waited for their naval squadron led by the 1,200 ton flagship Confiance to defeat the American force. Commodore Thomas MacDonough aboard the 700 ton American flagship Saratog, positioned his fleet at anchor in Cumberland Bay and waited for the British. On the morning of 11 September 1814 the British, still working to complete their flagship, made their attack. The Battle of Plattsburgh Bay, an intense broadside to broadside action, gave the Americans a decisive victory which secured the lake and helped negotiate a close to the wider war.

The American fleet and captured British vessels were transported to the naval base at Whitehall, New York where time and rot threatened to bring them to the bottom. In 1958 a group of historically minded citizens managed to raise (in three pieces) the naval schooner Ticonderoga. This survivor of the Battle of Plattsburgh is particularly interesting because the hull was begun in 1813 by the Lake Champlain Steamboat Company with the intention that it become the lake's second steamboat. After MacDonough arrived he converted the partially completed vessel into a traditional schooner. The eroded hull now lies behind the Skenesboro Museum at Whitehall, New York.

In 1981 three War of 1812 warships, the

American twenty-gun brig *Eagle*, the captured British brig *Linnet*, and the 75 ft (23 m) American gunboat *Allen* were relocated in a backwater near Whitehall. A full-scale multi-year historical and archaeological documentation project focused on the 117 ft (36 m) long *Eagle*. In 1995, through a grant from the Naval Historical Center, the in-water study of the other two vessels was completed in a joint University of Vermont–Texas A&M University field school.

Although 110 ft (33.5 m) sub-chasers (SCs) were built at Shelburne Shipyard during World War II, for all intents and purposes the lake's military era ended with MacDonough's victory at the Battle of Plattsburgh Bay, and the lake's commercial period began to bloom. Some old warships were converted to peaceful commerce, but with roads almost non-existent, the lake remained the primary means of transportation and a new class of lake sloop began to emerge. To date an early example of this class has not been located, but it was described in 1867 as having 'adopted the style of vessel built at New London [Conn.], which accounts for the superior models of the sloops here, which will be observed are not like the heavy Dutch sloops of those days, in use on the Hudson, but like the clipper vessels which were built at New London, New Haven, and Hartford to sail to New York, through Sound, for passengers, before the days of steamers'. This description seems to hold for commercial vessels of a later period. The schooner *Sarah Ellen* was built in 1849 on Isle La Motte, Vermont, one of the beautiful islands in the northern lake. Sinking in over 90 m of water in 1860, the 73 ft (22.25 m) long by 15 ft 10 in (4.87 m) beam fully intact hull gives the sleek appearance of the sloops described from an earlier time.

Another interesting example of a commercial schooner is the vessel **Water Witch**, although no insight can be gleaned regarding traditional sailing design because *Water Witch* was originally built as a steamboat in 1832. Emerging into a crowded competitive field, its builder, Jehaziel Sherman, seemed to expect the diminutive steamer – it was 80 ft (24.4 m) long – to be hastily purchased by the competition. To his surprise and disappointment it took until 1836 for that consolidation to happen. The Champlain Steamboat Company did not need the steamer and they converted it to a schooner. *Water Witch* carried cargo for the next thirty years, finally meeting its end in 1866 while hauling a load of iron ore. The sinking claimed the life of the Thomas Mock family's infant child, baby Roa.

The lake contains the oldest known surviving steamboat hull in the world. **Phoenix** was laid down in 1814, just after the American victory at Plattsburgh Bay, and joined the lake's first steamer *Vermont I* (1809) in competition with the established sailing interests. The 146 ft (44.5 m) long *Phoenix* travelled the full length of the lake from

A colonial era reproduction bateau ready for launch. (Courtesy of Lake Champlain Maritime Museum, Basin Harbor, Vermont)

Whitehall in the south to St Johns, Quebec in the north, stopping at all the principal ports en route. On the evening of 4 September 1819 *Phoenix* left Burlington, Vermont for Canada and mid-crossing while on the 'broad lake' was discovered to be on fire. In the night-time confusion, six people lost their lives as the helpless *Phoenix* drifted up on a shoal and burned to the waterline. The valuable steam engines and boilers were recovered and placed in the new *Phoenix II* (1820), while winter ice moved the discarded hulk of the original *Phoenix* into 18 to 33 m of water. *Phoenix* was documented in 1981 and from this study emerged a plausible theory for the cause of the fire having been intentional and resulting from the rivalry between established sail and new steam interests (see Davison).

In 1823 a new canal was completed, connecting the waters of Lake Champlain to those of the Hudson River. This 100 km 'Northern Canal' stimulated a huge increase in maritime commerce throughout the region, and triggered the Federally financed construction of lighthouses and breakwaters to support the rapidly growing number of

lake watercraft. Scores of standard canal boats, designed and sized to fit through the locks, appeared and quickly became the most common vessel type. Alongside the standard canal boat, which had no independent means of propulsion and was towed by horses and mules on the canal and steam-driven vessels on lakes and rivers, emerged the Lake Champlain sailing canal boat. These hybrid boats could sail upon the lake with centreboard and masts stepped above deck in a tabernacle, and upon reaching the canal transform into a canal boat ready to transit the locks. They first appeared in 1823, but were only rediscovered in the early 1980s with the locating and study of *General Butler* (1862). This schooner rigged vessel, 88 ft (26.8 m) long with a 14 ft 6 in (4.4 m) beam, had evolved its size and shape to fit the expanded locks on the Champlain Canal. Since the discovery of *General Butler*, at least half a dozen other examples of sailing canal boats have been located.

From the beginning of Champlain Valley settlement, right up until the present time, ferries have played an important role in moving people and freight through the region. The first ferries were canoes, rafts, and scows – almost anything qualified which floated and could get people across narrow expanses of lake. In the early part of the 19th century a new technology emerged: horse-powered watercraft. A technological rival to newly developed steam power, horse-powered vessels appeared on the Hudson River and Lake Champlain between 1814 and 1840. The only known surviving horse-powered ferry has been located and documented in Burlington Bay, Vermont. The 2 hp turntable-type drive mechanism is a tangible reflection of a short-lived technological era.

The **Horse Ferry Wreck**, resting in 15 m of water, along with the steamboat *Phoenix*, the canal schooner *General Butler*, and two standard canal boats are now part of the Vermont's Underwater Historic Preserve system. This programme was developed in 1985 to provide the diving public with access to these underwater sites. The preserve programme provides seasonal moorings at each site to make diving safer, while protecting the fragile sites from anchor damage. The preserves also provide guidelines for safe and proper usage of these extraordinary shipwrecks.

To date, several hundred submerged watercraft have been located under the waters of Lake Champlain. Unfortunately, the recent discovery of zebra mussels has triggered great concern for this historic collection, particularly the yet undiscovered shipwrecks that lie on the 90 per cent of the lake bottom that has never been explored. The Lake Champlain Maritime Museum at Basin Harbor, Vermont, a museum dedicated to the preservation and public interpretation of the lake's special heritage, has initiated an accelerated lake surveying project (see **Precollegiate education**). During the 1996 season 100 sq. km of new lake bottom have been examined and at least ten new shipwrecks have been located.

The rich collection of archaeological sites on the bottom of Lake Champlain reflects on the origins of the country as well as the region. This special legacy requires a stewardship perspective which looks forward to future generations and challenges us to preserve this non-renewable and precious public resource. A.B.C.

ADDITIONAL READING

Bourne, E.G., 1922, *The Voyages and Explorations of Samuel de Champlain, 1604–1616*, New York.

Cohn, A.B., 1995, *The 1992 Fort Ticonderoga-Mount Independence Submerged Cultural Resource Survey*, Basin Harbor.

Cohn, A.B. and True, M., 1992, 'The Wreck of the *General Butler* and the Mystery of Lake Champlain's Sailing Canal Boats', *Vermont History Magazine*, 60, 1, 29-45

Crisman, K.J., 1983, *The History and Construction of the United States Schooner Ticonderoga*, Alexandria, Virginia.

Crisman, K.J., 1987, *The Eagle, An American Brig on Lake Champlain during the War of 1812*, Shelburne.

Crisman, K.J. and Cohn. A.B., 1993, *The Burlington Bay Horse Ferry Wreck and the Era of Horse-Powered Watercraft*, Montpelier.

Crisman, K.J. and Cohn, A.B., 1993, *The Lake Champlain Schooner Water Witch*, Montpelier.

Davison, R., 1981, *The Phoenix Project*, Burlington.

Hill, R.N., 1995, *Lake Champlain, Key to Liberty*, Woodstock, Vermont.

Kalm, P., 1972, *Travels Into North America*, Barre, Massachusetts.

Krueger, J.W., *et al.*, 1985, 'The Fort Ticonderoga Shipyard Excavation', *Bulletin of the Fort Ticonderoga Museum*, 14, 6, 335-40.

Lundeberg, P.K., 1995, *The Gunboat Philadelphia and the Defense of Lake Champlain in 1776*, Basin Harbor.

Lake Garda Galley

Galley deliberately burned and sunk in 1509 by the Republic of Venice, together with a smaller boat, in Lake Garda in northern Italy. The boats had been constructed to give the Venetians naval power on the lake during wars with Milan and are unique examples of Venetian vessels relatively well preserved in fresh water. Initial exploration and excavation between 1962 and 1965 by Enrico Scandurra located the wreck site and revealed the galley in *c.* 27 m of water. The preserved length of the hull under a mass of heavy stones was *c.* 30 m and the frames were *c.* 25 cm apart; the excavators found two four-pronged iron anchors as well. Further work has been carried out in the 1990s by Dr Marco D'Agostino. H.W.

ADDITIONAL READING

Scandurra, E., 1972, 'The Maritime Republics: Medieval and Renaissance Ships in Italy', in G.F. Bass (ed.), *A History of Seafaring Based on Underwater Archaeology*, London, 209–10.

Lake Morat

see **Lake Neuchâtel**

Lake Nemi Ships

Two of the largest ancient ships ever recovered, excavated from Lake Nemi, Italy, after it was drained in 1929, though well known since the 15th century. Dating to Caligula's reign, their dimensions were 71.3 × 20 m and 73 × 24 m, and they probably had a sacral function. They had flat-bottomed

One of the Roman boats from Lake Nemi. (E. Felice)

hulls, and the pine wooden planking was mortised, externally covered with tarred wool, and lead sheathed. The smaller ship had some buildings on the main deck, with gilt copper tiled roofs and floors and walls covered with marble and mosaics. Fluted columns were also on board. The superstructures of the hulls were artistically adorned with bronze rings decorated by wild animal figures and apotropaic hands covered the heads of beams and helms. Bronze herms from balustrades, terracotta relief friezes, crockery, silver and gilt plate were also found. Among the collected materials were stamped bricks and terracotta pipes, lead water pipes stamped with Caligula's name, a bronze water tap, arms, coins, keys, and many ship fittings, among them bilge pumps, a large block, and some

wooden and iron anchors. The ships were placed in a local museum, but were burned (perhaps deliberately) on 31 May 1944. Only some metallic parts survive. E.F.

ADDITIONAL READING

Rubin de Cervin, G.B., 1955, 'Mysteries and Nemesis of the Nemi Ships', *Mariner's Mirror*, 41, 38–43.

Speziale, G.C., 1929, 'The Roman Galleys in the Lake of Nemi', *Mariner's Mirror*, 15, 333–46.

Speziale, G.C., 1931, 'The Roman Anchors Found at Nemi', *Mariner's Mirror*, 17, 309–20.

Ucelli, G., 1950, *Le navi di Nemi*, Rome.

Lake Neuchâtel

Lake in Switzerland containing the remains of prehistoric settlements. Termed the largest Swiss lake because of its location entirely within Switzerland's borders (Lake Geneva and Lake Constance are shared by Switzerland with neighbouring countries), Lake Neuchâtel stretches nearly 50 km along the southern faces of the Jura Mountains. Linked together with the smaller neighbouring lakes of Bienne and Morát by the rivers Thielle and Broye, Lake Neuchâtel forms the Jura Lakes. This lake system has been the location of some of the earliest human habitation in Switzerland – from the Upper Paleolithic (*c.* 12,000 BC) to the Roman conquest in 58 BC.

'In the Lake of Neuchâtel also exists pilings at Port Chevron (sic), Corcelettes, Auvernier and Columbier': thus Ferdinand Keller in his seminal exposition on the newly discovered Swiss lake villages, *The Celtic Pile Dwellings in the Swiss Lakes* (1854; see **Lake Zürich**). Edouard Desor, a Swiss geologist writing in 1865, noted that the presence of the ancient villages had long been recognized by the local fishermen who had 'veritable mountains of their remains' (pots, stone and metal finds, etc.). The value of these relics increased significantly after Keller brought them to the attention of the 19th-century world. Indeed, a cottage industry in the trafficking of artefacts sprang up and flourished well into the 20th century.

These and previously unknown sites were later exposed by the 'First Correction of the Jura Waters'. This engineering project, undertaken between 1868 and 1888, lowered the level of the Jura Lakes by an average of 2.5 m in an effort to control flooding. Edmund von Fellenberg (1838–1902), geologist and later Director of the Historic Museum of Bern, prepared a report on his 1873-4 work at Mörigen (Late Bronze Age), Lüscherz, and Schafis (Neolithic) on Lake Bienne, which included the first stratigraphic profile of a lake village. Unfortunately, this was the exception rather than the rule. With the lowering of the lakes, collection and sale of artefacts became a second vocation for many fishermen. For certain types of artefacts, there was such a demand that gangs of forgers grew up around the Jura Lakes. In 1862 the authorities forbade unlicensed excavation and the public interest in the lake dwellings led to the formation of archaeological societies (such as the Swiss Society for Prehistory) and academic positions in universities.

Along with Édouard Desor and von Fellenberg, the best-known antiquarian of the period was Colonel Frédéric Schwab (1803–69). Schwab's most famous discovery was the Iron Age site of La Tène at Marin-Epagnier on Lake Neuchâtel. La Tène is the eponymous site for the 'Second Iron Age' in Europe (450–58 BC). This site, like with the nearby site of Cornaux-Les Sauges found during the 'Second Correction of Jura Waters' (1962–73), was a collapsed bridge together with its victims – Iron Age Celts whose skeletons, weapons, and accoutrements were found among the ruins in the mud. The Iron Age sites of La Tène and Cornaux notwithstanding, the majority of the archaeological sites on Lake Neuchâtel and its vicinity are Neolithic and Bronze Age settlements. More specifically these sites range from the Middle Neolithic to the Late Bronze Ages, c. 3900 to 900 BC. There is a lacuna in this temporal range spanning the Middle Bronze Age, c. 1500–1200 BC, which is probably related more to high lake levels than to cultural reasons.

Modern scientific excavation of the Lake Neuchâtel archaeological sites began with Paul Vouga at the Bay of Auvernier in 1919. Vouga carried out large-scale stratigraphic excavations, documenting and mapping all artefacts, features, and levels within the site. These excavations established the basic cultural chronology for Lake Neuchâtel and the Jura Lakes. They are shown in the following table:

Date (BC)	Period	Culture
3850	Middle Neolithic	Cortaillod 'Late', Cortaillod 'Classic'
3300	Late Neolithic	Horgen
2850	Eneolithic/Chalcolithic	Auvernier, Lüscherz (corded ware groups), Saône-Rhône/'Bell Beaker' Horgen
1800	Early Bronze Age	North Alpine Bronze
1250	Late Bronze Age	Urnfield/'Rhine-Swiss-France Group'

Vouga was a pioneer in the excavation of those sites still underwater after the Correction of the Jura Waters. At Auvernier he used a barrel-like caisson to excavate inundated sites. The iron device, composed of barrel-shaped sections, was lowered to the lake bottom and the water pumped out. Vouga then clambered inside with a safety rope and proceeded to carefully excavate the cultural layers he encountered. At Auvernier and other sites investigated after Vouga's day, workers have reported the 'aureoles' left in the sediments by the caisson. He also tried a square version that allowed the excavation of up to 4 sq. m. Neither proved safe enough and were eventually abandoned by the archaeologist.

Lake Neuchâtel, although named for the canton and city, is bordered by the three other federal cantons – Vaud, Fribourg, and Bern. Lake Bienne is entirely within the canton of Bern, while Lake Morat is shared between the cantons of Vaud and Fribourg. While there can be jurisdictional disputes between these states, the practice of archaeology has been little affected. As with the underwater sites in Lake Zürich and elsewhere in Europe, every relic found is damp or soaked with water. Owing to its excellent preservation, the amount of surviving material is staggering. The site of Auvernier-Nord (8th century BC) alone produced over a tonne of pottery, 405 bronze items, and 150 baskets. Over 5 tonnes of pottery was recovered from Hauterive-Champréveyres. At Auvernier over 8,000 pilings were recovered and dated with dendrochronology. The data is diverse and extensive. The Swiss have been challenged to develop conservation and storage procedures to meet this need.

The most important sites are listed below.

1. Auvernier (Lake Neuchâtel; Neolithic, Chalcolithic and Late Bronze Age). Actually a suite of ten sites excavated first by Paul Vouga then, in response to road-building, during the modern era (1964-75). The site of Auvernier-La Saunerie has allowed a more complete evaluation of Vouga's 'Culture d' Auvernier' such as its cultural relationship to the Saône-Rhône culture of eastern France and western Switzerland's Jura Mountains and the Saône-Rhône valleys.

2. Bevaix (Lake Neuchâtel; Neolithic and Late Bronze Age). Located in the bay of Bevaix, this site remains largely unexcavated. It has produced several whole or partial dugouts. The upper (late) cultural layers have been eroded since the second Correction of the Jura Waters.

3. Concise (Lake Neuchâtel; Neolithic and Bronze Age). Located east of Corcelettes, Concise has produced some of the most impressive bronze ornaments and swords from the Late Bronze Age. Recent excavations have produced the remains of wheeled carts from Late Neolithic levels.

4. Cortaillod (Lake Neuchâtel; Neolithic and Bronze Age). The eponymous type-site for the Middle Neolithic culture, first named by Paul Vouga (1929) and later (1934) expanded by Emil Vogt to a pan-Swiss cultural horizon. It displays a rich burnished ceramic tradition – brown to black – along with polished stone and basketry. The Late Bronze Age site of Cortaillod-Est was completely excavated by the Cantonal Archaeological Service of Neuchâtel in 1981-3. The adjacent site of Cortaillod-les Esserts survives, although in a badly eroded state.

5. Estavayer-le-lac (Lake Neuchâtel; Neolithic, Bronze and Iron Age). Several sites are located in the bay formed south of Estavayer-le-lac. The most famous find is a Late Hallstatt (First Iron Age) dagger with an anthropomorphic 'antennae' handle done in iron and bronze. It epitomizes the mastery of metalworking and growing wealth of the people in prehistoric transalpine Europe.

6. Hauterive–Champréveyres (Lake Neuchâtel; Upper Paleolithic, Neolithic, and Bronze Age. The location of five villages ranging from three Magdalenian encampments in the 13th millennium BC to later Cortaillod, Horgen, and early Hallstatt settlements. The open-air Paleolithic site was a total surprise and the first such underwater site in Switzerland. It has produced evidence of horse hunting and mobile art which defines this Paleolithic culture. The excavation in the mid-1980s was conducted within a 2 hectare **Cofferdam**.

7. La Tène (Lake Neuchâtel; Second Iron Age). La Tène was extensively excavated (1874–85, 1907–17). Over 150 iron swords, 270 spear/lance points, 22 shield bosses, 7 shields, 385 fibulae, 50 phalerae, tools, coins, and wooden objects including a yoke and a wheel, though little pottery, was found. Current thinking considers it a bridge crossing of some military significance destroyed by a sudden flood.

8. Lüscherz (Lake Bienne; Neolithic and Bronze Age). This is the type-site of the Late Neolithic phase of the Saône-Rhône culture. The ceramics are characterized by round bases and rectilinear decoration along with small button-like appliqués. The decoration

was engraved using pointed tools and fingers. Polished stone axes of the 'Battle-Axe' type are found as well.

9. Montilier (Lake Morat; Neolithic). Excavations in the 1980s and 1990s by the Archaeological Service of Fribourg have defined a Neolithic sequence of Cortaillod and Horgen cultures for this site known since 1860. At the site of Montilier-Platzbünden excavators recovered 1,200 axe sleeves from Horgen levels alone in 1986.

10. Portalban (Lake Neuchâtel; Neolithic/Chalcolithic and Bronze Age). Discovered in 1858, Portalban, like Montilier and Estavayer-le-lac, are in Fribourg canton. It is a collection of sites like many other of these locations. Much of the results of 19th-century work has been lost or so poorly reported as to be of little scientific value. Station II was excavated in 1975 and Portalban-les-Gréves has demonstrated rich Late Neolithic–Chalcolithic settlements belonging to the Lüscherz and Auvernier groups. The latter phase of the Saône-Rhône culture is characterized by corded ware and Grand Pressigny flint daggers, the flint having been traded from the Paris Basin of France.

11. St Blaise (Lake Neuchâtel; Neolithic/Chalcolithic). St Blaise-les-Bains was excavated from 1986 to 1989 by the Archaeological Service of Neuchâtel. The site was composed of three superimposed villages, each larger as one approaches the present. The oldest village belonged to the Horgen culture, the following two to the Lüscherz and Auvernier groups respectively.

12. Twann (Lake Bienne; Neolithic/Chalcolithic). Characterized by the complete sequence of the Swiss Neolithic, Twann has produced one of the most unique finds ever for a Swiss lake village – bread! The small loaves were preserved in the waterlogged sediments and indicate the serendipity of this unique archaeology. E.G.

ADDITIONAL READING

Desor, E., 1865, *Les palafittes on constructions lacustres du lac de Neuchâtel*, Paris.

Egloff, M., 1979, *Un village de 6000 ans: Préhistoire lacustre d'Auvernier*, Schaffhausen.

Egloff, M., 1983, 'Lake Dwellings in the Light of Modern Archaeology, *Swissair Gazette*, 2, 17–20.

Keller, F., 1854, 'Die keltishen Pfahlbauten in der Schweizerseen', *Mitteilungen der Antiquarischen Gesellschaft, Zurich*, Pfahlebambericht, MAGZ9, Heft 3, 68-85.

Ramseyer, D., 1992, *Les cites lacustres*, Treignes.

Sauter, M.R., 1976, *Switzerland: From Earliest Times to the Roman Conquest*, London.

Schwab, H., 1973, *Die Vergangenheit des Seelandes in neuem Licht*, Fribourg.

Speck, J., 1981, 'Pfahlbauten: Dichtung oder Wahrheit', *Helvetia Archaeologica*, 45/48, 98–138.

Lake Phelps Canoes

Over two dozen dugout canoes located in Lake Phelps, a large freshwater lake in eastern North Carolina. The 6,700 hectare lake is contained within the boundaries of Pettigrew State Park. No natural streams flow into or from the lake. Instead, the shallow basin that forms the lake is fed almost exclusively by precipitation, causing the water to be unusually clear for a lake in this region.

Lake Phelps canoe revealed by low water levels.
(North Carolina Dept. of Archives and History)

The lake water is highly acidic which contributes to the remarkable preservation of organic material there.

Two events occurred in the mid-1980s that caused a significant drop in the lake's water level. First, large quantities of water were pumped from the lake to extinguish an extensive forest and peat fire adjacent to the south and east shores. The pumping was followed by an extended drought, and by the autumn of 1985 water levels were nearly one metre below normal. During this period State Park personnel received reports that prehistoric artefacts, including dugout canoes, were visible lying in the shallow water along the lake's northern shoreline.

The discovery prompted a series of investigations by researchers from the North Carolina Division of Archives and History, and East Carolina University. That work resulted in the systematic collection of lithic and ceramic artefacts exposed on the lake bottom and the documentation of twenty-three dugout canoes. Four of the canoes were removed from the lake and preserved using sucrose treatment. Archaeologists recorded the location of the remaining canoes, performed limited excavation to allow for measurements and photographs, and recovered wood samples from each dugout. After excavation, the canoes were backfilled and allowed to return to their natural state where they remain today.

Analysis of wood samples determined that all of the canoes had been hollowed out of bald cypress; several still showed evidence of charring on the inside from the burn and scrape method of construction. While most of the canoes had only one surviving end, making it difficult to determine the vessel's original length, estimated lengths ranged from 5.5 to 11.3 m. The widths of the canoes varied from 0.6 to 0.9 m.

Nineteen of the dugouts were dated using the radiocarbon process; the age of the canoes varied from 2430 BC to AD 1400. Dr David Phelps of East Carolina University recognized a direct correlation between the distribution of canoes by cultural period and the known age of lithic and ceramic artefacts recovered from the lake. None of the canoes, and only a small number of the spear points, date to the earliest age of New World prehistory, from the late Paleo-Indian period to the Middle Archaic period (9000–3000 BC). It is likely that the groups that visited the lake during that time span were on hunting expeditions and built only temporary camps.

By the Late Archaic period (3000–1000 BC) the region's climate had warmed to reach modern conditions and food resources had become more abundant. Artefacts recovered from that period reflect more frequent and extended use of the lake. The Late Archaic assemblage includes spear points, a spear thrower weight, bifacial blades, and soapstone cooking vessel fragments. The three oldest canoes found in the lake date to the Late Archaic period.

The transition between the Archaic and the Woodland periods is marked, among other features, by the development of ceramic technology. Two of the discovered canoes date to the Early Woodland period (1000–300 BC). The broken remains of a ceramic pot, of a ceramic type known as Deep Creek net impressed, were found in one of these canoes.

The Middle Woodland period (300 BC–AD 800) was the time of the greatest use of the lake, as evidenced by the abundance of artefacts, including eleven canoes, dating to this period. During the Middle Woodland period family groups established seasonal bases along the northern and western shorelines of the lake and subsisted by fishing, hunting, and gathering wild plants. Artefacts dating to this period include a number of ceramic vessels of various sizes and shapes, polished stone gorgets, and triangular arrow points. Eight of the eleven canoes span the years AD 110 to 340 and are spaced between twenty and thirty years apart, perhaps representing the average lifespan of a dugout cypress canoe. If such were the case, one canoe would serve a family for one generation before becoming waterlogged or decaying.

Only three canoes were found to date to the Late Woodland period (AD 800–1650) with dates of 1200, 1390, and 1400. Likewise, fewer ceramic and lithic artefacts date to this period. No Native American presence was noted in the vicinity of Lake Phelps when the body of water was encountered by European settlers in 1755.

By 1988 the lake's water level had returned to normal, making it more difficult to examine the prehistoric artefacts located on the lake bottom. Nevertheless, archaeologists have continued periodic research at Lake Phelps. In 1992 a research team sponsored by the **National Geographic Society**, assisted by personnel from the North Carolina Division of Archives and History and Division of State Parks, conducted a ground-penetrating radar survey of portions of the lake bottom with promising results. Although no new canoes were located during the survey, the radar system was able to detect previously located dugouts. R.L.

ADDITIONAL READING
Phelps, D.S., 1989, *Ancient Pots and Dugout Canoes: Indian Life as Revealed by Archaeology at Lake Phelps*, Creswell, North Carolina.

Lake Zürich

Lake in Switzerland with shoreline remains of prehistoric villages. The remains of prehistoric settlements found along Lake Bienne in central Switzerland were reported in the decade between 1840 and 1850 during a series of dry periods which dropped the lake level several metres below normal. The ancient dwellings appeared as large (1–2 ha) areas of stumps with the debris among them consisting of broken ceramic vessels, objects of flint, metal (copper/bronze) implements, bone and horn items, as well as woven and plaited basketry and fabric. The impetus to study these villages as archaeological sites came from the Zürich archaeologist Ferdinand Keller (1800–81).

Keller did not discover the lake dwellings himself but was made aware of their presence by a local schoolteacher by the name of Johann Aeppli. Aeppli went on to discover the Neolithic site of Obermailen on the west shore of Lake Zürich during the winter of 1853–4. That winter seems to have been particularly cold and dry, with all of the lakes of the Swiss Plateau dropping to record low levels. Keller received several items from Aeppli and in 1854 published his now-famous work on this new archaeological phenomenon entitled *The Celtic Pile Dwellings in the Swiss Lakes*. In this work Keller advanced his 'pile dwelling hypothesis' which has influenced interpretations of these sites ever since. Today it is referred to as the 'pile dwelling problem'. To truly understand Swiss lake dwelling archaeology one must first confront Keller's seminal conceptualization of the phenomenon.

According to Keller, the discoveries 'made it manifest, that in the very earliest times groups of families, or probably whole tribes, subsisting by hunting and fishing, with some knowledge of agriculture, lived on the borders of the Swiss lakes, in huts built not on dry ground, but on a series of piles in the shallows near the shores'. Keller supplied a drawing illustrating the construction of the pile-dwellings in lakes Zürich and Bienne, based on drawings of the stilt village of Doreh Bah, West New Guinea, made in 1827–9 by the French explorer Jules S.C. Dumont d'Urville.

Keller's publications and his pile-dwelling hypothesis were accepted by investigators at Lake Bienne, such as Frédéric Schwab (1803–69), and by other researchers taking up the study of the Swiss lake dwellings. Edouard Desor, a geologist, began systematic work at **Lake Neuchâtel**, while University of Geneva professors François A. Forel, Frédéric Troyon and Adolphe von Morlot were busy at the site of Morges in Lake Geneva. It was at Morges that this trio of researchers began what surely is the first study of prehistoric sites using diving equipment. A watercolour immortalizes this in a scene from 24 August 1854 showing von Morlot wearing a simple surface-supplied air helmet, diving in three metres below the surface of Lake Geneva at Morges. Troyon is von Morlot's tender while Forel operates the air pump.

The eclectic nature of the backgrounds of these early researchers is pronounced; all the more so in the case of Johann Uhlmann, country doctor and naturalist who excavated sites at Lake Moosseedorf, and Jakob Messikommer, a farmer, who studied the famous Robenhausen site.

By 1926 Keller's hypothesis was under attack by scholars outside Switzerland – first by Heinrich Reinerth and then during World War II by Oskar Paret, both eminent German archaeologists. Reinerth interpreted the pile structures as having been erected on the shores of lakes or rivers on marshy soil or dry ground – not above the water. These were lake*shore* dwellings. Following Paret and Reinerth, but going further, was Walter Staudacher. Most Swiss workers, for reasons of academic and national pride, did not readily accept this view. Even Paul Vouga, pioneer of modern Swiss archaeology, was not completely dissuaded of Keller's view. It was not until the Zürich prehistorian Emil Zogt (1906–74) wrote a hundred-page paper supporting Paret's ideas in 1955 that the pile-dwelling hypothesis was effectively abandoned. Today the notion of lakeshore villages of farming and fishing societies is the most accepted paradigm, being the most parsimonious with the archaeological facts.

Lake dwelling sites are best known for their rich diversity of cultural materials preserved by the aerobic muds and relatively cold waters of the lakes. In Lake Zürich and its vicinity (Lakes Greiffen and Pfäffikon) forty-five sites have been found. If one could know the exact number of cultural components or occupations at each, then the number of 'villages' would probably be higher. The general stratigraphy of a lake dwelling site has at least one Neolithic and one Bronze Age habitation layer. In many there are three or more village occupations of different cultural periods – 'Early' Neolithic, Middle Neolithic, Late Neolithic, Early and Late Bronze Age. In fact, in the broader context of the European Neolithic period, Switzerland has few sites that predate the 4th millennium BC: the earliest Neolithic culture in Switzerland is termed the Egolzwil culture and even its demonstrated contemporaneity with the late 'Band Keramik' Rössen culture of south Germany places it in the Early–Middle Neolithic. Few, if any, Egolzwil levels have been demonstrated in lake dwellings sites. Likewise, Middle Bronze Age occupations are not seen as well. The latter absence is largely due to high water levels in the Lake Zürich area during that period. The type site was built on the small shallow Lake Wauwil, now dried up, in Luzern canton.

The most prevalent cultural groups in Lake Zürich sites are (in chronological order) the Cortaillod culture (Middle Neolithic), the Zürich Group, the Horgen culture (Late–Middle Neolithic), the Pfyn culture (Middle Neolithic), the Schnurkeramik or Corded Ware culture (Late Neolithic/Chalcolithic), Early Bronze Age, and Late Bronze Age. These cultures span three millennia from 3900 BC to 900 BC.

Dredging and construction activities at the northern end of Lake Zürich, where the Limmat River flows out of the lake and through the city of Zürich, precipitated several modern studies. Feldmeilen, near its historically famous neighbour of Obermeilen, was excavated using a metal sheet-pile **Cofferdam** to allow dry-land excavation of the underwater site. The coffer-cell was sealed and pumped continuously to permit excavations of Neolithic and Bronze Age components. With the formation of the City Bureau of Archaeology in Zürich, the first truly underwater excavations of these sites began. Ulrich Rüiff directed excavations at the site of Grösser Hafner beginning in the winter of 1969. This site had three reoccupations during Cortaillod times, two during Horgen, and a final settlement in the Late Bronze Age. Near Grösser Hafner is the site Kleiner Hafner. Kleiner Hafner had as its earliest levels the remains of Egolzwil villages. Above the Egolzwil level was a thick deposit of a Cortaillod–Zürich Group village. Still higher are two Horgen villages and finally a Late Bronze Age component. The total depth of the profile at Kleiner Hafner exceeds 2 m.

It was at these sites that Zürich archaeologists began to use large submersible pumps and piping to create artificial currents across the face of their underwater trenches for the removal of turbidity caused by excavation. Using dry suits and surface-supplied air the Zürich teams could work year-round. The systematic and rigorous nature of modern underwater excavation was demonstrated to a somewhat dubious Swiss archaeological community. Underwater studies continue in the Zürich area today, including the phenomenal preservation of more than two dozen of the houses. E.G.

ADDITIONAL READING

Keller, F., 1854, *Die keltischen Pfahlbauten in den Schweizerseen*, Mittelungen der Antiquarischen Gesellschaft, Zürich.

Paret, O., 1946, *Das neue Bild der Vorgeschichte*, Stuttgart.

Ruoff, U. *et al.*, 'Zürcher Seeufersiedlungern', *Helvetia Archaeologica*, 48, 19-61.

Sauter, M.-R., 1976, *Switzerland from Earliest Times to the Roman Conquest*, London.

Staudacher, W., 1925, 'Gab es in vorgeschichtlicher Zeit am Federsee wirklich Pfahlbauten?' *Prähist. Zeitschrift*, 16, 45ff.

Vogt, E., 1955, *Pfahlbaustudien*, *'Pfahlbauproblem'*, Monographien zur Ur- und Frühgeschichte der Schweiz 11.

La Madonnina Wreck

A Greek merchant ship carrying three large stone anchors found off the coast of southern Italy about 50 km to the east of Taranto (ancient Tarentum). The type of pyramidal, truncated, stone anchor with a single hole carried by the vessel had previously been thought to be unique to Greece and to Greek warships. The La Madonnina anchors are significant for they can be dated to about 350 BC by the pottery finds, which also indicate that they belonged to a merchant vessel.

The wreck was found in 1965 by Peter Throckmorton and was published in 1972 by A.M. McCann. No further published investigation of the wreck site has occurred. Recently, nine similar pyramidal stone anchors were found by D. Kourkoumelis off the eastern coast of the Greek island of Cythera. Pottery appears to date these anchors to the end of the 4th or beginning of the 3rd century BC.

The La Madonnina Wreck is marked by the three heavy stone anchors and a mound of Greco-Italic amphora fragments. Found off the shore of the fishing village of Campomarino, the wreck was named after the little chapel of Maria SS di Altomare, locally known as 'La Madonnina', that stands on top of an ancient site on the shore. The wreck lies on a reef about 200 m offshore at a depth of about 10 m. No remains of the ship itself were found. But the presence of the anchors lying close together, around which amphora fragments and other pottery were scattered over an area of about 18 by 50 m running southwest–northeast, makes it reasonably certain that all belong to the same wreck.

Two of the pyramidal anchors (B and C) are exactly the same size with a height of *c.* 63 cm, a width at the base of *c.* 45 cm narrowing to *c.* 24 cm at the top, and a depth of *c.* 36 cm narrowing to *c.* 19 cm at the top. The round hole has a circumference of *c.* 13 cm. The third anchor (A) is larger with a height of *c.* 69 cm, a width at the base of *c.* 49 cm narrowing to *c.* 33 cm at the top, and a depth of *c.* 36 cm narrowing to *c.* 26 cm at the top. The hole has a circumference of *c.* 18 cm. Cut into the top surface of each are remains of lead fittings for securing rings. This type of stone-hole pyramidal anchor goes back at least to early Egyptian times, as it is pictured on a relief from the pyramid of King Sahure of about 2500 BC. La Madonnina gives evidence that they continued in use at least until the 4th century BC.

Other finds from the ship are a metal fitting, a brailing ring, and two sounding leads. The ship was carrying two distinctly different types of amphora jars. Type A has a horizontal or slightly sloping rim with a knob-shaped toe. Seventeen distinguishable fragments of this type were catalogued, with two Greek stamps. One stamp is trapezoidal with a delta and an unidentified letter, the other is rectangular with a theta and an epsilon. Such stamps occur in the Agora of Athens and the shape relates to an earlier Attic 5th-century BC form. The second type of jar, Type B, has a widely bevelled lip that overlaps the heavy outward-curving handles. The reddish-gray grog with augite is filled with large grains of sand in an unusual composition for amphoras. The short conical-shaped foot is flat on the bottom. Koehler relates this form to Corinth (Type A), dated to the 4th century BC, but the coarse clay of La Madonnina amphoras is unlike the Corinthian fabric. Both La Madonnina amphora shapes appear to derive from Greek forms, one Attic and one Corinthian, but were of local manufacture.

The most important piece of pottery for dating the wreck is a black-glazed Greek lamp with a horizontal band handle. A well-marked groove sets off the rim from the sides. This type is similar to ones found both at Corinth and in the Athenian Agora. The form (Type 25 A) has been dated to the second quarter of the 4th to the first quarter of the 3rd century BC. The slanting rim, however, is an early feature, pointing to a date of about 350 BC. A fragment of the local black-glazed Gnathian ware further secures a mid-4th-century date for the wreck.

La Madonnina belongs to the last commercial years of Magna Graecia (South Italy) which still in the 4th century looked to ancient Tarentum as its chief trading and defensive city. Tarentum was the last of the great Greek cities to fall to Rome in 272 BC, following the defeat of Pyrrhus of Epirus at Beneventum. A.M.M.

ADDITIONAL READING

Koehler, C.G., 1981, 'Corinthian Developments in the Study of Trade in the Fifth Century', *Hesperia*, 50, 4, 449-58.

McCann, A.M., 1972, 'A Fourth Century BC Shipwreck Near Taranto', *Archaeology*, 25, 3, 180-87.

Land Tortoise

British colonial vessel found in Lake George, New York, the only one of her class yet found, and the oldest intact warship in North America. During the French and Indian War (1755–63), control of lakes George and Champlain determined control of the North American continent. In July

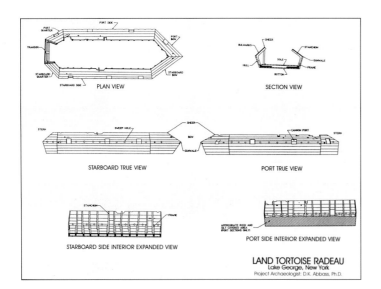

Plan of the Land Tortoise *radeau. (Bateaux Below Inc.)*

1758, following a disastrous defeat by the French at Carillon (Ticonderoga), the British returned to the southern end of Lake George and built vessels for a further assault on Ticonderoga. In September Maine shipwright Samuel Cobb began building a radeau. Connecticut colonel Henry Champion sketched the radeau in his journal and noted: 'It is 51 ft [15.5 m] in length, about 16 or 18 [4.9 or 5.5 m] wide. The name of this creature is Land Tortoise.' In October, Cobb launched *Land Tortoise* and another radeau; his journal indicates that they 'Rowed well they went with 26 Oars'.

The British then sank their fleet for winter storage, intending to raise it the following spring. However, in 1759 they constructed another radeau, *Invincible*, the only radeau present on Lake George that year. *Land Tortoise* was never mentioned again.

In 1990, members of the group that became Bateaux Below, Inc. discovered a radeau in 33 m of water at the centre of Lake George's southern basin. It is approximately 15.8 m long, with a 5.5 m beam, and has seven cannon ports and twenty-six sweep holes. Undoubtedly, this is the lost *Land Tortoise*. Its depth is probably why the British did not retrieve it in 1759. It also is why it has survived environmental hazards, wayward fishing gear, and artefact hunters.

Following its discovery, Bateaux Below, Inc., completed a study of *Land Tortoise*'s construction features, and identified the fish and marine growth associated with the site. It is an unkeeled seven-sided vessel made of flat panels supported by massive grown frames and stanchions; it is fastened with treenails and what appear to be hand-wrought metal nails or drifts. The profile is unusual and the quality of workmanship is

sometimes crude, but the parts fit together in a traditional manner.

Until this study, little was known about the radeau form. Although possibly related to barges, flats, and ferries, the radeau class was limited primarily to the protected waters of Lakes George and Champlain, and apparently did not survive past the American Revolutionary War. *Land Tortoise* suggests that its ability to fire while under sail was limited. The radeau's main purpose was to provide a stable and movable platform for ordnance. Following the end of hostilities, there would be no use for such an unwieldy vessel, so the form was abandoned.

The *Land Tortoise* project was unusual in that dedicated volunteer historians, archaeologists, and divers carried out the research, publishing professional and popular monographs, books, and articles. Regional and national interest in the vessel led to the creation in 1994 of *Land Tortoise* radeau shipwreck preserve. D.K.A., J.Z.

ADDITIONAL READING

Abbass, D.K., Cembrola, R., and Zarzynski, J.W., 1992, 'The Lake George Radeau: An Intact Vessel of 1758', in D.H. Keith and T.L. Carrell (eds), *Underwater Archaeology of Proceedings from the Society for Historical Archaeology Conference, Kingston, Jamaica*, Ann Arbor.

Bellico, R.P., 1993, *Sails and Steam in the Mountains: A Maritime and Military History of Lake George and Lake Champlain*, New York.

Champion, H., 1891, 'The Journal of Colonel Henry Champion', in F.B. Trowbridge, *Champion Genealogy*, New Haven.

Chapelle, H.I., 1946, *The History of American Sailing Ships*, New York.

Cobb, S., 1981, 'The Journal of Captain Samuel Cobb', *Bulletin of the Fort Ticonderoga Museum*, 14.

Zarzynski, J.W., Abbass, D.K., and Bellico, R.P.,

1994, 'Strange Bedfellows: Research and Politics of the *Land Tortoise*, Lake George's 1758 *Radeau* Shipwreck', in R.P Woodward and C.D. Moore (eds), *Underwater Archaeology Proceedings from the Society for Historical Archaeology Conference, Vancouver, British Columbia*, Ann Arbor.

La Pérouse Ships

French expedition to the Pacific consisting of *Boussole* and *Astrolabe*, both of which were wrecked on the island of Vanikoro in the Santa Cruz group of the Solomon Islands in 1788. In the second half of the 18th century the leading European powers sent voyages of discovery into the Pacific. France's major contribution was the voyage of the explorer Jean-François de la Pérouse, which set out from Brest in 1785. It was a meticulously planned naval operation that enjoyed the full support of Louis XVI and his ministers.

In choosing his ships, La Pérouse followed the example of James Cook: to better accommodate the scientific personnel, their collections, equipment, and libraries, he selected transport vessels for the voyage. Commissioned as 'frigates', the 550 ton *Boussole* and *Astrolabe*, built in 1782, shared the same dimensions, 42 m long and 6 m wide. Two illustrations from the voyage provide a idea of their appearance, one by Duché de Vancy drawn in Lituya Bay (Port des Français), Alaska, the other by Blondela of the ships anchored off Maui.

The voyage covered the length and breadth of the Pacific. After rounding Cape Horn and visiting Easter Island, Maui, the northwest coast of America, and California, the expedition crossed the ocean to Manila and to explore the coasts of China, Japan, and Russia before heading south to the Samoan Islands and Australia. After the stopover in Botany Bay, from where letters and journals were sent home via English ships, La Pérouse intended to sail along the north and west coasts of Australia before crossing the Indian Ocean to the Ile de France (Mauritius) and rounding Africa for Europe. But the expedition disappeared and it was close to forty years before traces of the ships were found on the reefs of Vanikoro, north of New Caledonia. A search and rescue expedition under the command of Bruny d'Entrecasteaux in the early 1790s failed to locate any sign of La Pérouse in the mass of islands north and east of Australia, although it sailed past Vanikoro.

Evidence of the location of the shipwrecks, in the form of a silver sword-guard and other European-made items, and stories of the loss of two ships, was finally uncovered by the Irish trader Peter Dillon on the neighbouring island of Tikopia in May 1826. Prevented by bad weather from extending his investigations to Vanikoro, Dillon sailed to Calcutta from where an exploratory expedition was launched. It arrived at Vanikoro in September 1827. Although some Frenchmen seem to have survived the cyclone and shipwreck that had ended their voyage, none was still living. But stories from local natives and the collection on shore of pieces from the ships and numerous other articles confirmed that here indeed was the site of the tragedy. On his return to Europe, Dillon took his relics to Paris in early 1829 where they were identified, and he was received and honoured by Charles X.

Meanwhile the French Navy had sponsored another expedition to follow up reports from whalers that items of French manufacture had been seen in New Caledonia and the Louisiade Archipelago. In Hobart, Tasmania, the commander Dumont d'Urville heard reports of Dillon's discoveries; six months after the Irishman, in February 1828, he reached Vanikoro. More articles were collected from the natives and, more importantly, the actual remains of one of the wrecks, probably *Astrolabe*, were located in a false pass through the reef; an anchor and some guns, still retaining their identification marks, were recovered. The materials collected by Dillon and d'Urville were exhibited in Paris, where today the Musée de la Marine holds the major collection of artefacts recovered from the wrecks. In 1883 an expedition sponsored by the Governor of New Caledonia recovered the anchors and guns that now sit at the base of the monument to the explorer in his birthplace of Albi in southern France.

Vanikoro's reefs guarded further secrets of the wrecks until after World War II. The technological breakthrough of the **SCUBA** and subsequent advances in equipment revolutionized diving and encouraged development of the discipline of underwater archaeology. The New Zealand-born salvage expert Reece Discombe, based in Vila (Vanuatu), explored d'Urville's old site in 1958 and 1959. Using explosives to dislodge the coral, he recovered numerous pieces of ships' equipment and armament. Discombe returned to Vanikoro in 1962. His close reading of Dillon and d'Urville's accounts and a comparison of their charts with modern maps led him to search for a second wreck site along the outside of the reef. Nearly 2 km from the false pass he found a number of large objects – anchors, cannon, and ballast blocks. Further investigation of a large gully confirmed that he had discovered

another wreck site. The French Navy sent an expedition in 1964 which concentrated on this site; among the objects recovered were the arc and maker's plaque from the expedition's large quadrant. This would almost certainly have been on *Boussole*.

Indiscriminate pilfering of the sites during the 1960s and 1970s compromised their archaeological integrity. In 1981 the Association Solomon was founded in Noumena, New Caledonia, to research the enigma of Vanikoro. More objects were recovered in a visit to the island that preceded the first professional investigation of the wrecks – primarily *Boussole* – by a French/New Caledonia/Australia team led

Voyage of La Perouse. Atlas, Plate 14. (Museum of London)

by Ron Coleman of the Queensland Museum. A second expedition from Noumena in 1990 was characterized by a continuation of a professional approach to documentation, retrieval, and conservation.

Major collections of artefacts from Vanikoro now exist in Paris, Noumena, Brisbane, and Lata, capital of the Solomon Islands' province of Temotu. Discombe has given a number of objects from his personal collection to the Association Lapérouse in Albi and to the Lapérouse Museum in Botany Bay, Australia. Although countless pieces remain unaccounted for in private hands, remarkable treasures from bells to buttons, cannons to coins, ceramics, pewter plates and goblets, geological specimens, personal items, and sections of navigational instruments have been recovered in the public interest. Much remains, however, for further professional work.

The evidence of the wreck sites confirms the theory that, caught on the reef in a cyclone, *Boussole* twisted and broke up on impact; *Astrolabe* lasted longer, spilling much of her contents over the false pass into the lagoon. There were survivors from the latter

ship who built a camp on land (dug in 1986 and 1990) and launched a small boat. Whether or not they escaped Vanikoro only to be wrecked a second time or to be murdered by natives on another island remains in the realm of speculation. Their unknown fate, along with those artefacts still remaining on the reefs of Vanikoro, continues to contribute to the enduring mystery of the La Pérouse expedition. R.R.I.

ADDITIONAL READING

Brossard, M., 1964, *Rendez-vous avec Lapérouse à Vanikoro*, Paris.

Dunmore, J., 1985, *Pacific Explorer: The Life and Times of Jean-François de la Pérouse, 1741–1788*, Annapolis.

Dunmore, J. (ed.),1994–5, *The Journal of Jean-François de Galaup de la Pérouse 1785–1788*, London.

Lapérouse, Vanikoro., 1992, 'Campagne de Recherches 1990', *Bulletin Scientifique de la Societé d'Etudes Historiques de Nouvelle-Caledonie*, 90, 1-62.

Shelton, R., 1987, *From Hudson Bay to Botany Bay: The Lost Frigates of Lapérouse*, Toronto.

La Trinidad Valencera

Member of the Levant squadron of the **Spanish Armada** wrecked in Kinnagoe Bay, Co. Donegal, Ireland. *Valencera* was a Venetian merchant ship, probably a bulk grain-carrier, embargoed in Sicily in 1586 to transport war stores and troops to Lisbon, where the Armada was being prepared. On arrival she was requisitioned to take part in the campaign, and in the fleet muster of May 1588 was rated as an 1,100 tonner with a complement of 79 mariners and 281 soldiers. The latter were members of the *tercio* (regiment) of Naples. The regiment's colonel, Don Alonso de Luzon, was the senior officer aboard. The ship's forty-two guns included four 40 pounder siege *canones* for the campaign in England, supplied complete with land carriages and limbers (two full sets for each gun) and the associated paraphernalia of a heavy artillery train.

It appears that *Valencera* was one of the fleet's heavily gunned troubleshooters, and played an active part in the Channel battles. As with so many other Armada ships the damage she received was not debilitating at the time, but proved her downfall on the homeward voyage. Separated from the main body of the fleet, and taking on water, *Valencera* ran for the north coast of Ireland and grounded in Kinnagoe Bay. Over the next two days, with the help of locals, Don Alonso and most of his men came safely ashore. On 16 September the ship broke apart, drowning the remaining Spaniards and a number of Irishmen who were engaged in looting the stranded hull.

The survivors were rounded up by the local English garrison, and many of them were massacred. A few escaped in the confusion, while the officers – including Don Alonso – were spared for ransom. After lengthy negotiations he and some others were repatriated. Of the rest, a handful eventually made it home via Scotland. Two of them – Juan de Nova and Francisco de Borja – subsequently left a graphic and harrowing account of their experiences.

The wreck was discovered in 1971 by members of the City of Derry Sub-Aqua Club, who found bronze guns, anchors, and spoked wooden siege-carriage wheels lying partly buried in a flat sandy seabed next to the shallow reef on which the ship had grounded and broken up. Two of the guns were 40 pounder siege *canones* whose descriptions and weight-marks matched information provided by *Valencera*'s lading manifest, so confirming the wreck's identity. A third gun of this type, also with matching weight-marks, was recovered later in 1986. At the Derry Sub-Aqua Club's invitation the survey and subsequent partial excavation of the site was directed by Colin Martin between 1971 and 1984, in association with the Ulster Museum and the **Scottish Institute of Maritime Studies** at St Andrews University.

Although the wreck is much broken up and dispersed, a wide range of material, including substantial organic deposits, has been preserved on the site. It appears that while the hull was still partially intact scour-pits formed in its vicinity, and these attracted accumulations of organics and other material. The hull seems to have broken up relatively rapidly and, when it did, the natural seabed stability reasserted itself, filling the scour-pits and encapsulating the material they contained. A number of hull components have been identified, though none occur as articulated assemblies. This may be

Philip II's arms on the breech of a bronze siege canon recovered from the wreck of La Trinidad Valencera. *(Colin Martin)*

explained by the exclusive use of iron fastenings in the ship's construction, a feature characteristic of contemporary Adriatic bulk carriers. The technique maximized maintenance over a short but intensive working life (hulls remained strong and tight so long as the iron was sound). When serious iron corrosion set in, typically within ten years or so, the vessel was simply discarded and replaced. These characteristics may explain why the hull broke up so quickly, thus ensuring the random burial and preservation of much associated material.

After a preliminary survey and assessments with probe and metal detector it was decided to open sample areas of the site, especially those which showed signs of organic deposition. Excavation was conducted within the framework of a reference grid, and a light **Water dredge** was used to remove spoil. The resultant collection of material, in addition to explaining the site's formation characteristics, constituted an unusually wide sampling of the vessel's contents. This information was greatly enhanced by the extensive lading documentation which was discovered in Spanish archival sources. Several items of artillery were recovered, including the siege guns, Venetian pieces, and a composite bronze and wrought-iron breechloading swivel gun. In addition to land-carriage elements a long-trailed two-wheeled Italian sea-carriage was identified, which has thrown light on contemporary gun-handling techniques. Two types of incendiary weapon – *alcancias*, or ceramic firepots, and *bombas*, a kind of

offensive firework – were found. Soldiers' weaponry and accoutrements included parts of muskets, arquebuses, and pikes, together with concreted steel helmets (with pine needle padding), powder flasks, a sword belt, and items of clothing and footwear. A wide range of personal and domestic items included wooden lanterns, musical instruments, and utensils of wood, pewter, and pottery. Military stores included part of a tent (of nettle fibre), wooden handspikes, trimmed saplings for the construction of defences, a shovel, and gunnery instruments. Considerable quantities of barrel components, cordage, and ship's fittings were found across the site.

Conservation of this material was carried out by the Ulster Museum, where the material is currently housed pending its transfer to a new museum in Londonderry. The site is protected under the Republic of Ireland's historic shipwreck legislation. C.M.

ADDITIONAL READING

Martin, C.J.M., 1975, *Full Fathom Five: Wrecks of the Spanish Armada*, London and New York, 189–224.

Martin, C.J.M., 1979, '*La Trinidad Valencera*: An Armada Invasion Transport Lost off Donegal', *International Journal of Nautical Archaeology*, 8, 1, 13–38.

Martin, C.J.M., 1988, 'A 16th Century Siege Train: The Battery Ordnance of the 1588 Spanish Armada', *International Journal of Nautical Archaeology*, 17, 1, 57–73.

Martin, C.J.M., 1994, 'Incendiary Weapons from the Spanish Armada Wreck *La Trinidad Valencera*, 1588', *International Journal of Nautical Archaeology*, 23, 3, 207–17.

Lawrence
see **Niagara**

Leonora

A ship owned by the infamous blackbirder and rogue William Henry (Bully) Hayes, which sank during a storm in Utwa Harbor, Kusaie (now Kosrae), Micronesia in 1874. The ship was a 218 ton brigantine originally built for the opium trade. Although its construction date is unclear, it first appeared in Micronesia under the name *Water Lily* after being purchased in 1868 in Honolulu. It went through a series of legal title changes before ending up solely in the possession of Hayes at the time of its sinking. During this time it went through a name change and was briefly known as *Pioneer*.

Leonora, otherwise an unremarkable ship, achieved a measure of fame and notoriety because of the legendary nature of its owner at the time of its loss. Bully Hayes left a convoluted legacy in which fact is entangled with fiction. The Cleveland-born American was undoubtedly a swindler, trader in human cargo (perhaps not exactly slaves), and a bigamist. On several occasions he seems to have relieved other men of both their ships and their wives, usually more by the wiles of a confidence man than by violence. There is no hard evidence of him being a pirate. He was killed during a quarrel with the cook of *Lotus* in transit from Jaluit to Kosrae.

In 1967 a Scripps Oceanographic Institution research vessel visited Kosrae and some of its divers visited the wreck site of what was suspected to be *Leonora*. They removed several artefacts including a bronze gudgeon which were subsequently turned over to the Star of India Museum in San Diego. The site was reportedly again visited in the 1970s by an unknown group which removed numerous artefacts, according to villagers.

In 1981 the US National Park Service (NPS) **Submerged Cultural Resources Unit** surveyed the site at the behest of the Kosraens and the Office of the Trust Territories of the Pacific Islands (TTPI). The team, consisting of Dan Lenihan, Larry Murphy, and Toni Carrell from the NPS, Teddy John from Kosrae, Ross Cordy (TTPI), Paul Ehrlich and Bob Adair (Peace Corps), documented all surface material and found a site significantly impacted since the visit of the Scripps vessel over a decade earlier. They concluded the site was largely intact under river-borne sediments, however, and recommended protection in place until there were sufficient assets available for a proper excavation.

Lenihan later visited the Star of India Museum in San Diego and documented the artefacts in their possession. The Submerged Cultural Resources Unit then produced a report on their findings in the field and included the inventory of material from San Diego. The report was later incorporated in its entirety into a Micronesian Archaeological Survey document edited by Russell Scott.

D.J.L.

ADDITIONAL READING

Becke, L., 1899, 'The Wreck of the *Leonora*: A Memory of Bully Hayes', in *Ridan The Devil and other Stories*, Philadelphia.

Lenihan, D.J., Carrell, T., and Murphy, L., 1981, *The Utwa Harbor Wreck Site: A Shipwreck Evaluation and Management Report*, United States Department of the Interior, National Park Service, Submerged Cultural Resources Unit, Santa Fe.

Michener, J.A. and Day, A.G, 1957, *Rascals in Paradise*, New York.

Russell, S. (ed.), 1982, *Of Wooden Ships and Iron Men: An Historical and Archaeological Survey of the Brig Leonora*, Micronesian Archaeological Survey Report 15, Saipan.

Liburnian Sewn Boat

Remains of a 1st century AD boat discovered off the Adriatic port of Zaton in Croatia. The Adriatic coast of Croatia was inhabited in ancient times by the Liburnians, a seafaring people who ruled the eastern Adriatic as far south as Corfu and portions of the western Adriatic before falling under Roman domination and becoming part of the province of Dalmatia.

Between 1982 and 1996, archaeological survey of the ancient Liburnian/Roman port of Aenona, 2.5 km south of Nin, near the present-day town of Zaton, discovered submerged remains of the port, including a large Roman pier and two shipwrecks. The wrecks were found buried in mud in 2 m of water. One vessel, 6.5 m long, was partially preserved. The second, an 8 m long vessel, retained twenty-seven frames, keel, and hull planking. Both vessels were excavated and raised in 1996 and underwent conservation at the Centre for Conservation of Hydro-archaeological Findings in Zadar.

Both boats were carvel-planked, with the planks caulked with tar and organic matter and sewn together with rope made from flax and Spanish broom. There is no evidence of iron fastenings. Two parallel timbers with slots for a mast and several blocks were found in the larger boat, which suggested to the Croatian archaeological team that the mast may have been bipedal and similar to those found in epigraphic representations of Egyptian craft. Fragments of leather excavated from the site also suggested that the sail may have been leather. The archaeological evidence led to the identification of the boats as Liburnian *serilia*, or sewn boats. Coins found inside the hulls were dated to the 1st century AD. J.P.D.

ADDITIONAL READING

Brusic, Z., and Domjan, M., 1985, 'Liburnian Boats' in S. McGrail and E. Kentley (eds) *Sewn Plank Boats*, Oxford, BAR.S. 276, 67-86.

Brusic, Z. *et al.*, 1996, 'Serilia Liburnica (Liburnian Sewn Boat) 1st Century AD–1st Century AD Reconstruction Project', in A. Kisic *et.al.*, *Wooden Shipbuilding in Croatia*, Dubrovnik.

Lisht timbers

Planks and framing components buried around the Middle Kingdom pyramid of Senwosret I (*c.* 1959–1914 BC) at Lisht, about 45 km south of Cairo, Egypt. Excavations by the Metropolitan Museum of Art at Lisht uncovered nearly a hundred timbers from watercraft broken apart and reused as foundations for causeways and ramps in and around the early Twelfth Dynasty pyramid complex. Made of locally available acacia and tamarisk, the Lisht timbers were originally edge-fastened with deep mortise-and-tenon fastenings and sewing. Unlike the cedar-built hulls of the **Khufu Ships** or **Dashur Boats**, the Lisht timbers can reasonably be identified as coming from a working boat or boats and offer another perspective on ancient Egyptian hull construction. In addition, the only planked boat model known from ancient Egypt has been found at Lisht, buried in sand outside the tomb of Imhotep, one of Senwosret I's officials. It mirrors the Dashur hull design but is only 2 m long.

Despite differences between the Khufu (2600 BC) and Dashur hulls (*c.* 1860 BC) and the Lisht hull components, they also share characteristics that establish a direct relationship with the shipbuilding technology used in all three groups. Khufu and Dashur hull planks are longer, more regularly shaped, and thinner than Lisht planks which have intricately joggled edges and planks more than half as thick as they are broad. (Joggles are the notches or projecting pieces used to create joints between two planks formed by a notch on one plank and the fitting projection on another.) Freight boats built with the construction features demonstrated by the Lisht timbers would efficiently support the elaborate building programmes of the ancient Egyptians who, as early as the Fourth Dynasty (*c.* 2600 BC), transported a 70 ton granite block more than 1,200 km down the Nile from the quarries at Aswan to the pyramid of Khufu at Giza. The little known about working boats in ancient Egypt comes from a few illustrations which feature the transportation of granite columns and obelisks, so physical evidence of this hull type is particularly helpful.

Several other Middle Kingdom pyramid sites also had hull timbers reused as building material but only the timbers at Lisht have been recorded and examined in detail. At Lisht, the timbers were laid onto a prepared surface with the outer planking surface uppermost before being covered with a mixture of plaster and limestone chips. The hardened mixture protected the timbers from damage, and there are no wear marks on the planks. Preservation varies; some timbers were little more than traces in the sand while others are sound. Grain and knot patterns indicate efforts to use wood economically while avoiding large knots, a potential source of structural weakness very common in both tamarisk and acacia wood.

When looking at the Lisht timbers, the unusual shapes and elaborate fashioning of plank edges stand out. Almost all of the planks have joggled edges. The planks measure 1.01–2.6 m long; their width ranges from 12 to 40 cm but in most cases planks are 16 to 20 cm wide. Their thickness of 9 to 18 cm, most commonly 12 to 15, means that the cross-section of most planks is squat and nearly square. Like other ancient Egyptian hull planks, the Lisht planks have holes for fastenings only on their inner surfaces and on plank edges.

Mortise-and-tenon joints, placed singly or in pairs in the plank edges, are so deep that they often pass the halfway point of the plank width. A number of tenon fragments remain in mortises, and some of these preserve traces of the slips about 1 sq. cm that were driven in beside the tenon to prevent longitudinal slippage. Even after 4,000 years, tenons fit so closely that it was extremely difficult to extract them for study. Like mortise-and-tenon joints in all other ancient Egyptian hulls, the Lisht examples were unpegged.

The builders of the Lisht hull also relied on ligatures, possibly to secure battens over plank seams. L-shaped lashing holes (65–95 × 50 × 10 mm) cut on the inner face and edges of most planks held a flat plaited strip woven from halfa grass (probably *Desmotchya bipinnata*). Placement of the ligatures is very similar to the pattern of ligatures on Khufu I and to the pattern of former ligatures (now dovetail tenons) on the Dashur watercraft.

One frame and several frame components were found in one of the timber groups at Lisht. The frame was originally believed to be part of a rocker assembly for moving stones but it is unquestionably from a boat. The composite Lisht frame spans about 2.4 m and consists of a curved floor timber and two smaller top timbers fastened to it with mortise-and-tenon joints and lashing. It has three holes, possibly for treenails to fasten the frame to the bottom planking in its lower face. A 50 cm wide cutting on the upper face of the floor timber, and a similar gap between the ends of the two top timbers, suggests that a hull member at least 50 × 30 cm long once rested here. On the basis of evidence from models of the same period, it is likely that this was a longitudinal timber analogous in function but stronger and lower in the hull than the carling that ran along the Khufu hull's centreline.

As found, the Lisht frame was incomplete, as a number of empty mortises on its upper timbers testify. Other elements found near it can be arranged to create a massive structure resembling a bulkhead more than 8 m wide. No evidence for placement in the hull exists, but we can imagine a hull designed with a thick shell of planking, relying on beams to support a deck load and frames like the Lisht assemblage to support each beam.

A recent study of barges built like the Khufu I hull showed that a hull built more lightly than the Lisht freighter(s) could carry 1,440 tons, the weight of two gigantic New Kingdom statues known as the Colossi of Memnon. A 70 × 24 m hull, built like cargo-carriers as exemplified by the Lisht material with planks 15–20 cm thick and supported internally by massive carlings and frames fastened to beams, would require no complicated engineering that had not already been tested by at least 500 years of shipbuilders. C.H.

ADDITIONAL READING

Haldane, C.W., 1992, 'The Lisht Timbers: A Preliminary Report', in D. Arnold (ed.), *The Pyramid Complex of Senwosret I at Lisht: Metropolitan Museum of Art Egyptian Expedition XXV, The Southern Cemeteries at Lisht III*, New York, 102–12 and plates.

Patch, D.C. and Haldane, C.W., 1990, *The Pharaoh's Boat at The Carnegie*, Pittsburgh.

Wehausen, J.V. *et al.*, 1988, 'The Colossi of Memnon and Egyptian Barges', *International Journal of Nautical Archaeology*, 17, 295–310.

Lithic artefacts

Stone tools and the debris that results from their manufacture, modification, and use. This class of artefact is frequently found in prehistoric archaeological sites, and in Africa they predate the appearance of pottery by over two million years. Lithic artefacts are particularly important as site preservation factors often eliminate all traces of human activity except for the stone artefacts that are present. This can be critical when trying to determine whether stratigraphic layers are natural or cultural. The analysis of lithic artefacts from underwater and intertidal contexts is successfully used to assist in the interpretation of **Site formation processes**, to determine the age and nature of archaeological deposits, and to provide insights into environmental conditions for the period the site was occupied.

The study of site formation processes seeks to understand the natural and cultural forces that cause archaeological materials to be found where they are. Some reasons for finding lithic artefacts in an underwater or intertidal context could include discard, accidental loss, shipwreck and the loss of cargo, the erosion of terrestrial sites, or changes in the sea-level resulting in the inundation of land sites. Pristine lithic artefacts found in an underwater context suggest the site was either rapidly inundated by a rising sea-level or the archaeological materials were buried by protective sediments prior to inundation.

The pre-pottery Neolithic site of Atlit-Yam, located off the coast of Israel near Haifa, is an example of an underwater site where pristine lithic artefacts were recovered. The condition of the lithic artefacts in combination with other materials, such as well-preserved human burials, house foundations, and other features, helped archaeologists determine that Atlit-Yam was buried in sand prior to its inundation by the **Mediterranean Sea**.

Lithic artefacts recovered from archaeological sites that are gradually inundated by the sea tend to be badly weathered or water-rounded owing to their prolonged exposure to the weather and tides. Lithic artefacts

Mesolithic tranchet axe found on the beach at Herne Bay, Kent, England. (Courtesy of the Trustees of the British Museum)

that are exposed for very long periods may become unrecognizable as the natural forces acting upon them completely erode any indications of their cultural nature.

The position that lithic artefacts are found in is also critical when interpreting site formation processes. For example, whether artefacts are horizontally or vertically bedded within the matrix may indicate the degree of post-depositional disturbance the site has undergone since it was formed. Horizontally bedded artefacts suggest a stable living surface with few, if any, post-depositional disturbances, while a mixture of horizontally and vertically bedded artefacts in the same stratigraphic layer suggests some level of post-depositional disturbance.

Like other classes of artefacts, lithics can sometimes be used to estimate the age of cultural deposits. In some instances specific artefact types from a geographically restricted area can be dated by their style or by specific attributes. An example of this could be a nephrite adze blade from southwestern British Columbia, Canada. Data from a series of excavations have determined that this particular artefact type was used between 2,500 and 200 BP. At a nearby undated site where the same artefact occurs, this information can then be used to estimate the relative age of the artefact and associated materials recovered from the same stratigraphic layer. Caution should be used when applying this technique: it can be problematic for certain areas or periods.

In rarer circumstances, the approximate age of lithic artefacts can be determined by dating materials that are found adhering to them. An example of this is lithic artefacts that are exposed in an intertidal environment, then later buried or immersed in deeper water by a change in sea-level. Under these conditions barnacles may adhere to the artefacts prior to their immersion or burial. These barnacles are extremely robust and can be radiocarbon dated using the accelerated mass spectrometry (AMS) method. This technique was used at the Arrow Creek 2 site, Haida Gwaii, Canada; here a radiocarbon date derived from a barnacle adhering to a basalt flake provided an age of 9,200 BP, thus indicating both the time the artefact was exposed in the intertidal zone and a *terminus ante quem* for the artefact's age.

The degree of weathering or water rounding is a very poor indicator of the age of artefacts as they can survive in pristine condition, even if underwater, for hundreds of thousands of years. In contrast, a storm beach, or other high energy environment, can produce considerable damage to artefacts very quickly. Experimental research into the effects of water rounding (e.g. by Harding and others) may one day allow archaeologists to estimate the relative ages of lithic artefacts by the degree of damage or water rounding. However, at present it is not possible to make generalizations beyond a restricted area or site.

Lithics are also valuable for their ability to provide information about the nature of human occupations, and their durability makes them particularly well suited for this purpose. For example, the recovery of a great number of cores, large primary reduction flakes, and low numbers of tools might suggest a location was used as a lithic raw material quarry where the acquisition of stone suitable for the manufacture of tools was the dominant activity. In contrast, a site containing high frequencies of edge trimming flakes might represent artefact maintenance and curation activities. Caution should be used when relying exclusively upon lithic artefacts to interpret the function of sites, however, as their durability can bias the composition of artefact assemblages when the preservation of non-lithic artefacts is poor.

Information concerning paleoenvironmental conditions at a site may also be reflected in assemblages of lithic artefacts from underwater and intertidal archaeological sites. For example, barnacle remains

on the surface of a number of lithic artefacts might indicate a now subtidal site was once intertidal. By dating these barnacle remains, the timing of the sea-level change could then be calculated and compared with other environmental data to determine the rate or nature of the sea-level fluctuation and the effect it may have had on the local population. These data could be used to demonstrate how the general environment and/or function of a site changed through time.

Other research projects have recovered lithic artefacts from intertidal and subtidal peat deposits. At Hartlepool Bay, England, pollen spectra drawn from organic material adhering to a stone flake have been used to reconstruct the nature of the environment as well as the use of this environmental niche by its occupants. Organic materials found associated with lithic artefacts in such environments can often be radiocarbon dated to assist in determining the age of the occupation and to aid with the reconstruction of the paleoenvironment.

Apart from the work of Apland, Harding, and others, the problems associated with studying lithic artefacts from intertidal and subtidal contexts has largely been ignored by archaeologists. Project reports tend to describe these artefacts as either waterworn or pristine without considering the processes necessary for them to remain pristine or to become worn. Similarly, few attempts have been made to construct a typology of waterworn artefacts or to develop methods for identifying lithic artefacts in advanced stages of wear. These are some of the basic issues that need to be addressed before substantive advances in the study of lithic artefacts from underwater and intertidal contexts can be made. Perhaps continued experimentation and the analysis of waterworn lithic artefacts from a wide variety of environmental contexts can begin to address some of these shortcomings. A.M.

ADDITIONAL READING
Apland, B., 1982, 'Chipped Stone Assemblages from the Beach Sites of the Central Coast', in P.M. Hobler (ed.), *Papers on Central Coast Archaeology*, Department of Archaeology Publication 10, Simon Fraser University, Burnaby, 13–63.
Crabtree, D.E., 1972, *An Introduction to Flintworking*, Occasional Papers of the Idaho State University Museum 28, Pocatello,.Idaho.
Easton, N.A. and Moore, C.D., 1991, 'Test Excavations of Subtidal Deposits at Montague Harbour, British Columbia, Canada: 1989', *International Journal of Nautical Archaeology*, 20, 4, 269–80.
Fedje, D.W. *et al.*, 1996, 'Early Holocene Archaeology and Paleoecology at the Arrow

Creek Sites in Gwaii Hanaas', *Arctic Anthropology*, 33, 1, 116–42.
Fedje, D.W. *et al.*, 1996, 'Early Period Archaeology in Gwaii Hanaas: Results of the 1993 Field Program', in R.L. Carlson and L. Dalla Bona (eds), *Early Human Occupation in British Columbia*, Vancouver, 133–50.
Galili, E. *et al.*, 1993, 'Atlit-Yam: A Prehistoric Site on the Sea Floor off the Israeli Coast', *Journal of Field Archaeology*, 20, 2, 133–57.
Harding, P. *et al.*, 1987, 'The Transport and Abrasion of Flint Handaxes in a Gravel-bed River', in G. de G. Sieveking and M.H. Newcomer (eds), *The Human Uses of Flint and Chert: Proceedings of the Fourth International Flint Symposium, Brighton, April 1983*, Cambridge, 115–26.
Josenhans, H. *et al.*, 1995, 'Post Glacial Sea-levels on the Western Canadian Continental Shelf: Evidence for Rapid Change, Extensive Subaerial Exposure, and Early Human Habitation', *Marine Geology*, 125, 73–94.
Masters, P.M. and Flemming, N.C. (eds), 1983, *Quaternary Coastlines and Marine Archaeology: Towards the Prehistory of Land Bridges and Continental Shelves*, Toronto.
Tooley, M.J., 1978, 'The History of Hartlepool Bay', *International Journal of Nautical Archaeology*, 7, 1, 71–5.

Little Salt Spring

Submerged prehistoric site in southwest Florida, United States. First explored by sport divers in the 1950s, Little Salt Spring became the focus of intense archaeological investigations in the 1970s. The spring is a shallow water basin overlying a deep underwater cavern. High concentrations of dissolved minerals and a lack of oxygen gives an anaerobic quality to the water, ideal for maintaining prehistoric materials in an excellent state of preservation.

Carl J. Clausen, the principal investigator during excavations in the 1970s, found the site to be rich in **Human remains**, cultural materials, and extinct megafauna and flora. Radiocarbon dating of selected materials suggest two periods of intense occupation, during the early Paleo-Indian period of 12,000 to 9,000 BP and the Archaic Indian period from 6,800 to 5,200 BP. In addition to the spring, the site includes a mucky slough that contains an estimated one thousand Archaic Indian burials. Materials of note encountered during the investigations of the 1970s included remains of a giant land tortoise, a sharpened wooden stake found in direct association with the tortoise that has been radiocarbon dated to 12,030 BP, portions of an immature mammoth or masto-don, extinct bison bones, and fragments of a non-returning Paleo-Indian boomerang.

The site is now held in trust by the University of Miami as an archaeological and ecological preserve. Archaeological investigations, halted between 1980 and 1985, were resumed by John A. Gifford of the University of Miami in 1986. Samples of neural tissue from a skull were retrieved from the site during the 1986 field season. Radiocarbon dated to 7,000 BP, the tissue's mitochondrial DNA sequences were successfully reconstructed. Work in the early 1990s consisted of coring for paleoenvironmental analysis. Core samples brought up oyster shell and large wood fragments, some of which appeared to have worked surfaces. D.J.L., A.A, M.R.3

ADDITIONAL READING

Clausen, C.J. *et al.*, 1979, 'Little Salt Spring, Florida: A Unique Underwater Site', *Science*, 203, 609–14.

Gifford, J.A., 1990, 'Underwater Archaeology at Little Salt Spring', *Context: Boston University Center for Archaeological Studies*, 9:16–18.0.

Lomellina

Wreck discovered in 1979 at a depth of 18 m in the middle of the Bay of Villefranche-sur-mer, near Nice, **France**. The initial survey of the site dated the wreck to the first half of the 16th century. Between 1982 and 1990 excavation of the site was conducted under the direction of Captain Max Guérout with the support of the Groupe de Recherche en Archéologie Navale (GRAN) and the collaboration of Eric Rieth and Jean-Marie Gassend from the Centre National de la Recherche Scientifique (CNRS). More than 4,500 dives were performed to study the site.

After test excavation, the wreck's date was confirmed and a Genoese origin appeared to be very probable. Considering the importance and the state of preservation of the hull remains, it was decided to proceed to an *in situ* study of the wreck, limiting the recovery of samples of the structure to only those that contributed to an understanding of the ship's construction. The research design was to study the ship's structure (description, methods, and principles of building, hull shape, nautical characteristics, and timber work), the ordnance, and the ship's equipment.

Remains of the ship's structure are spread out over a length of 35 m and a width of 10 m, buried in a mixed sand and mud sediment. The wreck leans 45 degrees to port. The keel is 33.38 m long and the total length of the ship is estimated at 46.5 m, with a width of 14 m and a depth of 4.4 m. The calculated tonnage is therefore about 825 tonnes. The keel is preserved from stem to stern except for one element, probably dredged away by modern anchors. On the

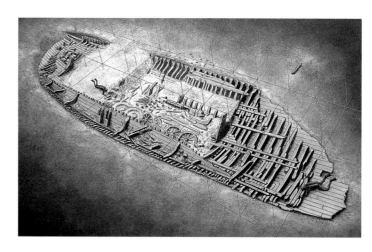

General view of the Lomellina wreck site. (© GRAN/N. Blotti)

View of the central part of the Lomellina wreck: on the right, lower deck and carriage wheels; in the centre, orlop deck with wrought-iron gun and carriage; on the left, structures of the bottom. (© GRAN/CNRS/J.C. Hurteau)

port side, two decks are preserved. The hold was filled with ballast made either of gravel or pebbles. After seven years of excavation and the discovery of an important document in the archives of Genoa, the comparison between archaeological data and several historical options led to the identification of the wreck as *Lomellina*, a Genoese *nave* which sank in a hurricane on 15 September 1516, together with its cargo of guns.

Navi formed the backbone of the Genoese fleet, used mainly to transport heavy cargoes over long distances in the Mediterranean and to northwest Europe, but were also used as warships if necessary. Between ten and fifteen *navi* were armed in the port of Genoa in the first quarter of the 16th century. Moored in the Bay of Villefranche, *Lomellina* was under repairs; capstan and jeer bitts were found dismantled on the lower deck, and sawdust and chips were found between the floor frames with a trying plane.

Numerous important equipment from the ship was studied and occasionally recovered. These included the rudder, capstan, jeer bitts (formed of three different elements with a total length of 8.22 m), lateen mast head, feet and dales of the pumps, powder hold, and portholes – probably the first archaeological observation of side portholes which first appeared around 1500.

The study of the remains of the mast-step led to the main scientific contribution of the excavation. Although the wreck was a round ship, the mast-step was similar to those of galleys and chebecs and different from all known mast-steps made according to the Atlantic Ocean shipbuilding tradition. These observations were reinforced by the discovery of contracts established for the building of Genoese *navi*, whose vocabulary was the same as for galley building and description. As the same vocabulary fits the same working method and the same type of structures, we can say that if the Mediterranean shipbuilding tradition of galleys was still alive in the 18th century, the shipbuilding tradition of Mediterranean round ships, observed here for the first time, disappeared at an unknown time.

Among thousands of artefacts illustrating the everyday life on board, some individual and collective weapons must be mentioned. Hand grenades of four different types illustrate weapons present in ships' inventories but rarely observed. Fifteen wrought-iron composite guns, some of them with their carriages, have been detected, some of which were retrieved for conservation treatment. Several pairs of carriage wheels were probably part of transported artillery. Gun shots of stone, iron, lead, and lead with iron cubes, in twenty-one different diameters, were found, the largest one being 27.3 cm in diameter.

Data recovered during the excavation is still being studied, but it already represents an important step in our knowledge of a turning-point in shipbuilding history. M.G.

ADDITIONAL READING

Calegari, M., 1970, 'Navi e barche tra il XV e il XVI secolo', in *Miscellanea storica ligure: Guerra e commercio nell'evoluzione della marina genovese tra XV e XVII secolo*, Genoa, 13–55.

Gatti, L., 1975, 'Construzioni navali in Liguria fra XV e XVI secolo', in *Studi di storia navale*, Florence, 25–72.

Guérout, M., Rieth, E., and Gassend, J.M., 1990,
   *Le navire gênois de Villefranche: Un naufrage de
   1516?*, Archeonautica vol. 9.
Rieth, E., 1991, 'L'emplanture du grand-mât de
   l'épave due début du XVIème siècle de
   Villefranche-sur-Mer: Un exemple
   d'emplanture de tradition méditerranéenne',
   in C. Villain-Gandossi, S. Busuttil, and
   P. Adam, *Medieval Ships and the Birth of
   Technological Societies*, Malta, 179–96.
Rieth, E., 1991, 'L'épave du début du XVIème
   siècle de Villefranche-sur-Mer', in K. Paul
   (ed.), *Carvel Construction Technique*, Oxbow
   Monograph 12, Oxford, 47–55.

London waterfront
see **River Thames**

Lord Western

The oldest located shipwreck in British
Columbia, Canada. Well known to natives of
the area, its wreck site in Adventure Cove,
Sydney Inlet, 32 km northeast of Tofino, was
first dived in 1957, but its identity was not
determined until 1988. For years its well-
preserved hull and cargo of fir piles was
known as the Sydney Inlet Mystery Wreck.

In 1957 a group of divers led by Dr
George Cotrell of Portland, Oregon recovered several artefacts while on an expedition
for John Jacob Astor's ill-fated *Tonquin*. The
excellent artefact preservation led the Royal
Canadian Navy to mount expeditions to the
site in 1959, 1960, and 1962. Using mine-
sweepers and Navy divers, a large number of
artefacts were raised for the new Maritime
Museum of British Columbia in Victoria.
These artefacts included a 63 ft 4 in (19.3
m) long mast, anchor, capstan, pumps,
spars, rigging hardware, hull planking, windlass, nails, hawse pipe, viewing port, and a
copper penny beneath the mast-step. Today
only the anchor remains; the rest, uncon-
served, became piles of rust and dust within
a few years.

In 1985 the **Underwater Archaeological Society of
British Columbia** (UASBC) began documenting
the shipwreck site in response to the proposed construction of a log dump and
booming ground over the site. Excavation
under a provincial permit in June 1987 confirmed that the wreck had a teak hull and
deck, iron deck knees, and three mahogany
masts. Artefacts recovered included a
leather shoe, and a brass 'day and night'
telescope with lenses intact.

With site measurements and research by
local marine historian Dick Wells, the
UASBC identified the ship as the three-
masted barque *Lord Western*, lost on
4 December 1853. En route from Sooke to
San Francisco, *Lord Western* became water-

Diver swims over the log
cargo of Lord Western.
(UASBC/Mike Paris)

Telescope from Lord Western.
(UASBC/Mike Paris)

logged in a storm off Cape Flattery and
drifted north to Sydney Inlet. As she was one
of the first ships to export logs from British
Columbia, and as her artefacts, preserved in
heavy silt, were so rich, in March 1988 the
UASBC convinced the Province to designate
the site as a heritage site and the log company to move its log dump away from the
site.

Lord Western was built in Aberdeen, Scotland by Alexander Hall and Sons and
launched on 5 March 1840. Her hull measurements were 118 ft 4 in (36.1 m) by 25 ft
5 in (7.7 m) by 19 ft 5 in (5.9 m) and her
tonnage was 530 938/1000. She was carvel-
built, with a square stern and single quarter
galleries. From 1840 to 1852 *Lord Western*
sailed out of India. In 1842 she was condemned at Calcutta and developed a reputation as a leaky ship, a foreshadowing of her
eventual fate. In July 1852 she arrived at San
Francisco with 293 Chinese immigrants, her
first voyage to America. *Lord Western*'s return
trip lasted only ten days when she turned
back due to leaks.

In June 1988 the UASBC mapped the site
using a **Sonic High Accuracy Ranging and Positioning
System** (SHARPS). Excavation of the hull
permitted accurate measurements of scantling, rider keelson, frame, and ceiling
planking which helped confirm the wreck's

identification. All artefacts recovered in
the 1987 and 1988 excavations have been
conserved and stored at the Vancouver
Maritime Museum.

The mystery was solved and the wreck was
saved but much remains to be learned from
this site rich in artefacts from the mid-19th
century. T.F.B.

ADDITIONAL READING

Jacques, M., 1988, *A Report on the Sydney Inlet
   Mystery Wreck for the British Columbia Heritage
   Trust*, Vancouver.
Jacques, M., 1989, *Exploring the Lord Western*,
   Vancouver.
Wells, R.E., 1988, unpublished MS, *The Sydney
   Inlet Mystery Wreck*, Sooke.
Wells, R.E., 1989, addendum to unpublished
   MS, *The Sydney Inlet Mystery Wreck*, Sooke.

L'Orient

French flagship sunk in action in Aboukir
Bay, Egypt in 1798. On 1 July 1798 the
French Army landed on the shore of Egypt,
west of Alexandria. The French fleet of thirteen ships of the line and four frigates
under the command of Vice-Admiral Brueys
reached Aboukir Bay after the landing. One
month later Admiral Nelson discovered and
engaged Brueys's fleet moored in the bay.
After a furious fight, nine French ships were
taken and four sunk. Among the latter was
the flagship *L'Orient*, built at Toulon in 1791
and rated at 120 guns. The ship was 63 m
long, 16.25 m wide, and carried a crew of
850.

The wreck was discovered on 2 July 1983
by Jacques Dumas, helped by the French
Navy minehunter *Vinh Long* using a hull
sonar and a radio navigation system
installed on shore. Under his direction, two
expeditions were organized. After the death
of Dumas in 1984, another team was authorized to work on the site by the Egyptian
Organization of Antiquities (EOA). During
these three expeditions about 400 artefacts

L'Orient *blowing up during the Battle of the Nile, 1 August 1798: painting by Arnold George. (© National Maritime Museum Picture Library)*

were retrieved from the site, although there was no true research design. Because there have been no scientific publications, no general plan of the site and of the excavation area is known.

Among the artefacts recovered is the 14 m long rudder, whose bronze brace bears the inscription *Dauphin Royal*, the former name of the vessel, which was changed during the Revolution to *Sans Culotte* and then to *L'Orient*. Arabic printing types were also recovered, which had been taken from the Vatican printery; they recall Bonaparte's intention to print proclamations and advertisements in different languages. M.G.

Louisbourg Wrecks

Several 18th-century shipwrecks in or near the harbour of Louisbourg, on the Island of Cape Breton in eastern Nova Scotia, Canada. The Fortress of Louisbourg was built by France in the first half of the 18th century. It stood as a symbol of French dominance in the New World until 1758, when it was captured and totally destroyed by British forces. Since 1960 the fortress has undergone a massive reconstruction funded by the Federal Government of Canada through the National Historic Parks and Sites programme. Its staff of researchers have to date produced hundreds of reports on a wide variety of research topics.

Twenty-six ships have been documented as sunk in or near the harbour of Louisbourg between 1713 and 1758. Most were small merchant or fishing schooners, blown ashore in storms and quickly destroyed by the pounding surf. However, the siege of 1758 stands out as being responsible for the largest number of shipwrecks at any one time. The exact number sunk at this time is open to debate, although prior to the sinking of the seventy-four-gun *Prudent*, it is known that the townspeople witnessed the destruction of *Entreprenant*, *Capricieux*, and *Célèbre*. In addition, five smaller vessels were deliberately scuttled in the harbour entrance to block the English advance.

The first systematic attempt to survey the submerged cultural resources of Louisbourg Harbour was undertaken in 1961–2 by a group of divers from Acadia University in Nova Scotia. The group was directed by professors Erik S. Hansen and J. Sherman Bleakney. The group's efforts were concentrated on investigating those areas reported to contain shipwrecks or shipwreck material, such as cannon. As a result, the survey was successful in locating eight 18th-century shipwrecks. Four of these sites have since been surveyed by the Marine Archaeology Section of Parks Canada, and are further detailed below; two of them have been archaeologically mapped.

The 18th-century shipwrecks of Louisbourg are managed by the Federal Department of Canadian Heritage with the cooperation of Transport Canada. A permit

to operate diving charters within the harbour is required from the harbour master. Dive tour operators and divers must follow a number of visitation guidelines established by Parks Canada.

Description of shipwrecks

Célèbre, a sixty-four-gun, 150 ft (45.7 m) French warship built in Brest in 1755, sank on 21 July 1758. The wreck is located in approximately 7 m of water in the southwest arm of Louisbourg Harbour. It consists of a large mound of ballast, limited structure, and a variety of shipboard artefacts, extending over an area measuring 50 by 12 m.

The bow of the wreck is identified by the remains of several structural elements. One of these is the stemson, a badly eroded timber which extends 3 m out from the ballast mound with a slight upward curve. Other structural remains in the bow include floor timbers, partially visible below the forward end of the keelson. Very near the bow, on the port side, a small segment of ceiling planking overlies several framing timbers. The planking is badly abraded and worm eaten, making it impossible to take precise dimensions. The ends of the framing timbers, which extend 4 to 6 m outwards from the centreline of the ship, are all burnt. The burning coincides with the historical documentation and description of the siege (see McLennan, p. 28).

The midship area is notable for the surviving sections of pump well, pumps, mast-step and mainmast. The pump well was a planked, box-like structure surrounding the mainmast and the ship's pumps. The surviving elements include portions of the lower planking and the bottoms of six stanchions. The remains of two wooden pump tubes are located within the well on the port side of the mainmast. These stump-like features protrude approximately 25 cm out of a bottom cover of beach rock ballast. Forward of the pump well was the shot locker. Its remains reveal the outline of two equal sized compartments. The base or stump of the mainmast rises over 1 m above the ballast mound and is approximately 1 m in diameter.

The stern of the wreck is poorly represented. Visible remains are limited to a small section of what appears to be deadwood. Other features include several large cannon spread out over a mound of concreted rock and coral, and a series of badly eroded framing timbers. The lack of visible evidence for the stern structure is quite surprising and may be indicative of considerable pre-sinking destruction.

The most conspicuous of artefacts on the wreck site are the cannon. Thirty-three complete and four broken cannon of various calibres are spread out over the length of the site. All are heavily corroded and, although appearing quite massive and indestructible, are in fact very fragile. The site is littered with cannonballs and bar shot. Two types of pulley block sheaves are represented: metal sheaves and wooden sheaves. A small anchor, heavily corroded and extremely fragile, is located in the bow area. Five iron structural support pieces are visible. Two are complete and resemble breasthooks or knees. Both shingle and shifting ballast are found on the site. Other artefact types include ceramic and glass sherds, rope fragments, small sections of lead and copper sheathing, and one large cargo hook.

Prudent, a seventy-four-gun, 175 ft (53.3 m) French warship built in 1753 at Rochefort, sank on 25 July 1758. The wreck is located a short distance off Careening Point in approximately 5 m of water. Much of the remains are now encased in hard protective coral and are not as fragile as those of *Célèbre*. Noteworthy is the large number of exposed floor timbers. The wreck also has numerous blocks of shifting ballast and broken cannon. One of the more interesting features of the wreck site is the mast-step/shot locker area. Here a large mound of concreted cannonballs surrounds an open cavity where the mainmast once stood. The cavity still contains remnants of the burned-out mast. The size of the mound suggests that *Prudent* had an ample supply of shot remaining when she was destroyed.

Two wrecks are located in Barachois Cove, at the end of the southwest arm of Louisbourg Harbour, in approximately 4 m of water. *Entreprenant* and *Capricieux*, seventy-four-gun and sixty-four-gun French warships, *c.* 175 ft (53 m) and 150 ft (46 m) respectively, sank on 21 July 1758. Exposure to the northeast winds, subsequent wave action, and shallow water have created a ditch- or moat-like effect along the eastern perimeter of the site. Sand has been pushed up and over the wrecks, forming a mound which covers most of the remains. Material culture items were limited to two partial cannon and several piles of concreted cannonballs. W.S.

ADDITIONAL READING

Grenier, R., 1993, 'Le concept du musée sous le mer de Louisbourg', *Actes des Colloques de la Direction du Patrimoine: Le patrimoine maritime et fluvial*, Paris, 397–401.

Hansen, E.S. and Bleakney, J.S., 1962, *Underwater Survey of Louisbourg Harbour for Relics of the Siege of 1758*, Wolfville.

McLennan, J.S., 1919, *Louisbourg From its Foundation to its Fall*, London.

Stevens, E.W., 1989, unpublished MS, *Louisbourg Submerged Cultural Resource Survey*, Federal Archaeology Office, Parks Canada, Ottawa.

Lucerne

Wreck of a 19th-century schooner located near Long Island, Wisconsin, on Lake Superior. The site was surveyed by underwater archaeologists in 1990, under a joint project of the State Historical Society of Wisconsin, East Carolina University, the National Park Service, and the University of Wisconsin Sea Grant Institute, under the direction of Wisconsin State underwater archaeologist David Cooper.

Lucerne was a gaff-rigged, three-masted **Great Lakes** topsail schooner, 194.9 ft (59.4 m) in length, with a sharp clipper hull. She was built for the Great Lakes grain trade by the firm of Parsons and Humble of Tonawanda, New York, and was launched on 23 April 1873. She was owned and operated by the Winslow fleet out of Cleveland, Ohio. *Lucerne* was one of the new class of 200 ft (61 m) long Great Lakes schooners built in the early 1870s. The increased size was in response to the completion of the new St Clair Flats ship canal in 1871, allowing larger Great Lakes vessels to trade between the upper and lower lakes. After a fifteen-year career in the grain and coal trade, *Lucerne* was lost on her first season carrying Lake Superior iron ore, stranding in a blinding snowstorm in November 1886. The frozen bodies of three crewmen were found lashed to the sunken wreck's protruding masts, with 15 cm of ice on their bodies. There were no survivors.

Archaeological evidence from the 1990 survey indicates that the vessel was probably riding the storm out at anchor, when the vessel's lowered centreboard struck bottom off Long Island, breaking her back. Amateur archaeological excavations in the 1970s under the direction of Minnesota diver LaMonte Florentz revealed a wealth of extremely well-preserved artefacts, including clothing, food remains, personal effects, and ship's furnishings and equipment. Although the site was heavily collected by sport divers, and few artefacts now remain at the site, the Florentz collection is on display at the Duluth Canal Park Marine Museum and the Apostle Islands National Lakeshore in Bayfield. The 1970s *Lucerne* project also has the distinction of being Wisconsin's first underwater archaeological excavation.

The wreck of *Lucerne* is well preserved and

The wreck site of *Lucerne*, Long Island, Lake Superior. (D. Cooper) is a popular sport diving destination. Although her masts, cabins, and most of her decks are missing, much of the partially buried hull is intact, including the bow, stern, most of the sides, and the centre-board trunk. An Emerson and Walker patent windlass is located on her fo'c'sle deck, and much of her cargo of iron ore is in place. The site is easily accessed, being located in 6 m of water, and is generally favoured with good underwater visibility. Due to her well-preserved hull and collection of artefacts, the *Lucerne* site and collection are a significant source of information on Great Lakes schooner architecture and shipboard life. The site is listed in the **National Register of Historic Places**, and is protected by the State of Wisconsin and the US National Park Service. D.J.C.

ADDITIONAL READING

Cooper, D.J. (ed.),1991, *By Fire, Storm, and Ice: Underwater Archeological Investigations in the Apostle Islands*, Office of the State Archaeologist, Technical Publication no. 3, Madison.

Keller, J.M., 1984, *The 'Unholy' Apostles: Tales of Chequamegon Shipwrecks*, Bayfield.

Nelson, R., 1992, 'The Loss of the *Lucerne*', *Lake Superior Magazine*, October–November, 45–7.

Lusitania

British liner torpedoed in the Atlantic by a German U-boat in World War I. Built between 1905 and 1907 for the Cunard Steamship Company's Liverpool–New York service, *Lusitania* was the world's first quadruple-screw turbine-driven liner. At 785 ft (239 m) long overall and 30,396 gross tons, she set new standards for size and luxury, eclipsing by far all other passenger ships of her day. She was built to compete directly with the German ships that had ruled the Atlantic for nearly a decade, and was among the first liners to use steam turbine engines, high-tensile steel construction, and forced-air heating. She quickly established a high reputation among the travelling public, being the first ship in history to cross the Atlantic in under five days.

Construction funds and an operating subsidy for *Lusitania* and her sistership *Mauretania* were provided by the British Government, which in turn stipulated that the vessels were to be built using certain features of warship design and that they were subject to requisition as armed naval auxiliaries in times of national crisis. In 1914, at the outbreak of World War I, many British liners were withdrawn from commercial service and placed at the disposal of the Royal Navy. By the spring of 1915, *Lusitania* remained as the only large liner running

The New Cunard Atlantic liner Lusitania *under way. (Vancouver Maritime Museum)*

between Britain and the United States. Since passenger revenue was down sharply, in order to prevent running her at a loss, one of her four boiler rooms was shut down in an effort to conserve coal, thus reducing her maximum speed from 26 to 21 knots.

Lusitania departed New York on her 202nd crossing on 1 May 1915, with 1,959 passengers and crew. That same day, the German Embassy placed an advertisement in many of the New York newspapers warning that all British ships were liable to immediate destruction once they entered the war zone around Britain. It was an uneventful voyage until the afternoon of 7 May. At 2.10 p.m. the ship was about 18 km from the Old Head of Kinsale on the southern coast of Ireland when Captain Walter Schwieger of the German submarine U-20 fired a single torpedo into the side of the liner. The exact point of impact has never been positively ascertained although Schwieger stated in his log-book that the torpedo struck just behind the bridge.

The explosion of the torpedo was quickly followed by a second more powerful blast. This second explosion is universally believed to have sounded the death knell for the liner. To this day, its origin has not been satisfactorily explained although various theories have been advanced, such as boiler, munitions, and coal dust explosions. Within seconds *Lusitania* took a dramatic list to starboard and began to settle by the bow. In just eighteen minutes she had disappeared from view, with a loss of over 1,200 passengers and crew. The sinking shocked the American public and contributed to the entry of the United States into World War I on the side of Britain.

Despite the historical importance of the ship, the mystery surrounding her loss, and the relatively shallow depth of 90 m at which the wreck lies, *Lusitania* has been visited very infrequently over the years. In mid-1935 the ship was located using an early form of echo sounding, and later that same year a diver reached the wreck for the first time, becoming the first person to see the ship in twenty years.

Lusitania then lay silent for nearly three decades. In the early 1960s an American diver, John Light, bought the wreck from the British Government and began a series of diving operations in an effort to determine what caused her to sink. His team made over a hundred dives to the ship, but in the late 1960s, because of the limitations of diving technology at the time, operations at the wreck site ended before he was able to make positive conclusions.

In autumn 1982 a consortium headed by Oceaneering International spent over a month at the wreck, and the first known salvage work was done. Among the artefacts recovered were one of the ship's whistles, a docking telegraph, three propellers, portholes, windows, dining plates and utensils, and many other smaller items, including several hundred military fuses, proving beyond a doubt that the ship had been carrying illegal munitions. Although Oceaneering claims that the vessel was lost through the detonation of munitions, the company declines to make its documentation public, preventing independent analysis.

Over a decade later, in August 1993, the

next expedition was mounted. The leader was Dr Robert Ballard, the scientist who had located the wrecks of **Titanic** and **Bismarck**. This expedition disproved most of the conclusions reached by the Oceaneering team and gave the world its first good look at the ship in nearly eighty years. Despite the thousands of still photos and over sixty hours of video brought back by Ballard, nothing conclusive was found that could pinpoint the reason she sank. It is in fact doubtful that further examination of the wreck will shed any light on why she foundered, not only because the wreck lies on her starboard side (where the torpedo damage is) but because of the wreck's advanced state of decay. In the eighty years since her loss, tides and currents have taken their toll, and except for the hull, little of the ship is left that is easily recognizable.

The future of the wreck at present is uncertain. Late in 1994 a court battle began over the ownership of *Lusitania*. In March 1995, after several months of hearings, the United States District Court in Norfolk, Virginia, awarded ownership of the wreck and certain salvage rights to a New Mexico businessman, who claims to have bought John Light's title to *Lusitania*. Only the ship and her appurtenances were included in the court's award; personal effects of passengers and crew as well as cargo were not.

This American court decision is not recognized by the Irish Government because the ship lies within Irish territorial waters. To prohibit further tampering with the wreck, the Irish Minister of Arts and Culture placed an Underwater Heritage Order on the ship, which prohibits diving to or recovering artefacts from *Lusitania* without the sanction of the Irish authorities. E.S., B.S.

ADDITIONAL READING

Bailey, T.A. and Ryan, P.B., 1975, *The Lusitania Disaster*, New York.

Ballard, R.D. and Dunmore, S., 1995, *Exploring the Lusitania*, New York and Toronto.

Hickey, D. and Smith, G., 1981, *Seven Days to Disaster*, New York.

Hoehling, A.A. and Hoehling, M., 1956, *The Last Voyage of the Lusitania*, London.

Lauriat, C.E., Jr, 1915, *The Lusitania's Last Voyage*, Boston.

Sauder, E. and Marschall, K., 1991, *R.M.S Lusitania: Triumph of the Edwardian Age*, Palm Springs.

Lydia

Buried ship in San Francisco, discovered during excavation for a sewer line in 1978, partially removed after archaeological study, and later determined to be the former whaler *Lydia*, buried in landfill at the site in

Excavation of Lydia *in San Francisco, 1978 . (J.P. Delgado)*

1908. The 329 ton, 104 ft (31.7 m) long barque *Lydia* was built at Rochester, Massachusetts in 1840. *Lydia*'s entire career at sea was spent whaling, first from the eastern seaboard of the United States, and after 1870 from San Francisco, which had become the principal whaling port in the US. *Lydia*'s final whaling voyage, to the Arctic, was in 1897. The vessel was laid up at Oakland Creek, on San Francisco Bay, in 1901, when *Lydia* was sold. In May 1901 a newspaper account reported the vessel was being refitted for use as a barge.

Archaeological evidence suggests *Lydia* caught fire and sank, with the bow high in the air and the stern in the mud. In March 1907 the San Francisco newspapers reported that the partially submerged hulk was being pounded apart with sledges. In 1908 the construction of a seawall and landfill buried the ship's remains.

The buried remains of *Lydia* were encountered by sewer construction workers along the alignment of King Street, south of Market Street, on 13 June 1978. The battered remains, greatly damaged by the sewer's excavation, consisted of the bottom of the hull roughly midships; it was angled, which showed that the vessel had heeled to port, with the bow rising. After cleaning and documentation by a team led by project archaeologist Allen Pastron and maritime historian Roger Olmsted, a portion of the hull was cut free for preservation, and work on the sewer continued. Probing beyond the lagging for the sewer trench, the archaeologists found more substantial remains of the hull, rising above the turn of the bilge, which suggested a greater degree of preservation than initially suspected.

A follow-up excavation of the site adjacent to the sewer line in March 1980 disclosed that the starboard bow was largely intact, with foremast chain-plates and deck beams remaining in place. Working with the architectural data, a reconstruction of the ship prepared by naval architect Raymond Aker, and the San Francisco newspapers, Olmsted was finally able to identify the wreck as *Lydia*. The site was listed in the **National Register of Historic Places**, since despite the damage done in 1978 the buried hulk of *Lydia* is the most substantial surviving American whaling ship of the early 19th century, other than the preserved whaler *Charles W. Morgan*, a floating exhibit at Mystic Seaport, Connecticut. J.P.D.

ADDITIONAL READING

Pastron, A.G., Prichett, J. and Zeibarth, M. (eds), 1981, *Behind the Seawall: Historical Archaeology Along the San Francisco Waterfront* I, San Francisco.

Ma'agan Mikhael Ship
see **Israel**

Machault

French frigate sunk in 1760 during the Battle of Restigouche, Canada. In the autumn of 1759 New France was on the verge of capitulation to the British. Montreal, its morale at a low ebb owing to the recent surrender of Quebec City and Louisbourg, was rapidly running out of military supplies and funds and in desperate need of French assistance. After prolonged haggling between civilian businessmen and the State, a six-ship fleet was hastily assembled at Bordeaux and outfitted to sail for Canada. The flagship of the fleet was *Machault*. It had been built in Bayonne, France, in 1757 as a 550 *tonneaux* merchant frigate and later converted to a 500 *tonneaux* frigate-at-war. Initially pierced for twenty-six guns, it could have carried as many as thirty-two on its last voyage.

On 11 April 1760, one day after leaving port, the fleet was scattered by two British ships, and only three ships – *Machault*, *Marquis de Malauze* and *Bienfaisant* – were able to make contact and continue their journey. By mid-May the French had reached the Gulf of St Lawrence, where they captured a British ship and learned that the British had preceded them upriver. The decision was made to head for the safety of the Bay of Chaleur, where they arrived with a number of British ships they had captured en route. The French set up camp on the bank of the Restigouche River and dispatched a messenger to Montreal for instructions.

The British response to news of their presence was decisive. A flotilla commanded by Captain Byron, which included *Fame* (seventy-four guns), *Dorsetshire* (seventy guns), *Achilles* (sixty guns), and the frigates *Repulse* (thirty-two guns), and *Scarborough* (twenty guns) quickly set sail with orders to find and destroy the French ships. On 22 June the British contacted the enemy fleet. The French, retreating upriver, attempted to prevent the British ships from following by sinking small boats across the channel, and at strategic points set up shore batteries with weapons removed from their ships. After approximately two weeks of manoeuvring and sporadic fighting, the final engagement occurred on 8 July 1760. When surrender became inevitable, Captain Giraudais of *Machault* ordered all hands to remove as

Machault ceramics on display at the Restigouche interpretation centre. (Parks Canada)

much cargo from the ships as possible. With a dwindling powder supply and with water in its hold, *Machault* was defenceless and the order was given to abandon and scuttle it. *Bienfaisant* suffered the same fate and later in the day the British boarded and burned the abandoned *Marquis de Malauze*.

The Battle of Restigouche, the last naval engagement between France and Britain for the possession of North America, was a turning point in Canadian history. Montreal, denied its much-needed supplies and morale booster, now had neither the means nor the will to attempt to re-take Quebec City or properly defend itself. In short, the loss of the remains of the fleet contributed to the British conquest of New France.

In 1966 the Canadian national parks service, Parks Canada, was persuaded that a survey and excavation of the wrecks might answer questions on the attribution and dating of artefacts being recovered from Canadian land sites with French occupation dates of roughly the same period. In addition, questions could perhaps be answered concerning maritime transportation and trade that could not be dealt with so directly in other ways. Although one ship, *Marquis de Malauze*, was known to have been disturbed, it was expected that a great deal of 18th-century French material would still be contained on the other wrecks and that these artefacts could be used for comparative dating and to indicate the kinds of products that France was exporting to its North American colonies. In addition to the cargo remains, it was hoped that items that could be related to the crew would shed some light on a seaman's life in the mid-18th century. Efforts to find the remains of the fleet were begun.

In 1967 a preliminary underwater search located the remains of *Bienfaisant*. During the winters of 1968 and 1969, systematic **Magnetometer** surveys over the ice led to the discovery of *Machault*. In the summer of

1969, led by Parks Canada marine archaeologist Walter Zacharchuk, a full-scale excavation of the vessel was initiated. Extending over a four-year period, the Restigouche Project was, in its time, one of the largest underwater archaeological projects in the world.

Diving conditions in the Restigouche River were far from ideal. Strong currents, a lack of visibility, polluted waters and a bottom littered with the debris of fifty years of logging made diving a challenging enterprise. Despite these impediments, over 5,000 hours were logged underwater throughout the course of the project. To carry out the excavation a vast array of specialized equipment was utilized. A large purpose-built diving barge, housing compressors, pumps, generators, a deck crane, kitchen, and office space, proved indispensable to the project. **Airlifts**, for removing the overlying sediments, became the excavation tool of choice. To systematically control the progress of the excavation, a rigid grid system divided into 5 ft (1.5 m) square units was installed over the site.

Actual excavation on the site lasted for four years. During 1972, the fourth year of the project, the emphasis was on raising selected portions of the ship's hull for detailed surface recording and eventual display. Using submersible chain saws, elements of the bow and stern plus a large midship section were detached from the hull and brought to the surface. The raised hull timbers were extremely well preserved, with both the stem- and sternpost clearly exhibiting incised roman numeral draught marks.

Although the historical record indicated that the French had removed much of the supplies from the frigate prior to its sinking, the enormous number of artefacts recovered during excavation indicated that a great deal of material had been left on board. Common items included ceramics, glass, clay pipes, leather shoes, shot, and other munitions. Also recovered were a variety of rigging elements, cables and rope, sailmaker's tools, a selection of carpenter's tools, plus foodstuffs. Rarer items included such things as religious objects, personal possessions, articles of clothing, surgical equipment, small arms, and navigational instruments. Upon analysis, researchers discovered unexpected quantities of certain types of artefacts that one would not normally associate with a military relief effort. Unusually high quantities of Chinese export porcelain and a variety of other refined and decorated tablewares suggested a cache of private venture merchandise belonging to some enterprising person on the vessel. The diverse collection of artefacts from *Machault* have revealed a wealth of information on aspects of 18th-century maritime travel, trade, defence at sea, and a variety of daily human activities.

The history of the battle, a selection of artefacts, and sections of *Machault* can be experienced at Parks Canada's visitor reception centre at Pointe-à-la-Croix, Quebec, overlooking the site of the Battle of the Restigouche. W.S.

ADDITIONAL READING

Beattie, J. and Pothier, B., 1996, *The Battle of the Restigouche*, Studies in Archaeology, Architecture and History, Ottawa.

was rediscovered and documented in 1990. USS *Macon* was a 785 ft (239 m) long, 133 ft (40.5 m) diameter dirigible built by the Goodyear-Zeppelin Company of Akron, Ohio in 1933. The hull was framed with Duralumin, an aluminium alloy, and was covered with cotton cloth painted with six layers of aircraft varnish or 'dope'. Lift was provided by twelve helium-filled gas cells and eight 560 hp German Maybach engines mounted inboard along the keels, four to a side. The engines each drove a geared, three-bladed propeller that could be tilted as much as 90 degrees. Fuel tanks, water bal-

tear loose and rupture the helium cells. *Macon*, based at Moffett Field at Sunnyvale, California, on San Francisco Bay, was returning from patrolling the coast when a gust of wind struck the ship on the evening of 12 February 1935. The damaged dirigible shot up nearly 1,500 m before dropping tail first into the sea off Point Sur, 160 km south of San Francisco. Two crew members were lost, but the remainder of the crew launched life rafts. Nearby Navy cruisers on manoeuvres rescued them, but within forty minutes *Macon* collapsed and sank in deep water. The loss of *Macon* ended the US

USS Macon *in flight over New York City, c. 1933–4. (US Naval Historical Center)*

Bryce, D., 1984, *Weaponry from the Machault, an 18th-century French Frigate*, Studies in Archaeology, Architecture and History, Ottawa.

Sullivan, C., 1986, *Legacy of the Machault: A Collection of 18th-century Artefacts*, Studies in Archaeology, Architecture and History, Ottawa.

Zacharchuk, W. and Waddell, P.J.A., 1984, *The Excavation of the Machault, an 18th-century French Frigate*, Studies in Archaeology, Architecture and History, Ottawa.

USS *Macon*

Submerged wreck of a **US Navy** dirigible which crashed off the California coast in 1935, and

last stored in fabric bags, living quarters for the eighty-three man crew, and a hanger for aircraft were located in the hull. A control car, located below the ship and near the bow, housed the navigational equipment and controls for the engines, rudders, elevators, and ballast. *Macon* carried five F9C-2 Sparrowhawk biplane aircraft that were hoisted and deployed from a retracting 'trapeze' that hooked onto a ring on the upper wing of the planes.

Built for the US Navy, *Macon* was the largest aircraft in the world when launched to serve as flying aircraft carrier. The dirigible was lost when strong winds damaged the frames near the stern, allowing a tail fin to

Navy's use of lighter-than-air ships as offensive weapons.

A local fisherman snagged a piece of the wreck in 1980, but it was not until 1990–91 that the submerged dirigible was relocated and surveyed. At the instigation of the National Museum of Naval Aviation Foundation, Pensacola, Florida, the US Navy sent its three-man **Submersible** *Sea Cliff* to investigate the site where the fisherman had snagged the wreckage. The remains of USS *Macon* were found in 440 m of water in June 1990. Officials from the Monterey Bay Aquarium Research Institute (MBARI) mounted a return expedition to the site in February 1991 to survey the site by remotely operated vehicle. The wreck lies collapsed in three major debris fields, roughly incorporating the bow, midships, and stern of *Macon*. Four Sparrowhawk aircraft were found in the wreckage. Plans to recover the aircraft for the National Museum of Aviation have been discussed, but not yet undertaken. Title to the wreck and the aircraft remains with the US Navy, and any recovery will be done to archaeological standards. J.P.D.

ADDITIONAL READING

Vaeth, G.J., 1992, 'USS *Macon*: Lost and Found', *National Geographic*, 181, 1, 114–27.

Madrague de Giens Wreck

Roman wreck discovered off the small fishing port of La Madrague, located on the northwest coast of the Giens peninsula, not far from Toulon, France. Of the numerous wrecks from the Mediterranean, the Roman wreck from the Madrague de Giens is particularly important as a result of the interest of the site itself and the extent of the excavations of which it has been the subject.

The wreck, which lies at a depth of 20 m, was discovered in 1967 by divers from the French Navy. It was largely covered by a thick layer of Poseidon weed which protected the integrity of the site. Only a small part of the wreck was visible at the time of its discovery, so a **Magnetometer** survey prior to the excavation was carried out to define the contours of the find. The site was 40 m long and 12 m wide and was therefore one of the largest known ancient wrecks yet to be found. From 1972 the wreck was the object of a series of important excavations organized by a team from the Centre National de la Recherche Scientifique (CNRS) and the University of Provence under the direction of André Tchernia and Patrice Pomey. The work ended in 1982 after eleven seasons which comprised the most important underwater archaeological excavation in the **Mediterranean Sea**. During the excavation stereophotogrammetry (see **Photogrammetry**) was employed for mapping, and a computerized system for the recording of archaeological data was also established.

The ship's cargo included about 6,000 to 6,500 wine amphoras (Dressel Type 1B) from Italy. The excavation showed that they were stacked in staggered rows in three layers reaching a height of 3 m. Most of the amphoras displayed potter's stamps of which the most frequent was that of Publius Veveius Papus; this allowed archaeologists to trace their origin to Terracina, to the south of Rome. Other amphoras of various types may have been part of the cargo or for on board consumption. A secondary cargo of black-glazed ceramics (Campanian) and of

Left: General view of the Madrague de Giens Wreck during the excavation: foreground, the hull; background, the cargo of amphoras. (A. Chéné, Centre Camille Jullian, CNRS)

common wares was placed in boxes above the amphoras. Towards the stern, the cabin area was noted for the presence of table wares, kitchen wares, and other various objects. The cargo, the artefacts, and the coins found on board allow archaeologists to date the shipwreck to between 75 and 60 BC. Curiously, a number of local ballast stones were found in large voids in the cargo. It seems that divers used these stones to descend and recover part of the cargo soon after the shipwreck. Thus was found, for the first time, evidence of the work of these divers, the *urinatores*, who are well attested in ancient texts.

The hull is well preserved and can be reconstructed as being 40 m in length, 9 m in width and with a depth of hold of 4.5 m. These dimensions imply a total cargo weight of 400 tonnes, with a ship displacement of about 520 tonnes. With such a capacity, the Madrague de Giens Wreck is one of the largest merchant ships used in antiquity, known by the name of *myriophoroi*, in other words capable of carrying 10,000 amphoras.

The hull seems particularly well built and robust, conforming to the imposing size of the ship. Of classical structure for a Roman vessel, it comprised a strong axial framing composed of numerous elements (keel, fore foot, stempost, cutwater, sternpost, inner post, false post), double planking, assembled entirely by mortise-and-tenon joints pegged from the inside, and covered with a sheet of lead. The frame is comprised of regularly alternated floor timbers and half frames. A large keelson, playing the

role of mast-step timber, doubles the axial frame, while the stringers, nailed on the frames, reinforced the hull longitudinally. These were alternated with movable ceiling planks.

The study of the hull construction demonstrates that the ship was built according to a shell technique where the planking plays the primary structural role. It is highly likely, therefore, that the construction processes are very close to the shell-first method in which the planking is assembled before the frames.

The ship's form is characterized by a central section with a sharp bottom and a prominent keel. Aft, the overhanging stern is doubled by a prominent false post. Fore, the keel is extended by a long fore foot which ended with a concave stempost tilted towards the back. This stempost is reinforced towards the front by an imposing cutwater in the form of a ram. These peculiar shapes confer a characteristic of the ship that is found on a number of iconographic documents, notably the mosaic from the thermal baths of Themetra in Tunisia, which depicts a sailing ship with shape and proportions resembling the ship from the Madrague de Giens. These documents give precise indications that allow us to reconstruct the upper parts and the rigging of the Madrague de Giens Wreck. Equipped with a very elaborate hull and powerful square sails carried by two (perhaps three) masts, the Madrague de Giens Ship, despite its large size and substantial tonnage, must have possessed good nautical qualities and have been an impressive sailing ship. P.P.

ADDITIONAL READING

Pomey, P., 1982, 'Le navire romain de la Madrague de Giens', *Comptes Rendus de l'Académie des Inscriptions et Belles-Lettres*, Jan–Mar, 133–54.

Tchernia, A., 1982, 'Roman Divers' Salvage at La Madrague de Giens', in *The Sixth International Scientific Symposium of the World Underwater Federation*, London.

Tchernia, A., 1987, 'The Madrague de Giens Wreck: A Roman Freighter Yields its Secrets', *UNESCO Courier*, 11, 11.

Tchernia, A., Pomey, P., and Hesnard, A., 1978, *L'épave romaine de la Madrague de Giens*, Supplement 34 of *Gallia*, Paris.

Magnetometer

An instrument that measures the magnetic field of the earth. Buried or submerged ferromagnetic materials, such as iron, distort the earth's field on a local level, such distortions often being called anomalies. Magnetometers are one of the most important survey tools used in underwater archaeology because they can detect ferromagnetic materials buried or encrusted in the sea floor.

The magnetic needle of a compass rotates and aligns itself with the magnetic field of the earth. The direction and magnitude of the earth's field can vary from point to point on the earth's surface. The field will likely have a dip, or inclination, angle relative to horizontal and will also have a rotation angle relative to the north–south direction. The magnetic poles of the earth are displaced from the geographic poles by about 18 degrees of latitude.

The most common unit of magnetic field intensity used in underwater archaeology is the gamma. A gamma is equivalent to one nanotesla in the MKSA system of units. The maximum intensity of the earth's magnetic field is approximately 50,000 gammas.

The earth's magnetic field is constantly changing. Secular changes take place over a period of decades or centuries. On a regular basis, the earth's field is changing to the order of 50 gammas per year. Of more importance to the user of a magnetometer are shorter-term variations. Most important is the diurnal variation. These field variations have a period of about a day and have an average amplitude of approximately 25 gammas. Magnetic storms are also a source of interfering magnetic noise. These storms, which correlate well with sunspot activity, can create short-term variations that have amplitudes as large as 1,000 gammas.

An anomaly in the earth's field is caused by an induced field being created in a ferromagnetic object. This induced field can either constructively add to the earth's field and create a positive anomaly or it can destructively add to it, causing a negative anomaly. The magnitude of the field induced in an object depends on the size, shape, orientation, and magnetic susceptibility of the object. The direction and intensity of the earth's field also influences the magnitude of the induced field. The magnitude of the anomaly depends on the depth of burial of the object, distance to the magnetometer, and orientation of the magnetometer.

In the early days of geophysical exploration, magnetometers were high-precision mechanical devices. The Schmidt Balance is a sensitive mechanical balance consisting of a permanent magnet that rotates and cre-

Contour logging using a magnetometer, at the site of King Philip. *(J.P. Delgado)*

ates a torque about its pivot point. The sensitivity of these mechanical instruments is about 10 gammas. Immediately before World War II, several types of electronic flux-gate magnetometers were being developed as magnetic geophysical exploration tools. The threat of submarine warfare diverted this development to airborne submarine detection systems. A good example of this effort is the AN/ASQ-3A that was developed by Bell Laboratories and the Naval Ordinance Laboratory. The sensitivity of these instruments is about one gamma.

The proton precession magnetometer was developed in the mid-1950s by Packard and Varian. This magnetometer was the most important development in magnetometry. The proton precession device has no moving parts and was ideally suited for airborne, land, and underwater surveys. Most elements have a magnetic moment. The spinning atoms will align themselves with the earth's magnetic field. Consider an externally applied magnetic field perpendicular to earth's field. The spinning atoms will align themselves with the resultant field consisting of the applied field and the earth's field. When the external field is removed, the spinning atoms will precess back to the alignment of the earth's field. The precession is similar to that of a gyroscope; its frequency is $w = \gamma H$, and is typically around 2,000 Hz. The precession frequency is directly proportional to the earth's field. A frequency counter is used to measure the frequency and turn it into a field value. Typical proton precession magnetometers can take a new reading approximately every one to two seconds and have a sensitivity of approximately one tenth of a gamma.

To date, caesium magnetometers are the most sensitive and fastest devices on the commercial market. The caesium magnetometer uses an infrared light source to optically pump the excited electrons in a caesium vapour. The population of the various energy levels in the caesium atom is related to the ambient earth's magnetic field. A caesium magnetometer can produce up to 100 readings per second and has a sensitivity of the order of milligammas.

Magnetic reference stations are commonly used to eliminate much of the short-term variations. A magnetic reference station, or base station, is a second magnetometer positioned at a stationary point close to the ongoing survey. Because this station is fixed, variations in the measured field are due to interference such as diurnal and magnetic storm variations. The base station records these transients which can be used later to correct the field data for signals caused by noise.

Global Positioning Systems (GPS) are commonly used to time and position stamp each magnetometer reading. This is particularly useful for offshore maritime surveys. The spatially referenced data is then easily analysed and contour plotted. In addition, suspected targets can be readily relocated.

Difficulties arise in interpreting data obtained from magnetic field surveys because a unique set of parameter values cannot be determined from a measurement of magnetic field patterns. In other words, a large number of parameter value combinations can produce an observed magnetic anomaly, and it is very difficult to reconstruct a physically valid image of the buried objects causing the anomaly. This problem of data interpretation is common to many geophysical techniques. An often used semi-empirical approach to magnetic data interpretation involves the use of simple models which mini-mize the number of parameters involved. For example, if it appears that the object is not too elongated then the use of a solid iron sphere model may be justified.

Gradiometers are sometimes used in mar-itime surveys. A gradiometer survey requires two closely spaced magnetometers. The readings from each are subtracted from the other. It is assumed that large-scale varia-tions in the earth's field and magnetic noise are identical at each magnetometer and the gradient will be zero. Anomalies caused by small objects will be different at each mag-netometer and will show up as a non-zero gradient value. s.s.

The Magor Pill Boat, on its lifting cradle within a holding tank, looking towards the bow. (National Museums & Galleries of Wales)

ADDITIONAL READING

Arnold, J. Barto III and Clausen, C.J., 1975, 'A Magnetometer Survey with Electronic Positioning Control and Calculator Plotting System', *International Journal of Nautical Archaeology*, 3, 353–66.

Breiner, S., 1973, *Applications Manual for Portable Magnetometers*, Sunnyvale, California.

Clausen, C.J. and Arnold, J. Barto III, 1976, 'The Magnetometer and Underwater Archaeology, Magnetic Delineation of Individual Shipwreck Sites: A New Technique', *International Journal of Nautical Archaeology*, 5, 159–69.

Dean, M. *et al.* (eds), 1992, *Archaeology Underwater: The NAS Guide to Principles and Practice*, London.

Magor Pill Boat

Medieval boat discovered in 1994 by an amateur archaeologist walking the intertidal mudflats of the Severn Estuary at Magor Pill, to the east of Newport, South Wales. The Severn Levels are renowned for the remark-able range of archaeological sites preserved in the mud, from prehistoric and medieval trackways and Iron Age house structures to medieval fishtraps and the remains of boats.

The wreck was excavated at low tides by the Glamorgan-Gwent Archaeological Trust Ltd, funded by Cadw: Welsh Historic Monu-ments. Following its excavation a collabora-tive team comprising Laing-GTM, GGAT, and the National Museums & Galleries of Wales recovered the hull, raising it intact on a cradle and transporting it to dedicated conservation facilities in Cardiff. Full record-ing was carried out while the hull was sup-ported in the lifting cradle in a custom-built tank, prior to the dismantling of the timbers for cleaning and conservation pre-treatment.

The forward section of the clinker-built boat survived for a length of about 7 m (width 3.3 m). All the main timbers were of oak. The last surviving ring on dendro-chronologically examined samples provided

a felling date of 1240. A rabbeted keel, broken in the midships area, ran to the bow end, where it was scarfed to an eroded and incomplete stempost. Thin ceiling planking lay above floor timbers and futtocks; outer planking was of radially split oak, fastened together with iron nails and roves. Floor tim-bers were joggled to match the underlying planks, and attached with treenails to the hull planking, but not the keel. The boat can be reconstructed as a 'keel' within the north-ern European tradition of shipbuilding, having an overall length of between 13.2 and 14.3 m and a beam of 3.7 m. An analysis of the 'language' of construction raises the pos-sibility that she was built somewhere on the shore of the Severn Estuary in the 13th cen-tury. The boat would have had a single square sail rig and been capable of coastal, inter-estuarine, and short sea voyages. Part of her cargo, iron ore, survived in the hull above a wattle hurdle.

The boat is important in providing a rare opportunity to study the fairly complete remains of a medieval ship from the west of Britain, from a period otherwise represented largely by boat fragments reused within waterfront structures. The boat was donated by the Duke of Beaufort to the National Museums and Galleries of Wales, and will be reconstructed in a gallery in Cardiff. M.R.

ADDITIONAL READING

Nayling, N., 1995, 'The Excavation, Recovery and Provisional Analysis of a Medieval Wreck from Magor Pill, Gwent Levels', *Archaeology of the Severn Estuary*, 6, 85–95.

Redknap, M. and Nayling, N., in press, 'Coastal Transport in 13th-century Wales, with Special Reference to the Magor Pill Boat: A Preliminary Statement', pre-printed paper of the Medieval Europe 1997 Bruges International Conference.

Mahdia Wreck

The first ancient wreck in the **Mediterranean Sea** to be scientifically excavated, either a Greek or Roman merchantman of the late 2nd or 1st century BC which sank off Tunisia. In 1907 Greek sponge divers working some 5 km northeast of Cape Africa (within the har-bour town of Mahdia) at a depth of 39 m noticed ancient works of art and retrieved some, selling them in Tunisia. This was noticed by A. Merlin, in charge of the Antiq-uities Service of the French protectorate of Tunisia, who realized that a major find of Late Hellenistic art (2nd/1st century BC) had been discovered, and traced the site.

From 1908 to 1913 he conducted the first underwater excavation ever performed. He never dived himself, but did his best to retrieve data from questioning the divers about their finds, and documented them, even reconstructing a site plan (which was unpublished and is now lost). The finds form a main source for the study of Hel-lenistic art. Stylistic datings varied within a span of about fifty years, which affected the dating of the shipwreck. Pottery from the wreck was only evaluated in the 1990s, resulting in a later date (second quarter of the 1st century BC) than had previously been thought.

Merlin realized that the works of art only formed an addition to the ship's bulk cargo of some seventy columns of Greek marble in an unfinished condition, and a large number of amphoras. Merlin salvaged all works of art recognized by his divers, and some metal items of the ship's equipment. He removed a number of marble columns that encumbered the salvage of works of art. Some timbers were recovered and identified as pine.

In 1948 Jacques-Yves Cousteau revisited

the site with **SCUBA**-divers. His main achievement appears to have been the removal of two lead anchor stocks. In 1953–4 G. de Frondeville investigated the site again, with two campaigns of professional underwater excavation. His interest was focused on the ship itself. In order to reach its floor (containing elm wood), de Frondeville removed some columns left in place by his predecessors. He salvaged much of the keel and dozens of plank fragments (in the Bardo Museum, Tunis). There is no final report, but his publications give an idea of the construction of the hull.

During preparations for the Mahdia exhibition at Bonn, the German Society for Underwater Archaeology (DEGUWA) and the Tunisian National Institute for the Patrimony (INP), with Mensun Bound of **Oxford University MARE**, resurveyed the site in a joint operation in 1993. The divers found parts of the bottom still preserved, but hardly any amphoras. A major new survey of the wreck was undertaken in the late 1990s.

The most significant part of the ship known is the keel, of a stepped cross-section indicating that the garboards met the keel at a Y (forming a V bilge), and that the bottom was double planked, with a lead sheathing. The keel sections preserved at Tunis are straight, without any scarfs. The lower parts of the stem- and sternposts seem to have been preserved but reliable data is lacking. According to S. Hechmi of the de Frondeville team nothing like a keelson or a mast-step was found in 1953–4.

The measurements of the hull and the shape of the hold's bottom may be gleaned from the position of the columns, as plotted by de Frondeville, and the position of the anchor stocks plotted by Merlin. The columns had been stowed in several groups, one tightly after the other except for one wider interval. They did not cover the north (stern) section of the hull, where Merlin's divers had noticed numerous amphoras. It should be noted that Merlin described the position of five lead anchor-stocks in a line as 'right in front of the southernmost columns'. Their lengths add up to some 10 m, markedly more than the bottom's width, as suggested by the columns. The anchors rested on the fo'c'sle when the ship sank, showing the deck was wider than the bottom. This implies that the sides inclined, suggesting a tapered or clipper stem rather than a 'false ram' like that on the **Madrague de Giens Wreck**.

The anchor-stocks in their relation to the columns give an idea of the ship's deck plan and overall dimensions (length *c.* 40.6 m, beam *c.* 13.8 m). The length/beam ratio of 2.92 is low though credible: the ship seems to have been short and squat, which would have improved its rigidity in the longitudinal axis, suggesting it was conceived for carrying heavy cargo.

The same impression may be derived from frame sections of 15 cm square. De Frondeville mentions one frame as being 'far stronger than the rest', but fails to give either its measurements or its position. Double planking with a thick inner shell assembled by mortises and tenons also demonstrates the ship's stout construction. There should also have been strong deck beams, possibly in the interstices between the groups of columns.

A cabin on the quarter-deck is suggested by the bronze hinges of a door. Some flat clay tiles might be connected with it, or with hatch covers. Bronze bearings of a pump exist, as do parts of catapults, perhaps from the cargo. We do not know if there was a mast where two groups of columns (perhaps placed below the hatches) leave space for a mast-bench. A light foremast (artemo), pivoted for doubling as a derrick, is likely; a few brailing rings exist, perhaps from an artemo sail. In theory, the ship might have been towed by oared vessels, as seems to have been practised in antiquity.

Many features of the Mahdia Wreck (keel, double planking, copper nails, lead sheathing, a bilge pump, use of elm wood) recur at Madrague de Giens, but this gives no clue to its home country. Most of its cargo came from Greece, and was probably bound for Italy, but there also are lead ingots from Spain, and pottery from North Africa. O.H.

ADDITIONAL READING

Baumer, U. *et al.*, 1995, 'Neue Forschungen zum antiken Schiffsfund von Mahdia', in *In Poseidons Reich*, Antike Welt 26, Mainz.

de Frondeville, G., 1956, *Les visiteurs de la mer*, Paris.

Gagsteiger, G. *et al.*, 1994, 'Neue Forschungen zum antiken Schiffsfund von Mahdia', in G. Hellenkemper Salies, H.-H. von Prittwitz und Gaffron, G. Bauchhenss, *Das Wrack*, vol. 1, Bonn.

Hellenkemper Salies, G. and H.-H. von Prittwitz und Gaffron, G. Bauchhenss (eds), 1994, *Das Wrack*, 2 vols, exhibition handbook, Rheinisches Landesmuseum Bonn.

Höckmann, O., 1994, 'Das Schiff', in G. Hellenkemper Salies and H.-H. von Prittwitz und Gaffron, G. Bauchhenss (eds), *Das Wrack*, vol. 1, Bonn.

Merlin, A., 1911, 'Les recherches sous-marines de Mahdia (Tunisie), *Comptes Rendus Académie Inscriptions et Belles-Lettres*, 556–65.

Rotroff, S.I., 1994, 'The Pottery', in G. Hellenkemper Salies, H.-H. von Prittwitz und Gaffron, G. Bauchhenss (eds), *Das Wrack*, vol. 1, Bonn.

Mainz Boats

Several ancient boats found at Mainz, Germany. Once a Roman legion's camp and later the capital of Germania Superior, Mainz is strategically sited on the River Rhine opposite the mouth of the River Main. Its early navigational importance is clear from the discovery of two ancient merchant harbours, and one ancient warship harbour.

In 1967 a boat was discovered when part of the warship harbour ('Brand') was found. In the winter of 1981/2 at a construction site close by the 'Brand', the remains of a wooden pier and wrecks of five 4th-century AD vessels and the 'ghost' of a sixth, embedded in a concrete wall, came to light. The

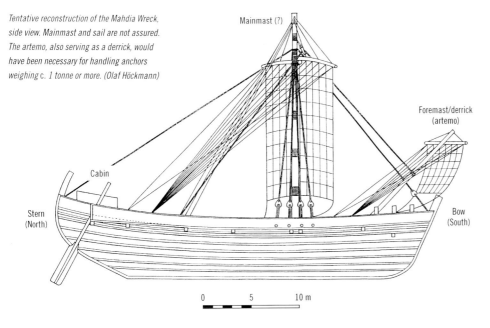

Tentative reconstruction of the Mahdia Wreck, side view. Mainmast and sail are not assured. The artemo, also serving as a derrick, would have been necessary for handling anchors weighing c. 1 tonne or more. (Olaf Höckmann)

Mainmast (?)

Foremast/derrick (artemo)

Cabin

Stern (North)

Bow (South)

0   5   10 m

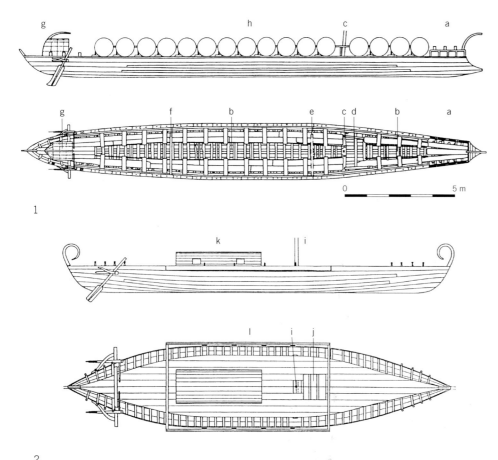

1 *Mainz Boats, Type A (boats 1, 4, 7, 9)*: a *low bow castle* (conjecture based e.g. on amber model from Cologne); b '*hold*'; c *mast-step, mast;* d *working space for handling mast;* e *beam (position conjectural; or combined with mast-bench?);* f *beam;* g *helmsman's cabin (conjecture based on representations, e.g. from Neumagen);* h *shields on rack (stanchion holes in gunwale extant).*
2 *Mainz Boats, Type B (boat 3)*: i *mast-step, mast;* j *bailing hatch in deck (conjecture);* k *passenger cabin (conjecture based on model from Rethel);* l *thole frame (beam conjecture).*

Zwammerdam type, they are unusual for their light construction. O.H.

ADDITIONAL READING

Esser, H., 1975, *10 Jahre Ausgrabungen in Mainz, 1965–1974*, Mainz.

Höckmann, O., 1982, 'Spätrömische Schiffsfunde in Mainz', *Archäologisches Korrespondenzblatt*, 12, 131–50.

Höckmann, O., 1984, 'Zur Bauweise, Funktion und Typologie der Mainzer Schiffe', in G. Rupprecht (ed.), 1984, *Die Mainzer Römerschiffe*, 3rd edn, Mainz, 44–77.

Höckmann, O., 1985, 'Late Roman River Craft from Mainz, Germany', in O.L. Filgueiras (ed.), *Local Boats: Fourth International Symposium on Boat and Ship Archaeology, Porto*, BAR 438, Oxford, 23–34.

Höckmann, O., 1993, 'Late Roman Rhine Vessels from Mainz, Germany', *International Journal of Nautical Archaeology*, 22, 125–35.

Höckmann, O., 1995, 'Reste römischer Prähme und Hafenanlagen vom Kappelhof in Mainz', *Mainzer Archäologische Zeitschrift*, 2, 131–66.

Rupprecht, G. (ed.), 1984, *Die Mainzer Römerschiffe*, 3rd edn, Mainz.

Malcolm Boat

A late 18th-century colonial sloop that was abandoned in a slough off the Ashley River about 12 km from Charleston, South Carolina. The 1780 edition of Falconers Marine Dictionary (Falconer 1970) defines a sloop as 'a small vessel furnished with one mast, the main-sail of which is attached to a gaff above, to the mast on its foremost edge, and to a long boom below; by which it is occasionally shifted to either quarter'. The 1815 edition adds, 'having a fixed steering bowsprit, and a jib-stay' (Falconer 1970a). The Malcolm Boat matches this contemporary description of a sloop. The published works of William Avery Baker and Howard I. Chapelle have summarized the evolution and role of the sloop in American colonial history, while those of P.C. Coker and Rusty Fleetwood have placed these watercraft in a regional perspective.

The Malcolm Boat was discovered in 1974 by a fossil hunter, after whom the site is named, who noticed timbers protruding from the marsh owing to erosion of the river bank. Archaeologists from the South Carolina

Monument Service, under G. Rupprecht, documented them *in situ*, in unfavourable conditions, and salvaged them. They are now in the Museum für antike Schiffahrt at Mainz, where the preserved remains are shown next to full-size replicas of both types. The ghost, *c.* 10 m long and differing from the other boats, whose length is *c.* 22 m, was not recovered.

The four hulls represent a type (A) of very sleek, shallow-draught, and low-sided undecked river warships with fifteen oars per side, of the *lusoria* type, which in the 4th century was the standard warship for defending the Late Empire's river borders (i.e. the rivers Rhine and Danube) against Barbarians, most of them of Germanic stock. The type goes back to oared cargo-boats in Egypt, and apparently was introduced to the Rhine by the secessionist 'Emperor of Gaul', Postumus, *c.* AD 260.

All boats consist of oak (the outer sides coated with pitch), as opposed to the general **Mediterranean** practice where pine or fir predominated, apart from oak keels; in this they resembled earlier merchantmen of the Celtic tradition around the English Channel. The same seems to apply to strakes fixed by clenched iron nails. Drilled holes closed by pegs (covered by frames), how-

ever, indicate there had been a stage when strakes had been fastened to temporary moulds for forming a shell into which composite frames could be inserted (Mediterranean shell-first fashion). The Mainz 'mould-first' technique unites Celtic and Southern traditions. It would have eased mass production by following standard plans, defined by the moulds.

Conspicuous features of Type A are the mast-step (preserved in Boat 9), formed by an enlarged floor timber, and narrow 'holds' in the centre line, with vertical sides. The mast insertion is inclined forward; this, and the foreship position, may suggest a lateen rig. The 'hold', useful for supplying Roman outposts on the enemy bank, might derive from merchant *lusoriae*.

Type B is represented by Boat 3. It is shorter and wider than the *lusoriae*, but is not a cargo boat. There is a mast-step, but internal timbers were removed in antiquity (as is the case in all the boats). Reconstruction as a state 'yacht' for taking officials to their places of duty (compare a model from Rethel, France) is conjectural.

In April 1982 two cargo prams (dating to the end of the 1st century AD) came to light at a merchant harbour *c.* 500 m upstream of the former site. Generally conforming to the

Institute of Archaeology and Anthropology at the University of South Carolina excavated and stabilized the site in 1992. Analysis of the artefacts and context in which the craft was found reveals that the boat was stripped and abandoned towards the end of the 18th century after a lengthy career. Study of the remains reveals a round-hulled keeled vessel with a transom stern. The reconstructed hull is 41 ft 10^1/$_4$ in (12.8 m) long, has a beam of approximately 11 ft 9^1/$_4$ in (3.6 m) and an estimated depth of hold of 4 ft 11 in (1.5 m). A displacement of approximately 24 tons is suggested. The vessel had a fairly sharp entry below the waterline and was roomy above. She had a full-bodied midsection that carried aft to the narrow transom. Construction features observed on the hull suggest a boat designed for strength and with the ability to carry heavy loads. A transom stern would have enhanced the vessel's cargo carrying capacity and seaworthiness for offshore voyages and appears to have been the stern of choice of colonial shipwrights in South Carolina. Yet the hull would have had a graceful shape and was no doubt pleasing to the eye.

The hull was fashioned entirely from woods locally available and abundant in South Carolina's coastal region. These included Southern yellow pine keel, keelson and planks, cypress garboards, and posts and frames fashioned from both live oak and white oak.

The Malcolm Boat is one of a number of archaeological finds of boat remains in South Carolina that date back to the mid- to late 18th century. These include the **Brown's Ferry Vessel**, a riverine and coastal schooner, and the **Clydesdale Plantation Vessel**, a similar craft which had been incorporated into a dike on the Savannah River during the late 18th century. Each vessel type was suited to a slightly different role in varied environmental conditions. Their significance lies in what these hulls can tell us about the watercraft and the people who built them. These small vessels were constructed using traditional methods handed down from generations of boat-builders; drawn plans for them are virtually non-existent. The Malcolm Boat represents one of the earliest examples in the Southeast of a round-hulled craft built locally using conventional European design and construction techniques that had the capability of being used for long passages in open sea conditions and of conducting trade as far away as the Caribbean and South America. C.A.

ADDITIONAL READING

Amer, C.F. *et al.*, 1993, *The Malcolm Boat (38CH803): Discovery, Stabilization, Excavation, and Preservation of an Historic Sea Going Small Craft in the Ashley River, Charleston County, South Carolina*, Research Manuscript Series no. 217, Columbia, South Carolina.

Baker, W.A., 1966, *Sloops and Shallops*, Columbia, South Carolina.

Chapelle, H.I., 1935, *The History of American Sailing Ships*, New York.

Chapelle, H.I., 1951, *American Small Sailing Craft*, New York.

Documenting the Malcolm Boat. (SCIAA)

Coker, P.C., III, 1987, *Charleston's Maritime Heritage, 1670–1865*, Charleston, South Carolina.

Falconer, W.A., 1970, *A Universal Dictionary of the Marine*, New York.

Falconer, W.A., 1970a, *A New Universal Dictionary of the Marine*, modernized by Dr William Burney, London.

Fleetwood, R., 1982, *Tidecraft: The Boats of Lower South Carolina and Georgia*, Savannah, Georgia.

Hocker, F.M., 1992, 'The Brown's Ferry Vessel: An Interim Hull Report', in D.H. Keith and T.L. Carrell (eds), *Underwater Archaeology Proceedings from the Society for Historical Archaeology Conference*, Ann Arbor, Michigan.

Steffy, J.R., 1994, *Wooden Ship Building and the Interpretation of Shipwrecks*, College Station, Texas.

Mallorytown Wreck
see Brown's Bay Vessel

Mallows Bay

A shallow 1.6 km wide embayment in Maryland, USA which contains the remains of at least 154 ships; it is thus the largest ships' graveyard in North America and possibly the world. In addition to a collection of 18th- and 19th-century vessels, including some dating to the American Revolution, Mallow's Bay holds ninety-two ships of the World War I Emergency Fleet. These wooden steamships, the last and largest in the world, were constructed in order to freight aid to Europe, running the German blockade. The majority of hull remains are exposed at low tide and have acted as polders capturing sufficient soil and seeds to encourage plant growth. Some vessels have become virtual islands and are home to diverse floral and faunal communities. The unique combination of environmental and cultural attributes led to the decision to make Mallow's Bay Maryland's second historic shipwreck preserve.

Of the more than 700 vessels commissioned by the **US Navy** from a dozen west coast shipyards in World War I, only 322 were completed. Of these, 296 were wooden vessels designed by chief naval architect Theodore Ferris and known as Ferris ships, and twenty-six were composites of wood and steel. The ships weighed between 3,000 and 4,000 deadweight tons, with a few as large as 4,500 tons, and cost between $750,000 and one million dollars each. Produced rapidly with green wood, and with alterations to their designs made even while under construction, the vessels suffered severely from leakage. This was exacerbated by engine vibration and resulted in the use of tons of concrete both to plug holes and to deaden the shaking, particularly around the propeller shafts.

Three hundred and nine ships actually saw service, but all in the Pacific; none went to Europe. At the close of the war the vessels were offered for sale several times and finally, in 1922, 234 were sold for a total of $750,000 (the cost of constructing one) to the Virginia firm Western Marine and Salvage Co., which brought 218 of them to the Potomac River. The ships were held off Widewater, Virginia and taken a few at a time to Alexandria to be stripped of engines and other valuable components before the hulks were returned downstream for final destruction by fire. Unfortunately, on more than one occasion vessels caught fire and, being rafted together, numerous ships burned before being salvaged. At other times vessels broke loose and created navigational hazards. This led to the decision to corral the hulls in Mallow's Bay.

The wrecking process continued until 1932 when the salvage company closed. During the Great Depression many wildcat salvage operations flowered in the bay; at one point wrecking at Mallow's was providing 15 per cent of the per capita income for the county. At this time other vessels were introduced to the bay, some as dormitory ships, such as the *Obak* and the four-masted schooner *Ida S. Dow*; others included floating brothels called Potomac River arks.

With the outbreak of World War II there was renewed industrial interest in the remains and Bethlehem Steel obtained a contract to continue salvage efforts. It was at this time that the burning basin and marine railways were constructed. Because of concern that the hulls could still drift out of the bay in storms, they were filled with rocks and soil and formed polders which over time caught more soil and plant matter from wind, water, and bird activity; elliptical islands began to form. Most of the remains are visible at low tide standing 3.0–4.5 m proud of the bottom. After World War II more vessels were abandoned there, such as the Menhaden fishing vessel *Mermenthau* and the last known Hog Island steel hull, *Accomack*, which had been converted to a vehicle ferry.

Maritime historian Donald Shomette, with a grant from the Maryland Historical Trust and working with the St Clement's Island Potomac River Museum, has undertaken a comprehensive survey of the remains in the bay and noted many of the associated terrestrial sites as well. Although there are Civil War battlements, prehistoric sites, and remnants of the pre- and post-war fishing industry in the vicinity, these are on private property and have not yet been completely documented.

The islands play an integral environmental role in the region, providing a habitat for diverse flora and fauna including some endangered entomological species. Great blue herons and cormorants proliferate and bald eagles in the area have increased over three summers from three to seven. Some hulls support trees 15 cm in diameter and 8 m tall as well as healthy shipboard populations of beaver, nutria, muskrat, and deer. The potential significance for both cultural and environmental educational uses of the resource base was recognized immediately. The preserve is scheduled to open formally in mid-1997 and will emphasize low-impact recreational activities such as diving, fishing, and canoeing. S.B.M.L.

ADDITIONAL READING

Shomette, D.G., 1994, *The Shipwrecks of Mallow's Bay: An Historic Overview*, Mallow's Bay, Maryland Submerged Cultural Resources Survey, on file, Maryland Historical Trust, Maryland.

Shomette, D.G., 1996, *The Ghost Fleet of Mallow's Bay and Other Discoveries of the Lost Chesapeake*, Centreville, Maryland.

Marco Polo

Nineteenth-century Canadian ship sunk off Cavendish Beach, Prince Edward Island National Park. Two outstanding examples of Canadian-built ships which gained international fame are *Bluenose* and *Marco Polo*. The wreck of the former lies in Haitian waters; whatever is left of its remains is virtually out of reach as a submerged cultural resource to Canada. *Marco Polo* was caught in a storm on 25 July 1883 in the Gulf of St Lawrence. As she began to sink, she was run in towards the shore by her captain, who beached the vessel. The crew was saved, but within a month the ship had sunk completely.

Marco Polo lies in approximately 5 m of water, 640 m off Cavendish Beach. The shipwreck represents a very large wooden vessel (the exterior planking measures 15 cm thick) with visible remains extending 40 m north–south by 24 m east–west, both ends of the wreck disappearing into the surrounding sands. The site consists of two main components, a large section of the starboard hull and a still larger section of the port hull. Both components exhibit a long row of broken futtocks curving upwards and which in some places are 2 m proud of the bottom sands. There is also a large portion of what appears to be a major section of the port side upper hull. This section is lying parallel to and outboard of the port side. It is lying flat and measures over 25 m long by 4 m wide. No loose material cultural items of any sort are visible on the site. Not even the smallest fragments of pottery or rigging are to be seen. There is a large amount of ballast stone, as well as a large concreted mass of chain links and a section of a mast. Several brass fastening pins are firmly embedded in the ship's timbers.

There are no surviving plans of *Marco Polo*. The wreck site is all that remains of this once internationally famous ship, built near St John, New Brunswick in 1851, which was once proclaimed by its captain to be the fastest ship in the world. Its career has been declared of national historic significance by the Historic Sites and Monuments Board of Canada. The secret of its speed, unexplained to this day, may lie within the shape of the bottom of the hull. W.S.

Marguerite

French warship sunk at Conche (now La Conche), Newfoundland, Canada in 1707, and rediscovered and surveyed by the New-foundland Marine Archaeology Society between 1977 and 1979. The twenty-six gun, 200 ton warship *Marguerite* was part of a five-vessel French fleet defeated in battle by a superior British fleet on 4 August 1707, at Conche. *Marguerite* was trapped in Martinique Bay and burned along with the larger thirty-two gun *Marina*. Residents of the fishing village of Conche, 100 km north of St John's, retained a strong oral tradition of the engagement and the loss of the two ships. Working from villagers' accounts, the Newfoundland Marine Archaeology Society (NMAS) relocated the wreck of *Marguerite* in 6 m of water in 1977. The site is marked by a ballast pile and twenty cannon.

In 1978 and 1979 limited test excavation of the wreck was undertaken by the NMAS. Ceramic sherds, copper sheet fragments, wood samples, and concretions were recovered and another cannon was discovered and documented. J.P.D.

ADDITIONAL READING

Barber, J.M., Barber, V.C., and Wheeler, R., 1981, 'A Trial Excavation of the *Marguerite*, and a Search for the *Murinet*, both St Malo Vessels Sunk in 1707 at Conche, Newfoundland', *International Journal of Nautical Archaeology*, 10, 1, 29–39.

Barber, V.C. *et al.*, 1979, 'An Initial Survey of a Wreck, Thought to be a St Malo Vessel, the *Marguerite*, Sunk in 1707 at Conche, Newfoundland', *International Journal of Nautical Archaeology*, 8, 1, 39–44.

Maria Louisa

A wooden tern-schooner constructed in 1884 by E.M. Miner & Son of Madison, Connecticut. En route to Genoa, Italy from Pensacola, Florida with a cargo of lumber, it stranded in the Dry Tortugas, Florida on 27 April 1917. The site was discovered as part of the **Dry Tortugas National Park** Survey in 1993. Archaeological investigation during July and August 1995, directed by Brenda Lanzendorf, concentrated on site documentation as part of the collaboration between National Park Service **Submerged Cultural Resources Unit** and Brown University. Archaeological evidence suggests the vessel stranded on a shallow bank while passing south of Garden Key. The crew off-loaded ballast to refloat the vessel. Temporarily freeing it, *Maria Louisa* stranded a second time in 5 m of water approximately 200 m southeast of the original point of contact. An attempt to 'kedge' the vessel off was unsuccessful.

Insurance records from the Bureau of American Shipping aided in identifying the vessel by detailing the types of material used in the construction of *Maria Louisa*. Furthermore, on 17 May 1917 the US Department of Commerce conducted a 'third order' coast and geodetic survey that shot angles from Hospital Key, Loggerhead Key, and the mainmast of a wrecked schooner. This order of survey gave highly accurate horizontal and vertical controls for the technology available at the time. In August 1995 the positioning data, taken in latitude and longitude, was converted into Universal Transverse Mercator (UTM) coordinates. The coordinates place the mainmast of the schooner approximately 5 m west of the site. This information helped to analyse effects of underwater post-depositional factors on the contextual integrity of the site over the seventy-eight-year period preceding the wreck.

The Coast Guard Casualty Report not only substantiated the identification of the vessel but detailed the wrecking sequence. As an example of the complementary aspects that historical documents and archaeological evidence can offer each other, in the Casualty Report the ship's master did not mention the first stranding and the off-loading of ballast or an attempt to kedge the vessel during the second grounding. Presumably this was because these two tactics were standard procedures that did not need to be mentioned. However, the captain did state that the deck load was 'jettisoned'. The deck load was lumber, a perishable cargo. The report also mentioned that the Light House tender *Ivy* pulled the vessel twice, and broke the hawser each time.

In 1981 the National Oceanic and Atmospheric Administration published geodetic survey records that included additional notes from the 1917 survey. Concerning *Maria Louisa* it stated that within five months after the wreck, the masts of the schooner were removed while the hull of the schooner remained in position. Of particular interest is the comment that the schooner's masts were removed: the presence of three mast caps at the site contradicts this statement. Would salvors have climbed the masts, manually removed the mast caps, and then thrown them overboard? If the masts were detached from the hull, it is more likely that they were simply cut down. In a case like this, using historical narrative to aid in the interpretation of an archaeological site, 'removed' means something different from 'detached'.

The wreck of *Maria Louisa* provided an opportunity to contrast the relationship between historical and archaeological evidence. Many archaeologists criticize the use of historical documents as a form of evidence because of inherent bias. Archaeological assemblages, however, exist within evidential constraints (i.e. once post-depositional factors have been considered, the distribution of artefacts exhibits contextual integrity). But archaeological records are often fragmentary. Historical documents can serve to corroborate, contradict, or complement the archaeological record. Used collectively, the two forms of evidence can produce a more reliable interpretation of archaeological sites. This is apparent with the wreck of *Maria Louisa*. B.L.

ADDITIONAL READING

Gould, R., 1995, 'The Bird Key Wreck, Dry Tortugas National Park, Florida', *Bulletin of the Australian Institute for Maritime Archaeology*, 19, 2, 7–16.

Lanzendorf, B., 1996, 'The Grounding and Abandonment of the Maria Louisa: A Behaviorist Approach', Master's research paper, Brown University, Providence, RI.

Murphy, L.E. (ed.), 1993, *Dry Tortugas National Park: Submerged Cultural Resources Assessment*, Santa Fe, New Mexico.

Maritime archaeology

The study of human interaction with the sea, lakes, and rivers through the archaeological study of material manifestations of maritime culture, including vessels, shoreside facilities, cargoes, and even **Human remains**. Maritime archaeology should not be confused with **Underwater archaeology**, which describes the study of the past through any submerged remains. Maritime archaeology is in part a speciality within underwater archaeology, although the material remains of maritime activity are not always submerged. Maritime archaeological work has included the study of **Beached shipwreck sites**, **Ship burials**, waterfront communities such as fishing villages and industrial neighbourhoods, including **Shipyard archaeology**, floating vessels, and, of course, sunken wrecks.

Similarly, maritime archaeology should not be confused with nautical archaeology, which examines the specifics of vessel construction and use. Nautical archaeology is a speciality within maritime archaeology. The late Keith Muckelroy, in defining maritime archaeology, elaborated that 'the primary object of study is man ... and not the ships, cargoes, fittings or instruments with which the researcher is immediately confronted' (1978, p. 4). Muckelroy argued, and the discipline has generally agreed, that maritime archaeology is concerned with maritime culture, 'not just technical matters, but also social, economic, political, religious and a host of other aspects' (*ibid.*).

This approach has found wider expression and support in the archaeological community, particularly among adherents of **Shipwreck anthropology**, who have advocated and expanded avenues of scientific enquiry to include, for example, the examination of groups of sites, such as the large number of wrecks in a specific geographic region or area (e.g. the work of the US National Park Service at the **Dry Tortugas National Park** in Florida) and how these wrecks are regional indicators (see **Regional approach**), for example the collaborative work of several scientists who are assessing the **Great Lakes** of North America. Other research has included a thematic approach (see **Thematic studies**), such as the examination of sites associated with specific trades or events. Examples are the Dutch East India Company (VOC), the English East India Company, or the California Gold Rush; research on the last of these examines the role of ships and maritime culture on the Gold Rush through the study of sites ranging from ships pulled ashore for use as storehouses, such as *Niantic*, ships that served as floating buildings, such as *LaGrange*, wrecked passenger vessels, such as *Tennessee*, and waterfront maritime businesses, such as **Hoff's Store**.

Muckelroy, in advocating a theory of maritime archaeology, suggested a three-tier hierarchy, beginning with the archaeology of shipwrecks, in which wreck sites and their environments were assessed. The maritime archaeologist first needs to understand the process of wrecking, which involves both **Filtering processes** and scrambling processes. Filtering processes include the floating away of material when a ship is wrecked, salvage operations, and the disintegration of perishables, all of which may remove materials and artefacts from the **Archaeological record**. Scrambling processes include the breaking up of a vessel on the surface, through the action of waves or war, for example, or the gradual distribution of scattered elements from a ship that has struck a rock and then sailed on before sinking, and the gradual disintegration of a ship on the bottom.

Post-depositional seabed movement, such as the shifting of bottom sediments, join other **Site formation processes** to create what Muckelroy called continuous (in which the remains are concentrated more or less in one area) and discontinuous (where the remains are scattered) sites. Examples of continuous sites include the **Kyrenia Ship**, *Vasa*, *Mary Rose*, and USS *Monitor*. The maritime archaeologist must understand the processes of site formation, so that the remains excavated can be properly interpreted. This approach is what makes possible **Reconstructions** such as those on some ancient wrecks, where the presence of tiles has provided evidence of a roofed structure aboard the ship, or Ballard's reconstruction of the sinking of **Bismarck**, which he argues was a scuttled and fully flooded hull which capsized, dumped its turrets, and then plunged bow first into the abyss, striking the slopes of sea mount and sliding down in an avalanche of bottom sediments.

Muckelroy's second tier is an archaeology of ships, in which the archaeological research focuses on the ship as a machine, the ship as an element in a military or economic system, and then, in a focus of particular interest to shipwreck anthropologists, as a closed community. The ship as a machine is a highly developed means of transport, that Muckelroy notes must meet two basic requirements: (1) it must be able to float in all the conditions it is likely to encounter; and (2) it must be able to move efficiently and in a controlled manner.

Much of our modern knowledge of the origin and development of ships comes from the archaeological record, particularly the work of nautical archaeologists who have studied not only the development of hull forms and construction methods, but also the intricacies of rigging, ship fittings such as pumps, steering apparatus, navigational instruments, and mechanical propulsion (for the most part focused on early marine steam engines on sites such as **Beaver** or SS **Xantho**). Thanks to the work of these archaeologists, a detailed understanding of prehistoric, ancient, and medieval craft is emerging, and emphasis from the 1980s on post-medieval wrecks, including ships of relatively recent vintage, has provided new and significant information. This includes the analysis of the structural failure of RMS **Titanic**'s hull after its collision with the iceberg, and the assessment of ship types specific to the world's largest inland body of water, the Great Lakes of North America.

Muckelroy also argued that ships basically fit into two systems – military and economic. Muckelroy acknowledged, but did not address, remains of ships with a ceremonial or recreational use (see **Small craft studies**), nor did he discuss the potential of fishing vessel sites to yield information, since as of 1978 'no such remains have yet been discovered; it may be that the special nature of the cargoes here positively impedes preservation' (1978, p. 219) However, since 1978, substantial work has been done with small craft, ceremonial vessels (such as the **Khufu Ships**), recreational vessels (such as the Royal Yacht **Mary**, and **Cleopatra's Barge**), and fishing vessels (such as the **Terence Bay Wreck**). Considerable work has been done with ships of war, the

specialized nature of their construction and use, and the circumstances of their loss, including such sites as the World War II wrecks of *Bismarck*, USS **Arizona**, and the **Cross-roads Wrecks** sunk in the atomic weapons tests at Bikini Atoll.

Muckelroy also stressed the ship as a closed community, noting that shipwreck sites have the potential to contain artefacts that would yield information about the lifestyles of those aboard, be they passengers or crew. This is the study of **Shipboard society**. The nature of shipboard discipline and command, with a marked division between the officers and the men, provides a unique archaeological perspective on the role and nature of hierarchies. Areas of research into shipboard life include the analysis of foodstuffs, health aboard ships (both usually through **Faunal studies**), the study of personal effects and belongings, and even the analysis of human remains, which may reveal traumas from injuries or illnesses endemic to seamen.

Muckelroy suggested as his third tier an archaeology of maritime cultures, in which nautical technology, naval warfare, maritime trade, shipboard societies, and incidental contributions to archaeology in general were all considered. Two-thirds of the world is covered by water, so endeavours to travel by water are among the oldest, longest lasting, and most prevalent of human activities. The ship was the largest and most complex machine built and used by many societies. Finally, ships carried a broad range of cargoes and materials, not just specialized maritime-unique artefacts, and the study of these sites has greatly aided land archaeology and the understanding of the past. The study of cargoes from ancient wrecks, for example, has provided the typology for amphoras, the spread of trade goods and items throughout the Mediterranean, and, in the case of the wreck at **Uluburun**, the best collection of medieval Islamic glass in existence.

Maritime sites have two special factors that encourage a higher level of preservation of the archaeological record than sites on land. The first is the high levels of preservation of materials, including organic remains, in water and in bottom sediments. Material thousands of years old survives in wet environments much better than it does in dry environments. The second factor is that shipwrecks usually sank beyond the reach of human interference or salvage, and thus are often regarded as 'time capsules' of the past. Filtering, scrambling, and differential levels of preservation on various sites argue against wrecks being 'time capsules', however; one scholar has suggested that they be termed 'cracked time capsules'.

Maritime archaeology, within a short time frame of a few decades, has become one of the major areas of archaeological study in the world. Advances in maritime archaeology since the late 1980s have included the use of new technologies to find, survey, and excavate maritime sites; the inclusion of sites for study other than sunken ships, such as beached wrecks, shipyards, waterfront communities, and structures such as ship chandleries, canneries, boarding houses, and manufacturing sites; the rise of anthropological approaches to sites and the use of **Research designs**, particularly with a shift away from the study and recovery of 'famous' or 'treasure' wrecks to thematic and regional studies of sites; the rise of **Experimental archaeology** with a maritime emphasis; and the analysis of vernacular types of small craft. J.P.D.

ADDITIONAL READING

Bass, George F. (ed.), 1972, *A History of Seafaring Based on Underwater Archaeology*, London.

Bass, George F. (ed.), 1988, *Ships and Shipwrecks of the Americas: A History Based on Underwater Archaeology*, London.

Blackman, D.J. (ed.), 1973, *Marine Archaeology*, London.

Frost, H., 1963, *Under the Mediterranean*, London.

Gould, R.A. (ed.), 1983, *Shipwreck Anthropology*, Albuquerque, New Mexico.

Greenhill, B. and Morrison, J., 1995, *The Archaeology of Boats and Ships*, London.

Hasslof, O., Henningson, H., and Christensen, A.E. (eds) 1972, *Ships and Shipyards, Sailors and Fishermen: An Introduction to Maritime Ethnology*, trans. M. Knight and H. Young, Copenhagen.

Henderson, G., 1986, *Maritime Archaeology in Australia*, Nedlands, Western Australia.

Johnstone, P., 1974, *The Archaeology of Ships*, London.

Muckelroy, K., 1978, *Maritime Archaeology*, Cambridge and London.

Muckelroy, K. (ed.), 1980, *Archaeology Under Water: An Atlas of the World's Submerged Sites*, Maidenhead, Berkshire and New York.

Throckmorton, P. (ed.), 1987, *The Sea Remembers: Shipwrecks and Archaeology*, New York and London.

Underwater Archaeology: A Nascent Discipline, 1972, UNESCO, Paris.

Marsala Punic Warship

Ancient vessel found off western Sicily. Phoenicio-Punic alphabetic signs painted onto this hull, which sank when new, show it to have been built by the western Phoenicians, whose capital was Carthage. It contrasts with all other Mediterranean wrecks of Classical antiquity which are of 'round' merchantmen, for although this ship shares their basic mortise-and-tenon construction, its design, contents and context show it to have been a 'long' oared vessel, probably a Liburnion, of the period of the first Punic War (264–241 BC). Victory went to the Romans at the naval battle of the Egadi Islands, which lie off the Sicilian coast to the north of Punic Lilybaeum (modern Marsala) where, in the course of commercial sand dredging, Diego Boninni identified a zone filled with ancient wrecks.

A connection between the Battle of the Egadi Islands and the Marsala wrecks is likely, for after the ships of the line had been routed the wind changed, so that any surviving ancillary craft might easily have made for the shelter of Lilybaeum (then still Punic territory).

After the zone had been surveyed in 1969, the wreck in question was excavated (1970–74) at the invitation of the Sicilian authorities by Honor Frost (on behalf of the British School in Rome). Only its aft end had survived, but by a stroke of luck, after the excavation was over, the unpredictable movement of a sandbank revealed a prow with a ram belonging to another wreck. A brief sounding showed that it bore the same kind of painted letter as the excavated wreck and was associated with the same kind of pottery. Of the contemporary kinds of rams mentioned by Polybius (I, 50, 6–7) this one tallies with the 'beaked' variety designed to pierce enemy hulls, rather than spring their planking apart by battering them at their waterline. The 'Colonna rostrata', a victory column set up in Rome during the First Punic War, was decorated with both types.

The timbers of the excavated ship were raised, then conserved with polyethelene-glycol (thanks to the collaboration of Dr Pietro Alagna, and the industrial infrastructure of Marsala's wine trade). During the late 1970s and early 1980s the treated wood was reassembled in a historic, but dilapidated, building that had been expropriated as a ship museum. The remains had to be protected by a plastic tent, under which they can still be glimpsed; the building was renamed the Museum of Regional Antiquities.

Structural details of the ship are as follows: the 3–4 cm thick planking is sawn lengthwise through trunks of pine. Sixteen strakes (or planks joined lengthwise) survive above the keel on the port side, and four on the starboard. Plank ends are joined by diagonal scarfs up to strake number 11. Thereafter, from the turn of the bilge towards the waterline, scarfs (which are S-shaped) coincide with an external feature unique to this wreck. The usual saw-marks still show on the inside of these planks (which are thicker

than the rest), but on the outside they are shaped by adze. Consequently, although still assembled by mortise-and-tenon like the rest of the smooth-skinned hull, the outer surfaces of strakes 12 to 16 look like clinkers, or overlapping planking (a form of construction unknown in the Mediterranean before the Middle Ages). The purpose of this belt of corrugation was probably to throw off the water which, at certain speeds, creeps up the sides of fast, smooth-skinned vessels and spills into them.

The keel, like the planks, is pinewood. The internal timbers are mostly oak, and the rise of the stern is maple. The latter prolongs the keel, turning upward to form a knee which is reinforced on the outside by a sternpost (also maple). About a third of the

The Marsala Punic Warship: sternpost. (H. Frost)

Warship with lead sheathing depicted on a mosaic. (Themetra, Tunisia)

keel (9 m) is still attached to the remains of the port strakes (whose overall length ends some metres beyond it). In addition, some 8.8 m of oak wale was found detached and broken in two: one half was on the site, the other was buried on the nearby beach. Since the wale's curve flattens out, part of it must have belonged to the (otherwise missing) parallel midships section of the hull. Wale and prow had been broken off in antiquity, while the stern had been driven down into the bottom where it remained lodged at an

angle of 7°; consequently, the water being shallow, the prow would have protruded above the surface and soon been carried away by the sea. Lead sheathing covered the hull, probably as on representations of warships of later date, such as a mosaic from the thermal baths of Themetra in Tunisia.

Epigraphic studies by Prof. William Johnstone (Aberdeen University) show the design of the vessel to have been preconceived. That several workmen were literate is implied by the fact that Phoenician letter WAW is written in seven different ways. An alphabetical sequence set out along the port face of the keel is repeated inside the hull where it marked the positions of the skeletal timbers. In addition, two Phoenicio-Punic words, as well as guidelines (both painted and incised) and also spills of paint, the imprints of a paint-pot and other marks, combine to explain the sequence of construction.

Unlike the usual consignments of identical amphoras and heavy kitchen equipment found on cargo ships, the pottery on this wreck consisted of small receptacles together with a few amphoras of various kinds, sufficient only for men on operational duty. Bones, plant material, ballast stones, and metals were studied respectively by, among others: F. Popelin, Museum d'Histoire Naturelle, Paris; the Jodrell Laboratory and Herbarium, Royal Botanical Gardens, Kew; G. Mascle, Department of Structural Geology, University of Paris VI; the late R.F. Tylecote, Institute of Archaeology, London. Carbon 14 measurements were taken by the Nuclear Physics Division, AERE, Harwell and the British Museum.

Animal bones (some butcher-cut) confirm the meat diet of the Carthaginians. A fragment of human long bone attests one casualty; it was found among tumbled ballast-stones with the bone from a small dog. Besides olives, nuts and other edibles, kitchen remains contained one surprising ingredient: *Cannabis sativa*. Quantities of plant material came from the dunnage (leafy branches laid over hulls to protect the wood from heavy objects). The preservation of organic matter was outstanding: some leaves caught under timbers and embedded in putty were still green. Like the carpenter's shavings mingled with the ballast, such leaves imply that the ship was built in haste and sank when new. A fern foreign to North Africa, combined with stones of northern origin, pottery and lead isotopic identifications, suggest that the ship had been built in some pocket of Italian territory still influenced by the erstwhile Carthagenian–Etruscan alliance. H.F.

ADDITIONAL READING

Basch, L., 1996, 'Notes sur l'épron', *Tropis*, 4, 31–102.

Basch, L. and Frost, H., 1975, 'A Typological Sketch and the Ram from Marsala', *International Journal of Nautical Archaeology*, 4, 2, 201–28.

Crumlin-Pedersen, O., 1993, 'Les lignes élégantes du navire de guerre de Marsala', *Les Dossiers d'Archéologie*, 183, 58–65.

Frost, H. *et al.*, 1981, *The Punic Ship: Final Excavation Report*, supplement to *Notizie degli Scavi di Antichità*, 8th series, 30, 1976, Accademia Nazionale dei Lincei, Rome.

Johnstone, W., 1978, 'Cursive Phoenician and the Archaic Greek Alphabet', *Kadmos*, 17, 2, 151–66.

Johnstone, W., 1983, 'The Epigraphy of the Marsala Punic Warship', *Acts of the First Congress of Phoenician and Punic Studies*, 3, Rome.

Marseille Bourse Wreck

Wreck discovered in 1974 during the excavation of the northeast extremity of the ancient harbour of Marseille, on the location of the future 'Centre Bourse'. The ship, empty of all cargo, was apparently deliberately abandoned during the first third of the 3rd century AD, after which some pieces,

including the mast-step timber, had been salvaged.

The wreck, about 20 m by 8 m, corresponds to a large merchant ship, the original dimensions of which can be estimated at 23 m in length and 9 m in width with a capacity of about 130 tons burden. The structure includes an axial frame composed of the whole keel, a great part of the sternpost and, towards the bow, a fore foot on which was fastened the stempost which is now missing. Inside, the axial frame is reinforced at its central part by two lateral keelsons which supported the mast-step timber. The framing, flat at the midships section, consists of alternating floor-timbers and half-frames (often overstepping the keel under the mast-step) extended by futtocks. These elements, of various lengths, are treenailed to the planking and are not fastened together, nor to the keel. The exception are seven floor-timbers bolted to the keel. The strakes of the planking are joined by tenons pegged on mortises in accordance with the traditional method of Greco-Roman shipbuilding. Lastly, a very great variety of wood species (at least twelve different species of resinous, evergreen, or broad-leaved trees) were used for the hull construction.

The characteristics of the structure suggest that a new method of shipbuilding was used, which has been called 'construction alternée' by J.-M. Gassend. A first series of short floor-timbers would have been fitted on the keel to be used as a partial skeleton to set up the first strakes. Then longer floor-timbers, half-frames, and lastly futtocks would have been used in turn for the progressive assembly of the planking. At each construction phase the planking would be assembled on a partial skeleton, contrary to the shell-first method of shipbuilding

assumed until then for all ancient ships. This method remains hypothetical and has not been demonstrated effectively. On the other hand, the ship obviously proceeds from a shell structural conception, and if we can suppose the use of active frames for the upper part of the hull, it seems more likely that the main part of the planking had been assembled first according to the shell-first method, and possibly strengthened during its progressive assembly by partial elements of frames.

The wreck was consolidated by an atmospheric pressure freeze-drying treatment, and is now exhibited in the History Museum of Marseille. P.P.

ADDITIONAL READING

Gassend, J.-M., 1982, *Le navire antique du Lacydon*, Marseille.

Pomey, P., 1988, 'Principes et méthodes de construction en architecture navale antique', *Cahiers d'Histoire*, 33, 3, 4, 397–412.

Mary

Wreck of the Royal Yacht of Charles II, lost in 1675 and rediscovered in 1971. When Charles II returned to England after his enforced stay in Holland, he was presented with a splendid *jacht*, a type of vessel which was only to be found in the Netherlands. *Mary* thus became the first such ship to be operated outside Holland, but she soon proved to be unsuitable for British conditions and after only one year, in 1661, she was transferred to the Royal Navy for general service.

On her final voyage from Dublin to Chester, *Mary* lost her position in the fog and in the early hours of 25 March 1675 she hit a

The three types of bronze gun recovered from Mary.
(Peter N. Davies)

submerged part of the Skerries – a rocky outcrop situated off the coast of Anglesey. *Mary* immediately took a heavy list and would have capsized completely except that her long mast rested on the rocks. This enabled thirty-nine of those on board to climb to safety but a further thirty-five were lost. The isolation of the site, strong tides, and bad weather all then helped to preserve the wreck from interference and it was not until July 1971 that it was accidentally relocated.

With the support of what is now the Merseyside Maritime Museum, a joint expedition made up of members of the Chorley and Merseyside branches of the British Sub Aqua Club was quickly organized. When they arrived on the site it was obvious that the wreck was being systematically looted and four of the eight bronze guns had been removed. While these were subsequently to be recovered it was clear that what was planned as a scientific investigation needed to be replaced by a rescue operation. The principal artefacts were, therefore, removed and taken to Liverpool, which was the nearest place where conservation facilities were available. While the threat to the site then diminished, it was only finally removed when *Mary* was scheduled under the 1973 **Protection of Wrecks Act (UK)**.

Subsequent excavation over the ensuing twenty years was concerned almost entirely with a mound measuring $4 \times 3 \times 1$ m. This consisted of the lead pigs and old cannon balls with which *Mary* had been ballasted. A small space was discovered between the concreted mass and the seabed which had originally been occupied by the now decayed deck timbers. These had been trapped when the yacht had turned over after her mast had finally broken. A second layer of concretion lay within this space and it was there that most artefacts were to be found. Excavation proved to be a very slow process, for although the depth of water was never more than 14 m the strength of the tide restricted diving to an hour or so each side of slack water. Delay was also caused by the hardness of the ballast mound, for it was impracticable to break into it by hand and an air-hammer proved difficult to control. A partial solution was to employ minute quantities of explosives to crack off pieces of concretion which could then be raised and examined in a better environment.

These techniques enabled slow progress to be maintained, and in addition to the ordnance many personal items were recovered. These included several gold lockets, rings, silver, candlesticks, and the Captain's plate, spoon, and fork. The remains of two individuals were also found, but little timber was discovered. This supports the view that once *Mary* had turned over and deposited her ballast the remains of her now lightened hull drifted away.

Mary's significance can be judged on several planes. She was the first yacht outside Holland and therefore the original (British) royal yacht. Her construction, history, service, and loss are extremely well documented; her set of matching bronze guns are amongst the finest surviving from the 17th century; and the problem of protecting the site was an important factor in promoting new and effective legislation.

The situation in the 1990s is that although no further diving is anticipated the wreck is still protected and so cannot be disturbed. All the artefacts remain in the care of Merseyside Maritime Museum where they are either on exhibition or undergoing conservation. P.D.

ADDITIONAL READING

Davies, P.N., 1973, 'The Mary, Charles II's Yacht: The Discovery of the Wreck', *International Journal of Nautical Archaeology*, 2, 1, 59–73.

Davies, P.N., 1978, 'The Discovery and Excavation of the Royal Yacht Mary', *Maritime Wales*, 3, 25–32.

McBride, P.W.J., 1973, 'Her History, Importance and Ordnance', *International Journal of Nautical Archaeology*, 2, 1, 59–73.

McElvogue, D.M., 1997, '1996 Royal Yacht Mary Topographical Survey', *Nautical Archaeology*, Spring 1997, 5–7.

Priestman, K. 1973, 'Conservation of Finds', *International Journal of Nautical Archaeology*, 2, 1, 59–73.

Tanner, M., 1997, 'Museum Diving Operations on the Royal Yacht Mary', *Mermaid: The Journal of the Friends of Merseyside Maritime Museum*, 41.

Mary Celestia

Confederate steamer wrecked in 1864 off Bermuda. Shortly after the outbreak of the American Civil War in 1861, a blockade of the ports of the Confederacy from Virginia to Mexico was declared by the Union. As the blockade took effect, the Confederates began to use fast steamers operating out of Havana in Cuba, Nassau in the Bahamas, and St George's in Bermuda. Goods, mostly items of war, were shipped to these ports from Europe in larger and much slower vessels and then transferred to the blockade runners for the shorter journey into the Confederacy. The

Paddlewheel from Mary Celestia. *(Bermuda Maritime Museum)*

trade out of Bermuda ceased after the fall of Wilmington, North Carolina, in early 1865, by which time two of the blockade runners had been lost on the reefs of the island.

Mary Celestia began service out of the town of St George's in late May 1864, having been launched as a 207 ton vessel that February at Liverpool. Cleared on the 23rd for Nassau, the fast steamer made the first of five successful runs into the port of Wilmington within a period of three months. On 6 September 1864 the ship was wrecked on a reef off the south shore of Bermuda less than 1 km from the Gibbs Hill Lighthouse.

The remains of the vessel are located in about 20 m of water. The paddle wheels, boilers, and some parts of the hull are visible, but most of the steamer is buried in the sand, surrounded by reefs. It was equipped with feathering paddle wheels and twin oscillating cylinder steam engines. The site was investigated by archaeologist Gordon P. Watts, Jr in the 1980s. See also **Shipwreck anthropology**. E.C.H.

ADDITIONAL READING

Wise, S.R., 1988, *Lifeline of the Confederacy: Blockade Running During the Civil War*, Columbia, South Carolina.

Mary Rose

King Henry VIII's warship, sunk in 1545 and raised in 1982. *Mary Rose* was built in Portsmouth, Hampshire, England in 1509–10. Documentary evidence indicates that she was a successful ship engaged for thirty-five years in policing the English Channel, keeping this vital sea passage clear of French warships and maintaining communications with Calais, then an English town.

In 1512 she served as the flagship for Sir Edward Howard at the Battle of Brest, and contemporary accounts refer to her as a fine sailing ship, but no plans or drawings survive from this period. Lists of her armament show that even at this early date she was fully armed with muzzle-loading and chambered bronze guns as well as breech-loading wrought-iron guns. In 1536 she was rebuilt and uprated from 600 to 700 tons. At this time the hull was strengthened with riders and a series of diagonal braces. These served to stiffen the hull below the waterline and allowed the introduction of heavier guns on the main gun deck.

In 1545 she sank with disastrous loss of life while engaging a French invasion fleet in the Solent channel between Portsmouth and the Isle of Wight. Over the next few years several guns were recovered and the ship was then abandoned. The wreck was rediscovered briefly in 1836 and the site was explored by pioneer salvage divers who recovered guns, longbows, and isolated

structural timbers. These were sold at public auction and the site was again abandoned.

The modern search was initiated in 1965 by Alexander McKee, who carried out a series of exploratory dives in the general area of the wreck site. In 1967 the late Professor Harold Edgerton of the Massachusetts Institute of Technology located an acoustic anomaly, which later proved to be the wreck, using a **Sub-bottom profiler** and **Side scan sonar**. The ship lay totally buried in the seabed and unproductive diver surveys of the seabed continued until 1971 when a combination of equinoctial spring tides and severe gales removed one metre of the light modern seabed sediments. Eight timbers were revealed, running at an angle of 15 degrees east. These proved to be the floor timbers and first futtocks on the starboard quarter.

Limited excavation continued over the next eight years to assess the integrity and cultural value of the surviving hull structure and its contents. Each season the work was confined to a predetermined programme aimed at defining the status of the hull and its contents with the minimum of interference. By 1979 it was clear that the ship lay on her starboard side at 60 degrees from the vertical and that the remains of four decks were preserved *in situ*. Excavations at the stern and the bow confirmed that the ship lay stern down by 5 degrees and there was no evidence to suggest that the starboard side was physically incoherent.

The Mary Rose Trust, a registered charity and limited company, was formed in 1979 to manage a full-time programme of work to excavate, survey, empty the hull, and, if feasible, to bring the empty hull ashore for study, conservation, and display. An intense full-time programme of underwater survey and excavation over the next four years culminated in the recovery of the ship. During

this period, many methods of salvaging the hull were proposed, reviewed, and rejected. The oak timbers of the hull and the elm keel had high mechanical strength and the outer planks were secured to the frames with oak treenails with only a relatively small number of iron fastenings securing the butt ends of the planks. By contrast, most of the internal fastenings were iron, which were much degraded by corrosion, and migration

The only contemporary illustration of Mary Rose, which comes from the Anthony Roll, a list of King Henry VIII's vessels completed in 1546. (By kind permission of the Master and Fellows of Magdalene College, Cambridge)

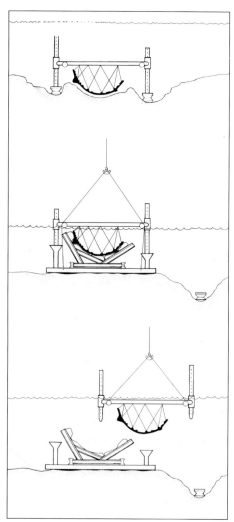

How Mary Rose was raised. Top: the hull ready for lifting, with wires attached to the tubular steel lifting frame (Sept. 1982); middle: the hull in suspension from the lifting frame, being transferred underwater to the support cradle (9 Oct. 1982); bottom: the cradle with the hull ready for the lift into the air: the lifting frame now acts as a spreader for the wire strops from the crane hook (11 Oct 1982). (Mary Rose Trust)

of the iron into the planks left voids. It became clear that the internal structure was only held in place by severely weakened iron nails and the surrounding mud. Consequently, each timber was surveyed and removed as the excavation progressed.

The first essential requirement was to design and fabricate a steel cradle which conformed to the shape of the hull. This was required to support the hull when it was lifted from the seabed into the air. The second essential requirement was a steel lifting frame to spread the load of the empty hull as it was lifted from the seabed. This lifting frame was constructed of tubular steel and its weight could be adjusted by flooding the tubes with seawater or pumping them dry. The frame sat above the wreck supported by four legs; it could be raised and lowered using hydraulic jacks fitted to the legs.

A series of iron bolts was passed through the hull timbers and attached by steel wires to the transoms of the lifting frame. The

The hull of Mary Rose *in the Ship Hall. The reinstatement of timbers surveyed and removed underwater was completed prior to the start of active conservation in September 1994. (Mary Rose Trust)*

The main deck of Mary Rose *looking from the bow; a rare uncluttered view photographed in July 1992 before work started on the upper deck above. (Mary Rose Trust)*

selection of the site for each of the 170 lifting bolts was critical as each lifting bolt performed two essential functions. Firstly, it passed through three or more elements and secured them together. As a minimum it passed through outer planking frame and inner planking or stringer, but whenever possible the bolt also passed through a hanging or rising knee. Secondly, it distributed the weight of the hull equally between all the pick-up points. After the hull was lowered into the cradle, the entire package – cradle, hull, and lifting frame – were lifted into the air and placed on a barge. The steel cradle still serves as the support for the hull, which was rotated through sixty degrees in 1985.

The hull now stands upright and most of

the internal timbers which were found *in situ* have been replaced within it. While *Mary Rose* remained buried in the anoxic mud of the seabed, the hull timbers and the organic artefacts were protected from macro- and microbiological organisms. After recovery and exposure to aerobic conditions and airborne contaminants, it was imperative that chemical, physical, and biological degradation was minimized. The ship was placed in a disused dry dock roofed with an insulated membrane, and an environment of 2–6 degrees and an atmosphere of 95 per cent relative humidity was maintained by irrigating the ship with chilled fresh water. This passive, non-destructive regime allowed the study of the ship to continue as the internal

timbers which were removed underwater were restored to their original position.

A programme of research to determine the most appropriate method of long-term conservation was begun in 1982. It was demonstrated by light and electron microscopy that the timbers have a decayed outer zone, a transitional zone containing decayed and sound wood, and a sound inner core. Most of the decay in the outer zone can be attributed to soft rot and bacterial attack in the past. Little active decay was observed. As most of the cultural and technical evidence for the construction, use, and modification of the ship is exhibited in the outer decayed zone, it was essential that any conservation technique ensured the stability of the outer surface of each timber. Carpenters' race marks, score and attrition marks, and small nail holes would all be lost if dimensional changes were allowed to occur. In late 1994 a three-stage active conservation programme was initiated. The first phase involves spraying the hull at ambient temperatures (17–18 degrees C) with an aqueous solution of low molecular weight polyethylene glycol. This will be followed by high molecular weight polyethylene glycol as a bulking agent. It is expected that these two phases will take at least twenty years. The third phase involves slow drying out in a controlled environment.

Over 22,000 registered finds are being analysed and prepared for publication. They range from environmental material including insect, fish, mammalian, and botanical remains to the massive guns and the people who sailed and fought on board the warship. Weed seeds caught in worsted clothing and grasses used as dunnage and mattress packing provide unique evidence for 17th-century agriculture. The weapons include bronze muzzle-loading and wrought-iron breech-loading guns, many of which were recovered with their carriages from action stations on the starboard side of the ship. Smaller breech-loading wrought-iron swivel guns were recovered from the bow and stern castles. Shot of iron, stone, and lead were recovered, together with composite shot of lead and iron, and wooden cannister shot containing sharp flint flakes.

Gun-furniture, including a copper alloy gunner's rule and wooden ring gauges, powder scoops, powder flasks, and reamers, were probably the personal possessions of the gunners. The linstocks used to apply the lint or slow match to the powder in the touch hole were crude hand-carved objects and highly personalized. More than 3,500 arrows and 138 yew longbows were recovered and many were associated with the remains of archers. Many of the **Human remains** were associated with fragmentary clothing, weapons, and other personal possessions. Groupings of material within a closely defined archaeological context within the ship often allows deductions to be made about social status or the occupation of the men within that group. A study of the human skeletal material by Stirland has identified individual traits associated with occupational stress.

Ship's equipment included spare running rigging in the stores on the orlop deck; and sections of standing rigging, including dead-eyes and chains, were found *in situ* beneath the starboard side of the stern castle. Navigation equipment included three steering compasses, a slate protractor, lead sounds, and dividers. A log reel and sand glasses were used to measure distance travelled within a fixed period of time. Many of the finds and the ship workshop are on display to the public in the Mary Rose Museum within the Royal Naval Base in Portsmouth, Hampshire. The work of conservation and interpretation continues, and the Trust is heavily dependent on public support. M.R.2

ADDITIONAL READING

Jones, A.M. and Rule, M.H., 1991, 'Preserving the Wreck of the Mary Rose', in P. Hoffman (ed.), *Proceedings of the 4th ICOM Group on Wet Organic Archaeological Materials Conference*, Bremerhaven, 25–48.

McKee, A., 1972, *King Henry VIII's Mary Rose*, London.

Rule, M.H., 1982, *The Mary Rose: The Excavation and Raising of Henry VIII's Flagship*, London.

Rule, M.H., 1994, *The Mary Rose: A Guide to the Exhibition and the Ship*, Portsmouth.

Stirland, A., 1991, 'The Diagnosis of Occupationally Related Paleopathology', in D.J. Ortner and A.D. Aufderheide (eds), *Current Synthesis and Future Options*, Washington, DC, 40–47.

USS *Massachusetts*

Pre-Dreadnought American battleship, sunk as an artillery target in 1921 off Pensacola, Florida and established as Florida's fourth Underwater Archaeological Preserve in 1993. USS *Massachusetts* was one of three Indiana class sea-going coastal battleships authorized in 1890 by the United States Congress to be built for the new 'steel navy'. Among the most powerful ships of their time, *Indiana*, *Massachusetts*, and *Oregon* were the first heavy-calibre, heavy-armour battleships built by the United States, and the first to be given hull numbers. Commissioned

USS Massachusetts, *photographed on 7 May 1900. (Courtesy of the Naval Historical Foundation, Washington, DC. US Naval Historical Center)*

in 1896, *Massachusetts* (BB-2) was just over 350 ft (107 m) long, with a beam of 69 ft (21 m), and a draft of 24 ft (7.3 m). Designed to cruise at a maximum of 15 knots, the battleship was armed with two heavy 13 in gun batteries and four 8 in secondary batteries, as well as smaller ordnance. Together with four torpedo tubes and a host of small arms, the ship's combined firepower was a force to be reckoned with. To protect the ship, an armoured belt of nickel case-hardened steel, in some places 18 in thick, ran along the water line, in addition to side and deck armour plates. *Massachusetts*'s firepower and armour were propelled through the water by vertical triple expansion steam engines driving two shafts at almost 10,000 hp. The crew consisted of 32 officers and 441 enlisted men.

The new battleship was engaged in combat in Cuba during the Spanish–American War (1898) and later performed a variety of duties. During a winter cruise in 1903 off Culebra, a premature detonation in one of the 8 in turrets caused the death of nine sailors and a change in naval gunnery practices. Decommissioned in 1906, *Massachusetts* was refitted in 1910 with a caged mainmast and other modern hardware and put back into commission; in 1914 she was decommissioned a second time. After the declaration of war with Germany, the nation's oldest battleship was recommissioned in 1917 to serve as a gunnery practice ship. Decommissioned

for the final time in 1919, the obsolete warship was loaned to the War Department as a target to test coastal defence artillery. Stripped of her guns and towed to Pensacola, Florida in January 1921, *Massachusetts* was scuttled in shallow water and subjected to over a hundred rounds of artillery fire. Left to the whims of the sea, the ship sat peacefully in the Gulf of Mexico attracting fish and fisherman alike until 1956, when several scrap companies joined forces to salvage the wreck. With the support of the people of Pensacola, the State filed an injunction to prevent the salvage; when the case was brought before the Supreme Court, title to *Massachusetts* was awarded to the State of Florida.

After spending seventy of her one hundred years in the sea, the battleship has become a giant artificial reef. In 1990 *Massachusetts* was nominated by a local diver to be considered as an underwater archaeological preserve. State archaeologists gathered historical data and ship's plans; explored, recorded, and mapped the ship's features; and made a formal proposal to the people of Pensacola for a cooperative project to establish the preserve. A group called Friends of the USS *Massachusetts* was formed to oversee the new preserve, to develop brochures and laminated field guides, and to design a bronze plaque to be placed on the ship. As a living underwater museum of American naval technology, the preserve was dedicated on 10 June 1993, on the centenary of the ship's launching. R.S.

ADDITIONAL READING

Alden, J.D., 1972, *The American Steel Navy: A Photographic History of the US Navy from the Introduction of the Steel Hull in 1883 to the Cruise of the Great White Fleet, 1907–1909*, Annapolis, Maryland.

Gibbons, T., 1983, *The Complete Encyclopedia of Battleships: A Technical Directory of Capital Ships from 1860 to the Present Day*, New York.

Harris, B., 1965, *The Age of the Battleship: 1890–1922*, New York.

Pater, A.F., 1968, *United States Battleships: A History of America's Greatest Fighting Fleet*, Beverly Hills, California.

Reilly, J.C. and Scheina, R.L., 1980, *American Battleships, 1886–1923: Pre-dreadnought Design and Construction*, Annapolis, Maryland.

Smith, R.C., 1991, 'Florida's Underwater Archaeological Preserves', in J.D. Broadwater (ed.), *Underwater Archaeology Proceedings from the Society for Historical Archaeology, Richmond*, Ann Arbor, Michigan.

Maud

Wreck of an Arctic exploration vessel lying off Cambridge Bay, Victoria Island in Canada's Northwest Territories (Nunavut) and documented between 1995 and 1996. The Polarskibet (polar ship) *Maud* was built in 1917 at Asker, Norway for explorer Roald Amundsen. She was used by Amundsen on his Polar expedition of 1918–23, and for the second transit of the Northeast Passage across the top of Russia. After an aborted return to the eastern Arctic in 1925, the ship was sold at auction in Seattle, Washington when Amundsen declared bankruptcy. Purchased by the Hudson's Bay Company and renamed *Baymaud*, the ship returned to the Arctic in 1926–7 as a supply vessel, and in 1928 was moored off Cambridge Bay as a floating warehouse, machine shop, and wireless station. *Bay-*

maud sank at her moorings in 1930 and was partially salvaged before slipping into deeper water.

The wreck lies canted on her port side in 10 m of water, parallel to the shore, with a portion of the starboard hull visible at low tide. *Maud* was documented by a team led by James Delgado in 1995 and 1996, the first wreck archaeologically documented in the **Arctic**. The ship is substantially intact to the level of the main deck, which was removed along with the superstructure and engines during salvage. The forecastle deck, with windlass, is intact, and the anchor cable runs through the hawsepipe to the seabed. The

Starboard hull of Maud *at the waterline. (Vancouver Maritime Museum/Mike Paris)*

Maud's windlass at the bow. (Vancouver Maritime Museum/Mike Paris)

hull is sound, and the massive ice beams, iron-sheathed bow and stern, retractable rudder, and double-planked hull evidences the special construction of the ship for Arctic voyages. J.P.D.

ADDITIONAL READING

Delgado, J.P., 1997, *Made for the Ice: The Wreck of the Polar Exploration Ship Maud*, Vancouver.

Mauritius

One of the oldest wrecks of the Dutch East India Company (VOC) that has been located and excavated to date. On 19 March

1609, seven years after the founding of the VOC, *Mauritius* sunk less than a kilometre off Cape Lopes Goncalves, near what is now Port Gentil, in Gabon, West Africa. The 700 ton VOC ship was on a homeward-bound voyage to Amsterdam. The wreck was discovered in 1985 during a geophysical survey by the oil company Elf Gabon at a depth of 10 to 15 m. In 1986 a large-scale underwater excavation was executed.

The site consisted of a large tumulus of metal ingots covered with madrepores which was 39 m long and 19 m wide. On the top and rear of the tumulus seven bronze guns and seven iron guns were exposed on the surface. Another fourteen guns were recovered beneath the tumulus; these were originally stocked in the hold across the axis of the keel. Of the twenty-eight guns which *Mauritius* had on board as armament or ballast, nine were made of bronze and nineteen were made of iron. They had been manufactured in England, Spain, Portuguese Goa, and Holland. An interesting specimen made by Henricus Meurs bore the inscription 'De Oude Oost Indische Compagnie', the name of one of the Dutch East India Companies that preceded the VOC.

The cargo of *Mauritius* appears to have largely consisted of small planoconvex metal ingots, their weights ranging from 1 to 13.5 kg. The total number of ingots on board has been estimated at 18,000 to 22,000, weighing approximately 122 tonnes. Archival information revealed that the ingots were made of a metal called *toutenague* or *tutanego* and that they were originally part of the cargo of *San Antonio*. This Portuguese carrack was captured in 1605 by the Dutch at Patani on the coast of Malesia. Metallographic analysis indicated that the metal was pure zinc, which contained only a few traces of lead, arsenic, antimony, iron, and cadmium. The exact place of origin of these ingots is not clear. According to their shape they might have come from China, but isotopic analysis points to a Japanese origin. Nevertheless, the excavation of *Mauritius* provided the first accurate data on the composition of these shipments of *toutenague* metal, which were mentioned frequently in historical documents from the beginning of the 17th century. The actual metallographic nature of these products, however, seemed not to have been fully understood at that time, as zinc was not identified and produced in Europe until the middle of the 18th century.

The presence of peppercorns, which were coagulated on the zinc ingots, indicated that *Mauritius* also carried spices. The pepper cargo had been packed in bags, of which some fragments were archaeologically retrieved. Although most of the pepper had disintegrated, paleobotanical analysis identified three different types of peppercorns from the Patani region. A small amount of blue and white Ming porcelain from the Wan Li period was also recovered. Some finds had unique shapes and decorations which were previously unknown in collections of Chinese export ceramics in European museums.

Finally, *Mauritius* afforded a fine opportunity to study the ship's construction, since the ingots had protected and preserved significant elements of the hull. This yielded important information on the ship's shell-first construction and double outer planking. M.L'H.

ADDITIONAL READING

L'Hour, M., Long, L., and Rieth, E., 1989, *Le Mauritius: La mémoire engloutie*, Paris.

L'Hour, M., Long, L., and Rieth, E., 1990, 'The Wreck of an "Experimental" Ship of the Oost-Indishe Companie: The *Mauritius* (1609)', *International Journal of Nautical Archaeology*, 19, 63–73.

Mediterranean Sea

A nearly tideless body of water 4,000 km long with an average width of 800 km, bounded by Europe on the north, Asia on the east, Africa on the south, and the Atlantic Ocean on the west. Clockwise from the west, the modern nations on its shores are Spain, **France**, Monaco, **Italy**, the former Yugoslavia, Albania, **Greece**, Turkey, Syria, Lebanon, **Israel**, Egypt, Libya, Tunisia, Algeria, and Morocco. Although it is fed by the Black Sea and many rivers, including the Ebro in Spain, the Rhône in France, the Po in Italy, and the Nile in Egypt, the sea's great

rate of evaporation, due to heat, causes its surface to lie slightly lower than that of the Atlantic, which flows into it through the Straits of Gibraltar.

The sea is divided into the western Mediterranean and the eastern Mediterranean by the island of Sicily and the boot of Italy, passage between the two basins being only through the Straits of Messina (between Sicily and Italy) or the Straits of Sicily (between Sicily and Tunisia). Other large islands are Majorca, Corsica, and Sardinia in the western Mediterranean, and Cyprus and Crete in the eastern Mediterranean.

The northern Mediterranean is broken into a number of smaller seas by islands and protruding land masses. These are the Ligurian Sea north of Corsica; the Tyrrhenian Sea between Corsica, Sardinia, Sicily, and the Italian mainland; the Adriatic Sea between Italy and the Dalmatian coast; the Ionian Sea to the west of Greece (with the Mediterranean's greatest depth, 4,900 m); and the Aegean Sea between Greece and Asia Minor. The modern names are based on those of a larger number of seas named in antiquity.

Throughout Classical antiquity, weather in each of the seasons dictated when mariners dared set sail. Storms and uncertain winds kept small craft beached and held larger commercial vessels in port during winter months, the time of *mare clausum* (when 'the sea was closed'). Spring and autumn were deemed less dangerous, and hardier seamen set sail from the beginning of March until the middle of November, although it was between 27 May and 14 September that the

winds were considered most suitable for navigation. Summer winds are predictable in the eastern Mediterranean with the etesians (modern Greek *meltemi* or Turkish *meltem*) blowing regularly from the north or northwest; there is no such prevailing wind in the western Mediterranean, although there is a predominance of east winds. In spring and autumn, there are many local winds, notably the mistral that blows from the mountains into the Ligurian Sea, the bora in the Adriatic, and the sirocco of the Maghreb. Sailors also took advantage of strong offshore breezes in the evenings. It was not until the development of the full-rigged ship, around 1500, that vessels regularly sailed year-round in the Mediterranean.

Currents also played a role in navigation. Generally there are anticlockwise current patterns in each of the two halves of the Mediterranean, western and eastern. Currents that especially affected ships were in the Straits of Messina and in the Euripus between the Greek mainland and the island of Euboea, as well as the strong currents into the Mediterranean from the Black Sea and Atlantic, although coastal countercurrents within the Straits of Gibraltar allowed greater flexibility of navigation there.

Prehistory

From very early times, the Mediterranean Sea has served as a highway over which people, goods, and ideas have moved. By 9,000 BC seafarers were travelling to the Aegean island of Melos for obsidian, a hard volcanic stone that was brought back to the mainland to be fashioned into tools, as

Phoenician galley depicted on a stone relief from the palace of the Assyrian king Sennacherib (704–681 BC) at Nineveh. (Courtesy of the Trustees of the British Museum)

revealed in southern Greece's Franchi Cave. Cyprus seems to have been colonized about the same time, perhaps 500 years later. The excavated bones of large fish and dolphins show that fishermen were pursuing their catches far from the shores of both Greece and Sicily at least as early as 8,000 BC. After the introduction of agriculture and animal husbandry to the Aegean, Crete was colonized around 6,000 BC by humans bringing sheep, goats, pigs, cattle, and dogs that must have required a significant fleet of some type, and Sardinia to the west was settled not much later. By the middle of the 5th millennium BC the earliest large stone buildings anywhere were being built on the centrally located island of Malta.

Navigation continued throughout prehistoric times, with a pattern of archaeological finds suggesting that Mesopotamian influences during the Late Neolithic period (late 4th millennium BC) reached the Mediterranean coast of Syria over land and continued to Egypt by sea.

In the Early Bronze Age, approximately the 3rd millennium BC, Egyptian sailors sailed to Lebanon for cedar timber in ships that may have attained lengths approaching 50 m; stone reliefs show the ships' bipod masts and the thick rope hogging trusses that ran from stem to stern to prevent those ends from sagging into the troughs of waves. In this earliest era of metallurgy, the search for metals rather than wood may well have led to seaborne expansion in the Aegean, where the Early Bronze Age cultures are called by archaeologists Early Helladic in Greece, Early Minoan on Crete, and Early Cycladic throughout the Cyclades (the islands between Crete and the Greek mainland). Cycladic artefacts have been found as far away as the Dalmatian coast and Sicily. The ceramic remains of an Early Helladic or Early Cycladic cargo have been excavated off the tiny island of Dokos, near larger Hydra, by the Hellenic Institute of Marine Archaeology, but it is only from depictions incised on pottery or from crude lead and clay models that we know the appearance of contemporary hulls, which look like long paddled canoes. This is also the time of almost identical gold treasures from Troy II in Asia and Poliochni on the neighbouring island of Lemnos, one of many indications of sea traffic between the two areas.

In the Middle Bronze Age, Minoan civilization flowered on Crete. Tradition holds that King Minos, after whom archaeologists named the Bronze Age culture of Crete, had the first navy, but whether he actually controlled the sea, as suggested by the lack of fortifications around most Minoan sites,

remains a subject of scholarly debate. Minoan colonies in the Aegean islands and on the west coast of Asia Minor, and Minoan trade goods spread from Sicily to the Levant, all point to maritime activity. The clearest depictions of ships and boats of the period are in a mural found at Bronze Age Akrotiri on **Thera** (Santorini), north of Crete, which was covered by deep ash from a volcanic eruption *c.* 1600 BC. Some of the vessels are rowed, others paddled, and still others have raised square sails. A ceramic cargo that has been tentatively dated to this time was excavated from the **Sheytan Deresi Wreck** in Turkey by the **Institute of Nautical Archae-**

Mesopotamian cylinder seal of hematite from the Kaş wreck at Uluburun, Turkey, and its impression in clay. (© INA)

ology (INA), but as at Dokos no hull remains were found.

By the Late Bronze Age (*c.* 1600–1100 BC) the Mediterranean was traversed from one end to the other. Mycenaean (another name for Late Helladic) pottery spread throughout the Levant and as far west as Spain, where two Mycenaean sherds have been found. Contemporary pottery from Cyprus has similarly been found all the way from the Syro-Palestinian coast to Egypt to Sicily and Sardinia. It once was believed that the Mycenaeans were the major sea power of this time, but the Late Bronze Age shipwrecks at **Cape Gelidonya** and **Uluburun** in Turkey, and at Iria in the Bay of Argos in Greece, excavated by the University of Pennsylvania Museum, the Institute of Nautical Archaeology, and the **Hellenic Institute of Marine Archaeology**, respectively, have led to a re-examination of the evidence, with much of it pointing to a larger role for Syrian and/or Cypriot seafarers than previously supposed; the two hulls in Turkey were both built of planks held together by pegged mortise-and-tenon joints, like those in Classical Greek and Roman hulls, and both carried heavy stone weight-anchors.

The Late Bronze Age in the eastern Mediterranean came to a rather sudden end around 1200 BC with the destruction and

subsequent depopulation of Mycenaean sites in Greece, the collapse of Hittite civilization in Anatolia (Turkey), and the violent destruction of cities on Cyprus and among Canaanite and other cities along the Syro-Palestinian coast. The destroyers, called by the Egyptians simply 'Peoples of the Sea', were eventually defeated by an Egyptian naval force in a battle commemorated in a relief of Ramesses III. It is not thought, however, that they were the original invaders, for these 'Sea Peoples' seem to have included refugees from Greece and/or Anatolia, driven from their homes by unknown forces or causes. That Egypt still sent ships to the Lebanon for timber is known from the Tale of Wen-Amon, preserved on papyrus, but it also reflects the decline in Egyptian power and influence by around 1100 BC.

The great seafarers in the succeeding Iron Age were the Phoenicians, descendants of the Canaanites. Because the Phoenicians did not leave a great literary legacy, their exploits are known today largely from archaeological finds and from Greek written sources, from which we learn that Phoenicians may well have circumnavigated Africa by 600 BC; there is no doubt that western Phoenicians from Carthage were colonizing the Atlantic coast of North Africa by the 6th century BC. Greek seafarers were scarcely less active, however, for it was also during the Iron Age that Greeks colonized the Black Sea, the western coast of Asia Minor, and much of southern Italy and eastern Sicily by sea.

A major development in naval warfare took place in this period, for in the 9th century BC the introduction of the ram transformed warships from simple troop transports like those that had carried Homer's heroes from Greece to Troy, or fighting platforms like those in the Ramesses III relief, into actual weapons. By the following century depictions of both Greek and Phoenician ships with rams were common. The need for more rowers on these war galleys led to the invention around 700 BC, either by Phoenicians or Greeks, of ships on which the number of rowers per side could be doubled by having some of the rowers sit at a higher level. In the second half of the 6th century BC the number of levels seems to have increased to three, with 170 men manning the oars of what came to be known as triremes.

6th–4th century BC: Greece, Etruria, and Carthage

Greece, not being a particularly fertile land, prospered between the 6th and 4th centuries BC largely because of its mercantile and military fleets, the former bringing grain from Italy and the Black Sea, and the latter, following its defeat of the Persian fleet at the Battle of Salamis in 480 BC, controlling the eastern Mediterranean. The economic and legal aspects of commercial voyages are known from written records. Merchants (often foreigners) financed their overseas ventures by borrowing from wealthy citizens who could make a profit when the loan plus interest were paid at the end of a successful voyage; it was a gamble, however, for the lender lost everything if the ship and its cargo were lost at sea.

Depictions of the single-masted Classical Greek vessels that were involved in this trade are surprisingly rare. Archaeology, however, is gradually revealing the hulls and cargoes of such merchantmen. A partial 5th-century Greek cargo has been raised by **Oxford University MARE** (Marine Archaeological Research) near Panarea in the Aeolian Islands, a Classical Greek ship of the late 5th or early 4th century BC has been excavated by the University of Pennsylvania Museum at Porticello (see **Straits of Messina Wreck**), and the remains of a much larger ship have been located and partly excavated by the Greek Archaeological Service at Alonissos in the northern Sporades. An exceptionally well-preserved Greek ship from a century later, excavated off Kyrenia, Cyprus, by the University of Pennsylvania Museum, was then restored by the INA and replicated and tested by the Hellenic Institute for the Preservation of the Maritime Tradition. The **Kyrenia Ship**'s lead-sheathed hull was held together by 4,000 pegged mortise-and-tenon joints, she was steered by a pair of quarter rudders, and her square sail could be adjusted into a fair imitation of a fore-and-aft sail by brailing lines that ran through nearly 200 lead brailing-rings sewn to the fabric. Another 4th-century BC Greek wreck, containing Punic finds, was partly excavated at El Sec, Palma Bay, Majorca.

The major rowed warships of this period,

Canaanite amphora which contained terebinth, from the Kaş Wreck at Uluburun, Turkey. (© INA)

triremes, are known, however, only through a very few depictions and ambiguous written descriptions, although the remains of the shipsheds that housed triremes, studied in the port of Athens at Piraeus and elsewhere, have provided evidence of dimensions. From such clues, John Morrison of Cambridge University and John Coates designed a modern **Reconstruction** which, having been built by the Greek Government for the British Trireme Trust, has been tested at sea by full complements of 170 volunteer rowers working their oars through outriggers that run the length of each side of the ship. Tactics used by triremes included the *diekplous*, by which ships ran straight through the enemy line, perhaps damaging the outriggers of opposing ships, and the *periplous*, by which ships went around the flanks of the enemy line; both allowed the attacking ships to turn and ram enemy vessels from the rear.

To the west, the Etruscans of northwest Italy also launched large fleets. Etruscan warships, with their peculiar bows, are known only from depictions, but several wrecks of probably Etruscan commercial ships have been found, with subsequent excavations of the 6th-century BC **Bon-Porté Wreck** by a French team and of the **Giglio Wreck** from about 600 BC at Giglio in Italy by Oxford University MARE. The hulls of these vessels were lashed or stitched together in a technique that would reappear half a millennium later in the northern Adriatic, where it would continue into medieval

times, but it is too early to say that lashing, or lacing, was typically Etruscan; one of two 6th- or early 5th-century BC Greek boats found underground in Marseille is lashed, whereas the other is mortise-and-tenon joined. A well-preserved hull of around 400 BC, of uncertain origin, excavated near Kibbutz Ma'agan Mikhael in Israel by the Centre for Maritime Studies (CMS) of Haifa University, shows a mixture of the two construction techniques, being built much like the Kyrenia Ship except at its lashed ends. A rare 6th-century BC tomb painting of an Etruscan merchantman shows it with an equally rare two masts.

Carthaginians, descendants of Phoenicians who settled in present-day Tunisia, continued the maritime tradition of their forebears, but firsthand evidence of their early ships is limited to scattered 7th- or 6th-century BC cargoes of Punic pottery at Cadiz, Spain, and Coltellazzo, Italy.

Alexander the Great left no heirs on his death in 323 BC. His empire was therefore divided among three of his generals. Thus began the two-hundred year period of separate kingdoms called Hellenistic. Hellenistic ships were sometimes immense, over a hundred metres in length, with crews of 3,000 to 4,000. Although names of these vessel types are preserved ('sixteens', 'twenties', 'thirties', and 'forties'), it is not known how they are rowed. Written evidence suggests that some were catamarans. These giants allowed the on-board construction of high fighting towers for archers, and the use of heavy war machines such as ballistas that could damage or sink other ships by hurling balls of lead or stone, or pots filled with combustible materials. Although physical evidence of these remain to be discovered, a Hellenistic ship's ram of the 2nd century BC was recovered near Athlit, Israel, and studied by CMS (see **Athlit Ram**); this unique find, the largest surviving ancient bronze cast in a single piece, was meant not to pierce an enemy ship's hull, but to crush and open the seams of its mortise-and-tenon joined planking. Two Hellenistic cargo carriers have been located and partly excavated by INA, one at **Serçe Limanı**, Turkey, and the other at Secca di Capistello, Lipari, Italy.

3rd century BC–4th century AD: Rome

The Romans of the Republic were not at first a seafaring people, having to depend on Greek ships and crews, but during the First Punic War in the middle of the 3rd century BC necessity led them to build and man their own navy, which soon was to rule the Mediterranean. Rome's foes in the Punic Wars were the Carthaginians or western Phoenicians, who by the middle of the

3rd century BC ruled the coasts of North Africa, southern Spain, Sardinia, Corsica, and western Sicily. The remains of a Carthaginian ship of about the same time (late third to first half of the 2nd century BC; see **Marsala Punic Warship**) was excavated and restored at Marsala, Sicily by Honor Frost, who also studied a neighbouring sister ship. The nearby harbour at Motya is one example of the artificial basins, called cothons, that the Carthaginians uniquely dug out to form parts of their harbours; on an island in the middle of the round cothon at Carthage in Tunisia were shipsheds, radiating like spokes, for over 220 warships.

From the earliest days of the Roman Empire at the end of the 1st century BC, the Romans realized the importance of a large permanent fleet to protect their commercial sea lanes from pirates and other enemies – for Rome depended on ships to bring her food, construction materials, and luxury goods (the last from as far away as India and China). Naval vessels still included the trireme and other types of large battleships, but were joined by the swift Liburnian, rowed from two levels, which was named after pirates from the Adriatic coast opposite Italy.

Commercial voyages were, as in earlier times, financed by maritime loans; merchants, shipowners and seamen continued to come from lower classes than the lenders. Commercial vessels were large – grain ships could be 55 m long – with curving swan necks typically placed behind stern cabins. They could be either double-ended or with straight stems that sometimes curved out to form ram-like cutwaters. Their hulls, especially those of larger ships, could be sheathed with lead. Merchant ships were usually driven by square sails, one on the mainmast and the other, called an *artemon*, on a raking mast at the bow (a unique three-master, depicted in a mosaic, carries in addition a mizzen), but a few representations of fore-and-aft sails exist, usually sprit sails but in one instance a lateen sail. Top average speed on voyages with favorable winds was 6 knots. Roman merchantmen were steered by a pair of quarter rudders, resembling great oars, one on either side. Typical Roman anchors were at first wooden, with lead stocks perpendicular to the arms and with lead collars that prevented those wooden arms from splaying away from their wooden shanks; myriad lead stocks and collars found on the floor of the Mediterranean point to the heavy maritime traffic at the time when they were in use. By the 3rd century BC, iron anchors appeared alongside wooden anchors, but did not immediately replace them.

Sailing from the East, Roman merchantmen brought back the lifeblood of Rome – African grain from Alexandria. A 2nd-century AD merchant ship built specially to carry grain has been excavated by the Direction des Recherches Archéologiques Sous-Marines at L'Anse des Laurons in France, its carefully waterproofed ceiling (interior planking) and unusually large chain pump providing evidence of the efforts taken to keep dampness from the grain, some of which was recovered from the wreck; in addition, this is the only ancient wreck with extensive preservation of its deck and bulwarks, and the first to provide examples of ancient dead-eyes.

As perishable grain does not leave a permanent record to be spotted on the seabed, most Roman wrecks are located and identi-

Greek bronze statue of the 5th century BC found in the Mediterranean off Calabria. (Ancient Art and Architecture Collection)

fied by cargoes of stone, tiles, bricks, metals in ingot form, works of art, and especially such things as wine, oil, and fish sauce (*garum*) that were carried in ceramic containers, especially two-handled amphoras and huge jars called *dolia*. A.J. Parker of Bristol University has collected information on nearly 700 Roman wrecks found in the Mediterranean, and the vast majority are of amphora carriers. The largest and most thoroughly studied of these is that of the 1st-century BC **Madrague de Giens Wreck**, near Toulon, France, with its 6,000 to 6,500 amphoras, which was excavated by scholars from the University of Aix-en-Provence for DRASSM and other French agencies.

Other Roman-period wrecks range from those of the tubby *corbitas* to the slender *pontos* and hybrid types. One of the most remarkably preserved was not found technically in the Mediterranean, but near it, in the Sea of Galilee, where a fishing boat of the time of Christ was salvaged and preserved by the Israel Department of Antiquities and Museums (see **Sea of Galilee Wreck**).

Stone was essential for the building of Rome, and non-perishable cargoes of stone from Asia Minor and Greece have been studied by the University of Pennsylvania Museum at Methone in southwest Greece, and at San Pietro and Torre Sgarrata on the heel of Italy; several of these show how sarcophagi were shipped with their decorated faces only roughly hewn, to be carefully finished at their destinations. Sunken cargoes of millstones are commonplace; one 2nd-century BC ship lost near Isla Pedrosa, Spain, carried nearly two hundred. Intended for the construction of buildings, shipments of stone columns and blocks have been found off the coasts of Tunisia, Libya, Croatia, Turkey, Italy and Sicily, Spain, and France, and the terracotta tiles meant to roof these buildings appear off most of these same coasts. Roman traffic in metals was especially heavy in the western Mediterranean, as revealed by sunken cargoes of tin, copper, iron, and lead ingots off the same coasts as well as those of Algeria and Morocco.

Probably the wrecks best known to the public, however, are those that have yielded works of art, as in the Bay of Marathon and the harbour at Piraeus. Shipments of art works in Italian waters are known from Bari, Riace, and those places in the Tyrrhenian and Adriatic seas, respectively, where fishermen netted the Piombino Apollo now in the Louvre, and the bronze Youth now in the Getty Museum. A ship wrecked off Tunisia carried marble and bronze statuary and marble architectural fragments (see **Mahdia Wreck**). Somewhere between the Greek island of Kalymnos and the Turkish mainland a fisherman netted the bronze statue of a woman, whereas in nearby Turkish waters outside Yalikavak Turkish sponge draggers netted the statue of an African youth and a bronze statuette of Fortuna. Off southern Turkey, not far from Serçe Limani, another sponger netted the bronze bust of a mourning lady.

The sea lanes all led to Rome, but not directly. In Republican times cargoes were unloaded at Puteoli, near Naples, and carted to Rome. Under Emperor Claudius, however, the outer harbour of the great port of Ostia at the mouth of the River Tiber was built; Trajan added an inner, hexagonal harbour. At Ostia cargoes were transferred onto lighters from freighters anchored offshore, or carried directly ashore after rowed tugboats pulled the large sailing vessels alongside stone quays. Produce and goods were then towed from paths on the banks of the Tiber upstream to Rome. The extent of this traffic is suggested by the estimate that Rome needed 200,000 tonnes of grain a year, and by the statement of a 2nd-century AD author that merchant ships arrived every hour of every day.

All harbours face the danger of becoming clogged with silt; the wreck of a vessel used for harbour dredging, found at Marseille, provides first-hand evidence of the Roman battle against it. Other Roman harbours show how efforts were made to avoid silting up by building quays on arches, which allowed currents to circulate beneath them. Hydraulic cement, invented in Roman times, was sometimes poured into **Cofferdams** in the sea to form piers and other supports, as described by Vitruvius, the Roman writer on architecture. Roman harbours that have been published thoroughly after intensive archaeological study include those at **Cosa** (under the auspices of the American Academy in Rome) and Ostia in Italy, the Corinthian harbour at **Kenchreai** in Greece (universities of Chicago and Indiana), and Herod's great harbour at **Caesarea Maritima** in Israel (Israel Antiquities Authority and the University of Maryland). The last was described by the Jewish historian Josephus, who told how Herod overcame the hostility of the nearly unbroken coast between Egypt and Phoenicia by having stone foundation blocks up to 15 m long lowered into the sea to depths of 35 m in order to start the construction of his breakwaters.

Lighthouses guided ships to the ports. The most famous was the 3rd-century BC Pharos at **Alexandria**, one of the Seven Wonders of the World as conceived during the Hellenistic period. The Pharos was in ruins in the 14th century, after having been damaged over the centuries by earthquakes, but its remains are being studied in the harbour of Alexandria by the Egyptian Supreme Council of Antiquities and the French Centre d'Etudes Alexandrines. Like others known from their remains or from ancient depictions, the Pharos was built in tiers of decreasing size with a flat top on which the fire burned.

Rome ruled the Mediterranean for 500 years, until internal strife and barbarian invasions in the 3rd century AD so weakened the empire that the Roman fleet withered; state revenues were needed to pay for the

Divers survey the Iskandil Burnu Shipwreck. (© INA)

army that faced the enemy tribes at Rome's borders. A renewal of piracy showed that the Mediterranean was no longer a Roman lake. By the time the Goths invaded the Aegean in the second half of the century, the Roman fleet was almost non-existent. The situation in Rome deteriorated so badly that in the 4th century Constantine the Great moved the capital to Byzantium (renamed by him Constantinople). An amphora carrier of around AD 400 has been carefully excavated by French archaeologists at Port Vendres in France.

5th–13th century

At first the Byzantines lacked a strong navy. In the 5th century Vandals captured Carthage and ruled a western Mediterranean kingdom that included Spain, the Balearics, Sardinia, and Corsica, and Ostrogoths had their own kingdom in Italy. In defence, perhaps, a new type of fighting ship appeared at this time in the Byzantine navy: the single-banked *dromon* ('runner'), which was exceptionally manoeuvrable because of its lateen rig, the favoured rig in the medieval Mediterranean. No warship of this time has been found, but a late 4th- or early 5th-century wine-carrier excavated by the University of Pennsylvania Museum off **Yassiada** in Turkey reveals the early stages of the slow evolution from hull-first ship construction to frame-first (or skeletal) construction.

In the 6th century, under Emperor Justinian, the Byzantine navy was able to capture Carthage and eventually end Vandal and Ostrogothic power in the Mediterranean. At this time Constantinople, like Rome earlier, still depended on shipments from abroad, especially shipments of grain from Egypt. The remains of several merchant ships from the 6th century have been found.

One, carrying the prefabricated marble elements for a Byzantine church, was excavated by Gerhard Kapitän off Marzamemi in south-east Sicily, and another, carrying pottery from Palestine, was studied by the INA off **Iskandil Burnu** in Turkey.

An early 7th-century hull excavated by M.-P. Jézégou at Saint Gervais, France, may be skeleton built unlike earlier Mediterranean ships – that is, its planks were nailed to a skeleton of frames rather than attached one to another by mortise-and-tenon joints as in the earlier practice – but this interpretation remains controversial. A contemporary hull being uncovered in the harbour of Dor, Israel, by CMS of Haifa University and INA seems to be a more certain example of a hull built in this modern manner, its small size making frame-first construction possible. In the early 7th century, as known from another wine-carrier excavated by the University of Pennsylvania Museum off Yassiada, the move towards modern hull construction was still evolving in larger vessels, for this seagoing ship was built in the ancient manner, with mortise-and-tenon joints, below the waterline, but in the modern frame-first manner above it.

The 7th century also saw the rapid rise of Islam. By the middle of the century, Byzantium faced a powerful new naval power that would help make possible the Arab domination of not only the eastern end of the Mediterranean, but of all of North Africa and Spain. At first the Arabs had to depend on experienced Christian shipwrights and seamen for their fleets. Nevertheless, they were able to defeat a Byzantine fleet of perhaps a thousand vessels in the Battle of the Masts in 655, and in 673 attacked Constantinople itself. It was only the use of Greek fire – a secret substance used in a kind of flame-thrower – that saved the city and was to drive the Arabs out of the Aegean.

The 8th and 9th centuries saw a decline in Byzantium's naval fortunes. Muslim forces conquered the major islands – Sicily, Crete, Corsica, Sardinia, and the Balearics – and were to remain powerful at sea until the 11th century. Even so, Byzantine maritime commerce was not halted. Not much is known of the ships of this time. From the end of the 9th century comes the earliest known depiction of a triangular lateen sail of the type that was to see such popularity in the Mediterranean, although it had probably been in common use for some time prior to the painting. The excavation of the 9th-century **Bozburun Wreck**, Turkey, begun by the INA in 1995, should reveal more about the development of ships and their rigging in this century.

At the end of the 10th century a Byzantine fleet of more than 3,000 ships began the reconquest of some of the empire's losses, a reconquest that continued into the first half of the 11th century. Around 1025 a Byzantine ship that had probably sailed from near Constantinople to somewhere near Caesarea in modern Israel sank with a cargo of three tonnes of raw and broken glass at Serçe Limani, Turkey. The excavation of the ship by the INA at Texas A&M University revealed what is the earliest fully excavated and studied example of a seagoing vessel built entirely in the modern frame-first manner; she probably sported two lateen sails. Her ultimate destination, perhaps Constantinople, remains unknown, although documents reveal that in the 13th century Byzantium's client, Venice, received similar shipments of broken glass from the Levant.

In the Christian reconquests of the 11th century, Pisa and Genoa helped free Corsica and Sardinia from the Muslims; by 1100 these and other maritime cities of a reawakened Italy were true naval powers. At the end of the 11th century the Byzantine call for aid against the Seljuk Turks, resulting in the First Crusade, further stimulated the growth of these Italian navies because of the use of their ships by Crusaders on their way to the Holy Land. But as they prospered from East–West commerce, these new maritime republics fought among themselves until Venice eventually became pre-eminent.

Fire-shooting Byzantine *dromon*s were rowed, like some Classical warships, from two levels, but without the benefit of outriggers. Shortly before 1300, however, these ships were replaced in Italian navies by galleys with rowers sitting on just one level, but with two or three men sharing single benches; each man on a bench pulled his own oar, with the oars from each bench pivoting close together on an outrigger similar to the outriggers of Classical times. At Camarina, Italy, the remains of a slim vessel, perhaps of the 12th century, have been found; they could be of a galley, perhaps a horse transport.

Throughout earlier periods seafarers had tried, when feasible, to stay within sight of land in order to navigate by landmarks, for further out at sea they had only celestial bodies and winds to give them an idea of direction. Navigational improvements in the 13th century allowed sailing during extended periods of overcast skies, and this was a major factor in voyages being undertaken at any time of the year. The improvements included the invention or introduction from the East of the compass; the introduction of portulans, or books of

sailing directions with bearings and distances; and the oldest known marine charts. To use these new navigational aids, a means for keeping accurate time was needed, and it was in the 13th century that the hour-glass was probably introduced. All of these advances helped make the Mediterranean a Latin lake again, for neither the Muslims or Byzantines kept up with the advances in maritime technology. It was at this time that the use of maritime insurance, bills of exchange, and manuals of foreign trade also aided maritime commerce.

During the time of the Crusades, from the end of the 11th century to the end of the 13th, it was not only warriors who needed transport. The growth of more populated towns in Europe meant a greater market for Oriental goods such as spices, aromatics, and silk, for which European merchants traded both manufactured goods and raw materials, and even slaves from the Black Sea. By the 13th century technically improved Venetian, Genoese, and Catalan merchantmen, in spite of papal pressure against Christian trade with Muslims, sailed year round to the Muslim Levant for pepper, ginger, cloves, cinnamon, frankincense, cotton, and the alkali needed in the production of soap and glass.

14th–18th century

The volume of Italian trade with the Near East fluctuated with continued papal pressure and prohibitions during the 14th century, but in the second half of the century regular trade resumed, with Venice emerging as the dominant European trading partner. Venetian cogs and galleys carried eastward vast quantities of European copper, tin, and lead, as well as olive oil, honey, fruits, nuts, and such luxury goods as furs, coral, and ambergris, but European cloth was the favoured object of trade. Between the 14th and 16th centuries great merchant galleys, probably introduced to provide pilgrims with quicker and safer passage to the Holy Land, sped goods faster than could sails, but at greater expense; a Venetian galley might have had 180 oarsmen, whereas a cog required on average only fifty seamen overall. Some contemporary galleys could haul 200 to 250 tonnes of merchandise, and some also carried three masts to take advantage of favourable winds. The role of great merchant galleys in the Italian textile trade with northern Europe, and in the Black Sea for grain and wax, was immense. The skeleton-built hull of a 14th-century merchant galley was excavated at Cala Culip in Catalonia, Spain, by a new department of underwater archaeology at the Centre for Archaeological Investigations in Girona.

The 14th century brought other innovations to Mediterranean seafaring, including the addition of guns to ships, and the adoption by Italian fleets of the stern rudder that had accompanied northern cogs into the Mediterranean. There were other changes based on these clinker-built, single-masted, square-rigged cogs with their high castles at bow and stern, resulting in the two-masted carrack.

The three-masted 15th-century carrack was the culmination of this mixture of northern and Mediterranean maritime traditions. Southern mariners added their familiar lateen sail, as a mizzen for greater manoeuvrability, to the single square sail of the northern cog, as well as a square headsail. With a redesigned hull this new merchant ship saw action from the Mediterranean to northern Europe throughout the 15th century. By this time heavy naval artillery was standard, and early in the next century gunports came into being. Oared ships continued in use. The most thoroughly studied remains of a fighting galley of the 15th century were found by Enrico Scandurra not in the Mediterranean, but at the bottom of inland **Lake Garda** in Italy, where the ship had been carried overland from Venice during a war against Milan in 1439, and scuttled during a different engagement in 1509.

Galleys in the 16th century were still rowed by several men to a bench, but now the men on each bench, sitting abreast, pulled the same huge oar rather than individual oars. The largest military galleys, called galliasses, were rowed by up to seven men per oar who sat under thick decks that supported heavy cannons and other artillery. Able to inflict damage on their enemies from great distances, galliasses helped the Christians defeat the Turks in the 1571 Battle of Lepanto, the last great naval battle fought with oared ships. The wreck of a 16th-century Mediterranean galliass (see *Girona*) built in Naples was excavated by Robert Stenuit off the coast of northern Ireland where it had sunk in a storm while fleeing with other vessels of the defeated **Spanish Armada**. The wreck of a vessel that was probably built and armed in Genoa (see *Lomellina*) at the beginning of the 16th century has also been excavated, with civic support and backing from the Ministry of Culture, off the French coast near the roadstead of Villefrance. And an Ottoman wreck of a possible warship from the same century, when Spain and Ottoman Turkey were the two major sea powers, has been excavated by the INA off Turkey (see **Yassiada Wrecks**).

In the 16th and 17th centuries Atlantic trade became more important to the major European powers, and it is in the New World, not the Mediterranean, that most shipwrecks of the period have been located, especially those of newly introduced men-of-war called galleons. This does not mean that the Mediterranean was emptied of vessels. Regular crossings of the sea occurred, which took one or two weeks from north to south, and two or three months from one end to the other. There has been, however, less archaeological interest in later ships in the Mediterranean than elsewhere.

Among later wrecks studied in the Mediterranean is that of the 18th-century *Slava Rossii*, sunk at Ile du Levant not far from St Tropez, France. Excavated by the Groupe de Recherche en Archéologie Navale, the wreck has yielded not only the expected armaments, but a unique collection of eighty bronze and brass icons that reveal new information about Russian culture and religion at the time of Catherine the Great.

The study of shipwrecks has added greatly to the history of the Mediterranean, the ships that crossed it, and the lands that border it. Even greater knowledge of the sea's past, unfortunately, has been lost forever. For every carefully excavated and published wreck, dozens have been destroyed by ignorant or greedy looters, some looking for souvenirs and others seeking profit. Such looting is illegal, but is as hard to stop as the growing illegal traffic in antiquities that destroys ancient sites on land. All countries bordering the Mediterranean have antiquities laws intended to protect antiquities, including those in the sea, but just as helpful for future research are the new or expanding programmes of nautical archaeology in almost all of these same countries, for they will set the examples for future generations to follow. G.F.B.

ADDITIONAL READING

Ahrweiler, H., 1966, *Byzance et la mer: La marine de guerre, la politique et les institutions maritimes de Byzance aux VIIe–XVe siècles*, Paris.

Archaeonautica, 1977–, Paris.

Ashtor, E., 1983, *Levant Trade in the Later Middle Ages*, Princeton, New Jersey.

Basch, L., 1987, *Le musée imaginaire de la marine antique*, Athens.

Bass, G.F. (ed.), 1972, *A History of Seafaring Based on Underwater Archaeology*, London and New York.

Bound, M. (ed.), 1995, *Archaeology of Ships of War*, Oswestry, Shropshire.

Braudel, F., 1972, *The Mediterranean and the Mediterranean World in the Age of Philip II*, trans. S. Reynolds, New York.

Calhoun, G.M., 1926, *The Business Life of Ancient Athens*, Chicago.

Casson, L., 1964, *Illustrated History of Ships and Boats*, Garden City, New York.

Casson, L., 1991, *The Ancient Mariners*, 2nd edn, Princeton, New Jersey.

Casson, L., 1994, *Ships and Seafaring in Ancient Times*, Austin, Texas.

Casson, L., 1995, *Ships and Seamanship in the Ancient World*, 2nd edn, Baltimore.

Enalia, 1989–, Athens.

Gardiner, R. (ed.), 1995, *The Age of the Galley: Mediterranean Oared Vessels Since Pre-Classical Times*, London.

Heyd, W., 1885–6, *Histoire du commerce du Levant au moyen âge*, trans. F. Raynaud, Leipzig.

INA Quarterly (formerly *INA Newsletter*), 1974–

International Journal of Nautical Archaeology, 1972–

Lane, F.C., 1934, *Venetian Ships and Shipbuilders of the Renaissance*, Baltimore.

Lewis, A., 1951, *Naval Power and Trade in the Mediterranean AD 500–1100*, Princeton, New Jersey.

Lewis, A.R. and Runyan, T.J., 1985, *European Naval and Maritime History, 300–1500*, Bloomington, Indiana.

McCann, A.M., 1987, *The Roman Port and Fishery of Cosa*, Princeton, New Jersey.

Meijer, F. and van Nijf, O., 1992, *Trade, Transport and Society in the Ancient World*, London and New York.

Morrison, J.S. and Coates, J.F., 1986, *The Athenian Trireme: The History and Reconstruction of an Ancient Greek Warship*, Cambridge.

Morrison, J.S. and Williams, R.T., 1968, *Greek Oared Ships 900–322 BC*, Cambridge.

Parker, A.J, 1992, *Ancient Shipwrecks of the Mediterranean and the Roman Provinces*, Oxford.

Prieto, J.N. *et al.*, 1989, *Excavacions arqueològiques subaquàtiques a Cala Culip*, Girona.

Raban, A. (ed.), 1985, *Harbour Archaeology*, Oxford.

Rougé, J., 1966, *Recherches sur l'organisation du commerce maritime sous l'empire romain*, Paris.

Rougé, J., 1981, *Ships and Fleets of the Ancient Mediterranean*, trans. S. Frazier, Middleton, Connecticut.

Throckmorton, P. (ed.), 1987, *The Sea Remembers: Shipwrecks and Archaeology*, London and New York.

Wachsmann, S., 1996, *Seagoing Ships and Seamanship in the Bronze Age Levant*, College Station, Texas.

Meresteyn

Dutch East India Company vessel wrecked on Jutten Island, at the entrance to Saldanha Bay, near Cape Town in 1702. *Meresteyn*, a pinnace of 826 tons, was carrying a cargo from Texel, the Netherlands, intended for trade in the East Indies and a complement of Dutch soldiers bound for the Company's military forts in Cape Town and Asia. The site is comprised of anchors, bronze swivel guns, iron cannon, lead ingots, and concreted coinage scattered over a shallow reef. Divers have illegally collected artefacts from this site since the 1970s, most of which have been sold at local and international auctions. In 1975 local museum curator Lalou Meltzer and numismatist Frank Mitchell managed to catalogue and publish reports on part of the collection. These items included ordnance, military hardware, cutlery, shoes, and navigation instruments. A small portion of the collection, primarily Dutch silver coins, was donated to the South Africa Cultural History Museum and Simons Town Museum in Cape Town and the Africana Museum in Johannesburg.

In 1983 *Meresteyn* was among twenty-three wrecks declared as national monuments by the National Monuments Council (NMC). This provisional declaration lasted five years, when all shipwrecks in South African waters were given equal protection by the 1986 amendment to the Act. A salvage permit was issued to Reginald and William Dodds by the NMC, who recovered the bronze guns and lead ingots. The NMC database contains the required salvage activity reports, a preliminary site map, and correspondence listing the artefacts that were donated to various museums. L.H., T.D.

ADDITIONAL READING

Leibrandt, H.C.V., 1896, trans. in *Precis of the Archives of the Cape of Good Hope, Journal, 1699–1732*, VC 16, Cape Archives.

Marsden, P., 1976, 'The *Meresteyn*, Wrecked in 1702, near Cape Town, South Africa', *International Journal of Nautical Archaeology*, 5, 3, 201–19.

Mitchell, F.K., 1972, 'Sea Treasure from the Wreck of the *Meeresteijn*', *South African Numismatic Journal*, 7 (Nov).

Mexico

Country in North America with a rich and complex blend of Indian and Spanish cultures. Part of this heritage remains at the bottom of its waters. Underwater archaeological sites can be divided mainly into two categories: those in inland waters which belong primary to the pre-Hispanic period, and those in marine waters where the historical shipwrecks occurred. Although the cultural richness in these marine waters belongs mainly to the Colonial period, there is evidence of pre-Hispanic coastal navigation.

Mexico has more than 10,000 km of coastline and has jurisdiction over 200 nautical miles (370 km) known as the Economic Exclusion Zone. It is surrounded by the Pacific Ocean to the west and the Gulf of Mexico and the Mexican Caribbean to the east. In addition to its major rivers, the longest one being the Rio Grande, called the Rio Bravo del Norte, which extends along the Mexican–USA border, there are numerous lakes, lagoons, springs, and *cenotes* or sink holes.

Owing to the fact that indigenous cultures established themselves next to inland waters, or along the coastline, there is a large number of pre-Hispanic submerged

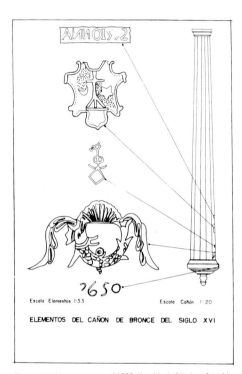

Twelve-sided bronze cannon of 1552, the oldest of its type found in the western hemisphere. Campeche, Mexico. (P.L. Erreguenerena)

cultural sites. Many of them were used as sacred places where the Olmecs, Mayas, Zapotecs, Mixtecs, Otomies, and Totonacas, among others, performed ceremonies during which they offered incense, semiprecious stones, textiles, gold, ceramic, copper, wood, and bone objects and, in many cases, human beings, to the deities of the water, whose names changed according to each culture. Other places contain remains of items of daily use, and sometimes evidence of riverine and seafaring trading activities. In some cases prehistoric fauna have been found in the same area where pre-Hispanic objects were located, as at the spring of Media Luna, in the State of San Luis Potosi, in central Mexico.

The historical submerged heritage includes a high number of shipwrecks that occurred during the period when the Spanish fleets would travel from the Old to the New World, and vice-versa, carrying not only people but supplies for the new settlements and all the riches that these colonies produced for the Spanish realm. For several centuries the ocean was the only means of communication possible between the two continents, and the hardships and dangers were many: storms, pirates, fires, ships' deterioration, lack of accurate maps and inexperienced pilots, among others.

During the 1950s, 1960s, and 1970s several treasure-hunters and sport divers – indigenous and foreign – dedicated themselves to explore sites and recover artefacts, which in many cases were taken outside the country. As diving technology improved, there was an increasing interest in undertaking projects that were more salvage than underwater archaeology. The main goal of these salvages was the recovery of materials, not the knowledge that a scientific study can provide. There were times, however, when objects were returned to the relevant authorities, and some information was published, mostly in magazines and newspapers. In none of these cases was conservation considered. This resulted in the deterioration and sometimes the complete destruction of the recovered objects.

There were other cases in which Mexican archaeologists directed or collaborated in underwater projects but, since they did not dive, they could not excavate the sites or make a systematic record underwater. In some of these projects the water level was lowered and archaeological land techniques were applied, as in the Cenote of Sacrifice or Sacred Well of **Chichén Itzá** in northern Yucatan during 1960–61 and 1967–8, and the Cenote of Agua Azul in Chinkultic, Chiapas, during four field seasons in 1966, 1968, 1969, and 1970.

Although there are activities that can be considered as the antecedents of Mexican underwater archaeology, it was not until 1980 that the National Institute of Anthropology and History (INAH) created its Underwater Archaeology Department (DAS) in order to protect, investigate, conserve, and make known the pre-Hispanic and historical submerged heritage of the country. Since the creation of the DAS, projects encompassing both categories – inland and marine waters – have taken place, with the assistance of Mexican and foreign institutions and such specialists as the Mexican Navy, the Ministry of Education, the National Autonomous University of Mexico (UNAM), and the national petroleum company PEMEX, as well as the **Institute of Nautical Archaeology** (INA) of College Station, Texas, the Institute of Ships of Exploration and Discovery Research (SEDR) of Corpus Christi, Texas and East Carolina University, and the

US National Park Service. Among the main projects that were carried out are:

1. The Cayo Nuevo Wrecks (1979–83). This project started after two Louisiana divers had located some cannon and anchors in the Cayo Nuevo Reef, off the coast of Campeche, in the Gulf of Mexico. Two colonial wrecks were distinguished, one from the 16th century and the other from the 18th century. During four field seasons, a survey and test excavations were conducted and some objects were recovered. Among these, the most significant is a demi-culverin, a twelve-sided bronze cannon apparently inscribed with the date 1552. This is the oldest cannon of its type ever recovered in the western hemisphere; it is now exhibited at the Regional Museum in Campeche City.

2. The Media Luna Spring (1981–2). This spring, located near the town of Rio Verde, San Luis Potosi, is considered to be a paradise for divers, so it has been continually ravaged since the 1950s. In 1981 the DAS conducted a project with two main goals: the study of the spring itself from an archaeological and biological perspective, and the correlation of the terrestrial and the underwater archaeological sites. In spite of the fact that thousands of artefacts had been looted, some pieces and two burials were recovered *in situ*. These were identified as belonging to the Chichimeca culture, between AD 600 and 900.

3. The **Bahía Mujeres Wreck** (1983, 1984, 1990). In the late 1950s and early 1960s important artillery pieces and anchors dating from the 16th century were recovered from this site by the local Lima family, a CEDAM team (a Mexican avocational group), Edwin Link, and the Mexican Navy; they believed that it was *La Nicolasa*, one of the conquistador Francisco de Montejo's ships. A joint effort among INAH, INA, and SEDR was made to relocate, survey, and excavate the remains of this shipwreck, in a reef between Can-Cun and Isla Mujeres, in the state of Quintana Roo. However, it was discovered that it was not *La Nicolasa*. In the last field season, a group of marine biologists from the UNAM studied the area, removed the corals where the diggings were going to happen, and replaced them after the archaeologists ended their research.

4. Pre-Hispanic Navigational Aids along the Coast of Quintana Roo (1984, 1985, 1988, 1989). Several surveys were made along the Yucatan coast of Quintana Roo in order to locate pre-Hispanic structures which might have served as navigational aids during Maya riverine and seafaring trading activities. While many of these structures are visible from the sea, others are located in the interior; some of them are near *cenotes* and modern lighthouses. During the 1985 field season, this project had support from the **National Geographic Society** and from the INA through a grant from the Kempner Fund, as well as the valuable assistance of several professionals. Michael Creamer conducted an experiment in the structure known as El Castillo, at Tulum, placing butane gas lamps inside the upper tower. It was noticed that the alignment of the light, as seen from the sea, coincided with a natural opening in the offshore reef. In other cases the structures seemed to be signalling harbour entrances or rocky points. Many of the structures are still used by local sailors as points of reference.

5. Cozumel's Submerged Cave (1987–8). A group of Mexican and American divers – some of them speleologists – discovered and explored a submerged cave at Cozumel Island in Quintana Roo. Maya ceramic objects and a jade axe were found there. The DAS was informed, and these artefacts were recovered in 1987. One year later a survey was conducted, a map was made, and some other fragments were found. The ceramics were dated between AD 600 and 1200, thus belonging to the Late Classic Period. It was concluded that the site was a Maya offering well. This well is part of a large submerged cave system, which has been already explored and mapped by local and foreign speleologists.

One of the DAS objectives, an ambitious long-term project, has been to produce an underwater archaeological atlas which will incude all submerged sites in Mexican waters. Another goal is to prepare Mexican underwater archaeologists for the challenge of uncovering their country's vast submerged richness. Thus the first underwater archaeology diploma conference was held in Mexico from May to November 1994, with the participation of well-known local and foreign professionals.

Although Mexico has had laws that protected its cultural heritage since 1827, no specific mention has been made in these laws regarding underwater remains. The first time that the Mexican authorities defended their ownership rights on artefacts recovered from a submerged site was in the 1920s in a legal case against Edward H. Thompson, the United States consul in Yucatan, who owned the old hacienda of Chichén Itzá and removed a large number of Maya objects from the Sacred Well located within his property, donating them to the Peabody Museum at Harvard University. The Mexican Government was adamant that, no matter if Thompson was the owner of the land, the pre-Hispanic remains belonged to the nation. Mexican laws now encompass the country's submerged cultural heritage, and in the 1970s the Mexican regulations for archaeological research specifically included this heritage.

Any archaeological project – terrestrial or underwater – must be presented before the INAH's Council of Archaeology. Each project should follow the requirements of the above-mentioned regulations, which include three main criteria: (1) it must be a scientific research project; (2) the project's director has to be an archaeologist supported by an academic institution; and (3) all recovered objects belong to and will remain in Mexico.

In 1995 the INAH Underwater Archaeology Department became a Sub-Directorate and started an important project to survey a large area in the Gulf of Mexico, in order to locate some of the nineteen vessels that comprised the New Spain fleet of 1631. This fleet departed from Veracruz in October 1631 and a few days later several of its ships were wrecked in a storm on the banks of the Bay of Campeche, off the Yucatan Peninsula. The first stage of this project involved research in Mexico as well as Spain. The first field season has been planned for 1997; the project director is archaeologist Pilar Luna Erreguerena, head of the Sub-Directorate.

Such projects have helped to create an important international network, mainly with government and academic institutions from the United States and Canada, as well as the practice of national collaboration among official entities, academic institutions, specialists in other disciplines, and archaeologists from the INAH and other agencies. The way Mexico is protecting its submerged cultural remains is beginning to be followed by other Latin American countries. Today, Mexico's position is quite clear: her underwater heritage is as important as her terrestrial heritage, it is not for sale, and it cannot be negotiated under any circumstances. Serious national and international scientific projects are welcome to share in the promising future of underwater archaeology in this part of the world. P.L.E.

ADDITIONAL READING

Andrews, A.P. and Corletta, R., 1995, 'A Brief History of Underwater Archaeology in the Maya Area', *Ancient Mesoamerica*, 6, 2, 101–17.

Creamer, M., 1986, 'Maritime Secrets of the Maya', *INA Newsletter, Institute of Nautical Archaeology*, 13, 2, 4–6.

Garcia-Bárcena, J. and Luna Erreguerena, P., 1987, 'El patrimonio cultural submarino', *Antropologia documentos*, Instituto Nacional de Antropologia e Historia, Mexico, Nueva época, 17, 1–12.

Luna Erreguerena, M. del Pilar, 1982, *La arquelogía subacuática*, thesis, ENAH-UNAM, Mexico.

Olivé Negrete, J.C., 1991, 'Legislación sobre arqueología subacuática', *Arqueología*, Segunda época, 8, 137–45.

Micronesia

Grouping of Pacific islands just north of the equator and stretching 1,930 km from west to east. The islands have loose cultural affiliations and are united under one rubric primarily as a function of Western sociopolitical convenience. 'Micro' refers to the cumulative land mass which is extremely small for such a large geopolitical entity. The approximately twelve million sq. km of Pacific Ocean which is called Micronesia has a combined land surface of less than 3,200 sq. km. Political status has changed frequently, as have place names, particularly since the end of World War II. Micronesia is now composed of Guam, the Commonwealth of the Northern Marianas (CNMI), the Republic of Belau (formerly Palau), the Federated States of Micronesia (FSM), the Marshall Islands, and the Gilbert Islands.

Underwater archaeology in this part of the world has been minimal; it primarily consists of site survey and documentation carried out by the US National Park Service's **Submerged Cultural Resources Unit** (SCRU) and recovery operations conducted by salvors on some Spanish shipwrecks of the 1600s.

Pre-European contact settlement patterns were dominated by migrations from Melanesia and Asiatic incursions, primarily through the **Philippines**. Early cultural expressions include megalithic stone architecture at Pohn Pei (formerly Ponape) and Kosrae (formerly Kusaie). At the former, a ceremonial complex now referred to as Nan Madol has some underwater components. In 1992 the SCRU determined that what were thought to be manmade pillars outside the seawall are in fact natural coral formations. Some quarried basaltic pieces have been reported in shallow waters fringing the complex. Legends of a 'bone hole', where defleshed human bones were deposited near the village of Lele at Kosrae, were not substantiated during an archaeological reconnaissance by SCRU in 1992.

The earliest European influences in Micronesia include the Spanish, who developed a trade between Manila and Acapulco that passed through Micronesia. Consequently some of the earliest shipwrecks in the area, and those most sought after by salvors, are vessels that were involved in the Manila trade. Spanish vessels that have become the focus of salvage permits and lengthy litigation and some successful recovery efforts include *Nuestra Señora del Pilar*, wrecked off Guam in 1690, and **Nuestra Señora de la Concepción**, wrecked off Saipan in 1638. The latter was the focus of a long recovery operation by Pacific Sea Resources under

Nan Madol site, Micronesia. (NPS/John Brooks)

the direction of Charles Mathers. It resulted in a collection of artefacts that is now owned by a Japanese resort company known as Apex Corporation. The collection is still in private ownership, although the owners have indicated they may donate the material to the government of Saipan in the year 2030. The site of the *Pilar* wreck off the south side of Guam was the subject of a Territory of Guam sanctioned salvage operation carried out by Davey Jones Archaeology Inc., after intense litigation with Robert Marx, who also desired to work the site. Thus far the work carried out on *Pilar* has been primarily motivated by treasure salvage interests, guided by a salvage contract, as opposed to archaeological concerns.

Although European influence on Micronesia was initially dominated by the Spanish, there were significant incursions by English missionaries and commercial enterprises in Copra. Later followed English, American, and eventually Australian whalers. Germany played an increasingly strong role until the end of World War I. Subsequently, Japanese influence strengthened as prior German possessions in the Pacific were taken over by the latter as spoils of war. American control became dominant after World War II, with the formation of the Trust Territories of the Pacific Islands.

There are vessels related to the whaling trade and missionary activities sunk in Micronesian waters in harbours and lagoons where they are accessible to standard diving technology. In Micronesia, ship losses any distance seaward from the fringing or barrier reefs are usually too deep for access by any but the most sophisticated and expensive underwater technology. In 1981 SCRU conducted a survey of a wreck that they confirmed to be **Leonora** in Utwa Harbour, Kosrae. *Leonora*, captained by the notorious blackbirder and rogue Bully Hayes, was sunk in 1874. Results of the survey were compiled into a limited distribution report by Lenihan, Carrell and Murphy and later published in their entirety in a monograph entitled *Of Wooden Ships and Iron Men*, edited by Scott Russell.

Extensive documentation of World War II sites and some whaling and prehistoric sites was conducted by the SCRU in Guam, Palau, Rota, Saipan, Chuuk, Kosrae, Pohnpei, and Majuro during the 1980s and early 1990s. Most of the projects were under the direction of Daniel J. Lenihan, with others being led by Larry Murphy or Toni Carrell. Dirk Spenneman, while acting as Historic Preservation Officer in Majuro, conducted research on a B-24 bomber that has resulted in a major report. Comprehensive discussions of World War II shipwreck populations in various islands include work by Klauss Lindemann in Truk (now Chuuk) Lagoon (see **Truk Lagoon Wrecks**) and in Palau.

In 1989 and 1990 the SCRU conducted a resurvey of the ships sunk during Operation Crossroads, the 1946 atomic bomb tests in Bikini Atoll (see **Crossroads Wrecks**). SCRU chief Daniel Lenihan led the survey and subsequently recommended the ships be integrated into a marine park open to sport diving as a mechanism to help build an economic base for the resettlement of Bikinians on the atoll. The utilization of World War II shipwrecks as the focus of diving-based tourism was first pioneered at Truk Lagoon and has become a significant factor in Palau, the Marianas, and increasingly in the Marshalls.

A particularly compelling site in the historical/recreational sense is that of the *Cormoran* and *Tokai Maru* on the island of Guam. SMS *Cormoran*, a World War I German raider, was scuttled in Apra Harbour by her skipper on the day the US entered the war in 1917. Almost on top of the *Cormoran* is a World War II Japanese transport, *Tokai Maru*, which was damaged at sea by a US submarine and finally sunk by another one while in the harbour in 1943. The result was the creation of a unique archaeological site in which a vessel from what was originally known as 'the war to end all wars' is symbolically overlaid with a ship from World War II.

The *Cormoran/Tokai* site was first mapped by the SCRU in 1983, since when it has become the focus of many recreational divers who visit Guam from the US and Japan. The Territorial Government of Guam and the local sport diving community have worked with the US Navy and the National Park Service to make the site accessible to sport divers. They have printed and distributed plastic underwater maps both of this site and that of the nearby *Kisagawa Maru*, another Japanese transport casualty, through local retail outlets. The same government entities cooperated in the teaching of underwater historic preservation courses in Guam. As a project, one of the classes in 1987 took on the mapping of another transport, *Aratama Maru*, in Talofofo Bay, Guam. Maps and narrative descriptions of all these sites and other sites in Guam are presented in the SCRU assessment of Micronesia edited by Toni Carrell.

The SCRU assessment also covers underwater archaeological operations conducted by the National Park Service team in association with the US Navy in the Republic of Belau as part of a cooperative inter-agency arrangement known as 'Project Seamark'. Coordinated by the Belauan Office of Historic Preservation, over 200 **US Navy** Reserve and Active Duty personnel were

cycled through the archipelago for a period of three months in 1988. During that time, under the direction of SCRU archaeologists, six Japanese vessel casualties of World War II were mapped and numerous other sites visited and photographically documented.

Not yet found, but of particular archaeological importance in Belau, would be the site of the East India packet *Antelope*, the wreck of which (in 1783) introduced this Micronesian archipelago to the European world. Of interest on the near end of the timeline would be the documentation of an armed Japanese trawler sunk by a US Navy plane piloted by an ensign who would become president of the United States: George Bush sank this vessel in 1944. There have been reports in the popular press of this trawler having been located and visited by sport divers. D.J.L.

ADDITIONAL READING

Carrell, T. (ed.), 1991, *Submerged Cultural Resources Assessment of Micronesia*, Southwest Cultural Resources Center Professional Papers 36, Santa Fe, New Mexico.

Delgado, J.P., Lenihan, D.J., and Murphy, L.E., 1991, *The Archaeology of the Atomic Bomb: A Submerged Cultural Resources Assessment of the Sunken Fleet of Operation Crossroads at Bikini and Kwajalein Atoll Lagoons*, Southwest Cultural Resources Center Professional Papers 37, Santa Fe, New Mexico.

Lindemann, K., 1991, *Desecrate 1*, Belleville, Ontario.

Lindemann, K., 1991, *Hailstorm over Truk Lagoon*, Belleville, Ontario.

Mathers, W.M., Parker III, H.S., and Copus, K.A. (eds), 1990, *Archaeological Report: The Recovery of the Nuestra Señora de la Concepcion*, Sutton, Vermont.

Russell, S., 1982, *Of Wooden Ships and Iron Men*, Micronesian Archaeological Survey Series, Report no. 15, Saipan.

Millecoquins Wreck
see **Great Lakes**

Minimum impact archaeology

The methodology of extracting the most archaeological data from a site with the least physical disturbance. It is based on conservation archaeology's basic tenet, which recognizes that rapidly diminishing archaeological resources are finite, non-renewable, and should not be disturbed (excavated) without ample justification. Minimum impact archaeology is distinguished from non-impact archaeology, which does not include disturbance of any kind.

Because of the increasingly rapid attrition of the maritime archaeological database,

emphasis arguably must be upon preservation as the most defensible management alternative to excavation as standard archaeological data recovery. Exemplary academic archaeology can be conducted by focusing on visible remains and extracting all relevant information possible from minimal disturbance of surface deposits. **Research design** formulation is fundamental to this process. Research designs pose specific questions that can be answered from data collected without excavation. Because it is impossible to collect 'all the data' even from exposed remains, research designs are necessary to focus on specific questions and research domains.

Minimum impact archaeology does not necessarily mean that systematic site testing or disturbance of any kind is always avoided. Minimum impact methodology should be a normal part of a total documentation strategy designed to produce cumulative data by exhausting non-invasive options before disturbing sub-surface sediments. Emphasis on **Remote sensing** as an alternative to test **Excavation** is one step in the cumulative hierarchical investigative approach to archaeological inquiry developed as part of minimum impact methodology. Examining surface remains also bolsters incorporation of multi-disciplinary operations into fieldwork at every level to refine analytical description.

Minimum impact methodology for underwater archaeology accepts the implicit conclusion that ephemeral surface materials contribute to archaeological inference. This conclusion has helped direct research interests away from the total excavation of single, usually spectacular, wreck sites to an investigation of the nature of the behaviour reflected in remains that were often previously ignored, such as regional stranding, salvaging, repair, and anchorage activity areas. It has also reinforced investigation of the formation processes responsible for the surface remains.

A longtime advocate of minimum impact approaches is the National Park Service's (NPS) **Submerged Cultural Resources Unit** (SCRU). From its inception, SCRU's policy has been to conduct minimum impact archaeology. The rationale is that unless one can exhaust data potential from visible remains, there is scant justification for excavation. SCRU projects thus generally rely on surface material as the primary archaeological data source. Fieldwork focuses on getting maximum results from minimum impact. Most SCRU research is conducted without disturbing sub-surface sediments or collecting artefacts. Working within the management framework of the NPS, this approach is not only highly successful but also cost-effective and congruent with the NPS mission and basic preservation philosophy.

It is within the strict parameters of preservation that methodological refinement of archaeological field investigations has taken place. There are two reasons excavation might take place in protected areas such as national parks: either the site is threatened with destruction, or there are compelling research questions that could be answered by excavation that could not be answered on sites outside protected jurisdiction. Intensive surface investigation is no substitute for excavation, but it precedes responsible excavation in all cases. Minimum impact archaeology conducted on protected sites contributes to the refinement of data collection methodologies complementary to more intrusive investigations, and there really should be little separation between these approaches in the collection of quality data. Minimum impact approaches require the consideration of archaeological questions that may be addressed in this format.

Outside protected areas, increasing financial constraints make sampling and non-destructive methodology attractive alternatives to excavation as the principal source of archaeological data. Excavation has its place under certain conditions, especially when there is insufficient information from surface remains to answer evaluation and research questions. It is sometimes difficult for archaeologists outside preservation agencies to accept the concept that long-term preservation is the primary objective of archaeological inquiry conducted within a management framework directed to reducing information loss about the past. Recent indications are that this situation is changing in American archaeology. Ethical concerns have altered academic archaeological training; in the 1990s less than one quarter of archaeological dissertations are based on excavation projects conducted by students, and the use of museum information has doubled. L.E.M., M.A.R.

ADDITIONAL READING

Terrell, B.G., n.d., *Fathoming our Past: Historical Contexts of the National Marine Sanctuaries*, Newport News, Virginia.

Modern Greece

British steam screw freighter which sank in 1862. Built by Richardson's of Stockton, England, for the Hull–Baltic timber trade, and pressed into the service of blockade-running in the American Civil War by its owner Pearson and Company of London, *Modern Greece* was a 753 ton vessel, 210 ft (64 m) in length, 29 ft (8.8 m) in breadth,

and drew 17 ft 2 in (5.2 m) of water. Unlike vessels chosen later in the war for their swiftness and ability to transport goods over shoal areas associated with many Southern ports, *Modern Greece* appeared early in the war before the skills and strategies of blockade-running were fully developed (see **Cape Fear Civil War Shipwreck District**).

The career of *Modern Greece* as a blockade-runner only lasted about six months. With her movements cloaked in secrecy, little is known of *Modern Greece*'s activities until she mysteriously appeared near land about 5 km north of Fort Fisher and New Inlet, North Carolina on 27 June 1862, only one day after an article appeared in the *Wilmington Journal* describing how 'the steamer *Modern Greece*, fitted out at Hull, sailed from Falmouth 28th April ostensibly for Tampico'. The Union blockader USS *Cambridge* fired on *Modern Greece* which hastened parallel to the shore to reach the protection of Fort Fisher's big guns. Under heavy fire, she ran hard aground nearly 1 km north of the fort. (There is some speculation that the heavily laden deep-draft vessel may not have been successful in entering New Inlet, whose channel was maintained at only 3.7 m.)

USS *Cambridge* and USS *Stars and Stripes* shelled *Modern Greece* once she was aground, striking her several times before being driven back by the guns at Fort Fisher. Solid shot was fired from the fort into *Modern Greece* to prevent Union forces from pulling her off and salvaging her, and to prevent gunpowder thought to be on board from exploding.

Salvage efforts by the Confederates at Fort Fisher began immediately and continued for some time. Though intelligence reports by both Union and Confederates vary widely, they indicate that at least four 12 pounder Whitworth rifled cannon were salvaged along with 5,000 small arms, powder, whisky, boxes, bales of clothing, and a large assortment of household goods. The wreckage of *Modern Greece* gradually settled into the ocean floor and was forgotten for a hundred years until found by divers after a storm uncovered it in 1962. That discovery, early in the celebration of the Civil War Centennial, sparked renewed interest in the vessel which prompted the State of North Carolina and the US Navy to salvage more than 10,000 artefacts from *Modern Greece* along with her anchors and capstans. These were preserved for study and display at a nearby museum and visitors centre built at the Fort Fisher State Historic Site. Now protected by North Carolina shipwreck salvage laws, the wreck remains today where she sank approximately 275 m offshore in

about 7.5 m of water near Fort Fisher, North Carolina. L.S.B.

ADDITIONAL READING

Bright, L., 1977, *The Blockade Runner Modern Greece and the Cargo*, Raleigh, N. Carolina.

Molasses Reef Wreck

Early 16th-century New World shipwreck, thought to be the earliest shipwreck discovered in the western hemisphere. It is named for the reef in the Turks and Caicos Islands on which it was found. Complete excavation of the site produced Spanish ceramics typical of the late 15th and early 16th centuries as well as early-style wrought-iron, breech-loading ordnance. Most of the hull of the ship had disintegrated in the shallow wave-swept waters of the reef, but about 2 per cent remained trapped beneath the stone ballast. In a better state of preservation were the ship's armament: swivel guns, cannon, shoulder arms, crossbows, swords, shot, and grenades. Following cleaning, conservation, and analysis in the US, the entire artefact collection was returned to the Islands where it forms the nucleus of the Turks and Caicos National Museum.

Like many other **Caribbean** shipwreck sites, the Molasses Reef Wreck was first discovered by treasure-hunters rather than by archaeologists. Although fishermen from the Caicos Islands, who free-dive for conch and lobster, must have visited the site many times over the years, its flattened, camouflaged condition prevented them from recognizing it. In 1976 a pair of underwater explorers methodically searching Molasses Reef for salvageable material spotted the site and realized that it was an early shipwreck. They stayed long enough to raise a few artefacts, then returned to Miami.

Four years later in 1980, under the name of 'Caribbean Ventures', the men applied to the Government of the Turks and Caicos, a British Crown Colony, seeking permission to prospect for and salvage shipwrecks on the Caicos Bank. When permission was granted they announced that they had found the wreck of Columbus's caravel, *Pinta*, and that they expected to make $100,000,000 from marketing it and from mining other treasure-bearing shipwrecks near by. The salvors' argument that the wreck on Molasses Reef was Columbus's *Pinta* was, at best, thinly supported. Not at all convinced by the Caribbean Ventures prospectus, the Governor of the Turks and Caicos Islands invited Dr Colin Martin of the **Scottish Institute of Maritime Studies** to visit the site and offer a second opinion on its scientific significance. Dr Martin's report urged the government to insist that an archaeologist be present

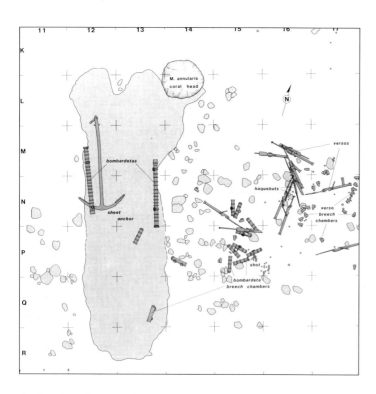

Molasses Reef Wreck: ordnance
distribution plan. Lightly shaded
areas are ballast. (© Ships of
Discovery)

Molasses Reef Wreck: reconstruction of
a bombardeta 'bed stock' carriage in
the Turks and Caicos National Museum.
(© Ships of Discovery/Joe Simmons)

during the salvage, and suggested the Texas A&M-based **Institute of Nautical Archaeology**. A year later, another band of salvors calling itself 'Nomad Treasure Seekers' showed up, claiming it had 'inherited' the site from the original discoverers – who had been jailed in the US for poaching on another treasure-hunter's site. When Nomad began visiting different shipwreck sites, hauling up cannon, anchors, and other artefacts at random without permission, the Government lost its patience, revoked the salvage permit, and invited maritime archaeologists from the Institute to excavate the Molasses Reef Wreck.

The reef's remote location, more than 28 km from the nearest inhabited island, meant that a seagoing vessel was necessary to work the site. Captain Sumner Gerard made his Miami-based 33 m research vessel *Morning Watch* available and an excavation team was hastily assembled. Arriving at Molasses Reef on 4 April 1982, the archaeologists had an unpleasant surprise: a huge crater, made by explosives and enlarged by frenzied digging, occupied the centre of the ballast mound. The remains of home-made pipe bombs and many intentionally mutilated artefacts lay scattered across the seabed. Fortunately, the site had been accurately mapped two years previously by a reconnaissance team, so the provenances of the most salient artefacts were known. Most of the wreck lay in water less than 6 m deep, in a depression between three 'fingers' of the reef covering an area of some 6,000 sq. m.

A natural **Ship trap**, Molasses Reef had captured other victims as well, and the remains of these later maritime disasters overlay parts of the site.

Six months of excavation on the reef, spread over three years, produced more than 10 tonnes of artefacts, all of which were shipped more than 4,000 km back to Texas. Pioneering studies in ballast analysis, metallography, and sclerochronology (counting the accumulation of annual growth rings) were undertaken during the artefact cleaning, documentation, conservation, and analysis phase of the project, which took seven years.

An intensive study of the ship's ballast undertaken by geologist William R. Lamb managed to trace some of the stones from the ship to their most likely place of origin: Lisbon, Portugal. Experiments carried out by Joe J. Simmons III discovered how the wrought-iron breech-loading artillery was constructed and how the mysterious lead-iron 'composite' shot were made. Dr Dick Dodge of Nova University attempted to date the site by sclerochronology in core samples extracted from a large coral head growing on top of the ballast mound. Unfortunately, the coral head proved to be only about 250 years old, much younger than the site.

The vessel's gross dimensions were revealed by combining clues provided by the scant remains of the ship's wooden hull, the distribution of ballast, and curious grooves gouged into the seabed by structures which had entirely disintegrated. It was a medium-sized ship of the period – about 19 m long, 5 to 6 m wide, and 6.2 m or slightly more in draft. Preserved portions of the hull included ceiling planking, first futtocks, and hull planking from one side of the ship at about the level of the turn of the bilge. No trace of the keel, keelson, or endposts survived. The remains of the fragmentary hull preserved several construction features commonly found on 15th- and 16th-century Spanish ships: dovetail-joined, transversely treenailed floors and futtocks, 'fillers' closing the gaps between floors and futtocks, and the use of white oak for every major component of the hull. The presence of two different sizes of iron hearteye straps suggests that the ship had at least three masts: square-rigged fore and mainmasts and at least one other mast which probably carried a lateen sail.

The ship's capacity is more difficult to estimate. The stone ballast in the ship's hold was carefully measured at 40 tonnes, to which must be added the mass of the armament, cargo, crew, and stores. The 'permanent' ballast-large stones placed in the bottom of the ship when it was built to balance its trim included black limestone originating near Bristol, England, and alkali-olivine basalt similar to that found in the mid-Atlantic islands; however, one of the most prevalent types of stone, high alumina basalt, appears to have originated in Lisbon, Portugal. Another prevalent type, Miocene limestone, is also found in the Lisbon area. While the evidence of the ballast study by itself cannot indicate where the ship was built, it does indicate a strong connection with Lisbon.

The ship was heavily armed, but most of the armament was stored and not loaded. A surprising dearth of ceramic sherds suggests that most of the ship's provisions were carried in wooden casks and barrels. The crew's modest possessions were predominantly utilitarian – even the tableware was spartan. No coins or other absolutely datable objects were found, but the characteristics of the artefact assemblage, particularly the pottery and firearms, indicate that the ship ran aground on Molasses Reef in the second or third decade of the 16th century (1510–30). Tiny glass beads may be indicators of trade with the Indians. Several sets of leg irons, some of them locked, may have been part of the ship's normal complement of disciplinary gear, or they may have been used to immobilize captives. Most of the crew apparently survived, although no one ever returned to salvage the ship.

Although scores of caravels and other types of exploratory vessels were abandoned, wrecked, or lost at sea during the early years of exploration and discovery in the New World, only three have been located. Of these, the Molasses Reef Wreck is the oldest, the most complete, and the most carefully studied. But even after analysis, the identity of the Molasses Reef Wreck remains a mystery. The wreck does not appear to match any of the more than 120 European ships known to have been lost in the Americas before 1520. Early maps show that Spanish navigators knew of, and had often visited, the Turks and Caicos Islands. The purpose of such voyages was to capture Lucayans, the Indians living in the Bahamas and Turks and Caicos Islands when the first Europeans arrived, to work as slaves in the mines and fields of Spanish Hispaniola. It is highly probable that the ship which came to grief on Molasses Reef was engaged in this 'grey market' enterprise. Departing from Santo Domingo or one of the other Spanish ports in the Greater Antilles, the ship left no record of its final voyage in Old World archives.

In 1988, responsibility for completing the project passed from the Institute of Nautical Archaeology to Ships of Discovery, a publicly funded non-profit-making research institute formed by the graduate students who had initiated and carried out the project from the beginning. From its new base of operations in Dallas, Ships of Discovery completed the conservation and study of the artefacts and designed the exhibits that would house them in the Turks and Caicos

National Museum. All the artefacts and original data resulting from the excavation were shipped to the museum in 1990 where they now occupy the entire ground floor, and comprise the museum's primary attraction. In spite of numerous impediments, the Molasses Reef Wreck remains one of very few New World archaeological shipwreck projects actually carried through to completion. D.H.K.

ADDITIONAL READING

Keith, D.H., 1983, 'The Molasses Reef Wreck: A Study in the Essential Elements of Nautical

Archaeology in the Caribbean', in C.R. Cummings (ed.), *Proceedings of the Fourteenth Annual Conference on Underwater Archaeology*, Fathom Eight, San Marino, California.

Keith, D.H., 1988, 'Shipwrecks of the Explorers', in G.F. Bass (ed.), *Ships and Shipwrecks in the Americas*, London.

Keith, D.H., 1993–4, 'Tiger by the Tail', *Times of the Islands*, Winter, 24–9.

Keith, D.H. *et al.*, 1984, 'The Molasses Reef Wreck, Turks and Caicos Islands, B.W.I.: A Preliminary Report', *International Journal of Nautical Archaeology*, 13, 1, 45–63.

Lamb, W.R., Keith, D.H., and Judy, S.A., 1990, 'Analysis of the Ballast of the Molasses Reef Wreck', *National Geographic Research*, 6, 3, 291–305.

Macaulay, D., 1992, *Ship*, New York.

Oertling, T.J., 1987, 'A Suction Pump from an Early Sixteenth-century Shipwreck', *Technology and Culture*, 3, 3, 584–94.

The Molasses Reef Wreck: coring a coral head on the ballast mound for sclerochronology. (© Ships of Discovery)Dennis Denton)

Oertling, T.J., 1989, 'The Molasses Reef Wreck Hull Analysis: Final Report', *International Journal of Nautical Archaeology*, 18, 229–43.

Simmons J.J., III, 1988, 'Wrought-iron Ordnance: Revealing Discoveries from the New World', *International Journal of Nautical Archaeology*, 17, 1, 25–34; also published in *Guns from the Sea: Ships' Armaments in the Age of Discovery*, Current Research and New Discoveries in Early Artillery, London, 25–34.

USS *Monitor*

Wreck of an American Civil War ironclad. The prototype of a revolutionary class of steam-powered, ironclad, turreted warships, USS *Monitor* was one of the most famous and significant warships in United States Navy history. She was designed and built by Swedish-American inventor John Ericsson (1803–89). Employing radical design and innovative construction methods, Ericsson was able to deliver the vessel in less than four months in order to counter the threat of the Confederate ironclad CSS *Virginia*. *Monitor* was commissioned at the Brooklyn (New York) Navy Yard on 25 February 1862, barely a week after the commissioning of *Virginia*.

Monitor was unique in many respects and was a striking contrast to the hulking Confederate ironclad CSS *Virginia* which was built on the damaged hull of USS *Merrimack*, a wooden warship. In fact, *Monitor*'s appearance was quite unlike that of any other warship afloat, being almost completely submerged and with no superstructure except for an armoured 'tower' or gun turret amidships and a small raised pilot house forward. The vessel was constructed primarily of iron, although the main deck and armour belt were wood protected by iron plating. Instead of the conventional battery of cannon lined along one or more gun decks, *Monitor*'s armament consisted of only two 11 inch Dahlgren smooth bore cannon, mounted side-by-side in the turret. Sceptics – both North and South – doubted the capabilities of this radical design, giving the ship such derisive nicknames as the 'cheesebox on a raft' and 'tin can on a shingle'.

On 9 March 1862, *Monitor* battled *Virginia* to a virtual draw in a four-hour conflict at Hampton Roads, Virginia, the first confrontation between steam-powered, iron-clad warships. The two ironclads bombarded each other at close range, seeking structural weaknesses, but inflicting little damage. The outcome of this naval engagement was widely reported. Indeed, this first-ever confrontation between ironclad vessels dramatically demonstrated that wooden, sail-powered warships would soon be obsolete.

That first engagement proved to be the only meeting between the ironclads. *Monitor* spent the spring of 1862 lying idly at Hampton Roads, under presidential orders to avoid a reengagement with *Virginia*. President Lincoln was afraid that *Monitor* might be sunk, thus jeopardizing the planned Union attack on the Southern capital at Richmond. Finally, in December, *Monitor* received orders to join the Union blockade of Charleston, South Carolina. However on New Year's Eve, while being towed south, the little ironclad sank during a severe storm off Cape Hatteras, North Carolina.

Monitor lay relatively undisturbed, its exact location unknown, until 1973 when the wreckage was located off Cape Hatteras by a scientific team aboard the research vessel *Eastward* from the Duke University Marine Laboratory at Beaufort, North Carolina. The wreck lies in 70 m of water, *c.* 30 km south-southeast of Cape Hatteras Lighthouse. *Monitor's* hull rests upside-down, partially buried in bottom sediment. The lower hull, which is now the highest part of the wreck, has collapsed forward of midships and the stern armour belt and associated structure has deteriorated badly. The displaced turret lies beneath the port quarter, suspending the stern and port side of the hull above the seabed. This unique configuration creates a severe stress on the hull. *Monitor's* hull exhibits extensive deterioration and structural damage, due primarily to three factors: damage that occurred at the time of sinking, deterioration caused by more than a century of stress and exposure to a seawater environment, and damage resulting from human action. It is widely believed that depth-charging during World War II damaged the lower hull, and possibly the stern armour belt. In addition, there is evidence that the wreck was damaged by vessels anchoring and fishing on the site.

In 1975 *Monitor* was designated by the Secretary of Commerce as America's first **National Marine Sanctuary**. Since its designation, *Monitor* has been protected and managed by the Sanctuaries and Reserves Division of the National Oceanic and Atmospheric Administration (NOAA), US Department of Commerce. *Monitor* is listed in the **National Register of Historic Places** and is also a National Historic Landmark. Since 1975 NOAA has gathered a considerable amount of data at the site. The unique characteristics and location of the site have made it the object of studies by a wide range of scientists, including archaeologists, oceanographers, geologists, biologists, corrosion specialists, structural engineers, and marine salvors.

Since 1990 increasing numbers of private researchers have studied the site. Observations during the early 1990s have revealed an increase in the rate of hull deterioration. When NOAA began revising the management plan for the sanctuary in 1992, it was recognized that additional site data were needed in order to complete long-range planning.

Responding to this need, NOAA conducted scientific expeditions on the site during 1993 and 1995. Results from NOAA studies were supplemented by data from private research. As a result of these studies NOAA concluded that *Monitor's* hull cannot be recovered owing to its fragile condition and to the prohibitive costs associated with conservation and long-term curation of the remains. NOAA further concluded that the accelerating rate of deterioration of the hull and its contents is cause for concern and called for the implementation of a long-range plan for the recovery, conservation, and display of key hull components and artefacts. Since *Monitor* was a prototype for scores of 'monitor class' vessels, much of its equipment was innovative and unique. The other 'monitor class' wreck available for detailed archaeological study and recovery, USS ***Tecumseh***, is a later vessel with many differences.

Among the objects being considered for recovery from *Monitor* are the turret, cannon, propeller, engine, and auxiliary machinery, including the bilge pumps, forced-air blowers, and turret drive mechanism. The Mariners' Museum, Newport News, Virginia, through a long-term cooperative agreement with NOAA, is the principal museum for curation of the *Monitor* collection of artefacts and documents. The museum also maintains a permanent exhibition on *Monitor* that can be expanded to include additional objects recovered from the site. J.D.B.

ADDITIONAL READING

Delgado, J.P., 1988, *A Symbol of American Ingenuity: Assessing the Significance of USS Monitor*, prepared for the US Department of Commerce, National Oceanic and Atmospheric Administration, National Park Service, Washington, DC.

Miller, E.M., 1978, *USS Monitor: The Ship that Launched a Modern Navy*, Annapolis, Maryland.

National Oceanic and Atmospheric Administration, Sanctuaries and Reserves Division, 1995, *A Look at the Monitor National Marine Sanctuary: Past, Present and Future*, Silver Spring, Maryland.

National Oceanic and Atmospheric Administration, 1995, *National Marine*

Anchor of USS *Monitor before conservation. (J.P. Delgado)*

Sanctuary Regulations, 15 CFR Part 922, published in the *Federal Register*, 27 December.

Newton, J., 1975, 'How We Found the Monitor', *National Geographic*, 147, 1, 48–61.

Watts, G.P., Jr, 1975, 'Location and Identification of the Ironclad USS *Monitor*', *International Journal of Nautical Archaeology*, 4, 2.

Watts, G.P., Jr, 1985, 'Deep-Water Archaeological Investigation and Site Testing in the Monitor National Marine Sanctuary', *Journal of Field Archaeology*, 12, 315–32.

White, W.C. and White, R., 1957, *Tin Can on a Shingle*, New York.

Montague Harbour

A well-protected embayment on the southwest shore of Galiano Island, one of a chain known as the Gulf Islands in the southern Georgia Strait of British Columbia, Canada. Its shoreline and submerged archaeological components have been excavated to investigate the effects of coastal transgression on prehistoric midden deposits.

Mitchell's excavation of shoreline deposits in 1971 defined the prehistoric culture type chronology for the region: Gulf of Georgia (AD 400–1800), Marpole (400 BC–AD 400), and Locarno (1400–400 BC), which is preceded by Charles culture (2500–1400 BC) at other regional sites. In collaboration with the **Underwater Archaeological Society of British Columbia**, underwater and intertidal zone excavations contiguous to the harbour's principal land site were directed by N.A. Easton between 1989 and 1992.

The Montague Harbour Underwater Archaeology Project was designed to test the hypothesis that archaeological remains related to maritime cultural adaptations have been inundated by rising sea-levels during the post-glacial period on the Pacific coast and to develop methods of excavation and interpretation of such remains. Field methods included: sediment coring to obtain data on the rate and scale of local

Holocene sea-level rise; intertidal excavation of beaches fronting **Shell middens**, to document the effects of transgression; and controlled excavation of submarine sediments. A series of metal retaining boxes (2.4 m square) was used to successfully excavate to depths of 2.5 m within the underwater sediments with minimum contaminating slumpage of surrounding deposits. Extensive sampling with 20 cm cores was designed to allow a range of post-excavation analyses to generate a multi-faceted data set for interpretation. Besides basic artefact and radiocarbon analysis, this has included **Foraminifera** and pollen identification, macro floral and fauna analysis, morphological and chemical sediment analysis, and experimentation on artefact decay due to water and sediment erosion.

Upper intertidal deposits were found to be deep (over 2 m), well stratified below beach gravels, and to contain a variety of lenses and artefacts related both typologically and by radiocarbon dates to the Marpole culture period. Middle and lower intertidal zone deposits are similarly deep but cultural stratification becomes less clear, correlated to increased bivalve bioturbation of the sediments. However, there remains a clear penultimate stratum above the basal clays, which runs through the entire intertidal zone, consisting of shell-free mineral soils. Artefacts recovered from this undated stratum included two robust bifacial points.

While the submarine deposits are clearly mixed by **Benthic bioturbation**, discrete strata are identifiable both in profile and through detailed analysis of level samples. This suggests that bioturbation may be restricted to specific depositional periods and zones and that stratigraphic principles may be applied to the deposits.

The project demonstrated that archaeological remains are in fact present in both the intertidal and submarine sediments of the harbour; several dozen bones and over four hundred **Lithic artefacts**, principally lithic debris, but including projectile points, scrapers, stone beads, net and line sinkers, and hammer stones, were recovered, as well as a nearly complete antler harpoon point dated to 3,458 ± 128 calibrated radiocarbon years (cybp). Radiocarbon dates of the deposits range from 400 to 7,000 years BP.

Sediment cores, excavation profiles, and foraminifera analyses suggest continuous transgression within the harbour from about 7,000 years ago, from at least 7 m below current sea-level, with two periods of rapid rise during the late Holocene, interpreted as caused by two tectonic events that caused relative subsidence within the harbour at

about 3,458 ± 128 cybp and between 1,100 and 2,500 cybp. The former date is consistent with geological evidence of a large interplate or intraplate earthquake reported from nearby Victoria, B.C. about 3,600 years BP, while the latter dates bracket a second earthquake which may have occurred at 1,900 years BP. While the social-cultural impact of such 'mega-quakes' on prehistoric inhabitants of the region can only be speculative at the present time, it is notable that each occurred close to major culture-type boundaries found in the archaeological record, namely between Charles and

Montague Harbour: intertidal fieldwork on a submerged Native midden site. (UASBC/Norman Easton)

Locarno, at about 3,500 years BP, and Marpole and Gulf of Georgia, at about 1,500 years BP, and that rapid shoreline subsidence of greater than one metre must have affected maritime shoreline settlements.

Faunal studies have focused on attempting to distinguish cultural midden remains from natural benthic deposits, the apparent effect of prehistoric benthic populations on subsided deposits, and the documentation of an expected 'reverse littoral sequence' in submarine deposits reflecting changing environmental conditions during site transformation from a shoreline to a benthic environment. The latter consists of statistically significant changes in the vertical distribution of intertidal fauna in the underwater sediments, in which the lower levels contain increasing percentages of upper- and supra-littoral species. This is most clearly seen in the vertical distribution of large bivalves versus barnacle remains.

Analysis of the data collected from Montague Harbour is continuing; the goal is to develop an understanding of the depositional and post-depositional formation of inundated coastal sites, through the integration of data from terrestrial, intertidal, and underwater excavation within a single coextensive site, using a battery of analytical

techniques drawn from a variety of disciplines. The development and testing through additional field research of such **Site formation processes** are critical to the ability to confidently interpret submarine prehistoric archaeological deposits. N.A.E.

ADDITIONAL READING

Easton, N.A., 1992, *Underwater Archaeology in Montague Harbour: Interim Report on the 1992 Field Investigations*, vol. 1: *Field and Technical Reports*, vol. 2: *Artefact Catalogue of the 1992 Collections*, Occasional Papers of the Northern Research Institute, Research Report no. 4, Yukon College, Whitehorse.

Easton, N.A. and Moore, C.D., 1991, 'Test Excavations of Subtidal Deposits at Montague Harbour, British Columbia, Canada: 1989', *International Journal of Nautical Archaeology*, 20, 4, 269–80.

Mitchell, D.H., 1971, *Archaeology of the Gulf of Georgia Area, a Natural Region and its Culture Types, Syesis*, 4, 1, supplement 1.

Reinhardt, E.G., Easton, N.A., and Patterson, R.T., 1996, 'Foraminiferal Evidence of Late Holocene Sea-level Change and Amerindian Site Distribution at Montague Harbour, British Columbia', *Géographie Physique et Quaternaire*, 50, 1, 35–46.

Monte Cristi Wreck

A northern European merchant vessel located in Monte Cristi Bay, on the north coast of the Dominican Republic. The wreck became well known in 1966 when a local fisher retrieved numerous ceramics and clay tobacco pipes from the site. Preliminary analyses suggested that the English-built vessel, carrying what appears to be a cargo of Amsterdam manufacture, sank between 1652 and 1656.

Seven distinct heel marks have been identified from among the more than 2,000 pipes recovered to date. One, a floral design, is similar to the Type 49 heel stamp from pipes at the Dutch-American settlement at Fort Orange (1624–75) in present-day New York. Imitation Native American funnel elbow-angled pipes, manufactured in Amsterdam, have also been found.

Silver *ocho reales* from the Potosi (Peru) and Santa Fe de Bogotá (Columbia) mints have established a *terminus post quem* of 1652. The Potosi coins were devalued by a variety of counterstamps similar to those on pieces of eight from **Vergulde Draeck** (1656), *Maravillas* (1656), and the Chanduy Reef Wreck (1654).

Many items – including funnel elbow-angled pipes, glass beads, and cooking pots – were probably intended for trade with Native Americans from Virginia to the Hudson River Valley. It is currently hypothesized that the ship, en route from Europe to North America via the Caribbean, may have entered Monte Cristi Bay to load salt from the nearby pans, or to trade with the buccaneers who were prevalent along the northern coast of Hispaniola. J.L.H.

See also **Faunal studies** (Vertebrates).

ADDITIONAL READING

Hall, J.L., 1994, 'Spanish Coins, German Weights, Dutch Clay Pipes, and an English Ship: The 1993 Monte Cristi Shipwreck Project Interim Report', in R. Woodward and C. Moore (eds), *Proceedings from 27th Annual Conference on Historical and Underwater Archaeology, Vancouver, British Columbia*, Ann Arbor, Michigan.

Huey, P.R., 1988, *Aspects of Continuity and Change in Colonial Dutch Material Culture at Fort Orange, 1624–1644*, PhD dissertation, University of Pennsylvania.

Monumental City

Nineteenth-century shipwreck site in the State of Victoria, **Australia**. The archaeological remains are situated close to the south side of Tullaberga Island, near the Victoria/New South Wales border. The propeller, propeller shaft, and remains of the engines lie in one to five metres of water in a series of sand-filled gullies between large boulders and outcrops of flat limestone reef. Kelp growing on the site often obscures the archaeological remains, and excellent weather conditions are needed to access the site as it is exposed to the prevailing south-westerly winds. The site has been inspected and surveyed by the Maritime Heritage Unit of Heritage Victoria (formerly the Maritime Archaeological Unit of the Victoria Archaeological Survey).

SS *Monumental City* was a wooden-hulled screw steamship of 737 tons built in 1850 by Murray and Hazlehurst at Baltimore, Maryland, USA. She was equipped with two

direct-acting oscillating engines powering a single Smith's (English patent) cast-iron propeller. The vessel's maiden voyage from Baltimore to San Francisco via Cape Horn took 112 days and was marred by bad weather and engine breakdowns. SS *Monumental City* made four voyages from Panama to San Francisco between mid-1851 and early 1853, but attempts to establish the vessel in regular service on the Panama route were unsuccessful largely owing to the unreliability of the engines. The vessel then made a voyage from San Francisco to Sydney, carrying passengers destined for the Australian Gold Rush, thus becoming the first steamship to cross the Pacific Ocean.

SS *Monumental City* was wrecked with the loss of thirty-seven lives on Tullaberga Island early on the morning of 15 May 1853 during a voyage from Melbourne to Sydney. As a direct result of this disaster a lighthouse was established on nearby Gabo Island and later the powers and responsibilities of the Steam Navigation Board of Enquiry were considerably expanded. The wreck site of SS *Monumental City* was found by **SCUBA**-divers in the 1960s and many small artefacts were removed from the site. It was declared as a historic shipwreck under the **Australian Historic Shipwrecks Act** in 1982. M.S.2

ADDITIONAL READING

Staniforth, M., 1986, *S.S. Monumental City: First Steamship to Cross the Pacific*, Victoria Archaeological Survey, Occasional Reports Series no. 24, Melbourne.

Mulan Wreck

An early 17th-century wreck at Mulan Island, near the sea route passing the Hanko peninsula on the southern coast of Finland. The wreck was investigated by the National Maritime Museum of Finland in 1988. The site, situated just 50 m north of the island, at a depth of 10 to 14 m, has been known since the 1970s. Since the 18th century a Swedish name for Mulan Island was 'Klockskär' or 'Bell Skerry': when the investigation of the wreck started, the first items lifted from it were two bronze church bells.

The bottom part of the vessel is preserved on the site. The ship's structure indicates it was a clinker-built vessel, originally 20 to 22 m long, with a width of 7 m. It evidently had two, possibly three masts, at least one of these rigged for a square sail. The ship was carrying bricks, thousands of which remain stacked in the hold. The bricks were evidently from one or several old buildings which had been dismantled. This was not an unusual practice in the 17th century to get access to building materials. The wreck contained a rich array of artefacts including a chafing-dish of bronze, a pair of spectacles, powder horns, a cuirass of iron, and a lead seal from a bale of cloth.

Coins found in the wreck indicate that the ship sank in 1611 or 1612. One of the church bells, according to an inscription on it, was cast in 1596 for the monastery of Derevyanitski, near Novgorod, Russia. Some of the finds, especially the church bells, as well as Russian coins and also other items, indicate that the ship was sailing from east to west, from an area of Russia which at the time had been conquered by Sweden. The vessel also contained objects of a west or central European origin, some of which appear to have belonged to soldiers as well as people of a higher social rank.

No contemporary written evidence has so far been found to identify the ship. One hypothesis is that it was a Swedish naval transport carrying taxation goods or loot from conquered areas in the east to Sweden. C.O.C.

A diver swims past one of the engines at the Monumental City *site. (Maritime Heritage Unit)*

ADDITIONAL READING

Heporauta, A., 1991, 'The Mulan Wreck: What Type of Vessel Was it?', *Maritime Museum of Finland Annual Report*, 58–72.

Sammallahti, L., 1989–90, 'Investigations by the Maritime Museum of Finland on the Mulan Wreck in Hanko', *Maritime Museum of Finland Annual Report*, 64–73.

Sammallahti, L., 1991, 'The Mulan Wreck in Hanko: The Wreck Site and Some of the Finds', *Maritime Museum of Finland Annual Report*, 73–7.

Museum display

The exhibition of shipwrecks and related artefacts in museums worldwide. Virtually every maritime museum has bits and pieces of shipwrecks, or images of them (paintings, drawings, prints, photographs) on display or in storage. Many other types of museums also contain shipwreck materials – for example, nearly all of the original bronze and marble statues from the Classical period of ancient Greece, as seen in the National Archaeological Museum in Athens and the British Museum in London (among others), were found on shipwrecks. Types of collections might range from a single coin or ancient Greek amphora to entire hulls with intact artefact assemblages, votive paintings or postcards of famous shipwrecks. In many cases, museums have been collecting these souvenirs since the 18th or 19th centuries; in other instances, new museums have been built to contain and display an individual ship or group of wrecks. Indeed, it is a museum's major responsibility to share its collections with public audiences and serve as a responsible repository for its collections for the foreseeable future. One way or another the public usually pays for the research and curation of public collections, and the presentation and interpretation of the materials have a major impact upon how audiences perceive a shipwreck and its treatment, both physically and conceptually.

There are too many significant shipwrecks in museums worldwide to list them individually; moreover, many of them are treated as separate topics elsewhere in this volume. Nearly all historic periods, cultures, and ship types are represented somewhere in one form or another; what follows are some examples illustrating highlights or notable milestones in international maritime heritage, arranged chronologically whenever possible. Preserved historic ships that were not shipwrecked, as well as replicas of historic ships, are generally excluded, although of course they are relevant to nautical archaeology. In theory, a dedicated museum visitor could select a particular period, cul-ture, ship type, cargo, category of armament, or other criterion and find at least one example preserved, if not several.

Pride of place goes to the Bodrum Museum of Underwater Archaeology in Bodrum, Turkey, where artefacts from the earliest scientifically excavated shipwreck may be seen: the **Uluburun** wreck of the 14th century BC, which sank off the southern coast of Turkey with a cargo of rare and valuable artworks, metal ingots, and other unique materials. The Bodrum Museum also exhibits artefacts from the **Cape Gelidonya** shipwreck (12th century BC), the **Yassiada Wrecks** (4th and 7th centuries AD) and the **Serçe Limani** wreck (11th century AD). The latter ship's hull has been fully reconstructed in a special gallery, on account of its pivotal position in the transitional period between the ancient shell-building method of hull construction and the more modern frame-first technique. Also unique is the ship's principal cargo of raw and finished glass products, displayed around the gallery perimeter with other artefacts.

The three **Ferriby Boats**, also dating to the late 2nd millennium BC, were excavated near Hull, England from 1937 to 1963. These craft reside at the National Maritime Museum in London and the Hull Museum. The former institution also houses the **Brigg 'Raft'** of *c.* AD 800 and a replica of the **Sutton Hoo** burial vessel (early 7th century AD), of which the original artefacts are on display at the British Museum. Also at the National Maritime Museum are the **Graveney Boat** (late 9th century AD) and portions of watercraft from the Middle Ages.

The hull and other materials from the **Kyrenia Ship** of the late 4th century BC are reconstructed and on exhibit at the Kyrenia Ship Museum, a Crusader castle in Kyrenia, Cyprus, near where the ship sank. The Kyrenia Ship was the first hull from the ancient world to be raised, fully conserved, and reconstructed in a museum setting; slightly more than 75 per cent of its structure is preserved.

The famous bronze **Athlit Ram**, from the bow of an ancient warship stylistically dated to the early 2nd century BC, is the only attributable hull section from a warship of the ancient world. It resides at the National Maritime Museum in Haifa, Israel, along with other shipwreck materials from the Israeli coastline ranging in date from the Canaanite to the Mamluk periods (14th century BC to 15th century AD). The **Sea of Galilee Wreck** or Kinneret Boat from the late 1st century BC, excavated from the shore of the Sea of Galilee and undergoing conservation in the 1990s, will be exhibited in Israel when treatment is complete.

Unfortunately, the first museum built exclusively for shipwrecks is no longer. This was the famous Roman Ship Museum at Lake Nemi, outside Rome, which was burned in a fire started on 31 May 1944 by a retreating German Army force. Completed in 1939, the museum housed two immense pleasure barges of the early Roman Imperial period, raised from the lake between 1928 and 1932 (see **Lake Nemi Ships**). Another smaller Nemi museum was built in the 1950s, housing models and some of the more durable artefacts that survived the conflagration, but the ships themselves were destroyed.

Several Viking ships have survived the centuries in remarkably good condition since they sank or were buried or lost, and they are on display at several museums throughout Scandinavia and its environs. Most notable among these are the Iron Age **Hjortspring Boat** (*c.* 300 BC) at the Nationalmuseet in Copenhagen; the **Nydam Boat** (AD 350–400) at the Schleswig-Holsteinisches Landesmuseum in Schleswig (Germany); the Kvalsund boat (*c.* AD 600) at the Bergens Sjøfartsmuseum; the oceangoing **Oseberg Ship** (*c.* AD 800), the **Gokstad Ship** (10th century), and the **Tune Ship** (10th century) at the Viking Ship Museum in Oslo; and the five **Skuldelev Ships** (11th century) at the Viking Ship Museum in Roskilde, Denmark. The latter institution, like others mentioned above, was especially built to display the Roskilde finds, and its staff continue to conduct research on regional wreck sites. As a group, these Scandinavian craft form an almost unbroken lineage from the Iron Age through the great age of the Vikings – a degree of preservation unparalleled by other regional traditions.

The European Middle Ages are also represented in museum galleries, particularly in the Netherlands and Germany. In the Netherlands, where old ships were often used as landfill, new discoveries are frequently made, aggressively documented, and placed on exhibit. For example, the Rijksmuseum for Ship Archaeology, originally in Dronten but now in Lelystad, houses an intact Roman canoe and two entire ships – a 16th-century ventjager and a 17th-century pinnace – as well as artefact assemblages from several other craft. Another highlight is the late 12th-century Utrecht Vessel at the Town Museum in Leiden. The late 14th-century **Bremen Cog** on exhibit at the Deutsches Schiffartsmuseum at Bremerhaven is unique among museum displays: the intact vessel is displayed in an immense clear tank filled with polyethylene glycol (PEG), in which it is undergoing active conservation in full view of the visitors. Once the PEG has replaced all of the water in the ship timbers, the tank will be drained and removed and the ship displayed in a dry state.

Royal Dockyard No. 3 at Portsmouth, England, converted into a wet conservation facility not far from Nelson's *Victory*, houses one of the world's best known shipwrecks – King Henry VIII's **Mary Rose**. Built in 1509–10 at an adjacent dock and raised in 1982, the famous warship was sealed into No. 3 with a long-term sprinkler system to keep the ship wet and eventually replace the water in her timbers with PEG. The humid environment creates a dramatic, foggy effect imbuing the ship remains with a ghostly aura; nearby, in a more conventional setting, over a thousand objects from the ship are on exhibit.

From around the same time is the **Molasses Reef Wreck**, found in the Turks and Caicos island group in the British West Indies and the earliest known shipwreck in the western hemisphere. Unfortunately, the site was looted by treasure salvors prior to scientific archaeological excavation. However, the remains of this heavily armed ship have been installed as the centrepiece of the new Turks and Caicos National Museum on Grand Turk Island.

The jewel in the crown of museum displays of shipwrecks is inarguably the royal Swedish flagship **Vasa**, which sank on her 1628 maiden voyage in Stockholm and was raised in 1961. She was placed on public exhibit the following year while the timbers were hand-sprayed with a preservative, and in 1965 a pioneering automatic sprinkler system was developed to preserve the big warship intact. In 1990 a new museum on the Stockholm waterfront dedicated to *Vasa* opened, complete with dramatic stage lighting and surrounded by artefacts and other exhibits. A marketing survey of foreign tourists has indicated that the ship brings visitors for one extra day to Sweden, and that this extra trip on the itinerary generates a million dollars in annual revenues.

Of the several European East India companies, the English and Dutch were the strongest and most durable. Wrecks of the latter (the Dutch East India Company or VOC), which lasted from 1602 to 1799, are particularly well represented in museums from Australia to the Netherlands. Materials from the 1629 wreck of **Batavia**, the first VOC ship wrecked in Australia, as well as **Vergulde Draeck**, wrecked in 1656, may be seen at the Western Australian Maritime Museum in Perth – the principal Australian museum for that nation's shipwreck research and exhibition. The wreck of the VOC's **Amsterdam**, which grounded on the coast of England at

Hastings in 1749 and has been the subject of a unique British/Netherlands scientifc agreement, is undergoing long-term analysis and conservation in Amsterdam, where portions are on public exhibition at the Nederlands Scheepvaart Museum.

Wrecked warships from the American Revolution to World War II are well represented in museums on the western side of the Atlantic as well. From the Revolution, the Smithsonian Institution's National Museum of American History displays the intact Continental gunboat **Philadelphia**, sunk by the British during a battle on Lake

Boat loft, Bermuda Maritime Museum. (Bermuda Maritime Museum)

Champlain (between Vermont and New York) in 1776 and raised in 1935. At Vergennes, Vermont, visitors may sail on a replica of *Philadelphia* and other historic regional craft at the Lake Champlain Maritime Museum, whose staff conduct ongoing archaeological research of the historic lake's shipping and military heritage. In Yorktown, Virginia, both the Visitors Center and the Victory Center display shipwreck artefacts from the Revolution's Battle of Yorktown, before which British General Cornwallis sank a line of ships along the York River shore to prevent an amphibious attack by the allied French and American forces (see **Yorktown Shipwrecks**). The Mariners' Museum in Newport News also exhibits materials from this last battle of the War for Independence, recovered for the museum in the 1930s. Artefacts from the Revolutionary privateer brig **Defence**, a member of the ill-fated 1779 Bagaduce Expedition from Boston to Maine, are on display at the Maine State Museum in Augusta. Items from Joshua Barney's **Chesapeake Flotilla** of the War of 1812, scuttled off Pig's Point, Maryland in 1814 to prevent its seizure by the British, are on exhibition at

the Calvert Marine Museum in Solomons, Maryland.

Naval shipwrecks of the American Civil War are also well represented in museums. From the Union side, artefacts from the iconic ironclad USS **Monitor** are on view at the Mariners' Museum in Virginia, and the City class USS **Cairo** is on open-air display at Vicksburg, Mississippi. Missing portions of *Cairo's* hull and casemate are outlined with heavy timber to fill out the vessel's profile, providing an excellent sense of scale. The Confederate Navy is even better represented by such vessels as the ironclad ram CSS *Jackson* and Maury class gunboat CSS **Chattahoochee** at the Confederate Naval Museum in Columbus, Georgia and the ram CSS **Neuse** at the Caswell-Neuse State Historic site in Kinston, North Carolina. Nearly every old maritime museum on the American east coast has souvenirs of CSS *Virginia* (ex-*Merrimac*), obtained during her partial 1874 salvage near Craney Island, Virginia or when the ship was flattened as a hazard to navigation by the Army Corps of Engineers in the 1930s; her bent and twisted propeller shaft is on outdoor display at the Confederate Museum in Richmond, Virginia. The Confederate raider CSS **Alabama** also is gradually offering up her contents to a French avocational team, who found her wreck off the French coast in 1984. After recovery and conservation, the artefacts are going to the Navy Memorial Museum at the Washington Navy Yard in Washington, DC, where many are already on display.

American merchant vessels, both sail and engine-powered and ranging from the colonial period to the 20th century, are also preserved at various institutions. Early sailing ships are represented by the little 17th-century colonial craft popularly named **Sparrow Hawk** at Pilgrim Hall in Plymouth, Massachusetts. The heyday of the mid-19th-century whaling era and the California Gold Rush are seen in the 4,000 artefacts from the whaler **Niantic** at the San Francisco Maritime Museum, found in landfill in 1978 during excavation for the foundations of an office building. The famous clipper **Snow Squall** was found in a wharf at Port Stanley in the Falkland Islands; portions of it have gone to various museums, including the National Maritime Museum, San Francisco and the Maine Maritime Museum in Bath.

Early American engine-power is also well represented in museum displays of shipwrecks. Remains of the early Great Lakes screw steamships *Independence* (1841) and **Indiana** (1848) are on display at the Whitefish Point Shipwreck Museum in Michigan and the Smithsonian Institution's National Museum of American History, respectively. Portions of the first steamboat in the Pacific Ocean, the sidewheeler **Beaver** (1835), are at the Vancouver Maritime Museum in British Columbia; the archetypal Mississippi River-type steamboat is represented by the 1864 sternwheeler **Bertrand**, which wrecked in the Missouri River shortly after construction and is preserved at the DeSoto National Wildlife Refuge in Nebraska.

Dozens of other wreck sites are displayed in myriad other institutions. Many well-known shipwrecks are undergoing conservation and analysis prior to public exhibition in museum settings. Prominent examples include the mid-17th-century Basque whaler *San Juan* found and excavated in **Red Bay**, Labrador and now in a laboratory in Ottawa, and the early 18th-century **Brown's Ferry Vessel** found in South Carolina, both of which are due to complete treatment and study in the late 1990s.

A few salvors also have constructed their own museums as profit centres, displaying intrinsically valuable artefacts from their wreck sites and often selling artefacts and replicas to visitors. The Treasures of the Steamboat Arabia Museum in Kansas City, Missouri (see **Arabia**) and the Mel Fisher Maritime Heritage Society in Key West, Florida, are examples of this sort of enterprise, and others are likely to emerge in the near future. In response to the issues raised by treasure salvors and the sale of artefacts from shipwrecks, professional museum and archaeological associations have drafted ethical policies, based upon international laws and heritage preservation guidelines, preventing their membership institutions from acquiring or displaying artefacts from commercially exploited sites (see **Professional ethics**). These guidelines are designed to prevent museum audiences from perceiving institutions ostensibly dedicated to preserv-

ing heritage as supporting and condoning its destruction for personal gain, and to curb the market for such artefacts.

There is a growing ethic within the archaeological community not to raise or recover entire wreck sites, but to document them *in situ* and cover them over again with sand after research. There are a variety of reasons for this, including the expense, space requirements for storage and/or exhibit, and other factors. Following this theory, only those sites at imminent risk of loss should be excavated thoroughly. Some archaeologists are adopting this position; others are urging a more particularistic approach to the subject, advocating a review of each site's own specific circumstances and potential for a significant advance in knowledge. In either case, a wealth of shipwrecks is on display throughout the globe, and more are added to the list each year. P.F.J.

ADDITIONAL READING

Allen, J.E. (ed.), 1995, *Membership of the International Congress of Maritime Museums*, Philadelphia, Pennsylvania.

Brouwer, N.J., 1985, *International Register of Historic Ships*, Annapolis, Maryland.

Delgado, J.P. and Candace Clifford, J., 1991, *Great American Ships*, Washington, DC.

Howe, H.E., 1987, *North America's Maritime Museums: An Annotated Guide*, New York.

Johnston, P.F., 1993, 'Treasure Salvage, Archaeological Ethics and Maritime Museums', *International Journal of Nautical Archaeology*, 22, 1, 53–60.

National Museums and Galleries on Merseyside, 1993, *A Repertory of Maritime Museums*, Liverpool.

Neill, P. (ed.), 1984, *Directory of Maritime Heritage Resources*, Washington, DC.

Rand, A.G. (ed.), 1995, *Membership Roster: The Council of American Maritime Museums*, Charlestown, Massachusetts.

Stanford, P. (ed.), 1990, *Sea History's Guide to American and Canadian Maritime Museums*, Croton-on-Hudson, New York.

Nagato

see **Crossroads Wrecks**

Nanking Cargo Wreck

A wreck, properly identified as the Dutch East Indiaman *Geldermalsen*, which lies at an undisclosed location in the South China Sea, believed by many authorities to be in sovereign Indonesian waters. Built in 1747 in the Netherlands, the Dutch East India Company's (VOC) *Geldermalsen* arrived at Guangzhou (Canton, China) in July 1751 laden with tin and cotton from Jakarta (Batavia), a major VOC trading post on the island of Java (off Indonesia). At Canton she loaded a cargo of tea, silks, spices, lacquerware, porcelain, and gold, clearing for home in late December under Captain Jan Morel. On 3 January 1752 *Geldermalsen* struck Admiral Stellingwerf Reef owing to a navigational error, and drifted for a time before sinking. Her papers and 32 crew survived, leading to an inquiry into the causes of the incident and the possible removal of some of the gold cargo during the wrecking.

In 1985 the site was located by Michael Hatcher, a British salvor in Singapore who had earlier found a 1640s Chinese junk in the same region and auctioned 23,000 pieces of its porcelain cargo through Christie's Amsterdam for more than $2 million. From *Geldermalsen*, Hatcher recovered some 160,000 pieces of Chinese export porcelain, 126 gold ingots, and a few other artefacts, which were also sent to Christie's Amsterdam for 'cleaning' and auction. Christie's undertook a massive publicity campaign, resulting in a sale in 1986, only a year after the wreck's discovery. The auctioned material is believed to represent approximately 5 per cent of the cargo, the majority of which was tea. Since historical research on the wreck was completed before the auction, it appears that both the salvor and Christie's may have known of the ship's identity prior to the sale. The Netherlands government, as heir of the VOC, claims ownership of all its shipwrecks.

The vast majority of the Chinese export porcelain salvaged consisted of dinner services, tableware, and teaware manufactured at Jingdezhen in Jiangxi Province and destined for Dutch middle-class dining rooms. Mostly blue and white in various patterns, it was incorrectly called 'Nanking' or 'Nankeen' at the time, after the city where

Europeans believed it was manufactured. Interestingly, Jörg's study of the preserved ship's records revealed that of a single category of cargo (cups and saucers), some 32,500 were left behind on the seabed.

The shoe-shaped gold ingots, or 'sycees', are of the 10 tael size, ranging in weight between 364 and 371 g (a full tael was 38 g). Cast in mud pits, they are in the traditional form of Chinese women's slippers. They were found outside the hull in a discrete group, probably indicating that the crew tried unsuccessfully to salvage them at the time of sinking (supporting the VOC inquiry). Gold was slightly cheaper in China than elsewhere at the time, so Captain Morel probably bought it at Canton for resale at Jakarta.

European materials salvaged number approximately a hundred examples of jugs, bottles, ceramics, and glass, along with a metal candlestick, a bell (dated 1747), cooking pots, and a chisel, probably for use by the ship's crew. Added to the auction at the last minute but not in the catalogue were two bronze cannon clearly identified by the Dutch East India Company's mark. A lawsuit brought by the Indonesian Government over the wreck was still unresolved at the end of 1996. P.F.J.

ADDITIONAL READING

Christie's, 1985, *The Nanking Cargo/Chinese Export Porcelain and Gold/European Glass and Stoneware Recovered by Captain Michael Hatcher from a European Merchant Ship Wrecked in the South China Seas*, Auction catalogue, 28 April–2 May 1986, Amsterdam.

Dyson, J., 1986, 'Captain Hatcher's Richest Find', *Reader's Digest*, 129, 5, 111–15.

Green, J., 1988, Reviews of Christie's, Jörg and Thorncroft volumes in *International Journal of Nautical Archaeology*, 17, 4, 357–9.

Green, J., 1990, Review of Sheaf and Kilburn, *International Journal of Nautical Archaeology*, 19, 4, 353–4.

Hatcher, M., de Rham, M., and Thorncroft, A., 1987, *Geldermalsen: The Nanking Cargo*, London.

Jörg, C.J.A., 1986, *The Geldermalsen: History and Porcelain*, Groningen.

Miller, G.L., 1987, 'The Second Destruction of the Geldermalsen', *American Neptune*, 47, 4, 275–81.

Sheaf, C. and Kilburn, R., 1986, *The Hatcher Porcelain Cargoes: The Complete Record*, Oxford.

Thorncroft, A., Hatcher, M., and de Rham, M., 1987, *The Nanking Cargo*, London.

Nassau

One of four wrecks from the Battle of Cape Rachado (1606), Bambek Shoal, Straits of Malacca, rediscovered in 1993. In May 1605, the Dutch East India Company (then only three years old) sent a fleet of nine ships under admiral Cornelius Matelief to capture Malacca, the leading emporium of Southeast Asia. By taking Malacca they hoped to be able to wrest control of the lucrative spice trade from the Portuguese, who had dominated the spice trade for most of the preceding century.

The fleet arrived at Malacca on 30 April 1606, and began their siege of the city. After three months Matelief learned of the approach of a large squadron of Portuguese ships under the command of the Viceroy of Goa. Matelief immediately broke off the siege, shipped his guns and set out to meet the Portuguese. The two sides met in the Straits on 17 August near Cape Rachado. Shots were exchanged but it was late in the day and soon hostilities ceased as the two fleets anchored for the night. The main battle commenced the following day when the Portuguese caught the Dutch vessel *Nassau* still at anchor. She was attacked on one side by *Santa Cruz* and on the other by *Nossa Senhora de Conceicao*. After failing to take her by storm (the favoured tactic of the Portuguese) they set her on fire. *Nassau* went down, holed and burning furiously.

The other main engagement involved the Dutch ship *Middleburg* which was grappled on one side by *Sao Salvador* and on the other by a vessel known only as 'Dom Duarte's Galleon'. Eventually all three ships caught fire and went down still grappled together. Approximately 600 people died in this particularly fierce engagement.

In 1993 the underwater salvage and engineering company Transea (Director Soo Hin Ong) found all four of the wrecks while searching the Bambek Shoal for the wreck of the British merchant ship *Caroline* which had been lost on the shoal in the early 19th century. Dutch and Portuguese cannon were raised which confirmed their identification.

In 1995 a survey and excavation of the wreck of *Nassau* was carried out for the National Museum of Malaysia by Transea, Oxford University and the National University of Malaysia (UKM). The excavation was directed by Mensun Bound of **Oxford University MARE**, using funding provided by the Federal Government of Malaysia. A special 180 ft (54.8 m) maritime archaeological diving vessel was designed in Singapore. Work began on the site in August 1995. Because of the severe currents and near zero-visibility, the dive team consisted mainly of professional hard-hat divers specially trained in the techniques of underwater excavation. Air was supplied via an umbilical from the surface and there was continuous video and hard-wire communication between the divers and the command station above. Decompression took place in a chamber on the deck. The project, which ran for nearly six months, was the largest since that of *Mary Rose* in the early 1980s.

Finds included bronze and iron cannon (two dated to 1604 and bearing the name and decorative device of the VOC), several thousand Spanish silver reals, musket shot (many impacted), Chinese porcelain, a range of North European tablewares, and navigational instruments. Evidence of the fire was found throughout the wreck in the form of burnt wood, melted metal, and charred rope.

The other three battle wrecks were also examined and were found to be situated directly alongside each other. Evidently they had ended up on the seabed grappled together just as they had sunk. One of the bronze cannon raised from the group of three had an iron cannon ball embedded in its side. M.B.

ADDITIONAL READING

Bound, M., Ong, S.H., and Pickford, N.,1997, 'The Excavation of the Nassau', *Excavating Ships of War*, International Maritime Archaeology Series, vol. 2, 63-87.

National Geographic Society

Society organized on 17 February 1888 at Columbia University, Washington, DC. In his introductory address, Society president Gardiner Greene Hubbard concluded: 'When we embark on the great ocean of discovery, the horizon of the unknown advances with us and surrounds us wherever we go. The more we know, the greater we find is our ignorance. Because we know so little we have formed this society for the increase and diffusion of geographical knowledge.' Since that time, the Society has been associated with hundreds of geographical, geological, and archaeological expeditions. Reports and photographs recording these explorative undertakings, and many others, are published in the society's *National Geographic Magazine*, which appears monthly and prints more than 1,600 pages annually. The Society also produces a technical reports journal, television documentaries, books, exhibits, and educational outreach programmes related to geographic topics. Among the many fields of endeavour supported and promoted by the Society is underwater archaeology.

In April 1952 the Society became actively engaged in the field of underwater archaeology when it provided its cooperative support to the pioneering undersea explorations of Captain Jacques-Yves Cousteau and his controversial excavation of 1st- and 2nd-century BC shipwrecks at **Grand Congloué**, off Marseille,

France. By the 1960s the Society was providing ever-increasing financial support for underwater archaeological investigations. In association with the Smithsonian Institution, the Society supported the first organized underwater research on the drowned city of **Port Royal, Jamaica**, in a project directed by Edwin Link. In concert with the Republic of Mexico, the Society supported the exploration of the **Chichén Itzá Cenote**, Yucatan, Mexico. In February 1961 the first of twenty-six research grants, eventually totalling nearly $560,000, was awarded to George Bass to conduct archaeological investigations of the 4th- and 7th-century AD **Yassiada Wrecks** in the Mediterranean. Further support for Dr Bass's work included funding of explorations to locate Hellenistic and Byzantine shipwrecks, a search for the ancient city of Helice, the excavation of a 5th/6th-century AD shipwreck for seafaring pottery, the first use of a **Submersible** in underwater archaeology, the organized investigation of shipwrecks using closed circuit television, and the excavation of the 14th-century BC Bronze Age shipwreck at **Uluburun** (Kaş), Turkey, the oldest shipwreck discovered to date.

In addition to projects which receive financial support from the Society through grants, by 1963 *National Geographic Magazine* had begun to report on many underwater archaeological investigations not specifically supported by the institution, but of interest to its readers. The magazine published on such widely diverse efforts as: the archaeological investigations to recover artefacts of the Canadian voyageurs in the rivers of Ontario, Canada and Minnesota; the discovery of the **Kublai Khan Fleet** in the Straits of Tsushima; the search for and discovery of the lost ships of the **Spanish Armada**; the excavation of a 14th-century Korean cargo ship laden with pottery; and the discovery of a unique early 19th-century horse-powered paddle-wheel steamboat in Burlington Bay, Vermont. Coverage of landmark marine archaeological projects included: the excavation, recovery, and restoration of the **Kyrenia Ship**; the raising of Henry VIII's *Mary Rose*; the survey of HMS *Pandora* on Australia's Great Barrier Reef; the excavation of the **Yorktown Shipwrecks**, Virginia; the *Kronan* project; and such significant deep water discoveries as the USS *Monitor*, *Titanic*, and the German battleship *Bismarck*.

National Geographic Magazine staff photographers, including Emory Kristof, Luis Marden, Bates Littlehales, and Bill Curtsinger, pioneered advances in the field of under-water photographic recording of archaeological sites in such areas as stereo-photogrammetry, 3-D photography and

video, and underwater lighting systems. On occasion, the magazine's photographers and writers have made significant archaeological finds. Marden's discovery of the wreck of HMS *Bounty* while on assignment at Pitcairn Island received international acclaim.

Through cooperative ventures between the National Geographic Society and other research institutions, museums, and even national governments, numerous underwater archaeological investigations have

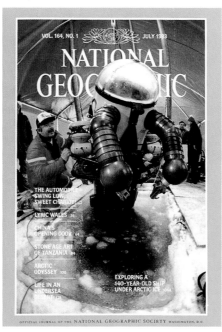

National Geographic Magazine, *vol. 164, no. 1, July 1983, featuring a diver in the Wasp suit (see* Breadalbane*). (National Geographic Society)*

benefited from both direct and indirect assistance in securing logistical, technological, and monetary aid. In May 1982, in concert with the Ontario Heritage Foundation, and the Province of Ontario Ministry of Citizenship and Culture, the Society sponsored the Hamilton–Scourge Foundation in conducting a comprehensive remotely operated vehicle (ROV) photographic survey of the intact War of 1812 warships *Hamilton* and *Scourge* lying in 91 m of water in Lake Erie. The effort was the first to employ surface-deployed ROVs for archaeological photographic recordation. In 1986, this time utilizing its own fleet of ROVs, the Society provided direct field assistance to the National Park Service in photographically inventorying, on film and video, numerous historical deep water shipwreck sites around Isle Royale National Park, in Lake Superior, Michigan (see **Isle Royale Shipwrecks**). The following year, in concert with the State of Maryland, and

assisted by the **US Navy**, the National Oceanic and Atmospheric Administration, and numerous private organizations, the Society supported the first systematic robotic underwater archaeological survey of a shipwreck utilizing ROV-mounted short-baseline sonar, on the 1870 wreck of the steamboat *New Jersey*, in Chesapeake Bay. The same project also resulted in the ultrasonic mapping of the wrecks of the 19th-century schooners *Henrietta Bach* and *Dashaway*, in the first successful open-water survey of a site using the **Sonic High Accuracy Ranging and Positioning System**. In 1993 the Society provided personnel, equipment, and technical assistance to the State of North Carolina to test the feasibility of employing sub-surface radar to detect the prehistoric **Lake Phelps Canoes**, together with their pottery and lithics, beneath the bottom of Lake Phelps. D.G.S.

ADDITIONAL READING

Ballard, R.D., 1985, 'How We Found Titanic', *National Geographic*, 168, 6, 696–718.

Cousteau, J.-Y., 1954, 'Fish Men Discover a 2,200-year-old Greek Ship', *National Geographic Magazine*, 55, 1, 1–36.

Lenihan, D.J. (ed.), 1987, *Submerged Cultural Resources Study: Isle Royale National Park*, Southwest Cultural Resources Centre Professional Papers 8, National Park Service, Santa Fe, New Mexico.

Payne, M.M., '75 Years Exploring Earth, Sea, and Sky', *National Geographic*, 123, 1, 1–43.

Shomette, D.G., 1988, 'The *New Jersey* Project: Robots and Ultra-Sonics in Underwater Archaeological Survey', in J.P. Delgado (ed.), *Underwater Archaeology Proceedings from the Society for Historical Archaeology Conference, Reno, Nevada*, Ann Arbor, Michigan.

National Marine Sanctuaries

Diverse marine protected areas in the United States, administered by the Sanctuaries and Reserves Division of the National Oceanic and Atmospheric Administration (NOAA), US Department of Commerce. In 1972 Congress passed the Marine Protection, Research, and Sanctuaries Act to ensure the comprehensive protection and management of resources within discrete areas of the nation's marine environment. Sites are chosen for designation as National Marine Sanctuaries based on the uniqueness and significance of their ecological, historical, recreational, and aesthetic resources. The National Marine Sanctuary Program recognizes the importance of both natural and cultural resources, and sanctuary regulations emphasize that, to the extent practicable, NOAA will manage cultural resources within the sanctuaries in a manner consistent with the Federal Archaeological Program.

In 1975 the wreck of the Civil War ironclad USS **Monitor** became the United States' first marine sanctuary. There are now twelve sanctuaries, protecting diverse marine areas on the Atlantic and Pacific coasts, in the Gulf of Mexico, and in Hawaii and American Samoa. Characteristics range from nearshore coral reefs to open ocean, encompassing areas from less than one to over 4,000 square nautical miles. The sanctuaries comprise (proceeding clockwise from New England): Stellwagen Bank (Massachusetts), *Monitor* (North Carolina), Gray's Reef (Georgia), Florida Keys (Florida), Flower Garden Banks (Texas), Channel Islands, Monterey Bay, Gulf of the Farallones, and Cordell Bank (California), Olympic Coast (Washington); also, in the Pacific, the Hawaiian Islands Humpback Whale (Hawaii) and Fagatele Bay (American Samoa). In addition to the diverse flora and fauna found in these protected areas, there is a wide range of historic and prehistoric archaeological sites.

NOAA's Sanctuaries and Reserves Division is committed to a policy of stewardship of all sanctuary resources. Although the *Monitor* National Marine Sanctuary is the only site to be designated exclusively for its cultural resources, NOAA recognizes the significance of historical and archaeological resources in all the sanctuaries. Potentially destructive activities are regulated within sanctuary boundaries, and permits must be obtained before cultural resources can be disturbed. Regulations specifically state NOAA's preference for non-destructive, *in situ* research on historic and prehistoric submerged archaeological resources, and explain the procedure to be followed for obtaining a permit for the disturbance of those resources.

The National Marine Sanctuary Program attempts to balance its mandate for resource protection with that of providing for public access and enjoyment of those resources. Among the most popular uses of sanctuary resources are recreational activities, including sport fishing, diving, and boating, and valuable commercial uses, such as fishing and kelp harvesting. NOAA strives for a program of sustainable multiple use, maintained through education, outreach, and, when necessary, enforcement.

In 1995 NOAA initiated a programme to locate and inventory all historic resources within each sanctuary, including all properties and sites containing historical, archaeological, or paleontological remains. The inventory is being entered into a computer database for use by programme managers and researchers. That same year, the agency's maritime historian and archaeologist published *Fathoming Our Past: Historical Contexts of the National Marine Sanctuaries*, a study summarizing the history that took place in the vicinity of each sanctuary, describing known sanctuary resources, and suggesting topics for further research. Three broad contexts are developed in the study: native peoples (approximately 20,000 years before present to the 18th century), European colonial period (16th to 19th century), and American period (18th to early 20th century). The historical contexts study provides a framework for the identification, protection, and management of cultural resources within the sanctuaries.

In order to promote and foster research in the sanctuaries, NOAA has formed partnerships with numerous governmental and private organizations for a wide range of scientific studies; private research is also encouraged. Through this active research programme, archaeological investigations have been conducted at the *Monitor*, Florida Keys, Channel Islands, Gulf of the Farallones, and Olympic Coast sanctuaries, and others are planned.

Within the Sanctuaries and Reserves Division is a parallel programme designed to promote the protection and study of special estuarine areas, those fertile and productive areas where rivers meet the sea. The National Estuarine Research Reserve System includes twenty-four discrete estuary preserves in seventeen states and Puerto Rico. Because these preserves encompass a wide variety of navigable waterways and their shorelines, all in coastal areas, most have high potential for containing significant submerged cultural resources, including inundated prehistoric and historic sites and shipwrecks. A cultural resources educational directory is being planned for the estuarine reserves to assist the sites with the public interpretation of their unique cultural and historical resources. J.D.B.

ADDITIONAL READING

Terrell, B.G., 1995, *Fathoming Our Past: Historical Contexts of the National Marine Sanctuaries*, Newport News, Virginia.

US Department of Commerce, National Oceanic and Atmospheric Administration, 1993, *A Tour of the Reserves*, Silver Spring, Maryland.

National parks

Lands set aside by a nation for preservation of natural and cultural resources, scenic and recreational values. Access is usually controlled and monitored to ensure a minimum of activities occur that detract from the relatively natural state of the landscape and the natural and archaeological values found therein.

An inherent tension in the managing of parks is the opposing forces of preservation and visitor use. The US national park system was created in 1872 when Congress established Yellowstone National Park. Enabling legislation explicitly addressed this issue by recognizing that although the service must 'provide for the enjoyment' of the resources, it was only in so far as they could be left 'unimpaired' for future generations.

In many cases park boundaries wholly or partially encompass submerged lands and consequently sites of former human occupation. Some marine, great lakes, and riverine parks contain historic shipwreck sites. Often these sites have been unintentionally included in areas set aside for natural resource or terrestrial cultural resource management purposes. Only a comparatively small number have been set aside specifically for shipwreck preservation and diving visitation. Consequently, a recurring issue in parks and other marine protected areas is the manner in which historic shipwrecks should be accommodated in management frameworks not originally designed for them.

The establishment of marine parks and preserves specifically to address underwater archaeological issues has occurred in several nations including **Israel**, **Australia**, the **United States** and Canada. In the US, USS *Arizona*, a warship sunk in the attack on **Pearl Harbor**, is still owned by the US Navy but managed by the park service. The Civil War ironclad USS **Monitor** is managed under the auspices of the marine sanctuary programme. In the US the NOAA **National Marine Sanctuary** programme encompasses major tracts of submerged lands that are governed under special protective regulations.

In some nations, such as the United States and Canada, the premier natural and cultural resource governmental preservation infrastructures are located in park management agencies. For example, Parks Canada and the US National Park Service both house the respective nations' main Federal underwater archaeological capabilities. The US team of underwater archaeologists is called the **Submerged Cultural Resources Unit** (SCRU), based in Santa Fe, New Mexico. Parks Canada has a Marine Archaeology Unit based out of Ottawa.

The US national park system has upwards of sixty areas that contain underwater sites ranging from prehistoric habitation sites to Spanish galleons and the battleship USS

Arizona. Underwater archaeology conducted on park lands in the US follows a strict conservation philosophy. Excavation is only undertaken when it is necessary for identifying and evaluating sites. They are banked for future research if fragile and unique, but most wrecks are open to visitation by the diving public.

A sample of US national parks that include historic shipwrecks are: Cape Cod National Seashore, Biscayne National Park, **Dry Tortugas National Park, Padre Island** National Seashore, Channel Islands National Park, Point Reyes National Seashore, **Isle Royale** National Park, and Apostle Islands National Lakeshore.

Among the Canadian parks that cater to wreck-diving visitors are Fathom Five National Marine Park in Georgian Bay, Ontario and Pacific Rim National Marine Park Reserve on Vancouver Island. Between them they offer dozens of wrecks for controlled diving enjoyment by sport divers. The Louisbourg Underwater Museum in Louisbourg Harbor is an advanced concept in underwater archaeological park management which requires close cooperation between archaeologists, park managers, and the private sector.

Parks in these cases serve as outdoor classrooms and underwater sites have been the focus of number of interpretation strategies. These include mooring buoys, underwater trails, and ranger guided tours. In some cases underwater earphones are being provided to divers for reception of voiced information for assisting in guiding them about shipwreck sites. The sender can be a diving ranger or a shore-based interpreter. This is being done on an experimental basis at Dry Tortugas National Park.

Reservoir Recreation Areas are a component of the US national park system that have been the source of unique submerged cultural resources management issues. Prehistoric sites including Anasazi Indian sites in the Southwest and significant historic period structures have been inundated and are the target of many recreational divers.

Perhaps the most unusual park dedicated to shipwrecks is the collection of ships sunk at Bikini Atoll as a result of atomic bomb testing in 1946 (see **Crossroads Wrecks**). The US Submerged Cultural Resources Unit documented and evaluated these vessels in 1989 and 1990 and recommended they become the focus of a nuclear park. In 1995 the Bikinian people had an infrastructure in place to accommodate small groups of advanced divers and are now in the process of implementing the first stages of a park management plan. D.J.L.

National Register of Historic Places

The United States' official listing of historic and archaeological sites deemed to be significant under a uniform set of criteria. The National Register was established by the United States Department of the Interior, National Park Service, after Congress passed the National Historic Preservation Act of 1966.

The National Register lists more than 70,000 sites, structures, buildings, and objects in the United States that have been nominated by individuals, institutions, organizations, and government agencies. A National Register nomination is first submitted to a State Historic Preservation Officer (SHPO) for a first level of review. If it passes the SHPO's review, the nomination is forwarded to the Keeper of the National Register, in Washington, DC for final review.

To be listed in the National Register, properties must meet at least one of four criteria. Under criterion A, they must be associated with events that have made a significant contribution to the broad patterns of US history. Under criterion B, they must be associated with the lives of persons significant in US history. Under criterion C, they must be representative of a type, or characteristic of a type or style, method of construction, or represent the work of a master. Under criterion D, they must have yielded, or be likely to yield, information important in history or prehistory.

A large number of archaeological sites in the US are listed in the National Register, including submerged sites such as **Warm Mineral Springs**. Shipwrecks are defined by the National Register as 'any vessel that has foundered, stranded, wrecked or been scuttled so that the vessel no longer survives as a floating entity. This includes vessels that exist as scattered components on the sea bed, lake bed, river bed, or beaches, and/or intact hulls beneath the water, buried, or exposed on mudflats or other shorelines.'

Nearly 200 shipwrecks in the United States or its territories are listed in the National Register. These include well-known wrecks, such as CSS **Hunley**, **Defence**, **Indiana**, **Bertrand**, USS **Cairo**, and the **Padre Island Wrecks**. The greatest number of shipwreck sites listed in the National Register are those listed as part of nominations of groups of shipwrecks, usually associated with each other geographically or thematically. These include the **Yorktown Wrecks**, Virginia, scuttled by the defeated British in 1782 during the final campaign of the American Revolutionary War; the **Cape Fear Civil War Shipwreck District** congregated near the mouth of North Carolina's Cape Fear River; shipwrecks and

buried ships associated with the California Gold Rush, including SS **Tennessee**, SS **Winfield Scott**, **Frolic**, and **Niantic**; a number of scuttled and abandoned wrecks of the 19th and 20th centuries near Wilmington, North Carolina; Japanese naval and merchant vessels sunk at **Truk Lagoon**; the **Isle Royale Shipwrecks** on Lake Superior; shipwrecks within the boundaries of Biscayne National Park, Florida; and the **Wiawaka Bateaux Cluster** in Lake George, New York.

A small group of shipwrecks are also designated National Historic Landmarks (NHL), or sites of exceptional significance in American history. National Historic Landmarks are usually recommended for designation by the Secretary of the Interior after a detailed study of any and all pertinent sites, structures, or objects is completed by the National Park Service. The first individually designated NHL shipwreck in the United States was USS **Monitor**, in 1986. Other NHL shipwrecks are USS **Arizona** and USS **Utah** at Pearl Harbor. Wartime shipwrecks at Kiska Harbor, Alaska, and at Truk Lagoon contribute elements to NHL districts there. In 1995 the National Park Service's National Maritime Initiative began a National Landmark theme study of Civil War shipwrecks, recommending designation of a number of them. J.P.D.

ADDITIONAL READING

Delgado, J.P., 1987, 'The National Register of Historic Places and Maritime Preservation', *The Association for Preservation Technology Bulletin*, 9, 1, 34–9.

Delgado, J.P. *et al.*, 1987, *Nominating Historic Ships and Shipwrecks to the National Register of Historic Places*, National Register Bulletin Number 20, National Park Service, Washington, DC.

National Reservoir Inundation Study (US)

A five-year project to determine the effects of reservoir construction on archaeological sites in the United States. The programme was prompted by federal managers who noted a proliferation of markedly different, often contradictory, conclusions to Environmental Impact Studies (EISs) focused on water impoundment projects. Such studies and their resulting mitigation recommendations were becoming increasingly common in the US during the early 1970s due to the enactment of various environmental laws.

The National Environmental Policy Act (NEPA) and associated historic preservation legislation mandated that archaeological research and recovery was necessary to mitigate impacts to dam building projects. One law (the amended 1960 Reservoir Salvage Act) actually authorized the dam construction agencies to spend up to 1 per cent of the project engineering costs on compliance with these preservation requirements.

In 1975 several agencies entered a cooperative agreement with the National Park Service (NPS) to conduct a major study aimed at gaining some consistency in the expectations for archaeological mitigation. The US Army Corp of Engineers, the Bureau of Reclamation, and the Soil Conservation Service provided most of the fund-

The trail marker to Capulin Canyon is submerged by the flooding of the Cochiti Reservoir. (National Park Service)

ing for work which was carried out by a team of NPS diving archaeologists. From 1975 to 1980 the Inundation Study team gathered background data on water impoundment dynamics, visited reservoirs in various stages of construction, and conducted tests to determine the impact of various inundation processes on archaeology in the affected sites. Effects of immersion, wave action, and increased ease of access by the public to remote sites in impounded areas were among the factors studied.

Because it had never been done before, the team was forced specifically to define archaeological values in a manner that would allow explicit testing of anticipated impacts. Classes of cultural material such as bone, ceramics, lithics, wood, vegetable fibres, and glass were isolated for separate examination, as were aspects of the archaeological process that might be harmed. The latter included analytical techniques such as soil-chemistry analysis, palynology, and source-identification techniques. Impacts of immersion on dating techniques such as carbon-14, dendrochronology, and obsidian hydration were also tested.

A model was then developed for understanding and measuring detrimental effects to these resources from the dam building,

water impoundment, and operational phases of the reservoir construction process. A **Research design** that posed hundreds of testable hypotheses about the nature of predicted impacts to archaeological values was published in the project's 1977 preliminary report. The use of a hypothetico-deductive model for this major research effort was a first in underwater archaeology.

Diving conditions in the many reservoirs dived by project personnel included limited visibility, cold, ceilings and overhangs, entanglement hazards, high altitude and occasionally extreme depth exposures. The diving technology and procedures employed by the team, therefore, borrowed heavily from the cave-diving and emergent 'technical' diving communities. Rigorous standards developed for the NPS divers during this study, and a continuing interaction with the technical diving community, have set a precedent for all subsequent development in NPS research diving protocols.

Among the major findings of the study was the observation that the zone of greatest physical impact was not the area of deepest inundation as many had previously hypothesized. The area of water-level fluctuation in what is known as the drawdown zone was the most adversely affected by mechanical, chemical, and human processes. In some cases massive deflation of banks had totally destroyed all site provenance and large cultural features were obliterated. Unfortunately, even in those cases where sites were quickly covered by deep water and there was no subsequent dry-cycling, the comparatively unaffected material culture was covered by heavy siltation. Even assuming that the water would eventually be removed during the life of the reservoir, future access to the sites was heavily compromised by the accumulation of heavy sediments. Further, Inundation Study researchers found that the quality of the locational data from most archaeological site reports often made relocation of sites difficult even before impoundment. If locational data were not improved in the reservoir impact mitigation projects still ongoing, the possibility of accessing these 'data banks' after they had been covered by a water column and silt was remote.

Some dating and analytic techniques were also found to be adversely impacted, including thermoluminescent dating and fission track and alpha recoil techniques (see **Absolute dating**). Some of the most popular dating techniques, however, did not seem to be affected by inundation. These included carbon-14 dating, obsidian hydration, and archeomagnetism. The use of intra-site soil

chemistry techniques to determine activity patterns was obviated due to total homogenization of soil values from the flooding.

Depending on such variables as type of clay, temper, and heat of firing, ceramics were found to suffer some degree of degradation from inundation, the worst of it occurring in the first few months. Lithics were only adversely affected in some of the analytic procedures performed on them by archaeologists. Of special interest to reservoir managers was the conclusion that the area just outside the flood pool which was never slated for inundation was an area of high impact. Access to what had often been remote wilderness areas was now open to increasing numbers of power boaters.

The study team also took the archaeological and managerial communities to task in the report for not communicating sufficiently to develop truly viable and rational long-range plans for mitigation. They pointed out that the standard archaeological response to use available funds to conduct massive full site excavations of the most dramatic sites in a reservoir impact zone was counterproductive. The study urged that research designs for new mitigation projects address the comparative impact level on different archaeological resources as gleaned from the results of the National Reservoir Inundation Study (NRIS) and other sources. Because the study improved our understanding of the effect of reservoir construction and flooding on archaeological sites, this improved understanding should be considered, along with a better understanding of the archaeological potential of these sites to yield information, in planning for future research.

In 1981 the Final Report of the National Reservoir Inundation Study was completed and distributed to all construction agencies and many universities. It became the primary reference for all archaeological studies conducted in the United States for the purpose of mitigating adverse effects of reservoir construction. It has also received much attention internationally, particularly in English-speaking nations. The study was directed by Daniel Lenihan, and other members of the core team included Toni Carrel, Stephen Fosberg, Tom Hopkins, Larry Murphy, Wayne Prokopetz, Sandra Rayl, Catherine Tarasovic, and John Ware. The original proposal for the study was conceived by NPS archaeologist Calvin R. Cummings. The Inundation Study provided the equipment and personnel infrastructure that in 1980 was transformed into the **Submerged Cultural Resources Unit**, National Service. D.J.L.

ADDITIONAL READING

Lenihan, D.J. *et al..*, 1977, *Preliminary Report of the National Reservoir Inundation Study*, Santa Fe, New Mexico.

Lenihan, D.J., *et al.*, 1981, *Final Report of the National Reservoir Inundation Study*, Santa Fe, New Mexico.

Lenihan, D.J., 1993, 'Damming the Past', *Natural History Magazine*, 102, 11, 40–47.

Ware, J.A., 1989, *Archaeological Inundation Studies: Manual for Reservoir Managers*, Museum of New Mexico contract report EL-89-4, Santa Fe, New Mexico.

National Trust

Organization founded in 1895 to preserve places of historic interest or natural beauty permanently for the benefit of the nation in England, Wales, and Northern Ireland (there is a separate National Trust for Scotland). As a registered charity, independent of government, the Trust relies on support from members and the public. Over 240,000 hectares of countryside are owned to date, together with historic houses, archaeological sites of all periods, and a range of coastal landscapes.

Enterprise Neptune is the Trust's coastal campaign, launched in 1965 as a special fund to acquire coastline threatened by development. Through Enterprise Neptune and earlier acquisitions the Trust now owns about a sixth of the nation's coastline (excluding Scotland), more than 885 km (550 miles) in length, with adjacent coastal land. Properties thus protected include parts of the White Cliffs of Dover, the Needles (Isle of Wight), Cape Cornwall, the Farne Islands (Northumberland) and the Giant's Causeway (Northern Ireland), a World Heritage Site. The campaign continues with the aim of protecting more of the finest areas of the coastline.

As far as possible the Trust aims to preserve whole coastal landscapes, combining historical and natural interest, and taking full account of the historic structures and associations of coastal areas, based on a systematic programme of surveys. Normally National Trust ownership extends only to the high water mark, but in some areas it includes tidal estuaries and intertidal land. Increasingly the Trust works with other bodies to take account of the significance of the marine zone as a whole.

Through its programme of archaeological and historic landscape surveys the Trust aims to identify and manage sites representing coastal history including the archaeology of historic communications, industry, defence, fishing, shipping, and transport. Defence works, for example, range from Iron Age cliff forts to the 20th-century ruins of the Atomic Weapons Research Establishment at Orford Ness (Suffolk). At Ravenscar (North Yorkshire) the Trust has conserved and opened to the public Britain's best preserved historic alum works, dating from the 17th century – an early example of a historic industrial chemical process site.

Priorities for Enterprise Neptune in the late 1990s include raising public awareness of the threats to Britain's estuaries from development, recreational, and other pressures; and focusing on historic structures such as lighthouses, which, as they are demanned and replaced by new technology, require new measures for their long-term protection.

Further information may be obtained from the Enterprise Neptune Appeal Manager, The National Trust, Attingham Park, Shrewsbury, Shropshire SY4 4TP, England. P.D.C.

National Underwater and Marine Agency (NUMA)

Privately funded US agency set up to preserve maritime heritage by discovering, surveying, and identifying shipwrecks of historic significance before they are lost forever. After a wreck site is found by NUMA's professional marine archaeologists, the resulting reports and all recovered artefacts are turned over to State and Federal authorities, or donated to museums and universities.

NUMA was founded by best-selling author Clive Cussler in 1978. Incorporated as a non-profit foundation in the State of Texas, its name was taken from the fictional Federal agency used in Cussler's novels. Although Cussler was not keen on the idea himself, the trustees, consisting of Dr Harold Edgerton, Peter Throckmorton, and Commander Don Walsh, out-voted him.

To date, NUMA has not been involved with any treasure expeditions. Nothing of value that is recovered and preserved is kept by any foundation members or project volunteers. Almost all funding comes through Cussler's royalties from his fiction adventure novels, with supplementary donations by a few private individuals and corporations. NUMA has no offices or salaried employees.

NUMA has achieved an outstanding record of success, discovering over sixty wreck sites of historic importance, including the Confederate submarine **H.L. Hunley**, the Vanderbilt steamer *Lexington*; the famous Confederate raider **Florida**; the destroyer of **Lusitania**, the German submarine U-20; USS **Cumberland**, sunk by CSS *Virginia*; the Republic of Texas Navy steamship *Zavala*; and the Belgian troopship *Leopoldville* that sank, killing 800 American GIs, on Christmas Eve 1944. C.C.

ADDITIONAL READING

Cussler, C. and Dirgo, C., 1996, *The Sea Hunters*, New York.

Nautical archaeology

see **Maritime archaeology**; **Underwater archaeology**

Nautical Archaeology Society

International society, based in London, founded in 1981 to further research in all aspects of nautical archaeology and to ensure publication of the results. It aims to advance education in nautical archaeology at all levels; to improve techniques in reporting, excavating, and conservation; and to encourage participation by members of the public. The Society is committed to the protection of the underwater cultural heritage throughout the world and to the increase of

An NAS instructor sets out a recording exercise in the swimming pool for trainee underwater archaeologists. (Colin Martin)

public appreciation of it. It publishes the **International Journal of Nautical Archaeology**, which since 1972 has been the main outlet for scholarly articles on underwater archaeology and related topics, and members receive a regular newsletter.

The Society's most notable achievement is its structured certification scheme. This consists of four ascending levels, or 'Parts'. Part I is an introduction which can be completed in a weekend. Part II is a practical course, modular in structure, which builds on the theory and techniques introduced in Part I with a more advanced series of lectures, a set of survey exercises leading to the production of a short report, and a requirement for conference attendance. Part III consists of an advanced underwater archaeology field school, the aim of which is to produce competent fieldworkers with sufficient skills and background knowledge to be assets on any project. The ultimate qualification represented by Part IV requires evidence of substantial experience of fieldwork and the submission of either a dissertation or a portfolio of practical work together with a report prepared to full publication standards.

Further information about membership of the Nautical Archaeology Society and details of its certification scheme may be obtained from the *NAS Guide to Principles and Practice*. C.M.

ADDITIONAL READING

Dean, M. *et al.* (eds), 1992, *Archaeology Underwater: The NAS Guide to Principles and Practice*, London.

Netherlands Institute for Ship and Underwater Archaeology (NISA/ROB)

Organization established on 12 April 1995, a combination of the former Centrum voor Scheepsarcheologie (Centre for Nautical Archaeology, successor of the Ship Archaeological Department of the Scientific Division of the IJsselmeerpolders Development Authority, or RIJP) in Ketelhaven, Province of Flevoland, and the Department of Underwater Archaeology of the former Ministry of Culture, Recreation and Social Works, in Aalphen aan de Rijn, Province of South Holland. The NISA is under the administration of the Rijksdienst voor het Oudheidkundig Bodemonderzoek (ROB; National Archaeological Service) in the Ministry of Education, Culture and Science, and is responsible for the investigation, conservation, analysis, and management of shipwrecks and related finds for the Netherlands.

Until 1998, when a newly constructed central facility comes into use in Lelystad (Flevoland), the staff assigned to terrestrial sites are headquartered in Ketelhaven, where facilities for the recording, conservation, analysis, and storage of ship remains and artefacts are allied to a moderately sized museum, and staff assigned to underwater sites are based in Aalphen aan de Rijn. The **Conservation** laboratory in Ketelhaven is one of the largest in Europe and treats finds from both terrestrial and underwater sites.

The Underwater Division, under the direction of Thijs Maarleveld, is best known for a series of excavations of late medieval and early modern ships in the vicinity of the island of Texel. These wrecks, excavated in both the North and Wadden Seas, have produced well-preserved hull remains and cargoes. The Underwater Division has also

pioneered the development of new tools for recording wreck remains in the difficult conditions of the North Sea, and has been one of the primary teams involved in the field development of Direct Survey Measurement.

The Ship Archaeological Division in Ketelhaven has its origins in the Zuiderzee Project, the large-scale damming and draining of the arm of the North Sea that had for seven centuries been the central waterway of the northern Netherlands. The Zuiderzee Project was initially conceived in the late 19th century as a means of increasing the arable land of the Netherlands and easing the population pressure in the cities of the most densely populated country in Europe. Work commenced in the 1920s with the construction of the first segment of the great Aftsluitdijk, the dike closing off the Zuiderzee at its narrowest point and turning it into the fresh water IJsselmeer, and the construction of a small, experimental polder (a parcel of reclaimed land surrounded by a dike to keep the sea out) to test the proposed methods of turning the land to be reclaimed into productive farmland. The first of the four large polders was drained in 1930, the last in 1968. In all, an area of 166,000 hectares was drained and converted to farmland and new towns. Management of all aspects of the project was vested in a single government agency, originally the Zuiderzee Project Directorate, eventually the Rijksdienst voor de IJsselmeerpolders (IJsselmeerpolders Development Authority, frequently known as the RIJP).

During the planning stages of the project, it had been anticipated that draining would reveal the remains of drowned, early medieval villages, and archaeologists have been contacted as early as 1940 to assist in the investigation of the polders. During the development of the new land, it rapidly became apparent that the bottom of the former sea did not hold many lost villages, but was littered with wrecks dating back to the Middle Ages. (See also **IJsselmeerpolders Wrecks**.) The digging of drainage ditches at close, regular intervals throughout the polders was, in effect, an archaeological survey of colossal proportions. The first of these wrecks to be investigated and published archaeologically, a small cog in the Noordoostpolder (Northeast Polder), was excavated in 1942. During World War II, a small archaeological team was added to the Zuiderzee Project Directorate, eventually the Scientific Division of the RIJP, and this team, initially headquartered on the former island of Schokland, began the investigation of wrecks discovered by development crews.

Since that time, the staff of this unit have registered and investigated 435 wrecks dating from the 13th to the early 20th centuries; over 150 of these have been excavated in their entirety and another 100 preserved in place to await later excavation. Finds were catalogued by the plot of land (*kavel*) in which they were found, so most of the wrecks are known by short alphanumeric codes; the small cog excavated in 1944 is thus NM 107 (Noordoostpolder M 107) or a 17th-century *beurtschip* excavated in the town of Lelystad is OB 71 (Oostelijk [eastern] Flevoland B 71). Recovered material was initially housed in the mainland town of Kampen and then in the old medieval church on Schokland, until the conversion of a granary in Ketelhaven, where the Museum voor Scheepsarcheologie was opened in 1971.

The archaeological work was initially directed by P.J.R. Modderman. In 1945, he was succeeded by G.D. van der Heide. Under van der Heide, the Museum developed many of the techniques that eventually became standard procedure for excavating and documenting ship finds. The staff also expended a great deal of effort in developing an accurate picture of the stratigraphy of the old bottom sediments which would allow at least general dating of finds. Under his successor, Reinder Reinders (1974–89), the Ship Archaeological Department devoted more time to the analysis of the large collection of finds, the development of procedures for excavation and documentation of ship finds, and initiated a systematic programme of publication in the *Flevobericht* series, technical publications of the scientific activities of the RIJP. Under the directorship of Jaap Morel (1991–), the museum has gone through an administrative restructuring. With the completion of the Zuiderzee Project, the RIJP was dissolved in the late 1980s, and the Ship Archaeological Department transferred to the jurisdiction of the ROB in the early 1990s. The latter move included the renaming of the unit as Centrum and Rijksmuseum (National Museum) voor Scheepsarcheologie.

Wrecks investigated by the NISA on terrestrial sites are generally treated in one of three ways. Those judged to be of great importance but which cannot be excavated immediately may be surveyed and then recovered in a manner that artificially raises the water table. Quite a few wrecks were treated this way in the 1970s and early 1980s. Wrecks that have to be moved may be excavated and recorded, the artefacts transported back to Ketelhaven for conservation and storage, and the hull remains reburied in a special preserve (the 'ship cemetery') where the water table is still quite high and the land has been set aside for this purpose (such wrecks were formerly recorded and then discarded). A small number of wrecks have been raised and conserved for display.

Since the development work has been completed, the rate of discoveries has fallen and the Centrum has been able to devote more resources to the excavation of previously discovered sites and the publication of older excavations. These projects have revealed that the anaerobic conditions in the polder mud that has in the past guaranteed outstanding preservation are disappearing. The lowering of the water table to facilitate agriculture has allowed unprotected sites to dry out and deterioration to accelerate. F.M.H., K.V.

ADDITIONAL READING

Modderman, P.J.R., 1945, *Over de wording en beteekenis van het Zuiderzeegebeid*, Gronigen.

Reinders, H.R., 1982, *Shipwrecks of the Zuiderzee*, Flevobericht 197, Lelystad.

van Duin, R.H.A. and de Kaste, G., n.d., *The Pocket Guide to the Zuiderzee Project*, Lelystad.

CSS *Neuse*

Ironclad gunboat built by the Confederate States Navy during the American Civil War to strengthen the southern defences and prevent Union occupation of the sounds and rivers of North Carolina. One of twenty-two ironclad warships commissioned by the Confederacy during the war, *Neuse* was designed by John L. Porter, naval contractor, and was built by Howard and Ellis, shipbuilders of New Bern, near the little town of White Hall near Goldsboro on the Neuse River in North Carolina. A sister ship, *Albermarle*, was built simultaneously on the Roanoke River. The ironclad concept was a relatively new innovation proven in the battle between USS **Monitor** and CSS *Virginia* at Hampton Roads in the spring of 1862. Construction of these superior armoured floating batteries, designed with a built-on ram, was intended to reduce the advantage of the much larger US Navy fleet of warships.

Work began on the gunboat *Neuse* in November 1862, and was to be completed and ready for machinery and armour by 1 March 1863. By early spring the finished hull was turned over to the Confederate Navy and towed down river to Kinston where armour-plating was to be installed. Progress slowed owing to the inability to get iron for the armour-plating. The Navy requested railroad iron to be rolled into plating, but it was ruled the Army needed it more for transporting troops. Finally, North

Bow view of the hull of CSS Neuse, *on display at Kinston in 1964. (US Naval Historical Center)*

Carolina governor Zebulon B. Vance secured iron from several railroad companies operating in the State. The rails were probably shipped to Atlanta, Georgia and rolled into 2 in (50 mm) armour-plating. It was not until April 1864 that *Neuse* was made ready for service with only one layer of armour. On 27 April, in an attempt to navigate downstream and to retake New Bern which had fallen into Union hands, *Neuse* grounded on a sandbar a kilometre below Kinston. It remained stuck there for more than a month. During this period, its support troops were transferred from Kinston to Virginia, preventing a second attempt to retake New Bern when *Neuse* was finally freed. As the Confederacy collapsed on 12 March 1865, Commander Joseph Price, on orders from General Braxton Bragg, ordered his crew to shell advancing enemy cavalry and then destroy *Neuse* by burning to prevent its capture. Before fire consumed the vessel, a loaded gun discharged, blowing a hole in *Neuse*, which sank rapidly.

Shortly after the war, machinery and armour were salvaged from *Neuse*. After settling into the river bottom, the ship lay undisturbed save for shifting sands and slight exposure during periods of low water until 1961. In that year, driven by curiosity and a rumour that a barrel of gold was to be found on the old gunboat, three Kinston men set forth a salvage project that lasted until 19 June 1993. Before *Neuse* was cut into three sections and transported 8 km to Governor Caswell Park in Kinston, a great number of citizens, groups, clubs, and political leaders, including the Governor of North Carolina, had contributed in some way to the recovery of *Neuse*. The remains are now on display at CSS Neuse State Historic Site in Kinston, North Carolina. L.S.B.

ADDITIONAL READING

Bright, L.S., Rowland, W.H., and Bardon, J.C., 1981, *CSS Neuse: A Question of Iron and Time*, Raleigh, N. Carolina.

Still, W.N., Jr, 1969, *Confederate Shipbuilding*, Athens, Georgia.

Still, W.N., Jr, 1971, *Iron Afloat*, Nashville, Tennessee.

New Guy's House Boat

Remains of a 2nd-century AD boat discovered in March 1958 while workers excavated a trench for the foundations for an addition to New Guy's House, a London hospital. The boat was found 4.85 m below ground level, lying beneath 2.1 m of silt and a 2.75 m layer of post-medieval rubbish. The boat lay in what had been a shallow creek in the marshes to the east of the Roman settlement near London Bridge. A layer of silt inside the boat, along with freshwater molluscs and accumulated driftwood, showed that it had been abandoned on the site and was subsequently buried by additional silting and landfill.

There was little opportunity to record the remains of the vessel *in situ* when it was discovered on 8 March 1958. The archaeologist on site, Peter Marsden, felt that the wreck was Roman because a nearby trench had disclosed Roman pottery sherds at the same level. The trench exposed the northern end of a broad, barge-like vessel. In all, only 6.7 m of the hull was documented in two separate excavations. The first, in 1958, exposed planks and frames near the end of the boat. Dug by the contractors, the first trench was roughly excavated and much detail was lost. In 1960 Marsden returned to the site and excavated a small trench at the extreme north end of the boat, exposing what may be either the bow or stern.

Working from his on site observations of 1960, and from pieces of frames and planks

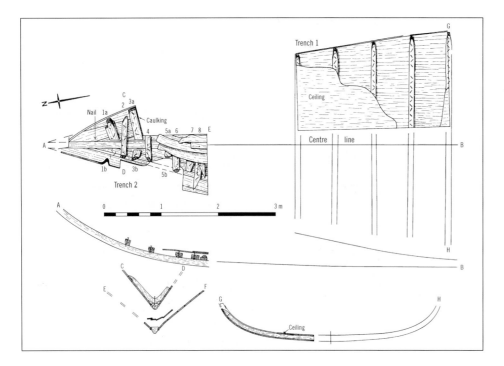

The New Guy's House Boat. (Museum of London)

cut away in 1958 and preserved at the Cummings Museum, Southwark, and the Shipwreck Heritage Centre at Hastings, Marsden published his initial findings in 1965 and revised them in 1994. Based on pottery dating from AD 190 to 225 found on the site, Marsden dates the wreck to the end of the 2nd century, and ascribes it to the Romano-Celtic family of shipbuilding. (See also **Barland's Farm Boat** and **Guernsey Wreck**).

An 'endpost' (so termed because the identity of bow and stern has yet to be determined) was rabbeted to accommodate the ends of planks laid end to end and fastened in place with flat-headed, square-shank iron nails. The planks were caulked with hazel shavings, and coated with pine resin. There was some evidence that not every plank was caulked, and that caulking was a feature of later repair or maintenance.

Some frames, apparently cut from the quarter of a tree branch, had limber holes similar to those seen on the **Blackfriars I** wreck and probably indicated that they followed the tapering end of a keel-plank. The frames at the end of the boat were U-shaped crooks fashioned from naturally grown trees. Some scarf joints, which were probably later repairs, were noted. Oak ceiling planks were fastened to the frames by iron nails.

Marsden reconstructs the New Guy's House Boat as a probable 16 m long, double-ended craft with a beam of approximately 4.25 m and only about 1 m deep amidships, although there was some sheer, with the gunwale rising at the north end.

The vessel was built frame first. Marsden postulates, given the low freeboard, that the boat was a locally built craft probably constructed on the Thames or one of its tributaries in the mid-2nd century for use as a river barge. After a long life, with several repairs, the vessel was abandoned. The limited excavations of the wreck, and damage to the boat when initially exposed, limit the amount of information about the ship available for reconstruction. Because a look at the exterior of the hull, the southern end, and its fittings was not possible, only a minimal reconstruction of the boat was undertaken.

The boat was threatened by future construction after 1958, largely because it could not be designated under existing ancient sites and monuments legislation as 'chattel' or movable property. Protection for the wreck was sought by Marsden and others, resulting in new legislation in 1979 that included buried and wrecked vessels. The Department of the Environment scheduled the boat as a protected monument in June 1983. Fearing a slow drying of the formerly waterlogged boat because the level of groundwater that once protected the boat has dropped, Marsden hopes that work to excavate fully and study the New Guy's House Boat will occur soon. J.P.D.

ADDITIONAL READING
Marsden, P., 1994, *Ships of the Port of London: First to Eleventh Centuries AD*, London.

Niagara

A **US Navy** twenty-gun brig built at Presque Isle (now Erie), Pennsylvania for service on Lake Erie during the Anglo-American War of 1812. *Niagara* and its sister brig *Lawrence* were constructed by New York shipwright Noah Brown during the late winter and spring of 1813 for the squadron of Master Commandant Oliver Hazard Perry. The warships were launched in early June, but outfitting each of them with rigging, ballast, stores, two 12-pounder long guns and eighteen 32-pounder carronades required until mid-July; crews for Perry's squadron were also in short supply, but *Niagara* was eventually manned by 155 sailors and US Army soldiers.

The new brigs entered the lake on 6 August, accompanied by eight smaller craft carrying between one and four cannon apiece; five weeks later, on 10 September, the US ships met the Royal Navy squadron in the western end of the lake and fought the Battle of Lake Erie. The American flagship *Lawrence* bore the brunt of the fight until its guns were put out of action, whereupon Perry crossed to the relatively undamaged *Niagara* in a small boat and then swiftly defeated his opponents. The US Navy's victory on the lake allowed the US Army to regain the initiative in the west, and made an enduring hero out of Perry.

Niagara was in service on the upper lakes until the conclusion of the war in early 1815, and then served as a receiving ship until 1818 when it was sunk for preservation alongside *Lawrence* and two captured British warships at Misery Bay, Lake Erie. The submerged hulls were sold to salvors in 1825. The hull of one brig, believed to be *Lawrence*, was salvaged in 1876 for display in the American Centennial Exposition at Philadelphia. A second wreck, identified as *Niagara*, was raised in 1913 as part of the centennial celebration of the Battle of Lake Erie. The hull was disassembled and then reassembled using much new timber and a questionable set of reconstruction plans (original plans for Perry's brigs have never been found). The vessel was subsequently acquired by the State of Pennsylvania, extensively rebuilt in 1933 using reconstruction plans prepared by Howard Chapelle, and placed on display ashore at Erie, Pennsylvania. By the 1980s *Niagara* had greatly deteriorated, and so was broken up once again and rebuilt from the keel up by naval architect and shipwright Melbourne Smith. The reborn *Niagara* was launched in 1988 and has since sailed the lakes.

Niagara's hull was inadequately documented in 1913, and little of the original vessel existed after the 1933 rebuilding. Wood identifications made at the time of recovery indicate that the frames were fashioned from oak, poplar, cucumber, ash, cedar, and walnut. Photographs of the salvaged hull suggest it was similar in size and appearance to the Brown-built Lake Champlain brig **Eagle** (1814), although *Niagara* differed in having its deck structure reinforced with knees and by the addition of small openings in the bulwarks, called sweep ports, for propelling the vessel by sweeps. K.C.

ADDITIONAL READING

Carone, A., 1988, 'Preserving the US Brig *Niagara*, 1913–1988', *Journal of Erie Studies*, 17, 103–12.

Chapelle, H.I., 1949, *The History of the American Sailing Navy*, New York.

Crisman, K., 1987, *The Eagle: An American Brig on Lake Champlain During the War of 1812*, Annapolis, Maryland, and Shelburne, Vermont.

Malcomson, T. and Malcomson, R., 1990, *HMS Detroit: The Battle for Lake Erie*, Annapolis, Maryland.

Rosenberg, M., 1987, *The Building of Perry's Fleet on Lake Erie*, Harrisburg, Pennsylvania.

Niantic

Buried ship discovered in San Francisco and partially excavated and removed in 1978. Built in 1833 for the China trade, *Niantic*'s career included several years as a whaler before being caught up in the California Gold Rush. Arriving at San Francisco in July 1849, the ship was hauled in close to shore and beached on the mudflats off the San Francisco waterfront. The ballast and masts were removed, and piles were driven alongside to stabilize the ship. The '*Niantic* storeship' was subdivided into warehouses and stores, with offices built into a large 'barn' that covered the deck. The *Niantic* storeship remained in business until destroyed by a fire on 4 May 1851, which burned *Niantic* to the waterline. The cargo of unburned merchandise was covered by collapsing burnt debris and later that year the entire hull was buried under a layer of sand to allow for the construction of a building on the site.

The remains of *Niantic* were exposed by construction work in late April 1978 at the corner of Clay and Sansome streets. Approximately 27 m of the vessel's hull was exposed from the stern to a point aft of the bow, extended beneath a concrete bulkhead and into an adjacent undeveloped lot. The exposed remains were slated for demolition to allow the construction work to continue,

so an arrangement was made with the San Francisco Maritime Museum for a 'rapid rescue dig' to recover several thousand artefacts, many of which were located where they had been stored inside *Niantic*. These materials were taken into the collections of what is now the National Maritime Museum, San Francisco.

The *Niantic* collection includes stationery and printing materials, firearms, tools, furnishings, food, intact crates of champagne, ceramics, barrels, crates and chests, miners' personal effects stored aboard the ship, and

The Niantic site. (National Park Service)

Cover of Niantic's logbook, 1848-9, showing the ship embarking passengers for San Francisco. (San Francisco Maritime National Historical Park)

parts of the vessel itself. While some items were charred, the burial of the ship and artefacts in wet mud and sand kept many items such as shoes, leather coats, and food in excellent condition.

The site and its collections, described as a 'Gold Rush Pompeii', comprises a detailed and well-preserved accumulation of materials imported to San Francisco from European and American markets in the first year of the California Gold Rush. The (albeit hasty) archaeological recovery of the *Niantic* cargo offered the first opportunity to analyse and interpret archaeologically a San Francisco storeship and life on the Gold Rush waterfront.

The collection was analysed by archaeologist Mary Hilderman Smith between 1979 and 1981. Smith found that the *Niantic* collection's largely foreign points of origin pointed to a cosmopolitan, world-class city reliant on maritime trade and serving as a cultural depot and dispersion point; 'the historical accident of gold's discovery in 1848 to the northeast of San Francisco served to *intensify* the frontier process already in motion at this location. This intensification catapulted San Francisco from a proto or fledgling city into a maturing metropolis.' J.P.D.

ADDITIONAL READING

Bullen, I., 1979, 'A Glimpse into the *Niantic*'s Hold', *California History*, 63, 4, 326–33.

Delgado, J.P., 1979, 'No Longer a Buoyant Ship: Unearthing the Gold Rush Storeship *Niantic*', *California History*, 63, 4, 316–25.

Delgado, J.P., 1983, 'A Gold Rush Enterprise: Sam Ward, Charles Mersch, and the Storeship *Niantic*', *Huntington Library Quarterly*, 46, 4, 321–30.

Parker, J., 1980, 'Invincible Amphibian: The Story of the Ship *Niantic*', *American West*, 17, 6, 48–53.

Smith, M.H., 1981, *An Interpretive Study of the Collection Recovered from the Storeship Niantic*, M.A. thesis, San Francisco State University.

Nieuwe Rhoon

A homeward-bound Dutch East Indiaman wrecked in Table Bay, Cape Town in 1776. In 1970 workmen building a civic centre on the city's reclaimed foreshore uncovered the structural wreckage of this vessel, consisting of the lower hull on either side of the keelson. With support from the University of Cape Town, Bob Lightley, a building inspector and ship model builder, meticulously exposed, recorded, and recovered timbers and artefacts from the buried ship. Items recovered included a large variety of shot, Kwangtung Chinese porcelain bowls, and clay pipes bearing factory marks with a date range between 1730 and 1780. This could be regarded as the first effort at maritime archaeology in South Africa.

Although each timber was individually tagged with the intention of reconstruction and display, many were subsequently lost in the absence of a formal infrastructure and policies to deal with this unique situation at that time. Some of the timbers and shot are housed in the South African Maritime Museum and photographs of the timbers and excavation are available. L.H., T.D.

ADDITIONAL READING

African Notes and News, March 1944, 1, 2.

Bruin, J.R., Gaastra, F.S., and Schoffer, I., 1979, *Dutch Asiatic Shipping in the 17th and 18th Century,* vol. 3, The Hague.

Lightley, R., 1976, 'An Eighteenth Century Dutch East Indiaman Found at the Cape', *International Journal of Nautical Archaeology,* 5, 4, 305–16.

Noquebay

Late 19th-century schooner-barge sunk in a shallow bay off Stockton Island in Apostle Islands National Seashore, Wisconsin. She lay undisturbed and nearly forgotten for nearly eighty years until spotted during a small plane overflight of the region in 1985. The discovery of the schooner-barge reopened a largely ignored chapter of **Great Lakes** maritime history.

Great Lakes schooners and schooner-barges evolved to meet the need for the movement of general cargo and bulk freight throughout the region during the second half of the 19th century. By 1870 more than 2,000 sailing ships were listed on the upper lakes, 80 per cent of these being schooners. Incorporating the tow system and using the steam donkey engine to expedite the unloading of bulk cargoes, shippers accelerated the demand for bigger, more efficient ships capable of carrying larger cargoes. The result was the development of the schooner-barge.

The schooner-barge differed from other barges in that it carried some sails on masts that were smaller than those on a traditionally rigged schooner. The sails provided additional power to move the tow and were used if the vessel broke free or had to be cast loose during an emergency. Because of the limited sail carried by the schooner-barge, usually nothing above the lower courses and a fore staysail, fewer crew members were required. The savings to the owners on crew wages and the increased capacity of a multi-barge tow resulted in the rapid demise of the sailing schooner for bulk cargo transport. By the time the last fully rigged schooner was launched at Manitowoc in 1889, the success of the consort system (towing barges with schooner-barges) was unquestioned.

Built in 1872 by Alvin A. Turner of Trenton, Michigan, *Noquebay* was specifically constructed as a schooner-barge for the lumber and coal trades. At 205 ft (62.5 m) in length, and capable of carrying 1,024,000 board feet of lumber or 1,350 tons of coal, it was typical of the schooner-barges of the day. The ship was active in the lumber trade, which reached a peak in 1882, and also transported coal and bulk salt across the lakes.

Noquebay's last voyage began routinely on 6 October 1905, with *Mautenee,* in tow of *Lizzie Madden,* bound for Bay City, Michigan. Loaded with hemlock, the trio travelled 32 km east of Bayfield, Wisconsin, when a fire was discovered in the area of the donkey boiler. It was reported in contemporary newspaper accounts that the fire started while the crew were eating their noon meal in the aft deckhouse. As a result, the smouldering flames were not noticed until they were widespread. Efforts to quell the blaze were unsuccessful; *Noquebay* eventually burned to the waterline, coming to rest in a shallow sandy bay. No effort was made to salvage the ship as, by the time of its loss, it was past its prime both economically and technologically.

The wreck was documented by local **Avocational** (amateur) archaeologists and the National Park Service's **Submerged Cultural Resource Unit** in 1985. T.L.C.

ADDITIONAL READING

Barry, J.D., 1973, *Ships of the Great Lakes: 300 Years of Navigation,* Berkeley, California.

Carrell, T.L., 1985, *Submerged Cultural Resources Site Report: Noquebay,* Southwest Cultural Resources Centre Professional Papers 7, Santa Fe, New Mexico.

Ericson, B.E., 1962, *The Evolution of Ships on the Great Lakes, Part I: Early History,* Niagara, Ontario.

Ericson, B.E., 1968, *The Evolution of Ships on the Great Lakes, Part II: Steam and Steel,* Cleveland, Ohio.

Mansfield, J.B., 1899, *History of the Great Lakes,* vol. 1, Chicago, repr. Cleveland, Ohio.

Morris, P.C., 1984, *Schooners and Schooner Barges,* Orleans, Massachusetts.

Nossa Senhora de Atalaia do Pinheiro

Portuguese carrack wrecked north of East London near the Cintsa River, South Africa, during a homeward voyage from Goa in 1647. She was voyaging with **Santissimo Sacramento**. The wreck site was located in 1978 during a comprehensive survey by the East London Museum under the supervision of Graham Bell-Cross to identify shipwreck sites along the southeast coast of Africa. Twenty-three cannon, part of a cargo consignment of spices, pewter, and porcelain, a sounding lead, anchors, and disarticulated timbers were found on the site. The museum staff attempted to establish some archaeological controls, but many problems with surf and low visibility were experienced.

Much of the initial recovery on the site was conducted prior to legislation and the museum's involvement through the permitting process. The museum was later assisted in this project by commercial salvors Peter Sachs and Sean Mitchley. To recover working costs, divers melted down bronze cannon for scrap value after attempting unsuccessfully to sell the cannon to museums. The artefact collection from this wreck, including some of the nine remaining cannon, is now housed in the East London Museum. L.H., T.D.

ADDITIONAL READING

Axelson, E. (ed.), 1988, *Dias and his Successors,* Cape Town.

Feyo, Bento Teyxera, 1650, *Relacam do naufragio que fizeram as naos Sacramento & Nossa Senhora da Atalaya vindo da India para o Reyno, no Cabo Esperanca,* Lisbon. Translated into English in G.M. Theal, *Records of South Eastern Africa,* 8, 295–360.

Sachs, P.N., 1980, *Interim Salvage Report on the Wreck of the Nossa Senhora de Atalaia do Pinheiro (1697),* Cape Town.

Nuestra Señora de Atocha

Spanish *almiranta* (vice-flagship) sunk in 1622 off Florida Keys. On 4 September 1622, twenty-eight ships composing the yearly *Tierra Firme* fleet left Havana, Cuba for Spain loaded with several thousand passengers and their belongings, appropriate provisions, and many tons of private and royal treasure. Within two days, eight of these ships were sunk in a hurricane along the western expanse of the Florida Keys, including the *almiranta* of the fleet *Nuestra Señora de Atocha*.

Various and limited remains of the 500 ton Spanish guard galleon, including nine bronze cannon, came to light in the 1970s and early 1980s when the commercial salvage firm Treasure Salvors, Inc. began recovery operations some 50 km west of Key West, Florida.

However, it was not until 1985, following a survey of approximately 12 km of secondary scatter trail, that the lower hull and primary deposit of cultural material was located. Prior to the location of this deposit, scatter provenance was recorded via a positioning system. Following this major discovery of greater arte-

fact concentrations, recoveries were plotted utilizing basic baseline triangulation and offsets, plumb bobs and line levels, and small grids where appropriate.

Simply explained, the wrecking sequence occurred in two phases. The original storm forced the vessel onto and over the outer reef in a north-northwesterly direction, leaving a trail of material approximately half a kilometre long to the point where the galleon settled. One month later a second storm of even greater intensity struck the area and broke the ship completely apart, scattering wreck debris along the bottom toward the west-northwest for many miles.

What remained of the lower hull was pinned down with ballast stones, hundreds of copper and silver ingots, and numerous wooden crates of coins and worked silver and gold. Also recovered from this area were the thousands of requisite wrought-iron fasteners, barrel hoops, ceramic containers of varying types and associated sherds, wooden dunnage, raw emeralds, and numerous other items representative of early 17th-century Spanish colonial endeavours. One significant find has been identified as the pilot's chest containing or closely provenanced with several bags of coins, three astrolabes, and the second earliest wooden cross-staff ever found.

One of the more fascinating phases of the excavation was the investigation and recording of the structural remains of this typical Spanish treasure galleon. Constructed in Havana, Cuba, by Alonso Ferrera, *Atocha* was the last of four 550 *tonalada* galleons built between 1616 and 1620 under the same contract specifically to carry royal treasure for the Spanish gov-

ernment. The original shipwright's contract (AGI Contracion 4895) was fortunately located in Spain by Dr Eugene Lyon and has afforded the rare opportunity to conduct a comparative analysis between early shipbuilding theory and actual practice. For example, the mortise-and-tenon

Left: One of four plants (Bidens alba) which sprouted from seeds excavated from beneath Atocha*'s hull structure. (David Moore)*

Right: Two silver ewers (before and after conservation) recovered from Atocha *in 1985. (Dylan Kibler)*

lap joint between framing components which had been previously recorded on two other galleons examined in Florida waters (*Santa Margarita*, 1622, and *San Martin*, 1618), was also specified in the *Atocha* contract. As expected, this characteristic was observed in *Atocha*'s frames as well, though with interesting variations. In addition, there were some discrepancies between fastener specifications and that recorded on the structure.

One surprising aspect of the post-excavation laboratory work was the sprouting of four seeds recovered from samples of organic material and bottom sediments previously removed from beneath a section of contiguous ceiling planks. The seeds, identified as *Bidens alba* and possibly utilized as animal fodder, were retrieved from a thick matrix of sand, other seeds, bones, insect fragments, etc., utilizing typical procedures, albeit with a denser sugar water flotation medium.

The interpretation and analysis on the *Nuestra Señora de Atocha* slowly progresses; a series of monographs are planned. D.M.2

ADDITIONAL READING

Kane, R.E. *et al.*, 1989, 'Emerald and Gold Treasures of the Spanish Galleon *Nuestra Señora Atocha*', *Gems and Gemology*, 25, 4.

Lyon, E., 1979, *The Search for the Atocha*, New York. Reprinted 1989 with additional material as *Search for the Motherlode of the Atocha*, Port Salerno, Florida.

Marken, M.W., 1994, *Pottery from Spanish Shipwrecks, 1500–1800*, Gainesville, Florida.

Mathewson, R.D., III, 1977, *Method and Theory in New World Historic Wreck Archaeology: Hypothesis Testing on the Site of Nuestra Señora de Atocha, Marquesas Keys, Florida*, M.A. thesis, Florida Atlantic University, Boca Raton, Florida.

Mathewson, R.D., III, 1986, *Treasure of the Atocha*, New York.

Moore, D.D., 1995, *Heritage in Wood: A Comparative Examination of the Structural Evidence of Three Seventeenth Century Spanish Galleons*, unpublished MS.

EDITOR'S NOTE: This site is included because it is well known and widely reported in the popular media and press. However, sites such as this have primarily been the focus of commercially oriented activity that has often resulted in the sale of recovered artefacts to private owners, the transfer of artefacts to private investors, or the splitting of artefacts between a government and a private salvor. Despite the presence of an archaeologist on the site, or the recovery of any archaeological data, the long-term potential of a site to yield meaningful information is compromised when the collection of artefacts – the primary data of any archaeological site – has been dispersed. Furthermore, the sale of artefacts from shipwreck sites endorses the concept that the archaeological past and antiquities are commodities for sale on the open market, which has proved detrimental to the protection and study of the past. The inclusion of this site in this encyclopaedia does not sanction or condone this type of activity.

Nuestra Señora de la Concepción

Spanish *almiranta* (vice-flagship) which sank in 1641 on the remote and dangerous Silver Shoals and became a legend in the annals of treasure hunting. The 600 ton ship was over twenty years old when she was converted to serve as convoy escort of a fleet which departed Spain for Mexico in 1640. There, the ships spent a year rotting in tropical waters before embarking with precious cargoes for Havana and home. At sea, dangerously late in the season, the convoy had passed the dangerous Florida reefs when a hurricane struck the fleet. Separated by the storm, the *almiranta* drifted out of control under a single mizzen sail, heavy with seawater despite constant pumping. After steerage was finally regained, Admiral Villavicencio and his pilots decided to head for Puerto Rico to save their lives and the ship's cargo. But during the following days the pilots changed course several times, finally settling on a heading of due south in search of land.

Having previously navigated in the same waters, Villavicencio insisted the course would lead them onto the dangerous coral banks north of Hispaniola, but under Spanish regulations, the pilots' decisions were supreme. Several nights later *Concepción* suddenly lurched into a series of submerged reefs, her waterlogged hull jamming between two coral heads. Only one of the ship's boats had survived the ordeal, and in the following days, eight rafts were built as the ship gradually sank. The pilots loaded two of the rafts and set a course for where they thought Puerto Rico lay; the remainder of the people headed southwards. Some of the rafts, including the admiral's boat, reached the north shore of Hispaniola; the others were never heard from again. Of the 532 people who sailed on *Concepción*, only 194 survived.

From Santo Domingo, Admiral Villavicencio attempted two separate salvage expeditions to the wrecked *almiranta* but each time he was foiled. The weather drove him off the shoals, corsairs seized his boats, his ship was wrecked; eventually the admiral gave up, but the treasure lost under his command was not forgotten.

Private expeditions were attempted in 1650, 1652, 1667, and 1673; each was unsuccessful. Boston sea captain William Phips found the remains of *Concepción* in 1687, some forty-five years after she was lost. Although the wreck was almost completely covered by coral, Phips managed to salvage treasure worth a quarter of a million pounds sterling; this treasure he brought to England, receiving a knighthood and the post of Governor of Massachusetts. In modern times, others continued to search for 'Phips's Wreck': Alexandre Korganoff sailed for the Silver Shoals in 1952; he was followed a few years later by Edwin Link, and in 1968 by Jacques Cousteau; all failed to find the remains of the lost *almiranta*.

American treasure hunter Burt Webber took up the quest in 1977; with a licence from the Dominican Government, his team scoured the remote shoals, turning up thirteen different wreck sites with the help of modern remote sensing instruments, but no sign of the lost galleon was found. Meanwhile, historian Peter Earle had discovered the logbook of Phips's salvage ship *Henry* in English archives. With the logbook's locational data, Webber's team found a trail of ballast stones that led to the remains of *Concepción*. Using hydraulic jacks, divers dug through refuse of Phips's expedition, mostly rum bottles and tools, into pockets in the reef where Spanish deposits were hidden. The galleon had broken its back on a steep coral promontory and spilled its contents in the valleys below. Phips had found the stern deposit at the base of the reef, but Webber soon located another deposit representing the remainder of the wreckage. Cutting through centuries of coral with underwater chainsaws, divers penetrated to deep cavities containing *Concepción*'s cargo. Silver and ceramics, glass beads and wooden cups, an astrolabe dated 1632, a marble statue, and gold chains marked the galleon's grave. In a sand-filled cavity in the coral divers unearthed a wooden trunk, the baggage of a wealthy passenger. Inside were stacked porcelain cups and silver tablewares, arranged as originally packed by their owner. The trunk had a false floor, under which were found 1,440 coins, carefully concealed contraband that had cemented together to form a solid silver mass.

The variety and quality of the artefacts recovered by the modern salvors constituted a major collection of archaeological and numismatic value. The Dominican portion of the recoveries is housed as a unique exhibit at the Museo de las Casas Reales in Santo Domingo; a travelling exhibition toured the United States to promote the sale of coins and other precious objects. But portions of *Concepción*'s coral-encrusted cargo may still lie buried in the Silver Shoals; treasure hunters are continuing to scour the grave of the famous *almiranta*.
R.C.S.

ADDITIONAL READING

Borrell, P., 1983, *Historia y rescate del galeon Nuestra Señora de la Concepción*, Santo Domingo.

Borrell, P., 1985, *Inventario del rescate del galeon Concepción*, Santo Domingo.

Cousteau, J. and Diolé, P., 1971, *Diving for Sunken Treasure*, Garden City, New York.

Earle, P., 1979, *The Wreck of the Almiranta*, London.

Grissim, J., 1980, *The Lost Treasure of the Concepción*, New York.

Karraker, C., 1934, *The Hispaniola Treasure*, Philadelphia.

Peterson, M., 1980, *The Treasure of the Concepción*, Chicago.

Smith, R.C., 1988, 'The Iberian-American Maritime Empires', in G.F. Bass (ed.), *Ships and Shipwrecks in the Americas: A History Based on Underwater Archaeology*, London.

EDITOR'S NOTE: This site is included because it is well known and widely reported in the popular media and press. However, sites such as this have primarily been the focus of commercially oriented activity that has often resulted in the sale of recovered artefacts to private owners, the transfer of artefacts to private investors, or the splitting of artefacts between a government and a private salvor. Despite the presence of an archaeologist on the site, or the recovery of any archaeological data, the long-term potential of a site to yield meaningful information is compromised when the collection of artefacts – the primary data of any archaeological site – has been dispersed. Furthermore, the sale of artefacts from shipwreck sites endorses the concept that the archaeological past and antiquities are commodities for sale on the open market, which has proved detrimental to the protection and study of the past. The inclusion of this site in this encyclopaedia does not sanction or condone this type of activity.

Nuevo Constante
see *El Nuevo Constante*

NUMA
see National Underwater and Marine Agency

Nydam Boat
Fourth-century AD boat excavated at Nydam, near Schleswig, Germany. The first systematic excavation of a boat-find was done by Conrad Englehardt between 1859 and 1863, at the site of two 4th-century AD boats, one built of pine, the other of oak, at Nydam, which was then part of Denmark. The vessels were interpreted as a sacrificial offering of war equipment from a defeated military force, probably from southern Scandinavia. The pine boat was destroyed by invading Prussian troops in 1864, but the oak boat, placed on display first at Kiel, and now in the Schleswig-Holsteinisches Landesmuseum at Schloss Gottorf, Schleswig, has survived. The Nydam Boat is particularly significant in that it is an early example of an oared boat built in clinker construction with iron fastenings. Such a vessel may have carried the Angles and Saxons to Britain (see Crumlin-Pederson and Rieck). (See also **Baltic Sea**.)

A series of researchers have offered reconstructions of the boat: Englehardt in 1865, Johannesen in 1924, and Harald Akerlund in 1963. The Nydam Boat has been dated to AD 350–400. It has five strakes on each side, attached to a light keel. The principal dimensions of the Nydam Boat are controversial: Arne Emil Christensen estimates planks 25 m long and 0.5 m wide, fastened with iron rivets clenched on the inside of the hull with square iron roves. The frames or ribs were cut from curved branches and lashed to cleats on the planking. Rowlocks for thirty oars were lashed to the gunwale. A large steering oar was found with the boat, but how it was fastened is not known (see Christensen).

Englehardt's work was terminated in 1864 because of the outbreak of war between Denmark and Germany. Archaeologists under the direction of Flemming Rieck commenced new excavations at Nydam Mose in 1994 and 1995. Excavators discovered five or six additional rowlocks and a section of gunwale from the pine boat, and precisely re-identified where Englehardt discovered the oak boat in 1863. Iron rivets and an undisturbed rowlock from the boat were found. In addition, large quantities of equipment from the pine boat were excavated in 1995, including bows, arrows, spear- and lance-poles, axe- and knife-shafts, and shields, some with traces of paint. Metal objects, in poor condition and almost completely corroded, included two swords and a lancehead. A sword sheath with a silver and inlaid stone mounting and runes was also recovered. The runic inscription 'harkilaR ahti' has been tentatively translated by Marie Stoklund as a man's name followed by what may be the word 'owns'.

The new excavations at Nydam, combined with a remeasuring of the boat in a collaborative German–Danish effort, has demonstrated that the finds at Nydam represent a series of deposits over a range of centuries and that the vessel had been subjected to considerable repair and replacement of planks in antiquity. A new **Reconstruction**, working with the recent finds at Nydam, the remeasurement, and a comparison of the Nydam Boat with the **Skuldelev Ships**, are planned. J.P.D.

ADDITIONAL READING

Akerlund, H., 1963, *Nydamskeppen: En studie i titig skandinavisk skepps-byggnadskonst*, Goteborg.

Arenhold, L., 1914, 'The Nydam Boat at Kiel', *Mariner's Mirror*, 4, 182–5.

Christensen, A.E., 1972, 'Scandinavian Ships from Earliest Times to the Vikings', in G.F. Bass (ed.), *A History of Seafaring Based on Underwater Archaeology*, New York.

Crumlin-Pederson, O. and Rieck, F., 1993, 'The Nydam Ships: Old and New Investigations at a Classic Site', in J. Coles, V. Fenwick, and G. Hutchinson (eds), *A Spirit of Enquiry: Essays for Ted Wright*, Exeter.

Englehardt, C., 1865, *Nydam Mosefund*, Copenhagen.

Gothche, M., 1995, 'Measuring the Nydam Boat', *Maritime Archaeology Newsletter*, 5, 18–20.

Muckelroy, K., 1978, *Maritime Archaeology*, London.

Rieck, F., 1994, *Jernalderkrigernes skibe: Ny og gamle udgravninger i Nydam Mose*, Roskilde.

Shetelig, H., 1930, 'Das Nydamschiff', *Acta Archaeologica*, 1–30.

Steffy, J.R., 1994, *Wooden Shipbuilding and the Interpretation of Shipwrecks*, College Station, Texas.

Ontario marine heritage conservation organizations

Three organizations in Ontario, Canada, are directly involved in underwater archaeology and marine heritage conservation: Save Ontario Shipwrecks (SOS); Preserve Our Wrecks (Kingston) (POW); and the Ontario Marine Heritage Committee (OMHC). The Ontario government operates the Ontario Marine Heritage Conservation Program.

SOS is a province-wide marine heritage conservation society incorporated in 1981, divided into local chapters. POW, also incorporated in 1981, is a local marine heritage conservation society based in Kingston, Ontario. Both societies were formed in response to endemic looting of submerged sites in the **Great Lakes**, and are composed of sport divers, and **Avocational** archaeologists and historians. Diver education and resource protection are the central aims of both SOS and POW. In addition, members of both societies have undertaken or participated in numerous archaeological surveys in the myriad lakes and rivers of Ontario. Surveys have been directed primarily at historic shipwrecks, but prehistoric sites and historic structures have also been investigated. In 1982, an archaeological survey of the schooner *Annie Falconer* (1867–1904) lost near False Duck Island, Lake Ontario, was undertaken by POW members in conjunction with provincial archaeologists; one of the first projects of its kind in Ontario, it helped lay the foundation for cooperation between provincial heritage agencies and avocational archaeologists within the sport diving community. The project led directly to the formation of the provincial Government's Ontario Marine Heritage Conservation Program in 1983, whose archaeologists provide guidance and assistance with archaeological fieldwork undertaken by SOS and POW, as well as delivering marine archaeology training seminars. In 1983 the Quinte chapter of SOS continued a survey of *Annie Falconer*, and since 1990 POW members have monitored and surveyed the deterioration of the vessel's hull. Between 1983 and 1987, members of both SOS and POW assisted provincial archaeologists at South Lake, Ontario with underwater survey and excavation of a multi-component prehistoric

The Nydam Boat. (Schleswig-Holsteinisches Landesmuseum)

site (c. 300 BC to AD 1450). In 1988, POW members surveyed the remains of four warships built at Kingston, Ontario during the War of 1812, and later abandoned at Kingston, including the *St Lawrence* (1814–32). Extensive **Side-scan sonar** surveys of the Pelee Passage in western Lake Erie have been undertaken by the Windsor chapter of SOS since 1988, resulting in the discovery of fifty-six new sites. Other notable SOS projects include surveys of the following sites: the schooner *Lillie Parsons* (1868–77); the side-wheel steamer *Rothesay* (1868–89); the screw-steamer *Conestoga* (1878–1922), all three lost in the St Lawrence River; and a schooner known as the Cedardale East Wreck (date unknown) lost in Lake Ontario near Presqu'ile, Ontario.

The OMHC, formed in 1975 and based in Tobermory, Ontario, is a group of professional and amateur archaeologists and marine historians. Archaeological investigations by the OMHC began in 1975 with a survey of the early 19th-century naval ship at Penetanguishene, Ontario, which was followed later by a survey of a Durham boat and the brigantine *Newash* (early/mid- 19th century), also near Penetanguishene. Other notable archaeological projects include the following: survey of the schooner *Marquette* (1856–67) lost near Hope Island, Georgian Bay; investigation of the barge *Concord* lost off Lion's Head, Georgian Bay in 1888; investigation of the schooner *Nimrod*, lost in Lake Erie; the survey of an unidentified schooner in Lake Erie off Port Stanley, Ontario; and a comparative survey of Great Lakes schooner rudder types. Ongoing projects in the 1990s include the Submerged Prehistoric Shoreline Survey in Georgian Bay and a survey of the Atherley Narrows fish weirs near Orillia, Ontario. J.D.M.

ADDITIONAL READING

Hibbert, A. (ed.), 1993, *A Diver's Guide to Ontario's Marine Heritage*, Save Ontario Shipwrecks, Willowdale, Ontario.

Oseberg Ship

Ninth-century ship from the Viking Age, with an inhumation burial, found at Oseberg farm in Slagen, Vestfold, south Norway. Fragments of two female skeletons were found in the ship, along with rich equipment. Analysis of the skeletons indicates that one person was fifty to sixty years old at the time of burial, the other was twenty to thirty years old.

The ship was placed in a trench cut in the ground on low-lying land about one to two kilometres from the Viking Age shoreline, and a mound around 50 m in diameter was built to cover the burial. A four-wheeled wagon, four sleds, two tents, kitchen equipment, wooden buckets, iron-bound chests, weaving tools, textiles, shoes, and much more was placed in the ship and the specially built burial chamber on board. At least twelve horses, four dogs, and two oxen were sacrificed. Many of the wooden artefacts are richly decorated with carving. The large tumulus erected over the grave was built of blue clay and tightly stacked turves. This resulted in extremely good preservation of all organic material. The grave was plundered; no jewellery was found, the skeletons are incomplete, and much of the grave goods fragmentary.

The grave was scientifically excavated in 1904. This extremely difficult work was led by Gabriel Gustafson, Professor of Archaeology at the University of Oslo. The finds are now in the Viking Ship Museum, Oslo. It has been suggested that the two women are a queen and a female slave. The name of the farm, Oseberg, has been connected to a Queen Åsa, mentioned in Snorri Sturlusson's saga of the Norwegian kings. It is uncertain whether the old or the young person is the main one in the burial. The reliability of Snorri as a historical source for the 9th century has been questioned, and it is best to let the 'Oseberg queen' remain nameless. The extremely rich grave goods show that she was a person of top rank, probably both a religious and political leader.

The ship is the oldest vessel from the Viking Age found in Scandinavia, and also the oldest vessel of Norse type with a mast and sail. Recent dating by dendrochronology gives the felling date for the ship's timbers of c. AD 815–20. Timber used to build the burial chamber was cut in the summer of 834. The dated wood is oak. As Viking Age woodworkers seem to have used unseasoned wood, the felling dates are accepted as the date for building the ship and for the burial. The ship is 22 m long overall, with a maximum beam amidships of 5.2 m. The height from the underside of the keel to the sheerstrake amidships is 1.6 m. The ship is built of oak, with beech used for the carved ends of the upper strake near the stems. The deckboards and oars are of pine. The 19.8 m long keel is scarfed from two pieces. The longer, forward part is 15.8 m in length. The keel is T-shaped, with the first (garboard) strake fastened to the 'wings' of the keel with iron rivets. Near stem and stern, the T-shape changes into a rabbet for the plank ends. The stems are made from naturally curved timbers. The stemtop is decorated with a coiled snake. The original was badly damaged by the grave robbers, and a replica has been placed on the ship. The stems and the end of the top strakes near the stems are richly decorated with intertwining animals. The top of the sternpost was missing, and has been reconstructed. The reconstruction is based on the stem, and contemporary ship pictures on standing stones and coins.

The ship has twelve strakes on each side. The strakes overlap and are fastened together by iron nails riveted over square roves in the standard clinker-building manner. All planks were made by splitting large logs. There is no indication that saws were used for converting timber or for building the ship. The first eight strakes have been shaped with cleats on the inside. The ribs were lashed to the cleats through holes in cleat and rib. The lashing material was strips of baleen. At the waterline, the ends of the ribs rest against a low triangular cleat on the ninth strake where the top of the rib is fastened with an iron rivet. The tenth strake has a cross-section like an inverted L. Its substantial dimensions give strength to the hull at the transition from bottom to topside. It is believed that this extra strong strake was named *meginhufr* ('the strong or mighty strake') in Old Norse. At this level, crossbeams span the hull from side to side. The beams are rabbeted for the deckboards. Around the mast and near the stems, the boards are loose, giving access to the ship's bottom; in the rest of the ship, small treenails fasten the deckboards to the beams. Above the *meginhufr* two more strakes are fitted in a nearly vertical position. They are supported by naturally grown 'knees' resting on the crossbeams. The knees are not lashed, but fastened with iron nails and treenails to beam and strakes. The top strake is pierced with holes for fifteen oars on each side. On the outside, the strake has a slender lath along the upper edge with openings for mounting shields.

The mast is supported by two heavy timbers, a short keelson spanning two ribs and a 'mast partner' resting on four crossbeams. The mast partner has a slit in the aft part which permits the mast to be raised or lowered. The ship was steered by a quarter rudder on the starboard side, secured to an extra sturdy frame aft. The rudder was secured by a flexible withy, which permitted the blade to be turned on its own axis, and a plaited leather band around the upper part of the rudder.

A large shovel-like bailer and a gangplank are part of the ship's equipment. Numerous fragments of ropes with different diameters were found. The material is the inner bark from basswood. Many of the ropes were probably for the two tents included in the grave goods, some may be from the rigging, but little definite evidence exists, apart from cleats on the upper strakes, which in all probability were for fastening running rigging. Some of the ropes had knots that are still in use in maritime context, like the sheet bend and reef knot. Apart from the ropes and knots, the artefacts offer little information on rigging. Contemporary ship pictures show one square sail on the mast amidships. The sail was spread by a yard along the upper edge. A parrel was found with the Oseberg Ship, a curved piece of wood that kept the yard to the mast. Of the rigging, a stay to the stem, and shrouds to the ship's side supporting the mast are shown in most pictures. A bowline from the front edge of the sail to the stem is clearly shown on some pictures. Standing stones on Gotland in the Baltic also show a complicated system of crossing ropes under the sail which has not been satisfactorily explained. It has been suggested that it is a system of shrouds for controlling the sail, or ropes for diminishing sail surface on the principle of a venetian blind. Other later pictures show two sheets from the lower corners of the sail, as was usual in later square-rigged boats. Braces to control the ends of the yard are today considered absolutely necessary for handling a square sail, but they are not shown on the Viking Age ship pictures. Sailcloth is believed to have been woven from wool.

A replica of the Oseberg Ship built in 1987 was equipped with a sail of 100 sq. m, later reduced to 90 sq. m. The sail was based on the rigging used by 19th-century north and west Norwegian square-rigged boats. The replica sailed well, but proved to be unstable at 10 knots speed and 10 degrees heel. In this situation, the bow wave flooded the hull. The replica was fitted with extra washstrakes for safe sailing. It is not certain whether this defect is also present in the original Oseberg hull.

When compared to the older Iron Age vessels found in Scandinavia and England, the Oseberg Ship shows considerable improvement in hull shape. The changes are best explained as adaptions that were found necessary when ships were equipped with mast and sail. The keel is more developed, and the cross-section has been changed from a round shape, well suited to rowing, to a V-shape, which gives better lateral resistance when sailing, especially when tacking against the wind. The ship's side is higher above the waterline, and permanent crossbeams help to absorb the stresses set up

in the hull when sailing. The older rowing vessels had permanent seats for the rowers, while there are none in the Oseberg, **Gokstad**, and **Tune** ships. It has been suggested that the crew sat on their sea-chests when rowing. Replica chests have been tried when rowing the ship replicas, and this system works well. In written sources from the early Middle Ages, warship sizes are given by the number of rowing benches, in Old Norse *sess*. The size of one type of ship mentioned in the Old Norse written sources, the *karve*, is given in a different manner, by the number of men rowing along one side of the ship. The explicit omission of *sess* when a *karve* is mentioned has led to the theory that these ships had loose seats, and that the Oseberg, Gokstad, and Tune ships are of this type.

The low freeboard, richly decorated stems and the less seaworthy shape when compared to the Gokstad Ship has led to the theory that the Oseberg Ship was a yacht intended only for inshore voyages in fair weather. Another view, put forward by Christensen, is that the ship is typical of the ships used in the early Viking Age, and that the differences seen between the Oseberg and Gokstad ships are improvements resulting from the experience collected on voyages across the North Sea and along the European coasts in the 9th century. A.E.C.

ADDITIONAL READING

Christensen, A.E. *et al.*, 1992, *Osebergdronningens grav*, Oslo.

Shetelig, H., 1917, *Skibet*, Osebergfunder I, Oslo.

Oxford University MARE

A unit of Oxford University specializing in Maritime Archaeological Research and Excavation, created in 1984 and the oldest academic unit of its kind in England.

Oxford University MARE grew out of the successful **Giglio Wreck** excavations of 1981–6; by the second half of the 1990s it was one of the largest maritime archaeological field units in the world. Alone or in collaboration with other organizations, MARE has surveyed or excavated sites around the world, some of which are noted below.

Mediterranean

Excavation of the Etruscan or Greek *Giglio Wreck*, and Roman and Hellenistic ships, off Giglio in the Tuscan Archipelago. It is believed that MARE's excavation of a 6th century BC wreck at Galbucino, Giglio was the first to use a remotely-operated vehicle (see also **Submersibles**). A large number of Punic, North African, Eastern Mediterranean and Spanish amphorae were excavated in the ancient harbour of Lilybaeum (modern Marsala), Western Sicily in 1982–3. An

excavation of a 2nd/3rd century BC wreck situated in 50–65 m of water off the tip of Devil's Point, Island of Montecristo, Tuscan Archipelago (1985–6) is believed to have been the first to use 'mixed-gas' diving.

In Greek waters MARE's projects have included the excavation of a possible 16th-century vessel that went down on a reef just outside the main port of Zakynthos in the Ionian Islands with a cargo of hazelnuts and blank silver coins. At Panarea in the Aeolian Isles to the north of Sicily, MARE excavated the *Dattilo Wreck*, a Late Classical wreck with a cargo of black-painted finewares, and in the 1990s the team has been collaborating on the **Mahdia Wreck**.

MARE's work at Gibraltar, begun in 1992, has concentrated on a large cannon deposit beside the detached mole that is believed (but not yet proved) to be the remains of one of the Spanish '**Battering' Ships** from the Great Siege of Gibraltar (1779–82).

Northern Europe

Survey of the late Elizabethan **Alderney wreck** in the English Channel (1992–4). A survey of bronze and iron cannon from *Wrangels Palais*, a Swedish forty-six-gun frigate lost off Bound Skerry, Shetland Islands. Since 1996 MARE has been collaborating with a French group led by Max Guérout in the search for *Cordelière* and *Regent*. These ships were sunk in 1512 when Henry VIII, in support of the Pope and the Spanish monarchy against the French King, sent a fleet across the Channel which engaged the French off Brest.

South America

MARE has been involved in surveying and excavating a number of important sites in and around the River Plate, Uruguay including *Admiral Graf Spee*; HMS *Agamemnon*; *Salvador*, a Spanish troopship lost during a storm in 1812, in which a wide range of military apparel and equipment typical of the Napoleonic era, as well as **Human remains**, have been found; the Bristol slave ship *Sea Horse*, carrying silver bullion; and the 18th-century Cabo Polonia Wreck, containing a large number of concreted boxes, one of which was found to be full of crucifixes and religious icons.

South East Asia

Nassau, Dutch East Indiaman, Straits of Malacca.

Nassau was one of a squadron of Dutch East Indiamen that in 1604 attempted to take the Portuguese trading-post of Malacca by siege. The siege was broken when a large fleet of Portuguese ships arrived from Goa. *Nassau* was lost during the fighting. The wreck was found by the marine salvage company Transea in 1993 and was excavated in 1995. *Nassau* is the oldest Dutch East Indiaman to be examined by archaeologists.

In 1997 MARE began excavations on the Cu Lao Cham Wreck in very deep water (65 m) off the coast of Vietnam. The ship was carrying a cargo of Vietnamese porcelain of 15th-16th century date.

South Atlantic

Like so many of the Atlantic islands the Cape Verde archipelago has a particularly rich submerged cultural heritage. Since 1996 MARE has been collaborating with the Portuguese maritime archaeological group Arqueonautas to carry out surveys of wrecks around the islands.

The finest collection of hulked 19th- and 20th-century square riggers from the final years of deep-water sail are to be found around the beaches of the Falklands, South Georgia and Patagonia (see **Falkland wrecks and hulks**). These are mostly vessels that have tried and failed to get around Cape Horn in the face of the prevailing westerlies. They range in date from the 1840s to the second decade of the 20th century. The survey, which was started by Mensun Bound in the late 1970s, became part of the MARE programme in the mid- 1980s. Work has mainly focused on *Charles Cooper* in Port Stanley harbour, *Garland* at Goose Green and *Ambassador* in the Straits of Magellan.

West Indies

Survey of HMS *Endymion*, Turks and Caicos Islands, West Indies (1992). *Endymion* was a 44 gun frigate built at Limehouse in 1779; she fought at the Battle of the Saints in April 1782 and was lost on an uncharted reef in June 1790. Her remains consist of a line of cannon, ballast and the lower hull. The site has been made a national park by the Turks and Caicos Government and has become a popular diving site. M.B.

Padre Island wrecks

Wrecks on Padre Island in Texas, USA of ships from the New Spain flota of 1554 returning to Spain. The flota, part of Carreno's outbound fleet of 1552, consisted of four ships: *San Andres*, *San Esteban*, *Espiritu Santo*, and *Santa Maria de Yciar*. On 9 April 1554 the flota sailed from Vera Cruz, Mexico, and twenty days later the last three listed ships wrecked on Padre Island in Texas, blown into shallow water and stranded by a storm. *San Andres* made it to Havana in sinking condition.

The Spanish had a salvage expedition on site in less than two months and recovered about half the cargo of primarily silver coin and bullion. One of the co-captains of the salvage expedition was Angel de Villafane, the man who later led the expedition to Pensacola Bay in relief of Luna's colony. This provides an interesting link to the **Emanuel Point Ship**, one of Luna's ships, excavated by the State of Florida.

In 1967 *Espiritu Santo* was located by treasure salvors and the artefacts removed without archaeological recording. An eighteen-year long lawsuit, known as the Platoro suit, ensued. The State of Texas ultimately retained title to the collection but had to pay a salvage award of about $350,000. After the Platoro incident, Texas enacted a strong antiquities law.

In the early 1970s the Texas Historical Commission and its now defunct sister agency the Texas Antiquities Committee conducted underwater archaeological excavations of *San Esteban*. The site was thoroughly published and continues to generate new detailed studies of various parts of the collection. There was a major travelling exhibition, several small travelling exhibitions, and now a major permanent exhibition. The Corpus Christi Museum of Science and History curated the collections and established the permanent exhibition.

Santa Maria de Yciar was at least partly destroyed when the artificial Mansfield Cut was dredged through Padre Island in the late 1940s or early 1950s. The US Army Corps of Engineers, Galveston District, contracted for several survey and testing projects that thus far have not located the remains of the site. J.B.A.

ADDITIONAL READING

Arnold, J.Barto, III and Weddle, R.S., 1978, *The Nautical Archeology of Padre Island: The Spanish Shipwrecks of 1554*, New York.

Arnold, J.Barto, III and McDonald, D., 1979, *Documentary Sources for the Wreck of the New Spain Fleet of 1554*, Austin, Texas.

Rosloff, J. and Arnold, J.Barto, III, 1984, 'The Keel of the *San Esteban* (1554): Continued Analysis', *International Journal of Nautical Archaeology*, 13, 287–96.

Palos Verdes anchor stones

Grouping of perforated stones on a shallow reef offshore near Los Angeles, USA. The main stone concentration occurs at a depth of about 6 m and covers a 100 m diameter area some 200 m offshore. A smaller grouping is found near by at a depth of 18 m. No shipwreck debris or artefacts have yet been documented in association with these enigmatic stones.

In 1975 **SCUBA**-divers Robert Meistrell and Wayne Baldwin discovered the stones and began investigations into their origin. Some thirty-five stones are presently known from this site and although a few scattered examples have been reported elsewhere from the California coastline, this concentration remains unique and unexplained. The site has intrigued popular authors and serious researchers since the announcement of its discovery.

The anchor stones can be grouped into two basic shapes – tabloid and cylindrical, the latter far in the majority. Both types are characterized as having symmetrical 9 to 15 cm holes through their centres. The cylinders are drilled through their long axis and several have holes only partway through. Two specimens have grooves around their circumference. The basic mineralogy of these stones is sedimentary, although at least one tabular example may be metamorphic in composition. Weights vary from 16 to 470 kg among those recovered. Several larger specimens remain in place. Contradictory findings have been published as to whether the anchors derive from imported or local shale.

Local Native American water craft carried stone anchors, but not of the size represented at this site, and can be eliminated as a potential source. Three prominent theories have emerged to account for the anchors. They are: Chinese transpacific voyagers from as early as AD 500 (Moriarty and Pierson), 19th-century Chinese-American fishing net weights and mooring devices (Frost), and whale carcass mooring weights from 19th-century Portuguese shore whalers (Chace). Unfortunately, research efforts have yet to prove the cultural origin and subsequent archaeological meaning of these objects. McCaslin and Orzech have conducted only

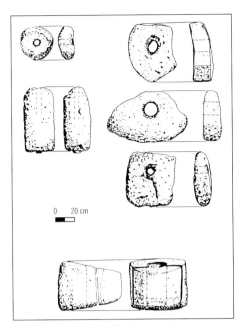

Palos Verdes anchor stones. (John Foster, after Pierson and Moriarty 1980)

preliminary underwater surveys at the Palos Verdes site. Stickel has published a research programme paradigm for resolving the mystery, but the site itself has yet to be intensely studied and interpreted. G.J.H., J.W.F.

ADDITIONAL READING

Chace, P., 1983, 'Chinese Stone Anchors: Research Design Validation', *Sixteenth Annual Meeting of the Society for Historical Archaeology*, Denver, Colorado.

Frost, H.J., 1982, 'The Palos Verdes Chinese Anchor Mystery', *Archaeology*, 35, 1, 20–28.

McCaslin, D.E. and Orzech, J.K., 1988, 'Romancing the Stones: The Worked Stone Objects off the Palos Verdes Peninsula, Los Angeles, California', in J.W. Foster and S.O. Smith (eds), *Archaeology in Solution: Proceedings of the Seventeenth Annual Conference on Underwater Archaeology*, Salinas, California.

Pierson, L.J. and Moriarty, J.R., 1980, 'Stone Anchors: Asiatic Shipwrecks off the California Coast', *Anthropological Journal of Canada*, 18, 17–23.

Stickel, G.E., 1983, 'The Mystery of the Prehistoric "Chinese Anchors": Toward Research Designs for Underwater Archaeology', in R.A. Gould (ed.), *Shipwreck Anthropology*, Albuquerque.

HMS *Pandora*

The frigate that the British Admiralty sent to the South Pacific in 1790 to recapture **Bounty** and bring to justice the men who had seized her. Arriving in Tahiti on 23 March 1791, *Pandora* spent five weeks at anchor in Matavai Bay. During this time fourteen of *Bounty*'s crew were taken prisoner. *Pandora*

then spent nearly four months searching the South Pacific for the leader of the mutiny, Fletcher Christian, and his followers. The search was unsuccessful and on 29 August 1791 *Pandora* was wrecked on the Great Barrier Reef, while searching for a passage through the reef to Torres Strait. Four of the prisoners and thirty-one of *Pandora*'s crew died when their ship sank.

The wreck was rediscovered in November 1977 and proclaimed a protected site under the **Australian Historic Shipwrecks Act** in 1979. Since 1982 day-to-day management of the wreck has been the Queensland Museum's responsibility. A number of excavations of the wreck have been carried out by the Queensland Museum with assistance from the Australian Historic Shipwrecks Programme. These have established that an extremely important collection of artefacts and a substantial portion of the wrecked hull are buried in the seabed in an excellent state of preservation; approximately 80 per cent of the site has yet to be excavated.

The wreck is located within Pandora Entrance approximately 5 km to the northwest of Moulter Cay. This sand cay is on the outer Great Barrier Reef 96 km east of Cape York. Although the wreck lies well inside the entrance, it is exposed to the full force of ocean swells generated by prevailing easterly winds in the Coral Sea. Directly to the east, southeast, and west, the site is surrounded by three small submerged reefs which give some protection against swells. These reefs also deflect the flow of tidal currents across the site. The pattern of these currents has not yet been determined, although divers have experienced their strength and unpredictability. Consequently, conditions for underwater archaeological operations are difficult, and further complicated by depths of between 30 and 34 m.

Excavation of Pandora site.
(© Queensland Museum/Patrick Baker)

The circumstances of *Pandora*'s loss are well documented. Eyewitness accounts (by George Hamilton, *Pandora*'s surgeon, and others) describe in considerable detail the wrecking of the ship. The ordered distribution of wreckage on the seabed attests that the hull was intact after sinking and that it settled on its starboard side where a portion of it was gradually buried by deposits of coralline sand. However, as sand was burying the lower parts of the hull, the exposed upper structure appears to have disintegrated owing to the combined effects of marine borers and current action.

The hull remains and the bulk of the artefact **Assemblage** lie within an area of 20 by 50 m. The outline and orientation of the hull remains are well delineated. This applies especially to the stern of the hull which is indicated by the large readily identifiable section of copper sheathing which had been tacked on to the lower hull as an anti-fouling measure. Draft marks (in embossed Roman numerals) are clearly visible on the sheathing, indicating that at least 3 m of the sternpost sheathing is buried.

Although several attempts, using a **Sub-bottom profiler**, have been made to determine the extent and condition of the hull remains, these efforts have only succeeded in giving indications suggesting that between 25 and 30 per cent of the hull has been preserved. A definitive assessment of the structural integrity and condition of the buried hull remains can only be made after archaeological excavation has retrieved the coherent artefact assemblage lying buried within the sediment layer covering the hull remains. It is estimated that approximately 780 cu. m of sediment will require excavation in order to expose the hull remains. There are also indications that suggest that currents may have dispersed some of *Pandora*'s lighter contents.

Left: Bottles found on
Pandora. (© Queensland
Museum/Patrick Baker)

dence which can answer a host of questions pertaining to late 18th-century European material culture and the material reality of maritime discovery. It will provide evidence which will enable researchers to formulate

in the course of any archaeological excavation. The research design outlined for *Pandora* to date contains several relevant questions which have evolved from consideration of the artefact collection retrieved so far.

Right: Mortar from Pandora,
as found. (© Queensland
Museum/Patrick Baker)

It is assumed that a dispersal trail, consisting primarily of light artefacts, will lead away from the wreck in the direction of the strongest current set.

The *Pandora* wreck is of historic significance because of its direct association with the mutiny on *Bounty*. The mutiny has been characterized as one of the most well-known and romanticized sea stories in the annals of maritime history. *Pandora*'s last voyage and the exploits of her crew are well documented. Written and pictorial primary sources not only relate the details of the voyage and depict the circumstances of *Pandora*'s wrecking, but also provide data for comparative research of 18th-century European maritime discovery in the Pacific Ocean. European maritime discovery in the Pacific was carried out by many nations and is extremely well documented. Its historiography is of long standing and it is a subject which continues to command attention and stimulate research.

The wreck site is of archaeological importance, not only because it presents a good opportunity to study marine archaeological **Site formation processes**, but more significantly, the wreck contains an extremely well-preserved and coherent artefact assemblage, which clearly has not suffered substantial transformation since its deposition. Using Muckelroy's criteria, the wreck should definitely be considered a first-class shipwreck site.

As such, it offers archaeologists a unique opportunity to retrieve from its functional context a precisely datable collection of late 18th-century British material culture and nautical technology. Archaeological excavation of *Pandora* will provide material evi-

new questions which hitherto could not be contemplated, or, because of the paucity of information in the written record, could only be speculated upon. For instance, artefacts from the wreck can elucidate aspects of early contact between European and Oceanic societies and provide data for comparative research of the evolution of material culture and nautical technology pertaining to life on board European sailing ships engaged on long inter-ocean voyages.

The investigation of environmental factors affecting the wreck is required for various reasons. For instance, a study of the wreck's stability in terms of the impacts of archaeological excavation; in particular, to determine whether backfilling techniques are effective means of consolidating overburden and thereby protecting the wreck's fabric, especially organic materials, from possible accelerated deterioration caused by biological agents.

The analysis of the biological characteristics of the sediments in which the wreck is buried is particularly important to determine whether a different rate or type of microbiological activity is occurring under backfilled areas. If so, what are the differences and how are they affecting the longevity of buried artefacts and the hull remains? Have detrimental effects been introduced or accelerated under backfilled areas? If so, how can they most effectively be counteracted or mitigated?

A **Research design** usually outlines a summary of possible directions for future research. Initial directions are generally not intended to claim primacy as they may be overtaken by other directions which can become apparent

Several specific questions have been formulated about the research potential of the crew's personal possessions. After all, the ability to retrieve from its functional context material evidence reflecting the ship's social fabric is probably the most salient justification to excavate and retrieve *Pandora*'s contents (see also **Shipboard society**). This class of artefact constitutes evidence of the crew's daily life on board. Its analysis, using anthropological, sociological or ethnological models and methodologies, can therefore elucidate aspects of late 18th-century British material culture.

For instance, given that British society in the 18th century consisted of class-determined subcultures, analysis of possible differences between personal possessions retrieved from officers' quarters and ratings' quarters can contribute answers to what extent a late 18th-century Royal Navy sailor's material possessions reflected his social position. Thus, assuming that possessions can be indicative of social position or a reflection of an individual's attitudes, to what extent do differences between a warrant officer's, a commissioned officer's, and a petty officer's personal possessions make visible statements about accepted values and expected behaviour in the Royal Navy during the 1790s? Alternatively, to what extent do a petty officer's personal belongings reflect the achieved status attributable to his rank?

Research directions have also been set for the impressive array of items of Polynesian origin (referred to as 'artificial curiosities' during the 18th century) retrieved from the wreck. This collection provides objects for ethnological research. In many instances, other 18th-century collections of Polynesian material culture cannot be precisely dated. The significance of the 'curiosities' from *Pandora* is that their exact time and place of collection can be firmly established. Their analysis can therefore answer such questions as, to what extent do objects retrieved from *Pandora* exhibit stylistic similarities or differences in manufacture to objects collected by scientists and sailors during James Cook's voyages of discovery in the 1770s? These answers can lead on to other questions: for instance, if changes or differences are apparent, to what extent can they be attributed to the impact of European technology on traditional manufacturing methods? Alternatively, are there appreciable differences between the 'curiosity' collections made by *Pandora*'s officers and by her ratings? If so, can differences be attributed to the Royal Navy hierarchy?

Because of the enormous scale and corresponding expense of a proposed series of excavations which the Queensland Museum intends to conduct between 1996 and 2001, priorities have been set. The museum's primary objective is to recover material which will reflect daily life on board. Consequently, a plan has been developed to finish excavation of the officers' accommodation and store areas in the stern and then concentrate on the bow area, where the lower ranks of the crew were accommodated. Excavation of the midships area has been assigned a lower priority because it is felt that hold spaces at midships will primarily contain material relating to late 18th-century nautical technology, a subject which is already relatively well documented. P.G.

ADDITIONAL READING

Dening, G., 1992, *Mr. Bligh's Bad Language: Passion, Power and Theatre on the Bounty*, Cambridge.

Gesner, P., 1991, *Pandora: An Archaeological Perspective*, Brisbane.

Guthrie, J. *et al*., 1994, 'Wrecks and Microbiology', *Bulletin of the Australian Institute for Maritime Archaeology*, 18, 2, 19–24.

Henderson, G., 1986, *Maritime Archaeology in Australia*, Nedlands, W. Australia.

Kaeppler, A.L., 1978, *Artificial Curiosities: An Exposition of Native Manufactures*, Honolulu.

Marden, L., 1985, 'Wreck of the HMS *Pandora*', *National Geographic*, 168, 4, 423–51.

McKay, J. and Coleman, R., 1992, *The Anatomy of the Ship: The 24-Gun Frigate Pandora, 1779*, London.

Muckleroy, K., 1978, *Maritime Archaeology*, Cambridge.

Rawson, G., 1963, *Pandora's Last Voyage*, New York.

Pearl Harbor

Site of the historic attack on Oahu by the Japanese on 7 December 1941. Most underwater archaeological work at Pearl Harbor has been confined to the World War II remains, which comprise the most dramatic material residues of the event. Although some vestiges of the attack are visible on land, such as the strafing gouges preserved in the masonry of barracks at Hickam Field, the majority of artefactual remains are found underwater.

The largest specific sites are the mostly submerged hulks of USS **Arizona** and USS **Utah**. In addition to the work carried out by the US National Park Service and the US Navy on these sites, the same two agencies cooperated on general underwater surveys of the inner and outer harbour in a series of short projects during the late 1980s and early 1990s. These surveys concentrated on searching for Japanese aircraft and midget submarines lost during the attack. The search for the aircraft involved use of **Side-scan sonar** and **Magnetometers**. The National Park Service **Submerged Cultural Resources Unit** (SCRU) archaeologist Larry Murphy was the key liaison with US Navy personnel for these projects. Many nondescript pieces of metal, including possible portions of airframes, were located but nothing definitive or positively related to planes from the attack was found.

In 1991 a deep water search (up to 365 m) for a midget sub in the outer harbour defensive perimeter also had negative

Chart of Pearl Harbor and environs depicting historical crash sites and areas surveyed in 1988. (Daniel Lenihan)

results. This project again included cooperation of SCRU and Navy personnel with the addition this time of a team sponsored by the **National Geographic Society** (NGS). Chris Nicholson from NGS and Dan Lenihan of SCRU were co-project directors and Larry Murphy was Operations Officer for the National Park Service. A promising target found in 1988 could not be relocated but numerous other contacts were examined by remote operated vehicle (ROV). Among the items located and positioned were trucks, small craft, and several vintage aircraft.

Ironically, a portion of a Japanese midget submarine was discovered by a University of Hawaii submarine while transporting a client from the Oregon Air Museum to the location of the planes as reported by the National Park Service/Navy/NGS team. The stern piece was judged by other archaeologists and historians to be unrelated to the Pearl Harbor attack. Why it resides in the search area is still a mystery.

In 1995 National Park Service archaeologists Daniel Lenihan and James Adams also dived the hulks of landing craft in West Loch. These remain from the massive disaster that occurred here on 21 May 1944. West Loch was a staging area for invasions of the western Pacific, and a number of LSTs were being loaded with ammunition and supplies when there was an enormous explosion that took 163 lives, wounded 396, and sank many vessels. Several landing craft of various classes were found largely intact in the loch by the NPS and Navy divers. These might be a future target for Project Seamark operations.

The greater part of the work conducted in

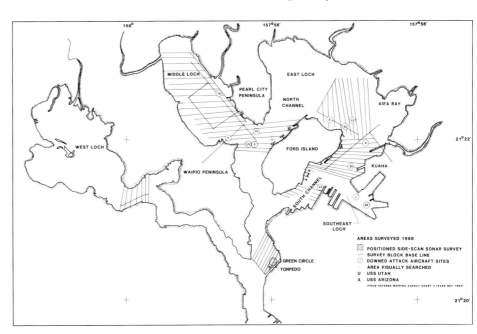

Pearl Harbor by the National Park Service in partnership with the US Navy took place before 1990; it is fully reported by Lenihan (1989). D.J.L.

ADDITIONAL READING

Delgado, J.P., 1991, *Pearl Harbor Recalled: New Images of the Day of Infamy*, Annapolis, Maryland.

Lenihan, D.J., 1989, *Submerged Cultural Resources Study of USS Arizona: Memorial and Pearl Harbor National Historic Landmark*, Southwest Cultural Resources Centre Professional Papers 23, Santa Fe, New Mexico.

Lenihan, D.J., 1991, 'The Arizona Revisited', *Natural History Magazine*, November, 64–72.

Wallin, H.N., 1968, *Pearl Harbor: Why, How, Fleet Salvage and Final Appraisal*, Washington, DC.

Penobscot Expedition

Revolutionary War expedition that has left the remains of more than thirty early American Navy vessels in the waters of Penobscot Bay and River in Maine, USA. The sites are important national cultural resources, one of which, the privateer *Defence*, has been fully investigated; a new search effort has located four additional sites.

In 1779, during the American Revolution, the British Crown and military command decided to build a fortification in Majabagaduce along the Penobscot River (now Castine, Maine). Maine had been a problem to the British, who wanted southern protection for Halifax, Nova Scotia and a possible new colony for British loyalists. On 17 June 1779 a British force began building Fort George at the top of the hill at Castine.

The Americans reacted swiftly. Any victory was welcomed in those desperate days of the war and the impending battle looked like a sure win. The new Continental Navy could only provide a few ships, but Massachusetts assembled a large number of warships and transports from both public and private sources. Historical records are not clear about the number of vessels in the expedition; estimates have varied from thirty-seven to forty-one ships. Although small in size, the many ships carried approximately 400 Continental Marines, 1,000 militia, and the necessary artillery and supplies for the expedition.

The Penobscot Expedition arrived before Castine on 24 July 1779, landed artillery on a small island at the harbour entrance, and shortly thereafter the marines led an heroic attack up a defended bluff, eventually taking the high ground west of the fort. The combatants soon found themselves in a siege situation, with the Americans making very slow progress. In mid-August the American hopes were destroyed by the arrival of the six warships of a British relief squadron in the bay.

Believing the expedition lost, the Americans returned to their ships and withdrew up river. The withdrawal was not orderly, the command structure had disintegrated, and most of the crews grounded and set their ships ablaze. The Penobscot Expedition ended with most crew members walking home. The British captured two warships and a number (five to ten) of transports; the American crews had scuttled the rest.

The American Revolution was one of the most important events in US history, and the Penobscot Expedition, the largest naval action of the war, was one of the largest naval disasters in US history. Yet little is known about the history of the expedition or the people and equipment involved. Historians cannot determine how many ships or people were involved and who they were. Questions exist about the design, construction, and outfitting of the revolutionary Continental Navy, individual state's navies, and private vessels of war. Questions exist about the sailors, marines, and militia as well as their supplies, equipment, their relationships to each other, lives at sea, and lives at home. Many of these questions could be answered by continued historical research and archaeological investigation of the Penobscot Expedition sites.

Although archaeological investigations of the remains of the Penobscot Expedition have been limited to the investigation of a single ship, *Defence*, in 1975 the four partners also dedicated some limited resources to a quick survey of the Penobscot River in a brief attempt to locate the remains of the other Revolutionary War ships. Some possibilities were noted in their remote sensing data, but no remains were located.

In 1994 the University of Maine began a new research programme, Penobscot Expedition II, directed by Dr Warren Riess. Riess's team, assisted by Maine Maritime Academy, is trying to locate the remaining ship sites using continued historical research, remote sensing, interviews with local people, and underwater inspections. Long-term plans include further site investigations and in-depth historical studies of the people involved in the expedition. W.R.

ADDITIONAL READING

Smith, S.O., 1986, *The Defence: Life at Sea as Reflected in an Archaeological Assemblage from an Eighteenth-Century Privateer*, unpublished Ph.D. thesis, University of Pennsylvania.

Switzer, D. and Ford, B., 1982, *Underwater Dig: The Excavation of a Revolutionary War Privateer*, London.

Peru

see **South America**

Philadelphia

The oldest preserved American warship (1776), sunk in **Lake Champlain** and raised in 1935. In May 1775 Brigadier-General Benedict Arnold and Ethan Allen captured Fort Ticonderoga and Crown Point on Lake Champlain, unused since the French and Indian War but still packed with British cannon and munitions. They planned to ship the guns to Boston to defend the besieged city, and to protect the water route between Quebec and New York from British invasion. From their Lake Champlain base, they raided the British in Canada, capturing Montreal, St John's, and several British warships. In response, the British amassed sizeable armies on Long Island, New York and in Quebec, planning to execute a pincer movement through New York and New England and join forces at Albany. With the arrival of winter and British reinforcements, the North American army was forced to abandon St John's and Montreal.

For the British plan to succeed, Sir Guy Carleton, Royal Governor of Quebec, had to control the critical Lake Champlain/ Hudson River corridor. He assembled a sizeable fleet at St John's, at the lake head. To counter it, General Arnold developed two new ship designs, luring 400 shipwrights and carpenters to Skenesborough, NY (in southern Lake Champlain) to build them and other, more familiar vessel types. One of his new designs was for a gondola or gunboat, based on a flat-bottomed rowing boat of the same name, with square sails used for transporting produce along New England rivers. Eight of these were built in the summer of 1776, along with the other types. Historians consider this hastily built squadron as the first American navy, although technically, it was part of the Continental Army.

Philadelphia was one of the eight gondolas constructed of local timber. Measuring 53 ft 4 in by 15 ft 6 in by 3 ft 10 in (16.16 by 4.72 by 1.16 m) and weighing 29 tons, she was framed and planked in white oak, built heavier than her commercial paradigm owing to the armament. Double-ended and flat-bottomed, she had a keelson but no keel; massive white pine deck beams and stanchions supported the midships gundeck. Thwartships benches were also of white pine. A lightly built wooden framework bore a canvas canopy over her after section from mast to tiller to protect the crew from the elements; they were shielded from enemy fire by fascines, or bundles of saplings lashed along her gunwales. A single fir mast and topmast carried two square sails, but *Philadelphia*'s manoeuvrability depended upon fourteen oars or sweeps of

The reproduction Revolutionary War gunboat Philadelphia II *is launched. (Courtesy of Lake Champlain Maritime Museum, Basin Harbor, Vermont)*

white ash. Unpainted owing to a paint shortage, the hull was tarred to inhibit marine growth and leakage and preserve the wood.

Philadelphia's armament comprised three large cannon and eight swivel guns mounted along the rails. On each side of the midship gundeck was a 9-pound broadside cannon on a carriage, already seventy-five years old when mounted. These were probably cast in Sweden. At the bow was a 12-pound smooth-bore *finbanker*, named after the Swedish town of Finsborg where it also had been cast about a century before. This gun was mounted on an old-style slide carriage on a rail or groove – some of *Philadelphia*'s sister ships were fitted with newer rotating slide carriages. The stem was cut low and the forestay was split to both sides to allow the gun to extend over the bow. Along the gunwales were eight ¾-pound British swivel guns. All of *Philadelphia*'s stone ballast was aft, to offset the weight of the ordnance.

After construction at Skenesborough, Arnold's flotilla was fitted out, rigged, and armed. On 10 August *Philadelphia*'s captain, 25-year-old Pennsylvanian Benjamin Rue, mustered aboard forty-four men from among what General Arnold had called 'a wretched motley crew'; included were a lieutenant, mate, boatswain and mate, gunner and mate, two sergeants, two corporals, eleven privates, and twenty-two marreans (seamen). Nearly two-thirds of the crew were from New Hampshire regiments. The fleet moved to the northern end of Lake Champlain and began patrolling the area, but near the end of September, Arnold

received word that the British fleet was preparing to move from St John's into lower Lake Champlain. Since it was too late in the year to retake Fort Ticonderoga and proceed to Albany, Governor Carleton's 1776 objectives had shrunk to Lake Champlain, 'to clean that place of the Rebels'. Recognizing that the British fleet of twenty-nine vessels with a combined total of eighty-nine guns firing 1,023 lb (weight of metal in one round) outweighed his squadron of fifteen ships with eighty-eight guns delivering 645 lb, Arnold chose a defensive strategy. He moved his squadron south to a sheltered cove at Valcour Island, one kilometre off the New York shoreline, and waited.

On the morning of 11 October 1776, the British fleet under Captain Thomas Pringle rounded the southern end of Valcour Island, spotting the American flotilla anchored to windward. The narrow space and wind direction only permitted a portion of the British fleet to beat to windward, as Arnold had planned. The two fleets engaged from 11.30 a.m. until 5.00 p.m., when the British withdrew to the southern end of the passage between the island and shore. By the day's end, the Americans had lost the schooner *Royal Savage* and gunboat *Philadelphia*, which took a 24-pound ball in her bow (among others) and sank an hour after the engagement ended. That night, fog and darkness permitted Arnold's squadron to slip southward along the shore around the British, but Carleton caught up with it on the 13th and destroyed it. All that remained were four vessels that escaped to Fort Ticonderoga. Carleton pressed his victory, capturing Crown Point and testing Fort Ticonderoga's firepower, but on 2 November he withdrew to St John's for the winter. Although he had won the battle, Arnold's fleet had delayed the British advance until the following year, when the Continental Army was larger, stronger, and better prepared. It defeated General John Burgoyne's forces at Saratoga in October 1777; this resulted in a French–American alliance, and ultimately independence four years later.

Philadelphia lay upright and undisturbed in 18 m of water off Valcour Island until 2 August 1935, when New York salvage engineer Lorenzo F. Hagglund raised her. Finding her perfectly preserved by the cold dark fresh water, he painted her guns with linseed oil, set her on a barge and for the next quarter century sailed her around Lake Champlain as a tourist attraction. Acquired in 1961 after Hagglund's death by the Smithsonian Institution's National Museum of American History, *Philadelphia*'s hull was sprayed with a mixture of polyethylene

glycol, water, and alcohol, and then coated with liquid nylon. Other donated artefacts include navigational instruments (dividers, sand glass), elements of rigging (hooks, eyes, dead-eyes, blocks, pitch brush and dish, cleat, drain plug, fasteners), armaments (musket parts, balls, buckshot, bayonets, gunflints, ramrod, cartouche-box block, cannon balls, shot gauges, tompions, langrage, gunner's worm), tools (serving mallet, chisels, augers, axes, shovel, knives, hinges), and personal items (fragmentary shoes and buckles, knee buckle, pewter spoons, ceramic cup). *Philadelphia* has been on permanent exhibition at the National Museum of American History in Washington, DC since it opened in 1964.

In 1989 the Lake Champlain Maritime Museum at Basin Harbor, Vermont began construction of a replica of the Smithsonian's Revolutionary War gunboat; launched on 18 August 1991, *Philadelphia II* is sailed regularly. P.F.J.

ADDITIONAL READING

Chapelle, H.I., 1949, *History of the American Sailing Navy*, New York.

Hagglund, L.F., 1949, *A Page from the Past: The Story of the Continental Gundelo 'Philadelphia' on Lake Champlain, 1776–1949*, Lake George, New York.

Hoffman, H.P., 1984, 'The Gunboat *Philadelphia*: A Continental Gondola of 1776 and her Model', *Nautical Research Journal*, 30, 2, 55–67.

Lundeberg, P.K., 1995, *The Continental Gunboat Philadelphia and the Defence of Lake Champlain in 1776*, Basin Harbor, Vermont.

National Museum of American History, 1991, *Philadelphia (1st) Gunboat*, The Smithsonian Collection of Warship Plans, Smithsonian Institution, Washington, DC.

Philippines

Group of islands where the Pacific Ocean meets the South China Sea. Located in the tropics, the country is often battered by strong storms and typhoons. Ferdinand Magellan claimed to have discovered it in 1521, and it was subsequently named after King Philip II of Spain. The Philippines, strategically positioned in Southeast Asia, was then one of several countries regularly visited by the early European maritime explorers. However, even before the 'discovery' by Magellan of this country and as early as the 9th century AD, this group of islands was already known to Southeast Asian mariners and traders such as the Thai, Vietnamese, Malaysian, Indonesian, Cambodian, as well as the southern Chinese peoples. Through time, because of strong typhoons and other hazardous navigational factors such as unknown atolls and dangerous coral reefs, accidents must have occurred which resulted in many shipwrecks surrounding the Philippine archipelago. Hence, this vital location of the Philippines offers a wide opportunity for underwater and maritime archaeology.

Underwater and maritime archaeology in the Philippines is a rather recent development compared to the land-based archaeology in the islands which started in the beginning of the 20th century. Underwater archaeology specifically makes use of **SCUBA** diving equipment or other forms of diving apparatus in the field of research; an example of underwater archaeology is the research work on the wreckage of the galleon **San Diego**. Maritime archaeology can be done without the use of scuba diving equipment on marshlands, shallow riverbanks, and former coastlines and waterlogged deposits; an example of maritime archaeology is the research work on the **Butuan Boat**, located in northwestern Mindanao in the Philippines. Other research includes the reconstruction of ancient maritime life-ways, such as the development of boat-building technology, maritime adaptations, and the traces of trade route patterns and the volume of trade goods transacted by the merchants with the local inhabitants. Attempts have been made to integrate underwater and maritime archaeology with land-based or terrestrial archaeology in the Philippines.

Permission to conduct underwater archaeology in the Philippines is necessary under Philippine law. Underwater archaeology can only be done through a cooperative venture with the National Museum of the Philippines. In 1988 its Archaeology Division, and the Underwater Archaeology Section, formulated and instituted rules and regulations on the practice of underwater archaeology. Proponents who wish to conduct underwater archaeology in the Philippines are required to follow the procedures of the rules and regulations and sign a memorandum of agreement which is intermittently reviewed by the archaeologists of National Museum of the Philippines for further improvement.

The use of scuba equipment in archaeological–historical investigation in the Philippines started in 1967 at Nabasagan Point, Santo Domingo, Albay Province, about 500 kilometres south of Manila. A search for a Spanish galleon, wrecked in about 40 to 65 m of water, was carried out. Two huge anchors, each weighing about 3 tons, with a forging date of 1649 were recovered. A bronze butterfly hinge, pottery sherds, copper plates and nails, chain links, capstan,

planking, and the centre bolt of an auxiliary mast were also found. The presence of copper sheathing does not fit with the picture of a 17th-century Spanish galleon: according to Peterson, until the latter part of the 18th century ships generally were not sheathed with metal. As sheets became available with the application of steam power to rolling mills, this material began to be used to sheathe the better constructed ships. The entire British battle fleet was sheathed during the American Revolution. At the turn of the 19th century even merchant ships of the better sort were protected in this manner. On wreck sites of these ships numerous small tapered-head copper nails were found along with fragments of copper sheathing. This suggests that there may have been two wrecks in the same site – a Spanish galleon and a British vessel.

In 1970 another vessel, believed to be a British steamship, was discovered off the coast of Guimaras Island in Iloilo City by a joint team of the Philippine Navy Coast Guard and the Philippine Constabulary Sea Patrol Group, assisted by the Ministry of Tourism which was deputized by the National Museum. Later the site was worked by the **US Navy**. The vessel was about 20 m long and 7.6 m wide. It was found in the shallow waters of Arevalo Shoal at an average depth of 5 m below the water surface. The associated cultural materials recovered were porcelain wares consisting of blue and white bowls and plates bearing the labels 'Perkin, R.C. & Co., Glasgow, England'. The other artefacts found were labelled 'Alexandria' and had Arabic designs.

The National Museum of the Philippines participated to a limited extent on these first two underwater semi-archaeological activities because at that time it did not have a trained underwater archaeologist on its staff. Diving operations were more of a recovery effort of artefactual remains than a systematic recording of archaeological data. In 1979 the Underwater Archaeology Unit was established in the Anthropology Division of the National Museum of the Philippines as a result of the Southeast Asian Ministry of Education Organization (SEAMEO) Special Projects in Archaeology and Fine Arts (SPAFA) training course in underwater archaeology in Bangkok, Thailand from December 1978 to March 1979. The Archaeology Section branched off from the Anthropology Division in 1988. This resulted in the upgrading of all member units, including the Underwater Archaeology Unit, into a section of the newly organized Archaeology Division. Consequently, the change paved the way for more specialized learning opportunities

abroad for local underwater archaeological researchers. Some National Museum staff members were sent to France and Thailand for technical training in underwater archaeological methods.

Between 1982 and 1995 more than twenty underwater archaeological sites were visited, assessed, and worked by some project proponents in coordination with the National Museum of the Philippines. Some of the more famous underwater archaeological sites are the following: *Royal Captain*, a 1773 East India Company vessel which was wrecked at the Royal Captain Shoal (after its name) at the western area off Palawan Island; *Griffin*, a 1760 British East India Company vessel which was wrecked on a rock northwest of Basilan Island and rested at the depth of 4 m below the water; *San Jose*, a 1694 Spanish galleon, which lies approximately 10 m below sea-level, near Lubang Island, off Mindoro; *San Diego*, a 1600 Spanish galleon converted into a warship, which sank offshore between Fortune Island and Nasugbu, Batangas, in 50 m of water; and an Indo-Chinese vessel of the 14th century, found in 40 m of water, between the southern tip of Palawan main island and Pandanan Island.

The methods for searching underwater sites in the Philippines vary from the simple snorkelling and diving on reported accidental finds of shipwrecks by local fishermen, to the more sophisticated use of modern technology such as computers, proton **Magnetometers**, **Sub-bottom profilers**, remotely operated vehicles (ROV) or robots, and submarine equipment, with the aid of **Global Positioning Systems** (GPS).

Documentary evidence from the historical period is helpful in providing clues concerning the area where shipwrecks may have occurred. There are times, however, when the documentary historical records do not match the archaeological evidence. A good example of this is the wreck of *San Diego*, which was sunk by the Dutch ship *Mauritius* on 14 December 1600; its admiral, Antonio de Morga, wrote that its position was about 12 kilometres away from Fortune Island. During the underwater archaeological survey, however, the shipwreck was located only 900 m northeast of Fortune Island with the use of a magnetometer in the systematic survey and the aid of GPS. For a variety of reasons, there can be a disparity between the historical record and the archaeological data, although in most cases the archaeological remains verify the historical documents. However, sometimes the archaeological evidence can contradict historical documents, as in the case of *San Diego*.

Some new terrestrial maritime archaeological sites in the group of islands in the Batanes area, particularly Ibuhos Island, were discovered in 1994 and are currently being surveyed. These included boat-shaped stone grave markers located on a hill adjacent to the castle-like formation on the western portion of Ibuhos Island. The significance of these grave markers is that they represent the first archaeological evidence of people adapted to a maritime environment, whose behaviour, including their burial practices, was influenced by boat culture. Philippine society is based on the concept of a *barangay* community wherein the basic political unit is organized rather like a group of people working on a boat. *Barangay* (or *balangay*) was one of the first native words the Spaniards learned in the Philippines. When the Spaniards reached Luzon, they found this word for boat also being used for the smallest political unit of Filipino society. E.D.

ADDITIONAL READING

Dizon, E.Z., 1992, 'Status of Philippine Underwater Archaeological Researchers from 1989–91: Prospects for 1992', *Bulletin of the Australian Institute for Maritime Archaeology*, 16, 1, 41–7.

Dizon, E.Z., 1993, 'War at Sea: Piecing Together the San Diego Puzzle', in *Saga of the San Diego (A.D. 1600)*, Manila.

Dizon, E.Z. and Santiago, R.A., 1995, 'Preliminary Report on the Archaeological Explorations in Batan, Sabtang and Ibuhos Islands, Batanes Province, Northern Philippines', in Yeung Chung-tong and B. Li Wai-ling (eds), *Archaeology in Southeast Asia*, Hong Kong.

Goddio, F., 1988, *Discovery and Archaeological Excavation of a 16th Century Trading Vessel in the Philippines*, Manila.

Goddio, F., 1994, *Le mystère du San Diego: Histoire et découverte d'un trésor englouti en mer de Chine*, Paris.

Goddio, F. and Jay, E., 1988, *18th Century Relics of the Griffin Shipwreck*, Manila.

Goddio, F. and Kristoff, E., 1994, 'The Tale of the San Diego', *National Geographic*, 186, 1, 34–57.

Peterson, M., 1965, *History Under the Sea: A Handbook for Underwater Exploration*, Washington, DC.

Ronquillo, W.P., 1993, 'The Archaeology of the San Diego: A Summary of the Activities from 1991–1993', in *Saga of the San Diego (A.D. 1600)*, Manila.

Scott, W.H., 1994, *Barangay: Sixteenth Century Philippine Culture and Society*, Quezon City, Philippines.

Phoenix

The second steamboat built on **Lake Champlain**, and to date the earliest steamer wreck to be

archaeologically studied. *Phoenix* was built in 1815, eight years after Robert Fulton launched the first commercially successful steamer on the Hudson River. Built at a cost of $45,000 by the Lake Champlain Steamboat Company at Vergennes, Vermont, *Phoenix* measured 147 ft (44.8 m) in length, 27 ft (8.2 m) in beam, and was powered at 8 miles (15 km) per hour by a 45 hp steam engine. The vessel entered into a lucrative passenger and freight service between opposite ends of the lake, making bi-weekly passages between Whitehall, New York and St Jean, Quebec. By all accounts the steamer was profitable, but it proved under-powered, a problem that was solved by purchasing a new engine in 1816. In 1817 *Phoenix* carried President James Monroe on his inaugural tour of the northern states; the following year it transported the exhumed body of Revolutionary War general Richard Montgomery, which was being returned from Quebec for formal burial in New York City.

The end of *Phoenix* occurred on 4 September 1819. That evening the vessel departed from Burlington, Vermont for Canada with forty-six passengers and crew. Shortly after midnight a fire broke out amidships, and in the ensuing panic the steamer's two boats were cast off before they were fully loaded, stranding eleven passengers and crew on board the flaming vessel. The captain assisted the remaining people into the water

Left: Steamboat Phoenix *broadside. (Courtesy of Lake Champlain Maritime Museum, Basin Harbor, Vermont)*

Below: Interior view of Phoenix*'s hull, showing charred wood. (Courtesy of Lake Champlain Maritime Museum, Basin Harbor, Vermont)*

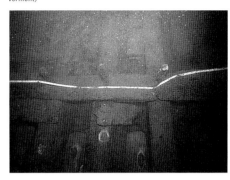

on planks and furniture, and then floated on a table leaf for two hours before being picked up. Six persons drowned in the lake. The Steamboat Company blamed a candle left burning in the galley for the disaster.

The burned-out hull of *Phoenix* drifted onto Colchester Shoal, where the engine and boiler were salvaged and installed in *Phoenix II*. The wreck subsequently drifted off the shoal and sank in deeper water. It was discovered in 1978 by sport divers, and was relatively intact (although charred) from the waterline down. The former location of the boiler and engine, about one-third of the vessel's length aft of the stem, could be identified by heavy longitudinal support timbers, several through-hull pipes, large iron bolts, and a scattering of bricks. A mass of stoneware crock and bottle fragments forward of the engine space showed where foodstuffs were stowed in the bow, while fused pieces of blue-transfer ware ceramics abaft the engine indicated the location of the passenger dining area.

Phoenix underwent preliminary archaeological recording by the Champlain Maritime Society in August 1980, and a set of wreck plans were prepared at that time; a second project by the Society in 1984 recovered ceramics, bottle glass, a stack of fused coins, and other artefacts for study and display. The wreck was incorporated in the Vermont Division for Historic Preservation's 'Underwater Preserve' programme in 1985, and is visited by scores of sport divers every year. K.C.

ADDITIONAL READING

Davison, R. (ed.), 1981, *The Phoenix Project*, Burlington, Vermont.

Simmons, J.J., 1988, 'Steamboats on Inland Waterways: Prime Movers of Manifest Destiny', in G.F. Bass (ed.), *Ships and Shipwrecks of the Americas*, London.

Photogrammetry

The generation of precise three-dimensional measurements from overlapping pairs of stereometric photographs (stereo pairs). Stereoscopes create a three-dimensional image perception from overlapping photographs taken from slightly different positions by allowing each eye to focus on one of the stereo pairs. Very small features can be distinguished on three-dimensional images, consequently stereo images are important in mapping. Stereoplotters combined with photogrammetric techniques currently produce most topographic maps from paired aerial images. Aerial mapping is the most common photogrammetric application, and its techniques were taken underwater by archaeologists. Multiple images are useful for mapping, scale drawing, and measuring archaeological features that increase documentation accuracy and can reduce time underwater.

Stereophotogrammetry demands exact camera placement, and stereoplotting typically requires a skilled photogrammetrist; many underwater projects have used professionals to post-plot maps. Photogrammetry should not be confused with **Photomosaics**, which are two-dimensional, planimetric images pieced together from multiple photographs that together cover an area larger than a single photograph. Mosaics provide vertical-perspective and horizontal dimensions only, whereas three-dimensional stereo images provide true shape and size.

Stereophotogrammetry underwater was first suggested by the photographic pioneer Dimitri Rebikoff in the 1950s and was made possible by the development of the Ivanoff-Rebikoff lens, patented in 1956, which corrects for plan diopter aberration of water. Rebikoff began making stereophotogrammetric mosaics before 1958. Underwater archaeological stereophotogrammetry began in 1963 when Julian Whittlesey used a horizontal bar to position cameras on the **Yassiada** Byzantine wreck. Photogrammetry has also been used for documenting terrestrial maritime sites.

Stereophotogrammetry uses dual, overlapping images produced either from identical twin cameras or a single camera held in a locational framework to position dual images precisely. Accurate camera positioning is critical; distances from the subject and between strictly parallel lenses must be exactly maintained to produce accurate measurements. Archaeologists have developed several camera-holding systems, and each requires considerable engineering and underwater preparation. However, when executed properly in good visibility

conditions, photogrammetry produces remarkable results. Canadian Park Service excavators found that orthographic projection of *San Juan* hull timbers (see **Red Bay**) produced photogrammetrically were more consistent and reliable than hand measurements.

Underwater vehicles have been used like aeroplanes to obtain stereoimages. Rebikoff developed the *Pegasus,* a diver propulsion vehicle mounted with stereo cameras that was effectively producing stereophotogrammetric mosaics by 1958. In 1964 Karius, Merrifield, and Rosencrantz used the submarine **Asherah** outfitted with dual aerial survey cameras mounted by Rebikoff to obtain stereophotogrammetric images of the Yassiada Roman wreck. These were used to produce a site map with elevations. The pictures were taken in half an hour, but it took fifty-six hours to assemble them into a mosaic.

One of the most promising developments is combining precise navigation with stereoscopic imaging aboard a remotely operated vehicle (ROV). Examples of stereophotogrammetry production on wrecks are the NOAA **Monitor** Project and the European Institute of Underwater Archaeology and **National Geographic Society** documentation of **San Diego**. Sophisticated integrated navigation-imaging systems for ROV mounting are available. Marquest recently carried the system a step further by combining it with the three-dimensional visualization software used by the Woods Hole Oceanographic Institute **Jason** ROV for imaging wrecks and geological features. This system has ten-second navigation updates, three-dimensional imaging, pre-plottable courses, high-resolution digital imaging, and stereo measurement capabilities.

Late 20th century advances in computer capability, software development, digital image capture technology, and digital cameras have made production of three-dimensional computer models from underwater images much easier. Convergent photogrammetry uses measurements obtained from images to determine the camera location when the image was made, which eliminates the rigid camera positioning requirements of stereophotogrammetry. The software uses the camera position – distance and angle to the object – to project straight lines or rays from the camera out into space. Linear equation calculations provide three-dimensional positions for points from intersecting or converging rays.

Simply, any point that appears on three or more intersecting images can be positioned in three dimensions by convergent pho-

togrammetric techniques. The object of photographing for this procedure is to have as many views as necessary from as many angles as required to obtain the desired details. Hand-held, roughly 90 degree angles are adequate, positioning is not critical, and close-up views can be combined with full-coverage overviews. For highest accuracy, stadia, objects of known dimensions or control points, should appear in each image; no other field measurements are necessary.

To date, several software programs using two principal techniques are available. Some systems, like the Rolleimetric MR2 system, use the unsurpassed resolution of photographs combined with a digitizing board for selection and digitization of points of interest. Others, like Photomodeler, use digital images produced by CD, digital camera, or video, and are much less expensive. Both systems have camera calibration programmes and produce very accurate results – 1:2000 with 95 per cent probability can be achieved under field conditions. Accuracy depends on several variables: camera calibration, digitizer quality, camera and digitizer resolution, camera position geometry, number of images used, and number and accuracy of point selection. These variables can degrade accuracy to 1:500. Measurement consistency is very high, and all quantitative operations are done by the software.

During post-plotting a defining line is drawn by connecting selected points that are clearly visible on three or more images. The modeller indicates to the software which points are the same on each image, and which points are connected. Zooming into digital images aids precise point selection (which is limited by pixel size). The lines joining selected multiple-image points produce a three-dimensional digital wireframe model of the object that is stored as a file. The file (usually dxf format) can be exported into a computer-assisted design (CAD) programme like AutoCAD for completion of scale drawings and three-dimensional imaging. External geodetic control can be added to the images, which allows inclusion into **Geographic Information Systems** (GIS) programs.

Convergent photogrammetry is very useful for mapping and positioning features, stratigraphy, and artefacts, recording excavation layers *in situ,* and minimizing dive time for documentation; essentially trading post-processing time for dive time. Photogrammetric images contain much data, and they can be consulted many times to enhance drawing details by selecting additional points and combining them with the model. These images also comprise an archival data source available for future queries for additional information not anticipated during original documentation.

The US National Oceanographic and Atmospheric Administration (NOAA) conducted the initial underwater test of the Rolleimetric system in 1992. The National Park Service **Submerged Cultural Resources Unit** (SCRU) tested this system in 1993. The SCRU has been using Photomodeler with both photographic and video imaging as part of the GIS-based survey of **Dry Tortugas National Park**. Photomodeler was selected because it can use screen-captured video images, which makes film developing in isolated areas unnecessary. Modern video camera resolution only slightly degrades photogrammetric accuracy. More than 125 georeferenced images, ranging from single objects to sites, have been successfully and accurately modelled.

Convergent photogrammetry is most

Photomosaic

A composite image made up of multiple photographs, each of which depicts a portion of the whole image. Because of the limited visibility encountered on underwater sites it is nearly impossible to photograph large areas in a single exposure. Therefore, photomosaics are often effective in producing overall images of such sites. Almost any set of overlapping photographic images can be used to create a photomosaic; however, the resulting mosaic will be of poor quality unless care is taken during the initial photography phase. For that reason, images used for creating photomosaics are generally produced in conjunction with a more comprehensive photogrammetric recording activity, that is, photographic site recording from which accurate measurements can be obtained.

The first step in producing a photomosaic of an underwater site is to establish a set of photographic references or a grid pattern over the site. The grid can be made

time, with each photograph overlapping the previous one by approximately 50 per cent.

The camera-to-subject distance must remain relatively constant in order to produce images of the same magnification. The resulting prints are fitted together in the same order as they were exposed, overlapping the prints until the images match and a composite photograph of the entire site is created. The large overlap is necessitated by the optical distortions that exist in underwater photography. High-quality lenses correct some, but not all, of these distortions. The centre portion of each image contains the best definition and the least distortion. One of the best known photomosaics, produced in 1974, is of the wreck of the civil war ironclad USS *Monitor*, lying off the coast of North Carolina in 70 m (230 ft) of water.

Since the 1950s, photomosaics of shipwrecks have been produced using underwater still cameras. Improvements in

effective when used in combination with direct observation and measurements that can be added to the scaled wireframe models to maximize efficiency of in-water observations and to produce final drawings. Combined convergent photogrammetric and GIS programs indicate the future direction for underwater photogrammetry. L.E.M.

ADDITIONAL READING

Green, J., 1990, *Maritime Archaeology: A Technical Handbook*, New York.

Mertens, L.E., 1969, *In-Water Photography: Theory and Practice*, New York.

UNESCO, 1972, *Underwater Archaeology: A Nascent Discipline*, Paris.

A photomosaic showing features confirmed as being part of the Union ironclad ship USS Monitor. *The mosaic is composed of photographs taken by the 35 mm cameras of the research vessel* Alcoa Seaprobe *during an evaluation cruise conducted by the US Navy during April 1974. (US Naval Historical Center)*

up of rows of parallel strings placed at right angles to each other, a series of markers or 'targets' placed around the site, or a rigid metal framework on which a camera stand is mounted. Grid spacing and camera height are determined by the size of the site and the ambient visibility. The site is then photographed, one small area at a

photographic equipment and computer technology since then have made it possible to produce photomosaics much more easily and accurately, using either still or video imaging techniques. The original images are digitized and the resulting 'image files' are merged into a composite image on desktop computers using commercially available software. A high degree of accuracy can be achieved using these techniques, but only if a sufficient number of photographic references have been placed on the site and accurately surveyed. Computers have the ability to adjust each image, based on references within the image, to correct for such distortions as parallax, lens distortions, and camera angle and height. Modern, high-speed computers and state-of-the-art software also permit the operator to 'cut-and-paste' images, changing parameters such as size and 'tilt' in real time, thus greatly enhancing the ability of researchers to produce quite accurate photomosaics on a very modest budget. J.D.B.

ADDITIONAL READING

Bass, G.F., 1966, *Archaeology Under Water*, London.

Dean, M., *et al.*, 1992, *Archaeology Underwater: The NAS Guide to Principles and Practice*, Dorchester.

Miller, E.M., 1978, *USS Monitor: The Ship That Launched a Modern Navy*, Annapolis, Maryland.

Newton, J., 1975, 'How We Found the *Monitor*', *National Geographic*, 147, 1, 48–61.

USS *Pilotfish*

see **Crossroads Wrecks**

Poland

European country bordered to the north by the **Baltic Sea**. The origins of nautical archaeology in Poland date to the second half of the 19th century, when shipwrecks and other ship-related artefacts were often found along the southern Baltic coast, then part of the Prussian state. Unfortunately, most of these remains were reused, either as fuel or building material. Even so, as early as 1869, news of shipwrecks and related material was occasionally included in general archaeological reports or the local newspapers. The discovery of an old lapstrake ship in Gdansk (then Danzig) in 1873 created such interest that this find is still cited in modern studies of northern European vessels. In 1895 Hugo Cowents, Director of the provincial museum in Gdansk, excavated the remains of a shipwreck at Bagart (then Baumgarth). In the same year, ship parts were excavated at Frombork (Frauenburg), on the shore of the Vistula lagoon. This find was interpreted at the time by Joseph Heydeck as a Viking ship.

In the years preceding World War I, Hugo Lemcke, conservator at the provincial museum in Szczecin (Stettin), published two wrecks found at Charbrowo (Charbrow); the first had been excavated and recovered in 1898, while the second was left in place and not surveyed in detail until 1931. A third wreck was surveyed in this area in 1934 and 1937 by Otto Lienau. Lienau, a naval engineer and professor at the polytechnic in Gdansk, had excavated and published three boat finds from the fields of Gdansk-Orunia (Danzig-Ohra). His

publication of these finds constituted a turning point in the development of nautical archaeology in the southern Baltic region. Previously, the reconstruction and analysis of ship remains had been carried out by archaeologists, conservators, or other public figures without any technical qualifications in ship design or construction. Lienau's work revealed the advantages of such qualifications in analysing ship remains.

The analysis of these and other ship remains formed the basis on which these investigators formulated a theory of Germanic or Scandinavian origin for southern Baltic shipbuilding. Following World War II and the return of eastern Prussia to Polish control, this theory was firmly rejected by the Polish school of research, whose adherents argued that the wrecks were vestiges of a Slavic or Wendish shipbuilding tradition. Their arguments were based more on historical assumptions than on the archaeological evidence; during the war, much of the primary evidence had been destroyed or badly damaged. In these conditions, renewed attempts were made to find and collect any material relevant to shipbuilding and seafaring in the southern Baltic region. In 1957, under the initiative of Wladislaw Filipowiak, director of the National Museum in Szczecin, the third wreck surveyed by Lienau at Charbrowo was excavated and removed to Szczecin. In 1962 excavations carried out by Tadeusz Wieczorowski at the medieval 'Produce Market' in Szczecin uncovered the remains of a lapstrake vessel. Built at the beginning of the 9th century AD, the boat seems to be one of the earliest planked vessels yet found in the southern Baltic region.

The need to raise awareness of Poland's maritime heritage led to the foundation, in 1960, of the Central Maritime Museum in Gdansk. Under Przemyslaw Smolarek, the new institution organized systematic underwater surveys in the Bay of Gdansk. The excavations of the 'copper wreck', a merchantman sunk in 1424 with a cargo of Hungarian copper, and of *Solen*, a Swedish warship sunk in the battle of Oliwa in 1627, are among the museum's most notable achievements. Between 1977 and 1996 the museum was also engaged in intermittent investigation of a large complex of underwater sites in Puck Bay, northwest of Gdansk. This complex, investigated by W. Stepien, I. Pomian, and J. Litwin, includes several early medieval shipwrecks and a defensive barrage of pilings. In the same period, Smolarek engaged the museum in the excavation on

land of several late medieval shipwrecks at Tolkmicko and participated in the analysis and interpretation of an early medieval wreck found at Lad in 1983. Upon Smolarek's death in 1991, he was succeeded as Director of the Central Maritime Museum by Andrzej Zbierski. The museum hosted the ninth ISBSA in 1997.

Although much of the nautical archaeological work conducted in Poland since 1960 has been carried out by the Central Maritime Museum, the National Museum in Szczecin, through its director Filipowiak, has also been active. In 1961 Filipowiak, K. Siuchninski, and R. Wolagiewicz conducted a series of underwater surveys in the Szczecin lagoon. The lengthy investigations at the medieval trading centre of Wolin brought to light no fewer than seven wrecks or derelict vessels, all dated between the 9th and 13th centuries. In 1984 a 13th-century wreck was excavated near Kamiern Pomorski, the medieval seat of the bishops of Pomerania.

These research efforts have been made possible not only by state funding support, but also by academic support provided by the Institute of Archaeology and Ethnology in Torun. Founded in 1975, the institute established, in cooperation with the Nicolaus Copernicus University, an academic programme with a specialization in underwater archaeology. Although much of the fieldwork undertaken by the programme has concentrated on the investigation of riverine structures, such as bridges and embankments, the technical and theoretical training provided by the programme has contributed to the growth of a core of well-trained professional nautical archaeologists, and underwater archaeology has been elevated to the rank of an independent discipline in Poland. Unfortunately, the socio-political changes in Eastern Europe since the late 1980s adversely affected public interest in archaeology and state funding for this kind of research, and in the late 1990s scholars and administrators involved in nautical archaeology had to adapt their research programmes to the new reality.

Although publication of Polish sites is fairly extensive, much of it is not easily accessible. Older publications are often in German regional journals, and post-war work is predominantly in Polish, although occasional articles appear in Western journals, including the *International Journal of Nautical Archaeology*, and several Polish scholars, including Smolarek and Litwin, have been regular attendees at international conferences. G.I.

Pontia

Island situated in the Tyrrhenian Sea, 33 km south of Cape Circe, the nearest point of land on the west coast of **Italy**. It is the main island of the Pontine group, consisting of two sub-groups some 35 km apart: the northwest group includes Pontia, Palmarola, Zannone, and Gavi; the southwest group includes Ventotene and Santo Stefano. Pontia owes its importance to the fact that it is the only one of the Pontine group with a natural harbour. The only other harbour in the Pontine Islands is a tiny port at Ventotene cut into live rock, an archaeological marvel but no competition for the harbour of Pontia.

The shape of the island, unique in the Tyrrhenian Sea, is that of a narrow, curving spine of limestone, 8 km in length, with ribs of rocky cliffs extending outward from side to side to form its many quiet coves. The widest point on the island is 1,700 m, the narrowest 200 m. Long lines of offshore rocks, labelled *faraglioni* or *scogliere* on Italian nautical charts, continue the contours of the coves out to sea in all directions. The cliffs rise steeply out of the sea to heights reaching up as high as 280 m at the southernmost tip of Punta della Guardia; the surfaces of the stone are striated in various colours and deeply corrugated with sharp-edged vertical cuts. The result is a seascape of powerful beauty and changing moods, as the waters reflect the different gradations of light and colour.

According to Livy, a Roman colony was established at Pontia in 313 BC, and it took on the character of a frontier outpost as Rome's political and commercial interests extended southward into Campania. The port of Pontia is located near the southern extremity of the island on its eastern coast. The headland, Punta della Madonna, extends northeast to enclose a large basin against the winds of the southeastern quadrant. This basin is bounded on the north by a lesser promontory at Santa Maria and its offshore line of rocks, the Scoglio Ravia. An inner harbour space is defined by a second line of rocks, the Scoglio di Frisio, extending due east from the shore in the middle of the harbour roadstead. A modern break-water extends northwest from the Punta della Madonna towards the Scoglio de Frisio, further protecting the inner harbour.

A reconstruction of the port completed in 1739 probably destroyed any remaining vestiges of the Roman moles and quays, for no ancient remains are visible today. Yet the location of the ancient port in this locality has been convincingly established by an underwater survey revealing the existence of great deposits of broken amphoras in the waters around the harbour. These deposits represent the accumulations from centuries of port traffic; the amphoras used in the shipment of various commodities would be discarded once the contents were transferred to smaller containers suitable for market.

A sampling of fifteen amphora fragments from the ancient dump sites around the harbour at the Punta della Madonna was taken

Chiaiadiluna (Chiardiluna), Pontia. (Vincent Bruno)

for further study to the work rooms of the American Academy in Rome at Cosa, where they were later examined by E. Will. Two samples found in a dump beneath the Faraglioni della Madonna and three more from the Scoglia Ravia belong to amphoras of Will Type 1a, which came into use in the late 4th century BC and were no longer manufactured after the beginning of the First Punic War in 264 BC. These five items, coinciding in date with the earliest period of the colony's history, provide clear evidence for the location of the colonial harbour in the Punta delle Madonna–Santa Maria area of the east coast. The remaining fragments sampled represent amphora types belonging to every period of Roman history from the Republic to the Late Empire, ranging over a period of more than 800 years. The latest example found was the neck of a so-called *spatheion*, a sword-shaped jar for olives and olive oil, belonging to the 5th century AD. (for a full discussion of the fragments, see Bruno and Will, 1985).

Another proof that the ancient port was in this particular location lies in the fact that there is a tunnel connecting this harbour to another bay on the opposite side of the island, facing west. This is the crescent-shaped bay called Chiaiadiluna (Chiardiluna on some charts). The tunnel itself is remarkable, a high vault 168 m in length carved through the rock, with an imposing series of light shafts cut through from above, and plenty of room to move men and material from one side of the island to the other. For ships approaching the island from the direction of Rome, the Chiaiadiluna would have been a convenient landing place, especially during easterly and southeasterly gales (the sirocco). These winds make circling the island by sea an arduous and dangerous undertaking, owing to the numerous offshore rocks, many of which are submerged. On such occasions, the Chiaiadiluna would certainly present itself as a calm and attractive refuge. Its smooth crescent of beach, with deep water reaching close to shore, would make it ideal for beaching vessels; its only drawback is that it is completely sealed off from the outside world by a wall of high cliffs embracing the entire crescent. Hence the tunnel, which made the port facilities of the main harbour at Punta della Madonna available to crews arriving at Chiaiadiluna from the north and west.

During the Augustan period, Pontia became an island of luxurious villas whose terraces spread over much of the best available land on the island. The construction of these villas may have resulted in the destruction of the earlier port town. The villa above Punta della Madonna has an interesting structure identified as a small theatre or *odeion* for the performance of music (Vitruvius 5.9). Also belonging to this villa is a rock-cut pool located outside the root of the modern breakwater, called by the natives the Bagno di Pilato. Such pools, carved into live rock, are mentioned by Calumella (*De re rustica* 8.17) as a great rarity on the coasts of Italy.

Other ancient remains include a system of underground aqueducts that carried water from a group of cisterns near the northern end of the island to the port area. As the Augustan villas are on a higher level, an earlier Republican date is assumed for the system. A large bronze cock from one of the ancient water pipes at Pontia is in the Naples Museum.

The island of Pontia seems to be the obvious choice for the location of Circe's palace, as Virgil envisioned it in his *Aeneid*. So believed Maiuri, who wrote: 'The island … with its shadowy mirrors hung all round with polychrome rocks or frightening precipices … must of necessity call up better than elsewhere the fabled voyage of Ulysses and the enchanted abode of Circe.' This enchantment with the island must have been felt as strongly by the ancients. Horace, as well as Virgil, is known to have travelled through the region. The characteristic shapes of the rock formations of the Faraglioni della Madonna and the Faraglioni di Calzone Muto appear in a variety of ancient paintings, and it is surely no accident that Tiberius filled a cave on the sea beside his villa at Sperlonga with sculptures representing scenes from the *Odyssey*. Pontia and its surrounding coasts and waters were clearly a special precinct of myth and the supernatural in the minds of those in antiquity who knew them. V.J.B.

ADDITIONAL READING

Bruno, V.J., 1976, 'Pontia', in R. Stillwell (ed.), *The Princeton Encyclopedia of Classical Sites*, 728.

Bruno, V.J. and Will, E.L., 1985, 'The Island of Pontia: A Nautical Survey', *Archaeology*, 38, January/February, 40–47.

Buchner, G., 1949, 'Isole Ponziane-Campania', *Notiziario Rivista Scienze Preistoriche*, 4, 225.

Castaldi, F., 1958, 'L'Isola di Ponza', *Annali dell' Istituto Superiore di Scienze e Lettere Santa Chiara*, 8, 167–215. List of ancient sources, 167–8.

Dies, L.M., 1950, *Ponza: Perla di Roma*.

Ghetti, M.F.A., 1968, *L'archipelago Pontine nella storia del medio Tirreno*, 1–59 and 309–15.

Guerrini, L., 1965, *Enciclopedia dell'Arte Antica*, 6.

Jacono, L., 1926, 'Solarium' di una villa romana', *Notizie degli Scavi di Antichita*, 219–32.

Jacono, L., 1927, 'Ponza', *Enciclopedia italiana*, 27, 907.

Jacono, L., 1935, 'Un porto duomillenario', *Istituto di Studi Romani: Atti del III Congresso Nazionale*, 318–24.

Maiuri, A., 1926, 'Ricognizioni archeologiche nell'isola di Ponza', *Bolletino d'Arte*, 224–32.

Radmilli, A.M., 1954, 'Le isole Pontine e il commercio dell'ossidiano nel continente durante il periodo neo-eneolitico', in M.G. Baserga (ed.), *Origines: Scritti*, 115 ff.

Tricoli, G., 1859, *Monografia per le isole del gruppo Ponziano*.

Port Royal, Jamaica

Town that sank into Kingston Harbour during a disastrous earthquake on 7 June 1692. At the time of the earthquake Port Royal was one of the most significant 17th-century English towns in the New World. It differs from most archaeological sites in that it is a 'catastrophic site'. More usually, the archaeologist has to deal with a situation where over a span of time houses, shops, warehouses, churches, and other buildings were constructed, expanded, neglected, abandoned, eventually collapsed, were razed and then possibly built over. Port Royal is strikingly different; after only thirty-seven years of existence much of this bustling seaport sank into the harbour in only a matter of minutes. It is the only sunken city in the New World.

In the middle of the 17th century Jamaica was a backwater possession of Spain. This was to come to an end when an invasion force sent out by Oliver Cromwell, Lord Protector of England, failed to capture Hispaniola. The force turned to Jamaica, easily capturing it in May 1655 as a consolation prize to appease Cromwell. Port Royal began as a defensive fortification built at the tip of the sand spit separating Kingston Harbour from the Caribbean. The fort, situated at the narrow entrance, controlled all access to the harbour. Since the harbour surrounding the fortification was ideal for anchoring and unloading ships, a small settlement known as the Point, or Point Cagway, formed. When the monarchy was restored and King Charles II was placed on the throne of England in 1660, the Point was renamed Port Royal.

Because of Port Royal's location within a well-protected harbour, its flat topography, and deep water close to shore, large ships could be easily serviced, loaded, and unloaded. Ships' captains, mariners, merchants, craftsmen, and privateers established themselves in Port Royal to take advantage of the trading and outfitting opportunities. As Jamaica's economy grew, Port Royal developed faster than any town founded by the English in the New World. This growth coincided with the period, between 1660 and 1671, of officially sanctioned privateering for which the city was so notorious. Privateering and/or piracy throughout the 17th century brought in a steady flow of Spanish money, gold, silver, and goods into the coffers of Port Royal and it became the mercantile centre of the Caribbean with an active trade in slaves, sugar, and raw materials. Vast amounts of goods flowed in and out of the port through an expansive trade network, that included extensive trading, and/or looting of coastal Spanish towns throughout Spanish America. Coinage circulated freely and the majority of the gold and silver coming into England passed through the hands of the merchants and privateers of Port Royal.

Throughout most of Port Royal's early history it was the *de facto* capital of the island and was Jamaica's only legal port of entry until its destruction in 1692. The merchants of the town controlled the economic affairs of the island. The profits of the merchants were used to finance the sugar plantations that dominated the economical and political affairs of Jamaica throughout the 18th century. By the 1690s it was the most affluent and largest English town in the New World with a population of between 6,500 and 7,000. Some 2,000 buildings, many constructed of brick and as high as four storeys, were crowded together on some 20 hectares of unconsolidated sand at the tip of the spit. Because of the ways of many of its inhabitants, the town had the reputation of being the 'wickedest city in Christendom'. All who have excavated on the submerged town have used some form of this quote, for it attracts attention to this once famous pirate port. Admittedly, it was a very loose and free-wheeling place; however, the quote slights the multi-faceted importance of Port Royal in the 17th century. What stands out is the affluence and importance of the town when compared to other contemporary English colonial towns.

The geological setting of Port Royal played a major role in its development and in its eventual destruction and preservation. The town was constructed on the widened end of a long, narrow sand spit. The spit separates Kingston Harbour from the Caribbean, but constructing buildings on unconsolidated, waterlogged sand in an earthquake-prone area proved to be a mistake. Shortly before noon on 7 June 1692, 13 hectares (66 per cent) of the 'storehouse and treasury of the West Indies' that lay along the old shore line slid, jumbled, and sank into Kingston Harbour in a disastrous earthquake. It is estimated that 2,000 persons were killed immediately by the earthquake and the seismic sea waves that followed, while an additional 3,000 citizens died of injuries and disease in the following weeks. Some two-thirds of the town and its population were lost. Salvage and outright looting began almost immediately and continued off and on for years. Sections of the town situated away from the harbour sank vertically with minimal horizontal disturbance during the earthquake through a geological process called liquefaction. Entire streets, blocks, and buildings along with their occupants and contents disappeared beneath the water with amazingly little distortion to walls and floors.

A diver examines the brick floor of a large building at Port Royal, Jamaica. (Donny Hamilton)

Unlike other 17th-century sites, at Port Royal the archaeologist deals with artefact **Assemblages** within the rooms and buildings where they were used. On some occasions the occupants of the rooms are found where they were trapped by fallen brick walls. This situation is in marked contrast to most terrestrial sites where archaeologists deal with discarded trash and discarded items – although this component is present also in Port Royal. In addition, because the part of Port Royal being excavated is under water, a considerable amount of perishable organic artefacts that are missing from most terrestrial sites are preserved. With intact artefacts and a full range of cultural data present, artefact studies and patterns are more

meaningful. Interestingly, a pocket watch made *c.* 1686 by Paul Blondel, a Frenchman living in the Netherlands, was recovered in underwater excavations near Fort James by Edwin Link. The hands of the watch were frozen at 11:43 a.m., recording the time of the earthquake – a first for archaeology!

Port Royal never recovered from the 1692 earthquake. Several disasters in the form of fires and hurricanes followed over the next fifty years. Following a severe storm, a hurricane, and two earthquakes in 1722, the town went into a decline from which it never emerged. Today, as one walks along the narrow streets of the poor fishing village of Port Royal, it is hard to imagine that in the late 17th century it was the largest and most economically important English settlement in the Americas. Port Royal remains today as an isolated town of 1,800 inhabitants at the end of the spit across the harbour from Kingston, the present capital of Jamaica.

Equally important to the archaeology of Port Royal is the vast treasury of historical documents that survive in the archives, libraries, and public offices of Jamaica and England. Through the historic documents and the archaeological record, we are able to conduct a detailed study of Port Royal at the time of the town's destruction in 1692. Even though Port Royal is generally thought of as an underwater site, it is important to remember that it is a land site, a town that just happens to have some parts of it under water. However, because of the excellent array and preservation of the artefactual material the submerged sections of the town have attracted the most archaeological attention.

The first archaeological excavations worthy of the name were conducted by Edwin Link in 1956 and 1959 in the area where Fort James and Littleton's Tavern are submerged. Archaeologically, the Link excavations have relatively little value because of the excavation techniques used, although they did demonstrate the archaeological potential of the site.

The next series of underwater excavations were conducted by Robert Marx from 1966 to 1968. Marx's excavations were the most extensive and the artefacts he recovered comprise the single largest collection of material from the town. Most of the area he excavated was located along the former coastline of the town and much of this area of the town slid seaward as it sank into the harbour. Thus the buildings of this area are jumbled and the provenance of many of the artefacts is in doubt. The results of his excavations are presented in two popular books and various journal reports. The material

recovered by Marx continues to be studied and included in a series of theses and dissertations at a number of universities.

In the years between 1968 and 1981, there was a series of excavations on land, most of which have not been reported. The largest and most extensive land excavation was that of Philip Mayes, the first professional archaeologist to excavate at Port Royal. Mayes worked in the area of the old Naval Yard where most of the excavations were on 18th-century components and the sequential development of the base. Most significantly, he excavated a large part of the site of St Peter's Church which sank in the earthquake of 1692, and is now located 2.4 m below the surface.

Mayes was followed by Anthony Priddy, who in 1975 excavated a residential block on New Street located near the centre of the town. This area was occupied into the late 18th century and was densely packed with small buildings dating from the 17th century which survived the earthquake. A large amount of artefacts and architectural features dating from the 17th century were recovered, but it has never been adequately reported.

There were no excavations of note after Priddy until 1981, when Donny Hamilton of Texas A&M University in association with the **Institute of Nautical Archaeology** and the Jamaica National Heritage Trust started a ten-year underwater archaeology project in the business core of the town near the intersections of Lime Street with Queen and High Streets. The buildings located here were larger and much more substantial than those excavated by Priddy. The reports, theses, and dissertations on these excavations have produced the largest and most detailed body of data on all aspects of life in 17th-century Port Royal.

A total of eight buildings were excavated by Hamilton. The construction features of the investigated buildings exemplify a variety of architectural styles found in the centre of the town, which contrasts with the more compact, high-density area of the town excavated by Priddy. Some of the excavated buildings were well-built multi-storeyed brick structures, while others were simple earth-bound frame buildings hastily built with no intention that they should last for any length of time. In several instances a small core building was constructed, and then rooms were tacked on as the need arose, until the structure formed a complex. During the excavation of one brick building, it was found that a ship rammed through the front wall of the building skewing the walls and brick floor forward. The excavation of a ship that was rammed through a building by a seismic wave during an earthquake is another first for archaeology. It is believed that the remains of the ship might be *Swan*, which was being careened at the time of the earthquake and was tossed into the town. The data recovered are the most complete and significant information gathered on 17th-century town planning, architecture, diet, cooking activities, and other aspects of daily life at Port Royal. The emphasis on brick buildings contrasts with their general lack, or at least rarity, in other New World 17th-century English colonial sites. The array of recovered delftware, coarse earthenwares, Chinese porcelain, pewter utensils, glass stemware, lead and brass weights, tobacco pipes, hafted tools, cooking utensils, and faunal remains are impressive. The analysis and conservation of the material recovered from Port Royal continues. D.L.H.

ADDITIONAL READING

Dunn, R.S., 1972, *Sugar and Slaves: The Rise of the Planter Class in the English West Indies, 1624–1713*, New York.

Hamilton, D.L., 1992, 'Simon Benning, Pewterer of Port Royal', in B.J. Little (ed.), *Text-Aided Archaeology*, 39–53.

Hamilton, D.L. and Woodward, R.P., 1984, 'A Sunken 17th-Century City: Port Royal, Jamaica', *Archaeology*, 37, 1, 38–45.

Link, M.C., 1960, 'Exploring the Drowned City of Port Royal', *National Geographic*, 117, 1, 151–83.

Marx, R., 1973, *Port Royal Rediscovered*, New York.

Pawson, M. and Buisseret, D.J., 1975, *Port Royal, Jamaica*, Oxford.

Zahedieh, N., 1986, 'Trade, Plunder, and Economic Development in Early English Jamaica, 1655–89', *Economic History Review*, 2nd series, 39, 2, 205–22.

Porticello Wreck
see **Straits of Messina Wreck**

Positioning systems

Systems of determining the accurate positions of wrecks and wreck features; they are fundamental to any underwater archaeology field activity, whether a vessel search, aerial survey, or excavation. Some manual methods will be discussed, but most current positioning is done electronically as part of a computer-based data acquisition system that provides real-time navigation, collects, collates, and stores sensor data, and positions automatically. As more researchers incorporate systematic remote sensing data into **Geographic Information Systems (GIS)** formats, knowledge of positioning accuracy and digital collection parameters becomes critical

for accurate GIS functions. Although arbitrary grid systems may be adequate for some small surveys, geographic coordinates have become standard and increasingly necessary as GIS use becomes more common.

Research requirements should determine which of the many accuracy standards should be used. Past accuracy requirements have often been set by plottable accuracy. A pre-GIS rule was that an error smaller than about 1/10,000 was unplottable on a one metre sheet. Virtually any error can now be plotted by GIS programs that allow rapid scale change and zoom capabilities. Absolute accuracy, necessary for GIS applications, means production of geographic coordinates to a specific accuracy level for compatibility among data sets.

Accuracy is usually expressed as parts per units (e.g. 1:10,000) plottable accuracy; or as circle of error, which is an ellipse whose largest radius represents the root mean square error of a system (or set of measurements), and whose orientation shows directional uncertainty. The ellipse, centred on the true position, is typically at the 95 per cent statistical confidence level. The least squares method is becoming standard for positional accuracy determination. Inherent or instrumental accuracy is usually a device's optimum capability. Attainable accuracy is what the instruments provide under specific field conditions. Relative accuracy is repeatable accuracy. Some instruments, such as LORAN, may have low absolute accuracy, but usable repeatable accuracy for site relocation when using the same instrument.

Positioning systems can be shore-based, vessel-based, and satellite-based; they can be divided into visual, optical, electro-optical, and electronic. Many systems have been developed for different purposes, primarily ship navigation and geophysical survey: this discussion concentrates on those that have been used for, or that are appropriate for, archaeological applications.

Visual

Fixed locations can be repositioned using multiple shore-based ranges, which are pairs of permanent objects visible from the site. (European practice uses 'transits' for 'ranges'.) Ranges are selected such that precise visual alignment of shore objects produces a line of position across a target. An accurate fix requires at least two pairs of ranges; three are preferable. A vessel pilot can maintain a course by following a single range pair alignment. Concordance of range pairs and resulting lines of position produce the location fix. Temporary shore positions can be maintained to provide visual reference for navigation or search.

One problem encountered with ranges is loss or movement of range objects; geographic coordinates should be generated for any important location, and ranges should be photographically recorded.

A variation is to use **Trilateration**, which uses distance to determine fixes. A range finder measures distances to two or more known shore targets from the vessel. Stadiometers can also generate offshore distance and are quite accurate for distances less than 2,000 m. These instruments measure the observed height of a known shore object to determine offshore distance.

Optical

The simplest systems use optical instruments that measure angles: sextant, transit, and theodolite. Double horizontal sextant angles turned between three shore-based points have been successfully used for nearshore positioning from a vessel. Inexpensive plastic sextants with one-second resolution are available that will produce about 2 m of accuracy per kilometre from shore. Two sextant operators and a plotter can produce multiple positions per minute. Positions are plotted on a chart containing shore stations with a three-arm protractor or a station pointer to produce angle resection points. Relocation with sextant angles is difficult; two sextants make the job easier. Horizontal sextants were first used in this manner by Jeremy Green in 1969 during the survey of Cape Andreas, Cyprus.

A shore- or tower-based instrument operator in communication with a vessel can direct the vessel track along prearranged bearings. By far the most accurate instrument for this is the theodolite. Typical instruments measure angles with a resolution of 0.1 minute or better, and with 20–40 times magnification produce a view of 20–30 m at 1 km. Modern versions provide electronic readouts. Because bearings diverge as distance from the instrument increases, partial tracks must be planned at longer distances to maintain consistent transect coverage for surveys. While this method can ensure adequate coverage, positions are not produced unless distance (range) is collected. Geographic positions require horizontal control for the survey station.

Dual shore-based theodolites at each end of a baseline that approximates the vessel distance offshore can also generate positioning. Instrument and vessel operators must be in radio communication. Angles from the base line to the vessel are taken periodically at one operator's command. Horizontal control for shore stations allows generation of geographic coordinates. Accuracy generally exceeds dual sextants, and repositioning is easier with high relative accuracy. Both instruments set relocation angles from the baseline, and the vessel steers a course towards one instrument guided by the operator. When the vessel crosses the second instrument, the operator alerts the vessel to deploy a buoy.

Combinations of methods provide flexibility and accuracy. For example, a theodolite operator or range markers can be used to keep a vessel on course while periodic positions are collected by sextant or other means. For optical surveys, multiple techniques reduce mistakes and increase positions acquired per minute.

Electro-optical

These shore-based devices add distance measurements (ranges) to optical instruments. Laser or infra-red devices, called electronic distance measurers (EDMs), generate ranges electronically. EDMs generally use electromagnetic wave phase-measurement to determine time delay between signal generation and reception after reflection from a target, usually vessel-mounted prismatic mirror arrays. Some newer laser instruments incorporating inclinometer and optical fluxgate compasses do not require reflection to generate a range, azimuth, and elevation to target. Electronic total stations with automatic data collection and coordinate computation, known as electronic tacheometer instruments (ETI), are available with accuracies of 0.02 seconds and 1/200,000 over 1,000 m. Companies have combined a laser ETI with computer equipment to track the survey vessel automatically and telemeter geographic coordinates to the vessel in real time to be incorporated into the data acquisition system.

Electronic

Vessel-based

The most common vessel-based electronic positioning system is radar. Electro-optical instruments relying on reflected signals require ideal (calm) conditions and are difficult to use from a vessel. Radar can provide quick range and bearings from the vessel location to a shore-based target; when combined with the target's geographic position, this produces an absolute position. Radar ranges can maintain survey transects calculated as parallel distances offshore. Radars with ranges of 40 km or more have an accuracy of 1:5000–10,000. Radar bearings are generally much less accurate than ranges. Most radars can only measure a single range at a time, which reduces range/range measurement accuracy because of delays.

Developed in the 1960s, acoustic systems rely on seabed acoustic beacons or transponders that transmit signals to ship-based hydrophones. To produce geographic coordinates, a second positioning system must establish beacon locations; deep ocean surveys are thus generally more accurate relatively than absolutely. Searches for *Titanic* and *Bismarck*, and the USS *Monitor* documentation project of the mid-1980s relied on seabed positioning systems. Current deep-ocean systems have accuracies of 1–2 m and ranges to more than 20 km.

SHARPS (**Sonic High Accuracy Ranging and Positioning System**) is an acoustic system requiring hardwired surface connections and consequently is not applicable to dynamic vessel surveys. However, the system has been used by the **Institute of Nautical Archaeology** and the US National Park Service **Submerged Cultural Resource Unit** and others for site mapping. (A wireless version, EXACT, provides ten-times-per-second update with a 120 m range.) The Western Australian Maritime Museum developed a similar system called an acoustic EDM. The **National Geographic Society** and Woods Hole Oceanographic Institute has deployed the system to position remote operated vehicles (ROVs) for mapping and photogrammetric surveys. System resolution is 2 cm accuracy over 100 m. There are other systems, based on similar surface hardwired Sonardyne technology. At least one system, Datosonics' Aquanav, is not hardwired. Most systems have sub-centimetre accuracy. This technology still has a way to go; ideally it should be cheaper, wireless, and easier to deploy.

Diver-held sonar is becoming viable for accurate positioning. Some systems are in use as location devices – reflected sonar from near objects is read out as a variable pitch sound and digital range. Some units are sufficiently accurate to trilaterate to reflectors installed near a work site. Newer units with increased accuracy are applicable to archaeological applications. Lasers, particularly those in the blue-green range, also have potential for underwater use if ranging capability is developed.

Another important acoustic-based system uses a single vessel-mounted hydrophone and transponders placed on submersibles, divers, sites, or instruments. The wireless system produces range and bearing positions to the transponders at one metre accuracy. An example is ORE Trackpoint, which is often used to provide precise positioning of towed remote-sensing instruments during deep water surveys. Its ability to display multiple sensors has been used for surface tracking of complex diving operations using ROVs and submersibles. A variety of lower cost systems is becoming available.

Shore-based

Shore-based systems measure either phase or travel time of multiple-source electromagnetic waves to create lines of positions. LORAN C is a low-frequency (90–110 kHz), multiple-pulsed, phase-coded radio navigation system that measures sequenced signals from widely spaced transmitters. A primary station initiates a transmission sequence pulse, then two secondary stations respond. The receiver times arrival of the pulses in microseconds, known as time delays (TDs). A microsecond is equivalent to 983 ft (299.6 m); most receivers read to 0.1 microsecond.

The system, developed in the 1950s, became generally available on the US east coast after 1975 and remains widely used for vessel and aircraft navigation in the North Pacific, North Atlantic, Mediterranean, Persian Gulf, and Red Sea. There are plans to begin phasing out LORAN in the US after the year 2000, replacing it with the **Global Positioning System (GPS)**. Errors result from station geometry, weather, differences in land, water, and sky transmission speeds, daily and seasonal variables, interference, and reflection. Errors of 0.5 minutes may be consistent in an area, which reduces absolute accuracy to about a 500 m circle of error to a 2–4 km circle of error at 2,400 km. High repeatability, roughly 20–30 m, is possible. Consequently, LORAN is not sufficiently accurate for survey, but may be useful for site relocation.

Before the availability of GPS, microwave systems were state of the art for surveys within line-of-sight of shore. J. Barto Arnold's survey of the Texas coast for the 1554 Spanish Plate fleet (see **Padre Island Wrecks**) investigation was the first archaeological application of these systems. Microwave positioning uses receive/transmit stations on shore that respond to a vessel-mounted master station. The elapsed time of microwave round trips from master to shore stations produce range/range distances for generation of geographic coordinates in near real-time by computer, which also provides the pilot with graphic navigation information. Accurate geographic co-ordinates require precise horizontal control for the shore stations. Various station heights and high-gain antenna configurations allow operational ranges to 200 km, with an accuracy of a 2–5 m circle of error. Longer range units, some using VHF bands, have ranges to 800 km.

Some system drawbacks are determining appropriate locations for shore stations, which must be surveyed, and maintaining the stations' battery power. Full coverage of a study area requires line-of-site shore positions with offshore intersect angles between 50 and 150 degrees. Multiple station locations may be required. Motorola and Del Norte manufacture systems are often used for archaeological purposes.

Satellite-based

Satellite-based systems measure time signals from orbiting space vehicles. 'Transit' is a US Navy system that became available to civilians in 1967; Russia has a similar system called 'Tsicada'. There are six polar-orbiting satellites spaced such that a point is passed twice in twenty-four hours, which means a fix is available every one to two hours. Receivers measure the Doppler frequency shift of satellite transmissions to generate a position using satellite ranges based on a corrected satellite position. This system's geodetic capability is useful for positioning microwave shore stations to produce geographic coordinates. The NAVSTAR (NAVigation Satellite Time and Ranging) GPS system is replacing Transit and most other satellite navigation systems.

GPS has become the state of the art and will probably replace other systems for most applications. The US Department of Defense (DOD) developed the GPS system for military purposes; the Russian equivalent is GLONASS. These systems use **Trilateration** of satellite transmitted signals to determine position. GPS provides one-second updates with global coverage from twenty-one satellites, meaning four or more vehicles are continuously in view. The GPS is close to an ideal positioning system; it is accurate and continuously available on demand anywhere in the world under any weather conditions.

Autonomous civilian GPS receivers produce circles of error less than 30 m. The largest error component is known as 'selective availability' (SA), which is intentional dithering of the GPS signals by DOD that degrades the signal to an accuracy of 100 m. The satellites produce two signals, known as C/A code and P code frequency, the latter encrypted and available only to military users. However, real-time accuracy of 2–3 m is possible when using a base station to correct for SA and ionospheric propagation variables through differential GPS correction (DGPS). A base station set up on a surveyed point generates corrections and transmits them via a radio modem to the mobile survey instrument. Corrections with accuracies of 1 m are available from commercial suppliers, and the US Coast Guard is setting up stations throughout the US that will provide navigation accuracies of 10 m.

Geodetic controls of sub-centimetre accuracy can be obtained with GPS through static and kinematic survey techniques, which require occupation times of 2–40 minutes. The first archaeological application of GPS for geodetic control was by the US National Park Service **Submerged Cultural Resources Unit** in 1982. The latest GPS development to date is real-time kinematic (RTK) survey that produces sub-centimetre accuracy with dual frequency receivers and 5 cm with single-band receivers. RTK systems using multiple antennae that allow real-time position correction for vessel roll, pitch, and yaw produce the highest level of accuracy for hydrographic survey and represent the current state of the art. L.E.M.

ADDITIONAL READING

Arnold, J.B. and Weddle, R., 1978, *The Nautical Archaeology of Padre Island: The Spanish Shipwrecks of 1554*, New York.

Green, J., 1990, *Maritime Archaeology: A Technical Handbook*, London.

Potassium-argon dating
see Absolute dating

Precollegiate education

Courses and programmes for primary (elementary) and secondary schoolchildren that incorporate the principles and techniques of **Underwater archaeology**, appreciation of maritime history, and a sense of stewardship for related cultural resources. Since the late 1980s, institutions in the **United States**, Canada, and elsewhere have developed educational activities that use nautical archaeology and maritime history to teach younger students basic academic subjects and skills. These diverse programmes share a recognition that classroom instruction, educational curricula, and the learning process can be enhanced by studying maritime history and the methods of underwater archaeology. Because these programmes often focus on the local area, they teach young people to appreciate the resources around them. This, in turn, guides children towards understanding the larger roles that waterborne enterprise has played in the development of populations and cultures, as well as the issues that confront the preservation of maritime sites.

Several factors stimulated the emergence of activities for this audience. As university-based academic programmes in the discipline matured, the number of professionals able and willing to engage in public outreach increased. In addition, popular media began to emphasize the value of underwater sites as sources of cultural information rather than sources of **Treasure**, affording the public a more constructive view of maritime resources. However, two other concurrent trends were also vital ingredients: the rise of 'public archaeology' as a means of protecting and preserving archaeological sites, and various movements to improve school education. In some respects, the development of precollegiate nautical archaeology programmes cannot be understood outside the context of these two factors. K.C.S.

United Kingdom

There are no formal teaching programmes that incorporate underwater archaeology at primary or secondary level within schools. However, the UK National Curriculum does make reference to the use of archaeology as an important resource for History at Key Stage 2 (for children of 7–11 years). Also, maritime transport, overseas exploration, the **Spanish Armada**, and life in the merchant marine and the Navy are all mentioned within National Curriculum History topics for this age group in England; in Wales, 'Ships and Sailors' are an optional historical theme at Key Stage 2; and in Northern Ireland, shipbuilding, fishing, exploration, and trade are included in 'The Vikings'. The Scottish curriculum is less prescriptive, so although maritime topics are not specifically mentioned there is perhaps more scope to bring them into 'People in the Past' (i.e. history). At Key Stages 3 and 4 (11–14 years), historical themes include exploration and encounters, migration, and transport. In addition, many of the principles and techniques required in archaeological analysis can be used to cover Attainment Targets at these Key Stages, and the skills and techniques routinely used in archaeology cross over into a multitude of other subjects. In summary, the onus is on the teacher to incorporate archaeology into programmes at individual schools.

Archaeology is offered at GCSE, AS and A level, but not through all examination boards. In addition to period-orientated teaching of the Archaeology of the British Isles, the syllabus covers excavation methods, site interpretation and finds, site recording, finds conservation, heritage legislation, publication and dating. Although 'migration' and 'transport' are listed, there is no mention of nautical or underwater archaeology.

Although a number of museums offer archaeologically biased workshops, very few of these use underwater archaeology to stimulate visitors. The Mary Rose Exhibition in Portsmouth offers two pre-booked archaeological activities to school parties. These are designed to excite children into learning through the exploration of artefacts from the 16th-century shipwreck **Mary Rose**. In the 'Finds Bay', children are encouraged to be 'Time Detectives'. Acting as a 'Dive Team' they handle, record and discuss original and selected 'groups' of replica artefacts as though they are archaeologists on board the diving support vessel. Through the interrogation of primary evidence (diving records, a site plan, and the artefacts), they deduce what the objects are, and what function they may have had. Through observation and discussion they decide the possible trade of the person who owned the artefacts and his role on board the ship. The objects represent assemblages relating to the Cook, Archer, Pilot and Carpenter and include several items of reconstructed clothing, which can be worn. Each group makes a presentation of its findings to the others. Depending on skill levels, a personal archaeological record and object drawings may be completed. The second activity consists of excavating objects from a reproduction chest. The activity takes place in a small recreated gun-bay, dimly lit by a lantern. The objects within the chest suggest that the owner may have been a Gunner, and the group is then led through a mock gun drill using role play and a full-size model of a breechloading wrought-iron gun. A complete set of teacher's notes, exhibition worksheets (focused on the same characters), and follow-up work for the classroom is sent in advance of the visit.

Although primarily aimed at Key Stage 2 (7–11 years) to link into the 'Tudor Life' element of National Curriculum History, the activity can be stimulating for all ages and has been used by university students. The facility is made available to the general public on certain occasions. The activities are led by trained interpreters, many of whom are volunteers.

The Mary Rose Trust has also produced 'Outreach Packs' which are designed for use by children who cannot visit the *Mary Rose* Exhibition. The packs contain nineteen replica objects and additional resources such as books, posters, and a teacher's manual. They are deposited with ten education authorities around the United Kingdom and are available free of charge to schools. They are designed to be kept for a period of weeks, and consist of recording sheets, worksheets, illustrated source material, and many ideas for lesson plans, including the making of a scale model of a *Mary Rose* gun. There is great emphasis on archaeological skills, classification, analysis, sequencing, and evaluation together with drawing, measuring, and forming written reports. This is backed up with historical source material such as

copies of contemporary illustrations and descriptive text.

The Mary Rose Trust has also taken part in Young Archaeologists Day, organized yearly through the York Archaeological Trust's Young Archaeologists Club. Any young visitor is encouraged to participate in a number of tasks including simple surveying tasks on a simulated scattered wreck site. This is followed by the registration, recording, and drawing of the finds 'lifted'.

The National Maritime Museum in London has produced a video and teacher's resource pack entitled *Shipwrecks: Learning Through Underwater Archaeology*, designed to link in with the National Curriculum Key Stage 2 Attainment Targets in a cross-curricular format. The video explains the importance of underwater sites and demonstrates techniques of survey and excavation. The resource booklet is stimulating and educational.

Government heritage bodies are as aware as the archaeological community that education can be instrumental in preserving the cultural heritage both below and above water. The Department of National Heritage in England, CADW in Wales, Historic Scotland, and the Department of the Environment in Northern Ireland together fund the **Nautical Archaeology Society** Training Programme. This is primarily designed to educate divers in the skills of underwater archaeology. Even the introductory weekend course considers legislation, the difference between treasure-hunting and archaeology, and the need for conservation. Attendance is not restricted by age, but people partaking in diving must conform to their own federation's age restriction and must be the equivalent of CMAS 1 Star. The structure is modular, with courses ranging from **Remote sensing** to Tudor shipwrightry, with the emphasis on participation rather than spectating. The programme has been a great success, and courses are also available in the following countries: **Australia**, **USA**, Canada, Germany, Sweden, Holland, Switzerland, South Africa, **Mexico**, Belgium, and Turkey.

Underwater archaeology as a focus for diving-related activities is briefly covered in a number of Diving Federation manuals.

Education regarding legislation to protect both the owners of wrecks and the finders of wrecks is also undertaken. This is implemented by the Receiver of Wrecks and administered through the Coastguard Agency by means of presentations and attendance at diving and boat shows, backed up by a poster and leaflet campaign.

One annual conference is devoted to underwater archaeology. Held at Fort Bovisand in Devon, the first underwater archaeology weekend was in 1971. In this casual forum amateurs and professionals, archaeologists and archaeological salvors come together to present their work and to discuss their views. A.H.

United States of America

In the mid-1980s, archaeologists responded to a clarion call about the destruction of cultural properties through pot-hunting, treasure-hunting, vandalism, development, and ignorance. Recognizing the need to enlist the support of the lay public for resource protection, researchers began actively to involve **Avocationals** and volunteers in their projects and to encourage their participation in public decision-making. In the US, professional organizations such as the Society for American Archaeology and the Society for Historical Archaeology established education committees to promote public awareness of archaeological sites and provide resources for teachers, archaeologists, and interpreters. Federal agencies also developed public education initiatives, as mandated by 1988 amendments to the Archaeological Resources Protection Act of 1979. While most public involvement was geared toward terrestrial sites, aquatic resources were not ignored.

The passage of the **Abandoned Shipwreck Act** of 1987 caused a new wave of interaction between State historic preservation offices and recreational and commercial interests. Managers and researchers sought public involvement in the creation of publications, underwater parks and preserves, and preservation initiatives. To promote the value of submerged resources, particularly shipwrecks, underwater archaeologists offered workshops and conferences, and they also worked with diving organizations and clubs to find meaningful ways in which sport divers could contribute to scientific research.

Although many archaeologists were sceptical about public involvement, those who were committed were soon joined by site interpreters, museum and classroom educators, federal managers, and others in creating programmes and resources, not only for adults but also for children – the next generation of preservationists and decision-makers. Archaeology educators found that a few teachers had been using archaeology in their classrooms since the mid-1970s. More important, they discovered that many teachers were willing to explore the discipline as an instructional device, in part because of trends taking place in the field of education.

These trends were the result of a reform movement that swept the United States in the 1980s after the issue of several sobering reports about the poor quality of instruction in precollegiate social studies, history, and geography. To improve teaching and learning in these areas, educators were urged to adopt challenging, multidisciplinary core curricula; to move away from memorization and textbook-centred study; to develop methods to enhance critical thinking skills, co-operative learning, and the use of primary sources; and to highlight multicultural topics and contributions. Because of its methods, theory, and content, archaeology is ideally suited to meet these goals. Its interdisciplinary approach satisfies many core curriculum requirements – the skills and standards that students must achieve at given academic levels – in the primary precollegiate subjects of social studies, science, mathematics, language, and art. In addition, whether students are studying artefacts in a classroom or recording sites in the field, the interactive and experiential nature of archaeological activities tends to leave a stronger impression than information derived from textbooks.

Archaeological activities also promote critical thinking skills such as observation, inference, deduction, classification, analysis, sequencing, problem solving, and evaluation. Moreover, they enhance practical skills, from mapping and measuring to writing, drawing, and visualization, and many of these tasks must be completed cooperatively. Scientific processes of archaeology teach students about hypothesis, research, testing, and synthesis, and about the ancillary disciplines that contribute to research, such as geology, botany, and chemistry. In historical contexts, students discover the importance of primary materials as valuable sources of data. Finally, through the knowledge that archaeology yields about past populations – from the nature of societies to the consequences of behaviours – students become culturally informed and culturally aware. They also learn that they have a stake in the preservation of archaeological resources to ensure that information about the past is available in the future.

Programmes for children that focus on nautical archaeology and maritime history, although modest in number, are found all over the US. A semester-long course in San Francisco based on a shipwreck simulation, created by Marco Meniketti, provides an example. Meniketti's objectives characterize the effects and results that other precollegiate nautical archaeology programmes

Lake Champlain Maritime Museum conservator John Bratten explains the conservation process to visiting schoolchildren, pointing out the rare iron cannon undergoing electrolysis treatment. (Courtesy Lake Champlain Maritime Museum, Basin Harbour, Vermont)

strive to achieve. Measurable, criterion-based goals include acquainting students with principles and methods of archaeology, providing a conceptual model for archaeological processes, and imparting specific information about the era that the site (or sites) represents. Objectives relating to adolescent cognitive development include strengthening students' problem-solving and critical thinking skills; teaching students to appreciate teamwork as a crucial element of research; and teaching recognition of shipwrecks as archaeological sites and non-renewable sources of data.

The central component of Meniketti's simulation is a large-scale model of a galleon, complete with masts, sails, rigging, ballast, tiny cannon, and artefacts, which he builds and sinks in a tank at the onset of the course. During ensuing weeks, as students learn about archaeological theory and method through lectures and audio-visual presentations, they also observe the vessel's deterioration and the **Site formation processes**. Because they must ultimately identify the ship from five choices, student teams gather information from historic accounts and documents, study the historical periods of each candidate wreck, debate the merits of clues, and determine research questions and hypotheses. When the ship and the artefacts have become buried, the tank is drained, the site is gridded, and the students begin to excavate. Excavation takes several days, during which detailed unit maps are drawn to scale and a large site plan is created. Students are assessed on the basis of written reports. Students also spend two weeks creating Hypercard programmes on computers that allow them

to demonstrate mastery of concepts and knowledge.

A programme offered by the **Lake Champlain** Maritime Museum in Vermont also uses a simulated site. 'Digging, Diving, and Documenting: The Process of Nautical Archaeology' is one of several outreach and on-site projects that the museum uses to teach appreciation of maritime resources. Developed in 1993 by Laurie Eddy and other museum staff, 'Digging and Diving' is a two-and-a-half-hour experience at the museum, which teachers complement with classroom activities. The museum provides pre- and post-visit materials that enable teachers to prepare students for programme concepts and tasks; to assess student learning after the field trip; and, if they wish, to expand the unit to encompass other classroom topics. Although designed for grades 4 to 12, the programme has been presented successfully to adults.

During their museum visit, student teams examine **SCUBA** equipment and discuss the challenges of working and communicating under water, particularly in cold environments. The shipwreck simulator consists of a 4.8 m wooden rowing boat in a sand bed, over which a grid has been suspended. Student teams map assigned grid squares; gather information about artefacts and their scatter patterns; and document construction details that offer clues to the vessel's age, function, and demise. After the exercise, drawings from each grid are placed together to create a picture of the vessel and its contents. Through group discussion, students describe their findings, consider the significance of artefact distributions, and develop hypotheses about the wreck.

A companion activity that also emphasizes archaeological context is staged on the deck of *Philadelphia II* (see **Philadelphia**), a full-scale replica of an American gunboat that sank in battle against the British on Lake Champlain in 1776. Imagining that they are the hard-hat divers who recovered the original boat in 1935, students use contextual clues to identify and determine the meaning of artefacts and architectural elements.

'Hidden Beneath the Waves', a self-contained educational kit that is sent to schools, represents another genre of underwater archaeology programmes for children. It allows teachers to present nautical archaeology and maritime history even if field trips are not practicable. Developed in 1992 by Mark Wilde-Ramsing of the North Carolina Underwater Archaeology Unit, in association with educators and volunteers at the Cape Fear Museum in Wilmington, NC, the kit consists of an integrated set of classroom-tested activities, with introductory videotapes, which eighth-grade teachers borrow for four to six weeks. To prepare teachers, Wilde-Ramsing and museum staff conduct a one-day in-service.

Student teams are assigned one of six shipwrecks to investigate, based on actual sites in the area. Drawing on resources and documents in the kit, as well as independent research that they conduct in local libraries, teams record vital statistics about their wreck on a 'ship's log'. They also make a scale drawing; visit a museum or other location related to the site; and prepare a skit or rap song about some aspect of their vessel. Oral presentations at the end of the course inform other students about each group's findings. The kit's cornerstone activity is the 'Mystery Wreck Exercise' in which students identify a mystery wreck from about twenty candidates using artefacts, geographical and cartographical details, and a scale model.

A summer camp with a nautical archaeology theme was developed in 1989 by K.C. Smith of the Museum of Florida History in Tallahassee. 'From Dugouts to Doubloons: The Maritime Heritage of Florida' is an annual, week-long programme for 12 to 16 year-olds that combines classroom and field experiences. The programme tends to be flexible, with fast-paced, hands-on activities. The camp's objectives include acquainting children with research methods and techniques, heightening appreciation for Florida's maritime traditions, and instilling a sense of stewardship for underwater sites. While educational motives are not specifically targeted, many of the week's activities involve critical thinking skills, group learning, and multi-disciplinary topics.

Using replicas and unprovenanced shipwreck artefacts, Smith creates a 9 by 4.5 m 'mock site' in the classroom. Campers discuss the identity, distribution, and meaning of objects and features, and develop hypotheses about the people and cargo on board. To learn basic mapping and recording techniques, they establish a rope grid over the site, and a two-person team is assigned to each grid square. Children who finish their mapping quickly use books and

Philadelphia II. *(Courtesy Lake Champlain Maritime Museum, Basin Harbor, Vermont)*

resources in the classroom to try to date artefacts on the site.

The highlight of the week is a three-day trip to the Pensacola (Florida) Bay area, where participants visit a conservation laboratory, use a visit to Fort Pickens to assess the role of coastal fortifications in the defence of local waterways, and tour a modern warship. However, the focal point of the trip is the examination of several shallow-water shipwreck sites, where snorkellers put into practice the recording skills that they learned in class.

The four resources described above are among the more elaborate and well-established nautical archaeology programmes for young people, but they are not the only examples in the US. Twice a year the Texas Seaport Museum in Galveston offers a two-and-a-half-hour workshop called 'Maritime Mystery' which involves children in a simu-

lated shipwreck mapping activity. The Newport Beach (California) Maritime Museum is planning to institute a maritime education programme for grades K–12 that will include archaeology and anthropology components for grades 7 to 9. In creating these activities, executive director Sheli O. Smith adapted several programmes that she had previously presented at the Los Angeles Maritime Museum. Pam Wheat of the Texas Historical Commission is developing teacher in-service and student materials to complement the commission's current excavation of the French shipwreck **La Belle**. The Louisiana Division of Archaeology has assembled a classroom travelling kit with artefacts and hands-on exercises based on **El Nuevo Constante**, a Spanish wreck off the coast.

Conclusion

The diverse resources designed to bring nautical archaeology and maritime history to children generally share two important attributes. They are based on sound pedagogical theories and strive to provide challenging, child-centred experiences. In addition, in sharing underwater archaeological method and theory with young people, they emphasize not only underwater archaeological methods and the significance of archaeological sites, but also the personal role that young people can play in assuring the preservation of submerged cultural resources. K.C.S.

ADDITIONAL READING

United Kingdom

Corbishley, M., 1983, A*rchaeological Resources Handbook for Teachers*, London.

Corbishley, M. (ed.), 1992, *Archaeology in the National Curriculum*, York.

Council for British Archaeology, 1997, *GCSE and A Level Archaeology syllabuses*, Factsheet no. 7, York.

Council for British Archaeology, 1995, *The British Archaeological Yearbook*, York.

HMSO, 1991, *History in the National Curriculum*, London.

National Maritime Museum, 1993, *Shipwrecks: Learning Through Underwater Archaeology*, Greenwich.

Newbury, E., 1996, *What Happened Here? Tudor Warship*, London.

United States

Meniketti, M., 1993, 'Shipwrecks in a Bottle: A Simulation Strategy for Teaching Nautical Archaeology to Adolescents', in J. D. Broadwater, (ed.), *Underwater Archaeology Proceedings from the Society for Historical Archaeology Conference, Richmond, Virginia*, Ann Arbor, Michigan.

Nobles, C.H., Eddy, L.T., and Meniketti, M., 1995, 'Teaming Up to Teach Archaeology', in

Paul F. Johnston (ed.), *Underwater Archaeology Proceedings from the Society for Historical Archaeology Conference, Washington, DC*, Ann Arbor, Michigan.

Smith, G.S. and Ehrenhard, J.E.,1991, *Protecting the Past*, Boca Raton, Florida.

Wilde-Ramsing, M., 1995, 'North Carolina's Underwater Archaeology Educational Program: Hidden Beneath the Waves', *Public Archaeology Review*, 3, 1–2, 27–9.

Prehistoric archaeology

The investigation of the material remains and the environmental context of human cultures undocumented by written records, with the goal of reconstructing past lifeways and culture. Underwater investigation oriented to questions of prehistoric adaptations and movements of the human species is arguably one of the last great tasks in archaeology; certainly, it is one of the least developed. Its importance is clear. Maritime adaptations have played a role in our species' survival since at least the times of *Homo erectus*, as evidenced by shellfish gathering at Terra Amata during the middle Pleistocene (about 200,000 years ago). The use of littoral and marine resources also seems to have intensified during the critical social-cultural transition of the Mesolithic, as human societies began experimenting with new forms of social and economic organization, such as large-scale sedentary settlements and exploitation of semi-domestic crops and animals. Occurring during the last part of the Upper Pleistocene and early Holocene (from about 15,000 to 8,000 years ago), during a period when sea-levels were much lower (by more than 100 m in many regions), the Mesolithic is also the period in which the earliest evidence for ocean vessels and navigation is found. It is speculated that **Sea-level changes**, rising in most regions during the late Pleistocene to early Holocene period, were an important variable in the development of coastal Mesolithic and Neolithic village aggregations. Holocene (or post-glacial) rising sea-levels have certainly inundated a range of coastal sites not represented in the current dry-land archaeological record. More hypothetically, the early movement of prehistoric peoples, such as from Africa to Europe, Southeast Asia to Australia, and Eastern Asia to the New World, might best be explained by coastal migrations (see **Coastal migration theory**). The primary evidence for such migrations would now lie upon submerged paleo-shorelines. In all these cases, there are no written documentary remains to provide evidence and they remain largely unattended-to arenas of prehistoric archaeology.

Underwater explorers have recovered prehistoric artefacts haphazardly over the years, increasingly so since the widespread introduction of **SCUBA** technology in the 1950s. As early as 1915, for example, divers in California recovered pottery and **Lithic** (stone) **artefacts** in the shallow waters off San Diego. Pleistocene fauna remains have been regularly recovered over the years by drag-net fishers off the coast of the American Northeast and in the **Baltic Sea**, and Neolithic artefacts discovered on the seabed in the near coastal waters of the **Mediterranean Sea**. All such remains were spurious discoveries, however, in so far as they were accidental finds which were collected without archaeological control of their full environmental context. It was not until the 1970s that a few archaeologists began seriously to conduct field research on the potential of underwater remains to contribute to our interpretation of the prehistoric past.

This is not to say that archaeologists were unaware of this potential. There is a close and productive relationship between archaeology and the earth sciences; the data of archaeology, artefacts and the sites in which they are found, are embedded within and affected by local, regional, and world geological processes. Most archaeologists working within coastal areas have long been aware of the fact that changes in sea-levels throughout the Quaternary (approximately the last two million years) has undoubtedly affected the visibility and accessibility of the coastal archaeological record and that considerable archaeological evidence of human occupation must necessarily lie within the boundaries of the submarine continental shelf. However, most archaeologists have restricted the integration of this fact with their research methodologies to searching for archaeological sites along now terrestrial remnants of higher sea-level strand lines. Besides the difficulty of physically accessing similar locations under water, many have generally assumed that the dynamic geological processes associated with the inundation of terrestrial deposits by rising sea-levels are fundamentally erosionary in nature. If so, any archaeological remains which might be located underwater would fail to meet the disciplinary standard of site integrity (a recognizable stratigraphic and unambiguous association between artefacts and stratigraphy levels) necessary for confident interpretation; thus many archaeologists are sceptical whether the costs of the resources required to locate, excavate, and analyse underwater prehistoric remains are worth the effort.

This view is being challenged by a genera-

tion of researchers eager to expand the discipline into new arenas of intellectual challenge. Much of the recent research is exploratory and often equivocal, but the participants are aware of the need for the refinement of existing and development of new methodologies and procedures of analysis which address the unique context of underwater archaeology. Thus, for example, attention is being directed towards the actual, rather than the assumed, processes of coastal inundation and the identification of conditions of sediment deposition which might preserve archaeological remains (see **Site formation processes**). Such studies suggest that while erosion of a site does occur during the initial period of transgression by the sea, sites below about five to ten metres of water tend to accumulate sediments which provide protection from further erosion.

Most of the archaeologically sponsored research on prehistoric underwater deposits through the 1970s and 1980s was directed towards the development of predictive models of potential site location. The historic symposium sponsored by the Scripps Institution of Oceanography in October 1981 in order to 'bring together scholars of oceanography, archaeology, geology, and anthropology to examine intensively the factors determining human movements on the continental shelves during glacial low sea-levels', resulted in the first major publication on the topic (see Masters and Fleming). In the ensuing decade and a half since that meeting, some progress in developing a 'prehistory of continental shelves' has been made by a still small coterie, through generating theories and testing of methodologies for the location, excavation, and analysis of submarine archaeological sites of a variety of ages and conditions. Many important challenges remain to be resolved, however.

Prehistoric sites

The discovery of prehistoric sites underwater has occurred in three principal ways: through accidental discovery, most often by sport divers; by survey and excavation of areas immediately offshore existing terrestrial coastal archaeological sites; and through the application of increasingly sophisticated site prediction models and systematic survey on postulated paleo-shorelines.

Accidental discoveries have predominantly recovered isolated surface finds as opposed to sites, generally presumed to lack archaeological context. However, spatial distribution of such finds within a defined area can be analysed with methods similar to those applied to terrestrial surface finds, as was done with the distribution of stone mortars of the La Jollan culture (9,000–3,000 BP) off the southern Californian coast. Surface finds may also represent eroded and transported remains, signifying additional prehistoric deposits within the sediments they lie upon or nearby.

The examination of offshore areas of known terrestrial sites allows a measure of controlled comparison of inundated with dryland deposits within the same local geophysical zone, providing an opportunity for recognition of site formation factors and the development of methods of analysis. This has been the principal orientation of excavations at **Montague Harbour**, British Columbia.

Site prediction models have been applied in several areas, perhaps most extensively in the American Gulf of Mexico as part of the legislated mitigation requirements for offshore oil development. Such models examine the undersea topography with a view to the reconstruction of paleo-shorelines and apply a similar land-use pattern as recorded in the terrestrial archaeological record to predict where sites might have been located during times of lower sea-level. The limited success of these models in locating underwater sites may reflect the paucity of such sites or continuing theoretical and technological barriers to the ready identification of sites by the relatively simple models of paleo-shoreline reconstruction and the **Remote sensing** of site signatures by sonar and **Sub-bottom profiler** technologies.

However they are found, prehistoric underwater sites present additional challenges in recovery and understanding. In shipwreck excavation, the principal interest is in the ship as an artefact in itself and its contents as representative of the period of its use. In prehistoric sites, the environmental and relational contexts of cultural remains are critical to an interpretation of their use; thus, stratigraphic control or clearly recording horizontal and vertical relationships between sedimentary levels, artefacts, ecofacts (such as fauna and flora), and their relative ages is essential. The application of standard archaeological excavation procedures to accomplish this is possible in still-water conditions, as found in the **Warm Mineral Springs** site in Florida. However, anyone who has dug in seaside sands will realize that the more dynamic fluid environment created by a variety of ocean currents requires methods to mitigate the tendency for submarine deposits to seek their own level. The use of retaining walls has been shown to mitigate sediment slumpage into submarine excavations. Within such containment walls, vertical provenance control can be accom-

plished by arbitrary excavation of sequential levels of 10–30 cm of depth and horizontal provenance control by triangulation.

Sophisticated laboratory analyses have been developed for the interpretation of archaeological deposits. These include a range of sedimentological analyses, such as grain size, shape, and wear, and the identification of chemical and petrological constituents, which provide clues to the depositional processes at work on the site. The identification of micro-organisms, such as diatoms, **Foraminifera** and pollens, provide an appreciation of climatic factors, such as temperature and salinity. Large organic remains of flora and fauna may suggest local environments, cultural use, and possibly trade. Such analyses require samples which are statistically representative of the site, and more importantly the levels within it, in order to ensure both validity and reliability of extrapolations from the sample to the level or site as a whole. Core samples, of a meaningful size (20 sq. cm) of each excavated level are undoubtedly the most effective way of achieving this.

Similarly, there exists a wide number of technical analyses which may be applied to recovered artefacts. In prehistoric sites, these tend to be stone tools, or lithics, but they also include organic artefacts. Descriptive analysis examines the form of artefacts, while morphological analysis proposes their function. Descriptive data generates an appreciation of both the norm and the range of variation present in artefact classes and, by applying the principles of seriation, may order their change through time. Such data can also be compared with that of other sites, often allowing for the relative dating of a level containing a specific artefact type through cross-dating. Such dates are necessarily of low accuracy, allowing us to say only that it is younger, older, or about the same age as that with which it is compared.

More accurate dating of prehistoric sites is possible through some form of chronometric dating, principally radiometric, the most common being radiocarbon dating, although its effectiveness is limited to about 80,000 years. Organic artefacts of bone, antler, or wood may themselves be dated to the time of their death and presumed use by humans. Lithic artefacts cannot themselves be dated directly; instead organic remains found in association with artefacts are dated. 'Direct' association, as in the lithic being embedded in an animal bone, provides the greatest reliability that the organic date and the lithic date are truly covalent. Failing this, 'indirect' association with a suitable radiocarbon sample from within the same arbi-

trary or stratigraphic level is used; the further the distance the lower the reliability that the date of the sample is related to the date of the artefact.

The radiocarbon content of organic materials from the ocean is subject to two important confounding phenomena which must be taken into consideration. The first is known as the 'marine reservoir effect', caused by the contamination of the sample by the residual carbon content of the water. Measurement of this effect has been calculated for gross regions of the world; however, fluctuations from the regional estimate and that actually existing at a specific locality within it can be several hundred years and may contribute to apparent or real reversals in stratigraphic chronologies within a site. The continued refinement of calculations of the marine reservoir effect within local areas of research is needed.

The second important confounding phenomenon is the **Benthic bioturbation** caused by marine organisms within underwater sediments and their effect on the integrity of archaeological deposits. This is a subject of critical, though to date limited, field study.

The analysis of any prehistoric site requires a theoretical reconstruction of its excavated areas, extrapolation to the remainder of the site unexcavated, and the attempt to explain the distribution and relationship of its natural and cultural elements. The more data that are available to be integrated into the analysis, the more likely that the reconstruction will represent the actually occurring sequence of events. To date, few underwater excavations have incorporated the full range of available archaeological analyses which might assist in this reconstruction.

This is changing, however. The latter half of the 1990s will see the completion and publication of comprehensive analyses from a number of prehistoric sites which will undoubtedly establish new standards within prehistoric archaeology under water.

Nevertheless, the rate at which progress in this subject occurs will continue to be slow until more resources are harnessed to investigate the questions it poses. While the discovery and exploration of deep water continental shelf prehistoric sites is perhaps decades away yet, there remains much necessary research which can be undertaken on or which is related to sites currently known. Of fundamental importance is the orientation to and training of established and emerging archaeologists in the problems and methods of the study of underwater prehistoric archaeology, as well as an expansion of the inter-disciplinary capacity of research projects. Basic field research projects are essential to explore the actual conditions of variables involved in site formation processes, both biological and geological, and to test and refine paleo-shoreline models. Mechanically, the identification of remote signatures of archaeological sites and the development of increased electronic sensitivity to them in sub-bottom profiler technology may be feasible within this decade. Legislation and policy integration of submerged prehistoric sites with coastal resource management regimes is lacking in most countries.

Clearly we remain some way from a 'prehistory of the continental shelves' of the world, but there are exciting indications that the further immersion of archaeology to explore this frontier will soon generate important results. N.A.E.

ADDITIONAL READING

Johnson, L.L. and Stright, M., 1992, *Paleoshorelines and Prehistory: An Investigation of Method*, Boca Raton, Florida.

Kerber, J.E., 1991, *Coastal and Maritime Archaeology: A Bibliography*, Metuchen, New Jersey.

McGrail, S., 1987, *Ancient Boats in Northwest Europe: The Archaeology of Water Transport to A.D. 1500*, New York.

Masters, P.M. and Fleming, N.C., 1983, *Quaternary Coastlines and Marine Archaeology*, New York.

Preserve Our Wrecks (Kingston)
see **Ontario marine heritage organizations**

Pre-university education
see **Precollegiate education**

Prince de Conty

One of the few wrecks of the French East India Company that have been archaeologically investigated. Another example is *Saint-Geran* (1744) which was discovered off the Island of Mauritius in 1979. The wreck of *Prince de Conty* lies off the southern headland of Belle Isle, Brittany, in western France. *Prince de Conty*, a vessel of 600 tons, was lost in December 1746 only a few miles from its home port of Lorient after a voyage to China, Indonesia, and Brazil. In 1747 the company tried to salvage guns and ballast pigs with help from English prisoners and a diving bell. The cargo of tea and porcelain was no longer retrievable as it had been dispersed and damaged by storms. The wreck was relocated through archival research and in 1985 an archaeological excavation began. Several tens of thousands of sherds of blue and white Chinese porcelain from the Qian long period (1736–95) were recovered. The finds were of very fine quality and disproved the general idea that

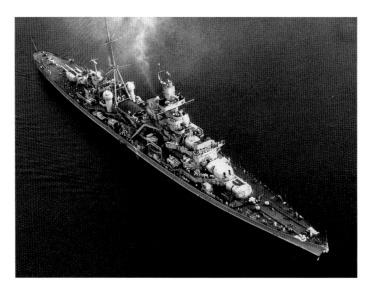

Opposite: Wreck of Prinz Eugen *lying partially submerged on the reef at Enubuj Island. (National Park Service/D.J. Lenihan)*

porcelain which was exported to Europe consisted of inferior products. They also allowed refinement of the dating system of these ceramics. The artefacts showed a large variety of essentially European shapes combined with typical Chinese decorations. The only archaeological remains of the tea cargo were some fragments of wooden chests lined with lead and a mass of brownish vegetable shreds. The wreck also contained trunks of *Pterocarpus santalignus*, an Asian dyewood which served as red pigment. Two types of small ingots of Chinese gold were found which were similar to those from the VOC ship *Geldermalsen* (see **Nanking Cargo Wreck**). They weighed 368.7 to 375.2 g and bore inscriptions of Chinese characters or ideograms. M.L.'H.

ADDITIONAL READING

L'Hour, M. and Richez, F., 1989, 'Le voyage inachevé du *Prince de Conty* (1746), vaisseau de la Compagnie des Indes Orientales', *Neptunia*, 173, 27–33.

L'Hour, M. and Richez, F., 1990, 'An XVIIIth century French East-Indiaman: the *Prince de Conty* (1746)', *International Journal of Nautical Archaeology*, 19, 75–9.

Prinz Eugen

A German heavy cruiser that now lies partially submerged on a reef at Kwajalein Atoll, in the Marshall Islands of Micronesia. *Prinz Eugen*, an Admiral Hipper Class heavy cruiser, was built at Krupp Germania Werft, Kiel, Germany, and commissioned on 1 August 1940. Named after Prince Eugene of Savoy, it displaced 14,800 tons, was 654 ft (199.4 m) in length, with a main armament of eight 8 inch guns in four turrets. *Prinz Eugen* is remembered primarily for scoring the first hits on HMS *Hood* while accompanying **Bismarck** on its ill-fated sortie into the

North Atlantic in May 1941. On 7 May 1945 *Prinz Eugen* surrendered to the British at Copenhagen, and was eventually turned over to the United States. On 17 June 1946 it joined a group of ships at Bikini Atoll (see **Crossroads Wrecks**) to serve as a target ship for a series of atomic bomb tests under the code name 'Operation Crossroads'. After surviving two bomb blasts *Prinz Eugen* was towed, along with approximately fifty other target ships, to Kwajalein Atoll, where the ships were anchored in the lagoon and inspected for bomb and radiation effects. On 22 December 1946, after developing leaks and being beached, this once-proud warship rolled over on its starboard side and sank on the reef at Enubuj Island, just northwest of Kwajalein Island.

Prinz Eugen is still an impressive sight, lying with part of its stern, rudder, and two propellers protruding above the water's surface, its bow at a depth of 33.5 m. Its sleek profile, gun turrets, and advanced fire-control equipment can be seen in the clear water where visibility often exceeds 30 m. A radiation survey in 1970 determined that the wreck poses no radiation hazard. Diving historians have documented the wreck, and in 1989 the US National Park Service's **Submerged Cultural Resources Unit** documented the wreck as part of a survey of ships participated in Operation Crossroads at Bikini Atoll. J.D.B.

ADDITIONAL READING

Bailey, D.E., 1992, *WWII Wrecks of the Kwajalein and Truk Lagoons*, Redding, California.

Broadwater, J.D., 1974, *Kwajalein: Lagoon of Found Ships*, Middlesboro, Kentucky.

Burdick, C., 1996, *The End of the Prinz Eugen (IX 300)*, Menlo Park, California.

Delgado, J.P., 1996, *Ghost Fleet: The Sunken Ships of Bikini Atoll*, Honolulu.

Dickey, G.L., Jr, 1969, 'The End of the *Prinz*',
    US Naval Institute Proceedings, August, 149–51.
Schmalenbach, D.P., 1971, *Kriegsmarine Prinz
    Eugen*, Warship Profile No. 6, Windsor.
Sieche, E.F., 1989, 'The German Heavy Cruiser
    Prinz Eugen: A Career under Two Flags',
    Warship, 49, 44–8.

Professional ethics

The ethical values and practices that form part of the professional standards of underwater archaeological practice. Underwater archaeologists, though they work on submerged sites and with techniques and technology that are often quite different from those of their terrestrial colleagues, share the ethical stance of land archaeology, a stance developed during more than a century of fieldwork on land. The ethical challenges particular to underwater archaeology derive in large part from the unusual nature of underwater sites, especially shipwrecks, and the commercial desirability of even the most mundane objects removed from such sites.

Underwater archaeologists work as government and agency specialists, curators, educators, and cultural resource consultants. Along with other professionals, they share specialized training and expertise, a high degree of autonomy, prestige, and a largely self-regulating organization. Also like members of other professions, underwater archaeologists provide important services to society, in the form of knowledge, education, and information needed for public policy decisions.

Professional standards in underwater archaeology have been evolving during the life of this relatively young discipline, and, as with other professions, ethical values in underwater archaeology are being formulated by its practitioners, who see their primary ethical obligation as belonging to the discipline of archaeology, not to the values of society in general; in fact, the latter may be at odds with professional values. Dilemmas and challenges arise when professional ethics come into conflict with other values espoused by a society with multiple interests. Archaeological ethics begin with the basic fact that archaeological sites and objects, whether on land or underwater, are the fragile, finite, and non-renewable material vestiges of the human past. As such, they represent important, and sometimes the sole, material evidence for vast segments of human history and experience. Archaeologists refer to archaeological remains as cultural resources, cultural heritage, or the archaeological heritage.

From these primary considerations emerge two basic principles of all professional archaeology: first, archaeologists study the shared cultural heritage of humanity, and the obtaining and provision of this knowledge is fundamentally in the public interest; and second, because of the fragility of the archaeological resource base, archaeological work must be conducted within a conservation ethic, not an ethic of exploitation. These primary archaeological values in turn lead to other important principles.

Archaeologists in the late 20th century have increasingly argued that the advancement of knowledge about the past is a public interest and that serving that public interest is a primary ethical duty. Archaeologists stress the obligation to provide access to archaeological data and findings to the public through articles, books, exhibitions, and education; and to colleagues and other researchers through data sharing. Many archaeologists also serve the public interest by offering their expertise in matters such as legislation and development policies.

The central value of stewardship – protecting and conserving the archaeological resource base – involves other important considerations. One is the principle of non-commerciality: archaeologists refrain from buying and selling artefacts, and from supporting commercially motivated ventures, because commercial interests result in the exploitation and destruction of the resource base as sites are looted to provide artefacts for the market. Another critical archaeological value linked to the conservation ethic is the importance of curating archaeological data, records, and artefacts in publicly accessible repositories. Permanent curation allows for public access and education, for reassessments of published findings, and for future research.

Underwater archaeologists share these general values with other archaeologists, but the special nature of underwater archaeology can generate certain ethical dilemmas seldom encountered in land archaeology. The fragility of archaeological sites and artefacts in an underwater environment imposes particular responsibilities on the excavator. The recovery of submerged artefacts without adequate facilities for their **Conservation**, for example, would be a clear violation of the conservation ethic. Another example is the partial **Excavation** of underwater sites, where agents of decay might be unintentionally introduced and adversely affect the integrity of the remainder of the site. Even the seemingly innocuous activity of underwater archaeological survey may have ethical consequences for the archaeologist, since the discovery of new underwater sites may lead to their eventual disturbance or destruction by treasure-hunters and site vandals.

The most visible conflicts are between underwater archaeology and **Treasure-hunting**, where scientific and historical interests are ignored by treasure-hunters, divers, and others concerned solely with the commercial value of objects removed, legally or illegally, from archaeological resources. These commercial interests enjoy a broad degree of public popularity, technological capabilities, investment-capital funding, and a misapplied historical tradition of maritime salvage (see **Salvage law**) supported by legal authority and sanction.

Much recent debate has centred on the ethical propriety of archaeologists collaborating with underwater salvors and treasure-hunters. Those who favour collaboration argue that, given the legality and popularity of commercial salvage, archaeologists must make the best of an undesirable situation and acquire whatever fragmentary data can be obtained in the circumstances. Archaeologists opposed to collaboration counter that participating in treasure-hunting violates the conservation and curation ethics, harms the public interest, and promotes uncritical public support for treasure-hunting by lending professional credibility to salvage projects. In recent years consensus has emerged that professional archaeologists must eschew collaboration with treasure-hunters; collaborators risk professional censure.

The protection of a dwindling underwater resource base from development and commercial predation is likely to remain the central challenge to underwater archaeologists in the future. Professional ethics in underwater archaeology will continue to evolve as the field further defines its values in the face of pressures from government, developers, employers, and commercial salvors. R.E.

ADDITIONAL READING

Archaeological Institute of America, 1994, 'Archaeological Institute of America, Code of Professional Standards', in K.D. Vitelli (ed.) *Archaeological Ethics*, Walnut Creek, California.

Elia, R.J., 1992, 'The Ethics of Collaboration: Archaeologists and the *Whydah* Project', *Historical Archaeology*, 22, 4, 105–17.

Institute of Field Archaeologists, 1988, *By-Laws of the Institute of Field Archaeologists: Code of Conduct*, Birmingham.

Lynott, M.J. and Wylie, A. (eds), 1995, *Ethics in American Archaeology: Challenges for the 1990s*, Society for American Archaeology Special Report, Washington, DC.

Society of Professional Archaeologists, 1988, 'Code of Ethics and Standards of Research Performance: Guide to the Society of Professional Archaeologists', in K.D. Vitelli (ed.), *Archaeological Ethics*, Walnut Creek, California.

Propwash deflection

A technique for excavating shipwrecks in shallow water. Propeller wash deflection was first largely reported by Florida treasure-hunters seeking a quick means to expose sand-buried shipwrecks. Variously known as a 'blower', 'duster', or 'mailbox', the system employs a custom-made solid metal cover that pivots over the transom of the boat, fits over the propeller(s) and angles toward the bottom. When the vessel is moored, the engines are revved to create a strong blast of water that pushes away sand and sediment, excavating the bottom. Effective in shallow water, propwash deflection can excavate a crater up to 7.5 m deep.

Propwash deflection, while fast, is not a tool for delicate **Excavation**. It is an effective tool for removing bottom sediments, but not for scientific, archaeological excavation. Keeping a stratigraphic record of artefacts is impossible, and many lighter artefacts are usually displaced by the heavy volume of water from the aptly nicknamed 'blaster'. As the pit excavated by the propwash deflection grows, larger and heavier artefacts also become displaced and tumble to the bottom of the excavation. Some archaeologists have employed propwash deflection to remove sand after coring has shown a substantial overburden of sand over cultural materials, or to expose more modern, sand-buried wrecks.

Sites excavated with propwash deflection, with some criticism, have included most Florida wrecks from the **Flota of 1715** and **Flota of 1733**, as well as early wrecks, such as *Nuestra Señora de Atocha* and *Whydah Galley*. J.P.D.

ADDITIONAL READING

Mathewson, R.D., III, 1986, *Treasure of the Atocha*, New York.

Meylach, M. and Whited, C., 1986, *Diving to a Flash of Gold*, Florida Classics Library, Port Salerno, Florida.

Protection of Military Remains Act (UK)

United Kingdom legislation of 1986 for the protection of the sanctity of military wrecks containing **Human remains**. The Act applies to certain vessels which have sunk or stranded while on military service, and any aircraft which has, at any time, crashed while in military service. Under the Act it is possible for the Secretary of State for Defence to designate a particular vessel, even if its location is not known, and also to designate certain areas as controlled sites. Both types of designation apply in the United Kingdom, in the territorial waters of the United Kingdom, or in international waters. However, in international waters offences under the Act will only be committed if the acts or omissions constituting the offence are committed on board a British-controlled ship, or by a British national.

Before the 1986 Act, the term 'war grave', although commonly used, had no formal significance or legal basis. Nonetheless, it was exploited by the Ministry of Defence to discourage diving on wartime wrecks. In the early 1980s the conflict with Argentina over the Falkland Islands heightened the British public's sensitivity concerning the sanctity of human remains. This fact, together with unauthorized interference with HMS *Hampshire*, which sank during World War I with the loss of many military personnel, made the Ministry of Defence realize that its unofficial war graves policy needed to be put on an official footing.

Under the 1986 Act the Secretary of State for Defence may designate any military vessel which sank or stranded on or after 4 August 1914, the outbreak of World War I. This includes vessels which were on British military service and vessels which were in the military service of another state, where those remains are in United Kingdom waters. The Act establishes 'protected places' to encompass the remains of all aircraft which have crashed while on military service and also the remains of designated vessels. Such protected places will, however, only be established in the United Kingdom, United Kingdom waters, or international waters. Under the Act it is an offence, *inter alia*, to tamper with, or damage the remains, or enter any hatch or other opening in the wreck, without the authority of a licence. Excavation, diving, and salvage operations are prohibited, if carried out for the above purposes. Liability for these offences depends on whether the defendant believed, or had reasonable grounds for suspecting, that the place comprised remains of a military aircraft or vessel. The reason that liability depends upon a particular state of mind is that the location of protected places will usually be unknown and divers will therefore have no means of checking whether or not they are entering a protected place.

In cases where the location of an aircraft or vessel is known, it is possible for the Secretary of State to designate an area as a 'controlled site'. This provision applies only where it appears to the Secretary of State that less than two hundred years have elapsed since the crash, sinking or stranding of the aircraft or vessel. Again, it is an offence, *inter alia*, to tamper with, or damage the remains, or enter any hatch or other opening in the wreck, without the authority of a licence. Excavation, diving, and salvage operations are prohibited if carried out for the purpose of investigating or recording details of any remains on the controlled site. In contrast to a protected place, the offences in relation to controlled sites are not dependent upon a particular state of mind on the part of the defendant. The location of controlled sites will be published in the Statutory Instrument designating the site and will be taken to be public knowledge. Therefore, a diver who interferes with remains in a controlled site, whether or not they have actual knowledge that the site is designated under the Act, will commit an offence.

The Secretary of State for Defence has power to grant licences authorizing that which would otherwise be an offence and conditions may be imposed upon the licence for the purpose of protecting or preserving remains. Licences will be issued without prejudice to the rights of any owner of an interest in the remains. Usually the owner of a military wreck will be the Crown (whose rights will be exercised by the Ministry of Defence), or an overseas government, but some individuals may have bought military wrecks, or salvage rights in military wrecks, from the original owner. Such rights are retained *vis-à-vis* any licensee. Where licensees do not have ownership rights, they retain their ordinary salvage rights and are required to declare material brought ashore in the United Kingdom to the Receiver of Wreck under the Merchant Shipping Act 1995. In the case of British military remains administered by the Ministry of Defence, it was stressed in the parliamentary debates on the Act that a licence under the Act is not a salvage contract, but that separate salvage contracts could be negotiated with the Ministry of Defence. Also, during the debates, an assurance was given that authority under the 1986 Act to dive would not be 'withheld unreasonably from genuine scientific and archaeological research groups'.

The Act makes one further provision which may have wide implications for divers and marine archaeologists. Excavations anywhere in the United Kingdom or United Kingdom waters are prohibited if they are undertaken to discover whether the place comprises any remains of an aircraft or vessel which has crashed, sunk, or been stranded while in military service. This provision relates to all aircraft or vessels on military service, whenever the casualty took place. Taken at its widest, it appears to prohibit any archaeological excavations on a wreck which either is, or may be, a military vessel (of any nationality), since one purpose of such excavations inevitably will be to establish the identity of the vessel. If this is the case, where there is any possibility that a wreck may have been a military vessel, a licence should be obtained under the Act before archaeological excavations take place.

A person guilty of an offence under the provisions of the 1986 Act may, in certain cases, be liable to pay an unlimited fine.

The provisions of the 1986 Act may be applied to World War I and World War II aircraft and shipwrecks and, in the case of controlled sites, wrecks up to 200 years old. Clearly, therefore, this may include wrecks of historical significance. Although not its specific purpose, the Act could in practice provide significant and valuable protection

to such wrecks. Its provisions in some respects are wider than those of the 1973 **Protection of Wrecks Act**, the statute specifically designed to protect wrecks of historical importance. First of all, the 1986 Act extends protection to aircraft, which the 1973 Act does not, and therefore provides a mechanism for protection of historic military aircraft, especially those which have crashed at sea. Secondly, under the 1986 Act it is possible to designate wrecks without knowing their location and therefore afford them protection from the moment their location is first discovered. By contrast, under the 1973 Act it is necessary to know the position of a wreck in order to designate it. Furthermore, a wreck cannot be afforded designated status under the 1973 Act until its 'historical, archaeological or artistic importance' has been assessed, which may be some considerable time after its discovery. In the meantime, it could be tampered with freely. Finally, whereas the 1973 Act applies only to United Kingdom waters, the 1986 Act provides some measure of protection for the wrecks of British military vessels situated in international waters. S.D.

ADDITIONAL READING

Dromgoole, S., 1996, 'Military Remains on and around the Coast of the United Kingdom: Statutory Mechanisms of Protection', *International Journal of Marine and Coastal Law*, 23–45.

Dromgoole, S. and Gaskell, N., 1993, 'Who Has a Right to Historic Wrecks and Wreckage?', *International Journal of Cultural Property*, 2, 217–73.

Protection of Wrecks Act (UK)

United Kingdom legislation for the protection of wrecks of historical, archaeological, or artistic importance. The Act's sole aim in respect of historic wrecks is to control salvage operations on certain sites of special importance and to secure the protection of these wrecks from unauthorized interference. The Act also includes a provision prohibiting interference with certain dangerous wrecks.

The Act was precipitated by the growth in popularity of sport diving in the 1970s which led to the discovery and plundering of certain wrecks of immense historical importance. These wrecks included the Dutch East Indiamen *Hollandia*, *de Leifde* and *Amsterdam*, and the wreck of *Mary*, a yacht belonging to King Charles II. However, it was the plight of HMS *Association* that was the eventual catalyst. This British warship was returning home in 1707 from a successful campaign in the Mediterranean when she struck rocks near the Scilly Isles and

sank. She was carrying a large quantity of gold and silver coins. When the wreck site was discovered in 1967, news of the find was reported in the press and amateur and professional divers from all over the world converged on the site. The extent of the damage and looting was such that, when the 1973 Act came into force, the site of *Association* was no longer considered worth protecting.

The Act provides for the designation of sites in United Kingdom territorial waters which are, or may prove to be, the site of a wreck which – on account of its historical, archaeological, or artistic importance – ought to be protected from unauthorized interference. Designated sites include those of King Henry VIII's flagship, *Mary Rose*, which sank in 1545, and the Dutch East Indiaman *Amsterdam*, which was wrecked in 1749. A more recent vessel deemed worthy of designation is *Iona II*, a passenger ferry which sank in 1864. A restricted area, varying from 50 to 300 m, is imposed around the wrecks. Within this area it is an offence, *inter alia*, to tamper with, damage, or remove a wreck lying on or in the seabed, or to carry out diving or salvage operations to explore such wrecks, without the authority of a licence. Someone who causes or permits any of the above to be done by others without the authority of a licence also commits an offence. The Act makes provision for an emergency designation order to be made in a case of immediate urgency where, for example, a wreck has recently been located and has become subject to interference from, and conflict between, different diving teams. Such orders can be implemented within a matter of days and at a later stage revoked if found to be unwarranted.

Licences will be granted only to persons who appear to be competent and properly equipped to carry out salvage operations in a manner appropriate to the importance of the wreck. In practice, this has included amateur as well as professional diving teams and in many cases the licensee will be the finder of the site. In general, licences are issued annually for the diving season. A licence may be granted subject to conditions or restrictions, and may be varied or, in extreme circumstances, revoked. In practice, two types of licence are issued: first, a licence to survey and, secondly, a licence to excavate. The aim of the licence to survey is to test the ability of the licensee to work in a disciplined manner. Such a licence precludes the raising of any part of the wreck or any artefacts, except for small items which may help to identify or date the wreck. Applicants for a licence to survey must prove that they have access to archaeological expertise in the form of a named archaeological adviser, who can verify the information recovered but who need not be a diver. The requirements for an excavation licence are more rigorous than those for a licence to survey. Generally, excavation licences are only granted once the site has been fully and satisfactorily surveyed. An excavation director must be nominated who should have underwater archaeological experience and be prepared to take an active on-site role in directing and supervising the excavation work. Details must be submitted of an operations programme and of the resources and equipment available to the team. A conservation specialist must also be nominated, and on-site and support conservation facilities must be available. At the end of the diving season, a licensee must submit a detailed report of work undertaken, including duration of time spent on the site, methods of operation, equipment used, and a log of finds. The issue of a further licence to the licensee depends, to a large extent, upon a satisfactory report being submitted promptly. Licensees are encouraged to publish their findings. It is an offence for any person to obstruct, or cause or permit the obstruction of, a licensee in carrying out authorized diving or salvage operations. A licence therefore provides the licensee with exclusive rights to work on a particular site and protects the licensee from interference by competing diving teams.

A person guilty of an offence under the Act may, in certain cases, be liable to pay an unlimited fine.

The award of a licence under the 1973 Act does not affect ownership rights. Where licensees do not themselves have ownership rights in a wreck, they retain their ordinary salvage rights and are required to declare material brought ashore in the United Kingdom to the Receiver of Wreck under the Merchant Shipping Act 1894 (as amended by the Merchant Shipping (Salvage and Pollution) Act 1994). This Act provides a one-year period in which ownership claims can be made. If items remain unclaimed after this period, the practice is that they will either be returned to the licensee (or other finder) in lieu of a salvage reward, or sold and the full proceeds paid as a salvage reward. This practice deprives the Crown of its statutory right under the 1894 Act to the unclaimed wreck.

The 1973 Act is administered by the Department of National Heritage, advised by a committee of experts. This non-statutory committee meets three times a year to select sites to recommend for designation and to consider licence applications and renewals. A full-time archaeological diving team provides the department and the committee with first-hand information concerning sites. The primary responsibilities of the diving team are to examine and assess the importance of specific undesignated sites with a view to their designation and to assess the work of licensees on designated sites. A secondary role is to provide licensees with advice in order to encourage high standards of survey and excavation work. S.D.

ADDITIONAL READING

Dromgoole, S., 1989, 'Protection of Historic Wrecks: The UK Approach', *International Journal of Estuarine and Coastal Law*, 4, 26–51, 95–116.

Dromgoole, S. and Gaskell, N., 1993, 'Who Has a Right to Historic Wrecks and Wreckage?', *International Journal of Cultural Property*, 2, 217–73.

Prudent
see **Louisbourg Wrecks**

Puerto Rico

Island in the Caribbean Sea. The Underwater Archaeological Council of Puerto Rico, instituted in 1987 under Law 10 of the Estado Libre Asociado de Puerto Rico, is currently involved in the compilation of a registry of submerged archaeological sites within the island's coastal waters. Archival research has produced in excess of 200 shipwrecks in the area of Puerto Rico. To date, nautical archaeologists have recorded twelve sites.

Two projects, ongoing since 1991, include an unidentified 18th-century vessel and *Alicante*, a Spanish steamship that sank in 1881 off the southwest coast of the island. Several shipwrecks in Cerro Gordo, a small bay located on the northern coast, have led researchers to hypothesize that the area was a centre, albeit of small scale, for ship construction between the 17th and 19th centuries.

The Underwater Archaeological Council is currently working to procure adequate conservation facilities for future research projects. The office of Historic Preservation of Puerto Rico has nominated to the **National Register of Historical Places** the Spanish steamship *Antonio Lopez*, which sank off the north coast of Puerto Rica in the Spanish–American War of 1898. R.F.A.

ADDITIONAL READING

Cardona Bonet, W., 1989, *Shipwrecks in Puerto Rico's History, I: 1502-1650*, Puerto Rico.

Fontánez Aldea, R., 1993, 'Documentación del pecio El Alicante, La Parguera, Puerto Rico: Proyecto de registro de sitios', *Actas del XV Congreso Internacional de Arqueología del Caribe*, San Juan.

Pulaski Site

Site of a wreck on Pulaski Shoals in the Dry Tortugas. It was found in 1993 during the **Dry Tortugas National Park** survey conducted by the **Submerged Cultural Resources Unit** (SCRU), under the direction of Larry Murphy. The site was documented as part of project collaboration between SCRU and Brown University; Donna Souza was principal investigator. The observed seabed distribution contained within the Pulaski Site covers an area of approximately 12,000 sq. m. Other features determined to be associated with the site are located as far as 450 m away. Diagnostic elements observed at the site, such as anchors, anchor-chain cables, and hawsepipes, indicate that this site is the wreck of a square-rigged merchant sailing vessel of approximately 350 to 400 gross tons that dates from the mid- to late 19th century. The wreck has been tentatively identified as that of the American brigantine *Shannon* built in Millbridge, Maine in 1867 and lost in 1892.

Materials observed include a large steam-operated windlass, a steam-operated capstan, a small steam engine, and a donkey boiler. The steam engine has been identified as a type originally designed for small textile or farm auxiliary equipment. Other artefacts documented at this site include an abundance of frame fasteners and drift bolts, chainplates and rigging, tools, bitts, and winches. This is a significant site because it contains what is arguably the richest archaeological assemblage of deck machinery and related hardware of any shipwreck site known so far from this era and represents a crucial period in the development of steam-operated deck machinery during the transition from sail to steam.

The Pulaski Site was used by researchers at Brown University as the centrepiece of a comparative study of six shipwreck sites in the Dry Tortugas that addressed interrelated issues pertaining to 19th-century merchant marine technology and the capitalist system in which that technology functioned. In explaining the persistence of sail in the age of steam, the project explored the impact of economic demand factors in the bulk cargo trade and their relationship to anomalous rates of change in the adaptation of newly introduced technologies. The archaeological investigation and the data gathered during the project provided a sufficient data base to begin to analyse the cultural, economic, and technological factors that dictated the persistence of sail in the age of steam and why the sailing-ship building industry of the 19th century was especially resistant to change. It was determined that the sailing vessels that operated through the Dry Tortugas during this period carried bulk cargoes and operated in trades such as lumber and coal that produced low economic returns, but in order to turn a quicker profit, operated at high risk by taking short-cuts through areas known to be hazardous, overloading, keeping vessels in service longer than their safe use life, and by cutting costs on repairs and maintenance. Furthermore, as sailing vessel tonnage began to decline and steam tonnage continued to increase, the merchant sailing industry responded by integrating steam technology with existing deck machinery to operate rigging and ground tackle allowing them to operate larger vessels with fewer crew members. These innovations adapted to existing types of machines allowed the merchant sailing industry to compete economically with steamships while maintaining a traditional way of life under sail. D.J.S.

ADDITIONAL READING

Souza, D.J., 1997, 'The Persistence of Sail in the Age of Steam', Ph.D. thesis, Brown University, Providence, Rhode Island.

Gould, R., 1995, 'The Bird Key Wreck, Dry Tortugas National Park, Florida', *Bulletin of the Australian Institute for Maritime Archaeology*, 19, 2, 7–16.

Murphy, L.E. (ed.), 1993, *Dry Tortugas National Park Submerged Cultural Resources Assessment*, Santa Fe.

Punic Warship

see **Marsala Punic Warship**

Quanzhou Ship

A large sea-going wooden ship excavated in August 1974 from the shore of Hou-Zhu harbour, Quanzhou Bay, Fujian Province, China. Coins found on the site date the ship to the last decade of the Song Dynasty (AD 960–1279). The ship's hull was preserved from the waterline down, but all superstructure and deck planking had disappeared. Even so, the surviving portion of the intact hull was massive, measuring more than 24 m in length and 9 m in width. The excavators believe that its original length would have been about 35 m and its breadth about 10 m. The ship was unearthed in a field which had been a navigable waterway, but which had been covered by land in the seven centuries that had passed since the ship sank. It was dismantled and reassembled in a special exhibition hall within the compound of the Kaiyuan Temple in the city of Quanzhou, where it is the central exhibit in the Museum of Overseas Communication History. When details of the discovery were published, Western authorities on Chinese maritime architecture were astounded. Instead of the flat-bottomed, bluff-bowed, shallow-draft vessel they expected, the Quanzhou Ship displayed a deep V-shaped bottom, two-part keel, pointed bow, rectangular stern, and a hold divided into thirteen compartments by twelve bulkheads.

Disassembly of the ship revealed its remarkable construction details. It had been fastened with thousands of iron nails and hundreds of iron 'dogs' shaped like giant staples. Steps for the foremast and mainmast were found resting on the ship's keel in the first and sixth compartments respectively. The ship had no keelson. Iron L-shaped brackets and wooden frames like those used in the West held the bulkheads in place. The thirteenth compartment housed and protected the rudder, and was open to the sea. The rabbeted clinker-built hull is unlike any other ever discovered. The planking was two layers thick between the keel and the tenth strake, and three layers thick from the tenth strake to the main wale. The edge-to-edge joins between the strakes of the planks of the innermost layer were rabbeted, while those of the second and third layers were not. In addition, the planks in the first ten strakes were 'stepped' every third strake, giving the appearance of clinker construction, but without any strake overlap. The intricately fitted hull planks were covered with a water- and corrosion-proofing material called *chu-nam*.

The original carrying capacity of the ship was estimated at more than 200 tonnes. Artefacts on board (betel nut, cowries, peppercorns, aromatic wood, and turtle shell) seem to indicate that the ship was plying the trade route between the central coast of China and Southeast Asia. Quanzhou is the modern name for the port that Marco Polo called Zaitun. It is the same port that Columbus was hoping to find when he set out on his first voyage. With its unique well-preserved hull and revealing collection of artefacts, its careful excavation and reconstruction, and its artful display the Quanzhou Ship is without doubt one of the principal treasures of maritime archaeology and history. D.H.K.

ADDITIONAL READING

Green, J., 1983, 'The Song Dynasty Shipwreck at Quanzhou, Fujian Province, People's Republic of China', *International Journal of Nautical Archaeology*, 12, 3, 253–61.

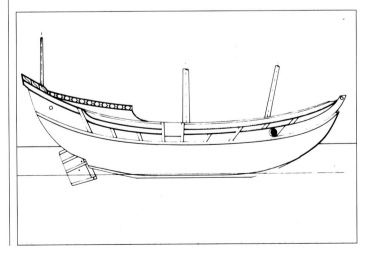

Reconstruction of the Quanzhou ship's profile. (Drawing by D. Keith)

Keith, D.H., 1979, 'A Fourteenth-Century Cargo Makes Port at Last', *National Geographic*, 156, 2, 230–43.

Keith, D.H., 1980, 'A Fourteenth Century Shipwreck at Shinan-gun', *Archaeology*, 33, 2, 33–43.

Keith, D.H. and Buys, C.J., 1981, 'New Light on Medieval Chinese Seagoing Ship Construction', *International Journal of Nautical Archaeology*, 10, 2, 119–32.

Li Guo.Qing, 1989, 'Archaeological Evidence for the Use of 'Chu-nam' on the 13th-century Quanzhou Ship, Fujian Province, China', *International Journal of Nautical Archaeology*, 18, 4, 277–98.

Merwin, D., trans., 1977, 'Selections from Wenwu on the Excavation of a Sung Dynasty Seagoing Vessel in Ch'uan-chou', *Chinese Sociology and Anthropology*, 4, 3, 6–106.

Needham, J., 1971, 'Civil Engineering and Nautics', *Science and Civilisation in China*, 4, 3.

Quaternary coastlines and land bridges

Former land areas now submerged due to post-glacial rises in sea-level. During the Pleistocene, periods of glacial building resulted in lower global sea-levels. The lower sea-levels exposed large areas of the continental shelves, resulting in altered coastline positions and land bridges between some land masses currently separated by the sea. The most recent glacial stage, the Wisconsinan or Würm, reached its last glacial maximum at approximately 19,000 BP (17,000 BC).

For any given area, the combined effects of eustatic sea-level change, isostatic adjustment, and tectonics have caused the position of the shoreline to change through time. Eustatic sea-level refers to the absolute changes in sea-level that result from water being removed from the ocean basins during glacial building, or added during glacial melting. Eustatic sea-level at the late Wisconsinan glacial maximum was approximately 120 m lower than present sea-level.

Isostatic adjustments refer to the differential depression or uplift of the earth's lithosphere in response to the weight of glacial ice and the amount of water in the ocean basins. The lithosphere beneath the areas formerly covered by glacial ice rebounded as the ice melted. The area of uplift around the margin of the ice masses, known as the glacial forebulge area, collapsed as the weight of the ice was released. The ocean basins subsided as a result of water loading due to glacial meltwater, and the continental margins uplifted in response to this subsidence. When these isostatic adjustments of the earth's lithosphere are combined with the effect of eustatic sea-level change and

with tectonic factors such as vertical movements along fault planes and subsidence from sediment loading, a very dynamic picture of global paleoshoreline positions emerges.

Data on former shoreline positions are obtained through radiocarbon dating of organic material from past shoreline features. A compilation of these age/elevation data points for a given geographic area is called a relative sea-level curve. In formerly glaciated areas that experienced isostatic rebound, shoreline positions from the glacial maximum are now tens to hundreds of metres above present sea-level. In areas far removed from the glacial ice masses, the glacial maximum shoreline position is well below the present sea-level. In areas not affected by isostatic adjustments or tectonics, the late Wisconsinan glacial maximum shoreline position will reflect only the drop in eustatic sea-level, and will be close to 120 m below present sea-level.

To determine where submerged archaeological sites might exist, it is first necessary to consult local relative sea-level curves. These curves allow determinations to be made regarding which areas were above sea-level and available for human habitation. Although the physical and cultural remains of prehistoric people might occur anywhere along these former land surfaces, archaeological sites are most often associated with landforms such as rivers, lakes, and embayments that fulfil basic human subsistence needs.

Archaeological sites exposed at the sea floor can be detected by **Side scan sonar**, followed by diver or remotely operated vehicle (ROV) investigations. Sites buried beneath the sea floor can be detected by **Sub-bottom profiler** which images the buried land surface and detects landforms with which sites are likely to be associated. Standard sedimentary analysis techniques can detect indicators of a buried archaeological site, even in the absence of recognizable artefacts.

Submerged Quaternary coastlines and land bridges are archaeologically important because archaeological sites located along these submerged features can provide information that is not available from terrestrial sites. Most sites that would demonstrate early prehistoric human adaptations to coastal environments are now submerged. Likewise, land bridges that would have provided easy migration routes between current land masses are also now submerged. Although raised Quaternary coastlines do exist, there may be few archaeological sites associated with these features because the rapid rate of isostatic rebound may have pre-

cluded the development of stable coastal ecosystems necessary to support human populations. M.J.S.

See also **Sea-level changes**.

Quebec Bateaux

The remains of eight bateaux discovered during the autumn and winter of 1984–5 and excavated for the Quebec Museum of Civilization in Quebec City. The excavation of the bateaux, the recording of three of the boats, and the recovery of portions of the boats was accomplished under the supervision of archaeologist Daniel La Roche in extreme field conditions. Frozen ground, inclement weather, and a flooding site kept workable by constant pumping plagued the archaeologists. The bateaux were found close together, on the buried former bank of the St Lawrence River, and beneath the foundation of a quay and a house built between 1751 and 1752. The five craft, all in deteriorated condition, were apparently abandoned on the site prior to 1751 and subsequently buried. The Quebec bateaux, along with the **James River Bateaux** and the **Wiawaka Bateaux Cluster**, are the only excavated and documented examples of these once common river craft in North America. J.P.D.

ADDITIONAL READING

La Roche, D., 1987, 'The Small Boat Finds at the "Musée de la Civilisation" in Quebec City', in A.B. Albright (ed.), *Underwater Archaeology Proceedings from the Society for Historical Archaeology Conference, Savannah, Georgia*, Ann Arbor, Michigan.

Quetico-Superior sites

A group of submerged sites representing spilled fur trade artefacts in the waters of the lakes and streams along the Minnesota (US) and Ontario (Canada) boundary. The **Great Lakes** of North America, the St Lawrence and Ottawa rivers, and thousands of smaller lakes and streams form an interconnected series of waterways rich in fur-bearing animals. Beginning in the late 16th century, and continuing to the early 19th century, the fur trade of North America was centred in this region, and led to the development of an ingenious system of communication and transportation based on the birchbark canoe.

In three centuries of fur trade activity, a number of canoe accidents spilled trade goods, traps, supplies, and weapons into the water, some of them in rapids or deep pools where they could not be retrieved. In 1960 the late Edward W. Davis, a University of Minnesota professor and fur trade specialist, convinced three **SCUBA**-divers to look for traces of the fur trade in the rapids along the old Grand Portage fur trade route, which stretched between the Canadian provinces of Manitoba and Ontario to the state of Minnesota. The divers searched Horsetail Rapids on the Granite River, 80 km northwest of Grand Marais, Minnesota, and promptly found a nest of seventeen complete brass kettles which are probably attributable to a British North West Company fur trade loss. This discovery spurred a thirteen–year initiative, the Quetico-Superior Underwater Research Project, which involved **Avocational** divers, archaeologists, and historians in Canada and the United States between 1960 and 1973. The project was organized by historian Robert C. Wheeler of the Minnesota Historical Society, and co-directed by the late Walter A. Kenyon, then with the Royal Ontario Museum in Toronto. The early work was in part funded with grants from the **National Geographic Society**.

The project, which has been aptly termed 'white-water archaeology', was marked by fast, turbulent waters and exceptional discoveries, many of them from crevices or deep pools where the currents did not carry the spilled goods away. The fresh water and burial in bottom sediments contributed to a usually excellent level of preservation. Few trade goods from the fur trade have survived in museum or private collections, and the artefacts have added considerably to our understanding of the material culture of the fur trade. Work on the project involved plotting and mapping discoveries, some excavation using an **Airlift**, and recovery.

Among the discoveries made were two bundles of thirty iron files, lead bale seals, brass kettles, kaolin trade pipes, iron axe heads, Northwest muskets, gun flints, lead musket balls, iron chisels, iron spears, a pewter trade pipe, beads, buttons, pigment, brass thimbles, glassware, knives, tin dishes, a spiked tomahawk, numerous wooden and birchbark canoe parts, shoes, and ceramics; in short, an extensive study collection for an important trade that had until then left little trace other than placenames, historical accounts, and occasional reminders of portages on land. One interesting discovery, recovered from the Granite River portage in June 1962, was the concreted and fused remains of what appeared to be a lost hunting pouch. The concreted mass, after conservation, held an iron axe blade, gunflint, gun worm, musket balls, what may have been a muskrat spear head, and lead shot.

The Quetico-Superior Underwater Research Project was one of the first underwater archaeological investigations in the United States, and attracted considerable public and professional attention. The project's directors organized the first underwater archaeological conference in the United States, in 1963, attracting an international audience, and set the stage for many fruitful years of work and professional development that followed. J.P.D.

ADDITIONAL READING

Olson, S. and Boyer, D.S., 1963, 'White Water Yields Relics of Canada's Voyageurs', *National Geographic*, 124, 412–35.

Wheeler, R.C. *et al.*, 1975, *Voices from the Rapids: An Underwater Search for Fur Trade Artifacts, 1960-1973*, St Paul, Minnesota.

R

Radiocarbon dating
see **Absolute dating**

Rapid

Early 19th-century American China trader wrecked on the northwest coast of Western Australia in 1811. The China traders of the early 19th century were the pride of the American fleet: they had to be large well-founded, speedy vessels for this rich but highly competitive and rigorous trade. *Rapid* is the first example of an outward-bound American China trader to be given archaeological attention, so aspects of that trade can now be re-examined from the archaeological perspective.

The 366 ton *Rapid* was built for the China trade at Braintree, just south of Boston in 1807, and sailed on its first voyage to China in 1809. A similar enterprise was undertaken the following year. The owners advertised, seeking the loan of Spanish dollars, and then loaded with 280,000 Spanish dollars. The intent was to buy cargo in China rather than to trade in goods, so no substantial cargo was loaded.

Rapid departed Boston for Canton on 28 September 1810. After rounding the Cape of Good Hope the vessel sailed across

Bell and coins from Rapid. *(© Western Australia Maritime Museum/Patrick Baker)*

Aerial photo of the Rapid site.
(© Western Australia
Maritime Museum/Patrick
Baker)

Underwater survey of Rapid.
(© Western Australia
Maritime Museum/Brian
Richards)

the southern Indian Ocean and then north-east towards North West Cape on the Australian coast. It looked like being a fast voyage, but disaster struck on the ninety-eighth day, when *Rapid* crashed onto the reef at Point Cloates. The next day a storm was raging and the crew set fire to the ship, sacrificing everything so that the wreck would not appear above water and attract other ships to the scene before the Captain could return to save the $280,000. The twenty-two crew sailed to Java in the ship's boats, and from there returned to Philadelphia. Another vessel was sent from Philadelphia to the Western Australian coast to salvage the treasure.

The wreck was found by a spearfishing group in 1978. During three seasons of excavation between 1979 and 1982 archaeologists from the Western Australian Maritime Museum under the direction of Graeme Henderson surveyed the ship's timbers and removed the artefacts from within the hull, including some 20,000 remaining Spanish silver dollars.

The excavation provided a picture of the life on board one of these fast ships. Ship's fittings, provisions, and the personal possessions of crew members had survived in reasonable condition on the site. The hull survey provided sufficiently comprehensive data for the lines of the vessel to be reconstructed, giving information about a vessel type often referred to in the literature but never comprehensively described. G.H.

ADDITIONAL READING

Henderson, G., 1981, 'The American China Trader *Rapid* (1811): An Early Western Australian Shipwreck Identified', *The Great Circle*, 3, 2, 125–32.

Reader's Point Wreck

British merchant sloop dating to the late 18th century, excavated off the north coast of Jamaica. The Reader's Point vessel is one of six colonial shipwrecks in St Ann's Bay discovered by archaeologists from the Jamaica National Heritage Trust and the **Institute of Nautical Archaeology** at Texas A&M University. These sites indicate that the bay was utilized as a ship graveyard where derelict vessels were scuttled after long careers as merchant traders.

The Reader's Point sloop is the first of these vessels to be excavated. Hull remains are well preserved below deck, measuring 59 ft (18 m) in length and 15 ft (4.5 m) wide. Evidence of wear, numerous repairs, and damaged timbers attest to the heavy use typically expected of these vessels. Most of the valuable objects had been removed from the ship before it was scuttled, although sufficient artefacts remain to indicate that the vessel sank around the time of the American Revolutionary War. Identifications of the wood used in the construction of the vessel suggest that the ship was built in North America, probably on the northeast coast. Most of the repairs, however, are made from tropical hardwoods, implying a substantial amount of trading in the West Indies and Central America. Sloops plying the coastal and island trades played a major role in the commerce of colonial economies. They provided a lifeline for small plantations hungry for manufactured items and affordable transport for raw goods to profitable markets. G.D.C.

ADDITIONAL READING

Goldenburg, J., 1976, *Shipbuilding in Colonial America*, Charlottesville, Virginia.

Baker, W.A., 1966, *Sloops and Shallops*, Barre, Massachusetts.
Chapelle, H.I., 1967, *The Search for Speed Under Sail*, New York.
MacGregor, D., 1980, *Merchant Sailing Ships, 1775–1815; Their Design and Construction*, Annapolis, Maryland.

Reconstruction

The reassembly or recreation of watercraft. The term most commonly applies to the interpretation of the remains of shipwrecks or abandoned vessels. Reconstruction can range from a few details and dimensions of sparsely preserved wrecks to museum reassemblies and sailing reproductions of well-preserved ships or boats. In its broadest sense, however, the reconstruction of watercraft encompasses far more than structural data and assemblies. Details concerning builders and crews, cargo stowage, operation, and even the demise of some vessels might be included in their reconstructions.

Most reconstructions begin with archaeology. In fact, ship and boat reconstruction is taught as a sub-discipline of nautical archaeology in some academic programmes; it has also become part of the curriculum of many other maritime-related institutions. Regardless of the nature of the wreck site, the success of any reconstruction is dependent on the archaeological and research procedures that produce it. Most of the world's shipwreck excavations and surveys have produced sparsely preserved hull remains. Such timbers frequently remain on the bottom after they have been recorded, the wreck being covered with a protective overburden. Bottom recording is often limited because most of the hull surfaces that are pressed against the seabed (usually the outer hull surfaces) cannot be documented. Nevertheless, whatever is visible must be documented completely; no hull remains are so sparse that their record is unnecessary. In fact, some reconstruction is usually possible even where nothing of the hull has survived. Cargo distribution, artefacts, and the vessel's anchors or machinery often provide clues about the ship's dimensions and arrangement.

The process of recording wrecks that remain on the seabed includes detailed drawings, sketches, and photography. Dimensions of individual planks and timbers, identification of wood samples, related artefactual material, and site distribution round out the documentation of wrecks that have survived poorly. In cases where hull remains are removed from the site for study, conservation, storage, or display, seabed recording is less demanding because minute details are better recorded in the good visibility and more comfortable surroundings of a laboratory. However, site records, especially photographs and drawings, are still a necessity.

No matter where the recording of hull timbers is conducted, the results must include as complete a set of structural specifications as is possible and as many drawings and photographs as are necessary to produce a thorough reconstruction. This means that those who are recording wrecks should have a thorough knowledge of hull construction of the period represented by the wreck. Where hull remains present a previously unrecorded form of architecture, shipbuilding knowledge is equally imperative so that nothing is overlooked. Details of ship and boat construction have been published for most historical periods; for the last five centuries, contemporary records are sometimes available.

Recording for ship and boat reconstructions is not limited to dimensions and arrangements of the various hull timbers, however. Tool marks must be analysed to determine the types of tools used by the shipbuilders and, it is hoped, to discover something about their construction methodology. Wood samples must be analysed by a competent laboratory in order to understand hull strength and the nature of the timber trade at the time. Dendrochronology or carbon-14 methods can be used to confirm the approximate date that the trees were cut to supply wood for the hull (see **Absolute dating**). Metals should be analysed and their applications understood. Pitches, paints, sheathing, and other hull coatings reveal methods of protecting hulls

from the ravages of nature. The application of caulking or luting indicates the builder's method of preventing leakage. Anchors and anchor machinery, bilges and bilge pumps, sparring and rigging, and interior appointments are but a few of the many details to be recorded where such information has survived. The data supplied by a well-preserved ship are extensive, sometimes encompassing thousands of drawings and photographs and reams of field and laboratory notes. The use of computers and improved mechanical and electronic recording devices has now made the job of handling and storing all this information considerably less burdensome.

Processing all the information produced by the archaeological and recording phases is the next step in reconstructing ships and boats. **Archival research**, database analysis, marine drafting, **Experimental archaeology** utilizing models and full-scale reproductions, computer simulations (see **Computer Modelling**), and cooperative studies with other disciplines and laboratories are but a few of the avenues to be followed in turning waterlogged wooden remains into accurate records of whatever craft those remains represent. Ship research nearly always demands extensive archival access and specialized drafting equipment.

The meat of the reconstruction process – reassembly of the wreck and as much of its associated history as possible – follows research. Ship and boat reconstructions fall into one of three general categories: *graphic*, *three-dimensional*, and *physical*.

Graphic reconstructions are interpretations of hull remains in the form of verbal descriptions, lists of dimensions, or sketches and scaled drawings. Computer graphics have been included in this category, although some of the more sophisticated computer reconstructions could arguably be included in the three-dimensional grouping. Graphic reconstructions of sparsely preserved hulls that are left on the seabed might include comparisons with previously documented craft having similar features. Usually such remains are represented by a detailed site drawing or a construction drawing that has been developed as accurately and extensively as possible. Scantling lists (dimensions of timbers and planks) can be arranged in any logical sequence or they might follow contemporary scantling lists published by naval constructors of a couple centuries ago.

Graphic reconstructions of extensively preserved wrecks should reveal considerably more information. Hull shapes can be developed by means of partial or complete line drawings. Structural features of the hull are

illustrated separately on multi-view construction drawings. Rigging plans and detailed sketches of topside and below deck appointments might be included if the vessel has been preserved well enough to reveal such information. One good example of a graphic reconstruction is Kevin Crisman's elaborate study of the remains of the brig-of-war *Eagle*, which he helped to excavate in Lake Champlain. Extensive descriptions of the surviving timbers as well as sketches, hull lines, and construction plans were purchased. A final report, which was published in book form, provided historical accounts of *Eagle*'s operations and demise, the work of its shipbuilders, and interesting accounts of life in the area during the War of 1812.

Three-dimensional reconstructions extend the graphic data into three-dimensional form, thereby expanding a project's research and interpretive capabilities. Such reconstruction vehicles can range from simple working models of mast-steps or pumps to detailed scale models of wreck sites or original vessels. Models provide the reconstructor with a three-dimensional perspective that cannot be achieved in graphic form. They are made in a variety of ways using an equally wide variety of materials.

Parks Canada's **Red Bay** Project is a reconstruction of a 15th-century whaling ship that sank along the coast of Newfoundland. It is a typical example of a project that employed a faithfully reproduced construction model of the hull's remains both for study and illustrative purposes. Another dual purpose example is the 1:10 scale construction model of the port half of the Yassiada Byzantine trader, a small merchant vessel that sank off the Aegean coast of Turkey in the 7th century AD (see **Yassiada Wrecks**).

Full-size reproductions of ships and boats (sometimes called replicas) are the ultimate three-dimensional reconstructions, providing information that would be unavailable from any other source. Quite a few of them have been built to represent watercraft from the Classical period to the present century. A reproduction of the **Kyrenia Ship** has weathered severe storms and monotonous calms in tracing the Mediterranean routes of its prototype, which sank off the north coast of Cyprus in the 4th century BC. Even more adventurous and rigorous were the globe-girdling and transatlantic voyages of full-scale models of Viking ships displayed in museums in Oslo, Norway, and Roskilde, Denmark.

Physical reconstructions are actual reassemblies of the conserved remains of watercraft. They are usually housed in museum environments and require extensive funding and expertise for their conservation,

An early reconstruction model of an 18th-century American coaster. (J. Richard Steffy)

fabrication, and maintenance. Physical reconstructions normally require specialized housing features such as climate control, customized lighting, and protection from damage by visitors. Each vessel has different requirements, especially for structural support and display. Proper housing of reassembled shipwreck remains should really be considered part of the reconstruction process, even though it does not directly affect the vessel's interpretation. Physical reconstructions have the advantage of being available for analysis or reinterpretation at any time. Thus a wreck that has been reassembled might provide additional information at some later date when it is compared with new excavations that are better preserved in certain areas. Similarly, it might be used in the identification of a sparsely preserved wreck that contains obscure features that might not be recognized in drawings or models.

Quite a few reassembled hulls survive in museums around the world (see **Museum display**), representing a wide range of periods and hull types. The oldest, the Royal **Khufu Ship**, dates to about 2650 BC and was found disassembled in a pit near the Great Pyramid at Giza. It is nearly 44 m long and can be seen in a museum near its burial place. Four other Egyptian boats that were buried about eight centuries later are housed in museums in Cairo, Chicago, and Pittsburgh. Still another extensively preserved boat, the **Sea of Galilee Wreck**, dating approximately to the time of Christ, is now on display at Lake Kinneret in Israel. The 4th-century BC Greek merchantman at Kyrenia, Cyprus (see **Kyrenia Ship**) and an 11th-century glass carrier at Bodrum, Turkey, are reassemblies of Mediterranean freighters. Five reassembled Viking vessels can be found in one museum at Roskilde,

Denmark (see **Skuldelev Ships**) and several more in the Viking Museum in Oslo. The largely intact **Bremen Cog** has been reconstructed in its museum in Bremerhaven, while a major part of the hull of Henry VIII's warship **Mary Rose** is on display while undergoing conservation, partial assembly, and study at Portsmouth, England. A large and well-preserved hull known as the Lelystad Buertschip provides physical evidence for Zuiderzee navigation in the Netherlands; it dates to about 1620. A 35 m long vessel, probably built in the 13th century, has been reassembled in a museum in Quanzhou, People's Republic of China (see **Quanzhou Ship**).

The physical reconstructions listed above are but a few of the preserved vessels displayed as living representatives of a broad variety of maritime ventures. Some were found nearly intact and needed only superficial additions; others required considerable research and experimentation before reassembly was possible. Even the best-preserved hulls always require some form of reconstruction, however. An example is *Vasa*, a 1,400 ton warship that sank in Stockholm harbour in 1628. Its recovery was more a salvage project than an archaeological one because the vessel was nearly intact, although its conservation and recording followed the same processes as many of the physical reconstructions listed above. But while the main hull remained solid and nearly complete, a lot of reconstruction still had to be done. It can be appreciated most in the marvellous museum displays that surround the fully restored hull. Exhibits highlight almost anything imaginable about the 17th-century vessel and the people involved with its conception and construction. Wood carvings, shipwrights, and even politics are included among the many subjects featured

in supporting displays that fully document *Vasa*'s world. All of them merely add spice to the reconstruction, however. The gigantic hull, with its elaborate decorations, rows of gunports, and huge, whipstaff-controlled rudder, rules the multistoreyed museum like a wooden monarch. R.S.2

ADDITIONAL READING

Bass, G.F. *et al.*, 1982, *Yassi Ada.: A Seventh-Century Byzantine Shipwreck*, College Station, Texas.

Crisman, C.J., 1987, *The Eagle: An American Brig on Lake Champlain During the War of 1812*, Annapolis, Maryland.

Hocker, F.M., 1991, 'The Lelystad *Beurtschip*. Preliminary Report on the Hull Construction', in R. Reinders and R. Oosting (eds), *Scheepsarcheologie: prioriteiten en lopend onderzoek*, Flevobericht 322, Lelystad.

Steffy, J.R., 1985, 'The Role of Three-dimensional Research in the Kyrenia Ship Reconstruction, in H. Tzalas (ed.), *Tropis I: Proceedings of the 1st International Symposium on Ship Construction in Antiquity*, Athens.

Steffy, J.R., 1994, *Wooden Ship Building and the Interpretation of Shipwrecks*, College Station, Texas.

Van de Moortel, A.M., 1991, *A Cog-like Vessel from the Netherlands*, Flevobericht 331, Lelystad.

Wachsmann, S. *et al.*, 1990, 'The Excavations of an Ancient Boat on the Sea of Galilee (Lake Kinneret)', *Atiqot*, English series, 19, Jerusalem.

Red Bay

A small inshore fishing community located on the south coast of Labrador in Canada's easternmost province of Newfoundland and Labrador. The first Red Bay ship, representative of 16th-century Basque whaling exploits in the New World, was discovered in the autumn of 1978. Over the course of the next six years two additional ships and four boats, all relating to the Basque whaling enterprises, were discovered in the clear cold water of Red Bay harbour. This article describes the highlights of the largest and most comprehensive marine archaeological project ever undertaken in Canada.

In the autumn of 1978 a marine archaeological survey team, led by Robert Grenier from Parks Canada's Marine Archaeology Section, travelled to Red Bay in search of *San Juan*, a 16th-century Basque whaling galleon. Archival research identified Red Bay as a major Basque whaling outpost and the site of the *San Juan*'s sinking in 1565. On the first day of towed searches the faint outline of a wreck was located in approximately 10 m of water. Test excavations revealed well-preserved oak timbers, a large quantity of barrel staves, and an oak capstan with a large whale mandible pinned beneath. These discoveries provided sufficient evidence to warrant further investigation in an attempt to identify the wreck's provenance. The following year thousands of barrel staves, head pieces, and wooden hoops were uncovered. Many of the staves had a white oily substance adhering to their interior sides. Of equal importance was the discovery of limestone ballast, a long overhanging stem, a sharply ranked sternpost, and a large section of the transom with a square tuck design and a reversed V-shaped planking pattern, all characteristic of 16th-century ship design. In addition, a verso primed and ready to fire was found off the starboard bow, an anchor was recovered, as were several heart blocks, the predecessor of dead-eyes. Finally, the most predominant of artefact types were the thousands of fragments of coarse earthenware roofing tiles, a testament to the numerous Basque tryworks and other onshore structures identified through land site excavations undertaken by Memorial University of Newfoundland. Having confirmed the discovery of a 16th-century shipwreck the decision was made to proceed with excavation, in what was to become a six-year, multi-disciplinary, marine archaeological research project. Total diving time exceeded 14,100 hours with 7,000 individual dives logged.

The Red Bay Project was designed to be much more than the excavation of a single shipwreck. It was a comprehensive submerged cultural resource study, encompassing the investigation of the entire underwater area of Red Bay harbour. The project was also carried out in conjunction with an extensive land site archaeological excavation programme, conducted by Dr James Tuck from Memorial University of Newfoundland. Throughout the investigation of the submerged traces of the whaling activities and technologies in the harbour of Red Bay, the hull of the whaling ship stands out as the single most important artefact discovery. The sheer volume and unique quality of the preservation of the lower hull remains has led to a better understanding of the history of ship design and shipbuilding technology of the mid-16th century.

The hull remains were located approximately 30 m offshore from Saddle Island, the site of a number of 16th-century Basque tryworks and related structures. The transom assembly was lying flat on the harbour bottom with its lower V-shaped transom located behind and below the broken end of the sternpost. Other loose timbers recovered included fragmented futtocks, deck beams, knees, waterways, wales, carlings,

and spacer planks. Pieces of exterior planking were scattered throughout the area. A 7.3 m section of an oak mast and a portion of the bowsprit were also recovered.

The starboard stern consisted of articulated hull structure up to and including a portion of the third futtocks, while the port stern was limited to the first futtocks. The rudder was found partially pinned beneath the collapsed hull while a deck beam uncovered incorporated the mizzen mast-step. The articulated structure in the bow extended to just beyond the first deck level. Some of the more important structural ele-

Macrophotography of the ship's timbers, Red Bay.
(Parks Canada/Peter Waddell)

ments uncovered in the bow area included Y-shaped floors, the stem, foremast step, and a hawse hole. Ceiling planking formed the bottom of the hold, consisting of five planks on either side of the keelson including the limber boards.

Material cultural items included pewter, ceramic, and treen fragments, leather footwear, numerous rigging components, and tool handles. A sand glass, a possible log reel, the ship's compass, a binnacle, and a possible log-chip make up a near complete navigation kit. Other important finds were the detailed etching of a ship at anchor, knights' heads, and, along the port side, seven pairs of heart blocks corresponding to the mainmast shroud assembly.

A modelling project, designed to reconstitute the structural remains through a 1:10 archaeological model, was originally envisioned to be formulated around a two-dimen-

sional 'as found' data perspective. However, with the decision to disassemble the hull, record the timbers on the surface, and rebury underwater, modelling could now be carried out from a three-dimensional data perspective. In marine archaeology, this methodological shift marks a transition in research emphasis from a 'raise it intact' theme to a 'raise, record, rebury' approach.

The disassembly of the ship took place over six years of excavation from 1979 to 1984. The initial stimulus to disassemble came from the fact that a chalupa or small whaleboat had been pinned below the star-

board stern quarter. The only reasonable way to excavate the chalupa safely was to disassemble the structure above it. Disassembly further permitted complete stratigraphic analysis throughout the site and the recovery of artefacts below the hull. Other information uniquely available through disassembly relates to the study of the hull itself. Tool marks, construction marks, as well as detailed dimensions and cross-sectional shapes are either not available or are not completely available on integral seabed structures.

Following the hull disassembly and recording, the major task was to rebury permanently the entire complement of the ship's timbers. A sandbag dyked area, measuring 14 by 16 by 1 m, was built within the seabed depression created by the excavation and disassembly of the wreck. The reburial methodology was designed by conservation scientists as a means to preserve and protect the timbers cost-effectively. Approximately 3,000 timbers were systematically reburied, spread out over three layers, and entombed

One-to-ten scale archaeological model of the Red Bay galleon. (Parks Canada/Rock Chan)

Ship's compass in situ at Red Bay. (Parks Canada/Denis Pagé)

in 320 tonnes of sand. The entire assemblage was then blanketed with an industrial hypalon tarpaulin and weighted down with over 60 concrete-filled tyres. In order to monitor the success or failure of the reburial, which was to create a sealed and anaerobic environment, water analysis tubes and controlled wood samples were randomly distributed throughout the enclosed area. To date, all sampling has shown it to be a definite success.

The one whaling ship, believed to be *San Juan*, remains the most complete and best preserved witness anywhere of the importance of the mid-16th century in the evolution of shipbuilding. Its unusual carved keel, made more or less in the Viking ship style, and other carved features, exhibit the last of the vanishing remnants of the old technique of the dugout boat going back thousands of years. The overall building technique of the Red Bay vessel illustrates a developing stage of the frame-first construction usually associated with modern times. In fact, this ship, with its free-floating frames, is still partially built with a shell-first process. In this case, the shell-first construction concept is applied through a system where the outer shell, normally used to define the hull lines and hold the frames in place, is replaced in this function by a complex network of battens and batten-like planks. As such, this ship illustrates extremely well some of the basic techniques used to build caravels and *naos* during the 15th and 16th centuries.

Through the wealth of archaeological data recovered and transposed onto the archaeological model, we can now perceive that the Basque shipwrights of the 16th century had already achieved a very high degree of sophistication and integration of the various components of the shipbuilding trades. W.S.

ADDITIONAL READING

Barkham, M., 1981, *Report on the 16th-Century Spanish Basque Shipbuilding circa 1550 to circa 1600*, Canadian Parks Service Manuscript Report Series 422, Ottawa.

Barkham, M., 1981, 'Life on Board a 16th-Century Basque Whaler', Canadian Parks Service Microfiche Report Series 75, Ottawa.

Barkham, S., 1978, 'The Basques: Filling a Gap in Our History between Jacques Cartier and Champlain', *Canadian Geographic*, February/March, 8–19.

Barkham, S., 1980, 'Finding Sources of Canadian History in Spain', *Canadian Geographic*, June, 66–73.

Barkham, S., 1982, 'The Documentary Evidence for Basque Whaling Ships in the Strait of Belle Isle', in G.M. Story (ed.), *Early European Settlement and Exploitation in Atlantic Canada*, St. John's, Newfoundland.

Bradley, C., 1982. 'Preliminary Analysis of the Staved Container Remains Recovered From the 1981 Underwater Excavations at Red Bay', *Canadian Parks Service Microfiche Report Series 260*, Ottawa.

Grenier, R., 1985, 'Excavating a 400 Year-Old Basque Galleon, *National Geographic*, 168, 1, 58–68.

Grenier, R., 1988, 'Basque Whalers in the New World: The Red Bay Wrecks', in G.F. Bass (ed.), *Ships and Shipwrecks of the Americas*, London.

Grenier, R., 1991, 'The Red Bay Wreck: Discovery and Excavation', in C. Renfrew and P. Bahn (eds), *Archaeology: Theories, Methods and Practice*, London.

Grenier, R. and Tuck., J., 1981, 'A 16th-Century Basque Whaling Station in Labrador', *Scientific American*, 245, 5, 180–88.

Grenier, R. and Tuck., J., 1988, *Red Bay, Labrador: World Whaling Capital 1550–1600*, St John's, Newfoundland.

Izaguirre, M., 1985, 'El rescate del galeon Vasco', *Viajar*, 7, 70, 60–68.

de Javierre, I., 1985, 'La pesca vizcaina', *El Campo*, July, 99, 21–26.

Otero, X., 1985, 'Tras la huella de los balleneros vascos', *Natura*, 23, 20–24.

Otero, X., 1991, *Euskaldunen Labrador de los vascos des Basques*, Euskal Herria.

Ross, L., 1985, 16th-Century Spanish Basque Coopering', *Historical Archaeology*, 19, 1, 1–31.

Tuck, J., 1981, *Basque Whalers in Southern Labrador: Early European Exploitation of the Northern Atlantic 800–1700*, Groningen, Netherlands.

Tuck, J., 1982, 'A 16th-Century Whaling Station at Red Bay, Labrador', in G. Story (ed.), *Early European Settlement and Exploitation in Atlantic Canada*, St John's, Newfoundland.

Tuck, J., 1985, 'Unearthing Red Bay's Whaling History', *National Geographic*, 168, 1, 50–57.

Tuck, J.A. and Grenier, R., 1981, 'A Sixteenth-Century Basque Whaling Station in Labrador', *Scientific American*, 11, 180–90.

Wadell, P.J.A., 1986, 'The Disassembly of a 16th-Century Galleon', *International Journal of Nautical Archaeology*, 15, 137–48.

Reef netting

A salmon fishing technique practised by the Straits Salish, a linguistic and social sub-division of the Coast Salish language family, in the Pacific Northwest of Canada, dated by underwater survey of anchor stones. This unique technique was practised at various locations throughout the southern Gulf of Georgia. Large nets were laid to simulate a rising reef along the established paths of salmon migration. The nets were anchored by large stones and the anchor stones themselves were abandoned at the end of each season, resulting in significant accumulations of these stones at reef-net locations. The technology was used at sites owned by particular families, required the hiring of large numbers of fishers and processors, and produced large surpluses of salmon which contributed to the establishment of extensive trade and other networks through the exchange of surplus salmon for other goods and social prestige through potlatches.

N.A. Easton located and surveyed the apparent numbers of underwater anchor stones at two sites in an attempt to provide an estimate of their age: DeRt-118 at Bedwell Harbour, Pender Islands was calculated to date to the latter half of the 18th century; DbRv-11, off Smythe Head, at the eastern entrance to Becher Bay, Vancouver Island, was dated to AD 1500 ± 50 years. The underwater archaeology of reef netting was subsequently integrated into an analysis of late prehistoric Straits Salish political economy. This fieldwork, which was undertaken in 1983–5, represented the first hypothesis-based underwater archaeological fieldwork in the Northwest coast culture area on a question of anthropological prehistory. N.A.E.

ADDITIONAL READING

Boxberger, D.L., 1989, *To Fish in Common: The Ethnohistory of Lummi Indian Salmon Fishing*, Seattle.

Easton, N.A., 1985, *The Underwater Archaeology of Straits Salish Reef-Netting*, MA thesis, University of Victoria, British Columbia.

Easton, N.A., 1990, 'The Archaeology of Straits Salish Reef-netting: Past and Future Research Strategies', *Northwest Anthropological Research Notes*, 24, 2, 161–77.

Suttles, W., 1951, *The Economic Life of the Coast Salish of Haro and Rosario Straits*, Ph.D. thesis, University of Washington, Seattle. Reprinted in 1974 in *American Indian Ethnology: Coast Salish Indians*, vol. 1, New York, 41–570.

Regional approach

A research approach directed at an entire geographic area or culture. An archaeological region in terrestrial site research is a discrete geographical area containing multiple sites that are related, patterned, and distinctive compared to other bounded areas. Terrestrial archaeologists have been conducting regional-scale research since the 1940s when Gordon Willey surveyed the Viru Valley of Peru and focused on questions about the nature of settlement patterns. Settlement pattern refers to the distribution of archaeological sites in the region, and its study focuses upon the interaction of humans and the environment.

Regions may vary spatially over time when dealing with more or less homogeneous human behaviour. For example, in historical archaeology, a region may be an administrative or military boundary, whereas in prehistoric archaeology it is generally a geographic region, such as a valley, drainage or river basin. Region is the scale of intersite comparisons, and may itself be an analytical entity for interregional comparisons.

In **Prehistoric archaeology** region is tied to two other concepts: archaeological culture and culture area. An archaeological culture is a repetitive occurrence of a particular assemblage discernable in different contemporary sites generally assumed to reflect a single human society. A culture area is a usually large geographic area in which archaeological assemblages characteristic of an archaeological culture occur. For example, one can speak of both a Mycenaean culture area and a Mycenaean cultural system. To gain a reasonable perspective on Mycenaean culture, numerous Mycenaean sites would need to be investigated because the range of cultural variability would not be located within a single site. Regional research approaches typically incorporate systematic investigation of an entire geographic area directed towards larger questions and issues than found within a single site. For example, research domains include the investigation of ecological variables in relationship to settlement patterns or community interactions, among other questions that potentially involve the whole archaeological culture.

One assumption inherent in terrestrial regional archaeological analysis that does not necessarily obtain in maritime archaeology is that interaction and proximity are directly related. Maritime interaction may be over great distances and bypass proximal areas. Terrestrial archaeology assumes regions are spatially discrete, and in some measure closed, although this is a matter of some debate. Maritime systems are, in contrast, open-ended.

The object of regional study is characterizing and explaining relationships among, usually, contemporary sites reflecting a multi-community society. Because it is generally impractical to study all the sites of a region, some sort of **Sampling** must take place, and for that to be practical, regional boundaries must be established. Regional boundary delineation can be difficult even for contemporary terrestrial sites associated with apparently discrete physiographic features. For maritime sites, it can be very difficult to establish cultural affiliation. Seafaring is a wide-ranging activity, and shipwrecks may be scattered wherever a maritime culture has been active. Consequently, cultural spatial relationships can be widely disparate. Individual maritime societies are not tightly bounded, closed entities amenable to independent analysis in the way a terrestrial region may be; a modification of terrestrial approaches is therefore necessary for maritime regions.

Two basic approaches to maritime regional analysis can be distinguished. One, a cultural approach, researches a single maritime culture. The second, a geographic approach, looks at maritime activities, single or multi-cultural, in a geographic region. Both approaches can be pursued synchronically or diachronically. A regional approach to maritime sites, then, can encompass all the maritime cultures active in a geographic area, or all the areas where a single maritime culture is active. The former is a more-or-less bounded geographic entity, the latter a region bounded by the extent of a single culture's maritime activity during the period of study. In both, the primary research objective is understanding the interrelationships between sites.

Cultural resources management (CRM) requirements fuelled regional studies in terrestrial archaeology, and the same has been true for maritime archaeology. The 1979 investigation of submerged sites within the proposed Tennessee–Tombigbee Waterway in Alabama and Mississippi was apparently the first explicitly regional study in maritime archaeology; it was also the first large-scale investigation of riverine sites. Sites, mostly western-river steamboats, were evaluated by Murphy and Saltus for significance in terms of their contribution to understanding social processes within the Tombigbee River valley. The Tombigbee region was also compared to other regional transportation systems, particularly that of the Mississippi River trunk system. Questions about how riverine transportation affected regional adaptation and settlement patterns, particularly ports, landings, and other related terrestrial sites, were developed to aid site interpretation and significance evaluation.

Other examples of regional riverine investigations have since been published. Australian researchers have incorporated regional approaches in investigating shipping on the River Murray, a major continental river system more than 2,500 km long. Kenderdine's important study examined the full range of related sites in the basin besides wrecks, including wharves, jetties, landings, locks, and weirs. Principal research questions involved economic, technological, and environmental adaptations within the Murray River region. A similar approach, which is in its early stages, has been used in examining more than 300 years of maritime activity on the Mersey Estuary in Liverpool Bay, England (see Stammers).

The National Park Service **Submerged Cultural Resources Unit's** (SCRU) survey of Point Reyes National Seashore, California (see Murphy), the Goodwins Archaeological Survey in Great Britain (see Redknap and Fleming), and the Texas Antiquity Committee's survey of Galveston, Texas (see Arnold) are some early examples of electronically positioned marine surveys conducted from a regional approach.

Great Lakes research has also taken a regional approach. In the initial study, NPS-SCRU utilized a strong regional perspective in analysing the **Isle Royale shipwrecks** (see Lenihan). Ten sites were interpreted in a regional context with particular emphasis on sociocultural effects on vessel development and site patterning; inter-regional comparisons, particularly with the Atlantic seaboard, informed site analysis. Other researchers have produced regional studies, notably Allen R. Saltus, who has conducted several studies of southern Louisiana waterways, and Patrick Labadie, who studied Pictured Rocks in Lake Superior. The **Dry Tortugas National Park** Survey employed a regional approach in design and site interpretation (see Murphy). Some states besides Texas have begun conducting regional based research, for example, Wisconsin (see Cooper) and Florida (see Franklin, Morris, and Smith) which represent progressive moves toward regional level investigations.

A regional approach is an appropriate methodology for expanding maritime archaeological enquiry to include broader anthropological and historical issues than can be addressed on the single-site scale. The maritime archaeological record is structured by behavioural and cultural processes that operate at different scales, from the repair of a vessel's hull to wide-area trade networks. The archaeological record is patterned because the human behaviour that created it was patterned – shipping routes are prime examples of patterned behavioural repetition. Shipping routes are structured by the trade networks of which they are a part, and they reflect the processes that structure that network. Regional-scale study of vessels wrecked while participating in a trade network can inform on processes such as cycles of trade, competition, conflict, adaptation, and market vagaries that affect networks. Questions involving the operation of large-scale spatial systems and local, regional, and interregional responses must be answered with regional-scale data. Understanding long-term change in regional trade patterns is an example of the kind of problem archaeology is uniquely suited to address. Practical regional-level studies are not easy, and this approach is relatively new to maritime archaeology. But, as methodological refinements are made, regional-level studies will probably be among the most important contributions maritime archaeology makes towards understanding the full range of past human behaviour. L.E.M.

ADDITIONAL READING

Arnold, J.B., III, 1986, *A Marine Magnetometer Survey of Archeological Materials found near Galveston*, Texas Antiquities Committee Publication 10, Austin.

Cooper, D.J. (ed.), 1991, *By Fire, Storm, and Ice: Underwater Archeological Investigations in the Apostle Islands*, Madison.

Franklin, M., Morris, J.W., and Smith, R.C., 1991, *Submerged Historical Resources of Pensacola Bay, Florida*, Tallahassee.

Kenderine, S.K., 1993, 'Historic Shipping on the River Murray, Australia: A Guide to the Shipwreck Resource', *International Journal of Nautical Archaeology*, 23, 3, 173–88.

Labadie, C.P., 1989, *Submerged Cultural Resources Study: Pictured Rocks National Lakeshore*, Santa Fe.

Lenihan, D.J. (ed.), 1987/1996, *Shipwrecks of Isle Royale National Park: The Archeological Survey*, Duluth.

Murphy, L.E. (ed.), 1982, *Submerged Cultural Resources Survey of Portions of Point Reyes National Seashore and Point Reyes-Farallon Islands National Marine Sanctuary: Phase I Reconnaissance*, Santa Fe.

Murphy, L. and Saltus, A.R., 1981, *Phase II Identification and Evaluation of Submerged Cultural Resources in the Tombigbee River Multi-Resource District, Alabama and Mississippi*, University of Alabama Office of Archaeological Research Report of Investigations 17, Tuscaloosa.

Murphy, L.E., 1993, *Dry Tortugas National Park: Submerged Cultural Resources Assessment*, Santa Fe.

Redknap, M. and Fleming, M., 1985, 'The Goodwins Archaeological Survey: Towards a Regional Marine Site Register in Britain', *World Archaeology*, 16, 3.

Saltus, A.R., 1991, *Submerged Cultural Resources: Investigation of a Portion of the Tchefuncta River SRM 4.5 to SRM 10*, Southeastern Louisiana University Department of Regional Studies.

Stammers, M.K., 1993, 'The Archaeology of the Mersey Estuary: Past Work and Future Potential', *International Journal of Nautical Archaeology*, 23, 1, 27–33.

Terrell, B.G., 1994, *Fathoming Our Past: Historical Contexts of the National Marine Sanctuaries*, Newport News, Virginia.

Remotely Operated Vehicles (ROVs)

see **Submersibles**

Remote sensing

The non-destructive detection, evaluation, or production of useful measurements and observations through electrical and optical sensors of an object or area without physically touching it. When the term was coined in 1960, and currently in most applications, 'remote sensing' refers specifically to the use of aerial electromagnetic radiation sensors to characterize the earth. In underwater archaeological practice, 'remote sensing' generally encompasses both remote sensing and geophysical instruments and techniques. Other synonyms such as archaeogeophysics may be encountered; 'archaeological prospection' is often used in European practice.

Many archaeological methods derive from geophysical techniques; consequently, familiarization with geophysics is important to archaeological practitioners. Geophysics is the application of physics to measuring the earth's physical, electrical, and chemical properties to determine specific characteristics. Geophysical measurements detect material property contrasts, such as magnetic susceptibility, acoustic transmissity, and chemical composition. This article follows the general, more inclusive, archaeological use of 'remote sensing'. Chemical, constituent, and provenance analyses, which many include as part of geophysics, are omitted.

Remote sensors currently applicable to maritime and underwater archaeology include electromagnetic radiation, field measurement, and acoustic devices. Remote sensing instruments provide non-invasive archaeological data on more than just site location, although that is currently their main application. Systematic deployment of appropriate remote sensors or archived remote sensing data procurement, as a part of archaeological methodology, can be useful to distinguish and delimit intrasite features and intersite spatial relations and to portray environmental context. Remote sensing's practical and cost-effective utility stems from its ability to characterize systematically the **Archaeological record** and its context to develop a representation of its structure before designing and initiating sampling and strategies. As non-destructive archaeology becomes more important, archaeological fieldwork increasingly supports remote sensing through signature development and target verification rather than continuing as the sole means of site discovery and documentation.

Basic remote sensing applications are site location, environmental context characterization, site delineation, and documentation. Remote sensing instrumentation can be divided into passive and active sensors. Magnetic and photographic-based sensors are passive, while most other sensors are active, as they generate data from an induced electromagnetic field and analyse alterations resulting from its contact with physical objects. Images are continuous, such as photographs, or discrete, such as radar images. Discrete images are collected in a digital format.

Post-processing is fundamental to remote sensing – few data are directly usable as collected. Continuous images such as photographs can be enhanced, differentially enlarged, or subjected to spatial and directional filtering processes to aid visual interpretation or combined as stereo pairs for mapping. Many inexpensive software programs are becoming available that are useful for processing continuous images.

Computers can classify geographic regions by remotely sensed spectral responses in much the same way as visual images are classified by vegetation or geology. Computer classification relies on discrete images, which are composed of pixels (from 'picture element'). Remote sensing resolution is typically specified in pixel size – a 20 m pixel means each image pixel is equivalent to a 20 × 20 m square of ground surface. Remote sensing instruments ascribe numerical electromagnetic intensity or other values to pixels, which allows computer processing. Digital analyses include a wide range of, generally interactive, procedures including image and radiometric correction, geometric rectification, haze and shade suppression, contrast manipulation, density slicing, spatial filtering operations, and data classification that may be critical for interpretation.

Geophysical data post-processing, which combines instrument data with spatial control, also allows computer manipulation, analysis, and quantified data display, which is typically necessary for interpretation. Successful remote sensing data utilization often depends on the availability and acquisition of ancillary support data and direct access to appropriate post-processing hardware and software tools. Discrete images and digital geophysical data sets are most useful when combined as themes in a **Geographic information system (GIS)**.

Remote sensing instruments

Most remote sensors detect or measure electromagnetic radiation reflected from objects. Various electromagnetic radiation wavelengths provide different information about the surface of an object. The first step in remote sensing is to decide which portion of the spectrum contains data pertinent to one's application. Aspects of scale, accuracy, precision, and data processing are important in deciding sensor appropriateness. Remote sensing data must be generated, or they can be acquired from the growing body of archived commercial and government data sets. Government-generated data are rapidly becoming available on CD and through Internet sources. Many countries have a remote sensing data centre that should be queried for available data.

Underwater archaeology is interested in characterizing the water surface, water column, and seabed, although some inundated terrestrial site research focuses upon recognition of ancient drainage systems and other exposed landforms. Water surface data provides information on wind, current, and wave conditions allowing the determination and modelling of oceanographic characteristics. Water column interest centres on depth. Seabed depiction can provide site locations, environmental context, and evidence of changes over time.

Aerial photography is the oldest remote sensing technique. Archaeological applications date to the early 1920s, using supports, balloons, kites, and later, aeroplanes. Photointerpretation for inundated Mediterranean port analysis predates World War II. Shipwreck searches date to 1971, although Carl Clausen used aerial images in 1965 as

an adjunct to mapping a 1715 Spanish wreck site. Photointerpretation is now included as part of the US National Park Service **Dry Tortugas National Park** Survey.

Site location depends upon the development of an area-specific signature for sites and impact scars. Once a specific signature is developed, its attributes can be used by others for site location. Signature attributes to be considered include size (scale dependent), shape, topographic context, tone (quality of light reflectance, influenced by wreck materials or biota), texture (related to image coarseness that allows tone differentiation), pattern, shadow, and image resolution.

Aerial photography relies upon light transmittance through water; proper film/filter combinations must be selected to maximize penetration. Clear ocean water transmits maximum light around 480 nanometers; coastal waters typically shift towards green with a peak at about 550 nanometers. Film particularly sensitive to these wavelengths should be considered. Ektachrome EF Aerograph film with a Wratten 3 filter has produced good results. There has been some promising experimentation with blue-insensitive emulsions, and recently J. Barto Arnold of the Texas Historical Commission recognized shallow vessels in turbid water on colour-infrared transparencies of the Sabine River in Texas. Low altitude, large-scale images at low solar incidence, which minimizes reflected light, are typically best for seabed investigation.

Overlapping pairs of aerial photographs can provide three-dimensional views that enhance shape recognition. Stereopairs require at least 60 per cent overlap and 65–75 per cent may be necessary. Stereoscopes, which use visual parallax, enhance aerial feature interpretation, and, when connected to digitizing tablets and plotters, provide accurate topographic feature mapping. A refraction correction of 0.3 per cent should be added to apparent depth to obtain true vertical depth. Terrestrial archaeological structures have been mapped with contour plots from aerial stereopairs, which has direct application underwater. Orthophotographs are images derived from stereo models in which all elements are in correct horizontal relationship, that is, they are rectified. Orthophotographs can be extremely useful for accurately mapping a study area.

Thermal infrared imagery has been used by terrestrial archaeologists to locate buried features by detecting subtle temperature changes. Although there is no water penetration in the thermal bands, there are thermal applications for underwater archae-

ology. Submerged applications include the determination of current direction and volume, sediment load, and oceanographic processes. In the 1970s Florida used aerial thermal scanner imagery to locate submerged cave systems. The device is also useful for locating inundated sinks, which are probable human activity loci during lower sea-level stands.

Airborne radar, or SLAR for side-looking airborne radar also using SAR technology, is another rapidly growing data set that may be of archaeological use. The high-resolution instrument depicts ground features through heavy cloud cover. Radar images can be mosaiced for cartography, geomorphological characterization, and soil moisture analysis. SLAR has been tracking sea ice since the 1980s.

Aerial deployed infrared/blue-green laser scanning systems can rapidly collect accurate bathymetric data to 50 m depths through measuring differences between surface and bottom laser pulse reflections. These systems, known as Lidar or LADS (Laser Airborne Depth Sounder) have a 0.2 m resolution and sample on a 10–30 m grid pattern to provide digital data collection at aeroplane speeds of 200 knots; horizontal positioning is provided by differential **Global positioning system (GPS)** equipment. Data generated by these systems should be available for many areas in the late 1990s.

Satellite imagery can be very useful for developing site context; its application to site identification is limited. The Earth Resources Technology Satellite (ERTS-1) was the first operational orbiting platform for remote sensing data collection. ERTS-1 became Landsat in 1975. Landsat satellites have been producing multispectral imagery on 128 channels ever since, and it is the most readily available imagery. Landsat imagery is produced with 80 m pixel size in 180 km swaths with a repeat time of eighteen days. Multispectral sensors detect radiation in several narrow wavelength bands to differentiate various earth surface conditions. Landsat uses a multispectral scanning system (MSS) with an 80 m pixel size, a 30 m pixel, a seven-band thematic mapper (TM), or a return-beam vidicon (RBV), also of about 30 m. These data sets are widely used for mapping landcover, but also have oceanographic applications. North and South America, Europe, Asia, and Australia have large Landsat sensor data bases.

Other Earth resources satellites have produced large databases potentially useful to archaeology. In 1978 the NIMBUS-7 began producing Coastal Zone Color Scanner data designed for optimal water property mapping with a pixel size of 800 m and a six-day repeat; water penetration is 20–40 m. The French SPOT satellite carries High Resolution Visible (HRV) scanners with pixel resolution of 20 m for three bands and a 10 m resolution panchromatic band very useful for cartography. Synthetic Aperture Radar (SAR) imagery has also been generated from satellite platforms, such as the short-lived SEASAT, which produced imagery with 25 m resolution of US, UK, and Canadian waters. SAR is especially useful for sea surface characterization.

Now declassified radar data from the US Navy's GEOSAT spacecraft generated in 1985 has been used to produce a detailed model of the seafloor to a resolution of between 5 and 10 km, a task estimated to take more than a century with conventional acoustic means. Additional classified very high-resolution satellite imagery may become available from the US government which may be applicable to archaeological purposes. Weather satellites generate nearly continuous meteorological data that can now be computer downloaded from nearly anywhere on the globe. Both aeroplane and satellite imagery are available for most of the earth's surface.

Geophysical instruments
Magnetometers
Magnetometers are instruments that measure the earth's magnetic field. Magnetic resolution for archaeological application should be about one nanotesla (nT) or gamma (synonymous units of magnetic field measurement) in about 70,000 gammas. The object of magnetic survey is location of anomalies in the earth's ambient geomagnetic field, which normally ranges between 25,000–70,000 nT.

Three types of magnetometers are in general use: fluxgate gradiometers, alkali or optically pumped magnetometers (cesium and rubidium), and proton-precession magnetometers, which are most common. Magnetometers, developed in the 1940s and 50s, were first used to locate shipwrecks in 1952 by Ed Link. Fluxgate magnetometers are continuous readout instruments that measure magnetic gradients, the other two measure full-field magnetic intensity at various cycle rates. Sensitivities are variable, current proton magnetometers can resolve 1 nT in 60,000 at once per second; cesium magnetometers have sensitivities between 1–.01 nT and cycle ten times or more per second. Some instruments are deployed in a multiple-sensor configuration, called gradiometers, designed to measure local changes in magnetic gradients, rather than variations from the ambient field.

Anomaly sources are features and objects having magnetic susceptibility contrasts with background soils. Magnetic anomalies are typically from ferrous material or thermoremnant features, which result from material being heated to a sufficiently high temperature to allow reorientation of magnetic particles parallel with the earth's field. Common examples are fire pits and ceramic

High Accuracy Control Survey for Sites
• this procedure involves post-processing of data.

BASE   REMOTE   Tethered Buoy with GPS Antenna

NPS

concentrations. Archaeological features can be detected by both an increase or decrease in total field output. For example, a fire pit would generate a positive anomaly, a sandstone wall covered with magnetite-rich silt would be a negative anomaly. Ferrous objects produce the largest magnetic anomalies, and they are the chief target for locating shipwrecks.

There are numerous examples of both terrestrial and hydrographic magnetic searches and surveys. Terrestrial applications typically involve taking a reading at gridded intervals, frequently 1–3 m, to locate culturally derived magnetic features like fire pits, kilns, tombs, foundations, and pottery concentrations. Terrestrial techniques have not been used underwater, but they are likely to be productive for inundated sites, anchorages and disposal areas.

Hydrographic surveys utilize a towed sensor along traverses or transects, the transect or lane spacing being determined by target mass size. Sensor proximity to target mass is important because magnetic intensity declines as a cube of the sensor distance from the object. This means, for example, a ton of iron at 30 m gives 1 nT, at 10 m 62 nT and 6 m 220 nT. In the 1970s, Barto Arnold determined colonial (US) period

vessels could be reliably detected on 50–metre transects, and this spacing has become standard for many offshore surveys. The US National Park Service **Submerged Cultural Resources Unit** adopted 30–metre transects in 1981 to ensure detection of isolated objects. Effective riverine searches typically reduce transects further to detect small watercraft.

Positioning a point using kinematric GPS. (National Park Service Submerged Cultural Resources Unit)

Opposite: Sub-bottom profiler sensor rigged for shallow-water survey.
(NPS/Tim Smith)

Metal detectors are small, normally hand-held devices utilizing a wire coil that induces an electrical field that is received by a secondary coil; some units use a single coil. Magnetic and metallic objects alter instrument field characteristics and are thus detectable. Currently the most effective detectors are pulse induced. Good metal detectors are able to detect ferrous and non-ferrous metals of tens of grams over tens of centimetres. Detection distances are in the range of four times the largest dimension of an object. Consequently, metal detectors are most useful for intrasite surveys for shallow buried metallic materials. Their use has become common since work on the **Kyrenia Ship** and *Amsterdam* in the late 1960s and early 1970s. Far more effective for ferrous objects over larger distances are submersible, hand-held magnetometers. Primary types for this application are rubidium and cesium, optically pumped magnetometers. Current resolution for these instruments are in the order of .1 nT.

Acoustic Instruments
The most common acoustic instruments are fathometers, which use submerged transducers to measure a sound pulse's round trip to the bottom to provide water depth. Recent advances include very high resolu-

tion, video displays and digital output useful for incorporation into computer-based survey systems. Wide-swath multibeam survey systems using several transducers are available that cover kilometres of seabed in a single pass.

Acoustic bottom classification instruments can be connected to fathometers to provide an unambiguous, real-time, numerically quantified seabed characterization. For example, the RoxAnn compares multiple fathometer returns to quantify seabed roughness and hardness.

Digital data is recorded and displayed in colour representing bottom-type classifications. This instrument has been in use by the National Park Service Submerged Cultural Resources Unit since 1994 for characterization of bottom context for archaeological sites.

Side scan sonar uses reflection of micropulses of sound (generally 100–500kHz) emitted multiple-times-per-second to characterize the seabed and objects on or above it. Sound generation and reception are through hull-mounted or over-the-side mounted transducers or, most common, dual sensors incorporated into a 'towfish.' Side scan sonars generate a vertically narrow, horizontally wide swath sound beam and measures variations in acoustic backscatter reflecting from the seabed and objects protruding from it. Variations are recorded as intensity and time of return; dark returns are strong reflections, lightest returns indicate acoustical shadows.

Surface readouts are either electrosensitive paper, or increasingly common, video monitor screen with digital recording, which adds colour to intensity to aid target recognition. Continuous data lines produce a sonograph, which is a topographic-like rendition of the bottom; sonographs can be combined to produce accurate seabed maps. Side scan sonar is very useful for low visibility searches because sound is unaffected by low-light and visibility conditions. Typical ranges extend to 600 m a side for 100 kHz instruments. The best resolution is generated by lower scan widths, 25–50 m, and higher frequencies 400–500 kHz. Sector scanning sonar is a similar device, but uses a rotating, high frequency sensor allowing effective shallow searches with boats and remotely operated vehicles (ROVs).

Current state-of-the-art includes miniaturized, portable instruments, very high resolution, digital manipulation and automated mosaic production, seabed sediment classification, and utilization of sonar signature generation for pinpointing particular targets. Video displays offer expansion of selected record portions for independent magnified examination with additional target colour enhancement. Integrated side-scan and multibeam bathymetry can produce geometrically corrected three-dimensional and stereo seabed modelling of large areas.

The **Sub-bottom profiler** also uses sound, but directs it downward rather than sideways. Low frequency sound (3.5–15 kHz) pene-

trates the seabed to be differentially reflected from underlying strata, each of which has a particular speed of sound transmission that is a function of density. The record depicts sound travel time and variable sediment reflective intensity. The current state-of-the-art is a CHIRP system that transmits a computer-generated digital wideband swept FM pulse (200 Hz to 30kHz) allowing quantitative evaluation and surficial bottom sediment classification. A particular advantage of CHIRP is essentially noise-free images to about 100 m in depth, which is of archaeological interest. Single-pulse profilers often compress and distort these upper sediment layers. The **Institute of Nautical Archaeology** used a CHIRP profiler in an attempt to locate Columbus' ships sunk during his fourth voyage in Queen Ann's Bay, Jamaica. Sub-bottom profilers sample a narrow path, so close transects must be conducted for full coverage. Consequently, sub-bottom is rarely used as an effective site location device, but rather to determine overburden depth and to depict the subsurface strata.

Towfish combining multiple sensors are becoming more common. For example, wide-swath bathymetry combined with side scan sonar for three-dimensional seabed imaging, or side scan with sub-bottom to provide three-channel data, and side scan with magnetometer. Multiple-sensor instruments may be less expensive than separate devices.

Site delineation and documentation

Most of the instruments discussed above are useful for site delineation in a high-resolution mode. For example, project-specific aerial imagery collected at low altitudes at varying view angles; sonar run slowly at optimal resolution and angle; and magnetic survey with close and perpendicular transects. Combinations of techniques may be most useful to archaeologists working under water.

One of the earliest combination surveys in underwater archaeology was by McKee and Edgerton who used a side scan sonar combined with a sub-bottom profiler in 1967 to develop a three-dimensional characterization of *Mary Rose*. More recent examples are the multi-instrument characterization of CSS *Georgia* and USS *Monitor*.

There are remote sensing instruments less appropriate for survey that have potential for site documentation, including quantitative spatial measurements and digital manipulation. An example of high-resolution site mosaic production utilizing ROVs, SHARPS (**Sonic High Accuracy Ranging and Positioning System**), and laser stadia is the 1994 European Institute of Underwater Archaeology and **National**

Results of remote sensing integrated into a GIS. (National Park Service Submerged Cultural Resources Unit)

Geographic Society maps of the Spanish wreck *San Diego*.

Laser sensors using argon laser line-scan technology that minimizes backscatter can produce very high resolution images in low visibility, high turbid conditions. The image is built up a pixel at a time until a 640 or 2,048 pixel line of video is generated; stereo images can also be produced. The Westinghouse SM2000 is available in a towed sensor configuration that produces very high monochromatic images at distances to 20 m, a view swath of 8–23 m at speeds up to four knots.

Experimental range-gated laser camera development is encouraging, although their power requirements lend only to ROV deployment. These devices minimize scatter by only recording laser light that has been reflected from an object for a few nanoseconds, rather than the entire time the light is travelling from the source to the receiver. The receiver is a cooled charged coupled device (CCD) that functions like a video. These devices image objects three to five times the distance of a conventional intensified-light camera with floodlights. Lasers offer some of the most promising advances of any current technology for turbid-water imaging. Similar non-laser technology using slow-scan CCDs with one hundred times the sensitivity of 1000 ASA film can generate high-resolution, low noise images in extremely low light conditions.

High resolution sector-scanning sonar mounted on ROVs has been useful for site documentation. Some examples are the 1987 **Monitor** Project, where wreck cross-sections, contours, and three-dimensional models were constructed from sector-scanning sonar data, and the *Hamilton* and *Scourge* project in the Great Lakes where detailed mosaic imaging was done with a ROV incorporating digital camera images and sonar data.

Like any scientific technique, effective remote sensing results depend upon appropriateness, which is a function of the investigator's understanding of instrument attributes, on applications to particular local conditions; and on the nature of research questions posed. Combined remote sensing data sets, including electronic charts, accessible through GIS are in the 1990s among the most powerful analytical tools available to underwater archaeologists.

In the early 1980s the Queensland Museum of Northern Australia HMS *Pandora* Excavation Project combined remote sensing, geophysical information, historical plans, excavation layers, and artefact plots into a computer-assisted design (CAD) programme that greatly assisted site analysis. This early, pre-GIS application of computer techniques illustrates the future potential for underwater archaeologists who combine multiple data sets with computer analyses. L.E.M.

ADDITIONAL READING

Breiner, S., 1973, *Applications Manual for Portable Magnetometers*, Sunnyvale, California.

Duel, L., 1969, *Flights into Yesterday*, New York.

Fish, J.P. and Carr, H.A., 1990, *Sound Underwater Images: A Guide to the Generation and Interpretation of Side Scan Sonar Data*, Catumet, Massachusetts.

National Park Service, 1977, *Remote Sensing: A Handbook for Archaeologists and Cultural Resource Managers*, Washington, DC.

Replicas

see **Experimental archaeology**; **Reconstruction**

Research design

An organized way of using scientifically grounded principles and controlled procedures in order to evaluate research results. Due partly to the influence of the 'new archaeology' during the 1960s and 1970s, research designs have become a normal part

of the conduct of land archaeology. The trend towards designed research, along with new analytical approaches, is also playing a greater role in **Maritime archaeology**. The first requirement in any archaeological research design is a willingness to frame expectations that can be tested. Earlier descriptive approaches in archaeology lacked such opportunities for testing and relied upon the element of discovery instead. 'Discovery-mode' maritime archaeology still occurs, most often in relation to shipwrecks associated with historically famous events or personalities. It usually centres on the collection of artefacts, especially items with special artistic or historical significance. A problem with discovery-mode, artefact-oriented archaeology is that finds are difficult to evaluate and can be atypical of the culture that produced them. Famous wrecks such as *Vasa*, *Mary Rose*, and *Titanic* are spectacular but are not necessarily representative of the ships of their period or of the activities they undertook.

To begin the testing process, a research design needs to develop an organized set of expectations, sometimes called hypotheses. For prehistoric or undocumented shipwrecks, these expectations may be based on other archaeological findings, usually resulting from land-based research. For example, the initial arrival of the human species in Australia is of special interest to maritime archaeologists. The findings of land archaeology indicate that this migration took place across a significant body of water, beyond sight of land. Although world sea-levels were lower during the Pleistocene, when this movement took place (estimates vary from around 35,000 to 65,000 years ago), the open water between the Southeast Asian islands and mainland and the Australian-Tasmanian-New Guinea continental land mass has existed for several million years. The presence of 30,000+ year-old sites in Australia shows that this was probably the earliest long-distance voyage in human prehistory. But no direct evidence for it has yet been found in the form of wrecked watercraft or land sites belonging to the earliest colonists.

So far, the testing process for this inference has consisted of excavations and dating of Pleistocene-age sites on offshore islands that were then part of the Australian mainland. Early dates from these island sites makes it clear that the remote ancestors of the Australian Aborigines once inhabited these surviving remnants of the original continental shelf. Further testing, by looking for submerged rock art sites and other inundated remains of these early colonists, is continuing. Had no sites or remains earlier than about 12,000 years old been found on these offshore remnants, this inference would have been disproved.

For maritime archaeologists with access to historical documents, the testing process is no less important. Written records provide a basis for constructing expectations that can direct archaeological investigations. Discovery-mode archaeology characteristically sought confirmation of the documentary accounts by archaeological research, mainly to obtain historic relics and to support the historicity of the events described in those accounts. But no amount of confirmatory evidence can actually prove that historical events occurred as described, nor can it resolve disputes about why these events occurred as they did. Only successive attempts to disprove the historical version of events and the ability of that version to withstand these attempts can give credibility to such historical accounts.

Maritime archaeology provides circumstantial evidence in the form of material associations, most often in the form of shipwreck sites, that can be evaluated in relation to historical accounts. The first step in any such evaluation is the recognition and control of post-depositional factors affecting site associations. Historical documents can then be used to frame questions that can be addressed archaeologically. The archaeological record is co-equal with the historical record, so archaeology can provide information and explanations not always available from documentary sources. An example of such an approach would be Colin Martin's analysis of the guns of the **Spanish Armada** armed transport *El Gran Grifon*. Historians had debated the competency of the Duke of Medina Sidonia, who was appointed to lead the Armada by Philip II of Spain on short notice following the death of Admiral Santa Cruz, who had originally been picked to lead the assault. Sidonia was not an experienced sailor or military leader, and some historians have blamed him for the Armada's failure in 1588. But Martin's analysis showed that the types and disposition of guns aboard the wreck of *El Gran Grifon* were consistent with the defensive requirements of an armed transport as opposed to a first-class fighting ship. This demonstrated that Sidonia was competent in distributing guns among the different Armada ships just before they departed – a point about Sidonia's behaviour that historians had been unable to resolve.

Good research design can lead to seemingly counter-intuitive approaches to underwater research. We usually think of conservation as the final step in the recovery of shipwreck remains, following surveys and excavation. But Michael McCarthy's research on the wreck of *Xantho*, the first steamship to operate commercially in Western Australia, shows the value of considering conservation first instead of last. He notes that the conservation of the ship's engine was an integral part of the excavation process. Systematic deconcretion and removal of salts enabled McCarthy and conservator Ian MacLeod to discover technical features of the engine that showed the *ad hoc* nature of its installation and use in a remote colonial setting. One of the most important results to emerge from McCarthy and MacLeod's work was the value of having conservators participate in the underwater survey and excavation from the beginning. The relationship of conservation to the overall research plan was established during the design phase of the research, before on-site studies began.

Regional and site survey is another aspect of research that requires planning in relation to an overall design. This is especially important with respect to **Sampling** strategies. Maritime archaeologists must be able to establish how representative the sample of materials observed in a survey is in relation to the total population from which it was derived. Various methods involving random and stratified sampling techniques are widely used in land archaeology. To achieve controlled results in such sampling efforts, archaeologists use techniques that enable one to survey an area so that, at the completion of the survey, one can say with assurance to a given level of probability that a failure to find items meant that they were not there. This is the opposite of discovery-mode archaeology, which evaluated the success of a search within an area according to the number of finds. Searches of this kind, however, do not resolve the matter of whether or to what extent the failure to find items was due to that fact that they were not present or were due to a failure in the search. In other words, searches – as opposed to surveys – are inconclusive and have no place in well-designed archaeological research.

Excavation, too, is subject to the controls and constraints of good research design (see also **Minimum impact archaeology**). In a growing number of cases, detailed non-destructive site recording has proved preferable to excavation, as shown by the efforts of the National Park Service at the USS *Arizona* Memorial at **Pearl Harbor**, Hawaii. Forty years after the Japanese attack in 1941, the US National Park Service team, led by Daniel Lenihan and Larry Murphy, produced a detailed and highly informative record of the shipwreck site without having to remove any artefacts or to penetrate the ship's hull. The site is a shrine to members of the ship's company entombed within the hull. This non-intrusive approach answered important questions about the ship's loss without violating the sanctity of the memorial site.

When excavation is required, initial use of non-destructive approaches makes it possible to be selective about what and how much to excavate. Rarely now do archaeologists attempt total excavation and removal of materials from a shipwreck site. Good research designs encourage archaeologists to excavate only those portions of a wreck that can answer questions or test hypotheses. From a preservationist point of view, good research design is as essential to maintaining shipwrecks as submerged cultural resources as it is to understanding them better. R.A.G.

ADDITIONAL READING

Muckelroy, K. 1978, *Maritime Archaeology*, Cambridge.

Nance, J.D., 1983, 'Regional Sampling in Archaeological Survey: The Statistical Perspective', in M.B. Schiffer (ed.), *Advances in Archaeological Method and Theory*, vol. 6, New York.

Resurgam

The world's first mechanically powered submarine. Its remains rest in 12–18 m of water off Rhyl, North Wales. The invention of a Victorian curate, Reverend George Garrett, it sank while under tow during a storm in 1880. The discovery of the wreck in 1995, and its subsequent designation as a Historic Wreck in 1996 under the 1973 **Protection of Wrecks Act**, will ensure that *Resurgam* is granted the historical recognition it deserves.

Resurgam was built at the Britannia Iron Works at Birkenhead and launched in 1879. Trials suggested that *Resurgam* could remain submerged for 10–12 miles (18–24 km) with a speed of 2–3 knots. The submarine supported a crew of three and was armed with two spring-mounted Whitehead torpedoes. During December of 1879 Garrett began a voyage to Portsmouth with *Resurgam* under steam to demonstrate the vessel's capabilities to the Admiralty. Delays and bad weather prompted Garrett to purchase a steam yacht to tow *Resurgam* to Portsmouth. Caught in a storm off Great Orme's Head, the submarine crew transferred to the yacht to help keep her afloat. It is assumed that the safety feature incorporated into the submarine's design preventing the closing of the hatch from the outside sealed her fate. Filling with water, the vessel became heavy and eventually broke the towing hawser and sank.

Innovative features of the vessel included a closed steam system using superheated water to provide up to four hours of steam without the need for a furnace. The engine type, patented in 1872 by Eugene Lamm, utilized water stored at 200 psi, which, when directed, produced a flash explosion of steam at 100 psi to drive the engine. *Resurgam*'s accumulator delivered 150 psi for a single boiler return connecting rod engine.

Constructional details suggest a length of 45 ft (13.77 m), a beam of 10 ft (3.1 m) and a displacement of 30 tons. Hull construction featured iron plates fastened over an iron lattice of stringers and frames. The central section of the hull was clad with wood retained by iron straps. Hydroplanes fitted to the central hull section enabled submersion once the vessel was moving forwards.

Garrett not only adapted existing machines for use in his submarine, but also designed and created breathing apparatus four decades ahead of the acclaimed Haldane. Termed the 'Garrett pneumataphore', this used caustic soda to scrub oxygen-exhausted air for re-use (similar in concept to modern rebreathers).

Modern directed searches for *Resurgam* began in 1975 as a collaboration between the Oxford Laboratory for Archaeology and the Welsh Association of Sub Aqua Clubs. A proton **Magnetometer** was used, without success. In 1981 magnetometer searches under Royal Navy leadership again failed to find *Resurgam*. Further searches by the Marine Archaeology Survey organization in 1987, this time also using a **Side scan sonar**, also failed. Surveys continued to produce negative results in 1988, 1989, 1992, and 1993; many of these attempts were funded and attended by William Garrett, great-grandson of the inventor.

The initial location of the submarine in October 1995 is attributed to net snagging and verification by sports diving. Following attempts by the finders to 'sell' the location of the submarine, the **Archaeological Diving Unit** carried out searches within a large area, and located a magnetic anomaly. Further investigation by American Underwater Search and Survey Ltd, using an Edgetech side scan sonar, located the submarine in 1996. The find was verified by ROV and diver survey.

The submarine is incredibly vulnerable, lying three-quarters proud of the seabed in an area expected to be subject to beam trawling on a large scale. Two substantial holes exist in the port side near the bow, and the lower cladding on the port side is missing. The three propeller blades are snapped off and the port hydroplane is missing. The hatch for the conning tower is also

missing and there is impact damage on the port side, restricting access to the inside via the conning tower.

Despite attempts to seal the conning tower in 1996, in the week between the location of the vessel and the Designation Order being placed, portable items were taken off the submarine and the conning tower steering wheel was broken.

A detailed predisturbance survey combined with a marine species identification survey and analysis of the corrosion potential of the vessel is scheduled for 1997. This will incorporate aspects of archaeological training within the **Nautical Archaeology Society** training programme. Internal excavation and recovery of the submarine depends on finding a suitable institution and dedicated funding. Only then may *Resurgam* live up to her name, 'I shall rise again'. A.H.

ADDITIONAL READING

Murphy, W. S., 1987, *Father of the Submarine*, London.

The Georgia Archaeological Institute, 1996, *The Resurgam, Predisturbance Survey and Recovery*, Research MS UKS–015, Augustus, Georgia.

Risdam

Dutch East Indies vessel which sank 500 m north of Pulau Batu Gajah, near Mersing, State of Johore, Peninsular Malaysia, in 1727. On 6 May 1984 a vessel was intercepted by Royal Malaysian Customs while engaged in looting a wreck site near Mersing on the east coast of Malaysia. This was the first public announcement relating to the wreck site which is now thought to be *Risdam*. There followed a brief expedition to the site by the Muzium Negara and a Royal Malay Navy diving team, which recovered over 110 tin ingots, 40 elephant tusks, and other material. Later, material recovered by the looters and impounded in Singapore was returned to Malaysia by the Singapore authorities (5 tin ingots and 61 elephant's tusks).

Risdam was built for the Chamber of Hoorn in 1713. She made two voyages to the Indies. The first departed for the Chamber of Amsterdam on 27 September 1714, arriving at Batavia on 22 April 1715, with a total complement of 119 people. *Risdam* returned to the Netherlands for the Chamber of Enckhuisen on 30 July 1718, with a complement of 87. She departed again on 16 November 1718 and arrived on 13 August 1719 in Batavia, with a complement of 162.

The vessel is described as a fluit, 130 voet (36.8 m) long and 100 last, in the Uitgezeilde schepen (8 November 1673–23 February 1796). According to the records the vessel loaded tin at Ligor and then went

to Ayutthaya on 29–30 November 1726(?) where she loaded sappanwood, barrels of ginger, forty pots of achar, thirty pots of klak (possibly kalk or lime, the 'a' and 'l' having been transposed, or alternatively lak), and 150 empty glazed pots. The vessel left Ayutthaya in a leaking condition on 8 December. When the leak became substantial *Risdam* was intentionally run aground on 1 January 1727 near Pulau Batu Gajah to save the lives of the crew.

Because the survey yacht (with an **Airlift**) was available for only two days, it was decided to airlift a shallow trench across the site. The objective was not to carry out any major excavation work but to expose the archaeological layer and investigate the extent and nature of the site; detailed survey work would then follow. A jackstay was laid, and a narrow trench was run across the site. Some structural timber was revealed, and a systematic probe survey recorded the western extremity of the hull. It was noted that there were a number of iron stakes, possibly left by looters, in the northern region of the site. The pegs were surveyed using a compass and tape to get an initial plan of the site. Later, a more accurate survey was made of all the survey pegs using three-tape **Trilateration**.

An exploratory Airlift trench was made along the west side of the site. The airlift was used to uncover the top of the hull structure which had been found by probing. This revealed part of the hull of the ship, with the tops of the frames, outer planking, sheathing, and ceiling. The sheathing was 30 mm thick, the outer planking 120 mm thick, the frames were 250 mm thick by 200 mm wide, and the ceiling was 100 mm thick. It was noted that the ceiling lay at an angle of 60 degrees to the horizontal. Heavy riders or chocks were noted in some places lying on top of the ceiling.

Meanwhile the pegs and exposed outline of the hull were surveyed using three-point trilateration. The next objective was to determine the location of the bow and stern and the depth at which the hull was buried under the surface of the seabed. Up to this point all excavation had been confined to removing the inert or sterile mud overburden to reveal the surface of the archaeological level.

Three test trenches were delineated. In the south a jackstay was laid across the site. In the middle of the site heavy riders had been found; these served to guide an approximate midship trench. A jackstay was also laid across the north of the site. The area at the stern proved to be a section of hull structure that had collapsed and separated from the main hull. It is extremely complex and badly eroded. While it is not exactly certain what part of the ship it belongs to, it may be connected with the stern structure. Excavation of this area revealed two sets of frames converging to a point towards the south. It is thought that this represents the deadwood of the stern, very close to the sternpost.

A trench 5 m long by about 2 m wide was made across the middle of the site at the position of the rider-chock complex. The objective was to excavate a profile across the site up to the keelson. The trench proved to be difficult to excavate because of the large quantity of wooden logs, presumably sappanwood, in the layer 1 m below the sterile mud. The keelson was located and a profile of the trench was made using a spirit-level and ruler to establish the levels across the ceiling. Individual ceiling planks were also measured, together with the thickness of the keelson and the details below the ceiling at the keelson. Next to the keelson a round hole was found, thought to be a pump hole which allows access to the bilge below the ceiling. The hole facilitated measurements below the ceiling planking of the thickness of the ceiling planking frames and keelson; timber holes were noted in the frames next to the keelson, but were not measured.

The survey clearly shows that the vessel is leaning at an angle of 15 degrees to the starboard and suggests that the starboard side will be better preserved to a depth of about 3.5 m. During the excavation a tin ingot was found close to the keelson. Parallel to the keelson was a vertical partition made up of clinker-laid planks supported by a vertical beam. This may be some form of hold partition to contain the cargo. Excavation work in the bow area indicated that the trench was slightly aft of the bow. A large concretion, which included elephant tusks and possibly a cannon, lay across the main axis of the hull. Two large beams, possibly breast hooks, were surveyed, together with a bulkhead. A large three-sheave pulley block was found at the bottom of the trench. On one of the large beams on the starboard part of the hull in this area, possibly a hanging knee or rider, the letters SB1 were carved onto the forward face. The significance of this is at present not clear. On the southern side of the excavation face a partition was noted, which could be part of the lateral partitioning of the hold of the vessel. From the site plan it appears that the site is about 37 m long which corresponds closely with the known length of the vessel of 130 Amsterdam voet (1 voet = 0.283 m), i.e. 36.8 m. It seems that the width, 10.8 m, is a little large against the figures from van Dam of a fluit in 1696 of 130 voet with a width of 33 voet 6.5 duim., i.e. 9.5 m. The discrepancy may reflect the fact that there has been a certain amount of outward collapse of the hull structure, or that the width of the vessel was measured at the main deck, and due to the tumblehome the width at the waterline is slightly greater. However, the figures are generally consistent with *Risdam*.

The survey indicates that there is more than 500 cu. m of internal hull which may contain archaeological material. There may well be collapsed material on either side of the vessel. Above the archaeological horizon there is about 1.5 m of sterile overburden. The vessel has been strongly constructed with regular sets of riders and chocks set on top of the ceiling. This is consistent with the 17th-century shipbuilding manual by N. Witsen (1690) who states that fluits that went to the Indies were strongly built. J.G.

ADDITIONAL READING

Green, J.N., 1986, 'The Survey of the VOC *Fluit Risdam* (1727), Malaysia', *International Journal of Nautical Archaeology*, 15, 2, 93–104.

River Thames

English river, the site of much nautical, underwater, and harbour archaeology. Many ancient vessels have been recovered from the Thames and its tributaries, including at least twenty-two logboats: these range in date from the Neolithic, the Iron Age, Roman, mid- and Late Saxon to the 13th century. Roman plank-built wrecks have been recovered from three sites in and around the City of London; a Roman wreck is presumably represented by the nine pewter ingots found at Battersea between 1859 and 1996; a Saxon boat was excavated on the Graveney marshes in Kent; there are two 14th- to 15th-century and one 17th-century wreck from the City, and a late 16th- or early 17th-century boat from Walthamstow on the River Lea; substantial remains of the late 15th- to early 16th-century *Sovreign* were recorded at Woolwich; while cannon thought to be from the 17th-century warship *London* have been raised from a site near Nore in the outer estuary. The two oldest surviving complete craft from the Thames are probably Queen Mary's shallop (*c.* 1689) and Prince Frederick's barge (*c.* 1732), both in the collection held by the National Maritime Museum, Greenwich.

Urban waterfront excavations have produced significant vessel fragments of 10th- to 14th-century date from the City, of later medieval date from Southwark and Kingston, and of 17th-century date from the City and at Rotherhithe to the east. They represent over twenty vessels of a range of types including boats, barges, and ships, but not all have been published. Early modern material has been recovered from sites in the inter-tidal zone, as at Bermondsey just east of the City, where the remains of an 18th-century foreshore shipyard has been recorded. Foreshore hulks of 19th-century date or later are now being recorded in Greater London, while others remain further downstream, as yet uninvestigated, such as the Danish schooner *Hans Egede* hulked at Cliffe in Kent. Hulks are also known from the Thames estuary and tributaries such as those from Whitewall Creek on the River Medway in Kent.

Underwater survey work has been conducted in the Thames at Henley, where 12th-century bridge remains have been examined. More activity has been undertaken in the outer estuary where the Marine Archaeological Survey group undertook remote sensing surveys from 1983 to 1989, for example. Sites include the Roman wreck at Pudding Pan, the 16th-century Girdler Sands Wreck, 18th-century wrecks such as ***Stirling Castle*** and *Northumberland* which sank in 1703, and ***Albion***, wrecked in 1765.

Most of the enclosed docks on the Thames, a complex which had once been part of the largest port in the world, were closed from 1968 to 1981. The demise of the docks also triggered a major redevelopment of the City's waterfront, when obsolete warehouses were replaced by new offices. This provided a unique archaeological opportunity for archaeologists from the Museum of London to excavate the ancient harbour sites which lay beneath the basements of the later warehouses, and from 1972 to 1995 a remarkable range of waterlogged waterfront sites of Roman, Saxon, and late medieval date were excavated. They revealed the remains of harbourworks, riverfront revetments, jetties, bridges, and warehouses, telling us much about the history of encroachment, the development of commerce, ancient river levels, and changing waterfront technologies.

The natural riverbank was located between 100 and 150 m north of the present-day river wall, and the first major waterfront development comprised a piled embankment dated by dendrochronology to the AD 50s. This was replaced by the first of a series of very substantial timber-faced quay structures a decade later. Similar structures of 2nd- and early 3rd-century date were recorded, most incorporating a braced front wall of five or six horizontally stacked squared oak baulks, each one up to 600 ×

400 mm in cross-section. Some were open-work quays or landing stages which would have supported a timber decking, but most were infilled with silts, oyster shells, or gravel. Associated with some of these developments, principally in the area around the bridgehead, were several examples of open-fronted warehouses or transit sheds, while large quantities of imported pottery including a high percentage of amphora fragments, were also recovered from the waterfront. Although the development of the harbour facilities was clearly a major initiative, there is little evidence that these structures were being actively maintained by the 4th century, although occupation in the town as a whole continued at an apparently reduced level into the early 5th.

The mid-Saxon port of Ludenwic was established on a new site to the west of Londinium from about AD 600 to 900, and was famously described by the Venerable Bede in the 730s as a 'mart of many nations, resorting to it by land and sea'. There have as yet been few opportunities to examine the contemporary waterfront, although a 7th-century embankment has been recorded. Presumably as a consequence of Viking raids, the town was moved inside the more readily defensible Roman town walls in the last decades of the 9th century. Thereafter, excavation has revealed how the waterfront was regularly extended, encroaching ever southwards as a series of embankments and revetments were built over the old foreshore to win more land. Many of the timber structures have been dated by dendrochronology, representing activity from the 10th to the 17th centuries.

Evidence of such ancient encroachment is now commonplace, and has also been demonstrated archaeologically at several sites outside the City, as at Southwark to the south and Kingston to the west. Study of these closely datable developments, while interesting in their own right, can also facilitate the calculation of ancient river levels at a particular time, as has been attempted for the Roman and medieval periods.

The remains of a possible Roman timber bridge were found in London, while the stone abutments of medieval bridges have been excavated in Southwark and Kingston. The remains of medieval warehouses and other waterfront structures have also been excavated, including 12th- and 13th-century dyehouses, a 12th-century hall associated with the Hanseatic merchants, and part of a post-medieval tidal mill, while an 18th-century whaling station was recorded at the Greenland Dock, near Surrey Quays, in 1996.

The study of ancient waterfront sites on the Thames merges into the subdiscipline known as industrial archaeology, which includes the study of the more recent docks, warehouses, shipyards, and factories situated on and by the river. The port of London was once supported by the extensive system of enclosed docks built up between about 1800 and 1920. From 1968 to 1981 the entire dock complex west of Tilbury was closed down, together with acres of warehouses and related industries. Regeneration has been patchy, but the recording of the buildings representing this major chapter in London's long history has barely kept pace with dereliction or demolition.

It has been estimated that some 5,000 ships were built on the Thames between 1512 and 1915 for the Royal Navy or for commerce: the number of boats and barges which were river-built is less well known. Study of this major long-lived industry has focused on the documentary evidence for the extensive developments at the Royal dockyards or at the major private yards at Blackwall. However, this subject can be much enhanced by archaeological study, both on waterfront excavations such as those at Rotherhithe or Woolwich in the 1970s, and more recently on intertidal zone sites, as at Bermondsey. Archaeological survey on the foreshore has helped identify sites of the humble boat and barge building/repair yards, as well as those of the neglected industry of ship-breaking: that veteran of Trafalgar, *Temeraire* (immortalized in Turner's paintings), was broken up on the foreshore at Rotherhithe, for example. G.M.

ADDITIONAL READING
Banbury, P., 1971, *Shipbuilders of the Thames and Medway*, Newton Abbot, Devon.
Carr, R. (ed.), 1986, *Dockland*, London.
Courtney, T., 1974, 'Excavations at the Royal Dockyard, Woolwich, 1972–3', *Post Medieval Archaeology*, 8, 1–28.
Courtney, T., 1975, 'Excavations at the Royal Dockyard, Woolwich, 1972–3, Part 2: The Central Area', *Post Medieval Archaeology*, 9, 42–102.
Good, G., Jones, R., and Ponsford, M., 1991, *Waterfront Archaeology*, Council for British Archaeology Research Report 74, London.
Marsden, P., 1994, *Ships of the Port of London: 1st to 12th Centuries AD*, English Heritage Archaeological Report no. 3, London.
Marsden, P., 1996, *Ships of the Port of London: 12th to 17th Centuries AD*, English Heritage Archaeological Report no. 5, London.
Milne, G., 1993, *The Port of Roman London*, 2nd edn, London.
Milne, G., in press, *Nautical Archaeology on the Foreshore*, Royal Commission on the Historic Monuments of England, London.
Milne, G. and Hobley, B., 1981, *Waterfront Archaeology in Britain and Northern Europe*, Council for British Archaeology Research Report 41, London.
Royal Commission for Historical Monuments of England, *Thames Gateway: recording Historic Building and Landscapes on the Thames Estuary*, Swindon.

Rockaway

Great Lakes scow-schooner site in lower Lake Michigan, Allegan County, Michigan, USA. *Rockaway* was built by Brower A. Morgan and launched in November 1866 at Oswego, New York, Lake Ontario for Chandler, Alvord, and Company. Historical records describe the vessel as 164.48 gross tons, 156.85 net tons, 106 ft 2 in (31.3 m) long, 24 ft 2 in (7.3 m) broad, and 7 ft (2.1 m) deep. *Rockaway* carried produce, packaged goods, and bulk freights of lumber, coal, and iron ore throughout the lakes region from 1866 to 1879. In 1880 she was transferred to the upper lakes region at Muskegon, Michigan, and engaged in the lumber trade until foundering in a storm off South Haven in November 1891.

The *Rockaway* site was discovered in September 1983. Archaeological fieldwork was directed from 1984 to 1991 by the Michigan Maritime Museum in cooperation with the Bureau of Michigan History and Michigan Department of Natural Resources. The site contained the ship's hull and an artefact assemblage of operational and maintenance tools, rigging and navigational equipment, galley wares, fasteners, containers, and personal effects. Study of the ship structure addressed the economics of vessel design and construction, and the cultural and environmental conditions that influenced **Great Lakes** designers, shipping financiers, and shipwrights to build and use large numbers of scow-schooners in the 19th century. Artefact analyses focused on an examination of the ship's equipment and supplies and hypotheses concerning the economics of shipboard life. Historical research included the documentation of *Rockaway*'s commercial career, the development and interpretation of a database on more than five hundred Great Lakes scow-schooners, and analyses of economic records for Great Lakes schooners active between 1860 and 1900.

Research showed that Great Lakes scow-schooners represented a vessel class of more varied design, construction, and capability than some historical characterizations suggest, and that vessel function was as important an influence in the minds of *Rockaway*'s designers and builders as cost of construction. The database revealed relevant patterns of scow-schooner development and use. The artefact **Assemblage** and historical research provided insights into the skills of the crew, ship maintenance routines, and the importance of adaptive reuse of materials during a period when the economic viability of commercial sail was in decline. Historical data also revealed the nature and significance of work routines performed on ship by schooner officers and crew when in port, as compared to the hiring of specialized craftsmen such as riggers, sailmakers, carpenters, blacksmiths, and other labourers. K.R.P.

ADDITIONAL READING

Inches, H.C. and Partlow, C.J., 1964, 'Great Lakes Driftwood Schooner-Scows', *Inland Seas*, 20, 4, 289–94.

Mansfield, J.B., 1899, *History of the Great Lakes*, Vol. 1, Chicago.

Pott, K.R., 1985, 'Investigating a Lake Michigan Shipwreck', *Michigan History*, 69, 4, 36–42.

Pott, K.R., 1993, 'The Wreck of the *Rockaway*: The Archaeology of a Great Lakes Scow Schooner', in S.O. Smith (ed.), *Underwater Archaeology Proceedings from the Society for Historical Archaeology Conference, Kansas City, Missouri*, Ann Arbor, Michigan.

Ronson Ship

An early 18th-century merchant ship located in a Manhattan landfill and excavated in 1982. The investigation indicated that it was an American-built ship whose design may be a mixture of British and Dutch standard types. The artefacts, which related to colonial New York, and the ship's bow were saved and conserved.

In 1981 developer Howard Ronson applied to the city of New York to construct a thirty-storey office building which would cover the entire block of 175 Water Street. He was required by the New York Landmarks Commission to conduct a preconstruction archaeological investigation of the site. Ronson contracted with Soil Systems, Inc. to conduct the investigation, which included the archaeological excavation of approximately 15 per cent of the block. In the rest of the site they dug deep test holes and checked the stratigraphy to compare it to the stratigraphy in the area that was carefully excavated. In the last deep test to be made, in the eastern part of the block, the eastern wall of the hole fell away to reveal the outside of the hull of a buried ship.

Shortly after discovering the ship Soil Systems called in Warren Riess and Sheli Smith to co-direct the site investigation. Riess and Smith realized that the ship was an almost intact early 18th-century merchant vessel. Since no such vessel had been found in the

The Ronson Ship, New York City. (© The Mariner's Museum/Warren Reiss)

Americas, the site was extremely significant. The developer agreed to underwrite the site investigation and postpone construction for one month (February 1982). A team of forty-six archaeologists was formed to excavate the site. The crew worked through snow storms, freezing rain, and logistical problems while construction began on the office building 150 m to the west. As they excavated and recorded the site, the excavation team raised ship pieces to a timber recording crew. All diagnostic artefacts were recovered and 10 per cent of the fill was saved for analysis. By the end of February the archaeologists reached the keelson, 6.4 m below street level.

After the first two weeks it was evident that the ship had been stripped of its contents and hardware and spiked to some pilings to become part of the landfill process on the east side of Manhattan. The ship lay almost parallel to the present shoreline, one block away, at the east end of the block. Layers of excess ballast and associated artefacts from other ships almost filled its hull. Layers of beach stones, coral sand, volcanic black sand, and English flint composed most of the fill in the hull. These in turn were covered by a layer of dirt, waste artefacts, and mud from the river. Evidence of a crude rock fireplace, a small loading crane, and excessive wear to the upper deck indicate it was used as a harbour wharf or quay for some time before the next landfill project left it inshore.

Only approximately half of the ship was

accessible to the archaeologists since the ship lay partly under Front Street. The bow was heading into the block a little, so that all of the bow, most of the port side, and very little of the stern was in the block. The starboard side and stern were outside the block and therefore off limits to the crew. Much of that portion may have been destroyed by street and utility construction under Front Street. In addition, four transverse sections of the site could not be excavated because the safety engineers felt that these sections were keeping the hull from collapsing.

The New York City Landmarks Commission asked for the bow to be saved, so the team dismantled the bow, piece by piece, and began a conservation process on the timbers. They planned to remove the first 7.6 m of the bow, but while they were removing it at night the mud walls started to slump and they stopped at approximately 5.5 m.

Analysis and interpretation of the ship suggested some answers to old problems and raised new questions. She was 82 ft (25 m) long on the lower deck (approximately 100 ft (30.5 m) overall), had a beam of 26 ft (7.9 m), and would have been registered in America at between 150 and 210 tons. She was larger than the average colonial merchantman, yet not as large as the great East India ships. Three southern latitude species of shipworms were found in her outer wood sheathing, indicating that she had sailed at least once to southern waters.

The bow of the ship was so full as to be almost square and had a massive, fully intact beak protruding 3 m in front. The foremast, now gone, was stepped far forward. Three bitts remained standing directly behind the foremast and an intact, all-wood capstan lay unstepped on the lower deck forward of the mast. Just aft of the bow area a section of the upper deck also remained, collapsed onto the lower deck. The cargo hold was extensive – 7 ft 6 in (2.25 m) high and at least 50 ft (15.2 m) long with no indication of any cargo-separating bulkheads, except in the bow.

A ballast pump was still in place and internal lower deck scuppers, which directed rain and splash water from the lower deck to the bilge pumps, were positioned just below three gunports along the port side. The gun ports indicated that the ship had been armed with six 6 pounder cannon on the lower deck, and probably more smaller guns above. Tongue-and-groove panelling lined the cabin area in the stern, pierced at one spot where a lead pistol ball still remained in it. Beneath a shelf in the cabin area was an 18th-century rum bottle, intact but empty.

The hull timbers were mostly oak, probably

much of it southern live oak. Many other species of wood were also used, including southern yellow pine. Although wood specialists cannot be certain of some of the key species because of the wood's condition, it appears that the only place all of the species were easily available in the early 18th century was the Chesapeake region. There is no archival data indicating the shipping of large amounts of southern hardwoods or yellow pine for long distances in America. However, English tobacco companies sent English shipwrights to the Chesapeake to build tobacco ships in the late 17th and early 18th centuries.

The Ronson Ship fits easily into this story. She was larger than most ships of her day, yet the normal size for a transatlantic tobacco ship. Moreover, the builder's attention to detail, something noted during the excavation, was typical of English rather than colonial shipwrights. Finally, she was probably made of a variety of woods natural only to the Chesapeake region. Riess's hypothesis, therefore, is that the ship was built as a tobacco ship in the Chesapeake, probably Virginia, for an English or Scottish tobacco company. At some time the Ronson ship may have been sent to New York to participate in the growing flour trade. There, she may have been condemned as unfit for a return voyage. After the ship was spiked into place and filled, New Yorkers appear to have used her as a wharf for a while, placing a small capstan in her bow and using the vessel's mizzen (rear) mast as a cargo boom. Eventually the shoreline was extended out another block and the ship was covered with 2.4 m of rubble and asphalt until it was found again in 1982.

To test this hypothesis Riess has studied the New York and much of the Chesapeake port records in an attempt to identify the ship, but as of August 1995 he had only narrowed the search down to four possibilities. Background research in America and Britain has bolstered the tobacco ship hypothesis with circumstantial evidence, but no hard proof exists for this solution. In fact, further research may lead to an entirely different explanation for the ship's history.

Riess's study of the ship's design led him to conclude that the designer used the geometric technique, often referred to as Deane's Method, with different fractions of the keel length to those that Deane published. He also concluded that the anonymous designer created a hybrid of an English merchant frigate and a Dutch flyboat. This design may have given the British Empire a distinct advantage in transportation efficiency, although this is the only example of such a design yet discovered.

The bow timbers were conserved using polyethylene glycol and slow drying. They are curated at the Mariners' Museum, Newport News, Virginia along with the artefact collection, data, and photographs. W.R.

ADDITIONAL READING

Riess, W., 1987, *The Ronson Ship: The Study of an Eighteenth-Century Merchantman Excavated in Manhattan, New York, in 1982*, unpublished Ph.D. thesis, University of New Hampshire.

Riess,W., 1989, 'Design and Construction of the Ronson Ship', *Proceedings of the International Symposium on Boat and Ship Archaeology, Amsterdam, 1988*, 176–83.

Rosloff, J., 1986, *The Water Street Ship:Preliminary Analysis of an Eighteenth-Century Merchant Ship's Bow*, unpublished MS thesis, Texas A&M University, College Station.

Roskilde Fjord wrecks
see **Skuldelev Ships**

ROVs
see **Submersibles**

Russia and the ex-Soviet Union

The development of underwater and maritime archaeology in Russia and the former USSR was in four stages: the emergence and formation of investigation techniques (18th century–mid-1930s), the elaboration and formulation of the foundations of methodology (mid-1930s–mid-1950s), the development and formation of the foundations of methodology (mid-1950s–1980s), and finally acquiring experience and improving scientific methods (1980s–1990s).

Interest in underwater sites as an integral part of human culture and material activities began in 1718 when Peter the Great signed an edict to collect and protect historical articles found in the ground and under water. Before the 20th century individual finds were collected for museum display. In most cases, museums initiated underwater investigations, among them partially submerged ancient towns on the Black Sea – Dioscuria (1876), Feodosiya (1905), Olbia (1909) – as well as examinations and measurements of a vessel found in Chudskoye Lake and supposed to date from the 15th century (1902). The first underwater filming of objects took place in 1930–31 during the search for the remains of the submerged ancient town of Chersonese. Professor R.A. Orbeli (1880–1943) invited military divers to examine submerged parts of northern Black Sea towns – Chersonese, Olbia (1937), Feodosiya, Kerch (1939), the Strait of Kerch, Koktebel Bay (1939) – as well as inland waters. These activities resulted in the find in the Bug of a dugout boat dating from the middle of the 1st millennium BC.

Orbeli's activities assisted in developing the scientific approach to underwater archaeological sites. He was the first in the Soviet Union to formulate objectives for the new scientific discipline – underwater historical geography, the concept of an underwater archaeology museum and institute – and to develop new approaches to underwater archaeological investigations, employing the methods of other sciences, such as geology, biology, and geography.

The elaboration of the foundations of general methodology gradually developed during scientific expeditions. Availability of light diving equipment made it possible to transfer from search and raising to complex and thorough investigations. Underwater sites in the Soviet Union were excavated layer by layer in a similar way to surface field archaeology, the archaeologists using metal detectors, geoacoustic equipment, and aerial photos. **Avocational** underwater expeditions guided by professional underwater archaeologists also began. The most important work was carried out by Professor V.D. Blavatski. In 1957–8 his expedition examined a submerged part of ancient Thanagoria and mapped its layout; in 1959 the town was excavated. In 1961 certain structures in submerged Olbia were examined with geoacoustics. In 1959–60 Blavatski examined a military shipwreck from the end of the 18th century in the Strait of Kerch. In 1964 and 1965 the remains of a ship dating from 4/3 BC were examined by Blavatski and his team. In 1972–7 an expedition of the Ukrainian Institute of Archaeology, headed by S.D. Kryzhitski, continued fieldwork at Olbia. After six years it produced a detailed town layout, revealed its stratigraphy, and recovered thousands of finds.

In 1968 systematic examination of the medieval settlement of Byandovan on the Caspian Sea commenced. Investigations continued of medieval structures on the bottom of Lake Issyk Kul (1958–61, 1975–8), medieval settlements, a Bronze Age site, and an 18th-century vessel in the Dnieper (1970). In 1979 the State Hermitage organized an underwater archaeological expedition. Several years of its activities discovered and examined a number of pile settlements of the 3rd–2nd millennium BC in lakes of the Pskov and Smolensk regions.

The 1980s brought improvement to investigation methods. In 1982 and 1984 the first All-Union Working Conferences were held, attended by amateur divers, professional archaeologists, historians, public and natural scientists, and museum workers. Regulations for examination and preservation of underwater cultural sites were developed. In 1988–9 A.V. Okorokov and V.N. Taskayev published methods of underwater archaeological examinations and excavations, and in 1991 A.K. Stanyukovich offered a geophysical prospecting concept for subsurface and underwater sites.

Among the most significant fieldworks in the 1980s and 1990s were the location and investigation of ancient Akra and Korokondama on the Black Sea (1983–6), which revealed the remains of buildings, a 16th–19th-century settlement at Kurshski Bay on the Baltic Sea (1983, 1994), the examination of 16th–19th-century sites on the White Sea (1988–90), and excavations at the Bering expedition camp on Bering Island (1979, 1981, 1991). Short-term projects were carried out in Byelorussian lakes, on the Dnestr, and the Volga.

At the beginning of the 1990s the formation of a new state (Russia) and the resultant political and economic changes shifted established attitudes to history and culture. Since the beginning of the 1990s the Centre for Complex Underwater Studies of the Scientific and Research Institute of Culture (founded in 1989) has carried out the most important work within Russia. This has included the examination of the submerged ancient settlement of Patrei (since 1990). Surface and underwater excavations conducted together with the Institute of Archaeology revealed its layout, remains of structures, and a rich collection of ancient vessels. A.V.O.

ADDITIONAL READING

Blavatski, V.D. and Koshelenko, G.A., 1963, *Otkrytiye zatonuvshego mira*, Moscow.

Len'kov, V.D., Silant'ev, G.L., and Stanyukovich, A.K., 1988, *Komandorskiy Lager Ekspeditsii Beringa* (*Opyt kompleksnogo izucheniya*), Moscow.

Len'kov, V.D., Silant'ev, G.L., and Stanyukovich, A.K., 1992, *The Komandorkii Camp of the Bering Expedition: An Experiment in Complex Study*, Anchorage.

Melnik, A.N. and Shatunova, N.V., 1987, 'Otechestvennaya gidroarkheologiya: istoriya i progress', in *Metody yestestvennykh nauk v arkheologii*, Moscow.

Okorokov, A.V., 1992, *History of Examination and Protection of Domestic Hydroarchaeological Sites: Emergence and Formation of Scientific Investigation Methods*, Moscow.

Okorokov, A.V., 1993, *Istoriya izucheniya i okhrany otechestvennykh pamyatnikov gidroarkheologii razrabotka i formirovaniye osnov metodologii*, Moscow.

Okorokov, A.V. and Taskayev, A.N., 1988, *Podvodnaya razvedka pamyatnikov istorii i kultury*, Moscow.

Okorokov, A.V. and Taskayev, A.N., 1989, *Podnodnye raskopki pamyatnikov istorii i kultury*, Moscow.

Orbeli, R.A., 1947, *Issledovaniya i izyskaniya*, Moscow.

Stanyukovich, A.K., 1991, *Issledovaniye anomality geomagnitnogo polya ot iskusstvennykh podzemnykh i podvodnykh obyektov*, Moscow.

St John's Bahamas Wreck

An unidentified wrecked Spanish sailing ship dating from the 16th century, the subject of an archaeological investigation in the 1990s. The vessel met its fate in 5 m of water on the southwestern edge of the Little Bahama Bank, approximately 37 km north-northwest of West End, Grand Bahama Island. This area is located along the eastern side of the Gulf Stream current as it passes between Florida and the Bahama Islands.

The site was discovered in July 1991 by the Florida-based marine salvage corporation St John's Expeditions during the survey of an area of sea bottom leased to them by the Bahaman Government for the right to explore the remains of sunken ships. When this particular site was discovered, archaeologists and historians familiar with colonial ships and maritime affairs, including a representative from the Mel Fisher Maritime Heritage Society (MFMHS) in Key West, Florida, were consulted for an assessment of the wreck. All concluded that this site dated from the 16th century and could contribute to a better understanding of the early colonization of the Americas. In December 1991 St John's Expeditions and the MFMHS formed an alliance to conduct an archaeological examination of the wreck. Under their agreement, all of the materials recovered from the site will be housed at the Key West facility as an intact and permanent collection open to both the public and interested researchers. The alliance continues to thrive and since its formation four periods of **Excavation** have been conducted, which have provided considerable insight to the long-lost ship and the era it represents.

Much of the data collected during the excavation of over 150 sq. m. of the site awaits analysis, but it has become evident that most of what remains of the ship has survived intact. In general, artefacts appear to have moved little since their initial deposition and are able to provide significant insight to the internal arrangements and loading practices on board this ship, such as the location of the galley, the stowage of various classes of arms and artillery, and the storage of supplies, among others. Lamentably, some damage did occur to the wreck during earlier, undocumented explorations by treasure-hunters, most significantly to

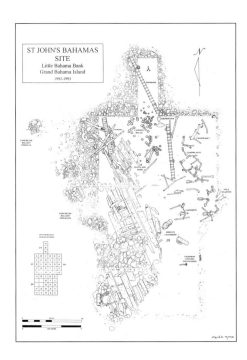

St John's Bahamas site with bombard type cannon to the right and verso nest to the left. (Dylan Kibler)

Site plan of the St John's Bahamas Wreck. (Mel Fisher Maritime Heritage Society)

areas of the lower hull structure. The absence of **Treasure** on this site has kept the incentive for any such venture at a low level and can account for the relative lack of disturbance that has been encountered.

The remains of the ship itself are quite fragile. They have generally been found in their original context, but are quite abraded and soft from the long immersion. The structure has been recorded through drawings and photographs before being reburied as it was found. The excavation has revealed, for the most part, exterior hull planking which is sporadically intersected by badly degraded framing components. These were once joined by combinations of iron fasteners and wooden dowels. A small section of what is thought to be the keel or some closely related structure has been found as well. The *in situ* structure that has been encountered indicates the ship had a minimum overall length of 19.9 m, though the actual measurement is certainly greater considering neither end of the vessel has been positively identified.

Nearly 1,000 individually tagged artefacts have been recovered, along with thousands of earthenware storage jar body sherds and hundreds of iron spikes and barrel hoop fragments. Large collections have been made of different classes of items, revealing the material culture on board this ship. Weapons, including a battery of three *bombardetas* and seven *versos*, nine crossbows, pole arms, and swords, provided the crew with a variety of military options. The many styles and types of ceramics seen from this site reflect the tastes of colonial Spain and trading patterns of the times. The remains of nearly one hundred earthenware 'olive' jars along with various tin-glazed majolica vessels, including those from Andalusia and Italy, lead-glazed wares, brown Cologne

stoneware, various unglazed wares and a variety of burnished ceramics believed to be of Aztec origin, form the major part of this group. Other artefacts include a number of iron rigging components, a horseshoe, glass vials, a bronze enema syringe, lead cloth seals, an iron helmet, and the femur of a young crocodilian. Significantly, the combination of assayers' marks stamped on two small silver coins, which were minted in Mexico City, could have been found on the ship only if it had sailed sometime after 1554. Many more artefacts remain to be cleaned and researched before final conclusions can be made about this ship, but it is interesting to note that there has been no cargo evident from the site.

It can be said that this sizeable, well-armed Spanish ship was sailing in the mid-16th century and wrecked on a remote shoal while en route to Spain. The site that has resulted from this mishap is proving to be an exceptional archaeological resource not only because of the large and varied collection of materials recovered from it, but because of its integrity, which provides us with new insights into the construction and arrangement of such an early vessel. Ships such as this were the sole means of transport for the exchange of people, goods and ideas between the Old and New Worlds and understanding how they operated is fundamental to any comprehension of the formation of what we have come to know as 'the Americas'. The continued excavation and research of the vessel currently known as the St John's Bahamas Wreck is working towards that understanding. C.M.2

ADDITIONAL READING

Malcom, C., 1991, 'The St John's Bahamas Wreck: Research and Excavation Plan', on file at Mel Fisher Maritime Heritage Society, Key West, Florida.

Malcom, C., 1996, 'The St John's Bahamas Wreck: Interim Report 1: The Excavation and Artefacts, 1991–5', *Astrolabe – Journal of the Mel Fisher Maritime Heritage Society*, 9, 1.

St Mary

Last example of the 19th-century American 'downeaster' type of square-rigged merchant vessel, so-called because so many of them were built in Maine. Portions of the wreck lie at Kelp Lagoon in the Falkland Islands, while a section of hull is on display at the Maine State Museum in Augusta.

St Mary, launched in the spring of 1890 from the Charles V Minott yard in Phippsburg, Maine, ran ashore on East Falkland on her maiden voyage from New York to San Francisco. No lives were lost but the captain reputedly committed suicide. Much of the cargo was salvaged. The wreck remained where it grounded until a severe storm in 1970 broke it up, leaving a substantial portion of the starboard side in place. Other wreckage such as masts litter the nearby store.

In 1978 archaeologist Peter Throckmorton, with a crew of volunteers, chainsawed a 12 m section of the 'tweendeck into segments which could be towed off the beach to a local freighter. These were shipped back to Maine via England and have been reassembled as an example of Maine wooden shipbuilding. The only other example of material from such a vessel is the cabin of the Maine-built *Benjamin F. Packard* on exhibit at Mystic Seaport Museum in Connecticut. The *St Mary* hull section

Wreckage of St Mary. *(Nicholas Dean)*

exemplifies the massive construction of these vessels, built both from local timber and hard pine imported from the American South. N.D.

ADDITIONAL READING

Dean, N. and Miller, S., 1979, 'The Story of the *St Mary*', *Falkland Islands Journal*, 35–41.

Throckmorton, P., 1976, 'The American Heritage in the Falklands', *Sea History*, 4, 36–41.

Throckmorton, P., 1978, 'The Beast on the Beach', *Sea History*, 11, 28.

St Nikolai

The wreck of an old man of war located in the 1940s in the waters near the town of Kotka on the southeastern coast of Finland. The wreck was first subjected to extensive salvage by commercial divers, and was only later archaeologically investi-

gated and excavated by the National Maritime Museum of Finland. The wreck was assumed to be the Russian frigate *St Nikolai*, sunk in the second Battle of Routsinsalmi between the Swedish and the Russian skerry fleets on 9 July 1790, during the 1788–90 war between Sweden and Russia. This assumption was confirmed in 1990 through studies in Russian naval archival sources, then recently made accessible.

St Nikolai went down after having received numerous hits, taking the captain and almost the entire crew with it. The battle was a major victory for the Swedish Navy and many Russian vessels were sunk. *Nikolai* was the only large ship that went down in deep water (18 m), while four of its sister ships were taken as prizes. This type of frigate was at that time one of the largest types of vessels in the Russian skerry fleet. The first eight frigates of this type were built at Kronstadt naval base just before the Swedish-Russian war. *St Nikolai* was launched on 23 April 1790.

The hull of *St Nikolai* is still standing on the bottom, although one side has collapsed. Extensive underwater documentation performed on the wreck gives a good picture of its state. The length of the hull is 40.6 m and its width is 10 m. These dimensions are very near to the ones given for the *St Nikolai* in the Russian naval archives – 39.6 and 9.75 m. Portions of the main deck still survive and the interior is partly well preserved. Archaeologists have been able to conduct a detailed documentation in plans and drawings of the frigate's galley. Many artefacts have been raised from the wreck, both in connection with the early salvage operations, when the main partsof the guns were raised, and during the archaeological investigations. The finds consist both of pieces of the structure of the ship and its fittings, as well as artefacts from the crew's equipment and personal belongings. C.O.C.

ADDITIONAL READING

Ericsson, C., 1972, 'A Sunken Russian Frigate', *Archaeology*, June, 3, 173–9.

Ericsson, C., 1975, 'The Instruments from Her Imperial Majesty's Frigate *Nicholas*', *International Journal of Nautical Archaeology*, 4, 65–72.

Mattsson, R., 1990, 'The Frigate Sunk in the Battle of Routsinsalmi and Some Facts Revealed by Russian History', *Maritime Museum of Finland Annual Report 1989–1990*, Helsinki.

Sorvali, H., 1977, 'On the Design and

Dimensions of the Frigate Nicholas', *Maritime Museum of Finland Annual Report 1977*, Helsinki.

Salvador

A Spanish troopship of the Napoleonic era. The greatest maritime tragedy in the history of the River Plate occurred on the night of 31 August 1812, when *Salvador* (sometimes recorded as *San Salvador*) was lost during a storm, some 300 m from the beach in Maldonado Bay, near Punta del Este, Uruguay. The vessel was carrying infantry and dragoons from Spain to reinforce Spanish interests in and around Montevideo, which at the time was under threat from rebel activity. The precise loss of life has been impossible to determine, but it would seem that about 470 men, out of approximately 600 who sailed, were drowned.

The site was found in the early 1990s by Uruguayan divers Héctor Bado and Sergio Pronezuk. An archaeological evaluation was carried out by Mensun Bound of **Oxford University MARE** in November 1993, followed by a survey in February–March 1997. The wreck was found to be in two sections, about 35 m apart, which accords with descriptions of the disaster in Spanish archives. The identity of the wreck was confirmed by the military buttons (some of which read YNFANTERIA) on the uniforms that still survive on many of the skeletons (see **Human remains**). Further proof came from pouch and shako badges, muskets, bayonets, sabres, and numerous other items of military equipment and apparel. Several ornate bronze cannon were also recorded along with a large quantity of copper-alloy ball-shot and barshot of a type which was much used by the Spanish at the Battle of Trafalgar. Cargo items included slate-boards, glass goblets and tumblers, cruet sets, nest weights, tea pots, blue and white ware dishes, eating utensils, wire bobbins, thimbles, bottles, storage jars, and silver coins. Most of the cargo goods were probably intended for Callao, in Peru, the vessel's final destination. One of the skeletons, presumably that of the ship's doctor, had medical instruments with it.

Salvador is the richest known wreck from the Napoleonic era and is of particular importance to the histories of both Spain and Uruguay. M.B.

Salvage Law (historic wrecks)

Salvage is the rendering of assistance to vessels and their cargo in distress at sea, whether afloat, shipwrecked or sunken. The law of salvage gives the salvor a right to compensation for services rendered, on behalf of the owner, to the property, not title to the property salved, by allowing a lien against the property which is enforceable in admiralty court. The salvor has the duty of properly caring for the property while it is in his possession. The owner of property in distress or lost at sea is not divested of ownership. The salvor who rescues such property does so for the benefit of the owner. The salvor does not become the owner of the salved property by virtue of his services. He merely has a maritime lien granted by the general maritime law to ensure that his reward for saving property will be satisfied out of the property saved. The salvor does not have the right to simply keep the salved property; should he do so, the salvor would become subject to suit for conversion. Rather, the salvor has the duty to bring the salved property to a safe place, and failing agreement with the owner, must place the property in the custody of the admiralty court for determination of the reward. Wrecked or sunken property is subject to the salvage services of the first comer. If the owner of the property, or the master of the vessel, has expressly and reasonably prohibited salvage services, the salvor of that property is not entitled to an award. A salvor may be deprived of the whole or part of the award to the extent that the salvage operations have been rendered more difficult because of the fault or neglect of the salvor, or if the salvor has been guilty of fraud or other dishonest conduct.

Two international treaties have sought to unify national laws regarding salvage at sea.

The 1910 Brussels Convention reflects the traditional international admiralty principles that a salvor may be remunerated for salvage services only if successful ('no cure – no pay'), and that the salvage reward is limited to the value of the property salved. Consequently, modern salvage awards have not supported today's more costly salvage operations which require trained personnel and highly specialized equipment. As a result, those salvors still in business did not have adequate economic incentive to undertake operations in cases which entail the risk of appreciable environmental harm (e.g., tankers in distress) but are otherwise not commercially attractive.

The 1989 Salvage Convention incorporates the essential provisions of the 1910 Convention, while offering increased protection for the marine environment by requiring both the vessel owner and the salvor to use due care to protect the marine environment, and by permitting the salvor to be rewarded for preventing or minimizing damage to the environment during salvage operations.

The 1910 Convention has no provisions expressly addressing historic shipwrecks. The 1989 Convention permits a State Party to reserve the right not to apply its provisions to maritime cultural property of prehistoric, archaeological or historic interest that is situated on the seabed. Neither Convention requires the application of proper archaeological techniques to historic shipwrecks, or the preservation of the scientific, historic, and archaeological integrity and provenance of the wreck.

The 1910 Brussels Convention does not apply to warships or other government ships appropriated exclusively to a public service. The 1989 Salvage Convention also does not apply to warships or (in modern terminology) other non-commercial vessels owned or operated by a state and entitled, at the time of salvage operations, to sovereign immunity under generally recognized principles of international law, unless that state decides otherwise, and so notifies the IMO Secretary-General of the terms and conditions of such application.

The 1910 Convention remains in force for some seventy states. The 1989 Salvage Convention entered into force on 14 July 1996, with almost twenty parties. The 1989 Salvage Convention replaces the 1910 Convention for states party to both Conventions where their provisions are incompatible.

These two treaties do not address the law of finds. If the property is abandoned, the law of finds, rather than the law of salvage, applies, permitting the admiralty court to confer ownership of the property to the finder. Admiralty law favours the law of salvage, not the law of finds, because salvage law's purposes, assumptions, and rules, directed towards the protection and preservation of maritime property, are more consonant with societal needs and interests. Thus, the law of salvage applies as a general rule. It may be said that the law of finds applies only in two categories of cases: (1) where the owners have expressly and publicly abandoned their property; and (2) where items are recovered from an ancient shipwreck and no one comes forward to claim ownership of them. United States admiralty courts have not consistently applied these principles.

Some modern cases have applied the law of finds to instances of long-lost and abandoned wrecks. The Spanish galleon *Nuestra Senora de Atocha*, with a cargo of gold and other valuables, sank in a hurricane in 1622 off the coast of Florida. In 1972 the wreck was located. Gold, silver, artefacts, and armament valued at $6 million were recovered. US courts upheld the finders' ownership and possession against the claim of the United States. On the other hand, the law of salvage was applied in the case of SS *Central America*, a paddle wheel steamer lost in a hurricane in September 1857 off North Carolina with its cargo of gold.

In the United States neither the law of salvage nor the law of finds now applies to three categories of abandoned shipwrecks located in state waters (generally, out to three miles (4.8 km) from shore): (1) historic shipwrecks 'embedded' in submerged lands; (2) shipwrecks in coral formations; (3) shipwrecks listed on the US **National Register of Historic Places**. Under the Abandoned Shipwreck Act of 1987, the United States asserts title to all abandoned shipwrecks in these three categories, and that title is transferred to the State in which it is located. State law is necessary to give effect to that transfer of title.

If title to property is vested in the Federal or State government, no salvage award should be given to a salvor who has recovered the property without the government's express or implied consent as the government has full power to reject or prohibit such services.

The law has now evolved to the point where both salvors and finders of historic shipwrecks should be required to use proper archaeological techniques and to preserve the scientific, historic, and archaeological integrity and provenance of the wreck. To do so would be consistent with the traditional law of salvage, which considers the skill of the salvor when making a salvage award. J.A.R.

ADDITIONAL READING

Treaties and related official documents
Convention for the Unification of Certain Rules with Respect to Assistance and Salvage at Sea, Brussels, 23 September 1910. United States Statutes at Large, 37, 1658–73; Treaty Series 576; Bevans (Charles I., comp.), Treaties and Other International Agreements of the United States of America, 1776–1949, 1, 780–90.
'Message from the President of the United States Transmitting the International Convention on Salvage, 1989', 102nd Congress, first Session, Senate Treaty Document 102–12, 11 September 1991.
Books
Brice, G., 1993, *Maritime Law of Salvage*, London.
Kennedy, D.S. and Kennedy, F.R., 1985, *The Law of Salvage*, 5th edn., London.
Norris, M.J., 1989, *Benedict on Admiralty: The Law of Salvage*, 3A, 7th edn rev., New York.
Schoenbaum, T.J., 1994, Salvage, *Admiralty and Maritime Law*, 2, 16, St Paul, Minnesota.
Wildeboer, I.H., 1965, *The Brussels Salvage Convention*, Leyden.

Articles

Giorgi, M.C., 1991, 'Underwater Archaeological and Historical Objects', in R.-J. Dupuy and D. Vignes (eds), *A Handbook on the New Law of the Sea*.

Gold, E., 1989, 'Marine Salvage: Towards a New Regime', *Journal of Maritime Law and Commerce*, 20 October, 4, 487–503.

Kerr, D.A., 1989, 'The 1989 Salvage Convention: Expediency or Equity?' *Journal of Maritime Law and Commerce*, 20 October, 4, 505–20.

Kerr, M., 1990, 'The International Convention on Salvage 1989: How It Came To Be', *International and Comparative Law Quarterly*, July, 39, 3, 530–56.

Parks, A.A., 1983, 'The 1910 Brussels Convention, the United States Salvage Act of 1912, and Arbitration of Salvage Cases in the United States', *Tulane Law Review*, June, 57, 1457–90.

Rosa, F.M. Jr., 1989, 'International Convention on Salvage', [US] *Federal Bar News & Journal*, October, 36, 8, 347–8.

Cases

The *Atocha*: Treasure Salvors, Inc. vs. Unidentified Wrecked and Abandoned Sailing Vessel, 408 F. Supp. 907 (D. Fla. 1976), affirmed 569 F.2d 330 (5th *c.*1978) (Treasure Salvors I); Florida Department of State vs. Treasure Salvors, Inc., 621 F.2d 1340 (5th *c.*1980) (Treasure Salvors II), affirmed in part and reversed in part, 458 US 670 (1982), on remand 689 F.2d 1254 (5th *c.*1982); Treasure Salvors, Inc. vs. Unidentified Wrecked and Abandoned Sailing Vessel, 640 F.2d 560 (5th *c.*1981) (Treasure Salvors III), on remand 546 F. Supp. 919 (S.D. Fla. 1981); Treasure Salvors, Inc. vs. Unidentified, Wrecked and Abandoned Sailing Vessel, 556 F. Supp. 1319 (S.D. Fla. 1983) (Treasure Salvors IV).

SS *Central America*: Columbus-America Discovery Group vs. Atlantic Mutual Ins. Co., 974 F.2d 450 (4th *c.*1992).

Sampling

Archaeological sampling has two meanings: (1) removal or collection of small sections or portions of an object or stratum to investigate it through many laboratory procedures such as dating, palynology, trace analysis, geochemical or geophysical analysis to determine constituents or provenance; (2) investigation of part of a population universe to characterize the whole, when the whole cannot be investigated completely for reasons of limited time, resources, or access. Sampling is applicable to any scale of investigation such as artefact attributes, types, features, sites, or regions. This discussion centres on the second meaning.

Sampling has been a conscious part of ter-restrial archaeology since the early part of the 20th century, when archaeologists became aware that their inferences about the past were based on small samples. Richard Ford and Gordon Willey used sampling procedures in the 1950s to limit biases in their Viru Valley survey. In 1964 **Research designs** incorporating probability sampling were promoted by Lewis Binford as a dependable means of obtaining representative data without introducing unacceptable and untested biases. During the 1970s various archaeological sampling procedures were developed, and sampling became an accepted and common practice.

The goal of archaeological sampling is to generalize from a sample to the population as a whole. In a real sense, all scientific generalizations are statistical inferences because they are derived from limited observations. All archaeological inferences also result from sampling of one kind or another. The objective of sampling strategies is to generate reliable, unbiased data about more objects than those actually investigated.

There are two basic sampling strategies: non-probabilistic, or intuitive, sampling and probabilistic sampling. Non-probabilistic sampling involves relying on one's experience or perhaps convenience of access to determine what portion of the **Archaeological record** to investigate. This practice by earlier terrestrial archaeologists led to a concentration on spectacular or conspicuous sites, and reflected the researchers' bias. This practice is still common among maritime archaeologists. Another disadvantage of this approach is that generalizations so derived cannot be objectively judged as to their representativeness of the whole population. Archaeologists introduced probabilistic sampling to deal with this problem.

Probabilistic sampling is a set of techniques derived from statistics used to investigate a representation of an area or object set to ensure representative coverage and, ideally, inclusion of all categories of materials or attributes. Statistical sampling is the mathematical methodology that allows systematic generation of archaeological inferences about the whole (statistical population) from a part (statistical sample, also known as the sampling fraction). Statistical sampling techniques enable archaeological generalization from research data to a mathematically determined statistically significant confidence level. Results of a properly designed sampling strategy characterize the areal or site universe to a statistically definable confidence. Significance is the probability that the statistical inference is characteristic of the population from which the sample was drawn and not a chance occurrence.

For example, a researcher could be confident to a level of 95 per cent that if 15 per cent of the sample objects are of a certain type, then 15 per cent of the whole population is of the same type. Sampling is not a search or site discovery tool, it is a means to characterize with confidence a large population that cannot be completely investigated.

There are many systematic sampling procedures, and much archaeological debate centres on which technique provides superior representativeness. To use sampling effectively, an archaeologist must be familiar with the theoretical and statistical advantages of different procedures and fit the sampling design to the local conditions and questions being asked. Sample design determination must meet requirements of both statistical and archaeological parameters. Statistical requirements include: each sample must be selected independently from other samples; any sampling unit, whether sherd or site, has equal chance of selection. Archaeological parameters include clear definitions about what the sample represents, and the boundaries of the whole population.

Some examples of common archaeological probability sampling techniques include: (1) simple random sampling – a selection of several sampling units equal to the sampling fraction based on genuinely random selection, for example from a random number table; (2) systematic sampling – begins with a sample unit and selects others based on an interval that provides the proper sampling fraction, say every sixth unit; (3) stratified sampling – the most common technique. The sampling universe is divided into homogeneous strata that reflect the sample universe's range of variation. Strata can be environmental zones, elevation, artefact classes, water depths, bottom type or anything else characteristic of the sampling universe.

Representativeness is characterized in two ways: by sample fraction compared with the total population, and by the nature of the factors that bias the sample. Any partial sample can miss rare or unique occurrences of cultural materials. Archaeologists now recognize that, because of the nature of archaeological data – principally that the sample universe is typically unknown, which complicates sample fraction determination – large samples are necessary to be representative. Generally, the larger the archaeological sample, the more representative it is.

There is a basic question in all archaeological survey: can there ever be a 'full coverage' survey that locates all archaeological material in an area? There is strong argument that all archaeological survey, regardless of intensity, is sampling. Whether full coverage is ever possible or not, there are many reasons to apply sampling procedures to underwater and maritime archaeological enquiry. An example from **Maritime archaeology** is **Remote sensing** survey, which is a sampling procedure. No instrument offers really 'full coverage' for all detectable phenomena; what is detectable is determined by deployment and post-processing parameters. Ultimately all indications (contacts, anomalies, etc.) may not be investigated, and here is where bias is often found. Funds may be limited, for example, for magnetic anomaly investigation in a survey, so perhaps only the largest ones are investigated. This procedure, common in US **Cultural resource management** surveys, eliminates smaller and scattered vessels from the survey sample. A better sampling strategy would be to stratify anomalies into size categories with each stratum sampled to provide a representation of the full range of magnetic cultural materials in the survey area. Another application is sampling a buried site's perimeter to establish site boundaries. Typically, site extent is determined intuitively, and sampling offers an efficient test of site determination. Sampling, so far rarely used in maritime archaeology, may become an important addition to investigative tools in future fieldwork. L.E.M.

ADDITIONAL READING

Mueller, J.W. (ed.), 1975, *Sampling in Archaeology*, Tucson.

Orton, C., 1980, *Mathematics in Archaeology*, Cambridge.

Thomas, D.H., 1976, *Figuring Anthropology: First Principles of Probability and Statistics*.

San Agustin

Spanish exploring vessel driven ashore and lost in late November 1595. The shipwreck site and remains of *San Agustin* lie in the lee of Point Reyes in Drakes Bay, approximately 200 m offshore from Drakes Beach and to the west of the entrance to Drakes Estero, California, USA. **Magnetometer** survey of Drakes Bay in 1982 located several clusters of anomalies; one cluster is presumed to be the site of *San Agustin*'s wreck based on analysis of historical accounts and plotting wave and current patterns against artefact distribution patterns.

Spanish vessels, beginning in 1573, opened trans-Pacific trade and inaugurated Spain's control of that ocean for centuries.

Because of the 'Manila galleons', Spanish trade and commerce flourished, major ports prospered in what is now Mexico and Panama, and voyages of exploration probed the coasts of California, Oregon, Washington, and British Columbia, seeking suitable anchorages and harbours. The site and remains of *San Agustin* are of exceptional significance as a tangible entity associated with those voyages and the Manila trade; for the ship's association with early explorer Sebastian Rodriguez Cermeno; as the only known remains of a Manila trade 'galleon' in the US, a largely undocumented type of vessel for this period; and as a grouping of prehistoric and historic archaeological sites whose excavation has begun to yield significant information on Native American–European interaction and the nature of early Manila trade cargoes. Future excavation has the potential to add substantially to and revise our understanding of Manila 'galleons', Spanish trade in the Pacific, Spanish voyages of exploration in the 16th century, and the events of November 1595 at Drakes Bay.

San Agustin was a small wooden vessel of approximately 200 tons built in the Philippines in 1594. Apart from a naval architectural treatise of 1587, details of design and construction for vessels of this period are sketchy, and little is consequently known about *San Agustin*. Naval architect and maritime historian Raymond Aker, working from historical accounts and basic details of 16th-century vessel construction, has hypothesized that *San Agustin*'s length between perpendiculars was about 24 m, with a beam of 6.7 or 7 m, and a 4 or 4.3 m draft. When wrecked, *San Agustin* carried about 80 people and 130 tons of cargo. From this, Aker postulates that the ship had a 'tween deck, forecastle, and a half deck aft that formed a sterncastle with cabins. Since historical accounts note that a deck-load of large ceramic jars of provisions, hen-coops, and chests was thrown overboard during a storm on 13 August 1595, Aker indicates that *San Agustin* would have been built with a commodious waist and solid bulwarks to accommodate the deck cargo. The vessel was three-masted and square rigged with lower courses on the fore and mainmasts, topsails, a spritsail, and lateen mizzen.

Considerable archaeological evidence of the wreck of *San Agustin* has been found through excavation of Late Horizon prehistoric Aboriginal habitation site middens on the shores of Drakes Estero that were abandoned in the 17th century.

In the summers of 1940 and 1941, Dr Robert F. Heizer of the University of California, Berkeley, and Richard K. Beardsley, one of Heizer's graduate students, conducted two field seasons of excavations of the middens at six sites, revealing among the numerous prehistoric artefacts seventy-four fragments of porcelain and forty-nine iron ship's spikes, some found in direct association with burials, others in concentrations Heizer attributed to using planks from the wreck to cover the pit houses of the local Indians. The porcelain was analysed as being Chinese, some being generally determined to be 'Late Ming made for export' (c.1550–1664), while many others were more precisely identified as being from the 'Wan Li' period (1573–1619). One fragment was identified as being from the 'Chia Ching' period (1522–66). The iron spikes were analysed and determined to be 'ancient', predating the 19th century. Heizer published his results in 1942, based on the historical evidence and his archaeological discoveries, and noted that the evidence pointed strongly to Cermeno's expedition as the one which introduced these remains. Indications that planks, which might easily have been from the wrecked *San Agustin*, were gathered from the beach by the Indians and the dates of manufacture of the porcelain all point to the Cermeno expedition. Furthermore, the Indian village which once stood at the archaeological Estero site was occupied at the time of Cermeno's visit, and it is near this village that the *San Agustin* was wrecked.

In 1942, Alfred L. Kroeber, writing a preface to Heizer's first report on his work in Drakes Bay, noted:

. . . we have recovered convincing, direct, physical evidence of contact between California Indian Aborigines and exploring Europeans in 1595 – three hundred and forty six years ago . . . Heretofore, the earliest positive dating of Indian–European contact material [in California] has been the beginning of the Mission period, about 1775. Our chronology has now been pushed back almost two centuries.

In 1945 excavation of many of the sites continued under the direction of Adan E. Treganza, and in 1949 additional excavations at Drakes Estero were pursued by Clement W. Meighan, who summarized ten years of research in 1950. Additional fragments of porcelain and ship's spikes were recovered, and at one site, Mrn-307, new types of non-Aboriginal artefacts were found. These were several iron drifts, used to hold keel timbers together, and seven pieces of brown-glazed stoneware. In 1952 Heizer and Meighan co-published an assessment of archaeological work at Drakes Bay in which the stoneware was identified as fragments from a large vessel, possibly a water jar, fired in Indo-China and near-identical to specimens recovered from excavation of late 16th-century sites near Manila, 'say mostly 1570–1600 . . .'

By 1952 the archaeologically recovered 16th-century materials were described as 125 fragments of Ming blue-on-white porcelain, most of it 'Wan Li', fifty-nine hand-wrought iron ship's spikes, eleven fragments of stoneware, and six 2.5 cm diameter iron drifts. According to Aker, the drifts 'give evidence of coming from the stem of *San Agustin*. The 'S' shape of two of them indicates that they had been affected by a shearing action, such as would occur if the ship's bow had broken away and caused the stem and keelson to pull apart.' Aker feels that the flood tide drove pieces of debris into the estero to its eastern edge and along Limantour Spit (the direction of the littoral drift) where flotsam would have accumulated. Supporting this contention is the presence of the drifts at Mrn-307 and nearby Mrn-232's yield of fifty-three out of seventy-one spikes recovered. Winter storms have also exposed hundreds of pieces of porcelain and some stoneware on Limantour Spit, which is the major zone of concentration for this type of artefact.

There are currently some 700 known pieces of porcelain that have been recovered from twelve sites along the shores of Drakes Estero. Excavations by Adan Treganza in the mid-1960s recovered two copper coat buttons with a fleur-de-lis design from Mrn-216, as well as a copper cone that may be the tip of a weapon handle or shaft. Other 16th-century European artefacts have been recovered from Drakes Bay and the Marin County area, but their provenance is not well established. These include the 50 cm artefact described as the tip of a Javanese-manufactured halberd, found near Mrn-281 in 1955, an Elizabethan sixpence dated 1567 excavated at Olampali in 1974, and a brass apothecary's mortar with a Nurenburg maker's stamp that predates 1604, reportedly found during a church picnic in 1950 at Drakes Bay and now displayed at St Francis Episcopal Church in Novato, California. The numbers or date '1570' are crudely chiselled into one side of the mortar.

The archaeological evidence gathered from Drakes Bay offers the only material record of early European exploration on the Pacific coast, there being no positively identified or non-controversial artefacts dating to Cabrillo's (1542) or Drake's (1579) voyages. Of particular note is the reuse and assimilation of *San Agustin* wreckage and cargo by the local coastal Miwok. Planks from the ship's hull were used to cover the roofs of these people's pit houses, and the porcelain was kept locally, perhaps highly prized or not prized at all, since attempts to bore beads (eleven blanks having been located to date) were a failure. Yet several pieces show evidence of reuse, including pendants, scrapers, and the presence of iron spikes in some burials, perhaps a sign of high status. The modified porcelains and burial good spikes excavated at Drakes Bay offer the first, and earliest, positively dated material cultural record of cross-cultural contact on the Pacific coast of North America.

The analysis of the recovered porcelain and other ceramic sherds has provided insights into the quality and variety of one type of commodity in the first quarter century of the Manila trade. Edward von der Porten has shown that the cargo of *San Agustin* was apparently utility ware 'rice bowls, plates, large and small low bowls, and large, heavy deep bowls'. Presumably repacked in Manila, the porcelains include unusually shaped vessels, such as a Seto ware cup from Japan, a flat dish, and a possibly fluted vase neck, as well as diverse styles of decoration that ranged from crude to delicate that might indicate Chinese uncertainty over their 'new "barbarian" customers' tastes'. Work on the sherds, which can be more or less precisely dated, has added to the knowledge of Manila trade cargoes beyond the general 'ceramics' or 'porcelain' listed in manifests, as well as trade practices and potential insights into Spanish consumer behaviour, Chinese trade behaviour in a new market, and the impact of this alien technology in the New World.

While at least one formal effort to locate the submerged wreckage of *San Agustin* was undertaken in 1965, and several unauthorized searches reportedly have been made, systematic survey of Drakes Bay was not accomplished until 1982. Archaeological survey work conducted by the National Park Service **Submerged Cultural Resource Unit** (SCRU) between 23 August and 5 September and 4 and 14 October 1982, probably pinpointed the wreck location. A total area of 6.5 square kilometres was surveyed with a proton precession recording **Magnetometer**, producing 684 anomalous readings that can be grouped into more than 300 discrete anomalies greater than 10 gammas. These readings were analysed and forty-nine separate clusters of anomalies were detected; in addition, 26 square kilometres inside Drakes Bay were surveyed with **Side-scan sonar** and 48 linear kilometres were assessed with **Sub-bottom profiling** equipment.

Using Spanish 17th- and 18th-century maps to plot *San Agustin*'s presumed anchorage at 0.8 km offshore of the western point of the entrance to Drakes Estero, Raymond Aker placed the wreck site of *San Agustin* at a point near the mouth of the estero. Reanalysing Aker's data, the National Park Service Submerged Cultural Resource Unit places the wreckage as much as 2.4 km west of Aker's suggested site. This conclusion is based on the southeast wind that blew the vessel ashore combining with the west-northwest swell in the bay to drive *San Agustin* either directly onshore or slightly to the west, therefore placing the site between 0.8 and 2.4 km west of the estero mouth. This theory would place *San Agustin* almost squarely on the point where the magnetometer survey revealed a high-duration, low-level cluster of anomalies that is similar to anomaly clusters mapped during a magnetometer survey of three Spanish wrecks of 1554 at **Padre Island** National Seashore, Texas. The cluster most probably represents a shipwreck containing few major iron parts but considerable wreckage scatter, as would be expected from *San Agustin*. The cluster is also the logical dispersion point for porcelain carried by littoral sand transport along the beach to major concentrations on Limantour Spit and at the head of Bear Valley, where the creek interrupts sand transport and worn, tumbled porcelain fragments are concentrated. Excavation of this anomaly cluster will probably reveal the wreckage of *San Agustin* beneath 3.6 and 7.3 m of sediment.

National Park Service plans call for future testing and excavation of the anomalies to determine the extent and nature of *San Agustin*'s remains. The NPS plans faced a serious challenge in the mid-1980s from Florida-based treasure-hunter Robert F. Marx, who sought permission to excavate the site with **Propwash deflection** and finance his expedition through the sale of artefacts, primarily porcelain, recovered from the wreck. When the NPS denied permission, citing the significance of the wreck, its location in a **National park** and a national marine sanctuary, and scientific and ethical objections to the sale of the artefacts, Marx filed suit in admiralty court and sought permission from the State of California. While the State ultimately approved Marx's plans, the National Oceanic and Atmospheric Administration and the National Park Service successfully blocked excavation. Marx conducted a magnetometer survey of the area, resurveying the anomalies pinpointed by the NPS in 1982, but did not pursue further work. J.P.D.

ADDITIONAL READING

Aker, R., 1965, *The Cermeno Expedition at Drakes Bay, 1595*, Palo Alto, California.

Heizer, R.F., 1942, *Archaeological Evidence of Sebastian Rodrigues Cermeno's California Visit in 1595*, San Francisco.

Heizer, R.F. and Meighan, C.W., 1952, 'Archaeological Exploration of Sixteenth-Century Indian Mounds at Drakes Bay', *California Historical Society Quarterly*, June, 31,2.

Meighan, C.W., 1950, 'Excavations in Sixteenth Century Shellmounds at Drakes Bay, Marin County', *University of California Archaeological Survey Records*, 9, 28–9.

Murphy, L. (ed.), 1983, *Submerged Cultural Resources Survey, Portions of Point Reyes National Seashore and Point Reyes-Farallon Islands National Marine Sanctuary, Phase I-Reconnaissance*, Santa Fe, New Mexico.

Shangrew, C. and von der Porten, E., 1981, *The Drake and Cermeno Expeditions' Chinese Porcelain at Drakes Bay, California, 1579 and 1595*, Santa Rosa, California.

von der Porten, E., 1968, *Porcelains and Terra Cottas of Drakes Bay*, Palo Alto, California.

von der Porten, E., 1973, *Drake and Cermeno in California: Sixteenth Century Chinese Ceramics*, Point Reyes, California.

Wagner, H.R., 1924, 'The Voyage to California of Sebastian Rodriguez Cermeno in 1595', *California Historical Society Quarterly*, April, 3, 1, 3–24.

San Diego

Spanish galleon that sank on 14 December 1600 after ramming the Dutch ship *Mauritius* during a battle near the southern approach to Manila Bay on the southwestern coast of the Philippine Island of Luzon. Grossly overloaded and over-manned, the 35 m long *San Diego* sank in deep water, taking with it most of the 450 men on board. No salvage was attempted in antiquity. The remains of the 300 ton *San Diego* were discovered in 1991 by the Paris-based treasure-hunting and salvage company the 'European Institute of Underwater Archaeology'.

With the aid of a **Magnetometer**, the salvors found the site in 55 m of water approximately 1,500 m off the shore of Fortune Island. The salvage was conducted during two seasons in 1992 and 1993. Equipped with a submarine and an ROV the salvors also visited the site in person, wearing scuba and surface-tethered diving equipment. Among the finds were 14 cannon, 570 storage jars, 430 coins, jewellery, Chinese porcelain, an astrolabe, and the remains and personal possessions of the 450 men who had been on board. Archival documents report that *San Diego* was built as a merchant

galleon in a shipyard on the island of Cebu in the Philippines. Having been dispatched from Manila specifically to engage a marauding Dutch fleet, it carried neither treasure nor cargo.

During the second season the well-preserved bottom of the ship, which had been protected by its ballast, was uncovered and mapped. Although some of the hull members were raised and studied, most were left *in situ*, and reburied following the salvage.

Although at first denied, it now appears that the finds were divided between the salvors and the government of the **Philippines**. It is important to note that most archaeological excavations of shipwrecks require ten to twenty years to complete; *San Diego* was discovered, salvaged, published, and placed on exhibit in less than three years. D.H.K.

ADDITIONAL READING

Carré, D., Desroches, J.-P. and Goddio, F., 1994, *Le San Diego: un trésor sous la mer*, Paris.

Goddio, F., 1994, 'San Diego', *National Geographic*, 186, 1, 35–57.

San Juan
see **Red Bay**

San Juan de Sicilia

Member of the **Spanish Armada**'s Levant squadron which blew up and sank in Tobermory Bay on the Isle of Mull, off the west coast of Scotland in 1588. The ship originally came from Ragusa (modern Dubrovnik in Dalmatia), and was embargoed by Spanish authorities in Sicily in 1586. Like *La Trinidad Valencera*, it was probably a specialist grain-carrier, a type of ship required by the Armada because its bulk cargo capacity made it suitable for the transport of invasion stores, including heavy siege artillery. In the fleet muster held at Lisbon

Tobermory Harbour, off the Isle of Mull in western Scotland, where San Juan de Sicilia *blew up and sank. (Colin Martin)*

before the Armada sailed, it is rated at 800 tons, and listed with a complement of 26 guns, 63 marines, and 279 soldiers. During the battles in the English Channel, it was heavily engaged, and received, according to one of her crew, many shots '... alow and aloft and from the prow to the stern, and below the waterline in places difficult to repair ...'. Separated from the main body of the fleet during the voyage home, it limped into Tobermory Bay where its commander, Don Diego Tellez Enriquez, provided the local clan chief with a company of troops to sort out his local feuds in return for provisions and an opportunity to make repairs. After some days the ship inexplicably blew up and sank, probably through sabotage, although a Spanish source suggests that it may have been an accident. There were few survivors apart from those onshore, most of whom eventually escaped to Flanders via Edinburgh.

Within a few years a strong though erroneous belief sprang up that the ship contained a vast **Treasure**, and for almost four centuries attempts have been made to recover it. A good description of the wreck was made in 1677 by divers working from a bell, who found the hull embedded in sand, with much of the upper structure collapsed around it. In the 1730s a major effort was made to recover the illusory treasure: these operations were conducted from a remarkable sealed diving engine, and involved the systematic ripping apart of the hull. Little was found, although a bronze gun of the French king Francis I, now at Inveraray Castle, was probably recovered at this time. Further attempts in the early years of the

20th century yielded a bronze swivel gun and some other artefacts, but later efforts – the last of which was in the early 1980s – have produced little concrete result, though they have further damaged an archaeological context which, had it been left undisturbed, would almost certainly have contained the major part of a late 16th-century Ragusan argosy. It is probable that the lower hull of the vessel remains preserved some 8 m below the present seabed, and it is to be hoped that the site will be protected against yet further intrusion by treasure-seekers. C.M.

ADDITIONAL READING
McLeay, A., 1986, *The Tobermory Treasure*, London.

Sankt Mikael

The so-called Borstö Wreck, located in the early 1950s in 42 m of water when fishermen's nets caught in the ship's structure. When Navy divers were called in to check on the obstacle on the bottom, they found an old but well-preserved sailing ship with its three masts still standing. The wreck is situated south of Borstö island at the southwestern part of the Finnish coast.

In the years following the discovery Swedish **SCUBA**-divers brought up a large quantity of artefacts, among which were a number of luxury items including snuff boxes, clocks, gold jewellery, and silver. Judging from manufacture stamps, most of these items were made in Paris 1745–7. In the aft part of the ship two human skeletons were found. According to osteological analysis, one was a young woman, the other an elderly man. (See **Human remains**.)

The shipwreck was photographed and surveyed during the 1960s and plans and perspective drawings were produced. Archival research performed by Dr C. Ahlström of Helsinki has shown that the wreck, which measures 25 m in length and 7 m in width, had originally been the galliot *Sankt Mikael* or *Sankt Michel*. It sank in the autumn of 1747 on a voyage from Amsterdam to St Petersburg. The master of the ship was a Dutchman, Carl P. Amiel, but the ship was probably owned by Russians. *Sankt Mikael* carried tobacco, sugar, wine, oak timber, and a carriol, a two-wheeled cart. C.O.C.

ADDITIONAL READING
Ahlström, C., 1978, 'Documentary Research on the Baltic: Three Case Studies', *International Journal of Nautical Archaeology and Underwater Exploration*, 7, 2, 59–70.
Ahlström, C., 1995, 'Spår av hav, yxa och penna: Historiska sjöolyckor i östersjön avspeglade i marinarkeologiskt källmaterial, bidrag till kännedom av Finlands natur och folk',
Utgivna av Finska Vetenskaps-Societeten, 148, 152–68.
Ericsson, C. and Risto, H., 1971, 'The Dutch galjoot off Borstö, parish of Nauvo/Nagu', *Maritime Museum of Finland Annual Report*, 4–6.
Ericsson, C. and Risto, H., 1973, 'The Borstö Wreck: Advanced Research and Archive Work 1971–73', *Maritime Museum of Finland Annual Report*, 4–5.

San Salvador
see *Salvador*

Santa Lucia

The remains of a ship believed to be the Spanish dispatch vessel *Santa Lucia*, which sank in Bermuda in 1584. This wreck, site number IMHA3, was discovered in 1964 by local divers and sporadically salvaged over the ensuing twenty-five years.

Between 1988 and 1991 the site was excavated and the hull remains recovered by the Bermuda Maritime Museum (BMM) and the **East Carolina University Program in Maritime History and Nautical Archaeology** (ECU), Greenville, North Carolina, under the direction of Gordon P. Watts, Jr. Evidence indicated that the vessel struck a remote section of the Western Ledge Reef, part of Bermuda's massive fringing reef system, and sank in approximately 12 m of water.

The hull remains were in two sections. The larger section was an articulated segment of the lower hull measuring over nine metres in length, covered and protected by a partially intact mound of stone ballast. This section consisted of the keel, fourteen floor timbers, twenty-two first futtocks, exterior and interior planking, and mast-step. The smaller section was an articulated assemblage of stern timbers, including the sternpost, stern knee, wye pieces, first futtocks, exterior planking, and the lowermost gudgeon.

In 1991 the surviving hull components were disassembled, raised, and transported to specially fabricated storage tanks at the museum's conservation facility, where the timbers were individually recorded in detail. The timbers were recorded 1:1 on mylar drafting film, and all fastenings and surface features (tool marks, scribe marks, caulking, etc.) were added to the drawings; in addition, a complete photographic record was made of each timber.

The extant keel was a single oak timber, roughly triangular in cross-section, with a preserved length of 9.33 m from the stem scarf to a point 4.8 m aft of the master couple. The master couple was very evident, consisting of a floor timber with first fut-

tocks fayed to both the forward and aft sides. Forward of the master couple the first futtocks were fayed to the forward side of the floors, while those aft of the master couple were fayed to the after side of the floors. Floors and first futtocks were joined with shallow dovetail scarfs, fastened with spikes and treenails. All frames were oak, spaced approximately 35 cm apart. The mast step was very distinctive, consisting of a large oak timber notched to fit over the floors and supported on each side by three buttresses, set at right angles; a rectangular mortise was cut to step the mast. The hull bears many striking similarities to the Basque whaler believed to be *San Juan*, excavated in **Red Bay**, Labrador.

The vessel's original dimensions are estimated as follows: overall length between 18.5 and 23.5 m, maximum beam between 5 and 6 m, and tonnage between 118 and 191 *toneladas*. Hull construction and cultural material suggest that the site was a Spanish vessel, possibly a small *navio* or *patache*, from the last quarter of the 16th century. Research conducted in Spain by the museum produced documentation on a likely identity: *Santa Lucia*, a Spanish dispatch vessel, or *navio de adviso*, that was lost in Bermuda in 1584. J.D.B.

ADDITIONAL READING
Watts, G.P., Jr, 1993, 'The Western Ledge Reef Wreck: A Preliminary Report on the Investigation of a Sixteenth-Century Shipwreck in Bermuda', *International Journal of Nautical Archaeology and Underwater Exploration*, 22, 2, 103–24.
Watts, G.P., Jr *et al.*, 1994, 'A Preliminary Description of the Excavation, Timber Recording, Hull Construction, and Cultural Material Analysis of a Sixteenth-Century Vessel Wrecked on Western Ledge Reef, Bermuda', *Underwater Archaeology Proceedings from the Society for Historical Archaeology Conference, Tucson, Arizona*, Ann Arbor, Michigan, 47–62.

Santa Maria de la Rosa
Vice-flagship of the **Spanish Armada**'s Guipuzcoan squadron, wrecked in Blasket Sound, southwest Ireland. The ship was built in 1587 at San Sebastian for a local citizen, Martin de Villafranca, perhaps as a mother ship for the Newfoundland whale fishery. Before she could sail, however, she was embargoed for the Armada and brought to Lisbon. The ship was rated at 945 tons and carried twenty-six guns. Her complement included 64 mariners and 225 soldiers of the *tercio* (regiment) of Sicily. The owner's son (also called Martin) sailed as master. She was severely damaged in the storm that

forced the fleet to seek refuge in Corunna shortly after it sailed, and a new mainmast was fitted there. During the fighting her hull was penetrated by shot in four places, one of them close to the waterline. In the course of the voyage round Britain the ship became detached from the main body of the fleet. On 21 September 1588, in extreme distress, it sought shelter from a violent westerly gale in Blasket Sound, off the southwest tip of Ireland. Two other Armada ships were already at anchor there, and the commander of one of them – Marcos de Aramburu – has left a graphic account of her fate. Wind and tide dragged her to a reef in the middle of the Sound, which she struck, sinking almost immediately. There was only one survivor.

Aramburu's account prompted Sydney Wignall, a British pioneer of **Underwater archaeology**, to launch a search for *Santa Maria*'s remains in 1968. Following a swim-line search of unprecedented magnitude – in all, over ten square kilometres were covered – a ballast mound with associated timber structure was located towards the end of the season. The remains lay at a depth of 36.5 m in the eye of a fierce tide-rip.

Further work, including some limited excavation, was conducted in 1969. It appeared from this that only the forward bottom section of the hull had survived, pinned down by some 200 tonnes of stone ballast. The rest of the ship, having lost its bottom and shed its ballast, apparently detached itself to move with the running tide into deeper water where, presumably, its remains now lie.

This hypothesis explains the absence of guns on the site, and a general paucity of other artefactual material. Nonetheless the evidence recovered from the wreck is significant. There are strong structural parallels with the 16th-century Basque whaling ship at Red Bay, Labrador, notably in the mast-stepping arrangements. The finds have included shot of various calibres, lead ingots (for casting small shot), the remains of muskets and arquebuses, pottery, and several pieces of pewter. Two of the latter bear the name *Matute*, who can be identified from the fleet muster rolls as Captain Francisco Ruiz Matute, commander of a Sicilian infantry company aboard the ship. C.M.

ADDITIONAL READING

Martin, C.J.M., 1973, 'The Spanish Armada Expedition, 1968–70', in D.J. Blackman (ed.), *Marine Archaeology*, Colston Papers, 23, London.

Martin, C.J.M., 1975, *Full Fathom Five: Wrecks of the Spanish Armada*, London and New York.

Santíssimo Sacramento (1647)

Portuguese vessel that went aground during a winter storm at Schoenmakerskop, in the vicinity of Port Elizabeth, South Africa in 1647. The vessel was homeward bound for Lisbon from Goa carrying a consignment of bronze and iron cannon.

In 1977 a local diver, David Allen, and his group initiated discussion on legislation with the National Monuments Council primarily to protect their interests on the site. The Port Elizabeth Museum and the Port Elizabeth Historical Society became involved in monitoring the historical and archaeological aspects of the operation. Correspondence from the museum states that careful mapping and systematic investigation of the site was hindered by the 'ever present threat of piracy and consequent need for haste'. Thirty-eight of the cannon were properly recorded. The artefact collection, including Ming export porcelain, stoneware, ebony, ballast stones, rope grommets, and peppercorns, have been donated to the Port Elizabeth Museum. One of the cannon is on display at the Art Gallery.

In 1994, accurate mapping of the remaining iron cannon, including a **Magnetometer** survey, was conducted by local divers using conventional, acceptable archaeological principles. L.H., T.D.

ADDITIONAL READING

Allen, G. and D., 1978, *The Guns of Sacramento*, London.

Axelson, E. (ed.), 1988, *Dias and his Successors*, Cape Town.

Feyo, B.T., 1650, 'Relacam do naufragio que fizeram as Naos Sacramento & Nossa Senhora da Atalaya vindo da India para o Reyno, no Cabo Esperanca', Lisbon, translated into English in G.M. Theal, *Records of South Eastern Africa*, 8, 295–360.

Santíssimo Sacramento (1668)

Portuguese galleon bound for Brazil that sank in 1668 in the middle of the night at the entrance to Bahia with the loss of most of its passengers and crew. The sixty-gun *Santíssimo Sacramento* served as the principal armed escort for a fleet of fifty merchant ships departing Portugal for Brazil in 1668. Commanded by General Francisco Correa da Silva for the royal Companhia Geral do Comércio do Brasil, the flagship guarded the annual South Atlantic trading fleet against Dutch warships, which threatened the security of Portugal's maritime commerce in Brazilian sugar and gold. Bound from Lisbon to Bahia (São Salvador), the ships were carrying European manufactured goods and foodstuffs needed in the colony, and royal arms and ammunition for its pro-

tection. The fleet also carried many passengers en route to America with hopes of making their fortunes. On board *Sacramento* were over 1,000 people, 800 of whom were sailors and soldiers – many from distinguished families – and 200 of whom were civilians, including clergymen and civil servants.

Approaching the entrance to the Bay of all Saints late on the stormy afternoon of 5 May, *Sacramento*'s pilot decided to attempt the dangerous reef-strewn passage in the growing darkness, and the ship ran aground on a shallow shoal at the eastern edge of the channel. Although da Silva ordered cannons fired to signal the galleon's distress, due to the stormy weather, no captain would leave port to assist the stranded vessel. Shortly before midnight a sudden squall blew *Sacramento* off the shoal into deeper water, where it foundered and sank. There were only 70 survivors; among the victims was General da Silva.

The discovery in the mid-1970s of several unique colonial cannon in a modern Salvador salvage yard prompted Brazilian naval officials to seize them as national treasures, and trace their origin to an unknown offshore shipwreck. Dates and founder's marks on the cannon indicated the wreck had occurred sometime after 1653, and that it belonged to the Brazil Company. Joint archaeological investigations commenced in 1976 by the Ministry of the Navy and the Ministry of Education and Culture, under the supervision of Ulysses Pernambuco de Mello. The warship's grave, marked by a large mound of granite ballast stones surrounded by cannons, anchors, olive jars and encrusted porcelain, lay in 30 m of water on a gravel bottom. The cannons bore dates from the last decade of the 16th century to the mid-17th century; many included engraved armillary spheres with the Latin inscription SPERO IN DEO on the breech as well as COMPANHIA G^{I}DO BRASIL. Portuguese silver coins, mostly from the reign of João IV (1650–56), had been counter-struck in 1663 to raise their value, providing investigators with a more accurate *terminus post quem* for the shipwreck. Positive identification of the site as that of *Santíssimo Sacramento* was established by the discovery of several pieces of Portuguese majolica ceramics bearing the coat of arms of the da Silva family.

Although *Sacramento* was a warship, she also carried cargo; hundreds of brass sewing thimbles and wooden-handled razors were unearthed on the site. Evidence of a shipment of textiles was revealed by several types of lead baling seals; those from the City of

London suggested that the galleon carried English cloth as well. The majority of the ship's cargo, however, appeared to have comprised thousands of lead musket balls, packed in olive jars, which were more normally used to hold liquids and condiments. Among the wreckage was found the unlucky pilot's equipment: two brass astrolabes, a set of navigator's brass rules and dividers, and sounding leads. Other ship-related objects included ceramic tablewares with the Brazil Company emblem, as well as pewter candlesticks, bowls, and plates.

Forty-two cannon found on the wreck site were of various origins. The oldest were of English manufacture: two brass culverins from the middle of the 16th century and two demi-cannon inscribed by their founders, John and Richard Phellips, dated respectively 1590 and 1596. Two additional brass quarter-cannon bore the inscription: GEORGE ELKINE MADE THIS PIECE: 1597. All the English guns had been inscribed with the Brazil Company's logo. Other artillery was of Dutch manufacture: three brass falconets dated 1646 with the inscription HENRICVS VESTRINK FECIT CAMPIS and a demi-cannon with the founder's inscription COENRAED WEDEWAERT ME FECIT HAGAE 1649. Most of the Portuguese cannons had been cast by founder Matias Escartim and bore the same inscriptions and coats of arms; others were eventually traced to different founders.

Nearly half of the ordnance aboard *Sacramento* had been made of cast iron; its bronze artillery appears to have been mounted from available foreign pieces, since Portugal suffered from a shortage of weaponry following its independence from Spain in 1640. Examined by military historian John Guilmartin, the early bronze guns displayed manufacturing characteristics much more complicated and labour-intensive than previously thought. Their presence on a ship of the mid-17th century reflected the longevity of bronze artillery at sea, and suggested that the best bronze cannons of the 16th century were still considered to be effective and useful weapons almost a century later. R.S.

ADDITIONAL READING

Guilmartin, J.F., Jr, 1983, 'The Guns of the Santíssimo Sacramento', *Technology and Culture*, 24, 559–609.

Pernambucano de Mello, U., 1979, 'The Shipwreck of the Galleon *Sacramento* – 1668 off Brazil', *International Journal of Nautical Archaeology and Underwater Exploration*, 8, 211–23.

Smith, R.C., 1988, 'The Iberian-American Maritime Empires', in G.F. Bass (ed.), *Ships and Shipwrecks in the Americas: A History Based on Underwater Archaeology*, London.

Santo Antonio de Tanna

A forty-two gun Portuguese frigate built in 1681 in Goa and sunk off Kenya in 1697. It had sailed mostly in the Indian Ocean, with but one voyage as far as Lisbon and back (the *carreira de India*), when it was called to help relieve the siege by Omani Arabs of Fort Jesus. The fort, overlooking the harbour of Mombasa, was one of the fortified outposts built from Brazil around Africa to India and China to protect the Portuguese

A carved wooden angel which adorned the stern of the Portuguese warship Santo Antonio de Tanna. *(© INA)*

Portuguese faience jars, plates, and bottle decorated with bird and plant motifs from the Portuguese warship Santo Antonio de Tanna. *(© INA)*

route to the east. The Arabs, angered by Portuguese taxes in East Africa, attacked the fort early in 1696, but relief in the form of a squadron led by General Luis de Mello Sampaio aboard *Santo Antonio de Tanna*, upgraded to a 50 gun vessel, did not arrive for ten months, and then did not remain long. After unloading supplies and men, the general sailed to Mozambique. On its return nearly a year later, the frigate suffered badly from enemy action. After its mooring cables broke, it lost its rudder and ran aground before sinking on 20 October 1697.

The wreck was found independently by local divers Conway Plough and Peter Phillips in the early 1960s. Pottery raised from a depth of 13–16 m allowed James

Kirkman, Curator of Fort Jesus, to date the wreck to the late 17th century; subsequent finds satisfied them that the ship was probably *Santo Antonio de Tanna*.

In 1976 Hamo Sassoon, Dr Kirkman's successor, invited the **Institute of Nautical Archaeology** (INA) to investigate the wreck. Donald Frey and Robin Piercy, with advice from Plough and Phillips, surveyed the wreck with a metal detector and **Magnetometer**, estimating the ship to be about 38 m long with a beam of 8 m.

The National Museums of Kenya next asked INA to undertake a joint excavation of the site. Under the direction of Piercy there were four campaigns between 1976 and 1980, with excavators from the British Joint Services Sub Aqua Diving Centre, the Western Australian Museum, the Kenya Navy, Texas A&M University and INA; study of the hull and more than 15,000 artefacts continues.

The boatswain's store at the ship's stern included a wooden lamp with shell lights, two compasses, boxes of nails and bolts, a wooden bucket and barrels, sailmaker's palms, a wooden caulking hammer and unused caulking, a delousing comb, a dough paddle, several wooden powder flasks, cannon quoins, a roll of reed matting,

and much rope. A carved wooden Portuguese coat of arms was probably from the stern castle. The ship's wooden pumps were located just aft of the main mast-step.

Probably belonging to the officers were Portuguese faience jars, porcelain plates and bowls, a brass table bell, a pewter plate, and a silver-plated candlestick. A shipboard sacrament consisted of two small pewter jugs, a tray with a stoppered bottle, and two small lidded bowls. In the bow were Indian earthenware flasks and stoneware Martaban jars of Southeast Asian manufacture, all probably taken on at Goa (other ceramics seem to have been picked up at Mozambique during the frigate's visit). In the bow, too, were Portuguese faience ware and much iron shot.

Only three large iron cannon were found; most of the armament was saved by the Portuguese or salvaged by the Arabs. Even if most valuables were removed then, there were still 3,500 artefacts spilled down-slope of the wreck, including jet pendants and earrings, Chinese porcelain, Portuguese faience, unglazed flasks, silver buttons, and a bronze breech-loading gun. G.F.B.

ADDITIONAL READING

INA Newsletter 18, 2 (Summer 1991) is devoted to *Santo Antonio de Tanna*, with articles by different authors on The Weapons, Archival Research in India, The Hull, The Rigging, The Pumps, The Compasses, Smoking Pipes, The Portuguese Faience, The Martaban Jars, and Conservation.

Kirkman, J., 1972, 'A Portuguese Wreck off Mombasa', *International Journal of Nautical Archaeology*, 1, 153–7.

Piercy, R.C.M., 1977, 'Mombasa Wreck Excavation, Preliminary Report[s]', *International Journal of Nautical Archaeology*, 1977, 6, 331–47; 1978, 7, 301–19; 1979, 8, 303–9; 1981, 10, 109–18.

Piercy, R.C.M., Darroch, A., and Bass, G.F., 1992, 'The Wreck of the Santo Antonio de Tanna', *Archaeology*, 45, 3, 32–5.

Santorini
see **Thera**

São Bento

Wreck of a Portuguese *nao*, located on the southeast African coast (formerly the Transkei), and one of the earliest wrecks on the South African coastline. *São Bento* was on a homeward voyage from Cochin, India, when it wrecked in 1544. The site was discovered in 1968 by a local diver who recovered several bronze cannon. In 1977 the Archaeology Department at the Natal Museum, under the leadership of Tim Maggs and Chris Auret, supervised further fieldwork.

Artefacts recovered from the site include eighteen bronze cannon, jewellery, beads, and a large quantity of porcelain dating from 1530–60. The majority of the porcelain, which seems to be the main cargo component, is in the Natal Museum Collection. Repositories for other artefacts include the Natal Museum, the Durban Local History Museum, the East London Museum, and the Transkeu Museum in Umtata. There is an excellent primary source account of the wrecking and the survivors' 675 km journey to reach the nearest Portuguese settlement by Manual de Mesquito Perestrelo. L.H., T.D.

ADDITIONAL READING

Auret, C. and Maggs, T., 1982, 'The Great Ship

Sao Bento: Remains from a Mid-Sixteenth-Century Portuguese Wreck on the Pondoland Coast', *Annals of the Natal Museum*, 25, 1, 1–39.

Axelson, E. (ed.), 1988, *Dias and his Successors*, Cape Town.

Theal, G.M., 1898, *Records of South-Eastern Africa*, Cape Town.

HMS *Sapphire*

British warship wreck, lost in 1696 off Bay Bulls, Newfoundland. The second oldest shipwreck identified and archaeologically documented in Canada, it was surveyed and partially excavated by the Newfoundland Marine Archaeology Society in 1974. HMS *Sapphire*, a thirty-two gun, fifth-rate frigate, was built at Harwich in 1675. The 346 ton, 89 ft (27 m) long vessel convoyed two merchant ships to Newfoundland in 1696. On or around 11 September 1696 *Sapphire* was attacked by a superior French squadron of nine ships and sank in 16–20 m of water.

The wreck, although unidentified, became known to local divers around 1960, and a number of artefacts were recovered. In 1972, commercial divers removed and sold three of several cannon from the wreck. Partly in response to this incident, other more preservation-oriented divers formed the Newfoundland Marine Archaeology Society.

The wreck site was surveyed in 1973, and in September 1974 a trial excavation was undertaken under permit from the Province of Newfoundland. This project identified the wreck as *Sapphire*. At least ten cannon, wooden hull remains, and numerous concretions were documented at the site, and more than 3,000 smaller artefacts, including concretions, ceramics, and glassware, were recovered and conserved. A comparative study of the artefacts was done with the collection from the 1690 wreck **Dartmouth** in England. The *Sapphire* artefacts are now in the collections of the Newfoundland Museum in St John's. As a result of the work done by the Marine Archaeology Society, the wreck of *Sapphire* was declared a Provincial Historic Site in 1975, and was the first underwater historic site to be declared in Newfoundland. In 1977 responsibility for the site's future work was transferred to the Marine Archaeology Unit of Parks Canada. J.P.D.

ADDITIONAL READING

Barber, V.C., 1977, 'The *Sapphire*, a British Frigate, Sunk in Action at Bay Bulls, Newfoundland, in 1696', *International Journal of Nautical Archaeology*, 6, 4, 305–13.

USS *Saratoga*
see **Crossroads wrecks**

Save Ontario Shipwrecks
see **Ontario marine heritage organizations**

Schools education
see **Precollegiate education**

Scottish Institute of Maritime Studies

Institution associated with St Andrews University, founded in 1973 to further interdisciplinary teaching and research into the archaeology, ethnology, and history of humankind's relationship with the sea. It is particularly active in the field of underwater archaeology, and since 1986 has been the home base of the **Archaeological Diving Unit** which operates in conjunction with the UK Government's legislation on historic shipwrecks. This work includes aspects of **Cultural resource management** and the establishment of maritime-related databases. The institute also operates a Field Research Unit in support of its own research programmes, and has investigated a number of shipwreck sites around the British Isles. Its other major strength is experience and practical involvement in the preservation, restoration, and management of surviving historic ships, and it undertakes extensive contract work for government and other agencies in this specialized field.

The institute offers a graduate teaching programme which provides a foundation for researching and recording the maritime past. Practical skills are combined with intellectual rigour, and the programme aims at developing students' abilities to the point at which they can prepare their own research material, including illustrations, to publication standards. A core module introduces students to concepts of maritime studies, research methodologies, and the identification and use of sources. Another module considers principles and techniques of underwater archaeology within a context of wider interdisciplinary study. The syllabus for this module closely follows that set by the **Nautical Archaeology Society**. There are additional opportunities for those whose interests lie in historic ship management or museum work. The foundation element of the programme is a one-year taught diploma, upon which higher degrees up to PhD level can be built.

Further information can be obtained from the Admissions Officer, Scottish Institute of Maritime Studies, University of St Andrews, Fife KY16 9AJ, Scotland, UK. C.M.

Scottish Trust for Underwater Archaeology

Scottish body, with its headquarters at the University of Edinburgh. The STUA was formed to 'further the study of sunken settlements and watercraft, drowned ancient landscapes and other elements of the underwater heritage, and to encourage their protection and preservation'. Interdisciplinary in approach, the STUA's work includes research, exploration, surveys, and publication. J.P.D.

Scourge

see *Hamilton* and *Scourge*

SCUBA

see **Self-Contained Underwater Breathing Apparatus**

Seahawk

Team that investigated the site of what is believed to be the 17th-century *Buen Jesus y Nuestra Señora del Rosario*. In 1965 a small amount of shipwreck material was recovered by a fishing trawler approximately 32 km south of the Dry Tortugas, Florida, USA, in deep water. In 1972 the research vessel *Alcoa Seaprobe* was used to search for the site with negative results. A few months later salvor Robert Marx attempted to locate the wreck by dragging a cable along the bottom and between two vessels. A large anchor was reportedly snagged and briefly brought to the surface before slipping off the cable and dropping back to the seabed. In 1988 Seahawk Deep Ocean Technology, Inc. teamed with Marx and, using his locational information, **Side scan sonar**, and a small remotely operated vehicle or ROV (see **Submersibles**), located the wreck in approximately 400 m of water. Over the next couple of years the company developed a much larger state-of-the-art ROV with positioning, data recording, excavation, and recovery systems.

Positioning was accomplished with a system of four Sonardyne acoustic transponders and transducer. This provided an electronic grid over the site proper which allowed for both ROV navigation and artefact provenance recording with accuracy within 10 cm when properly calibrated. Most artefacts were recovered with a variety of suction devices, while actual excavation was effected via one of two **Water dredges** and associated spoil chambers. Two *Schilling* manipulator arms, one with seven functions, the other with five, were available to actuate the various recovery and mapping devices. The ROV was also equipped with banks of lights for illumination and eight cameras (five video and three still) for recording all phases of bottom operation.

Approximately 60 per cent of the remaining lower hull was excavated, revealing numerous structural features including both stem and sternposts (with associated rudder); the aft portion of the keelson with several stanchion steps (including one stan-

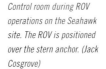

ROV Merlin *being launched from support vessel* Seahawk Retriever. *(Jack Cosgrove)*

Control room during ROV operations on the Seahawk site. The ROV is positioned over the stern anchor. *(Jack Cosgrove)*

chion stump); the lower ends of two bilge pump tubes and associated pump well; the octagonal stump of the mainmast; and the entire starboard side at the turn of the bilge. The vessel obviously reached the bottom in an upright position and came to rest with a starboard list. Consequently, the vast majority of the cultural material encountered was located on this side of the site. The ship's two bower anchors were located just forward of the stem and a smaller 8 ft (2.4 m) anchor was positioned just off the port quarter.

Thousands of artefacts were recovered including over 100 intact ceramic 'olive jars', most with imploded corks, an additional 100 or so jar rims with associated sherds, and numerous other ceramic vessel types. Approximately thirty examples of gold were located, including bars and small bits, one ring, and five gold chains looped together with a common link; approximately 4,000 silver coins; over 5,000 pearls

(some with extremely small drilled holes); numerous types of glass trade beads; lead firearm shot; a bronze bell; two bronze mortar/pestle sets and a millstone with associated stone pestle; a copper cauldron; three astrolabes (one inscribed DYAS); tortoiseshell; cannon balls; whetstones; an onyx inkwell and sand shaker; and organic material including numerous human teeth, various rigging elements, animal bones, seeds, squid beaks, and a wooden fid. One interesting aspect encountered was the comparatively small volume of ferrous material, particularly fasteners. Several fragments of planking and other structural components recovered indicated their original presence in large numbers. The few iron artefacts encountered were almost totally oxidized.

The site has been tentatively identified as *Buen Jesus y Nuestra Señora del Rosario* based on a set of circumstantial evidence including location, wreck size, timber scantlings, and the type and dating of artefacts. *Buen Jesus* was attached to the 1622 *Tierra Firme* fleet, which included **Nuestra Señora de Atocha** and swung through the Spanish South American pearl fisheries on the inbound voyage before eventually meeting the rest of the fleet in Havana. Documents indicate that *Buen Jesus*, under Captain Manuel Diaz, was Portuguese-built of 117 *tonaladas* and owned by Juan de la Torre Ayala. The ship was reported by survivors from another wreck to have foundered in deep water.

If *Nuestra Señora de Atocha* and galleons like her carrying royal treasure and affluent passengers can be viewed as 'white collar' vessels, then the site certainly represents the 'blue collar' parameter of the fleet and creates the potential for an interesting intra-fleet comparison and analysis. However, in 1991 the US Securities and Exchange Commission began an investigation into the activities of Seahawk Deep Ocean Technology, Inc. which effectively halted the excavation and recovery operations on the site short of completion and has subsequently prevented any comprehensive interpretation and analysis from taking place. D.M.

ADDITIONAL READING

Bascom, W., 1976, *Deep Water, Ancient Ships*, New York.

Gibbons, D., 1991, 'Archaeology in Deep Water: A Preliminary View', *International Journal of Nautical Archaeology*, 20, 2, 163–8.

Kelland, N.C., 1991, 'Acoustics as an Aid to Salvage Location and Recovery', *Hydrographic Journal*, 60, 27–32.

Marx, R. and Marx, J., 1994, *New World Shipwrecks, 1492–1825*, Dallas, Texas.

Pickford, N., 1994, *The Atlas of Shipwreck and Treasure*, London.

EDITOR'S NOTE: This site is included because it is well known and widely reported in the popular media and press. However, sites such as this have primarily been the focus of commercially oriented activity that has resulted in the sale of recovered artefacts at times to private owners, the transfer of artefacts to private investors, or the splitting of artefacts between a government and a private salvor. Despite the presence of an archaeologist on the site, or the recovery of any archaeological data, the long-term potential of a site to yield meaningful information is compromised when the collection of artefacts – the primary data of any archaeological site – has been dispersed. Furthermore, the sale of artefacts from shipwreck sites endorses the concept that the archaeological past and antiquities are commodities for sale on the open market, which has proved detrimental to the protection and study of the past. The inclusion of this site in this encyclopaedia does not sanction or condone this type of activity.

Sea Horse

see **Oxford University MARE**

Sea-level change

The variation in the real and apparent interface between the world's oceans and land masses. Sea-level plays a defining role in the formation and change of coastal landforms and, within the Quaternary period which encompasses human occupation on the earth, will have affected the location and deposition of evidence related to our use of coastal regions.

Sea-level changes on the earth have primarily resulted from three distinct but interacting factors: (1) tectonic deformation; (2) isostatic readjustment; (3) glacial-eustatic volume. A host of subsidiary variables may affect local relative sea-level.

Tectonic deformation is the massive movement of local or regional strata of the earth. These movements may raise or lower coastal lands. Sea floor spreading and crustal plate interactions may produce uplift or subsidence of coastal continental margins. Similar plate dynamics may produce mega-earthquakes of a force sufficient to displace shorelines. Volcanic activity may extend shorelines by lava flows or displace them by violent explosive eruptions. Tectonic forces are localized in effect; they do not operate simultaneously worldwide but regionally in discrete interludes.

Isostatic readjustment refers to the depression and uplift of sections of the earth's crust due, in the first case, to the compressing mass of continental glaciation and, in the second, to the rebounding of the crust following deglaciation. These movements are regionalized as well, directly related to the glacial history of the area, although during periods of worldwide glacial growth and decay, isostatic readjustment may occur more or less simultaneously around the globe in extreme latitudes.

Glacial-eustatic volume is determined by the total distribution of the earth's water within the hydrological cycle. The most significant variable for sea-level is the amount of water captured within ice sheets or glaciers.

Given the complexity of the forces determining it and the variations to be found around the earth it has been noted that sea-level is anything but level. The historic and continuing changes in sea-level are most dramatic in higher latitudes, which have been subject to all three primary factors; sea-levels in central latitudes are principally determined by glacial-eustatic volume and irregular tectonic activity. It is also critical to develop local sea-level histories for applica-tion to any specific archaeological site or question, since differences in sea-level history can be discerned between coastal points which lie within kilometres of each other.

The magnitude of sea-level changes in the Quaternary has important implications for **Underwater archaeology**. Since this period encompasses the time span of both the emergence of the human species and our diffusion across the globe and extensive glacial growth and decay, we can expect submerged coastal landforms to contain archaeological remains related to human occupation and use. The difficulties associated with the discovery and excavation of these remains constitute one of the most challenging and innovative arenas of archaeological research today. N.A.E.

See also **Quaternary coastlines and land bridges**.

ADDITIONAL READING

Kraft, J.C., Kayan, I., and Aschenbrenner, S.E., 1985, 'Geological Studies of Coastal Change Applied to Archaeological Settings', in G. Rapp, Jr and J.A. Gifford (eds), *Archaeological Geology*, New Haven, Connecticut.

Smith, D.E. and Dawson, A.G. (eds), 1983, *Shorelines and Isostacy*, Institute of British Geographers Special Publications 16, London.

Woodworth, P.L. *et al.* (eds), 1992, 'Sea-level Changes: Determination and Effects', *International Union of Geodesy and Geophysics*, Washington, DC.

Sea of Galilee Wreck

The hull of a boat entirely buried in the Sea of Galilee's muddy lake bed (Lake Kinneret). The vessel was discovered in 1986 by Moshe and Yuval Lufan at a time when it had been exposed by a severe drought, and an initial probe excavation carried out by the Israel Department of Antiquities and Museums (IDAM) revealed that much of the lower part of the hull survived in good condition and that the strakes had been edge-joined with mortise-and-tenon joinery.

The media immediately termed it the 'Jesus boat'. This began a chain of events that threatened the vessel's safety. To prevent this from happening, IDAM carried out a most unusual salvage **Excavation** at the culmination of which the boat was packaged in a cocoon of fibreglass frames and polyurethane and sailed to the nearby Yigal Allon Centre. There it was placed in a specially built **Conservation** pool. The polyethylene glycol conservation process was successfully completed in mid-1995. Plans are underway in 1997 to create a museum wing at the Yigal Allon Centre for the boat's exhibition.

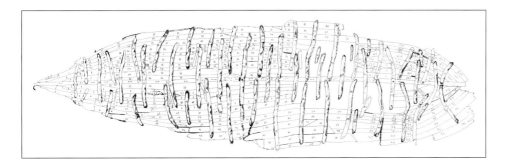

The Sea of Galilee Boat. (INA/J.R.Steffy)

The boat's date is based on a study of the techniques used in her construction, pottery found in the vicinity of the hull, a battery of radiocarbon dates, and historical considerations. These dating methods suggest that the boat's working life was sometime between 100 BC and AD 67.

The vessel was built in shell-first construction, typical of contemporaneous Mediterranean hull construction techniques. The boat has a preserved length of 8.2 m, a maximum breadth of 2.3 m and reaches a height of 1.2 m.

Either wood was extremely expensive in Galilee at this time, or the boat's owner was poor, for the hull is constructed with a large degree of recycled timbers, apparently removed from older boats. Furthermore, while most of planks examined are made of Lebanese cedar (*Cedrus*) and the frames of oak (*Quercus*), examples of five additional wood types were identified: siddar – also known as jujube or Christ thorn – (*Ziziphus spina-christi*), Aleppo pine (*Pinus halapensis*), hawthorn (*Crataegus*), willow (*Salix*) and redbud (*Cercis siliquastrum*).

Numerous repairs indicate that the boat had lived a relatively long working life, during which it was probably used primarily for fishing, particularly with a large seine net. Propelled by sail or oars, the boat could also serve as an all-purpose vessel to transport people and supplies.

Apparently after a long working life, the boat was brought ashore to an area of boat building construction and some parts of the hull were removed. These included the stem construction, the sternpost, mast-step and several frames, which were apparently intended for secondary use.

Based on a study of crew sizes, the boat apparently represents the type used by the Apostles (Mark 1:20; John 21:2–3) as well as the type of vessel in which Jews fought the Romans in the Battle of Migdal in AD 67 (Josephus *Jewish War*, 3, 522–31). There is no archaeological evidence, however, to connect this specific boat with any recorded events or persons. S.W.

ADDITIONAL READING

Steffy, J.R., 1987, 'The Kinneret Boat Project, Part II: Notes on the Construction of the Kinneret Boat', *International Journal of Nautical Archaeology*, 16, 325–9.

Steffy, J.R., 1994, *Wooden Ship Building and the Interpretation of Shipwrecks*, College Station, Texas.

Wachsmann, S., 1988, 'The Galilee Boat: 2,000-Year-Old Hull Recovered Intact', *Biblical Archaeology Review*, 14, 5, 18–33.

Wachsmann, S., 1995, *The Sea of Galilee Boat: An Extraordinary 2000-Year-Old Discovery*, New York and London.

Wachsmann, S. *et al.* 1990, 'The Excavations of an Ancient Boat in the Sea of Galilee (Lake Kinneret)', *Atiquot 19*, Jerusalem.

Wachsmann, S., Raveh, K., and Cohen, O., 1987, 'The Kinneret Boat Project, Part I: The Excavation and the Conservation of the Kinneret Boat', *International Journal of Nautical Archaeology*, 16, 233–45.

Sea Venture

Flagship of the Virginia Company's fleet. The colony of Jamestown, Virginia, was settled by the Virginia Company of London in 1607. Previous colonies sponsored by individual adventures had failed, but this time the risks were shared among a number of investors, and many of the company's leaders had experience with other distant enterprises in the East Indies and the Levant.

Despite the Virginia Company's advantages, the early years at Jamestown were difficult. The colonists struggled to survive. The winter of 1608–9 was particularly bad and the Virginia Company organized a relief fleet to carry supplies and additional colonists to Jamestown. This fleet of seven ships and two pinnaces, known as the Third Supply, sailed from Plymouth, England on 2 June 1609, with supplies and 600 settlers.

Sea Venture was built during an exciting period in English naval architecture. Design and construction had become recognizably English over the previous century, the result being the English galleon – the ship which helped crush the **Spanish Armada** in 1588 and carried the first English colonists to the New World.

Aboard the newly built flagship were Admiral Sir George Somers and Sir Thomas Gates, the new Lieutenant Governor of Virginia. In all, there were 150 passengers – gentlemen, tradesmen, servants and sailors. The captain of *Sea Venture*, Christopher Newport, was

Underwater view of Sea Venture. (Bermuda Maritime Museum)

making his fourth voyage across the Atlantic. On the advice of Sir George Somers, he took the fleet on a more northerly route to avoid the Spanish in the Caribbean.

After nearly two months, approximately eight days away from Jamestown, the fleet was struck by a hurricane. *Sea Venture* was separated from the rest of the fleet. Frantic bailing was relieved when land was sighted by Sir George and the captain was able to run the ship aground on a reef not far from the shore at the northeastern end of the Bermuda Islands.

The ship's company built shelters with the materials salvaged from the wreck, as well as cedar wood and palmetto leaves. They decked over the ship's longboat to make it seaworthy and sent a group of men off to Jamestown to take news of the shipwreck to the colonists there. The remaining survivors lit signal fires to guide rescuers to the island. None came; however, they found plenty of food – there were palmetto and cedar berries, wild hogs, and flocks of birds and their eggs. Turtles laid eggs on the sandy beaches, and the fish were so tame that reportedly they could be plucked out of the water by hand.

Using Bermuda cedar and timber, fittings and fastenings from *Sea Venture*, the castaways built two smaller vessels, *Deliverance* and *Patience*, and sailed for Virginia, arriving in Jamestown on 24 May 1610.

The wreck of *Sea Venture* marked the beginning of the permanent settlement of Bermuda, for several of the ship's crew remained on the island, to be joined in 1612 by sixty settlers sent out from England on *Plough*.

In 1610 news of the remarkable 'wreck and redemption' of *Sea Venture*'s company reached England. Two dramatic first-hand accounts described their grim struggle to stay afloat, and their miraculous deliverance onto an enchanted 'isle of devils' – Bermuda. The letters were apparently seen by William Shakespeare, possibly through his patron the Earl of Southampton, a backer of the Virginia enterprise. A year later Shakespeare wrote *The Tempest*.

The last known direct reference to the ship concerns Governor Butler (1619–22), who salvaged various items from the wreck site. Eventually, the hull remains were assimilated into the coral sands at the bottom of the gully and forgotten. The wreck was rediscovered in 1958 by Edmund Downing, an American descended from George Yeardley, *Sea Venture*'s captain of soldiery. Unable to research full time, Downing agreed that the Bermuda Government should employ Teddy Tucker to excavate the site. Every-

thing they found pointed to *Sea Venture* except a gun apparently dating from the 18th century.

The project subsequently lost momentum until the site was reinvestigated by the Bermuda Maritime Museum under Allan 'Smokey' Wingood. Wingood's team not only recovered additional material closely dated to *Sea Venture*'s time, but the offending gun was reassessed as 17th century after all. Pottery from the site was identified by Ivor Noël Hume as 'West of England', a type he was finding on the lost plantation of 'Martin's Hundred' in Virginia. He also found the whole **Assemblage** consistent with an English ship of the period, as opposed to those of other nations.

Subsequent research by the Sea Venture Trust revealed stratified deposits containing structural, artefactual, and environmental material. The surviving structure is largely an integral unit, primarily consisting of keel, floor timbers, futtocks, and ceiling. Together, they preserve much information on early 17th-century timber conversion, hull design, and construction. All indicate an English vessel very near the '300 tunnes' given in contemporary references. The contents include ceramic, metal, wood, leather, and bone objects, as well as faunal remains and organic residues. They characterized the cargo, stores and personal possessions carried aboard a colonial vessel, as distinct from a warship or merchant ship.

Sea Venture would therefore be important archaeologically, even without the historic and symbolic significance afforded by the Shakespeare connection, and a role in beginning Bermuda's permanent settlement. Ships like *Sea Venture* were the result of a period of profound change in English shipbuilding, yet one for which we have little evidence. *Sea Venture* provides one of the few maritime archaeological assemblages that can be integrated with the sparse historical and iconographic sources. The vessel makes a significant contribution to the early history of Bermuda, and to the archaeology of the whole colonial enterprise. It also illuminates wider issues underlying the design and use of ships, and related changes in society.

Sea Venture is contained in the Bermuda Maritime Museum, where there is a permanent display. E.C.H., J.R.A.

ADDITIONAL READING

Adams, J., 1985, '*Sea Venture*: A Second Interim Report, Part 1', *International Journal of Nautical Archaeology*, 14, 4, 275–99.
Lavery, B., 1988, *The Colonial Merchantman Susan Constant 1605*, London.
Peterson, M.L.R., 1988, 'The Sea Venture', *Mariner's Mirror*, 74, 37–48.
Steffy, J.R., 1994, *Wooden Ship Building and the Interpretation of Shipwrecks*, College Station, Texas.
Wingood, A.J., 1982, '*Sea Venture*: An Interim Report on an Early 17th-Century Shipwreck Lost in 1609', *International Journal of Nautical Archaeology*, 11, 4, 333–47.
Wingood, A.J., 1986, '*Sea Venture*: A Second Interim Report, Part 2', *International Journal of Nautical Archaeology*, 15, 2, 149–59.
Wright, L.B., 1967, *A Voyage to Virginia in 1609*, Charlottesville, Virginia.

Self-Contained Underwater Breathing Apparatus (SCUBA)

Underwater breathing apparatus. It is patent that the most critical technique for accomplishing work in **Underwater archaeology** is the use of Self-Contained Underwater Breathing Apparatus (SCUBA). The ability to enter the underwater world and remain at depth while completing archaeological projects is critical. A comparative examination of diving techniques can be drawn from the example of Edward Thompson, an American consul in Mexico, who, from 1904 to 1907, had divers working the **Chichén-Itzá Cenote**. The gear required was a helmet-diving system, supported from the surface by tenders who used a hand pump to provide a continuous flow of air to the diver. The logistics of helmet diving in a remote area were complex, requiring many personnel, gear such as helmets, diving dress, and hand-operated air pumps. Contrast the organization of such a dive with the first SCUBA dive accomplished in a Mayan cenote by the **National Geographic Society** photographer Luis Marden in 1958. Marden's SCUBA dive was performed in Dzibilchaltun, using a SCUBA system that required the standard mask, regulator, tanks, and compressor to supply the compressed air for the tanks, a much more mobile system. While it is true that neither Thompson's cenote dives nor Marden's were archaeological dives in the true sense of the word – Thompson recovered gold treasure; Marden documented the wells photographically – they illustrate the advantage to the underwater archaeologist of the freedom self-contained apparatus provided.

The most commonly used SCUBA is the open-circuit system in which a finite amount of compressed air is contained in tanks supported by the diver and exhausted into the underwater environment. This open-circuit technique has a long history; the concept of self-contained underwater breathing apparatus is seen in French engravings dating

Self-Contained Underwater Breathing Apparatus (SCUBA), the most important technological aid to underwater archaeological exploration. (Vancouver Maritime Museum/Mike Paris)

A SCUBA diver working on an archaeological site in the Dry Tortugas National Park. (NPS/John Brooks)

back to the early 1700s. A patent for a working SCUBA was filed in 1828 by a French inventor named d'Angerville, a system actually adopted by the French Navy. The first demand valves appear to have been patented in London in 1838 by Newton and in 1865 by the French Rouquayrol and Denayrouse. This latter apparatus was portrayed as the system used by Captain Nemo in Jules Verne's *Twenty Thousand Leagues Under the Sea* to enable his sailors to walk on the ocean bottom.

In 1926 the French naval officer LePrieur, working with Fernez, invented an aqualung which was successful but had the problem of a free-flow regulator which exhausted available air. The Fernez-LePrieur aqualung was improved by LePrieur himself in 1933 and another French inventor, Commheines, who

demonstrated his aqualung at the Paris Exposition in 1937. Commheines adapted a demand valve to his aqualung which conserved air. These developments set the stage for Gagnan and Cousteau, who in 1946 combined several features of the earlier inventions and developed a SCUBA with a demand valve which allowed the diver to breathe only when needed, thus eliminating the wasteful free flow of air. It was their system that provided the basis for modern SCUBA gear.

The breathing mix used in open-circuit SCUBA is compressed air, containing the normal percentages of nitrogen (78 per cent) and oxygen (21 per cent) with minute traces of other gases such as argon. It is general practice in recreational diving to set a depth limit of 39.6 m while using compressed air in SCUBA. More experienced divers, such as **US Navy**, National Park Service, and National Oceanic and Atmospheric Administration (NOAA) divers, may have an air diving depth limit of 57.9 m or more. These limits appear to fall within the vast majority of dive profiles required for underwater archaeology, within the standard decompression tables. Other factors such as water temperature, current, and visibility will be critical in planning dives to accomplish archaeological work, but again it appears that the use of SCUBA, along with standard protective gear such as a wetsuit, will be the equipment of choice in most underwater archaeological projects. A.J.B.

Serçe Limani

A natural harbour located on the Turkish coast directly north of the island and city of Rhodes; Serçe Limani means 'Sparrow Harbour'. The **Institute of Nautical Archaeology** (INA) excavated two shipwrecks within the harbour at an anchorage already used in the Bronze Age: an 11th-century Byzantine wreck in 1977–9 and a 3rd-century BC Hellenistic wreck in 1978–80.

The Hellenistic wreck, extensively covered by large boulders, was only partially excavated. The ship was carrying a wine cargo in at least 600 amphoras of two sizes. Their form and fabric, as well as stamps on some of the large ones, indicate that the wine was produced on the nearby Knidian peninsula. The profiles of the amphoras and some other pottery suggest a wreck date of about 280–275 BC. Small bulbous jars without handles, possibly containing scented oil, apparently represent a secondary cargo. The ship's hull was covered by lead sheathing laid over an inner lining of fabric impregnated with pitch or resin. Other ship-related finds included a wooden toggle for the quick attachment or release of a rigging line; two large rings, one marble and one lead, probably used to free fouled anchor cables or nets; and a lead pipe that may constitute the earliest remnant we have from an ancient ship's bilge-pump system.

The Byzantine wreck was entirely excavated and yielded sufficient hull remains to permit a fairly detailed reconstruction. The

Left: Excavation in progress on the Hellenistic wreck at Serçe Limani, Turkey. (INA)

Above: Part of the cargo of wine amphoras from the Hellenistic wreck at Serçe Limani. (INA)

vessel had an overall length of only 15.6 m, a moulded breadth of 5 m, and a midships hold depth of 1.6 m. Simple lines giving the hull a flat bottom, a tight turn of the bilge, and steep (72 degree), straight sides produced an extremely box-like hold that maximized capacity to about 35 tonnes.

Fractions and multiples of the Byzantine foot were used by the shipbuilder, while the framing pattern in the main body of the hull, in which floors with a long arm extending up through the turn of the bilge to port alternate with floors with a long arm to starboard, shows influence from central Europe, perhaps via the Danube. This suggests that the ship may have been built not too far from Constantinople.

The desired hull lines and dimensions were achieved in a manner that is possibly a recursor to the Mediterranean style of whole moulding recorded in the Venetian shipbuilding manuals of the 15th century. After keel, stem and sternpost were assembled, two full frames and eight partial frames (floor timbers) were erected amidships, and it is likely that a pair of robust half-frames near either end of the keel were erected at the same time. Five broad bottom planking strakes and the lowest side planking strake were then fastened in place, after which the remaining framing and planking were installed. Precise positioning and dimensioning of frames through careful measurement and the employment of simple geometric projections were the keys to obtaining the desired hull size and shape.

The ship was a two-masted lateener, with the mainmast set slightly aft of midships and the foremast with a somewhat smaller sail set

well forward in the bow. The pair of robust half-frames near either keel end appear to have supported bulkheads partitioning off the hold from a small bow compartment and a substantially larger stern compartment. Three iron anchors with wooden stocks were carried on the bow bulwarks, two to port and one to starboard; five spares were stacked on the deck between the masts. The anchors were small and thin in section, each weighing 48, 56 or 64 kg. The shank and arms formed an inverted Y, a then-universal Mediterranean anchor design that reduced length and thus the incidence of shank breakage. Even so, three of the anchors had shanks broken and then hastily repaired through forge-welding, very possibly during the voyage.

The ship had set sail with its cargoes from somewhere along the coast of present-day southern Lebanon or northern Israel, then part of the Moslem caliphate of the Fatimids. Commercial equipment on board included a Byzantine steelyard, three balances, two large sets of balance-pan weights, one Byzantine and the other Fatimid, and glass weights for weighing Fatimid gold and silver coins, some of them bearing legible dates, the latest being either 1024/5 or possibly 1021/2. The sinking therefore occurred in the third decade of the 11th century, a time of improving Fatimid –Byzantine relations. A paucity of coins – three Fatimid gold coins, fifteen clippings from Fatimid gold coins (substituting for silver coins), and some forty Byzantine copper coins – coupled with the presence of three Byzantine lead seals for documents, suggest the possible use of letters of credit.

The ship was carrying a variety of cargoes, some quite small, including some three tonnes of glass cullet, some eighty or more items of glassware, several dozen cooking pots, several dozen glazed bowls, several half-dozen lots of jugs and pitchers with

built-in filters (gargoulettes), raisins, sumac, and most of just over 100 Byzantine amphoras (almost all carrying wine). Such cargo diversity was then commonplace and served as a hedge against price fluctuations in a period of increasing free trade.

The glass cullet, two tonnes of raw glass and one tonne of broken glassware and glass-making waste transported in baskets had been stowed as ballast in the aftermost part of the hold. Glass cullet shipped cheaply as ballast often had a market at glass making centres near the sea, since it is far less expensive to melt glass already made than to produce new glass. The raisins and sumac had been placed above the glass cullet. Just over half of the cargo amphoras, as well as some of the gargoulettes, glazed bowls, and intact glassware, had been stowed within the stern compartment. Most of these amphoras had carved on them the letter M, which probably denoted Michael, perhaps the name of the ship's captain who had stowed his personal cargoes in the stern. What appear to be several other, much smaller, personal cargoes, which included some combination of amphoras, ceramics and glassware, were found in the midships area and, in one case, in the bow compartment. An unidentifiable perishable cargo had occupied the forward half of the hold.

Several hundred glass vessels have been restored from the broken glassware cullet. These vessels, along with the intact ones, constitute an unusually comprehensive collection of medieval Islamic glassware that now reveals that the Syrian regional glassware style at that time was characterized by a high incidence of vessels decorated with mould-blown geometric and vegetal patterns. Studies of the glassware and glazed bowls from this well-dated wreck have already led to important chronological revisions for medieval Islamic glassware and glazed wares.

The wine amphoras have yielded some remarkable new information on Byzantine metrology and economic life. Almost ninety of them are piriform and belong to over two-dozen distinct capacity sizes, some for red and others for white wine, ranging from 15 to 60 Byzantine pound (1 lb = 320 g) for wine and belonging to two interrelated capacity systems in which capacities increase at three- or five-pound intervals. Such a multiplicity of sizes stands in stark contrast to the few basic sizes employed before the Byzantine period and seems to imply profound changes in the marketing of wine. Although the amphoras differ considerably in size, almost all could have used standard stoppers of the same size, another innova-

The restored hull of the Byzantine wreck at Serçe Limani on display in the Bodrum Museum of Underwater Archaeology. (© INA)

tion. The owners of the amphoras were accustomed to using them over and over again as transport jars, selling the contents but keeping the jars and carving down damaged rims and handles to minimize further damage, yet another practice undocumented for earlier periods. Amphora graffiti give evidence suggesting that the amphoras and their owners were from a locale with a Byzantine–Slavic population, quite possibly on or near the Sea of Marmara, where piri-

Above: Two intact glass bottles, one with engraved decoration, from the Byzantine wreck at Serçe Limani. (© INA)

Right: Decorated bronze handle of an iron sword from the Byzantine wreck at Serçe Limani. (© INA)

form amphoras very similar to those from the wreck were made in kilns that have been discovered on the north coast.

Much has been learned about shipboard life (see **Shipboard society**). The vessel had been well maintained and was well equipped with all the tools (including perhaps the earliest known caulking irons), nails and tacks, and spare rigging parts that might be needed to make repairs during the voyage. Charcoal was used for cooking, and the menu included sheep or goat, pork, and fish. Fishing equipment included three large nets with floats, a smaller casting net, a multi-tined spear, netting needles for repairing the nets, and spindle whirls for making new line. Fish-net weights with Christian symbols and the consumption of pork suggest that at least some portion of those on board were Christian. Pastimes included chess and backgammon. One personal grooming kit contained scissors, razor, and delousing comb (along with some coins), and a small

amount of orpiment on board may have been used as a depilatory. Weapons used to defend the ship were javelins, thrusting spears, and swords, most of which were kept in the stern. One of the swords had a bronze hilt with an elaborately feathered hamsa bird decorating the guard on either side.
F.H.V.

ADDITIONAL READING

Bass, G.F., 1979, 'The Shipwreck at Serçe Limani, Turkey', *Archaeology*, 32, 36–43.

Bass, G.F., 1984, The Nature of the Serçe Limani Glass', *Journal of Glass Studies*, 23, 64–9.

Bass, G.F. and van Doorninck Jr, F.H., 1978, 'An 11th-Century Shipwreck at Serçe Limani, Turkey', *International Journal of Nautical Archaeology*, 7, 119–32.

Empereur, J.-Y. and Tuma, N., 1988, 'Zénon de Caunos et l'épave de Serçe Limani', *Bulletin de Correspondance Hellénique*, 112, 341–57.

Grace, V.R., 1986, 'Some Amphoras from a Hellenistic Wreck', in J.-Y. Empereur and Y. Garlan (eds), *Recherches sur les amphores grecques*, Bulletin de Correspondance Hellénique Supplément, 13, Paris, 551–65.

Günsenin, N., 1993, 'Ganos: Centre de production d'amphores à l'époque byzantine', *Anatolia Antiqua*, 2, 193–201.

Jenkins, M., 1992, 'Early Medieval Islamic pottery: The Eleventh Century Reconsidered', *Muqarnas*, 9, 56–66.

Pulak, C. and Townsend, R.F., 1987, 'The Hellenistic Shipwreck at Serçe Limani, Turkey: Preliminary Report', *American Journal of Archaeology*, 91, 31–57.

Steffy, J.R., 1994, *Wooden Shipbuilding and the Interpretation of Shipwrecks*, College Station, Texas.

van Doorninck, F.H., Jr, 1989, 'The Cargo Amphoras on the 7th-Century Yassiada and the 11th-Century Serçe Limani Shipwrecks: Two Examples of a Reuse of Byzantine Amphoras as Transport Jars', in V. Déroche and J.-M. Spieser (eds), *Recherches sur la céramique byzantine*, Bulletin de Correspondance Hellénique Supplément, 18, Paris, 247–57.

van Doorninck, F.H., Jr 1990, 'The Serçe Limani Shipwreck: An 11th-Century Cargo of Fatimid Glassware Cullet for Byzantine Glassmakers', *1st International Anatolian Glass Symposium 26–7 April 1988, Istanbul*, 58–63.

van Doorninck, F.H., Jr, 1993, 'Giving Good

Weight in 11th-Century Byzantium: The Metrology of the Glass Wreck Amphoras', *INA Quarterly*, 20, 2, 8–12.

van Doorninck, F.H., Jr *et al.*, 1988, 'The Glass Wreck: An 11th-Century Merchantman', *INA Quarterly*, 153, 1–31.

Severn Wrecks

Wrecks from the northern shores of the Severn Estuary in southeast Wales, ranging in date from the mid-2nd millennium BC to the late 19th century AD. As in the Humber region (see **Humber Wrecks**) the finds are from river and foreshore rather than underwater.

A 3.55 m fragment of oak planking, dated to *c.*1600 BC, from a former Severn tributary at Caldicot, is similar to planking from the **Ferriby Boats**, with cleats protruding from its inner face and stitch holes along its edges. It was probably the end of a sewn boat's second side strake, shaped so that it blended into a Ferriby-style bow or stern. From the same site, but dated to *c.*1100 BC, came another fragment from a plank similar to a **Brigg 'Raft'** bottom plank.

Two pieces of oak planking, with sewing holes at the edges and cleat ridges along the centre line, were also excavated from an inter-tidal site at Goldcliff and dated to *c.*1000 BC. They probably came from a Brigg-style of boat.

Substantial remains of an oak plank boat dated to the 3rd century AD were excavated from a site known as Barland's Farm, formerly a river flowing into the Severn (see **Barland's Farm Boat**). The two central planks projected below the outer bottom planks to form a plank-keel. A stem at the surviving end was positioned in a rabbet on this plank-keel and held there by a stout floor timber. The five strakes each side, and the bottom planks, were fastened to the stem and to approximately twenty-two sets of framing timbers by large iron nails, clenched by turning the point through 180 degrees back into the inboard face of the frames. Some of these framing units consist of two adjacent asymmetric timbers running across the bottom and up to the fifth side strake, one to port, one to starboard. Others are single floor timbers extending from third strake to third strake, with associated side timbers.

This boat and two contemporary seagoing ships, **Blackfriars Wreck** 1 from the River Thames in London, and St Peter Port 1 (see **Guernsey Wreck**), all members of the Romano-Celtic tradition, are the earliest known vessels built skeleton first: that is, the shape of their hull was determined by the framework; planking was added *after* the stems, plank-keel, and much of the framing had been assembled. These three vessels each had a

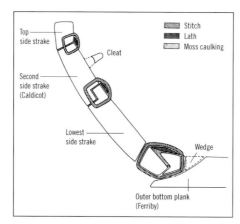

Part cross-section of a composite prehistoric sewn plank boat from the River Severn, with a Ferriby bottom and lowest side strake and a Caldicot second side strake. (Institute of Archaeology, Oxford)

mast-step about one-third the waterline length from the bow, an appropriate place for a fore-and-aft sail such as a lugsail. If this hypothesis is correct, this would be the earliest known European use of a non-square sail outside the Mediterranean. The Barland's boat probably originally measured 11.4 × 3.2 × 0.8 m, and could have carried *c.* 2 tonnes of cargo. She is housed in the Museum at Newport, southeast Wales.

The Tredunnoc boat was excavated from the river bed of a tidal section of the River Usk which flows into the Severn Estuary near Newport. This was a 19th-century inland barge, a type of vessel poorly documented. She measured 18 × 2.7 × 1.15 m, shaped like a lidless box which tapered to posts at the ends. Fifty-five transverse planks formed the bottom, on which was a keelson with a step for a towing mast one-third the waterline length from the bow. Knees were nailed to the outer edges of the bottom, and five strakes each side were nailed to bottom, posts, and knees. Bottom boards were fitted on which she could carry up to 24 tonnes of cargo. After a useful life, she was sunk at Tredunnoc as part of a training weir built to block a side channel of the River Usk. S.M.

ADDITIONAL READING

Bell, M., 1992, 'Field Survey and Excavation at Goldcliff, 1992', in M. Bell (ed.), *Severn Estuary Level Research Committee Annual Report*, 15–29.

McGrail, S. and Parry, S., 1991, 'A Flat-Bottomed Boat from the R. Usk at Tredunnoc, Gwent, Wales', in R. Reindeers and K. Paul (eds), *Carvel Construction Techniques*, Oxbow Monograph 12, Oxford, 161–70.

McGrail, S. and Parry, S., 1994, 'A Bronze Age Sewn Boat Fragment from Caldicot, Gwent, Wales', in C. Westerdahl (ed.), *Crossroad in*

Ancient Shipbuilding, Oxbow Monograph 40, Oxford, 21–28.

Nayling, N., Maynard, D., and McGrail, S., 1994, 'Barland's Farm, Magor, Gwent: A Romano-Celtic Boat', *Antiquity*, 68, 596–603.

SHARPS

see **Sonic High Accuracy Ranging and Positioning System**

Shell midden

An accumulation of refuse, principally shells, related to the occupation of shore-lines by prehistoric peoples. The use of the term 'midden' entered archaeology from the Danish *mödding* (dung or refuse heap) where it had been applied to the mounds of edible mollusc shells associated with prehistoric human habitations. Shell middens are one of the ubiquitous markers of maritime adaptations, resulting from intensive economic use of the resources within the littoral ecozone. Their size may range from small accumulations representing short-term camps to several hectares directly associated with large, permanent, or semi-permanent villages. In areas of transgressive coastlines, the midden may extend from above the shoreline into the intertidal and submarine zones, while in areas of regressive coastlines middens may be found a considerable distance inland from the contemporary seashore.

Besides direct evidence of exploited littoral fauna, shell middens often contain additional artefacts related to the prehistoric economic adaptation of coastal peoples, and thus their investigation is of great importance to our understanding of the development of human maritime adaptations. The literature on shell midden research is vast, and most of it is focused on the methodology and results of excavations located above the tide line. In recent years, however, increasing attention has been directed towards intertidal and submerged midden deposits which have been inundated by post-glacial rising sea-levels. In particular, current research is trying to develop an understanding of the effects of transgression on middens – in what ways are they changed by inundation and what implications do these changes have to intertidal or underwater excavation of submerged middens – and whether a culturally deposited midden has a recognizable signature which would distinguish it from natural accumulations of littoral molluscs. The resolution of these research questions is of critical importance to the successful location and interpretation of underwater prehistoric sites. N.A.E.

ADDITIONAL READING

Stein, J.K. (ed.), 1992, *Deciphering a Shell Midden*, San Diego.

Sheytan Deresi Wreck

Wreck in the Aegean, believed to date from the late Middle Bronze Age. In 1973 the newly founded **Institute of Nautical Archaeology** (INA) conducted its first systematic underwater survey of the Aegean coast of Turkey. A sponge diver led a team of divers and archaeologists to the site of Sheytan Deresi (Devil Creek) near Mazi, about 49 km east of Bodrum, where an assemblage of coarseware pottery was lying at a depth of approximately 30 m. Two complete pots, a krater and a pithos half-buried in the seabed, and sherds lying on the sand, were raised in 1973. Two years later full-scale **Excavation** took place.

Despite the absence of ship timbers, the location of the site off the eastern point of an open bay, the uniform fabric of most of the items, and the distribution of the material on the seabed, indicated that the assemblage represented a shipwreck. Made of similar clay were the remains of seventeen ceramic vessels, of which ten were restorable to their original, complete profiles. Other pieces, of different fabric, were obviously intrusive. Being coarseware utilitarian vessels, the pottery of the main group may have served as merchandise containers and/or constituted trade items, while some may have held the crew's food and drink supply. The vessel that carried them, most likely a small boat suitable for coastal trade, was probably rounding the cape into the bay when it was hit by one of the sudden and unpredictable gusts of wind that often sweep down the valley of Sheytan Deresi. It capsized, spilling the largest part of its cargo on the spot, then floated towards land, perhaps with a few items still trapped in the hull, and probably ended up breaking against the rocky shore, below which similar sherds were reported.

The large krater raised during the 1973 survey seemed to assign the find to the Archaic period (around 600 BC), but after excavation, conservation, and preliminary study of the material, project director George Bass dated the wreck to the late Middle Bronze Age and pointed to Minoan as well as Anatolian influences on the pottery. Although some have expressed scepticism, no scholar has yet refuted his arguments. While it is true that none of the Bronze Age analogues constitute exact parallels for any of the Sheytan Deresi ceramics, later periods do not provide any closer counterparts. In fact, a search for identical specimens could be futile since small-scale, local manufacture of pottery (as was probably practised at the beginning of the Late Bronze Age outside palatial centres), may have precluded the product uniformity concomitant with mass production. Thus, given the absence of better parallels, similarities between the Sheytan Deresi pots and their Bronze Age counterparts uphold the connection. Excavations since 1973 have brought to light material that supports a Middle Bronze Age dating for the assemblages and strengthens the case for the possibly Minoan or Minoanizing nature of the pottery. In addition, work in the eastern Aegean islands substantiates the tradition of colonization and intensive maritime activity by the Minoans in the region. The pottery from Sheytan Deresi may have been

Prof. George Bass and Ann Bass with the jars from Sheytan Deresi at the Bodrum Museum of Underwater Archaeology. (© INA)

made in a Minoan settlement of the eastern Aegean islands or a site on the Anatolian coast where Minoans lived and/or traded. R.E.M.

ADDITIONAL READING

Bass, G.F., 1974, 'Survey for Wrecks, 1973', *International Journal of Nautical Archaeology*, 3, 335–8.

Bass, G.F., 1976, 'Sheytan Deresi: Preliminary Report', *International Journal of Nautical Archaeology*, 5, 4, 293–303.

Bass, G.F., 1977, 'The Wreck at Sheytan Deresi', *Oceans*, 10, 1, 34–9.

Hägg, R. and Marinatos, N., 1984, *The Minoan Thalassocracy: Myth and Reality*, Stockholm.

Mee, C., 1978, 'Aegean Trade and Settlement in Anatolia in the Second Millennium BC', *Anatolian Studies*, 28, 121–56.

Shinan Gun Shipwreck

One of the most important and unique archaeological sites ever discovered in Korea. In the summer of 1975 fishermen found intact ceramic vessels in their nets after trawling the muddy seabed between two small islands in Shinan prefecture near the city of Mok'po on the Yellow Sea coast of Korea. When celadon bowls, plates, and jars began to come up, some of the fishermen rigged special nets to 'mine' the area. Others, realizing that they had discovered the site of an ancient shipwreck, convinced authorities in Seoul, the capital, to send someone to evaluate the finds. Archaeologists from the Cultural Properties Preservation Bureau (CPPB) positively identified the ceramics as Yüan Dynasty (1260–1368) and promptly reimbursed the fishermen for the value of the artefacts they recovered, thus saving this important archaeological site from destruction.

Excavation of the ship was initiated in 1976 by the CPPB assisted by divers and ships supplied by the Korean Navy. In spite of freezing, racing, turbid waters, the divers' descriptions and measurements of the shipwreck 20 m below the surface enabled archaeologists to determine that the site was that of a large ship, listing slightly and buried in the muddy seabed. The fact that the ship's hold was divided into eight compartments by seven watertight bulkheads aided the divers in determining where individual finds were made.

The quantity and quality of the finds was astonishing. Thousands of ceramic and wooden artefacts and more than seven million copper coins were recovered. Soon the archaeologists realized that this single site would give South Korea the largest collection of Yüan Dynasty celadon ware in the world. Wooden boxes were raised intact, the Chinese characters painted on their exteriors as plainly readable as the day they were packed. The ceramics contained inside were unblemished, still wrapped in paper and cushioned in perfectly preserved peppercorns.

The ship's cargo and probably the ship

Containers filled with celadon ware from the Shinan Gun Ship, awaiting conservation in the National Museum. (D. Keith)

Shinan Gun Ship: many of the boxes in which the celadons were packed were filled with peppercorns. (D. Keith)

itself originated in China. A bronze counterweight for a balance was inscribed *Qingyuanlu*, possibly a reference to the modern Chinese port of Ningpo. Of the 26.8 tons of copper Chinese coins found on board, none dated later than 1310, but a wooden cargo tag bore the date 1323, and that is thought to be the year the ship sank. A few of the artefacts found are definitely of Japanese origin. The excavators theorize that these could have been personal possessions of the crew. It seems most likely that the ship was a Chinese merchant vessel bound for Japan. Perhaps a storm drove it onto the jagged islands on the southwestern coast of Korea.

By 1989 the entire ship had been dismantled and raised. Most of the timbers were still undergoing conservation in 1997 in the Mok'po Conservation and Restoration Centre, and an analysis and reconstruction of the ship are planned. Although the Shinan Gun Ship shares some common construction characteristics with the somewhat earlier **Quanzhou Ship** (*c.*AD 1277), it is clear that their construction traditions are not closely related. D.H.K.

ADDITIONAL READING

Green, J., 1983, 'The Song Dynasty Shipwreck at Quanzhou, Fujian Province, People's Republic of China', *International Journal of Nautical Archaeology*, 12, 3, 253–61.

Green, J.N., 1983, 'The Shinan Excavation, Korea: An Interim Report on the Hull', *International Journal of Nautical Archaeology*, 12, 293–302.

Green, J. and Kim Zae Geun, 1989, 'The Shinan and Wando Sites, Korea: Further Information', *International Journal of Nautical Archaeology*, 18, 1, 33–41.

Keith, D.H., 1979, 'A Fourteenth-Century Cargo Makes Port at Last', *National Geographic*, 156, 2, 230–43.

Keith, D.H., 1980, 'A Fourteenth Century Shipwreck at Sinan-gun', *Archaeology*, 33, 2, 33–13.

Keith, D.H. and Buys, C., 1981, 'New Light on Medieval Chinese Seagoing Ship Construction', *International Journal of Nautical Archaeology*, 10, 2, 119–32.

Needham, J., 1971, 'Civil Engineering and Nautics', in *Science and Civilisation in China*, vol. 4, 3, Cambridge.

Zaine, C.M., 1979, 'The Sinan Shipwreck and Early Muromachi Art Collections', *Oriental Art*, 25, 1, 103–14.

Shipboard society

The social structure of the crew and passengers of a ship as revealed by its material remains. The term 'society' generally refers to an association of individuals gathered along political, economic, or cultural lines who can be seen as a distinct group. In social sciences such as anthropology and sociology the word often assumes a more precise meaning usually synonymous with 'social structure'. Social structure denotes the way a group of people differentiate and order themselves for the achievement of certain goals. In general, social structures can be characterized as existing along two intersecting continua. On one continuum, social structures range from highly differentiated, where every member of the group occupies a specific position and role, generally with variable access to power, to completely egalitarian, where all members participate equally in activities and have equal access to goods and power. On the other continuum, social structures range from rigid, where the degree of differentiation among members rarely or never changes, to loose, where differentiation is fluid and ranges from highly differentiated to loosely differentiated according to many variables. In short, it is possible to have many combinations of differentiation and egalitarian social structure: for example, a highly differentiated but changeable group, or an egalitarian group that maintains its structure rigidly and actively.

Many anthropologists studying social structures conclude that group organization is variable and largely instrumental, which means it is set up in a particular manner to address perceived and changeable group needs. In his work *Political Systems of Highland Burma*, anthropologist Edmund Leach documented how the Kachin highlanders altered their social structure from differentiated to egalitarian as they moved from one village site to another over a period of years. A particular group may be highly differentiated during periods of warfare or big game hunts, yet revert to egalitarian structure during more peaceful periods or while gathering food. Social structure for many groups, like the Kachin, is the result of a conscious attempt by group members to configure the group towards a certain perceived end. Clearly, as needs and perceptions change, the social structure changes in an attempt to meet the new conditions.

To further complicate the picture, groups are rarely unified in their perceptions, interpretation of variables, or conclusions regarding appropriate organizational structure. Often, different group members have competing ideas as to appropriate goals, as well as the proper organization that should exist to meet them. When differing ideas occur, the resulting social structure may be a compromise brought about by dynamic interaction of two or more competing subgroups holding differing views as to appropriate organization. In short, social structures exhibit varying degrees of volatility depending upon numerous factors, such as group size, goals to which the group is directed, and consensus of intended goal, with group change being more common than stasis.

When examining social structure, anthropologists and sociologists have found it useful to distinguish between the 'ideal' and the 'real', or, more simply, the way people believe things 'ought to be' and the way things are. Many groups professing an egalitarian social structure have, upon closer examination, a highly differentiated one. Similarly, some societies professing to be highly differentiated may turn out to be more egalitarian than its members acknowledge. In situations where there is disjuncture between the ideal and the real, it is often the case that ideology (a collectively held set of beliefs and presumptions) masks the disparity from members of the group. Among religious cults, for example, it is quite typical to profess equality before god and a strong commitment to this notion often blinds people to the reality that their group is, in fact, highly differentiated with large disparities in access to goods, information, and decision-making power.

Another distinction between the ideal and the real is that social scientists have found that, while a group may have specific roles to be fulfilled by its members, the individuals who are 'supposed' to fill these roles are often unwilling or unable to do so. When this situation occurs their responsibilities and duties are shifted to other members of the group. An incompetent captain of a ship, for example, might have some or most of his duties taken over by the first mate. Again, what 'ought to be' and what is may be disparate, and social scientists must be careful when drawing direct correlations between professed and actual social structure, whether the structure is reported through oral accounts or historical documents.

Typically, social structures fall along, reinforce, or create differentiation among other divisions apparent to group members, for example along such commonly observed social science categories as occupation, gender, race, ethnicity, religion, age, and socioeconomic status. These differentiations become important when they are used to separate one member of a group from another, or alternatively to unify a group under a common denominator, such as religion, to achieve a particular end.

In Americanist terrestrial archaeology, the study of social structure has been a research domain for more than thirty years. During the 1960s researchers such as Lewis Binford, James Deetz, William Longacre, and James Hill began using archaeological data to examine social structural questions such as prehistoric residence patterns, social organization and social interaction. These early studies were the foundation for later, more complex, less contentious, and methodologically more sophisticated work capable of producing convincing evidence of particular social structures in both prehistoric and historical groups.

Methodologically and epistemologically, an archaeological examination of social structure invariably draws upon other social sciences such as anthropology, history, or material culture studies. Reasons for this close association essentially revolve around the archaeologist's desire to move beyond artefact description of surface attributes like material and method of fabrication to the realm of meaning and its implication for inferences about social structure and behaviour. For this to be done convincingly, archaeologists must use auxiliary historical or anthropological data to demonstrate a particular culture, thought to be similar to the culture being studied archaeologically, used analogous artefact types as an indicator of abstract and intangible qualities like race, religion, or status, which might imply social differentiation. If this can be demonstrated, other elements of the social system may be inferred, albeit with less confidence than those elements indicated by the recovered artefacts. In short, the concrete presence of particular artefacts and associations can serve as a signature for more intangible social and cultural aspects of the society being studied archaeologically.

As discussed above, social structures typi-

Some of the many personal items excavated from Mary Rose, *including a thimble-ring, clasp, pocket sundial, whistle, purse-hanger, comb, coins, knife-handle, seal, and rosary; the stamp of the seal is marked 'G I' with holly surround. (© Mary Rose Trust)*

cally are built along divisional lines readily discernible by group members such as occupation, gender, race, ethnicity, religion, age, and socioeconomic status. Anthropologists and archaeologists have demonstrated that social divisions are not only reflected in material culture, but are also created, exacerbated, or maintained by them. For example, in a completely egalitarian group – one with little or no social differentiation – each group member generally has access to, and uses, similar material culture elements (artefacts). As a society becomes highly differentiated, typically there is increasingly variable access for group members to a more heterogeneous artefactual **Assemblage**. These variations are often represented archaeologically by differences among artefacts and associations in an assemblage, and through inter-assemblage comparisons that can yield disparities in physical attributes in entire classes of artefacts. In addition, variable access is usually reflected in the physical attributes of objects, such as material of construction and skill of manufacture, as well as where and how they are used.

There are numerous examples of the complex role of material objects and their social uses being discernible from ethnography and archaeology. British archaeologist Ian Hodder found that among the Ilchamus (a pastoral tribe in Kenya) decorative patterns on calabash milk gourds were used to estab-lish and maintain power among women of the tribe. In another example, archaeologist James Deetz used different decorative patterns on Arikara ceramics to demonstrate that recently married couples lived in the house of the wife's family (matrilocality). Beyond artefacts, social structure may be consciously manipulated in the built environment using such things as large and ornate buildings to emphasize the position of some group members, as well as the monopolization of private space by a select few such as the exclusivity and privacy of the captain's cabin often found on board a ship. In short, what ethnographic and historical research suggests is that artefacts such as religious icons, specialized tools or dress, ornate artefacts such as jewellery and weapons, exotic materials fashioned into artefacts, as well as differing design motifs and the variable allocation of space, all may be used as indicators of social differentiation. Investigation of archaeological materials pertaining to the intangible aspects of human culture, which are especially sensitive to masking by ideology, can tell us something about the society that produced them which may be otherwise unattainable through reference to historical documentation.

When looking at the maritime archaeology literature, it is remarkable that while shipboard ways of life are often cited as a research goal, so little work concerning social structure has been done. This may be partially due to the observation that archaeological data indicative of social structure are often more ambiguous than those denoting such things as ship construction and use, and thus produce less definitive and often less satisfying archaeological answers. Another difficulty may be that many archaeologists operate with the implicit assumption that shipboard societies exist in a rigidly differentiated manner as exemplified by the Western European maritime tradition, and thus need not be documented.

The Western European shipboard social configuration model needs to be demonstrated, not assumed; it represents an ideal that may or may not be borne out in reality. Even where demonstrated, variations of form and expression need to be delineated and examined, and this can be successfully done archaeologically. As discussed above, there is often a disparity between the ideal and the real, and demonstration of the model relies in most cases upon historical documents, which itself is problematic because they often report ideologically charged notions of how a society 'should be'. European sailors are a group given a history generated by dominant groups – merchants, naval officers, and more recently capitalists. Few social histories have been written about (or by) seamen, and generally sailors are not represented in historical documents. When mentioned in most Western historical documents, they are more often seen as a necessary evil, important only in moving a ship. In current literature, seafaring is often seen as a romantic pursuit: humans pitted against awesome oceanic elements aboard a frail wooden platform relying only on iron, rope, and sail. It was adventure that called crews to the sea, or so literary works would have us believe. These romantic images bear scant resemblance to the realities of seafaring, and ignore nautical traditions from other cultures stretching back thousands of years.

The social nature of seafaring and the particular nature of social relations that formed the framework of maritime behaviour comprise a realm of social science that has so far attracted little serious scholarly interest. What research has been done relies heavily on documents from the Western capitalist tradition, largely perpetuating ideals that benefit the few and mask reality for the many. The power of archaeology combined with materialist history is that it offers a baseline of evidence against which to evaluate the reported or assumed ideal. Where disparity between the observed and ideal emerges, interesting and unreported aspects of human behaviour can be exposed and demonstrated. It is here that archaeology can make significant contributions to the realm of social science in general.

From the earliest beginnings of seafaring to the start of the 19th century, most seamen were illiterate and their histories were written by non-sailors, representatives of the ruling elites, many of whom were unfamiliar with seamen. A study of the realities of seafaring life, like the study of many non- or poorly documented peoples, will be dependent upon new approaches and new directions in maritime archaeological enquiry. In formulating a new approach, archaeologists should be prepared to draw upon the widest range of social sciences – history, anthropology, sociology, etc. – to demonstrate that certain recovered artefacts and patterns may have been indicative of social differentiation on board the ship (or alternatively, indicative of a more egalitarian structure than had been previously assumed). A basic requirement for studying the 'society of the ship' is the formulation of material signatures for particular social structure and behaviour aboard ships. In the absence of external lines of evidence, archaeological questions pertaining to the society of the ship will either go unanswered or merely replicate contemporary assumptions.

When social scientists talk of the 'society of the ship', they generally are referring to the social structure of the crew, which should be differentiated from the society of the passengers, which may or many not be similar to the crew. In addition, the 'society of the ship' also produces a 'society of the shore', a particular social organization that emerges on land to fulfil the social and economic needs of those left behind and who must adapt to the absence of seafarers for the duration of their voyages, as well as accommodate them while ashore. The vessel often provides the rhythms and structure of the shore society through its comings and goings, work patterns, and shipboard structure. Community structure can also affect the society of the ship. For example, the labour recruitment practices of late 18th-century Nantucket merchants who manipulated credit to obligate sufficient labour for whaling ventures, set the tone for the whalers' social structure that emerged as a result.

When examining the society of the ship, archaeologists must avoid a simple reading of contemporary assumptions into the material record of the past. While many ships of the Western European nautical tradition evidenced a rigidly differential hierarchical social structure, some, such as pirate ships, did not. Pirates apparently were much more egalitarian, with a looser structure, which calls to question the assumption that rigid and differential structure is required for success at sea. In parts of the Southeast Asian maritime tradition, sailors signed on as trading partners and worked in exchange for a section of the cargo hold, which they used for their own enterprise. On the 'petticoat whalers' of the Pacific during the first half of the 19th century, captains commonly brought along their wives and sometimes their children, not only as companions, but occasionally as crew. In the British Royal Navy of the late 18th and early 19th century, women in the form of prostitutes, wives, and officers' girlfriends, as well as women disguised as men, were not an uncommon sight on board ships. British Supernumerary Lists indicate soldiers' and mariners' wives were sufficiently common to be considered in official victualling policy. Black Africans and other ethnic and racial minorities form a discernible presence on ships throughout history, from the earliest Nubians on Egyptian riverboats to African-American naval commanders from the Civil War to the present day. The challenge here is to generate clear signatures for gender and ethnicity contained within shipboard assemblages, and this can most profitably be done by drawing on ethnographies, histories, and contemporary practice for artefacts that may have analogues in the archaeology of a shipwreck.

In general, contrary to accepted belief, the society of a ship is less a generic hierarchy than a continuation of the land-based society from which it emerged, often reflecting similar positions on the scales of differentiation and rigidity. While it is true that shipboard life presents some unique challenges, the social structure arising to meet them does not come out of a social vacuum nor is it solely the reflection of the demands of ocean travel. Shipboard societies reflect, to various degrees, the larger society of which they are part – an egalitarian society tending to produce a more egalitarian crew, and a more rigidly differentiated society producing a more rigidly stratified crew – modified, as anthropologist Peter Lape observed, by such variables as ship size, voyage's purpose, distance travelled, and crew's ethnic make-up. Having said that, it is important to realize that the social structure of the ship will not have all the varieties of relations of the larger society, and will not strictly be a microcosm of the larger society. The challenge is to develop a methodology capable of producing an accurate reconstruction of shipboard social structure.

Methodologically the largest hurdle to a maritime archaeologist examining the material remains of the society of the ship lies in differentiating the crew's material assemblage from that of passengers and cargo. On a cargo vessel, such as the 7th-century AD shipwreck excavated by the **Institute of Nautical Archaeology** at **Yassiada**, Turkey, the artefacts associated with the crew were concentrated in an area towards what was interpreted as the stern, and they were relatively easily distinguishable from the cargo of amphoras. Elsewhere, as at the **Cape Gelidonya Wreck** in Turkey (also excavated by INA), artefacts associated with crew were less easily distinguished from the cargo, but could be discerned by use attributes such as fire blackening on lamps, which probably excluded them as items of trade.

On a passenger vessel, differentiation between the crew's personal possessions and those of the passengers may be more problematic, except in cases such as navigational instruments and other articles of specialized nautical equipment. In this case, archaeological associations and spatial patterning, interpreted from historical accounts of similar hull arrangements, may aid in the determination of site areas containing crew or passenger assemblages.

Once different artefact groups are isolated and attributed to shipborne groups, they can be examined for individual items providing signatures for things such as race, socioeconomic status, gender, and ethnicity, which groups typically use as convenient markers for internal differentiation. As an example, exotic Ming Dynasty china was found on the 1588 **Spanish Armada** wreck *La Trinidad Valencera*, and was an unexpected artefact indicating wealth and social position attributable to noblemen who made up the officers of the Spanish invasion forces. On the wreck of the *Girona*, another Spanish Armada ship, archaeologists found gold jewellery and other expensive personal possessions, reflecting the relative position of members of either the crew or passengers. A final example comes from the Late Bronze Age shipwreck at **Uluburun**, Turkey, where archaeologists found the remains of a Mycenaean-style sword and cloak pin, which strongly implies at least one Greek on board the ship.

From these and numerous other examples, it is clear that materials necessary to research anthropologically oriented questions pertaining to shipboard social structure probably exist on most shipwreck sites. Examination of questions involving social structure have long been a research domain for terrestrial archaeologists, and there are compelling examples of social structural interpretations based on archaeological remains. It is true that questions concerning social structure are rarely as definitively answered as those concerning other issues such as trading patterns and construction techniques, but this does not devalue the worthiness of their examination. Terrestrial archaeological examples provide models for

enquiry into the nature of the 'shipboard society'. Shipboard social structure represents a neglected and often ideologically masked element of human history, and it is one that maritime archaeologists are uniquely suited to examine. D.L.C./L.E.M

ADDITIONAL READING

Gould, R.A. (ed.), 1983, *Shipwreck Anthropology*, Albuquerque.

Ship burials

Burials in which a ship is used either as a container for the deceased and the grave goods, or as part of the grave goods themselves. In Bronze Age Egypt, ships were occasionally included as part of the grave goods of rich burials. The large **Khufu Ship I** found in a sealed pit beside the Cheops pyramid and the **Dashur boats** are the best known examples. In many Egyptian graves models take the place of the real ships. In these cases the vessels or models are part of very rich funeral equipment, together with other artefacts for use in the afterlife. However, the term ship burial is generally restricted to burials where a boat or ship is the main artefact, often used as a container for the dead person and the rest of the grave goods. This is a north European custom. The majority of the graves found are from the Viking Age (*c.*AD 800–1050). They are found in Sweden, Denmark, Norway, Iceland, part of Finland, and in Viking settlements in Scotland, the Isle of Man, Shetland, the Orkneys, and northern Russia. On the continent, there is one isolated example on the coast of Brittany. The majority of the Viking Age ship and boat burials are located in Norway, where they are found along the entire coast and more sparingly inland. The burials may be male or female, and both inhumation and cremation burials are found.

The vessels used for burial range in size from small boats 4-5 m in length, to large ships. The largest vessel found among properly excavated graves is the pre-Viking Age **Sutton Hoo** ship, with a total length of 27.1 m.

In the Viking Age, proof of boat and ship burials is in most cases the presence of the characteristic iron rivets which were used for fastening together the planks of clinker-built vessels. Inhumation burials sometimes give detailed information on the buried ship or boat. When wood is preserved as in the **Oseberg**, **Gokstad** and **Tune Ship** graves from Norway, and the Swedish **Årby** grave, the ships are our most important sources on Viking shipbuilding technique and hull shape. Even when all wood has disappeared, the rows of rivets and stains in the soil may give information on the length of the vessel, the number of strakes and other construction details,

like scarfs in the planking, fastenings between keel and stems, etc. If the rotting wood was well supported by the soil, the lines of the vessel may be recorded, sometimes with a high degree of precision. The best examples are the Danish Ladby grave from the 10th century, and the 7th-century grave at Sutton Hoo in East Anglia, England.

The shape of the Sutton Hoo ship was reconstructed as if the vessel had been intact. The position of every rivet was carefully recorded and plotted to give a set of lines where the run of every plank could be followed. Traces in the soil showed the position of ribs and rowlocks, and the cross-section of the shallow keel. In cremation graves, rivets show that a boat was present at the funeral fire, but it has been debated how many rivets should be present before the grave can be accepted as a boat grave. According to one author, one rivet is enough to call a grave a boat grave, while M. Müller-Wille rejects all graves with fewer than fifty rivets, and considers those with between fifty and a hundred rivets as uncertain. We can not ignore the fact that discarded boat timbers were used simply as fuel for the fire in cremation graves, and in such cases it would be wrong to speak of a boat grave, but a number of graves contain so many rivets that a complete vessel must have been burned.

Rivets were used as fasteners for other wooden structures, but those used in clinker boatbuilding are usually quite characteristic. Most of the rivets were used to hold the overlapping planks together and are of approximately the same length, corresponding to double planking thickness. If a smaller number of short rivets from plank scarfs, long rivets for fastening strakes to rib tops, and some nails for fastening plank ends to the stems are present together with the 'standard' plank rivets, the assembly must come from a clinker-built boat. There are examples of inhumation graves where a few planks or a clearly incomplete boat has been placed around the grave goods. In such cases, we must accept that the intention was to create a boat grave, even if a complete boat was not used. A similar situation can have existed when the grave was burned. One inhumation grave from northern Norway contained a double row of rivets with a lump of nails at each end. The excavator explained this as a boat where the first strake was riveted to the keel, and plank ends nailed to the stems, while the remaining fastenings were either treenails or lashings which had left no traces. Older, unprofessionally excavated finds may also contain far too few rivets, as these were either not found or discarded. As a result, every new find must be analysed and regarded as a possible boat grave even if fewer than fifty rivets are found.

The only eyewitness description we have of a Viking funeral tells about a cremation ship grave. The Arab traveller Ibn Fadlan happened to meet a party of Swedish Vikings in Russia around AD 920 and took part in the burial of their chief who had just died. The dead man was placed in a temporary grave during the preparations for the funeral, which took some days. The ship which had belonged to the dead man was pulled ashore, and a burial chamber was constructed on board. Rich equipment was placed in the ship and the dead man put to bed in the chamber, dressed in his best clothes. Animals and a female slave were sacrificed before the ship and its contents were set on fire. Afterwards, a large mound of earth was built over the ashes.

While ship and boat burials are most common in the Viking Age, the custom is older. One problem in recognizing boat graves is the difficulty of identifying a boat built without iron rivets. Iron fastenings for boats came into use in Scandinavia around AD 250–300. All boats before that time, and many after, were fastened by sewing or lashing the strakes together. On the Danish island of Bornholm, careful excavation of soil stains has proved that in the period between c.AD 100 and 250, 43 out of 467 inhumation graves on the Slusegaard burial field had coffins made from expanded dugout boats that had no metal fastenings. Few complete boats were found, but they seem to fall into three groups. The smallest boats were about 3 m long, and rather wide. An intermediate group were narrow boats of around 5 m in length, and there were fragments of a few larger boats, where the length could not be established. Similar graves from the Migration period have been found on the Anglo-Saxon cemetery at Snape in East Anglia, England. Here, the boats were probably ordinary dugouts, made from a large log, but not expanded.

A Viking Age female burial at Tuna-Badelunda in Uppland, Sweden was placed in an approximately 7 m long expanded dugout with lashed-on top-strakes. In this grave, wood was sufficiently well preserved to permit not only the identification of the boat type, but also conservation and exhibition of the boat. In the same grave field, graves were found where a boat-shaped trench had been dug into the ground, but no remains of the boat could be identified. On the evidence of the best-preserved grave, it is highly probable that the other graves

originally also contained similar boats. These finds make it likely that a number of boat graves have not been interpreted as such, when wood was not present or recognizable. A cremation burial where the boat had no metal fastenings is, of course, impossible to find archaeologically.

Sutton Hoo Mound I, the excavated ship, looking west towards the prow; the lines of plank fastenings are clearly visible running from bow to stern. (Courtesy of the Trustees of the British Museum)

A full continuity of the ship burial custom between the Slusegaard graves and the Viking Age is difficult to establish, but there are a few Migration period graves where rivets indicate boats. The majority are found in Norway. One, at Mølen, Vestfold, has been carbon-14 dated to AD 30–250 (uncalibrated).

In the 6th to 8th centuries, extremely well-equipped male graves at Ulltuna, Vendel, and Valsgärde in Uppland, Sweden were placed in boats. These graves are inhumations. Boat graves from the same period have also been found in Norway, where the majority of Viking Age graves, both burned and unburned, are to be found. In Norway, a couple of cremation graves, from Mølen and Ølbør, Rogaland, both with boat rivets among the grave goods, have boat-like stone settings as grave markers. Here, a boat was part of the grave goods, and the grave itself also has a boat shape.

Other boat-shaped stone monuments also contain graves. They can be dated either to the Late Bronze Age or to the Migration period – the Viking Age. They are found in

the countries around the Baltic and in Scandinavia and are generally interpreted as a special form of ship grave. Some are very large; others, like the late Viking Age graves from Lindholm Høye in Denmark, are only two to three metres long. Usually, two rows of raised stones are placed to indicate the curved sides of the ship, with taller stones marking the stem- and sternposts. There seems to be a span of several centuries between the early and late groups of these graves.

The distribution of ship and boat graves shows a marked majority along the coasts, but the custom is also found inland. In all probability, this reflects the different importance of boats in everyday life, regardless of the religious background of the custom.

The religious background of ship graves has been differently interpreted. In a few Norwegian graves without ship remains, a piece of silver has been found in the mouth of the dead person. This has been interpreted as a parallel to the Greek belief that Charon should be paid for ferrying the dead person across the River Styx. In maritime societies the idea could be taken one step further: a boat in the grave would make the dead person independent of the ferryman. Against this it has been maintained that our modest knowledge of heathen belief in Scandinavia does not contain any mention of travelling over water to the land of the dead. Other interpretations are that the ship or boat in the grave is a symbol of power, secular or religious. Ole Crumlin-Pedersen, who published work on the Slusegaard boats, has suggested that these boat burials belong to a dynasty of religious leaders, and are connected to the cult of the fertility gods Njord and Frey.

In the Viking Age, especially in Norway, many graves are well equipped with metal- or woodworking tools. We also find kitchen utensils, agricultural tools, and hunting and fishing gear, in addition to arms in male and jewellery in female graves. In such graves it is natural to interpret the vessel as just another tool: a large ship for the warrior chieftain, an ordinary small boat for the coastal farmer/fisherman. In both cases the vessel was intended for use in the afterlife, like the rest of the grave goods. The wide distribution of ship graves in time and space makes it quite possible that several different beliefs were behind the custom at different periods and places.

A variation of the ship burial custom mentioned in written sources, but which cannot be found by archaeological technique, is when the ship is sent out to sea. In the Anglo-Saxon poem *Beowulf*, which is generally dated to the 8th century, the burial of King Scyld Scefing is described. He was the legendary founder of the Scylding dynasty, kings of Denmark. The king had himself given instructions about how the burial should be arranged. He was carried to the beach and laid to rest by the mast of his splendid ship. Weapons, armour, and 'many treasures' were carried on board, before the ship was launched and given up to the ocean.

Younger members of the same dynasty selected similar burials, according to the Icelandic author and historian Snorri Sturluson. In his introduction to the saga of the Norwegian kings, he tells of the kings Haki and Sigurd Ring. They were both mortally wounded in battle. Ships were loaded with dead men and weapons. The dying kings boarded the ships and sailed out to sea as the vessels were set alight. In another work Snorri tells the legend of the burial of the heathen god Balder. He too is burned in his ship. It may be that the ship was sent out to sea, but the text is not clear. A.E.C.

ADDITIONAL READING

Crumlin-Pedersen, O., 1991, 'Bådgravene: Slusegårdgravpladsen III', *Jysk Arkeologisk Selskabs Skrifter*, 13, 3.

Müller-Wille, M., 1970, *Bestattung im Boot: Studien zu einer nordeuropäischen Grabsitte*, Neumünster.

Nylén, E. *et al.*, 1994, *Tuna i Badelunda I–II*, Västerås.

Ship trap

A maritime hazard with an extensive collection of shipwreck sites. Examples of ship traps are reefs jutting into narrow straits, as at **Yassiada** in Turkey, or into a stream of passing maritime commerce, as the **Dry Tortugas**, Florida. Other examples include Cape Iria in the Saronic Gulf of Greece, the Gulf of Fos off the French Mediterranean coast, and **Isle Royale** in Lake Superior. The idea of a ship trap helps explain why it is that nautical archaeologists often find numerous vessels in close proximity to each other.

Shipwrecks, in many cases, are less isolated events than they are the results of the natural and cultural processes which operate over extended periods and which pattern their deposition in non-random and archaeologically knowable ways. Many shipwrecks are the results of mariners taking risks and losing. For the individuals involved, shipwrecks come as unpleasant surprises; but evaluated from the historical perspective archaeology provides, ship traps can be seen as areas of poor odds for traversing seafarers, where the presence of wrecks is entirely predictable as the aggregate result of risk. Focusing on ship traps, as opposed to shipwrecks, stands in contrast to a traditional nautical archaeological approach that concentrates on a site as an isolated event rather than as the result of the intermeshed operation of cultural and natural systems. Through accumulated maritime knowledge transmitted via oral traditions and local histories, it is likely that the positions of many of these nautical hazards were known to sailors in the past, who developed routes to avoid them according to weather, time of year, and direction of travel. In non-literate traditions this knowledge is transmitted and retained via poems, songs, and apocryphal stories. Thus, while the monsters Scylla and Charybdis, voracious in the Sicilian Straits of Messina, are of dubious reality, they do speak of the underlying nautical hazards that make up the ship traps of the region. More recently, maritime hazards have been marked by lighthouses, buoys, and beacons with varying degrees of success. Even so, despite the best efforts of technology, shipwrecks continue to occur in predictable areas and for predictable reasons.

Ultimately, when one thinks about ship traps, perhaps a valid metaphor is a net, cast into the stream of passing maritime commerce. Some nets, like Yassiada, tend only to catch commerce travelling in one direction, while others may catch ships moving in two or more directions. Conceptually, there could be ship traps that work in three, four, or even all directions. Understanding these

ship traps and characterizing them should allow archaeologists to make informed statements regarding possible origins, destinations, and directions of travel for shipwrecks which do not have readily available auxiliary documentation. Delineating the directionality of the net extended into the stream of commerce feeds directly back into a characterization of this commerce and a reliable archaeological assessment of patterns of maritime trade. D.L.C.

ADDITIONAL READING

Murphy, L.E. (ed.), 1993, *Dry Tortugas National Park: Submerged Cultural Resources Assessment*, Santa Fe, New Mexico.

Shipwreck anthropology

The study of shipwrecks from an anthropological perspective. Although the idea of using anthropological concepts to explain shipwreck assemblages is relatively new, it is the product of a long-standing scholarly tradition. Anthropology began as a series of organized attempts to explain the origins of human social and cultural institutions through the use of ethnographic information about mainly non-Western societies. During the late 19th century, leading ethnologists like Lewis Henry Morgan in America and E.B. Tylor in England argued that all human societies evolved through a series of similar stages in the same order, though not necessarily at the same time. In Tylor's scheme, there was the notion that some societies evolved only to a certain stage and could be viewed as cases of arrested cultural development or 'survivals'. Morgan's framework influenced Friedrich Engels and was incorporated into a historical-evolutionary extension of Marxist social theory with stages that emphasized unequal distribution of goods, social stratification, and class struggle. All of these schemes were examples of unilineal *cultural evolution*, with their final stages approximating social conditions found in Victorian-era Europe and America.

Cultural evolutionism represented a form of conjectural history and was a major concern of early anthropology until a competing variety of conjectural history, *cultural diffusion*, gained importance in the early 20th century. Pioneered by scholars like Leo Frobenius, the German diffusionist approach (known as the *Kulturkreiselehre*) challenged earlier German *Anthropogeographie*, as presented by Friederich Ratzel and others, by replacing the study of human migrations with an interest in the spread, through culture contact, of ideas about patterned behaviour, including technologies and symbols. Diffusionist principles were widely adopted in America by anthropologists like Clark Wissler, who adapted the idea into his concept of 'culture areas' for different ethnographic North American Indian cultural groupings. Later he expanded this approach into his 'age-area hypothesis' by arguing that different groupings of cultural traits were the product of different episodes of diffusion at different times. Diffusionism also appeared in England in the form of the 'heliocentric theory' of cultural origins of traits derived from ancient Egypt, advocated by Grafton Eliot Smith.

All diffusionist theories had as their basic assumption the uninventiveness of the human species. Extreme diffusionists (especially the Germans and English) claimed that inventions occurred only once. Further occurrences of an invention or innovation, they argued, could only be due to the idea of the invention being passed from one group to another, forming a series of spreading waves of diffused culture complexes of associated traits. They rejected the notion of independent inventions of cultural traits, especially complicated ones like the 'lost-wax' technique in bronze-casting, or certain architectural and artistic styles. So, for example, German scholars noted the spread of the 'Melanesian Bow Culture' into the southwest Pacific region, where it was thought to have replaced cultures using spears, spear throwers, and other associated technologies. Like Tylor, they point to cultural 'survivals' in certain remote areas like Australia, where, they claimed, spear and spear thrower cultures persisted in isolation through lack of contact with later cultural diffusions. These ultra-diffusionist interpretations produced a kind of pseudo-stratigraphic picture of sequential trait complexes in different regions of the world.

Both cultural evolutionism and diffusionism were approaches that had chronological implications. Each developed into a theory of conjectural history about the origins, spread, and survival of cultural traits and institutions. Each approach depended upon ethnological findings to construct an idea of the human past, and it was these attempts to infer the past from the present that dominated early anthropology.

Conjectural history gradually fell out of favour in anthropology starting in the 1920s, especially due to the influence of social/cultural anthropologists like Bronislaw Malinowski and A.R. Radcliffe-Brown in England and Europe and Franz Boas in America. In various ways these scholars all sought to redirect anthropology towards explaining the operation and functioning of cultures in the present. They generally ignored or rejected conjectural history.

While conjectural history, in both its evolutionist and diffusionist modes, has persisted and even been revived in some quarters, the mainstream of anthropology has focused ever since on the present-day and short-term historical workings of human societies. Anthropological interests have tended to concentrate since then on understanding particular cultures, although there is a continuing interest in comparative anthropology as well.

At about the same time that conjectural history declined, modern stratigraphic archaeology emerged as the principal way of studying human prehistory. This shift reflects a willingness by anthropologists to accept principles of stratigraphy, superposition, and seriation and the use of appropriate archaeological controls and techniques as valid guides to understanding the human past. The transition from conjectural to empirical approaches in the study of human prehistory was accomplished in a relatively short time, mainly because archaeological techniques had been evolving since the mid-19th century and were achieving convincing results. The first indications of the possibilities for underwater archaeology had already appeared with the discovery of the Cortaillod Culture (Swiss Lake Dwellers) in 1853–4 and the initial recovery of ancient Maya Indian artefacts, including gold objects and wooden carvings, and evidence of human sacrifice at the Sacred Cenote (a water-filled limestone sinkhole) at **Chichén-Itzá** in the Yucatan region of Mexico in 1904. These early discoveries were not made in what would, today, be regarded as an archaeologically acceptable manner, but they did much to extend the domain of archaeology to underwater as well as land contexts.

In America, stratigraphic archaeology was readily incorporated into the discipline of anthropology, where it continues as a major sub-field. This did not happen in England or Europe, where archaeology is generally treated as a separate historical discipline or is combined with specialities like Egyptology or Classical Archaeology. Despite this institutional separation of archaeology as a form of history from anthropology, European and English scholars and, by extension, scholars in places like Africa, Australia, and New Zealand, continue to show a keen interest in anthropological findings. Maritime archaeology, too, has been allied predominantly with the discipline of history, even when dealing with prehistoric or undocumented shipwreck sites. Today, however, there is a parallel awareness and interest in anthropological approaches as a means of analysing shipwreck data in relation to social scientific issues.

Not all anthropological issues and approaches are appropriate for **Maritime archaeology**. Maritime archaeologists are encouraged to be critical and selective in their choices of relevant anthropological theory. The culture concept is one issue best approached with caution by maritime archaeologists. The general lack of consensus among anthropologists about the nature of culture or their ability to define culture provides many options but little guidance for maritime archaeology. Moving beyond definitions to the conduct of anthropology, we find ourselves on firmer ground. Anthropologists may disagree about the nature of culture, but they have developed useful approaches to the study of particular cultures. Some of these approaches can be extended to maritime studies.

Cultural relativism

This principle argues that non-Western cultures cannot be evaluated according to Western standards or expectations but must be viewed in their own terms. The early development of this view is firmly linked with Franz Boas, under whose influence this concept emerged as a dominant assumption of anthropology. This assumption is based on the necessity of establishing an insider's view of the culture being studied, through the use of appropriate linguistic and field techniques that seek to elicit native categories of knowledge and experience. This is done in the context of sustained, long-term field experience of *participant-observation*. The insider's view is commonly referred to as the *emic* perspective, from its historic connection with the phonemic approach used in modern linguistics to elicit sounds that are meaningful to the native speakers of a particular language. The outsider's point of view (especially when based on Western-derived, scientific, analytical methods) is often termed the *etic* perspective, from its association with earlier phonetic approaches to the study of language, like the International Phonetic Alphabet.

The emic approach, founded on anthropological concepts of cultural relativism, has proved useful in understanding non-Western methods of boatbuilding, seamanship, and navigation, most notably in the Pacific. Ethnographic studies on the islands of Puluwat and Satawal in Micronesia and Anuta in Polynesia provide detailed accounts of navigation by means of the star compass and sea indications like ocean swells and waves. Combined with studies of traditional boat construction and sailing practices, this research played a key role in the experimental voyages of the Polynesian double-hull canoe replica *Hokule'a* from

Hawaii to Tahiti and back. Mau Pialug, the Micronesian navigator on the trip, relied entirely upon traditional methods to conduct the Hawaii to Tahiti voyage, building upon his knowledge in the western Pacific to venture into new areas in eastern Polynesia. The success of the *Hokule'a* showed how purposeful voyages of colonization eastward against prevailing winds and current could have been accomplished by the ancient ancestors of the Polynesians. These experimental results were supported by archaeological findings showing the eastward spread of the Lapita culture, representing the earliest direct archaeological evidence for such initial settlement. Unique Lapita-style pottery and other materials appeared in a sequential series of radiocarbon-dated localities from approximately 3000 BC in the islands immediately northeast of New Guinea to eastern Polynesia, with later offshoots as far east as the Marquesas Islands sometime by at least the 1st century AD. So the concept of cultural relativism in anthropology extends beyond injunctions against making ethnocentric, Western-biased judgements about behaviour in non-Western cultures (such as 'Eating people is evil', or 'Australian Aboriginal art is primitive'). However one may feel personally about practices like cannibalism or may respond subjectively to Aboriginal art, the principle of cultural relativism positively requires that anthropologists make serious, organized efforts to understand these kinds of behaviour from the point of view and in the cultural terms of the people performing them.

Cultural presentism

Cultural processes studied by anthropologists are based on present-day observations of human behaviour and, in some cases, on recent culture history based upon historical accounts. So there is always the problem of applying present-day findings to the ancient human past without projecting present-day experience and observations into the past – 'the fallacy of affirming the consequent'. Anthropological awareness of cultural presentism teaches archaeologists to avoid constructing ideas about human history that merely create the past in the image of the present.

Archaeologists need to be able to confront and explain ancient cultures that have no modern or historic counterpart. Prehistory abounds with examples of this, and so does maritime archaeology. For example, there is the question of the initial arrival of the human species on the Australian continent. Evidence from land archaeology in Australia, Tasmania, and New Guinea shows that the ancestors of the modern and historic people living in these areas arrived over 30,000 years ago (with recent claims as high as 65,000 years ago). Although Australia, Tasmania, and New Guinea were joined as a single land mass during the Pleistocene, when world sea-levels were lower than today, they were not connected to either the islands or to the mainland of Southeast Asia. No land bridge has existed between Asia and Australia for millions of years, despite changes in sea-levels and land surfaces and shore-lines.

The implication is that the first migrants to Australia travelled beyond sight of land across a substantial body of water, with watercraft of some kind. Various alternative routes have been considered, with a strong argument in favour of early movement by sea from Timor to somewhere on Australia's northwest coast. No modern or historic Australian Aborigines produced watercraft that represent likely candidates for a voyage of this kind. This would be the earliest long-distance overwater voyage known so far in human prehistory, but no direct evidence of it (such as canoe remains or likely arrival sites) has yet been found. These watercraft were not necessarily sophisticated, but they had to be sufficiently large and strong to transport a viable colonizing population and their provisions. Nothing produced by the ethnographic Aborigines meets these requirements. Here is a case of ancient maritime behaviour inferred through archaeology that has no modern, living counterpart and that must be understood in relation to unique conditions that existed in the past.

Cross-cultural comparisons

Given the emic approaches favoured by most anthropologists, one can understand the difficulties encountered in making cross-cultural comparisons. If categories of knowledge and experience are viewed as unique to each culture, how can one effectively compare such knowledge, experiences, or anything else from one culture to another? Etic frameworks, on the other hand, permit controlled comparisons, at least for certain kinds of behaviour that can be observed and understood in relation to concrete situations. Exact equivalence from one culture to another should not be expected, nor is it necessary for useful results. Cross-cultural regularities of behaviour need to be explained in relation to the way they work and not merely as empirical generalizations, so a good 'insider's' view of the cultures involved in the comparison is still necessary, even if this must be achieved through the study of published ethnographies.

For example, a potentially useful hypothesis for cross-cultural testing by maritime archaeologists can be found in the concept of the 'society of the ship' (see **Shipboard society**). This idea posits that every human society that embarks upon long-distance voyaging will tend to evolve hierarchical, authoritarian systems of social control aboard the vessel, regardless of the social structure or level of technology of the parent culture. While direct evidence from shipwrecks to test such a proposition is scarce, ethnographic and historical accounts, especially from areas like Polynesia, Micronesia, Indonesia, and the Philippines, offer evidence of recent voyaging under such conditions. When Mau Pialug, the Micronesian navigator mentioned earlier in connection with the *Hokule'a* voyages, spoke of his relations with his crew while sailing on long canoe trips in Micronesia, he described them as being like his children. That is, he, like a father, was very much in charge and expected the members of his crew to follow his instructions without argument. But also, like a father towards his children, he recognized his responsibility to guide the canoe to its destination and to look after his crew's welfare during the voyage. In this case, the 'society of the ship' is presented in a kinship idiom emblematic of understood mutual obligations and responsibilities. In the case of a homogeneous society of voyagers aboard a Micronesian canoe, probably – as in Mau Pialug's case – from the same island, the idea of mutiny is unthinkable, since such behaviour would lead to ostracism and exclusion.

This concept has implications for maritime history and archaeology. How, for example, might a culture's social order be changed during the course of a long, open water voyage? Was it possible that people from relatively egalitarian societies who set off on such voyages might find their social order permanently altered into something more hierarchical after arriving at their destination and setting about establishing a new colony? Archaeologist Patrick Kirch has suggested such a possibility for Polynesia, and this could apply in other cases as well.

And what sorts of situational factors arise on long voyages that tend to select for quick decision-making and hierarchical control leading to the rapid implementation of those decisions? Voyaging is a process involving new and sometimes unexpected situations in an ever-changing environment. Yet quick decisions can sometimes be wrong decisions, and the study of shipwrecks, especially in relation to **Ship traps** like Bermuda and the **Dry Tortugas**, can provide examples of disasters resulting from over-adherence to this principle. Modern maritime history abounds with cases in which senior captains made bad decisions at sea with catastrophic results. The loss, in 1893, of the Royal Navy battleships HMS *Camperdown* and *Victoria*, following a collision at sea off the coast of Tripoli, represents a well-documented case of this kind. Vice-Admiral Sir George Tryon, Commander-in-Chief, Mediterranean, commanded a manoeuvre which the more junior officers saw would lead to a collision (made worse by the fact that these ships were equipped with ram bows which would increase the damage). But because of his seniority, no one challenged the Admiral's orders in time. The Admiral, along with 21 other officers and 339 seamen aboard *Victoria*, went down with the ship.

The wrecking of the Confederate blockade runner **Mary Celestia** on a reef close to the southwest shore of Bermuda during the American Civil War provides an example of flawed decision-making in the context of a hierarchical social system aboard the ship. Steaming close inshore, possibly to avoid a Federal squadron operating in the vicinity to intercept blockade runners, *Mary Celestia* was being steered at the time by a Bermuda pilot with the ship's regular captain on board as well.

Contemporary newspaper accounts indicate that a dispute arose between the captain and the pilot as the ship ventured closer to shore in an area of known danger near the Gibb Hill lighthouse. According to these accounts, the pilot insisted on continuing and overrode the captain. The ship struck the reef and sank only minutes later. *Mary Celestia* carried a cargo of rifles and uniforms, and speculation afterwards in the Bermudan press was that the pilot was secretly in the pay of the Federal forces. In this case the usual shipboard hierarchy was blurred by the relative status and authority of the pilot versus the captain, leading to a case of divided authority. The wreck of *Mary Celestia* has been documented archaeologically by a research team from East Carolina University and is a good example of this unique type of ship.

Conclusions

This description does not exhaust the possibilities for useful anthropological approaches to shipwreck studies. Anthropological perspectives have proved effective for the explanation of archaeological findings on land, and there is every reason to expect similarly useful results for maritime archaeology. Anthropological approaches encourage maritime archaeologists to look analytically at their results not only in relation to the specific details of maritime history but also to broader, social-scientific conclusions about human behaviour in relation to marine environments. R.A.G.

ADDITIONAL READING
Binford, L.R., 1962, 'Archaeology as Anthropology', *American Antiquity*, 28, 217–25.
Gould, R.A., 1983, *Shipwreck Anthropology*, Albuquerque.
Schuyler, R.L. (ed.), 1978, *Historical Archaeology: A Guide to Substantive and Theoretical Contributions*, New York.

Shipwreck protected areas

Shipwreck sites protected by law from theft, vandalism, and development activities. Thousands of shipwrecks are located within marine (ocean) and freshwater environments of the world. Shipwrecks are important to maritime and underwater archaeologists who develop knowledge of maritime history and past ways of life from the cultural materials remaining on these sites. Shipwrecks are also promoted as recreation attractions that enhance human development, and improve the economic wellbeing of coastal communities through tourism. The values associated with archaeological research, recreation, and tourism help demonstrate the need to protect, preserve, and manage shipwrecks and other underwater cultural resources for present and future generations. Options in management include the establishment of shipwreck protected areas (in particular, marine/freshwater parks and reserves, and shipwreck preserves).

The management of shipwrecks can be discussed in terms of four legal contexts: (1) general protection under national and Federal/State law; (2) marine/freshwater parks and reserves; (3) shipwreck preserves; (4) international agreements for the high seas.

Many governments worldwide have created laws to protect shipwrecks within inland lakes and streams, territorial waters, and exclusive economic zones from theft, vandalism, and development activities such as coastal construction, dredging, and harbour improvements. Law includes the development of statutes and regulations to guide human behaviour. Territorial waters may extend up to 12 nautical miles from a marine coast baseline. Coastal governments also have jurisdiction over submerged lands within the exclusive economic zone (EEZ). The EEZ may extend 200 (nautical) miles from a marine coast baseline, or to the edge of the continental shelf.

Shipwreck-related law can be created by national governments or, in federal systems, by state or provincial governments. In addition, local governments can influence the use of shipwrecks through zoning and other land use ordinances. Shipwreck-related law often establishes a permit system to allow commercial salvage, development activities, personal collection of artefacts, and scientific excavation of sites under certain conditions. Law may also provide for the establishment of parks and reserves for the management of shipwrecks and other marine/freshwater resources.

International waters or the high seas are located beyond territorial waters and are available for practically unrestricted use by all nations. Conventions or treaties have been developed among nations that provide some protection of shipwrecks within the high seas. Existing and proposed international conventions include the Convention on the Means of Prohibiting the Illicit Import, Export and Transfer of Ownership of Cultural Materials; the Model Treaty for the Prevention of Crimes that Infringe on the Cultural Heritage of Peoples in the Form of Movable Property; the International Convention on Underwater Cultural Heritage; and protocols for marine protected areas. The United Nations (especially the UN Educational, Scientific and Cultural Organization or UNESCO), the International Union for Nature and Natural Resources (IUCN), and the International Council on Monuments and Sites (**ICOMOS**) have been active in developing conventions that affect shipwrecks in the high seas.

Marine/freshwater parks and reserves

There is some agreement that development of marine parks and reserves began in the USA with the establishment of Fort Jefferson National Monument in Florida, and Green Island National Park in Australia during the 1930s. The ocean surrounding Fort Jefferson contains a number of historic shipwrecks managed by the US National Park Service. Marine parks and reserves were established during the 1930s to the 1950s primarily to protect coastal areas and nearby aquatic resources. Development of these areas was interrupted by World War II. Water-based or underwater parks and reserves began to be established during the late 1950s and early 1960s. These areas include Buck Island Reef National Monument in the Virgin Islands, John Pennekamp Coral Reef State Park and Key Largo Coral Reef Preserve in Florida, and Point Lobos Marine Reserve in California.

Diverse types of marine/freshwater parks and reserves were established throughout the world during the 1960s and 1970s. Many areas included shipwrecks and other underwater cultural resources. In the early 1970s, Fathom Five Provincial Park in Ontario, Canada became one of the first underwater parks created to protect shipwrecks and natural features in fresh water. By the mid-1970s, over fifty different names were given to marine/freshwater parks and reserves.

The development of these areas was stimulated by a number of international conferences, including the First World Conference on National Parks held in Seattle, USA, 1962; the International Conference on Marine Parks and Reserves held in Tokyo, Japan, 1975; and regional meetings on marine parks and reserves for the Mediterranean, 1973, Northern Indian Ocean (including the Red Sea and Persian Gulf), 1975, and South Pacific, 1975. Recommendation 15 at the First World Conference on National Parks in 1962 is recognized as the first international declaration in support of marine parks and reserves:

> The Conference invites the Governments of all those countries having marine frontiers, and other appropriate agencies, to examine as a matter of urgency the possibility of creating marine parks and reserves to defend underwater areas of special significance from all forms of human interference, and further recommends the extension of existing national parks and equivalent reserves with shore-lines, into the water to the ten fathom depth or the territorial limit or some other appropriate offshore boundary.

In general, parks were perceived at this time as having emphases in recreation and education. Reserves included areas established for special purposes such as scientific research, protection of aquatic organisms, preservation of habitat, or protection of cultural materials. Strict 'nature' reserves could prohibit all extractive uses, or exclude any human activities except under permit. Important functions of marine parks and reserves were defined by the IUCN in 1976 and included: protection of valuable archaeological, historical, and cultural sites; preservation of aesthetic values for present and future generations; interpretation for the purposes of tourism, recreation, and education of the public; and development as sites for the education and training of reserve managers.

By the late 1990s over 1,000 marine/freshwater parks and reserves had been established in about 100 countries around the world. These parks and reserves are now commonly referred to as protected areas. A marine/freshwater protected area is considered primarily an expanse of water with associated submerged lands and reefs. It may include a land component of islands and shore lands. Terrestrial parks and reserves containing or bordering water areas, estuaries, or wetlands are often considered marine/freshwater protected areas. In general, these protected areas include small highly protected reserves, and large multiple-use parks that are zoned for different types of use and levels of protection. A consideration of mission and objectives is more beneficial than 'names' in evaluating the purposes of marine/freshwater protected areas.

The International Union for Nature and Natural Resources classifies protected areas as: (1) scientific reserve/strict nature reserve; (2) national park; (3) natural monument/ national landmark; (4) nature conservation reserve/managed nature reserve/wildlife sanctuary; (5) protected landscape or seascape; (6) resource reserve (interim conservation unit); (7) natural biotic area/ anthropological reserve; (8) multiple-use management area/managed resource area; (9) biosphere reserves; and (10) world heritage sites. Most of the IUCN classes of protected areas may include shipwrecks, although a specific class is not provided for cultural resources.

The International Council on Monuments and Sites adopted a Charter for the Protection and Management of the Archaeological Heritage in 1990. The charter advocates the creation of archaeological reserves as part of governmental policies at international, national, regional and local levels. ICOMOS is a non-governmental organization that promotes collaboration in the conservation of the world's cultural heritage. It is currently developing international guidelines for the protection of underwater cultural heritage, and evaluates cultural properties nominated as world heritage sites.

Shipwreck preserves

Shipwreck preserves can be viewed as a type of protected area created primarily to enhance the preservation of sunken watercraft in archaeological context. Cultural materials affected predominantly by natural processes within aquatic ecosystems exist in archaeological context. Cultural materials used by society exist in systemic context. Maritime and underwater archaeologists study shipwrecks in archaeological context in order to better understand the systemic contexts of past societies.

Preservation can be viewed as actions by a contemporary society to slow the rate of deterioration and destruction of cultural materials. Impacts cause changes to shipwrecks and include marine and limnological processes, and the activities of humans. Negative effects are changes that decrease important values of a shipwreck site. An understanding of impacts and other formation processes is important to archaeologists in interpreting past human behaviour from cultural materials, and to resource managers in decision-making about present and future uses of the site.

Currently, the establishment of shipwreck preserves is most active in the **United States Of America**, Canada, the **United Kingdom**, and **Australia**. Shipwreck preserves vary by size, name, and purposes of management. Most management agencies encourage non-destructive recreational exploration, some level of tourism development, and support site documentation by volunteer and avocational organizations. The establishment of shipwreck preserves may soon be embraced by other nations worldwide.

The United States **Abandoned Shipwreck Act** of 1987 encourages states to develop underwater parks or areas to provide additional protection for shipwrecks. Shipwreck preserves have been established in Florida, Michigan, Vermont, and New York under state law. Florida's underwater archaeological preserves include the sites of *Urca de Lima* and *San Pedro*, vessels from Spanish treasure fleets of the 1700s. The **San Pedro** Underwater Archaeological Preserve has been enhanced for recreational diving by placing replica cannon and a historical marker on site, establishing an underwater interpretive trail, distributing information brochures, and by providing a mooring system for improved access to the site.

Vermont has established a number of underwater historic preserves since 1985, including the Coal Barge, the sailing canal boat *General Butler*, and the steamboat **Phoenix**. These watercraft were engaged in package freight trade and passenger service on freshwater **Lake Champlain**. An underwater historic preserve is confined to the shipwreck and a 60 m buffer zone. Action plans for preserves include a team process to select a site, detailed documentation of the site, recovery and conservation of exceptionally fragile or theft-prone artefacts, establishment of a mooring system, distribution of informational brochures, notification of emergency personnel, and promotion of the site.

The first sanctuary of the United States **National Marine Sanctuary** programme was established in 1975 to protect the Civil War ironclad USS **Monitor**. The site is one nautical mile in diameter; recreational diving is prohibited except under permit. A number of shipwrecks are included within other Federal sanctuaries and protected areas, including Channel Islands National Marine Sanctuary, Florida Keys National Marine Sanctuary, **Isle Royale** National Park, Biscayne National Park, and Fort Jefferson National Park.

Shipwreck sites are an important feature of Fathom Five National Marine Park in Lake Ontario, Canada, although the park was established for protection of many natural, cultural, and aesthetic resources. The marine parks of British Columbia also offer opportunities to explore shipwreck sites within their boundaries. The Canadian Parks Service and Department of Transport have developed guidelines for recreational exploration of significant historic shipwrecks located in Louisbourg Harbour (see **Louisbourg Wrecks**), Nova Scotia. Scuba-diving is restricted to licensed charter operations.

The United Kingdom **Protection of Wrecks Act** of 1973 was created to protect shipwreck sites of national historical, archaeological, and artistic importance. Over thirty sites have been designated, primarily on the south and southeast coasts. The United Kingdom **Archaeological Diving Unit** completes assessments of new sites, reviews licensed survey and excavation work, provides technical assistance to licensees, and evaluates impacts to the designated sites. Denmark maintains a Record of Marine and Maritime Sites as part of the National Record of Sites and Monuments.

Australia protects shipwrecks of particular heritage and historic significance under its Historic Shipwrecks Act of 1976. By 1997 about 150 sites had been declared historic shipwrecks. Management activities include survey, assessment, issuance of permits for scuba-diving in prohibited entry zones, development of site management plans, recovery and conservation of artefacts, education, and promotion. Management of historic shipwrecks is provided principally by state agencies in cooperation with non-profit organizations. K.J.V.

See also **National parks**.

Shipyard archaeology

The archaeology of shipyard and dockyard sites. Ships have often been studied for their performance as a specialized type of machine or for their role as part of a fleet, but few studies have been made of the shipyards and dockyards in which they were built and maintained. Yet shipyards remain significant historical and archaeological sites because they represent the places where ideas about function, speed and capacity were transformed into wood and metal ships.

Just as shipwrecks and their associated artefacts and historical records represent important aspects of the material culture of our maritime heritage, the material record left behind from ship construction and maintenance processes helps us to better understand an aspect of maritime activities that is often overlooked. The study of the layout of shipyards provides information on how shipbuilding developed as a construction process.

Shipbuilding in many areas began as small, single-owner businesses but these later developed or were consolidated into the large shipbuilding centres of the 19th century. Through the comparative analysis of shipwrecks and shipyards it is possible to establish a chronology of the technological changes incorporated into ship design and propulsion and to establish a correlation between ships, the infrastructure required to build and maintain them, and the resulting changes in the socio-cultural aspects of the shipbuilding industry.

Information that is collected about the process of ship construction at a shipyard site includes tool and equipment use and availability, preferences for specific kinds of tools and equipment, layout of equipment within ships or the yard as a whole, preferences of construction materials, points of origin, availability, and procurement of materials, materials handling, organization of the work with regard to sub-assemblies and final assembly, worker habits and lifestyles, and translation of data from design to production.

In wooden shipbuilding, highly skilled craftsmen built vessels based on traditional forms learned over many lifetimes of experience. Technological changes, such as the change from sail to steam propulsion, and from wood to iron construction, not only quickly altered the size of vessels and the fabrication techniques used to build them, but also the skills required of the workers. Men of varied skill backgrounds in metalworking, such as boilermakers and punch or shears operators, became essential to the shipyards. In many instances individuals were brought to the area from overseas for specialized trades or if the local workforce was too small.

Location was a critical element in the success of a shipyard. The amount of vessel traffic, the depth of water adjacent to the site, and the availability of timber resources were all factors in the development of a viable shipyard. Evaluation of the shipyard's layout provides information about how shipbuilding evolved as a process. In addition to the geographical, natural, and environmental factors, an understanding of man-made changes such as dredging channels or moorings is critical to a comprehensive interpretation of a shipyard site.

Many shipyard sites that built or repaired wooden ships resemble sawmill sites in overall appearance. Generally, facilities included sawmills, blacksmith's or ship smith's shops, tool sheds, oakum sheds, and timber storage yards and stocks. Facilities in the later iron and steel shipbuilding era evolved into large complexes with railways, cranes, pneumatic or electric tools, metalworking shops and engine works.

Fribrødre River Shipyard

Sections of a shipyard from around and shortly before 1100 excavated in Denmark by J. Skamby Madsen in a now-overgrown fjord system south of Stubbekøbing are among the earliest shipyard sites studied to date. The excavations indicate that ships were broken up on the site with the intention of reusing the planks and beams in new vessels. Finds and the local place names show a mixture of Danish and Slav elements, and the site is interpreted as that of a local Wendish colony under Danish control.

Pritchard's Shipyard

From the 17th century onwards South Carolina required an array of vessel types to support its growing trade and transportation network. Its vast timber resources, primarily live oak, pine, and cypress, made shipbuilding a lucrative economic enterprise by the 18th century. In 1778 Abraham Livingston and Paul Pritchard purchased the yard that had been known as Hobcaw Shipyard and changed the name to Pritchard's Shipyard. Previous owners included John Rose and James Stewart, who began the shipyard in 1753, and later William Begbie and Daniel Manson, who bought the property in 1769.

In 1993 preliminary investigations were conducted at Pritchard's Shipyard under the direction of archaeologists from the South Carolina Institute of Archaeology and Anthropology. Upon initial reconnaissance, two distinct areas on the foreshore were found to contain wood cribbing and pilings that were identified as the remains of two of the three slipways that are known to have been in use during the 18th and 19th centuries. Artefacts recovered during the excavation reflect the temporal range of historic occupation and utilization of the site as chronicled in archival records. Pipe stems and bowls indicate utilization of the area from 1750 to 1800, and ceramics and glass bottles are present from the 18th and 19th centuries. In addition, an adze, axe-heads, a pair of dividers, and a broken chain-plate all suggest activities associated with a shipyard.

Pritchard's Shipyard is a typical example of many shipyards where the building activity on the site continued even after several changes of ownership, presumably because of the quality of the location. The Commissioners of the Navy of South Carolina in 1778 acquired a three-quarters interest in the shipyard in part because of its facilities. They noted, 'There is on the Premises at Hobcaw a great deal of Store room, very Substantial good Wharves and Other Conveniences Sufficient to Heave down Three Vessels at the same time.'

The study of Pritchard's Shipyard is ongoing. There are sufficient exposed features and artefact distributions throughout the property to offer prospects of several possible investigation strategies that will lead to an understanding of the layout and operation of this site.

Buckler's Hard

The archaeology of the Solent in Great Britain and its rivers tells a story spanning thousands of years from the settlements of prehistoric hunters to the warships of World War II. The Beaulieu River was an integral part of the Solent maritime network before the advent of motorized transport. Buckler's Hard played an important role in the shipbuilding industry throughout the latter half of the 18th and into the 19th century, and

HMS Floating Dock Bermuda.
(Bermuda Maritime Museum)

was in use again during both world wars. This area is currently being investigated by researchers from the Department of Archaeology, University of Southampton, with sponsorship from the Hampshire and Wight Trust for Maritime Archaeology and the Hampshire County Council and the National Rivers Authority.

Many of the artefacts located at Buckler's Hard in 1994 can be simply classified as postwar shipyard rubbish. However, they are of great archaeological interest because they reflect river usage and the local community during that era. During underwater surveys of the slipways several features were located that include a rectangular boxgirder, large timbers, and treenails. The boxgirder structure was identified by the harbour master as part of the winding gear used in conjunction with the World War II slipway. On two other slipways, the timbers were located in a position where the ends of the slipways might lie, based on the lengths of the ships that were built in the 18th century. The treenails have been associated with the early shipbuilding era.

It is apparent from documentary records and archaeological investigations that there are three main periods of high activity associated with Buckler's Hard: (1) the initial creation and settlement; (2) the early period of shipbuilding in the 17th and 18th centuries; and (3) the activities during World War II.

Buckler's Hard exemplifies the potential for shipyard archaeology despite the destruction of a great deal of evidence during the years of World War II. Construction of gun emplacements, concrete walkways, and a reconstruction of a jetty obliterated some features of the site, but timbers remaining from the 17th century shipbuilding are still observable in the intertidal zone and below. Even with modern development over the surface of the shipyards, the sites are seldom destroyed in their entirety.

Artefacts located at Buckler's Hard are also typical finds for ship construction methods over the 18th century, especially for the copper sheath fragments and fasteners. Evidence of the scaffolding support systems and shores for stabilizing a hull while under construction add to our understanding of how these structures were erected.

Bermuda Dockyard and HMS Floating Dock *Bermuda*

To early Spanish mariners, the sighting of the Bermuda islands signalled that it was time to turn east in their trip back to Spain. The British recognized the strategic location and importance of these islands in the late 18th century when the United States of America was established. Construction of the Royal Naval Dockyard was begun in 1810 and additions and modification continued until the 20th century. Convict labour was used during most of the early phases of construction. The establishment of the Royal Naval Dockyard allowed Great

Britain to maintain a fleet of ships in the Atlantic in order to protect its interests in the Caribbean and Canada. Excavations at the Royal Naval Dockyard have provided valuable insights into construction methods, the living conditions of the convict labourers and the use of *ad hoc* underwater constructions to facilitate the transport of materials.

A key element of the Royal Naval Dockyard during the 19th and early 20th centuries was the great floating dock *Bermuda*. Designed and built in 1868 specifically for use in Bermuda, *Bermuda* was engineered with sixteen watertight compartments (eight on each side) with each of these divided transversely into three. By flooding these chambers with seawater the dock could be submerged to receive a ship for repairs. In addition, the floating dock was designed to be self-careening in order to facilitate repairs on its own hull when necessary. At the time it was built *Bermuda* was the largest floating dock in the world, capable of lifting any ship in the Royal Navy. *Bermuda* was a unique technological development designed to operate under special conditions imposed by the geography of Bermuda. The archaeological study of its remains has provided information important to the understanding of the processes of technological innovation and adaptation, defensive naval strategies, and preparations for war.

Detroit Dry Dock Company

The only shipyard known to be excavated in Michigan to date has been the Detroit Dry Dock Company's facility on Detroit's east river front. Excavations were conducted in 1984–5 by Gilbert/Commonwealth Inc. of Michigan for the City of Detroit. Principal investigator C. Stephan Demeter and his team opened seven test trenches, with their effort directed towards the oakum loft, Dry Dock No. 1, and potential beach line deposits. The team identified the clay puddling wall around the dry dock and exposed a portion of the dry dock itself. Estimated to have been in operation *c.*1857–1916, the dry dock consists of stepped yellow pine timbers which were found to be in an excellent state of preservation. This type of dry dock construction is unique as most were made of stone or early forms of concrete. Studying the area of the oakum shed, the team located sleeper planks and a partial board floor. Among the artefacts identified as shipyard-related were square and round spikes, wire nails, an unthreaded bolt, block staples (for use with keel and bilge blocks), horseshoe fragments, clay smoking pipe stems, and windows and bottle glass sherds.

Finding tablewares and extensive faunal remains in the area of the oakum loft suggests that the loft served as a luncheon site for the workers at the shipyard c.1850–70.

Charles Hare Ship-breaking Yard

The earliest site excavated on the Pacific coast of the USA with traces of shore-side maritime activity is the mid-1850s ship-breaking yard operated by Charles Hare at San Francisco's South Beach. Located immediately south of Rincon Point, and close to Gold Rush San Francisco's thriving metropolitan centre, Hare's yard disposed of dozens of ships that had arrived during the Gold Rush of 1849 and 1852 and then remained behind to clutter the crowded harbour.

Historical accounts, particularly secondary accounts and reminiscences, stress that the hulks were burned and their ashes sifted for scrap. While some vessels, particularly early in the yard's life, were burned, systematic excavation in 1988 by a team led by Allen G. Pastron allowed Pastron and J.P. Delgado to reconstruct a systematic and methodical ship-breaking process that left ten large clusters of vessel fragments and fittings at the site at the time of its abandonment sometime after 1857. This suggested reuse of timbers and fittings, a common maritime practice but one not until then associated with the California Gold Rush, when readily available materials and great wealth suggested to some that extensive disposal of material culture was the norm.

The majority of the excavated materials were portions of keels, keelsons, floors and half-floors, garboard strakes, outer hull planking, a stempost and a sternpost. In addition, sections of copper sheathing, a bar-style chain-plate, and a makeshift cant hook and a large breaking bar probably used to dismantle ships were also recovered.

Turner-Robertson Shipyard

The only other shipyard site on the Pacific Coast of the US to be surveyed and excavated was the former shipyard of Matthew Turner and James Robertson at Benicia, 43 km north of San Francisco at Carquinez Strait between San Francisco and Suisun bays. The yard was established by Turner in 1886, and later passed to James Robertson, who operated it until 1918. More than a hundred vessels, ranging from coastal schooners, bay ferries, and ocean-going sail and steam ships were built at the yard.

During a detailed survey of the yard site at extreme low tides in 1987, principal investigator James Delgado identified the remains of three rock and concrete ways, discarded lumber and timber and ship fastenings, a wooden marine railway, the foundations of shipyard buildings, a submerged wharfside boiler, pilings from the shipyard dock, a sub-

merged barge, perhaps used as a construction stage, and the substantially intact hull of the 1842-built whaling bark Stamboul, purchased by Turner and used as a sheer-hulk to step masts.

Test excavation of two metre-square test units inside Stamboul's hull disclosed an intact 'tween deck littered with wire rope and rigging fittings. The excavation of Stamboul was the first scientific underwater archaeological excavation in California. The project was largely accomplished with **Avocational** archaeologists and sport divers, including members of the Benicia Historical Society and the San Francisco Sport Divers Association. As a result of the project, the Turner-Robertson Yard was listed in the **National Register of Historic Places**, designated a State Historical Landmark, and preserved. The yard is a city park administered by the city of Benicia.

It is to be hoped that shipyards will be the focus of more analysis over the years as the importance of learning about *who* built ships and *how* they were built supplements the knowledge gained through shipwreck studies and historical research about vessels in our maritime heritage. D.J.S./S.M.P.

ADDITIONAL READING

Adams, J. (ed.), 1994, *Buckler's Hard: The Beaulieu River Project, Report Number 1*, unpublished report, University of Southampton.

Aldsworth, F.G., 1989, 'Excavations at the Former Royal Naval Dockyard, Bermuda: A Nineteenth Century Slave Hulk', *Bermuda Journal of Archaeology and Maritime History*, 1, 109–30.

Amer, C.F., 1995, 'Pritchard's Shipyard (38CH1049): Investigations at South Carolina's Largest Colonial Shipyard', in P.F. Johnston (ed.), *Underwater Archaeology Proceedings from the Society for Historical Archaeology Conference, Washington, DC*, Ann Arbor, Michigan.

Arnell, J., 1993, 'Bermuda as a Strategic Naval Base', *Bermuda Journal of Archaeology and Maritime History*, 5, 126–34.

Bream, J., 1992, 'Bermuda's Role in Sixteenth Century Navigation', in D.H. Keith and T.L. Carrell (eds), *Underwater Archaeology Proceedings from the Society for Historical Archaeology Conference, Kingston, Jamaica*, Ann Arbor, Michigan.

Crumlin-Pederson, O., 1993, 'Ships and Barriers', in S. Hvass and B. Storgaard (eds), *Digging into the Past: 25 Years of Archaeology in Denmark*, Copenhagen.

Demeter, C.S. and Weir, D., 1985, 'St Aubin Park Archeological Testing', Report 2724, Jackson, Michigan.

Gould, R., 1990, 'Underwater Construction at the Royal Naval Dockyard, Bermuda',

Bermuda Journal of Archaeology and Maritime History, 2, 71–86.

Gould, R. and Souza, D.J., 1995, 'HM Floating Dock *Bermuda*', *Bermuda Journal of Archaeology and Maritime History*, 6, 157-85.

Pastron, A.G. and Delgado, J.P., 1991, 'Archaeological Investigations of a Mid-19th-Century Ship-breaking Yard, San Francisco, California', *Historical Archaeology*, 25, 61–77.

Peters, S.M., 1993, 'Michigan Shipyards, 1850–1900: An Evolution', in S.O. Smith (ed.), *Underwater Archaeology Proceedings from the Society for Historical Archaeology Conference. Kansas City, Missouri*, Ann Arbor, Michigan.

Side scan sonar

A widely accepted tool for mapping the topography of the surface of the seabed and for detecting shipwrecks, artefacts, and other material of archaeological interest. Human vision would be the preferred method for underwater search, but optical visibility underwater via the eye, photography, or television, is severely limited. Under ideal conditions, the range of visibility in water is in the order of 30 m, but in many situations, this distance is reduced to less than 1 m.

Sonar (an abbreviation of Sound Navigation And Ranging) uses underwater sound which is capable of travelling relatively long distances. Side scan sonar is a specialized technique in which short pulses of acoustic energy are transmitted along the seabed in fan-shaped beams (narrow in the horizontal plane and wide in the vertical plane) from a moving vessel or an underwater towed vehicle. The return echoes from any objects in the path of these beams are electronically processed and continuously recorded side-by-side on a graphic display to create an image called a sonograph. These images frequently resemble large-scale aerial photographs. So, in a way, human vision is still used, but the sonar produces an image that the eye can interpret.

A typical side scan sonar system includes a towfish, a towing cable, and a graphic recorder. Additional accessories such as winches, tape recorders, and towing depressors are often used. The towfish contains piezoelectric transducers that convert electrical impulses into high-frequency sounds. These same transducers receive the acoustic echoes and convert these signals to electrical energy. The received signals are then amplified and filtered and sent up the tow cables to the graphic recorder on the ship. The graphic recorder further processes the signals and creates a permanent display on a paper chart.

Originally developed for military use in

the latter part of World War II, side scan sonar was first used for academic research in the late 1950s. Systems were developed at a number of academic institutions including the British National Institute of Oceanography, Hudson Laboratories of Columbia University, Bath University, and Scripps Institute of Oceanography. In 1960 Kelvin Hughes introduced the 'Fisherman's Asdic' (an abbreviation of Anti Submarine Detection Investigation Committee – an early term for

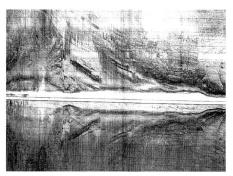

Side scan sonar image of the wreck of City of Rio de Janeiro. *(California State Lands Commission)*

Artist's concept of the side scan sonar technique. (Courtesy Klein Associates, Inc.)

antisubmarine sonar), which could be used as a side sonar. Then, in the mid-1960s, Hughes produced the 'Transit Sonar', a single-channel side scan sonar which used a 50 kHz fan-beam transducer that was mounted on a pipe off the side of the ship. In 1962 Professor Harold E. Edgerton of the Massachusetts Institute of Technology began using a 12kHz conical-beam echo sounder transducer aimed to look sideways in a side scan sonar mode. In 1964 Edgerton, Edward P. Curley and John Yules found the wreck of the *Vineyard Lightship* in Buzzards Bay, Massachusetts using this device.

In 1966 a team led by Martin Klein of E.G. & G. International, Inc. of Bedford, Massachusetts, introduced a single-channel towed side scan sonar, and in 1967 the first commercial dual-channel towed side scan sonar. Although intended for other research and commercial applications, the new system found some of its earliest use in assisting marine archaeologists. In August 1967 Dr George Bass used the system in an area 95 m deep off the coast of Turkey to locate a 2,000-year-old ship. Two months later Dr Edgerton, John Mills and Robert Henderson, working with Alexander McKee, used the side scan sonar in combination

with a sub-bottom profiler to locate King Henry VIII's flagship *Mary Rose* which sank in 1545.

Many other shipwrecks of archaeological interest have been subsequently located with the assistance of side scan sonar. Some of these include *Breadalbane* (found 1980), the War of 1812 schooners *Hamilton* and *Scourge* (found 1976), the Revolutionary War brig *Defence* (found 1972), several ships from the fleet of Lord Cornwallis at Yorktown, Vir-

ginia (found 1978), the Civil War ironclad *Monitor* (found 1973), the Swedish warship *Kronan* (found 1980), the *Land Tortoise* radeau (found 1990), *Titanic*, *Lusitania*, and many others.

Early side scan sonars used mechanical graphic recorders that utilized a rotating drum or a mechanical stylus to move an electrical point of contact on chemically treated recording paper. The popularization of facsimile instruments in the 1980s produced simpler and more reliable electronically scanned thermal graphic recorders. In modern side scan systems the sonar signals are converted to digital form, which allows for a wide variety of signal enhancements. Besides the 'hard copy' sonographs, sonar records may be displayed on computer cathode-ray-tubes, and colour may assist interpretation. Digital processing also allows the sonar images to be presented in a more geometrically correct fashion. Modern side scan systems may now be integrated with electronic positioning systems so that targets may be accurately positioned and relocated. Sonar survey information may now be stored on a variety of digital storage devices for later retrieval, analysis, and processing. M.K.

ADDITIONAL READING

Bass, G.F., 1968, 'New Tools for Undersea Archaeology', *National Geographic*, September, 134, 3.

Flemming, B.W., 1926, 'Side Scan Sonar: A Practical Guide', *International Hydrographic Review*, 53, 1, January.

Franzen, A., 1981, *HMS Kronan: The Search for a Great 17th Century Swedish Warship*, Stockholm.

Klein, M., 1967, 'Side Scan Sonar', *Undersea Technology*, April.

Klein, M. and Edgerton, H.E., 1968, 'Sonar: A Modern Technique for Ocean Exploitation', *IEEE Spectrum*, June.

Mazel, C., 1985, *Side Scan Sonar Training Manual*, Klein Associates, Salem, New Hampshire.

Nelson, D.A., 1983, '*Hamilton* and *Scourge*: Ghost Ships of the War of 1812' *National Geographic*, March, 163, 3.

Yules, J.A. and Edgerton, H.E., 1964, 'Bottom Sonar Search Techniques', *Undersea Technology*, November.

Sirius

The flagship of the eleven First Fleet ships that sailed from Great Britain to Australia in 1787 under the command of Governor Arthur Phillip. The ships that explored and established European settlements in the Pacific in the second half of the 18th century could not be described as a class. Nevertheless, maritime archaeological evidence and reinterpreted historical evidence is emphasizing the similarities between these vessels. In turn, this evidence is being used to support new theories about the reasons for the settlement of **Australia**.

Sirius was built at Rotherhithe on the Thames as the 511 ton Baltic trader *Berwick* in 1781. It was purchased by the British Navy and used as an armed storeship for several years. In 1786 the machinery to implement the British Government's decision to found a penal settlement at Botany Bay in New South Wales was put into motion. Various departmental officials set to work assembling the personnel and vessels for the expedition. *Berwick* was refitted and commissioned as a sixth rate by the name of *Sirius*.

As well as being the flagship, the vessel then took the role of principal naval defence vehicle for the fledgling colony, and the means of communication with the outside world. In 1790 Governor Phillip, short of food supplies for the colony, sent *Sirius* to Norfolk Island with 275 convicts and marines; the idea being that if the time came when there were no rations left, those sent to the island would have a better chance of living off the land than if they were in Sydney. However, *Sirius* was blown ashore and wrecked at Norfolk Island.

Pantograph from Sirius. (© Western Australia Maritime Museum/Patrick Baker)

The wreck site of Sirius, Kingston reef. (© Western Australia Maritime Museum/Patrick Baker)

During Australia's Bicentennial celebrations in 1988, G. Henderson led an expedition to Norfolk Island to find out if anything remained of the wreck of *Sirius*. Divers located the wreck and carried out several seasons of survey and limited excavation. The Sirius Museum was established on Norfolk Island to make accessible to the general public the research findings on the history of the ship.

Research is continuing on links between the archaeology of the wreck and theories on the colonization of Australia. The traditionally held theory is that Australia was colonized by a British Government with an 'out of sight, out of mind' approach to the social issue of crime: send them to the other end of the earth and forget them. *Sirius* was often used as a supporting element to this theory: it was argued that the vessel was a leaky old tub of a ship, quite inappropriate for a role in a sustained colonial enterprise.

More recently historians have questioned the traditional colonization view, arguing that the British Government had taken a long-term strategic approach to the settlement in Australia. The archaeologists involved with the *Sirius* wreck have joined the debate, focusing on the condition and suitability of the vessel for a more sustained role. The weight of evidence is supporting the modern interpretation, because it has been shown historically that the vessel was of similar type to such Pacific pioneers as Cook's *Endeavour*, and archaeologically that its outfit was of reasonable standard for the period. G.H.

ADDITIONAL READING
Henderson, G. and Stanbury, M., 1988, *The Sirius. Past and Present*, Sydney.

Site formation processes

Those factors that alter material culture as it becomes incorporated into the **Archaeological record**, including those affecting original deposition and those occurring between deposition and archaeological recovery. Material culture is simply all objects made, altered, or used by humans. Archaeologists, unlike other social scientists, do not have direct access to the object of their study, which is past human behaviour; specifically, interaction between behaviour and material objects. Rather, access is gained indirectly through study of the archaeological record from which past behaviour is inferred.

During the last quarter-century archaeologists became aware that the archaeological record was not a more-or-less complete fossilized representation of past societies that could be accessed directly, but rather an incomplete, materially dependent, differentially preserved and distorted record of human activity. Archaeologists have become increasingly concerned with understanding how the archaeological record is formed, and how it is affected by various disturbance processes in order to increase interpretive reliability. Maritime archaeologists, even when investigating well-preserved, deep wrecks, have also become increasingly aware that the archaeological record is incomplete and distorted. Limitations are particularly apparent in shallow-water shipwrecks that

can be a long way from what is implied in the notion of 'time capsule'.

The realization that the archaeological record does not directly reflect past societies prompted terrestrial archaeologists in the early 1970s to begin systematically investigating the transformational processes responsible for potential distortions. Rigorous examination of site formation processes was soon viewed as fundamental to reliable archaeological inference, and archaeology has become, by necessity, the interdisciplinary study of both society and nature.

Recognition of associations and patterns is basic to archaeological interpretation. Human behaviour in the past, natural processes, and archaeological method can each produce patterns in material residues. To confuse a pattern created by one process for another is to misinterpret seriously the archaeological record. The chief source of error in interpreting archaeological patterns and associations as if they directly represented past cultural activity is that what is interpreted as the result of cultural activity could well be the result of natural environmental processes. Accurate archaeological inference requires that transformational processes be completely accounted for in archaeological interpretation. The reason controlling for transformational processes is methodologically productive is that natural formation processes are uniformitarian and amenable to systematic scientific investigation. Transformation processes, which produce distinctive patterns, distort behavioural patterns in predictable ways. Consequently, natural formation process investigation relies heavily upon other disciplines such as chemistry, physics, geology, oceanography, and biology to provide laws that form the basic analytical tools for discerning site formation processes. Without these tools, correction of transformation processes would not be possible.

Archaeologists David L. Clarke from Great Britain and Michael B. Schiffer from the United States are associated with the early development of site formation processes as a principal research domain in archaeology. Both were concerned with what can be termed as the 'transformation view', which acknowledges the archaeological record is distorted, and they have contributed a substantial theoretical base for investigating formation processes and transformations.

David Clarke, in a 1973 paper entitled 'Archaeology: The Loss of Innocence', defined five theories employed by archaeologists in interpreting and reporting archaeological finds: pre-depositional and depositional theory incorporating human relations and social patterns; retrieval theory, which deals with sampling, and is concerned with the connection between what actually survives and what is recovered; analytical theory, concerned with analysis of recovered materials including classification, modelling and experimental studies; and interpretive theory, concerned with relations between observed archaeological patterns and past behaviour. He called for rigorous examination and refinement of these theories.

Michael Schiffer, pursuing a parallel track, has been a key developer of 'behavioural archaeology', which is defined as the study of human behaviour, which it attempts to explain in relation to material culture in all times and places. Much of Schiffer's and other behavioural archaeologists' research is directed towards refining archaeological inference by reducing, correcting or controlling for distortions inherent in the archaeological record. Much research has been directed towards the genesis of the archaeological record. Behavioural archaeologists make a basic distinction between systemic context, which refers to artefacts when part of a cultural system, and archaeological context, in which artefacts interact with the natural environment.

To strengthen archaeological inference, behavioural archaeologists attempt to establish correlates, usually expressed as statistical laws that reliably relate artefacts and archaeological associations to particular human behaviours. Effective utilization of correlates requires that formation processes intervening between systemic and archaeo-

logical context are completely accounted for to produce the most accurate statements about past cultural systems. Formation processes, which structure the archaeological record, are either cultural transformation processes, 'c-transforms', or natural formation processes called 'n-transforms'. C-transforms include things like use, discard, loss, reuse, salvage, and encompass processes that affect how material becomes part of the archaeological record, how later human behaviour affects that record, and how archaeologists interpret it. Natural processes like decay, currents, **Benthic bioturbation** and all other natural processes that directly affect the archaeological record are grouped under n-transforms (non-behavioural environmental record). The basic argument is that by understanding how archaeological material functioned in systemic context, became part of the **Archaeological record** and became transformed over time, archaeologists can reliably infer much about the original systemic context.

It is quite clear that a ship, which existed within a systemic context, is very different from a shipwreck. The range of intervening processes that account for the changes from ship to the widely variable shipwreck sites archaeologists investigate are site formation processes. Inundated terrestrial sites have also obviously undergone numerous changes. Systematic scientific enquiry is necessary to determine exactly what has been affected and how; untested common-sense notions will contribute little to sound archaeological inference.

Wreck formation processes were being systematically observed in the 1950s. Honor Frost discussed them in 1961 at the Annual Lecture to the Society for Nautical Research. Her lecture, 'Submarine Archaeology and Mediterranean Wreck Formations', was based upon Frederic Dumas's observations, published in *Deep-Water Archaeology* in 1962. Dumas discussed post-depositional processes such as burial rates and biological activity as well as depositional impact on amphoras and wood hulls. His discussion contains the first comparative observations on wreck sites in different environments, which led to his observation that most deeper wrecks stabilize in about ten years. Behavioural archaeologists Schiffer and Rathje first suggested transformation process analysis be applied to shipwreck research in 1973.

Keith Muckelroy, influenced by Clarke, conducted the first systematic study of site formation processes in the mid-1970s when he compared twenty wreck sites in Great Britain. By examining eleven variables such

as offshore fetch, winds, tides, water depth, slope, and sediment composition, among others, he determined general survivability factors affecting archaeological remains. Muckelroy developed an analysis of formation processes that divided them into extractive filters and scrambling devices. Extractive filters, which remove material from the archaeological record, include artefacts floating away, *in situ* deterioration, and contemporary salvage activities. Scrambling devices include the wrecking process and later seabed movement, which affect artefact preservation and associations through geologic and oceanographic processes that cause sediment mobility. Muckelroy stressed the need for interdisciplinary studies and recognized the possibilities for mutually beneficial cooperative research. For example, sedimentologists and biologists benefited from analysis of **Mary Rose** and its 400 years of cumulative data about the Solent.

Inundated site formation processes were being systematically investigated in the 1960s as a part of sea-level curve research. Nick Flemming examined more than seventy Aegean archaeological sites, and D.J. Blackman examined scores of mooring sites in Turkey to refine sea-level curves. One of the most comprehensive examinations of site formation process studies involved detailed examination of inundation impact on archaeological materials contained in river basins dammed for reservoir construction. An explicit research design was formulated and an extensive five-year study involving both field and laboratory projects investigated a wide range of natural and cultural impact on numerous categories of archaeological materials (see Lenihan).

Since the late 1970s there has been increasingly frequent mention of site formation processes, mostly centring on reconstruction of initial wreck depositional sequences. Less attention has been directed toward specific processes. However, research has now moved beyond wreck sequences to a range of post-depositional formation processes. International interest in site formation processes is increasing, and there is a small, slowly growing body of literature devoted to the subject. The *International Journal of Nautical Archaeology* has published numerous articles concerned with related subjects like encrustation processes, the influence of biogenic modifications of the seabed, and artefact associations. Ian Oxley and others of the **Scottish Institute of Maritime Studies** have been engaged in related research; Ian MacLeod of the Western Australian Maritime Museum has been systematically investigating formation processes on the steamship *Xantho* in Australia; and Larry Murphy of the **Submerged Cultural Resources Unit** has published research on formation processes of a dual component site off the east coast of Florida.

Unfortunately, very little research has been directed towards understanding formation processes deriving from cultural activities. Research into cultural processes promises to be among the most productive new approaches to maritime archaeology. Investigation of c-transforms includes such questions as refuse disposal aboard ship, reuse and recycling. The concept of a 'closed community', a frequent characterization of ship communities, glosses over things like overboard refuse discharge. C-transforms can be approached from a variety of scales from shipboard anchorages to the larger scale of wreck concentrations and regions. Collections of wrecks, which are currently treated as discrete, disparate, and unrelated sites, can be investigated as products of complex interrelated environmental and cultural factors. Shipwreck concentrations, studied as a group from a research framework focusing on formation processes, can provide a longitudinal perspective of maritime activity in an area providing information about such large-scale cultural activity as trade and settlement patterns, commercial and military relations, conflict and competition, which provide insight into how societies operate and change. Larger scale research informs on the present global economic system, which is fundamentally a maritime structure. The large-scale comparative approach may be the only way the historical sequences and social processes responsible for world system development, form, and operation can be elucidated.

Explicit research addressing site formation processes is critical to developing reliable archaeological inference on submerged terrestrial sites and maritime sites at a variety of scales. The realization of the inferential potential of the archaeological record lies in understanding the genesis of patterns and variability, and this research should be incorporated into every field project. L.E.M.

ADDITIONAL READING

Blackman, D.J., 1973, *Proceedings of the Twenty-Third Symposium of the Colston Research Society*, Hamden, Connecticut.

Dumas, F., 1962, *Deep-Water Archaeology*, London.

Lenihan, D.J. *et al.*, 1981, *The Final Report of the National Reservoir Inundation Study*, Santa Fe.

Muckelroy, K., 1977, *Maritime Archaeology*, Cambridge.

Muckelroy, K. (ed.), 1980, *Archaeology Underwater: An Atlas of the World's Submerged Sites*, New York.

Murphy, L.E., 1990, *8S117: Natural Site-Formation Processes of a Multiple-Component Underwater Site in Florida*, Santa Fe.

Schiffer, M.B., 1987, *Formation Processes of the Archaeological Record*, Albuquerque.

Schiffer, M.B., 1995, *Behavioural Archaeology: First Principles*, Salt Lake City.

Skerki Bank Wreck

see **Isis Wreck**

Skuldelev Ships

Five 11th-century ships found as part of a seaway blockade north of Roskilde, the former capital of Denmark. The Skuldelev ships were first recognized as Viking Age vessels when archaeologists started investigations of the blockade in the narrow channel 'Peberrenden' in the Roskilde Fjord in 1957. In 1962 the ships were recovered during a semi-wet excavation, where a **Cofferdam**, enclosing an area of 1,600 sq. m, was erected and drained. The ships were cleared from the stone cargo, which had constituted part of the blockade, and documented by **Photogrammetry** and photography.

During the **Excavation** the ships were numbered from 1 to 6 but later it has been demonstrated that numbers 2 and 4 are parts of the same ship. Heavily fragmented by the pressure of the stones, the ships were lifted piece by piece and later documented minutely in scale 1:1 drawings, which constituted a main element in the later reconstruction of the vessels. After conservation with polyethylene glycol, the ships were finally put on display in the Viking Ship Museum in Roskilde, where **Reconstruction** work started in 1968. The finding and excavation of the ships led to the creation of the Institute of Maritime Archaeology, a branch of the Danish National Museum and a centre for research into the history of north European seafaring.

The Skuldelev ships were all built in clinker fashion with iron rivets, inserted in decorative profiles. Their double-ended hulls had slender, T-shaped keels and curved stems. The frames were treenailed to the planking, but not to the keel and garbords, and had beams (*biti*) over every floor-timber. Stringers were attached directly to the planking. An indirectly secured keelson provided the mast-step for a centrally placed mast, braced with shrouds and stays and rigged with a single square sail. The reconstruction of the five ships has shown that at the close of the Viking Age an extensive specialization of Scandinavian crafts had already taken place. Two of the vessels, wrecks 1 and 3, were beamy, with few oars and probably designed for cargo carrying,

while two others, wrecks 2 and 5, were fast rowing vessels, longships. Wreck 6, the smallest of the vessels, is a large boat, suitable for multiple purposes.

The blockade had been constructed in two phases, and a wreck from each phase has been dated by dendrochronology. Wreck 5 was built from oaks felled 1030–40. Wrecks 3 and 1 originate from the same construction phase. Wreck 2 dates from *c.*1060. Wreck 6 was sunk at the same time as wreck 2.

Wreck 1

Preserved to *c.* 60 per cent. Reconstructed dimensions: length 15.9 m, beam 4.8 m, depth of hold 2.2 m. Calculated cargo capacity: *c.*24 tonnes. The ship has twelve strakes and it is planked with pine, while oak has been used for floor timbers, keel, most of the stem and stern timbers and for some bites. Other bites, as well as some side frames, are of lime, while fewer are made from pine. The hull has full ends and a distinct bottom shape, with the central part separated from the turn of the bilge by a near-vertical strake. Bites are low-lying, and supplementary beams are found only at the mast and fore and aft of the 5.5 m long hold. In the upper hull, side frames bisect the average 0.9 m distance between the frames. Fore and aft, manoeuvring decks are found, and heavy wooden clamps have formed seats for a beiteäss, a sailyard used for tacking. The wreck originates probably in western Norway, due to the wood species used, and it is believed to be a small representative of the *knarr*, a ship type known from the sagas as a seagoing cargo carrier in the 11th to 13th centuries. A replica of Skuldelev 1 circumnavigated the world between 1984 and 1986. Skuldelev 1 is most closely related to Wreck 3 from the Hedeby harbour, dendrochronologically dated to 1025.

Wreck 2

Preserved to *c.* 25 per cent with only parts of the bottom and the stern preserved. Reconstructed dimensions: length *c.* 30 m, beam *c.* 3.7 m, depth of hold 1.6 m. Calculated number of oars: about thirty pairs. The ship is constructed of oak grown in eastern Ireland and it was most probably built in **Dublin**. Willow has been used for side frames which extended under a stringer down over the upper bottom strakes. The frames are spaced only 0.7 m apart, and a full deck has been carried by the *biti*. The keelson is constructed of two timbers and extended over 13.3 m of the interior length of the vessel. At deck level, a mast partner probably made it possible to lower and rise the mast at sea. The ship was among the largest of its time, and it was probably referred to as a *draka* or a *snekkja*. Repairs carried out in Danish-grown oak attests that it spent a considerable part of its working life in Scandinavian waters.

Wreck 3

Preserved to *c.* 75 per cent, with most of the destruction taking place in the stern section. Reconstructed dimensions: length 13.85 m, beam 3.6 m, depth of hold 1.3 m. Calculated cargo capacity: *c.*4.5 tonnes. Oarports were found for seven oars in the uppermost, eighth strake. The hull form is very sharp toward the ends of the keel, and with an unpronounced turn at the bilge. Apart from the willow treenails and a few beach clamps, the vessel is built entirely of oak. The fully preserved, winged stem is made from one piece and it has been demonstrated that it was designed from a number of intersecting circles with radia in feet. Frames with multiple beams are found at the mast and in the fore and aft, where manoeuvring decks had also been present. The good state of preservation of the find allowed thorough reconstruction of the rigging of this vessel, based on the presence of fastening points and signs of wear around them.

Wreck 5

Preserved to *c.* 50 per cent, with the stern and most of the starboard side missing. Reconstructed dimensions: length 17.2 m, beam 2.6 m, depth of hold 1.1 m. Number of oars: twelve or thirteen pairs. Predominantly made of oak, but with planks in the upper three strakes made of ash and pine. Frames were situated at an average distance of 0.91 m. The *biti* carried a full deck, while the rowers were seated on a second level of beams. Two sets of stringers, one of them of alder, added to the longitudinal strength of the hull. An extensive reuse of ship timbers is seen in the hull; for example, a part of the gunwale strake shows two sets of oarholes, one of them being from the previous use of the plank in a vessel with a shorter distance between the frames. According to dendrochronology, the vessel originated in Denmark, and had a prolonged life with extensive repairs. This led to the interpretation of the find as a *leidangr* ship, a vessel built and kept by royal command for the defence of the local area and at the expense of the people living there. Skuldelev 5 is closely related to Skuldelev 3 in many constructional details, but it also resembles features found in the vessels deposited under similar conditions at the Fotevik blockade.

Wreck 6

Preserved to *c.* 50 per cent, with both stem and stern missing. Reconstructed dimensions: length 11.6 m, beam 2.5 m, depth of hold 1.16 m. The number of oars, if any, is not known. The vessel had originally been built with only six strakes, but the dimensions given above include an additional, seventh strake, secured with additional side frames of oak. Planks were made of pine, the keel of oak, and alder, pine and birch were used for various framing timbers. The keelson with the mast-step measures only approximately 1.3 m; it is secured to the mast frame and the keel only, and is made of birch. Due to the wood species and its small size, the vessel probably originated not too far north or east of Denmark, perhaps in western Sweden. It might have been a fishing or travelling boat.

The Skuldelev blockade consisted, apart from the ships and the stone filling dumped in them before and after their sinking, of a number of pole constructions and fascines which served to keep the ships in place and to encourage sedimentation. The first phase in the construction of the blockade probably originated in the 1070s, while the later phase may have been connected with fighting for the Danish throne in 1133, a war that also created the Fotevik blockade at Scania. Several other blockades in Roskilde Fjord are roughly contemporary with the Skuldelev blockade and most probably they were part of a larger defence system, including *warths* (observation and signalling posts) along the 40 km long waterway winding down the fiord to Roskilde. J.B.

ADDITIONAL READING

Crumlin-Pedersen, O., 1988, 'Gensyn med Skuldelev 5: Et ledingsskib?', *Festskrift til Olaf Olsen*, Copenhagen.

Crumlin-Pedersen, O., 1989, 'Wood Technology and the Forest Resources in the Light of Medieval Shipfinds', in C. Villain-Gandossi *et al.* (eds), *Medieval Ships and the Birth of Technological Societies*, 1, Malta.

Crumlin-Pedersen, O., 1991, *Aspects of Maritime Scandinavia* AD *200–1200*, Roskilde.

Crumlin-Pedersen, O. and Bonde, N., 1990, 'The Dating of Wreck 2, the Longship, from Skuldelev, Denmark', *Newswarp*, 7, 3–6.

Olsen, O. and Crumlin-Pedersen, O., 1968, 'The Skuldelev Ships II: A Report of the Final Underwater Excavation in 1959 and the Salvaging Operation in 1962', *Acta Archaeologica*, 38, 95–170.

Slot ter Hooge

Dutch East India Company (VOC) shipwreck of 1724, rediscovered in 1974 and salvaged by a team led by Robert Stenuit. The VOC ship *Slot ter Hooge*, named for a castle in today's Belgium, was a new vessel en route from Amsterdam to Batavia (Java) with a cargo of three tons of silver ingots and four chests of silver coin when it wrecked in the Madeira Islands on the evening of 19 November 1724. Blown off course by a storm, the ship attempted to find shelter off the island of Porto Santo, but was driven ashore. Only 33 from the complement of 254 passengers and crew survived.

Between 1725 and 1734 English salvor John Lethbridge, under contract to the VOC, recovered more than half of *Slot ter Hooge*'s treasure.

Working from historic accounts of the loss, Belgian treasure-hunter Robert Stenuit rediscovered the wreck in 18-22 m of water off Porto Santo's north coast in an inlet named the Porto de Guilherme. Working with an **Airlift**, Stenuit and his team recovered a number of artefacts – ceramics, glassware, pewter, and ship's fittings, as well as large numbers of silver coins of various nationalities. Stenuit also recovered a quantity of silver bars, including a group stacked inside the partially disintegrated remains of a wooden chest.

Stenuit's project, funded in part by the **National Geographic Society**, undertook some documentation of the site and the artefacts. Under terms of a contract with the Dutch government, which owned the wreck, Stenuit retained 75 per cent of his finds, which were sold at auction. No archaeological report was published, and the full nature of his discoveries is not known. Some of the finds are displayed at the Casa Colon in Porto Santo. J.P.D.

ADDITIONAL READING

Stenuit, R., 1975, 'The Treasure of Porto Santo', *National Geographic*, August, 260–75.

Small craft studies

The history, typology and investigation of indigenous or vernacular watercraft. Nearly all regions of the world hold a variety of types of waters ranging from small shallow creeks to large exposed sounds and treacherous inlets to the sea. Unique combinations of weather, geography, topography, and other environmental factors, together with cultural and economic circumstances have led to the development of boat types which are distinct from those of other maritime regions. Small craft which develop under these conditions are called indigenous watercraft, or sometimes vernacular watercraft, and are the products of individuals in remote or ethnic communities working with intuitive or acquired skills and concepts in response to restricted local or regionally specific requirements. They are normally very different from manufactured and 'standard' boat types which are produced by an industry or industrial process to suit a broader application.

Indigenous watercraft are seldom, if ever, built from plans or written specifications. How the shape and structure of the boat is achieved depends on the materials available for its construction, and the ingenuity of its builder in manipulating the materials. The skill or craft level depends on cultural factors such as tradition, native invention, economic resources and either intervention of outside resources, or the resultant effect of cultural or geographical isolation. Small craft are implements: they are means of moving people and their belongings around. They are unique sources of information about their builders and operators. Small craft afford an insight into times and technologies for which we have no other source.

A functional definition for small craft would be vessels built for and primarily used for inshore use, and not for long voyages offshore beyond shore support. Further, small craft studies are generally limited to those watercraft built prior to the middle to late 1950s, since this was about the time that large engines became commonly available, forcing design changes in boats that still prevail today. In general, small craft are in the range of 12 m in length or less.

Small craft evolution in many areas is indeed poorly understood. There are several basic reasons for this. Boatbuilding was often a backyard operation usually handed down orally from generation to generation. Personal papers, newspaper accounts, advertisements, etc. are simply not available to document even broad evolutionary developments. Another reason, as marine archaeologists have discovered, is that there is a lack of preserved small craft for study. This may be attributed to the general susceptibility of small craft to rot or decay, particularly since they were often left out in the weather throughout the year, and also to their low cost and expendable nature.

Although much of the history of small craft does not exist on library shelves or in museum storage areas, the information can be found. The remains of these vessels lie abandoned and forgotten in the waters and the bottom sediments of the lakes and rivers and watercourses where they were used. This is a difficult environment to work in, and until the 1980s professionals generally failed to search out those remains, or ignored them when they were found. Archaeologists have often been more interested in larger, more glamorous shipwrecks, while the interest of maritime museums around the country has been limited to historic small craft that were in good shape, either in a floating condition or existing in a stored condition in a boat shed or barn. Therefore, while many aspects of archaeology are well advanced, the field of **Underwater archaeology**, particularly when dealing with small craft, is in its infancy and only now are basic objectives being approached.

Three common questions facing archaeologists in the field upon confronting the remains of a small craft are: 'What is it?', 'How old is it?', and 'Is it significant?' These questions are not necessarily easily answered, since identification and evaluation are complex issues. Most often, the vessels in question are situated in underwater sites, and the archaeologist has gathered what little data as was possible under the most trying of conditions. The combination of limited visibility, hazardous currents, physical hardship, poor preservation, and usually largely obscured structural components conspire to prevent accurate observation of critical features.

Finding answers to these questions is made even more difficult if there happens to be no common language to describe small craft. Nomenclature of ship structures is often vague and ambiguous. In some aspects of vernacular boat types there may be no recognized standard nomenclature. Boatbuilding practices can vary widely from region to region, or even within the same general locale. In order to interpret small craft remains properly, the archaeologist must know what to look for, and then be able to communicate these observations to the other archaeologists and specialists for their review and input.

Therefore the initial step in interpreting small craft remains is establishing and then refining a chronological typology for vessels within a geographic region. A typology serves to reduce the maze of types, and variations within types, to a manageable number of related groupings, with key characteristics by which they may be identified. The features on which categories within a typology are established represent concepts based on a combination of field observation and historical records; none are speculative. They are generated from existing data collected from abandoned boats, boats stored in barns, pieces of boats lying in marshes or behind fish houses, and fragments of boats raised from underwater sites, and which is then combined with information found in historical accounts, records, and documents. Patterns and relationships emerge when examples are grouped by similarity of major elements, and when these elements are given a hierarchical status. The typology is an evolving system based on limited information.

After refinement the typology will eventually lead to a dichotomous key by which, through a series of simple choices between paired features, identification of a vessel's age, function, and significance may be accomplished. Such a key is a tool ideally suited to the needs of the archaeologist who is often dealing with deteriorated, partial remains, and who may lack the specialization required for identification and evaluation of the wide variety of vessels of diverse origins potentially residing in underwater sites.

A typology for regional small craft is most often based on key structural elements. The structural system recognizes the role of boatbuilding technology in the social and economic development of a societal group. As boat use and economic factors change in a community, shape, size, and arrangement of the boat and its equipment may alter, but the basic structural elements will evolve more slowly, because of the dependency of the building on the technology 'status quo' in a vernacular setting. A structural typology has the added advantage of being based on tactile, definitive objects that are readily recognizable and readable in the field.

The structural elements incorporated into a typology are planking style, keel morphology, and the system of transverse frames. A typology created for North Carolina small craft is based on the premise that structural systems are a more reliable indicator of origin and related cultural aspects than is shape, and what is usually referred to as the 'lines of a boat'. This concept may not be universally accepted as yet, but at least in the present situation it has removed several obstacles that had continually proved troublesome.

Acceptance of a typology based on structural morphology does not eliminate shape as a consideration. In the first place, boat shape is very much related to the methods and materials selected for construction. However, shape can and does vary to some degree within a type, and is also, like fad and fancy, subject to the whims of taste and the winds of change. A shape typology would probably have to begin with a classification separating hulls into the traditional three classes: round-bottom, V-bottom, and flat-bottom. Immediately, this invokes artificial criteria which will prejudice many future decisions regarding classification. True evolutionary lines, if present, will be camouflaged and may go undetected. There are other instances in which inconsequential factors conspire to confuse the issue when shape is used as a classification device.

**Typological hull classification
(North Caroline traditional construction)
(Alford 1989, revised 1995)**

I. Hollowed log shell (dugout, canoe, canoe-boat, kunner [coll.], periauger)
A. Single log, basic, trough-form or rudimentary
B. Single log, basic, modelled form
C. Single log, complex (inserted frames, modelled form)
D. Split, complex (inserted frames), extended, modelled form
E. Multiple log, complex, extended, modelled form (variant of 'D')

II. Plank-on-frame
A. Round bilge, moulded cross-section keel
    1. Transom stern
    2. Fantail stern
    3. Staved round stern
B. Round bilge, flat keel (or hog)
    1. Transom stern
    2. Round stern
C. Round bilge, lapstake
    1. Sharp stern
    2. Transom stern
        a. Skiff
        b. Deep keel, decked or partially decked
D. Deadrise bottom, longitudinally planked bottom, moulded cross-section keel marked
    1. Transom stern
E. Deadrise bottom, bottom planked longitudinally, flat or plank keel or no keel, slight or marked deadrise
    1. Transom stern
    2. Fantail stern
    3. Staved round stern
    4. Log forefoot
    5. Staved forefoot
    6. Planked forefoot
F. Flat bottom, longitudinally planked over frames, more or less rockered bottom
    1. Transom stern
    2. Staved round stern
    3. Sharp stern
    4. Square both ends
    5. Side frames moulded
    6. Side frames straight
    7. Side planked, narrow strakes
G. Plate bottom and knee, little or no bottom rocker (bateau construction)
    1. Sharp stern or transom stern
        a. Side frames moulded
        b. Side frames straight

III. Skiff constructed (slab and post, up to 70 ft in length)
A. Flat bottom skiff, bottom planked transversely
    1. Transom stern
    2. Sharp stern
    3. Round stern
    4. Swim head (square both ends)

IV. Flat, flatboats, and scows (square both ends)
A. Essentially skiff-built but larger and heavier construction
    1. Bottom planked transversely
    2. Bottom planked longitudinally
B. Archaic form (moulded side construction)

While such a typology is an essential tool to categorize, interpret, and determine the significance of individual small craft, caution is necessary. As previously stated, a typology is limited and experimental. It may also be oversimplified and there is some risk that in the field researchers may assume that if vessel remains do not immediately fit, that it indicates an insignificant vessel. The typology does not directly address significance, admittedly one of the initial objectives. On the other hand, it does say that vessels or remains that can be placed within the typology outline match certain minimum criteria for vernacular craft historically used in North Carolina. Every boat of vernacular origin is unique, each has significance of greater or lesser degree. Identification is nine-tenths of the significance questions, and the typology is a step towards identification.

Small craft finds in North Carolina are evaluated according to their potential contribution to refining the structural typology. In cases where no current examples exist, such as for sharpies, any example regardless of condition should be considered important. On the other hand, a prehistoric dugout or shad boat, even in good condition, may not be considered significant because it cannot contribute new information to the present typology, since so many of the same type exist and have been documented.

It should be remembered that the typology is based on structural features known or expected to have been employed historically during the construction of boat types native to North Carolina. Therefore, the remains of a craft may derive their significance solely from a singular feature, such as a certain framing pattern design.

The integrity of small craft remains is also a major consideration in assigning relative significance. When features are preserved to a degree that allows greater accuracy in observing and recording them when compared to other examples, a small craft's relative significance is amplified.

The emphasis of small craft studies is to refine and support a typology and accompanying chronology. The foremost priority therefore is to seek out and record as many small craft examples as possible. Widespread inventories are needed to sample areas throughout a region in order to record a variety of small craft in a thorough, systematic manner. Survey techniques can include various methods from simple visual inspections and interviews with local watermen to **Remote sensing** equipment using sophisticated position systems.

Surveys designed to cover a geographical unit systematically, such as a river drainage, will provide the database upon which to determine distributional patterns, which can lead to an understanding of natural hazard areas and human activities. Transportation routes, subsistence strategies, abandonment practices and other maritime activities taking place within a specific area may eventually come to light. The ultimate goal of archaeology is to view the underlying causes that precipitate change in human societies through time or explain cultural differences between coexisting societies. Small craft are especially suited to distributional studies due to their large numbers and expendable nature.

Recording consistent documentation for each individual small craft discovered during the survey, regardless of age, condition, or significance, is essential. This basic information gathering, often referred to as Level I documentation, encompasses a standard set of categories which are usually developed into a field form to insure thoroughness.

Level I – Investigations
Identification
    Project site number and name
    Investigator and affiliation
    Date recorded
Location
    Body of water
    Closest main body of water
    USGS Quad Map or NOAA chart
    Mark position on map, preferably
    Directions to the site.
Environment
    Describe marine environment (water depths, currents, bottom conditions)
    Describe associated uplands, if appropriate
Description
    Overall measurements (length, beam, depth of hold)
    Propulsion
    Hull configuration (round, deadrise, flat)
    Hull materials
    Prominent features
Condition of site
Historical research and/or informant interviews
Additional comments
A mid-range degree of field documentation, or Level II investigations, is necessary to

provide the basis on which to determine small craft remains that hold the greatest potential to contribute important data to the existing typology and thus be significant. Furthermore, it will help identify what features make an individual site significant and guide planning for mitigative measures and management in the future.

Level II – Investigations

1) Locate vessel on earth's surface using Universal Transverse Mercator or latitude/longitude coordinates.
2) Do a reconnaissance of the immediate area to understand the wreck's relationship to the surrounding environment.
3) Expose the wreck to the extent that it can be studied and collect associated artefacts.
4) Make a sketch map of the site with overall measurements.
5) Take basic measurements – establish a baseline down the keelson and locate all frames on a grid.
6) Record dimensional data on floors.
7) Take cross sections at critical places: midship, near the bow, and near the transom.
8) Note features such as the placement of mast-step and centreboard.
9) Sketch details such as shaft holes in the keel, the projected shaft clearance of the floors, heights of the engines, the shape of the keel log.
10) Take photographs whenever possible.
11) Recover samples for wood analysis and fastening identification.
12) Conduct historical research and inquiries of local people to solicit vessel identification, type, period of use, and so on.

As information is gathered and the typology strengthened, related contexts may be developed. More specific aspects of the structural typology, such as the evolution of the centreboard or the use of the log keel during the development of small craft, might stand as separate design contexts. In the future, small craft could be one aspect of an environmental context focusing on the factors that contribute to the building and use of vessels within a given region. They might also be incorporated in social contexts such as one aimed at revealing how maritime industries are organized and developed by viewing the consequences of economic strategies on the maritime archaeological record.

Small craft have been numerous and relatively expendable during man's reliance on the waterways for transportation and subsistence, a period beginning with the first inhabitants and continuing to the present.

They are particularly sensitive to changes in the environment, the economy, and social patterns. It stands to reason, then, that small craft remains must be recognized as a vital tool for answering a spectrum of anthropological research questions. These cultural resources should be afforded the recognition, attention, and protection comparable to the value they collectively possess. M.A., M.W.R.

ADDITIONAL READING

Alford, M.B., 1989, 'Small Craft Typology: A Tool for Archaeological Research', in J. Barto Arnold III (ed.) *Underwater Archaeology Proceedings from the Society for Historical Archaeology Conference*, Ann Arbor, Michigan.

Fleetwood, R., 1982, *Tidecraft*, Savannah, Georgia.

Gardner, J. (ed.), 1977, *The Classic Boat*, Time Life Library of Boating, New York.

Greenhill, B., 1976, *Archaeology of the Boat*, Middletown, Connecticut.

Johnston, P.F., 1980, *The Seacraft of Prehistory*, Cambridge, Massachusetts.

Lipke, P., Spectre, P. and Fuller, B.A.G. (eds), 1993, *Boats: A Manual for their Documentation*, Nashville, Tennessee.

Lonergan, E., 1988, 'A Waterman's Story', in J.L. Peacock and J.C. Sabella (eds), *Sea and Land: Cultural and Biological Adaptations in the Southern Coastal Plain*, Athens, Georgia.

McKee, E., 1983, *Working Boats of Britain*, London.

Snape Boat

Boat burial excavated in 1862 and 1863 as part of an investigation of a pagan Anglo-Saxon cemetery by Septimus Davidson. The cemetery lies 14 km northwest of **Sutton Hoo** and the status of the burial, which includes the Snape Ring, a fine Late Antique onyx intaglio in a gold Anglo-Saxon setting, suggests that, like the Sutton Hoo cemetery, it may have been a burial place of the East

Anglian dynasty. The 19th-century excavations revealed the remains of a clinker-built boat, approximately 20 m long, with eight or nine strakes a side, and similar in both size and proportions to the boat buried in Sutton Hoo Mound 2. No structural details were recorded at the time, but the rivets and bolts are identical to those used in the two Sutton Hoo vessels and show that the Snape Boat was built in the same tradition. A.C.E.

ADDITIONAL READING

Bruce-Mitford, R., 1974, 'The Snape Boat Grave', in R. Bruce-Mitford (ed.), *Aspects of Anglo-Saxon Archaeology*, London.

Snow Squall

The most intact example of an American clipper ship, built in Maine in 1851 and condemned in the Falkland Islands in the South Atlantic in 1864 (see **Falkland Islands wrecks and hulks**). Five expeditions (1982–87) excavated and recovered just over 10 m of the bow from keel to lower deck level for transport to South Portland, Maine. Initially **Conservation** of wet wood consisted of freshwater spraying at the Spring Point Museum but in 1995 hull elements selected for **Museum display** were dried over a period of several months in a lumber kiln, an apparently successful technique. Documentation of the hull and related artefacts consists of extensive field notes and photographs in addition to measured drawings and photographs made in 1992 and 1995 for the Historic American Engineering Record (HAER). These are on deposit at the Library of Congress. Major elements of *Snow Squall* are now at the Maine Maritime Museum (Bath), San Francisco Maritime National Historical Park, South Street Seaport Museum (New York), and the Spring Point Museum.

Vessels such as *Snow Squall*, with narrow, concave bows, a slender hull in proportion

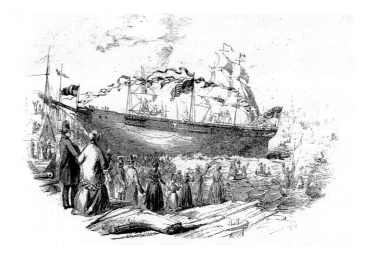

The clipper Snow Squall launched. From Gleason's Pictorial Drawing Room Companion. (Vancouver Maritime Museum)

Left: The bow of Snow Squall, Falkland Islands. (Nicholas Dean)

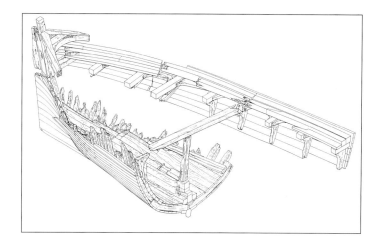

Right: Axonometric drawing of Snow Squall. (Historic American Engineering Record/Karl Bodensiek)

to length, and designed to carry a great deal of sail, were built in the mid-19th century with speed, rather than great cargo capacity, as the goal, primarily for trade between Atlantic American seaports and the Pacific, particularly California, Australia, and China. While many paintings of American clippers exist, little had been known about specifics of construction and materials, which in *Snow Squall*'s case involved at least ten species of hard and softwoods. Still in place on the hull are sheets of Muntz metal, a copper/zinc alloy which was intended to give protection against marine worms and fouling.

As built, *Snow Squall* was 157 ft (47.9 m) long. It was not possible to recover the after part of the hull as it lay buried under rockfill beneath a jetty. For the final 1987 recovery divers tunnelled under the keel to attach padded lifting chains linked to large air-filled bags, then severed the bow section from the rest of the hull with an air-powered chainsaw. A rising tide accomplished the lift. A tug towed the bow to a preassembled steel lifting frame, then a freighter's cranes lifted the bow, in its frame, aboard for transport to Maine. Previous expeditions had removed all above-water wood after tagging and photo documentation.

The first four *Snow Squall* Project expeditions were sponsored by Harvard University's Peabody Museum, the final bow recovery by the Spring Point Museum, where the bow and related artefacts remained until 1995. As happened with other projects which involved recovery of wet wood, long-term conservation costs proved far greater than expected, a burden to a small museum, hence the decision in 1995 to find new homes for the hull elements. N.D.

ADDITIONAL READING

Bass, G.F. (ed.), 1988, *Ships and Shipwrecks of the Americas*, New York.

Bayreuther, W.A., 1993, 'The Clipper Ship *Snow Squall*: Translating a Dream into Reality', *CRM*, 16, 3, 24–6.

Bayreuther, W.A. and Horvath, M.J., 1993, 'The *Snow Squall* Project: Saving the Last Yankee Clipper Ship', *Bermuda Journal of Archaeology and Maritime History*, 5, 99–109.

Switzer, D.C., 1992, 'The Clipper Ship *Snow Squall*: The Last of Her Breed', *Seaways*, November/December, 16–19.

Somers

Shipwreck from 1847 lying off the coast of **Mexico** near the port of Veracruz. *Somers* was laid down at the New York Navy Yard, Brooklyn for use as a sail training vessel for the United States Navy. Launched on 16 April 1842, the vessel was built to the Baltimore clipper model – sharp, fast, and heavily sparred. *Somers* was 100 ft (30.5 m) long between perpendiculars, with a 25 ft (7.6 m) beam, and displaced 259 tons. *Somers* was armed with twelve guns.

Somers gained national notoriety in 1842 on her second training voyage. Captain Alexander Slidell McKenzie allegedly discovered a plot to mutiny, kill the officers, and seize the brig for use as a pirate vessel. The purported ringleader, nineteen-year-old midshipman Philip Spencer, the scapegrace son of then Secretary of War John Canfield Spencer, was arrested along with two other accomplices. Fearing a spread of mutiny, McKenzie convened a hasty court martial and executed the three men by hanging them.

The 'mutiny' on *Somers* and Captain McKenzie's actions were controversial. The captain was court martialled on charges that the executions were not necessary, and he had murdered Spencer and his accomplices, but McKenzie was not convicted. The Navy abolished its system of training at sea in the wake of the '*Somers* Affair' and in 1845 the Secretary of the Navy established the United States Naval Academy at Annapolis, Mary-

land in its stead. The most famous outcome of the affair was the interest of Herman Melville, whose cousin, Guert Gansevoort, was first officer aboard *Somers*. Melville used the story of *Somers* in his last work, *Billy Budd*.

With the outbreak of war with Mexico in 1846, *Somers*, assigned to the Home Squadron, sailed into the Gulf under the command of Raphael Semmes, an officer who later gained fame as a Confederate admiral and commander of the most successful commerce raider in history, CSS **Alabama**. Under Semmes's command, *Somers* helped enforce the United States' blockade of Mexico's most important Gulf port, Veracruz. *Somers*'s war career was brief. On 8 December 1846, Semmes spotted a small vessel apparently trying to run the blockade. *Somers* gave chase as a squall blew up, striking the brig as she tacked. As the crew struggled to lower the sails, the brig capsized and sank instantly, drowning thirty-nine of the crew.

The wreck of *Somers* was rediscovered in 1986 by art dealer and explorer George Belcher of San Francisco under contract to the Mexican State of Veracruz. Following Mr Belcher's discovery, the governments of the United States and Mexico began a cooperative project to document the remains of the brig while diplomatically negotiating over ownership of the wreck.

An international team from both countries, constituted by the National Park Service's **Submerged Cultural Resources Unit**, the **US Navy**, Mr Belcher, and Mexico's Instituto Nacional de Antropologia e Historia (INAH), worked together in 1990 to complete a non-destructive documentation of the site. The remains of the brig visible on the site include: the copper-sheathed hull's port side, rudder and bow; anchors; nine cannon; the pumps; and the galley stove. A large number of fittings and equipment all lie inside the area bounded by the port side of the hull and the buried reaches of the starboard hull.

These all lie in the approximate space or area that they occupied on the ship when it was intact, indicating a **Site formation process** that was relatively undisturbed, allowing the disintegrating vessel to deposit its non-organic remains on the bottom in discrete patterns that conform to the ship's original layout. Excavation of the site would doubtless demonstrate artefact distribution in tight depositional stratigraphic contexts that demonstrate the ship's compartmentalization, as well as stowage of articles to port and starboard.

The *Somers* wreck also represents a unique archaeological resource as the only American naval shipwreck from the Mexican War available for study. Additionally, *Somers* represented a diplomatic and political challenge as the United States and Mexico, while agreeing to preserve and study the wreck, disputed each other's claims to sovereignty for the wreck. The *Somers* case, like that of the Confederate raider *Alabama*'s wreck in France, reflect a US Government policy to assert its ownership of warship wrecks, while emphasizing a cooperative international approach in their preservation, study, and interpretation. J.P.D.

ADDITIONAL READING

Belcher, G., 1988, 'The US Brig *Somers*: A Shipwreck from the Mexican War', in J.P. Delgado (ed.), *Underwater Archaeology Proceedings from the Society for Historical Archaeology Conference Reno, Nevada*, Ann Arbor, Michigan.

Chapelle, H.I., 1949, *The History of the American Sailing Navy: The Ships and their Development*, New York.

Delgado, J.P., in press, 'The Wreck of the Mexican War Brig *Somers*', in M. Bound (ed.), *Excavating the Ships of War*, Oswestry, Shropshire.

Delgado, J.P., 1994, 'Rediscovering the Somers', *Naval History*, 8, 28–31.

Hayford, H., 1959, *The Somers Mutiny Affair*, Englewood, New Jersey.

McFarland, P., 1985, *Sea Dangers: The Affair of the Somers*, New York.

Semmes, Lieut. R., USN, 1851, *Service Afloat and Ashore During the Mexican War*, Cincinnati.

Sonic High Accuracy Ranging and Positioning System (SHARPS)

A device for speeding up mapping and data-recording processes. Scientific archaeological techniques on land or underwater require that the size and location of structures, features, and artefacts on a site be

Diagram illustrating a typical SHARPS set-up: three transceivers, mounted on poles elevated above and surrounding a target, hardwired to a computer aboard a nearby vessel; a diver carrying a fourth transceiver also hardwired to the shipboard computer; and ultrasonic sound pulses being sent to the diver's transceiver as he surveys the site within the electronic net to provide XYZ coordinates within the net of any feature desired. (Courtesy Marine Sonic Technology, Inc.)

accurately measured and recorded if a complete database is to be provided for subsequent study and analysis. Difficult enough on a land site, accurate and repeatable measurements underwater have been an enormous problem, particularly on deep sites where bottom-time is precious. The invention of the Sonic High Accuracy Ranging and Positioning System (SHARPS) by Martin Wilcox, of the Applied Sonics Laboratory, of Gloucester, Virginia, was thus developed.

Dr Donald Frey of the **Institute of Nautical Archaeology** (INA) at Texas A&M University had faced all of these problems on ancient shipwreck sites under excavation in the eastern **Mediterranean Sea**. In January 1984 Frey first suggested to Wilcox that the problem of accurate measurement might be solved by using some type of ultrasonic measuring device similar to existing underwater navigation systems, but with improved accuracy. Navigation systems, Wilcox knew, operate at low ultrasonic frequencies over long distances and are accurate to within a metre or two. Measurement for mapping purposes, however, required improving that accuracy by a factor of one hundred.

From first-hand experience as a pioneer of medical ultrasonics technology, Wilcox was aware that under the pressure of intense international competition, medical ultrasonic equipment had become very good at producing highly detailed, real-time images of internal organs using the principle of 'pulse-echo reflection', or what the Navy refers to as 'active sonar'. Medical

imaging systems create their images with extremely short high-frequency pulses, the same technique used to locate submarines. The difference lay in the length and frequency of the pulse and the range to the target. When Wilcox formed Applied Sonics in 1983, though he had a strong background in medical ultrasonics, he had little experience in underwater technology. This inexperience, he later recalled, proved invaluable.

'We didn't know that almost every sonic navigation system uses the transponder principle to measure range. This means that the ship being navigated over the bottom sends a narrow-bandwidth (long-duration) sonic pulse to a group of transponders installed around the operating area. Each transponder detects this signal and replies with a narrow-bandwidth coded sonic pulse on a frequency unique to itself. The equipment on the ship times the return of these responses and triangulates the location of the ship in the net.'

Given Frey's original suggestion about improving the accuracy of navigation systems, knowledgeable underwater sound engineers would have started with the transponding approach. Although this technique is perfect for its intended task and permits the use of isolated, 'wireless' transponders, Wilcox's ignorance of it later proved to be fortunate.

Wilcox soon learned that most underwater archaeological sites such as shipwrecks rarely exceed 100 m in diameter. He thus decided to try a simple approach. After discovering experimentally that he could send very short high-frequency ultrasonic pulses over surprising distances underwater, he reasoned that he could set up a group or 'net' of ultrasonic transceivers around an underwater site connected by cables to a workboat anchored above. A diver or a remotely operated vehicle (ROV) would carry a portable transceiver that could be used as if it were an electronic 'pen'. As the diver or ROV outlined objects on the site, the 'pen' would emit short ultrasonic pulses. The pulses would be received at the other transceivers at times proportional to their distances from the 'pen'. Each transceiver would send a 'pulse received' message through the cable to a computer on the boat, which would gather the resulting data, make the necessary triangulation calculations, and display the resulting position points on its screen. The advantage of the system was that the sound pulse emitted from the diver's 'pen' transceiver makes a one-way trip to the net transceivers. Their response to the computer (which determines the range) is sent by cable at a large fraction of light speed instead of by return acoustic path used by the transponder system. This seemingly minor difference results in a major difference in performance. The short high-frequency pulses that can be used produce the required improvement in accuracy, and the one-way path produces immunity to the multi-path error problems that can plague a transponder system wherever large sound-reflecting surfaces are found near the site.

The first experimental unit, using software written by Dennis Hahn and Dr Glen Williams of Texas A&M University, was first field-tested at Yorktown site 44-YO-88, *Betsy,* and achieved distances over 30 m in clear water, resolving millimetres of movement, with overall accuracy of less than 1 cm. More than 600 XYZ points were taken on the wreck in less than an hour of diving, more than had been achieved in three months of traditional measurements using tape and grid. Further modifications and testing extended the range to over 100 m, with a corresponding reduction of accuracy to plus or minus 2 cm at maximum range.

The system in its first production form consisted of at least four stainless-steel-covered transceivers, each 22.9 cm long and weighing approximately 900 g, connected by underwater-grade coaxial cables to a junction box. The box was connected by a 90 cm multiple conductor cable to a control card that plugged into an input/output channel of a computer. A small power supply was connected to the control board to provide power for the transceivers. The

control board could operate up to six transceivers, and up to four control boards could be operated together to construct a net with as many as twenty-four transceivers. Software could set this maximum count to represent from 14 to 1,750 m. The diver transceiver 'gun' could be triggered by the diver in either a single-point or continuously running mode.

The first successful open water field tests of SHARPS were conducted in February 1987 in Chesapeake Bay on the wrecks of the steamboat *New Jersey* (1870) and the schooners *Henrietta Bach* (1883) and *Dashaway* (1883), under the direction of Donald Shomette, during the *New Jersey* Project, sponsored by the Maryland Geological Survey and the **National Geographic Society**, and in August 1987 in the Columbia River on the wreck of the brig **Isabella**, in a documentation project conducted by the US National Park Service's **Submerged Cultural Resources Unit**, led by Daniel Lenihan. D.G.S.

ADDITIONAL READING
Shomette, D.G., 1988, 'The *New Jersey* Project: Robots and Ultra-Sonics in Underwater Archaeological Survey', in J.P. Delgado (ed.), *Underwater Archaeology Proceedings from the Society for Historical Archaeology Conference, Reno, Nevada,* Ann Arbor, Michigan.

Shomette, D.G., 1993, *The Hunt for HMS De Braak: Legend and Legacy,* Durham, North Carolina.

South America

Southern part of America, which includes these countries of Latin-Iberian origin: Argentina, Bolivia, Brazil, Chile, Colombia, Ecuador, French Guyana, Guyana, Paraguay, Peru, Surinam, Uruguay, and Venezuela. The area of the continent covers 17.8 million sq. km; it stretches for about 7,400 km from north to south, and about 5,150 km from east to west. It is bounded by the Atlantic Ocean on the east and the Pacific Ocean on the west. To the north are the **Caribbean** Sea and Central America. To the south, the Drake Passage separates South America from Antarctica. In total, its coastline extends for 31,951 km. South America is the world's fourth largest continent, representing 12 per cent of the world's land mass.

South America has three main fluvial systems, the Orinoco, the Amazon, and the Parana. The Orinoco River in Venezuela is one of the most navigated rivers in the continent, and has been the setting for considerable human activity, especially in transporting huge quantities of iron ore. The Amazon is America's longest river, with a length of approximately 5,450 km to its mouth in the Atlantic. Human activity along

the Amazon has also been great. The river is navigable for ocean-going ships for almost 1,600 km, and vessels with drafts of 4 m or less can travel along it for about 3,700 km upriver. The Parana River system includes other major rivers such as the Paraguay, Uruguay, and Plata. The waters of the system drain into the Plata estuary, considered the entrance to the south of the continent, while Buenos Aires harbour is the gate of the fluvial system. Human activity has been associated with these rivers since 3,000 BC. The Parana River is navigable for ocean-going vessels as far as Rosario, Argentina; the whole river is navigable by small cargo and recreational vessels. Salto Grande is the head of navigation in the Uruguay River, but the main traffic of vessels is concentrated in the Plata River.

South America has three major lakes. Maracaibo Lake in Venezuela, connected to the Caribbean by a narrow inlet, is the largest body of water in the continent. It is mostly fresh water, shallow, and punctuated by petroleum derricks. Lake Titicaca is shared by Bolivia and Peru. At 3,810 m above sea-level, it is the highest navigable body of water in the world. Before the Spanish conquest it belonged to the Inca empire. Several islands in the lake have small populations; on Sun's Island, the inhabitants build Totora rafts (small boats made of Totora vegetable fibre). The boats are the same kind as those used by the Inca, and are now used for fishing and local transportation. Another important lake, Poopo, is located in southern Bolivia. It is a salt-water body 3,700 m above sea-level. In the southern part of the continent, in Patagonia, about 10,000 sq. km of the region consists of lakes and is shared by southwest Argentina and southeast Chile. This region is the result of Andean valleys being inundated by the drainage of melted snow and ice from the mountains. The lakes have very low salinity and very cold temperatures, with an average temperature of around 8 degrees C. The lakes vary in depth, but the deepest is 465 m.

The Caribbean has high temperatures and salinity. The seabed consists of very fine particles of sand. Coral concentrations and calcium concretions are frequently found together with the sand. These environmental conditions are not good for the conservation of submerged cultural remains. The main source of cultural material comes from the period after the Spanish conquest. Extensive European activity after Columbus's voyages, repeated storms, and the continual fights between Spain and other European countries trying to control the trading routes and the fleets carrying gold and silver, led to large numbers of shipwrecks. Important sites in the Caribbean date from the 15th to the 19th century, and are located in Colombia, French Guyana, Guyana, Surinam, and Venezuela.

The extended coastline of the Atlantic offers the best potential for underwater archaeological sites in South America. This area has one of the widest submarine platforms in the world with shallow waters. The range of temperatures and salinity is variable because of its location running from north to south and crossing the equator. In Brazilian waters the temperature ranges from 20 to 30 degrees C. The salinity of the sea is high, and the seabed is mostly fine particles of sand. Since Pedro Cabral landed in 1500, the shores of Brazil have been visited by sailors from every European country with a sailing tradition. Portugal had its principal colony here, while Holland held colonies to the north of Brazil. Both nations lost ships there.

The shores of Uruguay have different conditions; the main difference is temperatures ranging from 18 to 25 degrees C, owing to the influence of the cold water arriving from the Antarctic to the south. The low temperatures and salinity of the southern Atlantic coast do not allow shipworm to thrive. The seabed comprises alluvial deposits and sand. Average temperatures range from 2 to 20 degrees C and the conservation of archaeological finds is extremely good. Organic as well as inorganic material can be recovered from the sea, and objects are often found complete. Since Fernando de Magallanes sailed along the Patagonian shore in 1520–21 and found the strait that takes his name, sailors from around the world have passed through these waters and many ships have sunk there. Fernando de Magallanes suffered the first known wreck when he lost one of his ships during his stay in Patagonia in May 1520, near the estuary of the River Cruz. Since then, ships from many American and European countries have been lost there, particularly off Cape Horn in the 18th and 19th centuries. Until the opening of the Panama Canal in 1915, the only way of sailing from west to east and back was to go around Cape Horn or through the Magellan Strait. The main area of these shipwrecks is located in the south at Le Maire Strait, Staten Island, Magellan Strait, Beagle Channel, and Cape Horn.

The Pacific coast of South America, which lies off the Andes, is characterized by deep and very cold waters, with a very low rate of sedimentation. Even in the central area of the coastline in Peru, temperatures are low: during summer 15 degrees C is normal.

Because of the depth, this is the region of South America where the smallest number of underwater sites have been found. However, the materials recovered are in a good state of conservation. In Chilean waters it is normal to find organic materials such as wood, and, depending on the position, there is evidence of shipworm only in some areas, especially along the Peruvian coastline. Since the Spanish conquest, maritime activity on this coastline was prominent from Chile to Colombia as cargoes were sent to and from Europe. However, it is also believed that the area may contain submerged evidence of settlements from the Inca period.

There has been little scientific underwater archaeology carried out in South America. There are no official policies on underwater archaeology, nor on the preservation of the submerged cultural heritage. The absence of any legal authority for the protection of archaeological sites, and the promotion of commercial salvage, has encouraged the recovery of material with no scientific aim or methodology, many such operations being carried out by companies from the United States.

During the 1970s local Navy teams developed a scientific methodology while excavating wrecks in Brazilian waters. As a result, Dutch and Portuguese shipwrecks were scientifically studied. There are now two local teams working in the region, both based at the University of São Paulo. They are small, but are trying to increase their influence. The main problem they face is souvenir collecting by local and tourist sport divers. Easy access to the sea, and the existence of very poor people who use it daily as a source of food and other utilities, encourage this process. In the absence of official policies to promote scientific research, the environment has helped to protect the underwater cultural heritage through its very cold waters and isolated coastline (mainly in Patagonia), together with the large distances involved. It is very difficult and expensive to dive here, and as the sites are not expected to have gold or silver cargoes like those in the Caribbean there are no possibilities of profit for the treasure-hunting companies. In 1985 a technical team started to develop expertise in underwater archaeology with the support of the Argentine Committee of the International Council of Monuments and Sites (**ICOMOS**) and the provincial government. Field activities consisted of recording sites, including wreck sites and the remains of early settlements. Since 1991 other scientific teams, research groups, universities, and private foundations have been involved,

although unfortunately treasure-hunting has also taken place in Uruguayan waters.

The Pacific coast has seen very little archaeological work. There have been shipwreck finds in the four countries that have access to the sea (Chile, Colombia, Ecuador, and Peru). Searches for underwater sites have been conducted, though not always with scientific aims; technical language has often been used to hide treasure-hunting activities. At the same time, blatant treasure-hunting has occurred in every country. Foreign scientists have conducted archaeological research in Bolivia (Lake Titicaca) and Chile (in Antarctic waters). Although Japan and Spain have supported these projects with scientists, finance funds, and equipment, local development of resources for the preservation of the underwater cultural heritage has not been promoted.

Argentina

During 1978 archaeologist Jorge Fernández with a team of divers recovered a monoxile canoe from Nahuel-Huapi Lake. It was the first example of underwater archaeology in Argentina. Since then, Argentina has developed a regular programme of underwater archaeology. Two seminars were held to implement this programme. The Argentine Committee of ICOMOS promoted education, as recommended by both the World Heritage and UNESCO, initiating a plan for the region to fight against treasure-hunting activities. In 1985 the first team of local people was formed with the support of ICOMOS. The objective was to put into practice the techniques and methodology of underwater archaeology in an Argentinean context.

After several experiments in the sea and small lakes with different conditions of visibility, the team approached its first archaeological site, the wreck of HMS *Swift*, a sloop of war lost in March 1770 in the estuary of the River Deseado to the north of the province of Santa Cruz. Located in the middle of the Patagonian shore, the estuary contains a mixture of salt and fresh water. The wreck is 70 per cent complete, and the conservation of both organic and inorganic materials is very good. The local amateur divers who found it recovered ninety objects between 1982 and 1985. The scientific team carried out four seasons' work in three years to record and map the site. The work was done in very bad visibility (the average was 500 cm), strong currents (up to 2 knots), low temperatures (reaching 8 degrees C), and without adequate equipment.

During 1989 a field season in the River Parana took place. The aim was to survey

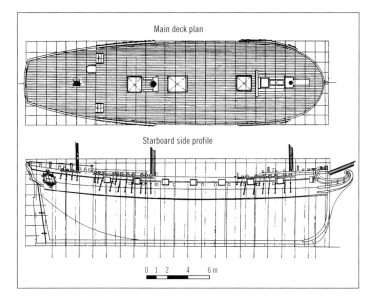

Main deck plan

Starboard side profile

0 1 2   4   6 m

Lines and deck plans of HMS Swift, wrecked in the River Deseado estuary, Argentina. (Eduardo Mangione)

Divers starting work at Santa Fe, La Vieja, San Javier River, Argentina. The poor visibility in the water is obvious. (Javier Garcia Cano)

the northern area of the river, searching for remnants of nautical activity from the 19th century. Visibility was zero. At the conclusion of the project, eleven sites with wrecks and other cultural objects were located. The finds dated from the end of the 19th century and the beginning of the 20th century, times in which the jungle in the north of the country was beginning to be exploited, and the colonists were establishing outposts.

During 1991, a non-profit private organization called the Albenga Foundation for the Preservation of Underwater Cultural Heritage was created to develop an underwater archaeological programme. Three projects have ensued to date. During 1994, the HMS *Swift* project was again pursued with personnel, equipment, and economical resources from Albenga. An up-to-date record was made and a documentary film was produced. Another project was to record ships wrecked and grounded in the Straits of Magellan. Nine ships were recorded, all of them from the 19th century. The last project is a survey in the ruins of the city of Santa Fe, founded in 1573 by the shore of San Javier River in the centre of the country. The project is being carried out in cooperation with the School of Anthropology of the National University of Rosario. Approximately one third of the town was inundated by the river and remains underwater to this day. Albenga has also cooperated with other institutions outside Argentina, in Holland, Malaysia, Sweden, and the **United Kingdom**. While there are no laws to protect the underwater cultural heritage in Argentina, two laws have been presented in the national parliament. Treasure-hunting activities are unknown, and the government does not have contracts with salvage companies.

Bolivia

Bolivia is one of the two inland countries in South America. While there has been no local development of underwater archaeology during the 1980s, a team of Japanese divers in a joint venture with archaeologist Max Portugal from the National Institute of Archaeology of Bolivia recovered ceramics and stone artefacts from Lake Titicaca. The project was financed by Asahi Television of Tokyo.

The site is located off the Sun's Island on the Bolivian side of the lake, at a depth of 20 m, and the objects belong to the Tiwanaku culture. Some of the artefacts were incense burners made of ceramics and having a feline shape; others were stone containers of cylindrical shape, perhaps offerings thrown into the waters as a gift for the gods. Conservation of the recovered ceramics was poor , and much of this material was not stabilized, resulting in high levels of deterioration. Some finds in Bolivia have been recovered by sport divers as souvenirs, but there is no precise information about the locations of finds. While the legal system protects the cultural heritage, it does not specifically mention underwater material.

Brazil

The first underwater archaeological fieldwork in Brazil was carried out by the Navy. In the late 1970s, it excavated a Portuguese galleon called *Santissimo Sacramento* (1668). Beginning in 1976, under the supervision of land archaeologist Ulysses Pernambucano de Mello Neto, many divers without experience in underwater archaeology recovered objects from the site. Bronze guns were taken to the surface and placed on exhibit.

In 1990 the Government created Archenave, a commission to study naval history, archaeology, and ethnography. The project did not go as far as had been anticipated. Archaeologist Gilson Rambelli works in the University of São Paulo in charge of underwater archaeology. There are few other experienced teams.

Treasure-hunting takes two forms in Brazil. The major salvage companies, who are frequently associated with foreign corporations, are one form. No major works have been carried out by these companies, although they have been granted permits by the government. The treasure-hunters frequently offer to share their profits with the authorities. The second form of treasure-hunting is the activities of local and foreign divers, who collect objects from the bottom, either to sell them on the black market or to take them back home as trophies of their holidays. Many of them do not know how significantly they are damaging the heritage of the country. Unfortunately, these activities are difficult to control on a very extended coastline, with the majority of the population living by or near the sea, and with a very high percentage of poor people. The poorest inhabitants can only see objects coming from the sea as a resource – only by selling them can they live. Some work to change this state of affairs has been done in the **National parks**, mainly in connection with the conservation of the natural environment. A specific law enacted in the 1960s protects shipwrecks, but the law has no possible application. The actions of people were not considered. Unfortunately, this destruction is less possible to control than that of the salvage companies, and there is no way of knowing how much damage has occurred or continues to occur. The submerged archaeological potential of this country is as big as the country itself, particularly when one considers the immense quantity of inland waters in Brazil.

Chile

Underwater archaeology in Chile has been conducted solely by Spanish scientists under the supervision of Dr Manuel Martin Bueno. The goal of Bueno's expeditions was a survey in Antarctic waters for the remains of an 18th-century Spanish ship, *San Talmo*, which sank in 1819. It is believed that this ship brought the first Europeans to the southern continent. The project did not find the wreck, but was the first underwater archaeology practised in Antarctica. Some Chilean archaeologists did work with the Spanish team, but the principal Chilean cooperation was offered by the Navy, who provided equipment, ships, and supplies. The last field season to date was in the summer of 1993.

Treasure-hunting in Chile began in the 1990s. In 1994 and 1995 a small private company searched for a 17th-century ship, *San Juan de Dios*. A Spanish vessel, it was sailing from Peru to Chile when it crashed ashore in 1684. The salvage company plans to recover a supposedly rich **Treasure**. It has a contract with the national government, who will share the profits. This is the first time that Chile's underwater cultural heritage has been threatened; the country's laws do not include the preservation of submerged cultural material, and there has been no declaration of intent to change the situation. The lakes in Chile, as in Argentina, are likely to hide a large number of important underwater sites.

Colombia

As one of the group of countries on the Caribbean coastline, Colombia has suffered from the strong influence of major treasure-hunting companies. There is no clear record of scientific work, although some of the treasure-hunters have been trying to explain their activities as 'archaeology'. The presence of Spanish ship *San Jose* found off Cartagena, which sank in 1706 with a reportedly rich cargo, spurred the imagination of many treasure-hunters about the possibility of profit from Colombia. After the United States of America passed the **Abandoned Shipwreck Act** in 1987, pressure by the salvage enterprises on the Colombian Government has increased considerably.

Treasure-hunters are regulated only by the contracts they sign with the local government.

Peru

The cold and deep waters of the Pacific Ocean off Peru have great potential for submerged cultural remains. Some local historians and sport divers have attempted to establish an underwater archaeological programme, but without success. One diver has found the remains of the Chilean Navy ship *San Martin*, a former English East Indiaman sunk in 1821. Built as *Cumberland*, she belonged to Chile's fleet during the war for independence. The hull is almost completely destroyed but some bronze guns were found where the wreck lies in front of Callao Harbour. Legislation does not cover the underwater cultural heritage, which thus has no protection. Some treasure-hunting has occurred, without major success, although some international companies have tried to establish a presence in the country. Dr Jorge Ortiz Sotelo, a historian with the Association of Ibero-American Maritime and Naval History, is trying to develop a local team for underwater archaeological work.

Uruguay

Uruguay has seen the most extensive damage from treasure-hunting in South America. Unfortunately, the national government has promoted these activities through several contracts with private international and local treasure-hunting companies. The legislation does not protect the submerged cultural heritage; on the contrary, it promotes searches that aim at commercial recovery. At least two important wrecks (*Nuestra Señora de Loreto*, and *Nuestra Señora de la Luz*) were destroyed by one company which, despite the opposition of some deputies, sold 18th-century artefacts at auction in London. The National Museum of Anthropology is the only institution which has tried to develop underwater archaeology and stop the destruction of the sites. The National Commission of Heritage is also trying to change this situation in Uruguay.

Venezuela

Venezuela has also suffered from treasure-hunting activities. There is no information on scientific work, although some foreign treasure-hunters try to pass themselves off as archaeologists. J.F.G.C.

ADDITIONAL READING

Archenave, 1990, *Patrimonia cultural naval do Brasil*, Comissao de Arqueologia, Historia e Etnografia Naval.

Garcia Cano, J. *et al.*, 1988, *HMS Swift Informe de Campaña*, GTPS, ICOMOS Argentina, Buenos Aires.

Guedes, M.J., n.d., *Arqueologia subaquático no Brasil*, Servico de Documentaçao Geral da Marinha Departamento de Museu Naval e Oceanográfico.

Nielsen, A., 1988, 'Descubrimientos arqueológicos en el lago Titicaca', *Revista de Historia*, 33.

Rodriguez, J.A. and Rodriguez, A.A., 1985, *Proyecto antropológico: Ecológico Santo Grande (primer informe)*, Universidad Nacional de Entre Rios.

Taiana, J.A., 1985, 'La aventura del Atlántico sur: Navegantes, descubridores y aventureros (siglos XVI–XVIII)', *El Ateneo*.

Southampton Centre for Maritime Archaeology

The Centre for Maritime Archaeology (CMA) is the focus for maritime archaeological research within the Department of Archaeology at the University of Southampton, UK. The CMA runs, or collaborates in, a number of maritime projects both in the UK and internationally as far afield as India, Scandinavia, the Channel Islands and Bermuda. It also provides the vehicle for field training of the department's students at undergraduate and postgraduate level, and incorporates a Special Branch of the British Sub Aqua Club. Within the university the CMA is involved in collaborative research with the Departments of Oceanography and Geology at the new Southampton Oceanography Centre, particularly in the field of high-resolution marine seismology. At a local level the CMA has close links with the Hampshire and Wight Trust for Maritime Archaeology, which – though an independent body – is also located within the university. The CMA is also linked to the **Nautical Archaeology Society**, incorporating NAS training courses within undergraduate and postgraduate programmes.

Further information can be obtained from: The Centre for Maritime Archaeology, Southampton, Highfield, Southampton, SO17 1BJ. J.R.A.

Sovereign immunity

The immunity of publicly owned property from the exercise of jurisdiction over it by any other government or private person or entity. Warships, naval auxiliaries, and other vessels owned or operated by a state and used only on government non-commercial service are state vessels. Aircraft used in military, customs, and police services are state aircraft. State vessels and aircraft, and their associated artefacts, whether or not sunken, are entitled to sovereign immunity. Title (i.e. ownership) of state vessels and aircraft is lost only by capture or sinking during battle (before sinking), by international agreement, or by an express act of abandonment, gift, or sale by the sovereign in accordance with relevant principles of international law and the law of the flag state governing the abandonment of government property. Once hostilities have ended, belligerents do not acquire any title to such vessels or aircraft through the act of sinking them. Likewise, title to such vessels and aircraft is not lost by mere passage of time.

A coastal state does not acquire any right of ownership to a sunken state vessel or aircraft by reason of its being located on or embedded in land or seabed over which it exercises sovereignty or jurisdiction. Access to such vessels and aircraft and their associated artefacts located on or embedded in the seabed of foreign archipelagic waters, territorial sea, or contiguous zones, is subject to coastal state control in accordance with international law. The policy of most governments is to honour requests from sovereign states to respect, or to authorize visits to, such sunken vessels and aircraft. Access to sunken state vessels and aircraft and their associated artefacts located on or embedded in the continental shelf seaward of twenty-four nautical miles from the baseline from which the breadth of the territorial sea is measured is subject to flag state control and is not subject to coastal state control. Access to sunken state vessels and aircraft and their associated artefacts located on or embedded in the seabed seaward of twenty-four nautical miles from the baseline is subject only to flag state control.

Except for opposing belligerents while hostilities continue, no person or state may salvage or attempt to salvage sunken state vessels or aircraft, or their associated artefacts, wherever located, without the express permission of the sovereign flag state, whether or not they are a war grave. Once hostilities have ended, sunken state vessels and aircraft containing crew remains are also entitled to special respect as war graves and must not be disturbed without the explicit permission of the sovereign state. The flag state is entitled to use all lawful means to prevent unauthorized disturbance of the wreck or crash site (including the debris field) or salvage of the wreck.

These rules do not affect the rights of a territorial sovereign to engage in legitimate operations, such as removal of navigational obstructions, prevention of damage to the marine environment, or other actions not prohibited by international law, ordinarily following notice to and in cooperation with the state owning the vessel or aircraft or otherwise entitled to assert the sovereign immunity of the wreck.

There is at present no multilateral treaty governing the treatment of sunken ships located in those areas beyond coastal state jurisdiction, nor is there any multilateral treaty governing the particular case of sunken warships or military aircraft, although UNESCO is considering the elaboration of an international convention on underwater cultural heritage. Consequently, the foregoing rules are based on a moderately well-developed body of customary international law governing the treatment of sunken warships and military aircraft. For example, in 1989, France and the United

States agreed that the United States owned the wreck and associated artefacts of the CSS *Alabama* sunk during the US Civil War in battle by USS *Kearsarge* on 19 June 1864 about 14.5 km off Cherbourg, France, waters which are now part of the territorial sea of France. The two states also agreed that access to and study of the wreck site had to comply with French law. US Federal Courts have upheld US ownership of the ship's bell salvaged by a US citizen without permission of the United States.

In 1952 the United Kingdom and Italy entered into an agreement concerning salvage of HMS *Spartan* sunk in Anzio Bay on 29 January 1944, recognizing British ownership of the wreck and Italian control of access to the site. The United Kingdom and South Africa entered into a similar agreement in 1989 concerning salvage of HMS *Birkenhead*, a Royal Navy troop ship, that sank off the Cape Colony in February 1852 with the loss of 445 lives. This latter agreement also safeguards the wreck's status as a war grave.

Ownership of the Russian cruiser *Admiral Nakhimov* passed to Japan by virtue of its capture on 28 May 1905, by the Japanese Imperial Navy during the Battle of the Japan Sea during the Russo-Japanese War of 1904–5. The ship sank an hour later in a high seas portion of the Korea Strait, which now forms part of the Japanese territorial sea. Japan rejected a 1980 Soviet objection to a Japanese project to salvage the ship on the grounds that the shipwreck was Japanese property by virtue of its capture in battle.

In 1980, the Singapore High Court affirmed German ownership of U-859, sunk by a British submarine in 1944 in international waters of the Straits of Malacca. J.A.R.

ADDITIONAL READING

'Abandoned or Sunken Vessels', 1986, *Digest of United States Practice in International Law*, US Government Printing Office.

'Agreement between the Government of the French Republic and the Government of the United States of America Concerning the Wreck of the CSS *Alabama*, Paris, 3 October 1989', TIAS 11687, 1992, UN Law of the Sea Bulletin, March, 20, 26.

'Agreement between the Government of the United Kingdom of Great Britain and Northern Ireland and the Government of the Republic of South Africa regarding the salvage of HMS *Birkenhead*, Pretoria, 27 September 1989', UK TS 3, 1990, Cm. 906, *British Yearbook of International Law 1989*, 60, 671–2.

'Diplomatic Correspondence Concerning Salvage of the Admiral Nakhimov and Awa Maru', *Japanese Annual of International Law*, 1986, 29, 114–15, 185–7; 1987, 30, 182–3.

'Exchange of Notes Constituting an Agreement between the Government of the United Kingdom of Great Britain and Northern Ireland and the Government of Italy Regarding the Salvage of HMS *Spartan*, 6 November 1952, Rome', 158, UNTS, 432.

Roach and Smith, 1996, 'United States Responses to Excessive Maritime Claims', *Kluwer Law International*, 466–78.

'Simon vs. Taylor and Another', 1980, 1 Malaysian Law Journal 236 (Singapore High Court 1975), 56 *International Law Reports 40*, (ownership of U-859).

United States vs. Steinmetz, 763 F. Supp. 1293, D.N.J. 1991, affirmed 973 F.2d 212, 3rd c.1992, cert. denied 113 S.Ct. 1578, 1993, (ownership of the ship's bell of CSS *Alabama*).

Soviet Union
see Russia and the ex-Soviet Union

Spanish Armada
Abortive attempt by Philip II to invade England which resulted in the wrecking of many ships on the voyage home, mainly on the coasts of Scotland and Ireland. The origins of the enterprise can be traced back to 1580, when Spain's annexation of Portugal secured the major Atlantic base of Lisbon. Three years later a self-contained amphibious operation, launched from Lisbon, successfully captured Terceira in the Azores, the last centre of Portuguese resistance. Meanwhile Philip was becoming increasingly concerned by the persecution of Catholics in England, by English support for the Dutch Revolt, and by increasingly bold incursions into the Caribbean and elsewhere in his dominions by English privateers like Sir Francis Drake.

In 1586 the Marquis of Santa Cruz, who had commanded the Terceira operation, was instructed by the king to prepare a plan for the invasion of England. The strategy he proposed was a self-contained task force – an Armada – on the Terceira model, but on a commensurably larger scale. In all, he reckoned, it would be necessary to put some 60,000 troops ashore in England, with provisions, munitions, a siege artillery train, and other supporting services sufficient for a six-month campaign. To get them there, and to counter any English attempt to stop them at sea, he calculated that he would need over 500 ships, of which nearly half would be substantial vessels. The fleet would adopt a formation by which it could defend itself without being deflected from progress towards its objective. Though the strategy posed monumental problems of logistics and funding, the strength of Santa Cruz's plan was its underlying simplicity – if the resources could be gathered together and set in motion, the whole vast entity would simply roll ponderously towards the landing-beaches of southeast England, smashing aside resistance until its goal had been achieved.

But the king had also asked his nephew Alexander Farnese, the Duke of Parma, for his views on how an invasion of England might best be conducted. Parma commanded Spain's formidable Army of Flanders in the Netherlands, and was unquestionably the foremost military commander of the time. His plan was as viable as Santa Cruz's, but very different in concept. If, under conditions of great secrecy, he could gather together a flotilla of barges containing some 20,000 of his veteran troops in the network of coastal canals close to the narrow channel which separated them from England, he believed that he could make the crossing under cover of darkness and achieve a surprise landing within striking distance of London. The quality of the troops at his disposal, and the weakness of England's land defences, should then assure a speedy victory.

To the outspoken dismay of his two senior commanders, however, the king decided to adopt elements of both plans in his final strategy. A much smaller Armada of 130 ships and 30,000 men (some 30 per cent of them mariners, the rest soldiers) would sail from Lisbon and rendezvous with 20,000 of Parma's barge-borne troops off Flanders. Protected by the Armada, the invasion force would then head for the Kent beaches shepherded by the fleet. Once the beach-head had been secured the Armada would land a back-up wave of troops with the munitions, provisions, and artillery necessary to achieve a break-out towards London. As the land forces advanced up the Thames Estuary in direction of the capital they would be supported on their flank by the fleet.

On paper the plan seemed workable, but it failed to take into account a number of practical difficulties. The most obvious was the stretch of shallow water off the Flemish coast which Parma's barges would have to cross before reaching the protection of the Armada's deep-draught warships. These shallows were dominated by fast and heavily armed rebel Dutch flyboats. More insidious, but just as serious, was the complexity of the king's strategy, compounded by the lack of any means of communication between the two component parts of the operation until they actually made contact. Parma required a lead time of at least a week to get his troops mustered and into their barges, but how was he to know when the Armada was actually going to arrive? Both Parma and Santa Cruz

voiced vigorous opposition to the combined plan, but Philip II's authority prevailed: he understood their concerns, he said, but since the enterprise was being conducted in God's cause the Almighty would surely enable these difficulties to be overcome.

Since to disagree with this logic would be tantamount to heresy, Parma and Santa Cruz began, with deep misgivings, to put the king's revised plan into effect. Ships, men, and stores began to assemble at Lisbon but the magnitude of the task was effectively beyond the capabilities and resources of a 16th-century administration, even one as massive as Spain's, and the enterprise began to bog down in a mire of rotting hulls, decaying provisions, and sick and dispirited men. The fleet was meant to sail in 1587, but after an interminable catalogue of disasters and postponements, Santa Cruz died of typhoid in February 1588, leaving the whole enterprise on the verge of collapse. It was rescued from chaos and oblivion by the man appointed by Philip II to succeed Santa Cruz, the much-maligned Duke of Medina Sidonia, a top-line administrator who in a few short months pulled the whole ramshackle affair into some sort of order and – miraculously – inculcated among his men a pious fervour for the crusade. In late May 1588 the Armada set sail for England from Lisbon.

Medina Sidonia's fleet was a polyglot affair. The most powerful squadron was composed of ten big Portuguese galleons which had been captured at the fall of Lisbon in 1580. Another squadron was made up of the escort galleons normally employed to protect the annual trans-Atlantic plate fleets. Four galleys and four galleasses completed the tally of royal ships. The remaining squadrons had been put together with ships requisitioned from a variety of sources: Basque-built merchantmen from Guipuzcoa and Biscay; vessels from the southern ports of Spain; big bulk-carriers from Italy and Dalmatia; and cargo hulks from the Baltic. They carried between them a total of almost 2,500 guns.

The Armada's intended tactics were simple, and based closely on Santa Cruz's original concept. When the fleet began its advance up the English Channel towards the rendezvous with Parma it would adopt a wide crescent-like formation in which each ship was required to keep rigid station. Within the fleet, however, twenty or so of the most powerful and nobly officered ships were given authority to act on their own initiatives whenever the formation as a whole was threatened. Thus, a defensive response was guaranteed, and self-regulating: no further orders would be needed to set it in

train. Meanwhile the formation as a whole would plod inexorably towards its objective, leaving gaps in its ranks to which the 'troubleshooters' could return once their business was complete.

After a pause to regroup and take on fresh supplies at Corunna the Armada entered the Channel on 30 July and shook itself into formation. A day later the main part of the English fleet, under Lord Howard and Sir Francis Drake, cleared its base at Plymouth and gained the Armada's weather gauge. The English were impressed by the Spaniards' tight defensive formation and matching discipline – 'we durst not adventure to put in amongst them, their fleet being so strong,' wrote Lord Admiral Howard in concerned frustration. In fact, the two fleets were tactically stalemated: the English, who had more manoeuvrable ships and heavier armament, could steer clear of danger and dictate the range at which they wished to fight, while the Spaniards sought close-range combat leading to boarding, in which their much greater military strength was likely to prevail. Naturally the English took pains to avoid this. In strategic terms, however, the Spaniards had the advantage, for their aim was not a decisive sea battle but unimpeded progress towards their objective.

The running fight which took place along the Channel over the following week, though not without incident, was little more than inconclusive sparring. But as Flanders drew closer, the Spanish plan began to disintegrate, just as Parma and Santa Cruz had predicted. On 7 August the Armada anchored off Calais, the last deep water anchorage available before the rendezvous. Parma was not ready to come out: he had been given insufficient warning and, moreover, he was not prepared to risk the annihilation of his army at the hands of Justin of Nassua's flyboats. At this point the English, now reinforced by ships from the Eastern Channel, took advantage of wind and tide to send in fireships. This stratagem at last broke Spanish resolve and discipline, albeit only temporarily, and the Armada scattered towards the waiting Flemish shoals.

A providential shift of wind saved the Spanish fleet from the sandbanks and pushed it northwards towards deep water, and it was here, off Gravelines, that Medina Sidonia revealed both his own mettle and the Armada's formidable strength. Somehow, from all the panic and disarray, discipline and formation were re-established (though one erring captain had to be hanged to encourage the others), and the Armada shook itself into its old defensive posture just in time to receive the English fleet's final, ferociously desperate assault. Howard's ships were running short of ammunition, and bereft of firepower they would have no further means of preventing the Spaniards from effecting a landing. All caution was thrown to the winds: for the first time the English went in hard and close, delivering salvoes of ship-smashing broadsides. But it was not enough to break the Armada's mutually-supportive formation, and at length the English had to disengage because their shot-lockers were empty. In reality, of course, the Spanish plan had already collapsed because the vital rendezvous had not been made. Each side had done all it could, and had nothing more to give. It was a draw, and the only thing left to do was to head for home.

The English bases were close at hand and to these, after shadowing the Spaniards for several days, they returned. But for the Spaniards, now well into the North Sea, there was no alternative but the perilous 'North-About' route around the top of Britain and so into the Atlantic for a southwards run to Spain. It was early autumn, and the equinoctial gales of that year – the Winds of God, as their Protestant adversaries would have it – blew early and with unusual violence. Many of the battle-damaged Spaniards were subsequently lost on the wild Atlantic coasts of Scotland and particularly Ireland.

No one knows exactly how many Armada ships were lost. The more important wrecks were recorded, but some lesser vessels vanished without trace or, if they were lucky, slipped into their home ports and oblivion. Of those that returned many were damaged beyond repair, and the human casualties – almost all from malnutrition and disease – were enormous. In overall terms about a third of the ships, and two thirds of the men, perished in the campaign.

Two ships, *San Juan de Sicilia* and *El Gran Grifon,* were lost in Scotland, and the whereabouts of their wrecks are known. There may have been two other wrecks in Scotland, probably off the western isles, and two more are thought to have been lost off Norway. Another vessel, *San Pedro Mayor*, was wrecked on Bolt Tail, on the southwest coast of England. But the great majority – perhaps as many as twenty-five – took place on the west coast of Ireland. The human toll was dreadful, both from the disasters themselves and from the waiting English garrisons.

Three of the wrecks – those of the galleass *Girona*, the Guipuzcoan vice-flagship *Santa Maria de la Rosa*, and the Levanter *La Trinidad Valencera* – have been discovered and archaeologically investigated in modern times. Three more,

English Ships and the Spanish Armada, 1588, *by an artist of the English school. (© National Maritime Museum Picture Library)*

all of the Levant squadron – *Juliana, Lavia,* and *Santa Maria de Vison* – were wrecked together off Streedagh Strand, Sligo. Their remains were discovered in 1986, and the site is now under a protection order from the Irish Government.

Archaeological investigation of the Armada shipwreck sites has proved fruitful not only for a fuller understanding of the historical events in which they took part but also, and more importantly, for the light it sheds on a much wider range of contemporary affairs. The very scale of the Armada – the years of planning and the administrative minutiae by which all the varied elements were brought together – has generated a vast bulk of documentation which complements the archaeological evidence derived from the wrecks. Thus, the Armada's siege train, represented by the three virtually identical 40-pounder bronze *canones* and associated equipment recovered from the wreck of *La Trinidad Valencera*, led to an investigation of their origins in the royal foundry at Malines, near Antwerp in 1556. The guns themselves were minutely compared to quantify the level of industrial repeatability their maker achieved. It was remarkably high. But this seems to have been an exception. Other guns recovered from the wrecks show a bewildering variety of specification and size, particularly in rela-

tion to bore and shot-weight. The apparently simple business of matching shot to gun appears to have been made inestimably complicated by an overall lack of standardization, further compounded by the use of several quite unrelated measuring systems and a widespread misunderstanding of basic arithmetical principles. This must have had an adverse effect on the offensive capability of the fleet as a whole, and may help to explain the Armada's poor artillery performance during the campaign. More than this, such a study provides a unique snapshot of the practical difficulties encountered by inhabitants of the early modern world as they struggled (however unwittingly) towards concepts of standardization and repeatability which would lead eventually to the present era of industrialization and mass production.

The Armada wrecks, with their associated documentation, offer many other microcosms of a world in the process of fundamental change. Maritime technologies, represented by the remains of the ships and their fittings, reflect the clash of old traditions rooted in Mediterranean-centred perspectives of ancient and medieval cultures with new challenges beyond the broad horizons of the great oceans. The shift of naval warfare from local to global theatres is also encapsulated by the Armada experience. If Spain nearly succeeded she did so with the last great amphibious operation in the medieval mould. England's narrow victory, on the other hand, was achieved with the unprecedented use of ships as mobile gun-platforms. Though the outcome was inconclusive and, for England, based on luck rather than judgement, it nevertheless heralded the shape of things to come.

Finally, as with all wrecks, the Armada has provided a rich and varied sampling of everyday things, made the more significant because each is part of a wider association, and everything was in contemporary use. The weaponry, accoutrements, and clothing of the soldiers are complemented by their domestic possessions, recreational items, and personal trinkets. Ordinary utensils reflect life on board and the campaign to come. And, beyond what they tell of the people who made and used them, the objects have a wider archaeological significance. Their closely dated contexts feed back into artefactual studies of significance to other, perhaps less well-dated, sites. Pottery from the Armada wrecks, for example, has made a major contribution to **Ceramic studies**. Some types are unique to particular ships, and can be related to their pre-Armada associations, while others are common to all the wrecks and can therefore be identified with official issues made before the fleet sailed. One piece tells a very particular story. It is a bowl of Ming porcelain, recovered intact from the wreck of *La Trinidad Valencera*. We may reasonably surmise that it was brought to Europe by way of the transpacific Manila galleons from the Philippines to Acapulco, whence it was mule-packed across the Isthmus of Panama to connect with the treasure fleets bound for Seville. There it came into the possession of a wealthy Spanish gentleman destined to sail with the Armada aboard a ship which would eventually founder in a lonely Irish bay. C.M.

ADDITIONAL READING

Gallagher, P. and Cruikshank, D. (eds), 1990, *God's Obvious Design*, London.

Martin, C., 1975, *Full Fathom Five: Wrecks of the Spanish Armada*, London and New York.

Martin, C.J.M., 1979, 'Spanish Armada Pottery', *International Journal of Nautical Archaeology*, 8, 4, 279–302.

Martin, C. and Parker, G., 1988, *The Spanish Armada*, London.

Pierson, P., 1989, *Commander of the Armada*, New Haven and London.

Sparrow Hawk

Remains of a hull believed to date to the 17th century. The bottom and lower part of the stern are all that survive of an old hull found on the east coast of Cape Cod at Pleasant Bay. Although it had been seen

from time to time in the 18th century, it was uncovered again by a storm in 1863. Shortly after that the remains were removed to Boston where they were reassembled and displayed briefly. The vessel's present and permanent home is in the Seventeenth-Century Ship Room in Pilgrim Hall, Plymouth, Massachusetts. Several reputable historians have presented evidence that this is what survives of *Sparrow Hawk*, a colonial ketch that wrecked on the east coast of Cape Cod in 1626 on its way to Plymouth. It is said to have carried forty people on board at the time. Although the identification has been disputed, the remains obviously represent a very old vessel. The arrangement of the extant timbers appears similar to documented construction of small seagoing vessels of the colonial American period. Its age and origin are fortified by the fact that all the hull structure is made from oak except the keel, which has been fashioned from English elm. Measurements taken from the remains in Pilgrim Hall reveal a hull that was no more than 40 ft (12 m) long. R.S.2

ADDITIONAL READING

Holly, H.H., 1969, 'Sparrow-Hawk: A Seventeenth Century Vessel in Twentieth Century America', Pilgrim Society, Plymouth, MA, reprinted from *American Neptune*, 1953, 13, 1.

Steffy, R.J., 1988, 'The Thirteen Colonies: English Settlers and Seafarers', in G.F. Bass (ed.), *Ships and Shipwrecks of the Americas*, London.

Steamboat archaeology in North America

The archaeological study of the steamboat era in North America (1811–1961). During this time there were an estimated 16,000 steamboats on the Mississippi River and its tributaries. In addition there were probably 3,500 more steamboats in the Canadian provinces, the Yukon Territory, California, Oregon, Washington, and Idaho. The steamboat's rapid rise in early 19th-century America attracted little contemporary historical limelight. Unlike railroading, steamboating's early history was minimally chronicled until much later and many glaring gaps remain throughout the literature.

Most people are not aware of how many different types of steamboats there were during the 19th century. Even though steamboats tended to have certain generic qualities, there were many regional differences in their architecture, construction, machinery, and aesthetics that gave them an incredible diversity. What is unusual about the steamboat is that it is the one purely American art and engineering form that evolved without European influences. The

huge, elegant side wheel steamboats of the Mississippi River during the 1860s and 1870s have become the icons of American history known throughout the world. Despite their massive size and speed, steamboats were surprisingly delicate ephemeral entities. Few steamboats survived a decade, for most were lost in fires and in sinkings.

As a result, the rivers of North America were filled with the wrecks of thousands of steamboats. The US Army Corps of Engineers routinely considered sunken steamboats hazards to navigation and quickly removed them with snag boats, dynamite, etc. without regard to their preservation or study.

Insurance companies immediately salvaged wrecked steamboats. If one was not salvaged, it was usually not worth the salvage effort. Salvaged boilers, pumps, engines, and other parts were normally recycled from one wrecked boat to another. After salvaging, many steamboat wreckages were left *in situ* when they were no longer obstructions in the navigational channels. Accordingly, a large number of steamboat wrecks were left undisturbed and forgotten for many years.

Unlike many fabled saltwater ships, steamboats seldom carried large precious cargoes. Because of this, steamboat wrecks usually involve historic artefacts instead of fabulous treasures. Anything worth taking was probably taken long ago, if it were accessible. Valuable cargoes were usually mercury, whisky, and gold. For the most part, steamboats handled mundane cargo items, especially when heading to frontier areas.

The free-flowing rivers of the United States are now few. Most navigable rivers have been improved with locks and dams to provide navigation and flood control. These improvements have inundated many steamboat wrecks from long ago that await discovery by underwater archaeologists. Our general knowledge of steamboating is surprisingly limited; and yet this seems incongruous in light of the literary attention that steamboating received in the 1880s when Samuel L. Clemens wrote his memoirs about his four years on the Mississippi, 1857–61.

Despite its noteworthy role in American literature, the steamboat's contribution to America's economy, engineering, and technology was appreciated by few contemporaries; and that oblivious tendency continues even today. The first writer to realize the steamboat's complex economic role was E.W. Gould. In 1889 he published *Gould's History of River Navigation*. He focused on the development of the steamboat and chronicled the steamboat industry with biographies of prominent figures of steamboating. Gould blazed a Herodotean trail generally overlooked by other historians.

A scholarly approach to steamboating history did not come until the 20th century. Much of the information was preserved in the river columns of newspapers and in government records; but researching these voluminous sources in the original materials or later microfilm is tedious and laborious. Few academics have ventured into the topic, mainly because of its staggering complexity. The study of steamboats is a large scholarly province that has yet to be fully researched. Acquiring a decent knowledge of steamboats usually takes a lifetime rather than the brief time needed for two advanced degrees. This is the reason that so few academics have dealt with the topic.

The late Captain Frederick Way, Jr (1901–92) was one of a handful of 20th-century historians who realized the steamboat's enormous role in American history. Way did much to systematize steamboating history and developed two useful directories for packets and towboats. Although Way was not a scholarly sort, he preserved much information and diligently collected photographs to document the steamboat's evolution.

Louis C. Hunter's monumental *Steamboats on the Western Rivers* of 1949 viewed the steamboat as an economic and engineering entity. Professor Hunter realized that a huge historic vacuum existed about this topic and took a definitive step to fill that void. Hunter was one of the few academics who left an indelible mark in steamboating research.

Synthesizing river history from the many fragmented sources is extremely time-consuming; however, it has been done with excellent results. For example, Captain William H. Tippitt (1900-) is now the oldest living steamboat pilot. He was a riverman, a collector, and a historian whose genius was viewing many historical sources that many others overlooked. What Captain Frederick Way, Jr was to the Upper Ohio River, Captain Tippitt is to the Mississippi from St Louis to New Orleans. A handful of serious collectors, such as the late Ray Samuel and Leonard Huber, both of New Orleans, Ruth Ferris of St Louis and Bert Fenn of Tell City, Indiana were instrumental in preserving steamboat artefacts. In their writings they viewed steamboats for historic accuracy rather than nostalgia.

Steamboats were generally built with a minimum of specifications and without blueprints in the modern sense until the advent of iron and steel hulls. As a result, it was difficult to fully understand and appreciate the design of steamboats until the 1950s. It was then that Alan L. Bates (1920–), a marine architect of Louisville, Kentucky, began using photogrammetric techniques to develop model plans for many steamboats that were not built with plans in the first place. Bates's contribution to steamboating research was to single-handedly enable steamboat design to become a form that could be studied.

Because steamboats were such pragmatic ephemeral entities, they were considered disposable. Although many steamboats were fondly remembered, they were not preserved. Occasionally snag boats would have display cases to show certain interesting artefacts found while destroying steamboat wrecks. As a result there was no such discipline as steamboat archaeology until the 1960s. Steamboat parts and machinery were so large that the most opulent collectors could not house large steamboat artefacts.

Even though many knew where certain steamboat wrecks were located, people tended to leave them alone; but there were occasional exploration of known wreckages. For example, the badly deteriorated remains of the Confederate *Charm* on the Black River in Mississippi were found in the 1960s. Many of *Charm*'s artefacts have been preserved at Grand Gulf, Mississippi.

In 1964 the late Dr Walter Johnston of Vicksburg, Mississippi, a giant figure in steamboat preservation, spearheaded a move to raise the remains of USS *Cairo* from the Yazoo River. Unfortunately, Dr Johnston lost his footing and fell overboard and drowned during that recovery. After a lengthy State vs. Federal government dispute over ownership, *Cairo*'s remains were eventually placed in a museum on the grounds of the Vicksburg Battlefield fifteen years after they were first raised. *Cairo* is probably the first legitimate effort that could be called 'steamboat archaeology'.

In 1968, *Bertrand*, a wreck of 1865, was found at Missouri Valley, Iowa, and the formal discipline of 'steamboat archaeology' began its rapid evolution. *Bertrand*'s cargo for a mining town gave considerable insight into contemporary frontier life of the 1860s and her intact hull provided incontrovertible evidence for steamboat construction. During the 1970s there were many scattered archaeological finds, though nothing nearly comparable to *Bertrand*'s discovery. Historic preservation became a more focused discipline in the late 1970s and legislation was gradually written to preserve steamboat wrecks. Throughout the 1980s many notable steamboat wrecks were located and surveyed. In 1987 low water near Memphis revealed a long-forgotten boneyard that contained several steamboat hulls and a model barge that had been deposited there long ago.

The most exciting steamboat archaeological find came in late 1987. It was then that the Hawley family of Independence, Missouri, found the remains of *Arabia*, a wreck of 1856, in a cornfield near the Missouri River. *Arabia* was 13.7 m below the ground and reaching her required lowering the water table with a number of diesel-powered pumps running around the clock. This was a privately funded archaeological effort and a stunning victory against staggering odds. The Hawleys established a superlative museum for the remains of *Arabia* at Kansas City, Missouri in 1991. The Arabia Steamboat Museum has drawn worldwide attention to steamboat archaeology.

In only thirty-two years 'steamboat archaeology' has become a distinct field of learning. Underwater archaeologists have amassed much knowledge about steamboats' construction, development, and technology.

The most propitious trend of the 1990s has been steamboat historians joining forces with archaeologist to share their knowledge and champion their mutual cause of learning more about the past. Steamboat archaeology still remains a relatively new field of learning. The inland rivers of North America have a tremendous number of boat wrecks eminently worthy of study. The problem is that there are so many that we can easily have dissertation topics to last for several centuries.

The important challenge for future underwater archaeologists is to understand the broad divisions and categories of steamboats. Instead of seeking to find every wreck, our greatest knowledge will come from studying the various types of steamboats, their evolution, their technology, their designers, and their builders. J.E.C.

ADDITIONAL READING

Bates, A.S., 1968, *The Western Rivers Steamboat Cyclopoedium*, Leonia, New Jersey.

Hawley, D.J., 1995, *Treasures of the Steamboat Arabia*, Kansas City, Missouri.

Hunter, L.C., 1949, *Steamboats on the Western Rivers: An Economic and Technological History*, Cambridge, Massachusetts.

Petsche, J.E., 1974, *The Steamboat Bertrand: History, Excavation and Architecture*, Washington DC.

Way, F., Jr, 1964, *Way's Steamboat Directory*, abridged pocket edn, Sewickley, Pennsylvania.

Sterling

Wreck of 1855 submerged in the Sacramento River, and the first shipwreck from the California Gold Rush discovered and documented on an inland waterway. Built in 1833 at Duxbury, Massachusetts, the brig *Sterling* was a 201 ton vessel engaged in the American eastern coastal trade. Like many other merchant vessels, *Sterling* was caught up in the California Gold Rush, sailing for San Francisco in January 1849 with seven passengers and cargo. The brig arrived at San Francisco in July. Within a month *Sterling* had sailed up the rivers that connected San Francisco Bay with the interior. By 1850 the brig was serving as a floating warehouse off the growing city of Sacramento, the 'gateway to the gold fields'. There the brig served until it sank at its moorings during the winter of 1855.

The remains of *Sterling* were discovered during a **Side scan sonar** survey of the Sacramento River in 1984. The remains of *Sterling* lie under 9 m of water, perpendicular to the shore on its port side. The port hull is buried beneath silt and sand; the starboard hull extends to a level just above the waterline near the sheerstrake. Inside the hull, which lies open because the decks are missing, at least one breast hook remains in place. The stub of the foremast is stepped into the keelson.

The remains of *Sterling*, like those of the nearby Gold Rush wreck *LaGrange*, are among a group of substantially well-preserved vessels from the California Gold Rush that include the buried hulks of *William Gray* and *Niantic* in San Francisco. These vessels, caught up in a massive maritime migration to California, are a sample of 'typical' American sailing craft of the mid-19th century and as such are a collection worthy of study to determine the characteristics and construction of these largely undocumented vessels. J.P.D.

ADDITIONAL READING

Delgado, J.P., 1996, *To California by Sea: A Maritime History of the Gold Rush*, Columbia, California.

Stirling Castle

British man of war wrecked off the east coast of England in the 'Great Gale' of 1703. *Stirling Castle* was a 70 gun third-rate ship built by John Shish in Deptford, one of four English line-of-battle ships wrecked on the Goodwin Sands, off the east coast of Kent, during the 'Great Gale' of November 1703 (other losses included the third-rates *Northumberland* and *Restoration*, and the fourth-rate *Mary*, flagship of Rear Admiral Sir Basil Beaumont's naval squadron). As a result of the dreadful weather conditions (described by Daniel Defoe) many merchantmen and naval ships were caught in the Downs, a favoured shelter between the Goodwin

Sands and the Kent coast. On 26 November 1703 the wind increased to hurricane force, and a large number of vessels were lost, the storm lasting from midnight until six the next morning. The storm cost the Navy fifteen warships, Admiral Beaumont, 1,500 seamen, and smaller craft. *Stirling Castle* was under the command of John Johnson; only 70 of her crew of 349 were saved.

The site was first investigated in 1979 by a group of local amateur divers in conjunction with the local archaeological society, the Isle of Thanet Archaeological Unit, following the investigation of a fisherman's net fastening in the area. At the time of discovery, winter gales had stripped a large part of the hull of the plateau of sand which had protected it, so that the remains stood about 6 m proud of the seabed. The structure had a length of approximately 55 m and maximum beam of approximately 18 m, greater than the recorded dimensions of *Stirling Castle* (46.33 × 12.34 × 5.38 m), indicative of hogging and partial collapse. In places, gun deck levels and gun ports could be seen, and some guns remained on their carriages.

A large number of artefacts were raised from the site; some are now in the National Maritime Museum, Greenwich, and some in the museum at Ramsgate. Finds included a bronze bell bearing the broad arrow mark, dated 1701; two large copper kettles; stone and brick from the galley area; a small bronze gun ornamented with a ship in full sail between breech and dolphins, and bearing the inscription ASWERUS KOSTER ME FECIT AMSTELREDAMI ANNO 1642, and a broad arrow chiselled onto it after capture. Other armament included musketoon barrels, musket stocks, lead shot, and brass sword hilts. Of particular importance are the remains of a wooden cross-staff, a Gunter's scale, nine pairs of dividers, and a complete set of sand glasses, one in working condition. Personal property was also recovered, including a large quantity of pewter, earthenware, stoneware, and clothing, much of it from the stern area.

The site was designated of archaeological and historical importance under the **Protection of Wrecks Act** (1973) in 1980. Since then the sands have moved, and the wreck has collapsed. In 1983 Marine Archaeological Surveys conducted a geophysical survey of the west side of the Goodwins, over the sites of *Stirling Castle* and *Northumberland*, in an assessment of the archaeological potential of the area. The site remains under licence for survey work, but diving conditions slow progress. M.R.

ADDITIONAL READING

Defoe, D., 1704, *The Storm: or A Collection of the Most Remarkable Casualties and Disasters which Happened in the Late Dreadful Tempest, Both by Sea and Land*, London.

Lyon, D.J., 1980, 'The Goodwins Wreck', *International Journal of Nautical Archaeology*, 9, 339–50.

Perkins, D.R.J., 1979, *Wreck of a British Man-of-war Discovered on the Goodwin Sands: Interim Report (1979)*, Isle of Thanet Archaeological Unit, Isle of Thanet.

Redknap, M. and Fleming, M., 1985, 'The Goodwins Archaeological Survey: Towards a Regional Maritime Register in Britain', *World Archaeology*, 16, 312–28.

Straits of Messina Wreck

The so-called Porticello Ship, a medium-size merchantman, possibly of Greek origin, which sank in the Straits of Messina about 400 BC near what is today the modern village of Porticello, Italy. The wreck was found in 1969 by Calabrese fishermen who were attracted by the large number of rock fish that lived around the remains of the ancient ship. These fishermen looted the site of approximately 100 amphoras, various small pieces of pottery, several anchors, and fragments of bronze sculpture, but after a falling-out among them over a divsion of the spoils, one of the looters revealed the location of the wreck to the authorities.

The site was first mapped by Franco Colosimo, who, upon realizing the importance of the site and that a scientific excavation was needed, requested that the superintendent of antiquities of Calabria, Dr Giuseppe Foti, enlist the aid of the University of Pennsylvania. David I. Owen, assistant curator of the University Museum's Underwater Archaeology Section, organized an expedition during the summer of 1970 with a team of sixteen divers.

Based on the distribution of the wreckage, the hull was estimated at 16 to 17 m long with a capacity of 30 tons. The hull remains were fragmentary, but enough remained to indicate that the hull planking was edge-joined in the Classical tradition with pegged mortise-and-tenon joints. The frames were attached to the strakes with copper nails which were driven in from the outer face of the planking and then clenched over the frames. In places where the frames were not flush with the planking, wedge-shaped shims were hammered between the planking and the lower faces of the frames. Small lead patches, the earliest evidence for lead sheathing, were nailed to the hull planking, probably to stop leaks, suggesting that the Porticello Ship had been sailing the Mediterranean for a number of years. The vessel was a typical merchant ship of the Classical period, modest in size but capable of sailing long distances.

Anchor fragments were found amidships on both the port and starboard sides and at the bow. The looters recovered lead cores of wood stocks weighing 125 kg, 350 kg, and 1,000 kg; previously, the earliest evidence for wooden stocks with lead cores was the mid-4th century BC. The shanks and arms of the anchors were made of wood, with bronze teeth attached to the ends of the arms.

The lack of hearth tiles or braziers make it impossible to determine if there was a galley or if cooking was even done on board, but the coarsewares used by the crew, which consist of bosals, lamps, *lopades*, a cup-skyphos, a *chytra*, an *oinochoe*, and a mortar, were found in the area believed to represent the stern of the ship. The bosals, oil lamps, and skyphos are of Athenian manufacture. The lopades and chytra are similar to Attic examples, but the mortar and oinochoe are clearly non-Attic and of unknown origin. Based on the coarsewares, the ship is dated to 415–385 BC. The stern area also yielded whetstones for sharpening knives and tools, cake ingots and nuggets of lead, and small lead weights for fishing to help supplement the crew's diet. The distribution of the fishing weights, cake ingots, and nuggets indicates that all were stored in the same area and probably in the same container. The ingots and nuggets, mainly of lead with a high concentration of silver, were probably used to make fishing weights, lead sheathing for the hull, brail rings for the rigging, anchor rings, and to repair or replace other items during the voyage. All of the Porticello lead, except for the anchor stocks, is from Laurion in Greece.

The thirty-three amphoras recovered by the archaeologists consist of four basic types, two from Mende and Byzantion in the northern Aegean, and two of a western Mediterranean tradition, Greek and Punic; the interiors of most were sealed with resin. The amphoras from Byzantion, Mende, and an as yet unidentified city are believed to have carried wine, while the Punic amphoras carried salted fish. The Mendean amphoras date to the end of the 5th century to the early 4th century BC.

The earliest examples of ink pots were also recovered from the wreck site. These baseless, spherical vessels with double mouths were intended to carry ink in either liquid or paste form. The cargo also contained an undetermined number of lead bar ingots, a number of which were melted down after being sold by the looters. All of the surviving bar ingots originated at the site of Laurion.

Twenty-two pieces of bronze statues were recovered. The composition of the bronze suggests that all the statues were cast in the same workshop. The stylistic unity between pieces also indicates a coherent group, which supports the hypothesis that all the pieces were commissioned from one workshop. The style of the statues dates them to

A life-size bronze head of a bearded male from the Straits of Messina Wreck. (© INA)

the third quarter of the 5th century, approximately twenty-five years before they were lost at sea. The location of the workshop is unknown, but it was probably in Greece proper or Magna Graecia, south Italy. It has been proposed that the statues were being sold for scrap, but it is also possible that they were originally commissioned for a buyer in Greece and years later were en route to a second buyer in Magna Graecia. The sculptures are believed to depict an elderly, and probably monstrous, mythological creature, at least two young men in athletic nudity, and possibly a third figure in a short garment, all forming a narrative group. It is unlikely, although also possible, that they were independent statues.

On its last voyage this ship may have been practising cabotage, starting by acquiring wine at Byzantion and then more wine at Mende, lead at Laurion, the bronze statues and more wine from unknown Greek ports, and then salted fish from a southern Italian or Sicilian port. S.M.2

ADDITIONAL READING
Eiseman, C.J., 1975, 'The Porticello Shipwreck', *INA Newsletter*, 2, 1, 1–4.

Eiseman, C.J. and Ridgway, B.S., 1987, *The Porticello Wreck: A Mediterranean Merchant Vessel of 415–385 BC*, College Station, Texas.
Owen, D., 1970, 'Picking Up the Pieces: The Salvage Excavation of a Looted Fifth Century BC Shipwreck in the Straits of Messina', *Expedition*, 13, 24–9.

Studland Bay Wreck

A lightly armed Spanish merchant vessel of *c.*1520–30 wrecked in 12 m of water just outside Poole Harbour on the south coast of England. It is similar to early 16th-century wrecks at **Molasses Reef**, **Highborn Cay**, Boudouse Cay, **Padre Island**, and the later **Red Bay** wreck, *San Juan*.

Nine seasons of fieldwork by Keith Jarvis and Ian Horsey took place between 1984 and 1922 when they excavated three areas of wreckage: area one (starboard side); area two (keel and floor timbers); and area three (ordnance and finds). The vessel probably lost heavy objects in area three and sank in area two. The starboard side probably moved along the seabed later.

G. Hutchinson has made an initial assessment of the area one wreck, which consists of the entire length of the carvel-built starboard side and is 22.5 m long and 3.5 m wide. All hull timbers are of oak, and treenails and nails were used to attach the planking to the frames. Various timbers have been preserved including the important keel/sternpost assembly and the floor/first futtock dovetail joint. L. Ladle's booklet *The Studland Bay Wreck* also summarizes results to date.

Wrought-iron ordnance includes four- and six-inch breech blocks and a six-inch gun with fragments of an oak carriage. Nine stone cannon balls have diameters of 2.25, 3, and 6 in (5.7, 7.6 and 15.3 cm).

One important find was the walnut foot and leather flapper of a pump, which can be compared with those from *Mary Rose* and Red Bay. Leather finds included three welted shoes and there were rare examples of straw matting. Wooden finds included a bowl, two boxwood combs, an ointment canister, and a beech book cover. More functional finds included a deadeye, an oak comb-like object and oak cask components. The pottery finds included many exotic Valencian lustrewares and Isabela polychrome plates. Also present are a Saintonge pegaux and a Breton rim. Merida-type Portuguese coarsewares include three red micaceous costrels and a costrel of Basque type. Other finds included an upper quern stone and 200 iron objects which are mainly nails but include a rigging chain linkage. The ballast, which is 55 per cent of Basque type, included four main types – granite, ironstone, limestone, and olivine dolerite. Some bone and wheat, fig, and pepper seeds were also recovered.

The finds of Spanish lustrewares and Sevillian Isabela polychrome are probably from a basket of cargo on the vessel's last voyage from southern Spain or Portugal. The date of the sinking is about 1520-30 and is based on the pottery and leather evidence. Merida-type and other coarsewares used by the crew suggest Iberian nationality.

The vessel construction is strikingly similar to the Basque Red Bay vessel and could suggest it was built in the Basque region. The oak used for the hull occurs in northern Europe down to central Spain. The ballast, of which some could be primary ballast from the construction, is also partly Basque. K.J.

ADDITIONAL READING

Hutchinson, G. (1991) 'The Early Sixteenth Century Wreck at Studland Bay, Dorset', in R. Reinders and K. Paul (eds), *Carvel Construction Technique Fiftieth International Symposium on Boat and Ship Archaeology, Amsterdam 1988*, Oxbow 12, 171-5.

Ladle, L. (1993) *The Studland Bay Wreck*, Poole Museum Heritage Series No. 1, Poole.

Sub-bottom profiler

An acoustic tool for mapping the sediments below the surface of the sea bed and for detecting shipwrecks, artefacts and other material of archaeological interest. The sub-bottom profiler is a specialized sonar technique in which short pulses of acoustic energy are transmitted directly at the sea bed in conical shaped beams from a moving vessel or an underwater towed vehicle. The return echoes from the seabed and from sediments below the seabed are electronically processed and continuously recorded on a graphic display to create an image called a sub-bottom profile. These images show the sediment layers in cross section, similar to viewing the side of a piece of layer cake.

A typical sub-bottom profiler system includes a towfish, a towing cable, and a graphic recorder. The towfish contains transducers that convert electrical impulses into low-frequency sounds. These same transducers may receive the acoustic echoes and convert these signals to electrical energy. Alternatively, a separate underwater hydro-phone may receive the signals. The received signals are then sent up the tow cable to the graphic recorder on the ship. The graphic recorder further processes the signals and creates a permanent display on a paper chart.

In general, lower acoustic frequencies tend to penetrate the bottom sediments more easily. However, the resolution of a sub-bottom profiler increases with higher frequencies. Therefore, profiler systems tend to be a compromise between penetration depth and resolution. Since cultural resources of archaeological interest tend to be in shallow sediments, sub-bottom profilers for archaeological use typically use relatively high frequencies (5–20 kHz). By contrast, sub-bottom profilers for other

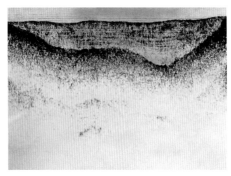

A typical high-resolution sub-bottom profile of the seabed showing sediment layers. (Courtesy Klein Associates, Inc.)

fields, such as oil exploration, use very low frequencies in order to penetrate deep into the bottom.

Sub-bottom profilers are an outgrowth of early sonar (an abbreviation for Sound Navigation And Ranging) systems which were used as depth-finders or echo-sounders to determine the water depth below a ship. Originally these units only had enough energy to detect the bottom echo. However, as the instruments increased in power, it was observed that some of the sound would penetrate the bottom and reflect off layers below the bottom.

In the late 1950s Professor Harold E. Edgerton of the Massachusetts Institute of Technology worked with Jacques Cousteau to lower a camera to the deepest part of the ocean. In order to position the camera, Edgerton used a precisely timed conical-beam 12 kHz echo-sounder transducer aimed at the bottom with a very short, high intensity sound beam. Edgerton observed that the sonar records revealed sub-bottom sediment layers. In October 1967 Dr Edgerton, John Mills and Robert Henderson, working with Alexander McKee, used a **Side scan sonar** in combination with a sub-bottom profiler to locate King Henry VIII's flagship *Mary Rose*, which sank in 1545.

Unlike side scan sonar, the sub-bottom profiler does not cover a wide swath, so it is not as effective as a primary search tool for submerged cultural resources. This is because the sub-bottom profiler only covers a relatively small area directly below the transducer. Also the profiler does not create the same kind of sonograph or sonar 'picture' as a side scan sonar, so that interpretation of the records is much more challenging. For this reason, the profiler is often used in conjunction with a side scan sonar or a metal detector or **Magnetometer**. Although it is a less effective search tool, the profiler can still be a very useful tool for pinpointing and determining the approximate size of a buried target whose location is closely known. The profiler may also help the archaeologist study near-bottom sedimentation patterns to determine the likelihood that targets may be buried. Buried artefacts may also be discovered by noting disturbances to the sedimentation patterns.

In modern sub-bottom profiler systems the sonar signals are converted to digital form, which allows for a wide variety of signal enhancements. Besides the 'hard copy', sonar records may be displayed on computer cathode-ray-tubes, and colour may assist interpretation. Digital processing also allows the images to be expanded to show additional details. Modern sub-bottom profiler systems may be integrated with side scan systems and with electronic positioning systems so that targets may be accurately positioned and relocated. Sonar survey information may now be stored on a variety of digital storage devices for later retrieval, analysis, and processing. M.K.

ADDITIONAL READING

Edgerton, H.E., Linder, E., and Klein, M., 1967, 'Sonar Search at Ashdod, Israel', *National Geographic Society Research Reports – 1967 Projects*, Washington, DC.

Edgerton, H.E. and Throckmorton, P., 1969, 'Exploring Subbottom Features of a Harbor with Sonar and Magnetometer', *National Geographic Society Research Reports – 1969 Projects*, Washington, DC.

Klein, M. and Edgerton, H.E., 1968, 'Sonar: A Modern Technique for Ocean Exploitation' *IEEE Spectrum*, June.

Milne, P.H., 1980, *Underwater Engineering Surveys*, London.

Pace, N.G. (ed.), 1983, *Conference Proceedings: Acoustics and the Seabed*, Bath, UK.

Trabant, P.K., 1984, *Applied High-Resolution Geophysical Methods*, Boston, Massachusetts.

Yules, J.A. and Edgerton, H.E., 1964, 'Bottom Sonar Search Techniques' *Undersea Technology*, November.

Submarine coring

A method of obtaining sediments, at and below the sediment-water interface, with a minimum of mixing or disturbance to the sedimentary section penetrated. The main types of coring equipment used for obtaining cohesive muddy sediments include the giant and standard piston corers, box corer, gravity corer, and stationary piston or fixed reference piston corer. Vibrocores use vibrating core heads to obtain samples of coarse sand and gravel, while rockcore drills are used for acquiring samples of consolidated sediments (bedrock). Gravity or piston coring is the most common method utilized when sampling sub-bottom unconsolidated sediments from the marine environment.

More than a hundred years ago, ocean sediment coring developed as a by-product of water depth measurements. The equipment then consisted of a tube with an added lead weight that was lowered to the ocean bottom with the aid of piano wire, called a Sigsbee machine. In 1935, Piggott further developed this same principle by manufacturing a steel tube that could be pushed into the sea-floor by means of a lead weight. Coring techniques continued to develop in response to unique requirements such as determination of depth of penetration or sediment type. In spite of these developments, sediment penetration and sample quality have remained below expectation.

Corers are simple but highly variable in design. They generally consist of a large headweight, to which is attached a steel barrel of varying lengths. A core cutter and a catcher are located within the lowermost pipe or barrel to both penetrate and retain the sediment acquired from the free-fall energy of the coring headweight. The standard piston corer, as developed by Kullenburg in 1947 to overcome depth penetration limitation within sediments, is still in use. This piston and split piston design permits the collection of virtually undisturbed, unconsolidated sediments, by the removal of residual water in the core pipe during coring operation. The piston is located above a core retainer at the bottom of the coring tube. A retrieving wire leads through the entire core barrel and head, where it is attached to a release mechanism. A safety pin prevents premature tripping of the corer before deployment. The coring tube is secured to the core head by a coupling. Gravity cores are frequently used as trigger weights for piston corers. In addition, they often obtain a more representative record of the surface sediment compared to that obtained by the main piston corer. Core barrel diameter may vary from between 7 and 11 cm internal diameter, to a maximum of 9 to 12 cm outside diameter. Overall coupled core length may vary from 2 to 60 m.

Although several models of corers are manufactured and in current use for different applications, the basic operating principles remain the same. A core head consists of a lead weight with guide vanes, hoisting plate, piston stop, and a nose onto which core barrels can be coupled. Several tubes may be coupled together, into which lengths of plastic liner (cellulose acetate butyrate) are deployed, to retain any acquired sediment. The lower portion of the last pipe is left open, to permit passage of sediments upon penetration. Once filled with sediments, a core catcher or core retainer's stainless steel fingers prevent the sediments from slipping out of the core barrel upon retrieval to the sea surface. The core head contains a tripping mechanism comprised of a trip arm and release, strategically placed to induce tripping by the fulcrum method. Measurements of physical lengths and angles of the various coring components determines the maximum head weights (average 1,000 kg), minimum and maximum corer penetration (up to 60 m), as well as the overall diameter and strength of the retrieving wire to be deployed. Mass physical and acoustic properties of the sediments obtained can be calculated utilizing these measurements.

Once retrieved, sediment cores retained in liners are carefully removed from the steel barrels, by pushing the sediment liners out of the coring pipe. Commencing with the uppermost pipe, cores are extruded from top to bottom sequentially. The core cutter and catcher are removed with the bottom portion of the extruded coreliner. Cores are stored vertically at all times and sealed to prevent further oxidation of the sediments. They may be refrigerated at 4° C to retard mould growth and desiccation. The sediments from the trigger weight corer are stored in a similar manner.

Principally stimulated by questions on global climate changes, new coring methods are being considered and evaluated, in an attempt to acquire deeper penetration of the sedimentary sections as well as improve recovery of sediment samples. Improvements in coring technology include the French Calypso, the Norwegian hydrostatically powered Selcore gravity corer system, the British Cambridge Kasten corer, STACOR (giant piston corer), bottom mounted remotely operated corers, accurate ship positioning, and high resolution seismic reflection of coring sites prior to actual core acquisition. Developments such as these will meet the demands for modelling ocean-atmosphere interaction, in order to reconstruct paleoclimate signals of previous glacial cycles. Corer penetration up to 60 m and core diameters sufficient to permit multiple sub-sampling across boundaries for climate change studies, will increase resolution from tens of millions of years to decadal time scales.

These improvements suggest increased utility of submarine coring to questions of direct archaeological concern, including improved mapping of submerged paleo-shorelines, and sampling of potential archaeological sites. I.A.H.

ADDITIONAL READING

Alpine Geophysical Associates, Inc., 1965, *Instruction Manual for Sediment Coring Apparatus, Models 202, 203, 204, 205, and 206.*

Benthos, Inc., 1968, *Instruction Manual Models 2170 and 2171 Gravity Corers IM2170,71,*

Buckley, D.E. *et al.,* 1994, 'Problems with Piston Core Sampling: Mechanical and Geochemical Diagnosis', *Marine Geology,* 117, 95–106.

Heintze, C., 1979, *The Bottom of the Sea and Beyond,* Nashville, Tennessee.

Kermabon, A. *et al.,* 1966, 'The "Sphincter" Corer: A Wide Diameter Corer with Watertight Core-catcher', *Marine Geology,* 4, 149–62.

Kullenberg, B., 1947, 'The Piston Core Sampler', *Svenska Hydrografisk-Biologiska Kommissionens Skrifter n.s. 3,* 1, 2, 1–46.

Kullenberg, B., 1955, 'Deep-sea Coring', *Report of the Swedish Deep-Sea Expedition,* 4, Bottom Investigation, 2, 37–96.

Nesje, A., 1992, 'A Piston Corer for Lacustrine and Marine Sediments', *Arctic and Alpine Research,* 24, 257–9.

Piggot, C.S., 1941, 'Factors Involved in Marine Core Sampling', *Bulletin of the Geological Society of America,* 52, 1513–24.

'Proceedings for Workshop', *International Coring for Global Change ICGC,* 28–30 June 1995, Kiel, Germany.

Sandvik, K.O. and Skinner, A., 1990, 'Offshore Diamond Coring Systems: A Review of Known Systems and a Comparison with the ODP Diamond Coring System', *Proceedings of the Ocean Drilling Program, Initial Report,* 124E–104, 41–4.

Seibold, E. and Berger, W.H., 1993, *The Sea Floor, an Introduction to Marine Geology.*

Walin, G.W. and Olsson, I., 1993, 'Professor Borje Kullenberg 1906–91', ICES International Council for the Exploration of the Sea, *ICES Journal of Marine Science,* 50, 1, 101–2.

Weaver, P.P.E. and Schultheiss, P.J., 1990, 'Current Methods for Obtaining, Logging and Splitting Marine Sediment Cores', *Marine Geophysical Researches,* 12, 1–2, 85–100.

Zangger, E. and McCave, I.N., 1990, 'A Redesigned Kasten Core Barrel and Sampling Technique', *Marine Geology,* 94, 165–71.

Submerged Cultural Resources Unit

The underwater archaeology team of the US National Park Service (NPS). The Submerged Cultural Resources Unit (SCRU) was formed in 1980 at the end of the **National Reservoir Inundation Study** (NRIS). When its task of assessing damage to archaeology from reservoir construction was completed, the NPS used the principal personnel and equipment assets of the NRIS in the establishment of a permanent capability to address underwater archaeology needs in the parks. Daniel Lenihan, former director of the NRIS, was named as first chief of the new unit and two archaeologists from the old study (Larry Murphy and Toni Carrell) also moved to the new team.

The SCRU is charged with conducting underwater research and resources management activities in the sixty-one areas of the US National Park System that have such needs. They have also worked on many sites in the present and former Trust Territories of the Pacific, in state waters, and on sites important to the American people in foreign waters. At the time of writing, they comprise the only operational field team of underwater archaeologists in the Federal government.

SCRU is composed of eight members including archaeologists, an underwater photographer, GIS and GPS survey specialists and a publications coordinator. They have become noted for a fast, accurate, yet minimally intrusive style of shipwreck investigation. Members of this team pioneered **Baseline trilateration** as a viable underwater technique during documentation studies of shipwrecks at **Isle Royale** National Park in Lake Superior and mapping large warships in **Pearl Harbor**. They have become leaders in the application of **Global Positioning System** (GPS) and **Geographic Information Systems** (GIS) technologies to shipwreck investigations.

The Submerged Cultural Resources Unit has actively used partnering with other entities as a strategy for accomplishing its historic preservation mission. The initial association with the **US Navy** in 1983 and 1984 to accomplish mapping goals on USS **Arizona** was later formalized into a relationship known as Project Seamark. This at first emphasized using small groups of Navy reservists on their active duty training exercises to augment SCRU diving staff and by 1988 had expanded to large projects employing hundreds of Navy divers on projects conducted in places as diverse as Koror Harbour in Palau and New York Harbour.

SCRU has at times also utilized large numbers of volunteer divers and engaged in cooperative ventures with the **National Geographic Society** and various museums. An example of the latter is work conducted in association with the Columbia River Maritime Museum on the 1830 wreck of *Isabella* on the Columbia River Bar. It was also on this site that the developing relationship between SCRU and the NPS National Maritime Initiative based out of its Washington office became formalized. James P. Delgado, chief maritime historian for the Service, worked closely with the archaeological team on this site and began officially serving as member of the team when he was engaged in archaeological activities. This internal arrangement in the NPS, as in its external partnerships, served to increase the impact of the small team of underwater specialists.

Major projects conducted by the unit include the documentation of ten shipwreck sites at Isle Royale, the mapping of the remains of USS *Arizona* and USS **Utah** in Pearl Harbor, the comprehensive underwater remote sensing survey of Biscayne and **Dry Tortugas National Park** and the resurvey of the ships sunk in Bikini Atoll Lagoon during Operation Crossroads, the US 1946 atomic bomb tests (see **Crossroads Wrecks**).

The unit also conducted a survey of Kiska Harbour in the Aleutian islands in 1989 in association with the US Navy and various surveys of park waters on the California coast. Included in the latter was work at Channel Islands National Park and Point Reyes National Seashore. In addition, SCRU has been active in shipwreck studies off Cape Cod and Fire Island National Seashores.

The first large-scale documentation project work undertaken by the unit was conducted on ten **Great Lakes** vessels sunk around Isle Royale National Park. They ranged in age from the 1870s to 1947, including wooden side wheelers and steel bulk freighters. Preservation of the ships was excellent given the deep, cold freshwater conditions.

The survey of the ships at Bikini Atoll resulted from a request by the Bikinian people via the US Department of Energy to the US Navy. Navy diving units accustomed to working with the SCRU on shipwreck projects requested that the archaeologists take over the Documentation task. After Navy divers had relocated the ships, SCRU personnel undertook mapping and photodocumentation of the sites. Operations included the detailed mapping of the aircraft carrier USS *Saratoga* and the generation of less detailed sketches and photo/video documentation of the Japanese battleship *Nagato*, US submarines *Pilotfish* and *Apogon*, US battleship *Arkansas* and several other ships sunk during the atomic bomb tests.

Large survey projects conducted by the SCRU focusing on the location, identification and evaluation of new shipwreck sites include the survey of Point Reyes National Seashore in 1982 and the most recent work conducted at Biscayne and Dry Tortugas National Parks. The underlying philosophy of unit leaders has been to engage in survey only where it is cumulative and reproducible. The 1982 work at Point Reyes and 1980 location of HMS *Fowey* at Biscayne was accomplished by SCRU utilizing microwave positioning systems. The major result of the Point Reyes survey was the location of the Spanish galleon **San Agustin**, the first known wreck on the Pacific coast of North America.

This state of the art approach at the time was determined to be marginally cost-effective and block survey of park lands became a low priority until technological advances in the late 1980s and early 1990s made it once more a major emphasis of NPS underwater archaeologists. Differential GPS made the data reproducible and cumulative and GIS made the acquired information increasingly relevant to resources stewardship. The unit devoted the early 1990s to honing their survey methodology into a package which was recognized in major industry publications as setting a new state of the art. The best discussion of this methodology to date is found in the *Submerged Cultural Resources Assessment of Dry Tortugas National Park* edited by Larry Murphy.

The unit has provided assistance to the former Pacific Trust Territories since its inception. In 1981, unit personnel investigated the site of the sinking of **Leonora** in Kosrae, Federal States of **Micronesia**. During several other expeditions to Micronesia unit personnel pursued investigations of a wide range of underwater sites, including World War II sites in Palau, the Marianas, Truk, Pohnpei, and the Marshalls. Also in Pohnpei, in 1992 the team proved conclusively that the pillars off the outer sea wall of the ancient ruins of Nan Madol were coral and not man-made basaltic columns.

During the 1990s the unit became increasingly involved with an interagency initiative to establish US Government interest in shipwrecks of importance to US naval history sunk in foreign waters. In 1990, members of the team worked with the Instituto Nacional de Antropologie e Historia of Mexico to document the remains of the US brig **Somers** which sank off Vera Cruz in 1846.

In 1993 a team of diving archaeologists and technicians from SCRU conducted a series of dives on CSS **Alabama**, a Confederate raider sunk off Cherbourg, France.

The group observed and evaluated the investigation of the site being undertaken by a French team under the direction of Max Guerout.

The unit has been active in creating dialogue on the theoretical aspects of underwater archaeology and in aggressively addressing impacts to underwater resources from treasure-hunting and vandalism. As early as 1982 the unit sponsored in association with the School of American Research the conduct of a seminar on the integration of shipwreck archaeology into the mainstream of anthropological theory. This resulted in publication of the book *Shipwreck Anthropology* edited by Richard Gould. D.J.L.

ADDITIONAL READING

Brooks, J., 1992, 'Swimming with History: From the National Park Service Dive Logs', in *Sea Frontiers*, October, 54-7.

Cederlund, C.O., 1992, 'Reports of the Submerged Cultural Resources Unit of the National Park Service', *International Journal of Nautical Archaeology*, 21, 37-8.

Lenihan, D.J. (ed.), 1994, *Shipwrecks of Isle Royale National Park: The Archeological Survey*, Lake Superior Port Cities Inc. Duluth, Minnesota

Murphy, L.E. and Smith, T.G., 1995, 'Submerged in the Past: Mapping the Beguiling Waters of Florida's Biscayne and Dry Tortugas National Parks', *Geographical Information Systems Magazine*, 5, 10.

Submersibles

Manned and unmanned submersible vehicles, which provide a means for archaeologists and historians to access the large volume of historically valuable material located beneath the surface of the world's water masses. Vehicles suitable for underwater exploration have existed for many years, originally designed to satisfy man's curiosity and further developed for military purposes. During the late 1960s, ocean exploration was viewed by many industrial corporations as providing opportunities similar to those envisioned for the exploration of space. As a result, a number of deep diving manned submersibles were constructed as a means of gaining ocean engineering experience and demonstrating the expertise necessary to participate in the expected market opportunities. Many of these submersibles were to be operated on a profit making basis in support of the expected plethora of scientific and industrial activities in the deep ocean. During this period, over a dozen submersibles such as Lockheed's *Deep Quest*, Rockwell's *Beaver*, Reynolds Aluminum's *Aluminaut*, General Motors' *Dowb*, and the Westinghouse *Deepstar*, were designed and constructed. Additionally, a myriad of vehi-

Diver entering the 1930s 'Iron Man' – a one-person, one-atmosphere submersible, predecessor to the modern 'Newtsuit'. (Vancouver Maritime Museum)

cles with shallower depth capabilities were produced, which tended to be designed for specific tasks and, frequently, were sold to companies providing services to the growing offshore oil and gas industry. It was at this time that the only submersible specifically designed for underwater archaeology, **Asherah**, was built.

The best known manned submersible constructed during that time is unquestionably the Deep Submergence Vehicle (DSV) *Alvin*. This vehicle, funded by the **US Navy**, was originally constructed by Litton Industries for operation by the Woods Hole Oceanographic Institution, Woods Hole, Massachusetts. *Alvin* was placed in service in 1964 with a depth rating of 1,828 m. The vehicle routinely carried two scientists and a pilot on 6–10 hour dives in support of deep ocean research by allowing scientists to make direct observations and manipulations on the sea floor. From then until the early seventies, *Alvin* made 60 to 80 dives per year from its catamaran support vessel, R/V *Lulu*, in support of science programmes. Its success caused it to be used as a model for the *Sea Cliff* and *Turtle* submersibles, vehicles constructed by General Dynamics Corporation for US Navy deep water search and retrieval tasks at depths of up to 2,000 m (6,500 ft).

Canada, England, France, Japan and Russia, in addition to the United States, also developed manned submersibles vehicles during the 1960s. However, by the late

1970s, the reality of attempting to operate complicated electro-mechanical devices in the hostile ocean environment had greatly decreased the number of operating vehicles. Only a small number of vehicles remained operational and, as with *Alvin*, many of those which survived were devoted to research activities. Examples are the French *Cyana* (launched in 1970), the Russian *Sever* 1 and 2, and Canada's *P2*.

A similar situation existed for manned submersibles designed for shallower operations. During the 1960s, many vehicles were designed and constructed for the purpose of supporting the offshore oil and gas industry. These were intended to provide the means for conducting the surveys and inspections associated with offshore drilling and production platforms as well as the necessary pipelines. Some of these submersibles provided a diver-lockout capability allowing them to serve as delivery vehicles for saturation divers. By the end of the decade, there were nearly 50 submersibles in existence; but, as with their deeper diving cousins, many proved uneconomical to operate and served primarily as prototypes for improved vehicles constructed in the 1970s. Two submersible manufacturers distinguished themselves with the design and construction of a large number of manned submersibles: Perry Submarine Builders of Riviera Beach, Florida, and HYCO Ltd., North Vancouver, BC, Canada. Between the two of them, they constructed close to 50 submersibles, some of which remain in use today. In addition, Harbor Branch Oceanographic Institution, Ft. Pierce, Florida, constructed the Johnson-Sea-Link I and II vehicles, both operational in 1997 and unique in their use of a clear pressure hull affording an unprecedented viewing capability. Numerous other submersibles were built by various organizations based upon the lessons learned by the pioneers of the 1960s, but by the end of the decade most had been removed from service as the cost of their operation became too great.

Manned submersibles were not the only undersea vehicles developed during the 1960s and 1970s. Unmanned remotely operated vehicles (ROVs) were constructed, controlled via electro-mechanical cable connections with their support ship. Initially, vehicles of this type consisted of little more than search systems with sonars and cameras in pressure-resistant housings, some having attached propellers to allow a degree of maneuverability. Dimitri Rebikoff, a pioneer in underwater photography and archaeology, developed the 'Poodle' ROV for locating deep wreck sites in the **Mediterranean Sea** and the oceanographer Willard Bascom constructed the 'Television Search and Salvage System' (TVSS). As time progressed, there was a constant development of increasingly capable ROVs with associated increases in complexity, sophistication, and cost. The hope was that ROVs could replace manned vehicles in conducting underwater industrial tasks and to some extent this was successful; during the late 1970s, the use of manned submersibles in support of offshore industrial activities declined and the major-

warmed by sub-surface volcanic activity, percolates up through the sea-floor rich in dissolved minerals. Surprisingly, these locations were found to be teeming with undersea life of various types existing as an ecosystem based on chemical synthesis. In 1979, *Alvin* returned to the Pacific, and this time hot-vents were discovered having water temperatures estimated at 350 degrees C. Although the biology was perhaps the most spectacular of the discoveries, geologists, geochemists, volcanologists, and others found

survey capability consisting of a set of cable controlled vehicles equipped with sophisticated sonar and imaging electronics. Under the guidance of Dr Robert Ballard, this group constructed *Argo* and **Jason** vehicles which were intended to be used simultaneously from a single support ship. *Argo* was a towed survey vehicle equipped with two types of sonar, down-looking and side-looking, plus a specially developed high altitude 'snap shot' video system. Additionally, *Argo* served as the garage for *Jason*, a smaller, fully manoeuverable ROV with sonar, film and video imaging systems designed for close-up, detailed work. The concept was to survey vast areas of the sea-floor using *Argo*, with stops for deployment of *Jason* whenever something warranting closer scrutiny was located.

Deploying an ROV for deep dives off Pearl Harbor. (NPS/Larry Murphy)

Chris Nicholson pilots the ROV from the control cabin on the surface. (NPS/D.J. Lenihan)

ity of the vehicles designed for this purpose ceased operations.

The 1980s began with few operational deep diving submersibles, most of which were employed in support of ocean research. Many of the world's shallow-depth submersibles, previously utilized in industrial activities, had been replaced with unmanned, remotely controlled devices. Those that continued to operate were also frequently engaged in scientific investigations. Hundreds of ROVs of every size and description were in routine use, most of the tethered, free-swimming variety with a depth capability of less than 1,000 m. In 1985, a plunge in the price of oil forced the discontinuation of much of the offshore production activities. Thus, the undersea service industry's operations were severely reduced, and development of new vehicles and equipment sharply declined. Only the few vehicles utilized for military and research purposes continued to operate as usual, and these applications provided one of the few avenues for progress in the design and development of deep-water submersibles.

Deep diving undersea research vehicles received a much needed boost when, in 1977, geologists utilizing the submersible *Alvin* in the eastern Pacific discovered warm-water vents. These are areas where water,

research in these areas to be extremely rewarding. As a result, the deep diving submersible became a valued and respected work horse of the oceanographic research community. During the 1980s, the American *Alvin* and French *Cyana* were joined by the Japanese *Shinkai 2000* and *Shinkai 6500*, the French *Nautile*, and the Russian *Mir 1* and *Mir 2* vehicles, all but the first having a depth capability of 6,000 m or greater. *Sea Cliff, Turtle,* and *Alvin* continued to operate in the United States, and each had been upgraded in depth capability, *Sea Cliff* to 6,000 m, *Turtle* to 3,000 m, and *Alvin* to 4,000 m.

During this same period the United States Navy funded the Deep Submergence Laboratory (DSL) of the Woods Hole Oceanographic Institution to develop a deep water

Development of these vehicles was a difficult and expensive task extending over many years. *Argo* was the first system to reach a point where an actual deep sea test was practical and warranted. The Deep Submergence Laboratory needed a site with a bottom terrain providing sufficient imaging targets, but plain enough to allow for testing *Argo*'s search capabilities. Many areas in the northern Atlantic were suitable, but to make the test more interesting, Dr Ballard chose the site believed to be the resting place of RMS **Titanic**. On 1 September 1985, *Argo* obtained images of *Titanic* resting on the bottom in close to 4,000 m of water.

As a step in the evolutionary development of *Jason*, a small vehicle originally constructed for the United States Navy was modified to allow deep water sensor evaluation. This vehicle was dubbed *Jason Jr.*; it was mated with Woods Hole's submersible *Alvin*, allowing the pilot to observe the ROV from within *Alvin* as he attempted to control its activities in deep water. Again, the test site was that of *Titanic* and in 1986 *Alvin* carried *Jason Jr.* to the wreck twelve times, where its maneuverability enabled it to obtain video and film images not previously possible.

Since that time *Argo/Jason* and other DSL developed vehicles have been utilized to locate and document the resting place of the German battleship **Bismarck**, the **Guadalcanal wrecks**, the **Lusitania** and *Britannic*. The systems have also been deployed in the central Mediterranean where they have allowed the location and documentation of numerous deep water wreck sites dating from Greco-Roman times. The best known is the 4th-century AD merchant ship located in approximately 2,500 ft of water and named **Isis** in honour of the mythological goddess of nature. Satellite image transmissions allowed thousands of students to observe

The submersible Argo, which found Bismarck, hauled aboard the
research ship Star Hercules. *(National Geographic Society/
Joseph H. Bailey)*

the exploration of this site as it occurred. In
1990 the *Jason* ROV was used for an archaeological investigation of two warships, **Hamilton and Scourge**, lost in a storm in Lake
Ontario during the War of 1812. Although
in only 90 m of water, this effort was unique
in that it demonstrated the results which
could be obtained at any depth by utilizing
the technology presently available with
modern submersibles and ROVs. A combination of centimetre accuracy vehicle navigation, fractional degree attitude sensors,
high frequency spot and scanning sonars,
plus high-resolution video imagining systems
allowed an unprecedented three-dimensional computer-based characterization of
the vessels. Similar results were obtained
when the scanning sonar system was used to
document USS **Monitor**, the sunken Civil War
ironclad, and when the US Navy's 3,000-ft
rated nuclear submarine NR-1 was used to
continue exploration of the ocean floor adjacent to the **Isis Wreck** in 1995. The success of
this latter investigation has resulted in the
planning of a return to the site in 1997 with
both the NR-1 and the *Jason* ROV.

A major trend in shallow water ROV development was begun by MiniROVER, a small
ROV developed by Deep Sea Systems International and costing approximately a tenth
of the price of similar devices available at
the time. This ROV was small, low maintenance, easily transported and deployed,
required little support equipment, and yet
provided both sonar and video search capabilities to depths of 260 m. The concept of

an inexpensive underwater vehicle was
extremely popular and many manufacturers
joined in the production of these devices.
Twenty to thirty unique models were
designed, and hundreds of individual units
produced. Noteworthy was the Phantom
series, begun in 1985 by Deep Ocean Engineering, with over two hundred sold by
1993. Vehicles of this nature are in demand
for shallow water search and salvage activities throughout the world. B.B.W.

ADDITIONAL READING
Kaharl, V.A., 1990, *Water Baby: The Story of Alvin*,
New York.
Piccard, J. and Dietz, R.M., 1961, *Seven Miles
Down: The Story of the Bathyscaphe Trieste*, New
York.

Sunken Fleet of 1758

see *Wiawaka Bateaux Cluster*

Sussex

Vessel of the English East India Company
(EIC), lost in 1738 on the reef of the French
atoll Bassa da India in the Channel of
Mozambique, Indian Ocean. To date, less
than ten English East Indiamen wrecks have
been studied, among which are *Trial* (1622),
Doddington (1758), and *Griffin* (1761). Despite
the fact that these vessels were the commercial carriers of the EIC during three centuries
and contributed to the success of this company, only scarce archaeological data is available. *Sussex* was wrecked on its return from
China. The ship hit the atoll which during
high tides was completely submerged and
therefore practically invisible. Some sailors
tried in vain to save the vessel after the commander had ordered them to abandon ship.

After its wrecking, *Sussex* was completely

destroyed by storms; thus the site is very
poorly preserved. In 1987 French archaeologists conducted a survey. Few remains have
been found: two anchors imbedded in concretion, some guns, cast-iron bars, and some
tens of thousands of Chinese porcelain
sherds which were scattered over approximately one square kilometre. Porcelain was
recovered which dated from the Yongzhen
period (1723–35). Among the finds were
dinner plates and serving dishes, saucers,
bowls, jars, and teapots. The quality of the
ceramic was mediocre. There were two
types: a glazed blue and white and a blue
and white with enamelled decorations. The
decorative patterns consisted mainly of landscapes or were derived from the Chinese
repertoire of symbolic motifs. M.L'H.

ADDITIONAL READING
Bousquet, G., L'Hour, M. and Richez, F., 1990,
'The Discovery of an English East-Indiaman at
Bassas da India, a French Atoll in the Indian
Ocean: the *Sussex* (1738)', *International
Journal of Nautical Archaeology*, 19, 81-5.
L'Hour, M., Richez, F. and Bousquet, G., 1992,
'Découverte d'un East-Indiaman de l'E.I.C. à
Bassas da India, atoll français de l'Océan
Indien: le *Sussex* (1738)', *Cahiers d'Archéologie
Subaquatique*, 10, 175-98.

Sutton Hoo

An early Anglo-Saxon ship burial, deep in
the sand on a promontory overlooking the
River Deben in Suffolk, England. The great
ship, which lay beneath Mound 1 in the
Sutton Hoo cemetery, is one of the most
remarkable artefacts to survive from the
early Anglo-Saxon period. The ship was used
as a coffin for an East Anglian royal burial;
the burial itself was laid out in a large chamber built amidships, and accompanying the
dead man was the richest assemblage of possessions yet excavated in Europe. It included
a magnificent helmet and shield, gold and
garnet sword fittings, belt buckles and
mounts, a purse-lid of ivory inlaid with gold
and garnet plaques, and a remarkable gold
buckle. The grave also contained silver tableware from east Mediterranean workshops
and three bronze hanging-bowls with exquis-
itely enamelled escutcheons from the Celtic
northwest. Two enigmatic objects, an iron
'stand' and a massive whetstone surmounted
by a bronze stag, are believed to be symbols
of the king's royal authority – the whetstone
is interpreted as a barbaric form of sceptre.
The purse contained a collection of 37
Merovingian gold *tremisses*, all from different
mints; the latest may have been minted in
the second decade of the 7th century AD.
The grave is popularly thought to be that of
Ræthwald (*c.* 596–625/6) who, after the

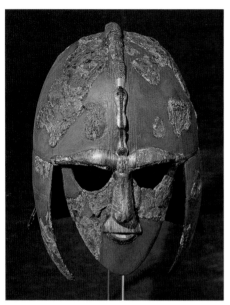

The Sutton Hoo helmet. (Courtesy of the Trustees of the British Museum)

death of Æthelbert of Kent in 616, assumed the mantle of 'overlord' of the English kingdoms south of the River Humber.

Excavations took place in the spring and summer of 1939, ending immediately before the outbreak of World War II. The ship, which survived only as an impression in the sand, was the first to be recorded using archaeological principles. She was surveyed and photographed by a team from the Science Museum in London but all the survey records and the field notebooks of the director, Lt Commander J.K.D. Hutchison, were destroyed in bombing raids on London and only twenty-two photographs and two provisional plans of the lines and structural details of the ship survived. Fortunately, several hundred photographs were also taken during the excavation of the ship by two amateur photographers, Miss Mercie Lack and Miss Barbara Wagstaff, both associates of the Royal Photographic Society, and these provide invaluable information about the ship's construction, particularly the cross-sections of the keel and endposts, as well as details of use and subsequent repair.

The ship was not backfilled at the end of the excavations and the use of the gravefield, in particular the excavation trench containing the ship, by the British Army resulted in massive damage to the stern gunwales and upper strakes. Between 1965 and 1967 the remains of the ship were re-excavated with the object of resolving questions posed by the Science Museum's plans and to record the relationship of the hull to the ship-trench and mound. After recording the position of each rivet and all extant details of the struc-

ture, a plaster cast was made and the battered remains were finally dug through to ensure that the ship had not concealed any part of the burial ritual. A fibreglass replica was made of the cast in 1968 and both remain in storage at the British Museum as permanent records of the hull.

The ship survived only as a fragile impression, with her sleek lines captured in the fine damp sand of the close-fitting burial trench. The oak planking had decayed to a thin dark skin, pierced by iron rivets which fastened the strake overlaps, and crossed at regular intervals by sandy casts of the twenty-six frames that strengthened the hull. Although no wood survived, details of the original planking and its carpentry remain on each iron fastening, preserved as wood-grain by the iron corrosion products. The lines of the hull also remained reasonably true despite some damage to the timbers when the ship was lowered into the ground. The ship was just over 27 m long with a maximum beam of 4.5 m and a depth amidships of 1.5 m. It had a broad keel-plank and low raking plank-on-edge endposts that swept up to an estimated height of 3.7 m above the waterline. It had nine strakes a side and was built of split oak planks 2 cm thick, with individual runs of up to 5.45 m amidships. The strakes were secured at the overlap by iron rivets and joined end to end by short rivets spaced evenly across the face of the plank. The spine of the ship was a massive keel-plank, which was originally attached to the stem and sternposts by wooden pegs although, when excavated, the after-scarf was fastened with iron rivets, replacements for the treenails and associated with a repair patch immediately to starboard of the scarf. The hull was strengthened by twenty-six square-sectioned frames riveted to the gunwale-strake and pegged to the planking. The three after-frames were closely spaced; two were club-headed to starboard and all three were probably associated with the fastenings of a heavy steering oar and designed to strengthen the hull against its drag.

Evidence for rowing positions survived outside the area of the burial chamber as dark shadows in the sand rising above the gunwale strake and as clusters of iron spikes that had secured the grown forks to the top of the strake. Amidships, where the construction of the burial chamber has distorted the evidence, tholes and gunwale spikes do not survive. Because of this, it is not clear if the rowing positions originally ran in an unbroken line along the gunwale strake, giving 20 oarsmen a side, or if they broke amidships, as they do on some later boats. It is also not clear if the ship was sail-

assisted: no sailing equipment was found during the excavations, but this should not necessarily be taken as evidence against the use of sail as the ship would probably have been stripped of all excess weight, including mast, keelson, and steering-oar, before its portage from the river to the gravefield. Also, although the Sutton Hoo ship has been interpreted as being more of a royal 'barge' than a practical seagoing vessel, computer projections suggest that the hull would be efficient under sail despite its abnormal length and the lack of a fully-formed keel.

The ship in Mound 1 is not the only one to be ceremonially buried in Anglo-Saxon England, although it is the largest. A large boat was buried beneath Mound 2 at Sutton Hoo, and a third of similar size was excavated at Snape (see **Snape Boat**). Newspaper reports record that Mound 2 was opened in the mid-19th century, although it may well have been robbed before this. It was excavated in 1938 by Basil Brown, when he found iron rivets and what he thought was a small boat with an iron-bound transom stern. This interpretation was rejected by subsequent scholars as contemporary clinker-built boats are invariably double-ended. When the mound was re-excavated as part of a research project (1983–91) to assess the cemetery, it was found that the boat had been destroyed and survived only as a scatter of rivets to either side of the earlier excavation pit with one rather doubtful cross-section.

However, as in Mound 1, details of the boat's structure are preserved in the proportions of the rivets and their ferrified wood grain. This information, together with the spread of the rivets across the mound, makes it possible to define the basic details of the boat. It was of typical double-ended and clinker-built construction with an overall length of c. 20 m, and probably similar in proportions to the mid-6th-century AD boat buried in the Anglo-Saxon cemetery at Snape. The oak planking was made in sections and fastened by short rivets placed across the overlapping ends of the plank. It is not known how the boat's keel and end-posts were constructed, how many strakes there were a side, how many frames strengthened the hull, nor how many rowing positions there were, but the rivets, gunwale spikes and rib-bolts show that in most structural details it was identical to the ship in Mound 1.

However, unlike the other ship, the boat in Mound 2 did not contain the burial but, in a complex ritual paralleled by the later Viking **Ship burial** at Hedeby, it had been dragged into place over a large rectangular burial chamber and then partially buried so that the end-posts would have been clearly visible outside the mound. Although only fragments of a once-rich grave assemblage survived, it is clear that the burial was of similar date and perhaps even approached the status of the royal burial in Mound 1. A.C.E.

ADDITIONAL READING

Evans, A.C., 1975, 'The Ship', in R. Bruce-Mitford (ed.), *The Sutton Hoo Ship Burial*, Cambridge.

Great gold belt buckle from the Sutton Hoo ship burial. (Courtesy of the Trustees of the British Museum)

Evans, A.C., 1994, *The Sutton Hoo Ship Burial*, London

Evans, A.C., forthcoming, 'Mound 2: The ship', in M.O.H. Carver (ed.), *The Sutton Hoo Cemetery and its Context*, London.

Swan
see **Duart Wreck**

Sweden
see **Baltic Sea**

Swedish Ancient Monuments Act

The Cultural Heritage Act (CHA), adopted by the Swedish Parliament in 1988, but incorporating elements dating as far back as the 17th century. The central state agency for cultural heritage management is the Central Board for National Antiquities and the National Historical Museums. Sweden is subdivided in 24 counties (*län*) and 287 local government districts (*kommuner*). The county administrations monitor compliance with the CHA and try applications for land or water use projects that might concern protected monuments, sites and listed historical buildings. They also administer the grant programmes within frames set for each county by the Central Board. The latter has coordinating and some supervisory functions vis-à-vis the county administrations, but these are not subordinate to the Central Board.

Physical planning powers rest basically with the local governments. The state has retained powers to intervene in local planning issues in order to prevent damage to certain national interests, among them heritage values, and to ascertain minimal environmental standards. Consequently, the county administration may nullify – but not alter – a plan adopted by a local government, if the plan runs contrary to national interests or minimum standards. There are some 1,700 areas in the country, which have been designated as areas of national heritage importance.

The CHA in its first paragraph states that ancient monuments which preserve the memory of the earlier inhabitants of the realm are placed under the protection of the law, and that no one, except by permission, may excavate, disturb, cover, or otherwise alter or damage or remove an ancient monument. The surveillance of ancient monuments is exercised by the state county administrations within the realm of each county.

The second chapter defines the types of permanent ancient monuments covered by the law. In this enumeration one finds burial structures, raised stones, and rock bases with inscriptions and other kinds of marks, crosses and other memorials, places for cult, trade and other purposes, remains of settlements, defence installations, votive springs and other cult places. Also included are remains of work sites abandoned in ancient times, as well as abandoned fortresses, castles, churches, and other noteworthy structures erected or constructed during ancient times. In addition disused roads, bridges and similar constructions are protected.

Remains of ancient settlements, water-based defences, fish traps, etc., which have once been built on the bottom, or on a shore which has later been inundated, are included in the definitions under Chapter 2 of the CHA in the same way as remains situated on land. Shipwrecks are also protected as ancient monuments, if a minimum of one hundred years have elapsed since the ship was wrecked.

Due to the growing number of skin-divers diving on wrecks since the 1950s and the increasing damage caused thereby, shipwrecks were added to the list of protected ancient monuments in 1967, and are now under the same premises as other protected archaeological remains under the CHA.

The general rules of the CHA include the following elements of protection:

An area on the ground or on the seabed or lake-bed, large enough to preserve an ancient monument belongs to the monument. It is prohibited to displace, remove, excavate, cover or, by building development, etc. to alter or damage a protected ancient monument. The Central Board and the state county administrations may take such measures as are necessary in order to protect and care for ancient monuments. The Central Board and state county administrations may examine an ancient monument, salvage a shipwreck being an ancient monument and investigate a place where archaeological finds have been discovered. The state county administration may grant some other agent permission to conduct such an investigation, on the conditions defined by the same administration. The state county administration may issue regulations for the protection of an ancient monument, for example by issuing a protection order for a place where archaeological finds have been discovered. Any person intending to erect a building or structure or to carry out any other enterprise should ascertain well in advance whether any ancient monument can be affected by the enterprise and, if such be the case, consult the state county administration. The county administrations have the right to order a special investigation in order to find unknown but suspected prehistoric monuments in the event of an exploitation. Any person wishing to displace, alter or remove an ancient monument must apply to the state county administration for permission. As conditions for permission under Chapter 12, the state county administration may make reasonable stipulations for a special investigation to record the ancient monument or to take special measures to preserve it.. The person conducting an enterprise affecting an ancient monument shall bear the cost of measures referred to in Chapter 13.

The CHA also contains special regulations concerning ancient archaeological finds. Such finds which do not have a known owner and are found in or at an ancient monument and have a connection with it belong to the state and have to be reported and delivered to the authorities. The same applies to ownerless finds which are found under other circumstances but which may be judged to be at least 100 years old and are completely or partly of gold, silver, copper, bronze or any other copper alloy; this also applies to finds which are constituted of two or more objects which presumably were deposited simultaneously.

Metal detectors may not be used except under certain circumstances or by representatives of authorized organizations. Nor may metal detectors be carried on archaeological sites except on public roads unless otherwise provided for.

A minimum of four years imprisonment or a fine may be imposed for an offence against the archaeological heritage. C.O.C.

ADDITIONAL READING

Aldercreutz, T., 1993, *Four Issues of Cultural Heritage Law in Six European Countries. (France, Germany, Hungary, Italy, Sweden and the United Kingdom)*, A report for the Council of Europe Programme Study Visits Abroad for Lawyers, Stockholm.

Sydney Cove

Merchant ship wrecked at Preservation Island, off the southeastern coast of **Australia**, on 9 February 1797, while carrying a speculative cargo from Calcutta to Port Jackson, New South Wales. Subsequent events connected with the loss of the vessel included the discovery and exploration of Bass Strait, separating the island of Tasmania from mainland Australia, and the establishment of a sealing industry in the region.

Since the rediscovery of the wreck by amateur divers in 1977, *Sydney Cove* has been the responsibility of the Tasmanian Parks and Wildlife Service. Early work on the site was a major stimulus for the development of a maritime heritage programme in Tasmania, and led to the State becoming a signatory to the **Australian Historic Shipwrecks Act** (1976) in 1983. The excavation of *Sydney Cove* was undertaken between 1991 and 1993, during which a total of 216 sq. m of the site was uncovered. While the majority of the artefact material located during the excavation was raised, the surviving hull structure and substantial quantities of dunnage (packing timbers) were recorded *in situ* before reburial. The conservation and subsequent man-

The Sydney Cove *wreck site. (Tasmanian Parks and Wildlife Service)*

agement of the artefact collection has been carried out by the Queen Victoria Museum, based in the northern Tasmanian city of Launceston.

While there is sparse documentary evidence regarding the history of the vessel the excavation has been able to confirm that *Sydney Cove* was constructed for use in the 'country' trade, carried out between Asian ports and the European colonies in the East. Built upon European lines, the 250 ton *Sydney Cove* had the light construction and shallow draft of a fast sailor designed for the short coastal voyages common to vessels of the country fleet. While the ship was constructed of locally obtained materials, the larger metal fittings found on the wreck, such as anchors, cannon, and rudder braces, were imported from Europe via the British East India Company. The rapid transfer of European technologies has also been demonstrated by the use of copper sheathing, in combination with more traditional Indian methods, to protect the vessel's hull.

The artefact collection has provided material evidence for the extensive trade networks which existed even during the earliest years of European settlement in Australia. While the cargo of alcohol, foodstuffs, and textiles was largely obtained from Calcutta and the hinterland of Bengal, European luxury goods as well as Chinese porcelain and tea were also included. The composition and generally poor quality of the excavated cargo confirms the dependency of the colonists on the choices of overseas mer-

Pottery from Sydney Cove. *(© Queen Victoria Museum, Launceston, Tasmania)*

chants. This is highlighted by the inclusion in the cargo of a large and varied quantity of alcoholic spirits, despite existing government regulations and the lack of more essential stores and equipment in the colony. As the artefacts from *Sydney Cove* are accurately dated the collection has also proved useful for comparative studies with early European settlement sites in the Sydney region. M.N.

ADDITIONAL READING

Henderson, G., 1986, *Maritime Archaeology in Australia*, Perth.

Nash, M., 1996, *Cargo for the Colony – The Wreck of the Merchant Ship* Sydney Cove, Sydney.

Strachan, S., 1986, *The History and Archaeology of the Sydney Cove Shipwreck (1797)*, Occasional Papers No. 5, Research School of Pacific Studies, Australian National University, Canberra.

USS *Tecumseh*

Wreck of a US Civil War ironclad 'monitor', lost during the battle of Mobile Bay on 5 August 1864. Rediscovered in 1967, the intact ironclad was the subject of several initiatives to raise and restore it. The principal effort, by the Smithsonian Institution, which discovered the wreck, was abandoned after seven years because of lawsuits and a lack of funds.

Tecumseh is intact, with its artefacts inside the hull retaining their original provenance. It is a unique, well-preserved warship wreck from the mid-19th century, and with the wreck of USS *Monitor*, one of two monitor-type wrecks available for study in the United States.

USS *Tecumseh* was a single-turret monitor built by Z. and C. Secor of New York in 1863. A refined version of the original American *Monitor*, designed and built by John Ericsson, *Tecumseh*, a *Canonicus* class monitor, incorporated improvements over the previous *Passaic* class monitors. Following the success of Ericsson's *Monitor*, the United States Government embarked on an ironclad construction programme during the Civil War that resulted in the construction of fifty-one such ships.

Tecumseh's iron hull, armoured deck, sides and turret displaced 2,100 tons. The ship was 225 ft (6.7 m) long, with a 43 ft 8 in (13.3 m) beam and a 13 ft 6 in (4.1 m) draft. The turret and pilot-house, the principal features on the flat, raft-like hull's deck, were armoured with 10 in (25.4 cm) of iron plate, while the sides were protected by a 5 in (12.7 cm) armour belt and the decks with 1½ in (3.8 cm) of iron. *Tecumseh* was powered by an Ericsson-designed, vibrating lever, 640 hp engine that drove a single, four-bladed propeller 14 ft (4.3 m) in diameter. The 9 ft (2.7 m) high, 21 ft (6.4 m) diameter revolving turret mounted two 15 in (38 cm) Dahlgren smoothbore, muzzle-loading guns.

Tecumseh was ordered by the US Navy in September 1862. The ship was launched on 12 September 1863, and accepted for service on 17 March 1864. The ironclad was commissioned on 19 April 1864 and ordered to join the North Atlantic Blockading Squadron at Hampton Roads, Virginia. After three months' service on Virginia's James River, *Tecumseh* was ordered to join the US Navy's Gulf Squadron in the summer. Under the command of Admiral David Glasgow Farragut, the Gulf Squadron pushed to seize Mobile Bay as a base of operations and close Mobile, one of the last ports remaining open to a flow of arms and supplies for the beleaguered Confederacy. On 5 August 1864, the attack on Mobile began with an assault on the harbour defences. Rounding the batteries of Fort Morgan, near the harbour entrance, *Tecumseh* led the fleet into Mobile Bay at 6.30 a.m.

The Confederate ram *Tennessee* made for Farragut's flagship, USS *Hartford*. Commander T. A. Craven, in *Tecumseh*, moved to intercept the Confederate ship. As *Tecumseh* swung to port, a large explosion from a submerged 'torpedo' (mine) erupted from the monitor's side, and *Tecumseh* capsized to port, sinking in less than a minute at approximately 7.30 a.m. Nearly the entire crew, ninety-two men in total, including Craven, were lost. Only twenty-one men out

The Destruction of Tecumseh by a Torpedo During the Battle of Mobile Bay, *sketch by Robert Weir. (US Naval Historical Center)*

of 114 survived. The US fleet faltered, but Farragut ordered, 'Damn the torpedoes! Full speed ahead!' The fleet continued into the bay and won the battle.

The wreck was rediscovered by the Smithsonian Institution in approximately 8.8 m of water in February 1967. The Smithsonian intended to raise and restore the ship as the centrepiece in a planned National Armed Forces Museum in Washington, DC. The wreck was discovered lying upside down, buried in silt with the exception of one bilge that protruded 46 cm from the mud. In July 1967 divers employed by the Smithsonian examined the exterior of the wreck, using dredges and water jets. They discovered that the wreck had turned over on sinking and was resting, intact, on its port gunwale, supported by the turret and pilot-house. The damage from the 'torpedo' that sank the ship was found to be an 2.4 by 1.5 m indentation, with small holes punched into the iron plate. The divers recovered metal and timber samples, some of the ironclad's ceramic dinnerware, a floor register or ventilator, and raised one of *Tecumseh*'s anchors. During survey dives in July 1968, brass bunk supports, stanchion rails, and a human scapula, the only human remains recovered from the wreck, were raised. In November 1968 divers were able to enter the engine room after cutting an access hole through the plate. They recovered a brass engine room gong and several burlap bags.

Despite the Smithsonian's plans to raise *Tecumseh*, ballooning estimates of the costs, fund-raising difficulties, and a lawsuit by the salvor hired to raise the ship, who success-fully recovered considerable out-of-pocket expenses, ended the project in 1973. It was formally abandoned in 1974. The wreck was listed in the **National Register of Historic Places** in 1975 to better ensure its protection as a federally owned resource. Efforts by the State of Alabama in 1975 to pursue raising and restoring *Tecumseh* did not come to fruition, and the wreck remains, buoyed but undisturbed, and protected by Federal law, just off Fort Morgan, now an Alabama State historical site. J.P.D.

ADDITIONAL READING

Smithsonian Institution, 1970, *USS* Tecumseh: *Capsule of History*, Smithsonian Institution, Washington, DC.

West, W. Wilson Jr., 1985, *The USS* Tecumseh, unpublished master's thesis, East Carolina University, Greenville, North Carolina.

Telephone booth

Nickname for an underwater 'communications centre' employed at the **Yassiada** site. Developed by archaeologists Michael and Susan Katzev, the 'telephone booth' was a Plexiglass hemisphere bolted to angle iron legs and weighted with 675 kg of steel ballast. Air was pumped into the hemisphere from a surface barge, creating a dry environment on a 41 m deep site where up to four divers could converse with each other, comparing notes, or talk to the surface by means of a telephone line to the barge. J.P.D.

ADDITIONAL READING

Bass, G. F., 1966, *Archaeology Under Water*, New York.

Bass, G. F., 1975, *Archaeology Beneath the Sea: A Personal Account*, New York.

Tennessee

Wreck of a Gold Rush side-wheel steamship which broke up in 1853 in California; it was archaeologically documented 1981–2. *Tennessee* was a 1,275 ton side-wheel steamship built in New York in 1848 that was pressed into passenger service on the Pacific during the California Gold Rush after being purchased by the Pacific Mail Steamship Company to operate between Panama City and San Francisco. The 'Panama Route' was one of the principal means of reaching California, and *Tennessee* served an important role during a brief three-year career on the Pacific, carrying passengers, mail, high-commodity freight, and gold specie. The ship was lost on 6 March 1853, running aground in fog en route to San Francisco, and was partially salvaged before breaking up in the surf.

The remains of *Tennessee* are buried at Tennessee Cove, a small, 366 m wide cove 6.4 km north of the Golden Gate on the northern California coast. The remains are buried in the coarse gravel and sand of the cove; the archaeological site composed of *Tennessee*'s remains extends beyond the surf line into the sub-aerial beach, where portions of the wreck were washed during the breaking up of the vessel.

Seasonal winter beach erosion exposed considerable remains of the ship and its engines in 1980–81, and more than 400 loose brass, copper, iron, and glass objects were found embedded in the rock and gravel shingle. These included ship fastenings, copper sheathing, parts of cast- and wrought-iron steam machinery, and glass and ceramic fragments.

A preliminary **Magnetometer** survey of the cove located a series of magnetic anomalies lying near the surf line which may be the principal concentration of wreckage from *Tennessee*, but high surf and limited

Side lever from Tennessee*'s engine. (J. P. Delgado)*

visibility have precluded any underwater work on the site.

The surviving remains of *Tennessee*'s side-lever steam engine comprise the earliest known remains of an American-built, ocean-going marine steam engine in the United States. The archaeological remains of *Tennessee*, and the 1853 wreck of the steamer **Winfield Scott** are the only archaeologically documented steamships from the California Gold Rush until work is done with the wrecks of **Central America** and *Brother Jonathan*. J.P.D.

ADDITIONAL READING

Delgado, J. P., 1995, 'The Wreck of the *Tennessee*', *Journal of the West*, October, 33, 4, 14–21.

Kemble, J. H., 1943, *The Panama Route: 1848–1869*, Berkeley and Los Angeles.

Ten Sail, Wreck of the

A shipwreck disaster involving HMS *Convert* and nine sail of a fifty-eight-ship merchant convoy. The vessels, homeward bound to Great Britain from Jamaica, were wrecked on the reefs of Grand Cayman on 8 February 1794, during the French Revolutionary Wars (1792–1802). The frigate *Convert*, formerly *L'Inconstante* of France, had been captured off Saint Domingue in November 1793, and remained outfitted with much original equipment, including the primary ordnance of French 12 pound cannon.

The disaster has been remembered for two centuries in Caymanian folklore as the *Wreck of the Ten Sail*. In the 1990s archaeologists conducted archival and archaeological research to verify the oral history. Among contemporary documents discovered in French, British, and Jamaican archives, are official correspondence, court records, captain's letters, court martial proceedings, ships' logs, muster rolls, ship registers, periodicals, prize-ship inventories, shipwreck salvage accounts, and ships' draughts. Archaeological remains were noted by the **Institute of Nautical Archaeology** in 1980, and further investigated between 1991 and 1993 under the auspices of the Cayman Islands National Museum.

The underwater sites of *Convert* and the merchantmen wrecks, in combination with associated terrestrial salvage campsites, constitute a significant cultural heritage zone. Although minimal excavations have been undertaken, surface artefacts have been mapped and controlled collections made. Among the materials present are ship-related objects, personal items, and ordnance, including 12-pounder cannon cast in 1781 at Forge-Neuve, an ironworks near

Angoulême in Charente, France. These long pattern cannon, cast according to the French Navy's Regulations of 1778–9, suggest that they are part of the original ordnance placed on board *L'Inconstante*, lost when the frigate was wrecked. Site management is ongoing, with future scientific investigations planned.

In commemoration of the 200th anniversary of the Wreck of the Ten Sail in 1994, an exhibition was presented at the Cayman Islands National Museum. It was viewed by Her Majesty Queen Elizabeth II and His Royal Highness Prince Philip during a visit to Grand Cayman. M.E.L.

ADDITIONAL READING

Leshikar, M.E., 1993, *The 1794 'Wreck of the Ten Sail', Cayman Islands, British West Indies: A Historical Study and Archaeological Survey*, Ph.D. dissertation, Texas A&M University, College Station, Texas.

Leshikar-Denton, M.E. (ed.), 1994, *Our Islands' Past, Volume II: The 'Wreck of the Ten Sail'*, Cayman Islands.

Smith, R.C., 1981, *The Maritime Heritage of the Cayman Islands: Contributions in Nautical Archaeology*, MA thesis, Texas A&M University, College Station, Texas.

Terence Bay Wreck

Wreck dating from *c*.1750, probably the remains of a New England fishing schooner, originally about 65 ft (19.8 m) long. It lies on its side in shallow water, in a cove on the Nova Scotian coast. The hull is intact from the rail to the turn of the bilge and almost from bow to stern. A volunteer team from the Underwater Archaeology Society of Nova Scotia partially excavated the site in the early 1980s, concentrating on the forecastle accommodation area.

This excavation found a typical assortment of contemporary domestic artefacts, including three English halfpennies, the latest dated 1752. Some clothing items were ornate, suggesting that they were from the crew's smart shore-going clothes. Fishing equipment found included lead weights and a leather 'barvel' or fisherman's apron. There were also many bricks from a galley fireplace which appears to have been of similar construction to the intact one found on the privateer *Defence* of 1779.

The site was most notable, however, for the very large number of fish bones found – a total of some 20,000 pieces. Most of these were from cod (*Gadus morhua*) which had been split for salting in the conventional manner. These fish had evidently been stowed in the hold and had been forced for-

Left: Excavation work on the Terence Bay Wreck in 1981. (Trevor Kenchington)

ward during the wrecking into the forecastle, where some intact skeletons were found. The remainder of the fish bones were either from mackerel (*Scomber scombrus*), probably used as bait, or from the skulls and other parts of the cod which were discarded during splitting. (See **Faunal studies**.)

The wreck's hull was built almost entirely of white oak, except for a pine deck. It had the expected structure for a colonial vessel of this size, with occasional mould frames and many disarticulated futtocks. Externally visible parts of the hull were carefully finished and showed traditional decorative elements, suggesting construction by a skilled shipwright. Internally, however, there was evidence of economical construction, including timbers of insufficient scantling to fill their spaces and bark left on a lodging knee where it would be visible to anyone in the hold. This quality of construction was obviously acceptable to the vessel's owner and crew. It may have been a rational response to the short working life expected of a schooner during wartime.

The site is of interest in that most of the information gathered during the excavation came from non-artefact sources. Conven-

tional artefacts revealed little more than the wreck's date and cultural origins. However, the fish bones showed her trade, a quantitative analysis of wood chips established where she was built and where she took on firewood, and geological examination of ballast stones refined this understanding of her origins, while study of the few mammal bones confirmed that the crew shared their home with rats. The relative importance of these kinds of data served as a powerful reminder that archaeology, as a quest for knowledge, should be concerned with all sources of relevant information – and not simply with artefacts. T.J.K.

Right: Cleithrum bones from cod, recovered from the Terence Bay Wreck; measurements from these bones were used to estimate the sizes of the fish and the total weight that had been stowed in the area excavated. (Trevor Kenchington)

ADDITIONAL READING

Carter, J.A. and Kenchington, T.J., 1985, 'The Terence Bay Wreck: Survey and Excavation of a Mid-18th Century Fishing Schooner', in P.F. Johnston (ed.), *Proceedings of the Sixteenth Conference on Underwater Archaeology*, Special Publications Series, 4, Society for Historical Archaeology, Ann Arbor, Michigan.

Kenchington, T.J., 1994, 'An 18th-Century Precursor of the Fishing Schooner's "Great Beam" or "Break Beam"?', *International Journal of Nautical Archaeology*, 23, 35–8.

Kenchington, T.J., Carter, J.A., and Rice, E.L., 1989, 'The Indispensibility of Non-Artefactual Data in Underwater Archaeology', in J. Barto Arnold III (ed.), *Underwater Archaeology Proceedings from the Society for Historical Archaeology Conference, Baltimore, Maryland*, Society for Historical Archaeology, Ann Arbor, Michigan.

Kenchington, T.J. and Kenchington, E.L.R., 1993, 'An Eighteenth-Century Commercial Length-Frequency Sample of Atlantic Cod, *Gadus morhua*, Based on Archaeological Data', *Fisheries Research*, 18, 335–47.

HMS *Terror*
see **Arctic; Franklin Expedition graves**

Texas A&M University, Nautical Archaeology Program

The first academic programme established in nautical archaeology. The basic philosophy of the Nautical Archaeology Program is that **Nautical archaeology** is more than just **Underwater archaeology**: it is the study of the history of seafaring and of humankind's relationship to the world's seas and waterways within the context of the history, economy, and social structure of the time period. In 1976 the academic discipline of nautical archaeology came of age when Dr George F. Bass, the founder of the **Institute of Nautical Archaeology**, affiliated the Institute with Texas

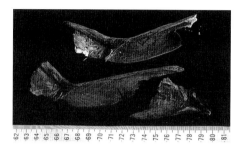

A&M University and started the Nautical Archaeology Program. This programme is the academic arm in this affiliation and the Institute of Nautical Archaeology is a private, non-profit research organization which provides the administrative, logistical, and fund-raising support for the various field projects. Some of the most significant shipwrecks over the past two decades have been excavated through their efforts, and the results have appeared in *National Geographic* articles and in television documentaries.

The Nautical Archaeology Program is part of the Department of Anthropology and students studying in the programme earn either Master of Arts or Doctor of Philosophy degrees in anthropology. In addition to being the first academic graduate programme in nautical archaeology, the Nautical Archaeology Program differs from similar academic programmes in nautical archaeology or maritime history because, through its affiliation with the Institute of Nautical Archaeology, it has an international focus. Because of this international focus, the faculty and the courses cover both the historic period and Old World archaeology. Students are required to take courses in basic archaeological method and theory and a variety of seminar courses which trace the history of seafaring in both the Old and New World. The courses concentrate on three areas of study: the history of seafaring and maritime trade, the history of shipbuilding, and **Conservation** of archaeological finds. Each of these courses looks at seafaring in its broader cultural context, both to see how the nature of the culture influences the design of ships, the structure of trade, and the nature of life aboard ships, and to see how seafaring, naval policy, and maritime trade contribute to the culture as a whole. Different courses deal with specific time periods, geographic and cultural areas.

The programme is internationally known for its research on ship construction and **Reconstruction**, and the conservation of material from underwater sites. A course on the history of wooden ships covers different conceptual approaches to shipbuilding, the major evolutionary building traditions in the **Mediterranean**, northern Europe, and the Far East, along with the relationship of shipbuilding to commercial economics and naval policy. The conservation courses are designed to introduce students to the basic techniques for the assessment and treatment of artefacts, with an emphasis on the treatment of artefacts recovered from the sea.

Because of the programme's connection to the Institute of Nautical Archaeology, the field schools offered in the summers and the theses and dissertations written by many of the students are related to the field excavations sponsored by these two entities. These excavations include the 11th-century Byzantine glass wreck at **Serçe Limani** in Turkey, the Bronze Age shipwreck at **Uluburun**, Turkey, the 9th-century shipwreck at **Cape Gelidonya**, the early 16th-century Spanish shipwreck at Turks and Caicos, the well-known sunken city of **Port Royal**, **Jamaica**, and extensive excavations on a variety of ships in **Lake Champlain**, Vermont. Students are also encouraged to initiate and direct their own projects.

In keeping with the international interests of the Nautical Archaeology Program, it has a varied and eclectic faculty that includes some of the leading personalities in the field of nautical archaeology. In 1996 there were six faculty and one emeritus faculty:

George F. Bass, the founder of both the Institute of Nautical Archaeology and the Nautical Archaeology Program at Texas A&M University. He is the former head of the programme and is best known for his excavations of Cape Gelidonya, **Yassiada**, Serçe Limani and Uluburun. He teaches Classical seafaring, preclassical and near-Eastern seafaring.

Kevin Crisman is best known for his excavations of numerous 18th- and 19th-century shipwrecks in Lake Champlain and the Great Lakes, such as *Eagle* and the Burlington horse-powered ferry. He teaches courses in New World seafaring and post-medieval seafaring.

Frederick H. van Doorninck is a specialist in medieval ship hulls and amphoras and has worked with Dr Bass on all of his excavations. He teaches courses on the history of seafaring, and post-medieval seafaring.

Donny L. Hamilton, the current head of the Nautical Archaeology Program and the Director of the Conservation Research Laboratory, is known for his conservation work on a number of archaeological projects, such as the 1554 Plate Fleet at **Padre Island**, and for his excavations of the sunken city of Port Royal, Jamaica. He teaches courses in historical archaeology and in artefact conservation.

Frederick M. Hocker, the current president of the Institute of Nautical Archaeology, specializes in the history of shipbuilding and medieval archaeology. He is known for his work on shipwrecks from the Netherlands, colonial South Carolina and for his ongoing excavations at the 9th-century **Bozburun Wreck**, Turkey. He teaches courses in ship construction, medieval seafaring, and post-medieval seafaring.

Shelley Wachsmann is a specialist in Bronze Age seafaring in the Levant and is best known for his excavation of the Kinneret boat (see **Sea of Galilee Wreck**). He teaches courses in biblical archaeology, preclassical, and near-Eastern seafaring.

J. Richard Steffy is an emeritus faculty who is known for pioneering many of the techniques used in ship reconstruction and for developing the ship courses now taught in the programme. He continues to work with the programme as an advisor.

Students from the programme have participated in shipwreck excavations on four continents, a host of countries, and a variety of states in the United States. Some of the graduates of the programme have academic positions, others have founded their own research organizations, and several are employed in Government service, as archaeologists for State or Federal departments, while some of the foreign students are archaeologists for their countries. D.L.H.

Thames, River
see **River Thames**

Thames Wrecks
see **Blackfriars Wrecks**

Thematic studies
The notion of collectively analysing and comparing archaeological sites having the same attribute. Thematic studies, long part of terrestrial archaeology, began to be conducted by maritime archaeologists in earnest in the 1980s. They can be con-

trasted with chronological studies, which often examine many related sites of different periods. One of the first thematic studies of underwater archaeological sites was the documentation of the 1588 **Spanish Armada** wrecks off the English and Irish coasts. Colin Martin's examination of these sites in the 1960s showed the importance of drawing from a larger database rather than a single site. Comparison of Armada vessel construction allowed observations that the Spanish craft may have been of inferior construction and not able to withstand the harsh nature of the North Atlantic. Hasty construction and faulty hull designs may have contributed more to Spanish vessel loss than British bombardment. This, among other conclusions resulting from a thematic approach, contributed directly to developing a more accurate, materially based history of the Armada engagement.

Other thematic studies include the historical and archaeological documentation of East India Company vessels and the work of Parks Canada on the Basque whaling operations in **Red Bay**, Labrador. The *International Journal of Nautical Archaeology* devoted a full issue (1990) to the former study, consisting of conference proceedings of the 'English East India Company and its Competitors' that included discussions and comparisons among British, French, and Dutch sites involved in East India commerce. The Parks Canada study examined Basque whaling, and is the first thematic study to include both terrestrial sites and shipwrecks. Earlier thematic approaches include three vessels from the 1554 Spanish Plate Fleet, near **Padre Island**, Texas, systematically excavated by the Texas Antiquities Committee in the 1970s. Some archaeologists questioned the quality of information retrievable from these scattered sites, but excavation proved that much could be learned from a collective, thematic analysis. Multiple vessel assemblage analysis produced several observations that would have been difficult had only one site been studied. For example, the wrecks' numismatic collection, mostly Mexico mint, provided a rare sample of a closely dated early Spanish New World monetary issue and informs on early practices; examination of the vessels' armament – wrought-iron, stave-built guns considered obsolete by 1554 – suggested that newer weapons were reserved for exclusive use in Europe, while New World exploration and colonization expeditions had to make do with older equipment, a clear indication of contemporary priorities.

In the US, historic context development has been an integral part of preservation planning and research since at least 1936. Historic property significance evaluation is typically conducted within historic themes. National and State guidelines have been developed to aid in laying out a framework of historical themes to describe an area's broad developmental patterns. Texas recently developed thematic contexts for maritime research in the state.

A basic assumption of the thematic approach is that decisions about identification, evaluation, registration, and treatment of historic and archaeological properties are most reliably made when information is organized into historic contexts. Resource classification is fundamental to their understanding and to the comparative analysis necessary for making judgements about relative significance and representativeness. The goal of most preservation programmes is to consider the full range of properties representing an area's history; development of comprehensive themes is an important tool in ensuring full representation of historical contexts and the most significant properties are recognized.

The **National Register of Historic Places**, the official list of the United States cultural resources worthy of preservation, provided impetus for several maritime thematic studies. The register is part of a national programme to coordinate public and private sector efforts to identify, assess, and protect the nation's historic and archaeological resources. Site nominations to the register can be made individually or in a group. Group nominations are made in several forms – geographic districts, discontinuous districts, or a thematic group nomination. Thematic nominations, which include sites related in 'a clearly distinguishable way', have served to protect a larger number of cultural resources by placing them on the register, as well as to develop several thematic shipwreck databases.

In the early 1980s, the National Park Service's **Submerged Cultural Resources Unit** conducted archaeological investigations of the **Isle Royale Shipwrecks**. The results of this work were used to develop the first thematic group nomination of shipwreck sites to the National Register. The study focused on the interrelating factors that affected Isle Royale wrecks from a regional context; socio-economic and cultural aspects were considered, as well as the maritime history of the Lake Superior region.

In 1985 the North Carolina Underwater Archaeology Unit (UAU) nominated shipwreck sites from the Civil War period to create the **Cape Fear Civil War Period Shipwreck District**, a thematic nomination based on analysis of numerous related sites (see Wilde-Ramsing). The nomination organized several scattered Civil War-era sites into a cohesive group to provide a management framework.

Nominations of thematic districts have several advantages over single nominations. Sites ineligible for nomination because of lack of individual historical significance or diminished archaeological integrity can qualify for the register when presented as an integral part of a thematic district. Initial district nominations do not need to be inclusive because thematic nominations allow for the addition of sites as they are discovered and researched. The National Park Service's National Historic Landmark Themes (NHL) provides guidelines for thematic studies. Its framework covers all sections of United States prehistory, history and cultural development and provides the context for evaluating the US sites of highest significance. The first shipwreck NHL thematic study was James Delgado's 1986 NHL nomination of California Gold Rush-era sites. This study examined vessels from California to the Falklands (see **Falklands wrecks and hulks**) that operated during the California Gold Rush, which has aided preservation of sites that otherwise would not have qualified for NHL status.

The **Dry Tortugas National Park** Survey is evaluating sites within several thematic contexts. One thematic research approach is examining wrecks associated with the construction of Fort Jefferson to investigate effects of ship transport on fort construction. This approach tested the hypothesis that capitalists, in an effort to maximize profit margins, push vessels beyond safe limits, particularly in transport of bulk trade, an aspect of the 'one more voyage' hypothesis. Documentation of fort construction-related vessels indicates old vessels were employed in 19th-century government contract work. Site documentation, conducted by Brown University under NPS auspices, includes three wreck sites to date containing construction materials such as bricks, cement, nails, and lime. Preliminary observations reveal structural elements with numerous repairs and patches and the use of low-quality ship's materials in vessel construction and rigging elements.

Thematic studies are an essential part of resource management-related archaeological research, and they have begun to be utilized by maritime archaeologist with good research results. Thematic approaches emphasizing comparative analysis can aid data generation about questions that might not be apparent from single-site analysis, which can serve as a springboard to understanding broad principles of maritime behaviour. L.E.M./A.A.

ADDITIONAL READING

Arnold, J. Barto III, 1989, 'Texas Shipwrecks: Overview of Historic Contexts', Technical Report 127, Texas Antiquity Committee, Austin.

Arnold, J. Barto III and Weddle, R., 1978, *The Nautical Archaeology of Padre Island*, New York.

Carrell, T., 1983, 'Shipwrecks of Isle Royale National Park', *Thematic Group Nomination to the National Register of Historic Places*, National Park Service, Washington, DC.

Delgado, J. P., 1986, *California Gold Rush Vessels*, National Historic Landmark Theme Study, Washington, DC.

Delgado J. P. *et al.*, 1985, *Nominating Historic Vessels and Shipwrecks to the National Register of Historic Places*, National Register Bulletin 20, National Park Service, Washington, DC.

Fenwick, V. and Redknap, M. (eds), 1990, *Ships, Cargoes and the East India Trade: The English East India Company and its Competitors*, special issue of *International Journal of Nautical Archaeology*, 19,1, 1-89.

Lenihan, D. J. (ed.), 1996, *Shipwrecks of Isle Royal National Park: The Archeological Survey*, Duluth.

Muckelroy, K. (ed.), 1980, *Archaeology Under Water*, New York.

Murphy, L.E., 1983, 'Shipwrecks as Data Base for Human Behavioral Studies', in R.A. Gould (ed.), *Shipwreck Anthropology*, Albuquerque.

Murphy, L.E. (ed.), 1993, *Dry Tortugas National Park: Submerged Cultural Resources Assessment*, National Park Service, Santa Fe.

Wilde-Ramsing, M., 1985, 'National Register Districts as a Management Tool for Underwater Resources', in P.F. Johnston (ed.), *Proceedings of the Sixteenth Conference on Underwater Archaeology, Boston, Massachusetts*, Ann Arbor, Michigan, special publications 4, 130–33.

Thera

The site on a Greek island in the Cyclades (also known as Santorini) of a wealthy and powerful Late Bronze Age town inundated by volcanic eruptions around 1520 BC. Often associated with the legendary civilization of Atlantis, the Late Minoan IA period site contains a dwelling known as the West or 'Admiral's' House, two rooms of which are decorated with maritime iconography. One (Room 4) has a repeating motif of eight Minoan-style ship *ikria*, or small stern deck cabins, ostensibly made of vertical posts covered with ox-hides and covered with a canopy. The posts terminate in large coloured finials and are decorated with floral swags.

The other (Room 5) contains elaborate marine murals on all four walls, unique to Late Bronze Age Greece. Known collectively as the 'Miniature Frescoes', they tell an intricately detailed story (or series of stories) probably from the homeowner's career; unfortunately, their fragmentary condition prevents a reliable sequential reconstruction, so they are generally interpreted as a series of events or a saga rather than a single tale. Consequently, a number of possible interpretations of the subject matter are possible, as demonstrated by the Additional Reading section below.

At two of the room's corners are two-thirds life-size fisher youths, each holding out strings of several fish. One of the smaller sections displays a number of youths and men on a hilltop, with running water around them. Another shows a building with men and women on top of it, with a small procession of men and women bearing spears or poles leaving it. Above them is a line of horned animals (possibly goats or sheep) with a shepherd at each end. Below the building is a body of white-coloured water with three fragmentary papyriform ships on it; three men are in the sea between the vessels, and their posture suggests that they are unconscious or dead. A third section portrays a long winding stream or river in a sub-tropical locale, with palm and papyrus trees, birds, a lion or griffin, and another sizeable feline. The longest and best-preserved mural strip has a town at either end, separated by a large body of water. The town on the left is circumscribed by two streams or rivers, which feed out of a larger one above it. Along the upper river's edge a lion chases three stags. The buildings in the town are populated with people in the windows and on the roofs; all but one are looking out to sea. A fleet of six large, slender papyriform ships propelled by a long line of paddlers along the side is leaving this town and proceeding towards another at the other end of the mural segment. All six are covered by canopies over most of their lengths, under which are seated several men. All the ships have floral and/or faunal emblems at the tip of the long, slender bows, and the stern of each is characterized by a horizontal member extending into the water. All have single crewmen seated in *ikria* at the stern and a crewman wielding a steering oar. Only one may be under auxiliary sail; the rest are all being paddled across the water, escorted by variegated porpoises cavorting around the ship hulls. The town on the right is larger than the other and is separated into two by a harbour in the middle. The buildings are higher and appear to be set on a hillside sloping down towards the harbour. Several small craft, also papyriform, ply the local waters; they are either rowed, poled or empty, but not paddled. As with the first

town, this one has people in the windows and on the rooftops, as well as a line of men along the shore, all watching the approaching fleet.

There are no comparable murals from other sites, nor are there any writings or inscriptions clarifying the scenes depicted in the Miniature Frescoes. As a consequence, it is possible only to speculate about their meaning. Spyridon Marinatos, who directed the excavations at Thera, hypothesized that the murals represented the return to Thera of a fleet of warships from Libya at the conclusion of a relatively peaceful expedition. The fleet was commanded by the house-owner, probably the admiral in command of the enterprise, who commissioned the mural to commemorate his mission's success. Other scholars have proposed a scene celebrating good relations between the Cretans and Achaeans; a race or procession connected with a cult pageant; a Minoan amphibian raid; a Minoan naval triumph; or a religious ceremony using watercraft that were archaic at the time. P.F.J.

ADDITIONAL READING

Casson, L., 1975, 'Bronze Age Ships: The Evidence of the Thera Wall Paintings', *International Journal of Nautical Archaeology*, 4, 1, 3–10.

Casson, L., 1978, 'The Thera Ships', *International Journal of Nautical Archaeology*, 7, 3, 232–3.

Doumas, C., 1992, *The Wall Paintings of Thera*, Athens.

Ernstson, J., 1985, 'The Ship Procession Fresco: The Pilots', *International Journal of Nautical Archaeology*, 14, 4, 315–20.

Giesecke, H.-E., 1983, 'The Akrotiri Ship Fresco', *International Journal of Nautical Archaeology*, 12, 2, 123–43.

Gillmer, T. C., 1975, 'The Thera Ship', *Mariner's Mirror*, 61, 4, 321–9.

Gillmer, T. C., 1978, 'The Thera Ships: A Reanalysis', *Mariner's Mirror*, 64, 2, 125–33.

Haider, P., 1979, 'Grundsätzliches und Sachliches zur historischen Auswertung des bronzezeitlichen Miniaturfrieses auf Thera', *Klio*, 61, 285–307.

Immerwahr, S., 1977, 'Mycenaeans at Thera: Some Reflections on the Paintings from the West House', in K.H. Kinzl (ed.), *Greece and the Eastern Mediterranean in Ancient History and Prehistory*, New York.

Kennedy, D. H., 1978, 'A Further Note on the Thera Ships', *Mariner's Mirror*, 64, 2, 135–7.

Marinatos, S., 1974, *Excavations at Thera VI*, Athens.

Marinatos, S., 1974, 'Das Schiffsfresko von Akrotiri, Thera', in Gray, D., *Seewesen*, 141–51.

Morgan, L., 1978, 'The Ship Procession in the Miniature Fresco', in C. Doumas (ed.), *Thera and the Aegean World*, vol. 1, London.

Morgan, L., 1988, *The Miniature Wall Paintings of Thera*, New York.

Raban, A., 1984, 'The Thera Ships: Another Interpretation', *American Journal of Archaeology*, 88, 11–19.

Reynolds, C. G., 1978, 'Note: The Thera Ships', *Mariner's Mirror*, 64, 2, 124.

Rubin de Cervin, G.B., 1977, The Thera Ships: Other Suggestions', *Mariner's Mirror*, 63, 2, 150–52.

Tilley, A.F. and Johnston, P., 1976, 'A Minoan Naval Triumph?', *International Journal of Nautical Archaeology*, 5, 4, 285–92.

Wachsmann, S., 1980, 'The Thera Waterborne Procession Reconsidered', *International Journal of Nautical Archaeology*, 9, 2, 287–95.

Warren, P., 1979, 'The Miniature Fresco from the West House at Akrotiri, Thera, and its Aegean Setting', *Journal of Hellenic Studies*, 99, 115–29.

Thermoluminescence dating
see **Absolute dating**

Titanic

Passenger liner that sank in 1912 in possibly the most famous maritime disaster of the 20th century. *Titanic* was the second ship of the Olympic class passenger liners to be constructed by the Harland and Wolff shipyard of Belfast, Northern Ireland for the White Star Line which was owned by the International Mercantile Marine syndicate, owned in turn by the American shipping magnate Pierpoint Morgan. She was the largest ship of her type when she began her maiden voyage from Southampton on 10 April 1912. En route to New York, she struck an iceberg at 2340 on 14 April 1912 and sank at 0220 the following morning. Mr Thomas Andrews, the managing director and chief naval architect of Harland and Wolff, spoke of her as being practically unsinkable, but the press dropped the word 'practically' in their glowing tributes of the new luxurious liner.

As *Titanic* made her way westward on 14 April 1912, she received nine ice-warning messages from ships that had encountered a very extensive ice field in her path. Captain Edward Smith made a course alteration at 1150 after receiving a message from the steamer *Baltic*, but due to an error in its transmission or copying he did not see an ice-warning message from *Mesaba* at 1950 which cautioned ships about large icebergs and an extensive ice field that was in the direct path of *Titanic*. Around 2330 lookouts Frederick Fleet and Reginald Lee spotted an ice mass some 1,365 m off *Titanic*'s starboard bow. The bridge was notified and in a desperate manoeuvre to avoid a collision, officer William Murdock ordered a full port turn, followed by a full-speed astern manoeuvre. *Titanic* turned slowly, but side-swiped the 80,000–300,000 ton iceberg, causing damage of less than 1.2 sq. m to the steel plates and riveted connections as well as punching some holes in the starboard side of the ship over a distance of 90 m of the bow section. The icy cold waters (−2 degrees C) had caused the mild steel plates and rivets to become more brittle and notch-sensitive to the impact with the iceberg and six fissure-like openings of 33 m in length formed in the plates and around rivet holes; rivets failed, and holes were formed about 6 m below the waterline that allowed seawater to flow in at different rates in the first six watertight compartments. The bow filled with some 7,450 tonnes of seawater in the first thirty minutes after the iceberg encounter. This forced the bow to trim down and contributed to a steady, progressive flooding which eventually caused the bow to be submerged and the stern to be upended at an angle of no more than 20 degrees. Around 0210 on 15 April 1912, there was a spectacular hull fracture between the second and third funnels, centred around an expansion joint. The stern settled back to the water surface, but a 15,450 ton deadweight pull of the now water-filled bow section caused the stern section to rise once again and plunge rather quickly below the water surface. During the sinking process, the bow and stern sections completely separated and came to rest some 600 m apart with a substantial debris field in between. At some distance below the water surface the stern section imploded, peeling back deck structure and bulging out the side shell. A third piece, that broke away during the sinking process, was discovered about 20 m in length and 200 m from the bow section.

In the worst peacetime maritime tragedy of the 20th century, only 705 of the 2,222 passengers and crew were rescued. Captain Smith and Mr Andrews went down with the ship. Some of the notable passengers who perished were John Guggenheim, Isidore Strauss and his wife, John Jacob Astor, Major Archibald Butt, a military aide to President Taft, John B. Thayer, and Charles Hays. Two investigations into this disaster, one held by a US committee under Senator William Smith of Michigan and the British Inquiry under Lord Mersey (Sir John Bigham), revealed that there were not enough lifeboats for the people who were aboard that fateful voyage or for the 3,200 people whom the vessel was designed to carry. The British Board of Trade lifeboat regulation of

Titanic sets out from Southampton, April 1912. (Vancouver Maritime Museum)

1890 was subsequently revised, as was the regulation that all ships were to have twenty-four-hour radio service.

The Cunard liner *Carpathia* arrived at the scene of *Titanic*'s demise shortly after 0430 to pick up the survivors. Another ship, SS *California*, remained motionless in the ice flow that night some 30 km northwest of the sinking site. Captain Stanley Lord decided to stop in the eastern edge of the ice flow. Although his crew reported seeing rockets being fired from what appeared to be a large liner that passed them earlier, he made no effort to determine what those rockets meant in the mistaken belief that they were part of a fireworks display at sea. It is very doubtful, however, that the *California* would have rescued any of *Titanic*'s passengers or crew because the coordinates given out in the SOS were incorrect, requiring *California* to proceed westward before heading back through the ice field to the site of the sinking.

Titanic had been the largest ship in the world, having a length of 880 ft (269 m), a beam of 92 ft (28 m), and a displacement of 53,256 tons. The ship was equipped with the latest safety devices and features that exhibited the lavish Edwardian splendour of the time. There have been seven expeditions to the site of the *Titanic* wreck over nine years, commencing with the 1985 joint expedition from Woods Hole Oceanographic Institution, Massachusetts, and the Institut Français de Recherches pour l'Exploitation de la Mer (IFREMER), France, led by Dr Robert Ballard and Jean-Louis Michel, which located the wreck. The 1991 IMAX and 1996 Discovery/Ellipse Expeditions brought back spectacular pictures and samples of the hull from the debris field. Metallurgical and chemical analysis of these

plates from both expeditions has proved that *Titanic*'s hull steel was brittle and notch-sensitive. The chemical analysis confirmed the significant content of sulphur and phosphorous, elements that make steel more notch-sensitive and brittle. The 1987, 1993, 1994, and 1996 expeditions have brought a significant number of artefacts from *Titanic*'s debris field which are a permanent exhibition at the National Maritime Museum at Greenwich, England. RMS *Titanic*, Inc. owns rights to those artefacts retrieved.

The *Titanic* tragedy created a legacy for mariners and ship designers that improved ship subdivision design, the provision of adequate lifeboat capacity, and the use of the radio at sea. An iceberg patrol began during the spring of 1914 and continues to the present day. W.H.G.

Litigation
Legal cases following the loss of RMS *Titanic*. Although a few cases were heard on both sides of the Atlantic in the months following the disaster, they were primarily concerned with compensation and limitation of liability. To a marine archaeologist the more recent cases are of most interest, since their subject matter is the allocation of salvage rights and ownership of any objects retrieved from the wreck.

In the United States the early cases concentrated on limitation of liability by the shipowners Oceanic (trading as the White Star Line) and they arrived at the US Supreme Court in <u>Oceanic Steam Navigation Company, Limited vs Mellor</u> in 1914. The question was whether American or English law applied – if the latter, the shipowner could not force all the US claimants to join in a single action or else be barred from any other action. The Supreme Court held that if a foreign ship is sued in the United States, the ship's owner can invoke the limitation of liability laws of the US. Consequently, a single class action could be insisted upon. This was significant because the only assets available in the limitation of liability fund to be split amongst all the claimants was $91,805.54 of freight and passage money yet to be paid, in addition to the rescued thirteen lifeboats and their equipment. At the same time in England, Ryan vs The Oceanic Steam Navigation Company, Limited was an action to which three others were joined in the names of O'Connell, Scanlon, and O'Brien, represented by relatives. All four were passengers travelling in steerage on *Titanic* and were drowned owing to the alleged negligence of the company's servants. The defendants argued that even if there was negligence, which they denied, they were excluded from liability by an exemption clause printed on the back of the passenger ticket. The court not only found that there had been negligence, but that insufficient notice of the exemption clause had been given to three of the four plaintiffs, and in any case the clause itself was found to be invalid according to the Merchant Shipping Act 1894. The relatives of each of the plaintiffs were awarded £100 in compensation.

Following these decisions, American claimants started to file actions in the English courts in the hope of better compensation, but while the actual negligence trial was continuing in the United States, further negotiations produced an out-of-court settlement on 28 July 1916. It was agreed that Oceanic would pay a total of $664,000 in damages for loss of life, personal injury, and loss of personal effects, provided that all claimants on both sides of the Atlantic dropped their actions, which totalled around $16,000,000. The actual payments were made by one of Oceanic's insurers, the Liverpool and London Steamship Protection and Indemnity Association Ltd.

Personal insurance was not very common in 1912 and many passengers travelled uninsured. Consequently, ownership of any personal items or cargo salvaged, and positively identified, could lie either with the insurance companies who paid out on any claims, or with any surviving passengers and relatives. Some pieces of jewellery found in a suitcase were identified as belonging to two survivors and returned to their descendants, and a survivor was recently presented with the watch that her father had been wearing when he drowned. By law the salvage com-

pany could claim a salvage award which, given the difficult and costly operation, would almost certainly be the entire value of the property, but for ethical and public relations reasons such a claim is unlikely ever to be made.

The modern litigation relating to *Titanic* may be found in two related cases: Marex Titanic Inc. vs The Wrecked and Abandoned Vessel, Its Engines etc., believed to be the RMS *Titanic* and RMS Titanic Inc. vs The Wrecked and Abandoned Vessel, Its Engines etc., believed to be the RMS *Titanic.* The Marex case arose in 1992, five years after salvage work had started at the wreck site, undertaken by IFREMER and Titanic Ventures Inc., a private American company. Marex Titanic sought a declaration of ownership, salvage, and injunctive relief over the site and, further, obtained a warrant of arrest covering not only the wreck but the 1,800-plus objects already salvaged, then in the custody of the French Government and undergoing **Conservation** work at laboratories in France. Once the case came to court, it was immediately obvious that Marex's original claim and the arrest warrant were based on serious factual misrepresentations. Titanic Ventures asked for the arrest to be withdrawn and for an injunction over Marex. The court issued a temporary restraining order which prevented the Marex vessel, which had by then reached the wreck site, from commencing diving operations. A few days later Marex, realizing 'the way the wind was blowing', requested that its case be dismissed, thus rendering all the court's actions, including the injunction and restraining order, null and void, but the court refused. At this point Titanic Ventures formally intervened and asked that it be declared the exclusive salvor of *Titanic*. Its claim was based upon its salvage operation in 1987 and a planned dive in the short weather window in 1993, as well as ongoing work with IFREMER on conservation, and a publicly declared interest in the site – most notably in discussions with the IMAX Corporation and its partners concerning a filming dive in 1991 – sufficient to demonstrate clear and continuous possession of the wreck. By the end of that day Marex's claim had been dismissed and it had been served with a permanent injunction, whilst Titanic Ventures was awarded the exclusive right to salvage the wreck. The district court's decision, refusing Marex voluntary dismissal, was overturned by the Court of Appeal the following year, since when nothing further has been heard to date from Marex Titanic Inc. However, the reversal of the decision

also had the effect of negating the award of salvage rights to Titanic Ventures Inc.

Consequently, the company, now reconstituted as RMS Titanic Inc., sought to establish its claim before all comers. It filed a motion for summary judgement in which Liverpool and London Steamship Protection and Indemnity Association wished to intervene, on the grounds that it had property rights in items on which it had paid insurance claims. Liverpool and London could not, however, show that it had paid a claim on any particular item, only that it had paid a lump sum in settlement of all claims directed against Oceanic, under the latter's liability insurance. This was insufficient to give Liverpool and London any proprietary rights under the principle of subrogation to any specific items recovered, even if it had been able to match any specific claim paid with items recovered.

Many maritime cases such as this are based on a legal fiction that the ship itself is the defendant. Since Liverpool and London's was the only other claim and that was dismissed at the joint request of the parties, there was no further opposition to RMS Titanic Inc.'s claim. A court order was thus issued on 7 June 1994, which found that RMS Titanic Inc. is the salvor in possession of the wreck and wreck site, including the hull, machinery, equipment, contents, and cargo, and that RMS Titanic Inc. is the true, sole, and exclusive owner of any objects salvaged, so long as it remains in possession. This means that even if another salvor should succeed in salvaging any objects from the site, its claim would be barred and it would not have ownership of the objects, so long as RMS Titanic Inc. remains salvor in possession.

What constitutes possession in salvage law depends to a large extent on the circumstances. Given the depth and position of the wreck site and the extremely hazardous and expensive nature of any salvage operations, RMS Titanic Inc. will not be expected to keep a constant human presence nor even to salvage objects every year, so long as it continues active operations in some form. This could consist of an exhaustive survey of the site and all the objects remaining in the debris field, scientific and photographic operations on the hull, or vigilance and consultation with any other expeditions interested in diving on the wreck, the 1991 IMAX/Shirshow Institute expedition being an example. In shallow waters buoys could be maintained over a wreck, but since this would be impossible at such depths, some form of electronic marking could perhaps be used.

A further problem may arise if other

salvors decide to work on the site, and there are intimations that this may already have happened. Although the American court order is binding upon all US nationals, both corporate and individual and US registered ships, it cannot be enforced anywhere else in the world or against nationals or ships of any other state. Rules of private international law state that there must be a direct connection between the property and/or persons involved and the state in which the order was made. The only alternative would be for RMS Titanic Inc. to fight an action for ownership in whichever state any objects may appear. In such a case there is no guarantee that US law would be applied. S.A.W.

ADDITIONAL READING

Ballard, R.D., 1987, *The Discovery of the Titanic*, London.

Biel, S., 1996, *Down with the Old Canoe: A Cultural History of the Titanic Disaster*, New York.

Garzke, W.H. Jr and Brown, D.K., 1996, 'How did the Titanic Really Sink?' *Naval History*, 10, 5 (Oct.), 15-19.

Hoffman, W. and Grimm, J., 1982, *Beyond Reach: The Search for the Titanic*, New York and Toronto.

Hutchinson, G., 1994, *The Wreck of the Titanic*, Greenwich.

Larsen, D.P., 1994, 'Ownership of Historic Shipwreck in US Law', *International Journal of Marine and Coastal Law*, 9, 31–56.

Lord, W. E., 1976, *A Night to Remember*, New York.

Lynch, D. and Marschall, K., 1992, *Titanic: An Illustrated History*, New York and Toronto.

MacInnis, J., 1992, *Titanic, In a New Light*, Charlottesville, Virginia.

Marex Titanic Inc. vs The Wrecked and Abandoned Vessel, Its Engines etc. Believed to be the *RMS Titanic*, 1993 AMC 1258, 1993 AMC 2799.

Montluçon, J. and Lacoudre, N., 1989, *Les objets du Titanic: La memoire des abîmes*, Paris.

Nafziger, J. A.R., 1988, 'Finding the *Titanic*', 12 Columbia, *VLA Journal of Law and the Arts*, 339–51.

Oceanic Steam Navigation Company, Limited vs Mellor, 1913, 233 US, 718.

RMS Titanic Inc. vs The Wrecked and Abandoned Vessel, Its Engines etc. Believed to be the *RMS Titanic*, Civil Action 2, 93cv902, 7 June 1994, unreported, heard in the US District Court, Eastern District of Virginia, Norfolk Division.

Ryan vs The Oceanic Steam Navigation Company, Limited, 1914, 3 Kings Bench, 731.

Timpany, M.S., 1986-7, 'Ownership Rights in the *Titanic*', *Case Western Reserve Law Review*, 37, 72–102.

Treasure

Loot, coins, precious metals, or gems found (or yet to be found) on shipwrecks. Treasure is in the eye of the beholder. For some, shipwrecks with marble statues (**Antikythera Wreck**, 70–80 BC) and bronze ingots (**Cape Gelidonya Wreck**, 1200 BC) might mean treasure, but to many people treasure means gold, silver, and gems. Some of the most widely dispersed (in terms of time and space) treasure-bearing wrecks are those associated with the empires of Spain and Portugal.

During the first 300 years of the Spanish New World (1492–1792) all money was either gold or silver but not in the form of coins as we know them today.

Until the 18th century, most money was cut from silver or gold plate and stamped with the seal of the royal treasury. This 'cut' money had neither perfectly round edges nor often a very legible inscription. It was in fact only one step removed from stamped ingots of precious metals that were so often shipped, and lost to pirates and storms, from the Indies to Spain.

The minted coins of the 18th century, and the cut money of earlier times, circulated in only ten denominations. These were the five types (half, one, two, four, eight) of *real*, a silver coin, and the five types of *escudo* (half, one, two, four, eight), a gold coin. The eight *real*, a silver, dollar-sized coin, was the famous 'piece of eight'. It, and lower denominations, remained legal tender in the US until 1857. The 'double valued' or 'doblon' four or eight *escudos* coins were the legendary coins that English speakers called 'doubloons'.

Except in the earliest decades, Spanish treasure was in silver. Shipped as ingots, coins, or the 'worked silver' as goblets, chains, and other artefacts, these formed the bulk of the cargo of the ships coming from the Indies. This is not to say that most ships didn't carry some gold, but Spanish gold was often from alluvial deposits that were labour-intensive to extract and yielded relatively little. Emeralds came from what is now the Republic of Colombia and pearls from various places throughout the colonial period (the island of Margarita, off the coast of northern South America, was one famous source). Portuguese traffic in precious metals and gems followed a very different path.

Portuguese merchants traded in New World silver (brought to the Orient via the Manila galleon from Acapulco) and African gold for the spices and gems of the East. Famous Portuguese wrecks carrying silver (*Madre de Deus* of 1609), gold (*Bacaim* of 1618), and even captured gem-encrusted thrones and other loot (*Flor de la Mar* of 1511) generated a very large contemporary

literature whose early publications are abundant in the libraries of Lisbon. But a fact often forgotten is that the treasure of the Portuguese overseas trade usually came, after the end of the 17th century, from the gold and diamond mines of Brazil. Indeed for many years in the 18th century, most of Europe's gold and diamonds came from the Portuguese colony of Brazil. Thanks to the destruction of Lisbon in the great earthquake of 1755, information about this trade is best found in the colonial archives of Brazil.

In this regard, Spanish repositories are much richer than those of Portugal for their description of the cargo and ships, collected testimony on ship loss and investigations into the salvage of lost ships. The investigator can find relevant records not only at the colonial record repository of the Archivo General de Indias (Seville, Spain) but also the Archivo General de Simancas (Spain), Museo Alvaro de Bazan (Viso del Marques, Spain) and the

Silver 8 reales of Philip IV of Spain, 1653: a 'piece of eight'.
(Courtesy of the Trustees of the British Museum)

Museo Naval (Madrid, Spain). Also of very great importance are the many provincial and local archives in Spain and the national archives of Spain's former colonies.

The great discoveries of gold in California, Australia and elsewhere in the 19th century frequently required ship transport to bring their precious metal to the financial centres of the world. Ships used in transporting these riches, like **Central America**, lost off the eastern coast of the United States and *General Grant*, lost south of New Zealand, have been the focus of treasure-hunting endeavours in recent years. World Wars I and II also resulted in enormous losses due to attacks of enemy surface and undersea raiders. The most famous salvaged World War treasure wreck is that of HMS *Edinburgh*, which went down in the Barents Sea with approximately four and a half tons of Russian gold. L.H.F.

ADDITIONAL READING

Burgess, R.F. and Clausen, C.J., 1976, *Gold, Galleons and Archaeology*, Indianapolis and New York.

Moreau, J.-P., 1988, *Guide des tresors archéologiques sous-marins des petites Antilles*, Clamart, France.

Pickford, N., 1994, *The Atlas of Ship Wrecks and Treasurer: The History, Location and Treasures of Ships Lost at Sea*, London and New York.

Records Related to Shipwrecks, Information Leaflet Number 65, 1986, Public Record Office, Kew, London.

Serrano Mangas, F., 1991, 'Naufragios y rescantes en el trafico indiano durantee el siglo XVII', *Fondo de Publicaciones*, Dreccion General de Intereses Maritimos, Lima, Peru.

Treasure-fleets

see **Flota of 1715**; **Flota of 1733**

Treasure-hunting

The search for intrinsically valuable objects from historic or archaeological sites for personal or private gain. Within the context of this encyclopaedia, the term is best defined as the search for and recovery of precious metals, jewellery, or other objects of monetary value from shipwrecks which can be sold or marketed for a profit. This is in direct contrast to scientific **Archaeology**, wherein the search is for a greater understanding of past history through the study of those same material cultural remains.

Treasure-hunting has taken a number of different forms throughout the centuries, ranging from simple beachcombers walking along the shore after storms to moonrakers, who tried to lure ships onto the shore with lanterns carried along the beach. Nowadays, the term can mean highly sophisticated and well-funded multinational corporations seeking specific shipwrecks for the booty they may contain. Most treasure-hunters, or salvors, as many of them prefer to be called, profit not from selling valuable artefacts, but by selling shares in limited partnerships to the public. When the public invests in these hunting expeditions, they are investing in a dream or fantasy rather than reality, much as the buyer of a lottery ticket. A close look at the investment prospectuses of such ventures reveals the risks, frequently buried in the fine print. An academic archaeologist, Ricardo Elia, recently described treasure-hunting as 'an industry that squanders precious archaeological resources in what amounts to an elaborate confidence game foisted on a gullible public by treasure-hunters, businessmen, the media, and sadly, even some who call themselves professional archaeologists'.

The subject of treasure-hunting has received ever-increasing media interest in the late 20th century, as salvors try to attract widespread publicity and thereby investors in their schemes. Image-conscious treasure-hunters are careful to portray themselves as swashbuckling, charismatic characters risking their lives on earth's last frontier, spending large sums of money to locate and retrieve treasure from the ocean's depths. Many sprinkle their conversations with archaeological jargon, stress the scientific aspects of their enterprise, and attempt to align themselves with academic institutions or professional archaeologists to legitimize their endeavours. The most direct method for ascertaining whether a project is scientific archaeology or treasure salvage is to learn who owns the artefacts and where they are going, since professional archaeologists do not keep or sell the artefacts they study.

Nowadays, the lower limit for the value of any wreck's treasure seems to hover around the $400 million mark, with several promising inflated values up to $1 billion. These astonishing figures are usually based upon the market value of the rarest, best-preserved piece of jewellery, coinage or bullion, multiplied by whatever number of them a salvor might hope to find. The promoters of these estimates do not mention the fact that a majority of the finds are of lesser condition or rarity, and that if the collection were sold or auctioned at the same time, such a large quantity would devalue the market.

The underwater technology used by salvors has improved exponentially, particularly in the areas of **Remote sensing** and recovery. This technology has filtered down to the public, mainly due to the end of the Cold War and the desire of the technology producers to develop new markets for their products. The remote sensing technology, which is applied to the search process, comprises mainly advances in magnetometry and sonar. Magnetometry detects fluctuations in the earth's magnetic fields, which can be caused by the presence of metals. Sonar bounces sound waves off submerged features and provides a detailed, graphic image of the target. The improved recovery capability consists of small manned submarines or remotely-operated vehicles (ROVs) with mechanical arms and hands that can grab objects and place them in baskets at great depths. The net effect of these technological improvements, which were first applied to the heavily publicized search for *Titanic* in the western Atlantic Ocean at a depth of some 3,800 m in the mid-1980s, permits treasure-hunters to locate and salvage deeper wrecks than was previously possible. Potentially valuable targets, previously inaccessible due to their depth, are now easily reached and recovered, as seen on such sites as *Titanic*, HMS *Edinburgh* and the California Gold Rush steamer **Central America**.

Modern salvage legislation, most often administered by admiralty courts, finds its origin in ancient British law. In many aspects it has changed very little since its early codification. In essence, salvage laws encourage salvors to help ships in distress by offering a reward based upon the value of the rescued ship or its cargo. Traditionally, these ships in distress may be at sea or onshore – the law does not distinguish. For centuries these regulations proved adequate, for there was no concept of the historical or archaeological value of a ship that might have been wrecked decades or centuries earlier. Only with the advent of underwater archaeology and increased public fascination with shipwrecks has the issue become more complex. Modern treasure-hunters invoke the law by declaring shipwrecks, regardless of how long ago they may have wrecked, to be at the same risk as a leaking oil tanker wrecked on a beach. In turn, judges have granted ownership to the salvors. International salvage law basically grants ownership of abandoned shipwrecks in international waters on the basis of 'finders-keepers' (see **Salvage Law**). Some salvors will trace a ship's original owners or their heirs and forge an agreement with them; others do not, sometimes because an owner may not be known (as for wrecks that may be hundreds of years old). In other cases, such as the sunken ocean liner *Andrea Doria*, owners may formally abandon a wreck for liability reasons, fearing that someone might be injured while diving on it.

Naval shipwrecks are a general exception to the rule. Most nations do not permit their wrecked warships to be salvaged by treasure-hunters, since the wrecks are frequently war graves worthy of veneration rather than desecration. Under certain circumstances, exceptions have been made (USS **Tecumseh**, **Hamilton** and **Scourge**, HMS *Edinburgh*, etc.), but they are rare.

Some salvors have hired archaeologists to assist with their salvage, in an effort to foster a public image of proper scientific enquiry. However, experience has shown that these archaeologists lack the authority to conduct field research to a high standard, usually on account of the costs involved. Extensive scientific excavation is time consuming, and therefore far more costly than simply salvaging artefacts. Consequently, salvors' 'archaeological' efforts are generally limited to recovery of treasure and minimal history. As a result, very few archaeologists are willing to work with salvors, and those who do commonly suffer declining reputations within the scientific community. In addition, there is seldom any funding set aside by the salvage community to conserve non-saleable artefacts or adequately publish the results of their research, even when they do employ archaeologists. As a result, whatever little information may be recovered is lost or unavailable to a wide audience.

As currently practised, treasure-hunting is incompatible with scientific archaeology, despite frequent statements by the salvage community to the contrary. An average shipwreck might contain an assemblage of several thousand artefacts, whose relationships to one another and to the ship itself must be understood and recorded to have any significant meaning. For example, the precise find-spot of a coin within a wreck site might tell an archaeologist whether it was part of the captain's private purse, a cargo item, or a common seaman's savings. However, if the provenance or context is not precisely recorded, as is usually the case with treasure-hunters unwilling to devote more resources than necessary to obtain the maximum return with minimum outlay, the information and interpretation potential are lost forever. When thousands of artefacts are multiplied by the thousands of possible relationships between them, and then multiplied again by the hundreds of salvaged shipwrecks, the large-scale loss of information is more easily perceived. Moreover, salvors are interested only in a tiny fraction of the total artefact assemblage; consequently, the remainder is ignored or destroyed. Examples of the hulls and contents of unique shipwrecks that have been pulled apart by hand, powerful machinery, or explosives are too numerous to cite individually. These artefacts, ranging from the hull itself to delicate organic finds or even the unique containers in which 'treasure' may have been stored for transport, are ablated forever. Unfortunately, it is often the artefacts of less monetary value which are rarest, and therefore of greater historic or archaeological significance than the 'treasure'. Historic shipwrecks are unique resources for understanding our past; along with many other marine resources like the whale or seal, they are non-renewable. Once a site is destroyed and dispersed, its contents can never be restored, studied, or shared with others.

As a result of these and other concerns, and in recognition of the severity of the problem, virtually every professional archaeological and museum association with published ethical guidelines throughout the globe has condemned treasure-hunting and

issued ethical policies for the treatment of submerged cultural resources. Among these are the International Council of Museums; the **International Congress of Maritime Museums**; the Society for Historical Archaeology; the **Council of American Maritime Museums**; the American Association of Museums; and the Archaeological Institute of America. In addition, new policies and regulations for underwater heritage have been drafted by the International Council on Monuments and Sites (**ICOMOS**) for review and passage by the United Nations. These new guidelines will severely curb future treasure salvage of historic resources in international waters and also have an impact on the market for trafficking in these properties.

Until these regulations are in place, wreck sites in international waters remain at risk. Wrecks within the waters of various nations fall under the jurisdictions of those countries, whose laws vary widely. For example, in the United States ownership of shipwrecks was turned over by the Federal Government to the individual States in 1988 with the passage of the **Abandoned Shipwreck Act**. Some States do not permit treasure salvage, while others allow it and take a share of the finds. As a result, a distressing trend is emerging, wherein salvors lose interest or their funding for a particular site and abandon them. In these cases, which include such ships as HMS *De Braak* in Delaware and the so-called *General Arnold* in Massachusetts, the salvaged wrecks and artefacts are abandoned to the States in whose waters they were found, and responsibility devolves upon the public for their management. Other nations, such as Greece, Turkey, and Sweden, do not permit treasure salvage under any circumstances. Some countries freely admit salvors and take a share of the finds; still others have no particular regulations governing underwater resources in place. It is towards these latter nations, with outdated or less-developed preservation laws, that treasure-hunters gravitate, in the hopes of cutting deals with governmental bureaucrats either uninterested or unaware of the historical potential in their national waters. However, this number is dwindling, partly as a result of the current revolution in global communications. In addition, the growing popularity of 'eco-tourism', wherein tourists can actually dive on historic shipwrecks, is beginning to put economic pressure on private one-time exploitation. The historic wrecks are beginning to be perceived as long-term marketable assets in protected shipwreck preserves, much like public parks that attract visitors and keep them coming back. Public education on the value of shipwrecks

is an essential goal within the historical and archaeological communities, and their operative phrase of 'take only pictures and leave only bubbles' hopefully will take root, preserving historic shipwrecks for future generations to learn from and enjoy. P.F.J.

ADDITIONAL READING

American Association of Museums, 1987, Statement Submitted by the American Association of Museums to the Subcommittee on Oceanography of the Committee on Merchant Marine and Fisheries, US House of Representatives on H.R. 74, The Abandoned Shipwreck Act, 21 April 1987, US Government Printing Office, Washington, DC., Serial No. 100–17, Printed for the Use of the Committee on Merchant Marine and Fisheries, 170–3.

Andrian, B. L., 1995, 'Treasure Trove, Wreck, and Salvage: Issues in the Reporting and Management of Discoveries Underwater in Britain', in P.F. Johnston (ed.), *Underwater Archaeology Proceedings from the Society for Historical Conference, Washington, DC.*, Society for Historical Archaeology, Washington DC.

Beaudry, M.C., 1988, 'Looting by Any Other Name: Archaeological Ethics and the Looting Problem', *Society for Historical Archaeology Newsletter*, 23, 1, 13–14.

Carrell, T.L., 1988, 'Ethics vs. Commercial Exploitation: What's It Worth to the Future?' Paper presented at the 54th annual meeting of the Society for American Archaeology, Atlanta, Georgia, 7 April.

Council of American Maritime Museums, 1990, Bylaws of the Council of American Maritime Museums, Inc., Council of American Maritime Museums, Mystic, Connecticut, Article VI, 3, Archaeological Standards.

Cummings, C. R., 1986, 'A Matter of Ethics', in C.R. Cummings (ed.), *Underwater Archaeology: The Proceedings of the Fourteenth Conference on Underwater Archaeology*, Fathom Eight, San Marino, California.

Cummings, C.R., 1988, 'National Professional Standards and Guidelines for Underwater Archaeology', in J.P. Delgado (ed.), *Underwater Archaeology Proceedings from the Society for Historical Archaeology Conference on Historical and Underwater Archaeology, Reno, Nevada*, Society for Historical Archaeology, Ann Arbor, Michigan.

Elia, R.J., 1990, 'Pirates Ahoy', *Boston Globe*, 10 September.

Elia, R.J., 1990–91, '*Whydah* Museum is not a Good Idea', *Context*, 9, 1–2, 19–20.

Elia, R.J., 1991, 'The Ethics of Collaboration: Archaeologists and the *Whydah* Project', *Historical Archaeology*, 26, 4.

Elia, R.J., 1995, 'Nautical Shenanigans', *Archaeology*, January/February, 81–4.

ICOMOS, 1990, *Charter for the Protection and*

Management of the Archaeological Heritage, International Committee on the Underwater Cultural Heritage.

Johnston, P.F., 1993, 'Treasure Salvage, Archaeological Ethics and Maritime Museums', *International Journal of Nautical Archaeology*, 22, 1, 53–60.

Keith, D.H., 1995, 'A True Adventure Among Pirates', review of Kiesling, *Antiquity*, 69, 263, 402–3.

Keisling, S., 1994, *Walking the Plank: A True Adventure Among Pirates*, Ashland, Oregon.

Miller, G.L., 1987, 'The Second Destruction of the *Geldermalsen*', book review article, *American Neptune*, 47, 4, 275–81.

Tarler, D. *et al.*, 1995, 'The National Park Service Archaeological Assistance Program and Submerged Cultural Resources Protection', in P.F. Johnston (ed.), *Underwater Archaeology Proceedings from the Society for Historical Conference, Washington, DC.*, Society for Historical Archaeology, Ann Arbor, Michigan.

Throckmorton, P., 1990, 'The World's Worst Investment: The Economics of Treasure-hunting with Real-life Comparisons', in T.L. Carrell (ed.), *Underwater Archaeology: Proceedings from the Society for Historical Conference Tucson, Arizona*, Society for Historical Archaeology, Ann Arbor, Michigan.

Vennochi, J., 1992, 'The Private Sector: Tourist Trap', *Boston Globe*, 19 June.

Trial

Australia's earliest known shipwreck. In 1621 the English East India Company (EEIC) dispatched the ship *Trial* to the Indies; during her outward voyage in May the following year she was wrecked on a reef off the coast of Western Australia. The wreck site of *Trial* was found in 1969 and is the earliest known wreck of an English East Indiaman.

Trial was lost as a result of a navigational error on the part of her master, who was following a new course to the Indies which had been learned from the Dutch East India Company (VOC) a few years earlier. This new fast route to the Indies took an easterly course from the Cape of Good Hope, and then a northerly one to the Indies. Following this course some VOC ships had sailed too far to the east and, as a result, in 1616 the coast of Western Australia had been discovered. There were numerous sightings of this land in the years that followed. Navigators of the time were faced with several problems, both because of uncertainty of the position of the land and the related difficulty in determining the ship's longitude. Inevitably ships ran into difficulties coming unexpectedly on this coast, particularly at night. It is indeed surprising that of all the ships that sailed to

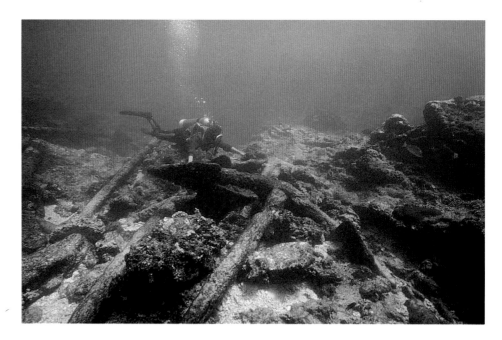

Trial: anchors on the probable wreck site.
(© Western Australia Maritime Museum/Patrick Baker)

the Indies in the 17th and 18th centuries, only five are known to have been lost on this coast, *Trial* on a remote reef off the northwest coast.

In the débâcle that followed, more than 100 men were lost, as well as most of the company's goods. Subsequently, there were serious allegations against the master: that he was negligent; that he had stolen some of the company's goods; that he was an incompetent navigator. Examinations of the records seem to indicate that the master falsified the location of the rocks to make it appear that he had been following orders, and so absolve himself of responsibility. Because of this falsification, Trial Rocks remained undiscovered for over 300 years, simply because they were not where they were said to be.

The subsequent career of the master is of interest, especially as the events reflect on his honesty. On the basis of his statements, now believed to be false, he was acquitted by the company of any blame, and was then given the command of the East Indiaman *Moone*, in which he returned home in 1624. In 1625 *Moone* was wrecked off Dover. The master was immediately imprisoned in Dover Castle for deliberately wrecking the ship. The court case dragged on for two years; finally he made a supplicative petition to the Company and the case was dropped.

By the 18th century there was complete confusion in the charts as to the position of Trial Rocks. At least four groups of non-existent islands were charted in the area, and it was not until the advent of accurate longi-

tude determination and the Admiralty Hydrographic Surveys in the late 18th and early 19th century that these anachronisms were sorted out.

Initially, the Admiralty officially declared Trial Rocks non-existent. Later their position was rather arbitrarily assigned to a group of islands in the general area. In 1934 the master's letters were published and showed that a reef known as Ritchie's Reef was in fact the reef on which *Trial* was lost. The Australia Pilot was amended and so finally Trial Rocks were officially and correctly located 314 years after their first tragic discovery.

In 1969 an expedition was mounted to locate the wreck site of *Trial*. On the first day of the search around the rocks, a wreck site was located and tentatively identified as that of *Trial*. Although four expeditions have visited the site since, no evidence has been found to identify the site conclusively, although circumstantial evidence indicates that the wreck site is that of *Trial*. J.G.

ADDITIONAL READING

Green, J.N., 1977, *Australia's Oldest Wreck: The Loss of the Trial, 1622*, BAR Supplementary Series 27, Oxford.

Green, J.N., 1986, 'The Survey and Identification of the English East India Company Ship *Trial* (1622)', *International Journal of Nautical Archaeology*, 15, 93–104.

Triangulation
see **Trilateration**

Trilateration

A technique for mapping the X, Y coordinates of points on a site using horizontal distance measurements from an unknown point to two or more points that have been already mapped and thus are of known co-odinates. The unknown point is then plotted using a scale rule and a compass on a plan view of the site. If three or more distances have been measured the three arcs intersect to make a 'cocked hat' or 'triangle of error', the size of the 'hat' being a measure of confidence in the plot. This technique is also known widely in the community as triangulation (although distances, not angles, are measured).

Refinements of the technique include the use of a plumb line to ascertain the distance below the plane of the primary datum points, **Baseline trilateration** which uses any known points on a line in order to gain the best geometry; and the **Direct Survey Method**, which is fully three-dimensional. N.R.

ADDITIONAL READING
Wilkes, B.S.T., 1971 *Nautical Archaeology*, Newton Abbott, Devon.

Truk Lagoon Wrecks

A substantial collection of World War II Japanese vessels sunk during a series of aerial raids in 1944–5. Truk Lagoon, a 64 km diameter atoll comprising 245 islands in the Central Pacific, is an exceptional natural anchorage. Truk, a German colony, was ceded to Japan after World War I and developed as a base for the Imperial Japanese Navy's Fourth Fleet. Known as the 'Japanese **Pearl Harbor**', Truk was fortified after 1940, when small repair and refuelling facilities and a scaplane base were built. Additional fortifications were added after January 1944 in anticipation of an Allied invasion, and Imperial Japanese Army troops arrived to garrison the islands. During the war, American radio broadcasts referred to Truk as the 'impregnable bastion of the Pacific'.

Between 1942 and 1944 the combined fleet of the Imperial Japanese Navy operated out of Truk, and many capital ships, including battleships, carriers, cruisers, and lesser combatants were based in the lagoon. A large number of Japanese merchant vessels, important to the war effort, also used Truk as a protected anchorage.

The Allies, using aircraft from carrier task forces, attacked and devastated Truk and its shipping in 1944–5. After an aerial reconnaissance, which unfortunately warned many of the Navy's capital ships, which fled, Truk was attacked on 16–17 February and 29–30 April 1944 by the United States Navy, and on 16 June 1945 by the British Royal Navy. US bombing raids, by B-24 and B-29

aircraft, also hit Truk. In 1944 US military planners also considered dropping the atomic bomb, then under development, on Truk's anchorage, but the plan was never acted upon.

After the war the US Strategic Bombing Survey concluded that the strikes against Truk had destroyed more than 416 aircraft, and sunk at least forty-three major ships, including three light cruisers, four destroyers, a seaplane tender, a patrol vessel, and numerous small craft. Many of the atoll's airstrips and naval facilities were crippled or destroyed. Truk had been neutralized as an extension of Japanese military power in the Pacific.

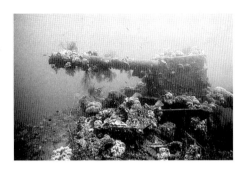

Truk Lagoon wreck: Fujikawa. *(NPS/Larry Murphy)*

Truk Lagoon wreck: a Japanese tank. (NPS/Jim Bradford)

The carrier raids and bombing of Truk left a substantial submerged material record in the form of sunken vessels, aircraft, and equipment. Truk Lagoon is today considered one of the world's top diving attractions because of its large number of World War II shipwrecks, but comparable collections of wrecks available for archaeological study and recreational diving are also found at Kwajalein and Bikini atolls (see **Crossroads Wrecks**), and at **Guadalcanal**.

The average depth of Truk Lagoon is 45–75 m, although it reaches 90 m in some places. More than forty wrecks have been

discovered by divers. Some of the wrecks protrude above the water, while others lie deep in the lagoon. The deep water wrecks have an incredible array of untouched material, including cargoes, armament and ordnance, and **Human remains**, although a concerted effort by Japanese groups has recovered many remains for cremation in funeral services ashore.

The wrecks of Truk Lagoon, including aircraft, were declared historical monuments by the Truk Legislature on 14 August 1971. Truk Lagoon is one of the world's few underwater **National parks** or **National marine sanctuaries** dedicated to shipwrecks, many of which are now incredible marine habitats. Sport diving is encouraged, and dive tourism is an important part of the Trukese economy, but the removal of artefacts from the wrecks and aircraft is prohibited.

Surveys and photographic documentation of the wrecks at Truk have been undertaken by diving researchers and historians, and in 1992 the US National Park Service's **Submerged Cultural Resources Unit**, at the request of the government of Truk, documented the impact of dynamite fishing and sport diving on a number of sites. Several documentary films, books, and articles in a number of magazines, including *National Geographic*, have greatly contributed to Truk's fame and popularity. J.P.D.

ADDITIONAL READING
Bailey, D.E., 1989, *World War II Wrecks of the Kwajalein and Truk Lagoons*, Redding, California.
Lindemann, K.P., 1982, *Hailstorm Over Truk Lagoon*, Singapore.
Rosenberg, P.A., 1981, *Shipwrecks of Truk*, USA.
Stewart, W.H., 1985, *Ghost Fleet of the Truk Lagoon*, Missoula, Montana.

USS *Tulip*

Union gunboat employed during the US Civil War. During the closing years of the Civil War the gunboat was assigned to the eclectic little fleet known as the Potomac Flotilla. USS *Tulip* was built in 1862. Originally called *Chih Kiang*, it was intended to serve the Chinese Government as a river patrol boat. In default of payment, it was renamed and sold to the **US Navy**. Impatient at the snail's pace, the captain ordered a defective boiler fired. Just upstream from the Piney Point lighthouse, St Mary's County, Maryland, the starboard boiler exploded, killing fifty-nine of the sixty-nine personnel aboard. Of the ten survivors rescued, two subsequently died.

During the Civil War, Maryland was in the awkward position of having southern sympathies while being federally occupied. In order to protect Washington, to control the north–south border, and to prevent blockade running, the Potomac Flotilla was created. The fleet patrolled not only the Potomac River but also portions of Chesapeake Bay around the mouths of important rivers such as the Rappahannock and the Piankatank.

The Navy purchased *Tulip* in 1863 for $30,000, acquiring its sister ship *Fuchsia* at the same time. It was refitted as a gunboat with two 24 pounder guns and a 20 pounder Parrott gun. The vessel saw action from August 1863 until July 1864, by which time its condition was deteriorating. In spite of repeated requests for repairs, the vessel continued in service. When two engineers finally refused to continue to run the ship, so concerned were they about the state of the boilers and engine, they were suspended then demoted.

By November the starboard boiler was so defective it could no longer be ignored and the ship was ordered upstream to Anacostia for repairs. After coating at St Inigoes, *Tulip* departed on 11 November 1864 at 3 p.m. with strict instructions not to use the starboard boiler. Heavily manned with returning military personnel, *Tulip* began to limp up the Potomac River to the Navy Yard near Washington, DC. However, when it took more than three hours to travel the comparatively short distance to pass Piney Point, Captain William Smith ordered the boiler to be fired; the official excuse was that the slow pace made the vessel vulnerable to Confederate attack. The fact of the matter was that there had been relatively little Confederate activity in the area for some time and *Tulip* carried two additional guns, making a total of five. It is more likely that the captain was keen to reach the yard because many of the personnel aboard were going to leave and he was himself to be met by his wife. The explosion took out most of the starboard side of the vessel and killed the majority of men just sitting down to dinner in the mess immediately above the engine room. Fifty-nine of the sixty-nine personnel aboard perished.

Tulip sank so quickly that the lifeboat could not be lowered and many of those who escaped the explosion died in the icy November waters. The explosion could be heard not only at St Inigoes but as far away as the prisoner of war camp at Point Lookout at the mouth of the Potomac almost thirty kilometres distant. The tug *Hudson* arrived on the scene in about an hour and picked up the ten survivors (two later died). Only eight bodies were recovered, and these were interred near St Inigoes at a site now marked as the smallest naval cemetery in the United States.

Prior to the existence of protective heritage legislation, the remains of *Tulip* were rediscovered and extensively collected in the 1960s and 1970s by local divers from Virginia. This was also before the US Navy had reasserted ownership and title to its submerged remains. It was 'officially' rediscovered in the 1980s using **Remote sensing** technology. In 1995 the Maryland Maritime Archaeology Programme (MMAP) of the Maryland Historical Trust's Office of Archaeology received a Department of Defense Resource Management Legacy Grant to study the remains and determine a plan for their management. Fieldwork was undertaken using volunteer divers working with State underwater archaeologists.

The remains are in only about fifteen metres of water but the strong currents and near-zero visibility complicate diving and recording, and severely limit photography. Work was completed on the site in October 1995. Results indicated that damage was severe in localized areas but that the overall structure of the vessel was sound. Collection of objects by divers was much more extensive than expected. Working with the original divers (then teenagers and now middle-aged) resulted in the return of more than 1,300 artefacts to the Navy. These included a glass decanter, brass lanterns with intact globes and wicks, a brass octant, a ewer and basin, as well as personal items like a comb, uniform buttons, ornamental brass pieces from an officer's sword, and hardware from mini balls to the vessel's speed log, and even an assortment of doorknobs; sadly all without provenance. The armament had not been recovered by the time of writing and disturbing reports were received that the individuals who raised those pieces also have in their possession human remains, which is a much more serious concern.

The site was still closed to recreational diving in 1997. Once the management study has been completed the Maryland Historical Trust will be in a better position to make recommendations to the Navy as to how best to deal with the resource. S.B.M.L.

ADDITIONAL READING

Morr, T., 1996, 'Blown to Atoms', *Naval History*, May/June, 10, 3.

Shomette, D., 1982, *Shipwrecks on the Chesapeake*, Centreville, Maryland.

Thompson, B., 1996, 'Legacy of a Fourth-Rate Steam Screw', *Naval History*, May/June.

Tune Ship

Early 10th-century ship burial from Haugen, Rolvsøy, Østfold, south Norway. The ship was excavated in 1867 and was the first Viking ship ever found. The local landowner found the ship while removing a large mound for agricultural purposes. The archaeological **Excavation** was led by Oluf Rygh, a professor of archaeology at the University of Oslo. The ship caused a sensation when found, and was taken to Oslo and exhibited in a special building. When the larger and better-preserved **Gokstad Ship** was excavated in 1880, the Tune Ship was put into the reserve collection of the University Museum, where it remained until 1930. It was then moved to the Viking Ship Museum, where it is exhibited with the **Oseberg** and **Gokstad Ships**.

The Tune Ship is not as well preserved as the Oseberg and Gokstad ships. The burial mound was partly made of blue clay, and partly of earth. Those parts of the find which were covered by clay are in excellent condition, while the rest disintegrated. Apart from the ship, only a few wooden objects were found. Important artefacts that helped identify the wreck are fragments of wood with carving in the Borre style, and the probable remains of a saddle. Based on these, the ship was dated to c.AD 900. Iron artefacts were observed only as rust stains during the excavation. A sword handle, spearhead, and the central iron boss for a wooden shield were identified. Before archaeological excavation started, the farmer had reportedly recovered human and animal bones. Small fragments of a burial chamber were found. Unlike the tent-like structures at Oseberg and Gokstad, the burial chamber of the Tune Ship seems to have been made by ramming vertical planks into the clay outside the ship's sides. The roof was probably flat. The weapons observed during excavation strongly indicate that this is a male grave.

After the excavation, the weakest part of the hull was strengthened by nailing on narrow iron bands, but **Reconstruction** was not attempted.

Dating by dendrochronology has now given felling dates for ship and burial chamber timbers from *c*.AD 910 and *c*.AD 910–20. This is contemporary with the Gokstad Ship. The two vessels are closely similar in construction, but not in hull shape. If the mast of the Tune Ship was placed at the midship frame as in the Gokstad Ship, the total length would have been about twenty metres. There are seven bottom strakes, a wedge-shaped transition strake and two top strakes above the crossbeams. There are no indications in the rib system of top timbers to support further strakes, as were found in the Gokstad Ship. There are no traces of oar holes in the fragments found of the tenth strake. If it did contain oar holes, it must have been very wide. The second to sixth strakes have lashing cleats for fastening the ribs. The rib tops rest against a low, triangular cleat on strake seven and are let into the underside of the crossbeams which rest against the wedge-shaped *meginhufr*, 'strong (or mighty) strake'. Knees on the crossbeams support strake nine and ten.

If the ship had only ten strakes, the maximum beam was *c*.4.5 m and the height from the underside of the keel to the sheerstrake amidships was approximately 1.3 m. This gives the ship a very low freeboard. This is compensated for by the strong outward slope of the two upper strakes. They would give good extra righting force when the ship heeled under sail. The keel is incomplete forward, but it was originally about fourteen metres long. Aft, the transition piece and a small fragment of the sternpost are still in place. The keel is T-shaped in cross-section, and is not as high as the Gokstad keel. The first strake is riveted to the 'wings' of the keel. The second to sixth strakes have lashing cleats for the ribs. Unlike the Oseberg and Gokstad ships, the ribs have only one hole for each cleat. The seventh strake has a low triangular cleat where the end of the ribs rest. The next strake is wedge-shaped, and similar to the *meginhufr* of the Gokstad ship. Above the *meginhufr*, there are two wide strakes, partly preserved. Crossbeams of pine span the hull at *meginhufr* level. The beams have rabbets for loose deck boards, but these were not found. Unlike the Oseberg and Gokstad Ships, there are no stanchions supporting the middle of the crossbeams. The sturdy rudder rib and rudder were found loose and both are of pine.

The mast support is a 3.15 m long keelson spanning four ribs and a 3.85 m long mast partner resting on five crossbeams. No rigging details were found apart from a short fragment of the mast still standing in the mast-step. The hull shape is shallower than the Gokstad Ship, with an open, flaring midship section. The robust keelson and mast partner clearly show that the ship was intended for serious sailing in spite of the low freeboard. The ship was found on the shore of a navigable river, about ten kilometres from the sea, and it has been suggested that its shape reflects the shallow conditions of the 'home harbour'. Reports of a ship found in the 18th century on one of the neighbouring farms and a large chamber grave on the same farm indicate that several members of a local Viking dynasty were buried in the area. Written sources are very vague for this part of Norway, and the buried man cannot be identified with any known historical person. A.E.C.

ADDITIONAL READING
Shetelig, H., 1917, *Tuneskibet*, Oslo.

Turtle Shell Wreck
see **Chesapeake Flotilla**

Tyjger

Colonial-period Dutch vessel whose remains were discovered buried beneath New York streets in 1916 and re-analysed in the 1990s. During construction of the Interborough Rapid Transit line's tunnels near the southern end of Manhattan Island in 1916, workers encountered the charred remains of a ship's bow. Bedded in charcoal were a keel, stem, keelson, floors, and several hull planks. A 2.6 m section of the remains was removed and ultimately placed within the collection of the Museum of the City of New York. Other portions of the ship were plotted in 1916 but not recovered, although several artefacts found in conjunction with the hull were removed. These included trade beads, clay pipes, blue and white pottery sherds, a cannon ball, a Dutch broad-headed axe, and chain. The artefacts have since disappeared.

Historians surmised – based on the location of the find near the original shoreline of Manhattan Island, the artefacts, and the ship's construction – that the remains were those of the Dutch ship *Tyjger* ('Tiger'). Under the command of Captain Adriaen Block, *Tyjger* was on a fourth trading voyage to Nieuw Amsterdam (New York) when she caught fire and burned in 1613 while loading for the return to Holland. The loss of the ship, prior to the establishment of a Dutch settlement on the island, stranded Block and his crew for the winter. Surviving with the help of the local Indians, they built a smaller ship, *Onrust* ('Restless'), and sailed for home in the spring of 1916.

Archaeologist J. Richard Steffy, studying the remains of the ship, and working with metallurgical evidence and carbon-dating of the timbers, as well as the construction of the timbers, dates the find to the early 17th century; hence the remains are probably those of *Tyjger*. The problems of working on buried ship remains in an urban setting are highlighted by *Tyjger*, however. Surmising that as much as 15.2 m or more of the wreck may have survived buried beneath Manhattan, archaeologists eagerly monitored the excavation of the site in 1968 for the construction of the World Trade Center, but nothing was found except two unassociated anchors. J.P.D.

Uluburun

Late Bronze Age shipwreck site southeast of
Kaş on the southern coast of Turkey. Dated
to the late 14th century BC, it is the source of
one of the largest assemblages of ancient
trade goods, both raw materials and manufactured items, yet discovered in the **Mediterranean Sea**. The ship was most likely of
Canaanite or Cypriot origin and probably
embarked from one such port for the
Aegean, with Mycenaeans aboard for some
part of the journey. Artefacts from at least
eleven different cultures attest the manifold,
far-reaching trade conducted in the Late
Bronze Age Mediterranean, and may help
refine some Late Bronze Age chronologies.

Discovered in 1982 by Turkish sponge
diver Mehmet Çakir some sixty to seventy
metres off the eastern face of Uluburun, or
'Grand Cape', the wreck lay between about
forty-two and sixty one metres deep on a
rocky slope. A preliminary survey in 1983
was followed by **Institute of Nautical Archaeology**
(INA) excavations between 1984 and 1994,
under the auspices of the Bodrum Museum
of Underwater Archaeology and the Republic of Turkey. Directed by George F. Bass in
1984 and 1985 and by Cemal Pulak between
1986 and 1994, archaeologists made 22,413
dives totalling 6,613 hours of bottom-time
on the site, which was completely excavated.

The ship's primary cargo comprised
approximately ten tons of copper and one
ton of tin. Terebinth (*Pistacia atlantica*)
resin, raw glass, hippopotamus and elephant
ivory, logs of *Dalbergia melanoxylon* (African
blackwood, called ebony by the Egyptians)
and Lebanese cedar, ostrich eggshells
(intended for use as containers), and murex
opercula (possibly an incense ingredient)
were also important cargo materials. Prior
to **Excavation**, most were known primarily or
only from cuneiform texts or Egyptian tomb
paintings. Almonds, pine seeds, figs, olives,
grapes (or wine or raisins), safflower, black
cumin, sumac, coriander, whole pomegranates, and wheat and barley found on the
wreck could have been trade goods or foodstuffs for passengers and crew.

Most of the copper cargo consisted of 354
four-handled or 'ox-hide' ingots weighing
an average of 24.61 kg and 130 plano-
convex discoid or 'bun' ingots. Given an
average weight of 25 kg per ox-hide ingot
on the wreck, 354 ingots would correspond
to approximately 325 talents of copper,

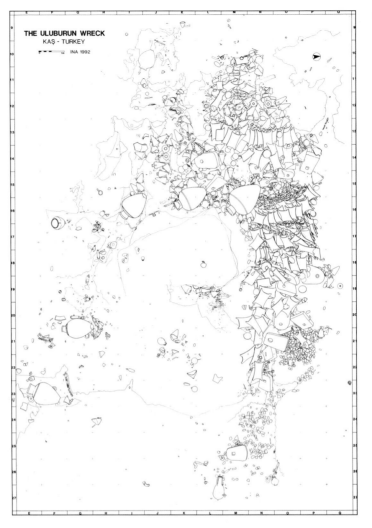

Site plan of the Kaş Wreck at
Uluburun. (© INA)

Excavation in progress in he
middle section of the Kaş
Wreck at Uluburun. Above a
stack of copper ingots lie a
row of stone weight-anchors.
(© INA)

recalling mention in the Amarna letters (British Museum, EA 34, 35) of shipments of 100 and 200 units of copper from Alashia to Egypt. Two groups of mould siblings (i.e. ingots cast in the same mould) have been found among those cleaned and studied. At least 160 ox-hide and nearly a quarter of the bun ingots bear marks of unknown meaning chiselled into their surfaces. Initial lead isotope analyses permit provisional association of the ox-hide ingots with Cypriot copper ores and some of the bun ingots with a hitherto unknown ore source.

The estimated one ton of tin ingots, cast mostly in the ox-hide form and later cut primarily into quarters (but also halves), are the earliest known securely dated tin ingots. At least one exhibits a mark found on some of the copper ingots.

Approximately one ton of resin chemically identified as terebinth was found within more than 145 Canaanite amphoras of a northern type. This may be what the Egyptians termed *sntr*, tribute the Egyptians are believed to have received chiefly from Canaan. In Egypt, *sntr* was primarily burned as incense. This resin may also provide an alternate translation for the Linear B word *ki-ta-no*, which was received annually in great quantities at Knossos and has been argued to mean terebinth fruits.

Some 175 glass ingots of discoid/truncated cone shape are cobalt blue, turquoise and, in one instance, lavender in colour. These are the earliest intact glass ingots known, and are probably the *mekku* and the *ehlipakku* on Ugaritic and Amarna tablets that list trade goods from the Syro-Palestinian coast. The cobalt blue glass is chemically identical to the blue glass of 18th-dynasty Egyptian core-formed vessels and to that of Mycenaean pendant beads, suggesting a common source of material.

The largest single group of manufactured items on the ship numbered at least 135 Cypriot pottery vessels: more than eighty finewares included White Slip II milk-bowls, White Shaved juglets, Base-ring II bowls, and Bucchero jugs; among the Cypriot coarsewares were *pithoi*, or large storage jars, oil lamps, trefoil-mouth pitchers, and wall brackets. Mycenaean objects included lentoid seals, nearly two dozen pieces of fine and utilitarian pottery, a long bronze pin, Baltic amber beads, glass pendant beads, razors, knives, spearheads, and swords. Among scrap and usable Canaanite gold and silver jewellery pieces were gold pectorals, medallions, pendants, beads, and a ring ingot. The head of a stone ceremonial sceptre-axe has its best parallel, though of bronze, in a hoard in modern Romania. A

stone parallel and a casting mould have been discovered in Bulgaria. Syrian, Assyrian, Kassite, and Old Babylonian cylinder seals were joined by Egyptian objects of gold, electrum, silver, and stone. The most important Egyptian artefact is a gold scarab inscribed with the name of Nefertiti, wife of the pharoah Akhenaten. The partial reversal of her name suggests to some scholars that late in Akhenaten's reign, or shortly after his death, Nefertiti was co-regent or pharaoh of Egypt. Various weapons and tools are Canaanite, Mycenaean, Near Eastern, Aegean coastal, and possibly southern Italian types.

Other noteworthy items from the wreck consist of copper or bronze cauldrons and bowls; at least five vessels made of tin, more than have been found previously across the entire Bronze Age Near East and Aegean regions; two ivory duck-shaped cosmetics containers with pivoting-wing covers, and an ivory trumpet in the form of a ram's horn; modified tortoise carapaces probably used as sound chambers for musical instruments; a large golden goblet or chalice; and thou-

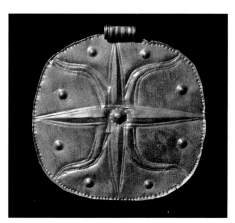

Gold medallion decorated with a star motif from the Kaş wreck at Uluburun. (© INA)

sands of beads of glass, faience, agate, carnelian, quartz, gold, bone, seashell, ostrich eggshell, and amber.

The largest set of Bronze Age zoomorphic pan-balance weights discovered to date includes a sphinx, bovines, waterfowl, frogs, lions, and a fly. Preliminary studies of over 120 additional stone and bronze weights of primarily sphenoid and domed shapes suggest that the dominant mass standard was probably based on the Egyptian *qedet* and averages 9.3 g, well within the range of the standard used along the Syro-Palestinian coast and Cyprus. From within one of the Cypriot pithoi emerged the oldest book, or diptych, yet known. Made of boxwood with a three-piece ivory hinge, it comprises two

leaves 6.2 cm wide by 9.5 cm long with inner faces slightly recessed and scored with cross-hatching to receive wax writing surfaces. One leaf of a second diptych was also recovered. Clearly, the folding writing tablets in Homer's *Iliad* (6.169) are not anachronistic.

The ship's hull, approximately 15-16 m long and built of cedar planks and oak tenons and pegs, constitutes the earliest known seagoing ship built with pegged mortise-and-tenon joinery. In this mode of construction, a shell of planks is assembled first, with framing elements added only after some or all planks are in place. Remarkably, no evidence for frames has yet been discerned among the hull fragments.

With regard to the nature of the Uluburun ship's voyage, five faience drinking cups, shaped like ram's heads, are probably the Near Eastern animal-head shaped cups often sent as value-laden gifts from one court to another. Collections of cylinder seals were often dispatched in a similar capacity and the Amarna Letters show that raw and worked ivory articles were gifts exchanged reciprocally. These factors, and the Canaanite, Mycenaean, Cypriot, Egyptian, Nubian, Baltic, northern Balkan, Old Babylonian, Kassite, Assyrian, eastern Near Eastern, and possibly Sicilian or southern Italian objects, indicate that the Uluburun ship was bearing an official offering of royal gifts, as well as items of international trade intended primarily for a single destination.

The ship's Canaanite or Cypriot origin is suggested by tools, a razor, amulets, and many other personal effects of those on board, in addition to most of the cargo having originated on the Syro-Palestinian coast. Further, a bronze female figurine, partly clad in gold, shares affinities with Syro-Palestinian figurines, and may have been intended to protect the ship and its passengers at sea. Among the galley wares were heavy, saucer-shaped Syro-Palestinian oil lamps with burned nozzles, presumably as a result of use aboard ship. The ship's twenty-four stone anchors, probably taken aboard in the ship's home port, are of a type well known in the eastern Mediterranean and practically unattested in the Aegean.

That the ship and crew were either Cypriot or Canaanite and appear to have been bound for the Aegean supports theories submitted by George F. Bass in his publication of the Late Bronze Age shipwreck at **Cape Gelidonya**. Bass argued for a significant east–west seaborne trade of copper, tin, and other raw materials from the eastern Mediterranean during the Late Bronze Age, and that eastern Mediterranean seafarers,

Duck-shaped cosmetic container of ivory from the Kaş wreck at Uluburun. (© INA)

not Mycenaeans, played a large, even dominant, role in that trade.

The Nefertiti scarab, the Mycenaean pottery, and absolute dendrochronological data from the Uluburun wreck are more consistent with the lower chronologies for Egyptian rulers. Thus the LHIIIA:2/LHIIIB:1 transition may be conservatively placed between 1320 and 1295 BC, after Akhenaten and some time before Horemheb.
M.A.F.

ADDITIONAL READING

Bass, G.F., 1986, 'A Bronze Age Shipwreck at Ulu Burun (Kaş): 1984 Campaign', *American Journal of Archaeology*, 90, 269–96.

Bass, G.F., 1987, 'Oldest Known Shipwreck Reveals Splendors of the Bronze Age', *National Geographic*, December, 172, 6, 692–733.

Bass, G.F., Frey, Donald A., and Pulak, Cemal, 1984, 'A Late Bronze Age Shipwreck at Kaş, Turkey', *International Journal of Nautical Archaeology*, 13, 271–9.

Bass, G.F. *et al.*, 1989, 'The Bronze Age Shipwreck at Uluburun: 1986 Campaign', *American Journal of Archaeology*, 93, 1–29.

Gale, N.H., 1991, 'Copper Oxhide Ingots: Their Origin and Their Place in the Bronze Age Trade in the Mediterranean', in Noël H. Gale (ed.), *Bronze Age Trade in the Mediterranean*, Jonsered, Sweden.

Haldane, C. Ward, 1990, 'Shipwrecked Plant Remains', *Biblical Archaeologist*, 53, 1, 55–60.

Haldane, C. Ward, 1993, 'Direct Evidence for Organic Cargoes in the Late Bronze Age', *World Archaeology*, 24, 348–60.

Mills, J.S. and White, R., 1989, 'The Identity of the Resins from the Late Bronze Age Shipwrecks at Ulu Burun (Kaş)', *Archaeometry*, 31, 37–44.

Payton, R., 1991, 'The Ulu Burun Writing-Board Set', *Anatolian Studies*, 41, 99, 106.

Pulak, C., 1988, 'The Bronze Age Shipwreck at Ulu Burun, Turkey: 1985 Campaign', *American Journal of Archaeology*, 92, 1–37.

Pulak, C. and Frey, D.A., 1985, 'The Search for a Bronze Age Shipwreck', *Archaeology*, 38, 4, 18–24.

Symington, D., 1991, 'Late Bronze Age Writing-Boards and their Uses: Textual Evidence from Anatolia and Syria', *Anatolian Studies*, 41, 111–23.

Warnock, P. and Pendleton, M., 1991, 'The Wood of the Ulu Burun Diptych', *Anatolian Studies*, 41, 107–10.

UN Law of the Sea Convention

A 1982 treaty that creates a structure for the governance and protection of all of the sea, including the airspace above and the seabed and subsoil below. In particular, the United Nations Convention on the Law of the Sea provides a framework for the allocation of jurisdiction, rights, and duties among states that carefully balances the interests of states in controlling activities off their own coasts and the interests of all states in protecting the freedom to use ocean spaces without undue interference.

The convention recognizes the maritime zones, details the regimes for dealing with the resources in these areas, including living marine resources (such as fishing), non-living resources (including those of the continental shelf and the deep seabed beyond the limits of national jurisdiction), and marine scientific research, and provides a framework for the protection and preservation of the marine environment of these areas. The convention contains various mechanisms for settling disputes regarding these provisions. Other provisions of the convention relate to maritime boundary delimitation, enclosed and semi-enclosed seas, landlocked and geographically disadvantaged states, and technology transfer, as well as definitions and the general and final provisions.

In setting out the various maritime zones, the convention addresses the balance of coastal and maritime interests with respect to all areas of the sea. From the absolute sovereignty that every state exercises over its land territory and superjacent airspace, the exclusive rights and control that the coastal state exercises over maritime areas off its coast diminish in stages as the distance from the coastal state increases. Conversely, the rights and freedoms of maritime states are at their maximum in regard to activities on the high seas and gradually diminish closer to the coastal state. The balance of interests between the coastal state and maritime states thus varies in each zone recognized by the convention.

The location of these zones under the convention may be summarized as follows:

(1) Internal waters are landward of the baselines along the coast. They include lakes, rivers and many bays.

(2) Archipelagic waters are encircled by archipelagic baselines established by independent archipelagic states.

The territorial sea extends seaward from the baselines to a fixed distance. The convention establishes twelve nautical miles as the maximum permissible breadth of the territorial sea. (One nautical mile equals 1,852 m or 6,067 ft; all further references to miles are to nautical miles.)

The contiguous zone, exclusive economic zone (EEZ), and continental shelf all begin at the seaward limit of the territorial sea. The contiguous zone may extend to a maximum distance of 24 miles from the baselines. The EEZ may extend to a maximum distance of 200 miles from the baselines.

The continental shelf may extend to a distance of 200 miles from the baselines or, if the continental margin extends beyond that limit, to the outer edge of the continental margin as defined by the convention. The regime of the continental shelf applies to the seabed and subsoil and does not affect the status of the superjacent waters or airspace. The regime of the high seas applies seaward of the EEZ; significant parts of that regime, including freedom of navigation and over-flight, also apply within the EEZ. The seabed beyond national jurisdiction, called the Area in the convention, comprises the seabed and subsoil beyond the seaward limit of the continental shelf.

Internal waters

Article 8(1) defines internal waters as the waters on the landward side of the baseline from which the breadth of the territorial sea is measured. This definition carries forward the traditional definition of internal waters found in Article 5 of the 1958 Geneva Convention on the Territorial Sea and the Contiguous Zone, 15 UST 1606, TIAS No. 5639, 516 UNTS 205.

Territorial sea

Article 2 describes the territorial sea as a belt of ocean which is measured seaward from the baseline of the coastal state and subject to its sovereignty. This sovereignty also extends to the airspace above and to the seabed and subsoil. It is exercised subject to the convention and other rules of international law relating to innocent passage, transit passage, archipelagic sea lanes passage, and protection of the marine environment. Under Article 3, the coastal state has the right to establish the breadth of its territorial sea up to a limit not exceeding 12 miles, measured from baselines determined in accordance with the convention.

The adoption of the convention has significantly influenced state practice. Prior to 1982, as many as twenty-five states claimed territorial seas broader than 12 miles (with attendant detriment to the freedoms of navigation and over-flight essential to national security and commercial interests), while thirty states, including the United States, claimed a territorial sea of less than twelve miles. Since 1983, state practice in asserting territorial sea claims has largely coalesced around the 12 mile maximum breadth set by the convention. As of 1 December 1995, 129 states claim a territorial sea of 12 miles or less; only seventeen states claim a territorial sea broader than 12 miles.

Contiguous zone

Article 33 recognizes the contiguous zone as an area adjacent to the territorial sea in which the coastal state may exercise the limited control necessary to prevent or punish infringement of its customs, fiscal, immigration, and sanitary laws and regulations that occurs within its territory or territorial sea. Unlike the territorial sea, the contiguous zone is not subject to coastal state sovereignty; vessels and aircraft enjoy the same high seas freedom of navigation and over-flight in the contiguous zone as in the EEZ. The maximum permissible breadth of the contiguous zone is 24 miles measured from the baseline from which the breadth of the territorial sea is measured. Fifty-eight states now claim a contiguous zone; only one of those states claims a contiguous zone broader than 24 miles.

Exclusive Economic Zone (EEZ)

The establishment of the EEZ in the convention represents a substantial change in the law of the sea. The underlying purpose of the EEZ regime is to balance the rights of coastal states to resources (e.g. fisheries and offshore oil and gas) and to protect the environment off their coasts with the interests of all states in preserving other high seas rights and freedoms.

Article 55 defines the EEZ as an area beyond and adjacent to the territorial sea, subject to the specific legal regime established in Part V, which elaborates the jurisdiction, rights, and duties of the coastal state and the rights, freedoms and duties of other states. Pursuant to Article 56, the coastal state exercises sovereign rights for the purpose of exploring and exploiting, conserving and managing the natural resources of the EEZ, whether living or non-living. It also has significant rights in the EEZ with respect to scientific research and the protection and preservation of the marine environment. The coastal state does not have sovereignty over the EEZ, and all states enjoy the high seas freedoms of navigation, over-flight, laying and maintenance of submarine cables and pipelines, and related uses in the EEZ, compatible with other convention provisions. However, all states have a duty, in the EEZ, to comply with the laws and regulations adopted by the coastal state in accordance with the convention and other compatible rules of international law.

Article 57 requires the seaward limit of the EEZ to be no more than 200 miles from the baseline from which the breadth of the territorial sea is measured. As of 1 December 1996, ninety-seven states claim an EEZ. No state claims an EEZ beyond 200 miles from its coastal baselines, although several states claim the right to restrict activities within their EEZs beyond that which the convention authorizes.

High seas

Pursuant to Article 86, the regime of the high seas applies seaward of the EEZ. The convention elaborates the regime of the high seas, including the principles of the freedom of the high seas, as it developed over centuries, and supplements the regime with new safety and environmental requirements and express recognition of the freedom of scientific research. The convention makes the right to fish on the high seas subject to significant additional requirements relating to conservation and to certain rights, duties and interests of coastal states.

Continental shelf

Pursuant to Article 76, the continental shelf of a coastal state comprises the seabed and subsoil of the submarine areas that extend beyond its territorial sea throughout the natural prolongation of its land territory to the outer edge of the continental margin, or to a distance of 200 miles from the baselines from which the breadth of the territorial sea is measured where the outer edge of the continental margin does not extend up to that distance. The coastal state alone exercises sovereign rights over the continental shelf for the purpose of exploring it and exploiting its natural resources. The natural resources of the continental shelf consist of the mineral and other non-living resources of the seabed and subsoil together with the living organisms belonging to sedentary species. Substantial deposits of oil and gas are located in the continental shelf off the coasts of a number of countries. Shipwrecks are not 'natural resources' as that term is defined in the convention.

The seabed beyond national jurisdiction

The convention defines as the Area the seabed and ocean floor and subsoil thereof beyond the limits of national jurisdiction. Possible exploration and development of the mineral resources found at or beneath the seabed of the Area are to be undertaken pursuant to the international regime established by the convention, as revised by the 1994 Agreement in Implementation of Part XI of the Convention, on the basis of the principle that these resources are the common heritage of mankind. The Area remains open to use by all states for the exercise of high seas freedoms for defence, scientific research, telecommunications, and other purposes. As shipwrecks are not included in the convention's definition of 'resources', shipwrecks located in the Area are not subject to the jurisdiction of the International Seabed Authority.

Airspace

The convention does not treat airspace as distinct zones. However, its provisions affirm that the sovereignty of a coastal state extends to the airspace over its land territory, internal waters, and territorial sea. The breadth of territorial airspace is necessarily the same as the breadth of the underlying territorial sea. International airspace begins at the outer limit of the territorial sea.

Archaeological and historical objects found at sea (Articles 33, 149, and 303)

Article 303 imposes a general duty on states to protect objects of an archaeological and historical nature found at sea and to cooperate for this purpose. The **United States** has implemented this obligation by the **Abandoned Shipwreck Act** of 1987, 42 USC §§ 2101–6, and implementing regulations 54 Fed. Reg. 13642 et seq.; the National Marine Sanctuary Act, 16 USC § 1431 et seq.; the Archaeological Resources Protection Act, 16 USC § 470aa–ll, and its uniform regulations 43 CFR Part 7, 36 CFR Part 296, 18 CFR Part 1312, 32 CFR Part 229; the National Historic Preservation Act, 16 USC. § 470, 36

CFR Part 800; the Antiquities Act of 1906, 16 USC. §§ 431–3; and the **National Register of Historic Places**, 36 CFR Parts 60, 63.

Coastal state competence to control the activities of foreign nationals and foreign flag ships in this regard is limited to internal waters, its territorial sea, and, if it elects, to its contiguous zone (Article 303[2]).

Under Article 149, all such objects found on the seabed beyond the limits of national jurisdiction must be preserved and disposed of for the benefit of mankind as a whole. Particular regard must be paid to the preferential rights of the state or country of origin, the state of cultural origin, or the state of historical or archaeological origin.

Article 303(3) clarifies that the convention is not intended to affect the rights of identifiable owners, admiralty law, and the laws and practices concerning cultural exchanges. Article 303 is without prejudice to other international agreements and rules of international law regarding the protection of objects of an archaeological and historical nature (Article 303[4]). For example, in 1989 the United States and France entered an agreement for the protection and study of the wreck of the CSS *Alabama*, sunk by USS *Kearsarge* on 19 June 1864, in waters now forming part of the French territorial sea (TIAS No. 11687).

The Third UN Conference on the Law of the Sea declined to authorize coastal states to exercise jurisdiction over such objects seaward of 24 miles from the baseline (i.e., the maximum breadth of the contiguous zone). Creation of a cultural heritage zone out to 200 miles (as is under consideration by UNESCO in its draft convention on underwater cultural heritage) would disrupt the existing balance of interests set out in the convention and encourage other unjustified maritime claims. Nevertheless, a few states have claimed jurisdiction over submerged cultural resources on their continental shelves or located within their EEZs seaward of twenty-four miles from the baseline: Australia (continental shelf, subject to the constraints of international law); Cape Verde (EEZ and continental shelf); Ireland (continental shelf); Jamaica (EEZ); Morocco (EEZ); Norway (continental shelf); Portugal (continental shelf); Spain (continental shelf); and the former Yugoslavia (continental shelf). In any event, a coastal state is not without power to provide protection to underwater cultural heritage located on or in its seabed more than 24 miles from the baseline as it may exercise jurisdiction over its nationals at sea, over vessels flying its flag, and over persons using its ports or otherwise located in its territory.

The term 'objects of an archaeological and historical nature' is not defined in the convention. While it does apply to some shipwrecks, it is not intended to apply to modern objects whatever their historical interest.

Relation to the 1958 Geneva Conventions

Article 311(1) of the LOS Convention provides that the convention will prevail, as between States Parties, over the four Geneva Conventions on the Law of the Sea of 29 April 1958: the Convention on the Territorial Sea and the Contiguous Zone, 15 UST. 1606, TIAS No. 5639, 516 UNTS 205 (entered into force 10 September 1964); the Convention on the High Seas, 13 UST 2312, TIAS No. 5200, 450 UNTS 82 (entered into force 30 September 1962); Convention on the Continental Shelf, 15 UST. 471, TIAS No. 5578, 499 UNTS 311 (entered into force 10 June 1964); and the Convention on Fishing and Conservation of Living Resources of the High Seas, 17 UST. 138, TIAS No. 5969, 559 UNTS 285 (entered into force 20 March 1966). Virtually all of the provisions of these conventions are either repeated, modified, or replaced by the provisions of the LOS Convention.

The LOS Convention opened for signature on 10 December 1982, and entered into force on 16 November 1994. As of 27 March 1997, one hundred and sixteen states have consented to be bound by the convention. Another twelve states have indicated their intention to consent to be bound upon completion of the necessary domestic procedures.

The Deep Seabed Mining provisions of the convention were modified by an Agreement to Implementation of Part XI of the convention that opened for signature on 16 July 1994 and entered into force on 28 July 1996. Seventy-eight states are now party.

J.A.R.

ADDITIONAL READING

Treaties and related official documents

United Nations Convention on the Law of the Sea, with Annexes, done at Montego Bay, 10 December 1982. UN Document A/CONF.62/122, 1982, reprinted in United Nations, Official Text of the United Nations Convention on the Law of the Sea with Annexes and Index, UN Sales No. E.83.V.5, 1983; International Legal Materials, 21, 6, 1261–1354.

Law of the Sea Convention: Letters of Transmittal and Submittal and Commentary. US Department of State Dispatch Supplement, 6, Supplement 1, February 1995, 1–52; International Legal Materials, 34, 6, November 1995, 1396–1447; Georgetown International Environmental Law Review, 7,

1, Fall 1994, 77–194; [US] Senate Treaty Document 103–39, 7 October, 1994, III–97.

Books

Center for Oceans Law and Policy University of Virginia, 1985–95, *United Nations Convention on the Law of the Sea 1982: A Commentary*, 5 vols, Dordrecht, Boston.

Churchill, R. and Lowe, V., 1988, *The Law of the Sea*, 2nd rev. edn, Manchester.

Dupuy, R.-J. and Vignes, D. (eds), *A Handbook on the New Law of the Sea*, 2 vols, Dordrecht, Boston.

Sohn, L. and Gustafson, K. G., 1984, *The Law of the Sea*, St Paul, Minnesota.

Underwater Archaeological Society of British Columbia

A 250-member group of primarily volunteer **Avocationals** and a number of professional underwater archaeologists. The majority of members are from British Columbia and the rest from across North America. The society is the largest diving organization, and one of the largest and most active heritage organizations, in the province.

The UASBC came about as a result of a course in **Underwater archaeology** offered by the Extension Department of the University of British Columbia in 1975. Upon completion of the course, the fourteen participants decided to continue the work they had started, and formed the UASBC with the mandate to conserve, preserve, and protect the maritime heritage lying beneath British Columbia's coastal and inland waters through education against artefact removal and exploration to assess artefact resources.

The UASBC was incorporated as a nonprofit society in 1975, and survey work began on four wreck sites in the Gulf of Georgia. The initial sites surveyed were the wrecks of *Panther*, *Zephyr*, *Del Norte* and *Iroquois*. There was some funding from the provincial government but the largest portion came from the participants themselves.

In 1980 the UASBC approached the Provincial Government's Heritage Conservation Branch and the British Columbia Heritage Trust with the idea of funding an ongoing programme of regional shipwreck surveys. The surveys would evaluate important wrecks in a given area, assess their current condition, and recommend action to ensure their preservation. This would provide the Archaeology Branch with baseline data on which to write policy. This programme became and remains the cornerstone of UASBC Explorations. In the absence of an Archaeology Branch 'underwater archaeology team', the UASBC serves that function. The society generally undertakes only non-destructive surveys, leaving artefacts *in situ*.

The Heritage Conservation Branch and the Trust agreed with the regional shipwreck programme and funded the first survey in 1980. To date, the UASBC has compiled and printed site surveys of the historic shipwrecks in five areas of the province: *The Historic Shipwrecks of the Gulf Islands, The Historic Shipwrecks of Barkley Sound, The Historic Shipwrecks of Nootka-Clayoquot, The Historic Shipwrecks of Southern Vancouver Island,* and *Vancouver's Undersea Heritage.*

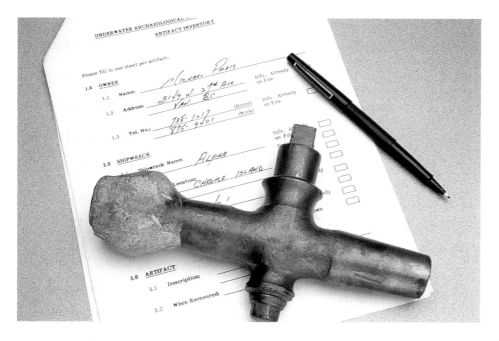

Brass valve from the wreck of Alpha *being recorded on an artefact inventory form by a member of the Underwater Archaeological Society of British Columbia. (Mike Paris/UASBC)*

The society has also completed four special studies: *The Search for the* Tonquin, *The* Ericsson, *Exploring the* Lord Western, 1989, and *The Underwater Heritage of Friendly Cove,* 1996. A reference book entitled *A Wreck Diver's Guide to Sailing Ship Artefacts of the Nineteenth Century,* 1993, has been written and produced for the sport diver who has an interest in shipwrecks and archaeology.

Three projects were under way in 1997. In the southern interior of British Columbia, the group is surveying wreck sites which include several paddle wheelers, steam tugs, and train wrecks that worked the lakes and rivers in the Kootenay region before and after the turn of the century.

The second project involves historic shipwrecks along the east coast of Vancouver Island from Campbell River north to Port Hardy. Further, in cooperation with the Vancouver Maritime Museum, the society is working on a special study of the wreck of the Hudson's Bay Company paddle wheeler, **Beaver**. *Beaver* is British Columbia's most historic shipwreck. It was the first steam-powered vessel on the west coast of North America.

Other exploration projects include placing underwater plaques on popular or protected wrecks, an educational underwater trail on the site of *Barnard Castle*, and a mooring buoy on SS *Del Norte* to protect against anchor damage. Surveyed sites are periodically monitored to ensure that artefacts are not being removed. At the society's instigation, the province has designated nine sites as specially protected heritage sites. The society is the prime contributor to the British Columbia Archaeology Branch Shipwreck Inventory, part of the nationwide Canadian Heritage Information Network computerized database. In all, some thirty projects had been completed by 1995.

From time to time the society undertakes special projects at the request of the Archaeology Branch. Two such projects are a bottom survey of a proposed car-ferry dock in Bella Bella, and the raising, photographing, drawing and return of a 300-year-old native canoe found in Lake Shuswap, British Columbia. The latter project was done in conjunction with the Archaeology Department of the University College of the Cariboo in Kamloops, BC. The UASBC also provides field workers for academic projects, as in the case of **Montague Harbour**, Restoration Bay, and **Maud**.

Projects have expanded beyond shipwrecks to submerged shore-side industrial facilities and First Nations habitation sites. Montague Harbour on Galiano Island was a three-year investigation into the methodology of excavating a site inundated by sea-level rise and was the first submerged First Nations site excavated on the west coast.

Alongside the exploration work by the society, education has developed into the other half of the UASBC's initiative. Early on, the society realized that laws and threats of prosecution would not work to protect wreck sites. This approach would only alienate the sport diving community and the pillaging of wreck sites would carry on unabated. The decision was made to pursue an instructional approach and inform divers about the importance of underwater heritage sites and the fact that wreck sites are not a renewable resource. Once they are disturbed, their story is lost to all future visitors to the site.

To this end, the society established links with maritime museums around the world, in particular the Vancouver Maritime Museum, and the Maritime Museum of British Columbia in Victoria, BC. Linkages were established as well with the commercial diving industry, universities, high-tech underwater exploration companies, and directly to sport divers through certification courses and the clubs – many of them eventually join upon completion of their courses.

Excellent links with the subsea industry have allowed the UASBC to make use of advanced technology to a degree unusual for avocational groups. The **Lord Western** project employed **Sonic High Accuracy Ranging and Positioning System** (SHARPS) mapping technology. The successful search to a depth of 111 m for the stern wheeler *City of Ainsworth* in Kootenay Lake employed sophisticated **Side scan sonar**.

These connections are also maintained through speaking engagements with diving clubs, community organizations and diving certification organizations, which have helped achieve a change of attitude. Trophy-taking is now much reduced. The society has a **Conservation** lab, the space donated by the Vancouver Maritime Museum, to provide basic treatment to artefacts previously taken by institutions or individuals and eventually donated to the society.

The society sponsors an annual shipwrecks conference which is directed at the general diving public and brings together speakers both local and from across North America to address and discuss with participants a wide variety of subjects that relate to heritage and the sea. The education programme includes collaborative work with universities, museums, and other heritage institutions to produce public exhibits, and brochures. The UASBC also links with other underwater organizations worldwide. In 1994 the UASBC co-sponsored, with the Archaeology Department of Simon Fraser University, the Society for Historical Archaeology Conference in Vancouver.

Part of the process has been educating the government on the value of undersea archaeological resources. The UASBC is regularly consulted on heritage issues, legislation, and applications for land and foreshore uses.

Educational services for members include monthly meetings which feature local speakers who cover a range of subjects related to history, the ocean, and diving. The society produces a quarterly publication, the *Foghorn*, which goes out to all members as well as to some of the diving shops in the province. The *Foghorn* is a vehicle for the society's business, as well as a forum for members to express opinions and reaction to relevant issues. The publication also carries articles and commentaries gleaned from other learned publications in the underwater archaeology field. The members also have full access to the society's archives, library, and computer bulletin board system.

In 1991 the society wrote and offered a course entitled Underwater Archaeology Search and Survey Techniques. The objective was to provide the **Avocational** archaeologist with the knowledge and ability to research, locate, and conduct a basic site survey on a shipwreck site. In 1995, with funding from the Federal government's Ministry of Heritage, this course was expanded and now follows the **Nautical Archaeology Society** (NAS) of Great Britain's Level One course. In 1995 the UASBC brought out three NAS instructors from the UK to teach the Level One instructor's course to twenty-six students from across Canada. In the spring of 1996 an NAS accredited Level One course was also offered to members, and eventually in cooperation with one of the local universities, Level Two, Three, and Four will be made available.

The society can be reached through the Vancouver Maritime Museum, 1905 Ogden Avenue, Vancouver, BC V6J 1A3. M.P.

Underwater archaeology

Archaeology practised in a submerged or underwater environment. This includes archaeological survey, documentation, and excavation performed in the ocean, lakes, rivers, streams, marshes, and cenotes, as well as reservoirs, canals, and other man-made bodies of water. The term refers to the environment in which the work is undertaken, as well as specific approaches required for working underwater, and the unique levels of preservation not usually found on dry land sites.

The discovery of submerged antiquities ultimately led to the practice of archaeology underwater, just as discoveries on land ultimately led to the development of archaeology as a discipline. Recoveries of cultural remains from submerged environments, at first accidental, in time became an intentional activity, particularly as technology provided the means for a more protracted human presence underwater. In some cases, the draining of bodies of water provided archaeologists with access to the high levels of preservation inherent in many submerged sites, such as the Roman ships of Emperor Caligula exposed after **Lake Nemi** was drained.

These early endeavours were at best salvage supervised by an archaeologist on the surface. Early work, such as the recovery of submerged artefacts at the **Antikythera Wreck** or at the **Chichén Itzá Cenote**, were undertaken by professional, hard-hat divers. Archaeological controls were non-existent, and archaeologists, not being trained divers, were placed more in the role of cataloguing and documenting artefacts without a detailed understanding of their spatial relationships or contexts.

The invention of **SCUBA** first opened the underwater world to archaeologists, although the first 'underwater' work was undertaken by divers who learned 'on the job' to become 'archaeologists'. These pioneers included Jacques Cousteau and Philippe Diole of France, who more than any other individuals popularized the nascent underwater archaeological 'profession'.

The first trained archaeologist to learn to dive, in order to work on a submerged site, was George Bass, of the University of Pennsylvania, who in 1960 went through basic scuba training before embarking on a project to survey and excavate the **Cape Gelidonya Wreck** with journalist, historian and diver Peter Throckmorton. Bass was the first to adapt standard archaeological techniques used on land to the underwater environment, and since then, new methods and technologies have been invented that have become standard aspects of underwater archaeological work, including the use of **Airlifts**, **Photomosaics**, lifting bags, and slates with clear mylar for taking field notes and measurements, for example.

Underwater archaeology in the late 20th century involves research in a variety of fields and areas, and is practised around the world in every ocean and body of water. Most underwater archaeology has been practised in lakes, in the shallow waters of the world's oceans, to depths of sixty metres or less, and in rivers. Underwater archaeology has expanded in recent decades to also include formerly dry-land sites submerged during reservoir construction in the United States, as well as work in deeper waters, including shipwrecks at great depth.

Prehistoric archaeology, and the reconstruction of paleo-environments, as well as work on Maya and other offerings made in North, Central, and South American waters by indigenous peoples, Classical archaeological research on submerged ancient cities and harbours, and shipwreck and other maritime archaeological research spanning ancient to modern cultures, is a recurrent and perennial activity.

Underwater archaeology has provided startling new evidence and major discoveries of material remains that otherwise would not have survived, and were archaeologically unknown prior to the development of underwater archaeological research. This has included the discovery in the 1990s of well-preserved paleolithic cave paintings at Cosquer, **France**; well-preserved faunal remains and wooden tools and implements from North American prehistoric sites; the preservation of human brain material from a burial at **Warm Mineral Springs**, Florida; Iron Age wooden settlements in Switzerland; a bronze warship ram from antiquity from Athlit (see **Athlit Ram**); early Polynesian ethnographic materials collected by British naval officers and preserved in the wreck of HMS *Pandora*; and well-preserved clothing, foodstuffs, and weapons from wrecks like *Vasa*, *Kronan*, and *Mary Rose*.

While a number of exciting new archaeological discoveries will doubtless continue to be made on land, underwater sites will yield the largest and greatest number of new finds over the next decades. Only one per cent of the world's oceans have been surveyed or explored, and many other water bodies have seen little exploration. With a vast, untouched resource, and the potential for high levels of preservation, the new frontier of archaeology is underwater. J.P.D.

ADDITIONAL READING

Bass, G., 1966, *Archaeology Under Water*, New York.

Muckelroy, K., 1980, *Archaeology Underwater, An Atlas of the World's Submerged Sites*, New York and London.

Underwater video

A common tool in underwater archaeological research in the 1990s. Diffused, low-contrast underwater lighting is ideally suited to television and video recording. Closed-circuit underwater television proved the

Left: Taking underwater video footage of HMS Fowey in Biscayne National Park, Florida. (NPS/John Brooks)

Right: Filming in the central hull of the Red Bay whaling ship. (Parks Canada)

medium's capability, but it was not until video tape recording that the real archaeological potential began to be realized. Video has the benefit of real-time viewing, immediate playback, non-destructive editing, and ease of operation.

Technological advances in resolution, low-light sensitivity, camera miniaturization, and digital formats since the 1980s have markedly increased video capability. Digital video imagery generated with digital cameras or through computer methods is the most important recent development in video technology. These images are now used for convergent photogrammetric mapping and coupled with **Global Positioning System** (GPS) location data, for incorporation into **Geographic information systems** (GIS). Digital video images are also being used for video mosaic and photogrammetric applications. High-resolution video images can be enhanced and manipulated in a similar way to aerial photographs to produce rectified and corrected imagery for analytic purposes. There are few underwater archaeological research projects that currently do not rely heavily upon video imaging in search, survey, and documentation operations.

Video application to underwater archaeological research began when Captain Jacques Cousteau suspended a steel-housed television camera from the surface during the excavation of a 2,200-year-old Greek vessel near **Grand Congloué** in 1953. Cousteau

immediately recognized the importance of surface communication, which allows excavation and documentation to be directed from the surface. Archaeologists were slow to adopt closed-circuit television for more than a decade. The Minnesota Historical Society used television to search for fur trade sites in 1967 during the **Quetico-Superior** project, and George Bass and Donald Rosencrantz used it for Mediterranean searches in 1968. However, it was not until 1975 that closed-circuit television coupled with video tape recording was fully integrated for the first time into the excavation and documentation plan of an underwater site. W.A. Cockrell recorded more than 120 hours of video tape of a 10,000 BP human burial site at **Warm Mineral Springs**, Florida. All excavation of the early strata was taped, and the cenote was systematically documented, including the interior of a cave at 70 m. Video has since been in use continually in many projects such as the *Mary Rose* excavation. Video deployment aboard remotely-operated vehicles (ROVs; see **Submersibles**) was recently instrumental in locating and documenting *Titanic* and *Bismarck* and shows the wide range of video use. Proliferation of **Underwater archaeology** commercial broadcast productions reflects widespread video use in field operations.

To date, video formats cover a wide range of options, including: VHS, S-VHS, 8 mm, Hi-8, Digital 6 mm, ³/4 in, ³/4 in SP, Beta,

Beta-SP, one inch, D-2, Digital Beta, W-VHS and High Definition Digital (HD-D). Several of these are slowly finding their way to the dusty shelves in the backroom because they are being replaced by newer technology. Certainly both the ³/4 in formats and Beta (not Beta SP) are included in the formats that are being phased out. VHS and 8 mm need not be considered for scientific work because of their low resolution of about 280 horizontal interlaced lines. Although this resolution may be sufficient for commercial television viewing, it is not sufficient for frame capture and computer manipulation. Video resolution is important because higher resolution images produce higher accuracy and precision levels in convergent photogrammetric measurement systems like PhotoModler. The one inch format and D-2 are not practical for most field applications because of equipment size and expense.

High Definition Digital equipment provides the ultimate video resolution. However, one must be able to afford the very high price, along with a very large and expensive housing or a dry submarine. HD-D video generates high-quality, photographic-like, still images from each video frame with a horizontal resolution of about 1200 lines. HD-D coupled with computer image enhancing techniques like line-hardening and line-doubling represent the present video state of the art.

Video resolution is measured in horizontal

lines, rather than pixels. It does have a vertical component that is made up of band width frequency times a constant factor. Occasionally this is portrayed as vertical resolution and, as in the case of HD-D, is reported as 1200 × 1000 lines of horizontal and vertical resolution. It should be noted that in the case of the vertical component this is not entirely an accurate measure. Other things such as the band width and signal to noise ratio are a more accurate measure of the video quality.

There are alternative high-definition formats, such as W-VHS (wide screen), which is available in Japan but yet to be marketed elsewhere. As high definition and wide screen technology becomes available elsewhere in the world, this format is sure to become more common. W-VHS has a horizontal resolution of 750 lines and a vertical component approaching HD-D, giving it an overall performance that is HD-like, but at a fraction of the cost. Woods Hole Oceanographic Institute already uses this format for video data collection.

The next step down from HD in resolution and price is Digital Beta. Digital Beta offers archival quality storage of visual data, multiple copies without generational loss, and high resolution images of more than 500 horizontal lines. Even though its horizontal resolution is not much better than plain Beta-SP, its overall appearance is much better due to an excellent signal to noise ratio of 62 and a band width that is flatter and wider than plain Beta-SP.

The non-digital Beta-SP has 500 lines of horizontal resolution, good storage under proper conditions and good duplication, but with some generational loss when going past third generation.

The coming high-resolution, low-cost champ is the mini 6 mm Digital format with 500 lines of horizontal resolution, or about 20 per cent more than Hi-8 or S-VHS, duplication with no generational loss, and good archival quality. It has sufficient resolution to exceed current broadcast standards and produce good computer manipulation results. Cost of the camera equipment will probably drop as supply and competition increases.

S-VHS and Hi-8, with resolutions of about 400–420 horizontal lines, is the minimum that should be considered for data collection when computer manipulation is required. Of these two formats, Hi-8 is better because of small equipment size and longer tape-playing time. The S-VHS comes in a smaller format, S-VHS C, but the tape is only thirty minutes long compared to two hours on Hi-8. Another benefit of Hi-8 is

metal-coated tape, which is more archivally stable than regular oxide tape. Sony produces a super-quality metal Hi-8 tape that is specially formulated for editing so it can be run back and forth without risk of damaging taped images. This tape should be used for field recording where video editing is anticipated, and it is necessary to keep video drop-out to a minimum.

Video format is far less complicated than still or motion-picture film. A diver with little photographic experience can get good usable images using video under most conditions. Reliable results from film media require much knowledge and experience for comparable results. Usually, video is much less expensive than 16 mm film, and in the case of Hi-8 or S-VHS, about the same cost as 35 mm still photography. If super-high resolution for large magnifications or high quality reproduction is required, the first choice remains film, either 35 mm or medium formats. For most applications, including computer manipulation, low cost digital video will work and generate consistent, dependable results. L.E.M, J.B.2

United Kingdom

European country with a long maritime history. The mainland and its offshore islands are situated on the continental shelf of northern Europe, a large area of which was dry land before the post-Flandrian marine transgression. A residual land bridge across what are now the Straits of Dover was probably breached as recently as 5000 BC. The present coastline is more than 17,700 km long and all of it has maritime archaeological potential. Coastal changes and the reclamation of land have buried old watercourses and sealed early shorelines and waterfronts beneath overlying deposits which may appear sterile. Strong currents, uncertain weather, and varied tidal ranges have in past centuries exacted a heavy toll of shipping losses. While late medieval to modern shipwrecks tend to be found in the sea, discoveries of early craft have invariably been made in excavations on land.

The creation of dock basins in the 19th century led to the discovery of numerous dugouts, as at Liverpool and Glasgow. During 20th-century redevelopment, single parts and whole sections of plank-built vessels used in the construction of successive medieval wharves have been found together with rich palaeo-environmental evidence. Other finds have been made in reclamation or drainage schemes in rural areas. Ship remains from non-waterlogged land sites, which rarely include the structural timber, consist of stains in the soil and rows of iron

fastenings. These have commonly been found beneath burial mounds where a boat has been used as a container for an inhumation, or has been burned as part of a cremation. The custom is of great antiquity, as was highlighted in 1989 by the discovery at Old Parkbury, Hertfordshire of a partly burned dugout containing a disarticulated body in a chest, dating to the 4th millennium BC. Boat-burials occurred in East Anglia in the 6th and 7th centuries AD and on the Isle of Man and Scottish islands in the Viking period. A discovery of iron rivets marking the stain of a Viking oak boat more than 7 m long in which three individuals had been interred was made in 1991 on an eroding beach on the Orkney island of Sanday.

Evolution of British archaeology

Early accounts contain incidental but tantalizing references to important boat discoveries, for instance to the seven boats found in gravel 3 m below the River Wantsum when the Fens were drained in 1642, or to the probable Roman vessel found outside the walls of Verulamium (St Albans) and described by a 13th-century monk. Nineteenth-century antiquarian interest in Britain's maritime past was focused on numerous finds of dugouts, invariably thought to be prehistoric, and of clinker vessels, invariably ascribed to the Vikings. Before the advent of modern dating techniques it seems that other types of vessel construction were disregarded. In 1820 a clinker-built barge 19 m long, from its finds now dated to the 16th century, was recovered from below a Kent riverbed and taken all the way to London for display as a 'Viking' ship.

Parallel with the descriptions of antiquarian investigations on land were those of antiquarian salvors, such as Archibald Miller who in 1683 published a description of a wreck he had seen in Tobermory Bay using a diving bell. This was probably the subsequently elusive wreck of the Armada ship *San Juan de Sicilia*.

The invention in the 1820s by the Deane brothers of the diving helmet transformed salvage work. In 1832 John Deane and William Edwards started work on the recovery of cannon and fragile items from *Royal George*, sunk in 1782, and in 1836 they started work on **Mary Rose**. Their recoveries were recorded in scaled coloured drawings of great sensitivity.

Serious study of ship discoveries developed rapidly after 1910 when the Society for Nautical Research was founded in London to foster the study of ships and seafaring throughout the world and in all ages. Its quarterly journal, *The Mariner's Mirror*, started publication the following year, to be for members 'a repository for their discoveries and as a medium whereby they may carry on their enquiries'. Thus the foundations were laid for the scholarly investigation of ancient ship structure. As far as the UK was concerned, interest focused particularly on the medieval period and the interpretation of the plentiful iconography. Members took part in the identification of two huge medieval hulks: in 1912 the 'Woolwich Ship' (probably Henry VIII's *Henry Grace à Dieu*), and in 1933 the Bursledon wreck (probably

education and sponsored a series of courses on underwater archaeological techniques at Fort Bovisand, Plymouth. Two publications of key importance were St John Wilkes's diving manual *Nautical Archaeology* (1971) and the **International Journal of Nautical Archaeology** (IJNA), which started the following year.

The 1970s saw a number of initiatives to develop university teaching and research. The unit set up in 1971 to record and conserve the **Graveney Boat** at the National Mar-

Logboat; and an evaluation of *Grace Dieu*. In the same year at the University of St Andrews a research **Institute of Maritime Studies** was created to offer an MA in maritime studies. Bristol University pioneered extra-mural practical courses and from 1976 offered **Maritime archaeology** as an undergraduate special course. Subsequently degrees and courses have been developed at Bangor, Oxford, London, and Southampton (see **Southampton Centre for Maritime Archaeology**).

In 1981 members of the CNA founded the **Nautical Archaeology Society** and in 1987, when the CNA was integrated with the Council for British Archaeology, ownership of the *International Journal of Nautical Archaeology* was transferred to NAS. Among the new society's achievements were the production of *Archaeology Underwater. The NAS Guide to Principles and Practice* and the development of carefully structured training courses, supported by government funding.

Concerned at the continuing disparity between the protection of archaeological sites on land and underwater, representatives of several interested bodies formed the Joint Nautical Archaeology Policy Committee and published recommendations in *Heritage at Sea*. Following this the Royal Commission on the Historical Monuments of England commenced a pilot project in

Henry V's *Grace Dieu*). An early society task was to preserve Nelson's *Victory* (1759) in dry dock at Portsmouth. It also campaigned, but unsuccessfully, to save *Implacable*, a French prize from Trafalgar, which was finally scuttled at sea in 1949. The society played a major part in establishing the National Maritime Museum in 1934. A bold project initiated in the same year but stalled by World War II was its survey of all of Britain's coastal craft.

After the war an increasing interest in shipwrecks by clearance and sport divers was facilitated by the development of **SCUBA**. Aware of the information which was being destroyed, Joan du Plat Taylor, based at London University's Institute of Archaeology, took the lead in fostering the nascent discipline of **Underwater archaeology**. In 1961 she presided over the inception of the institute's Underwater Research Group which was to play a continuing role in creating an interest among staff and students. Pool-training courses were followed by the creation, in conjunction with the British Sub-Aqua Club, of a training school at Swanage in 1965. She took part in the formation of the Council for Nautical Archaeology (CNA) which promoted diver

Dinnerware found in Mary Rose. (Cleveland Museum of Natural History/Bruce Frumker)

Divers excavating on the main deck at the stern of Mary Rose. Silt is being removed with an airlift. (Mary Rose Trust)

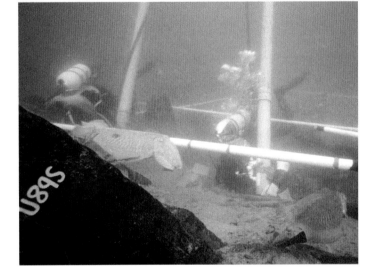

itime Museum was developed into the Archaeological Research Centre, both a national reference point for discoveries and research into the archaeology of the boat and a facility for the conservation of waterlogged wood. Before it was closed in 1985 the ARC's fieldwork included: the re-excavation of the **Brigg 'Raft'**; trial excavation on the **Ferriby** foreshore; the recovery of the **Hasholme**

maritime recording. In 1992 the English Commission and its counterparts in Scotland, Wales, and Northern Ireland extended their remit to the territorial seas. Maritime sections have since been added to the respective National Monuments Records.

Important discoveries

The earliest dated piece of boat equipment

from the UK is a birch paddle 16 in (42 cm) long found in a Mesolithic lakeside habitation site at Star Carr, Yorkshire. It may have been used to propel a reed, skin, or bark boat. Dugout finds of all periods from the Neolithic to the post-medieval are evidence for river transport. However, in the UK archaeological evidence for seacraft has not begun to illuminate the early maritime connections evinced by artefacts transported across rough stretches of water which separate its offshore islands, or imported from continental Europe. In contrast, for the Middle and Late Bronze Ages there are portions of stitched plank craft, unique in Europe, from the estuaries of the Humber at North Ferriby and the Severn at Caldicot (see **Humber Wrecks; Severn Wrecks**). In 1992 the seagoing capability of this type of construction seemed to be confirmed by a major portion of a variant type found on the coast during underpass construction in Dover, Kent (see **Dover Boat**). An earlier discovery by divers in nearby Langdon Bay comprised a large number of continental bronzes dating to the same period and the Dover Boat suggested that such cross-Channel trade in the Bronze Age took place in large plank-built craft.

In contrast with the preceding period, evidence for Iron Age seacraft is lacking, except indirectly: depicted on the coins of the native ruler Cunobelin; through descriptions by Classical writers such as Julius Caesar; from a rare find of an iron anchor from Bulbery, Dorset; and from discoveries of Roman period craft apparently built in a local tradition, using massive timbers and non-edge joined planking fastened with large hooked nails. Such a vessel dating to the 2nd century AD was found in 1960 beside Blackfriars Bridge in London, and other examples have subsequently been found at Newport, Gwent and St Peter Port, Guernsey (see **Blackfriars Wrecks; Guernsey Wreck**). In complete contrast to these is the only ship so far found in the UK which is built in a Mediterranean edge-fastened technique. This, the **County Hall Ship**, dates to the 3rd century AD and was found beside Westminster Bridge in 1910. It was also made of north European oak and so was presumably built locally by Roman shipwrights trained elsewhere. A Roman anchor stock from off Porth Felen, Gwynedd and pottery and amphoras trawled up from a number of locations are but slight indicators of extensive Roman naval and merchant shipping activity around the coast during more than four hundred years.

For the post-Roman 5th century in which large numbers of Anglo-Saxon immigrants voyaged across the North Sea, direct maritime evidence is altogether lacking. In their homeland clinker boatbuilding was practised and the boats of their descendants continued to be constructed in this way. A 6th-century 'ghost' of an Anglo-Saxon ship was recorded during amateur digging in a burial mound at Snape, Suffolk (see **Snape Boat**) as long ago as 1862. The grave had been robbed in antiquity and only rusted rows of rivets in the shape of the hull survived. However, in 1939 at **Sutton Hoo** a group of the country's most talented archaeologists took part in the meticulous excavation of an undisturbed 7th-century burial. From its impression in the sandy soil they were able to take the lines of a ship no less than 88 ft (27 m) long. It was bigger than the

Gold purse-lid from the Sutton Hoo Mound 1 ship burial. (Courtesy of the Trustees of the British Museum)

Viking **Oseberg** and **Gokstad Ships** and had been built by Anglo-Saxons some 250 years earlier than these perfectly preserved Scandinavian vessels.

While the ship impression and the artefacts contained in it required a radical re-evaluation of Anglo-Saxon technology, it was not until 1970 that wooden ship structure of this period was found – at Graveney on the north Kent coast, where about two-thirds of a merchant vessel about 50 ft (15 m) long lay beneath 2 m of marsh clay (see **Graveney Boat**). Careful study revealed that the square-sectioned iron fastenings of the clinker planks had been driven through wooden pegs filling predrilled holes. Wooden pegs were subsequently found used as fastenings in a number of fragments of clinker planking from waterfront excavations in London. Tree-ring analysis shows that all these boats were built in or near southeast England in the 10th century but the different techniques employed suggested that traditions were derived from both Scandinavia and northern Europe. Medieval planking from the London waterfront and from Southwold, Suffolk show that mixtures of wooden and metal plank fastenings came to be used together on individual vessels.

The ships in which waves of Norsemen reached the coast or worked their way up rivers have yet to be found, although in many instances the precise locations of landings and battles are chronicled. However, the meagre information from Viking period boat burials in the UK can easily be supplemented from numerous well-preserved craft which have been found in Scandinavia. In 1995 the after-end of a well-built clinker vessel was recovered from the eroding foreshore of the Severn Estuary at **Magor Pill**, Gwent. It dates to the 12th century and was possibly engaged in the transport of iron ore. Two clinker-built local craft, one a much-repaired fishing vessel, were briefly exposed during construction work in the bed of the Thames at Blackfriars in 1970 and dated to the 13th century. By way of contrast, huge and virtually undisturbed, the remains of the 15th-century carrack *Grace Dieu*, with a skin of three layers of clinker planking, still lies at Bursledon on the bank of the River Hamble in Hampshire. The medieval shipwrecks located on the seabed reflect foreign trade and contacts; the **Cattewater Wreck** and the **Studland Bay Wreck** have been the subject of careful recording and research. However, the largest and most intensive underwater excavation in UK waters was that of *Mary Rose*, for which a new **Direct survey method** of recording was devised (Rule 1989). The hull was finally raised in 1982 and placed in Portsmouth Historic Dockyard. A huge inventory of ordnance and artefacts was recovered and, like the hull, has been subjected to years of careful recording and conservation. The final publication will also include the environmental data and detailed evidence for the construction and refitting of a Tudor warship.

In 1964 the first Dutch East India Company (VOC) wreck was found in British waters. This was *De Liefde*, wrecked off the southern tip of the Out Skerries, Shetland in 1711 and located by Royal Navy divers.

Under archaeological supervision the site was surveyed and artefacts lodged in the local Lerwick Museum. The following decade saw unparalleled activity in the search for historic shipwrecks by treasure-hunters, untrained enthusiasts, and responsible groups, of both British and foreign nationality. In 1965 the search to relocate *Mary Rose* began and three years later a lease of the site from the Crown Estate, owners of the seabed, was obtained as a means of protecting the wreck from interference. The first ship of the **Spanish Armada** to be found was the fifty-gun Neapolitan galleass *Girona* located off the coast of County Antrim, Northern Ireland, in 1967. The ordnance recovered showed the potential for maritime archaeology to further the serious study of Spanish naval armament, and the 1970 search for *El Gran Grifon*, wrecked on Fair Isle, Shetland was undertaken specifically to obtain information on the armament of a second-line Armada vessel. In 1971 the wreck site of the first royal yacht, *Mary*, was for a time a bone of contention between rival teams and the CNA intervened to ensure that the artefacts were released by the Receiver of Wreck for conservation by Liverpool Museum. In 1973 the fifth-rate *Dartmouth* was found in the Sound of Mull and was carefully excavated over the following seasons. Meanwhile a university team had located *Kennemerland*, wrecked on the Out Skerries, Shetland in 1664, and there followed six further seasons of investigation on the site which also provided data for research on the distribution of objects on a scattered wreck site. Another scattered wreck site is that of *Pomone*, wrecked in 1811 on the Needles, Isle of Wight. The circumstances of the disaster were known and careful study of the distribution of the artefacts on the seabed showed that even in this apparently unpromising environment the material could reveal information on the wrecking process and the final orientation of the ship.

By 1974 six VOC shipwrecks had been identified in British waters, the oldest being that of the *fluitschip Lastdrager*, wrecked in 1653 off Yell, Shetland. A Dutch forty-four gun warship, the *Curaçao*, lost off Uist, Shetland in 1729, was located by a Belgo-French expedition in 1972. Among the 200 artefacts raised were a coil of rope and a fragment of a book with paper pages and vellum bands which showed the potential for the survival of fragile organic objects in an apparently hostile environment.

The use of explosives on historic wreck sites was a matter of contention, but in 1974 they were used responsibly on concretions

on the site of *Adelaar*, wrecked off the Isle of Barra, Outer Hebrides in 1728, and *Santo Christo de Castello*, a merchantman wrecked near the Lizard, Cornwall in 1667. Other sites were not so fortunate; particular targets in this period were the fleet of Sir Cloudesly Shovell wrecked on the Scillies in 1707, and *Anne* lost in 1690 during the Battle of Beachy Head. The VOC *Amsterdam*, which ran aground at Hastings, East Sussex in 1749, was damaged by mechanical excavators in 1969, but Anglo-Dutch excavations carried out between 1978 and 1988 showed her outstanding state of preservation. Most recently in the Scottish waters off Duart Point, Mull, superbly preserved artefacts and ship's carvings from a small 17th-century warship, probably *Swan*, have been excavated by the Scottish Institute of Maritime Studies (see **Duart Wreck**), and a Danish warship, *Wrangels Palais*, 1687, has been located off the Out Skerries, Shetland.

Submerged landscapes

In 1872 the geologist Geikie found evidence to link the Seine and Solent as part of an early river system, while important Palaeolithic and Early Mesolithic submerged peat sequences have been recorded and analysed over the past 50 years, chiefly in Southampton Water and Portsmouth Harbour. Recently oak trees eroding out of an underwater cliff on the north side of the Isle of Wight between 9 and 12 m below ordnance datum have been dated to 6500 BC. Extensive inter-tidal surveys have been undertaken on the coast of Essex, while in the Severn Estuary large-scale development has funded the collection of the greatest concentration of inter-tidal archaeological evidence in the UK by the Severn Estuary Levels Research Committee. Elsewhere an outstanding discovery, the result of erosion by the prop-wash of ferries, was made in Wootton Creek, Isle of Wight, where an exceptional sequence of prehistoric wooden features associated with superb **Lithic artefacts** extends below the low-water mark. Inland of the high-water mark English Heritage has funded four major wetland projects since 1973: the Somerset Levels; the Fenland Project; the North West Wetlands Survey; and the Humber Wetlands Project. The last is due to be completed in 2001. In Scotland and Wales **Crannogs**, former settlement sites on artificial islands in lakes and lochs have been investigated. In Northern Ireland the Maritime Archaeology Project was set up in 1993. It is based in the Queen's University of Belfast, and its fieldwork includes the investigation of early landing sites in Strangfold Lough.

Law and Management

By 1964 the need for legislation to protect the remains of vessels found either underwater or on dry land was clear and an *ad hoc* Committee (later Council) for Nautical Archaeology (CNA) was formed to campaign for this. Realization of the first aim was achieved in 1973; meanwhile sites such as *De Liefde*, were stripped of their artefacts while three separate groups obtained unlimited salvage rights to *Association*, a British warship wrecked on the Scilly Isles in 1707.

Section IX of the 1894 Merchant Shipping Act regulates salvage in territorial waters and does not distinguish historic from modern wreck. Salvaged items must be reported to the Receiver of Wreck. After one year, items for which an owner has not been found become the property of the Crown. The **Protection of Wrecks Act** 1973 enables a measure of protection to be conferred on shipwrecks of historic, archaeological, or artistic importance. All access to, and work on, designated sites requires a licence from the Department of National Heritage; since 1986 sites have been monitored by its **Archaeological Diving Unit**. Designation of shipwreck sites under the 1973 Act has been reactive rather than proactive and only 43 have been designated in 25 years. Three-quarters of these date to only three centuries (16th, 17th, and 18th) and twice as many warships as merchantmen are protected. All but eleven sites lie on the south coast of England.

The UK has been slow to take action to protect other types of underwater site of archaeological importance. In 1979 improved protection for all kinds of archaeological site was obtained with the Ancient Monuments and Archaeological Areas Act. Vessels on land have been scheduled but, although the legislation includes the territorial seas, as late as 1997 it had not been applied to hulks below the high-water mark or to any type of seabed site. The leasing of areas of seabed has been used by the Shetland Islands Council as a means of controlling important sites whilst permitting diver sightseeing. Environmental measures may confer protection on archaeological sites in the coastal zone; currently 34 per cent of the coast of England and Wales is designated Heritage Coast. There are two forms of marine protected area: Marine Nature Reserves (MNRs) which are statutory reserves; and Marine Consultation Areas (MCAs) which cover extensive areas. Sites of Special Scientific Interest (SSSIs) take archaeological features into account and an important precedent was set by the designation of the Upper Palaeolithic site at Boxgrove, Sussex.

Ports

Unlike the Mediterranean, the seas around the UK have a tidal range which allows flat-bottomed vessels simply to beach on suitable shores. Such informal landing places were used in prehistory and until quite recent times. However, during the Roman occupation substantial quays and jetties were constructed to serve not only military and naval bases, such as Dover, Kent and Caerleon, Gwent, but also the civilian settlement of London. In the post-Roman period at numerous towns small jetties, hards, and embankment sufficed and it is only later in the medieval period that deeper draught facilities in the form of docks, quays, and masonry waterfronts developed. During redevelopment in Hull, Yorkshire, a medieval warehouse, quay, and carefully levelled berth was discovered. A rural site which has never been built on is the early 18th-century Shipyard preserved at Buckler's Hard (Hampshire) which forms part of a project by Southampton University to survey the Beaulieu River (see **Shipyard archaeology**).

Dating and provenancing

Dendrochronology has made a major contribution to UK maritime archaeology in the late 20th century. Where suitable oak including outermost rings is present, a calendrical felling date for the tree(s) used can be obtained. Information on woodland management, the number of trees used in a vessel or structure, their age, and size, together with the identification of reused timber and repairs, is frequently possible. The application of computers to the measurement and processing of ring-width data in conjunction with a rigorous correlation with three or more independent chronologies has led to the establishment of many separate sequences for difference parts of Ireland and for southern, northern, and midland England; these in turn differ from Continental chronologies. The independent chronologies have proved particularly helpful in indicating the likely 'place of build' of an otherwise unidentifiable vessel. New finds continue to add to the extension of chronologies, which currently vary in length between one and four millennia. V.F.

ADDITIONAL READING

Note: The main source of information is the *International Journal of Nautical Archaeology*; this entry does not repeat entries found in the more detailed site articles elsewhere in the encyclopaedia.

Archaeological Diving Unit, 1994, *Guide to Historic Wreck Sites*, St Andrews, Scotland.

Bell, M. (ed.), 1990–94, *Severn Estuary Research Committee Annual Reports*, University of Wales, Lampeter.

Dean, M. *et al.*, 1992, *Archaeology Underwater: The NAS Guide to Principles and Practice*, London.

Joint Nautical Archaeology Policy Committee, 1989, *Heritage at Sea*, Greenwich.

Marsden, P., 1995–6, *Ships of the Port of London*, 2 vols, London.

Royal Commission on the Historical Monuments of England, 1996, *The National Inventory of Maritime Archaeology for England*, Swindon.

Rule, N., 1989, 'The Direct Survey Method (DSM) of Underwater Survey, and its Application Underwater', *International Journal of Nautical Archaeology*, 18, 157–62.

Van der Noort, R. and Ellis, S. (eds), 1995, *Wetland Heritage of Holderness: An Archaeological Survey*, University of Hull, Kingston upon Hull.

St John Wilkes, W., 1971, *Nautical Archaeology, A Handbook*, Newton Abbot, Devon.

United States of America

The United States of America holds a rich heritage in underwater material culture dating from prehistory through to modern times. European cultural remains date from the 1500s on the Pacific coasts and the Gulf

Alvin Clark *after 100 years of inundation in Lake Michigan.* (Daniel Lenihan)

of Mexico. The **Great Lakes** are also a rich repository of 19th- and 20th-century vessel remains and the nation's navigable rivers hold a well-preserved record of developments in river craft and support facilities.

Underwater archaeology in the United States tends to be practised in one of three schools: those pursuing the discipline as part of their general studies in anthropology; those involved in public archaeology or cultural resource management pro-

grammes; and those employing a historical particularist approach similar to that practised in much of Europe.

The Classical school has also had significant influence on the development of underwater archaeology in the United States. The work of Classical scholars such as George Bass on ancient shipwrecks in the **Mediterranean Sea** provided much of the inspiration and impetus for serious students of archaeology and maritime history in the Americas.

Environmental compliance legislation, including the National Historic Preservation Act, has provided a source of funding for many underwater survey and evaluation programmes. Land and resources management agencies, such as the Bureau of Land and Management and the Minerals Management Service, became prime movers in the conduct of offshore surveys in response to oil-lease development on the Outer Continental Shelf. The US Army Corps of Engineers has funded many inland surveys, particularly in riverine and harbour environments.

The National Park Service, which is the leading historic preservation agency in the US, established a permanent team of underwater archaeologists in 1980 called the **Submerged Cultural Resources Unit** (SCRU). Before the formation of the unit, the NPS had conducted occasional projects since the 1930s, including work at Colonial National Historic Park in Virginia (see **Yorktown Wrecks**) and the raising of USS *Cairo* in the 1960s. NPS archaeologists also conducted underwater investigations at Montzuma Well in 1968 and a number of national parks in Florida during the 1970s.

At the state level, the Minnesota Historical Society sponsored work on fur trade sites in the 1960s during the **Quetico-Superior** project and the State of Florida began archaeological studies at **Warm Mineral Springs** in 1972. Other early state-sponsored projects included work in Texas conducted by the Texas Antiquities

Cheese recovered from Alvin Clark. *(Daniel Lenihan)*

Committee on remains of the 1554 Spanish plate fleet (see **Padre Island Wrecks**).

US citizens and institutions were also responsible for early underwater excavations in other nations. In 1905 the Peabody Museum was the sponsor of excavations in the sacred **Chichén Itzá Cenote** in Mexico. From the 1960s to date, the work of the American **Institute of Nautical Archaeology** (INA) has been a significant force in Classical archaeology as practised in the Mediterranean. George F. Bass and later Donny Hamilton served as head of this institution, which is based at Texas A&M University at College Station, Texas.

Underwater archaeological sites in the US are found in salt and fresh water. Besides extensive coastlines on the Atlantic and Pacific shores and the Gulf of Mexico, the Great Lakes provide another significant maritime environment, as does the Chukchi Sea off Alaska and thousands of kilometres of navigable rivers in Alaska and the lower forty-eight states. Additional *loci* of underwater sites are the thousands of prehistoric sites now inundated in reservoirs as a result of dam construction. The inundation of prehistoric coastlines resulting from eustatic sea level rise (see **Quaternary coastlines and land bridges**) also contributes to the nation's underwater archaeological resource base.

The **Treasure-hunting** community in the US has been aggressive in seeking certain shipwrecks in territorial waters that they believe

carry cargoes of intrinsic value. They have engaged in rancorous disputes with underwater archaeologists and preservationists. This tension continues to have a significant dampening effect on institutional progress of the field in the US.

Legislation specific to historic shipwrecks was not enacted in the United States until 1987. The **Abandoned Shipwreck Act** specifically removed historic shipwrecks from the jurisdiction of admiralty. The US in one legislative action exerted title over all historic shipwrecks in its territorial waters and simultaneously passed title to the states except in specific cases such as national park lands.

Because the law also specifies that some accommodation be made to salvor interests, some states have opted to continue a policy of sanctioned removal of antiquities for profit. Most underwater archaeologists in the US consider the threat of treasure salvage and sanctioned antiquities trafficking to the resource base to be far greater than that presented by all natural processes combined.

Below is a discussion of the major underwater archaeological projects in the US arranged in the context of the range of eras and thematic groups within which they are usually studied.

Submerged prehistoric sites in the United States

Underwater archaeology has been conducted on prehistoric sites across the United States. Some of the best-known underwater prehistoric sites are located in freshwater sinkholes in Florida. Two of these, **Little Salt Spring** and Warm Mineral Springs, continue to produce, after more than two decades of investigation, ground-breaking information on regional prehistory.

Prehistoric sites were also examined off the Florida coast. The Douglas Beach Site (8SL17), an 18th-century Spanish shipwreck located above an Archaic period inundated terrestrial site, proved to be an excellent example of the viability of archaeological stratigraphy in underwater sites located in high-energy zones. Analysis of the site, which was found by treasure-hunters during their salvage of the 1715 Spanish plate fleet in 1978, was conducted by Larry E. Murphy. Murphy focused on **Site formation processes**, and his analysis of cores taken at the site provides a basis for identification of submerged prehistoric sites.

Other archaeological work off the coast of Florida has repeatedly confirmed the potential of underwater sites in high-energy zones. One example is Dr Reynold Ruppe's research on the Venice Beach Site (8SO26), a complex of prehistoric **Shell middens** and

mounds. Intact middens, running from above water, on the beach, to varying distances offshore, have provided the evidence. Research on the Venice Beach Site also tested predictive models for locating inundated sites offshore with **Remote sensing** equipment and contributed to knowledge of local prehistory and geomorphology of the Gulf of Mexico.

Work on the Venice Beach Site is not the only Florida project to extend to the conti-

Wilburn Cockrell holding skull from the Warm Mineral Springs site. (Wilburn A. Cockrell)

nental shelf. The Aucilla River Project (begun 1986), directed by Michael K. Faught, James S. Dunbar, and S. David Webb, documented human occupation in stratigraphic context on the inner continental shelf. Early research focused on visible segments of relict river channels in Florida and produced several offshore archaeological sites, including lithic quarries (8JE739), a middle Archaic shell midden and quarry (8TA139), and a possible early Archaic habitation site (8JE740). The pristine context of relict rivers is providing researchers with the opportunity to study materials undisturbed by humans for over 5,000 years.

Underwater archaeological investigations of prehistoric sites span the country. In the American Southwest, Montezuma Well, a component of Montezuma Castle National Monument in Arizona, in addition to being one of the first submerged prehistoric sites in the country to be examined, was the first submerged prehistoric site investigated by the NPS. The large limestone sink, investigated by NPS archaeologists George R. Fischer and Calvin Cummings in 1968, produced a collection of artefacts typical of the late Sinagua period of the Verde Valley (about AD 1450).

Prehistoric maritime craft have also been encountered. Twenty-two cypress carved

canoes were located by the Underwater Archaeology Unit of North Carolina during a survey of a small portion of **Lake Phelps**, North Carolina in 1986.

Numerous other prehistoric vessels have been excavated throughout the country, such as the Swan Lake Canoe. Found in 1989, the dugout canoe, dating from the late Mississippian Age (1500–1600) was uncovered during dredging operations of Steele Bayou in Washington County, Mississippi (Fuller 1992). The canoe was excavated and recorded by US Army Corps of Engineers archaeologists from the Vicksburg District. Once recorded, the canoe and artefacts associated with the site were recovered and transported to the Yazoo National Wildlife Refuge headquarters for conservation.

A unique research programme that emphasized prehistory but included some historical sites was the **National Reservoir Inundation Study** (NRIS) conducted by the NPS 1975–80.

Early European exploration and settlement

After the discovery of the New World by Columbus, Spanish maritime activity in the region increased rapidly. Gold and silver from Central and South America played a vital role in Spain's economy throughout the 16th century. Prevailing winds and currents in the **Caribbean** dictated the route treasure-laden galleons took when returning to Spain: through the Yucatán Channel into

the Gulf of Mexico, then eastward through the Straits of Florida into the Atlantic where the northward flow becomes the Gulf Stream. Spanish voyages of commerce used this route for centuries, resulting in a large collection of shipwrecks in the Gulf of Mexico, throughout the Florida Keys, and

Canoes exposed by low water levels at Lake Phelps. (North Carolina Dept. of Archives and History)

along Florida's east coast. In a particular, a number of flotas, groups of vessels sailing together for protection, were sunk by hurricanes over the centuries. Archaeological investigations of these early exploration and settlement sites began in the 1970s and continues to the present.

One of the earliest Spanish losses in the New World examined by archaeologists was a small fleet of vessels lost off **Padre Island**, on the Texas Gulf Coast, in 1554. Although one of the three wrecked vessels was destroyed in the late 1940s by dredging operations, the other two were located in 1967 by treasure-hunters, who began salvage operations on the wrecks. Growing public concern over the wrecks led to discontinuation of work by the salvors, and eventually resulted in state legislation protecting submerged cultural resources on Texas State bottom-lands. From 1972 to 1975, the Texas Antiquities Committee, first under the leadership of Carl J. Clausen and later J. Barto Arnold III, excavated a site believed to be *San Esteban*, which was the site least impacted by the treasure salvors (Arnold and Weddle 1978). Although only a small fragment of hull remains were extant, the site yielded a remarkable collection of ground tackle elements, armament, navigational aids and instruments, organic subsistence remains, personal possessions, and precious metals. In addition to material recovered during the excavation, the collection salvaged by the treasure-hunters was eventually returned to

the State, where it was conserved and curated.

Not long after the loss of the 1554 fleet, another disaster delayed Spanish settlement in what is now the southeastern United States. A 1559 expedition under Tristan de Luna, attempting to colonize northern Florida, was destroyed by a hurricane in what is now Pensacola Bay; at least six vessels were lost. In 1992 the State of Florida's Pensacola Shipwreck Survey staff discovered a small ballast pile during an underwater survey of the bay. Subsequent investigations revealed a well-preserved 16th-century sailing vessel and numerous 16th-century Spanish artefacts, probably associated with the failed de Luna expedition. From 1992 to 1995, the State of Florida team, directed by Dr Roger Smith, excavated the site, which is known as the **Emanuel Point Ship**.

Hurricanes wrought havoc on Spanish flotas again in 1622, 1715, and 1733, all of which left material remains on the seabed along the coast of Florida. Few shipwreck sites have received more popular attention than these plate fleets, which have been the object of commercial treasure-hunting activities since the 1960s. Despite decades of work on the flotas and numerous popular publications, very little scholarly work has been published on the sites since Carl J. Clausen published an analysis of artefacts from one of the 1715 fleet vessels in 1965. Most American archaeologists do not consider the wrecks suitable for comparative studies because archaeological fieldwork was compromised by the profit motive of modern salvors and the majority of materials from the sites have been sold to private collectors.

Sixteenth-century Spanish exploration and settlement was not limited to the southeastern United States. The Manila–Acapulco trade became important to the Spanish economy during the 16th century, which led to the first recorded shipwreck on the California coast. In 1595 the Manila galleon *San Agustin*, under the command of Sebastian Rodrequez Cermeno, was lost in what is now known as Drakes Bay, California. The NPS's Submerged Cultural Resources Unit conducted a remote-sensing survey of Drakes Bay, part of Point Reyes National Seashore, in 1982. One goal of this survey was to locate magnetically active areas that may represent historical shipwrecks, in particular, *San Agustin*.

The Spanish were not the only ones interested in establishing New World colonies in the 16th and 17th centuries. The French explorer La Salle attempted to claim and colonize the Mississippi River for France during the 1680s, with disastrous results. During his expedition, two vessels were lost in Matagorda Bay, Texas, including the frigate *La Belle*. In the summer of 1995 State of Texas Marine Archaeologist J. Barto Arnold III and a team from the Texas Historical Commission located the remains of *La Belle*.

18th-century sites

Many archaeological remains of watercraft dating from the 18th century are characterized by the wars in which they fought. Some of the vessels participating in the various French and English conflicts during the first half of the century were lightweight, shallow-draft craft called bateaux (see **James River Bateaux; Wiawaka Bateaux Cluster**). The archaeological remains of several bateaux have been investigated in Lake George, New York, **Lake Champlain**, and Richmond, Virginia.

Lake Champlain is also the resting place of numerous vessels. The remains of three mid-18th-century vessels were located during a 1983 underwater survey by Kevin J. Crisman and Arthur Cohn working with the Fort Ticonderoga Association, the Champlain Maritime Society, and the Vermont Division for Historic Preservation. The vessels, built by Royal Navy Captain Joshua Loring during the French and Indian War, were involved in one short, but successful, conflict with the French in October 1759. At the end of the war the vessels, stripped of their armament, slowly rotted and sank at their moorings at King's Dockyard below Fort Ticonderoga. The sixteen gun, 115 ton sloop *Boscawen* was the first of the three vessels to be investigated.

Interest in recovering information on vessels from the American Revolution predated work on *Boscawen* by more than fifty years. In the 1930s the schooner *Royal Savage* and gondola *Philadelphia* were raised from Lake Champlain by Lorenzo F. Hagglund, a salvage engineer. While little remained of *Royal Savage*, which was burned by the British in an action between Benedict Arnold's small fleet and British forces, *Philadelphia*, sunk during the same conflict, was relatively intact.

Perhaps the most well-known excavation of a Revolutionary War-era submerged site is **Betsy** (44YO88), a British supply vessel sunk at Yorktown in 1781 and rediscovered in 1978. In the same year, the Institute for Nautical Archaeology, under the direction of J. Richard Steffy, examined the remains of a large vessel on the Gloucester side of the York River. After further investigation of the site, it was determined to be the forty-four gun warship HMS *Charon*.

Action during the American Revolution was not limited to the smaller vessels such as *Royal Savage* and the gondola *Philadelphia*, nor to the larger vessels, such as the **Yorktown Shipwrecks**. Privateers, merchant vessels authorized to take enemy vessels for profit, aided the fight against the enemy and were a mainstay of the war. Some merchant vessels were quickly converted into privateers by the addition of armament, while others were built specifically for the task. The wreck of **Defence**, a vessel constructed as a privateer, whose career was cut short when it was scuttled by its crew during the ill-fated campaign by the colonists against the British outpost on Fort George, Penobscot Bay in 1779, was located by the Maine Maritime Academy and Massachusetts Institute of Technology in 1972. Excavation of the site was directed by David Switzer from 1975 to 1981; *Defence* was to be the first vessel from the American Revolution to be excavated under complete scientific controls.

Other sites dating from the Revolutionary War-era that have been investigated include the Crosswicks Creek vessels in Bordentown, New Jersey; the Mullica River wrecks, also located in New Jersey; a naval shipyard on the Chickahominy River; and the John's Island Site (0001EDS), a merchant vessel whose remains are located in Edenton, North Carolina.

In addition to vessels associated with various 18th-century conflicts, many merchant vessels operating on both the ocean and inland waterways have been examined archaeologically. Small vessels used for transporting supplies and passengers in the 18th century have been documented in various parts of the country.

Buried ships are frequently encountered at construction sites in port cities. In New York City, the hulk of an 18th-century vessel was uncovered during excavation of a building foundation. Known as both the Water Street Ship and the **Ronson Ship**, the site was examined by Warren Riess and Sheli O. Smith in 1982.

Other 18th-century sites located in rivers include the **Brown's Ferry Vessel**, a two-masted coaster, located in the Black River, South Carolina. In 1992 SCIAA also excavated a small ocean-going vessel dating from the last quarter of the 18th century and the first quarter of the 19th century. The site, called the **Malcolm Boat** (38CH803), was located in a mud bank of the Ashley River. The State of North Carolina's Underwater Archaeology Unit (UAU), led by Richard Lawrence, excavated two vessels from the 18th century. The Rose Hill Wreck, the charred remains of a 67 ft (20.4 m) long, 22 ft (6.7 m) wide, single-masted sailing craft, located in the North-east Cape Fear River, was investigated by the Unit in 1988. The second site, the Otter Creek Wreck, a coastal schooner, was excavated by UAU and Claude V. Jackson III, an East Carolina University graduate student, in 1988.

The archaeological remains of 18th-century vessels are not exclusive to the original colonies. Excavation of two vessels, a British Royal Navy vessel, nicknamed the Deadman's Shipwreck, dating from 1776–81, and the Town Point site (8SR983), a small British sloop or cutter of the same period, took place in Pensacola in the 1990s. Investigation of the Deadman's Shipwreck site was undertaken by the State of Florida, while a non-profit organization, Southern Oceans Archaeological Research (SOAR), undertook research of the Town Point site.

Other 18th-century British wrecks located in Florida waters include two within national parks. The site of the forty-four gun HMS *Fowey*, located in Biscayne National Park, became the first submerged archaeological site in a national park to be placed in a restricted zone. A preliminary investigation of the site was conducted by the South Eastern Archaeological Center (SEAC) and the Submerged Cultural Resources Unit (SCRU) of the NPS in 1980. Reinvestigation and full documentation of the site by NPS-SCRU and Dr John Seidel from 1993 to 1995 revealed a section of the side hull of the vessel with intact gunports and sweep ports. The wreck is currently undergoing site stabilization. The NPS-SCRU also investigated the remains of an 18th-century British warship in **Dry Tortugas National Park** in the 1990s. Preliminary research suggested its identity as the HMS *Tiger*, a fifty-gun ship wrecked near Garden Key in 1742.

HMS De Braak and **Whydah**, both 18th-century wrecks, were excavated by commercial treasure-hunters in the 1980s. These projects are more noteworthy for the division they caused between professional archaeologists and salvors, than archaeological merit. Some analysis of the sites took place, but their salvage proved examples of gross mismanagement of submerged cultural resources within the United States prior to the passage of the Abandoned Shipwreck Act in 1988.

War of 1812

Much of the naval action of the Anglo–American War of 1812 centred on the **Great Lakes** and Lake Champlain. Archaeological investigations have been carried out on a number of naval vessels from that conflict, both American and British, located in the freshwater lakes. Perhaps the most remarkable sites examined are the American armed schooners *Hamilton* **and** *Scourge*, located in Lake Ontario. Lost in a squall on 8 August 1813, the two converted merchantmen were located in 1973 by a dentist from St Catharines, Ontario, under the auspices of the Royal Ontario Museum.

Much of the naval action on the lakes during the War of 1812 was centred on ship-building races, with both American and British forces attempting to out-build the other. On Lake Ontario, this resulted in a fleet of vessels that never saw action. Many vessels were laid up after the war, and eventually rotted at their moorings and sank. Among these was the American brig *Jefferson*, which settled into the bottom of Sackets Harbor, New York. Its remains were discovered in the 1960s, and were considerably impacted by later marina construction. In 1985 an archaeological investigation sponsored by the New York State Bureau of Historic Sites, and directed by Kevin Crisman and Arthur Cohn, documented the site. Although the bow section was destroyed during marina construction, the vessel's aft portion was relatively intact, including the keel, keelson, sternpost and stern dead-wood, and most of the port side to the main deck level. Examination of the site led to a clearer understanding of the quickly-built fleet on Lake Ontario.

In Lake Champlain hastily constructed fleets on both sides participated in a decisive naval action in September 1814. Laid up in the southern end of the lake after the engagement, the American vessels did not see further action, and eventually sank at their moorings. Two of these vessels have received considerable attention from archaeologists. In 1958 the schooner *Ticonderoga*, a converted steamboat, was raised from Lake Champlain and put on display at the Skenesborough Museum in Whitehall, New York. Although badly damaged by exposure, the remains were recorded by Kevin Crisman in 1981. The lower hull to the turn of the bilge clearly display the vessel's steamboat origins, which probably did not make an ideal warship. The other vessel surveyed, the American brig *Eagle*, has provided invaluable information about wartime construction practices. The object of a two-year study by Kevin Crisman and Arthur Cohn, **Eagle** was found to be well preserved, with much of the lower hull and port side, including ten gunports, remaining. Investigation of the brigs *Eagle* and *Jefferson*, and the schooner *Ticonderoga*, have provided valuable insight into the design and construction of fleets of opportunity built during the War of 1812.

In addition, US gunboats on the Chesa-peake were examined by Donald Shomette and Ralph Eshelman in 1979 and 1980. (See **Chesapeake Flotilla**.) These studies have added to our understanding of previously undocumented facets of the War of 1812.

California Gold Rush

One of the largest migrations of humans since the Crusades, the California Gold Rush has been called by maritime historian James Delgado 'first and foremost a maritime event'. After President Polk's White House announced proof of the gold finds in California in December 1848, hundreds of fortune-seekers set off to the West coast. Only the hardiest chose the traditional over-land route during the harsh winter weather of 1848–9; the rest made their way to the gold fields by sea. They travelled to California by way of the Isthmus of Panama or made the long and arduous journey down the east coast and around Cape Horn.

The Port of San Francisco became the Gold Rush capital. Ideally located at the base of the river systems that led to the Sierra foothills and mines, San Francisco was first to receive the cargoes and passengers who had successfully made the voyage. More often than not, the vessels' journey ended there. Crews, captains, even vessel-owners caught up in the wave of gold fever, abandoned their vessels in the hope of striking it rich. The harbour in San Francisco became clogged with abandoned ships, but in a young city with few resources, the vessels were quickly put to use. Ships were stripped for materials, pulled ashore to be used as buildings, or sunk for landfill.

A number of Gold Rush sites have been studied and excavated. They include the **Niantic** site, found during excavation of a building in San Francisco's financial district in 1978; the *William Gray* site, excavated nearby in 1980; and the **Hoff's Store** site, excavated in 1986.

Another Gold Rush-era vessel was encountered during excavation of a tunnel for the city's subway system in December 1994. Constraints of the tunnel environment, which only allowed a 30 by 90 cm section to be viewed at a time, hampered the documentation process. James M. Allan, an archaeologist with the University of California at Berkeley, however, recorded visible sections on video and film. Preliminary research suggests that the site is the hulk of the *Roma* or *Rome*, built about 1820 and scuttled sometime in 1851 for landfill.

Gold Rush-era maritime-related sites have been found in both coastal and inland waterways. In the Sacramento River, across from the Old Sacramento Registered Historic District, archaeologists with Espey, Huston & Associates, Inc. located the remains of two ocean-going sailing vessels during a remote sensing survey in 1986 (James 1987). Historical and archaeological documentation suggest their identities as the barques *La Grange* and *Ninus*.

Sites discovered along the coast generally found their demise through accident. *Frolic*, an opium clipper sent to California to join in the lucrative trade opportunities, was wrecked in a small cove in Mendocino and was the subject of archaeological research in the 1980s.

Steam vessels are also included in the coastal wrecks. Sites studied to date are SS **Tennessee**, a vessel of the Pacific Mail Steamship Company that ran aground at Marin County in 1853, and the steam vessel **Winfield Scott**, which was wrecked off the Anacapa Island in 1853.

Civil War

The Civil War is perhaps the single most studied period in underwater archaeology in the United States. Shipwrecks from the war between the states have excited the imagination of the public and scholars alike. Although early attention, especially during the centennial celebrations of the early 1960s, was oriented more towards salvage and relic-hunting, many wrecks have received serious archaeological attention since the mid-1970s.

Probably the most visible and well-publicized, as well as the most voluminous, documentation has taken place on the ironclad USS **Monitor**. Several months after its celebrated battle with the CSS *Virginia*, *Monitor* was lost off the coast of North Carolina while under tow, en route to Beaufort, North Carolina. Lying upside down at a depth of 70 m, the ironclad was located in 1973 by a multi-disciplinary team aboard Duke University's research vessel *Eastward*. In 1975 the site was designated as the nation's first **National Marine Sanctuary**, administered by the National Oceanic and Atmospheric Administration (NOAA). Since then, numerous expeditions have visited the site.

During the 1960s Civil War centennial, several shipwrecks, both Union and Confederate, were raised for public display. Although the intentions of the salvagers were noble, the vessels were all severely damaged by salvage operations. Since these vessels were recovered, however, each has been the subject of archaeological documentation that has dramatically increased our knowledge of Civil War-era warship construction, especially Union and Confederate ironclads. The Union ironclad USS **Cairo**, sunk by a Confederate 'torpedo' (mine) in the Yazoo River, Mississippi, was the subject of extensive salvage before raising the vessel intact was attempted in 1964. Another Civil War gunboat, the Confederate ironclad CSS **Neuse**, burned by its crew in 1865 to prevent its capture by advancing Union forces in the Neuse River in eastern North Carolina,

CSS Neuse. (US Naval Historical Center)

was discovered by locals and salvaged between 1961 and 1963, and finally raised, obtained by the State, and transported to Caswell/ *Neuse* State Historic Site in 1964. This familiar story was repeated yet again in 1964, on the Chattahoochee River, near Columbus, Georgia. The remains of the Confederate gunboat CSS *Chattahoochee* and Confederate ironclad ram CSS *Jackson* were identified by the US Army Corps of Engineers as a navigational hazard to river traffic. Public interest in the wrecks led to their salvage and placement in the newly opened James W. Woodruff Confederate Naval Museum. While *Jackson* was recovered intact, *Chattahoochee*'s remains broke in half during lifting operations; only the stern was recovered. In 1984 the remainder of the gunboat's hull was relocated and recorded by staff and students from **East Carolina University Program in Maritime History and Nautical Archaeology**. Although the hull of CSS *Jackson* had suffered from exposure and a fire caused by a careless museum visitor, its remains were recorded in 1993 by an ECU team. Hindsight shows us that these vessels would have been better off left in their riverine graves. Nonetheless, conservation and display of these historic vessels, and archaeological research since their recovery, has expanded our knowledge of Civil War riverine ship construction and warfare.

Since the 1970s further archaeological examinations of Civil War shipwrecks on riverine and inland waterways, especially in North Carolina, have made significant contributions to the archaeological database. Union gunboats USS *Iron Age* and USS *Picket* (ex-*John F. Winslow*) were examined by archaeologists in the 1970s. Fuelled by the numerous wrecks in North Carolina waters and the proximity of East Carolina University's Program in Maritime History and Nautical Archaeology, many ECU students have teamed up with the staff of the North Carolina Underwater Archaeology Unit to study Civil War vessels. Some examples are the USS *Southfield*, an ex-New York ferryboat turned Union gunboat, a study which examined how vessels of opportunity were converted into warships; examination of the iron-hulled CSS *Curlew*; and the excavation of the Chicod Creek Wreck, a Confederate gunboat burned before completion. In addition, ECU spent several field seasons documenting *Maple Leaf*, a Union transport steamer lost in the St John's River, Jacksonville, Florida.

Another important site, the Confederate ironclad CSS **Georgia**, was the subject of extensive archaeological research between 1979 and 1984.

Several archaeological expeditions have examined Civil War vessels lost during naval operations at Mobile, Alabama. The Union monitor USS **Tecumseh**, Union gunboat USS *Philippi*, and Confederate gunboat CSS *Gaines*, were lost during the Battle of Mobile Bay in 1864; the blockade runner *Ivanhoe* was driven aground a month before the battle. Several remote sensing surveys were conducted in the bay in response to harbour development activities, but before a 1991 ECU survey, no material remains were observed. That survey identified the possible remains of *Philippi* and *Gaines*, and verified a magnetic anomaly located during a 1991 Florida State University terrestrial magnetometer survey for *Ivanhoe*. Work is continuing on the better preserved *Gaines* site.

Civil War blockade runners have received considerable attention in recent decades. Perhaps the earliest work on a blockade runner was the salvage of more than 11,000 artefacts from **Modern Greece**, near Fort Fisher, North Carolina in 1962 and 1963. Similarly, a collection of artefacts recovered from the blockade runner *Acadia*, wrecked near Galveston, Texas, during the late 1960s, was conserved and analysed by Frank Hole in the early 1970s. In 1994, as part of the NPS's Civil War Battlefield Protection Program, East Carolina University and the North Carolina Underwater Archaeology Unit continued a systematic investigation of the numerous blockade runners and other Civil War vessels wrecked off Fort Fisher and the mouth of the Cape Fear River. Many of these had been previously identified and included in a National Register thematic group nomination, the **Cape Fear Civil War Period Shipwreck District**. A recent survey of the Cape Fear River by the Underwater Archaeology Unit identified several more possible Civil War shipwreck sites, including the Confederate ironclad CSS *Raleigh*.

Confederate commerce raiders proved a particularly effective weapon against the Union and its merchant interests. Although several have been the focus of salvage operations by private parties, including CSS **Florida** and *Nashville*, only one, CSS *Alabama*, has received proper archaeological attention.

Sites related to commerce raiders have also been examined by archaeologists. The wreck of USS **Hatteras**, a Union blockade ship sunk by *Alabama* off the coast of Texas in 1863, has been the subject of a monitoring programme since 1992, and a preliminary map of the site was produced. Several whalers sunk by the commerce raider CSS *Shenandoah* have been examined in the Pacific by the NPS's Submerged Cultural Resources Unit (NPS-SCRU).

The Confederate submarine **H.L.Hunley**, lost in off Charleston, South Carolina in 1864 after becoming the first submarine successfully to sink a ship, has been the focus of several remote sensing surveys and much study after its 1995 discovery.

Riverine and lake sites

American river steamboats played an unique role in the opening of the Midwest and western interior. Transporting passengers, general cargo, and bulk freight along the western river systems, they were designed for specific purposes and environments. From small ferry craft, tow boats, dredge boats, to floating gambling palaces, steam vessels plied American waterways from the late 18th to the early 20th century (see **Steamboat archaeology in North America**).

The most popular steamboat configuration was the stern paddle wheeler. The 1860s riverboat *Bertrand*, wrecked in the Missouri River in what is now the Desoto National Wildlife Refuge, was one such vessel. Located by local salvors in 1968, *Bertrand* was excavated under the guidance of the NPS.

Charles H. Spencer, a paddle wheel steamboat wreck in Arizona's Lee's Ferry Historic District, a gold and coal mining operation located on the Colorado River, was documented by the NPS's Submerged Cultural Resources Unit in 1986.

Another stern paddle wheeler, *City of Hawkinsville*, located on the banks of the Suwannee River in Florida, was documented by archaeologists from the State of Florida in the early 1990s. The largest and last steamboat to travel the Suwannee River, *City of Hawkinsville*, was designed with a single smoke stack, square stern, moulded bow, two decks, and a length of 141 ft (42.9 m). Abandoned in 1922, the steamboat site has become one of Florida's Underwater Archaeological Preserves.

Black Cloud, a side wheel steamboat, located in the Trinity River in Texas, was one of the first sites documented by nautical archaeology graduate students at Texas A&M University. The vessel, which had transported cotton and assorted goods to and from Galveston, was in service for nine years before its abandonment in 1873. Rediscovered in 1965 during installation of a natural gas pipeline, its remains were documented during two surveys in the autumn of 1978.

The first large-scale archaeological survey of US rivers, the Tennessee-Tombigbee Waterway Project, took place from 1978 to 1979. An investigation of anomalies detected during a remote sensing operation along construction impact zones of the Tombigbee River, it was a precedent-setting project in underwater archaeology. Directed by Larry E. Murphy and Allen Saltus of Interagency Archaeological Services Atlanta and funded by the US Army Corps of Engineers, Mobile District, the project was the first to evaluate submerged sites from a regional perspective.

From 1989 to 1990 the remains of two cordwood barges in Emerald Bay, Lake Tahoe, California were documented by Sheli O. Smith. Mooring buoys and interpretive kiosks were placed on site and shore by the California Department of Parks and Recreation.

The cold, dark, fresh water of the **Great Lakes** has created a unique environment for shipwreck preservation. Many important archaeological investigations have taken place on these freshwater lakes that have expanded our knowledge of the evolution of Great Lakes vessels and the trades in which they served.

The 19th century on **Lake Champlain** was a time of wide commercial activity and expanding trades. A variety of vessel types were involved in lake-borne commerce, and many have left material remains on the bottom.

Pacific Coast vessels of commerce

Maritime activity on the Pacific coast was limited before the Gold Rush in 1848. Commerce and industry expanded rapidly during the 1850s and throughout the rest of the 19th century. The remains of many different vessel types involved in myriad trade activities have been studied on the Pacific coast, from southern California to Alaska.

One of the earliest known shipwrecks on the west coast after the initial period of Spanish exploration in the late 1500s is the wreck of the supply ship *Isabella* in 1830 on the Columbia Bar. This British-built brig, in the service of the Hudson Bay Company, was lost at the mouth of the Columbia in an effort to supply Fort Vancouver. Its remains were doc-

umented by the NPS-SCRU and the Columbia River Maritime Museum in 1987.

The remains of the medium-clipper *King Philip*, exposed and recorded on Ocean Beach, San Francisco in 1983, represents one of many 'environmentally exposed' shipwrecks examined in California.

Left: Sword hilt from USS *Huron, which was lost off the coast of North Carolina in 1877. (North Carolina Division of Archives and History)*

Opposite: Gun recovered from the wreck of USS *Huron. (North Carolina Division of Archives and History)*

Another naturally exposed shipwreck near San Francisco represents the remains of another significant vessel type, the Pacific coast lumber schooner. The schooner *Neptune* was involved in the lumber trade from 1882 to its loss in 1900. The archaeological documentation conducted by James Delgado is particularly important because this site is the most intact section of a Pacific coast lumber schooner recorded to date. Investigation of additional, highly scattered lumber schooner sites has also taken place in Channel Islands National Park.

Although little archaeological work has been done to date in Alaska, the potential

for maritime archaeology is great. Several historical studies have been undertaken to assess vessel losses in various Alaska regions. One area that has received attention is World War II losses in the **Aleutian** Islands. Several historic shipwrecks have been located by various Alaskan interests, including the whaler *Orca*, but nothing has been published about the projects to date.

Atlantic and Gulf coast ships of commerce and war

One of the most extensive underwater archaeological projects studying trade and commerce in the Gulf region is currently underway at **Dry Tortugas National Park**, 112 km west of Key West, Florida.

Another project undertaken in the Florida Keys is the documentation of a wreck believed to be USS *Alligator*, wrecked in 1822. This vessel has long been the focus of salvage and looting by Keys treasure-hunters and sport divers, but renewed interest in the vessel has been sparked by the Naval Historical Center in Washington, DC. The vessel is historically significant, and is the oldest United States naval vessel located in Florida waters. A multi-agency team of archaeologists visited the site in October 1995, and fieldwork took place in 1995-6.

Another significant US naval vessel on the

Atlantic coast, USS *Huron*, was documented by East Carolina University student Joe Friday, and later became the State of North Carolina's first shipwreck preserve.

World War II

Minimal underwater archaeological study has been conducted on World War I or World War II sites in the lower forty-eight states, although there has been work in Alaska and on US submerged bottoms in Hawaii and Guam. Most notable has been the efforts of the NPS-SCRU in these places.

A documentation project on the hulk of the USS *Arizona* at **Pearl Harbor** under the direction of Dan Lenihan began in 1983. It resulted in the eventual publication of a complete study of the underwater residues of the war in Pearl Harbor National Historic Landmark (Lenihan 1989). In addition to documentation and corrosion studies on *Arizona*, the only other World War II vessel remaining in the harbour from the attack, USS *Utah* was included in the project.

Studies of underwater sites in Guam and the Aleutian Islands, Alaska, were conducted by various SCRU personnel including Lenihan, Larry Murphy, and Toni Carrell during the 1980s. While surveying World War II wrecks in Apra Harbour, Guam, the team also mapped the wreck of the World War I German raider *Cormoran*. This vessel lies keel to keel on the bottom with the Japanese armed transport and WWII casualty *Tokai Maru*. SCRU operations in the far Pacific were reported in a special unit publication (see Carrell 1991).

SCRU personnel also surveyed Kiska Harbor in association with the US Navy in 1989. They located and documented a number of casualties from the Japanese occupation and American re-invasion.

Also during 1989 and 1990 the NPS team documented the ships sunk at Bikini Atoll in the atomic bomb tests known as 'Operation

Crossroads' (see **Crossroads Wrecks**). Dirk Spenneman also conducted work on World War II wrecks in the Marshall Islands with the most notable being the complete study of a B-24 off Majuro.

In addition to the work of SCRU in Palau and **Truk Lagoon**, these islands have been well documented for underwater remains of the World War II by Klauss Lindemann. D.J.L., A.A, M.R.3

ADDITIONAL READING

This list includes only those ADDITIONAL READINGS not cited in the various, more detailed entries found elsewhere in the encyclopaedia.

Submerged prehistoric sites in the United States

Murphy, L.E., 1990, *8SL17: Natural Site-Formation Process of a Multi-Component Underwater Site in Florida*, Southwest Cultural Resources Center Professional Papers, 39, Santa Fe.

European exploration and settlement

Clausen, C.J., 1965, 'A 1715 Spanish Treasure Ship', *Contributions of the Florida State Museum*, Gainesville, Florida.

18th-century sites

Morris, J.W. and Franklin, M., 1995, *An Archaeological Assessment of the Vessel Remains at Town Point, Site 8SR983*, Southern Oceans Archaeological Research, Inc., Site Report 1, Pensacola Bay.

Wilde-Ramsing, M.U. *et al.*, 1992, *The Rose Hill Wreck: Historical and Archaeological Investigation of an Eighteenth Century Vessel at a Colonial River Landing near Wilmington, North Carolina*, Underwater Archaeology Unit, Division of Archives and History, North Carolina Department of Cultural Resources, Kure Beach, N. Carolina.

War of 1812

Crisman, K.J., 1987, *The Eagle: An American Brig on Lake Champlain During the War of 1812*, Annapolis, Maryland.

California Gold Rush

Delgado, J.P., 1990, *To California by Sea*, Columbus.

Civil War

Hole, F., 1974, *The Acadia: Civil War Blockade Runner*, Houston, Texas.

Riverine and Lake Sites

Adams, R.M., 1980, *Survey of the Steamboat Black Cloud*, Department of Anthropology and Archaeology, Texas A&M University, College Station.

Smith, S. O., 1991, *Emerald Bay Barges Archaeological Survey 1989–1990*, California Department of Parks & Recreation and the Los Angeles Maritime Museum, Sacramento, California.

Pacific, Atlantic and Gulf coasts

Delgado, J.P., 1986, 'Documentation and Identification of the Two-Masted Schooner Neptune', *Historical Archaeology*, 20.

Murphy, L.E., 1993, *Dry Tortugas National Park: Submerged Cultural Resources Assessment*, Santa Fe.

World War II

Carrell, T. (ed.), 1991, *Micronesia Submerged Cultural Resources Assessment*, Santa Fe.

Uruguay

see **South America**

US Navy

The US Navy, through the Naval Historical Center (NHC) initiated an **Underwater archaeology** programme in 1993. The NHC had already been involved for some time on a

locate and access. The NHPA is incorporated into two important US Navy regulations, the Secretary of the Navy's Instruction 400.35 and Operating Naval Instruction 5090.IB. These regulations place the Navy's responsibilities for historic Navy ships, naval shipwrecks, and historic aircraft with the Naval Historical Center.

The Department of the Navy retains custody of its ship and aircraft wrecks by the principle of **Sovereign immunity**. Navy ownership is not affected by the passage of time, nor whether the wrecks are located in US, foreign, or international waters. These wrecks are not abandoned but remain the property

on the Law of the Sea (1982) the Convention on the Law of the Sea (1982), and established principles of international maritime law are the legal basis for Navy custody. These laws establish that right, title, or ownership of Federal property is not lost to the government due to the passage of time, or by neglect or inaction. Ultimately, abandonment of government-owned ships and aircraft occurs only through congressional action. United States court cases have supported this doctrine and established significant legal precedents in Hatteras Inc., vs the USS *Hatteras*, her engines, etc. *in rem* and the United States of America, *in personam* (1984

The recovery of the Dauntless SBD aircraft from Lake Michigan. (US Naval Historical Center)

case-by-case basis with managing historic Navy shipwrecks and sunken aircraft. This new programme originated from the responsibilities mandated to the Navy under Federal preservation laws, such as the National Historic Preservation Act of 1966 (NHPA), and the awareness that these historically significant ships and aircraft are in imminent danger from diverse interest groups. This danger is a direct result of recent advances in diving, **Remote sensing**, and **Global Positioning System** technologies that have made these sunken Navy wrecks easier to

of the government until specific formal action is taken to dispose of them and, thus, are immune from the law of salvage without authorization from the appropriate Navy authorities. This immunity is founded in historic principles of maritime law. These properties are not considered 'abandoned' in the **Abandoned Shipwreck Act** of 1987 (43 USC 2101–6) and did not transfer to the states with adoption of that Act. The property clause of the United States Constitution (Article IV, Section 3, Clause 2), Articles 95 and 96 of the United Nations Convention

A.M.C. 1094, aff'd, 698 F.2nd 1215, 5th Cir., [1982]) and US vs Richard Steinmetz (763 F. Supp. 1293, 1294, [D.N.J. 1991]; aff'd, 973 F.2nd 212, [3d Cir. 1992] cert. denied, 113 S. Ct. 1578 [1993]), also known as the '*Alabama* bell case'. The former is the most frequently cited legal precedent supporting the government's policy.

CSS *Alabama* and approximately 320 other Confederate naval vessels represent a special category of shipwrecks entitled to sovereign immunity since they now belong to the

United States Government based upon the principle that the present government by right of conquest succeeded to the property of the former Confederacy. Confederate naval shipwrecks are currently under the Administrator of the General Service Administration (GSA), a responsibility of GSA inherited from the Treasury Department. In some instances, the GSA has authorized the NHC to assume management responsibilities for significant shipwrecks under their jurisdiction. CSS Alabama, USS **Tecumseh**, and **H.L. Hunley** are examples of such.

There are several important reasons why continued United States Government ownership of its sunken warships and aircraft is important. These are listed in the Navy's policy fact sheet *Sunken Naval Vessels and Naval Aircraft Wreck Sites* (Naval Historic Center 1995) and include compliance with Federal preservation laws, protection of war graves, dangers to the public from ordnance and explosives, to deter commercial exploitation, and the recognition that these wrecks represent valuable historic properties to be held in the public trust.

Navy policy has been clear for some time where **Human remains** are concerned: 'Salvors should not presume that sunken US warships have been abandoned by the United States. Permission must be granted from the United States to salvage sunken US warships, and as a matter of policy, the United States Government does not grant such permission with respect to ships that contain the remains of deceased service men . . .' (DOS 1986; UNESCO 1994). This is not a new policy, as the Navy's involvement with USS *Tecumseh* illustrates. *Tecumseh* was lost in 1864 during the battle of Mobile Bay with ninety-two men drowned. In 1873 *Tecumseh* was sold for salvage, but after the purchase the salvor let it be known that he intended to use explosives to blast the wreck into salvageable pieces. The relatives of the men lost on *Tecumseh* petitioned Congress to stop this salvage. Congress acted quickly to do so and stipulated that any future salvage must provide for the removal and proper burial of the remains of the crew. This precedent was continued with other Navy shipwrecks. Another consideration for the Navy is those wrecks that still contain ordnance on board and present a danger to public safety.

The Naval Historical Center works in close cooperation with other Navy commands, such as the Navy's Federal Preservation Officer and the Admiralty Law staff of the Navy Judge Advocate General, and the various Navy active and reserve units. It also works in partnership with other Federal agencies, including the NPS, NOAA, the General Services Administration, and the Advisory Council on Historic Preservation.

Cooperative partnerships with a number of states, through their state preservation and archaeology offices, state universities, and local maritime museums are an integral method of managing Navy ship and aircraft wrecks lying within state waters. The benefits of NHC and state alliances are manifold: helping to create and refine the Navy's national inventory of naval wrecks, providing for site assessment and monitoring, developing management plans for specific wrecks or groups of wrecks, and recommendations for future protection and interpretation.

For Navy wrecks within foreign territorial waters, protection or scientific investigation depends upon cooperation between the United States and the coastal states. Management of CSS *Alabama* is one example of such international cooperation. CSS *Alabama* is the property of the United States, but the excavation of this site is carried out under the laws of the Republic of **France**. CSS *Alabama* is recognized as an important heritage resource of both nations and its administration set a precedent in international cooperation. A Joint French–American Scientific Committee was established to consider issues of protection and the terms under which archaeological exploration is conducted.

The Navy is responsible for a large number of aircraft wrecks. These represent unique underwater sites, which are quite different from shipwrecks. These submerged aircraft are often intact and can be relatively easily recovered, unlike shipwrecks. The high public interest in vintage aircraft creates special problems in preserving these underwater sites. Although acceptance of aircraft as archaeological sites is growing, it is a relatively new concept.

The NHC and the National Museum of Naval Aviation have been involved in the preservation of two very significant Navy aircraft. One of these is a Dauntless SBD (BuNo. 2106) recovered from Lake Michigan, which survived both the Japanese attack on Pearl Harbor and the Battle of Midway. The other aircraft is the only known example of a Torpedo Bomber Devastator, TBD-1, and may be a combat veteran of the Battle of the Coral Sea.

The Navy has reached out to the recreational diving community by providing for interpretation of naval wrecks through the development of shipwreck diving preserves. In 1993 the North Carolina Department of Cultural Resources and the US Navy entered into the first cooperative agreement to administer a diving preserve involving a Navy shipwreck, USS *Huron*, which sank in a storm in 1877 with great loss of life. Building on this effort, the Maryland Historical Trust and the Navy entered into a partnership to develop a Navy prize of war, the sunken German U-boat U-1105, or 'Black Panther', into a diving preserve. Diving preserves can provide both an experience that educates the public and recreational adventures.

Today, the Navy recognizes that it has under its jurisdiction some of the most significant historical properties within the United States. Many of the Navy's sunken warships are eligible for listing on the **National Register of Historic Places**, for these wrecks are the archaeological evidence of the actions and events that forged the nation. These sunken vessels and aircraft also represent the courageous actions of those Americans who have earned a permanent place in United States history and are the final resting place for many who sacrificed their lives for their country. R.S.N.

ADDITIONAL READING

Cooper, D.J., 1994, 'In the Drink: Naval Aviation Resources and Archaeology', in R.P. Woodward and C.D. Moore (eds), *Underwater Archaeology Proceedings from the Society for Historical Archaeology Conference, Vancouver, British Columbia*, Ann Arbor, Michigan.

Neyland, R.S., 1996, Sovereign Immunity and the Management of United States Naval Shipwrecks', in S.R. James and C. Stanley (eds), *Underwater Archaeology*, Ann Arbor, Michigan.

USSR

see **Russia and the ex-Soviet Union**

USS *Utah*

United States auxiliary gunnery training ship sunk during the carrier-based air raid by the Japanese Navy on US forces at **Pearl Harbor**, 7 December 1941. *Utah* is the only major warship survivor of the attack that still remains in the harbour with the notable exception of USS **Arizona** which has become a major American shrine. *Utah*, a lesser known memorial, was mapped and photo-documented by the NPS's **Submerged Cultural Resources Unit** (SCRU) with assistance from **US Navy** divers in 1986.

Utah was the second of the Florida class battleships (BB-31) built in 1909. Its main fire power was concentrated in five turrets that mounted a total of ten 12 in guns. In 1914 it played an important role in American landings at Vera Cruz, Mexico during a period of intense civil strife. *Utah* was redesignated as an auxiliary in 1931 and there-

Above: USS Utah *at Pearl Harbor. (NPS/C. Cummings)*

Right: Ladder on number 1 turret of USS Utah. *(NPS/D.J. Lenihan)*

after served as a target ship and finally as an anti-aircraft training ship for the Pacific fleet.

Larry Murphy supervised the work done on *Utah* in 1986. It was part of a combined project that had the dual purpose of further documenting *Arizona* while beginning efforts on *Utah*. Overall project director was Daniel Lenihan. Illustrator Jerry Livingston rendered a drawing of *Utah* from the mapping data which was later refined during several smaller projects over the next three years.

The 1986 work on *Utah* marked the first time the informal relationship between SCRU and US Navy divers was formalized and given the name of Project Seamark. The Navy divers came primarily from the reserve community and were under the command of Commander James K. 'Otto' Orzech. They worked under the auspices of Mobile Diving Salvage Unit 1, an active duty command led by Commander David McCampbell. Both of these officers would continue to help concentrate Navy assets on SCRU underwater historic preservation projects for the next decade.

Utah lies on its starboard side in 12 m of water with portions of its remaining superstructure and port gunwale breaking the surface. This splash zone is suffering the worst deterioration effects. Most of the hull is submerged and keeping closer to a state of equilibrium where degradation of the metal hull proceeds at a much slower pace.

Most of the hull is intact and all of *Utah*'s three anchors are in place in their hawse pipes with their associated chain extending along the deck to the chain locker. All of the

5 in guns which were mounted at the time of the attack are still intact except for the barrel of one which is missing. The 5 in 38 cal. anti-aircraft guns were placed on the old boarded-over turrets used to hold the 12 in guns when *Utah* served as a battleship. Heavy timbers used to protect the ship from

excavated in 1974. The construction of Utrecht I is dated by carbon-14 and dendrochronology to the 11th century; the sinking of Utrecht II is dated by stratigraphy to the second half of the 12th century. Neither vessel was found with any cargo or equipment, although a few small utilitarian

base log, while the long ribs are joggled over and fastened to the first side strake as well. A beam, possibly for attachment of a quarter rudder, was found with Utrecht I. All fastenings are treenails.

Earlier attempts to date Utrecht I had placed it in the Carolingian period, and the

Above: The remains of USS Utah. *(NPS/Jerry Livingston)*

the impact of dummy bombs during bombing practice are strewn about the deck.

Utah was designated as one of the first two shipwreck National Historic Landmarks in the United States. The successful nomination was prepared by NPS Maritime Historian James Delgado, working with a team from SCRU in 1990. *Utah* is still owned by the Navy, although there have been various proposals to have the ship managed by the NPS. D.J.L.

ADDITIONAL READING

Lenihan, D. (ed.), 1989, *Submerged Cultural Resources Study: USS Arizona Memorial and Pearl Harbor National Historic Landmark*, NPS Southwest Cultural Resources Center, Professional Papers 23, Santa Fe.

Utrecht Boats

Two large extended logboats of medieval date excavated in Utrecht, the Netherlands. The first vessel, sometimes known as Utrecht I, was excavated in 1930, conserved in creosote, and reassembled in the basement of the Central Museum of Utrecht, where it is currently on display. A second vessel, sometimes known as Utrecht II and sometimes as the Waterstraat Vessel, is smaller but of similar construction and was

objects and bones were found in the vicinity of Utrecht I.

Utrecht I is reconstructed at 17.2 m in length, 3.66 m in beam, and 1.3 m in depth amidships, with a deadweight capacity of *c.* 113 tonnes. The second vessel is somewhat smaller, with an estimated length of *c.* 13 m and beam of *c.* 3 m. Both hulls have round rockered bottoms that rise substantially at the ends. The form is largely dictated by the method of construction, as each hull is based on a bottom carved from a single immense oak log. In Utrecht I this log is extended at the ends by carved blocks. The sides are made up of an overlapping strake fastened to the upper edge of the log base, a heavy wale made from a half-log (in Utrecht I, the port and starboard wales were cut from the same tree) overlapping the strake and fastened to it, a sheerstrake fastened to the inner surface of the upper edge of the wale (sometimes referred to as 'reverse clinker' construction), and a rub rail fastened to the outer, upper edge of the sheerstrake. In Utrecht I the ends of these timbers are fastened to the extension blocks; in Utrecht II they are fastened directly to the ends of the log bottom. The bottom and sides are strengthened by a system of alternate long and short ribs. The short ribs extend only to the edges of the

vessel had been portrayed as an ancestor of the late medieval hulk, which was thought to be a large clinker-built vessel without a true keel, stem, or sternpost. The construction of Utrecht I, with its hollow bottom and planks fastened to blocks at the ends, rather than to posts, seemed an early manifestation of this tradition. Scholarship now links the Utrecht boats to a tradition of extended logboats known in northwestern Europe since at least Neolithic times, and largely discounts the association with the hulk. F.M.H.

ADDITIONAL READING

Hoekstra, T.J., 1975, 'Note on an Ancient Ship Found at Utrecht', *International Journal of Nautical Archaeology*, 4, 390–92.

Vlek, R., 1987, *The Medieval Utrecht Boat: The History and Evaluation of One of the First Nautical Archaeological Excavations and Reconstructions in the Low Countries*, BAR International Series 382, Oxford.

Valle Ponti Ship
see **Comacchio Wreck**

Varve dating
see **Absolute dating**

Vasa

Sixty-four gun Swedish man of war, lost in 1628 and raised in 1961. The ship is 69 m overall with the length of the hull between the prow and the stem 45.5m. *Vasa*'s maximum width is 11.7 m and the draught 5.5 m. The height from the keel to the top of the main mast was 52.5 m. The ship displaced 1,210 tons and had ten sails with a total area of 1,256 sq. m. The sailing crew is estimated to have been 145 men, and 300 soldiers to serve the cannon and make a fighting force on board the ship.

The salvage of *Vasa* in 1961 triggered a more widespread interest in marine archaeology in Scandinavia; the project also inspired considerable interest in many other countries. It was not a marine archaeological undertaking as we see it today, where the **Excavation** is performed underwater. This was a delicate salvage operation where the complete hull of the ship after 333 years underwater was lifted to the surface and only then subjected to an archaeological excavation.

Swedish king Gustavus Adolphus ordered the ship in early 1626. Since 1621 Sweden had been at war with Poland, where Gustavus Adolphus's cousin Sigismund was king. Sigismund had been deposed from the Swedish throne in 1599, but was still making claims to the Swedish kingship. The war was waged in Polish Livonia and Polish Russia. With the **Baltic Sea** between the war and his home country, the Swedish king wanted to keep its waters under control – thus the need for a strong fleet.

On the afternoon of Sunday, 10 August 1628, *Vasa* set sail on her maiden voyage to the naval base in the Stockholm archipelago. While in the harbour, a gust of wind caught the sails, the ship listed to port, water gushed in through the open gunports and *Vasa* sank 'with standing sails, flags, and all'. This is how the disaster was reported to the king. It was a critical loss as *Vasa* was one of the biggest ships in Europe at the time and would have played an important role in strengthening the Swedish Navy.

A big ship with a large amount of valuable bronze cannon attracted many adventurous

The Warship Vasa 1628, reconstruction drawing by I.N. Kowarsky, based upon all available information in July 1968. (© Kowarsky, Isacsons, Göteborg)

Vasa during transportation in 1961; the warship is mounted on a concrete pontoon in the framework of the aluminium building that housed her for twenty-eight years. (Courtesy of the Vasa Museum, Stockholm, Sweden)

men from different parts of Europe who wanted to make a fortune by bringing up the ship, or at least the cannon. They all tried in vain until the Swede Albrecht von Treileben in the 1660s introduced a simple diving-bell. With brave divers he managed to bring up most of *Vasa*'s cannon. After that, the ship was left more or less forgotten.

In the 1950s private researcher Anders Franzén was the first to draw the interesting and rather obvious conclusion from a fact that was well known to marine biologists – that the water in the Baltic Sea is not salty enough for the shipworm *Teredo navalis* to thrive there. He realized that this might be the only sea where big sunken men of war from the 16th and 17th centuries stand a chance of being preserved. Franzén started a search in the archives for the location of a number of lost large warships. The first on his list was *Vasa*.

In 1956 Franzén's search of the seabed with grapnel and a core-sampler produced results. A diver confirmed that there was a huge ship standing on its keel on the bottom at a depth of 32 m. In the darkness the diver could not see, but felt with his hands the ship's sides, which seemed to have no end in any direction.

The Neptune Salvage Company, a very experienced Swedish enterprise, was consulted about the salvage operation. They suggested that a conventional technique be used. Six tunnels were to be dug out under

the ship's hull for steel cables that would be attached to lifting pontoons. There was nationwide interest in the *Vasa* project, and the Swedish Navy provided divers and boats for support.

It was a very tough job for the divers. Because of mud on the bottom that whirled around with every move, they had to work blind, lying down in the tunnels, blowing their way through the clay under the ship with water jets from Zetterström nozzles. It was easy to get stuck, and above their heads was a 300-year-old ship weighing more than 1,000 tonnes and carrying stone ballast. It took two years to make the preparations for the first lift.

In August 1959 the ship was cradled with steel cables and the water was pumped out of the lifting pontoons. The clay bottom of the seabed released the ship. In sixteen stages the ship was lifted to shallower water. There, the preparations for the final lift (with jacks mounted on the pontoons), were performed. Damaged parts of the stem and the stern were closed in; the gunports were given new temporary lids; and thousands of holes from rusted-away iron bolts were plugged to make the ship watertight. *Vasa* had to float into dry dock on her own keel when brought up to the surface, as the ship with one pontoon on each side was too wide to pass through the dry dock's opening. On 24 April 1961 *Vasa* broke the surface.

With *Vasa* safe in the dry dock the archaeological excavation was carried out during the summer and autumn of 1961. The excavation was diligently planned and led by archaeologist (and later director of the National Maritime Museum) Per Lundström. The result was around 25,000 finds, of which about half were parts of the ship that formed a gigantic jigsaw puzzle ultimately leading to a restored vessel.

Between 1963 and 1967 every summer was devoted to a systematic search of the

harbour bottom around the cavity left from the *Vasa*. The most important finds from that period were more than 700 sculptures and sculptured parts that had fallen down into the clay when the nails holding them to the ship had rusted away. Thus they had been well protected and in most cases survived in very good condition.

The finds from the interior of the ship were as might have been expected – belongings of the crew members and equipment and ship stores. This being the maiden voyage, the brand new ship had evidently not yet taken on board all its stores or any hand weapons, with the exception of a few personal arms. These finds were also evidence of the lifestyle of the poor, and the kind of belongings that are not otherwise saved for posterity. There were all kinds of materials: textiles, leather, wood, ceramics, clay, glass, bronze, and pewter. There were all sorts of things: clothes, shoes, gloves, hats, bowls, plates, flasks, barrels, boxes, fishing-gear, a backgammon set, musket balls, cannonballs, etc. There were spare parts for the ship and, in a sail locker, the six original sails that were not set when *Vasa* sailed out.

A temporary museum and workshop for *Vasa* was built in 1961 and opened to the public early in 1962. The first problem to solve was the preservation of the ship, as nothing like it had been done before. No tried method was available. By chance, though, it was discovered that a patent owned

by the Swedish forestry company Mo & Domsjö, and worked out by Bertil Centervall och Rolf Morén, for treating fresh wood with polyethylene glycol, worked even better with waterlogged wood. An automatic sprinkling system was installed and *Vasa* was treated with polyethylene glycol for seventeen years before the wood was saturated and could be allowed to dry slowly. The process was followed and controlled all the way by taking bore samples for analysis. A **Conservation** laboratory was built where all the loose parts were treated. These thousands of wooden pieces, ranging from very small to heavy long beams, were treated in huge baths under controlled conditions, making it possible to cut down the time to completed preservation to one and a half years for oak and one year for pine. In the laboratory other materials were also taken care of and preserved.

Among the most interesting and also most difficult objects to save were the six original sails, folded and stored in the ship's sail locker. The fragile material had to be unfolded and cleaned under water. It was then dried in alcohol and xylene and affixed to fibreglass backing with a special plastic

Vasa's upper gundeck with the gun carriages standing on their places after the salvage in 1961. (Courtesy of the Vasa Museum)

made for the purpose by the preservation department.

The second big problem was the restoration of the ship. The reason why *Vasa's* hull had not collapsed while standing on the seabed with all its iron bolts and nails rusted away was that the hull was also held together by treenails, approximately forty per square

metre. First, some 5,000 new iron bolts had to be inserted in the empty bolt holes to stabilize the ship's hull. No drawings were used in shipbuilding in *Vasa's* time and no painting or engraving is known to picture the ship. But with patience and skill, the big jigsaw puzzle fell into place, and the ship was restored with the destroyed beak-head and stern-castle rebuilt and the standing lower rigging reconstructed, most of it with original parts.

The most delicate job was the handling and the preservation of the ship's 700 sculptures, a major collection of wooden sculptures from the late Renaissance and early Baroque. They have provided first-hand knowledge of the decoration of a man of war of this size and importance. An intriguing part of the restoration work was to establish where on the ship the sculptures had originally been placed. Studies have shown that the adornment of big warships was the result of well thought out programmes. The sculptures gave particular messages to the observer, speaking of king and country, of victory and glory, of virtue and strength, of life and death.

A further question was in what way the now-blackened sculptures were once painted. Some of the sculptures that were brought up from the seabed showed traces of gold leaf, but at the time there were no reliable means of analysing the colour. Science has since provided new opportunities. It is now possible to take samples from the sculptures and, using an electron microscope, establish what paint was used on the figures. The result of this analysis gives evidence of strong, bright colours made even stronger by using elements of gold – just like the altar pieces of the churches of the time.

The temporary museum of 1961–2 had to be replaced by a permanent arrangement where the climate could be well controlled. In June 1990 the new *Vasa* Museum was ready for inauguration by HM King Carl XVI Gustaf. The museum is well designed for the ship with a huge ship's hall where the visitor can experience *Vasa* fully. The ship is surrounded by basic exhibitions that place *Vasa* in its context. *Vasa* is the only preserved 17th-century ship in the world. It gives us important knowledge of its time, of shipbuilding and the society that produced the ship, of life on board and ashore. *Vasa* Museum has become the most visited museum in Scandinavia. L.-Å.K.

ADDITIONAL READING

Kvarning, L.-Å. and Ohrelius, B., 1973, *Swedish Warship Wasa*, London.

Landström, B., 1980, *The Royal Warship Vasa*, Stockholm.

Soop, H., 1992, *The Power and the Glory: The Sculptures of the Warship Vasa*, Stockholm.

Borgenstam, C. and Sandström, A., 1984, *Why Wasa Capsized*, Stockholm.

Kvarning, L-Å., 1993, 'Raising the Vasa', *Scientific American*, 269, 4.

During, E., 1994, *De dog på Vasa* (*They Died on the Vasa*, summary in English), Stockholm.

Vergulde Draeck

Wreck of a medium-sized East Indiaman, lost in 1656. On 4 October 1655, *Vergulde Draeck* of the Amsterdam Chamber of the Dutch East India Company (VOC) set sail from Texel, on what was to be its second and final voyage to Batavia (modern Jakarta) in the East Indies. The master was Pieter Albertsz and there was a crew of about 193 men, indicating a medium-size East Indiaman (the ship was occasionally referred to in contemporary texts as a yacht). It is recorded that the ship carried a cargo of trade goods worth 106,400 florins, together with eight chests of silver coin worth 78,600 florins. After stopping briefly at the Cape of Good Hope, the ship sailed east following the route to the East Indies established by Henrik Brouwer in 1611. This course followed the Roaring Forties east towards the southland, and then north to Batavia. On 28 April 1656 *Vergulde Draeck* struck a reef close to the Southland at the beginning of the first day watch, at a latitude 31Bo 16'. Seventy-five survivors, including the master and understeersman, reached shore, but all that could be saved from the ship were a few provisions. The master dispatched the under-steersman and six men to obtain assistance

Artefacts from Vergulde Draeck. *(© Western Australia Maritime Museum/Patrick Baker)*

from Batavia. Following their arrival, the company sent numerous expeditions to locate the survivors, but no traces of the survivors or the shipwreck were found.

For nearly 200 years the documents relating to *Vergulde Draeck* remained in the State Archives in Holland; the 19th-century publications in English of the loss stimulated much speculation as to the position of the wreck. In 1931 a young boy found about 40 silver coins in the sandhills near the site. These coins caused much excitement at the time as their dates ranged between 1619 and 1655, thus indicating that they could belong to the survivors of *Vergulde Draeck*. The first substantiated report of the discovery of the wreck came on 13 April 1963. A superficial examination of the site revealed cannons, anchors, ballast bricks and elephant tusks, thus clearly indicating an old wreck, and possibly *Vergulde Draeck*.

The first material raised was an elephant tusk and some ballast bricks. In the months following the discovery, a large amount of material was recovered. Unfortunately there are no accurate records of what exactly was raised. In October 1963 newspapers reported the first of several accounts of blasting on the wreck site. Since it was clear that the situation was getting out of control, and unique and valuable historical material was being destroyed, a group of the finders asked the state government to intervene. They claimed that in view of the immense historical value of this wreck it should become state property, be properly excavated, and be available for everyone to see.

The reef on which the wreck lies has numerous solution holes, caves, tunnels, and gullies. Except on the sand-shingle floors of these caves, it is extremely difficult to distinguish the wreck material from the bedrock. The more obvious wreck indications are five anchors and twelve iron cannons, which more or less delineate the wreck site. In some cases these cannons lie on the top of the reef (2–3 m deep) and in other places in deeper parts of the site. This is a difficult site to work, since it is exposed to the Indian Ocean swell.

The first museum excavation took place in 1972. The surface deposits were found to consist of loose jumbled ballast bricks and lumps of broken concretion. Below this was a sand layer containing loosely scattered ballast bricks. Bedrock was reached at a depth of about 0–1.5 m where animal bones and the remains of the staves of a wooden barrel were found. Since the bones have the marks of butchering, it was concluded that this was possibly the remains of provisions such as salt beef. Apart from the very deepest levels, no stratigraphy was noted, nor was there any indication of the ship's structure.

Examination of other areas on the wreck site indicated a similar situation. However, the work of looters, often using explosives, and the effects of severe storms, have confused much of this work. It was therefore concluded that detailed and systematic recording of individual items on this site was unnecessary at this point. The priority was to remove the surface layers of disturbed material and to try to uncover undisturbed levels. The results of this first phase confirmed the initial findings that the superficial levels were severely disturbed. However, in levels undisturbed by looters, very little structure or stratification was noted. In the eastern area of the trench some ship's structure was found. However, the timbers were badly broken up and almost unrecognizable. In some cases pottery and other small artefacts were found above and below the ballast brick layer. This tended to indicate that the ship had broken up violently and the wreckage was thoroughly mixed up.

Excavation continued recording only the significant material, by sketching on the accurate plan of the site the approximate position and depth at which it was found. It is likely that the ship broke up in a complex manner and material was therefore distributed at the time of the wreck in a confused pattern. Also, the subsequent action of the sea and of severe gales possibly caused a redistribution of the lighter material, and the effects of looting and blasting have added to the confusion. The one outstanding pattern that can immediately be recognized is that of the coins. These are exclusively confined to the north and main section of the trench. This has been the area most heavily worked by looters, but due to the weight of the individual coins, they have not been moved significantly by wave action, and therefore indicate something of their original distribution. With the ceramic material, it is likely that any intact stoneware jugs that were lying in superficial levels of the sand-ballast brick

Astrolabe from Vergulde Draeck. *(© Western Australia Maritime Museum/ Patrick Baker)*

areas had been removed by looters. It is interesting to note that apart from a few jugs in superficial levels, the majority were recovered from either deep levels or infilled underhangs. The large amount of animal bone recovered during the course of the excavation was invariably associated with the remains of wooden barrels. This presumably was part of the ship's victuals: salt beef and pork. Other bone remains include fish and, possibly, chicken.

In July 1981 twelve days were spent re-examining the site. The objectives were to excavate the main wreck site areas that had been left at the end of 1971–2. These areas comprised the large concretion in the centre of the site and the inside reef area. The concretion lump was exposed from the surrounding spoil using an **Airlift**. Work then commenced on breaking it up, a task which proved to be extremely difficult. By the end

of the season, only very limited progress had been made. Another iron gun was found in this area, bringing the total number of guns on the site to twenty. Work on the inside reef proved to be extremely difficult because of bad weather and limited time. A further season in 1983 was a great success due to long periods of unseasonable and unusually calm weather.

The initial objectives of the 1983 excavation were to clear the northern area of any large remaining rocks, excavate to sterile bedrock, and check for artefacts. Whilst this work was in progress, a **Photomosaic** of the southern area was carried out prior to excavation there. Once this was completed, the **Water dredge** was set up to excavate around the concretion lump. The lump was cleared of all sediments and overburden, so that the concretion was clearly exposed. The concretion lump was then seen to consist of a number of highly corroded boxes which originally contained iron bars. In some cases the boxes still had the wooden packing around the outside, but inside all consisted of a hard and brittle iron concretion-shell, surrounding a fragile and friable core of iron bars or strips. Extreme care was required to dismantle this concretion. The procedure finally arrived at, after some trial and error, was to use a car jack inserted under the concretion to separate the boxes. In general, the points where the boxes were

cemented to one another were weaker than their internal structure, so that by judicious selection of jacking points, it was possible to separate the boxes either in groups or individually. This was not totally successful, but out of about seven to eight boxes, two were recovered intact. Once the boxes were separated they were raised using lifting bags and moved to a storage site some distance off the site.

Later on, when the work boat was brought to the site, the boxes were raised on board and transported to Ledge Point, where a temporary gantry had been constructed on the beach. The boxes were unloaded in the shallow water and winched ashore using a power-operated winch on the front of the department's four wheel drive field vehicle. The boxes were then winched under the gantry and raised on a chain hoist. A truck was then backed underneath and the boxes lowered onto the truck. As a result, all the boxes were transported from the site to the **Conservation** Laboratory at Fremantle in one and a half days. The actual wreck site to truck time was about three hours.

During the 1983 excavation, because of the extremely calm conditions experienced on the site, it was possible for the first time to investigate the area on top of the reef and in fact to carry out an excavation there. During the first dive in this area, an astrolabe with its alidade and part of a bell were recovered, the astrolabe lying exposed on the top of the reef. In both seasons a number of highly interesting finds were made. It is surprising that a number of these finds were quite different from the bulk of material recovered in 1971–2. In particular, a number of fine ceramic objects were found, together with the very unusual pipe.
J.G.

ADDITIONAL READING

Green, J.N., 1973, 'The Wreck of the Dutch East Indiaman the *Vergulde Draeck* (1656)', *International Journal of Nautical Archaeology*, 2, 267-89.

Henderson, G.,1986, *Maritime Archaeology in Australia*, Nedlands, Western Australia.

Vicar of Bray

Dismasted, partially submerged hulk in the Falklands, and a rare surviving British merchant vessel from the mid-19th century. Built at Whitehaven, England in 1841 as a 281 ton barque, and subsequently rebuilt as a longer, 347 ton vessel, *Vicar of Bray* was home-ported in Liverpool and was actively engaged in British international trade. In 1849 the barque made a voyage to San Francisco during the California Gold Rush, arriving in November of that year with mining

Vicar of Bray *at Goose Green, 1982, showing her port side.*
(Nicholas Dean)

equipment. Leaving California in March 1850, the barque remained in active trade, ending her career in the copper ore trade between Chile and Great Britain. In 1870, en route to Chile with a load of coal, the barque was damaged and put into the Falkland Islands. Beyond repair, *Vicar of Bray* was condemned, and put to use as floating warehouse in Stanley Harbour. The dismasted hulk was finally incorporated into a now-dilapidated dock at Goose Green.

The partially decked hull of *Vicar of Bray* rests in approximately 3 m of water, parallel to shore and listing to port. Archaeological and architectural surveys of the barque's hull and fittings by Peter Throckmorton in 1976, and Eric Berryman in 1979, have included the probing of the silt-filled hull and the drafting of architectural plans. Like other hulks (**Egeria**, **Snow Squall**, St Mary, **Jhelum**, **Charles Cooper**, and **Actaeon**), *Vicar of Bray* is one of a unique collection of largely intact wrecks of 19th-century vessels, available for archaeological study because they are preserved by the cold, dry climate of the Falklands (see **Falklands wrecks and hulks**). J.P.D.

Video mosaic

An image, usually digital, formed by the composition of multiple smaller images, allowing a wider field of view than any of the component images, but hopefully maintaining their resolution. Mosaicking of underwater imagery has been performed since the early days of underwater photography. Digital mosaicking has only been feasible in recent years, due to limitations on readily available digital image collection and processing systems. This entry will concentrate on the digital formulation of mosaics made from underwater imagery, ignoring the important topic of acquisition of the digital imagery.

There are three fundamental difficulties which must be addressed in the formulation of a mosaic. These are: (1) provision of geometric control; (2) reconciliation of parallax induced geometric inconsistencies; (3) minimization of radiometric inconsistencies.

It is exceedingly rare in underwater work for geometric control accuracy to match the resolution of optical sensors. In deep water work, common positioning sensors have an accuracy on the order of metres. Even when highly sophisticated short-range systems are used, accuracy is rarely better than several centimetres. In comparison, sensor resolution in the target plane sometimes approaches one millimetre. Further, transfer of positions derived from navigation sensors to the camera focal position requires precise vehicle and sensor calibration, and a suite of accurate attitude sensors. These are rare in practice.

It is possible to orient photogrammetrically the constituent images in a mosaic, allowing for whatever control is possible. If sufficient overlap is present in the imagery, even a relative orientation (which is complete but for absolute position and scale) can be used to register the imagery, allowing rectification and accurate placement. If geometric control is available via targeted points, stretched strings, or other artificially introduced data, the rectified images can be scaled appropriately as well.

Another method which has been used in control of a mosaic is the use of preconceived models of the geometric shape of the mosaic subject. For example, if as-built plans of a wreck exist, and if the mosaicker is confident that significant portions of the wreck have not changed in shape, then the plans can be introduced as a base map for the mosaic. The potential pitfalls in this approach should be obvious.

The techniques just described could have been abstracted from a manual on aerial photo-interpretation and mosaicking. Some of the aspects are, indeed, identical. However, there is a crucial difference. The ratio of target range to height disparity in the subject is far greater in underwater work, since the vagaries of underwater imaging greatly reduce imaging range. Range-induced parallax forces extreme differences in multiple views of the same object. Were we simply to accept image placements and shapes as derived from geometric control, one result, no matter how accurate the control, would be great mismatches in features, obviating the reason for forming the mosaic.

One approach to reconciling the different views of the same object with the theoretically correct placement of images is to place correctly a portion of the controlled imagery throughout a pre-planned digital base map with a density great enough to provide reasonable overall control for the mosaic but sparse enough to avoid overlapping and irreconcilable views. The 'blank' spaces between the control images are filled by digitally warping non-controlled imagery to the base map. The warp is generally performed using a selection of tie points between the images, and a variety of parametric warps. Generally, low order polynomial warping is most successful.

This type of mosaicking has been used successfully in deep sea geological analyses. It is useful in that endeavour to produce digital image coverage base maps, allowing ready selection of images for mosaicking.

This type of mosaic formulation is highly interactive, requiring operator selection of multiple tie points and control of warps. No matter how well the registration works, however, there will still be geometric inconsistencies due to parallax. At this point, highly subjective mosaic area selection procedures are used. Two approaches are prevalent: cut-line selection and tapering, and digital airbrushing. Cut lines are created by operator selection of a boundary between images. Typically, the line would be chosen such that it follows a natural edge in the imagery, minimizing perception of a boundary between images. Edge-feathering techniques are often used. There have been successful attempts at automatically detecting appropriate cut lines in aerial and satellite imagery.

Airbrushing techniques have been drawn from the computer graphics arts communities, and use a digital brush to blend images together. Airbrushing allows a more visually pleasing product, but is even more subjective and interactive than cut-line specification.

The final obstacle to a visually pleasing mosaic is addressed by minimizing radiometric inconsistencies between images. Underwater imagery is usually characterized by uneven illumination. The illumination gradient can cause image edges to be prominent no matter how adept the airbrushing or cut-line selection. Adaptive histogram specification has proved to be a key

composite scenes, but many rely upon flat-plane or constant-parallax assumptions. Photogrammetric investigators, and some vision efforts, recognize the three-dimensional nature of the problem without ready solutions. J.H.

Villefranche-sur-mer Wreck
see *Lomellina*

HMS *Viper*
see HMS *Vixen*

Virolahti Boat
Clinker-built vessel dating to the 1st century AD. In 1977 the remains of a clinker-built vessel were reported, and also surveyed, in shallow water at the islet of Lapuri, parish of Virolahti, on the Finnish south coast near the sea border of what was then Soviet Russia. The vessel had been built of broad,

Eenil, J., 1991 'Keskiajan merenkulusta Itisell Suomenlahdella', *Suomen Museo*, 98, 47–76.

Ericsson, C., 1977, 'Viking-ship Remnants in Eastern Waters', *The Maritime Museum of Finland Annual Report*, 4–5.

HMS *Vixen*
Royal Navy gunboat of 1864, scuttled at Bermuda after 1896, and archaeologically documented and studied in 1986–8. Construction began on *Vixen* and two sister ships, *Viper* and *Waterwitch*, in England in 1864. These ships were intended to serve as 'armoured gunboats' in fleet actions at sea, and they incorporated many technological innovations that characterized the first generation of ironclads. *Vixen* was the first twin-screw ship to join the Royal Navy as well as the first composite ironclad to serve as a naval vessel. The ship was iron framed and iron hulled, with an outer

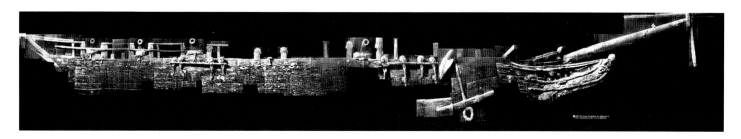

Video mosaic of Hamilton *formed using approximately one hundred digital still camera images, collected by ROV Jason of the Woods Hole Oceanographic Institution, 1990. (© Jason Foundation for Education and the City of Hamilton)*

technique in minimizing radiometric inconsistencies and allowing a visually pleasing mosaic. This image processing technique, which is quite common in the medical imaging field, uses the distribution of intensity levels in a local image neighbourhood in a sub-area of the local neighbourhood. Although it can exaggerate image noise in poor-quality imagery, the technique has proved extremely useful in minimizing illumination gradients. Other techniques involve forcing matches between histograms and other image statistics between mosaics and potential constituent imagery.

In practice, digital mosaicking can be an extremely laborious and expensive process. Batch-style image processing can be used with great effect to adjust radiometric intensities, but extensive operator interaction is usually necessary both in placing and rectifying imagery and in blending images together. Substantial research is ongoing in the computer vision community into automated formulation of mosaics and other

thin planks, joined in a classic Iron Age lapstrake technique. Parts of a keel with a T-shaped cross-section and floor timbers, loosened from the structure, seemed similar to the same structural members in earlier boat finds from the late Iron Age in Scandinavia. Later underwater investigations and salvage of the remains have shown that the thin board planks were held together with iron clench-nails. Carbon-dating of the cow hair used as caulking has given the date of AD 980 for the construction of the vessel.

The remains retrieved from the bottom are evidently from a slender, clinker-built, undecked oak hull. The vessel was 12–13.5 m long and had a width between 2.45 cm and 3 m. It has a reconstructed length–breadth ratio of 5.0–5.1:1.

As the vessel had a light structure and a slender shape, it is assumed that it was built for use in inland or coastal waters. The hypothesis has been put forward that this was a vessel which was used for traffic on the route from Sweden along the south coast of Finland to Russia and perhaps further to the Black Sea during the Viking Age. C.O.C.

ADDITIONAL READING

Alopaeus, H., 1984, 'Virolahden myhisrautakautinen alus', *Suomen Museo*, 91, 117–20.

cladding of 5½ in (14 cm) of teak over the entire hull. When launched in 1865, *Vixen* and her sister ships attracted interest from marine engineers owing to their unique design features, but their trials in 1867 were disappointing.

All three ships were slow. *Vixen*, with a top speed of only 9.06 knots, proved to be the slowest ironclad ship in the Royal Navy at that time. These ships were also unseaworthy. *Vixen* was nearly lost in a gale in the Irish Channel in 1867. *Vixen*'s coal bunkerage allowed for only twelve days of steam cruising, which was inadequate for continuous operations with the main battle fleet at sea. Like other seagoing ironclads of the 1860s, *Vixen* and her sister ships were masted and carried a full complement of sails as a way of conserving fuel during cruises. Steam power was generally limited to movements in and out of harbour, during periods of little or no wind, and for manoeuvring during battle.

The need to shift back and forth from sail to steam propulsion led to the adoption in *Vixen* and *Viper* of lifting screws, with vertical trunks in the stern to hold the screws while cruising under sail. This feature appeared in late wooden naval ships powered by steam and sail and in large ironclads like *Warrior*.

But *Vixen*, *Viper*, and the slightly later iron-clad *Penelope* had two vertical trunks to accommodate the twin screws.

These ships all had telescoping funnels which were lowered when under sail and raised while steaming. *Waterwitch* had the unique capability of changing direction by reversing the flow from its underwater jets produced by a hydraulic engine. Although *Vixen* and *Viper* could turn faster than the larger ironclads of the period, *Waterwitch*'s turning performance was worse, which was unfortunate, since *Waterwitch* was constructed as a double-ended ram (with a ram bow and stern). These poor results led to the abandonment of hydraulic propulsion for naval ships until the late 20th century. *Viper* resembled *Vixen* in all respects except that the ship lacked wooden outer cladding, making *Viper* lighter and slightly faster.

Vixen and *Viper* were towed to Bermuda, where they remained as coast defence ships for the remainder of their careers. Neither ship ever saw combat. They brought HM Floating Dock *Bermuda* from the Narrows to the Royal Navy Dockyard in Bermuda in 1869. Sometime after 1873, all masts and rigging were removed from both ships following suggestions to station them permanently in Bermuda. *Vixen* was struck from the Navy List in 1896. Uncertainty exists about the destruction of *Vixen*, but archaeological evidence indicates that the ship was scuttled with blasting charges to block the Chubb Cut Channel off Daniel's Head along Bermuda's west end. Documents show the existence of a plan to use a blockship in this area to augment the shore batteries. *Vixen* was that blockship, and the scuttling probably occurred in 1896.

Although stripped of its guns, engines, and portable artefacts, the wreck of *Vixen* retained most of its hull and deck structure. The wreck was recorded in 1986–8. The most conspicuous feature was a projecting ram bow, with massive reinforcing structures of iron within the forward hull to support the ram. Much of this structure did not appear in the original plans for these ships. *Vixen*'s main armour consisted of a box-like armoured citadel covering the mid-section of the ship to protect the engines. The wrought-iron armour was 4½ in (11 cm) thick, with a teakwood backing of 10 in (25 cm) and the wooden outer cladding described earlier. The main armour did not, however, protect the ship's four small guns (two 7 in rifled muzzle-loading guns and two 20 pounder breech-loading guns) on the exposed upper deck. Secondary armour belts of similar thickness extended fore and aft of the citadel along both sides of the

Hand-operated capstan on the bow deck of HMS Vixen.
(Richard A. Gould)

vessel which, together with some unique longitudinal frames, stiffened the hull against the shock of ramming.

Archaeological documentation of the wreck of HMS *Vixen* revealed a greater emphasis with respect to the ship's structure on the tactic of ramming than was apparent in the plans and other documents pertaining to these ships. Conversely, the light armament and the lack of armour to protect these guns challenged the documentary description of these ships as gunboats. The engineering and construction of *Vixen* and her sister ships suggests a degree of tactical indecision by the Admiralty during the mid-1860s about how best to use the new technologies of iron and steam in their earliest ironclad, with no clear choice yet between ramming and gunnery. R.A.G.

Warm Mineral Springs

North American prehistoric archaeological site. The formerly terrestrial and now uniquely inundated prehistoric archaeological site at Warm Mineral Springs has been the subject of research and analysis since 1972, under the direction of Wilburn A. Cockrell with support from the State of Florida's Division of Archives and History, private sponsors, and Florida State University.

The site contains well-preserved organic and other remains of the Paleolithic period in southeastern North America. Warm Mineral Springs' significance lies in the antiquity of the materials recovered (11,000 BP) and in the unique nature of these discoveries, including one of the oldest intentional human burials yet excavated in North America, the recovery of a shell spur from an *atlatl* (spearthrower), the oldest such artefact yet found in North America, and the unique mixture of organic and other materials which are providing the first detailed assessment of the now largely changed environment in which early humans of the region hunted and lived.

The deep, oxygen-free, mineralized waters, and the as yet substantially unexcavated debris mound at the bottom of the springs indicate the potential of this site to continue to add to and revise our understanding of the beginnings of the human experience in the area.

Site geology and hydrology

Warm Mineral Springs is located on the coastal plain of southwest Florida some 20 km from the Gulf of Mexico and southeast of Venice in Sarasota County. This area of the Florida peninsula is characterized by karst topography; Warm Mineral Springs is an uncommonly deep hourglass-shaped cenote (sinkhole). From bank to bank, on a north–south axis, the pool at the surface is 72 m in diameter. Descending in the water column to 3–5 m below the surface, at the first 'drop off', the width is 48 m. At 10–15 m below the surface, the cavity widens to about 55 m. The walls of the cenote then constrict again to form a nominal 13 m 'ledge' and a throat 20–30 m below the surface with a width of only 36 m. At 30 m below the surface the cavity widens to form the lower chamber of the 'hourglass' and continues to widen to 72 m at the maximum depth of 70 m below the surface.

The sinkhole is fed by one large warm water spring and several small cool and warm water springs, giving a normal surface temperature of 30–31 degrees C. The limestone bedrock in which the sinkhole formed is a marine rock known as the Hawthorn formation of the Miocene period, with an upper stratum age of 7,000,000 years, the lowest exposed level of the sinkhole dating to 20,000,000 BP.

A series of caverns was formed by dissolving limestone and the surrounding Pleistocene marl, creating the sinkhole during a time of lowered sea-level during the upper Pleistocene. The collapse of the solution cavity's roof at the site during lower sea-levels formed the sinkhole. At that time, well-preserved dripstone and flowstone formations in the sinkhole, now preserved underwater, were formed. These formations, numerous at Warm Mineral Springs, are rarely found at underwater sites but were preserved here because of the lack of dissolved oxygen in the water.

Prehistoric archaeological materials
While considerable natural features and fossils abound in the springs, the deposition of prehistoric archaeological material occurred after a 60–100 m lowering of the sea-level 12,000–14,000 years BP left a dry ledge some 13 m below the sinkhole's lip. Three archaeological components are present at the site: (1) a terrestrial component; (2) the once-dry 13 m below-surface ledge; and (3) a 70 m wide debris cone, comprising silt and organics that fell into the cenote, which rises to within 38 m of the surface. Archaeological and related paleo-environmental deposits in the three areas resulted from different behavioural and depositional mechanics and must be studied with that in view.

While it is known that Seminoles were in the vicinity in the 19th century and it may be assumed that the people at the time of European contact, the Calusa and related tribes, knew about the site, very few historic materials dating earlier than the 1930s have been recovered from any component; the earliest historic period artefacts are several fragments of hand-blown spirit bottles of the late 19th century.

Cockrell has ordered the site's prehistoric components into a Formative Stage (Historic period to c. 2,500 BP), Archaic Stage (c. 2,500 BP to c. 9,000 BP), and Paleoindian Stage (before c. 9,000 BP). It is felt that the Archaic to Paleoindian stage date is as yet inconclusive. So far, project research has uncovered evidence from all three stages in one or more components of the site, but with the greatest amount of evidence coming from the Paleoindian Stage, dating to c. 11,000 radiocarbon years before the present.

Excavation on the terrestrial component, in acidic sands, has recovered an unifaced scraper and pressure flaking debitage, in the same stratigraphic layer as mineralized terminal Pleistocene camel and horse remains. In the upper strata of the sand, archaeologists have found more debitage and a contracting stem biface fragment, a characteristic Archaic Stage tool. The limited testing so far has not yet encountered Formative Stage artefacts on dry land.

The 13 m ledge is composed of dry-deposited sediments accumulated during the mid- to early Holocene. Until the 1987 field season it had been believed that the ledge had been dry from c. 11,000 to c. 8,000 BP, but recent dating sequences have demonstrated dry deposited strata dating to c. 7,000 BP. This places the uppermost strata clearly within the Archaic Stage period. While it is possible that local SCUBA-divers may have recovered Archaic material in the 1950s and 1960s, their provenance is suspect; controlled excavation of the ledge to date has not recovered Archaic remains.

Paleoindian Stage material recovered from the 13 m ledge has been most constructive. In addition to broad paleo-environmental data, archaeologists recovered a c.10,300 radiocarbon year old intentional, flexed human burial with a carved shell spearthrower spur interred with the body as well as a human mandible from a stratum dated at c.11,000 radiocarbon years BP. Additionally, project archaeologists have documented the remains of at least eighteen other individuals from the 13 m ledge. Pollen and well-preserved macrobotanical remains indicate that an eastern deciduous forest was dominant at the time, rather than the pine barren interspersed with sabal palm and oak prevalent today.

In addition to existing faunal forms, ranging from rat to racoon, deer, and panther, the ledge also has produced ground sloth (*Megalonyx*) and sabre cat (*Smilodon*) radiocarbon dated at 11,000 BP. These stratigraphically related 13 m ledge finds from the 1970s mark the first time in North America that sabre cat, ground sloth, and humans were seen to be coeval; however, there is no direct evidence whatsoever of any contact between the people and these extinct faunal forms.

The debris cone on the bottom, being more than 30 m high and over 70 m wide at its base, and constantly covered by preservative anaerobic waters, holds the greatest promise of the three components. Here, in a mound of exceptionally well-preserved organic and mineral remains, is a stratified record representing surface and subsurface activities from the present back to the initial opening of the sinkhole, which is assumed to be at a time of Pleistocene sea-level lowering, first estimated at c. 20,000 BP. Cockrell has adopted as a working hypothesis that the sinkhole opened c. 30,000 years BP. In the future, planned sub-bottom profiles and coring will support or reject this hypothesis, as well as resolve the question of the configuration of the bedrock at the base of the debris cone. According to hydrologists who have examined the site, once these questions have been resolved, it should be possible to reconstruct with more certainty the formational sequence of the cavity.

Inasmuch as excavations to date have reached a level of only 3,300 years back into the cone, one would expect to find only Formative Stage materials *in situ*, with intrusive geological and possibly archaeological specimens from both younger and older strata redeposited from the surface and 13 m ledge deposits above. Aside from numerous Pleistocene fossil finds, archaeologists have located a deer bone pin, or awl, in the c. 2,000 BP stratum. It is believed that this artefact clearly dates from the early Formative Stage occupation of Warm Mineral Springs.

Project archaeologists continue to recover remarkably well-preserved wood, acorns, hickory nuts, seeds, occasional fish remains, and various faunal fragments. Excavation is accomplished using the bare hand as a tool, as the peat sediments are of the consistency of sponge cake, and it is expected that wooden artefacts, basketry, cordage, and perhaps animal soft tissues will ultimately be encountered. Additional human remains will probably also continue to be excavated. An as yet undated human humerus was recovered from the 55 m depth in the late 1970s; it was eroding out of a gully in the site created by cascading sand which had been trucked in as a beach for bathers, and subsequently redeposited over the ledge by waders. J.P.D., W.C.

ADDITIONAL READING
Cockrell, W.A. and Murphy, L.E., 1978, 'Pleistocene Man in Florida', *Archaeology of Eastern North America*, 6, Summer, 1-13.
Cockrell, W.A., 1980, 'The Belated Recognition of Inundated Sites', in K. Muckelroy (ed.), *Archeology Under Water: An Atlas of the World's Submerged Sites*, New York.
Rosenau, J.C. *et al.*, 1977, 'Springs of Florida', *Bulletin No. 31 (Revised)*, Department of Natural Resources, Tallahassee, Florida.

Water dredge

A tool for lifting sediments in underwater **Excavation**. The water dredge, like an **Airlift**, is used by a diver, and generally comprises a plastic or metal tube that works by pumping water through the mouth. Water dredges are more effective than airlifts at depths of less than 10 m, because the difference in pressure decreases in an airlift at shallow depths. The water dredge works by propelling water into a venturi tube (a tube with a 30 degree angle bend at the end), creating suction and drawing up water and sediment. While the airlift is worked vertically, a water dredge lies horizontally and is worked in this fashion.

Water dredges can be powerful; a 900 litre per minute pump, when linked to a 150 mm pipe, can lift water and sediment as high as 20 m and excavate approximately 7.5 cu. m of sediment or loose gravel in an hour. Dredges can be manufactured in varying sizes and hence made smaller and less powerful for more detailed work.

Originally used as a primary excavation tool, like the airlift, water dredges are now only recommended to remove spoil (sediments already excavated by hand) from a site. The powerful suction can take up smaller artefacts and break them if used improperly. At the spoils end of the dredge, a screen is recommended to catch any artefacts that may have been missed in the excavation, or to collect samples for analysis of faunal remains. J.P.D.

ADDITIONAL READING

Dean, M. *et al.* (eds), 1992, *Archaeology Underwater: The NAS Guide to Principles and Practices*, London.

St. John Wilkes, W., 1971, *Nautical Archaeology: A Handbook for Skin Divers*, New York.

Waterstraat Vessel

see **Utrecht Boats**

Water Witch

A small steamboat built by Jehaziel Sherman in 1832 at Vergennes, Vermont to compete with established steamboat lines on **Lake Champlain**. The intact wreck of this vessel, sunk in the central part of the lake, has yielded many details of 19th-century inland merchant steam and sailing vessels.

The keel for *Water Witch* was laid in 1831 and the completed vessel was launched early the following year. According to the original enrolment papers, *Water Witch* measured 80 ft (24 m) in length, 17 ft (5 m) in beam, 7 ft 4 in (2.2 m) depth of hold, and had a tonnage calculated at 91^{52}/95 tons. The side wheels were propelled by a 40 hp steam engine. The steamer's name may have been

Diver using a water dredge on the wreck of Ericsson.
(Neil McDaniel/UASBC)

inspired by the novel *Water Witch* published by James Fenimore Cooper in 1831. Captain Sherman put his new vessel into service as an 'opposition boat', that is, a passenger and freight carrying steamer that ran just ahead of other steamships and took their business by offering an earlier schedule and cheaper fares.

Water Witch competed with the Champlain Transportation Company (CTC) steamer *Phoenix II* in late 1832 and 1833, leading the captain of that vessel to refer to Sherman's boat as a 'pirate'. The CTC finally bought Sherman out in 1835 in exchange for cash, shares in the company's stock, and a place on the board of directors; due to a surplus of steamers on the lake *Water Witch* was stripped of boiler and engine, converted into a merchant schooner, and sold. For the next thirty years *Water Witch* sailed the lake with cargoes of manufactured goods and raw materials. While carrying a load of iron ore to Burlington, Vermont on 26 April 1866, the schooner was knocked over by a squall and sank in 30 m of water.

The wreck of *Water Witch* was discovered by a sport diver in 1977, upright and nearly intact with only the mainmast and a few spars missing, and the foremast broken at the partners and fallen to starboard. The schooner's small boat lies off the stern. The Vermont Division for Historic Preservation sponsored a preliminary survey in 1990, and the lines of the vessel were recorded during a joint Lake Champlain Maritime Museum-**Institute of Nautical Archaeology** project in 1993.

The extent of the rebuilding that took

place during the conversion from steam to sail is not known, but the wreck retains the same dimensions as the 1832 enrolment. As a schooner, *Water Witch* appears typical of sailing merchant craft that worked between Champlain's ports in the 19th century. Hull features include an extremely shallow hull and a centreboard amidships that provided stability under sail. Deck features include a log windlass at the bow, two small cargo hatches on the main deck, and a raised quarter deck with a small deck house covering the after cabin companionway. The schooner's gaff rig consisted of a bowsprit with club to extend the foot of the jib and a basic gaff rig on each of the two masts. Steering was accomplished with a long tiller, although some lake schooners had a wheel. K.C.

ADDITIONAL READING

Crisman, K. and Cohn, A., 1993, 'The Lake Champlain Schooner *Water Witch*', *Vermont Division for Historic Preservation Report*, Montpelier, Vermont.

Crisman, K., 1993, 'Relics of the Revolution and a Schooner Called *Water Witch*', *Institute of Nautical Archaeology Quarterly*, 19, 4, 22–30.

HMS *Waterwitch*

see **HMS *Vixen***

Whydah Galley

The only confirmed remains of a pirate vessel ever discovered. The words and date, '*The Whydah Galley* 1716**' (*sic*), moulded onto the ship's bell discovered on wreckage found in 1984 and located about 450 m off Wellfleet, Cape Cod, Massachusetts, established the identity of a pirate vessel long sought by New Englanders. Research into its historical background and artefacts, coupled with analyses of the natural and cultural processes of site transformation, have added significant details of our knowledge of the 'Golden Age of Piracy' of the late 17th and early 18th century. The best period references are *The Buccaneers of America* by John Exquemelin (1684) and *A General History of the Robberies and Murders of the Most Notorious Pirates* by Captain Charles Johnson (1724) generally believed to have been Daniel Defoe. The chapter dealing with *Whydah* within the Defoe book was found to be inconsistent with historical documents, but it still bears examination for some historical details, perspective, and personalities.

Whydah was apparently on its maiden voyage as a slave transport between Europe, the slave coast of West Africa, and Jamaica. On the final leg of its voyage and after two perfunctory cannon salvos in protest,

Whydah was captured by two pirate vessels in the Windward Passage off the Bahama Islands in February 1717. Samuel Bellamy, a crony of Edward Teach or Black Beard, was voted pirate Captain of *Whydah* in place of merchant Captain Edward Lawrence Prince. Prince was given £20 and one of the pirate vessels, subsequently sailing away with his merchant crew, minus eight to twelve men who were either forced to join or voluntarily joined the pirates. The pirate pair, led by *Whydah*, then sailed along the coast of North America robbing more vessels. Separating off the Capes of Virginia with plans to meet in Maine waters, *Whydah* sailed along to Cape Cod.

Caught in a storm on 27 April 1717 (Julian date), *Whydah* capsized upon a sand bar about 150 m from the beach. Breaking apart, the hull and items which could float were washed ashore. Upon hearing the news of the wreck, both Cape Codders and government agents from Boston rushed to the location. The Cape Codders won the race by about three days. During this period it is probable that some unknown quantity of the material from the wreck, then in less than 4 m of water, was retrieved by the locals. Cyprian Southack, the agent of the Royal Governor of Massachusetts, recovered only two cannon among other minor wreckage.

Southack and others variously describe *Whydah* as a London-built, ship-rigged galley of about 300 tons. Two hundred and seventy years and three hundred metres of eroded beach later, accompanied by an estimated 5 m drop in site elevation, the excavation yielded a debris field of about 1,820 sq. m (19,600 sq. ft) with a total area of controlled excavation of about 695 sq. m (7,478 sq. ft). Individual artefacts and concretions of sand, rocks, and artefacts surrounding ferrous cores of three, four and six pounder cannon, bow and kedge anchors, and various ship components and cargo, were discovered. The debris field was spread along a line about 24 m in length oriented northwest at the stern to southeast at the bow. The bow was marked by the ship's stove, bell, and anchors. Twenty-seven cannon were recovered; at least one remains on site.

Almost 110,000 artefacts were retrieved from *Whydah*, with all but about 8,000 (some 3,000 coins with most of the remainder being lead shot) having provenance data. The artefacts were then placed into 'Major Groups' and subdivided into 'Minor Groups'. The groups included 'Activities' (carpentry tools, fishing implements, measuring instruments, navigation instruments, restraining devices, and rigger/sail maker tools); 'Arms' (ammu-nition, small arms, cannon, and explosive ordinance); 'Cargo' (coins, jewellery, merchandise and storage containers); 'Galley' (faunal remains, galley/kitchenware and tableware); 'Personal' (apparel and recreation) and 'Ship Architecture' (hardware, ship structure, and rigging elements).

The wreck of *Whydah* provided a variety of artefacts. Analysis of individual artefacts revealed items from Europe, Africa as well as North and South America. Manufacturers of some of the artefacts were identified including pewterer John Robyns of Penzance, gun smith John Brooke of London, and tobacco pipe manufacturer Robert Tippet of Bristol. Also, over 9,000 coins, mostly Spanish *Real* cobs, West African Akan cast gold jewellery (the earliest collection of such material with provenance information), relatively large numbers of navigational instruments, plus an over-abundance of cannon and several types of trade muskets, pistols, and grenades, helped generate a profile of a pirate vessel which can be compared with other wrecks.

An example of the type of spatial analysis of the artefact distribution was a comparison of nineteen silver, versus sixty-four non-silver buttons, buckles, and cufflinks. The mean point of distribution of the silver clothing items was to the stern of the less valuable non-silver pieces. The results were interpreted to indicate that the wealth of the senior pirates, who would have resided towards the stern of the vessel, was greater than that of the common seamen whose quarters were towards the bow. These results contradict notions of pirate egalitarianism often noted in literature.

Another result of analysis on a pewter plate raises an intriguing question regarding the possible association of piracy of the period with the conflict over the throne of Great Britain. What can be interpreted to be the Freemason 'compass and square' was etched lightly onto the plate by one of its users. If one leaves aside objections such as the pirate identity of the maker of the mark, then the connection between early 18th-century piracy, Freemasonry of Scottish Rite affinity and the several Jacobite rebellions of the first half of the 18th century becomes compelling and worthy of further historical research. C.E.H.

ADDITIONAL READING

Defoe, D., 1972, *A General History of the Robberies and Murders of the Most Notorious Pirates*, rev. and ed. M. Schonhorn, Columbia, South Carolina.

Exquemelin, J., 1966, *The Buccaneers of America*, Baltimore, Maryland.

Hamilton, C. (ed.), 1992, *Final Report of Archaeological Data Recovery*, Report on file at the US Army Corps of Engineers, Waltham, Massachusetts and The Massachusetts Historical Commission, Boston, Massachusetts.

Vanderbilt, A.T. II, 1986, *Treasure Wreck: The Fortunes and Fate of the Pirate Ship* Whydah, Boston.

EDITOR'S NOTE: This site is included because it is well known and widely reported in the popular media and press. However, such sites have primarily been the focus of commercially oriented activity that resulted in the sale of recovered artefacts at times to private owners, the transfer of artefacts to private investors, or the splitting of artefacts between a government and a private salvor. Despite the presence of an archaeologist on the site, or the recovery of any archaeological data, the long-term potential of a site to yield meaningful information is compromised when the collection of artefacts – the primary data of any archaeological site – has been dispersed. Furthermore, the sale of artefacts from shipwreck sites endorses the concept that the archaeological past and antiquities are commodities for sale on the open market, which has proved detrimental to the protection and study of the past. The inclusion of this site in this encyclopaedia does not sanction or condone this type of activity.

Wiawaka Bateaux Cluster

Seven 30 ft (9 m) long French and Indian War (1755–63) shipwrecks located in Lake George, New York, USA. Dubbed the 'Wiawaka Bateaux Cluster' because of their location off the Wiawaka Holiday House, these vessels are part of the 1758 British and provincial (colonial) fleet at Lake George. The shipwrecks were nominated to the **National Register of Historic Places** by Bateaux Below, Inc., a not-for-profit education corporation, and the New York State Historic Preservation Field Services Bureau. They were listed in the National Register of Historic Places on 14 June 1992, and in 1993 became part of a New York State shipwreck preserve park.

The Wiawaka Bateaux Cluster represents a popular colonial American watercraft. The word 'bateau' is French for boat, but the prototype of the English bateaux probably was imported by the New York Dutch.

Colonial bateaux were flat-bottomed, shallow-draft boats broader at the bow than at the stern. They were constructed of pine planks and oak frames with plank-on-frame construction. Bateaux were used by both the French and English during the colonial era of North America. They averaged 30–35 ft (9–11 m) long, though some approached 50 ft (15 m) in length and others were as

One of the Wiawaka Bateaux Cluster. (Russell Bellico)

short as 18 ft (5.5 m). The width of bateaux varied, but those bateaux 30–32 ft (9–10 m) long, like most of the Wiawaka Bateaux Cluster, were up to 6 ft 6 in (2 m) wide.

Bateaux were powered by rowing, poling, and under certain circumstances by crude sail. Each bateau carried four to six oars. For steerage an oar was tied off the stern. French bateaux carried up to three tons of cargo, while British bateaux transported up to twenty-three men with a month's supplies.

During the French and Indian War, known in Europe as the Seven Years War (1756–63), bateaux transported British and provincial troops throughout the inland waters of the northeast region of the thirteen English colonies. The Albany-Schenectady, New York area was a key bateaux construction centre, providing the British with bateaux for use on the Hudson and Mohawk Rivers, Lake George, and Lake Champlain.

The Wiawaka bateaux were members of a large British and provincial fleet stationed at Lake George in 1758. In July 1758 British General James Abercromby and 15,000 British and provincial troops were defeated at Fort Carillon, a French fort on Lake Champlain which later was known as Ticonderoga, by a much smaller French force under the Marquis de Montcalm. In that expedition, Abercromby's troops used 900 bateaux. After the rout of Abercromby's army the British and provincials retreated to their base at the south end of Lake George and undertook a massive boat-building campaign, hoping to return to Carillon later in 1758.

With winter approaching, in the autumn of 1758 the British and provincials deliberately sank two radeaux (floating gun batteries), the sloop *Halifax*, at least two row galleys, and 260 bateaux for winter storage and protection against marauding French and their Indian allies. The British scuttled their fleet in the lake's shallows, planning retrieval the following year rather than leaving them ashore over the winter and defenceless to enemy attack.

Many of these bateaux and other warships were never raised in 1759, as the theatre of war moved swiftly from Lake George to nearby **Lake Champlain**. Two centuries later, in 1960, two scuba-divers located over a dozen bateaux sunk in Lake George. This suddenly gave archaeologists and historians an opportunity to examine previously unknown colonial bateaux. In September 1960 at least three bateaux were raised from the lake bed. After treatment with polyethylene glycol, one bateau was exhibited at the Adirondack Museum, Blue Mountain Lake, New York, and the rest were added to the collection of the New York State Museum.

Further study of these sunken vessels occurred during 'Operation Bateaux' in 1963–4. Armed with a State permit, Terry Crandall, an archaeological diver with the Adirondack Museum, found several dozen well-preserved bateaux. In 1965 New York State Police divers examined several Lake George bateaux. However, after 1965 no further research and fieldwork on Lake George's colonial sunken fleet was done until 1987. In that year the Lake George Bateaux Research Team, whose principals later renamed their group Bateaux Below, Inc., began a five-year study of the Wiawaka Bateaux Cluster.

During that project, each of the Wiawaka sites' seven bateaux was measured, photographed, videographed by divers and a **Submersible**, documented by Klein **Side scan sonar**, and detailed drawings of each vessel as well as a site map completed.

The Wiawaka Bateaux Cluster lies approximately 36 m offshore within a rectangular shape, with a boundary approximately 135 m long by 32 m wide. The warships lie in 6–14 m of water on a soft sediment slope. They have some bottom planks, transverse cleats, and frames protruding above the sediment. Rocks lie on or near each bateau, and were probably used to help sink them.

The Wiawaka Bateaux Cluster is protected by New York State Education Law Code 233. In September 1993 the State of New York created a Submerged Heritage Preserves programme, an underwater park for visiting sport divers. The Wiawaka Bateaux Cluster became one of the New York State's first two shipwreck preserves, both located in Lake George, and thus a pilot project for shipwreck preserves in other waterways around New York. The Wiawaka Bateaux Cluster preserve, named 'The Sunken Fleet of 1758', is administered by the New York State Department of Environmental Conservation with monitoring duties conducted by Bateaux Below, Inc. 'The Sunken Fleet of 1758' preserve is marked by a mooring buoy and a navigational aid buoy. Underwater signage and trail lines provide scuba-divers with public access, but in a controlled environment so as to promote preservation at the site. J.Z.

ADDITIONAL READING

Bellico, R.P., 1992, *Sails and Steam in the Mountains: A Maritime and Military History of Lake George and Lake Champlain*, New York.

Crisman, K.J., 1988, 'Struggle for a Continent: Naval Battles of the French and Indian Wars', in G.F. Bass (ed.), *Ships and Shipwrecks of the Americas: A History Based on Underwater Archaeology*, New York.

Gardner, J., 1967, 'Bateaus Played Key Role In American History', *National Fisherman*, April, 8A, 9A, 19A.

Gardner, J., 1987, *The Dory Book*, Mystic, Connecticut.

Hager, R.E., 1987, *Mohawk River Boats and Navigation Before 1820*, New York.

Peckham, M.L., 1992, 'Lake George Shipwrecks Nominated to National Register', *Preservation League of New York State Newsletter*, Spring issue, 2.

Zarzynski, J.W. and Farrell, J., 1994, 'Recent Underwater Archaeological Surveys at Lake George, New York', in D.R. Starbuck (ed.), *Archaeology of the French and Indian War: Military Sites of the Hudson River, Lake George, and Lake Champlain Corridor*, Glens Falls, New York.

William Salthouse

Shipwreck site in the State of Victoria, Australia. The archaeological remains are situated close to Port Phillip Heads at the entrance to the port of Melbourne. The lower part of the wooden hull, together with the remains of the cargo, including many partial and complete casks containing salted meat and fish (see **Faunal studies**), lie in approximately 12 m of water. Many of the cask heads are marked with brands, stencils and other markings, which provide information about the weight, quality, or grade of the contents. The name of the inspector, the city where it was inspected, the year and month of inspection and 'L.C.' for Lower Canada, are also branded on the cask heads. Analysis of the wooden cases as well as the bottles, corks and their contents has revealed details such as that the champagne came from the region of the village of Ay in the Champagne district and the muscat was shipped through the port of Cette on the Languedoc coast of France. Strong tidal flow restricts diving access to the wreck site to a short period at around slack water. The site has been inspected, surveyed, and a test excavation was carried out by the Maritime Heritage Unit of Heritage Victoria (formerly the Maritime Archaeological Unit of the Victoria Archaeological Survey).

William Salthouse was a wooden-hulled sailing vessel of 251 tons built for Salthouse and Company of Liverpool, England in 1824. A typical small British trading vessel of the first half of the 19th century, it carried mixed cargoes between Great Britain and the colonies in the West Indies and India for seventeen years. By 1841 it was owned by Green and Company, who dispatched the vessel from London to Montreal with a mixed cargo. The vessel then loaded a cargo in Montreal which included salted meat, salted fish, timber, cases of wine, and baskets of champagne and set out on the long voyage to the recently established settlement of Melbourne in the Australian colonies. *William Salthouse* struck a rock at Port Phillip Heads and sank without loss of life on the sandbank known as Pope's Eye.

The wreck site of *William Salthouse* was found by **SCUBA**-divers in August 1982. It was declared as an historic shipwreck under the Historic Shipwrecks Act 1981 (Victoria) in December 1982. A permit is required to dive on *William Salthouse* as the site lies within a protected zone which prohibits boating, fishing, and diving within 250 m. M.S.2

ADDITIONAL READING

English, A.J., 1990, 'Salted Meats from the Wreck of the *William Salthouse*: Archaeological Analysis of Nineteenth-Century Butchering Patterns', *Australian Journal of Historical Archaeology*, 8, 63–9.

Staniforth, M., 1987, 'Casks from the Wreck of the *William Salthouse*', *Australian Journal of Historical Archaeology*, 5, 21–8.

Staniforth, M. and Vickery, L., 1984, *The Test Excavation of the William Salthouse Wrecksite*, Australian Institute for Maritime Archaeology Special Publication no. 3, Fremantle, Victoria.

Winfield Scott

Wreck of a Gold Rush steamer lost off the California coast in 1853 and archaeologically studied since 1981. *Winfield Scott* was a 1,291 ton, 225 ft (68.6 m) long wooden-hulled side-wheel steamship built in New York in 1850. After operating between New York and New Orleans in 1851, the steamer was sent to the Pacific in 1852 to operate on the Panama Route, connecting Panama City and San Francisco on the principal oceanic link between the coasts during the California Gold Rush. *Winfield Scott* was lost en route from San Francisco to Panama on 2 December 1853, striking the rocks near Anacapa

SS Winfield Scott.
(San Francisco Maritime National Historical Park)

Island and sinking. Partial salvage of the ship and its contents haphazardly ensued for the next century. Pilfering of the site by divers seeking gold from passenger baggage has led to considerable damage to the wreck, and in the mid-1980s the US Government and the State of California successfully prosecuted a group of divers for damaging the wreck and removing artefacts since it lies in a national park and a national marine sanctuary.

The wreck site of SS *Winfield Scott* lies immediately offshore of the northeast corner of Middle Anacapa Island in the Channel Islands group along the central California coast. Anacapa Island is a unit of Channel Islands National Park, Ventura, California. The remains of the ship lie in variable depths of 4.5–9 m on a sand and rock bottom which is obscured at different times of the year by a heavy growth of kelp and sea grass.

Archaeological survey and reconnaissance by the National Park Service has disclosed that approximately 10 per cent of the area

of the ship is exposed on the seabed, notably the midships portion of the hull complete with the engine bed plates and substantial portions of the engines. Considerable wooden structure has survived, partially covered by sand and iron concretion. Through-hull fittings, yellow-metal drifts and spikes, wrought-iron diagonal strapping, and exposed copper sheathing can be observed. Frames and outer hull planking can be seen, and it is likely that inner hull planking (ceiling planking) has survived where protected by a sand overburden.

Substantial pieces of the engines remain on the site. Observed and identified remains include both paddle wheels, one paddle shaft, a crosshead with connecting rods attached, the base of a cylinder, a crosstail, numerous intermediate shafts, a substantial pile of anthracite coal, fire bricks, and a side lever; approximately 50 per cent of the large engine components, perhaps more, are in place on the site.

A large number of artefacts collected from the site over the past few decades by divers have been returned to the National Park Service, and have been analysed. They include ship fastenings, hardware (locking mechanisms, keyholes, brass skeleton keys, pivot hinges for salon doors, pull rings, portholes, and brass double hinges), ornamental pane glass, deck lights, brass steam gauge housings and steam pipes, as well as ceramic and glass artefacts, a brass luggage tag, firearms, gold and silver coins of various denominations, belt buckles and buttons (some military), gold jewellery, and gold flakes and nuggets. Unfortunately, all of these artefacts lack provenance and much of their information potential is diminished.

James Delgado with the paddlewheel of SS Winfield Scott.
(National Park Service)

However, despite 19th-century salvage activity and periodic sport diver collection activities, *Winfield Scott* retains a high level of resource integrity. The majority of the site lies beneath sand overburden which has not been excavated. The 10 per cent of the site which lies exposed on the rocks has not been 'picked clean' by sport divers and professional surveys in the 1980s and 1990s have disclosed intact glass bottles, copper ship fittings, and ceramics that await careful study and excavation.

Archaeological investigation of the remains of SS *Tennessee*, a Panama Route steamship lost the same year as *Winfield Scott*, would be particularly useful for comparison, and National Park Service archaeologists have already coordinated work on the two sites. J.P.D.

ADDITIONAL READING
Delgado, J.P., 1982, 'Water Soaked and Covered With Barnacles: The Wreck of the SS Winfield Scott', *Pacific Historian*, 27, 2.
Kemble, J.H., 1943, *The Panama Route, 1848–1869*, Berkeley and Los Angeles.
Morris, D.P. and Lima, J., 1996, *Channel Islands National Park and Channel Islands National Marine Sanctuary*, Submerged Cultural Resources Assessment, Intermountain Cultural Resource Centers Professional Papers no. 56, Santa Fe, New Mexico.

Witte Leeuw

Wreck of a Dutch East India Company ship, lost in 1613, and rediscovered in 1976 by Robert Stenuit. The ship *Witte Leeuw* (White

Lion) was built by and for the Council of Amsterdam prior to 1610. The three-masted, square rigged, 700 ton ship was approximately 160 ft (49 m) long. *Witte Leeuw* sailed from Texel, Holland in 1610 as part of a four-ship 'great fleet' en route to the Far East. Arriving in Indonesian waters in November 1610, *Witte Leeuw* traded through the Moluccas and in Java before embarking a cargo of spices, ceramics, and jewellery at Bantam, Java in December 1612.

Witte Leeuw, in company with three other Dutch ships and two English ships, put into St Helena for provisions in May 1613. They were attacked by Portuguese ships. While engaged in the battle, *Witte Leeuw* exploded and sank.

In June 1976 an expedition led by Robert Stenuit, working from archival accounts of the loss, surveyed Jamestown Bay on St Helena and discovered the wreck of *Witte Leeuw* in 33 m of water near Munden's Point. The wreck site was marked by brass cannon and ballast, but was largely buried in mud. Working with airlifts and on a rigorous decompression schedule, Stenuit's team excavated the wreck. Substantial remains of the ship's hull, primarily the bow and forward half of the vessel, were encountered, but documentation and study of them was deemed not to be possible due to time constraints. The team focused on the recovery of the ship's ordnance, cargo, instruments, and fittings. Stenuit noted that the discovery of a large quantity of Chinese trade porcelain on the site also influenced this decision. Ultimately, an area of approximately 400 sq. m was excavated, representing only a portion of the site.

Fifteen guns were observed on the site: twelve were iron guns that were left *in situ*; three bronze guns were recovered. A large number of artefacts, including samples of the spices carried as cargo, cooking and eating utensils, personal belongings, including a silver bosun's whistle, and the porcelain were recovered. The archaeological documentation of the site demonstrated that despite the loss of the ship by explosion, the wreck survived as both a substantial and well-preserved entity.

The recovered artefacts were sold at auction at Sotheby's in London and Amsterdam. The Rijksmuseum in Amsterdam purchased some of the collection at the auction, and later negotiated an agreement with Robert Stenuit that transferred the broken ceramics and sherds to the Rijksmuseum's collections in 1977. The Rijksmuseum assembled a working group under the direction of curator and archaeologist J.B. Kist to sort, reassemble, and document the 400 kg of broken ceramics. Their effort represents the only archaeological information, albeit incomplete because of the private sale of a number of artefacts, generated from the *Witte Leeuw* project. J.P.D.

ADDITIONAL READING
Pijl-Ketel, C.L. van der (ed.), 1982, *The Ceramic Load of the 'Witte Leeuw' (1613)*, Rijksmuseum, Amsterdam.

EDITOR'S NOTE: This site is included because it is well known and widely reported in the popular media and press. However, such sites have primarily been the focus of commercially oriented activity that resulted in the sale of recovered artefacts at times to private owners, the transfer of artefacts to private investors, or the splitting of artefacts between a government and a private salvor. Despite the presence of an archaeologist on the site, or the recovery of any archaeological data, the long-term potential of a site to yield meaningful information is compromised when the collection of artefacts – the primary data of any archaeological site – has been dispersed. Furthermore, the sale of artefacts from shipwreck sites endorses the concept that the archaeological past and antiquities are commodities for sale on the open market, which has proved detrimental to the protection and study of the past. The inclusion of this site in this encyclopaedia does not sanction or condone this type of activity.

Wrangels Palais
see **Oxford University MARE**

Xantho

Iron steamship discovered off the coast of Western Australia. In 1978 Keith Muckelroy stated that work on early steamships and the like, while interesting and sometimes 'furnishing useful displays for museums', was 'not archaeology' (Muckelroy, 1980). The **Excavation** of the wreck of Charles Broadhurst's iron steamship SS *Xantho* (1848–72) off the coast of Western Australia has proved that new information about both materials and people can be obtained from such work and that Muckelroy's position was too proscriptive to find much favour in modern **Maritime archaeology**. The project leader's methodological approach in the instance of *Xantho* is encompassed in the twin philosophies 'conservators underwater . . . archaeologists above' and 'the excavation continues . . . in the laboratory'.

An important development born of this approach has been the full pre-disturbance study of the wreck's biological and electrochemical properties that was conducted in 1983, giving concrete insights into the condition of the site.

The archaeological inspection of the wreck, conducted at the same time, showed that it was engineered not as expected with a new condensing, two-cylinder compound engine, but with a ten-year-old, 60 hp, non-condensing, double-acting, double-trunk engine, exhausting to the atmosphere. Built by John Penn for the Royal Navy's Crimean War gunboats of 1854–5, the type were most likely the first high-pressure, first high-revolution, and first mass-produced marine engines made (*Engineer*, 11 Feb. 1898). They were also suitable only for use in a naval context due to their huge appetite for coal and other problems that were solved only by constant maintenance.

Xantho itself was a former iron-hulled Scottish paddle steamer built in 1848 and was subsequently sold to a scrap metal merchant who, in 1871, had joined the aged hull with the second-hand ex-RN screw engine, new boilers and pumps, and offered the revamped hybrid lot for sale. Was Stewart dishonest, the marine equivalent of the shady horsedealer or today's crooked used-car dealer? These were early impressions. That the ship appeared on the Western Australian coast also posed the question what sort of person would buy it for use on the sparsely populated, poorly serviced coast, far from coal supplies and the nearest marine engine repair facilities at Adelaide and Surabaya?

Thus the *Xantho* programme came to focus on Charles Broadhurst, the owner of the ship, and how he came to make the apparently strange decision to purchase this odd vessel. The excavation of the stern section of the wreck which was completed in 1994, partly for these purposes, also included the recovery of the ship's engine.

The treatment and 'excavation' of the engine, begun in a **Conservation** laboratory soon after it was raised in 1985, was completed a decade later with the opening up of the last of the internal spaces and the freeing of all working parts. The success of that process and the technical and behavioural information that has been obtained have cemented the archaeologist's place in the conservation laboratory, especially in the deconcreting process. Even in the disassembly of the engine in the conservation laboratory, where nearly 2,000 kg of concretions were removed, was found evidence of both a technical nature and of the way Charles Broadhurst operated the ship. These findings in the laboratory and at the wreck allowed *Xantho* to provide an ideal vehicle to examine the utility of processual and post-processual approaches, commonly used in terrestrial archaeology, for 'explanation' in maritime archaeology. M.M.

ADDITIONAL READING

Carpenter, J., 1990, 'A Review of Physical Methods Used to Remove Concretions from Artefacts, Mainly Iron, Including Some Recent Ideas', *Bulletin of the Australian Institute for Maritime Archaeology*, 14, 1, 25–42.

McCarthy, M., 1986, 'Conservators Underwater', in H. Mansell (ed.), *Towards 2000: Papers from the Institute for the Conservation of Cultural Material Conference, Perth, 1985*, ICCM Bulletin, 12, 3 & 4, 21–6, Canberra.

McCarthy, M., 1986, 'SS *Xantho*: A 19th Century Lemon Turned Sweet', in P.F. Johnston (ed.), *Proceedings of the 16th Conference on Underwater Archaeology*, Society for Historical Archaeology, Ann Arbor, Michigan.

McCarthy, M., 1986, 'The Excavation and Raising of the SS *Xantho* Engine and Australia's First Practical and Theoretical Seminar on Iron and Steamship Archaeology', *International Journal of Nautical Archaeology*, 15, 2, 73–6.

McCarthy, M., 1988, 'SS *Xantho*: The Pre-disturbance, Assessment, Excavation and Management of an Iron Steam Shipwreck off the Coast of Western Australia', *International Journal of Nautical Archaeology*, 17, 4, 339–47.

McCarthy, M., 1989, 'The Excavation Continues . . . in the Laboratory', *Bulletin of the Australian Institute for the Conservation of Cultural Material*, 21–8.

McCarthy, M., 1990, 'Charles Edward Broadhurst, 1826–1905: A Remarkable 19th Century Failure', unpublished M.Phil. thesis, Murdoch University, Western Australia.

McCarthy, M., 1996, 'SS *Xantho*: An Integrated Approach to the Maritime Archaeology and Conservation of an Iron Steamship Wreck', unpublished Ph.D. thesis, James Cook University, Townsville.

MacLeod, I.D., 1992, 'Conservation Management of Iron Steamships: The SS *Xantho* (1872)', *Multi-Disciplinary Engineering Transactions*, G.E., 1, 45–51.

MacLeod, I.D., North, N.A., and Beegle, C.J., 1986, 'The Excavation, Conservation and Analysis of Shipwreck Sites', in *Preventative Measures During Excavation and Site Protection, Second ICCROM Conference on Conservation and Archaeological Excavation, Ghent, 1985*, 113–31.

Muckelroy, K., 1978, *Marine Archaeology*, New Studies in Archaeology, Cambridge.

Yamato

The largest battleship ever built. Two weeks short of the fortieth anniversary of Japan's surrender to the Pacific Allied Forces, the wreck site of *Yamato*, the pride and symbol of Japan's Imperial Navy, was located at 360 m, 300 km southwest of Kogoshima, Japan.

With the sinking of the invincible *Yamato* in Operation 'Ten' *ichigo* on 7 April 1945, the world witnessed the eclipse of naval floating fortresses. Her designers equipped the ship with awesome firepower and speed so that she could outfight and outrange any existing foreign battleship; however, the advent of aircraft carriers made her capabilities obsolete even before her commissioning in December 1941.

Yamato was 263 m in length and had a displacement of 72,000 tons when loaded. The main battery consisted of nine 46 cm guns mounted in triple turrets that alone weighed over 2,774 tonnes, as much as a destroyer. They were the largest naval guns ever made and had a range of 42–46 km. For her secondary battery, the ship was fitted with two triple batteries of 15.5 cm guns, and 12–12.6 cm guns in six, twin-enclosed batteries. The number of 25 mm machine guns was increased after her late 1944 refit, to a total of 152 triple and single guns. The unique shape of her hull reduced water resistance to a minimum and enabled her to reach a cruising speed of 27 knots. The designers made the massive armour plating an integral part of the hull structure to reduce weight. Finally, the superior nature of her optical equipment, sonar, and radar made *Yamato* a formidable opponent of the Allied Pacific Fleet.

In what was to be the last major naval encounter of the Pacific Theatre, the Japanese made one, final desperate attempt to dislodge US forces from Okinawa, and launched a naval kamikaze force consisting of *Yamato* and nine destroyers on 6 April 1945. Entering the China Sea on the morning of 7 April, *Yamato* steamed at full speed intending to either engage the US fleet off Okinawa, or beach itself and act as a shore battery to support the besieged Imperial Army. With no air support, the outcome of the mission was a foregone conclusion. Although the US planes were picked up on radar at 1000 hrs, the attack did not begin until 1220 hrs. The ship exploded and sank at 1423 hours after one of the 15.5 cm guns

Japanese battleship Yamato *fitted out at Kure, Japan, September 1941. (US Naval Historical Center)*

Japanese battleship Yamato *blows up, 7 April 1945. (US Naval Historical Center)*

was knocked out in the first raid; *Yamato* was never brought under control. A hit may have ignited the aft magazine, resulting in a massive explosion that tore the ship apart. Prior to its sinking, however, the ship was reported listing at 23 degrees, the decks torn sheets of red-hot metal and most of her guns inoperable. Only 280 of *Yamato*'s 2,778 crew survived. By 1500 hrs, when the attack was broken off, five of the nine escort ships had also been sunk.

Using coordinates supplied by the **US Navy**, the *Yamato* Society launched the first of three surveys to find the ship in 1978. A 1983 ROV survey of the largest sonar target revealed twisted metal wreckage littered with munitions and **Human remains**. The magnitude of the site suggested it was the battleship rather than one of the destroyer escorts. Plans were then made to mount a full-scale investigation with manned **Submersibles** in 1985, the fortieth anniversary of her sinking. Sponsored by the Tombstone of the Sea Committee, Research Submersibles Ltd's PISCES II, a Canadian-built, 1000 m, three-man submarine was chartered and operated from the deck of one of Fukada Salvage and Marine's ships.

The inverted stern section and one of the detached 46 cm triple-gun turrets of the ship were discovered at 335 m on the first

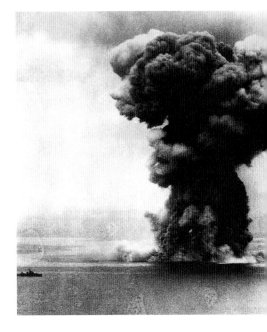

dive on 29 July 1985. The next day, submersibles following a second massive pile of twisted wreckage that formed the central section of the battleship, found the bow section rising at a 60 degree angle from the seabed on an 80 degree list to starboard. The capstans, anchors, anchor cables with chain stoppers, bollards, and fairleads were in place and clearly visible at 366 m. The glittering metre-wide, gilded wooden 'Kikusui' chrysanthemum crest (the emblem of Masashige Kusunoki, a 14th-century loyalist hero and martyr) is still affixed to the apex of the bow. *Yamato* was the only ship in the Imperial Navy awarded the honour of bearing this symbol.

With the identity of the site finally confirmed, there were six additional days of filming and documenting other unique and intact sections of this ship, such as the bulbous bow projection, the forward 46 cm gun turret, and related projectiles. The central section was found to be split open to such an extent that on one occasion the submarine sailed inside and between decks before it realized the peril. Personal effects, shoes, a desk lamp, sake bottles, plus munitions of various calibre were recovered. On the last day, one of the surviving crew members made a short dive to the site and deployed a floral tribute to the battleship, and a memorial service was held on the surface attended by the families of the lost crew.

NHK-TV produced a sixty-minute film which was the highlight of the 15 August 1985 VJ Day programming. No future dives are planned on the 'Giant of the East' as it is considered a memorial site. In the words of the Chairman of the Tombstone of the Sea Committee, 'The 1985 project was considered a Requiem for all souls, of all nations, lost at sea during battle.' R.P.W.

ADDITIONAL READING

Thornton, T., 1989, 'The Sinking of the *Yamato*', *Warship*, 145–55.

Yassiada Wrecks

Wrecks off Yassiada (Flat Island), a small southeastern Aegean island between Pserimos and the Turkish coast. Of over a dozen shipwrecks caused by a reef off the island, three have been excavated: a 7th-century Byzantine wreck in 1961–4; a 4th-century Byzantine wreck in 1967, 1969 and 1974; and a 16th-century Ottoman wreck in 1967, 1969, and 1982–3.

The 7th-century wreck underwent complete excavation, during which new mapping techniques including deep water stereo-photogrammetry were developed. Although little of the hull's forward half survived, the after half was sufficiently preserved to permit a close determination of overall hull shape and dimensions. The hull, with an on-deck length of about 20.52 m and moulded beam of 5.02 m, had a sharp bow, full stern, a deep wine glass shape in section, and a capacity of about 60 tons. Designed for speed, the vessel probably carried a single lateen sail.

The hull's construction was economical and not labour intensive. Wales and a majority of timbers lining the hull interior were little more than half-logs. The hull planking was not fastened to frames by wooden trunnels and clenched nails, as was commonly

Tablewares from the galley area of the 4th-century AD shipwreck at Yassiada. (© INA)

Lead-filled bronze counterweight cast as a bust of Athena, from the 7th century wreck at Yassiada. (© INA)

Raising amphoras from the 7th century Byzantine wreck, Yassiada, with the aid of an air-filled lifting balloon. (© INA)

done in earlier periods, but by light nails barely penetrating halfway into frames. Mortise-and-tenon joints that edge-joined hull planking together were extremely small, very widely spaced, not pegged, made only a negligible contribution to hull strength, and were used only below the waterline.

The ship was carrying eleven iron anchors. Four bower anchors with wooden stocks were on the bulwarks just forward of the mast, two on either side. Seven spare anchors and three iron stocks were stacked on the deck between them. Three bower anchors and three spares weighed about 100 Roman pounds (1 lb = 315 g) each; the other bower (best bower) and one spare, about 250 lb each; and the bottom three spare anchors (sheet anchors), about 350 lb each.

A galley set down in the hull at the stern had a tile firebox with iron grill and a deckhouse superstructure with a tile roof. It was equipped to prepare and serve food and drink to a considerable number of people,

remarkable in an age when passengers normally provisioned themselves. Utensils included twenty-one cooking pots, two cauldrons and a baking pan of copper, eighteen ceramic pitchers, and four or five table settings. A well-stocked larder contained sixteen pantry jars.

The larder was part of the ship's stores locker located immediately forward of the galley and secured with a padlock. Here were kept the finer tableware, spare lamps, a censer, a set of carpenter's tools, the ship's gold and copper coins, and weighing equipment including one of the most complete extant sets of Byzantine balance-pan weights and possibly the largest steelyard from antiquity. An inscription on the steelyard indicates that the captain, Georgios, was a priest. Just aft of the galley was the bosun's locker, which contained line- and net-fishing gear, a grapnel for the ship's boat, and digging and woodcutting tools used on land.

The ship may have belonged to the Church and been designed to transport both cargo and churchmen. Shortly after a Persian naval force withdrew from the Aegean in AD 626, she had set out from an eastern Aegean port with low grade wine in some 700 globular amphoras stacked three deep in the hold and some 100 small, cylindrical amphoras placed horizontally between the necks of the top layer. A new study of the amphoras currently in progress has raised the possibility that the wine was intended for troops then fighting against the Persians in the East.

The 4th-century wreck partly lay beyond a sharp drop-off on the seabed. Unexcavated portions of the wreck in deeper water may include the ship's anchors. The hull's port half was extensively preserved up to the waterline. These remains indicate that the ship had a moulded beam of just under 8 m, an overall length of about 20 m, but a keel length of no more than 7 m. The hull shape may have been like that of a Roman *corbita*. The mortise-and-tenon joints in the edge-joined hull planking were smaller, more loosely fitted, and more widely spaced than in comparable hulls of earlier date. A pair of

half-frames appears to have been erected amidships after only five planking strakes had been assembled. Perhaps this early erected midships frame assisted the shipwright in shaping the hull. A rather spacious galley set down in the stern had a rough stone hearth; tiles for a roof were not found. Galley equipment included pantry jars, cooking ware, tableware, possibly three steelyards, copper coins, a casting net, and some lamps. Ceramic wares, including a lamp signed KY from an Athenian workshop, place the shipwreck around the end of the 4th century. The ship was carrying approximately 1,100 amphoras of three types: bag-shaped, cylindrical, and smaller ovoid jars. Slight evidence indicates that the bag-shaped jars contained olive oil and the other jars, wine. The cargo was probably of Aegean origin. Lead from a hull patch appears to be from the Troad.

The Ottoman wreck, approximately 90 per cent excavated, is probably of a warship or naval supply ship 21–23 m long. The keel's latest growth ring, dating to 1572, and a 4-real piece of Philip II, dated to 1566–89, put the ship in the last quarter of the 16th century. Extensive keel damage and a paucity of finds suggests that the ship was aground on the reef long enough to be salvaged. Objects left behind include twelve pedestalled glazed

bowls, a lamp holder and gimballed treble hook possibly used together, musket shot, a few cast-iron and stone cannon balls, a hammer for dressing stone, and some pointed poles possibly designed to be hurled against enemies from the topcastle. Ship fittings include pulley-block bushings, a deadeye strap and pair of chains that anchored the forestay, and the rudder hardware for a curved sternpost. The primary hull framing consisted of floors and futtocks side-joined by hook scarfs fastened with clench-nails driven in both directions before the frames were mounted on the keel. F.H.V.

ADDITIONAL READING

Bass, G.F. and van Doorninck, Jr, F.H., 1971, 'A Fourth-Century Shipwreck at Yassiada', *American Journal of Archaeology*, 75, 27–37.

Bass, G.F. *et al.*, 1982, *Yassiada*, vol. 1: *A Seventh-Century Byzantine Shipwreck*, College Station, Texas.

Frost, H., 1963, *Under the Mediterranean*, Englewood Cliffs, New Jersey.

Pulak, C., 1992 and 1993, 'Ottoman Wreck', *International Nautical Archaeology Quarterly*, 19, 2, 17 and 20, 1, 16–17.

Steffy, J.R., 1994, *Wooden Ship Building and the Interpretation of Shipwrecks*, College Station, Texas.

van Doorninck Jr, F.H., 1976, 'The Fourth-Century Wreck at Yassiada: An Interim Report on the Hull', *International Journal of Nautical Archaeology*, 5, 2, 115–31.

van Doorninck Jr, F.H., 1989, 'The Cargo Amphoras on the 7th Century Yassiada and the 11th Century Serçe Limani Shipwrecks: Two Examples of a Reuse of Byzantine Amphoras as Transport Jars', in V. Déroche and J.-M. Spieser (eds), *Recherches sur la céramique byzantine*, Bulletin de Correspondance Hellénique Supplément, Paris, 18, 247–57.

Yorktown Shipwrecks

A group of British vessels sunk during the Battle of Yorktown, Virginia in 1781. By 1780, six years into the American War of Independence, Sir Henry Clinton, Commander of British forces in North America, had become frustrated by unsuccessful campaigns in the Carolinas. This frustration, coupled with his fears of an Allied assault on his position in New York, led Clinton to order several units of the Southern British Army, Major General Charles, Earl Cornwallis commanding, to retire north to strengthen his defences. When Cornwallis and his forces reached Virginia, however, Clinton revised his orders, directing Cornwallis to establish a fortified post with an ice-free port in the lower Chesapeake Bay, from which the Southern British Army and the British fleet, then in New York, could

safely remain during the winter before embarking on a new offensive in the Chesapeake region.

In late summer 1781 Cornwallis chose Yorktown, Virginia, a few kilometres up the York River from the mouth of the Chesapeake Bay, as a position that could be readily defended and that provided deep water access and an ample anchorage for a large number of ships. Cornwallis had at his disposal a large supply fleet consisting of five relatively small naval vessels, approximately fifty transports and armed merchantmen, seven captured prizes, and an assortment of small sloops, schooners, and rowing craft.

In September, when the British fleet under Admiral Thomas Graves attempted to join and reinforce Cornwallis at Yorktown, it was confronted at the mouth of the Chesapeake Bay by a French fleet responding to a request for assistance from American general George Washington. On 5 September the two fleets clashed in an indecisive engagement that came to be known as the Battle of the Capes. On 15 September, his ships damaged and outnumbered by the French, Graves retired with his fleet to New York, leaving Cornwallis to hold Yorktown until the fleet could be refurbished and reinforced. Soon realizing that he was trapped at Yorktown and that an attack on his position was imminent, Cornwallis ordered a group of transports to be scuttled along the Yorktown beach to obstruct an anticipated French amphibious landing.

On 9 October a combined French and American army commenced the siege of Yorktown. Almost immediately, several British vessels fell victim to shot which, according to an eyewitness, 'flew over our whole line and the city into the river, where they often struck through 1 and 2 ships'. HMS *Charon*, Cornwallis's largest warship, and the transport *Shipwright* were burned and sunk that first night. As the siege continued, additional vessels were damaged or sunk by cannon fire. When Cornwallis realized that defeat was imminent, he scuttled most of his remaining vessels and requested terms of surrender. At the time of the formal British surrender on 19 October 1781, the warships *Charon*, *Fowey*, and *Guadaloupe*, along with most of the transports, lay sunk near Yorktown, some with their masts still protruding from the water. During the winter *Guadaloupe* and several transports were refloated by the French, leaving an estimated twenty-six vessels unaccounted for and presumed abandoned on the bottom of the York River. In spite of sporadic salvage attempts over the years, the Yorktown shipwrecks lay relatively undis-

turbed until the advent of SCUBA equipment led to intrusions by sport divers and, eventually, a large-scale scientific investigation.

The Yorktown Shipwreck Archaeological Project, conducted in 1978–90, resulted in the discovery and investigation of nine shipwrecks from the Battle of Yorktown. The project was directed by John D. Broadwater, senior underwater archaeologist, Virginia Department of Historic Resources, and funded by the National Endowment for the Humanities, the US Department of the Interior, the Commonwealth of Virginia, and numerous foundations, corporations, and individuals.

Wrecks discovered during surveys in 1978–80 included two warships and seven transports. Preservation at the nine sites varied appreciably, due to differences in the hydrography of the river bottom in the area. Several wrecks lay in areas of strong currents and long-term erosion, while others were protected by a deep layer of silt. Shipwreck site 44GL136, located in shallow water near Gloucester Point, was identified as HMS *Charon* during a field school conducted by Texas A&M University and the Virginia Historic Landmarks Commission (now the Virginia Department of Historic Resources). Although *Charon* was poorly preserved, with less than 5 per cent of the hull surviving, its identification was made possible by comparing the limited hull remains with the as-built plans obtained from the National Maritime Museum in Greenwich, England. Additional evidence was present in the form of shipboard objects melted by an intense fire and copper hull sheathing, an innovation applied almost exclusively to warships in 1781. Wreck 44YO12, known as the **Cornwallis Cave Wreck**, is probably HMS *Fowey*, based on the hull dimensions and on the fact that several recovered artefacts from the ship's stores were marked with the 'broad arrow' of the British Board of Ordnance. This mark was placed on all Royal Navy property and is more likely to be found on the equipment of warships than on that of transports. Site 44GL106, located near the remains of HMS *Charon*, exhibits signs of a fire and is probably the transport *Shipwright* that was set alight when *Charon* struck it before sinking. Three transports near the Yorktown shore – 44YO88, 44YO89, and 44YO94 – were found to be exceptionally well preserved.

The primary focus of the Yorktown Project was Cornwallis's naval transports, almost all of them leased merchant vessels about which little is known. Merchant vessels constituted the backbone of the British mercantile system. By the time of the American Revolution, British and American merchant ships were engaged in a lively commerce between the Americas, the West Indies and Europe. Merchant shipping was essential to the survival and prosperity of the American colonies as well as an economic factor in British trade, since merchant vessels provided the means for exchanging American raw materials for English manufactured goods. These ships also served as the colonial link with the cultural and economic centres of the Old World. Despite the importance of merchantmen in commerce and war, most surviving documents deal with warships; very few British or American records describe typical merchant ships in detail. Those for which hull lines were recorded often represented radical rather than typical designs. The ships at Yorktown were viewed as a significant source of comparative information on merchant ship construction, differences between merchant ships and warships, and life aboard these important, but little-known, vessels.

Yorktown Shipwreck 44YO88 was fully excavated and documented during the period 1982–8. This site was chosen for excavation because a preliminary survey had shown that it was clearly a former merchant vessel, and also because of its excellent state of preservation. The presence of mast stumps, bulkheads, deck components, and the rudder promised to yield valuable information on naval architecture, interior configuration, and wartime usage. In an effort to offset the adverse diving conditions in the York River – strong currents, near-zero visibility, and stinging jellyfish – the **Excavation** was conducted within a **Cofferdam**, a steel enclosure which surrounded the site and within which the water was filtered and clarified. This structure, completed in 1982, proved to be an effective tool for underwater archaeological research. This was the first shipwreck excavation ever conducted underwater from within a cofferdam. The cofferdam and connecting pier also provided a rare opportunity for the public to observe an underwater excavation in progress.

Site 44YO88 proved to be the British collier brig *Betsy*, built in Whitehaven, Cumberland. *Betsy* was a boxy, heavily built vessel, typical of the English colliers that were so frequently chosen for the Transport Service of the Royal Navy during the 18th and 19th centuries. The vessel was rigged as a brig, a vessel with two masts, carrying square sails on both masts and, usually, a fore-and-aft 'driver' mainsail. Uniform buttons from the 43rd Regiment of Foot led to regimental documents that helped identify *Betsy*.

The cause of sinking was a hole cut through the hull below the waterline. The official records of the Royal Navy Board state that *Betsy* was employed as a victualler, that is, a transport that normally carried food supplies. Designation as a victualler would have been appropriate for *Betsy* in light of the Navy Board's policy of rejecting vessels of under 200 tons for the transport service, but often accepting these smaller vessels as victuallers. Archaeological evidence suggests that while at Yorktown, *Betsy* served as a 'floating factory', fabricating wooden components for the land fortifications, as well as constructing and repairing a variety of items from cannon trucks to shoes.

The Yorktown shipwrecks provided significant new information on 18th-century naval architecture and technology, hull construction details, rigging, stores and cargo, as well as a more complete picture of the Battle of Yorktown. J.D.B.

ADDITIONAL READING

Broadwater, J.D., 1970, 'The Yorktown Shipwreck Archaeological Project: Results from the 1978 Survey', *International Journal of Nautical Archaeology*, 9, 3, 227–35.

Broadwater, J.D., 1988, 'Secrets of a Yorktown Shipwreck', *National Geographic*, June, 173, 6, 804–23.

Broadwater, J.D., 1992, 'Shipwreck in a Swimming Pool: An Assessment of the Methodology and Technology Utilized on the Yorktown Shipwreck Archaeological Project', *Historical Archaeology*, 26, 4, 36–46.

Broadwater, J.D., 1995, 'In the Shadow of Wooden Walls: Naval Transports During the American War of Independence', in M. Bound (ed.), *The Archaeology of Ships of War*, Oswestry, Shropshire.

Broadwater, J.D., Adams, R.M., and Renner, M., 1985, 'The Yorktown Shipwreck Archaeological Project: An Interim Report on the Excavation of Shipwreck 44YO88', *International Journal of Nautical Archaeology*, 14, 19, 301–14.

Davis, B., 1970, *The Campaign that Won America: The Story of Yorktown*, New York

Fleming, T.J., 1963, *Beat the Last Drum: The Siege of Yorktown, 1781*, New York.

Mahan, A.T., 1913, *The Major Operations of the Navies in the War of American Independence*, London.

Sands, J.O., 1983, *Yorktown's Captive Fleet*, Charlottesville, Virginia.

Sands, J.O., 1988, 'Gunboats and Warships of the American Revolution', in G.F. Bass (ed.), *Ships and Shipwrecks of the Americas: A History Based on Underwater Archaeology*, London.

Syrett, D., 1970, *Shipping and the American War, 1775–83: A Study of the British Transport Organization*, London.

Z

Zeewijk

One of five East Indiamen constructed by the Dutch East India Company in 1725. On 7 November 1726 *Zeewijk* left Rammekens near Vlissingen in the Netherlands. She was bound for Batavia, Java, with a complement of 208 seamen and soldiers. On 13 November *Zeewijk* arrived at the Road of Downs off the English coast and ten days later, after having lost two anchors and one of her cables, finally set sail for the East Indies.

Zeewijk was a Zeeland ship, 40.6 m (145 ft) long with a draught of 5.53 m (19.75 ft) in her stern and 4.9 m (17.5 ft) forward. She was registered at 140 lasten (278 tonnes) and armed with thirty-six cannon and six small breech-loading swivel guns. The master carpenter and supervisor was Hendrick Rass. On her maiden voyage *Zeewijk* carried heavy ironwork, bricks, and cash money in ten chests amounting to 315,837 guilders. Provisions for the long journey to the East Indies included barrels and cases of meat, fish, groats, butter, cheeses, wine, and brandy. The originally appointed skipper, Jan Bogaard, was not on board. He was ill and unfit to sail, and Jan Steyns from Middelburg was nominated to take his place. This change of command was to be of great significance for the fate of *Zeewijk*. For Jan Steyns, *Zeewijk* was to be his first and last command.

After a journey of four and a half months, *Zeewijk* arrived at the Cape of Good Hope on 26 March 1727. There the crew brought ashore cargo which had been loaded for the Cape. It is not known what was actually brought ashore but the unloading took ten days. In a letter from the Governor and Council of the Cape of Good Hope to the Gentlemen XVII, it is stated that the goods and provisions carried in the company's ships for 1727 had been delivered in good order according to the invoices and bills of lading sent with them. However, in the letter there is a statement that 4,098 pieces of grey brick stones and one donkey, which had died on the voyage, had not been delivered. When the unloading was complete, ballast was taken on board and three days later, on 21 April 1727, *Zeewijk* slipped her cables and set sail for Batavia. It was on this leg of the voyage that Jan Steyns made an unfortunate decision – despite the protests of the steersman. The ship's log of 21 May 1727 reads: '. . . it was decided unanimously to

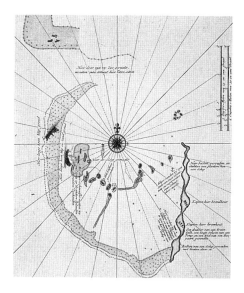

Gun Island, site of the Zeewyjk wreck.
(© Western Australia Maritime Museum/Patrick Baker)

Zeewyjk survivors' map, 1727.
(© Western Australia Maritime Museum)

steer ENE, if there is an opportunity, in order to, if feasible, call at the land of Eendracht' (Western Australia). This decision contravened the strict sailing orders of the Directorate of the Dutch East India Company, which warned skippers of the low offshore reefs and sandbanks off the Western Australian coast. According to the Governor-General and High Council of the Dutch East Indies, Jan Steyns took *Zeewijk* too close to the coast, thus causing the loss of the ship.

At 7.30 p.m. on 9 June 1727, with the small sail and foresail set and both topsails double-reefed, *Zeewijk* ran aground. The ship had struck on the northern edge of Half Moon reef in the Houtman Abrolhos, near the land of Eendracht. In the dusk the surf breaking on the reef had been mistaken for reflections from the sky. The ship crashed with full force. The rudder was knocked out of the helm port and the mainmast broke and fell overboard. As the second mate Adriaen van der Graeff made his way to the steerage he found that the ship had filled with 2.25 m of water. Outraged, the crew blamed their master Jan Steyns for having caused the disaster.

At daybreak the castaways observed ten to twelve islands lying approximately 4 km from the ship, which they assumed to be Frederick Houtman's Abrolhos. After having been exposed to the heavy swells and breakers on the reef for over a week, the crew finally managed to launch the longboat. Ninety-six members of the crew reached the shore of a nearby island, which is known today as Gun Island. This island is 800 m long and 350 m wide, approximately 64 km from the mainland – the land of Eendracht. It is a flat rocky limestone island with narrow sandy beaches situated on the inside of the reef where *Zeewijk* was wrecked. It is

treeless, has sparse vegetation and the highest point rises only about four metres above sea-level. However, to the survivors from the wreck of *Zeewijk* the most important factor was that the island had fresh water.

Soon after the camp was organized a group of eleven of the best seamen under the command of the First Officer Peter Langeweg decided to sail to Batavia for help. The longboat was put into order and on 10 July, a month after the disaster, they set sail for Batavia. No help was to come; the longboat never reached its destination. On Gun Island the castaways spent their time looking for fresh water and collecting food. Some caught seals or birds, while others, whenever possible, tried to get to the wreck to collect provisions. By the end of October it became obvious to the survivors that something must have happened to the longboat. On 29 October there is a significant passage in the journal: 'from the wreck we have, to the best of our ability, despatched a good deal of victuals . . . as well as timber, rope, and iron fittings, everything, in short, which could serve for the building of a new vessel for our rescue'. The forecastle and important features such as planks, beams, knees, and the spare mainmast and the mizzen mast stump were taken from *Zeewijk*. In addition, a group was sent out to search for timbers on the nearby islands.

On 7 November the keel was laid on what was to be their new boat, called *Sloepie*. Victuals, as much as were thought to be required for the voyage to Batavia, were collected and stored in a separate tent. On 16 November *Sloepie*'s sternpost was erected and two weeks later the stern. The vessel was launched on 28 February and the *Zeewijk*'s crew celebrated the event by consuming some of the wine that had been saved from the wreck.

During the following days the castaways warped their yacht, and the second mate Adriaen van der Graeff made an exploratory tour in the gig to plot *Sloepie*'s course through the shallows. Finally, on 26 March they weighed anchor and set sail for Batavia. On board were eighty-eight officers, seamen, and soldiers, 120 fewer than had left the Netherlands one and a half years earlier. The month-long journey to Batavia saw the deaths of another six men before finally, at 5 o'clock in the evening on 30 April 1728, *Sloepie* arrived at the Batavia Roads. The journey that had started on 7 November 1726 had at last come to an end.

Eighty-two of the crew and the cargo of money from *Zeewijk* had been salvaged. The skipper Jan Steyns, however, had to appear before the High Court of Justice at Batavia and take the consequences of his fateful decision to call at the land of Eendracht. In a letter from the Indies to the Gentlemen XVII the skipper Jan Steyns is accused of *Zeewijk*'s disaster by having 'approached the "Zuydland" too recklessly contrary to the known orders and the protests of the steersman'. He was also blamed for having tried to deceive the Governor-General and the High Council of the Dutch East Indies with altered or falsified journals, in order to cover, if possible, his significant role in the disaster. Jan Steyns was put under arrest and sued, and all his property and cash were confiscated. He was deprived of his office and salary and declared forever unable to serve the Honourable Company.

In addition, he was banished forever from the territories under the jurisdiction of the Company.

The last minutes of the proceedings and resolution of Gentlemen XVII concerning the fate of *Zeewijk* and its crew is dated 30 August 1729. It states that it had been approved and resolved that the earned monthly wages would be paid to the heirs of the men who had died in the *Zeewijk* disaster. In 1840, 113 years after *Zeewijk* was lost on the reefs and shallows of the Indian

Zeewyjk *hull timbers. (© Western Australia Maritime Museum/Patrick Baker)*

Ocean, the British survey ship HMS *Beagle* landed on the island where once the marooned survivors had camped. They found a brass four pounder swivel gun, with a breech block and the Dutch East India Company's initials VOC (Vereenigde Oost-Indische Compagnie) engraved on it; thus the island was named Gun Island. They also found ornamental brasswork for harnesses, the gilding still well preserved; two Dutch coins dated 1707 and 1720; clay pipes; and a number of stout Dutch wine bottles. Stokes, of HMS *Beagle*, who related this, also mentions that the bottles had been placed in a row, as if for the purpose of collecting water. He considered the bottles to be very large and capable of holding about twenty-five litres.

During his visits to the Abrolhos, Stokes observed guano deposits on some of the islands in the Pelsart group, among them Gun Island. Private enterprise soon started to

exploit the valuable guano, and it is known that from 1844 to 1850 at least four ships transported guano from the Abrolhos. In 1879 Deputy Surveyor-General John Forrest went ashore on Gun Island to locate and evaluate the guano deposits. He found scarcely any guano and stated that there were only a few tons to be procured. In the same report he mentions the remains of the *Zeewijk* survivors' campsite: 'Found the old encampment of the *Zeewijk* party in 1727. Number of broken bottles, iron, a cannon ball, broken wine glass, number of clay pipes in perfect preservation [and] also two coins, one of copper about the size of a half penny with "Hollandia 172" on it and the other the size of a four penny with "Zeelandia 1722" on it.'

In 1884, after having tested the quality of the guano on the islands, Charles Edward Broadhurst formed the partnership of Broadhurst and McNeil Guano Contractors. The firm leased Gun Island and nineteen other islands in the area for five years, a lease which was to be renewed several times during the following years. The guano diggers cleaned the topsoil of many islands and at times up to ninety vessels were chartered to transport the guano to various places throughout the world. The boom lasted to the turn of the century when the guano industry became uneconomic due to rising costs and the competition from chemical fertilizers. However, by that time the surface of Gun Island had been stripped to bare limestone rock except for a narrow strip of sand dunes on the western and northern ends of the island.

The deposits on Gun Island had been one of the most heavily mined in the Pelsart group, and as a result a large amount of *Zeewijk* relics were encountered. Fortunately the Broadhursts were interested in their discoveries and any artefact found during the course of digging was carefully collected and listed. Among the finds recovered during that period were musket and cannon balls, fish hooks and lead weights, kettles, jars, pots, bottles, wine glasses, tobacco boxes and clay pipes, and different types of silver and copper coins. In 1897, following the renewal of their leases for several times, the Broadhursts supplied a list of finds to the Royal Geographical Society of Australasia.

In the 20th century there have been various visits to Gun Island. In 1952 six cannon, three cylindrical pieces of iron, and two bundles of iron bars were located in the shallows on the inside of Half Moon reef. Three of the guns were raised and one twelve pounder and one eight pounder are now with the Western Australian Museum. The cannon might have been carried into the shallows by *Zeewijk*'s crew with the original intention of transporting them to Batavia. However, the presence of the cylindrical pieces of iron and the iron bars indicates that the cannon could probably originate from a major piece of wreckage that was washed over the reef when the ship broke up. Alternatively the cannon may have been jettisoned in an attempt to refloat *Zeewijk*. This could have happened but it seems unlikely as it is not mentioned in the ship's journal, and does not explain the presence of the other cannon on the top of the reef and in the shallows.

In 1963 the author and journalist Hugh Edwards, in cooperation with the *West Australian* newspaper, organized an expedition to the island. The shallows inside the reef were searched and digs were carried out at random on the island. In the shallows, five cannon, broken bottles, timbers, iron bars, lead. and cannon balls were found. Two iron cannon were raised. What was thought to be the old *Zeewijk* camp was located with a metal detector and barrel rungs, and metal fragments were found down to 1.5 m. During the course of digging, human bones, rosary beads, pottery and clay pipes were recovered, as well as fragments of broken glass and a glass bottle. A fisherman showed the expedition members a site on the island 'known' to contain artefacts, and after uncovering the surface of the place, a camp fire, a knife blade, a heap of barrel rungs, bones, and fragments of glass and pottery were revealed. In 1968 Hugh Edwards searched outside the reef for the main

Zeewyjk artefacts found during guano mining. (© Western Australia Maritime Museum)

Zuytdorp land excavation. (© Western Australia Maritime Museum/Jon Carpenter)

Begun in 1941, the investigations have been performed by a wide-ranging number of individuals and groups each driven by an equally wide range of motives or agenda, which in turn reflect contemporary trends and attitudes to terrestrial and underwater archaeological sites. While many were scholars of some repute, some were treasure-seekers known for their looting at other VOC and EEIC sites.

The site has also proved one of the most difficult and dangerous wrecks on the Australian coast. As a result, there has been high drama associated with this site since work began. There have been, for example,

wreck and in March discovered major wreckage consisting of anchors, cannons, and a large mound of conglomerate. In 1968 British Petroleum operated an unsuccessful oil rig on the island. During the construction work a guano camp on the east side of the island was demolished and several Dutch graves were unearthed on the west side. Two skeletons and the mask from a Bellarmine jug were found.

From 30 April to 17 May 1972, a combined underwater and land survey was carried out in the area by the Underwater Explorers Club under the supervision of a member from the Maritime Archaeological Department, Western Australian Museum. An investigation of the inside reef revealed five large conglomerates which appeared to be kegs of nails and a large quantity of metal tubing of different shapes and sizes. Various anchors and cannon, as well as a breech block, were also found. A random land-digging revealed bones, broken pottery, and fragments of glass and clay pipes. In 1976 the Maritime Archaeology Department at the Western Australian Museum commenced the 'Zeewijk Project' – a combined land and underwater survey of the *Zeewijk* site. The project plotted and recorded the remains of the wreck on both sides of Half Moon reef, and relocated and excavated the old *Zeewijk* encampment on Gun Island. J.G.

ADDITIONAL READING

Henderson, G., 1986, *Maritime Archaeology in Australia*, Nedlands, Western Australia.

Ingelman-Sundberg, C., 1977, 'The VOC Ship *Zeewijk* lost off the Western Australia Coast in 1727: An Interim Report on the First Survey', *International Journal of Nautical Archaeology*, 6, 3, 225–31.

Zuidersee Wrecks

see IJsselmeerpolders Wrecks

Zuytdorp

A large and well-equipped Dutch East India

Company (VOC) ship, lost without trace in the winter of 1712 en route from Holland to Batavia (now Jakarta) while carrying a rich cargo and silver bullion. Of the seven Dutch (VOC), British (EEIC), Portuguese, and American East India ships known to be lost off the coast of Western Australia, *Zuytdorp* is the only wreck from which survivors did not reach the nearest European settlement at Batavia to tell the tale. This makes the wreck of *Zuytdorp* unique in Western Australian waters and renders the remains on the seabed significant as they hold the only known clues to the fate of the ship's complement and the circumstances of the wreck. Remains, indicative of a Dutch camp adjacent to the wreck, also raised the possibility of a European occupation of the hinterland. A link with Aboriginal people, possibly even a genetic one, centres on the disease *Porphyria Variegata*, which began at the Cape of Good Hope in 1688, a few years prior to *Zuytdorp* calling in to recruit nearly 100 crew. In 1990 Dutch material was also found at Aboriginal camps in the hinterland.

near-drownings, some severe accidents, the fire-bombing of the museum's caravan and aviation near-misses.

The Western Australian Museum became legislatively responsible for the site in 1964 and began a series of salvage attempts focused on the removal of the remaining silver bullion. Some success followed these endeavours, though work at the site was put in abeyance due to other pressures. In 1986 research and fieldwork resumed and the process of tying the various existing investigative threads into a cohesive and comprehensible whole began. These investigations were then developed further by involving scholars, prehistorians, historical archaeologists, maritime archaeologists, geneticists, and others, notably geologist Dr Phillip Playford, who was responsible for most of the early archival research and terrestrial investigations, and chief diver Geoff Kimpton in the water. Given the dangers and difficulty of working the site, innovative recording and recovery strategies were devised and applied. Plans of the wreck have been produced using, in part, aerial photographs

Coins from Zuytdorp. (© Western Australia Maritime Museum/Patrick Baker)

Detail of the bronze gun from Zuytdorp. (© Western Australia Maritime Museum/Patrick Baker)

and other airborne photogrammetric techniques. Rapid diver deployment and material recovery strategies have also proved successful.

The central theme in the various studies since 1986 has been the activities of the people who appear to have survived the wreck, centring on the possibility that there were survivors and that they may have intermarried with Aborigines. Prehistorians have examined shell middens found near the site and identified them as Aboriginal, dating to around 4,000 BP; they pose as yet unanswered questions as to the interaction, if any, between the Aborigines and the Europeans. M.M.

ADDITIONAL READING

Henderson, G.J., 1978, *Unfinished Voyages*, vol. 1, *1622–1850*, Nedlands, Western Australia.

Kimpton, G. and McCarthy, M., 1988, *Zuytdorp (1701–1712) Report on Underwater and Other Work Conducted During the Period April 1986 to April 1988*, Report: Department of Maritime Archaeology, 30.

McCarthy, M., 1993, '*Zuytdorp*: The Search Continues', *Landscope: Western Australia's Conservation, Forests and Wildlife Magazine*, Autumn, 43–8.

Morse, K., 1988, 'The Archaeological Survey of Midden Sites Near the *Zuytdorp* Wreck, Western Australia', *Bulletin of the Australian Institute for Maritime Archaeology*, 12, 1, 37–40.

Playford, P.E., 1959, 'The Wreck of the *Zuytdorp* on the Western Australian Coast in 1712', *Journal and Proceedings of the Western Australian Historical Society*, 5, 5, 5–41.

Playford, P.E., 1996, *Carpet of Silver: The Wreck of the Zuytdorp*, Nedlands, Western Australia.

Zwammerdam

One of around twenty Roman forts on the south bank of the old River Rhine. Between 1968 and 1971, the Amsterdam University Institute for Pre- and Protohistoric Archaeology (IPP) excavated a Roman auxiliary fort on the south bank of the old River Rhine, since AD 47 the northern frontier of the district, since AD 88/9 the province of Germania Inferior. Zwammerdam – 'Nigropullo' on the Empire's map known as the Tabula Peutingeriana – was the sixteenth of about twenty forts (now excavated) downstream from the fortress at Xanten.

The fort at Zwammerdam had three dated building phases: AD 47–69, with timber buildings of military character; AD 70–175, a wooden fort (134.4 × 76.4 m); AD 175–260, rebuilding in stone (140.6 × 86 m) with a bath house outside its walls. Over 500 m long rows of late 1st-century quays were extended twice in the 2nd century and stretched along the fort and its *vicus*.

Roman period boats – three logboats, three barges, and a steering oar – were found in the 1971–4 excavations.

Log boat No. 1, about 7 m in length, was cut from an oak tree. It has a straight stem with a hole for a mooring post. A vertical timber is nailed to the stern. The three deck planks were fastened to transverse deck beams with iron nails and wooden pegs. A rectangular opening was sawn in the deck and the sides were perforated to let the water in to keep live fish.

Log boat No. 5, about 5.5 m in length, was cut from an oak tree. Its construction was the same as that of No. 1. On the deck of silver fir, a hatch with iron hinges was found. The sides were perforated.

Extended log boat No. 3, 10.4 m in length, was cut from an oak tree and is trough-shaped in section. The sides are raised with a silver fir plank. The forward extension board (with hole) is a separate piece of oak, adzed differently and fastened to the hull with iron nails. Cracks in the dugout were repaired before the ribs were placed in position. The ribs were fastened to the hull and the heightened sides with iron nails. There is a small mast-step.

Barge No. 2, 22.75 m in length, was built of oak timbers. The seven strakes are at their maximum 15 m in length. The L-shaped heavy chine is a raised clinker by one plank. The thirty-seven floor timbers are fork ended and placed in alternate positions. Separate uprights are slotted into the smooth ends of the floor timbers. An inner timber is fitted at the top of the side-board and has rectangular holes to slot the uprights and the forks. The light mast-step was possibly a towing post. The fastenings are large iron nails, partly clenched, and paired with treenails to join the floor timbers to the strakes. The ship's middle part is rectangular in plan.

Barge No. 4, 34 m in length, was built of oak timbers. The six strakes are at their maximum 21.6 m in length. The L-shaped heavy chine, its largest plank being 22.4 m in length, is a raised clinker by one plank. The ninety-three floor timbers are knee-ended, placed in pairs, and in alternate positions. The knee-ends and some loose uprights are nailed to or inserted in the inner timber at the top of the side-board. A large mast beam and mast-step point to a sailing rig. The fastenings are large iron nails, partly clenched. The ship's middle part is rectangular in shape.

Barge No. 6, 20.4 m in length, was built of oak timbers. The seven strakes are the ship's length at their maximum. The L-shaped heavy chine is heightened – in two cases with a mortise-and-tenon joint – edge-on-edge with one plank. This plank is a raised clinker by one plank. The thirty floor timbers are knee-ended and placed in alternate positions. Near the stem and stern, two crossed floor timbers were placed. Knee-ends – some of them enlarged – are inserted in the inner timber on top of the side-board. Near the stem, four transverse ribs were fastened on top of the board with swallow-tails. The mast-step indicates the ship was towed. All the fastenings are large iron nails, partly clenched. In plan the ship is gently curved. Stem and stern are over 2 m wide. The larboard side of the stem was strengthened with an iron corner.

The tripartite steering oar is oak and is 5.15 m in length. The length of the loom is 2.8 m, the blade is 1.24 m wide. The central part of the blade and the loom are of one piece of wood. Three holes in the central part of the blade were to fasten it to a ship. A rectangular hole at the top of the loom held the tiller. The blade is widened by two pieces, fastened to the central part with mortise-and-tenon joints, and at three of the four corners with an iron nail.

Marsden (1976) upgraded the Zwammerdam barges to a type: long, flat-bottomed, of very great size (19–40 m), with no keel, long and low; parallel, vertical sides built of overlapping planks; ribs of single pieces of L-shaped timber used singly or in pairs and attached to the strakes by iron nails, usually clenched; mast step cut in a keelson or a rib; the chines are built of planks, L-shaped in section, cut from a single piece of timber to form the right-angled junction between each side and the bottom of the craft.

In terms of water displacement of a barge's (rectangular) middle part, the cargo capacity is calculated at 30–105 tonnes. The recorded original cargoes include (at Zwammerdam) building materials for forts (tuffa, Schieffer, tiles), or grain (Woerden).

Relation to other Roman-period types

Maps and catalogues of Roman-period boats are found in Arnold (1992), Höckmann (1989), Marsden (1994), Parker (1992), and De Weerd (1988). For Roman period plank boats in Western and Central

Steering oar from Zwammerdam during excavation. (Instituut voor Pre- en Protohistorische Archeologie Albert Egges van Giffen, University of Amsterdam, The Netherlands)

Zwammerdam: barge no. 2 during excavation. (Instituut voor Pre- en Protohistorische Archeologie Albert Egges van Giffen, University of Amsterdam, The Netherlands)

Europe, Marsden (1976) sees four building methods: (1) Mediterranean (edge-joining by mortise-and-tenon); (2) **New Guy's House**; (3) **Blackfriars**/Bruges, and (4) Zwammerdam. McGrail (1995) sees the Romano-Celtic tradition as a polythethic grouping of different building methods and refers to new finds. Marsden (1966) and Ellmers (1969; 1983) defended a relationship (as to the building method with heavy transtra/flooring timbers and iron nails) between the vessels of the Celts (in 56 BC: Caesar, *De Bello Gallico* 3, 13) and the Blackfriars/New Guy's House boats. In this setting Zwammerdam barges, with their heavy chines and flooring timbers, were considered magnified small local Celtic prototypes. Nowadays over twenty types of Zwammerdam barges are recognized along the Rhine, in Switzerland and in Northern Gaul – most of them outside Celtic territory – but no small prototypes have come to

light. It can be argued that Zwammerdam barge-building took over the boat form of Northern Adriatic *sutiles naves* and replaced the sewing of planks and the insertion of half ribs by nailing and/or pegging ribs which bridged – and stiffened athwart – the full width of the flush flat-bottomed craft. In late Roman **Mainz** the *actus* is a new boat type.

Date and function

The barge's introduction at the end of the 1st century AD seems to be due to Roman military needs: e.g., the cheap transport of stone downstream to the estuary. Certainly, along with military transport, a civil use of barges also came into being. The 9th-century 14 × 2.50 m barge in Xanten has chines which, in a way, are reminiscent of Zwammerdam.

Metrology of Zwammerdam building procedures

Upon an analysis of plank lengths and scarf

positions, a prefab production of standardized plank length emerges in round numbers of multiples of five or ten Roman feet. When converted to Roman foot lengths, rib distances in Zwammerdam type barges furthermore show a pattern from which a phasing of rib insertion emerges. Such patterns are based on a repeated halving of rib distances set at standardized lengths. This type of insertion easily connects Zwammerdam non-edge-joined building technique to the erection of *Primärspanten* in early phases of shell constructed (edge-joined) Mediterranean vessels. Höckmann (1988) proves the Zwammerdam method and metrology of rib insertion in both the **Lake Nemi Ships**.

The Zwammerdam building technique, and especially its phased rib insertion at standardized Roman foot lengths, continued in the early Middle Ages. The barge Zwammerdam measuring system is found in the type Utrecht 11th-century extended log-based boats, the Roman type Utrecht small sized extended log boat (Zwammerdam 3) and in the 14th-century coglike vessel N5 in Flevolandpolder, published by Reinders (1980).

Our type of rib distance analysis is reviewed by Arnold (1990, 1992), McGrail (1992), and Fenwick (1995). They make the point that the statistics used are not convincing, but the argument can be reversed: a statistical analysis of a set of rib distances does not imply a scheme of rib insertion without any prior idea of such a scheme; our proposed scheme fits the data and explains the building method in plausible terms (De Weerd 1994).

Other Roman-period boat finds and maritime structures in the north

Quay-systems and small 'harbours'/quays undoubtedly accompanied the mid-1st- to mid-3rd-century frontier forts along the Rhine, but only parts of these structures are recorded at Valkenburg, Zwammerdam, Woerden, and Vechten.

At the legionary base (7 BC–AD 9) at Haltern, modern Germany, boathouses have been encountered.

The pre-frontier tranship harbour (with boathouses) and small legionary base (AD 15–37) at Velsen on the south bank of a northern branch of the Rhine produced shipbuilding and repair tools, ship timbers in the Mediterranean technique, fragments of rigging, and lead cladding. Extended riverine harbours in the provinces of Germania Inferior are only recorded with the legionary fortresses attached to civil towns in Xanten, Bonn and Cologne in Germany. Roman-period Zwammerdam type plank boats have been found in the Rhine estuary and upstream in Belgium and Northern France; many more undoubtedly await discovery. At Vechten, in 1892–3, a 12 m long boat was found, built in the Mediterranean technique. Other boats with mortise-and-tenon joined planks in western and central Europe are known from London, Zwammerdam (fragments) and Oberstimm (river Danube). The same method of joining has been reported in a boat in Ireland. M.D.W.

ADDITIONAL READING

Arnold, B., 1990, 'Some Objections to the Link Between Gallo-Roman Boats and the Roman Foot (*pes monetailis*)', *International Journal of Nautical Archaeology*, 19, 4, 273–7.

Arnold, B., 1992, 'Batellerie gallo-romaine sur le Lac de Neuchâtel', 2 vols, *Archéologie Neuchâteloise*, 12, 13.

Berkel, H. and Obladen-Kauder, J., 1992, 'Das römerzeitliche Schiff von Xanten-Wardt', *Archäologie im Rheinland 1991*, 74–77.

OhEailidhe, P., 1992, 'The Monk's Boat: A Roman Period Relic from Lough Lene, Co. Westmeath, Eire', *International Journal of Nautical Archaeology*, 21, 3, 185–190.

Ellmers, D., 1969, 'Keltishcher Schiffbau', *Jahrbuch des Römisch-Germanischen Zentralmuseums Mainz*, 16, 73–122.

Ellmers, D., 1983, 'Vor- und frühgeschichtlicher Boots- und Schiffbau in Europa nördlich der Alpen', in H. Jankuhn, (ed.), *Das Handwerk in vor- und frühgeschichtlicher Zeit*, vol. 2, 471–53, Göttingen.

Fenwick, F., 1995, 'Review Article of Arnold 1992', *International Journal of Nautical Archaeology*, 24, 167–70.

Haalebos, J.K., 1976, 'Nigrumpullum (Zwammerdam)', in R. Stillwell (ed.), *The Princeton Dictionary of Classical Sites*, Princeton, New Jersey.

Haalebos, J.K., 1977, 'Zwammerdam Nigrum Pullum', *Ein Auxiliarkastell am Niedergermanischen Limes*, Amsterdam (Cingula 3).

Höckmann, O., 1985, *Antike Seefahrt*, Münich.

Höckmann, O., 1988, 'Zwammerdam und Nemi: Zur Bauplanung römischer Schiffe', *Archäologisches Korrespondenzblatt*, 18, 389–96.

Höckmann, O., 1989, 'Römische Schiffsfunde westlich des Kastells Oberstimm', *Bericht der Römisch-Germanischen Kommission*, 70, 321–50.

Höckmann, O., 1994, 'Der erste römische Schiffsfund am Rhein', *Das Logbuch*, 30, 201–7.

Horn, H.G., 1987, *Die Römer in Nordrhein-Westfalen*, Stuttgart.

Hulst, R.A., 1993, 'Ship Remains', in R.M. van Dierendonck (ed.), *The Valkenburg Excavations 1985–1988*, Amersfoort, Netherlands.

Hüssen, C.-M., Rieder, K.H., and Schaaff, H., 1995, 'Die Römerschiffe in Oberstimm: Ausgrabung und Bergung', *Das Archäologische Jahr in Bayern 1994*, 112–16.

McGrail, S., 1992, 'Boat and Ship Archaeology in Roskilde: Sixth Meeting of the ISBSA, 2–5 September 1991', *International Journal of Nautical Archaeology*, 21, 61–4.

McGrail, S., 1995, 'Romano-Celtic Boats and Ships: Characteristic Features', *International Journal of Nautical Archaeology*, 24, 139–145.

Marsden, P.R.V., 1976, 'A Boat of the Roman Period, Found in Bruges, Belgium in 1899', *International Journal of Nautical Archaeology*, 5, 23–35.

Marsden, P.R.V., 1994, *Ships of the Port of London: 1st to 12th Centuries AD*, London.

Morel, J.-M.A.W., 1987, 'Frührömische Schiffshäuser in Haltern, Hofestatt', *Ausgrabungen und Funde in Westfalen-Lippe*, 5, 221–49.

Obladen-Kauder, J., 1994, 'Ein karolingischer Flusskahn aus Kalkar-Niedermormter', *Archaologie im Rheinland 1993*, 98–9.

Pals, J.P. and Hakbijl, T, 1992, 'Weed and insect infestation of a grain cargo in a ship at the Roman fort of Laurium in Woerden (Prov. of Zuid-Holland)', *Review of Palynology and Palaeobotany*, 73, 287–300.

Parker, A.J., 1992, *Ancient shipwrecks in the Mediterranean and the Northern Provinces*, BAR International Series 580, Oxford.

Reinders, H.R., 1980, 'Het onderzoek van een schip op kavel N5', *Flevobericht* 166, 6-15.

Vlek, R, 1987, *The Medieval Utrecht Boat*. BAR International Series 382, Oxford.

Weerd, M.D. de, 1987 (pub. 1989), 'Sind "keltische" Schiffe römisch? Zur angeblich keltischen Tradition des Schiffstyps Zwammerdam'. *Jahrbuch des Römisch-Germanischen Zentralmuseums Mainz* 34, 387-410.

Weerd, M.D. de, 1988, 'Schepen voor Zwammerdam'. Thesis, University of Amsterdam.

Weerd, MD. de, 1994, 'Rib insertion in phases: the type Zwammerdam shell-first building procedure 500 BC (?)-AD 1500', in C.

Westerdahl (ed.), *Crossroads in Ancient Shipbuilding*, Oxbow Monograph 40, 43-44.

Glossary of nautical terms

Abaft/Aft Towards the **stern** of a ship.

After-deck Short raised deck on a platform at the **stern**.

Amidships The middle of a vessel.

Apron Area of a wharf where cargo is unloaded, also a timber that makes up part of a ship's stem.

Back-stay A stay supporting a mast from the **aft**. See **fore-stay**.

Ballast Heavy material placed in a ship for stability.

Beam Extreme width of a vessel.

Bend To fix one thing to another e.g. 'bend' the sail to **yards** ready for hoisting.

Bilge The lowest part of a hull's interior.

Bipedal mast Two-legged mast.

Bonventure mast Fourth mast in a four-masted ship, located at the **stern**.

Boom The lower **yard** to which is fitted the foot of the sail.

Bow /s Front part of a vessel.

Bowlines Ropes attached to the middle parts of both **leeches** of a small sail; when a ship is sailing to windward one of the bowlines is pulled tight in order to keep the **weather leech** of the sail taut.

Bowline A knot which will not slip or get tighter under tension.

Bowsprit Spar protruding from the **bow** of a vessel, used as an attachment point for the **bowlines**. It extends the head sails and helps support the mast(s) through headstays.

Braces Ropes attached to the ends of a **yard** and led **aft**; 'bracing the yard' involves pulling a **brace** on one side of the ship taut, so that the end of the yard swings across to that side of the ship.

Brails Lines for shortening a loose-footed sail. Brails were secured to the foot, travelled up the forward surface through fairleads sewn in vertical rows, passed over the **yard**, and came down to the **aft** deck.

Break To unfurl flag with a quick motion. Also the name given to a sudden rise or fall of the ground level of the deck.

Bulwark The part of the hull which frames the deck.

Butt of oar Upper or handle end.

Calcet See **halyard-block**.

Capstan Revolving barrel with vertical axis, worked by men walking round and pushing horizontal levers, alternatively by steam power. For winding cable, **halyard**, etc.

Carling Short fore-and-aft timber or girder placed under a deck to stiffen it: for example, under mooring bits, winches, masts, etc.

Carvel-built Vessel in which the hull planks are laid flush edge to edge.

Cascabel The knob at the breech of a cannon.

Casemate Protected or armoured position for battery – of second armament of battleship.

Cat To hang anchor clear of hawsepipe: anchor was hoisted when 'catted'.

Cathead Sheeve and necklace doing job formerly done by '**davit**'.

Caulk To make the deck or side of a wooden construction watertight by forcing oakum (unravelled, tarred cordage) between planks.

Caulking Material used to fill and waterproof the seams between planks in a hull.

Central-shelf A narrow longitudinal timber following the middle of a vessel from **stern** to stern at deck level.

Chebec/Chebacco Boat A common North American inshore fishing boat until around 1820.

Chine/Chime Meeting of the bottom and side of the hull in a sharp line or projection.

Cleat Metal or wooden fitting firmly attached to vessel on a spar or gangway. It has two projecting horns round which light ropes can be wrapped for securing or can be used to give foothold.

Clench To secure a nail or rivet, by driving the point sideways when through.

Clinker-built/Lapstrake A method of boat building in which the lower edge of each plank overlaps the upper edge of the one below it.

Close-hauled A ship is said to be sailing 'close-hauled' when it is sailing as close as possible into the wind.

Cog One of a series of projections on the edge of a wheel or the side of a bar transferring motion by engaging with another series, also a medieval ship type.

Comb Semicircular flanges or rings below the **halyard-block** flanking the mast to which the lifts of the lower **yard** or **boom** are fixed.

Cotter Key, wedge or bolt, for securing parts of machinery etc, e.g. split pin which opens after passing through hole.

Cringles A short piece of rope worked **grommet**-fashion into the bolt-rope of a sail.

Cross-beam Horizontal timbers running from side-to-side of the vessel that support the deck and give lateral rigidity to the hull.

Davit Crane for hoisting and lowering boats and other gear.

Deadrise Vertical distance between **keel** and turn of **bilge**.

Deadwood Pieces of wood at each end of a boat or ship joining the **aprons** to the **keel** and to which the ends of the lower planks are fastened.

Deck A platform of planks extending from side to side of a vessel or part of it.

Draft A single sling of cargo, also the depth of water required by a ship to float freely.

Drag i) To search for objects on the seabed by dragging grapnel or other gear along it. ii) Retarding effect of shallow water.

Entrance Passage or channel leading to harbour or dock. Also the shape of the hull below the waterline – this relates to speed as well as appearance.

Finials The wooden extensions fitted to the **stem** and **stern** of a vessel.

Fore-deck A short, raised platform at the **bow**.

Foremast Mast set in the fore part of a ship.

Fore-stay Rope running from the mast-head and secured to the **bow**, supporting the mast.

Foreward The forewards or fore direction in a ship – towards the **bow**.

Frame Angle iron, bar or similar, forming main transverse strength-member of the hull structure running from keep to upper deck and conforming to shape of the hull.

Frames/framing Internal hull timbers, used to give shape and strength to the hull.

Furl The operation of taking in the sail and securing it with **gaskets** or by lashing.

Futtock One of the middle timbers in wooden vessel. **Futtock-plate** (in sailing ship) iron plate at edge of lower top to which lower end of **topmast** rigging is secured.

Gaff-rig Fore and aft, or schooner rig.

Gantry A raised wooden frame consisting of two upright posts joined by a cross-piece on which the mast could be rested when unstepped.

Garboard/strake Plank or line at bottom-plating next to **keel**, i.e. strake next to keel.

Gasket A rope or strip of canvas used to secure a sail when **furled** to a **yard** or **boom**.

Girdle-truss The rope that encircles a boat just below the **gunwales**.

Girt-rope The rope that encircled the prow and **stern** of the boat to which the **hogging-truss** was attached.

Grommet A strand of rope laid up in the form of a ring. One of its uses was to hold the oars to the **thole-pins** when rowing.

Gudgeon Metal loops or rings on the hull of a boat into which the pintles of the rudder fit.

Gunwale The upper edge of the **bulwark**.

Halyard-block/Calcet The block immediately below the mast-head, pierced with holes to take the halyards of the sail and the middle topping-lifts of the upper **yard**.

Halyards Ropes used to hoist or lower the sail.

Hermaphrodite brig Two-masted sailing vessel with the foremast square-rigged and the main mast fore-and-aft rigged.

Hogging-truss A heavy rope under tension secured around the hull at the **stem** and **stern** and supported at one or more stanchions above deck level. It provided longitudinal rigidity to the hull in the absence of a **keel**.

Jeer Tackle for hoisting and lowering **yards** with a double block at mast head and a single on yard.

Jib Triangular stay sail from outer end of jib-boom to fore topmast-head in large ships – from **bowsprit** to mast head in

smaller ones. Or to pull sail/**yard** round from one side to another.

Jib-stay Standing rigging – usually a strong rope or wire that runs from the foremast to the **bowsprit**.

Joggle Long slightly curved shackle to fit across any link of cable and with room for shackling on wire hawser.

Keel The lowest and most important timber in a hull, the 'backbone' of a vessel; the **frames** and **keelson** are normally attached to the keel.

Keelson Line of timber fastening the ship's floor timbers to the keel, inside the hull.

Kentledge Permanent pig-iron **ballast** – usually stowed next to the keel.

Kerf Slit made by cutting (esp. with a saw).

Knee Wooden fitting securing **thwart** to the side of boat, originally grown to shape, now laminated.

Larboard/Port side The left-hand side of the vessel looking forward.

Leech Vertical edge of a sail.

Lifts Ropes attached to the ends of a **yard**.

Limber Hole cut in floor timbers to drain water into pump-well.

Loom The part of an oar which extends from its point of pivot to the **butt**, i.e what is not in the water.

Loose-footed Term used of a sail the foot of which is not laced to a **boom**.

Lug A short piece of angle iron used to connect parts of an iron or steel ship.

Made mast Mast composed of several pieces of timber fitted together.

Mainmast The largest and most important mast in a ship.

Mast Vertical timber carrying a **yard** and a sail; masts are denoted by their position, thus even though a mainmast may have a main **topmast** and a main **topgallant mast** set above it, the whole assemblage is known as the '**mainmast**'.

Mast-step Point in a hull in which the lower end of a mast is set or 'stepped'.

Mast-support step The wooden support at deck level which gave lateral support to the mast. Also known as a 'knee', 'mast shoe' or 'tabernacle'.

Mizzenmast Mast set behind the mainmast.

Monitor Warship of moderate size and slow speed, armed with a small number of very heavy guns.

Não Early 16th century Portuguese and Spanish vessel.

Parral/Parrel-lashing Rope device used to

help hold a **yard** against a mast, and to allow it to move up and down in the wind.

'Passive' frame A curved timber-piece running from the hull bottom to the side rails. Often inserted after the shell of planking forming the hull had been set in place to provide extra lateral stiffening to the hull.

Pole mast Mast made from a single timber.

Quant A pole used for propelling a vessel through shallow water.

Rabbet Step-shaped channel cut along the edge of a face of protruding angle of wood – to receive edge of another.

Rake of ship, or of its **bow/stern**: Projection at upper part of bow or stern beyond the keel.

Ribs The timbers of a ship which rise from the **keel** to form the shape of the hull.

Rig General term for the masts and sail of a ship.

Rove A washer which secures a boat nail.

Rowlock A looped rope attached to the **gunwale** of a vessel to receive the oar while rowing.

Running rigging Lines or rope used to move and control the ship's **yards** and sails.

Scantling Dimensions of various parts of a ship's structure resulting in an indication of the general strength and weight of the vessel.

Scarf/Scarph A bevelled or wedge-shaped joint between two pieces of similar section at the join.

Scow-schooner Load carrier – flat bottomed boat.

Sheer The curve of the hull from stem to stern.

Sheets Ropes attached to the lower corners of a sail, and led **aft** (similar function as the braces).

Shell-first A method of boat building in which the shell-planking is put in place before the other strengthening members are fitted.

Shrouds The **standing rigging** of a sailing ship which gives a mast its lateral support.

Skeleton-first A method of boat building in which the **frames**, (ribs) are put in place before planking is attached.

Sloop i) Small single-masted sailing craft. ii) Small long-ranged warship. iii) Small square-rigged corvette with guns on an all-weather deck.

Spritsail Numerous definitions, the main one being, a sail carried on the sprit **yard** which was slung underneath the **bowsprit**.

Square rig/square sail Rectangular or

square-shaped sail, carried on a **yard** normally set at right-angles to the **yard**.

Standing rigging Rigging used to support the mast and spars.

Stem This can mean the front part of the ship in a general sense, or the foremost timber, the stempost.

Stempost See **stem**.

Stern This can mean the rear part of the ship in a general sense, or the rearmost timber, the sternpost.

Sternpost See **stern**.

Strake The individual planks which run the length of the ship's hull.

Tacks Ropes attached to the lower corners of a sail, and led forward.

Thole-pin A wooden pin fixed in the **gunwale** of a boat to which an oar is attached by means of a **grommet**.

Thwart Bench in a boat on which oarsmen sit.

Tie/tye/uptie Rope or ropes attached to the centre of a **yard** and used to raise or lower it.

Topmast Mast attached to the top of a larger lower mast.

Topgallant mast Mast attached to the top of a **topmast**.

Transom Athwartship timber at the **stern** of a vessel.

Treenail Pin of hard wood for securing planks.

Trim The way in which a vessel floats on the water in relation to her fore-and-aft line.

Uptie See **tie**.

Verso Small mounted cannon situated on the **bulwark** (16th century).

Wale Broad, thick timber along the side of a ship.

Washstrake A removable upper **strake** attached to the **gunwales** to keep out spray.

Weather-leech Vertical edge of a sail closest to the wind direction when a ship is sailing to windward.

Windlass Contraption for hoisting anchors and to warp slip or move a ship into harbour.

Wing Part of a ship's hold, next to the vessel's side.

Yard A spar to which a sail is attached.

Index

E

F

G

I

M

N

O

P